Century 21
Accounting

11e Advanced

Claudia Bienias Gilbertson, CPA
Retired
North Hennepin Community College
Brooklyn Park, Minnesota

Mark W. Lehman, CPA, CFE
Associate Professor Emeritus
Richard C. Adkerson School of Accountancy
Mississippi State University
Starkville, Mississippi

Australia • Brazil • Mexico • Singapore • United Kingdom • United States

Century 21 Accounting Advanced, Eleventh Edition

Claudia Bienias Gilbertson, CPA, PhD
Mark W. Lehman, CPA, CFE, PhD

SVP, GM Skills & Global Product Management: Jonathan Lau

Product Director: Matthew Seeley

Product Manager: Nicole Robinson

Executive Director, Content Design: Marah Bellegarde

Learning Design Director: Juliet Steiner

Learning Designer: Jennifer Starr

Senior Content Manager: Karen Caldwell

Product Assistant: Nicholas Scaglione

Vice President, Strategic Marketing Services: Jennifer Ann Baker

Marketing Manager: Abigail Hess

Senior Production Director: Wendy Troeger

Designer: Erin Griffin

Digital Delivery Lead: Jim Gilbert

Production Management and Composition: SPi Global

Cover image(s): s_maria/Shutterstock.com; CHAIWATPHOTOS/Shutterstock.com; THANAROT NGOENWILAI/Shutterstock.com

Design elements: Ethics in Action (Lady Justice): asharkyu/Shutterstock.com; Financial Literacy (magnifying glass): Zadorozhnyi Viktor/Shutterstock.com; Careers in Accounting (building): telesniuk/Shutterstock.com; Think Like Accountant (vortex): agsandrew/Shutterstock.com; FYI Box Icon: Blablo101/Shutterstock.com; Calculator Icon: Aleksandr Bryliaev/Shutterstock; Why Accounting? (dollar): Yorkman/Shutterstock.com; Look at Accounting Software: Sergey Nivens/Shutterstock.com; Explore Accounting (compass): allstars/Shutterstock.com; Remember box (post-it): Evgenii Bobrov/Shutterstock.com; Global Awareness (globe): kentoh/Shutterstock.com; Forensic Accounting (dollar): yurchello108/Shutterstock.com; Accounting in the Real World (World Map): Pyty/Shutterstock.com.

For product information and technology assistance, contact us at
Cengage Customer & Sales Support, 1-800-354-9706

For permission to use material from this text or product, submit all requests online at **www.cengage.com/permissions.**
Further permissions questions can be e-mailed to
permissionrequest@cengage.com

Library of Congress Control Number: 2019933600

Student Edition ISBN-13: 978-1-337-79880-8

Cengage

20 Channel Center Street

Boston, MA 02210

USA

Cengage is a leading provider of customized learning solutions with employees residing in nearly 40 different countries and sales in more than 125 countries around the world. Find your local representative at **www.cengage.com/repfinder**.

Cengage products are represented in Canada by Nelson Education, Ltd.

To learn more about Cengage platforms and services, register or access your online learning solution, or purchase materials for your course, visit **ngl.cengage.com**.

Notice to the Reader

Publisher does not warrant or guarantee any of the products described herein or perform any independent analysis in connection with any of the product information contained herein. Publisher does not assume, and expressly disclaims, any obligation to obtain and include information other than that provided to it by the manufacturer. The reader is expressly warned to consider and adopt all safety precautions that might be indicated by the activities described herein and to avoid all potential hazards. By following the instructions contained herein, the reader willingly assumes all risks in connection with such instructions. The publisher makes no representations or warranties of any kind, including but not limited to, the warranties of fitness for particular purpose or merchantability, nor are any such representations implied with respect to the material set forth herein, and the publisher takes no responsibility with respect to such material. The publisher shall not be liable for any special, consequential, or exemplary damages resulting, in whole or part, from the readers' use of, or reliance upon, this material.

Printed in the United States of America
Print Number: 01   Print Year: 2019

CONTENTS

PART 2

Accounting Adjustments and Valuation

PART 3 Corporation Accounting

PART 4

Management Accounting

PART 5
Internal Control and Other Organizational Structures

Reviewers

The authors would like to acknowledge and thank the numerous instructors and reviewers who have contributed their time and expertise in building the foundation for this edition.

Technical Reviewers for the 11ᵗʰ edition

Amy K. Gruenberg, CPA, Retired

Matthew Lowenkron, EA

About the Authors

Claudia B. Gilbertson, Certified Public Accountant, served as a highly effective high school instructor for 11 years and a community college instructor for 25 years. While retired from North Hennepin Community College, Ms. Gilbertson remains active in shaping today's educational processes as she serves as a respected and sought-after consultant for numerous online accounting learning solutions. She is active in the National Business Education Association, North Central Business Education Association, and Minnesota Business Educators, Inc.

Mark W. Lehman, assistant professor emeritus of Accountancy at the Richard C. Adkerson School of Accountancy at Mississippi State University, taught Accounting Information Systems and Forensic Accounting. A former auditor with PricewaterhouseCoopers, Dr. Lehman is a Certified Public Accountant and a Certified Fraud Examiner. He has written journal articles and has consulted with accountants on the use of software in fraud detection. He was awarded Outstanding Educator by the Mississippi Society of Certified Public Accountants in 2007.

This edition of **Century 21 Accounting Advanced** is aligned to Precision Exams' Accounting, Advanced (213) certification. The **Business and Marketing** pathway connects industry with skills taught in the classroom to help students successfully transition from high school to college and/or career. Working together, Precision Exams and National Geographic Learning/Cengage focus on preparing students for the workforce, with exams and content that is kept up to date and relevant to today's jobs. To access a corresponding correlation guide, visit the accompanying Instructor Companion Website for this title. For more information on how to administer the **Accounting, Advanced** exam or any of the 170+ exams available to your students, contact your local NGL/Cengage Sales Consultant.

Transform Your High School Accounting Course with Century 21 Accounting, from the leader in high school accounting education for 100+ years.

Input from educators, accounting professionals, content experts, and high school accounting students has shaped the 11th Edition of Century 21 Accounting. Newly refined content built on sound learning design principles is combined with relevant critical-thinking activities, real-world applications, and enhanced online learning solutions to help you transform your accounting course. For the 11th Edition, we are pleased to introduce MindTap for a complete online learning experience.

MINDTAP
From Cengage

▶ A focus on **learning design** ensures technical and pedagogical **content** clearly supports, and **assessments** accurately measure, **learning outcomes** to bolster student success in the 11th Edition.

▶ **An emphasis on conceptual understanding and financial statement analysis** encourages students to apply accounting concepts to real-world situations and develop higher-level thinking skills to make informed business decisions.

▶ **Critical thinking and technology use**, as defined by the Partnership for 21st Century Skills, are supported through these features to give students real-world practice and help them master valuable skills:

Forensic Accounting   *Think Like an Accountant*
Financial Literacy   *Why Accounting?*

▶ **Commercial technology** is integrated throughout the text to equip students to work with Microsoft Excel®, Sage 50 Accounting, Tableau, and QuickBooks®. Students are given step-by-step instructions and the flexibility to use a variety of popular commercial software. Students use Tableau's dynamic data visualizations to identify and interpret data trends impacting the business.

The Century 21 Accounting program provides students with a complete learning system designed to keep students on track and helps you measure outcomes.

The **organization** ensures clear student understanding. Students start with departmentalized accounting and then learn about corporation and management accounting, before concluding with internal control and other organizational structures.

The **step-by-step instructional approach** clearly reinforces text concepts, while the consistent use of T accounts increases student comprehension of journalizing transactions.

Validated Learning Objectives align technical content with end of lesson and chapter questions and problems, in addition to all supplementary assessments, to provide a clear pathway for learning. Learning objectives are identified at the point of introduction, throughout the chapter, and in the end-of-chapter problems, making it easier for students to stay on track. By paying attention to the Learning Objectives, students can focus on what is important and you can better measure outcomes.

"I believe you have provided us with just what we need to get the objectives introduced, practiced, and then mastered."

Kathleen O'Connor Ford,

Rochester Community Schools, Rochester Hills, MI

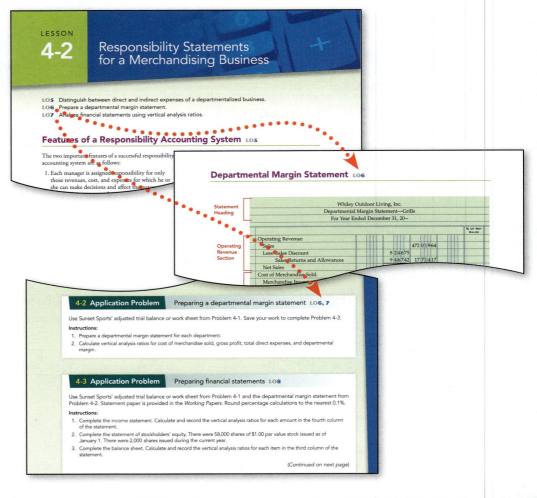

Measurable Outcomes

The **lesson structure** consists of two to four lessons per chapter and corresponding assessment activities. Each end-of-lesson section includes a **Work Together** problem and an **On Your Own** assignment. The Work Together problem allows you to demonstrate the new accounting concept to your class. Students can then check their understanding by completing the On Your Own assignment.

The **end-of-chapter material** includes short application problems to ensure students' understanding before they tackle the longer mastery and challenge problems.

> "The activities and problems at the end of the chapter do a great job of providing students with the chance to use their knowledge and skills from the chapter sections."
>
> *Kathleen Harenza, Mukwonago High School, Mukwonago, WI*

END OF LESSON — Review

LO5 Explain the purpose and process of recording purchases and purchase returns in a departmental accounting system.

LO6 Journalize departmental purchases of merchandise on account using a purchases journal.

LO7 Post merchandise purchases to an accounts payable ledger and a general ledger.

LO8 Journalize departmental purchases returns and allowances.

TERMS REVIEW

departmental accounting system
merchandising business
posting
debit memorandum
contra account

Audit your understanding LO5, 6, 8

1. Why should a business consider using a departmental accounting system?
2. When Whiley's grills department purchases merchandise on account, which general ledger accounts are affected, and how?
3. Which general ledger accounts are affected, and how, by a return of furniture department merchandise?

Work together 1-2 LO6, 7, 8

Journalizing and posting purchases on account and purchases returns and allowances Electronic Warehouse has two departments: Audio and Video. A purchases journal, general journal, and partial general and accounts payable ledgers are provided in the *Working Papers*. Source documents are abbreviated as follows: debit memorandum, DM; purchase invoice, P. Your instructor will guide you through the following examples.

1. Journalize the following transactions. Use page 6 of a purchases journal and page 6 of a general journal. Post the items that are to be posted individually.

   Transactions:
   June 3. Purchased audio equipment on account from Davis Corporation, $1,625.00. P243.
   5. Returned video equipment to TPC Supply, $42.50, from P239. DM38.
   8. Purchased video equipment on account from TPC Supply, $995.00. P244.
   12. Purchased audio equipment on account from National Industries, $1,100.00. P245.
   18. Received an allowance on audio equipment from National Industries, $165.80, from P245. DM39.
   23. Purchased audio equipment on account from Davis Corporation, $820.00. P246.

2. Prove and rule the purchases journal. Post the totals.

On your own 1-2 LO6, 7, 8

Journalizing and posting purchases on account and purchases returns and allowances Ashley's Fashions has two departments: Clothing and Shoes. A purchases journal, general journal, and partial general and accounts payable ledgers are provided in the *Working Papers*. Source documents are abbreviated as follows: debit memorandum, DM; purchase invoice, P. Work this problem independently.

1. Journalize the following transactions. Use page 7 of a purchases journal and page 7 of a general journal. Post the items that are to be posted individually.

   Transactions:
   July 2. Purchased clothing on account from Keller Corporation, $2,418.00. P366.
   7. Returned clothing to Keller Corporation, $185.90, from P366. DM45.
   9. Purchased clothing on account from Ackerman Supply, $1,680.00. P367.
   13. Received an allowance on shoes from Peters Company, $115.30, from P365. DM46.
   16. Purchased shoes on account from Peters Company, $1,150.00. P368.
   22. Purchased clothing on account from Keller Corporation, $925.00. P369.

2. Prove and rule the purchases journal. Post the totals.

Problem Solving *Creativity*

An emphasis on conceptual understanding and financial statement analysis balances coverage of accounting mechanics with how its application in executing business decisions.

CRITICAL THINKING ACTIVITIES

are infused throughout the text to provide more opportunities for higher-level thinking and analysis, preparing students for college and career readiness.

21ST CENTURY SKILLS

included in the end-of-chapter material, provides activities that cultivate mastery of essential skills such as problem solving, communication, and technology use as defined by the Partnership for 21st Century Learning. Acquisition of the knowledge and skills taught in this feature will prepare students to compete in a workplace that demands creativity and innovation.

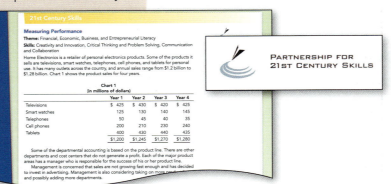

21st Century Skills

Measuring Performance

Theme: Financial, Economic, Business, and Entrepreneurial Literacy
Skills: Creativity and Innovation, Critical Thinking and Problem Solving, Communication and Collaboration

Home Electronics is a retailer of personal electronics products. Some of the products it sells are televisions, smart watches, telephones, cell phones, and tablets for personal use. It has many outlets across the country, and annual sales range from $1.2 billion to $1.28 billion. Chart 1 shows the product sales for four years.

Chart 1
(in millions of dollars)

	Year 1	Year 2	Year 3	Year 4
Televisions	$ 425	$ 430	$ 420	$ 425
Smart watches	125	130	140	145
Telephones	50	45	40	35
Cell phones	200	210	230	240
Tablets	400	430	440	435
	$1,200	$1,245	$1,270	$1,280

Some of the departmental accounting is based on the product line. There are other departments and cost centers that do not generate a profit. Each of the major product areas has a manager who is responsible for the success of his or her product line.

Management is concerned that sales are not growing fast enough and has decided to invest in advertising. Management is also considering taking on more product and possibly adding more departments.

PARTNERSHIP FOR 21ST CENTURY SKILLS

THINK LIKE AN ACCOUNTANT

presents challenging problems using Excel and Tableau that correspond to higher-level thinking skills based on the criteria established in Bloom's Taxonomy.

Excel and Tableau templates are provided on the Companion Website for students to use as an analysis tool.

...e returns can make determining ...amount of the purchases discount more difficult.

THINK LIKE AN ACCOUNTANT

Analyzing Purchases Discounts

The accounting procedures manual of Rackley Corporation includes the following statement regarding purchases discounts:

"The corporation strives to obtain purchase discount agreements with its merchandise vendors. Accounting personnel are responsible for processing cash payments on a timely basis to take advantage of all purchase discounts offered by merchandise vendors. Exceptions to this policy should be approved by an appropriate level of management."

Cheryl Rosario, an internal auditor for Rackley Corporation, is performing a review of the purchasing processes of the company. It's not unusual for Cheryl to notice a couple of instances where purchases discounts were not taken. After all, mistakes do occur. But on this review, she notices more than the typical number of lost discounts.

quantify the extent of purchase discounts lost during the current fiscal year.

OPEN THE SPREADSHEET TLA_CH01

The worksheet contains a list of cash payments for merchandise. The list includes the purchase discount percent offered by the vendor, if any, and the amount of discount taken. Follow the steps on the Instructions tab to analyze the cash payments and discounts lost. Use the analysis to answer the following questions:

1. What is the number of discounts taken?
2. What is the average, maximum, and total amount of discounts taken?
3. What is the number of discounts lost?
4. What is the average, maximum, and total amount of discounts lost?
5. Does the information collected suggest any

Communication
Information Literacy

FINANCIAL LITERACY

guides students in the exploration of both business finance issues and critical personal finance topics through engaging activities that provide opportunities for students to apply valued skills such as problem solving, critical thinking, and technology use as defined by the Partnership for 21st Century Skills.

GLOBAL AWARENESS

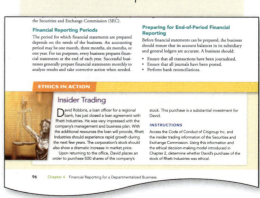

presents the role of accounting in a global environment and the cultural implications that occur as a result of the trans-migratory nature of the marketplace. It reflects current trends, concerns, and issues in global business, and cultural diversity in the workplace. Cultural topics will address both international and domestic issues.

ETHICS IN ACTION

responds to the increasing importance of ethics and personal character in accounting today. These ethical dilemmas assist students with decision-making and critical-thinking skills and challenge students' personal character development.

> "The use of Excel . . . is an extremely important skill. Many of my high school students who come back to visit while they are in college have said they wish they would have used Excel more in class, because it is something they are doing a lot of in college business courses."
>
> *Kevin Willson, York Suburban School District, York, PA*

Forensic Accounting presents criminal investigations involving fraud, providing students the opportunity to apply what they're learning in class to a real-world scenario. Students will examine the fraud scenarios using Excel® and Tableau to analyze the data and continue the investigation.

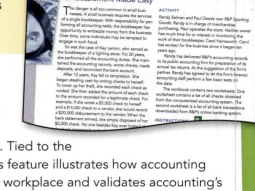

Why Accounting? provides examples of how accounting skills are applicable in a variety of business situations. Tied to the National Career Clusters, this feature illustrates how accounting knowledge transfers into the workplace and validates accounting's importance in the marketplace.

Careers in Accounting, designed to encourage students to think about their future in accounting, features a broad range of careers in the accounting field and promotes accounting as a profession through one-on-one interviews with various accounting professionals.

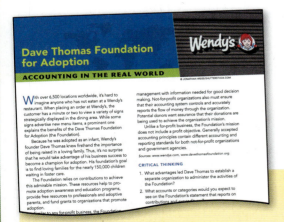

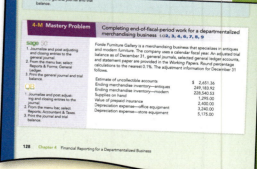

Accounting in the Real World: Fascinating chapter openers spotlight actual businesses that interest students, such as Wendy's, Ford Motor Company, and Kohl's Corporation, with intriguing questions that connect chapter topics to what's driving business decisions in today's organizations.

Commercial technology, integrated into the end of each chapter, equips students to work with **Microsoft Excel®, Sage 50c Accounting, Tableau, and QuickBooks®** with step-by-step instructions and the flexibility to use multiple versions of software.

Accounting Practices to Life

Bring Accounting Practices to Life with
Relevant Simulations

Simulations provide your students with hands-on, real-world experience in accounting practice.

First Year

Simulation 1: Red Carpet Events

Students encounter accounting principles and practical applications as they experience the challenges of operating an event-planning service business organized as a proprietorship. Students complete the simulation after Chapter 8. *Completion time 4-8 hours.*

Simulation 2: Authentic Threads

Students bring fashion trends into the world of accounting while they practice accounting applications in this dynamic merchandising business organized as a corporation. Students complete the simulation after Chapter 17. *Completion time 10-17 hours.*

Simulation 3: Digital Diversions

Students go digital in this engaging simulation with the latest retail software, cell phones, video cameras, music, and more in this merchandising business organized as a corporation. Students complete the simulation after Chapter 22. *Completion time 10-15 hours.*

Advanced

Simulation 1: Organic Aisles

Students sell organic produce and grocery items in Organic Aisles, a departmentalized grocery store organized as a corporation. Students complete the simulation after Chapter 4. *Completion time 10-20 hours.*

Simulation 2: Adventure Gear

Adventure rules as students bring adventure sport gear and accessories into the world of accounting within this merchandising business organized as a corporation. Students complete the simulation after Chapter 14. *Completion time 10-20 hours.*

Online Working Papers

Online Working Papers, available in MindTap, feature automatic grading for instructors and immediate feedback for students. C21 Accounting Online Working Papers mirror the print working papers and tests including online journals, ledgers, worksheets, financial statements, and other forms students use to complete their textbook problems and tests.

▶ Mirror the C21 Accounting Print Working Papers
▶ Immediate Feedback for Students
▶ Automatically Graded Assignments for Instructors
▶ Chapter Tests Included

Students who stay engaged with material put more effort into the course. Century 21 Online Working Papers give **students instant feedback**, making sure they are learning from each question while gaining a better understanding of accounting basics.

The Online Working Papers **automatically grade assignments**, relieving instructors of the burden of grading homework by hand. As students complete the assignments, the instructor receives a complete assessment of their work and comprehension levels, while their grades are instantly recorded in the instructor's online grade book.

The Online Working Papers keep instructors informed about student participation, progress, and performance through real-time graphical reports. Instructors can easily download, save, manipulate, print, and import student grades into their current grading program.

What Users Are Saying!

▶ **73%** say that **student performance has improved** in their class since using the Online Working Papers!
▶ **82%** report that their students are **more engaged** in the Accounting course.
▶ **75%** say their ability to **monitor student progress** has improved.
▶ **57%** say that after using Online Working Papers, their students are **more likely to enroll in further study in accounting** and/or other business education courses.

Visit https://ngl.cengage.com/digitalreview

Accounting MindTap

MindTap: Empower Your Students

MindTap is a platform that propels students from memorization to mastery. It gives you complete control of your course, so you can provide engaging content, challenge every learner, and build student confidence. Customize interactive syllabi to emphasize priority topics, then add your own material or notes to the ebook as desired. This outcomes-driven application gives you the tools needed to empower students and boost both understanding and performance.

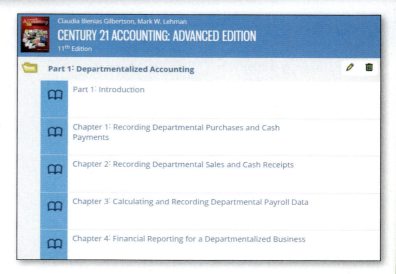

Claudia Bienias Gilbertson, Mark W. Lehman

CENTURY 21 ACCOUNTING: ADVANCED EDITION
11th Edition

Part 1: Departmentalized Accounting

Part 1: Introduction

Chapter 1: Recording Departmental Purchases and Cash Payments

Chapter 2: Recording Departmental Sales and Cash Receipts

Chapter 3: Calculating and Recording Departmental Payroll Data

Chapter 4: Financial Reporting for a Departmentalized Business

Twelve distinct metrics give you actionable insights into student engagement. Identify topics troubling your entire class and instantly communicate with students who are struggling. Students can track their scores to stay motivated toward their goals. Together, you can be unstoppable.

To request free review access to MindTap for Advanced Accounting, visit: **https://ngl.cengage.com/digitalreview**

Student and Teacher Companion Websites extend the learning experience with study tools, data files, and more. **www.c21accounting.com**

Getting Ready to Start Your Class? Need Help Getting Started?

National Geographic Learning, a part of Cengage, offers **NGLSync** access with every course. NGLSync is your portal to online courses, instructor and student resources, test banks, rostering, and more!

Find NGLSync User Guides and Video Trainings at **www.cengage.com/coursepages/NGL_DigitalFulfillmentSupport**.

Unsure whether you have access? Contact your Sales Consultant at **www.ngl.cengage.com/RepFinder**.

Transform Your Teaching Experience with **tools to make your job easier**

Automatic grading with Online Working Papers and MindTap, designed to minimize your time grading, while maximizing your impact within the classroom. Immediate feedback for students and automatic grading for you will save you time and give you an instant sense of each student's comprehension. Grades are automatically entered in an instructor's online gradebook.

Teacher's Resource Guide, located on the Instructor's Companion Website, includes comprehensive support previously included in the Wraparound Teacher's Edition, including:

▶ An overview of each accounting part

▶ Chapter Outlines

▶ Teaching tips to increase student engagement

▶ Suggested answers to critical thinking questions found in all chapter features

▶ Alternate activities for different learning styles

▶ Essential questions

*Written **by** high school accounting teachers, **for** high school accounting teachers.*

Written by high school accounting teachers, for high school accounting teachers.

Instructor's Companion Website includes comprehensive teaching resources all in one place, including:

▶ Working Paper and Recycling Problem solutions

▶ Chapter and Part Tests solutions

▶ Simulation keys

▶ Solutions to Sage 50c Accounting, QuickBooks®, Simulations

▶ Blackline masters (Full Color Illustrations)

▶ Interactive spreadsheets

▶ Chapter and Part Tests

▶ Teacher's MindTap Overview Video

Assessment Resources

▶ **Cognero® computerized test bank** allows you to easily create custom tests within minutes. Simply edit, add, delete, or rearrange questions with this easy-to-use software.

▶ **Chapter and Part Test Masters** Two separate test masters for every chapter and part include problems and objective questions.

▶ **Teacher's Edition Chapter and Part Tests** Provide solutions for convenient grading.

▶ **Print Working Papers** for Chapters 1-14 and 15-24.

NEW TO THIS EDITION

For the 11th Edition, all Online Working Papers will be available only in MindTap. The Learning Objectives have been fully revised throughout the text. The Wraparound Teacher's Edition has been replaced with the Teacher's Resource Guide, located on the Instructor's Companion Website.

Chapter 1
- *Accounting in the Real World* – changed highlighted company from Skechers to **The Kroger Co.**

Chapter 2
- *Accounting in the Real World* – changed highlighted company from Expedia, Inc. to **Exxon Mobile**
- Updated *Careers in Accounting*

Chapter 3
- *Accounting in the Real World* – changed highlighted company from Automatic Data Processing, Inc. to **Netchex**
- Updated tax tables
- *Forensic Accounting* - updated exercise to a Tableau exercise
- Updated *Explore Accounting*

Chapter 4
- *Accounting in the Real World* – changed highlighted company from Whole Planet Foundation to **Dave Thomas Foundation for Adoption**
- Updated federal income tax rates
- Updated *Careers in Accounting* and *Why Accounting?*

Chapter 5
- *Accounting in the Real World* – changed highlighted company from Johnson & Johnson to **Huntsman Corporation**
- Updated *21st Century Skills*

Chapter 6
- *Accounting in the Real World* – changed highlighted company from Target to **Chesapeake Energy Corp.**
- Updated *Careers in Accounting* and *Think Like an Accountant* – this is now a Tableau activity.

Chapter 7
- *Accounting in the Real World* – changed highlighted company from Union Pacific to **CSX Corporation**
- Updates to *Ethics in Action*, *Global Awareness*, and *Forensic Accounting* – this is now a Tableau activity.

Chapter 8
- *Accounting in the Real World* – changed highlighted company from Tanger Outlets to **One Liberty Properties, Inc.**

- Updated *Careers in Accounting*
- Added new *Explore Accounting* feature discussing alternative note payment options
- All new *21st Century Skills* feature

Chapter 9
- *Accounting in the Real World* – changed highlighted company from Southwest Airlines Co. to **Ford Motor Company**
- Updated *21st Century Skills*

Chapter 10
- *Accounting in the Real World* - changed highlighted company from DuPont to **ARMO BioSciences, Inc.**
- Updated *Careers in Accounting*

Chapter 11
- *Accounting in the Real World* – changed highlighted company from Pandora to **Wells Fargo & Company**
- Added new *Explore Accounting* feature to address mergers, acquisitions, and hostile takeovers

Chapter 12
- *Accounting in the Real World* – changed highlighted company from The U.S. Treasury Company to **Port of New Orleans**

Chapter 13
- *Accounting in the Real World* – changed highlighted company from Chipotle to **Kohl's**
- A new section discussing non-recurring items on the interest statement was added
- Updated *Forensic Accounting* - this is now a Tableau activity

Chapter 14
- *Accounting in the Real World* – changed highlighted company from EMC Corporation to **Apple, Inc.**
- Updated *Careers in Accounting* and *Explore Accounting*

Chapter 15
- *Accounting in the Real World* – changed highlighted company from Walmart to **Burlington Stores, Inc.**
- Updated content throughout chapter to reflect new federal income tax rates

Chapter 16
- *Accounting in the Real World* – changed highlighted company from Nintendo to **Samsung**
- Updated *Careers in Accounting* and *Think Like an Accountant* is now a Tableau activity

Chapter 17
- *Accounting in the Real World* – changed highlighted company from General Mills to **Donnelly Custom Manufacturing**
- Updated *21st Century Skills*

Chapter 18
- *Accounting in the Real World* - changed highlighted company from Verizon to **Macy's**
- All new *21st Century Skills*

Chapter 19
- *Accounting in the Real World* – changed highlighted company from Wm Wrigley Jr. Company to **General Mills**
- Updated *Global Awareness* and *Why Accounting?*
- Updated *Think Like an Accountant* and changed it to a Tableau activity

Chapter 20
- *Accounting in the Real World* - changed highlighted company from PetSmart to **ACL Services Ltd.** *Analyzing Nike's Financial Statements.*
- Updated *Financial Literacy*

Chapter 21
- *Accounting in the Real World* – changed highlighted company from Pricewaterhouse Cooper to **Ernst & Young**

Chapter 22
- *Accounting in the Real World* – changed highlighted company from PVR Partners, L.P. to **Valero Energy Partners LP**
- Updated *Careers in Accounting*

Chapter 23
- *Accounting in the Real World* – changed highlighted company from Amtrak to **MARTA**

Chapter 24
- *Accounting in the Real World* – changed highlighted company from the City of Tampa to the **City of Tulsa**
- Updated *Careers in Accounting*

Century 21
Accounting

11e   Advanced

Departmentalized Accounting

THE BUSINESS—

WHILEY OUTDOOR LIVING, INC.

Whiley Outdoor Living, Inc., is the business that will be used in the chapters in Part 1 to illustrate the accounting concepts and procedures for a departmentalized merchandising business organized as a corporation. Whiley has two sales departments: Grills and Furniture.

© ISTOCKPHOTO.COM/TIM ABRAMOWITZ

Chart of Accounts
WHILEY OUTDOOR LIVING, INC.

GENERAL LEDGER

Balance Sheet Accounts

(1000) ASSETS
1100–1400 Current Assets
1105 Cash
1110 Petty Cash
1205 Accounts Receivable
1210 Allowance for Uncollectible Accounts
1305 Merchandise Inventory—Grills
1310 Merchandise Inventory—Furniture
1405 Supplies
1410 Prepaid Insurance
1500 Plant Assets
1505 Office Equipment
1510 Accumulated Depreciation—Office Equipment
1515 Store Equipment
1520 Accumulated Depreciation—Store Equipment

(2000) LIABILITIES
2100–2300 Current Liabilities
2105 Accounts Payable
2110 Sales Tax Payable
2215 Employee Income Tax Payable—Federal
2220 Employee Income Tax Payable—State
2225 Social Security Tax Payable
2230 Medicare Tax Payable
2235 Medical Insurance Payable
2240 Retirement Plan Payable
2245 Unemployment Tax Payable—Federal
2250 Unemployment Tax Payable—State
2305 Federal Income Tax Payable
2310 Dividends Payable

(3000) STOCKHOLDERS' EQUITY
3105 Capital Stock
3110 Retained Earnings
3115 Dividends
3205 Income Summary

Income Statement Accounts

(4000) OPERATING REVENUE
4105 Sales—Grills
4110 Sales Discount—Grills
4115 Sales Returns and Allowances—Grills
4205 Sales—Furniture
4210 Sales Discount—Furniture
4215 Sales Returns and Allowances—Furniture

(5000) COST OF MERCHANDISE
5105 Purchases—Grills
5110 Purchases Discount—Grills
5115 Purchases Returns and Allowances—Grills
5205 Purchases—Furniture
5210 Purchases Discount—Furniture
5215 Purchases Returns and Allowances—Furniture

(6000) DIRECT EXPENSES
6100 DIRECT EXPENSES—GRILLS
6105 Advertising Expense—Grills
6110 Payroll Taxes Expense—Grills
6115 Salary Expense—Grills
6200 DIRECT EXPENSES—FURNITURE
6205 Advertising Expense—Furniture
6210 Payroll Taxes Expense—Furniture
6215 Salary Expense—Furniture

(7000) INDIRECT EXPENSES
7105 Credit Card Fee Expense
7110 Depreciation Expense—Office Equipment
7115 Depreciation Expense—Store Equipment
7120 Insurance Expense
7125 Miscellaneous Expense
7130 Payroll Taxes Expense—Administrative
7135 Phone Expense
7140 Rent Expense
7145 Salary Expense—Administrative
7150 Supplies Expense
7155 Uncollectible Accounts Expense
7160 Utilities Expense

(8000) INCOME TAX
8105 Federal Income Tax Expense

The chart of accounts for Whiley Outdoor Living, Inc., is illustrated above for ready reference as you study Part 1 of this textbook.

1 Recording Departmental Purchases and Cash Payments

LEARNING OBJECTIVES

After studying Chapter 1, in addition to defining key terms, you will be able to:

LO1 Explain how reporting information by department impacts accounting procedures.

LO2 Describe the relationship between assets, liabilities, and owners' equity in the accounting equation.

LO3 Describe the function and design of accounting records used by a business.

LO4 Explain the relationship between a subsidiary ledger and a controlling account.

LO5 Explain the purpose and process of recording purchases and purchase returns in a departmental accounting system.

LO6 Journalize departmental purchases of merchandise on account using a purchases journal.

LO7 Post merchandise purchases to an accounts payable ledger and a general ledger.

LO8 Journalize departmental purchases returns and allowances.

LO9 Journalize departmental cash payments using a cash payments journal.

LO10 Post cash payments to an accounts payable ledger and a general ledger.

© BLACKAKALIKO/SHUTTERSTOCK.COM

The Kroger Co.

What qualities are the hallmark of an innovative company? Being the first to introduce a new process or product? Expanding into new markets? Applying technology to solve problems and create new opportunities?

If you ask a group of people to identify some innovative companies, their list likely would include companies in technology, medicine, energy, and entertainment. But would their list include a grocery store? Probably not, but it should. Today's grocery stores differ dramatically from stores that consumers experienced over a century ago. The history of The Kroger Co. illustrates how innovation has shaped the grocery industry.

When Barney Kroger opened his first grocery store in 1883, he followed common industry practices of the time. Kroger's store did not sell meat; instead, customers shopped at a local butcher. Kroger purchased bread and produce from local bakeries and farms.

Driven to increase profits, Kroger began to innovate. His store became the first grocery in the country to bake its own bread. He purchased cabbage and enlisted his mother to make sauerkraut, a local favorite. Encouraged by this success, Kroger continued to expand the offering of "private-label" items produced in company-owned manufacturing facilities.

Kroger has continually expanded its product offerings to satisfy customer demands. A typical Kroger store now more closely resembles a shopping mall, offering departments such as floral, deli, cheese shop, pharmacy, and organic foods, just to name a few. Many Kroger stores also include a fuel station in the parking lot.

Because the Kroger Company sells so many products, reporting sales on its financial statements can be complicated. Financial information provided on Kroger's annual report to stockholders lists sales in five categories: perishable, non perishable, fuel, pharmacy, and other.

Source: www.kroger.com.

CRITICAL THINKING

1. The manager of a local Kroger store needs more detailed financial information than is reported to the stockholders: What products are selling well? What products are not meeting sales targets? Yet the manager cannot absorb a report containing too much detailed information. How would you suggest further dividing sales in the non perishable category?

2. Kroger has entered the meal kit market, offering customers a collection of perfectly proportioned ingredients and recipes for cooking a complete gourmet meal. Would you recommend that the sales and expenses of these products be reported as a separate category?

KEY TERMS

asset
liability
equities
owners' equity
stockholders' equity
accounting equation
source documents

double-entry accounting
journal
special journal
account
ledger
general ledger
subsidiary ledger

controlling account
file maintenance
departmental accounting
 system
merchandising business
posting
debit memorandum

contra account
cash discount
purchases discount
petty cash

Using Accounting Principles and Records

LO1 Explain how reporting information by department impacts accounting procedures.
LO2 Describe the relationship between assets, liabilities, and owners' equity in the accounting equation.
LO3 Describe the function and design of accounting records used by a business.
LO4 Explain the relationship between a subsidiary ledger and a controlling account.

Financial Reporting for Departments LO1

Financial information for a business can be recorded, summarized, and reported in a variety of ways. Accountants design accounting systems to meet the specific needs of the business. The way in which information is kept and reported in the accounting system is determined by the size, type, and complexity of the business. When designing financial records, the business should also consider the types of decisions that will be made, based on the financial statements.

If managers of individual departments want to use financial statements to assist in making decisions, information for each department must be recorded separately.

The types of information to be gathered by department include purchases, sales, and expenses. Payroll data may also be identified by department. Gathering information by department requires a somewhat different set of accounting procedures. Regardless of the accounting procedures used, the same accounting concepts and practices are followed.

If a business decides to record information by department, it must establish procedures to ensure that transactions are assigned to the correct department. The chart of accounts must contain departmental accounts for significant types of transactions, such as purchases, sales, and salary expense.

ETHICS IN ACTION

Researching Codes of Conduct

The Sarbanes-Oxley Act of 2002 requires publicly traded companies to have a code of conduct. Most companies make their codes available on the Internet. Companies title and link their codes differently. Accessing these codes on the Internet requires knowledge of common search terms and methods.

Begin your Internet search by visually scanning the available links on the company's home page. *Code of Conduct, Code of Ethics*, and *Corporate Governance* are common links. A company whose website is designed primarily to sell its product is

unlikely to have an ethics-related link on its home page. In this case, look at the top or bottom of the web page and find a link such as *Investor Relations*.

Most companies provide a search tool. Use the search tool to search for any of these terms: *ethics, code of conduct, code of ethics*, and *corporate governance*.

INSTRUCTIONS

Access the code of conduct for three publicly traded companies. Prepare a summary of the links and searches you used to access the code for each company.

Accounting Equation LO2

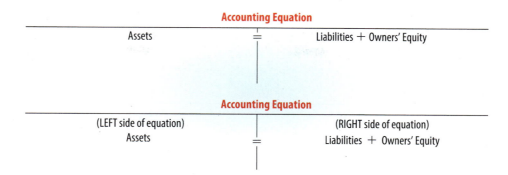

Accounting Equation

| Assets | = | Liabilities + Owners' Equity |

Accounting Equation

| (LEFT side of equation) Assets | = | (RIGHT side of equation) Liabilities + Owners' Equity |

Anything of value that is owned is called an **asset**. An amount owed by a business is called a **liability**. Financial rights to the assets of a business are called **equities**. The amount remaining after the value of all liabilities is subtracted from the value of all assets is called **owners' equity**. The owners' equity in a corporation is called **stockholders' equity**.

An equation showing the relationship among assets, liabilities, and owners' equity is called the **accounting equation**. The accounting equation may be stated as assets = equities. More commonly, the equation is stated as assets = liabilities + owners' equity.

The equation is often viewed as forming a "T." In the figure above, assets are listed on the left side of the T account and equities (liabilities and owners' equity) on the right side of the T account. Total assets must always equal total liabilities plus owners' equity.

Accounting Records LO3

Accounting records show changes and the current account balance of each asset, liability, and owners' equity (or stockholders' equity) account. Business transactions are reported in numbers that have common values—that is, using a common unit of measurement. If part of the information in the accounting records is financial and part is nonfinancial, the financial statements will not be clear. In the United States, the amounts are stated in dollars and cents. **>> App A: Unit of Measurement**

Accounting concepts are described throughout this textbook. When an application of a concept first occurs, it is explained. When additional applications occur, a concept reference, such as **>> App A: Business Entity**, is used to indicate an application of a specific accounting concept. A brief description of each accounting concept used in this text is also provided in Appendix A.

Source Documents

Business papers from which information is obtained for a journal entry are called **source documents**. Each journal entry must be supported by a source document proving that a transaction occurred. **>> App A: Objective Evidence** The source document is the original business paper indicating that the transaction did occur and that the amounts recorded in the accounting records are accurate and true. When accounting information reported on the financial statements needs to be verified, an accountant will first check the accounting record. If the details of an entry need further checking, an accountant will then check the source documents as objective evidence that the transaction did occur.

FYI The government's first regulation of accounting information occurred in 1917 with the Federal Reserve Board's publication of "Uniform Accounts."

General Journal

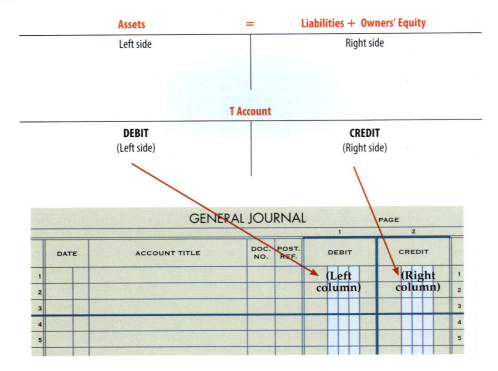

The recording of debit and credit parts of a transaction is called **double-entry accounting**. With every transaction, at least two accounts will change. Two accounting principles are common to double-entry accounting: (1) The total value of things owned by a business (assets) equals the total value of claims of outsiders (liabilities) and claims of owners (owners' equity). (2) Debits equal credits for each business transaction recorded.

A form for recording transactions in chronological order is called a **journal**. A general journal may be used to record all business transactions. A general journal includes amount columns for recording the dollars and cents of a transaction. **>>** App A: Unit of Measurement The general journal has two amount columns. The left amount column is labeled *Debit*. The right amount column is labeled *Credit*. An entry recorded in the debit column is known as a *debit*. Likewise, an entry recorded in the credit column is known as a *credit*. The "T" previously described in the accounting equation is also present in a general journal's debit and credit amount columns.

A journal used to record only one kind of transaction is called a **special journal**. A business with many daily transactions may use special journals. Special journals include amount columns used to record debits or credits to specific accounts. For example, a cash payments journal includes a Cash Credit amount column. Whiley uses four special journals along with a general journal to record its transactions:

1. Purchases journal—for all purchases of merchandise on account
2. Cash payments journal—for all cash payments
3. Sales journal—for all sales of merchandise on account
4. Cash receipts journal—for all cash receipts

Whiley uses a general journal to record all transactions that are not recorded in a special journal.

Remember Total assets must always equal total liabilities plus total owners' equity.

General Ledger Accounts

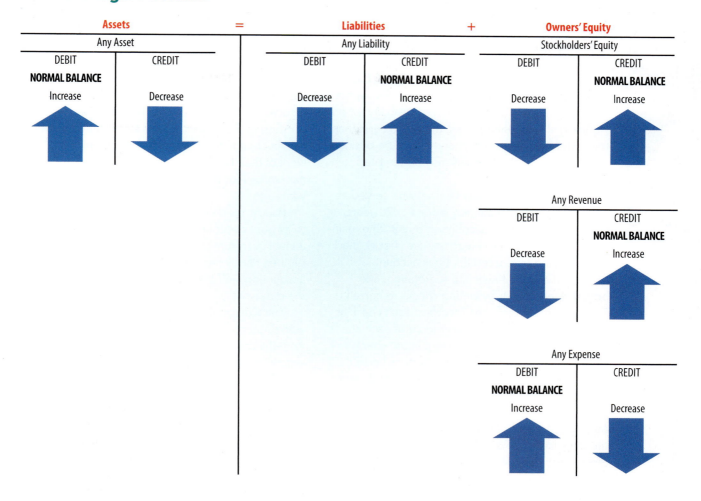

Transactions are journalized in chronological order. Periodically, information is sorted to summarize like kinds of information. A record that summarizes all the transactions pertaining to a single item in the accounting equation is called an **account**.

The amount in an account is known as an *account balance*. Each business transaction causes a change in two or more account balances. Increases in an account balance are recorded in the same column as its normal balance. Decreases in an account balance are recorded in the column opposite its normal balance. The normal balances of different classifications of accounts are shown in the figure above.

Asset account balances are increased by debits and decreased by credits. Liability and owners' equity account balances as well as revenue account balances are increased by credits and decreased by debits. Expense account balances are increased by debits and decreased by credits.

Remember Increases in revenue accounts increase owners' equity. Therefore, the normal credit balance of revenue accounts is the same as the normal balance of owners' equity. Increases in expense accounts decrease owners' equity. Therefore, the normal debit balance of expense accounts is opposite the normal balance of revenues or owners' equity.

Embezzlement Made Easy

The danger is all too common in small businesses. A small business requires the services of a single bookkeeper. With responsibility for performing all accounting tasks, the bookkeeper has opportunity to embezzle money from the business. Over time, some individuals may be tempted to engage in such fraud.

So was the case of Kay Lemon, who served as the bookkeeper of a lighting store. For 20 years, she performed all the accounting duties. She maintained the accounting records, wrote checks, made deposits, and reconciled the bank account.

After 12 years, Kay fell to temptation. She began stealing cash by writing checks to herself. To cover up her theft, she recorded each check as voided. She then added the amount of each check to the amount recorded for a legitimate check. For example, if she wrote a $5,000 check to herself and a $15,000 check to a vendor, she would record a $20,000 disbursement to the vendor. When the bank statement arrived, she simply disposed of her $5,000 check. No one besides Kay ever looked at the bank statements or bank reconciliations. Nor did the business ever count its inventory, an activity that would have revealed a large overstatement in its recorded value.

How was her theft discovered? For eight years, Kay lived under the pressure of her crime. Finally, she voluntarily confessed to embezzling $416,000 and served three years in prison.

ACTIVITY

Randy Selman and Paul Deeds own R&P Sporting Goods. Randy is in charge of merchandise purchasing. Paul operates the store. Neither owner has much time for or interest in monitoring the work of their bookkeeper, Carol Hainsworth. Carol has worked for the business since it began ten years ago.

Randy has delivered R&P's accounting records to its public accounting firm for preparation of its annual tax returns. At the suggestion of the firm's partner, Randy has agreed to let the firm's forensic accounting staff perform a few basic tests on the data.

The workbook contains two worksheets. One worksheet contains a list of all checks obtained from the computerized accounting system. The second worksheet is a list of all bank transactions downloaded from R&P's online banking system.

INSTRUCTIONS

Open the spreadsheet FA_CH01 and complete the steps on the Instructions tab. Use the spreadsheet to answer the following questions:

1. How many checks cleared the bank but were not recorded in R&P's accounting records?

2. What trends do you detect in the list?

Source: "Enemies Within," Joseph T. Wells, Journal of Accountancy, December 2001.

General and Subsidiary Ledgers LO4

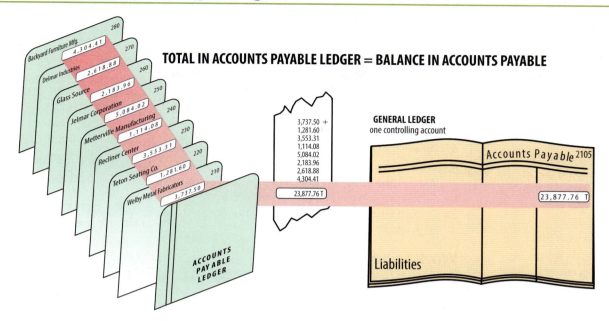

TOTAL IN ACCOUNTS PAYABLE LEDGER = BALANCE IN ACCOUNTS PAYABLE

A group of accounts is called a **ledger**. A ledger that contains all accounts needed to prepare financial statements is called a **general ledger**. A ledger that is summarized in a single general ledger account is called a **subsidiary ledger**. An account in a general ledger that summarizes all accounts in a subsidiary ledger is called a **controlling account**.

Two subsidiary ledgers and two general ledger controlling accounts are commonly used:

> **Subsidiary Ledgers**
> Accounts Receivable Ledger
> Accounts Payable Ledger
> **Controlling Accounts**
> Accounts Receivable
> Accounts Payable

Accounts for customers who buy merchandise on account are kept in an accounts receivable ledger. The corresponding controlling account is Accounts Receivable. Separate accounts are kept in an accounts payable ledger for vendors to whom money is owed. The corresponding controlling account is Accounts Payable. The total of the subsidiary ledger account balances should equal the balance of the controlling account.

General and Subsidiary Ledger File Maintenance

Whiley uses a general ledger account numbering system that meets three needs: (1) A separate numeric listing is provided for each ledger division. (2) A predesigned arrangement of numbers is provided within each ledger division. (3) Account number digits are spaced to allow the addition of new accounts. The procedure for arranging accounts in a general ledger, assigning account numbers, and keeping records current is called **file maintenance**.

The number assigned to Merchandise Inventory— Grills is analyzed above. Whiley's general ledger chart of accounts has eight divisions. The first digit of each four-digit account number shows the general ledger division in which the account is located. For example, asset accounts begin with the number 1.

The accounts in some divisions, such as Assets, are divided into categories. The second digit of the account number shows the category in which the account is located. Whiley assigns the number 3 to all inventory accounts. The categories are not necessarily labeled in the chart of accounts. However, an analysis of the accounts in a category should reveal the nature of a category. For example, all liability accounts in category 2 are related to payroll taxes and withholdings.

The last two digits show the location of a specific account with respect to other accounts in that division and category.

LO1 Explain how reporting information by department impacts accounting procedures.

LO2 Describe the relationship between assets, liabilities, and owners' equity in the accounting equation.

LO3 Describe the function and design of accounting records used by a business.

LO4 Explain the relationship between a subsidiary ledger and a controlling account.

TERMS REVIEW

asset

liability

equities

owners' equity

stockholders' equity

accounting equation

source documents

double-entry accounting

journal

special journal

account

ledger

general ledger

subsidiary ledger

controlling account

file maintenance

Audit your understanding LO1, 2, 3, 4

1. How does recording information by department impact the chart of accounts?
2. How is the accounting equation most commonly stated?
3. Describe how transaction amounts are recorded in a general journal.
4. Describe the function of a journal.
5. When is a transaction recorded in a special journal?
6. What is the normal balance of an asset account? A revenue account?
7. What is the relationship between an accounts payable subsidiary ledger and the Accounts Payable general ledger account?
8. What division of the Whiley's chart of accounts relates to Revenue and Direct Expenses?

Work together 1-1 LO3

Determining the normal balance, increase, and decrease sides for accounts Write the answers to the following problems in the *Working Papers*. Your instructor will guide you through the following examples.

Sales	Supplies
Prepaid Insurance	Trent Associates (an account receivable)
Pacific Supply (an account payable)	Capital Stock
Advertising Expense	Petty Cash

For each of the accounts above, complete the following.

1. Prepare a T account for each account. Enter the title of the account.
2. In parentheses to the right of the account title, identify the account as asset, liability, owners' equity, revenue, or expense.
3. Label the debit and credit sides.
4. Label each side of the T account using the labels *Normal Balance*, *Increase*, or *Decrease*.

On your own 1-1 LO3

Determining the normal balance, increase, and decrease sides for accounts Write the answers to the following problems in the *Working Papers*. Work this problem independently.

Rent Expense	Equipment
Utilities Expense	Mount Air Co. (an account receivable)
Sales	Pace Corp. (an account payable)
Cash	Retained Earnings

For each of the accounts above, complete the following.

1. Prepare a T account for each account. Enter the title of the account.
2. In parentheses to the right of the account title, identify the account as asset, liability, owners' equity, revenue, or expense.
3. Label the debit and credit sides.
4. Label each side of the T account using the labels *Normal Balance*, *Increase*, or *Decrease*.

Journalizing and Posting Purchases and Purchases Returns

LO5 Explain the purpose and process of recording purchases and purchase returns in a departmental accounting system.

LO6 Journalize departmental purchases of merchandise on account using a purchases journal.

LO7 Post merchandise purchases to an accounts payable ledger and a general ledger.

LO8 Journalize departmental purchases returns and allowances.

Departmental Accounting System LO5

Management decisions depend on accounting information about each phase of a business. When a business has two or more departments, accounting information can help management decide whether a department's performance is acceptable or unacceptable. Accounting information can also determine the kinds of merchandise that produce the greatest or the least profit.

An accounting system showing accounting information for two or more departments is called a **departmental accounting system**. In a departmental accounting system, gross profit is calculated for each department. The general ledger, therefore, must include a number of separate departmental accounts. Shoe stores, furniture stores, computer stores, department stores, and sporting goods stores are examples of firms that commonly organize on a departmental basis.

A business that purchases and sells goods is called a **merchandising business**. Whiley sells grills and outdoor furniture. The business is a corporation organized on a departmental basis.

Whiley uses a departmental accounting system. Accounting information is recorded and reported for two departments: (1) Grills and (2) Furniture. The separate departmental accounts for Whiley are in the chart of accounts at the beginning of Part 1. All accounts for the grills department include "Grills" in the account title. All accounts for the outdoor furniture department include "Furniture" in the account title. For example, the grills department's inventory account is titled Merchandise Inventory—Grills and is assigned number 1305. The first digit, 1, indicates that the account is an asset. The second digit, 3, shows the account is in the third category (inventory accounts) of the asset division. The last two digits, 05, show the location of the account with respect to the other accounts in the inventory account category.

All departmental purchases of merchandise on account are recorded in a purchases journal. A business with more than one department records a purchase on account in the same way as a business with a single department, except for two differences: (1) Each purchase invoice has a notation placed on it showing to which department the purchase applies. (2) Each department has a separate Purchases Debit column in the purchases journal. Whiley's purchases journal, shown on the next page, has special Purchases Debit columns for each department—Grills and Furniture. Purchase invoices are used as the source documents for all purchases on account. **>> App A: Objective Evidence**

FYI CPAs help small businesses avoid many of the pitfalls of doing business. Business owners rely on CPAs for advice in such areas as taxation, payroll requirements, banking policies, and business planning.

Journalizing Purchases on Account LO6

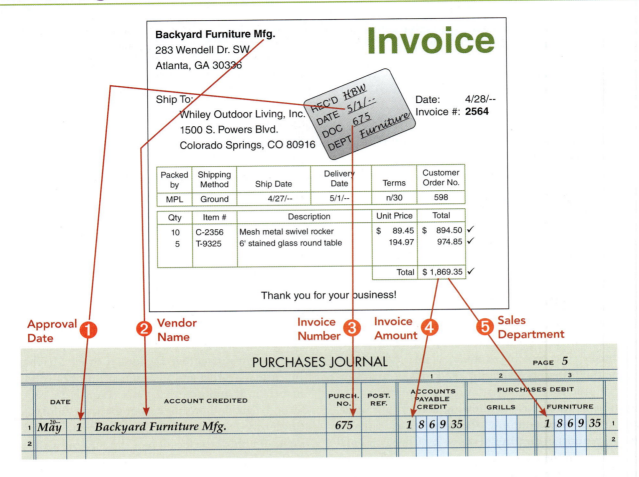

Backyard Furniture Mfg.
283 Wendell Dr. SW
Atlanta, GA 30336

Invoice

Ship To:
Whiley Outdoor Living, Inc.
1500 S. Powers Blvd.
Colorado Springs, CO 80916

REC'D *HBW*
DATE *5/1/--*
DOC *675*
DEPT *Furniture*

Date: 4/28/--
Invoice #: **2564**

Packed by	Shipping Method	Ship Date	Delivery Date	Terms	Customer Order No.
MPL	Ground	4/27/--	5/1/--	n/30	598

Qty	Item #	Description	Unit Price	Total	
10	C-2356	Mesh metal swivel rocker	$ 89.45	$ 894.50	✓
5	T-9325	6' stained glass round table	194.97	974.85	✓
			Total	$ 1,869.35	✓

Thank you for your business!

① Approval Date **②** Vendor Name **③** Invoice Number **④** Invoice Amount **⑤** Sales Department

PURCHASES JOURNAL   PAGE 5

	DATE		ACCOUNT CREDITED	PURCH. NO.	POST. REF.	ACCOUNTS PAYABLE CREDIT (1)	PURCHASES DEBIT GRILLS (2)	PURCHASES DEBIT FURNITURE (3)	
1	May 20--	1	*Backyard Furniture Mfg.*	675		1 8 6 9 35		1 8 6 9 35	1
2									2

GENERAL LEDGER
Purchases—Furniture

⬆ 1,869.35 |

Accounts Payable

| ⬆ 1,869.35

ACCOUNTS PAYABLE LEDGER
Backyard Furniture Mfg.

| ⬆ 1,869.35

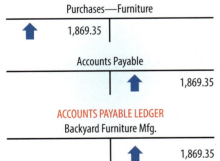

May 1. Purchased furniture on account from Backyard Furniture Mfg., $1,869.35. Purchase Invoice No. 675.

When a purchase invoice is received, an employee verifies the accuracy of the invoice. A stamp may be used to provide a place to enter his or her initials, the date the invoice is received, the purchase invoice number assigned, and the department.

≫ Journalizing a Purchase on Account

① Write the date the invoice was received and approved, **May 1**, in the Date column. Since this is the first entry on page 5, include the current year, **20--**.

② Enter the vendor name, **Backyard Furniture Mfg.**, in the Account Credited column.

③ Record the invoice number, **675**, in the Purch. No. column. Since only purchase invoice numbers are recorded in this column, no identifying letter is necessary.

④ Write the credit amount, **$1,869.35**, in the Accounts Payable Credit column.

⑤ Record the debit amount, **$1,869.35**, in the Purchases Debit Furniture column.

Posting from a Purchases Journal LO7

Whiley keeps vendor accounts in an accounts payable ledger. Transactions recorded in the purchases journal are posted individually to vendor accounts in the accounts payable ledger and in total to the general ledger.

Posting from a Purchases Journal to the Accounts Payable Ledger

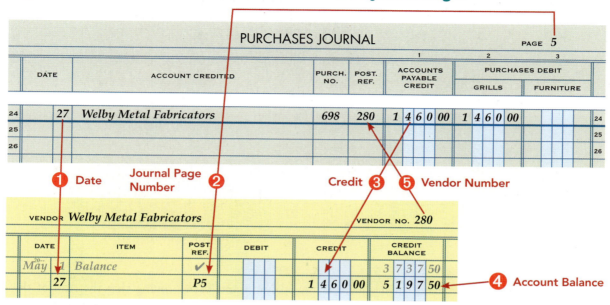

Transferring transaction information from a journal entry to a ledger account is called **posting**. Whiley keeps vendor accounts in an accounts payable ledger. Individual amounts in the Accounts Payable Credit column of the purchases journal are posted when the transaction is entered in the journal. Frequent posting helps ensure that vendor accounts are paid on time. By maintaining a reputation for paying its accounts on time, Whiley is able to continue purchasing goods and services on account.

The purchases journal is abbreviated as *P* in the Post. Ref. column of the ledger accounts. Posting from the Accounts Payable Credit column of the purchases journal to a ledger account is shown above.

>> Posting from the Purchases Journal to the Accounts Payable Ledger

❶ Write the date of the transaction, **27**, in the Date column of the ledger account.

❷ Enter the purchases journal page number, **P5**, in the Post. Ref. column of the ledger account.

❸ Record the credit amount, **$1,460.00**, in the Credit column of the account for Welby Metal Fabricators. All postings from the purchases journal to the ledger accounts will be to the Credit amount column of the ledger.

❹ Add the amount in the Credit amount column to the previous balance in the Credit Balance column. Write the new account balance, **$5,197.50**, in the Credit Balance column.

❺ Record the vendor number, **280**, in the Post. Ref. column of the journal. The vendor number shows that the posting for this entry is complete.

Remember
The number recorded on the invoice, *675*, is the unique number Whiley assigned to this invoice. This number should not be confused with the invoice number, *2564*, assigned by the vendor. Each vendor uses a different numbering system. Therefore, vendor invoice numbers would not be recorded in sequence.

Posting the Totals of a Purchases Journal to the General Ledger

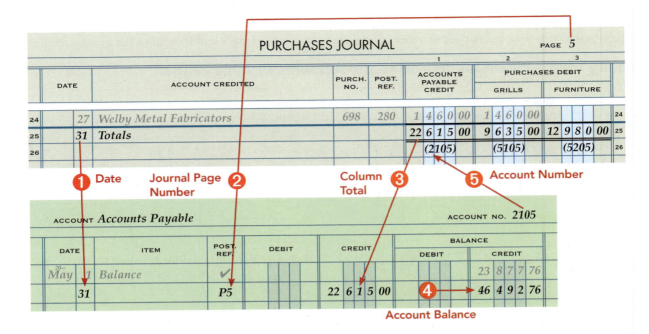

PURCHASES JOURNAL   PAGE 5

	DATE	ACCOUNT CREDITED	PURCH. NO.	POST. REF.	ACCOUNTS PAYABLE CREDIT (1)	PURCHASES DEBIT GRILLS (2)	PURCHASES DEBIT FURNITURE (3)	
24	27 Welby Metal Fabricators		698	280	1 4 6 0 00	1 4 6 0 00		24
25	31 Totals				22 6 1 5 00	9 6 3 5 00	12 9 8 0 00	25
26					(2105)	(5105)	(5205)	26

① Date   **Journal Page Number**   **②**   **Column Total**   **③**   **⑤**   **Account Number**

ACCOUNT **Accounts Payable**   ACCOUNT NO. **2105**

DATE	ITEM	POST. REF.	DEBIT	CREDIT	BALANCE DEBIT	BALANCE CREDIT
20-- May 1	Balance	✔				23 8 7 7 76
31		P5		22 6 1 5 00		46 4 9 2 76

④ →   **Account Balance**

The purchases journal is proved and ruled whenever a journal page is filled, and always at the end of each month. A purchases journal is proved by adding each column and then proving that the sum of the debit column totals equals the credit column totals, as shown below.

Credit Column Totals	Debit Column Totals	Credit Column Totals
Accounts Payable Credit		$22,615.00
Purchases Debit—Grills	$ 9,635.00	
Purchases Debit—Furniture	12,980.00	
Totals	$22,615.00	$22,615.00

Double lines are then ruled across the amount columns to show that the totals have been verified as correct. Each amount column total is posted to the general ledger account named in the column heading. The posting of the purchases journal's Accounts Payable Credit column total to the **Accounts Payable** account in the general ledger is shown above. The same procedure is used to post the totals of the Purchases Debit—Grills and the Purchases Debit—Furniture columns.

FYI

Every special journal is proved by comparing the totals of the debit and credit columns. After any errors are corrected, a double line is drawn to indicate the journal has been proved.

>> **Posting the Total of the Accounts Payable Column to the General Ledger**

❶ Write the date, **31**, in the Date column of the account.

❷ Write the purchases journal page number, **P5**, in the Post. Ref. column of the account.

❸ Write the Accounts Payable Credit column total, **$22,615.00**, in the Credit amount column of the Accounts Payable account.

❹ Calculate and record the new account balance, **$46,492.76**, in the Balance Credit column.

❺ Write the general ledger account number, **2105**, in parentheses below the column total in the purchases journal.

Journalizing Purchases Returns and Allowances LO8

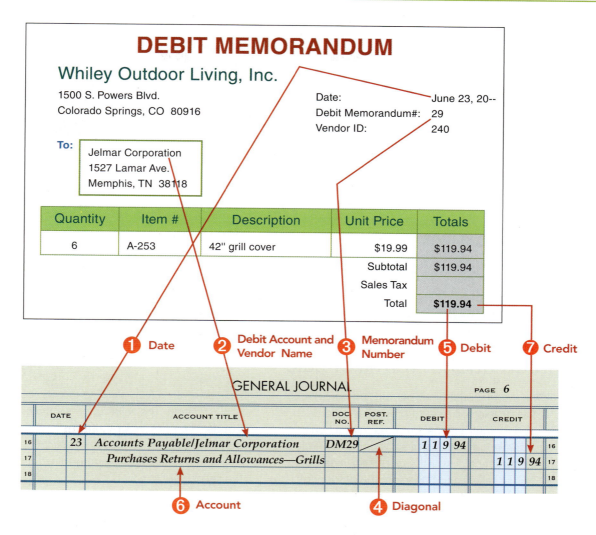

DEBIT MEMORANDUM

Whiley Outdoor Living, Inc.

1500 S. Powers Blvd.
Colorado Springs, CO 80916

Date: June 23, 20--
Debit Memorandum#: 29
Vendor ID: 240

To:
Jelmar Corporation
1527 Lamar Ave.
Memphis, TN 38118

Quantity	Item #	Description	Unit Price	Totals
6	A-253	42" grill cover	$19.99	$119.94
			Subtotal	$119.94
			Sales Tax	
			Total	**$119.94**

1 Date **2** Debit Account and Vendor Name **3** Memorandum Number **5** Debit **7** Credit

GENERAL JOURNAL PAGE **6**

DATE	ACCOUNT TITLE	DOC. NO.	POST. REF.	DEBIT	CREDIT	
16	23	*Accounts Payable/Jelmar Corporation*	DM29	/	1 1 9 94		16
17		*Purchases Returns and Allowances—Grills*				1 1 9 94	17
18							18

6 Account **4** Diagonal

When merchandise is returned to a vendor, the vendor's account and Accounts Payable are reduced by a debit. An allowance may also be given for merchandise that is not returned. A form prepared by the customer showing the price deduction taken by the customer for a return or an allowance is called a **debit memorandum**. The transaction illustrated above is described on the following page.

>> Journalizing a Purchases Return

1 Write the date, **23**, in the Date column of the general journal.

2 Write the titles of the accounts to be debited, **Accounts Payable/Jelmar Corporation**, in the Account Title column.

3 Record the debit memorandum number, **DM29**, in the Doc. No. column.

4 Draw a diagonal line in the Post. Ref. column to indicate that the single debit amount is posted to two accounts.

5 Write the debit amount, **$119.94**, in the Debit column.

6 Indent and write the title of the account to be credited, **Purchases Returns and Allowances—Grills**, in the Account Title column.

7 Record the credit amount, **$119.94**, in the Credit column.

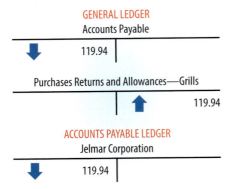

GENERAL LEDGER

Accounts Payable

⬇ 119.94	

Purchases Returns and Allowances—Grills

	⬆ 119.94

ACCOUNTS PAYABLE LEDGER

Jelmar Corporation

⬇ 119.94	

An account that reduces a related account on a financial statement is called a **contra account**. The purchases returns and allowances accounts are contra accounts to the purchases accounts.

In the general ledger, Accounts Payable decreases by a $119.94 debit. Purchases Returns and Allowances—Grills increases by a $119.94 credit. In the accounts payable ledger, Jelmar Corporation decreases by a $119.94 credit.

Whiley documents all purchases returns and allowances with a debit memorandum and records the transaction in a general journal.

> June 23. Returned six grill covers to Jelmar Corporation, $119.94. Debit Memorandum No. 29.

GLOBAL AWARENESS

International Terms of Sale

The International Chamber of Commerce (ICC) has developed a set of pre-defined words to be used for international business transactions. These terms are referred to as "Incoterms® Rules." The terms define clearly the responsibilities, costs, and risks of sellers and buyers for the delivery of goods under international sales contracts.

The ICC has updated regularly the first set of terms, established in 1936. The most recent set of terms is Incoterms® 2010, which went into effect January 1, 2011. New terms were under review when this book was published. They are expected to be introduced in 2020. Selected terms include:

CIF (Cost, Insurance, and Freight) to the named port of destination. The seller quotes a price for the goods. The price includes insurance, all transportation, and all miscellaneous charges to bring the goods to the port of destination. Once in port, all costs are the responsibility of the buyer.

DDP (Delivered Duty Paid) to the named place of destination. The seller quotes a price for the goods. The price includes all costs to bring the goods all the way to the final destination. This term places maximum responsibility for costs on the seller.

EXW (Ex Works) to the named place of delivery. This is the opposite of DDP. In EXW, the buyer is responsible for all costs from the named place of delivery, which is usually the seller's factory or warehouse.

CRITICAL THINKING

Other Incoterms® are FCA, CFR, and FAS. Use the Internet to find the rules for these terms. Write a brief summary of the rule for each term.

Source: www.iccwbo.org.

LO5 Explain the purpose and process of recording purchases and purchase returns in a departmental accounting system.

LO6 Journalize departmental purchases of merchandise on account using a purchases journal.

LO7 Post merchandise purchases to an accounts payable ledger and a general ledger.

LO8 Journalize departmental purchases returns and allowances.

TERMS REVIEW

departmental accounting system

merchandising business

posting

debit memorandum

contra account

Audit your understanding LO5, 6, 8

1. Why should a business consider using a departmental accounting system?
2. When Whiley's grills department purchases merchandise on account, which general ledger accounts are affected, and how?
3. Which general ledger accounts are affected, and how, by a return of furniture department merchandise?

Work together 1-2 LO6, 7, 8

Journalizing and posting purchases on account and purchases returns and allowances Electronic Warehouse has two departments: Audio and Video. A purchases journal, general journal, and partial general and accounts payable ledgers are provided in the *Working Papers*. Source documents are abbreviated as follows: debit memorandum, DM; purchase invoice, P. Your instructor will guide you through the following examples.

1. Journalize the following transactions. Use page 6 of a purchases journal and page 6 of a general journal. Post the items that are to be posted individually.

   Transactions:

   June 3. Purchased audio equipment on account from Davis Corporation, $1,625.00. P243.
   5. Returned video equipment to TPC Supply, $42.50, from P239. DM38.
   8. Purchased video equipment on account from TPC Supply, $995.00. P244.
   12. Purchased audio equipment on account from National Industries, $1,100.00. P245.
   18. Received an allowance on audio equipment from National Industries, $165.80, from P245. DM39.
   23. Purchased audio equipment on account from Davis Corporation, $820.00. P246.

2. Prove and rule the purchases journal. Post the totals.

On your own 1-2 LO6, 7, 8

Journalizing and posting purchases on account and purchases returns and allowances Ashley's Fashions has two departments: Clothing and Shoes. A purchases journal, general journal, and partial general and accounts payable ledgers are provided in the *Working Papers*. Source documents are abbreviated as follows: debit memorandum, DM; purchase invoice, P. Work this problem independently.

1. Journalize the following transactions. Use page 7 of a purchases journal and page 7 of a general journal. Post the items that are to be posted individually.

   Transactions:

   July 2. Purchased clothing on account from Keller Corporation, $2,418.00. P366.
   7. Returned clothing to Keller Corporation, $185.90, from P366. DM45.
   9. Purchased clothing on account from Ackerman Supply, $1,680.00. P367.
   13. Received an allowance on shoes from Peters Company, $115.30, from P365. DM46.
   16. Purchased shoes on account from Peters Company, $1,150.00. P368.
   22. Purchased clothing on account from Keller Corporation, $925.00. P369.

2. Prove and rule the purchases journal. Post the totals.

LO9 Journalize departmental cash payments using a cash payments journal.

LO10 Post cash payments to an accounts payable ledger and a general ledger.

Departmental Cash Payments LO9

Most of Whiley's cash payments are made by check. Therefore, checks are the source documents for most cash payments. **>> App A: Objective Evidence** All cash payments are recorded in the cash payments journal.

Purchases on account are expected to be paid within the stated credit period. A vendor may encourage early payment by allowing a deduction from the invoice amount. A deduction that a vendor allows on the invoice amount to encourage prompt payment is called a **cash discount**. When a company that has purchased merchandise on account takes a cash discount, this is called a **purchases discount**.

A purchases discount is usually stated as a percentage. For example, the terms of an invoice may be written as 2/10, n/30. The expression 2/10 means that 2% of the invoice amount may be deducted from the amount due if payment is made within 10 days of the invoice date. The expression n/30 means that payment of the total invoice amount must be made within 30 days of the invoice date.

A purchases discount reduces the net amount of cash paid for a purchase. Purchases discounts are kept in separate accounts from the purchases accounts. This procedure helps the business see what proportion of purchases on account were allowed purchases discounts.

WHY ACCOUNTING?

Microcredit

Finance · CareerClusters®
PATHWAYS TO COLLEGE & CAREER READINESS

Have you ever pictured yourself as a banker? You could serve in the role of a bank loan manager—making microloans to people in poverty in the United States and throughout the world.

The idea of microloans began in Bangladesh in 1974 when Muhammad Yunus served as a banker to 42 women who needed the money to support a small business. Muhammad lent the women approximately $27 (U.S.) at a low interest rate.

There are opportunities to make loans to people for a variety of projects. Most organizations that handle such loans allow the donor to pick the project to be funded. As a donor, you would play the role of a banker and look at the financial status of the project to determine if it can make enough income to repay the loan.

Some organizations may charge a low rate of interest, while others charge no interest. When the donor is repaid, that donor can choose to get the funds back or to loan them to another entrepreneur.

Microloans are not without controversy. Some recent studies show that results are less than expected. Many of these small loans have not raised the entrepreneur out of poverty as hoped. In addition, some microloan organizations have been found to charge very high interest rates.

CRITICAL THINKING

Search the Internet for microcredit organizations. Investigate one organization and write a short report that answers the following questions:

1. Does the organization charge interest on the microloans or make interest-free loans?
2. What happens to the money when the loan is repaid?
3. What percentage of loans is actually repaid?

Sources: www.economist.com, www.givewell.org, www.washingtonpost.com.

Journalizing a Purchases Discount

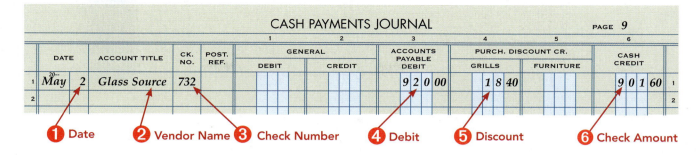

CASH PAYMENTS JOURNAL   PAGE **9**

| | | | | | GENERAL | | ACCOUNTS PAYABLE DEBIT | PURCH. DISCOUNT CR. | | CASH CREDIT | |
	DATE	ACCOUNT TITLE	CK. NO.	POST. REF.	DEBIT	CREDIT		GRILLS	FURNITURE		
1	May 2	Glass Source	732				9 20 00	1 8 40		9 01 60	1
2											2

❶ Date   **❷** Vendor Name   **❸** Check Number   **❹** Debit   **❺** Discount   **❻** Check Amount

GENERAL LEDGER
Accounts Payable
⬇ 920.00

Cash
⬇ 901.60

Purchases Discount—Grills
⬆ 18.40

ACCOUNTS PAYABLE LEDGER
Glass Source
⬇ 920.00

> **May 2. Paid cash on account to Glass Source, $901.60, covering Purchase Invoice No. 672 for $920.00, less 2% discount, $18.40. Check No. 732.**

The source document for this transaction is a check. ▶▶ App A: Objective Evidence

> ▶▶ **Journalizing a Cash Payment That Includes a Purchases Discount**

❶ Write the date, May 2, in the Date column.

❷ Enter the vendor name, Glass Source, in the Account Title column.

❸ Record the check number, 732, in the Ck. No. column.

❹ Write the debit amount, $920.00, in the Accounts Payable Debit column.

❺ Record the discount credit amount, $18.40, in the Purchases Discount Credit Grills column.

❻ Enter the check amount, $901.60, in the Cash Credit column.

Whiley's cash payments journal has two debit columns—General Debit and Accounts Payable Debit. The journal also has four credit columns—General Credit, a Purchases Discount Credit column for each of the two departments, and Cash Credit.

Taking a Discount After a Purchase Return

An additional calculation is necessary when a discount is taken after a purchase return or allowance has been granted. The discount is calculated on the amount owed at the time the invoice is paid. Therefore, the amount of the return or allowance must be deducted from the amount of the original purchase before the discount can be calculated.

Amount owned on invoice:

Original Purchase Invoice Amount (P670)	−	Purchases Return (DM28)	=	Purchase Invoice Amount After Return
$824.00	−	$182.00	=	$642.00

Purchases discount:

Purchase Invoice Amount After Return	×	Purchases Discount	=	Purchases Discount
$642.00	×	2%	=	$12.84

Amount due after purchases discount:

Purchase Invoice Amount After Return	−	Purchases Discount	=	Total Amount Due
$642.00	−	$12.84	=	$629.16

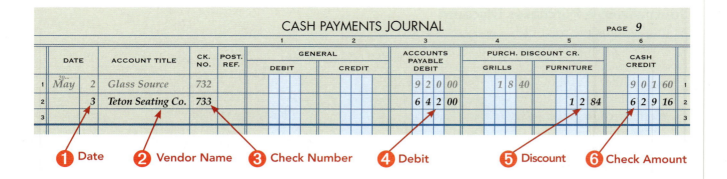

CASH PAYMENTS JOURNAL PAGE **9**

	DATE		ACCOUNT TITLE	CK. NO.	POST. REF.	GENERAL DEBIT	GENERAL CREDIT	ACCOUNTS PAYABLE DEBIT	PURCH. DISCOUNT CR. GRILLS	PURCH. DISCOUNT CR. FURNITURE	CASH CREDIT	
1	20-- May	2	Glass Source	732				9 2 0 00	1 8 40		9 0 1 60	1
2		3	Teton Seating Co.	733				6 4 2 00		1 2 84	6 2 9 16	2
3												3

❶ Date ❷ Vendor Name ❸ Check Number ❹ Debit ❺ Discount ❻ Check Amount

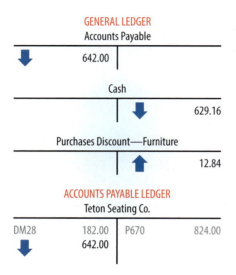

GENERAL LEDGER
Accounts Payable

⬇ 642.00 |

Cash

| 629.16 ⬇

Purchases Discount—Furniture

| 12.84 ⬆

ACCOUNTS PAYABLE LEDGER
Teton Seating Co.

DM28 182.00 | P670 824.00
⬇ 642.00 |

May 3. Paid cash on account to Teton Seating Co., $629.16, covering Purchase Invoice No. 670 for $824.00, less Debit Memorandum No. 28 for $182.00, and less 2% discount, $12.84. Check No. 733.

The source document for this transaction is a check. **>> App A: Objective Evidence** The total amount due for this purchase after the return and the discount is calculated as shown above on the previous page.

The T account for Teton Seating Co. shows the original purchase, $824.00, and the purchases return, $182.00. The two transactions result in a $642.00 outstanding account balance.

This transaction is journalized in the same way as a payment of cash when there is no purchases return or allowance. The only difference is the way in which the amounts are calculated.

>> Calculating a Discount After a Return or Allowance is Granted and Journalizing the Cash Payment

❶ Write the date, 3, in the Date column of the cash payments journal.

❷ Enter the vendor name, Teton Seating Co., in the Account Title column.

❸ Record the check number, 733, in the Ck. No. column.

❹ Write the debit amount, $642.00, in the Accounts Payable Debit column.

❺ Record the discount credit amount, $12.84, in the Purchases Discount Credit Furniture column.

❻ Enter the check amount, $629.16, in the Cash Credit column.

Purchases Discount and Purchases Returns and Allowances are both contra accounts to Purchases. The contra accounts are presented on the income statement, as shown below. Net purchases is determined by deducting the contra accounts from purchases.

Cost of Merchandise Sold:
 Merchandise Inventory, Jan. 1, 20-- . . . .
 Purchases. $154,865.35
 Less: Purchases Discount. $2,614.26
   Purchases Returns and Allowances. 5,148.95   7,763.21
 Net Purchases $147,102.14

Methods of Recording Cash Discounts

Whiley records the total of a purchase invoice in its purchases journal when the invoice is approved for payment. When the invoice is paid within the discount period, Whiley records a journal entry that includes a credit to Purchases Discount. This accounting procedure is referred to as the *gross price method* of recording purchasing invoices.

Some businesses elect to record the purchases discount when the purchase invoice is approved for payment. The amount recorded to Accounts Payable is the net of the invoice amount and the purchases discount. When the invoice is paid, the transaction debits Cash and credits Accounts Payable for the net amount. This accounting procedure is referred to as the *net price method* of recording purchasing invoices. The net price method can be an efficient accounting procedure for businesses that consistently take advantage of purchase discounts. The method also ensures that the purchases discount is recorded in the same accounting period as the purchase. However, purchase returns can make determining the final amount of the purchases discount more difficult.

THINK LIKE AN ACCOUNTANT

Analyzing Purchases Discounts

The accounting procedures manual of Rackley Corporation includes the following statement regarding purchases discounts:

"The corporation strives to obtain purchase discount agreements with its merchandise vendors. Accounting personnel are responsible for processing cash payments on a timely basis to take advantage of all purchase discounts offered by merchandise vendors. Exceptions to this policy should be approved by an appropriate level of management."

Cheryl Rosario, an internal auditor for Rackley Corporation, is performing a review of the purchasing processes of the company. It's not unusual for Cheryl to notice a couple of instances where purchases discounts were not taken. After all, mistakes do occur. But on this review, she notices more than the typical number of lost discounts.

Cheryl's audit manager directs her to perform a more in-depth analysis of cash payments. Before talking with accounting personnel, she decides to quantify the extent of purchase discounts lost during the current fiscal year.

OPEN THE SPREADSHEET TLA_CH01

The worksheet contains a list of cash payments for merchandise. The list includes the purchase discount percent offered by the vendor, if any, and the amount of discount taken. Follow the steps on the Instructions tab to analyze the cash payments and discounts lost. Use the analysis to answer the following questions:

1. What is the number of discounts taken?
2. What is the average, maximum, and total amount of discounts taken?
3. What is the number of discounts lost?
4. What is the average, maximum, and total amount of discounts lost?
5. Does the information collected suggest any reason for the unusually high number of discounts lost? Support your answer.

Recording Entries in a Cash Payments Journal

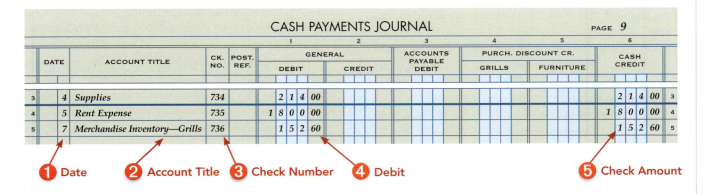

	DATE	ACCOUNT TITLE	CK. NO.	POST. REF.	GENERAL DEBIT	GENERAL CREDIT	ACCOUNTS PAYABLE DEBIT	PURCH. DISCOUNT CR. GRILLS	PURCH. DISCOUNT CR. FURNITURE	CASH CREDIT	
					1	2	3	4	5	6	
3	4	Supplies	734		2 1 4 00					2 1 4 00	3
4	5	Rent Expense	735		1 8 0 0 00					1 8 0 0 00	4
5	7	Merchandise Inventory—Grills	736		1 5 2 60					1 5 2 60	5

1 Date   **2** Account Title   **3** Check Number   **4** Debit   **5** Check Amount

---

May 4. Paid cash to Jenkins Co. for supplies, $214.00. Check No. 734.

>> Journalizing Buying Office Supplies for Cash

1 Write the date, **4**, in the Date column.

2 Enter the account title, **Supplies**, in the Account Title column.

3 Record the check number, **734**, in the Ck. No. column.

4 Write the debit amount, **$214.00**, in the General Debit column.

5 Record the credit amount, **$214.00**, in the Cash Credit column.

May 5. Paid cash to Rackley Properties for rent, $1,800.00. Check No. 735.

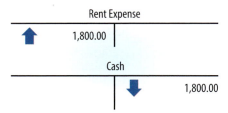

>> Journalizing the Cash Payment of an Expense

1 Write the date, **5**, in the Date column.

2 Enter the account title, **Rent Expense**, in the Account Title column.

3 Record the check number, **735**, in the Ck. No. column.

4 Write the debit amount, **$1,800.00**, in the General Debit column.

5 Record the credit amount, **$1,800.00**, in the Cash Credit column.

May 7. Paid cash to GH Patrick Industries for grill accessories, $152.60. Check No. 736.

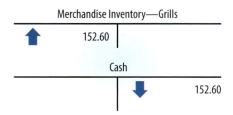

>> Journalizing the Cash Payment for Merchandise

1 Write the date, **7**, in the Date column.

2 Enter the account title, **Merchandise Inventory—Grills**, in the Account Title column.

3 Record the check number, **736**, in the Ck. No. column.

4 Write the debit amount, **$152.60**, in the General Debit column.

5 Record the credit amount, **$152.60**, in the Cash Credit column.

Cash Payment to Replenish Petty Cash

	DATE	ACCOUNT TITLE	CK. NO.	POST. REF.	GENERAL DEBIT	GENERAL CREDIT	ACCOUNTS PAYABLE DEBIT	PURCH. DISCOUNT CR. GRILLS	PURCH. DISCOUNT CR. FURNITURE	CASH CREDIT	
					1	**2**	**3**	**4**	**5**	**6**	
15	31	Supplies	742		3 5 75					1 2 0 70	15
16		Advertising Expense—Grills			5 0 00						16
17		Miscellaneous Expense			3 4 95						17

CASH PAYMENTS JOURNAL   PAGE **10**

❶ Date   ❷ Account Title   ❸ Check Number   ❹ Debit   ❺ Check Amount

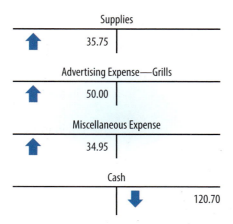

Supplies
⬆ 35.75

Advertising Expense—Grills
⬆ 50.00

Miscellaneous Expense
⬆ 34.95

Cash
⬇ 120.70

Business activities for an accounting period are summarized in financial statements. To adequately report how a business performed during an accounting period, all revenue earned as a result of business operations must be reported. Likewise, all expenses incurred in producing the revenue during the same accounting period must be reported. **>> App A: Matching Expenses with Revenue** The concept of matching expenses with revenue gives a true picture of business operations for an accounting period.

An amount of cash kept on hand and used for making small payments is called **petty cash**. Whiley's petty cash fund is $250.00. It replenishes petty cash whenever the fund drops below $100.00. In addition, the petty cash fund is replenished on the last business day of each fiscal period to ensure that all expenses are recorded during the fiscal period in which they occurred. **>> App A: Matching Expenses with Revenue**

> **May 31. Paid cash to replenish the petty cash fund, $120.70: supplies, $35.75; advertising expense—grills, $50.00; miscellaneous expense, $34.95. Check No. 742.**

To replenish petty cash, a check is written for the amount spent from the fund. The check is cashed and the money placed back in the fund.

>> Journalizing the Cash Payment to Replenish Petty Cash

❶ Write the date, **31**, in the Date column.

❷ Enter the account titles, **Supplies**, **Advertising Expense—Grills**, and **Miscellaneous Expense**, in the Account Title column.

❸ Record the check number, **742**, in the Ck. No. column on the first line of the entry.

❹ Write the debit amounts for the appropriate accounts, **$35.75**, **$50.00**, and **$34.95**, in the General Debit column.

❺ Record the check amount, **$120.70**, in the Cash Credit column on the first line of the entry.

Posting from a Cash Payments Journal LO10

CASH PAYMENTS JOURNAL

PAGE **10**

	DATE	ACCOUNT TITLE	CK. NO.	POST. REF.	GENERAL DEBIT (1)	GENERAL CREDIT (2)	ACCOUNTS PAYABLE DEBIT (3)	PURCH. DISCOUNT CR. GRILLS (4)	PURCH. DISCOUNT CR. FURNITURE (5)	CASH CREDIT (6)	
20	31	Delmar Industries	763	220			1 9 4 5 00	3 8 90		1 9 0 6 10	20
21	31	Purchases—Furniture	764	5205	6 8 7 00					6 8 7 00	21
22	31	Totals			8 1 9 4 42	1 6 4 4 20	28 4 9 1 52	1 2 4 68	3 0 4 84	34 6 1 2 22	22
23					(✔)	(✔)	(2105)	(5110)	(5120)	(1105)	23
24											24

2 Vendor Account   **1** Post to Vendor Account

VENDOR *Delmar Industries*   VENDOR NO. **220**

DATE	ITEM	POST. REF.	DEBIT	CREDIT	CREDIT BALANCE
May 22		P5		1 9 4 5 00	1 9 4 5 00
31		CP10	1 9 4 5 00		———

4 Account

Column Total **3**

ACCOUNT *Accounts Payable*   ACCOUNT NO. **2105**

DATE	ITEM	POST. REF.	DEBIT	CREDIT	BALANCE DEBIT	BALANCE CREDIT
31		P5		22 6 1 5 00		46 4 9 2 76
31		CP10	28 4 9 1 52			18 0 0 1 24

The accounting procedures for posting from a cash payments journal are the same as those followed for posting from the purchases journal. During the month, Whiley posts from the General Debit and General Credit columns to the general ledger when the transaction is entered in the journal. Whiley also posts from the Accounts Payable Debit column to the accounts payable ledger when the transaction is entered in the journal. This procedure permits Whiley to keep each vendor account balance in the accounts payable ledger up to date.

When the journal page is full or at the end of each month, the cash payments journal is proved and ruled. Totals of the special amount columns are posted to their respective accounts in the general ledger. The general ledger account number is written in parentheses immediately below the total. A check mark is recorded in parentheses below the totals of the General Debit and Credit columns to show that these totals are not posted.

Whiley's departmental cash payments journal is shown after all posting has been completed.

>> Posting from a Cash Payments Journal

1 Post individual amounts from the General Debit and General Credit columns to the appropriate accounts in the general ledger. Post individual vendor amounts from the Accounts Payable Debit column to the appropriate accounts in the accounts payable ledger. Do this when the transaction is journalized.

2 Record the account or vendor number in the Post. Ref. column of the journal. The number shows that the posting for this entry is complete. Do this when the transaction is journalized.

3 Post the total of each special amount column to the account named in the journal's column headings.

4 Write the account number in parentheses under the totals as a posting reference.

LO9 Journalize departmental cash payments using a cash payments journal.

LO10 Post cash payments to an accounts payable ledger and a general ledger.

TERMS REVIEW

cash discount

purchases discount

petty cash

Audit your understanding LO9, 10

1. Which general ledger accounts are affected, and how, by a cash payment on account for furniture that includes a purchases discount?
2. Where are cash payments affecting accounts that are not listed in the column headings recorded?
3. When are amounts recorded in the General Debit column posted to the accounts payable ledger?

Work together 1-3 LO9, 10

Journalizing and posting departmental cash payments Bass Craft Center has two departments: Crafts and Frames. Selected general ledger and accounts payable ledger accounts are provided in the *Working Papers*. Source documents are abbreviated as follows: check, C; debit memorandum, DM; and purchase invoice, P. Your instructor will guide you through the following examples.

1. Journalize the transactions completed during June of the current year. Use page 6 of a cash payments journal. Post the items that are to be posted individually.

   Transactions:

   June 3. Paid cash to Peterson Supply for a miscellaneous expense, $164.34. C345.
   5. Paid cash on account to Harris Industries for crafts purchased on P342, $2,141.00, less DM23 for $245.00, and less 2% discount. C346.
   12. Paid cash to Mason Office Source for supplies, $86.35. C347.
   18. Paid cash on account to Fulton Corporation covering P343 for frames, $2,840.00, less 2% discount. C348.
   22. Paid cash to Daniel Woodworks for frames, $580.00. C349.
   30. Paid cash to replenish the petty cash fund, $102.10: advertising for crafts, $50.00; miscellaneous expense, $32.60; supplies, $19.50. C350.

2. Prove and rule the cash payments journal. Post the totals.

On Your Own 1-3 LO9, 10

Journalizing and posting departmental cash payments Angela's Designs, Inc., has two departments: Ceramic and Stone. Selected general ledger and accounts payable ledger accounts are provided in the *Working Papers*. Source documents are abbreviated as follows: check, C; debit memorandum, DM; and purchase invoice, P. Work this problem independently.

1. Journalize the transactions completed during July of the current year. Use page 7 of a cash payments journal. Post the items that are to be posted individually.

   Transactions:

   July 4. Paid cash to Artistic Ceramics for ceramic tiles, $698.00. C422.
   8. Paid cash to Peterson Supply for a miscellaneous expense, $297.00. C423.
   11. Paid cash on account for ceramic tiles from Marris Ceramics covering P308 for $2,984.00, less 2% purchases discount. C424.
   14. Paid cash to Abraham Corporation for supplies, $109.35. C425.
   21. Paid cash on account for stone purchased from Overland Stone covering P312 for $2,351.00, less DM53 for $375.00, and less 2% discount. C426.
   26. Paid cash to Z&Z Landscaping for stone, $743.00. C427.
   31. Paid cash to replenish the petty cash fund, $99.10: advertising for stone, $45.00; miscellaneous expense, $22.90; supplies, $31.20. C428.

2. Prove and rule the cash payments journal. Post the totals.

A Look at **Accounting** Software

Setting Up Accounts for a Corporation

When Whiley Outdoor Living, Inc., was first organized, its accountants would have set up a computerized accounting system to record the company's financial transactions. Compared to the manual system you experienced in this chapter, an automated system (a) improves the efficiency of the accounting staff, (b) reduces the likelihood of errors, (c) allows for significantly greater detail in the data, (d) simplifies the search and retrieval of accounting information, and (e) makes the reporting of financial information incredibly fast and flexible.

Prior to setting up the chart of accounts, as illustrated in these windows, accountants would have entered general company information on the first tab. After setting up the accounts, they would proceed to set up the subsidiary ledgers for customers and vendors. Finally, as Whiley began to order inventory and hire employees, the accountants would set up inventory items to manage pricing, sales, and reorders and set up employees to account for salaries, wages, benefits, and payroll taxes.

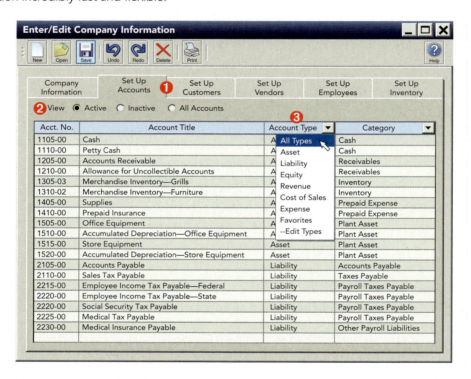

❶ The user selects the **Set Up Accounts** tab. The system lists a default set of accounts based upon the type of business chosen on the Company Information window. The user then modifies, adds, or deletes accounts to customize the list for the new business.

❷ The system selects the **View Active** button by default to list only active accounts. If the user wanted to view only accounts that had been deactivated, the **Inactive** button would be selected. The **All Accounts** button would show

both active and inactive accounts. When an account is no longer needed, it is made inactive. Accounts are rarely deleted because they contain historical data that may be needed for comparative financial reports.

❸ The account type describes where the account appears in the financial statements. Account categories are chosen by the accountant to simplify account search and retrieval and to facilitate the creation of financial reports. Account types and categories are set up or edited using their drop lists.

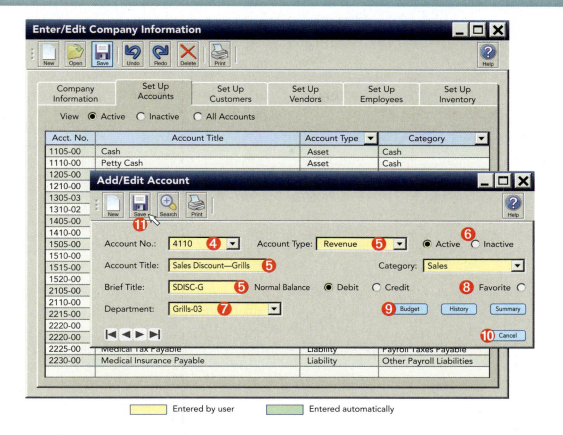

Entered by user   Entered automatically

④ To add a new account, the user would click on **New** on the menu bar. The system would open a blank pop-up window. The Add/Edit Account window could also be opened by double-clicking an account number or title in the account list. In that case, the pop-up window would appear with that account's data already entered, allowing it to be modified as needed. In this pop-up window, the accountant has entered a new account.

⑤ Drop lists are used to select the account type and category. The user continues by entering an account title and brief title. Abbreviations are useful for labeling accounts on financial reports where there isn't room for complete titles. The system applies a default setting for the account's normal balance. In this window, Credit would have been the default setting for Sales Discount because the user categorized it as a Sales account. The user has changed it to Debit because Sales Discount is a contra account to Sales.

⑥ The system default for a new account is *active*. As a business continues to operate over time, it undergoes changes that can affect the accounts it uses to record transactions. It will sometimes be

useful to set accounts to inactive so they no longer show up in reports or menu lists.

⑦ When setting up the type of business on the Company Information tab, the accountant would have selected *Departmental* and set up the departments. The system then sets departmental fields on transaction and report windows. In this window, the user selects the correct department from the drop list.

⑧ There are certain accounts that the accounting department may wish to give special attention. Perhaps a brief daily report would be used to show managers the status of those accounts. Marking an account as a favorite allows it to be easily selected.

⑨ To set up or view the budget for this account, or to view the account history or a summary statement of the account, the user would click on the appropriate button.

⑩ The user can click the **Cancel** button at any time to clear the data from the pop-up window and start over.

⑪ Clicking on **Save** records the new or edited account. Clicking on **New** clears all fields to enable the user to create another new account.

The accounting equation is often viewed as a "T" account with assets on the left side and equities (liabilities and owners' equity) on the right side. Debits are recorded on the left and credits on the right side of the accounting equation. The normal balance of asset accounts, on the left side of the accounting equation, is a debit. The normal balance of equity accounts, on the right side of the accounting equation, is a credit.

Accounting transactions are recorded in journals. Four special journals are used to record similar transactions. All other transactions are recorded in a general journal. Transactions impacting an account are posted to its general ledger account. Transactions impacting a controlling account are also posted to subsidiary ledger accounts.

A merchandising business that sells different types of products can benefit from using a departmental accounting system. Sales, merchandise purchases, and selected expense transactions are recorded in the general ledger by department.

The purchase of merchandise on account is efficiently recorded in the special amount columns of the purchases journal. The transaction is immediately posted in the vendor's accounts payable ledger account to update the amount owed to the vendor. The totals of the special columns of a completed purchases journal are posted to the general ledger. Purchase returns and allowances, journalized in a general ledger, reduce the amount owed to the vendor.

All cash payments are recorded in the cash payments journal. The journal contains special amount columns to efficiently record the many cash payments made for purchases on account. To encourage early payment, some vendors offer a cash discount that allows the customer to pay less than the full amount of the purchase invoice. The cash payments journal includes special amount columns for purchase discounts for each department. Cash payments for other purchases and expenses are also recorded in the cash payments journal. The totals of the special columns of a completed cash payments journal are posted to the general ledger.

EXPLORE ACCOUNTING

Accounting Certifications

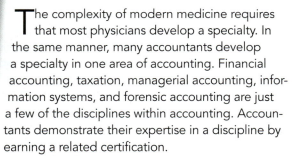

The complexity of modern medicine requires that most physicians develop a specialty. In the same manner, many accountants develop a specialty in one area of accounting. Financial accounting, taxation, managerial accounting, information systems, and forensic accounting are just a few of the disciplines within accounting. Accountants demonstrate their expertise in a discipline by earning a related certification.

The Certified Public Accountant (CPA) is the most widely recognized certification. To become a CPA, an individual must pass a certifying examination and meet the educational and experience requirements of the board of accountancy in the individual's state. A CPA is qualified to perform a variety of accounting functions, including auditing financial statements, preparing tax returns, and providing tax planning. Many CPAs focus in one of these areas.

A partial list of other accounting certifications follows:

Certified Management Accountant Responsible for the accounting information system; assists managers in using accounting information in decision making; works to provide the company with adequate financial resources to conduct business.

Certified Internal Auditor Audits the accounting information system and other operational reporting systems.

Certified Information Systems Auditor Evaluates the operations of an organization's information technology systems.

Certified Fraud Examiner Investigates alleged fraudulent activities by examining accounting records and interviewing personnel; prepares evidence for admission into court.

Enrolled Agent Represents taxpayers before the Internal Revenue Service on issues related to collections, audits, and appeals.

Certified Financial Planner Assists individuals in developing investment strategies to meet future financial needs, such as retirement.

Accredited in Business Valuation (a special CPA designation) Determines the value of businesses involved in acquisitions or dispositions.

INSTRUCTIONS

Identify an individual who has one of the certifications listed above. Ask the individual to describe how the certification has played a role in his or her professional career.

APPLY YOUR UNDERSTANDING

INSTRUCTIONS: Download problem instructions for Excel, QuickBooks, and Sage 50c from the textbook companion website at www.C21accounting.com.

1-1 Application Problem
Determining the normal balance, increase, and decrease sides for accounts LO3

Write the answers for the following problem in the *Working Papers*.

Prepaid Insurance
Advertising Expense
Capital Stock
Daniel Miller (an account receivable)

Northland Supply (an account payable)
Supplies
Sales—Video
Retained Earnings

1	2	3	4	5	6	7	8
Account Title	Account Classification	Account's Normal Balance		Increase Side		Decrease Side	
		Debit	Credit	Debit	Credit	Debit	Credit
Prepaid Insurance	Asset	✔		✔			✔

Instructions: Do the following steps for each account. The Prepaid Insurance account is given above as an example.

1. Write the account title in Column 1.
2. Write the account classification in Column 2.
3. Place a check mark in either Column 3 or 4 to indicate the normal balance of the account.
4. Place a check mark in either Column 5 or 6 to indicate the increase side of the account.
5. Place a check mark in either Column 7 or 8 to indicate the decrease side of the account.

1-2 Application Problem
Journalizing and posting departmental purchases on account and purchases returns and allowances LO6, 7, 8

Jessie's Landscapes has two departments: Flowers and Gifts. A purchases journal, general journal, and partial general and accounts payable ledgers are provided in the *Working Papers*. The balances are recorded as of August 1 of the current year. Post the following transactions when journalized: (1) transactions impacting the accounts payable subsidiary ledger and (2) transactions recorded on the general journal. Source documents are abbreviated as follows: debit memorandum, DM; purchase invoice, P.

Instructions:

1. Journalize the transactions completed during August of the current year. Use page 8 of a purchases journal and page 8 of a general journal. Post the items that are to be posted individually.
2. Prove and rule the purchases journal. Post the totals.

Transactions:

Aug. 4. Purchased statues on account from Tennessee Crafts, $4,165.00. P392.
5. The order from Tennessee Crafts contained broken statues, $68.45, from P390. DM41.
7. Purchased artwork on account from Glade Arts Center, $2,148.00. P393.
14. Returned dead plants to Marlon Nursery, $318.10, from P388. DM42.
16. Purchased cut flowers from Carson Growers, $3,269.00. P394.
21. Returned broken gifts to Tennessee Crafts, $265.00, from P392. DM43.
22. Took delivery of flowering plants from Marlon Nursery, $450.00. P395.
29. Purchased gifts on account from Glade Arts Center, $1,845.00. P396.

1-3 Application Problem Journalizing and posting departmental cash payments LO9, 10

sage 50

1. Journalize and post transactions to the cash disbursements journal.
2. From the menu bar, select Reports & Forms; Accounts Payable.
3. Make the selections to the print the purchase journal and the cash disbursements journal.

QB
Quick Books

1. Journalize and post payments to vendors on account in the Pay Bills window.
2. Journalize and post payments to vendors in the Write Checks window.
3. From the menu bar, select Reports; Banking, Check Detail.
4. From the menu bar, select Reports; Vendors and Payables, Vendor Balance Detail.

[x]

1. Journalize and post vendor transactions on account to the cash payments journal, accounts payable ledger, and general ledger.
2. Print the worksheets.

Step Music has two departments: Guitars and Keyboards. Post the following transactions when journalized: (1) transactions impacting the accounts payable subsidiary ledger and (2) cash payments entered in a general amount column of the cash payments journal. A cash payments journal and partial general and accounts payable ledgers are given in the *Working Papers*. The balances are recorded as of March 1 of the current year. Source documents are abbreviated as follows: check, C; debit memorandum, DM.

Instructions:

1. Journalize the transactions completed during March of the current year. Use page 3 of a cash payments journal. Post the items that are to be posted individually.
2. Prove and rule the cash payments journal. Post the totals.

Transactions:

Mar. 2. Paid cash to Z96 Radio, Inc., for advertising announcing a guitar sale, $350.00. C642
    5. Paid cash on account to Airways Music covering P584 for a keyboard, $1,980.60, less 2% discount. C643.
    9. Paid cash to C&C Supplies for office supplies, $145.60. C644.
    17. Paid cash on account to Campbell Guitar covering P592 for six bass guitars, $2,774.00, less DM32 for $368.00, less 2% discount. C645.
    24. Paid cash to Elon Accessories, Inc., for a keyboard stand, $235.95. C646.
    31. Paid cash to replenish the petty cash fund, $81.80: miscellaneous, $26.73; guitar strings (Purchases-Guitars), $12.95; supplies, $42.12. C647.

1-M Mastery Problem Journalizing departmental purchases and cash payments LO6, 7, 8, 9, 10

sage 50

1. Journalize and post vendor transactions on account to the purchase journal.
2. Journalize and post vendor transactions on account to the cash disbursements journal.
3. From the menu bar, select Reports & Forms; Accounts Payable.
4. Make the selections to the print the purchase journal and the cash disbursements journal.

QB
Quick Books

1. Journalize and post vendor transactions on account in the Enter Bills window.
2. Journalize and post payments to vendors on account in the Pay Bills window.
3. Journalize and post payments to vendors in the Write Checks window.
4. From the menu bar, select Reports; Banking, Check Detail.

Jan's Jewelry has two departments: Costume and Fine. Post the following transactions when journalized: (1) transactions impacting the accounts payable subsidiary ledger, (2) transactions recorded in the general journal, and (3) cash payments entered in a general amount column of the cash payments journal. Journals and partial general and accounts payable ledgers are given in the *Working Papers*. Source documents are abbreviated as follows: check, C; debit memorandum, DM; purchase invoice, P.

Instructions:

1. Journalize the transactions completed during August of the current year. Use page 8 of a purchases journal, page 8 of a general journal, and page 12 of a cash payments journal. Post the items that are to be posted individually.
2. Prove and rule the purchases journal. Post the totals.
3. Prove and rule the cash payments journal. Post the totals.

Transactions:

Aug. 1. Paid cash to Gallup Properties for rent, $2,400.00. C685.
    2. Purchased fine jewelry on account from Austin Creations, $4,367.00. P567.
    3. Paid cash to Davis Office Source for supplies, $123.14. C686.
    4. Returned costume jewelry to Destin Crafters, $109.50, from P562. DM46.
    6. Paid cash to Sanders Hardware for paint (miscellaneous expense), $56.34. C687.

1. Journalize the transactions to the purchases, cash payments, and general journals.
2. Post the transactions and journal totals to the accounts payable and general ledgers.
3. Print the worksheets.

9. Returned fine jewelry to Austin Creations, $98.00, from P567. DM47.
10. Paid cash on account to Austin Creations covering P567 for fine jewelry for $4,367.00, less DM47 for $98.00, less 2% discount. C688.
14. Paid cash to Williams Accessories for beads (costume jewelry), $275.00. C689.
16. Purchased costume jewelry on account from Jenkins Designs, $4,642.00. P568.
21. Paid cash to City Electric Department for the utility bill, $512.12. C690.
24. Paid cash on account to Jenkins Designs covering P568 for costume jewelry, $4,642.00, less 2% discount. C691.
25. Purchased costume jewelry on account from Ketler Krafts, $1,854.00. P569.
31. Paid cash to replenish the petty cash fund, $93.24: advertising for fine jewelry, $40.00; miscellaneous, $21.56; supplies, $31.68. C692.

1-C Challenge Problem   Establishing a departmental accounting system LO5

Each business in this chapter has illustrated a two-department accounting system. In real life, a company may elect to have more than two departments. Management must evaluate its operations and determine the information value of having multiple departments. Having too few departments may not provide enough information for making informed decisions. Yet the effort required to record transactions in too many departments may outweigh the value of the information provided to management.

Eupora Music currently uses two departments: Guitars and Other. The manager has asked that you suggest how the company could be divided into more focused departments. To assist in your decision, the manager has provided you with a list of recent inventory purchases.

Quantity	Description	Unit Cost	Sales Price
3	Guitar straps	$ 6.95	$ 12.95
1	5-string banjo	149.00	299.00
15	6-string nylon guitar strings	5.95	12.95
1	Acoustic guitar	1,495.98	2,399.00
50	Sheet music, recent publication mix	3.99	6.99
25	20' electric guitar cable	8.95	19.99
2	Wireless microphone	325.95	650.00
5	Effects pedal	99.99	209.95
6	Beginner guitar package	89.99	199.99
3	Harmonica with case	159.25	249.99
5	Bass guitar package	129.99	199.99
2	Tom drums with stand	109.95	189.99
6	Digital metronome	59.99	109.95
20	5B drumsticks	4.95	9.99
3	Acoustic electric guitar with gig bag	219.99	379.99
4	12-string nylon guitar strings	5.95	12.95
20	Microphone wind screens	2.99	4.95
4	100' 8-channel audio snake	129.99	259.99
2	Bass guitar with case	799.99	1,799.99
15	Ear plugs	2.95	5.95
12	5-string bass guitar strings	6.95	15.95
3	Drum set	495.95	795.95

Instructions:

Use the form in the *Working Papers* to assign the purchased parts into the following departments: acoustic guitars, other stringed instruments, drums, and other.

Mike's Discount Golf sells golf and tennis equipment. Journals and source documents related to the purchase and cash payments are provided in the *Working Papers*. Post the following transactions when journalized: (1) transactions impacting the accounts payable subsidiary ledger, (2) transactions recorded in the general journal, and (3) cash payments entered in a general amount column of the cash payments journal. Mike's Discount Golf uses a chart of accounts similar to Whiley Outdoor Living.

Instructions:

1. Journalize the transactions shown in the source documents, by date, using page 5 of a purchases journal, page 5 of a general journal, and page 7 of a cash payments journal. Some transactions may be related to more than one source document.
2. Prove and rule the purchases journal.
3. Prove and rule the cash payments journal.

21st Century Skills

Supplier Savvy

Theme: Financial, Economic, Business, and Entrepreneurial Literacy

Skills: Creativity and Innovation, Critical Thinking and Problem Solving, Communication and Collaboration, ICT Literacy

PARTNERSHIP FOR
21ST CENTURY SKILLS

Suppliers, or vendors, are essential to a merchandising business. Careful selection of suppliers can create a meaningful partnership that allows the business to flourish. Good business partners can help cut costs and improve products and services.

Suppliers can be divided into four categories:

Manufacturing—Some products are sold directly from the manufacturer, or from a sales representative for the manufacturer. This is usually the lowest-cost option; however, shipping can be costly.

Distributors/Wholesalers—A distributor usually buys large quantities from several manufacturers and places the merchandise in a warehouse to sell to retailers. The distributor's cost of merchandise is usually more than a manufacturer's, due to additional markup and selections.

Jobbers/Independent Craftspeople—These individuals usually make daily deliveries to grocery stores or present unique creations at trade shows.

Importer—Products are sent from another country and usually operate much like a domestic wholesaler.

APPLICATION

1. Juan Clemente has decided to sell insulated water bottles in his sporting goods store.
    a. Using the Internet, find three vendors (suppliers) and obtain the following information: product description, price, quantity discounts, additional charges such as art or setup charges, shipping costs, and estimated delivery time. Place this information in a spreadsheet.
    b. Write a letter to Mr. Clemente summarizing your findings and making a recommendation for purchase. Be sure to state the reasons for your conclusions.
2. Visit a small merchandising business in your local community or online. Examine the products available for sale. Then, with a partner, brainstorm three new products that you think would be beneficial for this business to sell.
    a. Present your findings to the class.
    b. Compose a letter to the business explaining your assignment and suggestions.

A manager at Lambert Industries just prepared the chart below, which lists all the account titles from the company's chart of accounts. For each account, a "+" or "−" was recorded in the appropriate debit and credit column to show the impact of a debit or credit to each account's balance. The last column indicates the normal balance for each account. The intent of creating the chart is to provide an easy reference tool to help new accounting clerks accurately record journal entries and calculate general ledger balances.

Review the manager's chart below. Make a new chart so that the reference tool is accurate.

Account Title	Debit	Credit	Normal Balance
Petty Cash	+	−	Dr.
Accounts Receivable	+	−	Dr.
Allowance for Uncollectible Accounts	+	−	Dr.
Merchandise Inventory	+	−	Dr.
Store Equipment	+	−	Dr.
Accumulated Depreciation—Store Equipment	−	+	Dr.
Accounts Payable	−	+	Cr.
Interest Payable	−	+	Cr.
Capital Stock	−	+	Cr.
Retained Earnings	+	−	Cr.
Dividends	+	−	Cr.
Sales	−	+	Cr.
Sales Returns and Allowances	−	+	Cr.
Purchases	+	−	Dr.
Purchases Discount	+	−	Dr.
Rent Expense	+	−	Dr.
Federal Income Tax Expense	+	−	Dr.

Analyzing Home Depot's Financial Statements

Selected published financial information for Home Depot, Inc., is reproduced in Appendix B of this textbook. Like many companies, Home Depot rounds dollar amounts when reporting financial data on various financial statements. It is very important when reviewing data in Home Depot's annual report to determine if the amounts presented have been rounded to the nearest million, nearest thousand, or not rounded at all. Look at page B-5 in Appendix B. Under the heading at the top of the page, notice the phrase "in millions, except per share data." This means that all dollar amounts above and including Net Earnings are rounded to the nearest million. For example, the reported fiscal year 2017 (ended on January 28, 2018) Net Sales amount of $100,904 actually represents $100,904,000,000. Actual dollar amounts on this page are calculated by multiplying the amount reported by 1,000,000 ($100,904 × 1,000,000 = $100,904,000,000).

INSTRUCTIONS

Refer to the Consolidated Balance Sheets and Consolidated Statements of Earnings in Appendix B on pages B-5 and B-6 to identify the following amounts:

1. List the actual dollar amount of Cost of Sales and Operating Income for fiscal year 2017.
2. List the actual dollar amount of Total Assets for fiscal year 2017.
3. List Home Depot's diluted earnings per share for fiscal year 2017.

Recording Departmental Sales and Cash Receipts

LEARNING OBJECTIVES

After studying Chapter 2, in addition to defining key terms, you will be able to:

LO1 Explain the purpose and process of recording purchases and purchase returns in a departmental accounting system.

LO2 Journalize departmental sales on account using a sales journal.

LO3 Post sales on account to an accounts receivable ledger and a general ledger.

LO4 Journalize departmental sales returns and allowances.

LO5 Post sales returns and allowances to an accounts receivable ledger and a general ledger.

LO6 Explain the impact of sales discounts on the collection of accounts receivable.

LO7 Journalize departmental cash receipts using a cash receipts journal.

LO8 Post cash receipts to an accounts receivable ledger and a general ledger.

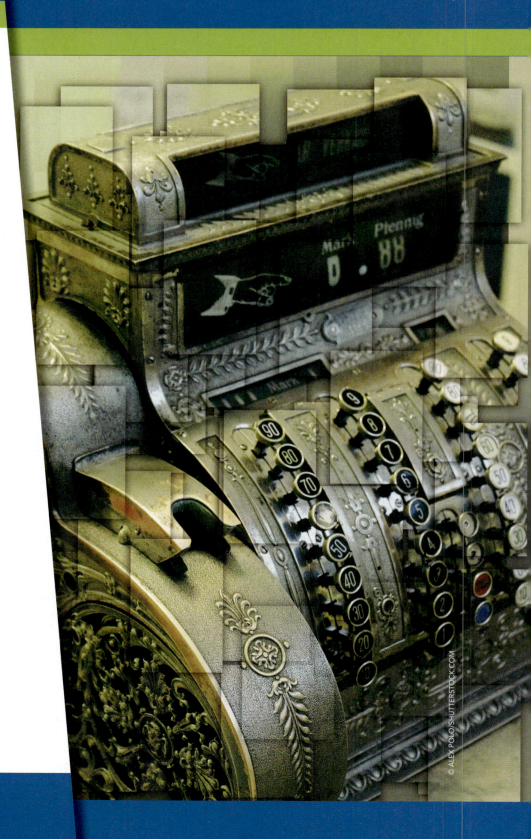

ExxonMobil

ACCOUNTING IN THE REAL WORLD

Drivers across the globe are familiar with gas stations with the brand names Exxon, Esso, and Mobil. These three brands are the most recognized part of the world's largest publicly traded international oil and gas company, ExxonMobil. Operating for more than 150 years, ExxonMobil has expanded into businesses that, unlike gas stations, are seldom visible to the average consumer. The remarkable evolution of ExxonMobil was influenced by scientific discovery, strategic business decisions, and government intervention.

For centuries, early scientists developed methods of making "rock oil" or "coal oil," a burnable fuel extracted from coal found on the earth's surface. The discovery that oil provided a better source for producing this type of burnable fuel led to kerosene, a more clean-burning fuel that is still available today. The growing nation's demand for kerosene during the 1850s required the discovery of a large source of oil.

In 1859 the Seneca Oil Company was the first oil exploration company to successfully drill an oil well. This discovery launched an oil boom in the United States and Canada. Recognizing the magnitude of this discovery, John D. Rockefeller led the formation of the Standard Oil Company. Through a series of acquisitions and controversial business practices, the company soon controlled most of the nation's oil production. In 1911, the United States Supreme Court ruled that Standard Oil was an illegal monopoly and forced the company to divide into 34 unrelated companies. Two of these independent companies would later be rebranded as Exxon and Mobil.

Over the next century, scientists discovered new products that could be refined from oil. Lubricating oils were developed for a variety of applications from power plants to commercial aircraft. Materials refined from oil or natural gas are used in the production of aspirin, cellular phones, eyeglasses, nail polish, house paint, tires, and more.

In the late 20th century, oil companies began to transform into energy companies. No longer were scientific advancements limited to generating fuels and other forms of energy solely from oil. Advances were made in creating energy using biofuels, wind, solar power, and geothermal sources. Creating clean energy and reducing emissions from the burning of fossil fuels became a priority.

In 1999, Exxon and Mobil merged to form a single company. Imagine the complexity of managing a business that manufactures such an extensive list of products from multiple energy sources. Complex companies such as ExxonMobil rely on departmental accounting to provide them with useful information about distinct parts of the business.

Generally accepted accounting principles have similar requirements for published financial statements. Corporations must report revenue and expenses for distinct parts of the business. These parts are known as segments. Typically, the number of segments within a company is significantly more limited than the level of departmental accounting used by management to control and monitor its operations.

Sources: www.corporate.exxonmobil.com, www.aoghs.org, www.energy.gov.

CRITICAL THINKING

1. Access the latest Form 10-K of ExxonMobil. Identify and describe the corporation's segments.

2. Identify a local business, school district, or university. Suggest the segments that the organization could use to report its financial activity.

KEY TERMS

credit memorandum
sales discount

point-of-sale (POS) terminal
terminal summary

LESSON 2-1

Departmental Sales on Account and Sales Returns and Allowances

LO1 Explain the purpose and process of recording purchases and purchase returns in a departmental accounting system.

LO2 Journalize departmental sales on account using a sales journal.

LO3 Post sales on account to an accounts receivable ledger and a general ledger.

LO4 Journalize departmental sales returns and allowances.

LO5 Post sales returns and allowances to an accounts receivable ledger and a general ledger.

Departmental Sales on Account LO1

Managers use departmental data to make decisions relating to business operations. Companies such as Whiley Outdoor Living, Inc., are often organized into departments, based on the different types of products or services they sell. In order to maximize business operations, Whiley identified two departments based on the two categories of merchandise it sells—Grills and Furniture. Whiley's management team uses departmental information to analyze the profitability of each department, set annual goals, evaluate managers, and determine company bonuses.

In order to have comprehensive departmental data, however, a business should record sales and cash receipts data separately for each department. For example, gross profit from operations for each department is one type of valuable information for management decision making. Departmental gross profit from operations helps business managers decide if each department is earning an appropriate profit. If not, departmental information can help managers determine which items are causing the problem. To determine departmental gross profit from operations, the business must keep records of sales and the cost of merchandise sold by department.

Chapter 1 presented how to account for purchases transactions for a departmental merchandising business. To have complete departmental data, Whiley also records all sales transactions by department. Whiley makes sales on account to individuals, business firms, and schools. It sells merchandise in two departments. The grills department sells home and commercial grills. The furniture department sells a variety of outdoor furniture, including chairs, chaise lounges, swings, and tables.

Whiley records all departmental sales on account in a sales journal. The sales journal has one debit column—Accounts Receivable Debit. The journal also has three credit columns—Sales Tax Payable Credit and special Sales Credit columns for Grills and Furniture.

The Sales Tax Payable Credit column is used to record all sales tax amounts that Whiley collects. Most states require vendors to collect sales tax from their customers. The city and state in which Whiley is located have a combined sales tax rate of 6.0%. Some customers are not required to pay a sales tax. Many agencies supported by local and state governments and not-for-profit organizations are exempt from paying a sales tax. For example, Central Community College is a tax-exempt customer of Whiley.

Whiley prepares sales invoices in duplicate for each sale on account. **>> App A: Objective Evidence** Each sales invoice shows the amount of merchandise sold by department. The customer receives the original copy of the sales invoice. The duplicate copy is the source document for journalizing the transaction.

Whiley records all departmental sales at the time of sale, regardless of when payment is made. **>> App A: Realization of Revenue** The *Realization of Revenue* concept states that revenue is recorded at the time goods or services are sold. A business may sell either goods or services. Cash may be received at the time of sale, or an agreement may be made to receive payment at a later date. Regardless of when the business actually receives cash, it records the sale amount in the accounting records at the time of sale. For example, during November a business sells office furniture on account for $2,000.00. The customer pays its account in January of the next fiscal year. The business records $2,000.00 of revenue in November, at the time of the sale, even though the $2,000.00 is collected later.

A Business Lunch Light on Business

As the sales manager for Natural Springs Hotel, Samantha Jones is responsible for selling conventions that use the hotel's grand ballroom. Samantha received a call from Lois Drucker, president of a 1,000-member national education association. Lois expressed interest in having her group's annual conference at the hotel. Therefore, Samantha invited Lois to lunch at the hotel's Sunset Lounge to sell her on the merits of Natural Springs Hotel.

Samantha likes to establish a relationship with the potential customer. So minutes into the lunch, Samantha and Lois discovered they grew up in the same town. Time flew by as they reminisced about their hometown. Before they knew it, the lunch hour was over without them discussing any business.

Samantha returned to her office and opened her expense report software. She entered all the facts of the lunch—date, guest's name, and amount spent. She paused as she stared at the Purpose of Expense box. After a moment, she entered "Preliminary meeting with president of." Only then did she realize that she never learned the name of Lois's organization. Not sure what to do, she continued by entering "National Association of Educators."

Did Samantha act in an ethical manner? Many models have been promoted to assist individuals in making ethical decisions. The ethical decision-making model used in this textbook has four steps:

1. Recognize you are facing an ethical dilemma.
2. Identify the action taken or the proposed action.
3. Analyze the action.
   a. Is the action illegal?
   b. Does the action violate company or professional standards?
   c. Who is affected, and how, by the action?
4. Determine if the action is ethical.

The first two steps often occur as the situation unfolds. If the action is either illegal or violates company or professional standards, the action should not be taken. However, it is often necessary to analyze the action further. The positive or negative impact on all stakeholders—individuals, groups of individuals, organizations, and businesses affected by the action—should be determined and analyzed.

INSTRUCTIONS

Access the *Business Corporate Guide* for Marriott International, Inc. Using this code as a guide, use the ethical model to help determine whether the action by Samantha demonstrates ethical behavior.

Journalizing Sales on Account LO2

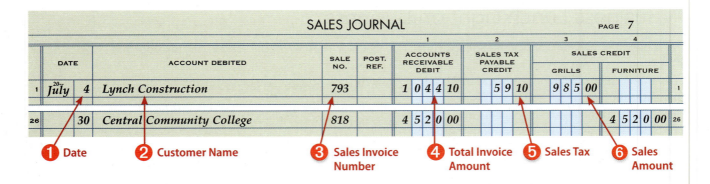

SALES JOURNAL PAGE 7

DATE		ACCOUNT DEBITED	SALE NO.	POST. REF.	ACCOUNTS RECEIVABLE DEBIT (1)	SALES TAX PAYABLE CREDIT (2)	SALES CREDIT GRILLS (3)	SALES CREDIT FURNITURE (4)	
1	20-- July 4	Lynch Construction	793		1 0 4 4 10	5 9 10	9 8 5 00		1
26	30	Central Community College	818		4 5 2 0 00			4 5 2 0 00	26

① **Date** ② **Customer Name** ③ **Sales Invoice Number** ④ **Total Invoice Amount** ⑤ **Sales Tax** ⑥ **Sales Amount**

> **July 4. Sold a grill on account to Lynch Construction, $985.00, plus sales tax, $59.10; total, $1,044.10. Sales Invoice No. 793.**

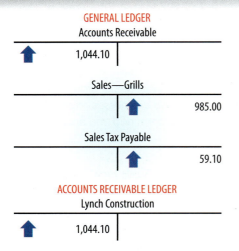

GENERAL LEDGER

Accounts Receivable

⬆ 1,044.10 |

Sales—Grills

| ⬆ 985.00

Sales Tax Payable

| ⬆ 59.10

ACCOUNTS RECEIVABLE LEDGER

Lynch Construction

⬆ 1,044.10 |

This transaction is recorded in the departmental sales journal. The source document for this transaction is a sales invoice. ❯❯ App A: Objective Evidence

In the general ledger, Accounts Receivable is increased by a $1,044.10 debit. The amount that the customer owes represents the price of the merchandise plus the sales tax. All sales tax received is later remitted to the state in which Whiley is located. Therefore, the liability account Sales Tax Payable is increased by a $59.10 credit. Sales—Grills is increased by a $985.00 credit. In the accounts receivable ledger, Lynch Construction is increased by a $1,044.10 debit.

The transaction on line 26 of the sales journal shows a transaction for a tax-exempt customer. Since Central Community College is an educational institution, it is not required by the state to pay sales tax.

> **❯❯ Recording Sales on Account in the Sales Journal**
> ❶ Write the date, **20--, July 4**, in the Date column.
> ❷ Write the customer name, **Lynch Construction**, in the Account Debited column.
> ❸ Record the sales invoice number, **793**, in the Sale No. column.
> ❹ Enter the total invoice amount, **$1,044.10**, in the Accounts Receivable Debit column.
> ❺ Enter the credit amount, **$59.10**, in the Sales Tax Payable Credit column.
> ❻ Enter the credit amount, **$985.00**, in the Sales Credit Grills column.

> **FYI**
> All businesses and not-for-profit entities that have employees must have a federal tax identification number. This number is used in much the same way that individuals use their social security numbers. The Internal Revenue Service identifies entities that are exempt from federal income tax by their federal identification numbers. States may require vendors to keep a written record of the federal tax identification numbers of their tax-exempt customers.

Posting from a Sales Journal LO3

The accounting procedures for posting from a sales journal are the same as those followed for posting from the purchases journal, as shown in Chapter 1.

Whiley keeps customer accounts in an accounts receivable ledger. Transactions recorded in the sales journal are posted individually to customer accounts in the accounts receivable ledger and in total to the general ledger.

Posting from a Sales Journal to the Accounts Receivable Ledger

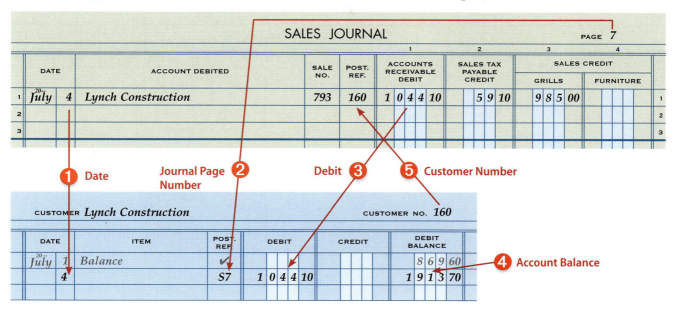

Individual amounts in the Accounts Receivable Debit column are posted when the transaction is recorded in the sales journal. This procedure keeps the customers'

accounts up to date. The sales journal is abbreviated as *S* in the Post. Ref. column of the ledger accounts.

>> Posting from the Sales Journal to the Accounts Receivable Ledger

❶ Write the date, **4**, in the account's Date column.

❷ Record **S7** in the Post. Ref. column of the subsidiary ledger account to indicate that the posting came from page 7 of the sales journal.

❸ Enter the debit amount, **$1,044.10**, in the account's Debit column. This is the total amount due from the customer. It includes the price of the grill and the sales tax.

❹ Add the amount in the debit column, **$1,044.10**, to the previous balance of **$869.60**. Write the new account balance, **$1,913.70**, in the Debit Balance column.

❺ Record the customer number, **160**, in the Post. Ref. column of the sales journal to show that posting is completed for this line.

FYI Sales taxes collected by businesses must be sent to the appropriate governmental agency. In many states, sales taxes are paid monthly. The payment is accompanied by a form that provides information such as total sales, sales tax collected, and sales exempt from sales tax.

Posting from a Sales Journal to a General Ledger Account

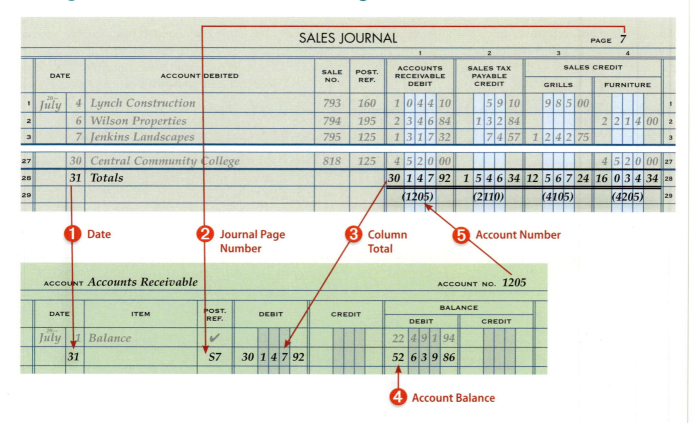

	DATE		ACCOUNT DEBITED	SALE NO.	POST. REF.	ACCOUNTS RECEIVABLE DEBIT (1)	SALES TAX PAYABLE CREDIT (2)	SALES CREDIT GRILLS (3)	SALES CREDIT FURNITURE (4)	
1	July 20--	4	Lynch Construction	793	160	1 0 4 4 10	5 9 10	9 8 5 00		1
2		6	Wilson Properties	794	195	2 3 4 6 84	1 3 2 84		2 2 1 4 00	2
3		7	Jenkins Landscapes	795	125	1 3 1 7 32	7 4 57	1 2 4 2 75		3
27		30	Central Community College	818	125	4 5 2 0 00			4 5 2 0 00	27
28		31	Totals			30 1 4 7 92	1 5 4 6 34	12 5 6 7 24	16 0 3 4 34	28
29						(1205)	(2110)	(4105)	(4205)	29

SALES JOURNAL   PAGE 7

① Date ② Journal Page Number ③ Column Total ⑤ Account Number

ACCOUNT **Accounts Receivable**   ACCOUNT NO. **1205**

DATE		ITEM	POST. REF.	DEBIT	CREDIT	BALANCE DEBIT	BALANCE CREDIT
July 20--	1	Balance	✔			22 4 9 1 94	
	31		S7	30 1 4 7 92		52 6 3 9 86	

④ Account Balance

The sales journal is proved and ruled when the page is filled and always at the end of each month. Each amount column total is posted to the general ledger account named in the column heading.

FYI Proving a journal means verifying that the total debits equal the total credits. To prove a journal:

1. Add each amount column and write the total.
2. Add the column totals for all debit columns.
3. Add the column totals for all credit columns.
4. Verify that total debits and total credits are equal. Once a journal is proved, it should be ruled.

>> **Posting a Column Total from the Sales Journal to the General Ledger**

① Write the date, **31**, in the account's Date column.

② Write **S7** in the Post. Ref. column of the ledger account to indicate that the posting came from page 7 of the sales journal.

③ Write the column total, **$30,147.92**, in the Debit column of the ledger account.

④ Add the amount in the Debit column, **$30,147.92**, to the previous debit balance of **$22,491.94**. Write the new debit balance, **$52,639.86**, in the Balance Debit column.

⑤ Write the general ledger account number, **1205**, in parentheses immediately below the column total in the sales journal to show that the amount has been posted.

Journalizing Sales Returns and Allowances LO4

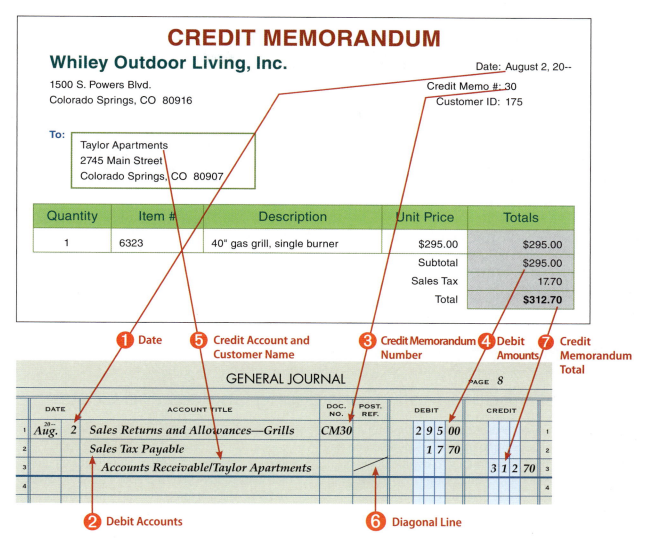

When merchandise is returned by a customer, the customer's account and Accounts Receivable are reduced by a credit. A form prepared by the vendor showing the amount deducted for returns and allowances is called a **credit memorandum**. >> App A: Objective Evidence Whiley records all sales returns and allowances in a general journal.

>> Recording a Sales Return and Allowance in a General Journal

❶ Write the date, 20-- and Aug. 2, in the Date column.

❷ Write the debit accounts, Sales Returns and Allowances—Grills and Sales Tax Payable, in the Account Title column.

❸ Record the credit memorandum number, CM30, in the Doc. No. column.

❹ Write the debit amounts, $295.00 and $17.70, in the Debit column.

❺ Indent and write Accounts Receivable and the customer name, Taylor Apartments, in the Account Title column.

❻ Draw a diagonal line in the Post. Ref. column to indicate that the single debit amount is posted to two accounts.

❼ Record the total of the credit memorandum, $312.70, in the Credit column.

An account that reduces a related account on a financial statement is known as a *contra account*. An account showing deductions from a sales account is a contra revenue account. Sales Returns and Allowances—Grills is a contra revenue account. Sales returns and allowances are kept in a separate account and not deducted directly from the sales account. This procedure helps the business see what proportion of the merchandise sold was returned by customers.

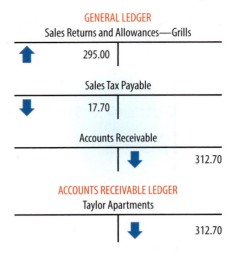

GENERAL LEDGER
Sales Returns and Allowances—Grills

295.00	

Sales Tax Payable

17.70	

Accounts Receivable

	312.70

ACCOUNTS RECEIVABLE LEDGER
Taylor Apartments

	312.70

> **August 2.** Granted credit to Taylor Apartments for the return of a gas grill, $295.00, plus sales tax, $17.70, from Sales Invoice No. 816; total, $312.70. Credit Memorandum No. 30.

When a sales return is accepted or an allowance is granted, the sales tax amount is no longer due. In the general ledger, Sales Returns and Allowances—Grills is increased by a $295.00 debit. Sales Tax Payable is decreased by a $17.70 debit. Accounts Receivable is decreased by a $312.70 credit. In the accounts receivable ledger, Taylor Apartments is decreased by a $312.70 credit.

FINANCIAL LITERACY

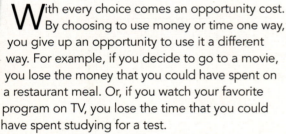

What's the Tradeoff? Considering Choices and Costs

With every choice comes an opportunity cost. By choosing to use money or time one way, you give up an opportunity to use it a different way. For example, if you decide to go to a movie, you lose the money that you could have spent on a restaurant meal. Or, if you watch your favorite program on TV, you lose the time that you could have spent studying for a test.

People evaluate opportunity costs differently. However, by recording your choices every day, you can decide how to better use your time and resources. A planning tool or a budget can help you make choices about how to use your money and time. Your decisions should be based on long-term as well as immediate effects.

ACTIVITIES

1. Using the Internet, search for a Roth IRA Savings Calculator. Use the following information to determine the opportunity cost of each listed item versus investing this money in a given retirement account. For example, to determine the opportunity cost of a daily cup of coffee, multiply the cost per day by the number of purchases over a 40-year career. Then, plug this figure into your savings calculator. Note that Roth IRA accounts require you to prepay estimated taxes of 25%, which is to be deducted from the savings investment. Also, assume a 6% return over the 40 years.

   a. Daily cup of coffee, $1.50 per day
   b. Weekly lunch at local fast-food restaurant, $8.00
   c. Weekly manicure, $15
   d. Music downloads, $20 per month
   e. Haircut, $35 per month

2. Record your spending for one day (or one week, if time permits). Create a spreadsheet of your spending and explain your opportunity costs. Then, use the Roth IRA Savings Calculator to determine the opportunity cost of the daily expenditure if you invested in a Roth IRA at 6% over a 40-year career.

   Explain your findings to the class.

Posting from a General Journal LO5

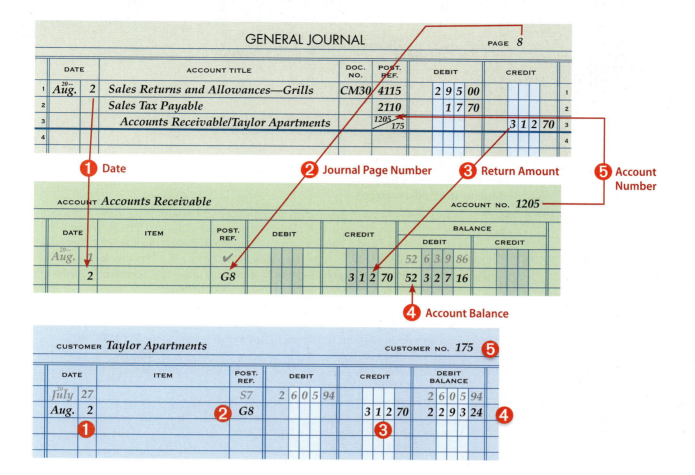

Sales returns and allowances are posted to the accounts receivable ledger and general ledger when the transaction is journalized. This procedure keeps an individual customer's account up to date.

When a sales return or allowance is granted after the customer has paid for the purchase, the customer account after posting may have a credit balance instead of a normal debit balance. The credit balance, a contra balance, reduces the amount to be received from a customer for future sales on account. When a three-column account form is used, a contra balance is shown by enclosing the amount in parentheses.

>> Posting Amounts from a General Journal

❶ Write the date in the Date column.

❷ Write G8 in the Post. Ref. column of the account to indicate that the posting came from page 8 of the general journal.

❸ Write the debit or credit amount in the appropriate column of the account.

❹ Record the updated account balance.

❺ Record the account numbers in the Post. Ref. column of the journal.

LO1 Explain the purpose and process of recording purchases and purchase returns in a departmental accounting system.

LO2 Journalize departmental sales on account using a sales journal.

LO3 Post sales on account to an accounts receivable ledger and a general ledger.

LO4 Journalize departmental sales returns and allowances.

LO5 Post sales returns and allowances to an accounts receivable ledger and a general ledger.

TERM REVIEW

credit memorandum

Audit your understanding   LO1, 4

1. What is a benefit of recording sales and expenses by department?
2. What is a tax-exempt customer? Give an example.
3. What is the source document for a sale on account?
4. How does the *Realization of Revenue* concept apply to the recording of sales?
5. For what purpose is a credit memorandum issued?

Work together 2-1   LO2, 3, 4, 5

Journalizing and posting departmental sales on account and sales returns and allowances

Back Office sells used office furniture in two departments: Chairs and Desks. Page 3 of a sales journal, page 6 of a general journal, and partial accounts receivable and general ledgers are provided in the *Working Papers*. Your instructor will guide you through the following examples.

1. Journalize the following transactions completed during September of the current year. Post the items that are to be posted individually. The sales tax rate is 8%. Source documents are abbreviated as follows: sales invoice, S; credit memorandum, CM.

    Transactions in September:
    3. Sold a desk on account to LKL Products Co. for $1,415.00, plus sales tax. S422.
    6. Sold a chair on account to United Charities (tax exempt) for $310.00. S423.
    11. Sold three desks on account to Grasson, Inc., for $2,400.00, plus sales tax. S424.
    16. Granted credit to Grasson, Inc., for one of the desks sold on S424, $800.00, plus sales tax. CM45.
    23. Sold 10 chairs on account to LKL Products Co. for $3,650.00, plus sales tax. S425.
    27. Granted credit to Davenport Corp. as an allowance for a defective chair, $75.00, plus sales tax from sales invoice S421. CM46.

2. Prove and rule the sales journal. Post the totals to the general ledger.

On your own 2-1   LO2, 3, 4, 5

Journalizing and posting departmental sales on account and sales returns and allowances

Danger Downhill has two departments: Equipment and Accessories. Page 10 of a sales journal, page 15 of a general journal, and partial accounts receivable and general ledgers are provided in the *Working Papers*. Work this problem independently.

1. Journalize the following transactions completed during October of the current year. Post the items that are to be posted individually. The sales tax rate is 8%. Source documents are abbreviated as follows: sales invoice, S; credit memorandum, CM.

    Transactions in October:
    2. Sold ski equipment on account to Mason Dent for $763.00, plus sales tax. S144.
    7. Sold 5 hand warmers on account to Sara Stennis for $35.00, plus sales tax. S145.
    12. Granted credit to Sara Stennis as an allowance for two defective hand warmers, $14.00, plus sales tax from sales invoice S145. CM16.
    18. Sold 10 sets of skis and boots on account to Mountain Pass High School, $4,250.00. No sales tax. S146.
    19. Granted credit to Mason Dent for the return of ski poles, $52.00, plus sales tax from sales invoice S144. CM17.
    27. Sold training videos (accessories) on account to Davis Reese for $375.00, plus sales tax. S147.

2. Prove and rule the sales journal. Post the totals to the general ledger.

LO6 Explain the impact of sales discounts on the collection of accounts receivable.

LO7 Journalize departmental cash receipts using a cash receipts journal.

LO8 Post cash receipts to an accounts receivable ledger and a general ledger.

Cash Receipts on Account LO6

Whiley keeps a record of all cash receipts. The sources of most cash receipts are (1) cash received from customer payments on account and (2) cash and credit card sales.

Each customer is expected to pay the amount due within the agreed credit terms. To encourage early payment, a business may grant a deduction on the invoice amount. A deduction that a vendor allows on the invoice amount to encourage prompt payment is known as a *cash discount*. A cash discount on a sale taken by the customer is called a **sales discount**. Whiley sells on account using 2/10, n/30 terms. The *2/10* means that a 2% sales

discount may be deducted if sales on account are paid within 10 days of the invoice date. All sales on account must be paid within 30 days of the invoice date, or *n*/30.

When a sale is made on account, the amount debited to Accounts Receivable reflects the total amount owed by the customer, including sales tax. Sales is credited only for the pretax selling price. An additional credit must be made to Sales Tax Payable for the sales tax liability on the total sales invoice amount. Whiley prepares a receipt as the source document for cash received on account. **>>** App A: Objective Evidence

---

WHY ACCOUNTING?

Distribution Impacts a Company's Goals

A famous ice cream company in New England had the goal of using local suppliers and making all of the ice cream locally. The company also strived to minimize its impact on the environment. These two goals seemed attainable at the start. Local dairies provided the cream. Local residents were hired to make the ice cream, and it was delivered to local shops via fuel-efficient trucks. This strategy worked until the demand for ice cream spread to the west coast.

The company realized that the environmental impact of shipping ice cream across country in refrigerated containers was too high. A decision had to be made: Continue making the product locally and harm the environment during shipping, or expand the production facilities to the west coast. An environmental audit was

performed, and the company decided to relax its "make ice cream locally" goal.

Not all companies use the effect on the environment to decide where to locate their production facilities. Oftentimes, the "bottom line" is the determining factor, meaning that the plants will be located where all costs of production are the lowest.

CRITICAL THINKING

1. Besides shipping costs, what other costs could be considered by a company when determining where to locate its production facility?

2. Name three non-accounting factors that must also be considered when deciding where to locate a production facility.

Journalizing Cash Receipts LO7

Whiley records all cash receipts in a cash receipts journal. A business with more than one department records a sales on account in the same way as a business with a single department, except each department has separate Sales Credit and Sales Discount Debit columns in the cash receipts journal.

Journalizing a Cash Receipt with a Sales Discount

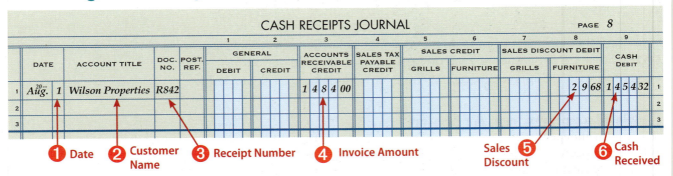

Whiley sold merchandise to Wilson Properties using 2/10, n/30 payment terms. The 2/10 means that a 2% discount may be deducted if a sale on account is paid within 10 days of the invoice date. The sale on account must be paid within 30 days of the invoice date, or n/30.

> **August 1. Received cash on account from Wilson Properties, $1,454.32, covering Sales Invoice No. 812 for outdoor furniture for $1,484.00 ($1,400.00 plus sales tax, $84.00), less 2% discount, $29.68. Receipt No. 842.**

The amount of cash received when payment is made within a discount period is calculated as follows:

Sales Amount	+	6.0% Sales Tax	=	Invoice Amount
$1,400.00	+	$84.00	=	$1,484.00

Invoice Amount	×	Discount Rate	=	Sales Discount
$1,484.00	×	2%	=	$29.68

Invoice Amount	−	Sales Discount	=	Amount Due
$1,484.00	−	$29.68	=	$1,454.32

Cash is increased by a $1,454.32 debit. The contra revenue account, Sales Discount—Furniture, is increased by a $29.68 debit. Using a separate account to record discounts allows the business to determine the proportion of available discounts that customers actually take. Accounts Receivable is decreased by a $1,484.00 credit. In the accounts receivable ledger, Wilson Properties is decreased by a $1,484.00 credit.

>> **Recording the Receipt of Cash When the Sales Discount is Taken**

1. Write the date, **20--** and **Aug. 1**, in the Date column.
2. Write the customer name, **Wilson Properties**, in the Account Title column.
3. Record the document number, **R842**, in the Doc. No. column.
4. Write the invoice amount, **$1,484.00**, in the Accounts Receivable Credit column.
5. Write the sales discount, **$29.68**, in the Sales Discount Debit Furniture column.
6. Write the amount of cash received, **$1,454.32**, in the Cash Debit column.

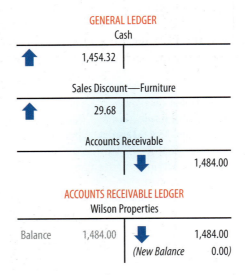

Journalizing Cash and Credit Card Sales

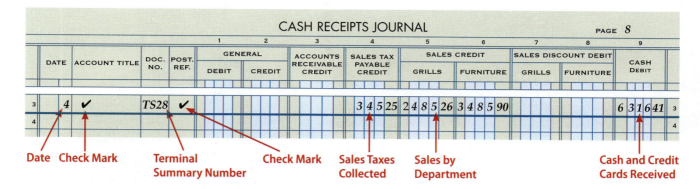

	DATE	ACCOUNT TITLE	DOC. NO.	POST. REF.	GENERAL DEBIT	GENERAL CREDIT	ACCOUNTS RECEIVABLE CREDIT	SALES TAX PAYABLE CREDIT	SALES CREDIT GRILLS	SALES CREDIT FURNITURE	SALES DISCOUNT DEBIT GRILLS	SALES DISCOUNT DEBIT FURNITURE	CASH DEBIT	
3	4	✔	TS28	✔				3 4 5 25	2 4 8 5 26	3 4 8 5 90			6 3 1 6 41	3
4														4

Date   Check Mark   Terminal Summary Number   Check Mark   Sales Taxes Collected   Sales by Department   Cash and Credit Cards Received

Whiley accepts cash or credit cards from its customers. An independent company or bank hired by Whiley to process credit card sales automatically deposits the daily total of credit card sales in Whiley's bank account. Because credit card sales are usually deposited in Whiley's account within two or three days, credit card sales and cash sales are recorded together in the cash receipts journal.

Both cash and credit card sales are entered into a modern version of a cash register. A specialized computer used to collect, store, and report all the information about a sales transaction is called a **point-of-sale (POS) terminal**. The POS terminal prints a receipt for the customer and internally accumulates data about total departmental sales. At least once a week, Whiley instructs the POS terminal to print a report of all cash and credit card sales. The report that summarizes the cash and credit card sales of a point-of-sale terminal is called a **terminal summary**. The terminal summary is identified with a *TS* and a sequential number. Whiley uses the terminal summary as the source document for cash and credit card sales. >> App A: Objective Evidence For a departmental business, the POS terminal would be programmed to report departmental sales on the terminal summary.

Cash increases by a $6,316.41 debit. Sales Tax Payable increases by a $345.25 credit. Sales—Grills increases by a $2,485.26 credit, and Sales—Furniture increases by a $3,485.90 credit.

GENERAL LEDGER

Cash
6,316.41 |

Sales Tax Payable
| 345.25

Sales—Grills
| 2,485.26

Sales—Furniture
| 3,485.90

The details of Terminal Summary No. 28 are recorded on line 3 of the cash receipts journal. The steps needed to record this transaction are similar to those required to record other cash receipts transactions. Place a check mark in the Account Title column to show that no account title needs to be written. Place a check mark in the Post. Ref. column to show that amounts on this line are not to be posted individually.

> **August 4.** Recorded cash and credit card sales: grills, $2,485.26; outdoor furniture, $3,485.90; plus sales tax, $345.25; total, $6,316.41. Terminal Summary No. 28.

FYI Cash and credit card sales may include sales to tax-exempt organizations. Thus, the sales tax payable amount may not equal total sales multiplied by the sales tax rate.

Careers In Accounting

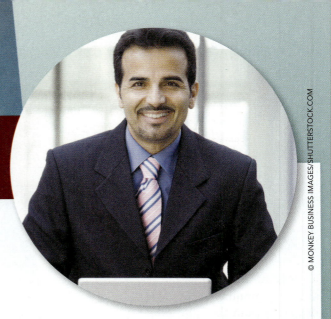

Ahmed Rucker
Owner of CPA Firm

Immediately out of college, Ahmed Rucker started working in a large accounting firm. He enjoyed his work, and after a few years, he started thinking that he would like to have his own accounting practice someday. Ahmed started by doing part-time work in the evenings and on weekends for a few small businesses. After about four years, he decided to quit his job with the large accounting firm and go on his own full time.

With the help of a mentor from the Small Business Administration (SBA), Ahmed developed a business plan. He hired an office administrator and rented a small office. At first, he needed to spend much of his daytime hours meeting with prospective new clients. Ahmed offered these new clients a full range of accounting services. For some clients, he did all of their recordkeeping, from recording transactions through preparing financial statements. Many clients hired Ahmed to prepare tax returns and give tax advice.

Some small businesses recorded their own transactions, hiring Ahmed to complete year-end work, such as adjusting entries and preparing financial statements. He found that he sometimes needed to advise and educate these clients on how to follow standard procedures for recording transactions. In the early years of his business, he also did payroll services. However, as he took on more and more accounting clients, he realized he couldn't do it all and gave up his payroll clients. When asked about those early years, Ahmed doesn't like to think about how much he made per hour. He will admit that he worked many hours and had some periods of negative cash flow.

As his business grew, Ahmed needed to spend less time meeting with potential new clients. Most of his new business was acquired by referrals from his current clients. He also found

that if he took the time to educate his clients up front, he could spend less time correcting errors and more time focusing on advisory services.

Today, Ahmed has two additional CPAs working for him. These assistants do much of the daily work of the firm. Ahmed focuses on scheduling projects for himself and his staff, meeting with major clients, and overseeing and finalizing the work of his assistants. However, he still has contact with all clients. He feels that this personal contact is very important to each client and a major reason why each client chose to work with a smaller accounting firm.

Looking back over the years, Ahmed feels all the hard work was very worthwhile. He enjoys his relationship with his clients. He feels good when he can give them advice and help them with accounting issues.

Salary Range: The salary range for the owner of a small accounting firm varies greatly, depending on several factors, such as geographic location, specialization of services, and number of employees.

Qualifications: The qualifications for the owner of a small accounting firm vary, based on the services offered. For broad-based services, the designation of CPA is required. Additional education in tax preparation is also required for tax preparers.

Occupational Outlook: The growth for accounting positions is projected to be higher than average (10% to 14%) for the period from 2016 to 2026.

Source: www.onetonline.org.

Taking a Discount after a Sales Return

CASH RECEIPTS JOURNAL													PAGE 8	
					1	2	3	4	5	6	7	8	9	
					GENERAL		ACCOUNTS RECEIVABLE CREDIT	SALES TAX PAYABLE CREDIT	SALES CREDIT		SALES DISCOUNT DEBIT		CASH DEBIT	
DATE	ACCOUNT TITLE	DOC. NO.	POST. REF.		DEBIT	CREDIT			GRILLS	FURNITURE	GRILLS	FURNITURE		
5	Taylor Apartments	R844	175				2 2 9 3 24				4 5 86		2 2 4 7 38	

Sales discounts are calculated on the amount owed at the time the invoice is paid. When a customer takes a discount after being granted a return or an allowance, the amount of the return or allowance must be deducted from the amount of the original sale before the discount can be calculated. To calculate the amount of cash received, (1) find the sales discount amount and (2) determine the amount of cash to be received. The calculation for these items is shown below.

This transaction is journalized the same way as a receipt of cash when there is no sales return or allowance. The only difference is the way in which the amounts are calculated. In the general ledger, Accounts Receivable is decreased by a $2,293.24 credit. The amount that the customer paid, $2,247.38, represents the customer's outstanding balance less the sales discount, $45.86. Therefore, Cash is increased by a $2,247.38 debit and the contra revenue account Sales Discount—Grills is increased by a $45.86 debit. In the accounts receivable ledger, Taylor Apartments is decreased by a $2,293.24 credit.

> **August 5.** Received cash on account from Taylor Apartments, $2,247.38, covering Sales Invoice No. 816 for $2,605.94 ($2,458.43 plus sales tax of 6.00%), less Credit Memorandum No. 30 for $312.70 ($295.00 plus sales tax, $17.70), less 2% discount, $45.86. Receipt No. 844.

GENERAL LEDGER

Cash
2,247.38	

Sales Discount—Grills
45.86	

Accounts Receivable
S816	2,605.94	CM30	312.70
			2,293.24

ACCOUNTS RECEIVABLE LEDGER

Taylor Apartments
S816	2,605.94	CM30	312.70
S864	1,627.62		2,293.24
(New Balance	1,627.62)		

	Sales Amount	+	Sales Tax	=	Invoice Amount
Original Sales Invoice Amount (S816)	$2,458.43	+	$147.51	=	$2,605.94
less Sales Return (CM30)	295.00	+	17.70	=	312.70
equals Sales Invoice Amount after Return	$2,163.43	+	$129.81	=	$2,293.24

Sales Invoice Amount after Return	×	Sales Discount Rate	=	Sales Discount
$2,293.24	×	2%	=	$45.86

Sales Invoice Amount after Return	−	Sales Discount	=	Net Sale (Cash Collected)
$2,293.24	−	$45.86	=	$2,247.38

Posting from a Cash Receipts Journal LO8

CASH RECEIPTS JOURNAL PAGE 8

	DATE	ACCOUNT TITLE	DOC. NO.	POST. REF.	GENERAL DEBIT	GENERAL CREDIT	ACCOUNTS RECEIVABLE CREDIT	SALES TAX PAYABLE CREDIT	SALES CREDIT GRILLS	SALES CREDIT FURNITURE	SALES DISCOUNT DEBIT GRILLS	SALES DISCOUNT DEBIT FURNITURE	CASH DEBIT	
					1	2	3	4	5	6	7	8	9	
1	5	Taylor Apartments	R844	175			2 2 9 3 24				4 5 8 6		2 2 4 7 38	1
25	30	Denison Landscapes	R860	125			1 3 5 9 00					2 7 18	1 3 3 1 82	25
26	31	Totals			—	—	28 9 4 8 16	8 5 9 18	7 4 1 5 95	9 1 4 8 25	3 4 8 19	46 0 2 3 35		26
27					(✔)	(✔)	(1205)	(2110)	(4105)	(4205)	(4110)	(4210)	(1105)	27
28														28

① Date **②** Journal Page Number **③** Column Total **⑤** Account Number

ACCOUNT Accounts Receivable — ACCOUNT NO. 1205

DATE	ITEM	POST. REF.	DEBIT	CREDIT	BALANCE DEBIT	BALANCE CREDIT
20-- Aug. 1	Balance	✔			52 6 3 9 86	
2		G8		3 1 2 70	52 3 2 7 16	
31		S8	27 1 6 4 69		79 4 9 1 85	
31		CR8		28 9 4 8 16	50 5 4 3 69	

④ Account Balance

CUSTOMER Taylor Apartments — CUSTOMER NO. 175 **⑤**

DATE	ITEM	POST. REF.	DEBIT	CREDIT	DEBIT BALANCE
20-- July 27	Balance	S7	2 6 0 5 94		2 6 0 5 94
Aug. 2		G8		3 1 2 70	2 2 9 3 24
4		S8	1 6 2 7 62		3 9 2 0 86
5		CR8		2 2 9 3 24	1 6 2 7 62

① **②** **③** **④**

When the journal page is full or at the end of the month, the cash receipts journal is proved and ruled. Proving cash before the journal's column totals are posted helps to identify any errors in recording transactions. The cash columns of the cash receipts and cash payments journals are used to calculate an updated cash balance. This balance should match the outstanding cash balance on the next unused check stub.

The steps for posting a cash receipt to an accounts receivable account are similar to the posting of sales on account. The letters CR and the journal page number are entered in the Post. Ref. column. Individual amounts in the Accounts Receivable Credit column are posted when the transaction is recorded in the cash receipts journal. This procedure keeps the customers' accounts up to date. The accounts receivable account for Taylor Apartments shows the history of the original sales invoice, the credit memorandum, and the cash receipt.

Totals of the special amount columns in the cash receipts journal are posted to their respective accounts in the general ledger. The general ledger account number is written in parentheses immediately below the total. A check mark is placed in parentheses below the totals of the General Debit and Credit columns to show that the totals are not posted.

>> Posting Amounts from the Cash Receipts Journal

① Write the date in the Date column.

② Write **CR8** in the Post. Ref. column of the account to indicate that the posting came from page 8 of the cash receipts journal.

③ Write the debit or credit amount in the appropriate column of the account.

④ Record the updated account balance.

⑤ Record the account numbers under the total of a special column or in the Post. Ref. column of the journal.

Evaluating Departmental Sales

Hua Wang was about to enter her first meeting with the board of directors of Breland Fashions. She had been hired just three days ago as Breland's first chief financial officer. Thus, she had to review quickly the following departmental sales report, which Bonita Alvarez, an accounting intern, had prepared for her:

Department	Budget	Actual	Budget Variance	
Children's Apparel	$ 65,000	$ 63,084	↑	$ (1,916)
Gifts	32,000	30,180	↑	(1,820)
Housewares	48,000	51,982	↑	3,982
Jewelry	69,000	54,382	↓	(14,618)
Men's Apparel	124,000	118,917	→	(5,083)
Men's Shoes	28,000	29,079	↑	1,079
Women's Apparel	223,000	214,932	→	(8,068)
Women's Shoes	87,000	79,847	→	(7,153)

Hua recognized that the arrows in the Budget Variance column had been created by Excel's conditional formatting tool. "A good use of technology," she said. "But its application may confuse the board. What does this green arrow mean to you?" she said, pointing to the negative Budget Variance amount for the gifts department. She paused to allow Bonita to consider the question. "I think most people think green is good," she continued, "so I wonder if they'll understand green arrows next to negative amounts."

OPEN THE SPREADSHEET TLA_CH02

Follow the steps on the Instructions tab. Modify the report to provide better information on actual departmental sales relative to the budget. Use the spreadsheet to answer the following questions:

1. Determine the range of values that would result in a red, yellow, and green arrow in the Over (Under) Budget column.

2. Which department(s) sold 105% or more of its budget?

3. Which department(s) sold 95% or less of its budget?

4. Compare the arrows in the original and revised reports. State how the original application of conditional formatting of the amount of the budget variance was misleading.

LO6 Explain the impact of sales discounts on the collection of accounts receivable.

LO7 Journalize departmental cash receipts using a cash receipts journal.

LO8 Post cash receipts to an accounts receivable ledger and a general ledger.

TERMS REVIEW

sales discount

point-of-sale (POS) terminal

terminal summary

Audit your understanding LO6, 7, 8

1. Why does a business offer cash discounts?
2. What does 2/10, n/30 mean?
3. What impact does a sales discount have on the amount recorded in the Sales account?
4. Why are credit card sales and cash sales recorded together in the sales journal?
5. How and when are entries in the Accounts Receivable Credit column posted?

Work together 2-2 LO7, 8
Journalizing and posting departmental cash receipts

Columbus Hardware has two departments: Hardware and Lumber. The company offers credit terms of 2/10, n/30. Page 5 of a cash receipts journal and partial accounts receivable and general ledgers are provided in the *Working Papers*.

1. Journalize the following transactions completed during March of the current year. Post the items that are to be posted individually. The sales tax rate is 7.5%. Assume sales tax was paid on all cash and credit card sales. Source documents are abbreviated as follows: credit memorandum, CM; receipt, R; sales invoice, S; terminal summary, TS.

   Transactions in March:
   3. Received cash on account from Andrews Homes for lumber purchased on S426 for $12,458.95, less discount. R445.
   4. Recorded cash and credit card sales for the week: hardware, $3,194.18; lumber, $8,418.69; plus sales tax. TS12.
   7. Received a check from Estate Housing for lumber on S428 for $9,248.17, less CM44 for $833.02, less discount. R446.
   18. Received a check from Lisle Construction for hardware on S435 for $2,473.61, less CM45 for $325.51, less discount. R447.
   22. Recorded cash and credit card sales for the week: hardware, $4,184.94; lumber, $6,148.71; plus sales tax. TS13.

2. Prove and rule the cash receipts journal. Post the totals to the general ledger.

On your own 2-2 LO7, 8
Journalizing and posting departmental cash receipts

Forde Growers has two departments: Flowers and Plants. The company offers credit terms of 1/10, n/30. Page 5 of a cash receipts journal and partial accounts receivable and general ledgers are provided in the *Working Papers*. Work this problem independently.

1. Journalize the following transactions completed during April of the current year. The sales tax rate is 6.5%; assume sales tax was paid on all cash and credit card sales. Source documents are abbreviated as follows: credit memorandum, CM; receipt, R; sales invoice, S; terminal summary, TS.

   Transactions in April:
   2. Received cash on account from Hillside Manor for flowers purchased on S297 for $615.17, less discount. R321.
   5. Recorded cash and credit card sales for the week: flowers, $624.89; plants, $1,048.69; plus sales tax. TS16.
   6. Received a check from Bakersville Gardens for plants purchased on S299 for $1,065.71, less discount. R322.
   15. Recorded cash and credit card sales for the week: flowers, $1,097.43; plants, $1,190.45; plus sales tax. TS17.
   21. Received a check from Grendon Clinic for plants purchased on March 22 on S278 for $229.61, less CM21 for $35.20, no discount. R323.
   26. Received a check from Platte Hotels for flowers purchased on S428 for $841.95, less CM22 for $294.33, less discount. R324.

2. Prove and rule the cash receipts journal. Post the totals to the general ledger.

Receiving a Payment on Account

Managing accounts receivable is an important accounting function. In large companies, accounts receivable (AR) is usually a department, with its own employees, within the larger accounting department. The accounts receivable staff would include a credit manager who decides which customers can be extended credit and how much credit they are allowed. When customers fall behind in their payments, it is the AR staff that sends reminders and makes phone calls in an effort to collect. Dealing with customer accounts is an important part of maintaining good customer relations. Errors in handling customer billings and receipts can damage customer relations.

There are several errors that AR could make in receiving a customer payment. (1) The payment could be applied to the wrong customer account. (2) The amount of the payment could be entered incorrectly. (3) The payment might not be applied against the invoices and credit memos intended by the customer. (4) An earned discount might not be given or might be calculated incorrectly. (5) The debit could be posted to the wrong general ledger account. While computerized accounting systems improve accuracy and efficiency over manual systems, only errors 4 and 5 might be avoided with an automated system. Ultimately, it is the accounting staff that must take responsibility for correctly processing customer payments, whether their system is manual or automated.

❶ On the **Received on Account** tab, the user selects (by number or name) the customer whose check is being received. The system enters the address, contact information, and a list of open items—invoices and credit memorandums.

❷ The current date is entered by the system, but it can be changed if the receipt occurred at an earlier date. The system automatically assigns the next sequential receipt number.

❸ The user selects the type of payment—cash, check, credit card, or EFT (electronic fund transfer)—and keys the amount of the receipt. The system deducts the payment from the customer account balance and displays the new balance. Double-clicking the account balance would display a pop-up window

with the customer's account. Clicking **New** on the menu bar would clear the window and allow the user to start over or enter another receipt.

❹ The system enters the default Cash account. If another account is to be debited, the user can change this account number. The system displays the account title.

❺ The system displays the new balance of account number 1105-00.

❻ The system is programmed to apply the payment to the customer's account in a logical sequence. First, it would look for an invoice matching the amount of the payment. In this case, no invoice matches the amount of the payment, so the system would apply the payment to the oldest invoice.

Receive Cash

New	Open	Save	Undo	Redo	Delete	Print	Help

Cash Sale | **Received on Account**

Customer No.: 120
Customer Name: Taylor Apartments

Taylor Apartments
101 Taylor Road
Colorado Springs, CO 80905
(555) 437-0101

Date Received: Aug. 5, 20--
Receipt No.: 844
Payment Method: Check
Amount Received: 2,247.38
Account Balance: 468.82

Account No.: 1105-00
Account Title: Cash
Account Balance: 24,093.17

P D	Inv. No.	Due Date	Amount Due	Disc.	Amt. Paid	Bal. Due	Memo
✔	816	Aug. 26, 20--	2,605.94	45.86	2,560.08	0.00	Paid by check #126913
✔	CM30		(312.70)		(312.70)	0.00	Applied on invoice #816
	837	Sep. 30, 20--	1,627.62		0.00	1,627.62	

☐ Entered by user   ☐ Entered automatically

7 The system is programmed to apply a cash discount of 2% within ten days of the invoice date (see page 51). When the payment was entered, the system applied the payment to the oldest invoice and calculated the discount. Since the payment was less than the invoice amount, the system calculated the discount based on the amount paid ($2,247.38 ÷ 0.98 = $2,293.24; $2,293.24 × 0.02 = $45.86). The balance due would then be $312.70 ($2,605.94 − $45.86 − $2,247.38).

8 Seeing that the customer had applied the credit memo to the payment, the user clicked on the **PD** box for credit memo CM30. The system then applied the amount of the credit memo to invoice #816, resulting in the balances shown in the illustration.

9 The user has entered notes about how the payment was applied. The notes will be helpful if a question is ever raised about the payment.

10 The user clicks on **Save** to record the transaction and clear the window for the next receipt.

CHAPTER SUMMARY

Managers use departmental data to make decisions relating to business operations. Sales on account are recorded in the sales journal. Cash collected from sales on account are recorded in the cash receipts journal. Departmental sales are recorded in the Sales Credit columns of each journal.

Individual amounts in the Accounts Receivable column of each journal are posted when the transaction is recorded. This procedure keeps customer accounts up to date.

Each special journal contains a Sales Tax Payable Credit column. Most states require vendors to collect sales tax on sales of merchandise and services. Government agencies and some not-for-profit organizations are typically exempt from paying sales taxes.

A business receives cash from collections of its sales on account and cash sales. To encourage early payment of sales on account, a business may grant a sales discount on the invoice amount. Many businesses offer terms of 2/10, n/30. A 2% discount off the amount owed is allowed when the invoice is paid within ten days. Sales discounts are recorded in a contra revenue account. A Sales Discount Debit account for each department is in the cash receipts journal.

Cash sales include sales to customers who paid with a credit or debit card. Department sales are recorded in Sales Credit columns from information contained in a terminal summary.

A credit memorandum is prepared to document the return of merchandise from a customer. The credit memorandum is the source document for an entry in a general journal. Sales returns and allowances are recorded in a contra revenue account. Sales returns and allowances are posted to the accounts receivable and general ledgers when the transactions are journalized.

The totals of the special columns of each special journal are posted to the general ledger.

Transfer Pricing

Departmental accounting allows managers to evaluate the performance of individual departments. Some companies use departmental income from operations as a basis for rewarding effective managers. A management incentive plan could base a manager's salary on the amount of departmental income from operations, the percentage of income to net sales, or some other measure of profitability.

This type of incentive program becomes difficult to administer when a manager is responsible for a department in which the product is transferred to another department. Consider the following example. Cement Art has two departments: Design and Casting. The design department creates molds used by the casting department to make a variety of cement statues, bird baths, and planters. The casting department purchases its molds from the design department, pours cement in the molds, and sells the finished product to retail stores. The manager of each department receives a bonus equal to 0.05% of the department's profit.

The incentive plan would seem to be a good idea. However, if the casting department is required to purchase molds from the design department at any price, the design department manager has no incentive to control production costs. Thus,

management must establish policies to determine the prices of molds transferred between the departments. Setting prices for the transfer of products between the departments is known as *transfer pricing*. Several transfer pricing methods are available:

1. Set the price consistent with the prices charged by other suppliers of the same or similar products.

2. Set the price based on the price for which the product could be sold to other companies.

3. If the product is unique, use a percentage markup. This method must include a provision for containing increases in production costs.

INSTRUCTIONS

With another student, assume the roles of the design and casting department managers. Assume that the current cost of producing a mold is $20.00, and the mold is sold to the casting department for $25.00. The casting department adds $10.00 of other materials and labor to the product and sells the finished product to customers for $60.00. Negotiate a transfer pricing policy that provides an incentive salary for each manager. The policy should include a provision for the design manager to increase the price of a mold for an increase in production costs.

APPLY YOUR UNDERSTANDING

INSTRUCTIONS: Download problem instructions for Excel, QuickBooks, and Sage 50c from the textbook companion website at www.C21accounting.com.

2-1 Application Problem
Journalizing and posting departmental sales on account and sales returns and allowances LO2, 3, 4, 5

The sales journal, general journal, and partial accounts receivable and general ledgers for Welch Furniture are provided in the *Working Papers*. Welch Furniture has two departments: Chairs and Tables. The general ledger and accounts receivable ledger are provided in the *Working Papers*.

Instructions:

1. Journalize the transactions completed during May of the current year. Use page 5 of a sales journal and page 8 of a general journal. Post the following transactions when journalized: (1) transactions affecting the accounts receivable subsidiary ledger and (2) transactions recorded in the general journal. The sales tax rate is 7%. Source documents are abbreviated as follows: sales invoice, S; credit memorandum, CM.

   Transactions in May:

   4. Sold six chairs for $259.00 each on account to Elrod Clinic, plus sales tax. S256.
   8. Elrod Clinic received credit for returning one of the chairs sold on S256, plus sales tax. CM27.
   12. Sold a table on account to Anna Patrick for $534.00, plus sales tax. S257.
   16. Sold 20 chairs for $219.00 each on account to Lincoln City Schools. No sales tax. S258.
   17. Granted credit to Anna Patrick for the return of the table sold on S257, plus sales tax. CM28.
   23. Sold a table on account to Keller Stendal for $1,259.00, plus sales tax. S259.

2. Prove and rule the sales journal. Post the totals to the general ledger.

2-2 Application Problem
Journalizing and posting departmental cash receipts LO7, 8

sage 50

1. Journalize and post customer transactions on account to the cash receipts journal.
2. From the menu bar, select Reports & Forms; Accounts Receivable.
3. Print the sales journal and cash receipts journal.

QB *QuickBooks*

1. Journalize and post customer transactions on account in the Receive Payments window.
2. From the menu bar, select Reports; Banking, Deposit Detail.
3. From the menu bar, select Reports; Customers & Receivables, Customer Balance Detail.

Excel

1. Journalize and post customer transactions on account to the cash receipts journal, accounts payable ledger and general ledger.
2. Print the worksheets.

The cash receipts journal, partial accounts receivable ledger, and partial general ledger for Nelson Auto Parts are provided in the *Working Papers*. Nelson Auto Parts has two departments: Parts and Tires. The company offers credit terms of 2/10, n/30.

Instructions:

1. Journalize the following transactions completed during June of the current year. Use page 7 of a cash receipts journal. The sales tax rate is 6.5%; assume sales tax was paid on all cash and credit card sales. Post transactions affecting the accounts receivable subsidiary ledger when journalized. Source documents are abbreviated as follows: credit memorandum, CM; receipt, R; sales invoice, S; terminal summary, TS.

   Transactions in June:

   3. Received cash on account from Sam's Service Station for parts purchased on S624 for $624.95, less discount. R668.
   4. Received a check from Foreign Car Center for parts purchased on S599 for $498.18, less CM57 for $173.99, no discount. R669.
   6. Recorded cash and credit card sales for the week: parts, $3,594.16; tires, $6,451.95; plus sales tax. TS21.
   8. Received a check from Bob's Auto Repair for parts purchased on S625 for $842.62, less discount. R670.
   20. Recorded cash and credit card sales for the week: parts, $5,148.19; tires, $8,144.08; plus sales tax. TS22.
   22. Received a check from Delta Transportation for tires purchased on S634 for $3,221.94, less CM58 for $280.17, less discount. R671.

2. Prove and rule the cash receipts journal. Post the totals to the general ledger.

2-M Mastery Problem

Journalizing departmental sales, sales returns and allowances, and cash receipts LO2, 3, 4, 5, 7, 8

sage 50

1. Journalize and post customer transactions on account to the sales journal and cash receipts journal.
2. From the menu bar, select Reports & Forms; Accounts Receivable.
3. Print the sales journal and cash receipts journal.

 QB Quick Books

1. Journalize and post customer transactions on account in the Create Invoices window.
2. Journalize and post customer transactions on account in the Receive Payments window.
3. From the menu bar, select Reports; Sales, Sales by Customer Detail.

X (Excel)

1. Journalize and post customer transactions on account to the sales journal and cash receipts journal. Journalize and post sales returns to the general journal.
2. Post the transactions and journal totals to the accounts receivable and general ledgers.
3. Print the worksheets.

The sales journal, cash receipts journal, general journal, and partial accounts receivable and partial general ledgers for Maynard Office Supply are provided in the *Working Papers*. Maynard has two departments: Equipment and Supplies. The company offers credit terms of 2/10, n/30.

Instructions:

1. Journalize the transactions completed during May of the current year. Use page 5 of a sales journal, page 6 of a general journal, and page 8 of a cash receipts journal. The sales tax rate is 5%. Assume sales tax was paid on all cash and credit card sales. Post transactions affecting the accounts receivable subsidiary ledger and transactions in the general journal when journalized. Source documents are abbreviated as follows: credit memorandum, CM; receipt, R; sales invoice, S; terminal summary, TS.

Transactions in May:

3. Received cash on account from Lakeland Church for supplies purchased on April 26 covering S575 for $315.74, less discount. R603.
4. Sold equipment on account to Eastern Realty, $1,842.25, plus sales tax. S578.
5. Recorded cash and credit card sales: equipment, $6,148.27; supplies, $2,481.19; plus sales tax. TS21.
7. Granted credit to Eastern Realty for equipment returned, $295.00, plus sales tax, from S578. CM38.
12. Sold supplies on account to BLC Storage, $425.00, plus sales tax. S579.
13. Received cash on account from Eastern Realty for equipment purchased on May 4 on S578, less CM38, less discount. R604.
20. Received cash on account from BLC Storage for supplies purchased on May 12 on S579, less discount. R605.
23. Received $1,500.00 cash on account from Natural Products for equipment purchased on April 22. R606.
24. Sold supplies on account to Lakeland Church, $614.00. Lakeland Church is exempt from sales taxes. S580.
25. Recorded cash and credit card sales: equipment, $2,894.96; supplies, $3,148.09; plus sales tax. TS22.
26. Granted credit to Lakeland Church for supplies returned, $62.50, from S580. CM39.

2. Prove and rule the sales journal. Post the totals to the general ledger.
3. Prove and rule the cash receipts journal. Post the totals to the general ledger.

2-S Source Documents Problem

Journalizing departmental sales, sales returns and allowances, and cash receipts LO2, 3, 4, 5, 7, 8

Ozark AV Shack sells audio and video equipment. Journals and source documents related to the sales and cash receipts are provided in the *Working Papers*. Post the following transactions when journalized: (1) transactions affecting the accounts receivable subsidiary ledger, (2) transactions recorded in the general journal, and (3) cash receipts entered in a general amount column of the cash payments journal. Ozark AV Shack uses a chart of accounts similar to the one Whiley Outdoor Living, Inc., uses.

Instructions:

1. Journalize the transactions shown in the source documents, by date, using page 11 of a sales journal, page 13 of a general journal, and page 14 of a cash receipts journal. All outstanding accounts receivable on November 1 relate to the sales of audio equipment. Post the items that are to be posted individually.
2. Prove and rule the sales journal. Post the totals.
3. Prove and rule the cash receipts journal. Post the totals.

Journalizing departmental sales, sales returns and allowances, and cash receipts LO7

Ellis Paint sells paint and paint supplies. Many customers purchase merchandise from both departments on a single sales invoice. Ellis Paint offers its customers terms of 2/10, n/30. Thus, any sales discount needs to be divided between the paint and supplies departments. Sales and sales return transactions are journalized in the sales and general journals shown below. A cash receipts journal is provided in the *Working Papers*.

SALES JOURNAL

PAGE 6

	DATE	ACCOUNT DEBITED	SALE NO.	POST. REF.	ACCOUNTS RECEIVABLE DEBIT	SALES TAX PAYABLE CREDIT	SALES CREDIT PAINT	SALES CREDIT SUPPLIES	
1	June 6	Daniel Painters	664	125	2 7 6 48	2 0 48	1 9 9 68	5 6 32	1
2	9	Hammond Construction	665	145	6 7 4 35	4 9 95	3 7 4 64	2 4 9 76	2
3	12	Rowell Designs	666	180	3 9 7 49	2 9 44	2 3 2 50	1 3 5 55	3

GENERAL JOURNAL

PAGE 12

	DATE	ACCOUNT TITLE	DOC. NO.	POST. REF.	DEBIT	CREDIT	
1	June 15	Sales Returns and Allowances—Supplies	CM55	4215	2 5 95		1
2		Sales Tax Payable		2110	2 08		2
3		Accounts Receivable/Rowell Designs		1205/180		2 8 03	3
4							4
5							5

Instructions:

Journalize the transactions completed during June of the current year. Use page 9 of a cash receipts journal. The sales tax rate is 8%. Source documents are abbreviated as follows: credit memorandum, CM; receipt, R; sales invoice, S.

Transactions:

June 12. Received cash on account from Daniel Painters covering S664, less discount. R701.

16. Received cash on account from Hammond Construction covering S665, less discount. R702.

20. Received cash on account from Rowell Designs covering S666, less CM55, less discount. R703.

Bug Appétit!

Theme: Financial, Economic, Business, and Entrepreneurial Literacy

Skills: Creativity and Innovation, Critical Thinking and Problem Solving, Communication and Collaboration, ICT Literacy

PARTNERSHIP FOR
21ST CENTURY SKILLS

While restaurants are winning customers with dishes like caramelized mealworms and fried arachnid, entrepreneurs are creating new business opportunities. Organic insects by World Entomophagy, scorpion suckers by Hotlix, or cricket protein bars by Exo are several of the new ventures.

Eating insects is actually an old tradition. Crickets, beetles, cicadas, and locusts are recorded in historical writings and have been consumed by humans for over ten thousand years. For example, fried winged termites are consumed in Ghana, grubs in New Guinea, and cicadas in Latin America. Experts say that insects are a food source for almost 80% of the world's population; yet Americans still prefer livestock.

Food preferences are usually determined by culture. Entomophagy, or eating insects, is gaining in popularity due to the nutritional value and environmental advantages. It could be the food of the future and an opportunity to increase sales. Perhaps the next time you eat BLTs, you will be eating beetles, locusts, and tarantulas!

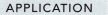

APPLICATION

1. You are in the livestock business. It is estimated that the world population is expected to reach 9 billion people by 2050, and insects could be a viable option for food. With a partner, brainstorm three business opportunities involving insects that could help you maintain sales. Share your findings with the class.

2. Using the Internet, research advantages of eating insects. Create a commercial convincing others to get over the "yuck" factor and consume insects.

Source: www.time.com/time/magazine/article/0,9171,1810336,00.html; www.businessweek.com/magazine/on-the-menu-stinkbugs-and-mealworms-11172011.html.

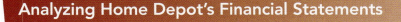

Analyzing Home Depot's Financial Statements

Published financial statements include notes that provide a better understanding of some of the amounts, terms, and accounting policies used in preparing them. Home Depot's Consolidated Balance Sheets contain the heading "Cash and Cash Equivalents." The reader of the financial statements must refer to Home Depot's notes to learn what it reports in this amount on its balance sheets.

INSTRUCTIONS

1. Using the Consolidated Balance Sheets in Appendix B on page B-5, identify the actual amount of Home Depot's cash and cash equivalents as of January 28, 2018.

2. Referring to the Notes to Consolidated Financial Statements in Appendix B beginning on page B-10, identify the types of financial instruments included in cash and cash equivalents.

3

CHAPTER 3

Calculating and Recording Departmental Payroll Data

LEARNING OBJECTIVES

After studying Chapter 3, in addition to defining key terms, you will be able to:

LO1 Explain how employees are paid.

LO2 Calculate employee earnings.

LO3 Prepare payroll reports.

LO4 Explain the procedures for the payment of a payroll.

LO5 Journalize the payment of a payroll.

LO6 Explain the process for calculating the four payroll taxes typically paid by employers.

LO7 Journalize the payment of payroll taxes.

© JIRSAK/SHUTTERSTOCK.COM.

Netchex

ACCOUNTING IN THE REAL WORLD

NETCHEXONLINE.COM

Paying employees for their labor is a fundamentally simple process. Multiply the hours worked by the hourly wage rate, and then prepare a check for that amount. But wait! Income taxes, Social Security, and Medicare taxes must be deducted and deposited with the appropriate government agency on a rigid time schedule. Health insurance, retirement contributions, and other voluntary deductions must be processed. At the end of the year, numerous tax forms must be on file and tax reports must be printed. In reality, payroll accounting can be complicated, tedious, and often confusing.

It's no surprise that when computers were first introduced last century, payroll applications were among the first to be automated. For decades large corporations have used in-house computer systems for payroll processing. Smaller companies often elected to "outsource" their payroll preparation to specialized service organizations. Outsourcing payroll processing does not relieve a business of its responsibilities. Accountants must understand payroll tax laws and procedures to ensure the business complies with all federal, state, and city tax regulations.

Formed little more than a decade ago, Netchex is a relative newcomer to the payroll outsourcing market. The company offers cloud-based solutions that use the latest computer and web technology to provide clients with more than the preparation of checks and tax forms. Its family of technology solutions supports recruiting, hiring, onboarding, human resources, and employee benefits. When the government enacts new laws, such as the Tax Cuts and Jobs Act of 2017, Netchex professionals quickly modify the software to ensure that their clients are in full compliance with the law.

Data analytics is an increasingly important component of the payroll function. Netchex solutions enable managers to access detailed payroll data. Using filter, sort, and dashboard tools, businesses gain insights into all aspects of employee management. Thus, *human capital management* has become the modern term for the software solutions and systems related to recruiting, hiring, and paying an organization's workforce.

Source: netchexonline.com.

CRITICAL THINKING

1. Search the Internet to identify the types of tasks involved in "onboarding."

2. Suggest some activities that would enable new employees to learn the social norms of the organization.

KEY TERMS

wage	payroll	tax base	automatic check deposit
salary	payroll taxes	payroll register	electronic funds transfer (EFT)
pay period	withholding allowance	employee earnings record	

LO1 Explain how employees are paid.
LO2 Calculate employee earnings.
LO3 Prepare payroll reports.

Paying Employees LO1

Employees are an essential element of the business world. Businesses depend on competent employees in order to operate successfully. Employees provide services to a business in exchange for money. The amount paid to an employee for every hour worked is called a **wage**. A fixed annual sum of money divided among equal pay periods is called a **salary**. Federal, state, and local laws require employers to keep accurate records of payments to employees and other payments related to employee services. Payroll records are maintained for the business and for each employee. The payroll system used differs among businesses. A business protects itself by keeping complete and accurate payroll records of all required information.

The number of days or weeks of work covered by an employee's paycheck is called a **pay period**. The total amount earned by all employees for a pay period is called a **payroll**. In addition to salaries, a business must pay taxes based on the payroll. Taxes based on the payroll of a business are called **payroll taxes**. The law also requires employers to withhold certain payroll taxes from employee salaries each pay period.

Periodically, employers must pay government agencies all payroll taxes withheld from employee salaries as well as the employer payroll taxes. A business must also provide a yearly report to each employee showing the total salary earned and the total taxes withheld. The yearly report is provided to each employee on Form W-2. Businesses must distribute this form to their employees by January 31, reporting earnings and amounts withheld for the previous calendar year. Therefore, a business must keep records of each employee's earnings, amounts withheld, and net amount paid. Payroll records also must show the total amount of payroll taxes that a business must pay.

ETHICS IN ACTION

The Danger of Social Media

Angela is recognized as the best salesclerk in the juniors clothing department at Chandler's Fashions. She has a special talent for selecting brands that best fit a customer's size and shape. Angela's regular customers often communicate with her via her personal social media account. A recent exchange follows:

Maggie: When are the Christiana summer styles arriving?

Angela: Probably early April.

Maggie: I hear the colors are really bright. Can't wait!

Angela: Don't get too excited.

Maggie: ???

Angela: Unless you're a supermodel, you're not going to be able to pull it off.

Maggie: ☹

INSTRUCTIONS

Access the *Business Conduct Guide* of Target Stores. Using this code and the ethical model, determine whether Angela's posts demonstrate ethical behavior.

Payroll Deductions

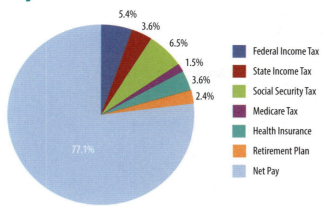

- 5.4% Federal Income Tax
- 3.6% State Income Tax
- 6.5% Social Security Tax
- 1.5% Medicare Tax
- 3.6% Health Insurance
- 2.4% Retirement Plan
- 77.1% Net Pay

Whiley is required by law to withhold federal income tax and two FICA taxes (Social Security tax and Medicare tax) from each employee's pay. *FICA* is the abbreviation for the Federal Insurance Contributions Act.

The total earnings, marital status, and number of withholding allowances claimed by an employee determine the federal income tax amount to be withheld. For each person supported, including the employee, an employee is entitled to a reduction in the amount on which income tax is calculated. A deduction from total earnings for each person legally supported by a taxpayer, including the employee, is called a **withholding allowance**.

FICA provides for a federal system of old age, survivors, disability, and hospital insurance. The Social Security tax finances the old age, survivors, and disability insurance portion. The Medicare tax finances the hospital insurance portion. Each of these taxes is reported separately. Social Security tax is calculated on employee earnings up to a maximum paid in a calendar year. The maximum amount of earnings on which a tax is calculated is called a **tax base**. Congress sets the tax base and the tax rates for Social Security tax. The Social Security tax rate and base used in this textbook are 6.2% of earnings up to a maximum of $128,400.00 in each calendar year. Medicare does not have a tax base. The Medicare tax rate used in this text is 1.45% of total employee earnings.

Some cities and states also require that employers deduct amounts for income and other taxes from employee earnings. Laws for handling state, city, and county taxes vary.

Some businesses also make deductions from employee earnings for health insurance, life insurance, retirement plans, and charitable contributions. Whiley makes deductions from its employee salaries for federal income tax, state income tax, Social Security tax, Medicare tax, health insurance, and retirement plans. The payroll components for Guiren L. Heng are shown in the graph above.

GLOBAL AWARENESS

International Clubs

Many students want to learn more about other cultures and peoples. Because of this, schools and colleges often sponsor international clubs or organizations. The focus of these clubs may vary, but most bring students together to promote understanding and appreciation of different cultures.

Club activities reflect the focus of the organization. Some clubs may sponsor and plan global awareness events featuring international art, food, dance, and speakers. Other clubs may enable students to practice speaking a foreign language—or help international students practice speaking English. Clubs can focus on support for international students, ranging from assistance on educational visas to helping them connect with other students from their homeland. Some clubs organize social events to foster new relationships. A popular activity is the celebration of holidays of different cultures, educating participants on the traditions and history of each holiday.

Many international clubs focus on travel by sponsoring study-abroad programs. Some study-abroad programs organize studies in a different foreign country each semester, with all participating students attending the same classes in that country. In other programs, each student is able to choose the foreign country in which he or she wishes to study.

CRITICAL THINKING

1. Search the Internet to find an international club in your community. List at least one goal and one activity of the club.

2. Search the Internet to find out about a study-abroad program in your area—at either the high school or college level. List the name of the program and the sponsoring organization.

Calculating Employee Earnings LO2

Hourly Employee Time Summary					
Pay Period:	6/29/20-- to 7/12/20--				
Prepared on:	7/14/20--				
Name	**ID**	**Week Ended**	**Regular**	**Overtime**	**Totals**
Denton, Juanita P.	14	7/5/20--	40	1	41
		7/12/20--	40	3	43
			80	4	84
Golden, Larry A.	35	7/5/20--	40		40
		7/12/20--	40		40
			80		80
Jewell, Mary B.	18	7/5/20--	37	2	39
		7/12/20--	35		35
			72	2	74

Whiley pays an hourly salary biweekly to most store and accounting department employees. Whiley's biweekly pay period is 80 hours, consisting of two regular 40-hour workweeks. The store is open six days a week. However, employees usually work only a five-day week of 40 hours. The pay rate for these employees is stated as an hourly rate.

Whiley uses an employee identification card scanner to log employee hours. All employees have badges with a magnetic strip coded to include their name and identification number. Employees slide the card through the card scanner when they begin and end each work period. At the end of a payroll period, a report listing employee hours worked provides the data for calculating employee earnings. The employee hours report for the biweekly period June 29 through July 12 is shown above.

The software that supports the card scanner can produce a variety of reports. For example, to monitor employee attendance, a report of the actual times an employee arrives and leaves can also be generated.

All time worked in excess of 8 hours a day or 40 hours in any one week is considered overtime. Employees are paid 1½ times the regular rate for overtime hours. However, managers are paid a base salary and commissions, so their hours worked are not presented on this report.

Employee regular earnings are calculated by multiplying the hourly rate by the number of regular hours. Employee overtime earnings are calculated by multiplying the regular rate by 1.5 and multiplying the result by the number of overtime hours. The calculations are shown below for Juanita P. Denton.

Regular Hours	×	Regular Rate		=	Regular Earnings	
80	×	$18.00		=	$1,440.00	

Overtime Hours	×	Regular Rate	×	1.5		= Overtime Earnings
4	×	$18.00	×	1.5	=	$108.00

Regular Earnings	+	Overtime Earnings	=	Total Earnings
$1,440.00	+	$108.00	=	$1,548.00

Commissions Record

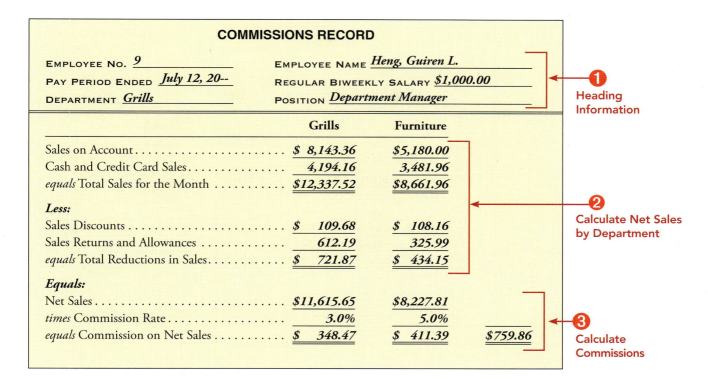

COMMISSIONS RECORD

EMPLOYEE NO. _9_ EMPLOYEE NAME _Heng, Guiren L._
PAY PERIOD ENDED _July 12, 20--_ REGULAR BIWEEKLY SALARY _$1,000.00_
DEPARTMENT _Grills_ POSITION _Department Manager_

❶ Heading Information

	Grills	Furniture	
Sales on Account......................	$ 8,143.36	$5,180.00	
Cash and Credit Card Sales..............	4,194.16	3,481.96	
equals Total Sales for the Month	$12,337.52	$8,661.96	
Less:			
Sales Discounts	$ 109.68	$ 108.16	
Sales Returns and Allowances	612.19	325.99	
equals Total Reductions in Sales...........	$ 721.87	$ 434.15	
Equals:			
Net Sales..............................	$11,615.65	$8,227.81	
times Commission Rate..................	3.0%	5.0%	
equals Commission on Net Sales	$ 348.47	$ 411.39	$759.86

❷ Calculate Net Sales by Department

❸ Calculate Commissions

Other types of earnings may supplement an employee's basic salary. For example, an employee may receive commissions, cost-of-living adjustments, a share of profits, or a bonus.

At Whiley, department managers are paid a biweekly salary. This salary compensates the managers for their responsibility for the operations and appearance of their department. They are not paid for overtime hours.

To encourage increased sales, the managers are paid a commission on their net sales. While serving a customer, each manager often sells merchandise from both departments. Thus, they receive a commission based on their sales of merchandise from each department.

The departments have different commission rates. Whiley recognizes that customers need more assistance with furniture purchases than with grill purchases. Thus, furniture sales have a higher commission rate, 5%, than the 3% earned for grills sales.

The point-of-sale system provides a detailed report of each supervisor's sales from credit card and cash sales during the pay period. Amounts related to credit sales are accumulated by an analysis of sales invoices and credit memoranda. These amounts are used on a commissions record to calculate each supervisor's commission.

▶▶ Preparing a Commissions Record

❶ Record the employee number, employee name, pay period, regular biweekly salary, department, and position at the top of the form.

❷ Calculate department net sales for the month:
  • Write the amount of sales on account for each department.
  • Write the amount of cash and credit card sales for the month.
  • Add the two sales amounts and write the total sales for the pay period.
  • Write the amount of sales discounts.

  • Write the amount of sales returns and allowances.
  • Write the total of sales discounts and sales returns and allowances.

❸ Calculate the commission on net sales for the month.
  • Calculate the difference between total sales for the month, less total sales discounts and returns and allowances. Write the amount of net sales.
  • Write the commission rate.
  • Multiply the commission rate times the net sales amount and write the commission on net sales.
  • The June commission for Guiren L. Heng is calculated as shown in the illustration.

Preparing Payroll Reports LO3

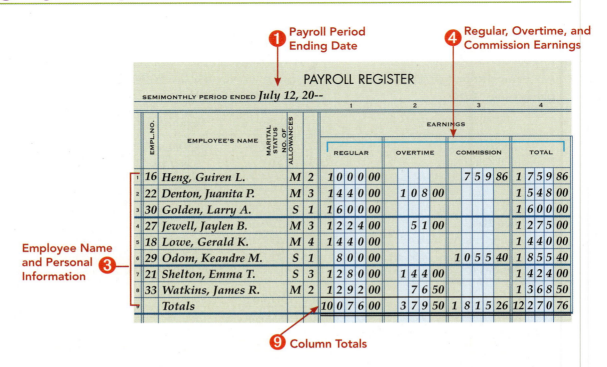

1 Payroll Period Ending Date

4 Regular, Overtime, and Commission Earnings

PAYROLL REGISTER

SEMIMONTHLY PERIOD ENDED *July 12, 20--*

Employee Name and Personal Information 3

	EMPL. NO.	EMPLOYEE'S NAME	MARITAL STATUS	NO. OF ALLOWANCES	EARNINGS			
					REGULAR	OVERTIME	COMMISSION	TOTAL
1	16	Heng, Guiren L.	M	2	1 0 0 0 00		7 5 9 86	1 7 5 9 86
2	22	Denton, Juanita P.	M	3	1 4 4 0 00	1 0 8 00		1 5 4 8 00
3	30	Golden, Larry A.	S	1	1 6 0 0 00			1 6 0 0 00
4	27	Jewell, Jaylen B.	M	3	1 2 2 4 00	5 1 00		1 2 7 5 00
5	18	Lowe, Gerald K.	M	4	1 4 4 0 00			1 4 4 0 00
6	29	Odom, Keandre M.	S	1	8 0 0 00		1 0 5 5 40	1 8 5 5 40
7	21	Shelton, Emma T.	S	3	1 2 8 0 00	1 4 4 00		1 4 2 4 00
8	33	Watkins, James R.	M	2	1 2 9 2 00	7 6 50		1 3 6 8 50
9		Totals			10 0 7 6 00	3 7 9 50	1 8 1 5 26	12 2 7 0 76

9 Column Totals

An accounting form that summarizes the earnings, deductions, and net pay of all employees for one pay period is called a **payroll register**. Whiley prepares a separate payroll register for each biweekly (every two weeks) payroll. Whiley's payroll register for the July 12 pay period is shown above and extends on to the next page.

To provide better cost control, Whiley separates employee earnings into three classifications: Grills Department, Furniture Department, and Administrative. The earnings of employees and departmental managers are recorded in their respective departmental classification. The earnings of the store manager and accounting and office employees are recorded in the Administrative classification.

>> Preparing a Payroll Register

For each pay period:

1 Enter the last day of the biweekly payroll period, July 12, 20--, at the top of the payroll register.

2 Record the date of payment, July 16, 20--, also at the top of the payroll register. The time between the end of a pay period and the date of payment is needed in order to prepare the payroll records and payroll checks.

For each employee:

3 Enter employee number, 16; name, Heng, Guiren L.; marital status, M; and number of allowances, 2. This information is taken from personnel records kept for each employee.

4 Write regular earnings, $1,000.00, and commissions, $759.86, in columns 1 and 3. An employee's overtime earnings would be entered in column 2. Write his total earnings, $1,759.86, in column 4.

The regular earnings are calculated for hourly employees. Manager salaries are recorded in the Regular Earnings column, column 1. Add the regular earnings, overtime earnings, and commission earnings together to determine the total earnings for the biweekly pay period.

5 Extend total earnings to the appropriate department column or Administrative Salaries.

PAYROLL REGISTER

DATE OF PAYMENT *July 16, 20--*

	5	6	7	8	9	10	11	12	13	14	15	
	DEPARTMENT			DEDUCTIONS								
	GRILLS	FURNITURE	ADMINIS-TRATIVE	FEDERAL INCOME TAX	STATE INCOME TAX	SOCIAL SECURITY TAX	MEDICARE TAX	HEALTH INSURANCE	RETIREMENT PLAN	TOTAL	NET PAY	CHECK NO.
1	1348.47	411.39		104.00	44.00	109.11	25.52	60.00	40.00	382.63	1377.23	1
2		1548.00		63.00	38.70	95.98	22.45	75.00	60.00	355.13	1192.87	2
3			1600.00	150.00	40.00	99.20	23.20	45.00	20.00	377.40	1222.60	3
4	1275.00			35.00	31.88	79.05	18.49	75.00	50.00	289.42	985.58	4
5			1440.00	35.00	36.00	89.28	20.88	90.00	60.00	331.16	1108.84	5
6	2293.37	1626.03		184.00	46.39	115.03	26.90	45.00	25.00	442.32	1413.08	6
7			1424.00	90.00	35.60	88.29	20.65	75.00	50.00	359.54	1064.46	7
8		1368.50		61.00	34.21	84.85	19.84	60.00	30.00	289.90	1078.60	8
9	2852.84	4953.92	4464.00	722.00	306.78	760.79	177.93	525.00	335.00	2827.50	9443.26	9

⑤ Earnings by Department ⑥ Payroll Deductions ⑦ Total Deductions ② Payment Date ⑧ Net Pay

>> Preparing a Payroll Register

⑥ Enter the payroll deductions: federal income tax, **$104.00**; state income tax, **$44.00**; Social Security tax, **$109.11**; Medicare tax, **$25.52**; health insurance, **$60.00**; and retirement plan, **$40.00**. Federal income tax withholding is calculated using withholding tables, such as the ones shown on pages 70–71. The state in which Whiley operates calculates state income tax at **2.5%** of total earnings. Guiren Heng's Social Security tax deduction for the biweekly pay period ended July 12 is calculated as shown here.

Total Earnings × Social Security Tax = Social Security Tax Deduction
$1,759.86 × 6.2% = $109.11

Guiren Heng's Medicare tax deduction for the biweekly pay period ended July 12 is calculated as shown here.

Total Earnings × Medicare Tax = Medicare Tax Deduction
$1,759.86 × 1.45% = $25.52

The number of dependents covered determines the health insurance deduction. A business determines what portion of monthly health insurance premium it requires its employees to pay.

Each employee determines the amount to be withheld for his or her contribution to the retirement plan.

⑦ Add the amounts for deductions and enter the total, **$382.63**, in column 14.

⑧ Subtract the total deductions from total earnings to determine net pay, **$1,377.23**. The net pay for Guiren Heng is calculated as shown here.

Total Earnings − Total Deductions = Net Pay
$1,759.86 − $382.63 = $1,377.23

At the end of the payroll period:

⑨ When the net pay has been entered for all employees, total each payroll register amount column. Subtract the Total Deductions column, **$2,827.50**, from the Total Earnings column, **$12,270.76**. The result should equal the total of the Net Pay column. If the totals do not agree, find and correct the errors. Rule the payroll register.

Using the Federal Income Tax Withholding Tables

Wage Bracket Method Tables for Income Tax Withholding

SINGLE Persons—**BIWEEKLY** Payroll Period

(For Wages Paid through December 31, 20--)

And the wages are—		And the number of withholding allowances claimed is—										
At least	But less than	0	1	2	3	4	5	6	7	8	9	10
		The amount of income tax to be withheld is—										
$960	$980	$92	$73	$54	$35	$19	$3	$0	$0	$0	$0	$0
980	1,000	94	75	56	37	21	5	0	0	0	0	0
1,000	1,020	97	78	58	39	23	7	0	0	0	0	0
1,020	1,040	99	80	61	42	25	9	0	0	0	0	0
1,040	1,060	102	82	63	44	27	11	0	0	0	0	0
1,060	1,080	104	85	66	47	29	13	0	0	0	0	0
1,080	1,100	106	87	68	49	31	15	0	0	0	0	0
1,100	1,120	109	90	70	51	33	17	1	0	0	0	0
1,120	1,140	111	92	73	54	35	19	3	0	0	0	0
1,140	1,160	114	94	75	56	37	21	5	0	0	0	0
1,160	1,180	116	97	78	59	39	23	7	0	0	0	0
1,180	1,200	118	99	80	61	42	25	9	0	0	0	0
1,200	1,220	121	102	82	63	44	27	11	0	0	0	0
1,220	1,240	123	104	85	66	47	29	13	0	0	0	0
1,240	1,260	126	106	87	68	49	31	15	0	0	0	0
1,260	1,280	128	109	90	71	51	33	17	1	0	0	0
1,280	1,300	130	111	92	73	54	35	19	3	0	0	0
1,300	1,320	133	114	94	75	56	37	21	5	0	0	0
1,320	1,340	135	116	97	78	59	39	23	7	0	0	0
1,340	1,360	138	118	99	80	61	42	25	9	0	0	0
1,360	1,380	140	121	102	83	63	44	27	11	0	0	0
1,380	1,400	142	123	104	85	66	47	29	13	0	0	0
1,400	1,420	145	126	106	87	68	49	31	15	0	0	0
1,420	1,440	147	128	109	90	71	51	33	17	1	0	0
1,440	1,460	150	130	111	92	73	54	35	19	3	0	0
1,460	1,480	152	133	114	95	75	56	37	21	5	0	0
1,480	1,500	154	135	116	97	78	59	39	23	7	0	0
1,500	1,520	157	138	118	99	80	61	42	25	9	0	0
1,520	1,540	159	140	121	102	83	63	44	27	11	0	0
1,540	1,560	162	142	123	104	85	66	47	29	13	0	0
1,560	1,580	164	145	126	107	87	68	49	31	15	0	0
1,580	1,600	166	147	128	109	90	71	51	33	17	1	0
1,600	1,620	169	150	130	111	92	73	54	35	19	3	0
1,620	1,640	171	152	133	114	95	75	56	37	21	5	0
1,640	1,660	176	154	135	116	97	78	59	40	23	7	0
1,660	1,680	180	157	138	119	99	80	61	42	25	9	0
1,680	1,700	184	159	140	121	102	83	63	44	27	11	0
1,700	1,720	189	162	142	123	104	85	66	47	29	13	0
1,720	1,740	193	164	145	126	107	87	68	49	31	15	0
1,740	1,760	198	166	147	128	109	90	71	52	33	17	1
1,760	1,780	202	169	150	131	111	92	73	54	35	19	3
1,780	1,800	206	171	152	133	114	95	75	56	37	21	5
1,800	1,820	211	176	154	135	116	97	78	59	40	23	7
1,820	1,840	215	180	157	138	119	99	80	61	42	25	9
1,840	1,860	220	184	159	140	121	102	83	64	44	27	11
1,860	1,880	224	189	162	143	123	104	85	66	47	29	13
1,880	1,900	228	193	164	145	126	107	87	68	49	31	15
1,900	1,920	233	198	166	147	128	109	90	71	52	33	17
1,920	1,940	237	202	169	150	131	111	92	73	54	35	19
1,940	1,960	242	206	171	152	133	114	95	76	56	37	21

FYI The taxes withheld from the earnings of single individuals are greater than those withheld from married individuals. For example, a single individual earning $1,800 with 2 allowances has $154 withheld. The same individual, if married, will have only $109 withheld. Depending on the spouse's earnings, the married individual may pay a higher annual tax bill. This unusual result of tax law has been dubbed the "marriage penalty."

Wage Bracket Method Tables for Income Tax Withholding
MARRIED Persons—BIWEEKLY Payroll Period
(For Wages Paid through December 31, 20--)

And the wages are—		And the number of withholding allowances claimed is—										
At least	But less than	0	1	2	3	4	5	6	7	8	9	10
		The amount of income tax to be withheld is—										
$865	$885	$43	$27	$11	$0	$0	$0	$0	$0	$0	$0	$0
885	905	45	29	13	0	0	0	0	0	0	0	0
905	925	47	31	15	0	0	0	0	0	0	0	0
925	945	49	33	17	1	0	0	0	0	0	0	0
945	965	51	35	19	3	0	0	0	0	0	0	0
965	985	53	37	21	5	0	0	0	0	0	0	0
985	1,005	55	39	23	7	0	0	0	0	0	0	0
1,005	1,025	57	41	25	9	0	0	0	0	0	0	0
1,025	1,045	59	43	27	11	0	0	0	0	0	0	0
1,045	1,065	61	45	29	13	0	0	0	0	0	0	0
1,065	1,085	63	47	31	15	0	0	0	0	0	0	0
1,085	1,105	65	49	33	17	1	0	0	0	0	0	0
1,105	1,125	67	51	35	19	3	0	0	0	0	0	0
1,125	1,145	69	53	37	21	5	0	0	0	0	0	0
1,145	1,165	71	55	39	23	7	0	0	0	0	0	0
1,165	1,185	73	57	41	25	9	0	0	0	0	0	0
1,185	1,205	75	59	43	27	11	0	0	0	0	0	0
1,205	1,225	78	61	45	29	13	0	0	0	0	0	0
1,225	1,245	80	63	47	31	15	0	0	0	0	0	0
1,245	1,265	83	65	49	33	17	1	0	0	0	0	0
1,265	1,285	85	67	51	35	19	3	0	0	0	0	0
1,285	1,305	87	69	53	37	21	5	0	0	0	0	0
1,305	1,325	90	71	55	39	23	7	0	0	0	0	0
1,325	1,345	92	73	57	41	25	9	0	0	0	0	0
1,345	1,365	95	75	59	43	27	11	0	0	0	0	0
1,365	1,385	97	78	61	45	29	13	0	0	0	0	0
1,385	1,405	99	80	63	47	31	15	0	0	0	0	0
1,405	1,425	102	83	65	49	33	17	1	0	0	0	0
1,425	1,445	104	85	67	51	35	19	3	0	0	0	0
1,445	1,465	107	87	69	53	37	21	5	0	0	0	0
1,465	1,485	109	90	71	55	39	23	7	0	0	0	0
1,485	1,505	111	92	73	57	41	25	9	0	0	0	0
1,505	1,525	114	95	76	59	43	27	11	0	0	0	0
1,525	1,545	116	97	78	61	45	29	13	0	0	0	0
1,545	1,565	119	99	80	63	47	31	15	0	0	0	0
1,565	1,585	121	102	83	65	49	33	17	1	0	0	0
1,585	1,605	123	104	85	67	51	35	19	3	0	0	0
1,605	1,625	126	107	88	69	53	37	21	5	0	0	0
1,625	1,645	128	109	90	71	55	39	23	7	0	0	0
1,645	1,665	131	111	92	73	57	41	25	9	0	0	0
1,665	1,685	133	114	95	76	59	43	27	11	0	0	0
1,685	1,705	135	116	97	78	61	45	29	13	0	0	0
1,705	1,725	138	119	100	80	63	47	31	15	0	0	0
1,725	1,745	140	121	102	83	65	49	33	17	1	0	0
1,745	1,765	143	123	104	85	67	51	35	19	3	0	0
1,765	1,785	145	126	107	88	69	53	37	21	5	0	0
1,785	1,805	147	128	109	90	71	55	39	23	7	0	0
1,805	1,825	150	131	112	92	73	57	41	25	9	0	0
1,825	1,845	152	133	114	95	76	59	43	27	11	0	0
1,845	1,865	155	135	116	97	78	61	45	29	13	0	0
1,865	1,885	157	138	119	100	80	63	47	31	15	0	0
1,885	1,905	159	140	121	102	83	65	49	33	17	1	0
1,905	1,925	162	143	124	104	85	67	51	35	19	3	0
1,925	1,945	164	145	126	107	88	69	53	37	21	5	0
1,945	1,965	167	147	128	109	90	71	55	39	23	7	0
1,965	1,985	169	150	131	112	92	73	57	41	25	9	0
1,985	2,005	171	152	133	114	95	76	59	43	27	11	0
2,005	2,025	174	155	136	116	97	78	61	45	29	13	0
2,025	2,045	176	157	138	119	100	80	63	47	31	15	0
2,045	2,065	179	159	140	121	102	83	65	49	33	17	1

EXAMPLE: Guiren Heng is married and claims 2 withholding allowances. His total earnings for the pay period are $1,759.86.

❶ Use the left two columns of the Biweekly Married Persons tax table shown here to locate the range containing the total earnings—At least $1,745 but less than $1,765.

❷ Find the column with the correct number of withholding allowances, 2.

❸ Find the intersection of the row and column. The amount of income tax to be withheld is $104.00.

Crazy Eddie

Crazy Eddie was a chain of retail electronics stores in the New York region. Formed in the early 1970s by members of the Antar family, including Eddie Antar, the company grew to 43 stores, with annual sales of over $350 million.

Eddie Antar was born into a family of retailers. Through the generations, the Antars had learned how to operate a successful business. But according to Eddie's cousin, Sam Antar, they also learned how to avoid paying income taxes. Sam Antar, a former CPA, was the chief financial officer of Crazy Eddie. He states that skimming cash was a regular business practice for the Antar family. Skimming is the theft of cash before the sales transaction is recorded in the accounting records. Lower sales means less income and, thus, less income taxes.

The cash that the Antars skimmed from Crazy Eddie was deposited in foreign bank accounts. The fraud went undetected until the Antars decided to take the company public. To make the stock attractive for potential investors, the company had to report strong growth in profits. The Antars decided to stop the skimming gradually. From 1980 to 1984, Crazy Eddie reduced its skimming from $3 million per year to nearly zero. Reported income began to soar. To fuel its income growth further, the company began bringing skimmed funds back into the country. The funds, received in the form of a check, were included in daily receipts and recorded as sales.

Sam Antar contends that an examination of the components of daily deposits from sales would have revealed the fraud. The amount of daily sales paid with credit cards, checks, and cash should have been relatively consistent. Both the skimming and the depositing of money back into the company would have resulted in significant fluctuations.

ACTIVITY

BRT Enterprises is considering the purchase of Artic Dollar Stores. The director of the review team knows the history of the Crazy Eddie fraud. As a result, the director has obtained the daily sales by payment method for a five-year period. You have been assigned the task of analyzing the data to identify whether there is any evidence to support the existence of a fraud.

INSTRUCTIONS ⊕ +ableau

The Tableau workbook FA_CH03 contains daily sales data for the years 2014 to 2018. Read the caption above each chart to understand the data presented. Use the charts to answer the following questions.

1. Review the Quarterly Reports worksheet. How would you describe the trend in quarterly sales over the five years?

2. Analyze the Quarterly Receipts by Method worksheet. Was the composition of sales divided consistently between cash, checks, and credit cards? Support your answer.

3. Use the Cash, Checks, and Credit Card worksheets to analyze the trends in sales from each payment method. Export to Excel any points of interest. Does this evidence support the existence of a skimming scheme similar to the Crazy Eddie fraud?

Source: www.whitecollarfraud.com.

Preparing an Employee Earnings Record

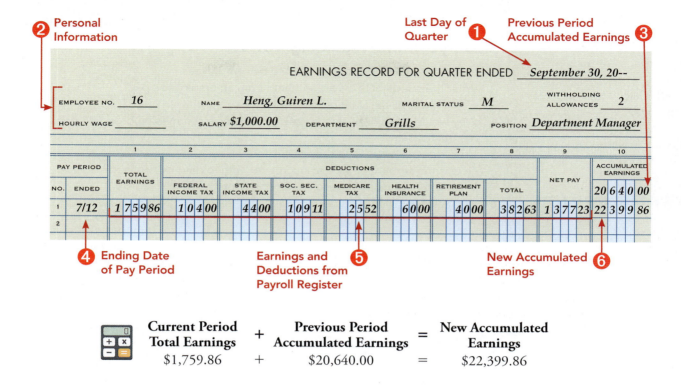

Personal Information ②

Last Day of Quarter ①   **Previous Period Accumulated Earnings** ③

EARNINGS RECORD FOR QUARTER ENDED *September 30, 20--*

EMPLOYEE NO. *16*   NAME *Heng, Guiren L.*   MARITAL STATUS *M*   WITHHOLDING ALLOWANCES *2*

HOURLY WAGE _____   SALARY *$1,000.00*   DEPARTMENT *Grills*   POSITION *Department Manager*

		1	2	3	4	5	6	7	8	9	10
PAY PERIOD		TOTAL EARNINGS	DEDUCTIONS							NET PAY	ACCUMULATED EARNINGS
NO.	ENDED		FEDERAL INCOME TAX	STATE INCOME TAX	SOC. SEC. TAX	MEDICARE TAX	HEALTH INSURANCE	RETIREMENT PLAN	TOTAL		20 640 00
1	7/12	1 759 86	104 00	44 00	109 11	25 52	60 00	40 00	382 63	1 377 23	22 399 86
2											

Ending Date of Pay Period ④

Earnings and Deductions from Payroll Register ⑤

New Accumulated Earnings ⑥

Current Period Total Earnings + Previous Period Accumulated Earnings = New Accumulated Earnings

$1,759.86 + $20,640.00 = $22,399.86

A business must send a quarterly report to federal and state governments showing employee taxable earnings and taxes withheld from these earnings. A business form used to record details of an employee's earnings and deductions is called an **employee earnings record**. An employee's total earnings and deductions for each pay period are summarized on one line of the employee earnings record.

Whiley prepares a new earnings record for each employee each quarter. Guiren Heng's earnings record for the third quarter is shown here.

Accumulated earnings are often referred to as *year-to-date earnings*. Accumulated earnings are needed for each employee because some payroll taxes do not apply after an employee's earnings reach a certain tax base.

>> Preparing an Employee Earnings Record

① Write the last day of the yearly quarter, September 30, 20--, at the top of the earnings record.

② Enter the employee's number, name, marital status, withholding allowances, hourly rate or salary, department, and position in the appropriate space. This information is taken from the employee's personnel records.

③ Record the fiscal year's accumulated earnings, $20,640.00, for the beginning of the current quarter. This information is taken from the ending accumulated earnings for the previous quarter. The Accumulated Earnings column of the employee

earnings record shows the accumulated earnings since the beginning of the fiscal year.

④ Write the ending date of the current pay period, 7/12.

⑤ Enter the total earnings, deductions, and net pay in the assigned columns of the earnings record. This information is taken from the current pay period's payroll register.

⑥ Calculate and record the new accumulated earnings, $22,399.86, on the same line as the other payroll information for the pay period ended July 12.

TERMS REVIEW

wage

salary

pay period

payroll

payroll taxes

withholding allowance

tax base

payroll register

employee earnings record

Audit your understanding LO1, 2, 3

1. Identify six types of earnings used to pay employees.
2. What three federal taxes are withheld from an employee's pay?
3. Explain how to calculate overtime earnings.
4. Why would a business elect to pay employees a commission based on departmental net sales?
5. How is a commission typically calculated?
6. How is the amount of federal income tax withholding determined?
7. What is the formula for calculating net pay on the payroll register?
8. What amount is added to the accumulated earnings to get the new accumulated earnings to date?

Work together 3-1 LO2, 3

Completing payroll records

Coastline Flooring's partial payroll register for the pay period ended July 3, 20--, to be paid July 7, 20--, and a blank earnings record form are provided in the *Working Papers*. Use the appropriate withholding tax tables shown in this lesson to determine the federal income tax. Deductions for all employees are 2% of total earnings for state income tax, 6.2% for Social Security tax, and 1.45% for Medicare tax. Your instructor will guide you through the following examples. Save your work to complete Work Together 3-2.

1. Prepare a commissions record for Nigella K. Panuska, employee No. 12 and carpet department manager, for June of the current year. Nigella's biweekly salary of $1,200.00 is assigned to the carpet department. She also receives a monthly commission of 4% of carpet net sales and 2% of tile net sales. Commissions for the previous month are paid in the first pay period of the current month. Accounting records for the month ended June 30 of the current year are as follows:

	Carpet	Tile
Sales on account	$6,148.19	$1,706.22
Cash and credit card sales	2,491.96	2,882.03
Sales discounts	104.15	28.11
Sales returns and allowances	321.06	418.95

2. Prepare the payroll register entries for the following two employees:

   a. On line 5: Nigella K. Panuska, employee number 12, carpet department manager, married, and two allowances. Use the commission calculated in instruction 1. Her health insurance premium is $60.00 and retirement plan contribution is $100.00.

   b. On line 6: Andrew T. Webber, employee number 8, tile department clerk, single, one allowance, regular salary of $16.00 per hour with overtime paid at 1½ times the regular rate. He worked 80 hours regular time and 6 hours overtime. His medical insurance premium is $50.00 and retirement plan contribution is $60.00.

3. Complete the payroll register by totaling each amount column.

4. Prepare Andrew's earnings record for the first pay period of the quarter ended September 30, 20--. Accumulated earnings for the quarter ended June 30, 20--, are $18,240.00.

On your own 3-1 LO2, 3

Completing payroll records

Parker Electronics' partial payroll register for the pay period ended October 8, to be paid October 11, 20--, and a blank earnings record form are provided in the *Working Papers*. Use the appropriate withholding tax tables to determine the federal income tax. Deductions for all employees are 4% of total earnings for state income tax, 6.2% for Social Security tax, and 1.45% for Medicare tax. Work this problem independently. Save your work to complete On Your Own 3-2.

1. Prepare a commissions record for Destiny P. Tarton, employee No. 6 and video department manager, for September of the current year. Destiny's biweekly salary of $900.00 is assigned to the video department. She also receives a monthly commission of 5% on audio net sales and 8% on video net sales. Commissions for the previous month are paid in the first pay period of the current month. Accounting records for the month ended September 30 of the current year are as follows:

	Audio	Video
Sales on account	$1,483.96	$ 945.68
Cash and credit card sales	5,148.39	4,184.19
Sales discounts	22.04	14.15
Sales returns and allowances	415.16	319.41

2. Prepare the payroll register entries for the following two employees:

   a. On line 5: Destiny P. Tarton, employee number 6, video department manager, single, and three allowances. Use the commission calculated in instruction 1. Her health insurance premium is $100.00 and retirement plan contribution is $200.00.

   b. On line 6: Becky G. Wise, employee number 9, audio department clerk, married, two allowances, regular salary of $14.00 per hour with overtime paid at 1½ times the regular rate. She worked 80 hours regular time and 8 hours overtime. Her medical insurance premium is $80.00 and retirement plan contribution is $75.00.

3. Complete the payroll register by totaling each amount column.

4. Prepare Becky's earnings record for the first pay period of the quarter ended December 31, 20--. Accumulated earnings for the quarter ended September 30, 20--, are $24,652.00.

Recording a Payroll and Payroll Taxes

LO4 Explain procedures for the payment of a payroll.
LO5 Journalize the payment of a payroll.
LO6 Explain the process for calculating the four payroll taxes typically paid by employers.
LO7 Journalize the payment of payroll taxes.

Payroll Bank Account LO4

Whiley pays its employees biweekly by check. A special payroll checking account and special payroll checks are used. After a biweekly payroll register has been completed, a check is written on Whiley's general checking account, payable to Payroll for the total net pay. This check is deposited in a special payroll checking account against which payroll checks are written for each employee's net pay. This account is reduced to zero as soon as all employees have cashed their payroll checks. Because the special payroll bank account has a balance only until all payroll checks are cashed, no special account is needed in the general ledger.

Automatic Check Deposit

Employees may authorize an employer to deposit payroll checks directly in their accounts at a specified bank.

Depositing payroll checks directly to an employee's checking or savings account is called **automatic check deposit**.

A computerized cash payments system that transfers funds without the use of checks, currency, or other paper documents is called **electronic funds transfer (EFT)**. Electronic funds transfer eliminates the need for preparing payroll checks. Under this system, each employee receives a statement of earnings and deductions similar to the detachable stub on a payroll check.

The use of automatic check deposit or electronic funds transfer for payroll does not change the accounting procedures for recording payroll. **>>** App A: Consistent Reporting

Journalizing Payment of a Payroll LO5

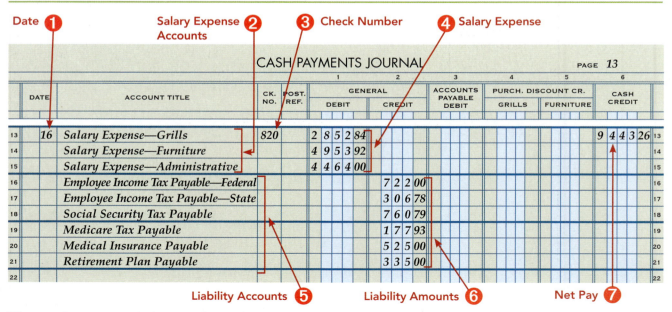

CASH PAYMENTS JOURNAL   PAGE **13**

	DATE	ACCOUNT TITLE	CK. NO.	POST. REF.	GENERAL DEBIT	GENERAL CREDIT	ACCOUNTS PAYABLE DEBIT	PURCH. DISCOUNT CR. GRILLS	PURCH. DISCOUNT CR. FURNITURE	CASH CREDIT	
13	16	Salary Expense—Grills	820		2 8 5 2 84					9 4 4 3 26	13
14		Salary Expense—Furniture			4 9 5 3 92						14
15		Salary Expense—Administrative			4 4 6 4 00						15
16		Employee Income Tax Payable—Federal				7 2 2 00					16
17		Employee Income Tax Payable—State				3 0 6 78					17
18		Social Security Tax Payable				7 6 0 79					18
19		Medicare Tax Payable				1 7 7 93					19
20		Medical Insurance Payable				5 2 5 00					20
21		Retirement Plan Payable				3 3 5 00					21
22											22

Whiley's payroll register contains the information needed to journalize a payroll as shown in the cash payments journal. The source document for journalizing a payroll payment is the check written for the net payroll amount. **>> App A: Objective Evidence**

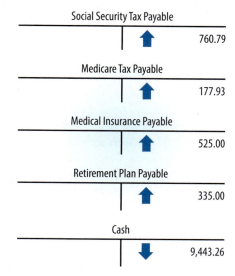

July 16. Paid cash for biweekly payroll, $9,443.26 (total payroll: grills, $2,852.84; furniture, $4,953.92; administrative, $4,464.00; less deductions: employee income tax—federal, $722.00; employee income tax—state, $306.78; Social Security tax, $760.79; Medicare tax, $177.93; medical insurance, $525.00; retirement plan, $335.00). Check No. 820.

Salary Expense—Grills

| ↑ 2,852.84 | |

Salary Expense—Furniture

| ↑ 4,953.92 | |

Salary Expense—Administrative

| ↑ 4,464.00 | |

Employee Income Tax Payable—Federal

| | ↑ 722.00 |

Employee Income Tax Payable—State

| | ↑ 306.78 |

Social Security Tax Payable

| | ↑ 760.79 |

Medicare Tax Payable

| | ↑ 177.93 |

Medical Insurance Payable

| | ↑ 525.00 |

Retirement Plan Payable

| | ↑ 335.00 |

Cash

| | ↓ 9,443.26 |

>> Journalizing Payment of a Payroll

❶ Write the date, **16**, in the Date column of the cash payments journal.

❷ Record the salary expense accounts, **Salary Expense—Grills**, **Salary Expense—Furniture**, and **Salary Expense—Administrative**, in the Account Title column.

❸ Enter the check number, **820**, in the Ck. No. column.

❹ Write the salary expense amounts, **$2,852.84**, **$4,953.92**, and **$4,464.00** in the General Debit column.

❺ Enter the liability accounts, **Employee Income Tax Payable—Federal**, **Employee Income Tax Payable—State**, **Social Security Tax Payable**, **Medicare Tax Payable**, **Medical Insurance Payable**, and **Retirement Plan Payable**, in the Account Title column.

❻ Record the liability amounts, **$722.00**, **$306.78**, **$760.79**, **$177.93**, **$525.00**, and **$335.00**, in the General Credit column.

❼ Write the net pay, **$9,443.26** in the Cash Credit column.

Employer Payroll Taxes LO6

Most employers have four separate payroll taxes:

1. Employer Social Security tax
2. Employer Medicare tax
3. Federal unemployment tax
4. State unemployment tax

Unemployment taxes are used to pay cash benefits to qualified workers for limited periods of unemployment.

Calculating Employer Payroll Taxes

Department	Social Security Earnings	Social Security 6.2%	Medicare 1.45%	FUTA Earnings	Federal Unemployment 0.6%	State Unemployment 5.4%	Total Payroll Taxes
Grills	$ 2,852.84	$176.88	$ 41.37	$1,275.00	$ 7.65	$ 68.85	$ 294.75
Furniture	4,953.92	307.14	71.83	1,548.00	9.29	83.59	471.85
Administrative	4,464.00	276.77	64.73	—	—	—	341.50
	$12,270.76	$760.79	$177.93	$2,823.00	$16.94	$152.44	$1,108.10

Employers must pay to the government the taxes withheld from employee earnings. Employers must also pay several of their own payroll taxes. Employers must match the Social Security and Medicare taxes withheld from employee earnings. Employers must also pay federal and state unemployment taxes. Only employers pay unemployment taxes.

Employer payroll taxes are based on a percentage of employee earnings. The earnings subject to Social Security and Medicare taxes are referred to as *Social Security earnings*. Congress sets the Social Security and Medicare tax rates for employees and employers. Congress often changes the tax rates and tax base. The Social Security tax rate used in this text is 6.2% of earnings up to the tax base—a maximum of $128,400.00 each calendar year. The Medicare tax rate used in this text is 1.45% of total employee earnings. The employer Social Security tax (6.2%) and Medicare tax (1.45%) rates are the same as the rates used for employees.

The calculation of Social Security and Medicare taxes for Whiley's latest payroll period is shown above. None of its employee's accumulated earnings has exceeded the $128,400.00 Social Security tax base. Therefore, the Social Security and Medicare taxes are calculated using total earnings for each department.

The federal unemployment tax used in this text is 6.0% of the first $7,000.00 earned by each employee. Earnings subject to unemployment taxes are referred to as *FUTA earnings*. An employer generally can deduct the amounts paid to state unemployment funds from federal unemployment payments. This deduction cannot be more than 5.4% of taxable earnings. The effective federal unemployment tax rate in most states is, therefore, 0.6% on the first $7,000.00 earned by each employee (6.0% federal − 5.4% deductible for state = 0.6%). The employer pays all of the unemployment tax on the first $7,000.00 of salary. State tax rates and tax bases vary by state.

The accumulated earnings for most of Whiley's employees exceeded $7,000.00 during the first quarter. Thus, no additional unemployment taxes must be paid for these employees during the second quarter. Whiley hired two employees during the second quarter. Neither employee's accumulated earnings exceeded $7,000.00 during the quarter. Whiley must pay unemployment on these earnings during the second quarter. The calculation of FUTA and SUTA taxes for Whiley's latest payroll period is shown above.

Whiley reports employee earnings by department to determine what expenses were incurred in earning each department's revenue. Payroll taxes are a direct result of the employees working in each department. Therefore, payroll tax expenses are also reported by department.

The salary column totals of the payroll register are used to calculate the employer's payroll taxes for each department. These calculations are summarized in the table at the top of the page. The calculations for the grills department are shown below as an example.

Rounding differences can occur when percentage calculations are performed on parts of a total amount and then compared with the percentage of the total. To correct the one-cent rounding error, add or subtract the rounding error to the larger of the department tax amounts.

	Total Taxable Earnings		Tax Rate		Grills Department Tax
Social Security	$2,852.84	×	6.20%	=	$176.88
Medicare	2,852.84	×	1.45%	=	41.37
Unemployment—Federal	1,275.00	×	0.60%	=	7.65
Unemployment—State	1,275.00	×	5.40%	=	68.85
Total Grills Department Payroll Tax Expense					$294.75

Journalizing Employer Payroll Taxes LO7

Employer payroll taxes are recognized as a liability when the payroll is processed. The timing for when each tax must be paid is established by the government agencies. A business must maintain accurate records of its payroll tax liabilities to ensure proper and timely payment.

Employer Payroll Tax Liability

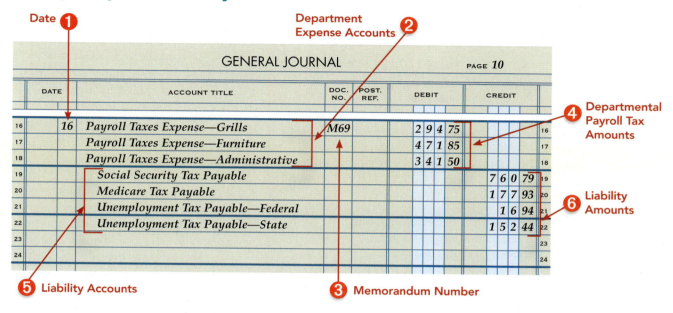

① Date
② Department Expense Accounts
④ Departmental Payroll Tax Amounts
⑥ Liability Amounts
⑤ Liability Accounts
③ Memorandum Number

July 16. Recorded employer payroll taxes for the biweekly pay period ended July 16. Taxes owed are Social Security tax, $760.79; Medicare tax, $177.93; federal unemployment tax, $16.94; state unemployment tax, $152.44; total payroll taxes by department are grills, $294.75; furniture, $471.85; and administrative, $341.50. Memorandum No. 69.

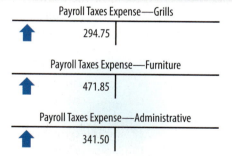

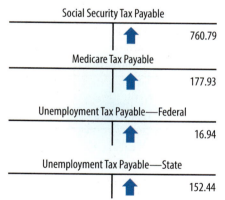

▶▶ Journalizing Employer Payroll Taxes

① Write the date, **16**, in the Date column of the general journal.

② Write the expense account titles, **Payroll Taxes Expense—Grills**, **Payroll Taxes Expense—Furniture**, and **Payroll Taxes Expense—Administrative**, in the Account Title column.

③ Enter the source document, **M69**, in the Doc. No. column.

④ Record each department's payroll taxes expense, **$294.75**, **$471.85**, and **$341.50**, in the Debit column.

⑤ Write the liability account titles, **Social Security Tax Payable**, **Medicare Tax Payable**, **Unemployment Tax Payable—Federal**, and **Unemployment Tax Payable—State**, in the Account Title column.

⑥ Enter the liability amounts, **$760.79**, **$177.93**, **$16.94**, and **$152.44**, in the Credit column.

Payment of Federal Income Tax, Social Security Tax, and Medicare Tax Liabilities

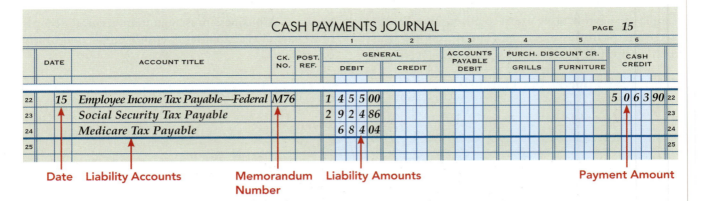

	DATE	ACCOUNT TITLE	CK. NO.	POST. REF.	GENERAL DEBIT	GENERAL CREDIT	ACCOUNTS PAYABLE DEBIT	PURCH. DISCOUNT CR. GRILLS	PURCH. DISCOUNT CR. FURNITURE	CASH CREDIT	
22	15	Employee Income Tax Payable—Federal	M76		1 4 5 5 00					5 0 6 3 90	22
23		Social Security Tax Payable			2 9 2 4 86						23
24		Medicare Tax Payable			6 8 4 04						24
25											25

Date   Liability Accounts   Memorandum Number   Liability Amounts   Payment Amount

Employers must pay to federal, state, and local governments all payroll taxes withheld from employee earnings as well as the employer payroll taxes. Federal and state laws govern the frequency of payments.

> **August 15.** Made a deposit using the EFTPS for payroll tax liabilities: employee federal income tax, $1,455.00, employees' and employer's Social Security tax, $2,924.86, and Medicare tax, $684.04; total, $5,063.90. Memorandum No. 76.

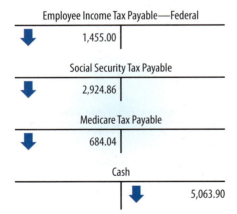

Employee Income Tax Payable—Federal
1,455.00

Social Security Tax Payable
2,924.86

Medicare Tax Payable
684.04

Cash
5,063.90

The total amount of tax paid each year determines the frequency and method of payment of employee and employer payroll taxes. The greater the amount of taxes owed, the more frequently the liability must be paid. Whiley is classified as a monthly schedule depositor. A monthly schedule depositor must deposit the taxes by the 15th day of the next month.

Most employers are required to deposit federal payroll taxes using the Electronic Federal Tax Payment System (EFTPS). Either by computer or telephone, the business can have the deposit transferred directly from its bank account to the government. The EFTPS allows the employer to print a receipt of the deposit. This receipt is attached to a memorandum to document the payment of cash. **>> App A: Objective Evidence**

Whiley's July biweekly pay periods end on July 12 and 26. The payroll taxes for these pay periods must be deposited by August 15.

Whiley's liability for state income tax withholding is paid at the end of each quarter.

> **FYI** Employers with large payroll tax liabilities must make more frequent deposits. A business that deposits more than $50,000 in a calendar year is classified as a semiweekly schedule depositor. If a payroll tax liability of $100,000 or more is accumulated on any day, the business must deposit the taxes on the next business day. Consult the most recent Internal Revenue Service publications for specific deposit rules.

ANDREY_POPOV/SHUTTERSTOCK.COM

Payment of Federal Unemployment Tax Liability

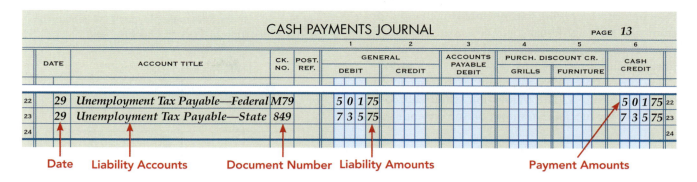

	DATE	ACCOUNT TITLE	CK. NO.	POST. REF.	GENERAL DEBIT	GENERAL CREDIT	ACCOUNTS PAYABLE DEBIT	PURCH. DISCOUNT CR. GRILLS	PURCH. DISCOUNT CR. FURNITURE	CASH CREDIT	
22	29	*Unemployment Tax Payable—Federal*	M79		5 0 1 75					5 0 1 75	22
23	29	*Unemployment Tax Payable—State*	849		7 3 5 75					7 3 5 75	23
24											24

Date — Liability Accounts — Document Number — Liability Amounts — Payment Amounts

If the federal unemployment tax liability for a business is $500.00 or more at the end of a quarter, it must pay the tax by the end of the following month. Any unpaid federal unemployment tax must be paid by January 31 of the following year.

Whiley's federal unemployment tax liability at the end of the first quarter did not exceed $500.00. Thus, no payment was made in April. The liability at the end of the second quarter is $501.75. Whiley must deposit this amount by the end of July, the following month.

Federal unemployment taxes are deposited using the EFTPS. A receipt of the deposit is attached to a memorandum to document the payment of cash. **>> App A: Objective Evidence**

> July 29. Paid cash for federal unemployment tax liability for quarter ended June 30, $501.75. Memorandum No. 79.

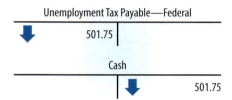

Unemployment Tax Payable—Federal
501.75

Cash
501.75

Labor Costs

The board of directors knows that the corporation will soon be required to renew its contract with its labor union. To ensure that management understands the money issues, the board asked the Accounting department to prepare an analysis of the labor costs. This analysis is to include all taxes and benefits paid.

Melinda Loggins, one of your colleagues, has prepared a first draft of the analysis. Her worksheet contains a schedule that calculates the employee and employer taxes for a worker having a $50,000 salary. The schedule also includes estimates of voluntary deductions, such as health insurance and retirement contributions. The corporation currently pays 60% of every employee's health insurance premiums. The corporation also matches the employee's retirement plan contributions.

"I used a pie chart, so that the board could see what portion of the total labor costs consists of employer taxes and contributions," Melinda stated proudly. "The supporting data, taken from the schedule, are to the right of the chart. So if you decide to make any changes, those are the data reflected in the chart."

OPEN THE SPREADSHEET TLA_CH03

The worksheet contains the pie chart and its supporting schedules. Follow the steps on the Instructions tab. Modify the chart to improve the information communicated to the board. Answer the following questions:

1. Which pie chart design provides the best information?
2. Prepare a brief statement that summarizes the information provided in the chart.
3. How does changing the chart type and format improve understanding?
4. What other changes would you propose?

Payment of State Unemployment Tax Liability

Requirements for paying state unemployment taxes vary from state to state. Usually, employers are required to pay the state unemployment tax during the month following each calendar quarter.

Whiley's state unemployment tax for the second quarter is $735.75. The transaction is journalized on the cash payments journal shown on the previous page.

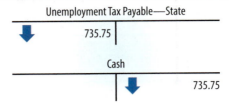

July 29. Paid cash for state unemployment tax liability for quarter ended June 30, $735.75. Check No. 849.

Unemployment Tax Payable—State

| | 735.75 |

Cash

| | 735.75 |

Executive Compensation

CareerClusters
PATHWAYS TO COLLEGE & CAREER READINESS
Business Management & Administration

When determining how to configure a compensation plan for a company executive, the human resource manager has to consider many things. A compensation plan should motivate the executive to take actions that are in the best interests of the company. However, the compensation plan must also contain items important to the executive.

The human resource manager must also understand that not all forms of compensation affect the company's financial statements in the same way. One example of this is how stock options have been treated over time.

Prior to 2006, many companies offered stock options to their executives. A stock option is the right to purchase a share of stock in the future at a set price. An executive would exercise his or her option if the value of the stock increased above the option price. The benefit to the company was that the value of the option was not counted as an expense in the company's records. Therefore, executives could receive this benefit with no negative impact on the company's net income.

In 2006, a new accounting rule was passed, FASB Statement No. 123, *Accounting for Stock-Based Compensation*. This rule required that stock options be expensed, thereby decreasing the company's net income. A human resource manager who was not aware of this accounting change might continue including stock options in compensation packages and greatly reduce the net income reported on the company's income statement.

Source: www.aicpa.org.

CRITICAL THINKING

1. At the time of publication, restricted stock was not required to be expensed. Write a one-paragraph description of restricted stock.

2. Besides actual salary, what other items should be included when calculating the cost of hiring one employee?

LO4 Explain procedures for the payment of a payroll.

LO5 Journalize the payment of a payroll.

LO6 Explain the process for calculating the four payroll taxes typically paid by employers.

LO7 Journalize the payment of payroll taxes.

TERMS REVIEW

automatic check deposit

electronic funds transfer (EFT)

Audit your understanding LO4, 5, 6

1. Explain how a payroll bank account is used to pay employees.
2. How does the use of automatic check deposit change the accounting procedures for recording payroll?
3. When a payroll is journalized, which account is credited for the total net amount paid to all employees?
4. What four separate payroll taxes do most employers have to pay?
5. What employer payroll taxes are subject to a limit for each employee?

Work together 3-2 LO5, 6, 7

Journalizing and paying payroll and payroll taxes

Use the solution from Work Together 3-1. A cash payments journal, page 15, and general journal, page 7, are provided in the *Working Papers*. Your instructor will guide you through the following examples.

1. Calculate departmental payroll taxes for the pay period ended July 3. No employees have earned more than the Social Security tax base. Unemployment taxes are due on the following earnings for this period: Carpet, $1,330.00; and Tile, $1,851.42.
2. Journalize the following transactions for July of the current year.

Transactions:

July	7.	Paid the July 3 payroll. Check No. **568**.
	7.	Recorded employer's payroll taxes for the pay period ended July 3. Memorandum No. 55.
	15.	Made a deposit using the EFTPS for employee and employer payroll taxes for the June pay periods: employee federal income tax withholding, $859.00; Social Security tax, $2,230.52; and Medicare tax, $521.67. Memorandum No. 56.
	29.	Made a deposit using the EFTPS for federal unemployment taxes for the first and second quarter, $523.69. Memorandum No. 57.
	29.	Paid state unemployment tax for the quarter ended June 30, $303.16. Check No. 579.

On your own 3-2 LO5, 6, 7

Journalizing and paying payroll and payroll taxes

Use the solution from On Your Own 3-1. A cash payments journal, page 18, and general journal, page 10, are provided in the *Working Papers*. Work independently to complete the following problem.

1. Calculate departmental payroll taxes for the pay period ended October 8. No employees have earned more than the Social Security tax base. Unemployment taxes are due on the following earnings for this period: Audio, $1,568.00; and Administrative, $1,628.00.
2. Journalize the following transactions for October of the current year.

Transactions:

Oct.	11.	Paid the October 8 payroll. Check No. 772.
	11.	Recorded employer's payroll taxes for the pay period ended October 8. Memorandum No. 68.
	15.	Made a deposit using the EFTPS for employee and employer payroll taxes for the September pay periods: employee federal income tax withholding, $978.00; Social Security tax, $2,243.48; and Medicare tax, $524.73. Memorandum No. 69.
	29.	Made a deposit using the EFTPS for federal unemployment taxes for the first three quarters, $508.84. Memorandum No. 73.
	29.	Paid state unemployment tax for the quarter ended September 30, $331.99. Check No. 785.

Managing Employee Information

In a manual accounting system, information needed for managing and paying employees is maintained on several forms. Some payroll information is maintained in employee earnings records. Other information required by government regulatory and taxing agencies is kept in a file for each employee. In larger companies, a Human Resources (HR) Department maintains these files.

A computerized accounting system maintains all employee information in the Manage Employees module.

Due to the confidentiality of the information, access to this module is strictly controlled by system security measures. Only authorized persons can view this information. Often, only a few individuals are authorized to enter and edit it.

The Set Up Accounts tab in the Enter/Edit Company Information window was illustrated in A Look at Accounting Software in Chapter 1. Many of the features on that tab operate in the same way on the Set Up Employees tab illustrated in this chapter.

1 The user clicks on the **Set Up Employees** tab in the Enter/Edit Company Information window.

2 The **View Active** button is the system default setting. The user can narrow the list of employees displayed by selecting **Inactive** or **All** and by using the drop-down lists in the Dept. and Position columns.

3 To set up a new employee, the user clicks **New** on the menu bar. In this illustration, the user has double-clicked on employee number 022 to open the Manage Employees window for Juanita Denton.

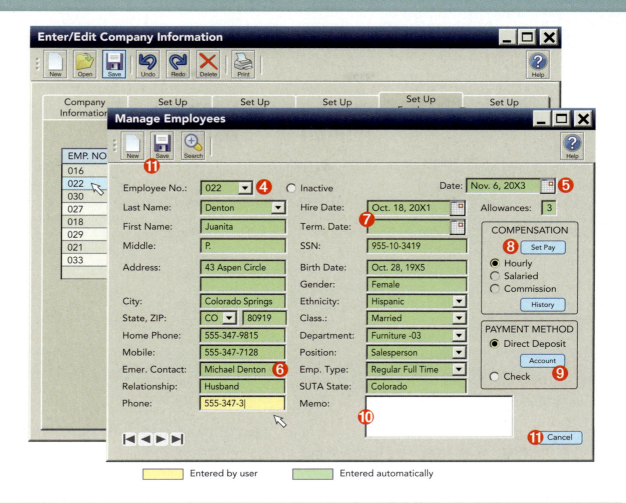

| Entered by user | Entered automatically |

4 If the user were entering a new employee, this pop-up window would be mostly empty. The date would be displayed along with the next sequential employee number set by the system. Some fields would display default settings, such as Hourly and Direct Deposit, which were determined to be most likely when management programmed the system. Since Juanita Denton is already an employee, this screen is displayed with all her current data. The Manage Employees window collects all the information necessary to (1) prepare the payroll and (2) comply with federal, state, and local tax codes.

5 The system date is displayed. It cannot be changed.

6 Whiley maintains emergency contact information for each employee as part of its emergency preparedness plan. The user is keying a new phone number for Juanita Denton's emergency contact.

7 Other key information, required by the federal government, is the hire date and termination date of each employee.

8 Compensation data are required by the system to process payroll. Either **Hourly** or **Salaried** can be selected, but **Commission** can be selected in addition to either of those. Clicking the **Set Pay** button would open another pop-up window to enter the rate of pay, overtime, vacation, and benefits. The **History** button would let the user view all year-to-date payments to the employee or to select a range of payments.

9 When direct deposit is set up for an employee, the user would click the **Account** button and enter the routing number and account number for the linked bank account.

10 The memo field allows the user to enter notes pertaining to employee issues, problems, training, advancement potential, etc.

11 Clicking **Cancel** erases any changes and clears the screen. Clicking **Save** records the new information and prepares the window for the entry of a new employee.

Businesses must keep accurate records of employee earnings and the related payroll taxes. Employers are required to withhold federal income, Social Security, and Medicare taxes from the employees' total earnings. Some employers must also withhold state and city income taxes. Employees can elect to have medical insurance, retirement contributions, and other items deducted from their total earnings. These withholdings are liabilities of the business until paid.

Hourly employees are paid a set wage rate for all hours worked. Most employers are required to pay employees overtime pay for hours worked over 40 hours per week. The overtime pay rate is typically $1\frac{1}{2}$ times the regular pay rate. Some employees earn a fixed salary each pay period. An employee's earnings can also include a commission on sales.

A payroll register summarizes the earnings, deductions, and net pay of all employees. A business can classify employee earnings by department. The payroll register is used to update an employee earnings record, a form useful in submitting quarterly and annual payroll tax reports to government agencies.

Employers must also pay payroll taxes. These taxes include Social Security, Medicare, federal unemployment, and state unemployment taxes. Employer payroll taxes can be classified by department. The federal government has rules that govern when and how taxes are to be deposited. Most employers must deposit employee and employer payroll taxes using the Electronic Federal Tax Payment System (EFTPS). Each state determines how its state taxes are deposited.

EXPLORE ACCOUNTING

Pretax Benefits

Federal income tax is a major expense for most families. Current laws permit employers to set up retirement and health care plans that allow employees to set aside a portion of their earnings on a pretax basis. Employees pay no taxes in that tax year on the amounts withheld.

RETIREMENT PLANS

For amounts placed in many qualified retirement accounts, income tax is "deferred" on earnings. Individuals will pay income taxes on the amounts withdrawn from their retirement accounts when they retire. Because of the income tax deferral, the amount available at retirement will be much larger. The general requirements of most pretax retirement plans include the following:

1. The employer withholds the specified amount and deposits it in qualified investments, such as mutual funds.

2. The amount of earnings an employee can defer each year is limited.

3. Employees are assessed penalties if they withdraw amounts from their retirement account before the age of 59½.

4. Withdrawals from retirement plan accounts must begin by the time the person reaches age 70½.

HEALTH CARE AND CHILDCARE PLANS

Employees may be permitted to have a portion of their pretax earnings deducted from their salaries. These amounts are then used to reimburse out-of-pocket medical or childcare expenses. The plans are referred to as flexible spending arrangements (FSA). The advantage of an FSA is that payment is made with pretax dollars. However, the amount of earnings withheld is available only for the purpose designated. For example, assume an employee authorizes $60.00 a month to be withheld for medical costs but uses only $500.00 during the year. Current tax laws limit the amount of unused FSA contributions that can be carried forward to the next year. Amounts over the limit are not paid back to the employee and cannot be used for childcare expenses.

INSTRUCTIONS

1. Why would Congress allow employees to defer taxes on contributions to a retirement plan?

2. Are there any disadvantages to participating in a tax-deferred retirement plan?

3. Are there any disadvantages to participating in a tax-deferred health care plan?

APPLY YOUR UNDERSTANDING

INSTRUCTIONS: Download problem instructions for Excel, QuickBooks, and Sage 50c from the textbook companion website at www.C21accounting.com.

3-1 Application Problem — Completing payroll records LO2, 3

Suburban Tractor's partial payroll register for the pay period ended July 8, 20--, payable on July 12, 20--, and a blank earnings record form are provided in the *Working Papers*. Use the appropriate withholding tax tables from this chapter to determine the federal income tax. Deductions for all employees are 5% of total earnings for state income tax, 6.2% for Social Security tax, and 1.45% for Medicare tax. Save your work to complete Application Problem 3-2.

Instructions:

1. Prepare a commissions record for Lien Y. Trang, employee No. 16 and equipment department manager, for June of the current year. Ms. Trang's biweekly salary of $1,000.00 is assigned to the equipment department. She also receives a monthly commission of 6% on equipment net sales and 1% on parts net sales. Commissions for the previous month are paid in the first pay period of the current month. Accounting records for the month ended June 30 of the current year are as follows:

	Equipment	Parts
Sales on account	$12,184.19	$3,149.62
Cash and credit card sales	3,148.22	4,107.15
Sales discounts	201.14	51.23
Sales returns and allowances	514.34	312.05

2. Prepare the payroll register entries for the following two employees:

   a. On line 4: Lien Y. Trang, employee number 16, equipment department manager, married, and three allowances. Use the commission calculated in instruction 1. Her health insurance premium is $100.00 and retirement plan contribution is $250.00.

   b. On line 5: Peter S. Valdez, employee number 20, parts department clerk, single, two allowances, regular salary of $18.00 per hour with overtime paid at 1½ times the regular rate. He worked 80 hours regular time and 1 hour of overtime. His medical insurance premium is $80.00 and retirement plan contribution is $100.00.

3. Complete the payroll register by totaling each amount column.

4. Prepare Peter Valdez's earnings record for the first pay period of the quarter ended September 30, 20--. Accumulated earnings for the quarter ended June 30, 20--, are $9,148.50.

3-2 Application Problem — Journalizing and paying payroll and payroll taxes LO5, 6, 7

Use the solution from Problem 3-1. A cash payments journal, page 12, and general journal, page 9, are provided in the *Working Papers*.

Instructions:

1. Calculate departmental payroll taxes for the pay period ended July 8. No employees have earned more than the Social Security tax base. Unemployment taxes are due on the following earnings for this period: Equipment, $1,162.00; and Parts, $921.16.

2. Journalize the following transactions for July of the current year.

Transactions:

July 12. Paid the July 8 payroll. Check No. 645.

12. Recorded employer's payroll taxes for the pay period ended July 8. Memorandum No. 50.

15. Made a deposit using the EFTPS for employee and employer payroll taxes for the June pay periods: employee federal income tax withholding, $967.00; Social Security tax, $2,102.43; and Medicare tax, $491.73. Memorandum No. 51.

30. Made a deposit using the EFTPS for federal unemployment taxes for the first three quarters, $529.16. Memorandum No. 54.

30. Paid state unemployment tax for the quarter ended June 30, $218.59. Check No. 653.

sage 50 ·

1. Journalize and post payroll transactions to the cash disbursements journal and general journal.
2. From the menu bar, select Reports & Forms; Accounts Payable, Cash Disbursements Journal.
3. From the menu bar, select Reports & Forms; General Ledger, General Journal.

QB
Quick Books

1. Journalize and post payroll transactions in the Write Checks window.
2. Journalize and post payroll transactions to the journal.
3. From the menu bar, select Reports; Banking, Check Detail.
4. From the menu bar, select Reports; Accountant & Taxes, Journal.

X

1. Complete the payroll register.
2. Journalize and post payroll transactions to the cash payments journal and the general journal.
3. Print the worksheets.

Coastline Flooring's partial payroll register for the pay period ended October 4, 20--, a blank earnings record form, page 13 of a cash payments journal, and page 7 of a general journal are provided in the *Working Papers*. Use the appropriate withholding tax tables shown in this chapter to determine the federal income tax. Deductions for all employees are 3% of total earnings for state income tax, 6.2% for Social Security tax, and 1.45% for Medicare tax.

Instructions:

1. Prepare a commissions record for DeShawn O. Ward, employee No. 4 and carpet department manager, for September of the current year. DeShawn's biweekly salary of $1,000.00 is assigned to the carpet department. He also receives a monthly commission of 10% of carpet net sales and 15% of drapery net sales. Commissions for the previous month are paid in the first pay period of the current month. Accounting records for the month ended September 30 of the current year are as follows:

	Carpet	Drapery
Sales on account	$6,092.77	$1,019.14
Cash and credit card sales	1,049.25	594.10
Sales discounts	84.19	19.11
Sales returns and allowances	21.49	42.08

2. Prepare the payroll register entries for the following two employees:

   a. On line 5: Shekeia M. Shipp, employee number 8, drapery cutter, married, two allowances, regular salary of $18.00 per hour with overtime paid at 1½ times the regular rate. She worked 80 hours regular time and 8 hours overtime. Her medical insurance premium is $75.00 and retirement plan contribution is $200.00.

   b. On line 6: DeShawn O. Ward, employee number 4, carpet department manager, single, and one allowance. Use the commission calculated in instruction 1. His health insurance premium is $50.00 and retirement plan contribution is $100.00.

3. Complete the payroll register by totaling each amount column.

4. Prepare Shekeia Shipp's earnings record for the first pay period of the quarter ended September 30, 20--. Accumulated earnings for the quarter ended June 30, 20--, are $16,948.00.

5. Calculate departmental payroll taxes for the pay period ended October 4. No employees have earned more than the Social Security tax base. Unemployment taxes are due on the following earnings for this period: Carpet, $973.00; and Administrative, $1,328.00.

6. Journalize the following transactions for October of the current year.

Transactions:

Oct. 7. Paid the October 4 payroll. Check No. 841.

7. Recorded employer's payroll taxes for the pay period ended October 4. Memorandum No. 44.

15. Made a deposit using the EFTPS for employee and employer payroll taxes for the September pay periods: employee federal income tax withholding, $1,018.00; Social Security tax, $2,285.70; and Medicare tax, $534.61. Memorandum No. 45.

29. Made a deposit using the EFTPS for federal unemployment taxes for the first three quarters, $541.16. Memorandum No. 49.

29. Paid state unemployment tax for the quarter ended September 30, $346.57. Check No. 854.

3-S Source Documents Problem

Completing payroll records, journalizing payment of a payroll, and journalizing payroll taxes LO2, 3, 5, 7

Exterior Design sells doors and windows. Journals and source documents related to payroll are provided in the *Working Papers*. Use the appropriate withholding tax tables shown in this chapter to determine the federal income tax. Deductions for all employees are 4% of total earnings for state income tax, 6.2% for social security tax, and 1.45% for Medicare tax.

Instructions:

1. Prepare the commissions records for Daniel C. Pizzo and May E. Verdell. Each manager's regular salary is assigned to the department he or she manages. The information required to complete the commissions records is obtained from a Commission Sales Report and the Personnel Report. Overtime is paid at 1½ times the regular rate for hours worked over 8 hours per day or 40 hours per week.
2. Prepare the payroll register using information presented on the Hourly Employee Time Summary, each Commission Sales Report, and the Personnel Report. Withholdings for health insurance are based on each employee's allowances: one allowance, $100.00; two allowances, $150.00, three allowances, $180.00; and four allowances, $200.00.
3. Complete the employee earnings records.
4. Calculate departmental payroll taxes for the pay period ended July 9. Three of the employees have earned more than the FUTA tax base.
5. Journalize the following transactions for July of the current year.

Transactions:

July 13. Paid the July 9 payroll. Check No. 905.

13. Recorded employer's payroll taxes for the pay period ended July 9. Memorandum No. 65.

15. Deposited payroll taxes for the June pay periods. Memorandum No. 66.

30. Deposited federal unemployment taxes. Memorandum No. 72.

30. Paid state unemployment taxes. Check No. 916.

The Internal Revenue Service only provides tax withholding tables for a range of earnings. The table for biweekly married persons stops at earnings of $3,085.00. The tax withholdings for a married taxpayer earning over $3,085.00 in a biweekly payroll period must be calculated using the percentage method. A portion of the tax rate table available when this text was written is shown below.

TABLE 2—BIWEEKLY Payroll Period

(a) SINGLE person (including head of household)—

If the amount of wages (after subtracting withholding allowances) is:

The amount of income tax to withhold is:

Not over $142 . . . . $0

Over—	But not over—		of excess over—
$142	—$509 . .	$0.00 plus 10%	—$142
$509	—$1,631 . .	$36.70 plus 12%	—$509
$1,631	—$3,315 . .	$171.34 plus 22%	—$1,631
$3,315	—$6,200 . .	$541.82 plus 24%	—$3,315
$6,200	—$7,835 . .	$1,234.22 plus 32%	—$6,200
$7,835	—$19,373 . .	$1,757.42 plus 35%	—$7,835
$19,373		$5,795.72 plus 37%	—$19,373

(b) MARRIED person—

If the amount of wages (after subtracting withholding allowances) is:

The amount of income tax to withhold is:

Not over $444 . . . . $0

Over—	But not over—		of excess over—
$444	—$1,177 . .	$0.00 plus 10%	—$444
$1,177	—$3,421 . .	$73.30 plus 12%	—$1,177
$3,421	—$6,790 . .	$342.58 plus 22%	—$3,421
$6,790	—$12,560 . .	$1,083.76 plus 24%	—$6,790
$12,560	—$15,829 . .	$2,468.56 plus 32%	—$12,560
$15,829	—$23,521 . .	$3,514.64 plus 35%	—$15,829
$23,521		$6,206.84 plus 37%	—$23,521

Adrianne Atkinson earns $5,000.00 each biweekly pay period. She is married and claims three withholding allowances. She is allowed to exclude $159.60 for each withholding allowance. Using the table above, her tax withholding is calculated as follows:

Total earnings		$ 5,000.00
Withholding allowance per person	$159.60	
Number of allowances	× 3	478.80
Earnings subject to withholding		$ 4,521.20
Minimum tax		$ 342.58
Additional tax ($4,521.20 − $3,421.00) × 22%		242.04
Taxes to be withheld		$ 584.62

Instructions:

Use the tax rate table above to calculate tax withholdings for five employees. A form is provided in the *Working Papers*. The amounts for Adrianne Atkinson are provided as a guide.

Kelly Sanders has prepared her first set of monthly commission records. She obtained sales data from the Commission Sales Report. The portion of the Commission Sales Report for Jane C. Kellogg and the commissions record Kelly prepared follow.

COMMISSION SALES REPORT

MONTH *August*

PREPARED ON *9/08/20--*

Name	Account Title	Computers	Printers
Kellogg, Jane C.	Sales on Account	$2,154.26	$1,089.66
	Cash and Credit Card Sales	9,142.36	3,048.15
	Sales Discounts	33.94	16.66
	Sales Returns and Allowances	648.16	319.90
	Commission Rate	5%	4%

COMMISSIONS RECORD

EMPLOYEE NO. *532*

PAY PERIOD ENDED *August 5, 20--*

DEPARTMENT *Computers*

EMPLOYEE NAME *Kellogg, Jane C.*

REGULAR BIWEEKLY SALARY *$1,000.00*

	Computers	Printers	
Sales on Account	$ 2,154.26	$1,089.66	
Cash and Credit Card Sales	9,124.36	3,048.15	
equals Total Sales for the Month	$11,278.62	$4,137.81	
Less:			
Sales Discounts	$ 33.94	$ 166.66	
Sales Returns and Allowances	648.16	319.90	
equals Total Reductions in Sales.	$ 682.10	$ 486.56	
Equals:			
Net Sales	$11,960.72	$3,651.25	
times Commission Rate	5.0%	4.0%	
equals Commission on Net Sales	$ 598.04	$ 279.26	$877.30

As the senior accounting clerk, you have responsibility for reviewing the work prepared by new hires. Examine the commissions record Kelly prepared. Identify any errors. Calculate the correct commission if errors are found.

Pay … Attention

PARTNERSHIP FOR
21ST CENTURY SKILLS

Theme: Financial, Economic, Business, and Entrepreneurial Literacy

Skills: Creativity and Innovation, Critical Thinking and Problem Solving, Communication and Collaboration,

ICT Literacy

When it comes to employee pay, most managers try to determine an affordable amount that will attract and retain a quality employee. Most employees are trying to find the company that offers the highest pay for the skills offered. However, managers and employees must consider the total compensation package.

Compensation is your total gross earnings plus your benefits, or perks, that have monetary value and are often paid for, either totally or in part, by the employer. One study showed that the benefits most valued by employees when considering a job offer (not including salary) were (in order of priority): vacation time / paid time off, corporate culture / work environment, career advancement potential, work-from-home options, and professional development / training. However, the results varied greatly by geographical region, gender, and age.

Premiums on the insurance plans alone can cost a company tens of thousands of dollars per year, adding significantly to the compensation package of an employee. Yet, employee benefits have become so necessary to the employee that offering an attractive benefits package can help recruit and retain the best talent for a company.

Source: www.rh-us.mediaroom.com.

APPLICATION

1. Use the Internet, make phone calls, or interview an adult to research benefits offered by three different companies. Compare your findings for similarities and differences.
2. Assume that you are a new start-up company. With a partner, create five benefits, or perks, that you could offer to your employees that would be attractive, yet inexpensive. Explain.

Analyzing Home Depot's Financial Statements

Expenses incurred in one fiscal period but not paid until a later date are called **accrued expenses**. During the last fiscal period of each year, Home Depot incurs salary and benefit expenses that are not paid until the following fiscal year. This occurs when a fiscal year ends in the middle of a payroll period. The accounting concept *Matching Revenue with Expenses* requires that financial statements must show all business expenses for a fiscal period. Consequently, Home Depot must report the unpaid salary and benefit amount even though it has not yet paid out cash. The unpaid amount owed for incurred employee salaries and benefits represents a liability. Use the material shown in Appendix B of this text to answer the questions below.

INSTRUCTIONS

1. Referring to the Consolidated Balance Sheets in Appendix B on page B-5, (a) list the title of the account that represents an amount owed for salaries and benefits and (b) list the amounts owed for this account on January 28, 2018, and January 29, 2017.

2. Referring to the Selected Financial Data on page B-20, identify one fact that would help explain the increase in this liability. List at least two other reasons that might explain the increase.

LEARNING OBJECTIVES

After studying Chapter 4, in addition to defining key terms, you will be able to:

LO1 Prove the accuracy of the subsidiary and general ledgers.

LO2 Journalize adjusting entries.

LO3 Prepare an adjusted trial balance.

LO4 Calculate the federal income tax adjustment.

LO5 Distinguish between direct and indirect expenses of a departmentalized business.

LO6 Prepare a departmental margin statement.

LO7 Analyze financial statements using vertical analysis ratios.

LO8 Prepare financial statements for a departmentalized merchandising business.

LO9 Journalize closing entries for a departmentalized merchandising business.

LO10 Prepare a post-closing trial balance.

LO11 Summarize the accounting cycle.

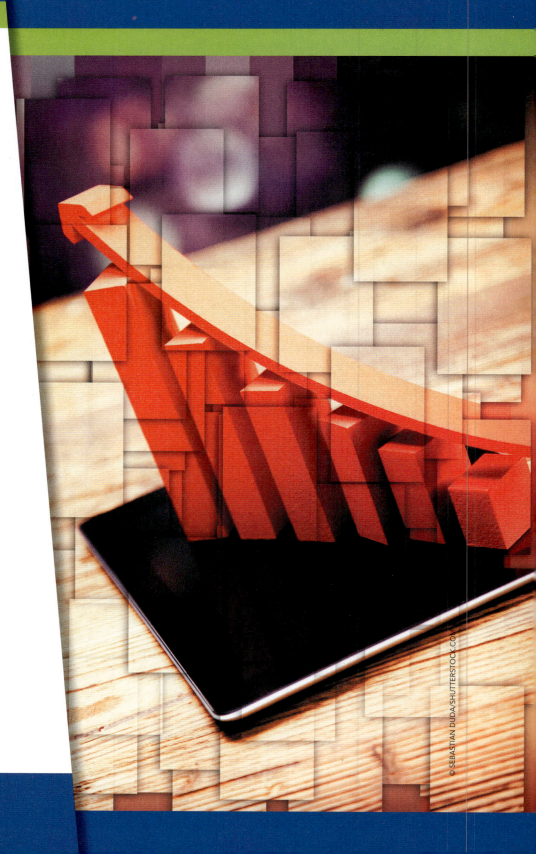

© SEBASTIAN DUDA/SHUTTERSTOCK.COM

Dave Thomas Foundation for Adoption

ACCOUNTING IN THE REAL WORLD

With over 6,500 locations worldwide, it's hard to imagine anyone who has not eaten at a Wendy's restaurant. When placing an order at Wendy's, the customer has a minute or two to view a variety of signs strategically displayed in the dining area. While some signs advertise new menu items, a prominent one explains the benefits of the Dave Thomas Foundation for Adoption (the Foundation).

Because he was adopted as an infant, Wendy's founder Dave Thomas knew firsthand the importance of being raised in a loving family. Thus, it's no surprise that he would take advantage of his business success to become a champion for adoption. His foundation's goal is to find loving families for the nearly 150,000 children waiting in foster care.

The Foundation relies on contributions to achieve this admirable mission. These resources help to promote adoption awareness and education programs, provide free resources to professionals and adoptive parents, and fund grants to organizations that promote adoption.

Similar to any for-profit business, the Foundation must maintain an accounting system that provides management with information needed for good decision making. Not-for-profit organizations also must ensure that their accounting system controls and accurately reports the flow of money through the organization. Potential donors want assurance that their donations are being used to achieve the organization's mission.

Unlike a for-profit business, the Foundation's mission does not include a profit objective. Generally accepted accounting principles contain different accounting and reporting standards for both not-for-profit organizations and government agencies.

Sources: www.wendys.com, www.davethomasfoundation.org.

CRITICAL THINKING

1. What advantages led Dave Thomas to establish a separate organization to administer the activities of the Foundation?

2. What accounts or categories would you expect to see on the Foundation's statement that reports on contributions and expenditures?

KEY TERMS

fiscal period
fiscal year
schedule of accounts
  receivable
schedule of accounts
  payable
trial balance
adjusting entries
unadjusted trial balance
plant assets

depreciation expense
adjusted trial balance
responsibility accounting
direct expense
indirect expense
responsibility statements
departmental margin
departmental margin
  statement

gross profit
financial ratio
vertical analysis
income statement
statement of stockholders'
  equity
capital stock
retained earnings
dividends

balance sheet
cash flow
statement of cash flows
operating activities
investing activities
financing activities
closing entries
post-closing trial balance
accounting cycle

LO1 Prove the accuracy of the subsidiary and general ledgers.

LO2 Journalize adjusting entries.

LO3 Prepare an adjusted trial balance.

LO4 Calculate the federal income tax adjustment.

Ensuring the Accuracy of Financial Statements LO1

Financial statements summarize the financial information that a business records. These statements are then analyzed to evaluate the financial position and progress of the business. The managers of a business use the statements to make financial decisions for future operations. A business also uses the financial statements in preparing tax reports and other reports, such as those required by the Securities and Exchange Commission (SEC).

Financial Reporting Periods

The period for which financial statements are prepared depends on the needs of the business. An accounting period may be one month, three months, six months, or one year. For tax purposes, every business prepares financial statements at the end of each year. Successful businesses generally prepare financial statements monthly to analyze results and take corrective action when needed.

The length of time for which a business summarizes its financial information and reports its financial performance is called a **fiscal period**. **>> App. A: Accounting Period Cycle** A fiscal period consisting of 12 consecutive months is called a **fiscal year**. Each business determines when its fiscal year ends. Whiley uses a fiscal year ending on December 31.

Preparing for End-of-Period Financial Reporting

Before financial statements can be prepared, the business should ensure that its account balances in its subsidiary and general ledgers are accurate. A business should:

- Ensure that all transactions have been journalized.
- Ensure that all journals have been posted.
- Perform bank reconciliations.

ETHICS IN ACTION

Insider Trading

David Robbins, a loan officer for a regional bank, has just closed a loan agreement with Rhett Industries. He was very impressed with the company's management and business plan. With the additional resources the loan will provide, Rhett Industries should experience rapid growth during the next few years. The corporation's stock should also show a dramatic increase in market price.

Upon returning to the office, David places an order to purchase 500 shares of the company's stock. This purchase is a substantial investment for David.

INSTRUCTIONS

Access the *Code of Conduct* of Citigroup Inc. and the insider trading information of the Securities and Exchange Commission. Using this information and the ethical decision-making model introduced in Chapter 2, determine whether David's purchase of the stock of Rhett Industries was ethical.

Proving the Accuracy of Subsidiary Ledgers

Whiley Outdoor Living, Inc.						
Schedule of Accounts Receivable						
December 31, 20--						
Barnes Construction	3	8	3	4	80
Central Community College	4	1	9	0	70
Franklin Landscaping	1	1	4	6	96
Jenkins Properties	2	6	3	6	54
Lynch Construction	2	8	9	8	49
Marist & Nelson, LLC	3	1	3	8	77
Pratte Real Estate	1	5	7	8	85
Taylor Apartments	2	6	0	5	95
Wilson Properties	1	4	8	4	21
Total Accounts Receivable	23	5	1	5	27

Another step in preparing financial statements is to determine the accuracy of customer and vendor accounts. The total of the accounts receivable and accounts payable subsidiary ledgers should equal the amount of the related controlling accounts in the general ledger. A **schedule of accounts receivable** is a listing of customer accounts, account balances, and total amount due from all customers. Whiley's schedule of accounts receivable is shown above. The total of the schedule must equal the balance of the general ledger controlling account, Accounts Receivable. Whiley should correct any differences before preparing financial statements.

Whiley also prepares a report showing the total of all accounts payable ledger accounts. A listing of vendor accounts, account balances, and the total amount due

all vendors is called a **schedule of accounts payable**. Some businesses call this listing an *accounts payable trial balance*. The total of the schedule must equal the balance of the general ledger controlling account, Accounts Payable.

Reconciling a Bank Statement

A bank reconciliation is the tool used to ensure that cash transactions are posted accurately. The receipts and expenditures processed by the bank provide a business an independent accounting of these transactions. Banks and computer systems provide forms that assist businesses in performing bank reconciliations. Although the format of these forms vary, the logic of a bank reconciliation is identical. The relationship of items used to reconcile a bank statement is shown in the following example.

Book Balance	$ 2,846.00	Bank Balance		$ 3,525.00
Deduct: Service Charges	25.00	Add: Outstanding Deposits		472.00
		Deduct: Outstanding Checks		1,167.00
Other: Posting Errors	9.00	Other: Posting Errors		
Adjusted Balance	$ 2,830.00	Adjusted Balance		$ 2,830.00

A business should notify the bank of any bank posting errors. Service charges identified on the bank statement should be journalized in the cash payments journal. Errors identified in how transactions were

journalized requires that a correcting entry be journalized. Errors in posting a correctly journalized transaction requires only that the post be corrected in the general ledger.

Proving the Accuracy of the General Ledger

Whiley Outdoor Living, Inc. Unadjusted Trial Balance December 31, 20--		
ACCOUNT TITLE	**DEBIT**	**CREDIT**
Cash	60 8 4 9 26	
Petty Cash	5 0 0 00	
Accounts Receivable	23 5 1 5 27	
Allowance for Uncollectible Accounts		9 5 69
Merchandise Inventory—Grills	86 1 4 8 68	
Merchandise Inventory—Furniture	106 7 3 1 89	
Supplies	7 6 1 0 87	
Prepaid Insurance	14 0 0 0 00	
Office Equipment	32 4 8 1 15	
Accumulated Depreciation—Office Equipment		14 1 5 0 00
Dividends Payable		5 0 0 0 00
Capital Stock		100 0 0 0 00
Retained Earnings		114 3 5 2 88
Dividends	19 2 5 0 00	
Income Summary—General		
Income Summary—Grills		
Income Summary—Furniture		
Sales—Grills		472 0 1 9 64
Sales Discount—Grills	8 2 4 6 75	
Sales Returns and Allowances—Grills	9 4 6 7 42	
Sales—Furniture		492 1 8 7 31
Sales Discount—Furniture	5 2 1 9 23	
Sales Returns and Allowances—Furniture	13 8 1 0 76	
Purchases—Grills	254 8 5 1 26	
Purchases Discount—Grills		3 1 0 5 48
Purchases Returns and Allowances—Grills		6 1 0 8 67
Purchases—Furniture	197 0 8 4 64	
Purchases Discount—Furniture		2 6 7 1 69
Purchases Returns and Allowances—Furniture		8 0 9 4 21
Advertising Expense—Grills	14 9 2 0 00	
Payroll Taxes Expense—Grills	6 4 5 3 36	
Salary Expense—Grills	73 0 1 1 20	
Advertising Expense—Furniture	5 6 5 0 00	
Payroll Taxes Expense—Furniture	10 9 2 6 17	
Salary Expense—Furniture	125 8 0 6 20	
Credit Card Fee Expense	6 8 4 2 20	
Depreciation Expense—Office Equipment		
Depreciation Expense—Store Equipment		
Insurance Expense		
Miscellaneous Expense	3 4 9 5 04	
Payroll Taxes Expense—Administrative	7 6 0 2 20	
Rent Expense	18 4 0 0 00	
Salary Expense—Administrative	88 0 2 8 80	
Supplies Expense		
Uncollectible Accounts Expense		
Utilities Expense	16 2 0 4 68	
Federal Income Tax Expense	16 0 0 0 00	
Totals	1297 2 9 1 10	1297 2 9 1 10

The process of preparing financial statements begins with a list of all general ledger accounts. A proof of the equality of debits and credits in a general ledger is called a **trial balance**. The trial balance lists all accounts, even those with a zero balance. Thus, it provides a complete list of accounts that may need to be adjusted.

Journal entries recorded to update general ledger accounts at the end of a fiscal period are called **adjusting entries**. A trial balance prepared before adjusting entries are posted is called an **unadjusted trial balance**. Beginning with the first account, a business should review each account to determine if an adjusting entry is required.

Journalizing Adjusting Entries LO2

The next step in the preparation of financial statements is to record adjusting entries to bring selected account balances up to date.

Adjustment Information

Whiley collected the following information necessary to prepare the adjusting entries.

Adjustment Information, December 31

Estimate of uncollectible accounts	$ 2,210.61
Ending merchandise inventory—grills	89,349.72
Ending merchandise inventory—furniture	102,915.36
Supplies on hand	2,430.00
Value of prepaid insurance	2,000.00
Depreciation expense—office equipment	7,320.00
Depreciation expense—store equipment	8,370.00

Uncollectible Accounts Adjustment

	DATE		ACCOUNT TITLE	DOC. NO.	POST. REF.	DEBIT	CREDIT	
1			*Adjusting Entries*					1
2	Dec.	31	*Uncollectible Accounts Expense*			2 1 1 4 92		2
3			*Allowance for Uncollectible Accounts*				2 1 1 4 92	3

GENERAL JOURNAL   PAGE 20

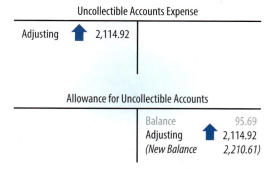

Uncollectible Accounts Expense

Adjusting ⬆ 2,114.92

Allowance for Uncollectible Accounts

Balance	95.69
Adjusting ⬆	2,114.92
(New Balance	2,210.61)

Merchandise is sometimes sold on account to customers who later are unable to pay the amounts owed. Amounts that cannot be collected from customers are business expenses. All expenses must be recorded in the fiscal period in which the expenses contribute to earning revenue. ≫ App. A: Matching Expenses with Revenue

The Allowance for Uncollectible Accounts balance represents the total estimated amount of accounts receivable that Whiley believes will never be collected. Whiley estimates that $2,210.61 of its accounts receivable will eventually be uncollectible. The current balance in Allowance for Uncollectible Accounts is a $95.69 credit. An adjusting entry for $2,114.92 ($2,210.61 required balance less $95.69 current credit balance) is required to increase the account balance to $2,210.61. Uncollectible Accounts Expense increases by $2,114.92. Allowance for Uncollectible Accounts, a contra asset account, increases by $2,114.92. Write the words *Adjusting Entries* in the Account Title column before the first adjusting entry.

Adjusting entries are immediately journalized in a general journal. Adjusting entries are not typically posted to general ledger accounts until all adjusting entries have been journalized.

Merchandise Inventory Adjustments

	DATE	ACCOUNT TITLE	DOC. NO.	POST. REF.	DEBIT	CREDIT	
				GENERAL JOURNAL		**PAGE 20**	
4	31	*Merchandise Inventory—Grills*			3 2 0 1 04		4
5		*Income Summary—Grills*				3 2 0 1 04	5
6	31	*Income Summary—Furniture*			3 8 1 6 53		6
7		*Merchandise Inventory—Furniture*				3 8 1 6 53	7
8							8

The merchandise inventory account balances in the trial balance are the beginning inventory amounts for a fiscal period. The amount of the ending inventory is determined by taking a periodic inventory at the end of a fiscal period.

The beginning merchandise inventory of grills, $86,148.68, is shown in the Debit column of the unadjusted trial balance. The periodic inventory taken on December 31 shows that the cost of the grills inventory is $89,349.72. To bring the grills inventory up to date, the balance of Merchandise Inventory—Grills needs to be increased by $3,201.04 ($89,349.72 ending inventory less $86,148.68 beginning inventory).

A similar adjusting entry is made for the furniture inventory. The $3,816.53 credit adjusting entry reduces the balance of Merchandise Inventory—Furniture.

Most accounts needing adjustment at the end of a fiscal period have a related expense account. Expense accounts are temporary accounts. For example, the adjustment to Allowance for Uncollectible Accounts included a debit to a related expense account, Uncollectible Accounts Expense. Merchandise Inventory, however, does not have a related expense account. Therefore, Income Summary, also a temporary account, is used to adjust Merchandise Inventory at the end of the fiscal year. Each department uses a separate income summary account.

Merchandise Inventory—Grills

Balance	86,148.68	
Adjusting	3,201.04	
(New Balance	89,349.72)	

Income Summary—Grills

	Adjusting	3,201.04

Income Summary—Furniture

Adjusting	3,816.53	

Merchandise Inventory—Furniture

Balance	106,731.89	Adjusting	3,816.53
(New Balance	102,915.36)		

Supplies Adjustment

	DATE	ACCOUNT TITLE	DOC. NO.	POST. REF.	DEBIT	CREDIT	
GENERAL JOURNAL						PAGE 20	
8	31	*Supplies Expense*			5 1 8 0 87		8
9		*Supplies*				5 1 8 0 87	9

The Supplies account balance in the unadjusted trial balance includes two items: (1) the account balance on January 1 and (2) the cost of supplies bought during the year. The account balance does not reflect the cost of any supplies used during the year, which is an operating expense. The amount of the ending inventory is determined by taking a periodic inventory at the end of a fiscal period.

The Supplies balance is $7,610.87. The estimate of supplies on hand on December 31 is $2,430.00. To bring the account up to date, the balance must be decreased by $5,180.87 (December 31 balance, $7,610.87, less the estimate of supplies on hand, $2,430.00).

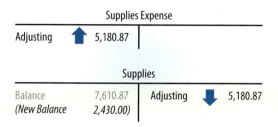

Prepaid Insurance Adjustment

	DATE	ACCOUNT TITLE	DOC. NO.	POST. REF.	DEBIT	CREDIT	
GENERAL JOURNAL						PAGE 20	
10	31	*Insurance Expense*			12 0 0 0 00		10
11		*Prepaid Insurance*				12 0 0 0 00	11
12							12

The Prepaid Insurance account balance in the unadjusted trial balance includes two items: (1) the account balance on January 1 and (2) the amount of insurance premiums paid during the year. The account balance does not reflect the amount of any insurance used during the year, which is an operating expense. The amount of unexpired insurance is determined at the end of a fiscal period.

The Prepaid Insurance account balance is $14,000.00. The estimate of unexpired insurance on December 31 is $2,000.00. To bring the account up to date, the balance of Prepaid Insurance must be decreased by $12,000.00 (December 31 balance, $14,000.00, less unexpired insurance, $2,000.00).

Depreciation Expense Adjustments

GENERAL JOURNAL
PAGE 20

	DATE	ACCOUNT TITLE	DOC. NO.	POST. REF.	DEBIT	CREDIT	
12	31	Depreciation Expense—Office Equipment			7 3 2 0 00		12
13		Accumulated Depreciation—Office Equipment				7 3 2 0 00	13
14	31	Depreciation Expense—Store Equipment			8 3 7 0 00		14
15		Accumulated Depreciation—Store Equipment				8 3 7 0 00	15
16							16

Depreciation Expense—Office Equipment

Adjusting ⬆ 7,320.00

Accumulated Depreciation—Office Equipment

Balance	14,150.00
Adjusting ⬆	7,320.00
(New Balance	21,470.00)

Depreciation Expense—Store Equipment

Adjusting ⬆ 8,370.00

Accumulated Depreciation—Store Equipment

Balance	34,550.00
Adjusting ⬆	8,370.00
(New Balance	42,920.00)

Physical assets that will be used for a number of years in the operation of a business are called **plant assets**. Plant assets are not bought for resale to customers in the normal course of business. Plant assets decrease in value because of use, the passage of time, and the availability of new models. The portion of a plant asset's cost that is transferred to an expense account in each fiscal period during that asset's useful life is called **depreciation expense**. The decrease in the value of equipment because of use and the passage of time is an operating expense.

>> App. A: Matching Expenses with Revenue

The amount of depreciation is an estimate. The actual decrease in equipment value is not known until equipment is disposed of or sold. For this reason, the estimated depreciation is recorded in a separate contra asset account for each type of equipment.

Whiley estimates that the annual depreciation on office equipment is $7,320.00. To adjust for the depreciation of office equipment, Depreciation Expense— Office Equipment increases by a $7,320.00 debit. The contra asset account, Accumulated Depreciation— Office Equipment, increases by a $7,320.00 credit.

A similar adjustment is made for Depreciation Expense—Store Equipment. Calculating the amount of depreciation is described more fully in Chapter 7.

© ISTOCKPHOTO.COM/HOCUS FOCUS STUDIO

Preparing an Adjusted Trial Balance LO3

ACCOUNT TITLE	DEBIT	CREDIT
Whiley Outdoor Living, Inc.		
Adjusted Trial Balance		
December 31, 20--		
Cash	60 8 4 9 26	
Petty Cash	5 0 0 00	
Accounts Receivable	23 5 1 5 27	
Dividends	19 2 5 0 00	
Income Summary—Grills		3 2 0 1 04
Income Summary—Furniture	3 8 1 6 53	
Sales—Grills		472 0 1 9 64
Sales Discount—Grills	8 2 4 6 75	
Sales Returns and Allowances—Grills	9 4 6 7 42	
Sales—Furniture		492 1 8 7 31
Sales Discount—Furniture	5 2 1 9 23	
Sales Returns and Allowances—Furniture	13 8 1 0 76	
Purchases—Grills	254 8 5 1 26	
Purchases Discount—Grills		3 1 0 5 48
Purchases Returns and Allowances—Grills		6 1 0 8 67
Purchases—Furniture	197 0 8 4 64	
Purchases Discount—Furniture		2 6 7 1 69
Purchases Returns and Allowances—Furniture		8 0 9 4 21
Advertising Expense—Grills	14 9 2 0 00	
Payroll Taxes Expense—Grills	6 4 5 3 36	
Salary Expense—Grills	73 0 1 1 20	
Advertising Expense—Furniture	5 6 5 0 00	
Payroll Taxes Expense—Furniture	10 9 2 6 17	
Salary Expense—Furniture	125 8 0 6 20	
Credit Card Fee Expense	6 8 4 2 20	
Depreciation Expense—Office Equipment	7 3 2 0 00	
Depreciation Expense—Store Equipment	8 3 7 0 00	
Insurance Expense	12 0 0 0 00	
Miscellaneous Expense	3 4 9 5 04	
Payroll Taxes Expense—Administrative	7 6 0 2 20	
Rent Expense	18 4 0 0 00	
Salary Expense—Administrative	88 0 2 8 80	
Supplies Expense	5 1 8 0 87	
Uncollectible Accounts Expense	2 1 1 4 92	
Utilities Expense	16 2 0 4 68	
Federal Income Tax Expense		

Account Titles ①

Account Balances ②

Income Statement Credit Accounts ③

Income Statement Debit Accounts ④

Total of income statement credit accounts	$987,388.04
Less total of income statement debit accounts, excluding federal income tax expense	904,822.23
Income before income taxes	$ 82,565.81

Income before Income Taxes ⑤

An updated trial balance is prepared once all adjusting entries are posted to the general ledger. A trial balance prepared after adjusting entries are posted is called an **adjusted trial balance**. The adjusted trial balance is prepared in two steps. In the first step, all account balances, except for Federal Income Tax Expense, are entered on the trial balance. This procedure allows for the calculation of income before income taxes.

>> Calculating Income before Income Taxes

❶ Enter the account titles of all general ledger accounts.

❷ Enter the account balances of all accounts except **Federal Income Tax Expense**.

❸ Calculate the total account balances of income statement credit accounts. Include the account balance of any **Income Summary** account having a credit balance.

❹ Calculate the total account balances of income statement debit accounts, excluding the balance of **Federal Income Tax Expense**. Include the account balance of any **Income Summary** account having a debit balance.

❺ Subtract the total of debits from the total of credits to calculate income before income taxes.

How Secure Is Social Security

Social Security is a mandatory deduction from most employees' paycheck. Currently, if employees work 40 quarters throughout their career, they will be eligible to receive Social Security benefits when they reach full retirement age (67 years old), and these benefits will continue for life.

As people live longer, financial stress is put on the Social Security system. The Social Security Administration warns that, within just a few years, Social Security benefit payments will begin to exceed Social Security tax income. Currently, more than 67 million people receive some type of Social Security benefits.

Social Security has changed over the years to meet people's needs, and some experts feel it must change again to meet future challenges. One proposed change is to privatize Social Security. Privatization could allow individuals to direct their benefits into a personal account. Other recommendations have been to (1) reduce benefits, (2) raise the payroll tax rate, (3) raise the payroll tax cap for wage-earner contributions, (4) increase the taxes on Social Security benefits, and (5) raise the retirement age.

ACTIVITIES

1. Research two of the recommended changes. Prepare a spreadsheet with the following information: (a) a summary of each recommendation, (b) its impact on the future recipient, and (c) its impact on either the employer or the employee (wage earner). Highlight the change you prefer and explain why.

2. Interview someone you know who is collecting Social Security and ask for his or her opinion. Share your findings with the class. Did this interview change your preference in question 1?

Source: www.ssa.gov.

Calculating the Federal Income Tax Adjustment LO4

		GENERAL JOURNAL										PAGE 20				
	DATE	ACCOUNT TITLE	DOC. NO.	POST. REF.			DEBIT						CREDIT			
16	31	*Federal Income Tax Expense*			1	3	3	8	82							16
17		*Federal Income Tax Payable*									1	3	3	8	82	17
18																18

Now that the amount of income before income taxes is known, the actual amount of federal income tax is calculated. The tax rate for corporations is 21% of income before income taxes. Whiley's income tax, $17,338.82, is calculated by multiplying the tax rate, 21%, by the income before income tax, $82,565.81. Corporations are required to make quarterly income tax payments to the government. Whiley made quarterly tax payments of $4,000.00 on the dates shown in the account. Therefore, an additional $1,338.82 needs to be paid and recorded as Federal Income Tax Expense.

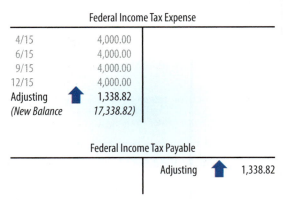

The adjusting entry increases Federal Income Tax Expense and increases the balance of Federal Income Tax Payable by $1,338.82. Whiley must pay an additional $1,338.82 when it files its tax return.

Careers In Accounting

Lian Vong
Junior Accountant/Senior Accountant

Lian Vong graduated from college with a degree in accounting. Although she hoped someday to pass the CPA (certified public accountant) exam, she knew she needed some work experience before she could get her license. She decided to study for the exam while working full-time in an accounting position. She got a job as a junior accountant in one of the major accounting firms.

A junior accountant is an entry-level position in most accounting firms, and it usually requires a degree in accounting. As a junior accountant, Lian performed many tasks to support senior accountants. She double-checked calculations, performed tax calculations, posted journal entries, gathered data for monthly reports, and worked with receivables and payables.

The accounting firm paid for Lian to take a CPA exam review. She completed the course and passed the exam. After four years with the firm, Lian, now a CPA, was promoted to the position of senior accountant.

As a senior accountant, Lian had more responsibilities and performed higher-level work. She coordinated auditing procedures, performed financial analyses, and prepared tax returns and financial reports. She also communicated directly with clients on a regular basis. In addition, she supervised a team of junior accountants, including their training and scheduling.

Lian enjoys public accounting and hopes to stay with her firm for many years. She likes the variety and the opportunity for advancement.

Salary Range: The range for a senior accountant is $58,500 to $111,500. The range for a junior accountant is $47,000 to $90,000 per year.

Qualifications: Both junior accountant and senior accountant positions require a degree in accounting. The position of senior accountant also usually requires three or more years of work experience and a CPA designation.

Occupational Outlook: Both junior and senior accounting positions are expected to experience faster than average growth (10% to 14%) from 2016 to 2026.

Sources: online.onetcenter.org; Ehow.com; Robert Half 2018 Salary Guide.

Completing the Adjusted Trial Balance

Whiley Outdoor Living, Inc.
Adjusted Trial Balance
December 31, 20--

ACCOUNT TITLE	DEBIT	CREDIT
Cash	60 8 4 9 26	
Petty Cash	5 0 0 00	
Accounts Receivable	23 5 1 5 27	
Allowance for Uncollectible Accounts		2 2 1 0 61
Merchandise Inventory—Grills	89 3 4 9 72	
Merchandise Inventory—Furniture	102 9 1 5 36	
Supplies	2 4 3 0 00	
Prepaid Insurance	2 0 0 0 00	
Office Equipment	32 4 8 1 15	
Accumulated Depreciation—Office Equipment		21 4 7 0 00
Store Equipment	64 1 8 4 07	
Accumulated Depreciation—Store Equipment		42 9 2 0 00
Accounts Payable		30 3 9 2 88
Sales Tax Payable		6 1 4 8 05
Employee Income Tax Payable—Federal		1 6 6 6 00
Employee Income Tax Payable—State		1 1 9 0 00
Social Security Tax Payable		2 9 5 0 80
Medicare Tax Payable		6 8 7 22
Medical Insurance Payable		1 0 5 0 00
Retirement Plan Payable		7 1 0 00
Unemployment Tax Payable—Federal		2 0 72
Unemployment Tax Payable—State		1 3 9 86
Federal Income Tax Payable		1 3 3 8 82
Depreciation Expense—Office Equipment	7 3 2 0 00	
Depreciation Expense—Store Equipment	8 3 7 0 00	
Insurance Expense	12 0 0 0 00	
Miscellaneous Expense	3 4 9 5 04	
Payroll Taxes Expense—Administrative	7 6 0 2 20	
Rent Expense	18 4 0 0 00	
Salary Expense—Administrative	88 0 2 8 80	
Supplies Expense	5 1 8 0 87	
Uncollectible Accounts Expense	2 1 1 4 92	
Utilities Expense	16 2 0 4 68	
Federal Income Tax Expense	17 3 3 8 82	
Totals	1319 6 3 5 88	1319 6 3 5 88

Federal Income Tax Amounts

Total, Prove, and Rule

After the income tax adjustment is posted, the balances for Federal Income Tax Payable and Federal Income Tax Expense are entered in the adjusted trial balance.

The trial balance is totaled, proved, and ruled. The trial balance provides the information necessary to prepare the financial statements.

LO1 Prove the accuracy of the subsidiary and general ledgers.

LO2 Journalize adjusting entries.

LO3 Prepare an adjusted trial balance.

LO4 Calculate the federal income tax adjustment.

TERMS REVIEW

fiscal period

fiscal year

schedule of accounts receivable

schedule of accounts payable

trial balance

adjusting entries

unadjusted trial balance

plant assets

depreciation expense

adjusted trial balance

Audit your understanding LO1, 2, 3

1. Identify the steps that should be completed before preparing financial statements.
2. How are outstanding deposits and checks used to reconcile a bank statement?
3. What two reports are prepared to prove the accuracy of posting to subsidiary ledgers?
4. Why are adjustments made to certain accounts at the end of the fiscal period?
5. Explain how income before income taxes is calculated using an adjusted trial balance.

Work together 4-1 LO2, 3, 4

Preparing an adjusted trial balance

Adjustment information for Foley's Interiors on December 31 is presented below.

Estimate of uncollectible accounts	$ 2,101.23
Ending merchandise inventory—kitchen	147,084.62
Ending merchandise inventory—bath	97,671.31
Supplies on hand	1,950.00
Value of prepaid insurance	2,500.00
Depreciation expense—office equipment	7,250.00
Depreciation expense—store equipment	8,490.00

A partially completed adjusted trial balance, a general journal, and selected accounts are provided in the *Working Papers*. Your instructor will guide you through the following examples. Save your work to complete Work Together 4-2.

1. Record the adjusting entries on page 20 of a general journal.
2. Post the adjusting entries to the general ledger accounts.
3. Enter the adjusted account balances on the adjusted trial balance.
4. Calculate federal income tax expense using the tax rate presented in the lesson. Prepare and post the adjusting entry for federal income tax expense.
5. Complete the adjusted trial balance.

On your own 4-1 LO2, 3, 4

Preparing an adjusted trial balance

Adjustment information for Mixon Auto Supplies on December 31 is presented below.

Estimate of uncollectible accounts	$ 3,123.53
Ending merchandise inventory—parts	254,285.38
Ending merchandise inventory—accessories	114,223.95
Supplies on hand	1,480.00
Value of prepaid insurance	3,000.00
Depreciation expense—office equipment	4,850.00
Depreciation expense—store equipment	6,490.00

A partially completed adjusted trial balance, a general journal, and selected accounts are provided in the *Working Papers*. Work this problem independently. Save your work to complete On Your Own 4-2.

1. Record the adjusting entries on page 22 of a general journal.
2. Post the adjusting entries to the general ledger accounts.
3. Enter the adjusted account balances on the adjusted trial balance.
4. Calculate federal income tax expense using the tax rate presented in the lesson. Prepare and post the adjusting entry for federal income tax expense.
5. Complete the adjusted trial balance.

Responsibility Statements for a Merchandising Business

LO5 Distinguish between direct and indirect expenses of a departmentalized business.

LO6 Prepare a departmental margin statement.

LO7 Analyze financial statements using vertical analysis ratios.

Features of a Responsibility Accounting System LO5

The two important features of a successful responsibility accounting system are as follows:

1. Each manager is assigned responsibility for only those revenues, cost, and expenses for which he or she can make decisions and affect the outcome.
2. The revenues, costs, and expenses for which a manager is responsible must be readily identifiable with the manager's unit. For example, if a manager is responsible for advertising expense, that manager should make decisions about advertising. In addition, a separate record should be kept for the manager's advertising expense. Thus, responsibility accounting traces revenues, costs, and expenses to the individual managers who are responsible for making decisions about those revenues, costs, and expenses.

Controlling costs is essential to a business's success. However, who should control a business's costs? Good management practices require that each manager be responsible for controlling all costs incurred by the manager's business unit. Assigning control of revenues, costs, and expenses to a specific manager is called **responsibility accounting**. Merchandising businesses with effective cost controls generally use some kind of responsibility accounting.

A typical merchandising business income statement reports net income earned during a fiscal period. However, the statement usually does not report specific information that a department manager can use to control departmental costs. Therefore, merchandising businesses often prepare departmental statements to show each department's contribution to net income.

In responsibility accounting, operating expenses are classified as either direct or indirect expenses. An operating expense identifiable with and chargeable to the operation of a specific department is called a **direct expense**. The cost of supplies used by a specific department is an example of a direct expense. An operating expense chargeable to overall business operations and not identifiable with a specific department is called an **indirect expense**. Therefore, the cost of electricity used by a business's overall operations is an example of an indirect expense. A department manager has little or no control over the use of electricity in the department.

Whiley uses responsibility accounting to help control costs and expenses. Whiley has two merchandising departments: Grills and Furniture. Each department's revenue, cost of merchandise sold, and direct expenses are recorded in separate departmental general ledger accounts as shown in Whiley's chart of accounts.

Each business develops a chart of accounts to meet its needs. Whiley groups its departmental accounts by type, such as operating revenue, cost of merchandise, direct expenses, and indirect expenses. For example, accounts under Direct Expenses—Grills are 6100 numbers. Accounts under Direct Expenses—Furniture are 6200 numbers.

Departmental Margin Statement LO6

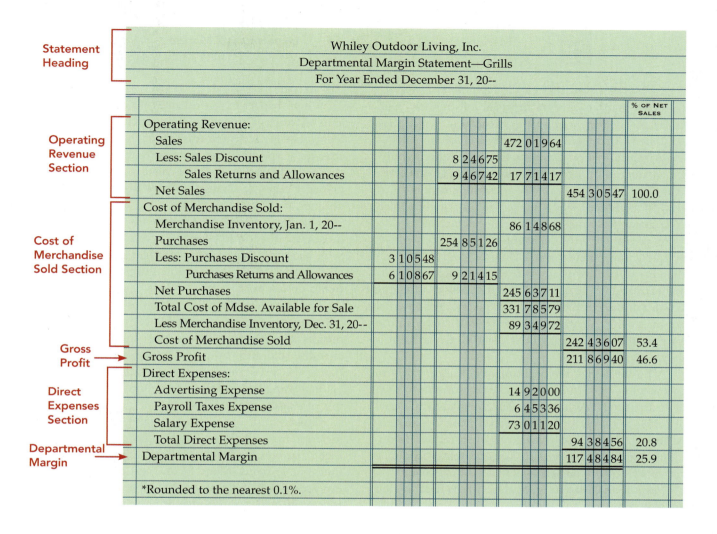

					% OF NET SALES
Operating Revenue:					
Sales			472 01 9 64		
Less: Sales Discount		8 24 6 75			
Sales Returns and Allowances		9 46 7 42	17 71 4 17		
Net Sales				454 30 5 47	100.0
Cost of Merchandise Sold:					
Merchandise Inventory, Jan. 1, 20--			86 14 8 68		
Purchases		254 85 1 26			
Less: Purchases Discount	3 10 5 48				
Purchases Returns and Allowances	6 10 8 67	9 21 4 15			
Net Purchases			245 63 7 11		
Total Cost of Mdse. Available for Sale			331 78 5 79		
Less Merchandise Inventory, Dec. 31, 20--			89 34 9 72		
Cost of Merchandise Sold				242 43 6 07	53.4
Gross Profit				211 86 9 40	46.6
Direct Expenses:					
Advertising Expense			14 92 0 00		
Payroll Taxes Expense			6 45 3 36		
Salary Expense			73 01 1 20		
Total Direct Expenses				94 38 4 56	20.8
Departmental Margin				117 48 4 84	25.9

Statement heading: Whiley Outdoor Living, Inc. / Departmental Margin Statement—Grills / For Year Ended December 31, 20--

*Rounded to the nearest 0.1%.

Financial statements reporting revenue, costs, and direct expenses under a specific department's control are called **responsibility statements**. Whiley prepares the usual end-of-fiscal-period financial statements. In addition, Whiley prepares a responsibility statement for each department.

The revenue earned by a department less its cost of merchandise sold and less its direct expenses is called **departmental margin**. A statement that reports departmental margin for a specific department is called a **departmental margin statement**.

Whiley's departmental margin statement—grills for the year ended December 31 is shown above. Information for this statement is obtained from the adjusted trial balance accounts having grills in the account title. The format of the statement is similar to an income statement. However, only direct expenses for the grills department are included on the departmental margin statement.

The operating revenue remaining after cost of merchandise sold has been deducted is called **gross profit**. Gross profit, therefore, shows the direct relationship between sales and sales price and merchandise inventory and the cost of merchandise inventory. By analyzing a department's gross profit data, managers can determine the amount of revenue remaining after the cost of merchandise has been deducted from net sales.

The departmental margin statements help department managers determine how revenue, costs, and direct expenses affect department results. With this knowledge, managers can make informed decisions to improve those results.

Vertical Analysis of Departmental Margin Statements LO7

$$\text{Departmental Margin} \div \text{Net Sales} = \text{Vertical Analysis Ratio for Departmental Margin}$$

$$\$117{,}484.84 \div \$454{,}305.47 = 25.9\%$$

To help a manager analyze financial information, relationships between items in a financial statement are calculated. A comparison between two components of financial information is called a **financial ratio**. Reporting an amount on a financial statement as a percentage of another item on the same financial statement is called **vertical analysis**. Vertical analysis ratios may be shown in a separate column on a financial statement.

Whiley analyzes its departmental margin statements by calculating vertical analysis ratios for cost of merchandise sold, gross profit, direct expenses, and departmental margin. The ratios are calculated by dividing the amount on selected lines by the amount of departmental net sales. The calculation of the vertical analysis ratio for the departmental margin of the grills department is shown above.

A business may set departmental margin goals to encourage and determine acceptable performance by each of its department. Whiley set a departmental margin goal of 25.5% to 27.5% for the grills department. Departmental goals are determined by reviewing many factors, including the department's previous achievements, economic and market trends, and changes in department costs.

Vertical analysis ratios for the current fiscal period are also compared to ratios for previous fiscal periods. The grills department's departmental margin ratios for the current and prior fiscal years are shown below.

	Current Year	Prior Year	Target Range
Cost of Merchandise Sold	53.4%	54.1%	53.0% – 54.0%
Gross Profit	46.6%	45.9%	46.0% – 47.0%
Direct Expenses	20.8%	20.4%	19.5% – 20.5%
Departmental Margin	25.9%	25.5%	25.5% – 27.5%

When changes in vertical analysis ratios occur for an item on the departmental margin statement, the department manager seeks the reasons for the changes. If the changes are positive, the policies resulting in favorable changes are continued. If the changes are negative, the manager seeks to change policies to prevent further declines.

The departmental margin ratio for the grills department increased from 25.5% to 25.9%, a favorable trend. Still, the grills department manager should examine other vertical analysis ratios to ensure that unfavorable trends do not exist.

The cost of merchandise sold ratios indicate that the grills department was successful in controlling its cost of merchandise, resulting in a decrease in the cost of merchandise sold ratio from 54.1% to 53.4%, a favorable trend. The cost of merchandise sold ratio will increase by (1) increasing sales prices and (2) purchasing merchandise at a discounted unit price.

However, the grills department's direct expenses increased from 20.4% to 20.8% of net sales. The department manager needs to investigate the reasons for this unfavorable trend. Many factors and events can cause expenses to be higher than expected. The department may have contracted excessive advertising, scheduled too many workers, or allowed employees to work overtime hours.

Without the information on the departmental margin statement, a department manager will not know which policies to continue and which to change. The statements also provide information to assist company officers to evaluate the performance of department managers.

FYI — Vertical analysis ratios are also known as *component percentages*.

TERMS REVIEW

responsibility accounting

direct expense

indirect expense

responsibility statements

departmental margin

departmental margin statement

gross profit

financial ratio

vertical analysis

Audit your understanding LO5, 6, 7

1. What two features are required if responsibility accounting is to be successful?
2. For what type of accounts does Whiley have separate departmental accounts in the general ledger?
3. Describe how departmental gross profit is calculated.
4. How are the vertical analysis ratios for departmental margin calculated?
5. The departmental margin ratio increased from 31.4% to 32.5%. Management has a target range of 32.4% to 33.2%. Is the trend favorable or unfavorable?
6. A department's direct expenses increased from 22.6% to 23.1% of net sales. Management has a target range of 21.8% to 22.4%. Is the trend favorable or unfavorable?

Work together 4-2 LO6, 7

Preparing a departmental margin statement

Foley's Interiors has two departments: Kitchen and Bath. Use the adjusted trial balance or work sheet from Work Together 4-1. Your instructor will guide you through the following examples. Save your work to complete Work Together 4-3.

1. Prepare a departmental margin statement for each department.
2. Calculate vertical analysis ratios for cost of merchandise sold, gross profit, total direct expenses, and departmental margin.

On your own 4-2 LO6, 7

Preparing a departmental margin statement

Mixon Auto Supplies has two departments: Parts and Accessories. Use the adjusted trial balance or work sheet from On Your Own 4-1. Work this problem independently. Save your work to complete On Your Own 4-3.

1. Prepare a departmental margin statement for each department.
2. Calculate vertical analysis ratios for cost of merchandise sold, gross profit, total direct expenses, and departmental margin.

Financial Statements for a Departmental Merchandising Business

LO8 Prepare financial statements for a departmentalized merchandising business.

Preparing Financial Statements for a Departmentalized Merchandising Business LO8

Whiley prepares four financial statements to report its results of operations and financial condition.

Income Statement with Departmental Margin

Statement Heading

Whiley Outdoor Living, Inc.
Income Statement
For Year Ended December 31, 20--

	DEPARTMENTAL		COMPANY	% OF NET SALES*
	GRILLS	FURNITURE		
Information from Departmental Margin Statements				
Net Sales	454 3 0 5 47	473 1 5 7 32	927 4 6 2 79	100.0
Cost of Merchandise Sold	242 4 3 6 07	190 1 3 5 27	432 5 7 1 34	46.6
Gross Profit	211 8 6 9 40	283 0 2 2 05	494 8 9 1 45	53.4
Direct Expenses	94 3 8 4 56	142 3 8 2 37	236 7 6 6 93	25.5
Departmental Margin	117 4 8 4 84	140 6 3 9 68	258 1 2 4 52	27.8
Indirect Expenses:				
Credit Card Fee Expense			6 8 4 2 20	
Depreciation Exp.—Office Equipment			7 3 2 0 00	
Depreciation Exp.—Store Equipment			8 3 7 0 00	
Insurance Expense			12 0 0 0 00	
Miscellaneous Expense			3 4 9 5 04	
Payroll Taxes Expense			7 6 0 2 20	
Rent Expense			18 4 0 0 00	
Salary Expense—Administrative			88 0 2 8 80	
Supplies Expense			5 1 8 0 87	
Uncollectible Accounts Expense			2 1 1 4 92	
Utilities Expense			16 2 0 4 68	
Total Indirect Expenses			175 5 5 8 71	18.9
Income before Income Tax			82 5 6 5 81	8.9
Less Federal Income Tax Expense			17 3 3 8 82	1.9
Net Income			65 2 2 6 99	7.0

*Rounded to the nearest 0.1%.

Vertical Analysis Ratios

Labels on left margin: **Indirect Expenses from Adjusted Trial Balance**, **Income Taxes and Net Income**

A financial statement showing the revenue and expenses for a fiscal period is called an **income statement**. Whiley's income statement for the year ended December 31 is shown on the previous page. The income statement is prepared with five columns: two for departmental amounts and three for company amounts and vertical analysis ratios.

The amounts for the first section are obtained from the departmental margin statements. The remaining accounts and balances are obtained from the adjusted trial balance. Vertical analysis ratios are calculated by dividing each amount by company net sales.

Statement of Stockholders' Equity

Statement Heading	Whiley Outdoor Living, Inc.	
	Statement of Stockholders' Equity	
	For Year Ended December 31, 20--	

Capital Stock Section	Capital Stock:		
	$1.00 Par Value		
	January 1, 20--, 95,000 Shares Issued	95 0 0 0 00	
	Issued during Current Year, 5,000 Shares	5 0 0 0 00	
	Balance, December 31, 20--, 100,000 Shares Issued		100 0 0 0 00
Beginning Retained Earnings →	Retained Earnings:		
	Balance, January 1, 20--	114 3 5 2 88	
	Net Income for 20--	65 2 2 6 99	
Change in Retained Earnings	Less Dividends Declared during 20--	19 2 5 0 00	
	Net Increase during 20--	45 9 7 6 99	
	Balance, December 31, 20--		160 3 2 9 87
	Total Stockholders' Equity, December 31, 20--		260 3 2 9 87

Total Stockholders' Equity

A financial statement that shows changes in a corporation's ownership for a fiscal period is called a **statement of stockholders' equity**. Whiley's statement of stockholders' equity for the fiscal year ended December 31 is shown above. Information for this statement is obtained from (1) the prior year's statement of stockholders' equity, (2) the income statement, and (3) the adjusted trial balance.

A statement of stockholders' equity contains two major sections:

1. Capital stock. Total shares of ownership in a corporation are called **capital stock**.
2. Retained earnings. An amount earned by a corporation and not yet distributed to stockholders is called **retained earnings**.

Net income increases the retained earnings of a corporation. A corporation may retain some income for business expansion. Some income may be distributed to stockholders as a return on their investment. Earnings distributed to stockholders are called **dividends**.

Balance Sheet

<table>
<tr><td colspan="5" align="center">Whiley Outdoor Living, Inc.</td></tr>
<tr><td colspan="5" align="center">Balance Sheet</td></tr>
<tr><td colspan="5" align="center">December 31, 20--</td></tr>
<tr><td></td><td></td><td></td><td></td><td>% OF ASSETS*</td></tr>
<tr><td colspan="5" align="center">ASSETS</td></tr>
<tr><td>Current Assets:</td><td></td><td></td><td></td><td></td></tr>
<tr><td>Cash</td><td></td><td>60 8 4 9 26</td><td></td><td></td></tr>
<tr><td>Petty Cash</td><td></td><td>5 0 0 00</td><td></td><td></td></tr>
<tr><td>Accounts Receivable</td><td>23 5 1 5 27</td><td></td><td></td><td></td></tr>
<tr><td>Less Allowance for Uncollectible Accounts</td><td>2 2 1 0 61</td><td>21 3 0 4 66</td><td></td><td></td></tr>
<tr><td>Merchandise Inventory—Grills</td><td></td><td>89 3 4 9 72</td><td></td><td></td></tr>
<tr><td>Merchandise Inventory—Furniture</td><td></td><td>102 9 1 5 36</td><td></td><td></td></tr>
<tr><td>Supplies</td><td></td><td>2 4 3 0 00</td><td></td><td></td></tr>
<tr><td>Prepaid Insurance</td><td></td><td>2 0 0 0 00</td><td></td><td></td></tr>
<tr><td>Total Current Assets</td><td></td><td></td><td>279 3 4 9 00</td><td>89.6</td></tr>
<tr><td>Plant Assets:</td><td></td><td></td><td></td><td></td></tr>
<tr><td>Office Equipment</td><td>32 4 8 1 15</td><td></td><td></td><td></td></tr>
<tr><td>Less Accumulated Depreciation—Office Equipment</td><td>21 4 7 0 00</td><td>11 0 1 1 15</td><td></td><td></td></tr>
<tr><td>Store Equipment</td><td>64 1 8 4 07</td><td></td><td></td><td></td></tr>
<tr><td>Less Accumulated Depreciation—Store Equipment</td><td>42 9 2 0 00</td><td>21 2 6 4 07</td><td></td><td></td></tr>
<tr><td>Total Plant Assets</td><td></td><td></td><td>32 2 7 5 22</td><td>10.4</td></tr>
<tr><td>Total Assets</td><td></td><td></td><td>311 6 2 4 22</td><td>100.0</td></tr>
<tr><td colspan="5" align="center">LIABILITIES</td></tr>
<tr><td>Current Liabilities:</td><td></td><td></td><td></td><td></td></tr>
<tr><td>Accounts Payable</td><td></td><td>30 3 9 2 88</td><td></td><td></td></tr>
<tr><td>Sales Tax Payable</td><td></td><td>6 1 4 8 05</td><td></td><td></td></tr>
<tr><td>Employee Income Tax Payable—Federal</td><td></td><td>1 6 6 6 00</td><td></td><td></td></tr>
<tr><td>Employee Income Tax Payable—State</td><td></td><td>1 1 9 0 00</td><td></td><td></td></tr>
<tr><td>Social Security Tax Payable</td><td></td><td>2 9 5 0 80</td><td></td><td></td></tr>
<tr><td>Medicare Tax Payable</td><td></td><td>6 8 7 22</td><td></td><td></td></tr>
<tr><td>Medical Insurance Payable</td><td></td><td>1 0 5 0 00</td><td></td><td></td></tr>
<tr><td>Retirement Plan Payable</td><td></td><td>7 1 0 00</td><td></td><td></td></tr>
<tr><td>Unemployment Tax Payable—Federal</td><td></td><td>2 0 72</td><td></td><td></td></tr>
<tr><td>Unemployment Tax Payable—State</td><td></td><td>1 3 9 86</td><td></td><td></td></tr>
<tr><td>Federal Income Tax Payable</td><td></td><td>1 3 3 8 82</td><td></td><td></td></tr>
<tr><td>Dividends Payable</td><td></td><td>5 0 0 0 00</td><td></td><td></td></tr>
<tr><td>Total Liabilities</td><td></td><td></td><td>51 2 9 4 35</td><td>16.5</td></tr>
<tr><td colspan="5" align="center">STOCKHOLDERS' EQUITY</td></tr>
<tr><td>Capital Stock</td><td></td><td>100 0 0 0 00</td><td></td><td></td></tr>
<tr><td>Retained Earnings</td><td></td><td>160 3 2 9 87</td><td></td><td></td></tr>
<tr><td>Total Stockholders' Equity</td><td></td><td></td><td>260 3 2 9 87</td><td>83.5</td></tr>
<tr><td>Total Liabilities and Stockholders' Equity</td><td></td><td></td><td>311 6 2 4 22</td><td>100.0</td></tr>
<tr><td colspan="5">*Rounded to the nearest 0.1%.</td></tr>
</table>

A financial statement that reports assets, liabilities, and owners' equity on a specific date is called a **balance sheet**. A balance sheet reports the financial condition of a business on a specific date. Whiley's balance sheet for December 31 is shown above.

The data used in preparing the asset and liability sections of a balance sheet come from the adjusted trial balance. Assets are divided into two categories: current assets and plant assets. Accounts receivable, office equipment, and store equipment each have a contra account. The balance of the contra account is subtracted from the

asset account. Liabilities are typically divided into two categories: current liabilities and long-term liabilities. Whiley does not currently have any long-term liabilities.

The data used in preparing the stockholders' equity section of a balance sheet come from the statement of stockholders' equity. Only the total amounts of capital stock and retained earnings are presented on the balance sheet. Information that is more detailed is available on the statement of stockholders' equity.

Vertical analysis ratios are calculated by dividing selected amounts by total assets.

Statement of Cash Flows

Whiley Outdoor Living, Inc.					
Statement of Cash Flows					
For Year Ended December 31, 20--					
Cash flows from operating activities:				
Cash receipts from customers		914 1 0 8 26	
Cash payments for:			
Inventory purchases	(429 1 0 5 18)		
Salaries and wages	(311 8 2 7 93)		
Rent	(18 4 0 0 00)		
Taxes	(16 2 0 4 18)		
Insurance	(14 0 0 0 00)		
Other operating expenses	(57 4 1 8 10)		
Total cash payments		(846 9 5 5 39)	
Net cash provided (used) by operating activities			67 1 5 2 87
Cash flows from investing activities:			
Sale of equipment		5 2 0 0 00	
Purchase of equipment		(18 5 2 0 00)	
Net cash provided (used) by investing activities			(13 3 2 0 00)
Cash flows from financing activities:			
Issuance of stock		5 0 0 0 00	
Payment of cash dividends		(21 2 0 0 00)	
Net cash provided (used) by financing activities			(16 2 0 0 00)
Net change in cash			37 6 3 2 87
Cash balance, January 1, 20--			23 2 1 6 39
Cash balance, December 31, 20--			60 8 4 9 26

The income statement, statement of stockholders' equity, and balance sheet are prepared using the accrual basis of accounting. Understanding how a business receives and spends its cash provides a different perspective into its operations. The cash receipts and cash payments of a company are called **cash flow**. A financial statement that summarizes cash receipts and cash payments resulting from business activities during a fiscal period is called a **statement of cash flows**.

The statement of cash flows is divided into three sections. The cash receipts and payments necessary to operate a business on a day-to-day basis are called **operating activities**. These activities include receiving cash from customers, purchasing merchandise, and paying expenses. Cash receipts and cash payments involving the sale or purchase of assets used to earn revenue over a period of time are called **investing activities**. These activities include the sale and purchase of plant assets. Cash receipts and payments involving debt or equity transactions are called **financing activities**. These activities usually involve borrowing money from creditors and repaying the principal or selling stock and paying dividends.

The preparation and use of the statement of cash flows is presented in greater depth in Chapter 14.

Audit your understanding LO8

1. Where does Whiley obtain the information to prepare the indirect expenses section of the income statement?
2. From where is the information to prepare the direct expenses section of the income statement obtained?
3. Where does Whiley obtain the stockholders' equity amounts reported on the balance sheet?

Work together 4-3 LO8

Preparing financial statements

Use the adjusted trial balance or work sheet for Foley's Interiors from Work Together 4-1 and the departmental margin statement from Work Together 4-2. Partially completed financial statements are provided in the *Working Papers*. Round percentage calculations to the nearest 0.1%. Save your work to complete Work Together 4-4.

1. Complete the income statement. Calculate and record the vertical analysis ratios for each amount in the fourth column of the statement.
2. Complete the statement of stockholders' equity. There were 74,000 shares of $1.00 par value stock issued as of January 1. There were 1,000 shares issued during the current year.
3. Complete the balance sheet. Calculate and record the vertical analysis ratios for each item in the third column of the statement.
4. Use the following information to complete the statement of cash flows. Foley's began the fiscal year with a cash balance of $375.14.

Cash received from:		Insurance	$ 16,000.00
Issuance of stock	$ 1,000.00	Inventory purchases	309,481.36
Sale of equipment	3,180.00	Other operating expenses	37,104.74
Sales to customers	697,018.61	Purchase of equipment	24,830.00
Cash payments for:		Rent	18,000.00
Dividends	16,000.00	Salaries and wages	231,648.69
Income taxes	14,048.17		

On your own 4-3 LO8

Preparing financial statements

Use the adjusted trial balance or work sheet for Mixon Auto Supplies from On Your Own 4-1 and the departmental margin statement from On Your Own 4-2. Partially completed financial statements are provided in the *Working Papers*. Round percentage calculations to the nearest 0.1%. Work this problem independently. Save your work to complete On Your Own 4-4.

1. Complete the income statement. Calculate and record the vertical analysis ratios for each amount in the fourth column of the statement.
2. Complete the statement of stockholders' equity. There were 19,500 shares of $10.00 par value stock issued as of January 1. There were 500 shares issued during the current year.
3. Complete the balance sheet. Calculate and record the vertical analysis ratios for each item in the third column of the statement.
4. Use the following information to complete the statement of cash flows. Mixon began the fiscal year with a cash balance of $11,826.01.

Cash received from:		Insurance	$ 13,000.00
Issuance of stock	$ 5,000.00	Inventory purchases	331,548.36
Sale of equipment	2,150.00	Other operating expenses	32,148.10
Sales to customers	701,483.39	Purchase of equipment	19,485.00
Cash payments for:		Rent	16,500.00
Dividends	36,000.00	Salaries and wages	201,483.17
Income taxes	12,940.74		

End-of-Period Work for a Departmentalized Business

LO9 Journalize closing entries for a departmentalized merchandising business.
LO10 Prepare a post-closing trial balance.
LO11 Summarize the accounting cycle.

Journalizing Closing Entries for a Departmentalized Business LO9

Heading

	DATE		ACCOUNT TITLE	DOC. NO.	POST. REF.	DEBIT	CREDIT	
1			*Closing Entries*					1
2	Dec.²⁰⁻⁻	31	Income Summary—Grills			3 2 0 1 04		2
3			Sales—Grills			472 0 1 9 64		3
4			Sales—Furniture			492 1 8 7 31		4
5			Purchases Discount—Grills			3 1 0 5 48		5
6			Purchases Returns and Allowances—Grills			2 6 7 1 69		6
7			Purchases Discount—Furniture			6 1 0 8 67		7
8			Purchases Returns and Allowances—Furniture			8 0 9 4 21		8
9			Income Summary—General				987 3 8 8 04	9

GENERAL JOURNAL   PAGE 21

Temporary Accounts With Credit Balances

Total of Credit Accounts

Journal entries used to prepare temporary accounts for a new fiscal period are called **closing entries**. Whiley's closing entries made on December 31 are shown above. The information to journalize closing entries is obtained from the adjusted trial balance and other closing entries.

At the end of each fiscal period, Whiley records the following four closing entries:

1. Closing entry for income statement accounts with credit balances (revenue and contra cost accounts).
2. Closing entry for income statement accounts with debit balances (cost, contra revenue, and expense accounts).
3. Closing entry to record net income or net loss in the retained earnings account and to close the income summary account.
4. Closing entry for the dividends account.

Closing Entry for Income Statement Accounts with Credit Balances

The closing entry for Whiley's income statement credit balance accounts on December 31 is shown above. The departmental income summary accounts with a credit balance are Income Summary—Grills and the revenue and contra cost accounts for each department. These accounts are closed to the account Income Summary—General. This account is used to collect the balances of all temporary accounts.

FYI Only temporary accounts are closed. Permanent account balances are needed to continue conducting business in the next accounting cycle.

Closing Entry for Income Statement Accounts with Debit Balances

	DATE	ACCOUNT TITLE	DOC. NO.	POST. REF.	DEBIT	CREDIT	
10	31	*Income Summary—General*			922 1 6 1 05		10
11		*Income Summary—Furniture*				3 8 1 6 53	11
12		*Sales Discount—Grills*				8 2 4 6 75	12
13		*Sales Returns and Allowances—Grills*				9 4 6 7 42	13
14		*Sales Discount—Furniture*				5 2 1 9 23	14
15		*Sales Returns and Allowances—Furniture*				13 8 1 0 76	15
16		*Purchases—Grills*				254 8 5 1 26	16
17		*Purchases—Furniture*				197 0 8 4 64	17
18		*Advertising Expense—Grills*				14 9 2 0 00	18
19		*Payroll Taxes Expense—Grills*				6 4 5 3 36	19
20		*Salary Expense—Grills*				73 0 1 1 20	20
21		*Advertising Expense—Furniture*				5 6 5 0 00	21
22		*Payroll Taxes Expense—Furniture*				10 9 2 6 17	22
23		*Salary Expense—Furniture*				125 8 0 6 20	23
32		*Supplies Expense*				5 1 8 0 87	32
33		*Uncollectible Accounts Expense*				2 1 1 4 92	33
34		*Utilities Expense*				16 2 0 4 68	34
35		*Federal Income Tax Expense*				17 3 3 8 82	35

A portion of the closing entry for Whiley's income statement debit balance accounts on December 31 is shown above. The departmental income summary accounts with a debit balance are Income Summary—Furniture, the contra revenue accounts of each department, and all expense accounts. Similar to the closing entry for the income statement credit accounts, the accounts are closed to the account Income Summary—General.

Closing Entry to Record Net Income or Net Loss

	DATE	ACCOUNT TITLE	DOC. NO.	POST. REF.	DEBIT	CREDIT	
36	31	*Income Summary—General*			65 2 2 6 99		36
37		*Retained Earnings*				65 2 2 6 99	37
38							38

GENERAL JOURNAL   PAGE 21

The closing entry to record Whiley's net income in the retained earnings account and to close Income Summary—General on December 31 is shown above. The balance of this account is the result of (1) closing all income statement credit accounts and (2) closing all income statement debit accounts. The difference between the two amounts is the net income.

After this closing entry is posted, Income Summary—General has a zero balance. The net income, $65,226.99, has been recorded as a credit to Retained Earnings. A corporation's net income increases its retained earnings.

Total of income statement credit accounts	$987,388.04
Total of income statement debit accounts	922,161.05
Net income	$ 65,226.99

THINK LIKE AN ACCOUNTANT

Allocating Corporate Expenses

Timeshare is an alternative way for individuals to vacation. In exchange for a one-time cost and annual maintenance fees, individuals purchase the right to occupy a vacation resort for a week every year. Some timeshare owners receive points that can be used to reserve a unit. The number of points required to book a reservation is based on the location of the resort, the season, the size of the unit, and the number of days being reserved. For example, a two-bedroom unit at a Florida beach in January will require more points than a one-bedroom unit in July.

Sunset Resorts operates 20 timeshare resorts in four southeastern states. Sunset Resorts' corporate office is located in Tampa, Florida. This office handles all management and accounting tasks that can be effectively performed from a central location. For example, it is more efficient for the corporate office to pay all vendors than for each division, or each resort, to process its own cash payments.

Corporate expenses are allocated to the company's five divisions. Corporate expenses are included in each division's income statement. Each division's net income has a direct impact on annual bonuses awarded to employees. Thus, each division manager wants his or her corporate expense allocation to be as small as possible.

For several years, some division managers have criticized how corporate expenses are allocated. The expenses of each department have been allocated based on the number of points redeemed at each location. The managers felt that more relevant measures should be used to allocate different departmental expenses. For example, the northern Florida region has, by far, the fewest number of complaints that might lead to lawsuits. Yet, that division is charged with nearly 17% of the legal department's expense.

OPEN THE SPREADSHEET TLA_CH04

The worksheet contains a schedule of departmental expenses and selected operational measures, including the points redeemed in each division. Follow the steps on the Instructions tab to calculate a more equitable allocation of corporate expenses. Prepare a statement that supports the method selected for allocating the Reservations departmental expense.

Closing Entry for the Dividends Account

		GENERAL JOURNAL				PAGE 21	
	DATE	ACCOUNT TITLE	DOC. NO.	POST. REF.	DEBIT	CREDIT	
38	31	Retained Earnings			19 2 5 0 00		38
39		Dividends				19 2 5 0 00	39

The closing entry for Whiley's Dividends account on December 31 is shown above. The debit balance of a Dividends account is the total amount of dividends declared during a fiscal period. Since dividends decrease the earnings that a corporation retains, the Dividends account is closed to Retained Earnings. The information needed for closing the Dividends account is obtained from the adjusted trial balance.

After the closing entry for the Dividends account is posted, Dividends has a zero balance. The amount of the dividends, $19,250.00, has been recorded as a debit to Retained Earnings.

After closing entries are posted, all temporary accounts have zero balances and are prepared for a new fiscal period.

Post-Closing Trial Balance LO10

Debits must always equal credits in general ledger accounts. The trial balance proves that debits equal credits before adjusting and closing entries are posted. After adjusting and closing entries are posted, the equality of general ledger debits and credits is proved again. This procedure ensures that the equality of debits and credits has been maintained in preparation for a new fiscal period.

A trial balance prepared after the closing entries are posted is called a **post-closing trial balance**. Whiley's post-closing trial balance prepared on December 31 is shown above. The total debit balances, $380,224.83, is the same as the total credit balances. The equality of general ledger debits and credits is proved. Whiley's general ledger is ready for the next fiscal period. >> App. A: Accounting Period Cycle

Whiley Outdoor Living, Inc.
Post-Closing Trial Balance
December 31, 20--

ACCOUNT TITLE	DEBIT	CREDIT
Cash	60 8 4 9 26	
Petty Cash	5 0 0 00	
Accounts Receivable	23 5 1 5 27	
Allowance for Uncollectible Accounts		2 2 1 0 61
Merchandise Inventory—Grills	89 3 4 9 72	
Merchandise Inventory—Furniture	102 9 1 5 36	
Supplies	2 4 3 0 00	
Prepaid Insurance	2 0 0 0 00	
Office Equipment	32 4 8 1 15	
Accumulated Depreciation—Office Equipment		21 4 7 0 00
Store Equipment	64 1 8 4 07	
Accumulated Depreciation—Store Equipment		42 9 2 0 00
Accounts Payable		30 3 9 2 88
Sales Tax Payable		6 1 4 8 05
Employee Income Tax Payable—Federal		1 6 6 6 00
Employee Income Tax Payable—State		1 1 9 0 00
Social Security Tax Payable		2 9 5 0 80
Medicare Tax Payable		6 8 7 22
Medical Insurance Payable		1 0 5 0 00
Retirement Plan Payable		7 1 0 00
Unemployment Tax Payable—Federal		2 0 72
Unemployment Tax Payable—State		1 3 9 86
Federal Income Tax Payable		1 3 3 8 82
Dividends Payable		5 0 0 0 00
Capital Stock		100 0 0 0 00
Retained Earnings		160 3 2 9 87
Totals	378 2 2 4 83	378 2 2 4 83

Summary of the Accounting Cycle LO11

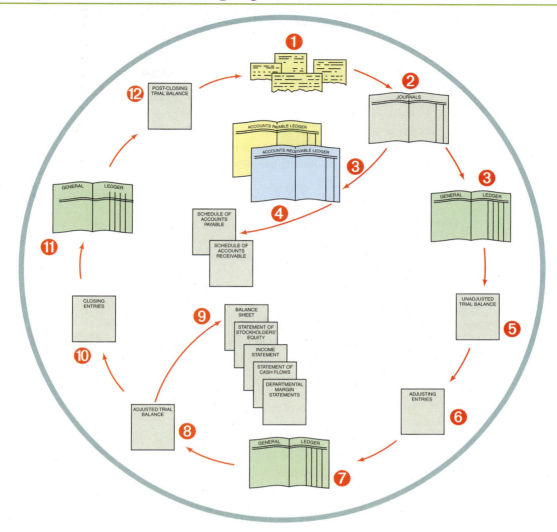

Accounting procedures used by Whiley, a departmentalized merchandising business, are described in Chapters 1 through 4. The same procedures are used from year to year. >> App. A: Consistent Reporting The series of accounting activities included in recording financial information for a fiscal period is called an **accounting cycle**. Whiley's complete accounting cycle is shown above. Accounting cycle procedures provide information for preparing interim and end-of-fiscal-period financial statements. >> App. A: Accounting Period Cycle

>> Accounting Activities in the Accounting Cycle for a Departmentalized Business

❶ Source documents are checked for accuracy, and transactions are analyzed into debit and credit parts.

❷ Transactions, from information on source documents, are recorded in journals.

❸ Journal entries are posted to the accounts payable ledger, the accounts receivable ledger, and the general ledger.

❹ Schedules of accounts payable and accounts receivable are prepared from the subsidiary ledgers.

❺ An unadjusted trial balance is prepared from the general ledger.

❻ Adjusting entries are journalized.

❼ Adjusting entries are posted to the general ledger.

❽ An adjusted trial balance is prepared from the general ledger.

❾ Financial statements are prepared from the adjusted trial balance.

❿ Closing entries are journalized.

⓫ Closing entries are posted to the general ledger.

⓬ A post-closing trial balance is prepared from the general ledger.

TERMS REVIEW

closing entries
post-closing trial balance
accounting cycle

Audit your understanding LO9, 10, 11

1. What is the purpose of closing entries?
2. What accounts are closed by each of the closing entries?
3. What is the purpose of a post-closing trial balance?
4. What accounts are presented on a post-closing trial balance?
5. What three types of entries are posted to the general ledger?
6. What step precedes the preparation of financial statements?

Work together 4-4 LO9

Journalizing closing entries

Use the adjusted trial balance or work sheet from Work Together 4-1. Page 21 of a general journal is provided in the *Working Papers*. Your instructor will guide you through this problem.

Journalize the closing entries for Foley's Interiors.

On your own 4-4 LO8

Journalizing closing entries

Use the adjusted trial balance or work sheet from On Your Own 4-1. Page 23 of a general journal is provided in the *Working Papers*. Work this problem independently.

Journalize the closing entries for Mixon Auto Supplies.

A Look at **Accounting** Software

Modifying a Report

Business managers and accountants need regular financial and operational reports in order to control their businesses. Ever since 1979, with the release of VisiCalc®, the first electronic spreadsheet, even users of manual accounting systems have been preparing reports with spreadsheet software. Spreadsheets today allow almost unlimited formatting capabilities—font styles, sizes, attributes, and colors; numbers with varying decimal places, rounding, and characteristics such as percentage and date forms; lines and symbols; and dozens of mathematical functions. However, with a manual accounting system, the data still must be keyed in, which can require a lot of time and is subject to error.

All computerized accounting systems provide some preprogrammed reports. Some provide report-writing modules with capabilities similar to spreadsheet software. The advantage to preparing a report in a computerized accounting system is that the data is already in the system, so a report can be displayed or printed in seconds. Changing the underlying data will immediately update the report.

No accounting system can ever provide all the reports that business managers or accountants may wish to see. That's why all accounting systems allow for some degree of report modification. All systems also allow report data to be exported to a spreadsheet where reports can be easily reformatted.

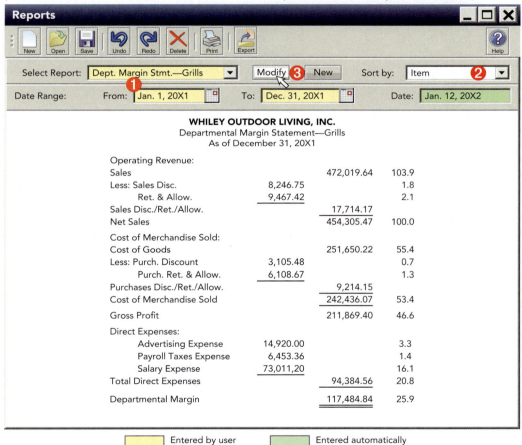

| | Entered by user | | Entered automatically |

❶ The user has selected a report and set a date range for the fiscal year.

❷ The **Sort by** selection block has been left in its default status (Item) to display the report in the order it was created. Options would include By account, By date, By amount/ascending, and By amount/descending. Sorting is most often used with custom reports.

❸ Clicking on the **New** button would allow the user to create a new report form. Here, the user is clicking on the **Modify** button to make changes to the departmental margin statement in the window.

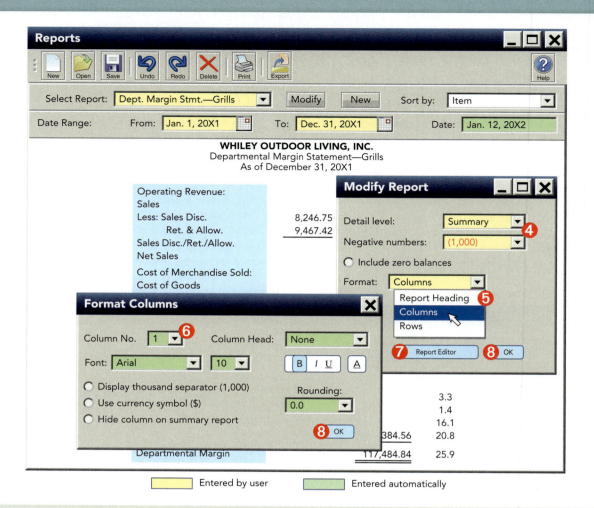

Entered by user		Entered automatically

④ The system has opened the Modify Report dialog box, and the user has selected the Summary detail level. The user also opted to have negative numbers displayed in parentheses and in red, although there are no negative numbers in the current report.

⑤ The user has selected Columns from the **Format** field drop-list, which opened the Format Columns dialog box with **Column No. 1** pre-selected. At the same time, the system highlighted column 1 on the report. The dialog box shows the formatting currently set for column 1. Any changes made by the user would apply to all items in the column.

⑥ Selecting **Column No. 2** would move the highlighted area to the second column and show the format in that column. Options available to the user with these formatting dialog boxes allow quick modifications, but the choices are

limited. For example, setting a column 1 format to an italic font would display all row headings in italic. It is not possible here to select just one row heading to display in italic.

⑦ If the user wanted to format the report at the field level—for example, the field for the heading **Operating Revenue** or the field for the amount of **Net Sales**—the report would have to be opened in the report editor. The report editor enables the coding of each individual cell for data content, format, calculation, and other attributes. The report editor would also be used for placing graphic elements, such as the underscores beneath the columns, in the report.

⑧ The user, having chosen not to change any column formats, would click the **OK** button or the **Close** box. Then, clicking **OK** on the Modify Report dialog box would accept the settings chosen by the user and display the modified report form.

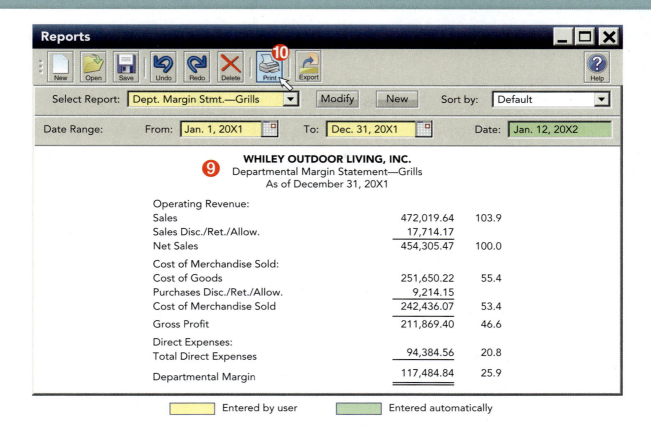

Reports

New | Open | Save | Undo | Redo | Delete | Print ⑩ | Export | Help

Select Report: | Dept. Margin Stmt.—Grills ▾ | Modify | New | Sort by: | Default ▾

Date Range: | From: Jan. 1, 20X1 | To: Dec. 31, 20X1 | Date: Jan. 12, 20X2

WHILEY OUTDOOR LIVING, INC.
⑨ Departmental Margin Statement—Grills
As of December 31, 20X1

Operating Revenue:		
Sales	472,019.64	103.9
Sales Disc./Ret./Allow.	17,714.17	
Net Sales	454,305.47	100.0
Cost of Merchandise Sold:		
Cost of Goods	251,650.22	55.4
Purchases Disc./Ret./Allow.	9,214.15	
Cost of Merchandise Sold	242,436.07	53.4
Gross Profit	211,869.40	46.6
Direct Expenses:		
Total Direct Expenses	94,384.56	20.8
Departmental Margin	117,484.84	25.9

☐ Entered by user   ☐ Entered automatically

⑨ The user chose to display a summary report form, the same financial statement in a more condensed format. These options allow a report to be presented at different levels of detail appropriate for different levels of management.

Attributes programmed in the report editor determine which rows get removed from the standard report to produce a summary report. The result is shown in the illustration above.

⑩ The user would click **Print** to print the report.

The preparation of financial statements at the end of the fiscal year begins with the preparation of an unadjusted trial balance. All accounts, even those having a zero balance, are entered. The unadjusted trial balance acts as a checklist, enabling the business to determine which accounts need to be adjusted to up-to-date balances. Adjustments in the balance of merchandise inventory are recorded in an income summary account. Other adjustments involve a balance sheet account, such as Supplies, and a related expense account, such as Supplies Expense.

An adjusted trial balance is prepared after adjusting entries are posted. The balance of Federal Income Tax Expense is not included so that income before income taxes can be calculated. The total of the income statement debit accounts is subtracted from the total of income statement credit accounts to determine the income before income taxes. After federal income taxes are calculated, adjusted, and posted, the adjusted trial balance is completed. The adjusted trial balance is the source of information for financial statements.

A company having distinct product groups should use a departmental accounting system. Departmental revenues, costs, and direct expenses are accounted for to enable management to evaluate the performance of each department. Only those revenues, costs, and expenses that can be controlled by a manager should be recorded by department. The dollar amounts and vertical analysis ratios of a departmental income statement enable a business to evaluate the performance of a department.

A corporation prepares the traditional four financial statements. The format of the income statement contains the departmental revenue, gross profit, and margins for each department. The other financial statements are similar to those of other corporations.

Closing entries are journalized and posted to prepare the accounting records for the next fiscal year.

EXPLORE ACCOUNTING

Exception Reports

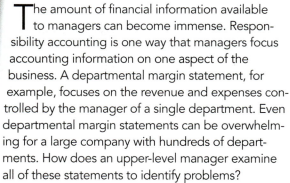

The amount of financial information available to managers can become immense. Responsibility accounting is one way that managers focus accounting information on one aspect of the business. A departmental margin statement, for example, focuses on the revenue and expenses controlled by the manager of a single department. Even departmental margin statements can be overwhelming for a large company with hundreds of departments. How does an upper-level manager examine all of these statements to identify problems?

Rather than reviewing every line of every departmental statement, a manager can instruct the computer system to prepare a report of only those accounts for which the actual results differ significantly from expected results. These reports, often called *exception reports*, should identify both positive and negative situations. For example, an exception report could identify those accounts that differ by more than 10% from departmental budgets. This shorter report would allow the manager to focus quickly on areas that deserve attention.

Managers must gather information and be objective when investigating the reasons for excessive expenses. Does salary expense exceeding budget by 20% indicate that workers lack discipline? Although this explanation is possible, other reasons could cause even the best employees to be unproductive. For example, note these factors:

1. Workers have not received adequate training.

2. Equipment is obsolete and often broken.

3. Parts are frequently out of stock.

It is natural for managers to focus on negative situations. The manager can work with the department manager to correct the problem. Too often, managers neglect to investigate the reasons for positive performances. If a department has generated sales 20% more than its budget, the manager should investigate what strategies and methods can account for the successful results. This information can then be shared with other departments to improve sales throughout the company.

INSTRUCTIONS

A manager of Midwest Textiles receives an exception report showing that fabric costs of its toddler department are 14% above the budget. List possible explanations for the apparent problem in the purchase and use of fabric.

APPLY YOUR UNDERSTANDING

INSTRUCTIONS: Download problem instructions for Excel, QuickBooks, and Sage 50c from the textbook companion website at www.C21accounting.com.

4-1 Application Problem — Preparing an adjusted trial balance LO2, 3, 4

Sunset Sports, Inc., is a merchandising business that sells golf and tennis equipment. The company uses a calendar fiscal year. The following adjustment information for December 31 is available:

Estimate of uncollectible accounts	$ 1,740.79	Value of prepaid insurance	$ 1,000.00
Ending merchandise inventory—golf	64,933.31	Depreciation expense—office equipment	3,190.00
Ending merchandise inventory—tennis	47,687.92	Depreciation expense—store equipment	6,280.00
Supplies on hand	670.00		

Instructions:

A partially completed adjusted trial balance, a general journal, and selected general ledger accounts are provided in the *Working Papers*. Save your work to complete Problems 4-2, 4-3, and 4-4.

1. Record the adjusting entries on page 18 of a general journal.
2. Post the adjusting entries to the general ledger accounts.
3. Enter the adjusted general ledger account balances on the adjusted trial balance.
4. Calculate federal income tax expense using the tax rate presented in the chapter. Prepare and post the adjusting entry for federal income tax expense.
5. Complete the adjusted trial balance.

4-2 Application Problem — Preparing a departmental margin statement LO6, 7

Use Sunset Sports' adjusted trial balance or work sheet from Problem 4-1. Save your work to complete Problem 4-3.

Instructions:

1. Prepare a departmental margin statement for each department.
2. Calculate vertical analysis ratios for cost of merchandise sold, gross profit, total direct expenses, and departmental margin.

4-3 Application Problem — Preparing financial statements LO8

Use Sunset Sports' adjusted trial balance or work sheet from Problem 4-1 and the departmental margin statement from Problem 4-2. Statement paper is provided in the *Working Papers*. Round percentage calculations to the nearest 0.1%.

Instructions:

1. Complete the income statement. Calculate and record the vertical analysis ratios for each amount in the fourth column of the statement.
2. Complete the statement of stockholders' equity. There were 58,000 shares of $1.00 par value stock issued as of January 1. There were 2,000 shares issued during the current year.
3. Complete the balance sheet. Calculate and record the vertical analysis ratios for each item in the third column of the statement.

(Continued on next page)

4. Use the following information to complete the statement of cash flows. Sunset Sports began the fiscal year with a cash balance of $26,534.33.

Cash received from:

Issuance of stock	$ 2,000.00	Insurance	$ 12,000.00
Sale of equipment	3,015.00	Inventory purchases	253,149.61
Sales to customers	567,148.14	Other operating expenses	27,841.09
Cash payments for:		Purchase of equipment	18,413.00
Dividends	23,400.00	Rent	14,250.00
Income taxes	9,914.62	Salaries and wages	186,414.68

4-4 Application Problem   Journalizing closing entries LO9

Use Sunset Sports' adjusted trial balance or work sheet from Problem 4-1. Page 19 of a general journal is provided in the *Working Papers*.

Instructions:

Journalize the closing entries for Sunset Sports, Inc.

sage 50

1. Journalize and post adjusting and closing entries to the general journal.
2. From the menu bar, select Reports & Forms; General Ledger.
3. Print the general journal and trial balance.

QB Quick Books

1. Journalize and post adjusting and closing entries to the journal.
2. From the menu bar, select Reports; Accountant & Taxes.
3. Print the journal and trial balance.

X (Excel)

1. Journalize closing entries in the general journal.
2. Print the worksheet.

4-M Mastery Problem   Completing end-of-fiscal-period work for a departmentalized merchandising business LO2, 3, 4, 6, 7, 8, 9

sage 50

1. Journalize and post adjusting and closing entries to the general journal.
2. From the menu bar, select Reports & Forms; General Ledger.
3. Print the general journal and trial balance.

QB Quick Books

1. Journalize and post adjusting and closing entries to the journal.
2. From the menu bar, select Reports; Accountant & Taxes.
3. Print the journal and trial balance.

Forde Furniture Gallery is a merchandising business that specializes in antiques and modern furniture. The company uses a calendar fiscal year. An adjusted trial balance as of December 31, general journals, selected general ledger accounts, and statement paper are provided in the *Working Papers*. Round percentage calculations to the nearest 0.1%. The adjustment information for December 31 follows.

Estimate of uncollectible accounts	$ 2,651.36
Ending merchandise inventory—antiques	249,183.92
Ending merchandise inventory—modern	228,540.53
Supplies on hand	1,295.00
Value of prepaid insurance	2,400.00
Depreciation expense—office equipment	3,240.00
Depreciation expense—store equipment	5,175.00

1. Journalize and post adjusting entries to the general journal.
2. Complete the departmental margin statements and other financial statements.
3. Journalize and post closing entries to the general journal.
4. Print the worksheets.

Instructions:

1. Record the adjusting entries on page 24 of a general journal.
2. Post the adjusting entries to the general ledger accounts.
3. Enter the adjusted general account balances on the adjusted trial balance.
4. Calculate federal income tax expense using the tax rate presented in the chapter. Prepare and post the adjusting entry for federal income tax expense.
5. Complete the adjusted trial balance.
6. Prepare a departmental margin statement for each department. Calculate vertical analysis ratios for cost of merchandise sold, gross profit, total direct expenses, and departmental margin.
7. Prepare the income statement, statement of stockholders' equity, and balance sheet. There were 11,800 shares of $25.00 par value stock issued as of January 1. There were 200 shares issued during the current year. Calculate and record the vertical analysis ratios for each amount in the fourth column of the income statement and third column of the balance sheet.
8. Use the following information to complete the statement of cash flows. Forde began the fiscal year with a cash balance of $36,569.20.

Cash received from:

Issuance of stock	$ 5,000.00	Insurance	$ 13,600.00
Sale of equipment	2,818.00	Inventory purchases	632,154.36
Sales to customers	1,318,614.61	Other operating expenses	62,184.98
		Purchase of equipment	48,450.00
Cash payments for:			
Dividends	60,000.00	Rent	22,500.00
Income taxes	49,148.50	Salaries and wages	400,915.61

9. Journalize the closing entries. Use page 25 of a general journal.

4-C Challenge Problem   Analyzing a departmental margin statement LO6, 7

The departmental margin statement for the chemicals department of Crystal Pools for the years 20X6 and 20X7 is provided in the *Working Papers*. The company has set a goal for the chemicals department to contribute a minimum of 25.0% departmental margin. For the years 20X1 through 20X6, the departmental margin for the chemicals department has varied from 24.9% to 26.8% of net sales.

Instructions:

1. For 20X7, calculate and record the vertical analysis ratios to compare to the ratios given for 20X6. Round percentage calculations to the nearest 0.1%.
2. Calculate the changes in ratios from 20X6 to 20X7 for the following items: (a) cost of merchandise sold, (b) gross profit, (c) total direct expenses, and (d) departmental margin.
3. From an analysis of the departmental margin statement and the amounts obtained from instructions 1 and 2, answer the following questions:
   a. Is the departmental margin for the chemicals department at a satisfactory percentage of sales? Explain why it is or is not satisfactory.
   b. Is the trend of the cost of merchandise sold percentage favorable or unfavorable? Explain why it is or is not favorable. Suggest some possible reasons for the change in the cost of merchandise sold from 20X6 to 20X7.
   c. Is the trend of the total direct departmental expenses percentage favorable or unfavorable? Explain why the trend is or is not favorable.

Measuring Performance

Theme: Financial, Economic, Business, and Entrepreneurial Literacy

Skills: Creativity and Innovation, Critical Thinking and Problem Solving, Communication and Collaboration

PARTNERSHIP FOR
21ST CENTURY SKILLS

Home Electronics is a retailer of personal electronics products. Some of the products it sells are televisions, smart watches, telephones, cell phones, and tablets for personal use. It has many outlets across the country, and annual sales range from $1.2 billion to $1.28 billion. Chart 1 shows the product sales for four years.

Chart 1
(in millions of dollars)

	Year 1	Year 2	Year 3	Year 4
Televisions	$ 425	$ 430	$ 420	$ 425
Smart watches	125	130	140	145
Telephones	50	45	40	35
Cell phones	200	210	230	240
Tablets	400	430	440	435
	$1,200	$1,245	$1,270	$1,280

Some of the departmental accounting is based on the product line. There are other departments and cost centers that do not generate a profit. Each of the major product areas has a manager who is responsible for the success of his or her product line.

Management is concerned that sales are not growing fast enough and has decided to invest in advertising. Management is also considering taking on more product lines and possibly adding more departments.

APPLICATION

1. Shannon is the product manager of the Telephones Department. She has learned that one of management's proposals is to invest $500,000 in advertising. To track costs and to aid in evaluating the departmental areas, the costs of advertising will be spread evenly across the product departments. Discuss why Shannon would be for or against this method of tracking costs. What other proposals could Shannon suggest?

2. To increase sales, management is considering adding video games to the product selection. Compare and contrast the advantages and disadvantages of adding another department for the new product area, instead of adding the new products to an existing product department.

A new accounting clerk for Lindsay Jewelry Company prepared the following post-closing trial balance:

Lindsay Jewelry Company
Post-Closing Trial Balance
December 31, 20--

ACCOUNT TITLE	DEBIT	CREDIT
Cash	36 1 5 4 21	
Accounts Receivable	42 1 0 8 62	
Allowance for Uncollectible Accounts	4 0 9 3 68	
Merchandise Inventory—Gold	301 5 8 9 36	
Merchandise Inventory—Silver	104 8 4 7 31	
Supplies	3 2 5 0 00	
Prepaid Insurance	4 8 0 0 00	
Office Equipment	21 6 7 4 95	
Accumulated Depreciation—Office Equipment		10 8 4 5 00
Store Equipment	42 1 0 9 98	
Accumulated Depreciation—Store Equipment		19 2 6 5 41
Accounts Payable		31 0 8 7 91
Employee Income Tax Payable—Federal		2 1 9 4 56
Social Security Tax Payable		3 7 1 5 25
Medicare Tax Payable		8 8 1 15
Unemployment Tax Payable—Federal		5 1 36
Federal Income Tax Payable		4 1 9 4 00
Dividends Payable	20 0 0 0 00	
Capital Stock		250 0 0 0 00
Retained Earnings		195 3 4 3 76
Income Summary		14 8 6 2 35

1. Identify any errors in the trial balance.
2. Calculate the correct column totals.

Analyzing Home Depot's Financial Statements

The cost of merchandise is a significant cost for all merchandising businesses. In order to maximize profits, management attempts to keep this cost as low as possible. In this chapter, you have learned that the amount of revenue from sales less the cost of goods sold is called *gross profit*. The vertical analysis ratio for gross profit, most often referred to as *gross margin*, is an important measure of how effectively management is controlling its merchandise costs. Managers can compare the current ratio to prior years' ratios. Investors and other interested individuals can compare the ratios of companies operating in the same industry. Online investing sites, financial news publications, and company annual reports report gross margins.

INSTRUCTIONS

Refer to the Selected Financial Data in Appendix B on page B-20 to answer the following questions:

1. Identify the term used by Home Depot to refer to its gross margin.
2. List the gross margin for each fiscal year presented.
3. Identify the term used by Home Depot to refer to its net income vertical analysis ratio.
4. List the net income vertical analysis ratio for each fiscal year presented.
5. Would you classify Home Depot's trends identified in the previous questions as favorable or unfavorable?

APPENDIX: Preparing a Work Sheet

Departmental Work Sheet

A work sheet is a columnar accounting form used to summarize the general ledger information needed to prepare financial statements. Prior to the use of computerized accounting systems, the work sheet was the most effective tool for collecting the information needed to prepare financial statements.

A 12-column work sheet prepared using Whiley's account balances on December 31 is shown here. The additional columns provide the information for departmental margin statements. The adjustments planned on the work sheet are journalized and posted after the work sheet is completed.

1 List all accounts, even those with zero balances.

3 Extend adjusted balances to appropriate statement columns.

Whiley Outdoor Living, Inc.
Work Sheet
December 31, 20--

#	ACCOUNT TITLE	TRIAL BALANCE DEBIT	TRIAL BALANCE CREDIT	ADJUSTMENTS DEBIT	ADJUSTMENTS CREDIT	GRILLS DEBIT	GRILLS CREDIT	FURNITURE DEBIT	FURNITURE CREDIT	INCOME STATEMENT DEBIT	INCOME STATEMENT CREDIT	BALANCE SHEET DEBIT	BALANCE SHEET CREDIT
1	Cash	60 849 26										60 849 26	
2	Petty Cash	500 00										500 00	
3	Accounts Receivable	23 515 27										23 515 27	
4	Allowance for Uncollectible Accounts		95 69		(a) 2 114 92								2 210 61
5	Merchandise Inventory—Grills	86 148 68		(b) 3 201 04								89 349 72	
6	Merchandise Inventory—Furniture	106 731 89			(c) 3 816 53							102 915 36	
7	Supplies	7 610 87			(d) 5 180 87							2 430 00	
8	Prepaid Insurance	14 000 00			(e) 12 000 00							2 000 00	
9	Office Equipment	32 481 15										32 481 15	
10	Accumulated Depreciation—Office Equipment		14 150 00		(f) 7 320 00								21 470 00
11	Store Equipment	64 184 07										64 184 07	
12	Accumulated Depreciation—Store Equipment		34 550 00		(g) 8 370 00								42 920 00
13	Accounts Payable		30 392 88										30 392 88
14	Sales Tax Payable		6 148 05										6 148 05
15	Employee Income Tax Payable—Federal		1 666 00										1 666 00
16	Employee Income Tax Payable—State		1 190 00										1 190 00
17	Social Security Tax Payable		2 950 80										2 950 80
18	Medicare Tax Payable		687 22										687 22
19	Medical Insurance Payable		1 050 00										1 050 00
20	Retirement Plan Payable		710 00										710 00
21	Unemployment Tax Payable—Federal		20 72										20 72
22	Unemployment Tax Payable—State		139 86										139 86
23	Federal Income Tax Payable				(h) 1 338 82								1 338 82
24	Dividends Payable		5 000 00										5 000 00
25	Capital Stock		100 000 00										100 000 00

Departmental Work Sheet (partial — lines 26–67)

#	Account Title	Trial Balance Dr	Trial Balance Cr	Adjustments Dr	Adjustments Cr	Income Statement—Grills Dr	Income Statement—Grills Cr	Income Statement—Furniture Dr	Income Statement—Furniture Cr	Income Statement Dr	Income Statement Cr	Balance Sheet Dr	Balance Sheet Cr
26	Retained Earnings		114,352.88										114,352.88
27	Dividends	19,250.00										19,250.00	
28	Income Summary—General				(b) 3,201.04		3,201.04						
29	Income Summary—Grills												
30	Income Summary—Furniture			(c) 3,816.53				3,816.53					
31	Sales—Grills		472,019.64				472,019.64						
32	Sales Discount—Grills	8,246.75				8,246.75							
33	Sales Returns and Allowances—Grills	9,467.42				9,467.42							
34	Sales—Furniture		492,187.31						492,187.31				
35	Sales Discount—Furniture	5,219.23						5,219.23					
36	Sales Returns and Allowances—Furniture	13,810.76						13,810.76					
37	Purchases—Grills	254,851.26				254,851.26							
38	Purchases Discount—Grills		3,105.48				3,105.48						
39	Purchases Returns and Allowances—Grills		6,108.67				6,108.67						
40	Purchases—Furniture	197,084.64						197,084.64					
41	Purchases Discount—Furniture		2,671.69						2,671.69				
42	Purchases Returns and Allowances—Furniture		8,094.21						8,094.21				
43	Advertising Expense—Grills	14,920.00				14,920.00							
44	Payroll Taxes Expense—Grills	6,453.36				6,453.36							
45	Salary Expense—Grills	73,011.20				73,011.20							
46	Advertising Expense—Furniture	5,650.00						5,650.00					
47	Payroll Taxes Expense—Furniture	10,926.17						10,926.17					
48	Salary Expense—Furniture	125,806.20						125,806.20					
49	Credit Card Fee Expense	6,842.20								6,842.20			
50	Depreciation Expense—Office Equipment			(f) 7,320.00						7,320.00			
51	Depreciation Expense—Store Equipment			(g) 8,370.00						8,370.00			
52	Insurance Expense			(e) 12,000.00						12,000.00			
53	Miscellaneous Expense	3,495.04								3,495.04			
54	Payroll Taxes Expense—Administrative	7,602.20								7,602.20			
55	Rent Expense	18,400.00								18,400.00			
56	Salary Expense—Administrative	88,028.80								88,028.80			
57	Supplies Expense			(d) 5,180.87						5,180.87			
58	Uncollectible Accounts Expense			(a) 2,114.92						2,114.92			
59	Utilities Expense	16,204.68								16,204.68			
60						366,949.99	484,434.83	362,313.53	502,953.21				
61	Department Margin—Grills					117,484.84					117,484.84		
62	Department Margin—Furniture							140,639.68			140,639.68		
63						484,434.83	484,434.83	502,953.21	502,953.21				
64	Federal Income Tax Expense	16,000.00		(h) 1,338.82						17,338.82			
65	Column Totals	1,297,291.10	1,297,291.10	43,342.18	43,342.18					192,897.53	258,124.52	397,474.83	332,247.84
66	Net Income									65,226.99			65,226.99
67										258,124.52	258,124.52	397,474.83	397,474.83

Callout notes:

2 — Plan adjustments and label using letters.

4 — Excess of departmental revenue over expenses.

5 — Adjust and extend Federal Income Tax Expense after calculating income before income tax.

6 — Credit less debit column total equals net income.

1 **Unadjusted trial balance**. Enter unadjusted account balances from the general ledger.

2 **Enter adjustments**. Adjustments are entered in the Adjustments columns. Letters are used to label each entry.

3 **Extend updated balances**. Adjusted account balances are extended to one of the four financial statement debit and credit columns. Asset, liability, and equity accounts are extended to the Balance Sheet Debit and Credit columns. Department revenue and expense accounts are extended to the appropriate department's debit and credit columns. All other revenue and expense accounts, except for Federal Income Tax Expense, are extended to the Income Statement Debit column.

4 **Calculate the difference of departmental revenue and expenses**. The department columns are totaled. The credit column total less the debit column total is the excess of departmental revenues over expenses. Enter the amount under

the debit column total and in the Income Statement Credit column. Enter Department Margin and the department name in the Account Title column.

5 **Record the adjustment for income taxes**. The total of the Income Statement Credit column less the Income Statement Debit column (excluding federal income tax expense) equals income before income tax. Calculate federal income tax expense, enter an adjustment for any taxes due, and extend the income tax accounts to the appropriate columns.

6 **Calculate net income**. Enter the total of the Income Statement and Balance Sheet columns. The total of the Income Statement Credit column less the Income Statement Debit column is the net income for the fiscal period. The net income is written under the work sheet's Income Statement Debit column and the Balance Sheet Credit column. The net income amount makes each statement's debit and credit columns totals balance.

INSTRUCTIONS: For each of the following Appendix Problems, prepare the work sheets as follows:
1. Enter the adjustments on the work sheet. Label each adjustment using consecutive letters, (a), (b), etc.
2. Extend the adjusted account balances to the appropriate columns of the work sheet.
3. Complete the work sheet.

4-1 Appendix Problem   Preparing a work sheet

A partially completed work sheet for Foley's Interiors, based on Work Together 4-1, is provided in the *Working Papers*. The adjustment information for December 31 is presented below.

Estimate of uncollectible accounts	$ 2,101.23	Value of prepaid insurance	$2,500.00
Ending merchandise inventory—kitchen	147,084.62	Depreciation expense—office equipment	7,250.00
Ending merchandise inventory—bath	97,671.31	Depreciation expense—store equipment	8,490.00
Supplies on hand	1,950.00	Federal income tax expense	2,367.12

4-2 Appendix Problem   Preparing a work sheet

A partially completed work sheet for Mixon Auto Supplies, based on On Your Own 4-1, is provided in the *Working Papers*. The adjustment information for December 31 is presented below.

Estimate of uncollectible accounts	$ 3,123.53	Value of prepaid insurance	$3,000.00
Ending merchandise inventory—parts	254,285.38	Depreciation expense—office equipment	4,850.00
Ending merchandise inventory—accessories	114,223.95	Depreciation expense—store equipment	6,490.00
Supplies on hand	1,480.00	Federal income tax expense	1,449.64

4-3 Appendix Problem   Preparing a work sheet

A partially completed work sheet for Sunset Sports, Inc., based on Problem 4-1, is provided in the *Working Papers*. The adjustment information for December 31 is presented below.

Estimate of uncollectible accounts	$ 1,740.79	Value of prepaid insurance	$1,000.00
Ending merchandise inventory—golf	64,933.31	Depreciation expense—office equipment	3,190.00
Ending merchandise inventory—tennis	47,687.92	Depreciation expense—store equipment	6,280.00
Supplies on hand	670.00	Federal income tax expense	3,071.36

Reinforcement Activity 1

Processing and Reporting Departmentalized Accounting Data

    sage 50

This activity reinforces selected learning from Part 1, Chapters 1 through 4. The complete accounting cycle is for a departmentalized merchandising business organized as a corporation.

Jewel's Kitchen, Inc.

Jewel's Kitchen, Inc., sells kitchen merchandise in two departments: Equipment and Accessories. Jewel's Kitchen is open for business Monday through Saturday. It pays a monthly rent on the building. The business owns office equipment and store equipment. Most customers pay with cash or a credit card. A small number of customers have arranged to purchase merchandise on account.

Jewel's Kitchen's fiscal year is January 1 through December 31. The company uses the chart of accounts shown at the end of this activity. The journals and ledgers are similar to those illustrated in Part 1. The journals and ledger forms are provided in the *Working Papers*. Beginning balances have been recorded in the ledgers.

Recording Transactions

INSTRUCTIONS

1. Use the appropriate journal to record the following transactions completed during December of the current year. Calculate and record sales tax on all sales and sales returns and allowances as described in Chapter 2. The sales tax rate is 5.0%. Post the following transactions when journalized: (1) transactions affecting the accounts receivable or accounts payable subsidiary ledgers, (2) transactions recorded in the general journal, and (3) cash payments entered in the general columns of the cash payments journal. Source documents are abbreviated as follows: check, C; credit memorandum, CM; debit memorandum, DM; memorandum, M; purchase invoice, P; receipt, R; sales invoice, S; terminal summary, TS.

Dec. 1. Paid cash to SBG Properties for rent, $2,300.00. C796.

2. Purchased equipment on account from Burkes Industries, $3,484.15. P261.

Dec. 2. Received cash on account from Denton Seafood, $4,108.62, covering S605 for accessories. R592.

4. Paid cash on account to Kitchen Concepts, $5,045.60, covering P258 for accessories for $5,148.57, less discount. C797.

4. Recorded cash and credit card sales: equipment, $6,148.26; accessories, $1,104.68; plus sales tax. TS48.

5. Sold accessories on account to Carlisle Steakhouse, $5,418.69, plus sales tax. S621.

6. Purchased accessories on account from Triangle Manufacturing, $6,148.17. P262.

6. Paid cash on account to Burkes Industries, $3,414.47, covering P260 for equipment for $3,484.15, less discount. C798.

8. Sold equipment on account to Virgie Berger, $614.25, plus sales tax. S622.

9. Paid cash for a miscellaneous expense, $275.00. C799.

9. Purchased accessories on account from Central Kitchen Supply, $5,174.68. P263.

10. Paid cash to Central Electric for a utility bill, $512.12. C800.

10. Sold accessories on account to Denton Seafood, $8,415.25, plus sales tax. S623.

11. Paid cash on account to Fulgham Pottery, $1,846.37, covering P257 for accessories. C801.

11. Granted credit to Virgie Berger for equipment returned, $120.00, plus sales tax, from S622. CM44.

13. Received cash on account from Carlisle Steakhouse, $5,575.83, covering S621 for accessories for $5,689.62, less discount. R593.

13. Returned accessories to Central Kitchen Supply, $614.62, from P263. DM55.

14. Purchased equipment on account from Specialty Supply, $4,914.74. P264.

14. Paid cash to Ganther Broadcasting for advertising a sale on accessories, $400.00. C802.

15. Received cash on account from Virgie Berger, $508.58, covering S622 for equipment for $644.96, less CM44 for $126.00, less discount. R594.

Dec. 15. Paid cash for liability for federal employee income tax, $524.00; Social Security tax, $961.85; Medicare tax, $224.95; total, $1,710.80. C803.

16. Sold accessories on account to LaFlore Café, $6,142.61, plus sales tax. S624.

16. Received cash on account from Hamilton Group, $2,000.00, in partial payment of its account. R595.

16. Paid cash on account to Hunley Equipment Co., $2,325.05, in partial payment of P255 for equipment. C804.

18. Paid cash on account to Central Kitchen Supply, $4,468.86, covering P263 for accessories for $5,174.68, less D55 for $614.62, less discount. C805.

18. Recorded cash and credit card sales: equipment, $7,813.25; accessories, $2,047.64; plus sales tax. TS49.

18. Declared a dividend of $0.50 per share on 15,000 shares outstanding. The dividend will be payable on January 18. M61.

21. Purchased accessories on account from Kitchen Concepts, $8,104.94. P265.

21. Sold accessories on account to Hamilton Group, $1,425.21, plus sales tax. S625.

22. Received cash on account from LaFlore Café, $6,320.75, covering S624 for accessories for $6,449.74, less discount. R596.

23. Received cash on account from Polk County Schools, $2,481.14, covering S618 for equipment. R597.

23. Sold equipment on account to Mary McCrory, $825.21, plus sales tax. S626.

27. Purchased accessories on account from Fulgham Pottery, $9,414.78. P266.

27. Sold accessories on account to Polk County Schools, $3,148.25; no sales tax. S627.

28. Paid cash to Davis Office Supply for supplies, $168.00. C806.

29. Paid cash on account to Triangle Manufacturing, $2,000.00, partially covering P262 for accessories. C807.

30. Sold accessories on account to LaFlore Café, $1,847.95, plus sales tax. S628.

Dec. 30. Paid credit card fee expense for December, $223.14. M62.

30. Recorded cash and credit card sales: equipment, $3,418.66; accessories, $845.60; plus sales tax. TS50.

30. Paid cash for monthly payroll, $5,017.56 (total payroll: equipment, $3,394.78; accessories, $2,801.69; administrative, $1,062.40; less deductions: employee income tax—federal, $498.00; employee income tax—state, $218.00; Social Security tax, $450.05; Medicare tax, $105.26; health insurance, $450.00; retirement contributions, $520.00). C808.

30. Recorded employer payroll taxes for the December pay period. Taxes owed are: Social Security tax, $450.05; Medicare tax, $105.26; federal unemployment tax, $2.80; state unemployment tax, $18.90. Payroll taxes are distributed among the departments as: equipment, $259.70; accessories, $236.04; and administrative, $81.27. M63.

2. Prove and total page 15 of the cash payments journal. Post the totals of the special columns to the general ledger.

3. Journalize the following transactions, applying the same posting procedures used above.

Dec. 31. Paid cash to H&L Computers for office equipment, $961.25. C809.

31. Paid cash to reimburse the petty cash fund, $203.83; advertising expense—accessories, $75.00; miscellaneous expense, $56.68; supplies, $72.15. C810.

4. Prove and rule the sales journal. Post the totals of the special columns.

5. Prove and rule the purchases journal. Post the totals of the special columns.

6. Prove the cash receipts journal and page 16 of the cash payments journal.

7. Prove cash. The balance on the next unused check stub is $46,712.48.

8. Rule the cash receipts journal. Post the totals of the special columns.

9. Rule page 16 of the cash payments journal. Post the totals of the special columns.

End-of-Fiscal-Period Work

INSTRUCTIONS

10. Prepare a schedule of accounts receivable and a schedule of accounts payable. Compare each schedule total with the balance of the controlling account in the general ledger. The total and the balance should be the same.

11. Record the adjusting entries on page 17 of a general journal.

Adjustment Information, December 31

Estimate of uncollectible accounts	$ 2,930.00
Ending merchandise inventory—equipment	89,626.86
Ending merchandise inventory—accessories	160,029.03
Supplies on hand	2,160.00
Value of prepaid insurance	1,400.00
Depreciation expense—office equipment	5,260.00
Depreciation expense—store equipment	6,120.00

12. Post the adjusting entries to the general ledger accounts.

13. Enter the general ledger account balances on the adjusted trial balance.

14. Calculate federal income tax expense using the tax rate presented in Chapter 4. Prepare and post the adjusting entry for federal income tax expense.

15. Complete the adjusted trial balance.

16. Prepare departmental margin statements for Jewel's Kitchen's equipment and accessories departments. Calculate and record component percentages for each amount in the fourth column of the statements. Round percentage calculations to the nearest 0.1%.

17. Prepare an income statement. Calculate and record the vertical analysis ratios for each amount in the fourth column of the statement. Round percentage calculations to the nearest 0.1%.

18. Prepare a statement of stockholders' equity. There were 14,000 shares of $10.00 par value stock issued as of January 1. There were 1,000 shares issued during the current year.

19. Prepare a balance sheet. Calculate and record the vertical analysis ratios for each item in the third column of the statement.

20. Use the following information to complete the statement of cash flows. Jewel's Kitchen began the fiscal year with a cash balance of $17,311.88.

Cash received from:

Issuance of stock	$ 10,000.00
Sale of equipment	3,150.00
Sales to customers	621,548.61

Cash payments for:

Dividends	28,500.00
Income taxes	10,942.00
Insurance	14,800.00
Inventory purchases	339,141.45
Other operating expenses	51,449.76
Purchase of equipment	24,168.00
Rent	27,600.00
Salaries and wages	108,696.80

21. Use page 18 of a general journal. Journalize and post the closing entries.

22. Prepare a post-closing trial balance.

Chart of Accounts
General Ledger

Balance Sheet Accounts

(1000) ASSETS
1100–1400 CURRENT ASSETS
1105 Cash
1110 Petty Cash
1205 Accounts Receivable
1210 Allowance for Uncollectible Accounts
1305 Merchandise Inventory—Equipment
1310 Merchandise Inventory—Accessories
1405 Supplies
1410 Prepaid Insurance
1500 PLANT ASSETS
1505 Office Equipment
1510 Accumulated Depreciation—Office Equipment
1515 Store Equipment
1520 Accumulated Depreciation—Store Equipment

(2000) LIABILITIES
2105 Accounts Payable
2110 Sales Tax Payable
2115 Employee Income Tax Payable—Federal
2120 Employee Income Tax Payable—State
2125 Social Security Tax Payable
2130 Medicare Tax Payable
2135 Medical Insurance Payable
2140 Retirement Plan Payable
2145 Unemployment Tax Payable—Federal
2150 Unemployment Tax Payable—State
2155 Federal Income Tax Payable
2160 Dividends Payable

(3000) STOCKHOLDERS' EQUITY
3105 Capital Stock
3110 Retained Earnings
3115 Dividends
3205 Income Summary—General
3210 Income Summary—Equipment
3215 Income Summary—Accessories

Income Statement Accounts

(4000) OPERATING REVENUE
4105 Sales—Equipment
4110 Sales Discount—Equipment
4115 Sales Returns and Allowances—Equipment
4205 Sales—Accessories
4210 Sales Discount—Accessories
4215 Sales Returns and Allowances—Accessories

(5000) COST OF MERCHANDISE
5105 Purchases—Equipment
5110 Purchases Discount—Equipment
5115 Purchases Returns and Allowances—Equipment
5205 Purchases—Accessories
5210 Purchases Discount—Accessories
5215 Purchases Returns and Allowances—Accessories

(6000) DIRECT EXPENSES
6100 DIRECT EXPENSES—EQUIPMENT
6105 Advertising Expense—Equipment
6110 Payroll Taxes Expense—Equipment
6115 Salary Expense—Equipment
6200 DIRECT EXPENSES—ACCESSORIES
6205 Advertising Expense—Accessories
6210 Payroll Taxes Expense—Accessories
6215 Salary Expense—Accessories

(7000) INDIRECT EXPENSES
7105 Credit Card Fee Expense
7110 Depreciation Expense—Office Equipment
7115 Depreciation Expense—Store Equipment
7120 Insurance Expense
7125 Miscellaneous Expense
7130 Payroll Taxes Expense—Administrative
7135 Rent Expense
7140 Salary Expense—Administrative
7145 Supplies Expense
7150 Uncollectible Accounts Expense
7155 Utilities Expense

(8000) INCOME TAX
8105 Federal Income Tax Expense

Subsidiary Ledgers

Accounts Receivable Ledger
110 Virgie Berger
120 Carlisle Steakhouse
130 Denton Seafood
140 Hamilton Group
150 LaFlore Café
160 Mary McCrory
170 Polk County Schools
180 Waukawy Country Club

Accounts Payable Ledger
210 Burkes Industries
220 Central Kitchen Supply
230 Fulgham Pottery
240 Hunley Equipment Co.
250 Kitchen Concepts
260 Specialty Supply
270 Triangle Manufacturing

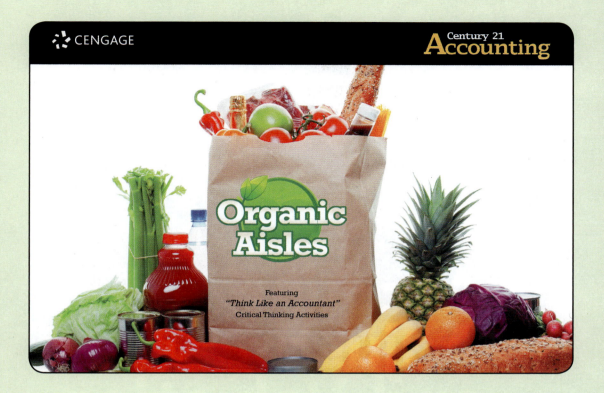

CENGAGE

Century 21
Accounting

Organic
Aisles

Featuring
"Think Like an Accountant"
Critical Thinking Activities

Organic Aisles is a departmentalized organic grocery store organized as a corporation. The company sells produce and grocery items. Separate accounting records are kept for two departments, Produce and Grocery. The activities included in the accounting cycle for Organic Aisles are listed here.

This automated simulation is completed in the General Ledger System, available in MindTap.

The following activities are included in this simulation:

1. Recording transactions in special journals and a general journal.

2. Calculating and recording departmental payroll data.

3. Posting items to be posted individually to a general ledger and subsidiary ledgers.

4. Proving and ruling journals.

5. Posting column totals to a general ledger.

6. Preparing schedules of accounts receivable and accounts payable.

7. Preparing a trial balance on a work sheet.

8. Planning adjustments and completing a work sheet.

9. Preparing financial statements.

10. Journalizing and posting adjusting entries.

11. Journalizing and posting closing entries.

12. Preparing a post-closing trial balance.

13. Completing Think Like an Accountant Financial Analysis.

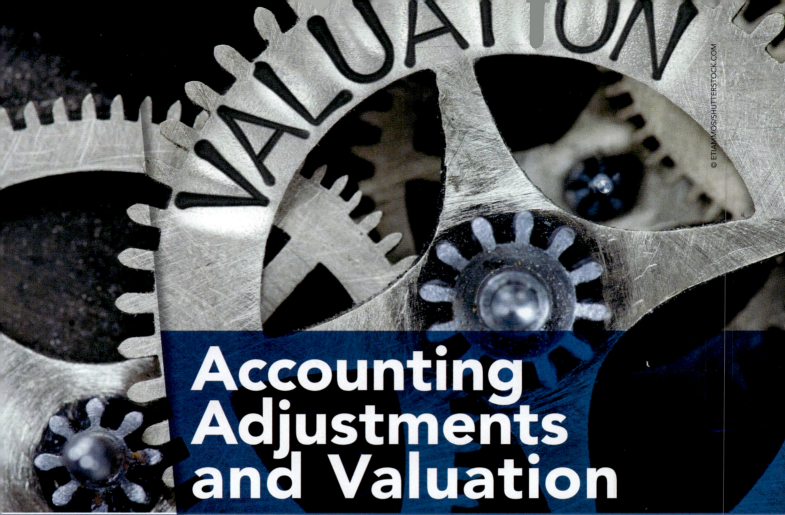

Accounting Adjustments and Valuation

THE BUSINESS—

VAUGHN DISTRIBUTORS, INC.

Vaughn Distributors, Inc., the business described in Part 2, purchases hand tools from foreign manufacturers and distributes the merchandise to independent hardware stores. Vaughn operates from a large warehouse, part of which it rents to other businesses.

Chart of Accounts
VAUGHN DISTRIBUTORS, INC.

GENERAL LEDGER

Balance Sheet Accounts

(1000) ASSETS
1100   Current Assets
1110   Cash
1115   Petty Cash
1120   Accounts Receivable
1125   Allowance for Uncollectible Accounts
1130   Merchandise Inventory
1140   Supplies
1150   Prepaid Insurance
1155   Prepaid Advertising
1160   Notes Receivable
1165   Interest Receivable
1200   Plant Assets
1210   Land
1220   Building
1225   Accumulated Depreciation—Building
1230   Office Equipment
1235   Accumulated Depreciation—Office Equipment
1240   Warehouse Equipment
1245   Accumulated Depreciation—Warehouse Equipment

(2000) LIABILITIES
2100   Current Liabilities
2105   Accounts Payable
2110   Salaries Payable
2115   Employee Income Tax Payable
2120   Social Security Tax Payable
2125   Medicare Tax Payable
2130   Unemployment Tax Payable—Federal
2135   Unemployment Tax Payable—State
2140   Unearned Rent
2150   Federal Income Tax Payable
2160   Notes Payable
2165   Interest Payable
2200   Long-Term Liabilities
2205   Mortgage Payable

(3000) STOCKHOLDERS' EQUITY
3105   Capital Stock
3110   Retained Earnings
3115   Dividends
3120   Income Summary

Income Statement Accounts

(4000) OPERATING REVENUE
4105   Sales
4110   Sales Discount
4115   Sales Returns and Allowances

(5000) COST OF MERCHANDISE
5105   Purchases
5110   Purchases Discount
5115   Purchases Returns and Allowances

(6000) OPERATING EXPENSE
6105   Advertising Expense
6110   Depreciation Expense—Building
6115   Depreciation Expense—Office Equipment
6120   Depreciation Expense—Warehouse Equipment
6125   Insurance Expense
6130   Miscellaneous Expense
6135   Payroll Taxes Expense
6140   Property Tax Expense
6145   Salary Expense
6150   Supplies Expense
6155   Uncollectible Accounts Expense

(7000) OTHER REVENUE
7105   Gain on Plant Assets
7110   Interest Income
7115   Rent Income

(8000) OTHER EXPENSES
8105   Interest Expense
8110   Loss on Plant Assets

(9000) INCOME TAX
9105   Federal Income Tax Expense

The chart of accounts for Vaughn Distributors, Inc., is illustrated above for ready reference as you study Part 2 of this textbook.

5

Inventory Planning and Valuation

LEARNING OBJECTIVES

After studying Chapter 5, in addition to defining key terms, you will be able to:

LO1 Describe the impact of merchandise inventory on financial reporting.

LO2 Account for the quantity of merchandise inventory.

LO3 Determine the cost of merchandise inventory using the FIFO, LIFO, and weighted-average inventory costing methods.

LO4 Describe the issues involved in selecting an inventory costing method.

LO5 Determine the reported cost of merchandise inventory using the lower of cost or market inventory costing method.

LO6 Estimate the cost of merchandise inventory using the gross profit and retail methods of estimating inventory.

LO7 Calculate and analyze the inventory turnover ratio and days' sales in inventory.

© TRONG NGUYEN/SHUTTERSTOCK.COM

Huntsman Corporation

ACCOUNTING IN THE REAL WORLD

Few corporations can brag that their products are found in a wide variety of markets, including transportation, home life, construction, energy and fuels, clothing, and footwear. Huntsman's products are present in so many consumer items, yet Huntsman is not a commonly recognized household name. Perhaps this unfamiliarity is due to Huntsman's products having names such as polyurethane, monomethylethanolamine, ethylene carbonate, and polyoxyalkyleneamine. Huntsman is an international supplier of chemicals used in the production process.

The purchase of goods and services is the largest expenditure for most businesses. Management must ensure that purchasing decisions are made in accordance with the company's standards and policies. Employees must be free of any relationships that improperly influence their purchasing decisions. A relationship that causes an employee to make a decision at odds with the goals of a business is called a *conflict of interest*. Unlike many corporations, Huntsman has a code of conduct for its vendors, in addition to a general code of conduct for its employees. Huntsman's *Vendor Code of Conduct* (the Code) clearly communicates that vendors are expected to follow Huntsman's values of honesty, integrity, respect, and responsibility.

Vendors frequently give small gifts to purchasing department employees with whom they do business.

The business community generally recognizes that entertainment, such as lunches and dinners, and modest gifts are customary in the normal course of business. However, giving valuable or extravagant gifts can, at a minimum, give the appearance of a conflict of interest. Whether these gifts influence purchasing employees' decisions and represent an actual conflict of interest is often difficult to determine.

Huntsman expects its vendors to "use good judgment and moderation when offering gifts or entertainment to Huntsman associates." The Code provides vendors with specific guidance on giving gifts to Huntsman employees. Vendor representatives are instructed to limit giving Huntsman associates an individual gift greater than $50 or multiple gifts totalling more than $125 during a 12-month period.

Source: www.huntsman.com.

CRITICAL THINKING

Many corporate codes of business conduct include sample situations of potential conflicts of interest. A sample situation might include a one-paragraph statement of the facts and then explain how the company would expect the employee to resolve the situation. Prepare a sample situation that could be added to the conflict of interest section of Huntsman's *Vendor Code of Conduct*.

KEY TERMS

consignment
consignee
consignor
stock record
stock ledger
inventory record
generally accepted
  accounting principles

first-in, first-out inventory
  costing method
last-in, first-out inventory
  costing method
weighted-average
  inventory costing
  method
inflation

deflation
international financial
  reporting standards
lower of cost or market
  inventory costing
  method
gross profit method of
  estimating inventory

retail method of estimating
  inventory
inventory turnover ratio
days' sales in inventory

LO1 Describe the impact of merchandise inventory on financial reporting.
LO2 Account for the quantity of merchandise inventory.

The Nature of Merchandise Inventory LO1

For most merchandising businesses, the cost of inventory sold is the largest cost of doing business. Merchandising businesses implement good control measures in managing their inventory. A successful business must maintain an adequate amount of merchandise inventory that customers are willing to buy. A business may fail if it keeps too much or too little merchandise inventory on hand.

Business managers frequently analyze sales and inventory transactions to assist them in planning future inventory purchases. From this analysis, managers can determine the items of inventory that are selling well and the items that are not selling well. Managers also examine sales and inventory transactions to identify any seasonal trends in sales. This information allows managers to order the right kinds of merchandise at the right time.

Most businesses now maintain their inventory records on a computer. Computerized inventory systems can keep more accurate records of the amount of inventory on hand. Computerized systems also provide more frequent inventory information to managers. Managers use this information to make effective business decisions.

ETHICS IN ACTION

Is Someone Reading Your E-mail?

Janice Tillman had just been escorted from the plant by security guards. Twenty minutes earlier, she lost her job because she sent e-mail messages containing threats directed toward Sylvia Hernandez, her supervisor. When confronted with the messages, Janice tried to dismiss them casually as a joke. When she realized that her argument wasn't working, she accused Sylvia of invading her privacy, claiming that she selected the "private message" option when sending the e-mails to a friend.

The company's code of conduct states, "E-mail communication on the company computer systems is subject to electronic monitoring. Employees are expected to limit the use of the company e-mail system for personal messages."

INSTRUCTIONS

Use the ethical model to evaluate Sylvia's decision to fire Janice.

Effects of Errors in Costing Merchandise Inventory on Net Income

	Correct Ending Inventory = $700		Incorrect Ending Inventory = $500	
Net Sales.............................		$6,000		$6,000
Cost of Merchandise Sold:				
Beginning Inventory...................	$ 600		$ 600	
Plus Net Purchases	3,200		3,200	
Cost of Merchandise Available for Sale..	$3,800		$3,800	
Less Ending Inventory	700		500	
Cost of Merchandise Sold		3,100		3,300
Gross Profit..........................		$2,900		$2,700
Operating Expenses		2,000		2,000
Net Income...........................		$ 900		$ 700

An accurate ending merchandise inventory cost must be determined to report adequately the financial progress and condition of a merchandising business. **>> App A: Full Disclosure** The cost is reported in the Assets section of the balance sheet. The cost is also used on the income statement to determine the cost of merchandise sold. Any error made in costing the ending inventory has a significant effect on the income statement. An abbreviated income statement for Erin Company is shown above. On the left side, the income statement reflects the correct cost of Erin's ending inventory, $700. The right side shows the effect of using an incorrect cost of $500 for the ending inventory. The $200 understatement causes the cost of merchandise sold to be overstated. This error also affects the gross profit and the net income, which are understated.

Effect of Errors in Costing Merchandise Inventory on Financial Statements

An error in the ending inventory also affects other financial statements. The table below summarizes the effect of the $200 understatement of Erin's ending inventory on selected amounts of three financial statements. The statement of cash flows is the only financial statement not affected by the error.

Reports and Items Affected	Correct Amount	Effect of Understating Ending Inventory	Misstated Amount
Income Statement			
Cost of Merchandise Sold	$3,100	$+200	$3,300
Gross Profit............................	2,900	−200	2,700
Net Income.............................	900	−200	700
Statement of Stockholders' Equity			
Net Income.............................	900	−200	700
Retained Earnings.......................	1,200	−200	1,000
Stockholders' Equity....................	1,700	−200	1,500
Balance Sheet			
Merchandise Inventory	700	−200	500
Total Assets............................	2,200	−200	2,000
Stockholders' Equity....................	1,700	−200	1,500

If the ending inventory is understated, the cost of merchandise sold will be overstated. The cost of merchandise sold overstatement results in an understatement of net income. Consequently, the understatement of net income results in an understatement of retained earnings and stockholders' equity. If the ending inventory is overstated, the reverse will be true, and additional income tax must be paid on the overstated income. In neither situation will the financial statements report accurate information. **>> App A: Full Disclosure**

Counting the Inventory LO2

Items in merchandise inventory are frequently referred to as *goods*. Typically, a business counts as part of its inventory all goods that it legally owns. The cost of these goods includes:

1. The price paid to vendors for the merchandise. This price is the purchase invoice amount less discounts, returns, and allowances granted by the vendors.
2. The cost of getting the goods to the place of business and ready for sale. This cost includes transportation charges paid by the buyer.

Merchandising businesses must know both the cost of the goods and the number of goods in inventory.

Businesses use two methods to determine the number of goods in inventory:

1. Taking a physical count of the items in inventory. All goods in inventory as of a given date are included in a physical inventory count.
2. Keeping a continuous record for each merchandise item showing the number purchased and the number sold. Using this method, a business can determine the number of goods in inventory at any point in time.

Goods In Transit

Merchandising businesses purchase goods and services from vendors. A vendor that sells merchandise to a merchandising business is often referred to as a *supplier*. The supplier ships the goods to the business. For goods in transit at the time of a physical count of inventory, the business must determine who holds title to the goods. When title to goods in transit passes from the supplier to the buyer, the goods become part of the buyer's inventory regardless of where they are physically located.

A supplier's terms of sale may include the provision *FOB shipping point*. FOB is an abbreviation for the phrase *Free on Board*. FOB shipping point means that the buyer pays the transportation charges. Under FOB shipping point terms, the title to the goods passes to the buyer as soon as the vendor delivers the goods to a shipping company. These goods in transit, not yet received by the buyer, are part of the *buyer's* inventory.

If the terms of sale are *FOB destination*, the vendor pays the transportation charges. Title to the goods passes to the buyer when the buyer receives the goods. These goods in transit, not yet received by the buyer, are part

of the *supplier's* inventory. The buyer does not include these goods in the cost of inventory.

Goods On Consignment

Goods that are given to a business to sell but for which title remains with the vendor are called a **consignment**. The person or business that receives goods on consignment is called the **consignee**. The person or business that gives goods on consignment is called the **consignor**.

The consignee agrees to receive, care for, and attempt to sell the consigned goods. If the goods are sold, the consignee deducts a commission from the sale amount and sends the remainder to the consignor. In a consignment, title to the goods does not pass to the consignee. The goods on consignment are part of the consignor's inventory. The consignee does not include consigned goods in the cost of its inventory.

A consignee agrees to care for the goods on consignment and to make adequate attempts to sell them. Therefore, a consignee has implied liabilities if anything should happen to the goods before they are sold. A consignee often reports the cost of consigned goods as a footnote to its balance sheet.

Maintaining a Stock Record for a Perpetual Inventory System LO2

Item Description ❶

Purchase Transactions ❹

Beginning Quantity ❷

Sales Transactions ❸

STOCK RECORD

Description *6-inch drill extension* Stock No. *D-1643*

Reorder *60* Minimum *20* Location *Bin 253*

1	2	3	4	5	6	7
INCREASES			DECREASES			BALANCE
DATE	PURCHASE INVOICE NO.	QUANTITY	DATE	SALES INVOICE NO.	QUANTITY	QUANTITY
Oct. 1						*38*
			Oct. 22	*2065*	*20*	*18*
			Oct. 31	*2156*	*10*	*8*
Nov. 5	*816*	*60*				*68*
			Nov. 14	*2215*	*30*	*38*
			Dec. 9	*2295*	*25*	*13*
Dec. 23	*881*	*60*				*73*

A continuous record of merchandise inventory increases and decreases and the balance on hand is known as a *perpetual inventory*. Vaughn Distributors maintains a perpetual inventory.

A perpetual inventory provides day-to-day records about the quantity of merchandise on hand. Based on the records, management knows when an item of inventory is low and needs to be reordered. For each inventory item, the record shows the number on hand, the number purchased, and the number sold. A form used to show the type of merchandise, quantity received, quantity sold, and balance on hand is called a **stock record**. A file of stock records for all merchandise on hand is called a **stock ledger**.

Vaughn's stock record for a 6-inch drill extension is shown above. It includes a notation of the minimum balance at which a reorder is to be placed. For example, Vaughn determines that two weeks are required to order and to receive a shipment from a vendor. In a two-week period, Vaughn will sell an average of 20 units. Therefore, Vaughn reorders the item when the inventory reaches 20 units. Each reorder is for 60 units. On October 22, the inventory balance falls below the reorder point. An order is immediately placed for 60 units. The order is received on November 5. A second order, placed on December 9, is received on December 23.

During the year, sales are recorded on the stock record when the sale is made. Purchases are recorded on the stock record when the goods are received. Unit prices are not recorded on the stock record. They are obtained from copies of the purchase invoices.

>> Maintaining a Stock Record

❶ Record the description of the inventory item, **6-inch drill extension**, the stock number, **D-1643**, the reorder quantity, **60**, the minimum number, **20**, and the warehouse location, **Bin 253**.

❷ Write the beginning quantity. On Oct. 1, 20--, the quantity on hand was **38**.

❸ Record all sales transactions in the Decreases columns of the stock record. For the October 22

sale, enter the date, **Oct. 22**, sales invoice number, **2065**, and quantity sold, **20**. Subtract the amount sold from the previous balance and enter the new balance, **18**.

❹ Enter all purchase transactions in the Increases columns of the stock record when the goods are received. Enter the date, purchase invoice number, quantity, and balance.

Inventory Record Used for the Physical Inventory

INVENTORY RECORD

DATE	December 31, 20--		ITEM	Drill Accessories	
1	**2**		**3**	**4**	**5**
STOCK NUMBER	DESCRIPTIONS		NO. OF UNITS ON HAND	UNIT PRICE	TOTAL COST
D-0643-3	3/16-in masonry bit		102	1.25	127.50
D-1643	6-in drill extension		47	40 @ 3.25 ⎱ 7 @ 3.20 ⎰	152.40
C-6432	Grout mixer		48	4.98	239.04
	Total				6,018.47

An inventory determined periodically by counting, weighing, or measuring items of merchandise on hand is known as a *physical inventory*. Counting, weighing, or measuring merchandise on hand for a physical inventory is commonly referred to as "taking an inventory." For businesses with a large quantity of merchandise on hand, taking an inventory is expensive. Therefore, businesses usually take an inventory only once each fiscal period.

Vaughn uses the perpetual inventory method to ensure that it maintains an adequate level of merchandise for sale. Errors can occur, however, even when the perpetual inventory method is used. Therefore, Vaughn takes a physical inventory once each year to check the accuracy of the perpetual inventory.

A form used during a physical inventory to record information about each item of merchandise on hand is called an **inventory record**. One inventory record is used for each item or category of items in inventory. When taking an inventory, Vaughn uses an inventory record for categories of merchandise as shown above.

The inventory count is compared to the perpetual inventory. Any differences are adjusted on the inventory records. If large differences are found, the business should review its recording and control procedures to ensure that the inventory and the inventory records are being properly maintained.

WHY ACCOUNTING?

CareerClusters
PATHWAYS TO COLLEGE & CAREER READINESS
Education & Training

Retraining after Workplace Injuries

The Bureau of Labor Statistics (BLS) is a government agency whose mission is "to collect, analyze, and disseminate essential economic information...." One item that the BLS tracks is the number of recordable injuries that occur in private industry each year. In 2016, there were nearly three million nonfatal injuries on the job.

An injured employee may have the right to collect payments through a workmen's compensation insurance program. These payments will continue until the employee recovers and is able to return to work. In many cases, the employee will never be able to return to the same position, and may be retrained for another position.

Retraining is feasible when the cost of the retraining is less than the cost of the continued workmen's compensation payments. This retraining may take place within the company, at an outside

training facility, or at a college or university. The retraining plan must be based on the limitations of the injured employee and the requirements of the new position. The plan needs to include the estimated cost of the retraining.

CRITICAL THINKING

Visit the Bureau of Labor Statistics website (www.bls.gov). Find the answers to the following questions:

1. The BLS is part of which federal government department?
2. Find one report published by the BLS. List the title of the report.
3. The BLS publishes a table of the fastest growing occupations. Search the website for the table and list the top occupation.

Source: Bureau of Labor Statistics (www.bls.gov/iif/).

Restatement at Rite Aid Corporation

If not for the country's fascination with Enron and WorldCom, the accounting fraud at the Rite Aid Corporation might have received more attention. About the same time that the Enron and WorldCom frauds were being revealed, the Securities and Exchange Commission (SEC) announced charges against several former senior Rite Aid executives. The SEC complaint alleged that Rite Aid overstated its net income by $1.6 billion between May 1997 and May 1999. When Rite Aid published corrected financial statements, it was the largest restatement ever recorded.

In a press release, the SEC outlined 13 different charges, ranging from improper accounting entries to false statements, abuse of vendor relationships, and improper related-party transactions. The extent of these frauds caused the regional director of the SEC's Northeast Regional Office to state:

> The charges announced today reveal a disturbing picture of dishonesty and misconduct at the highest level of a major corporation. Rite Aid's former senior management employed an extensive bag of tricks to manipulate the company's reported earnings and defraud its investors.

One of its "tricks" related to its transactions with vendors. Rite Aid was allowed to reduce amounts owed to vendors for the value of damaged and outdated products. Rite Aid overstated these amounts from vendors who did not require the unusable products to be returned to them. According to the SEC, Rite Aid overstated the value of damaged and outdated products by $36 million over a two-year period.

ACTIVITY

The internal auditors at Foster Stores are performing their regular examination of the purchasing function at each of the company's locations. A standard audit test is to search for any evidence that irregular transactions, such as those described here, are occurring.

The workbook contains two worksheets. One worksheet contains a list of all pharmaceutical items obtained from the computerized accounting system. The list includes the number of unit returns and purchases during the fiscal year for its Macon location. The list also contains an *Expire* column that provides instructions for how credit is obtained for outdated items. *None* indicates that the vendor does not accept credits for outdated items. *Return* indicates that the outdated items must be returned to the vendor for credit. *Discard* indicates that the vendor does not require the items to be returned in order to receive credit.

INSTRUCTIONS

Open the spreadsheet FA_CH05 and complete the steps on the Instructions tab.

Use your analysis to answer the following questions.

1. Does any evidence exist that suggests that the location is inflating its credits for outdated items?

2. Is there a significant difference in the return rate between vendors that require the items to be returned, as compared to those that do not allow any credit for outdated items?

Source: www.sec.gov/news/press/2002-92.htm.

LO1 Describe the impact of merchandise inventory on financial reporting.

LO2 Account for the quantity of merchandise inventory.

TERMS REVIEW

consignment

consignee

consignor

stock record

stock ledger

inventory record

Audit your understanding LO1, 2

1. What two elements are included in the cost of merchandise available for sale?
2. If the ending merchandise inventory is understated, will the net income be overstated or understated?
3. What two costs are included in the cost of merchandise inventory?
4. For goods shipped FOB shipping point, when does the title for goods in transit pass from the vendor to the buyer? Which party pays for the shipping costs?
5. Name and briefly discuss the two ways to determine the number of inventory items on hand.

Work together 5-1 LO2

Completing a stock record for a perpetual inventory system

A stock record form and an inventory record form for Harris Security are provided in the *Working Papers*. Your instructor will guide you through the following examples.

1. Fill in the top portion of the stock record form with the following information: Description, wireless monitoring camera; Stock No., C-4264; Reorder, 100; Minimum, 20; and Location, Bin 662.
2. Harris Security has 68 units of the item in stock on August 1. Record the following information. Save your work to complete On Your Own 5-1.

Date	Purchase Invoice No.	Sales Invoice No.	Quantity
Aug. 22		675	50
Aug. 31		712	12
Sept. 5	316		100
Sept. 14		785	18

On your own 5-1 LO2

Completing a stock record for a perpetual inventory system

Use the *Working Papers* from Work Together 5-1 above. Work independently to complete the following problem.

1. Record the remaining information for product number C-4264 on the stock record.

Date	Purchase Invoice No.	Sales Invoice No.	Quantity
Sept. 20		798	45
Sept. 22		802	30
Oct. 5	322		100
Oct. 26		834	25

2. Compare the ending balance in units from the stock record to the number of units on hand for item C-4264 in the inventory record. Make sure the quantities on the two records are equal.

LO3 Determine the cost of merchandise inventory using the FIFO, LIFO, and weighted-average inventory costing methods.

LO4 Describe the issues involved in selecting an inventory costing method.

LO5 Determine the reported cost of merchandise inventory using the lower of cost or market inventory costing method.

Assigning Unit Costs LO3

Three methods for assigning the cost of items in merchandise inventory are commonly used. Generally accepted accounting principles require that a business consistently apply the same method when reporting comparable financial statements.

First-In, First-Out Inventory Costing Method

FIFO Inventory Costing Method					
Purchase Dates	Units Purchased	Unit Price	Total Cost	FIFO Units on Hand	FIFO Cost
January 1, beginning inventory	20	$ 9.40	$ 188.00		
March 12, purchases	12	9.80	117.60		
June 22, purchases	28	10.20	285.60		
August 7, purchases	24	10.70	256.80	20	$214.00
December 2, purchases	16	10.75	172.00	16	172.00
Totals	100		$1,020.00	36	$386.00

- ② Units Needed to Equal the Total Units on Hand
- ① Units from Most Recent Purchase
- ③ Unit Price Times Units on Hand
- ④ Total Units on Hand and Total Cost

The standards and rules that accountants follow while recording and reporting financial activities are called **generally accepted accounting principles**. These standards and rules are often referred to as *GAAP*. GAAP permit a business to use one of several methods to cost its merchandise inventory.

Once Vaughn takes a physical inventory, it must determine a dollar cost for each item. **>> App A: Unit of Measurement** Using the price of merchandise purchased first to calculate the cost of merchandise sold first is called the **first-in, first-out inventory costing method**. *FIFO* is an abbreviation for first in, first out. The FIFO method assumes that the merchandise purchased first (first in) is the merchandise sold first (first out). Thus, the FIFO method uses the most recent purchase prices to determine the cost of merchandise inventory remaining. Vaughn's inventory of 36 drill sets would be costed as shown above.

>> Calculating Inventory Costs Using the FIFO Method

① Assign ending inventory units from the most recent purchase. The number of units in the ending inventory is 36. All **16** units from the December purchase are assigned to ending inventory.

② If all units of the ending inventory have not been assigned, assign units from the next most recent purchase, August. This purchase included 24 units. Assign the lesser of the unassigned units, 20, or the number of units of the purchase, 24. Enter **20** units from the August purchase. All 36 units in ending inventory have now been assigned.

③ Multiply the units in the FIFO Units on Hand column by the unit prices. Enter the results, **$214.00** and **$172.00**, in the FIFO Cost column.

④ Total the columns. The total number of units, **36**, is the number of units on hand. The total cost assigned to these units using the FIFO method is **$386.00**.

Last-In, First-Out Inventory Costing Method

				LIFO Units	
Purchase Dates	**Units Purchased**	**Unit Price**	**Total Cost**	**on Hand**	**LIFO Cost**
January 1, beginning inventory	20	$ 9.40	$ 188.00	20	$188.00
March 12, purchases	12	9.80	117.60	12	117.60
June 22, purchases	28	10.20	285.60	4	40.80
August 7, purchases	24	10.70	256.80		
December 2, purchases	16	10.75	172.00		
Totals	100		$1,020.00	36	$346.40

LIFO Inventory Costing Method

Beginning Inventory Units

Unit Price Times Units on Hand

Units Needed to Equal the Total Units on Hand

Total Units on Hand and Total Cost

Using the price of merchandise purchased last to calculate the cost of merchandise sold first is called the **last-in, first-out inventory costing method**. *LIFO* is an abbreviation for last in, first out. The LIFO method uses the earliest purchase prices to determine the cost of merchandise inventory. If Vaughn used the LIFO method, the 36 drill sets would be costed as shown above.

Of the 36 units on hand, 20 units are assumed to be the units in the beginning inventory at $9.40 per unit. Another 12 units are assumed to have been purchased on the next earliest date, March 12, at $9.80 each. The remaining four units are assumed to have been purchased on the next earliest date, June 22, at $10.20 each. The total cost is $346.40.

The remaining 24 units from the June purchase and the units from the August and December purchases are designated as the units that were sold. These drill sets are last in. Therefore, the business assumes that they are also the first out, or first sold.

THINK LIKE AN ACCOUNTANT

Helping a Client Avoid Penalties

Jermaine Johnson's construction business has done very well building starter homes for lower-income families. His advertisements guarantee the quality and timely completion of the house.

While preparing Jermaine's tax return, you notice an unusual expense item—Penalty Expense. Giving him a quick call, you learn that this account reflects the costs of missing contract completion dates. Jermaine's contracts include a $50.00-per-day penalty for every day the house is not completed on time. Digging deeper, you learn that few houses are completed on time.

When Jermaine comes to your office to sign his return, you take the opportunity to ask him about how he determines target completion dates. He states that he estimates it requires 135 workdays to build a house. Accounting for weekends, he estimates it takes 180 days, or six months, to complete a house.

It is clear to you that Jermaine's method does not adequately account for the weekends, nor does it consider holidays. Therefore, you invite Jermaine to help you create a spreadsheet to assist him in setting completion dates.

OPEN THE SPREADSHEET TLA_CH05

The worksheet contains an incomplete schedule for estimating the start and end time for each significant stage of home construction. Follow the steps on the Instructions tab to complete the schedule. Answer these questions:

1. What is the projected completion date for a house with a start date of February 16, 2018?

2. What is the projected completion date for a house with a start date of September 8, 2018?

3. What additional changes to the schedule would you suggest that would help Jermaine estimate the completion dates of new contracts?

Weighted-Average Inventory Costing Method

Weighted-Average Inventory Costing Method			
Purchase Dates	**Units Purchased**	**Unit Price**	**Total Cost**
January 1, beginning inventory	20	$ 9.40	$ 188.00
March 12, purchases	12	9.80	117.60
June 22, purchases	28	10.20	285.60
August 7, purchases	24	10.70	256.80
December 2, purchases	16	10.75	172.00
Totals	100		$1,020.00

Total Units and Cost of All Purchases

Total of Beginning Inventory and Purchases	÷	Total Units	=	Weighted-Average Price per Unit	Average Price per Unit
$1,020.00	÷	100	=	$10.20	

Units in Ending Inventory	×	Weighted-Average Price per Unit	=	Cost of Ending Inventory	Cost of Ending Inventory
36	×	$10.20	=	$367.20	

Using the average cost of the beginning inventory plus merchandise purchased during a fiscal period to calculate the cost of merchandise sold is called the **weighted-average inventory costing method**. This method is based on the assumption that the cost is an average of the price paid for similar items purchased during the fiscal period. If Vaughn used the weighted-average method, the 36 drill sets would be costed as shown above.

The total cost, $1,020.00, is divided by the total units purchased, 100, to calculate the weighted-average cost per unit, $10.20. The 36 units currently on hand are assumed to have been purchased at an average cost of $10.20 each. Therefore, the total cost of the ending merchandise inventory using the weighted-average method is $367.20. Vaughn would use the same weighted-average cost per unit, $10.20, to determine the cost of merchandise sold.

FYI Inventory management consists of determining the quantity of goods on hand and developing procedures for ordering, receiving, and maintaining the inventory.

Selecting an Inventory Costing Method LO4

A business must consider many factors when selecting an inventory costing method. The impact of changing prices, international accounting standards, and tax law must all be considered.

Purchases		FIFO Method		LIFO Method		Weighted-Average Method
Date	Unit Price	Units	Cost	Units	Cost	
Beginning Inventory............	$ 9.40			20	$188.00	
March	9.80			12	117.60	
June..........................	10.20			4	40.80	$ 10.20
August	10.70	20	$214.00			
December	10.75	16	172.00			
Totals		36	$386.00	36	$346.40	$367.20
If prices are rising:						
Ending Inventory		Highest		Lowest		Intermediate
Cost of Merchandise Sold		Lowest		Highest		Intermediate
Reported Net Income		Highest		Lowest		Intermediate

Costing Inventory During Periods of Increasing Prices

The rate at which the price for goods and services increases over time is called **inflation**. Inflation impacts the cost of the ending inventory calculated using each of the inventory costing methods. The cost of the ending inventory affects the cost of merchandise sold amount on the income statement. The higher the ending inventory, the lower the cost of merchandise sold amount, and vice versa.

The prices for the drill sets illustrated in this lesson increased from $9.40 to $10.75 per unit. Three ways of costing the inventory of 36 drill sets during a period of increasing prices are summarized above. During an inflationary period, the FIFO method usually results in the highest cost of inventory. The most recent purchases are used to cost the inventory.

During an inflationary period, the LIFO method usually results in the lowest cost of inventory. The beginning inventory and the early purchases are used to cost the inventory. Therefore, the LIFO method results in the highest cost of merchandise sold and the lowest reported net income.

Tax Limitations of Using LIFO

The rate of inflation is influenced by many economic factors and varies by country each year. The United States has experienced inflation in nearly every year since records have been maintained. Two periods of unusually high inflation occurred from 1917 to 1920 (16.6%) and 1979 to 1981 (11.7%).

In an inflationary period, a business would choose to use the FIFO method to prepare its financial statements. The FIFO method allows the business to report the highest level of net income. At the same time, a business would also choose to use the LIFO method to calculate its taxable income. The LIFO method would result in lower taxable income and a lower income tax liability.

Although lowering income taxes benefits a business, it also reduces tax revenues to the government. For this reason, early tax rules did not allow a business to use the LIFO method for calculating taxable income. During the late 1930s, Congress changed the tax laws to allow a business to use the LIFO method for calculating income taxes. However, it added an important requirement: the business must use the same method for financial and tax reporting.

Remember FIFO uses the prices of the most recent purchases to determine the cost of merchandise inventory.

Costing Inventory During Periods of Decreasing Prices

Purchases		FIFO Method		LIFO Method		Weighted-Average Method
Date	Unit Price	Units	Cost	Units	Cost	
Beginning Inventory............	$10.75			20	$215.00	
March	10.70			12	128.40	
June	10.20			4	40.80	$ 10.15
August	9.80	20	$196.00			
December	9.40	16	150.40			
Totals		36	$346.40	36	$384.20	$365.40
If prices are decreasing: Ending Inventory		Lowest		Highest		Intermediate
Cost of Merchandise Sold		Highest		Lowest		Intermediate
Reported Net Income		Lowest		Highest		Intermediate

The rate at which the price for goods and services decreases over time is called **deflation**. If Vaughn determined the cost of inventory during a period of decreasing prices, the three inventory costing methods would be summarized as shown above.

During a deflationary period, the FIFO method usually results in the lowest merchandise inventory cost. This lower inventory cost results in a higher cost of merchandise sold and a lower net income. In contrast, the LIFO method usually results in the highest ending inventory cost. This higher inventory cost results in a lower cost of merchandise sold and a higher net income.

The weighted-average method usually results in a total cost between the FIFO and LIFO total costs in both periods of increasing and decreasing prices. For businesses that purchase items with frequent fluctuations in price, the weighted-average method results in more consistent reporting of merchandise inventory costs.

Each business selects the method of costing merchandise inventory that best fits its policies and goals. Once selected, generally accepted accounting principles require that the business continue to use that method. In this way, the information on a series of financial statements can be compared easily. >> App A: Consistent Reporting

FYI

Computer prices have declined over time despite dramatic advancements in technology. Electronic equipment has traditionally experienced declining prices.

© DMITRY MOLCHANOV/SHUTTERSTOCK.COM.

Criticism of the LIFO Method

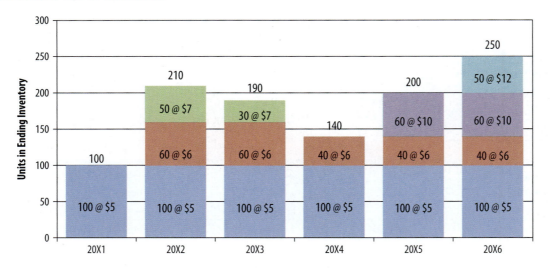

Inflation causes a conflict between the fair reporting of the cost of inventory and the cost of merchandise sold. In an inflationary period, the LIFO method more accurately presents the cost of merchandise sold but understates the cost of inventory.

In the example above, a company's first purchase of an item in 20X1 is 150 units @ $5.00 each. At the end of 20X1, the business has 100 units in inventory. The LIFO cost would be 100 units @ $5.00. In 20X2, the first two purchases are 60 units @ $6.00 and 180 units @ $7.00. At the end of 20X2, the business has 210 units in inventory. The LIFO cost would be 100 units @ $5.00, 60 units @ $6.00, and 50 units @ $7.00. In the years that follow the units in ending inventory vary between 140 and 250, but always stay above 100 units. Thus, the $5.00 unit cost continues to be used to cost 100 units, despite the fact that the latest market price has risen to $12.00.

Using the LIFO method, the cost of the 250 units in the 20X6 inventory is $1,940.00. If the FIFO method was used and the most recent purchase was for $12.00 per unit, the FIFO cost of these same units would be $3,000.00. The understatement of the cost of inventory grows over time. For a business selling the same product

for decades, such as an oil business, the understatement can become large enough to distort the amount reported on the balance sheet.

International Accounting Standards

The LIFO method has been criticized because of its understatement of inventory. As discussed earlier, the LIFO method was not initially accepted for the calculation of federal income taxes. In addition, the LIFO method has not been universally adopted in other countries.

The international financial community has also developed accounting standards. A set of accounting standards being adopted across the world is called **international financial reporting standards**, or *IFRS* (pronounced eye-fers). IFRS do not allow the LIFO method.

The Securities and Exchange Commission is committed to requiring publicly held corporations to submit financial statements prepared using IFRS rather than GAAP. However, businesses that are not publicly traded may still issue financial statements using GAAP. At the time this textbook was written, the LIFO method was still accepted for the calculation of federal income taxes.

 IFRS do not allow the LIFO method.

Lower of Cost or Market Inventory Costing Method LO5

Lower of Cost or Market Inventory Costing Method			
Costing Method	Cost	Market Value (36 units × $10.15) current market price)	Lower of Cost or Market
FIFO	$386.00	$365.40	$365.40
LIFO	346.40	365.40	346.40
Weighted-average	367.20	365.40	365.40

↑ Determine Cost ↑ Determine Market Price ↑ Lower of Cost or Market Price

Regardless of the method used to cost inventory, the amount reported on the financial statements should not exceed the market value of the inventory. Using the lower of cost or market price to calculate the cost of the ending merchandise inventory is called the **lower of cost or market inventory costing method**. In this context, market refers to the current replacement cost of the merchandise item. For example, Vaughn may currently have to pay a vendor $10.15 to purchase a drill set. The market price, therefore, is $10.15. When merchandise is purchased, the unit price is used to record inventory costs. **>> App A: Historical Cost** The historical cost concept states that the actual amount paid for merchandise or other items bought is recorded.

If the unit price is higher than the market price at the end of a fiscal period, the inventory cost is reduced to the current market price. However, if the unit price is lower than the market price, the inventory cost is maintained at the unit price.

Two amounts are needed to apply the lower of cost or market method:

1. The cost of the inventory using the FIFO, LIFO, or weighted-average method.
2. The current market price of the inventory.

These two amounts are then compared, and the lower of the two is used to cost the inventory. For example, Vaughn uses the weighted-average method of costing inventory. The weighted-average cost and the current market price for 36 drill sets are shown above. The weighted-average cost is $367.20, and the current market price is $365.40. Using the lower of cost or market method, the market price of the drill sets is lower than the weighted-average cost. Therefore, the market price of $365.40 is used as the cost of the drill sets.

If Vaughn used the FIFO method, the FIFO cost would be $386.00. The $365.40 market price is lower than the FIFO cost, so the market price would be used instead of the FIFO cost. If Vaughn used the LIFO method, the LIFO cost would be $346.40. The LIFO cost is lower than the market price, so the LIFO cost would be used to cost the inventory.

© URBANS/SHUTTERSTOCK.COM

> **FYI** The goal of the Japanese concept, the just-in-time (JIT) system, is to minimize inventory. Materials should be received only when they are needed for production; they should not be kept in inventory. The JIT system works well when vendors and buyers work together as business partners to plan inventory levels.

TERMS REVIEW

generally accepted
  accounting principles

first-in, first-out inventory
  costing method

last-in, first-out inventory
  costing method

weighted-average inven-
  tory costing method

inflation

deflation

international financial
  reporting standards

lower of cost or mar-
  ket inventory costing
  method

Audit your understanding LO3, 4, 5

1. Which inventory costing method uses the earliest purchase prices to determine the cost of merchandise inventory
2. What two amounts are used to calculate the weighted-average price per unit?
3. During an inflationary period, what inventory costing method will result in the highest reported net income?
4. What must a business do to qualify for using the LIFO method for tax reporting?
5. Which inventory costing method is not allowed by international financial reporting standards?
6. What two amounts are needed to apply the lower of cost or market inventory costing method?

Work together 5-2 LO3, 5

Costing ending inventory using FIFO, LIFO, and weighted-average

Forms for calculating inventory costs for Jensen Auto are provided in the *Working Papers*. Your instructor will guide you through the following examples.

Jensen Auto had the following beginning inventory and purchases for an air filter. At the end of the year, 34 units remained in the inventory. Determine the cost of the ending inventory using the FIFO, LIFO, and weighted-average inventory costing methods.

	Units	Unit Price
Beginning inventory	8	$ 9.96
February purchase	20	10.24
May purchase	20	10.36
August purchase	20	10.46
November purchase	20	10.54

On your own 5-2 LO3, 5

Costing ending inventory using FIFO, LIFO, and weighted-average

Forms for calculating inventory costs for Jensen Auto are provided in the *Working Papers*. Work independently to complete the following problem.

Jensen Auto had the following beginning inventory and purchases for an engine belt. At the end of the year, 226 units remained in the inventory. Determine the cost of the ending inventory using the FIFO, LIFO, and weighted-average inventory costing methods.

	Units	Unit Price
Beginning inventory	180	$4.00
February purchase	156	4.20
May purchase	160	4.50
August purchase	168	4.60
November purchase	176	4.80

Estimating the Inventory

LO6 Estimate the cost of merchandise inventory using the gross profit and retail methods of estimating inventory.

LO7 Calculate and analyze the inventory turnover ratio and days' sales in inventory.

Methods for Estimating the Cost of Merchandise Inventory LO6

A business needs to determine the cost of merchandise inventory to prepare monthly financial statements. Most merchandisers maintain a perpetual inventory using stock records or a computerized accounting system. The cost of the ending merchandise inventory can be obtained from accounting records.

For some small merchandisers, the cost of maintaining a perpetual inventory may exceed its benefit. Taking a monthly physical inventory is too expensive. A cost-effective alternative used by some small businesses is to estimate monthly ending inventories.

Gross Profit Method of Estimating Inventory

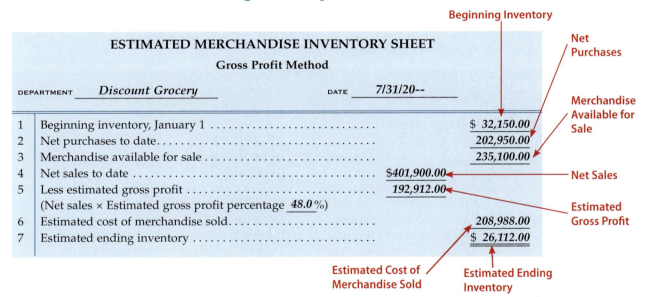

Estimating inventory by using the previous year's percentage of gross profit on operations is called the **gross profit method of estimating inventory**. This method assumes that a continuing relationship exists between gross profit and net sales. Based on experience in previous fiscal periods, a gross profit to net sales percentage is calculated.

Discount Grocery does not maintain a perpetual inventory system. Instead, it estimates its monthly cost of merchandise inventory by using last year's actual gross margin of 48.0%. An ending merchandise inventory calculated using the gross profit method is an estimate and is not accurate. However, for monthly financial statements, the estimated amount is sufficiently accurate without taking a physical inventory.

In the illustration above, the net purchases on line 2 is the purchases amount from the general ledger, reduced by purchases discounts and purchases returns and allowances. The net sales on line 4 is the sales amount reduced by sales discounts and sales returns and allowances.

Retail Method of Estimating Inventory

ESTIMATED MERCHANDISE INVENTORY SHEET

Retail Method

COMPANY _____F&G Stores_____ DATE _____7/31/20--_____

		Cost	Retail
1	Beginning inventory, January 1	$190,300.00	$325,300.00
2	Net purchases to date..................................	116,700.00	198,700.00
3	Merchandise available for sale	$307,000.00	$524,000.00
4	Net sales to date		208,600.00
5	Estimated ending inventory at retail....................		$315,400.00
6	Estimated ending inventory	$184,824.40	
	(Inventory at retail × Percentage _58.6_ %)		

Beginning Merchandise Inventory at Cost and Retail

Merchandise Purchased at Cost and Retail

Merchandise Available at Cost and Retail

Sales to Date

Estimated Ending Inventory at Retail

Estimated Ending Inventory Cost

Cost Divided by Retail

Estimating inventory by using a percentage based on both cost and retail prices is called the **retail method of estimating inventory**. The retail method may be used instead of the gross profit method. To use the retail method, a business must keep separate records of both cost and retail prices for net purchases, net sales, and the beginning merchandise inventory.

An estimated ending merchandise inventory for F&G Stores, using the retail method, is shown above.

In this illustration, the percentage used to estimate the ending inventory, 58.6%, is calculated by dividing the merchandise available for sale at cost, $307,000.00, by the merchandise available for sale at retail, $524,000.00.

Many businesses that need to estimate the ending merchandise inventory use the gross profit method rather than the retail method. The gross profit method does not require separate records for cost and retail prices.

GLOBAL AWARENESS

Work/Holiday Visa

If you are interested in working in a foreign country, you will most likely have to obtain a work visa, also called a *work/holiday visa*. This visa allows you to hold a temporary job in that country. Its purpose is to encourage an understanding of other countries.

Many countries put age restrictions and time limits on work/holiday visas. For example, Australia limits them to people aged 18 to 30, with a time limit of 12 months. Many countries allow work/holiday visas based on reciprocal agreements between countries. Because the United States does not usually grant work/holiday visas for citizens of other countries, U.S. citizens are limited in their options.

If you would like to live and work in a foreign country on a more permanent basis, further restrictions apply. Many countries require you to have a job before you can apply for a work permit. This is further complicated because, in many countries, you cannot enter the country

to look for work. This means that you must be able to find a job and be hired without entering the country.

Some countries only allow work visas for positions that cannot be filled by a citizen of the country. In these cases, the employer must apply for the work visa for the new foreign employee. The employer must show evidence of unsuccessful attempts to fill the position with citizens of the country.

CRITICAL THINKING

1. Pick a country in which you would like to work while traveling. Use the Internet to determine:
   a. Can a U.S. citizen apply for a work/holiday visa for that country?
   b. What is the maximum length of time a work visa is valid?
   c. What are the age restrictions for a work/holiday visa?
2. Summarize your findings in a short written report.

Sources: www.travel.state.gov; www.australia.gov.au; www.newzealandnow.govt.nz.

Financial Analysis of Merchandise Inventory LO7

The more rapidly a business sells merchandise, the more chance it has to make a satisfactory net income. For example, more revenue results from selling 100 drill sets per day than from selling 60 drill sets per day. Two measures of the speed with which merchandise inventory is sold are:

1. Inventory turnover ratio.
2. Days' sales in inventory.

Inventory Turnover Ratio

January 1 Merchandise Inventory	+	December 31 Merchandise Inventory	÷	2	=	Average Merchandise Inventory
($154,813.36	+	$162,048.14)	÷	2	=	$158,430.75

Cost of Merchandise Sold	÷	Average Merchandise Inventory	=	Inventory Turnover Ratio
$924,871.46	÷	$158,430.75	=	5.84

The number of times the average amount of merchandise inventory is sold during a specific period of time is called the **inventory turnover ratio**. An inventory turnover ratio expresses a relationship between an average inventory and the cost of merchandise sold. Merchandise inventory represents a large investment for most merchandising businesses. Therefore, a low inventory turnover ratio usually indicates a low return on investment.

A 5.84 inventory turnover ratio means that the business sold the average merchandise inventory 5.84 times during the current year. National trade associations and financial organizations publish average ratios for businesses in specific industries. Vaughn can compare its ratio with the ratio for similar businesses, which have an average inventory turnover ratio of 6.25 times. Vaughn's turnover ratio of 5.84 is below the industry standard of 6.25. To correct this situation, Vaughn's managers should consider taking action to better control the quantity of merchandise inventory on hand.

Days' Sales In Inventory

The time needed to sell an average amount of merchandise inventory is called the **days' sales in inventory**. The days' sales in inventory, based on a 5.84 USD inventory turnover ratio, is calculated as shown below.

Days in Year	÷	Inventory Turnover Ratio	=	Days' Sales in Inventory
365	÷	5.84	=	63 Days

The number of days' sales in inventory is rounded to the nearest day. This level of accuracy provides managers with adequate information to make sound business decisions.

An average of 63 days means that, on average, each item in inventory is sold 63 days after it is purchased. Published averages show that businesses similar to Vaughn have an average number of days' sales in inventory of 58. Vaughn's management should seek ways to increase its turnover of inventory.

The higher the number of days in inventory, the longer merchandise tends to remain unsold. A business can increase the inventory turnover ratio and reduce the number of days' sales in inventory by reducing the size of the inventory kept on hand. However, a lower inventory level may not allow a business to meet customers' demands. A business also can improve its turnover ratio and the number of days' sales in inventory by increasing the amount of merchandise sold during a month or a year.

LO6 Estimate the cost of merchandise inventory using the gross profit and retail methods of estimating inventory.

LO7 Calculate and analyze the inventory turnover ratio and days' sales in inventory.

TERMS REVIEW

gross profit method of estimating inventory

retail method of estimating inventory

inventory turnover ratio

days' sales in inventory

Audit your understanding LO6, 7

1. On what assumptions are the gross profit method of estimating inventory based?
2. To use the retail method of estimating inventory, what records must be kept?
3. Explain an inventory turnover ratio of 5.0.
4. Explain a days' sales in inventory of 60.

Work together 5-3 LO6, 7

Estimating inventory using the gross profit and retail methods; financial analysis of merchandise inventory

The following information is available for Debbie's Fabrics for the month of October. Estimated merchandise inventory sheets are provided in the *Working Papers*. Your instructor will guide you through the following examples.

	Cost	Retail
Beginning inventory, October 1	$96,850.00	$205,190.00
Net purchases for October	19,480.00	40,750.00
Net sales for October		40,510.00
Gross profit percentage	52.6%	

1. Estimate the ending inventory using the gross profit method.
2. Estimate the ending inventory using the retail method. Round the percentage to the nearest 0.1%.
3. The inventory for Debbie's Fabrics was $92,890.00 on January 1 and $101,700.00 on December 31. The cost of merchandise sold for the year was $496,710.00. Calculate the inventory turnover ratio and the days' sales in inventory. Round the inventory turnover ratio to two decimal places and the days' sales in inventory to the nearest day.

On your own 5-3 LO6, 7

Estimating inventory using the gross profit and retail methods; financial analysis of merchandise inventory

The following information is available for Kelly Music for the month of July. Estimated merchandise inventory sheets are provided in the *Working Papers*. Work independently to complete the following problem.

	Cost	Retail
Beginning inventory, July 1	$65,180.00	$159,750.00
Net purchases for July	24,740.00	58,900.00
Net sales for July		62,730.00
Gross profit percentage	58.4%	

1. Estimate the ending inventory using the gross profit method.
2. Estimate the ending inventory using the retail method. Round the percentage to the nearest 0.1%.
3. Kelly Music's inventory was $63,250.00 on January 1 and $70,960.00 on December 31. The cost of merchandise sold for the year was $289,210.00. Calculate the inventory turnover ratio and the days' sales in inventory. Round the inventory turnover ratio to two decimal places and the days' sales in inventory to the nearest day.

A Look at **Accounting** Software

Setting Prices

In a manual accounting system, price lists would generally be maintained in a spreadsheet file and then printed out for use by sales staff, customers, and the accounting department. When a sales invoice was being prepared, the price sheet would be consulted to determine the prices to be charged. If variations to a listed price were needed for a particular type of customer or for a particular situation, all that would be required would be a written approval from an authorized manager.

Pricing is much more complicated in a computerized accounting system, but the business benefits by achieving much faster and more accurate recording of sales. The sales function of the accounting system is linked to the inventory function, and invoicing is done automatically. Therefore, it is necessary to set detailed rules for the way prices are to be charged when a sale is entered. Special situations need to be anticipated and rules set for alternate pricing in those situations.

The pricing function of a computerized accounting system is normally accessed from the primary navigation window. In this system, that is called the System Manager. Access to the price controls is strictly limited to only a few trusted individuals. While most users would be given the privilege of viewing prices, they would be unable to change them.

① The authorized user clicked on the **Manage Pricing** option from the System Manager, and the system opened a navigation pane providing access to the various parts of the pricing utility.

② To calculate default selling prices on individual inventory items, the system uses four variables: Pricing Methods, Units of Measure, Price Levels, and Price Groups.

③ To set the price for an inventory item, the user would click on the **Item Pricing** button. Clicking the **Sale Pricing** button would enable the user to set temporary sale prices on selected groups of products without affecting normal selling prices.

④ Price lists for List Prices, Group Selling Prices, or special Sale Prices can be printed by selecting Print Price List. Sales price tags could also be printed for use on the sales floor.

⑤ The user has opened the Price Groups dialog box to set up a new Electric Tools price group.

	Entered by user		Entered automatically

6 The system limits the length of some labels and sets their format. The Price Group label is formatted as all capital letters and is limited to ten characters, so the user has created the label ELEC TOOLS and entered its description.

7 Setting price levels allows the business to maintain different prices on the same inventory items. The user selected RETAIL. Values for Unit of Measure, Pricing Method, and Percent are entered automatically. The user wanted to see how the other price levels were set up and clicked on the **Price Level** label to open the Set Price Levels dialog box.

8 A merchandising business that sells to both wholesale and retail customers would have different price levels for each type of customer. Businesses might also sell to individual customers on a contract basis, where item prices are set by agreement with the customer.

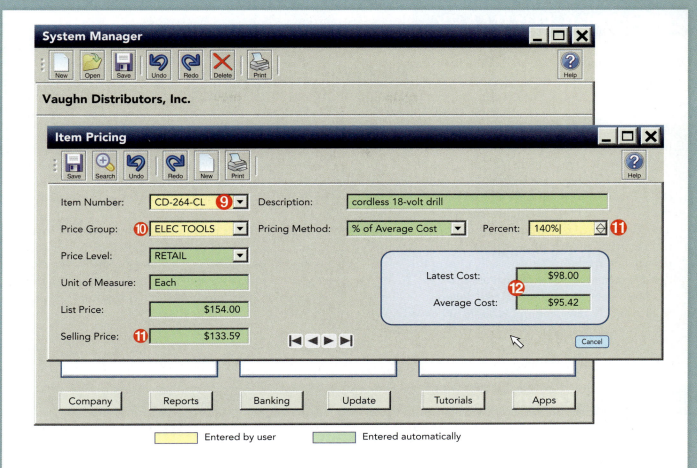

| Entered by user | | Entered automatically |

9 Having set up the ELEC TOOLS price group, the user returned to the Manage Pricing navigation pane and opened the Item Pricing dialog box. The user now is beginning the process of assigning individual inventory items to the new price group and has selected the cordless 18-volt drill.

10 When ELEC TOOLS is selected, the system populates all the other fields with their default values. These defaults can be changed by an authorized user. Price groups speed up the process of setting prices, and they maintain more uniformity in pricing.

11 The default Percent would have been entered as 160% (as seen in the Set Up Price Groups dialog box). If a sale were entered for this drill, the system would automatically use a selling price of $152.67 ($95.42 × 160%). Perhaps this drill has not sold well or a competitor is selling it for less. To reduce the regular selling price, the user changed Percent from 160% to 140%, and the selling price went down to $133.59 ($95.42 × 140%).

12 Computerized accounting systems maintain detailed records of the costs of each item purchased. Vaughn Distributors uses the FIFO method of inventory costing, and the accounting system maintains a perpetual inventory. Therefore, as each sale is made, the older items are deducted from inventory first. Also with each sale, the average cost of each item in inventory may change. This system displays both the average cost and the latest cost to assist the user in setting the item's price.

CHAPTER SUMMARY

The cost of merchandise sold is the largest expense of most retail merchandising businesses. The amount is determined by subtracting the cost assigned to the ending inventory from the total cost of merchandise available for sale. Any error in the calculation of the ending inventory also causes the cost of merchandise sold and net income to be misstated.

Generally accepted accounting principles allow the cost of merchandise inventory to be determined using the LIFO, FIFO, or weighted-average costing method. The cost assigned to each item in inventory is compared to its current market price. The amount of inventory reported on the balance sheet is the total of the lower of the cost or market value of each item.

The method used to cost merchandise inventory results in different amounts as unit prices increase or decrease. The LIFO method results in the lowest cost of merchandise inventory during an inflationary period. As a result, the LIFO method yields the highest cost of merchandise sold and the lowest net income of the three methods.

The LIFO method has not been universally accepted. U.S. tax law only allows the use of the LIFO method for tax reporting if the method is also used for financial reporting. International financial reporting standards do not permit the use of the LIFO method.

A business that does not maintain perpetual inventory records can use the gross profit method or retail method to estimate its merchandise inventory. Financial ratios used to analyze activity in merchandise inventory include the inventory turnover ratio and days' sales in inventory.

EXPLORE ACCOUNTING

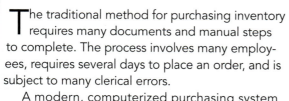

Computerized Purchasing Systems

The traditional method for purchasing inventory requires many documents and manual steps to complete. The process involves many employees, requires several days to place an order, and is subject to many clerical errors.

A modern, computerized purchasing system might work as follows: The company's computer continually monitors stock levels against minimum quantities established by management. When the quantity of any inventory item falls below its reorder point, the computer automatically sends a message to a vendor's computer with the order information. (Management frequently enters into long-term contracts with selected vendors that govern prices and delivery schedules.) The vendor's computer immediately informs its warehouse to ship the items. When the items are received, the company's computer sends a message to its bank's computer instructing the bank to transfer funds to the vendor's account.

The direct transfer of information between computers of two or more companies is called *electronic data interchange (EDI)*. EDI reduces the cost of placing an order by reducing paperwork and labor costs. The most important advantage, however, results from improved delivery times. The traditional manual ordering system required several days or weeks to process an order. An EDI system can have the order in transit on the same day the order is placed. Improved delivery time allows companies to reduce inventory levels, which results in substantial cost savings.

INSTRUCTIONS

Contact a local business and inquire if its computer system automatically contacts a vendor's computer with an order.

APPLY YOUR UNDERSTANDING

INSTRUCTIONS: Download problem instructions for Excel, QuickBooks, and Sage 50c from the textbook companion website at www.C21accounting.com.

5-1 Application Problem — Keeping perpetual inventory records LO2

Lambert Tools sells construction equipment to homebuilders. The company maintains a perpetual inventory system. Source documents are abbreviated as follows: purchase invoice, P; sales invoice, S.

Instructions:

1. Complete the heading of a stock record for the following inventory item: description, scaffolding; stock number A-32; reorder quantity, 60; minimum quantity, 15; and location, aisle 6. Lambert has 32 units on hand on May 1.
2. Record on the stock record the merchandise items received and sold during May of the current year.

Transactions:

May 2. Sold 9 units of scaffolding to Schmidt Construction. S322

3. Sold 10 units of scaffolding to Davidson Homebuilders. S333

11. Central State University bought 7 units of scaffolding. S348

12. Received 60 units of scaffolding from Betts Manufacturing. P195

15. Twenty more units of scaffolding were sold to Schmidt Construction. S352

19. Sold 25 units of scaffolding to Kisner Contracting. S360

25. Received 60 units of scaffolding from Betts Manufacturing. P199

5-2 Application Problem — Determining inventory cost using FIFO, LIFO, weighted-average, and lower of cost or market LO3, 5

sage 50

1. Journalize and post purchases of inventory in the Purchases/ Receive Inventory window.
2. Print the purchase journal, sales journal and item costing report.

QB Quick Books

1. Journalize and post purchases of inventory in the Enter Bills window.
2. From the menu bar, select Reports; Inventory.
3. Print the inventory valuation summary and inventory valuation detail reports.

X‍‍

1. Use the inventory costing methods to calculate year-end inventory.
2. Print the worksheet.

Forms containing the purchases and market prices of three inventory items of Bridges, Inc., are presented in the *Working Papers*. Units in the December 31 inventory and the market prices are shown below.

Stock Item	Quantity of Units on Hand	Market Price
B26	24	$ 6.90
C45	80	8.80
D55	18	11.75

Instructions:

1. For each item, calculate the inventory cost using the FIFO, LIFO, and weighted-average inventory costing methods. Identify whether the unit prices are increasing or decreasing. Identify whether each method results in the highest, lowest, or intermediate cost for ending inventory, cost of merchandise sold, and reported net income.
2. Assume that Bridges uses the FIFO method at the lower of cost or market. Complete the form in the *Working Papers* to determine the reported cost of the merchandise inventory.

5-3 Application Problem

Estimating cost of merchandise inventory; financial analysis of merchandise inventory LO6, 7

The following information is available for Cagle Company for the month of August. Estimated merchandise inventory sheets are provided in the *Working Papers*.

Item	Cost	Retail
Beginning inventory, August 1	$82,680.00	$173,690.00
Net purchases in August	26,150.00	54,930.00
Net sales in August		64,340.00
Gross profit percentage	52.4%	

Instructions:

1. Calculate the corporation's estimated ending inventory using the gross profit method of estimating inventory.
2. Calculate the corporation's estimated ending inventory using the retail method of estimating inventory. Round the percentage to the nearest 0.1%.
3. Cagle Company's inventory was $83,930.00 on January 1 and $82,750.00 on December 31. Cost of merchandise sold for the year was $369,940.00. Calculate the inventory turnover ratio and the days' sales in inventory. Round the inventory turnover ratio to two decimal places and the days' sales in inventory to the nearest day.

5-M Mastery Problem

Costing and financial analysis of merchandise inventory LO3, 5, 6, 7

Quick Books

1. Journalize and post purchases of inventory in the Enter Bills window.
2. From the menu bar, select Reports; Inventory.
3. Print the inventory valuation summary and inventory valuation detail reports.

1. Use the inventory costing methods to calculate year-end inventory.
2. Print the worksheet.

On December 31 of the current year, Covert, Inc., took a physical inventory. Units in the December 31 inventory and the market prices are shown below.

Stock Item	Quantity of Units on Hand	Market Price
1548-C	23	$10.05
5324-B	60	6.85
0234-H	21	8.45

Instructions:

1. Calculate the inventory costs using the FIFO, LIFO, and weighted-average inventory costing methods. Use the form in the *Working Papers*.
2. Covert uses the LIFO inventory costing method to determine the cost of inventory. Use the market price given in the form at the beginning of the problem to determine the cost of inventory using the lower of cost or market. Total the Lower of Cost or Market column. Use the form in the *Working Papers*.
3. Calculate the corporation's estimated ending inventory using the gross profit method of estimating inventory. The corporation's records show the following on December 31 of the current year.

Item	Cost	Retail
Beginning inventory, January 1	$ 64,120.00	$132,950.00
Net purchases for year	164,260.00	336,180.00
Net sales for year		392,480.00
Gross profit percentage	51.6%	

4. Calculate the corporation's estimated ending inventory using the retail method of estimating inventory. Round the percentage to the nearest 0.1%.

5. Use the information and the estimated inventory calculated using the gross profit method. Calculate the corporation's inventory turnover ratio. Round the ratio to two decimal places.

6. Calculate the corporation's days' sales in inventory. Round the amount to the nearest day.

5-C Challenge Problem · Financial analysis of merchandise inventory LO7

Selected information for three corporations follows.

	Corporation		
Item	A	B	C
Beginning merchandise inventory	$ 6,500.00	$ 121,510.00	$ 65,180.00
Ending merchandise inventory	6,200.00	116,480.00	68,350.00
Cost of merchandise sold	294,910.00	351,490.00	998,450.00

Instructions:

1. For each corporation, calculate the inventory turnover ratio. Round the ratio to two decimal places.

2. For each corporation, calculate the days' sales in inventory. Round the amount to the nearest day.

3. Using your knowledge of retail stores gained from being a consumer, identify which corporation is most likely a grocery store, a gas station, and an auto parts store.

Auditing for Errors LO6

On the evening of September 23, Douglass Music Store was heavily damaged by fire. Inventory with an estimated cost of $12,625.00 was salvaged. The remainder of the inventory was either burned or incurred heavy smoke damage. Many of the accounting records were also lost in the fire.

Based on the prior year's financial statements, Douglass began the fiscal year with inventory of $45,750.00. Using bank records, the company determined that its sales and inventory purchases through the date of the fire were $563,180.00 and $264,890.00, respectively. During the prior fiscal year, the company had a gross profit percentage of 53.8%.

Using this information, the bookkeeper prepared the following analysis to be submitted to the insurance company. Verify the numbers on the report, including the bookkeeper's additional items at the bottom of the report. List any errors and the correct amounts.

ESTIMATED MERCHANDISE INVENTORY SHEET
Gross Profit Method

DEPARTMENT **Douglas Music Store**   DATE   9/23/20--

1	Beginning inventory....................................		$ 45,750.00
2	Net purchases to date..................................		246,890.00
3	Merchandise available for sale		$292,640.00
4	Net sales to date	$563,180.00	
5	Less estimated gross profit	308,622.64	
	(Net sales × Estimated gross profit percentage _53.8_ %)		
6	Estimated cost of merchandise sold....................		254,557.36
7	Estimated ending inventory		$ 38,082.64
	Salvaged inventory		12,625.00
	Inventory lost in fire		26,457.64

A Shrinking Dilemma

PARTNERSHIP FOR
21ST CENTURY SKILLS

Theme: Financial, Economic, Business, and Entrepreneurial Literacy

Skills: Creativity and Innovation, Critical Thinking and Problem Solving, Communication and Collaboration, ICT Literacy

Inventory shrinkage, when the physical count of inventory is less than the accounting records, costs U.S. retailers over $48.9 billion a year. This shrinkage is approximately 1.44% of sales revenue. Lost profits have forced some retailers out of business.

There are four primary sources for inventory shrinkage in retail:

1. The major source of inventory shrinkage is shoplifting (36.5%). Shoplifting consists of altering price tags as well as removing the merchandise from the store by concealment.

2. The second source of inventory shrinkage is from employee theft (30.0%). Employees will often fake refunds, process fraudulent credit card sales, and manipulate inventory records.

3. The third source of inventory shrinkage is administrative errors (21.3%). Administrative errors include pricing mistakes and inaccuracies in paperwork.

4. The fourth source of inventory shrinkage is vendor fraud (5.4%). Vendor fraud consists of receiving smaller shipments than invoiced.

APPLICATION

1. Using the Internet, find at least five loss prevention strategies that you would implement for your retail establishment to reduce inventory shrinkage.

2. Write a letter to your manager, describing new strategies that you would suggest for reducing inventory shrinkage.

3. Shrinkage affects the profitability of a business, but it also affects others. Describe at least two other stakeholders that could be affected by inventory shrinkage. Explain.

Source: 2017 National Retail Security Survey, conducted by the University of Florida.

Analyzing Home Depot's Financial Statements

Most companies include information about inventory in the first note to the financial statements, *Summary of Significant Accounting Policies*. This note usually tells the reader which method the company uses to value the cost of its ending inventory.

INSTRUCTIONS

1. Using Note 1, beginning on page B-10 of Appendix B, locate the paragraph titled *Merchandise Inventories*. List the method Home Depot uses to value the majority of its merchandise inventory.

2. Identify the inventory turnover for each year reported in the Selected Financial Data on page B-20. Use the inventory turnover ratios to calculate the days' sales in inventory for each year.

3. Go to Home Depot's website (www.homedepot.com) and locate the financial statements for the most current year available. (Look for "Investor Relations" or a similar link.) Calculate Home Depot's inventory turnover ratio and days' sales in inventory for the most recent fiscal year.

4. Did these measures improve or worsen since fiscal year 2017?

6

Accounting for Uncollectible Accounts

LEARNING OBJECTIVES

After studying Chapter 6, in addition to defining key terms, you will be able to:

LO1 Record entries for uncollectible accounts using the direct write-off method.

LO2 Explain how to select a method for accounting for uncollectible accounts.

LO3 Record entries for uncollectible accounts expense using the allowance method.

LO4 Calculate the accounts receivable turnover ratio and days' sales in accounts receivable.

LO5 Analyze accounts receivable using the accounts receivable turnover ratio and days' sales in accounts receivable.

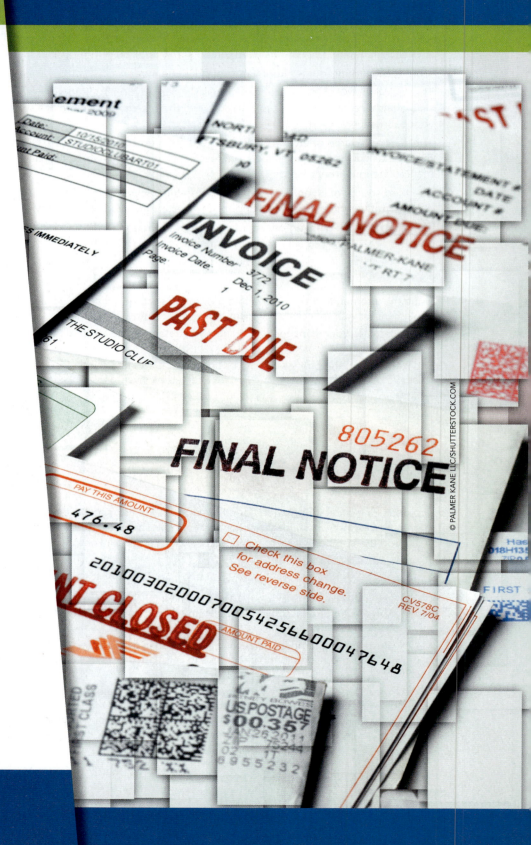

© PALMER KANE LLC/SHUTTERSTOCK.COM

Chesapeake Energy Corporation

ACCOUNTING IN THE REAL WORLD

CHESAPEAKE
ENERGY

OWNER RELATIONS   INVESTORS

LATEST PRESENTATION

We are focused on reducing debt, ir
and increasing cash flow generatio

SOURCE: CHESAPEAKE ENERGY CORPORATION

What comes to mind when you think of an oil company? Likely your first image is the local gas station. Maybe you recall a deep-water oil rig you have seen in one of several popular movies. Depending on where you live, you might be familiar with pipelines, oil refineries, or working wells. However, you may not be as familiar with the process that makes gas available to you as a consumer.

The supply chain that brings gas to your local service station has many distinct stages. It begins with the discovery of an oil field and then progresses to drilling for oil, transporting the oil to a refinery, refining the oil into gas, transporting the gas to stores, and selling the gas to the final consumer. The fact is, only a few of the world's largest oil companies are involved in all stages of the oil business, from exploration to the gas pump. Most oil companies focus on only one or two stages of the supply chain.

Chesapeake Energy Corporation focuses on the first stages of the supply chain. According to Chesapeake, its operations "are focused on discovering and developing its large and geographically diverse resource base of unconventional oil and natural gas assets onshore in the United States." In other words, Chesapeake sells oil, natural gas, and natural gas liquids to companies involved in refining and retail distribution.

Sales of its products on account result in accounts receivable. When sales are made on account it's possible that a customer will be unable to pay its account. Chesapeake uses a dual approach to reducing the probability of having an account become uncollectible. First, Chesapeake continually monitors the creditworthiness of its customers. More importantly, Chesapeake often requires the customer to have a letter of credit or parent guarantee to ensure timely payment. A letter of credit involves a customer entering into an arrangement with a financial institution to guarantee payment of the customer's account. A customer that is partially owned by another company, known as the parent company, might be required to have its parent company guarantee payment.

As a result of its efforts to monitor its customers, Chesapeake experiences a relatively small amount of bad debts. During 2017, 2016, and 2015, Chesapeake recorded $9 million, $10 million, and $4 million, respectively, of bad debt expense related to uncollectible receivables. Its allowance for uncollectible accounts, reflected in Accounts Receivable, Net, on the Consolidated Balance Sheets, was $30 and $32 million for 2017 and 2016, respectively.

Source: www.chk.com.

CRITICAL THINKING

1. What criteria could a credit manager use to assess the creditworthiness of a potential new customer?

2. Chesapeake's balance sheet presents accounts receivable net of the allowance for uncollectible accounts. The amount of the allowance is only shown in the notes to the financial statements. Do you agree with this presentation? Support your answer.

KEY TERMS

uncollectible accounts
writing off an account
direct write-off method
allowance method

book value
aging accounts receivable
accounts receivable turnover ratio
days' sales in accounts receivable

Direct Write-Off Method of Recording Uncollectible Accounts

LO1 Record entries for uncollectible accounts using the direct write-off method.

Accounting for Losses from Uncollectible Accounts LO1

Many business transactions are completed on account rather than for cash. Businesses offer credit terms to attract new customers, increase sales to current customers, and encourage customer loyalty. Before a business sells merchandise on account, it should investigate the customer's credit rating to ensure that the customer will pay promptly.

Regardless of the care taken in granting credit, some customers will not pay when payment is due. Accounts receivable that cannot be collected are called **uncollectible accounts**. Uncollectible accounts are sometimes referred to as *bad debts*.

When a business makes a sale on account to a customer, it records the amount in a general ledger account

titled Accounts Receivable. The amount remains recorded in this asset account until it is paid or until it is specifically known to be uncollectible.

When a customer account is believed to be uncollectible, it should be removed from the company's books. An uncollectible account should be canceled and removed from the assets of the business. Canceling the balance of a customer account because the customer does not pay is called **writing off an account**.

Occasionally, an account that has been written off is collected. The account balance is restored and the receipt of cash is recorded. A complete history of the transactions for each customer is maintained.

ETHICS IN ACTION

Integrity in Management Accounting

The Institute of Management Accountants (IMA) is an organization dedicated to providing its members with professional development opportunities in management accounting, financial management, and information management. The institute supports lifelong learning by its members through self-study courses, seminars, conferences, and webcasts. Members are encouraged to demonstrate their knowledge by becoming a Certified Management Accountant (CMA).

An important element of the IMA's mission is to encourage its members and their organizations to

adopt ethical business practices. The IMA's *Statement of Ethical Professional Practice* states that IMA members must act ethically. Specific guidance is provided in the areas of competence, confidentiality, integrity, and credibility.

INSTRUCTIONS

Access the IMA's *Statement of Ethical Professional Practice*. What does the IMA state related to integrity?

Source: www.imanet.org.

Recording Uncollectible Accounts Expense—Direct Write-Off Method

	DATE	ACCOUNT TITLE	DOC. NO.	POST. REF.	DEBIT	CREDIT	
		GENERAL JOURNAL				**PAGE 11**	
4	4	*Uncollectible Accounts Expense*	M62		1 8 2 00		4
5		*Accounts Receivable/Plaza Electronics*				1 8 2 00	5
6							6

An amount owed by a specific customer is part of the Accounts Receivable account balance until it is paid or is written off as uncollectible. An uncollectible account is closed by transferring the balance to a general ledger account titled Uncollectible Accounts Expense.

Riverside Café operates a restaurant and catering business. Most of Riverside's sales are made for cash or are paid with a credit card. Riverside periodically makes a sale on account to cater an event for a business customer. Riverside has a small number of accounts receivable and very few of these accounts become uncollectible. Therefore, Riverside records uncollectible accounts expense only when a specific account is actually known to be uncollectible. Recording uncollectible accounts expense only when an amount is actually known to be uncollectible is called the **direct write-off method** of recording losses from uncollectible accounts.

On November 4, Riverside Café learned that Plaza Electronics is unable to pay its account. Riverside decides that Plaza Electronics' account is uncollectible.

> November 4. Wrote off Plaza Electronics' account as uncollectible, $182.00. Memorandum No. 62.

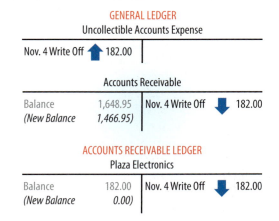

After this entry is journalized and posted, the balance of Accounts Receivable no longer includes the $182.00 as part of the business's assets. Also, Plaza Electronics' account has a zero balance and is written off.

THINK LIKE AN ACCOUNTANT

Evaluating Credit Policies

Sales at Petaland Company had been increasing only modestly in past years. New management believed it could accelerate sales growth best by loosening its credit requirements for customers. Now three years later, the board of directors has requested an analysis of how the new credit policy has impacted sales and the collection of receivables.

OPEN THE TABLEAU WORKBOOK TLA_CH06

The Tableau workbook contains sales and collection data for a three-year period. Read the caption above each chart to gain an understanding

of the data presented. Use the charts to answer the following questions.

1. Review the Sales by Credit Score worksheet. How does the credit score appear to impact sales and gross profit?

2. Based on the Collections by Credit Score worksheet, should the company restrict its credit requirements by requiring a higher credit score?

3. Review the Collections by Score Change worksheet. Is there any evidence that there is a relationship between account collections and a change in a customer's credit score?

Collecting a Written-Off Account—Direct Write-Off Method

Reopen the Account ❶

Record the Cash Receipt ❷

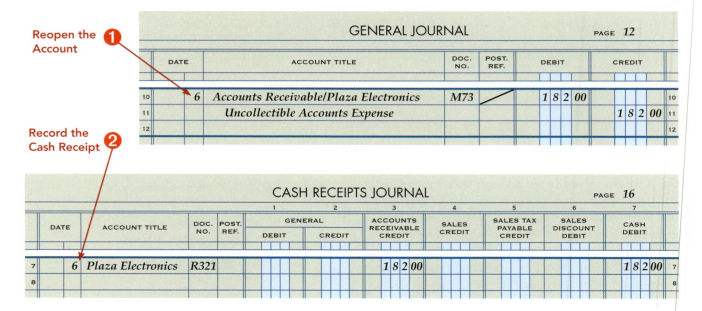

A business should continue its efforts to collect an account even after it has been written off. If the account is later collected, a credit is recorded to Uncollectible Accounts Expense. The credit offsets the debit recorded when the account was written off. The write-off and collection also result in no impact on the balance of Uncollectible Accounts Expense.

> **December 6.** Received cash in full payment of Plaza Electronics' account, previously written off as uncollectible, $182.00. Memorandum No. 73 and Receipt No. 321.

Riverside Café needs a complete history of each customer's credit activities. Therefore, two journal entries are recorded for the collection of a written-off account receivable as shown above.

1. A general journal entry to reopen the customer account.
2. A cash receipts journal entry to record the cash received on account.

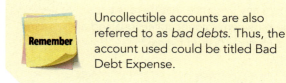

Uncollectible accounts are also referred to as *bad debts*. Thus, the account used could be titled Bad Debt Expense.

Remember

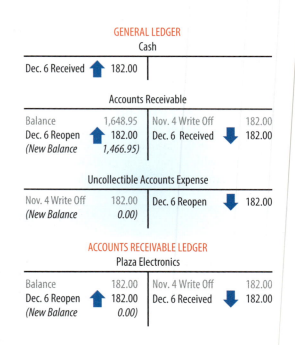

GENERAL LEDGER
Cash

Dec. 6 Received ⬆	182.00		

Accounts Receivable

Balance	1,648.95	Nov. 4 Write Off	182.00
Dec. 6 Reopen ⬆	182.00	Dec. 6 Received ⬇	182.00
(New Balance	1,466.95)		

Uncollectible Accounts Expense

Nov. 4 Write Off	182.00	Dec. 6 Reopen ⬇	182.00
(New Balance	0.00)		

ACCOUNTS RECEIVABLE LEDGER
Plaza Electronics

Balance	182.00	Nov. 4 Write Off	182.00
Dec. 6 Reopen ⬆	182.00	Dec. 6 Received ⬇	182.00
(New Balance	0.00)		

>> **Collecting a Written-Off Account Using the Direct Write-Off Method**

❶ Record an entry in the general journal to debit **Accounts Receivable/Plaza Electronics** and credit **Uncollectible Accounts Expense** for the amount of the receipt, **$182.00**.

❷ Record an entry in the cash receipts journal to debit **Cash** and credit **Accounts Receivable** for the amount of the receipt, **$182.00**.

LO1 Record entries for uncollectible accounts using the direct write-off method.

TERMS REVIEW

uncollectible accounts

writing off an account

direct write-off method

Audit your understanding LO1

1. Why should the amount of an uncollectible account be removed from the assets of a business?
2. In the direct write-off method, how is an uncollectible account closed?
3. Why is the customer account reopened when cash is received for an account previously written off as uncollectible?

Work together 6-1 LO1

Journalizing entries to write off uncollectible accounts—direct write-off method

Winters, Inc., uses the direct write-off method of recording uncollectible accounts expense. A general journal and a cash receipts journal are provided in the *Working Papers*. Use page 2 of a general journal and page 4 of a cash receipts journal. Source documents are abbreviated as follows: memorandum, M; receipt, R. Your instructor will guide you through the following examples.

Transactions:

Feb. 3. Wrote off Loper Company's past due account as uncollectible, $115.81. M33.

Apr. 24. Wrote off Polk Supply's past due account as uncollectible, $95.00. M42.

May 14. Received cash in full payment of Loper Company's account, previously written off as uncollectible, $115.81. M51 and R221.

June 8. Received cash in full payment of Polk Supply's account, previously written off as uncollectible, $95.00. M64 and R259.

On your own 6-1 LO1

Journalizing entries to write off uncollectible accounts—direct write-off method

NorthStar, Inc., uses the direct write-off method of recording uncollectible accounts expense. A general journal and a cash receipts journal are provided in the *Working Papers*. Use page 1 of a general journal and page 3 of a cash receipts journal. Source documents are abbreviated as follows: memorandum, M; receipt, R. Work this problem independently.

Transactions:

Jan. 14. Wrote off Sylvia Mendoza's past due account as uncollectible, $92.45. M25.

Feb. 12. Wrote off Conisha Martin's past due account as uncollectible, $62.48. M31.

June 20. Received cash in full payment of Sylvia Mendoza's account, previously written off as uncollectible, $92.45. M54 and R148.

Aug. 25. Received cash in full payment of Conisha Martin's account, previously written off as uncollectible, $62.48. M89 and R195.

LO2 Explain how to select a method for accounting for uncollectible accounts.

LO3 Record entries for uncollectible accounts expense using the allowance method.

Selecting a Method for Accounting for Uncollectible Accounts LO2

The direct write-off method of recording losses from uncollectible accounts is easy to apply. A business that uses this method only records the expense when a specific customer account is determined to be uncollectible. Thus, the expense may be recorded in a fiscal period different from the period of the sale. For this reason, the direct write-off method usually is not allowed under generally accepted accounting principles.

Uncollectible accounts expense should be recorded in the same fiscal period in which the sales revenue is received. >> App. A: Matching Expenses with Revenue However, at the time sales on account are made, a business has no way to know for sure which customer will not pay an amount due. Therefore, the business makes an estimate based on its past history of uncollectible accounts. Crediting the estimated value of uncollectible accounts to a contra account is called the **allowance method** of recording losses from uncollectible accounts.

Business activities creating dollar amounts large enough to affect business decisions should be recorded in the accounting records using generally accepted accounting principles. [Business Concept: Materiality] An item that is not large enough to affect business decisions is referred to as being *immaterial*.

Accounts receivable must be reported on the balance sheet at their net realizable value. Only the allowance method achieves this reporting objective. However, a business can use the direct write-off method if the difference between using the two methods is immaterial.

Businesses having a small number and dollar amount of accounts receivable may be able to use the direct write-off method. Riverside Café, the business in Lesson 6-1, uses the direct write-off method. Most of its customers pay with cash or a credit card. Riverside only accepts credit sales for catering events with business customers. Thus, Riverside has a small number of accounts receivable and very few of these accounts become uncollectible.

Estimating Uncollectible Accounts Expense Using the Allowance Method LO3

Two methods are commonly used to estimate uncollectible accounts expense:

1. Percentage of sales method.
2. Percentage of accounts receivable method.

The percentage of sales method assumes that a percentage of each sales dollar will become an uncollectible account. The percentage of accounts receivable method assumes that a percentage of accounts receivable at the fiscal year-end will become uncollectible. Regardless of

the method used, the estimated amount is charged to Uncollectible Accounts Expense.

The difference between an asset's account balance and its related contra account balance is called **book value**. The book value of accounts receivable, reported on the balance sheet, represents an estimate of the total amount of accounts receivable the business expects to collect. When the accounts receivable are collected, the actual amount collected is said to have been realized. For this reason, the book value is often referred to as the *net realizable value*.

Adjustment Using the Percentage of Sales Method

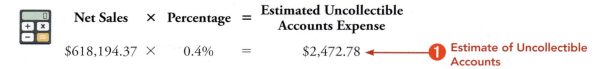

$$\text{Net Sales} \times \text{Percentage} = \text{Estimated Uncollectible Accounts Expense}$$

$$\$618,194.37 \times 0.4\% = \$2,472.78 \quad \longleftarrow \quad \textbf{1} \text{ Estimate of Uncollectible Accounts}$$

GENERAL JOURNAL   PAGE *16*

	DATE		ACCOUNT TITLE	DOC. NO.	POST. REF.	DEBIT	CREDIT	
1			*Adjusting Entries*					1
2	Dec.	31	*Uncollectible Accounts Expense*	M62		2 4 7 2 78		2
3			*Allowance for Uncollectible Accounts*				2 4 7 2 78	3
4								4

2 Adjusting Entry

Past experience of Noland Company indicates that approximately 0.4% of its net sales will prove to be uncollectible. On December 31, Noland estimated that 0.4% of its $618,194.37 net sales, $2,472.78, eventually will prove to be uncollectible.

At the end of a fiscal period, an adjustment for uncollectible accounts expense is journalized on the general journal. Before the adjustment is made, Noland's general ledger shows **Allowance for Uncollectible Accounts** with a $225.60 credit balance. This balance is what remains of estimates made in previous fiscal periods but not yet specifically identified by customer. The new balance, $2,698.38, is an estimate of the accounts receivable that will become uncollectible.

The balance of **Allowance for Uncollectible Accounts** may increase from year to year. A large increase may indicate that an incorrect percentage is being used to calculate the uncollectible amount. When this occurs, a new percentage should be calculated based on actual experience for the past two or three years. Other factors, such as an economic downturn, may cause a business to change the percentage.

Regardless of the percentage used, the estimate of the **Allowance for Uncollectible Accounts** must result in a reasonable and unbiased estimate of the money a business expects to collect in the future. A business must not change any estimate to achieve some other goal, such as reducing net income to avoid income taxes. It must make accounting estimates that are free from bias.
>> App. A: Neutrality

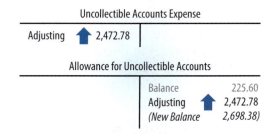

Uncollectible Accounts Expense

Adjusting ⬆ 2,472.78

Allowance for Uncollectible Accounts

Balance	225.60
Adjusting ⬆	2,472.78
(New Balance	*2,698.38)*

>> Estimating Uncollectible Accounts Expense by Using the Percentage of Sales Method

1 Compute the estimated uncollectible accounts expense by multiplying net sales, $618,194.37, by the percentage estimate, 0.4%, which equals $2,472.78.

2 Record a debit to **Uncollectible Accounts Expense** and a credit to **Allowance for Uncollectible Accounts** for the amount of $2,472.78.

FYI A company can elect to base its estimate of uncollectible accounts expense on a percentage of total sales on account. The calculation of the allowance amount is the same as when total net sales is used.

Aging of Accounts Receivable

Customer	Account Balance	Current	Days Account Balance Past Due			
			1–30	31–60	61–90	Over 90
Anderson Stores	$ 3,670.92	$ 2,184.61	$1,486.31			
Campbell Hardware	2,769.05		2,084.36	$ 684.69		
Vance Corporation	495.31					$ 495.31
Wallis Supply	1,068.68				$1,068.68	
York Tools	5,227.38	4,162.68	1,064.70			
	$31,098.44	$12,914.68	$8,436.81	$3,481.69	$2,084.31	$4,180.95
Percentages		2.0%	5.0%	10.0%	40.0%	80.0%

The percentage of accounts receivable method assumes that a percentage of the Accounts Receivable account balance is uncollectible. Therefore, emphasis is placed on estimating a percentage of accounts receivable that will not be collected. An amount that will bring the balance of Allowance for Uncollectible Accounts up to the estimated amount is recorded in that account.

Analyzing accounts receivable according to when they are due is called **aging accounts receivable**. Vaughn Distributors, Inc., ages accounts receivable at the end of each fiscal period, as shown above, to provide information for the uncollectible accounts expense adjustment. Vaughn sells on terms of 2/10, n/30. Vaughn offers customers a 2% discount for paying within 10 days. Vaughn expects customers to pay in full within 30 days.

FINANCIAL LITERACY

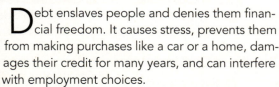

Avoid Debt Distress

Debt enslaves people and denies them financial freedom. It causes stress, prevents them from making purchases like a car or a home, damages their credit for many years, and can interfere with employment choices.

One of the leading reasons for debt problems in the United States is credit cards. Total credit card debt in the United States is estimated at $931 billion, while the average household has $15,983 in credit card debt. Credit cards are not bad when used appropriately. However, some of the following tactics used by credit card companies are often the culprits for excessive debt.

- Minimum monthly payment—Paying a minimum monthly payment allows the balance to grow steadily with interest charges.
- Low introductory rate—This gimmick will hook you and then switch your lower rate to a much higher rate, resulting in more interest charges.

- Fees—Many credit card companies tack on late payment fees, even if you are only a day late.
- Universal default—Sometimes your credit card company will increase your interest rate, based on one late payment with another company.

ACTIVITIES

1. Search through local newspapers or on the Internet for three advertisements that use any of these tactics. Share with the class.

2. Obtain three different credit card applications. Read the fine print on the application. Then, draw a Venn diagram to compare/contrast the similarities and differences in interest rate, introductory interest rate, fees, universal default rules, and amount of minimum payment.

Source: www.247wallst.com.

Calculating the Adjustment Amount Using Percentage of Accounts Receivable

Age Group	Amount	Percentage	Uncollectible	
Current	$12,914.68	2.0%	$ 258.29	
1–30	8,436.81	5.0%	421.84	
31–60	3,481.69	10.0%	348.17	➊ Estimate for Each Age Group
61–90	2,084.31	40.0%	833.72	
Over 90	4,180.95	80.0%	3,344.76	
	$31,098.44		$5,206.78	➋ Total Estimate
Current Balance of Allowance for Uncollectible Accounts			308.64	
Estimated Addition to Allowance for Uncollectible Accounts			$4,898.14	➌ Addition to Allowance Account

Vaughn Distributors expects customers to pay in full within 30 days. If Vaughn has not received cash within 30 days, it mails reminders to the customers. If the business has not collected an amount from a customer after 90 days, it may stop selling on account to that customer until collection has been made.

Vaughn determines that a percentage of each accounts receivable age group will become uncollectible in the future. The percentages are based on past collection history and adjusted for current economic conditions. For example, 10.0% of the accounts receivable overdue 31–60 days will probably become uncollectible.

Using these percentages, Vaughn calculates the total amount of estimated uncollectible accounts receivable, as shown above. Of the total accounts receivable on December 31, $31,098.44, the business estimates that $5,206.78 will prove to be uncollectible in the future.

Vaughn's general ledger shows that Allowance for Uncollectible Accounts has a $308.64 credit balance. This balance is what remains of estimates made in previous fiscal periods but not yet specifically identified by customer. The allowance account is increased by a $4,898.14 credit. The new balance of the allowance account, $5,206.78 (previous balance, $308.64, plus adjustment, $4,898.14), equals the estimate of uncollectible accounts.

> **Estimating the Balance of Uncollectible Accounts Expense Using the Percentage of Accounts Receivable Method**

➊ Compute the estimate for each age group. Multiply the amount of each age group by the percentage estimate.

➋ Compute the total, **$5,206.78**, of the uncollectible estimates.

➌ Subtract the current balance, **$308.64**, from the total estimate to determine the addition to the allowance account, **$4,898.14**. (If the allowance account has a debit balance, add the current balance to the total estimate.)

FYI

A *credit rating* is an evaluation of the willingness and ability of an individual or a business to pay debts on a timely basis. Credit ratings are maintained by a several credit bureaus.

Writing Off an Uncollectible Account—Allowance Method

		GENERAL JOURNAL						PAGE 1	
	DATE	ACCOUNT TITLE	DOC. NO.	POST. REF.		DEBIT		CREDIT	
4	23	*Allowance for Uncollectible Accounts*	M121			4 9 5 31			4
5		*Accounts Receivable/Vance Corporation*		/				4 9 5 31	5
6									6

The procedures for writing off an account are the same regardless of the method used to calculate the estimated uncollectible accounts expense. When a specific customer account is thought to be uncollectible, the account balance is written off as shown above. Vaughn Distributors, Inc., determined that Vance Corporation will probably not pay the amount it owes, $495.31. The balance is no longer estimated to be uncollectible; it is actually determined to be uncollectible.

> **January 23. Wrote off Vance Corporation's past due account as uncollectible, $495.31. Memorandum No. 121.**

After this entry is journalized and posted, Vance Corporation's account has a zero balance. Uncollectible Accounts Expense is not affected by this entry.

Vaughn did not notify Vance Corporation that it wrote off its account. Although Vaughn believes the account is probably uncollectible, it may continue its attempts to collect the account. In some cases, customers do subsequently pay accounts that have been written off.

In a previous fiscal period, an adjusting entry was recorded for estimated uncollectible accounts expense resulting in an Allowance for Uncollectible Accounts balance of $5,206.78. This balance is the estimated amount of uncollectible accounts. The $495.31 debit entry in this account removes an actual amount that is no longer estimated. As shown in the next column, the book value of accounts receivable is not affected by writing off an account.

GENERAL LEDGER

Allowance for Uncollectible Accounts

Jan. 23 Write off	495.31	Balance	5,206.78
		(New Balance	4,711.47)

Accounts Receivable

Balance	31,098.44	Jan. 23 Write off	495.31
(New Balance	30,603.13)		

ACCOUNTS RECEIVABLE LEDGER

Vance Corporation

Balance	495.31	Jan. 23 Write off	495.31
(New Balance	0.00)		

	Before Account Written Off	After Account Written Off
Accounts Receivable	$31,098.44	$30,603.13
Allowance for Uncollectible Accounts	5,206.78	4,711.47
Book Value	$25,891.66	$25,891.66

> **FYI**
>
> Proper internal control requires that the custody, recording, and authority for a transaction be segregated. The employee responsible for writing off an account should not also have access to the cash received from customers paying their accounts.

Collecting a Written-Off Account—Allowance Method

Reopen the Account **1**

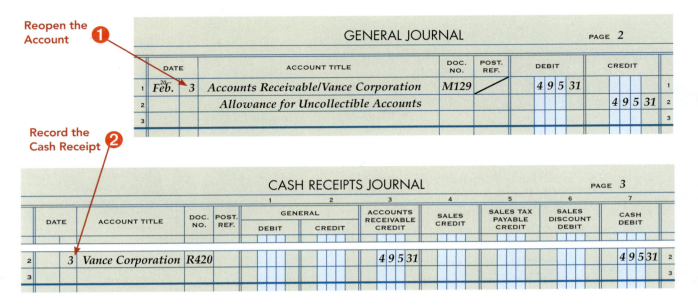

GENERAL JOURNAL PAGE 2

	DATE		ACCOUNT TITLE	DOC. NO.	POST. REF.	DEBIT	CREDIT	
1	Feb. ²⁰⁻⁻	3	Accounts Receivable/Vance Corporation	M129	✓	4 9 5 31		1
2			Allowance for Uncollectible Accounts				4 9 5 31	2
3								3

Record the Cash Receipt **2**

CASH RECEIPTS JOURNAL PAGE 3

					1	2	3	4	5	6	7	
	DATE	ACCOUNT TITLE	DOC. NO.	POST. REF.	GENERAL DEBIT	GENERAL CREDIT	ACCOUNTS RECEIVABLE CREDIT	SALES CREDIT	SALES TAX PAYABLE CREDIT	SALES DISCOUNT DEBIT	CASH DEBIT	
2	3	Vance Corporation	R420				4 9 5 31				4 9 5 31	2
3												3

February 3. Received cash in full payment of Vance Corporation's account, previously written off as uncollectible, $495.31. Memorandum No. 129 and Receipt No. 420.

GENERAL LEDGER

Cash

Feb. 3 Received ⬆	495.31	

Accounts Receivable

Balance	31,098.44	Jan. 23 Write off	495.31	
Feb. 3 Reopen ⬆	495.31	Feb. 3 Received ⬇	495.31	
(New Balance	30,603.13)			

Allowance for Uncollectible Accounts

Jan. 23 Write off	495.31	Balance	5,206.78	
		Feb. 3 Reopen ⬆	495.31	
		(New Balance	5,206.78)	

ACCOUNTS RECEIVABLE LEDGER

Vance Corporation

Balance	495.31	Jan. 23 Write off	495.31	
Feb. 3 Reopen ⬆	495.31	Feb. 3 Received ⬇	495.31	
(New Balance	0.00)			

Later in the year, Vaughn Distributors received a check in full payment of the amount owed by Vance Corporation.

Vaughn Distributors' records must show a complete history of Vance Corporation's credit dealings. The collection of a written-off account receivable involves two journal entries as shown above.

A general journal entry is recorded to reopen the customer account. The $495.31 debit increases Accounts Receivable and Vance Corporation's account in the accounts receivable ledger. The account balances now appear as they were before Vance Corporation's account was written off as uncollectible.

The cash received from Vance Corporation is then recorded in the cash receipts journal. The $495.31 credit decreases Accounts Receivable and Vance Corporation's account in the accounts receivable ledger.

Remember

Entries for the collection of a written-off account present evidence of the customer's credit history. Managers can use this information to make informed decisions about extending credit to the customer in the future.

>> Journalizing the Collection of a Written-Off Account—Allowance Method

1 Reopen the account by debiting Accounts Receivable and crediting Allowance for Uncollectible Accounts for the amount of the receipt, **$495.31**.

2 Record an entry in the cash receipts journal to debit Cash and credit Accounts Receivable for the amount of the receipt, **$495.31**.

Careers In Accounting

Abu Sarr
Accounting Advisory Specialist

Abu Sarr works for a major international accounting firm, but he does not perform audits. He is an accounting advisory specialist who is part of a large staff of consultants that provide advisory services to businesses. His company offers advisory services in many areas, including accounting, risk management, performance improvement, tax, global expansion, and corporate leadership and development.

Abu graduated from a public college with a degree in accounting. He went to work in a regional public accounting firm, where he served as a junior accountant for three years. During that time, he became a CPA. He was hired by his current company in an entry-level accounting consulting position. After four years with the company, he was promoted to a senior consultant.

Abu has worked in many areas, including lease financing and the implementation of International Financial Reporting Standards (IFRS). Most recently, he has concentrated on mergers and acquisitions (M&A). In M&A, he helps companies make decisions about what companies to acquire and how to organize the merged companies. Because most M&As are quite complex, he works on a team with investment bankers, lawyers, financial analysts, tax specialists, and other consultants.

Abu took public speaking while in college and feels that this skill is very beneficial in his current position. He often must present complex issues to his clients and do so at a level that the client will understand.

Salary Range: Salaries for senior managers in the management services area average $103,500 to $210,250.

Qualifications: Extensive accounting knowledge, usually including the CPA designation, is required. In addition, the consultant must have excellent communication and presentation skills and must be able to work effectively in a team environment.

Occupational Outlook: As a career area, accounting is expected to experience faster than average growth (10% to 14%) from 2016 to 2026.

Sources: www.onetonline.org; Robert Half 2017 Salary Guide.

LO2 Explain how to select a method for accounting for uncollectible accounts.

LO3 Record entries for uncollectible accounts expense using the allowance method.

TERMS REVIEW

allowance method

book value

aging accounts receivable

Audit your understanding LO2, 3

1. What would justify a business to use the direct write-off method rather than the allowance method?
2. What are the two methods commonly used to estimate uncollectible accounts expense using the allowance method?
3. What is the formula for estimating uncollectible accounts expense based on net sales?
4. How is the addition to allowance for uncollectible accounts calculated using the percentage of accounts receivable method?
5. What is the impact on Uncollectible Accounts Expense when writing off an account using the allowance method?
6. Compare the journal entries to collect an account that was written off using the direct write-off and allowance methods.

Work together 6-2 LO3

Estimating amount of uncollectible accounts expense; journalizing the adjusting entry General journals and a cash receipts journal are provided in the *Working Papers*. Your instructor will guide you through the following independent examples.

1. Lycum, Inc., had net sales of $642,453.29 during the current year ended December 31. It estimates that the amount of uncollectible accounts expense is equal to 0.8% of net sales. Record the adjusting entry for uncollectible accounts expense on December 31.
2. The aging of accounts receivable for Rollins, Inc., as of December 31 of the current year and estimated percentages of uncollectible accounts by age group are presented in the *Working Papers*. Calculate the estimated balance of Allowance for Uncollectible Accounts. Record the adjusting entry for uncollectible accounts expense. The balance of Allowance for Uncollectible Accounts on December 31 before adjusting entries are recorded is a $148.68 debit.
3. Journalize the following transactions completed during the current year.

   Transactions:
   Jan.   6. Wrote off Marcia Ayers' past due account as uncollectible, $621.23. Memorandum No. 225.
   Apr. 14. Received cash in full payment of Marcia Ayers' account, previously written off as uncollectible, $621.23. Memorandum No. 259 and Receipt No. 630.

On your own 6-2 LO3

Estimating amount of uncollectible accounts expense; journalizing the adjusting entry General journals and a cash receipts journal are provided in the *Working Papers*. Work this problem independently.

1. Goodrum, Inc., had net sales of $868,540.95 during the current year ended December 31. It estimates that the amount of uncollectible accounts expense is equal to 0.6% of net sales. Record the adjusting entry for uncollectible accounts expense.
2. The aging of accounts receivable for Nichols Supply is presented in the *Working Papers*. Record the adjusting entry for uncollectible accounts expense. The balance of Allowance for Uncollectible Accounts on December 31 before adjusting entries are recorded is a $248.68 credit.
3. Journalize the following transactions completed during the current year.

   Transactions:
   Jan.   4. Wrote off Patricia Webb's past due account as uncollectible, $492.16. Memorandum No. 123.
   Mar. 29. Received a partial payment on Patricia Webb's account, previously written off as uncollectible, $200.00. Memorandum No. 162 and Receipt No. 456.

LESSON 6-3

Financial Analysis of Accounts Receivable

LO4 Calculate the accounts receivable turnover ratio and days' sales in accounts receivable.

LO5 Analyze accounts receivable using the accounts receivable turnover ratio and days' sales in accounts receivable.

Accounts Receivable Ratios LO4

A business needs cash to purchase additional merchandise and pay for operating expenses. If it does not collect amounts due from customers promptly, too large a share of the assets of the business will be in accounts receivable and not immediately usable. A business selling on account needs prompt collection from credit customers.

Accounts Receivable Turnover Ratio

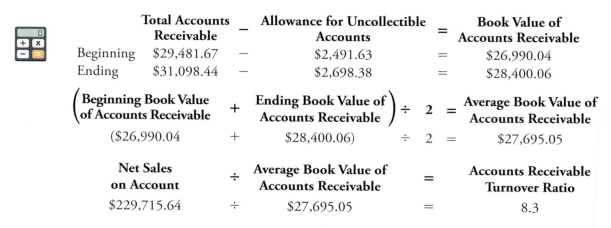

	Total Accounts Receivable	−	Allowance for Uncollectible Accounts	=	Book Value of Accounts Receivable
Beginning	$29,481.67	−	$2,491.63	=	$26,990.04
Ending	$31,098.44	−	$2,698.38	=	$28,400.06

$$\left(\begin{array}{c}\text{Beginning Book Value}\\\text{of Accounts Receivable}\end{array} + \begin{array}{c}\text{Ending Book Value of}\\\text{Accounts Receivable}\end{array}\right) \div 2 = \begin{array}{c}\text{Average Book Value of}\\\text{Accounts Receivable}\end{array}$$

$$(\$26,990.04 + \$28,400.06) \div 2 = \$27,695.05$$

Net Sales on Account	÷	Average Book Value of Accounts Receivable	=	Accounts Receivable Turnover Ratio
$229,715.64	÷	$27,695.05	=	8.3

The number of times the average amount of accounts receivable is collected during a specified period is called the **accounts receivable turnover ratio**. The accounts receivable turnover ratio is calculated by dividing net sales on account by the average book value of accounts receivable. Vaughn Distributors' accounts receivable turnover ratio is calculated as shown above.

An accounts receivable turnover ratio of 8.3 times means that Vaughn Distributors turns over (or collects) its average accounts receivable 8.3 times a year.

Days' Sales in Accounts Receivable

The average period of time to collect an account receivable is called the **days' sales in accounts receivable**. The ratio is also referred to as *days' sales outstanding*. The days' sales in accounts receivable based on an 8.3 accounts receivable turnover ratio is calculated as shown in the next column.

Days in Year	÷	Accounts Receivable Turnover Ratio	=	Days' Sales in Accounts Receivable
365	÷	8.3	=	44

The number of days' sales in accounts receivable is rounded to the nearest day. This level of accuracy provides managers with adequate information to make sound business decisions.

The terms of sale a business offers its credit customers influence its days' sales in accounts receivable. Vaughn offers 2/10, n/30 terms to its credit customers. Thus, Vaughn expects most of its customers to take advantage of the 2% discount and pay within 10 days. Some customers pay the net amount in 30 days and others have past due accounts. The longer time required to collect these accounts explains why Vaughn's average collection period is 44 days.

Analyzing Accounts Receivable Ratios LO5

Year	20X1	20X2	20X3	20X4	20X5	20X6	20X7
Accounts receivable turnover ratio	7.4	7.5	7.7	7.5	7.9	8.2	8.3
Days' sales in accounts receivable	49	49	47	49	46	45	44

The accounts receivable turnover ratio and days' sales in accounts receivable enable a business to analyze how frequently customers make payments on account. If customers are not paying promptly, the business can adopt new procedures to encourage more prompt collections.

From 20X1 through 20X7, Vaughn Distributors' accounts receivable turnover ratio increased from 7.4 to 8.3 times, as shown above. In 20X1, customers took an average of 49 days to pay their accounts in full. In 20X7, customers took an average of 44 days to pay their accounts in full, 5 days less than in 20X1.

With the exception of 20X4, the turnover ratio has been steadily increasing. On the average, customers have been paying their accounts in five fewer days over the seven-year period. Vaughn wants this favorable trend to continue.

However, Vaughn's days' sales in accounts receivable is still higher than would be expected. With 2/10,

n/30 credit terms, a minimum goal should be to have a turnover ratio of 12.0 times (365 days/12.0 accounts receivable turnover ratio equals an average of 30 days for payment). The business might take several steps to create a more favorable accounts receivable turnover ratio.

1. Send account statements to customers more often, including a request for prompt payment.
2. Not sell on account to any customer who has an account for which payment is overdue more than 30 days.
3. Conduct a more rigorous credit check on new customers before extending credit to them.

Sometimes the demand for quicker payment can result in a loss of business. Some customers might start buying from competitors. A business must weigh a change in credit policies against the effect the change will have on total sales.

WHY ACCOUNTING?

Cost of Preventing Workplace Injuries

Health Science

Public health professionals in Minnesota worked with Minnesota teachers to develop a curriculum targeted to the health and safety of adolescents (under age 18) in the workplace. The curriculum, called *Work Safe Work Smart,* describes ways to protect the employee, such as adequate training, protective gear, and using shields and guards with dangerous machinery.

Steps taken to prevent workplace injuries usually come with a price tag. How much the employer is willing to pay to prevent injuries is dependent on a number of factors, including the likelihood of injury, the seriousness of the possible injury, the cost of preventive measures, and the losses that the

company would incur if an injury occurs. Company personnel from many areas, such as accounting, human resources, risk management, operations, and upper management, need to work together to calculate these costs and determine what preventive measures to take.

CRITICAL THINKING

Select a workplace (yours or a friend's or relative's) and identify its required work safety procedures/equipment. Explain why you think these procedures/equipment are or are not useful.

Sources: www.health.state.mn.us.

LO4 Calculate the accounts receivable turnover ratio and days' sales in accounts receivable.

LO5 Analyze accounts receivable using the accounts receivable turnover ratio and days' sales in accounts receivable.

TERMS REVIEW

accounts receivable turnover ratio

days' sales in accounts receivable

Audit your understanding LO4, 5

1. What is the formula for calculating the accounts receivable turnover ratio?
2. What is the meaning of a days' sales in accounts receivable of 50?
3. How would you interpret the situation of a business that desires an accounts receivable turnover ratio of 12.0 times but actually has a turnover ratio of 6.0 times?
4. How can extremely restrictive credit terms have a negative impact on a business?

Work together 6-3 LO4, 5

Financial analysis of accounts receivable

LMK Industries offers its customers n/30 credit terms. The turnover ratio for the prior year was 6.4. The following account balances were obtained from LMK Industries' records for the current year. Your instructor will guide you through the following examples.

	January 1	December 31
Accounts Receivable	$126,468.15	$135,643.58
Allowance for Uncollectible Accounts	4,123.27	5,754.77
Net Sales on Account		847,386.56

1. Calculate the accounts receivable turnover ratio for the current year.
2. Calculate the days' sales in accounts receivable.
3. Is LMK Industries effective in collecting its accounts receivable?

On your own 6-3 LO4, 5

Financial analysis of accounts receivable

Yang Supply offers its customers 2/10, n/30 credit terms. The turnover ratio for the prior year was 15.9. The following account balances were obtained from the records of Yang Supply for the current year. Work this problem independently.

	January 1	December 31
Accounts Receivable	$65,856.05	$ 67,643.48
Allowance for Uncollectible Accounts	3,535.12	3,635.36
Net Sales on Account		982,435.94

1. Calculate the accounts receivable turnover ratio for the current year.
2. Calculate the days' sales in accounts receivable.
3. Is Yang Supply effective in collecting its accounts receivable?

A Look at **Accounting** Software

Setting Credit Limits

To minimize the number of write-offs of receivables, businesses take steps to reduce the risk of uncollectible accounts. One of the more important steps is determining the creditworthiness of each customer and limiting the amount of credit extended. In a manual accounting system, the credit limit would probably be written on a customer's ledger card. Before each credit sale, an accounting department employee would review the customer's account to be certain that the sale was within the customer's limit.

In a computerized accounting system, a business enters credit terms into each customer's record. The customer's credit limit is checked automatically prior to each sale. This process speeds credit sales and minimizes the chances of customers exceeding their credit limit.

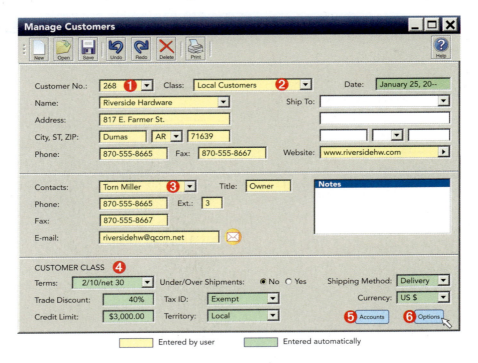

① The accountant for Vaughn Distributors is setting up a new customer account for Riverside Hardware. On the Manage Customers window, the accountant accepted the next sequential customer number offered by the system.

② The accountant selected Local Customers as the classification for Riverside Hardware. Having classifications allows the system to assign default settings for different types of customers.

③ After entering the customer's name, address, phone, fax, and website, the accountant entered the contact information for the customer's employee responsible for purchasing.

④ The Customer Class section of the window displays the default settings for the classification set in

Step 2. The accountant can accept or change the settings. In addition to payment terms and trade discount, these settings indicate whether the customer will accept under- or over-shipments, the normal method of delivery, the amount of sales tax to collect (if any), the type of currency (for export sales), and the territory (for managing sales by salesperson or sales manager).

⑤ The **Accounts** button would be clicked to open a window where general ledger accounts could be assigned for handling transactions with this customer. Those accounts are assigned by default and would only be accessed to change them.

⑥ The accountant accepted all the defaults and clicked on the **Options** button to open the Credit Options dialog box.

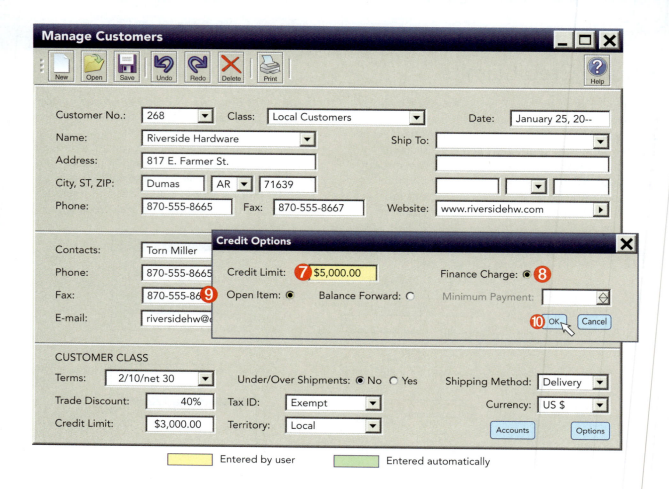

Entered by user	Entered automatically

❼ The accountant has changed the $3,000.00 default credit limit for local customers to $5,000.00 for Riverside Hardware.

❽ Many businesses have a policy of assessing finance charges on customer balances when payments are late. The default setting is "on," but it can be turned off for select customers.

❾ There are two methods of maintaining customer accounts—open item and balance forward. Open

Item is the default. Under that method, the customer is expected to pay each invoice in full within the terms of payment. Some customers may be offered a Balance Forward account. Those customers can purchase merchandise up to their credit limit and are expected to pay a prescribed minimum amount of their account balance each period.

❿ The accountant clicks **OK** to accept the settings and return to the main window.

A business may offer credit terms to attract new customers, increase sales to current customers, and encourage customer loyalty. The business will likely have some customers that will be unable to pay their accounts. An uncollectible account is no longer an asset and should be written off.

The two methods used to account for uncollectible accounts are the (1) direct write-off and (2) allowance methods. The direct write-off method recognizes an uncollectible account expense at the time the account is considered uncollectible. Although the method is easy to apply, it fails to always match the expense of the uncollectible account in the same accounting period as the related sale. For this reason, the method is not a generally accepted accounting principle. However, a business having an immaterial amount of uncollectible accounts may be able to use the direct write-off method.

A business using the allowance method records an estimate of uncollectible accounts expense in the same period as the related sales. Two methods of calculating an estimate are commonly used. The percentage of sales method assumes that a percentage of each sales dollar will become uncollectible. The percentage of accounts receivable method assumes that a percentage of accounts receivable at the fiscal year-end will become uncollectible. This method applies a series of percentages to age groups on an aging of accounts receivable. The accounts of the adjusting journal entry are the same regardless of the method used to estimate uncollectible accounts.

The accounts receivable turnover ratio and the days' sales in accounts receivable enable a business to analyze its effectiveness in collecting accounts receivable. The accounts receivable turnover ratio is calculated by dividing net sales on account by the average book value of accounts receivable. The days' sales in accounts receivable is calculated by dividing 365 by the accounts receivable turnover ratio. The ratio, stated in days, indicates the average length of time to collect an account.

EXPLORE ACCOUNTING

Credit Scoring Systems

To help reduce the amount of uncollectible accounts, a business should evaluate the creditworthiness of potential customers before granting credit. The most widely used credit score for individuals used in the United States is the FICO score. FICO stands for Fair Isaac Corporation, the company that developed the scoring model used to calculate credit scores.

The FICO score ranges between 300 and 850. The higher the score, the more creditworthy the customer. U.S. law enables individuals to obtain their credit score, free of charge, from three national credit bureaus. Each bureau collects financial information on individuals, such as payment history, types of credit, and use of credit. These data are entered into the FICO scoring model to calculate the FICO score. Since each bureau's financial information may vary, the FICO scores are often different.

Although individuals can obtain their credit scores free of charge, a business must pay a fee to the credit bureaus to obtain the same information.

Similar sources of information are available for a business to evaluate the creditworthiness of business customers. A business must weigh the cost of evaluating a customer's creditworthiness against the benefit of reducing uncollectible accounts expense. The benefit of reducing uncollectible accounts expense should exceed the costs of performing credit evaluations. A business should not, for example, spend $60,000 in salaries and bureau fees to evaluate credit if the business can only reduce its annual uncollectible accounts expense by $40,000. Regardless of how credit is evaluated, a company must ensure that its decisions are consistent. Federal laws exist to ensure that individuals and businesses have equal access to credit.

INSTRUCTIONS

Research the FICO score. Identify the weight of each type of financial information used in the FICO score.

Source: myFICO.com.

APPLY YOUR UNDERSTANDING

INSTRUCTIONS: Download problem instructions for Excel, QuickBooks, and Sage 50c from the textbook companion website at www.C21accounting.com.

6-1 Application Problem

Journalizing entries to write off uncollectible accounts—direct write-off method LO1

Stallworth Company uses the direct write-off method of recording uncollectible accounts expense. A general journal and cash receipts journal are provided in the *Working Papers*.

Instructions:

Journalize the following transactions completed during the current year. Use page 4 of a general journal and page 6 of a cash receipts journal. Source documents are abbreviated as follows: memorandum, M; receipt, R.

Transactions:

Jan. 23. Rochelle Company's legal counsel notified Stallworth of its plans to declare bankruptcy. Write off the $325.15 account balance as uncollectible. M42.

Mar. 6. Received a $168.25 check from Norris Industries in full payment of its account. Norris Industries was never notified that Stallworth previously wrote off the account as uncollectible. M62 and R432.

May 9. Based on conversations with managers at Guice Corporation, the account is expected to become uncollectible, $421.05. M73.

July 30. Received a check from Zimmer Supply as a partial payment on its account that was previously written off as uncollectible, $250.00. M85 and R503.

6-2 Application Problem

Estimating amount of uncollectible accounts expense; journalizing the adjusting entry LO3

sage 50

1. Journalize and post transactions related to allowance for uncollectible accounts to the cash receipts journal.
2. Journalize and post accounts receivable transactions previously written off as uncollectible to the sales journal and cash receipts journal.
3. Print the sales journal and cash receipts journal.

QB Quick Books

1. Journalize and post transactions related to allowance for uncollectible accounts to the journal.
2. Journalize and post accounts receivable transactions previously written off in the Create Invoices window and the Receive Payments window.
3. Print the journal and customer balance detail report.

General journals and a cash receipts journal are provided in the *Working Papers*.

Instructions:

1. eSystems, Inc. estimates that its uncollectible accounts expense will be approximately 0.9% of net sales. The current year's net sales is $514,815.35. Use page 20 of a general journal to record the adjusting entry for uncollectible accounts expense on December 31 of the current year.

2. Wimberly Corporation's aging of accounts receivable as of December 31 of the current year is presented in the *Working Papers*. Use the estimated percentages by age group to estimate the required balance of Allowance for Uncollectible Accounts. The balance of Allowance for Uncollectible Accounts on December 31 before adjusting entries are recorded is a $342.05 credit. Use page 13 of a general journal to record the adjusting entry for uncollectible accounts expense.

3. Journalize the following transactions for Wimberly Corporation completed during the current year. Use page 1 of a general journal and page 3 of a cash receipts journal. Source documents are abbreviated as follows: memorandum, M; receipt, R.

1. Estimate the required balance of Allowance for Uncollectible Accounts to journalize the adjusting entry for December 31.

2. Journalize transactions related to allowance for uncollectible accounts.

3. Print the worksheets.

Transactions:

Jan. 9. Concluded that Queen Industries is unable to pay its $450.00 outstanding account receivable. M148.

Mar. 3. Received a partial payment on Davis Manufacturing's account, previously written off as uncollectible, $800.00. M162 and R710.

May 14. Windle Supply has closed its doors. Write off its $900.00 account as uncollectible. M179.

June 22. Received a $580.00 check from Mattie Company in full payment of its account. The account was previously written off as uncollectible. M190 and R832.

6-3 Application Problem   Financial analysis of accounts receivable   LO4, 5

LampLight Industries offers its customers n/30 credit terms. The turnover ratio for the prior year was 11.0. The following account balances were obtained from LampLight Industries' records for the current year:

	January 1	December 31
Accounts Receivable	$45,364.23	$ 47,153.65
Allowance for Uncollectible Accounts	3,015.85	3,384.08
Net Sales on Account		484,047.53

Instructions:

1. Calculate the accounts receivable turnover ratio for the current year.

2. Calculate the days' sales in accounts receivable.

3. Is LampLight Industries effective in collecting its accounts receivable?

6-M Mastery Problem   Journalizing entries for uncollectible accounts—allowance method; calculating and journalizing the adjusting entry for uncollectible accounts expense   LO 3, 4, 5

West River, Inc., uses the allowance method of recording uncollectible accounts expense. The following information was obtained from West River's records for the current year:

	January 1	December 31
Accounts Receivable	$65,184.26	$ 72,184.95
Allowance for Doubtful Accounts	3,481.62	4,048.78
Net Sales on Account		847,386.56

A general journal and cash receipts journal are provided in the *Working Papers*.

Transactions:

Feb. 2. A phone call to Alex Yarber, president of Yarber Supply, confirmed that the company is intending to file bankruptcy. Alex stated that no money would likely be available to pay Yarber Supply's creditors. The Yarber account of $6,215.48 is over 180 days past due. M166.

Mar. 24. Last year, you wrote off the $2,084.65 balance of Innovation Central. The account was over 180 days past due and collection seemed doubtful. Today, you received a $2,084.65 check from Innovation Central along with a letter stating that the company wished to reestablish a credit account with your company. M178 and R555.

June 12. Received a reply to a collection request letter sent to Dennis Raborne. Dennis refuses to pay the remaining $62.00 of his bill, stating that the original bill was larger than the agreed-upon price. Although your records clearly indicate the $62.00 was an appropriate charge, your manager believes that further efforts to collect this account are pointless. M192.

Oct. 17. The U.S. Postal Service was unable to deliver a collection letter to Nancy Givens. Nancy owed $123.54 from an invoice dated January 16. M210.

Nov. 3. Today you received a $1,243.10 check from Yarber Supply. In the enclosed letter, Alex stated that the bankruptcy court ordered the company to pay 20 cents for every dollar owed to its creditors. Thus, the $1,243.10 is the only amount that Yarber Supply would ever be able to pay of its original account balance of $6,215.48. M222 and R621.

Instructions:

1. Journalize the selected transactions above that were completed during the current year. Use page 1 of a general journal and page 1 of a cash receipts journal. Source documents are abbreviated as follows: memorandum, M; receipt, R.

2. Journalize the adjusting entry for uncollectible accounts expense on December 31 of the current year. West River estimates that the amount of uncollectible accounts expense is equal to 1% of its net sales of $915,084.62.

3. Compute the accounts receivable turnover and days' sales in accounts receivable.

sage 50

1. Journalize and post transactions related to allowance for uncollectible accounts to the cash receipts journal.

2. Journalize and post accounts receivable transactions previously written off as uncollectible to the sales journal and cash receipts journal.

3. Print the sales journal and cash receipts journal.

QB
Quick Books

1. Journalize and post transactions related to allowance for uncollectible accounts to the journal.

2. Journalize and post accounts receivable transactions previously written off in the Create Invoices window and the Receive Payments window.

3. Print the journal and customer balance detail report.

6-C Challenge Problem Estimating amount of uncollectible accounts expense; journalizing the adjusting entry **LO3**

A form and general journal are provided in the *Working Papers*. A complete list of the accounts receivable, as of December 31, of Destin Warehouse follows:

Account	Amount	Invoice Date
Ballard Corporation	$2,383.70	August 11
Colister Company	3,874.80	October 12
Eads & Godfrey	1,260.30	November 19
Garrett, Inc.	2,031.00	September 16
Jeffries Distributors	1,406.50	August 14
McEwen Industries	2,722.10	November 5
Perryman Company	2,047.20	December 3
Ruffin Associates	3,615.20	October 23
Turnage Supply	5,664.80	December 14

Instructions:

1. Age the accounts receivable by determining the age group for each invoice and totaling the invoice amounts in each age group category. Destin Warehouse's credit terms are n/30.

2. Calculate the estimated balance of Allowance for Uncollectible Accounts, using the following percentages: not yet due, 0.5%; 1–30 days past due, 2.0%; 31–60 days, 5.0%; 61–90 days, 30%; and over 90 days, 60%.

3. Journalize the adjusting entry for uncollectible accounts expense on December 31 of the current year. Use page 12 of a general journal. The Allowance for Uncollectible Accounts has a debit balance of $221.68 on December 31 of the current year before adjusting entries are recorded.

College Choices beyond Ramen Noodles

Theme: Financial, Economic, Business, and Entrepreneurial Literacy

Skills: Creativity and Innovation, Critical Thinking and Problem Solving, Communication and Collaboration, ICT Literacy

PARTNERSHIP FOR
21ST CENTURY SKILLS

Student loans now exceed credit card debt and total more than $1.3 trillion. Due to increases in the cost of college, students are relying more heavily on these loans to pay for their education, with the average student debt exceeding $37,000.

Any debt removes the financial freedom that a young person can have when starting a career. The debt can delay the purchase of a car or a home or impact lifestyle decisions, such as marriage or having children. The Department of Education estimates a student loan default rate of 11.5%, damaging an individual's credit report for many years.

Students should consider the return on their investment. For instance, if they attend an expensive school but choose a career that does not have high earning potential, it may take years for them to pay off their debt.

Sources: www.forbes.com; www.ed.gov.

APPLICATION

1. In addition to tuition and fees, students must budget other costs for attending college.
   a. Using the Internet, research three colleges of your choice to determine the breakdown in costs. Be sure to include at least three other areas of costs in addition to tuition and fees. Prepare a spreadsheet of your findings.
   b. Research the starting salary for a career of your choice. Determine which of the schools you researched would be the best choice. Explain why.
2. List three alternative ways you could pay for college besides student loans.
3. Interview a college graduate who has a student loan. Ask this person how the loan has impacted his or her lifestyle upon graduation and any advice he or she would provide to future students. Prepare a presentation using video, audio, or print, informing other students of the dangers and risks of student loan debt.

Analyzing Home Depot's Financial Statements

As shown in the financial statements in Appendix B of this textbook, Home Depot's Consolidated Balance Sheets list "Receivables, net" under the heading "Current assets." This amount represents Home Depot's receivables after the allowance for uncollectible accounts estimate has been deducted. Additional information about these amounts is presented in Note 1, "Summary of Significant Accounting Policies."

INSTRUCTIONS

1. Refer to the Consolidated Balance Sheets on page B-5 to identify the net amount of accounts receivable on January 28, 2018, and January 29, 2017.
2. Using Note 1, beginning on page B-10, locate the paragraph titled "Receivables." Summarize the three types of accounts receivable described in the note.
3. How does the note describe the amount of the allowance for uncollectible accounts at the end of fiscal 2017 or 2016?

7

Accounting for Plant Assets

CHAPTER 7

LEARNING OBJECTIVES

After studying Chapter 7, in addition to defining key terms, you will be able to:

LO1 Record the purchase of plant assets.

LO2 Describe how asset purchases are recorded using International Financial Accounting Standards.

LO3 Identify the three items often used in calculating depreciation.

LO4 Calculate depreciation expense using the straight-line method.

LO5 Record depreciation expense.

LO6 Describe how to account for repair and maintenance payments.

LO7 Journalize the disposal of plant assets.

LO8 Calculate depreciation expense using the declining-balance method.

LO9 Calculate depreciation expense using the units-of-production method.

LO10 Calculate depreciation expense for income tax reporting.

LO11 Compare annual depreciation expense for three depreciation methods.

LO12 Calculate depletion of a natural resource.

CSX Corporation

ACCOUNTING IN THE REAL WORLD

For nearly two centuries, railroads have been an integral part of the nation's transportation system. Railroads are an efficient and environmentally friendly method for transporting bulk commodities over land. One of the nation's largest railroad companies, CSX Corporation (CSX), operates more than 21,000 miles of track in 23 states east of the Mississippi River, the District of Columbia, and the Canadian provinces of Ontario and Quebec.

CSX operates three primary lines of business: merchandise, coal, and intermodel. The merchandise business transports bulk items such as chemicals, automobiles, grain, fertilizer, and forest products. The coal business transports bulk shipments of coal, coke, (coal residue used as fuel), and iron ore.

The intermodal business combines water, rail, and truck transportation to deliver products from oversea sources to destinations across the country. Containers received at port are loaded on CSX flatcars and delivered to intermodal terminals across the country. The containers are then loaded on truck trailers for delivery to their final destinations. The goods never leave the containers until final delivery. The company transports containers inland from ports along the Atlantic Ocean, Gulf of Mexico, Mississippi River, Great Lakes, and St. Lawrence Seaway.

Operating a railroad requires a huge investment in rails, engines, and cars. Nearly 90% of CSX's assets are plant assets. A business must establish accounting policies for assigning the useful life to different types of plant assets. These useful lives are used to determine annual depreciation expense. Computer equipment, for example, might have a three-year useful life, even though computers often are used for more than three years. Most companies assign useful lives based on tables provided by the Internal Revenue Service or other reliable sources. In contrast, businesses with many plant assets (known as plant asset-intensive businesses) such as CSX make the effort to reflect the actual useful lives of their assets.

Unlike most businesses, CSX does not depreciate most of its fixed assets individually. Instead, CSX uses a group-life method. The estimated useful life of a locomotive is 29 years. Using a group-life method, CSX recognizes the annual depreciation expense of 3.5% (calculated by dividing 1 by 29 years) of the total cost of all locomotives. The estimated useful life of its freight cars is 35 years, resulting in an annual depreciation rate of 2.9% (1/35 years). CSX uses this method to depreciate 86% of its fixed assets. The company regularly conducts studies to determine the actual service lives of its equipment. Management analyzes the results of these studies to adjust the useful lives used to calculate depreciation expense in later years.

Source: www.csx.com.

CRITICAL THINKING

1. What factors might cause the useful life of a locomotive to increase? Decrease?

2. Identify another plant asset–intensive business. Suggest how the business might assign a useful life and explain what factors could cause the useful life to increase or decrease.

KEY TERMS

current assets	salvage value	modified half-year	Modified Accelerated
plant asset record	straight-line method of	convention	Cost Recovery System
real property	depreciation	declining-balance method	(MACRS)
personal property	book value of a	of depreciation	depletion
assessed value	plant asset	units-of-production	
millage rate	half-year convention	method of depreciation	

LO1   Record the purchase of plant assets.

LO2   Describe how asset purchases are recorded using International Financial Accounting Standards.

Recording the Purchase of Plant Assets LO1

A business owns a variety of assets, all of which are used to help it earn a profit. Cash and other assets expected to be exchanged for cash or consumed within a year are called **current assets**.

Other assets, such as land, buildings, and equipment, are expected to help the business earn a profit for more than one year. Assets that will be used for a number of years in the operation of a business are known as *plant assets*. Plant assets are sometimes referred to as *fixed assets* or *long-term assets*.

Financial statements are prepared with the expectation that a business will remain in operation indefinitely. **>> App A: Going Concern** The going concern concept enables a business to record the cost of plant assets on the balance sheet. The cost of plant assets is recognized over many years through the recording of depreciation expense. Without the going concern concept, plant assets would have to be reported at the value for which they could be sold within the fiscal year.

All costs necessary to get the plant asset ready for its intended use are included in the cost of a plant asset. For example, the cost of equipment would include freight and installation. The cost of land would include surveying and realtor fees. Renovation costs to ensure compliance with fire codes and accessibility laws would be included in the cost of a building.

ETHICS IN ACTION

The Land of Opportunity?

As the director of corporate development, Kelly Maben is completing a proposal to locate a resort in Gulf Shores, Alabama. The beach resort would include a conference center complete with fine and casual dining options, a day spa, and a water park with entertainment experiences for every age. Rooms in the 500-unit tower would be equipped with the latest technology.

Confident the proposal will be approved, Kelly is considering the purchase of a family-owned restaurant across the street from the proposed building site. The restaurant operates a lunch and dinner buffet offering classic southern cooking with a New Orleans flare.

INSTRUCTIONS

Obtain the *Code of Business Conduct and Ethics* of Hyatt Hotels Corporation. Using this information and the ethical model, provide Kelly with guidance on her proposed restaurant purchase. Is Kelly violating her company's code of conduct or simply seizing an opportunity?

Buying a Plant Asset for Cash

					1	2	3	4	5	
	DATE	ACCOUNT TITLE	CK. NO.	POST. REF.	GENERAL DEBIT	GENERAL CREDIT	ACCOUNTS PAYABLE DEBIT	PURCHASES DISCOUNT CREDIT	CASH CREDIT	
CASH PAYMENTS JOURNAL									**PAGE 5**	
14	14	*Warehouse Equipment*	416		16 850 00				16 850 00	14
15	16	*Warehouse Equipment*	417		2 800 00				2 800 00	15
16										16

Vaughn Distributors, Inc., purchased an industrial storage system. The system will be used in the warehouse to store a new line of chemicals.

> **March 14. Paid cash to Metal Fabricators for a storage system, $16,850.00. Check No. 416.**

Warehouse Equipment

| Mar. 14 ⬆ | 16,850.00 | |
| Mar. 16 | 2,800.00 | |

Cash

| | Mar. 14 ⬇ | 16,850.00 |
| | Mar. 16 | 2,800.00 |

The storage system requires assembly, including the services of a welder and an electrician. The assembly is required to get the system ready for its intended use. Thus, the cost of the assembly is part of the cost of the storage system.

> **March 16. Paid cash to Preston Construction to assemble the storage system, $2,800.00. Check No. 417.**

Both transactions increase the cost of warehouse equipment, as shown in the T accounts.

Accounting for Environmental Costs in Agriculture

CareerClusters
PATHWAYS TO COLLEGE & CAREER READINESS
Agriculture, Food & Natural Resources

As with any business, a farmer must estimate all costs and revenues when deciding what products to sell. A grain farmer will have different costs than a dairy farmer. If some costs are omitted from the estimate, the farmer's net income will be less than the estimated amount.

The market price for any farm product is the result of a combination of factors, one of which is the cost to produce the product. The ideal market price will cover all costs plus an adequate net income for the farmer.

Current costing methods for farmers do not include any environmental cost. For example, assume that a farmer applies a pesticide to a field, and the runoff from the pesticide flows into a nearby river. If the farmer does nothing to return the river to an undamaged state, the cost of repairing the river is not reflected in the cost of the farmer's products. Instead, the cost is passed on to someone down river, such as a fishery, where the fish die as a result of the chemicals in the river.

Many groups around the world are encouraging all businesses to include environmental costs when calculating the cost of products.

CRITICAL THINKING

List one industry that could impact the environment during the production of its product. List the possible environmental costs due to production.

Source: International Institute for Sustainable Development (www.iisd.org).

Buying a Plant Asset on Account

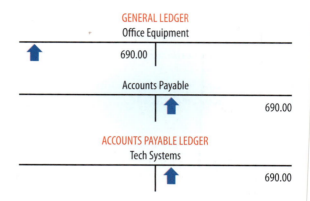

	DATE	ACCOUNT TITLE	DOC. NO.	POST. REF.	DEBIT	CREDIT	
4	6	*Office Equipment*	M23		6 9 0 00		4
5		*Accounts Payable/Tech Systems*				6 9 0 00	5
6							6

GENERAL JOURNAL   PAGE *3*

Not all plant assets are bought for cash. Vaughn Distributors sometimes buys a plant asset on one date and pays for it on a later date.

March 6. Bought on account new monitors for three office computers from Tech Systems, $690.00. Memorandum No. 23.

This transaction does not involve the purchase of merchandise. Therefore, the entry is not recorded in a purchases journal. It is recorded in the general journal as shown above. The entry is posted to both the general ledger and the accounts payable ledger.

GENERAL LEDGER
Office Equipment

690.00 |

Accounts Payable

| 690.00

ACCOUNTS PAYABLE LEDGER
Tech Systems

| 690.00

GLOBAL AWARENESS

Applying for a Passport

International travel usually requires a passport. A passport is a formal document that allows exit from and reentry into a country. It proves citizenship and provides identity for the traveler.

Currently, a person may apply for a passport book, a passport card, or both a book and a card. The passport book is good for all travel. The passport card is only good for land and sea border crossing between the United States and Canada, Mexico, Bermuda, and the Caribbean. The passport card is not good for international air travel.

In the United States, first-time passport applicants over the age of 16 must present the following items:

1. Completed application form, which can be obtained online.
2. Proof of U.S. citizenship such as a certified birth certificate or a naturalization certificate.
3. Proof of identity, such as a driver's license or government ID.
4. A photocopy of the identification document.
5. A passport photo that meets specific criteria. Many local photo studios and photo centers offer passport photo services.
6. Fee.

Those items must be presented in person at an Acceptance Facility or Passport Agency. The locations of these offices and further information may be found at the U.S. Department of State, Bureau of Consular Affairs website.

Source: www.travel.state.gov.

CRITICAL THINKING

Search the Internet to find the following:

1. How much are passport fees?
   a. Fees for a first-time passport book.
   b. Fees for a first-time passport card.
   c. Fees for both if ordered together.
2. How long is a passport valid?
3. Do passport renewals have to be done in person?

Allocating the Cost of Plant Assets

GENERAL JOURNAL

PAGE 3

	DATE	ACCOUNT TITLE	DOC. NO.	POST. REF.	DEBIT	CREDIT	
16	12	Land	M26		56 0 0 0 00		16
17		Building			224 0 0 0 00		17
18		Notes Payable				280 0 0 0 00	18
19							19

Plants assets can be purchased as a group. Vaughn agreed to purchase a distribution center from NexTra Industries for $280,000.00. The purchase includes the land and building. NexTra is financing the purchase, allowing Vaughn to pay for the distribution center over 10 years.

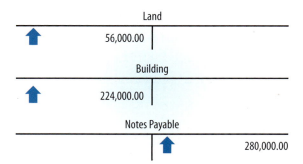

Land
56,000.00

Building
224,000.00

Notes Payable
280,000.00

> **March 12. Purchased a distribution center from NexTra Industries, signing a 10-year note. Memorandum No. 26.**

To help assign a cost to each plant asset, Vaughn hired an appraiser to assign market values to each item. The appraiser assigned a value of $60,000.00 to the land and $240,000.00 to the building. Thus, the total appraised value of the distribution center is $300,000.00. The appraised values are used to allocate the $280,000.00 cost to the land and building, as shown below.

	Appraised Value	Percentage of Total Appraised Value	Assigned Cost
Land	$ 60,000.00	20%	$ 56,000.00
Building	240,000.00	80%	224,000.00
Total	$300,000.00		$280,000.00

The land's appraised value is 20% of the total appraised value of $300,000.00. Thus, land is assigned 20% of the actual purchase price of the distribution center, as shown below.

Appraised Value	÷	Total Appraised Value	=	Percentage of Total Appraised Value
$60,000.00	÷	$300,000.00	=	20%

Percentage of Total Appraised Value	×	Total Purchase Price	=	Cost Allocated to Land
20%	×	$280,000.00	=	$56,000.00

Plant Asset Record

PLANT ASSET RECORD No. **215** General Ledger Account No. **1230**

Description **Copy machine** General Ledger Account **Office Equipment**

Date Bought **August 2, 20--**		Serial Number **642-34632-63C**		Original Cost **$1,400.00**	
Estimated Useful Life **5 years**		Estimated Salvage Value **$200.00**		Depreciation Method **Straight-line**	

Completed When Asset Is Purchased

Disposed of: Discarded _____ Sold _____ Traded _____

Date _____ Disposal Amount _____

Completed When Asset Is Disposed of

Year	Annual Depreciation Expense	Accumulated Depreciation	Ending Book Value

Completed Each Year to Record Depreciation

A business keeps a separate record of each plant asset it owns. An accounting form on which a business records information about each plant asset is called a **plant asset record**. Vaughn Distributors uses a printed card as its plant asset record as shown above.

Vaughn Distributors' plant asset record has three sections. Section 1 is prepared when the company buys a plant asset. Information in this section shows a description of the item, the general ledger account title and number, date bought, serial number, and information needed to calculate annual depreciation expense for the plant asset. Section 2 provides space for recording the disposition of the plant asset. Section 3 provides space for recording annual depreciation expense.

Calculating depreciation and disposing of plant assets are described later in this chapter.

Property Taxes

In most states, businesses have to pay taxes on plant assets. For tax purposes, state and federal governments define two kinds of property. Land and anything attached to it is called **real property**. Real property is sometimes referred to as *real estate*. All property not classified as real property is called **personal property**.

The value of an asset determined by tax authorities for the purpose of calculating taxes is called the **assessed value**. Assessed value is usually based on the judgment of persons referred to as assessors. Assessors are elected by citizens or are specially trained employees of a governmental unit.

The assessed value is assigned to an asset for tax purposes only. Often, the assessed value is only a part of the true value of the asset. Most governmental units with taxing power have a tax based on the value of real property. The tax rate used to calculate property taxes is called a **millage rate**. Some governmental units also tax personal property such as cars, boats, trailers, and airplanes. The millage rate is multiplied by an asset's assessed value to determine the property tax.

Payment of property taxes is necessary if a firm is to continue in business. Therefore, Vaughn Distributors classifies property tax as an operating expense. The transaction is journalized using the same steps as other operating expenses.

International Accounting Standards LO2

	DATE	ACCOUNT TITLE	CK. NO.	POST. REF.	GENERAL DEBIT	GENERAL CREDIT	ACCOUNTS PAYABLE DEBIT	PURCHASES DISCOUNT CREDIT	CASH CREDIT	
					1	2	3	4	5	
17	7	Truck—Frame	523		23 1 0 0 00				30 0 0 0 00	17
18		Truck—Transmission			4 5 0 0 00					18
19		Truck—Tires			2 4 0 0 00					19
20										20
21										21

CASH PAYMENTS JOURNAL — PAGE 6

Generally accepted accounting principles (GAAP) require that the cost of similar plant assets be accumulated in individual accounts. Common plant asset accounts include land, buildings, trucks, cars, and office equipment.

International financial reporting standards (IFRS) require a similar method of accounting for plant assets. However, IFRS are more aggressive in their requirements. IFRS recognize that components of a single plant asset may be used by the business for different periods of time. Thus, each significant component of a plant asset is assigned a cost and recorded in different plant asset accounts.

Bethune Company purchased a delivery truck for $30,000.00. Using generally accepted accounting principles, Bethune would record the entire $30,000.00 purchase price in its Trucks plant asset account. However, Bethune prepares its financial statements using IFRS. The business recognizes that the transmission will have to be replaced after four years. In addition, the tires will only last for two years. Thus, Bethune records the truck in three plant asset accounts.

> **June 7.** Bethune Company pays cash for a $30,000.00 delivery truck. Check No. 523.

The cost of the delivery truck is assigned in the same manner as Vaughn Distributors assigned the costs of its distribution center. An estimate of each component of the truck is used to allocate the total cost, as shown below.

	Appraised Value	Percentage of Total Appraised Value	Assigned Cost
Frame	$24,640.00	77%	$23,100.00
Transmission	4,800.00	15%	4,500.00
Tires	2,560.00	8%	2,400.00
Total	$32,000.00		$30,000.00

A set of replacement tires currently costs $2,560.00. This cost represents 8% of the total estimated value of the truck ($2,560.00 ÷ $32,000.00 = 8%). The tires are assigned 8% of the actual cost of the truck, $2,400.00 (8% × $30,000.00).

FYI It is not uncommon for the purchase price of a group of assets to be less than would be required to purchase the items individually.

DEAN DROBOT/SHUTTERSTOCK.COM

LO1 Record the purchase of plant assets.

LO2 Describe how asset purchases are recorded using International Financial Accounting Standards.

TERMS REVIEW

current assets

plant asset record

real property

personal property

assessed value

millage rate

Audit your understanding LO1, 2

1. What costs are included in the cost of a plant asset?
2. How is the cost assigned to plant assets purchased as a group?
3. What are the three sections of a plant asset record?
4. How is the amount of property tax determined?
5. How is the purchase of plant assets accounted for using IFRS?

Work together 7-1 LO1

Journalizing asset purchase transactions

Kellgren Corporation depreciates all plant assets using the straight-line method. Plant asset records, a general journal, and a cash payments journal are provided in the *Working Papers*. Source documents are abbreviated as: check, C; memorandum, M. Your instructor will guide you through the following examples.

Transactions:

Jan. 3. Paid cash for printer (plant asset no. 321), $840.00: no estimated salvage value; estimated useful life, three years; serial no. BO634BRE. C610.

Apr. 5. Bought a conveyor table (plant asset no. 326) on account from Packing Systems, $1,800.00: estimated salvage value, $200.00; estimated useful life, five years; serial no. HE26-3464. M67.

Oct. 8. Purchased a warehouse for $300,000.00. The building was appraised for $240,000.00 and the land for $80,000.00. The building has a useful life of 25 years and an estimated salvage value of $25,000.00; plant assets no. 341 and 342. C920.

1. Journalize the transactions completed during 20X1. General ledger accounts are: Land, 1210; Building, 1220; Office Equipment, 1230; and Warehouse Equipment, 1240.
2. Complete section 1 of a plant asset record for new asset purchases. Save your work to complete Work Together 7-2.

On your own 7-1 LO1

Journalizing asset purchase transactions

Hairston Stores depreciates all plant assets using the straight-line method. Depreciate all plant assets using the straight-line method. Plant asset records, a general journal, and a cash payments journal are provided in the *Working Papers*. Source documents are abbreviated as: check, C; memorandum, M. Work independently to complete the following problem.

Transactions:

Jan. 7. Bought a tablet computer (plant asset no. 403) on account from Computer Source, $650.00: no salvage value; estimated useful life, five years; serial no. 26-BT-327. M43.

July 12. Paid cash for a point-of-sale system (plant asset no. 410), $2,500.00: estimated salvage value, $500.00; estimated useful life, five years; serial no. 62-838C. C743.

Sept. 28. Purchased a store building for $200,000.00. The building was appraised for $132,000.00 and the land for $88,000.00. The building has a useful life of 25 years and an estimated salvage value of $20,000.00; plant assets no.≈448 and 449. C993.

1. Journalize the transactions completed during 20X1. General ledger accounts are: Land, 1210; Building, 1220; Office Equipment, 1230; and Store Equipment, 1240.
2. Complete section 1 of a plant asset record for new asset purchases. Save your work to complete On Your Own 7-2.

LO3 Identify the three items often used in calculating depreciation.
LO4 Calculate depreciation expense using the straight-line method.
LO5 Record depreciation expense.
LO6 Describe how to account for repair and maintenance payments.

Factors Used to Calculate Depreciation **LO3**

Plant assets may wear out, may no longer be needed in the operation of a business, or may become outdated by new models. To match revenue with the expenses incurred to earn it, the cost of a plant asset should be allocated to an expense account over the useful life of the plant asset. **>> App A: Matching Expenses with Revenue** As explained in Chapter 4, the portion of a plant asset's cost that is transferred to an expense account in each fiscal period during a plant asset's useful life is called *depreciation expense*.

Because of its permanent nature, land is not subject to depreciation. Increases or decreases in land value are usually recorded only when land is sold or otherwise disposed of.

Three factors are used to calculate a plant asset's annual depreciation expense:

1. Original cost.
2. Estimated salvage value.
3. Estimated useful life.

Original Cost

The original cost of a plant asset includes all costs paid to make the asset usable to a business. These costs include the purchase price, delivery costs, and any necessary installation costs. **>> App A: Historical Cost**

Estimated Salvage Value

When a plant asset is disposed of, some part of its original value may remain. When a plant asset is bought, its final value can only be estimated. The estimated **salvage value** is the amount that will be received for an asset at the time of its disposal. Salvage value is also referred to as *residual value*, *scrap value*, or *trade-in value*.

Until a plant asset is disposed of, most businesses have difficulty determining its exact salvage value. Thus, until actually disposed of, a plant asset's salvage value can only

be estimated. Because salvage value is used to calculate a plant asset's annual depreciation, the most accurate estimate possible is made when a plant asset is bought.

Estimated Useful Life

The estimated useful life of a plant asset is the number of years it is expected to be useful to a business. A plant asset's useful life differs from one situation to another. Most businesses use past experience as the basis for estimating a plant asset's useful life. If a calculator usually lasts five years for a specific business, then the business uses five years as the estimated useful life of a new calculator. Sometimes, however, a business has difficulty estimating a plant asset's useful life. In these cases, it may use the Internal Revenue Service's guidelines that give the estimated useful life for many plant assets. **>> App A: Neutrality**

Depreciation Methods

Various depreciation methods are illustrated in this chapter. A business should select the depreciation method that provides the best financial information. A business typically uses the same depreciation method for all assets within a plant asset category.

Straight-Line Depreciation LO4

DEPRECIATION TABLE

Plant Asset:	Computer	Estimated Salvage Value:	$1,000.00
Depreciation Method:	Straight-line	Estimated Useful Life:	3 years
Original Cost:	$4,000.00		

Year	Beginning Book Value	Annual Depreciation	Accumulated Depreciation	Ending Book Value
1	$4,000.00	$600.00	$ 600.00	$3,400.00
2	3,400.00	600.00	1,200.00	2,800.00
3	2,800.00	600.00	1,800.00	2,200.00
4	2,200.00	600.00	2,400.00	1,600.00
5	1,600.00	600.00	3,000.00	1,000.00

Recording an equal amount of depreciation expense for a plant asset in each year of its useful life is called the **straight-line method of depreciation**.

On January 2, 20X1, Vaughn Distributors bought a computer for $4,000.00 with an estimated salvage value of $1,000.00 and an estimated useful life of five years. The details of the purchase and the depreciation amounts for each year of the asset's estimated useful life are shown above.

The estimated total depreciation expense is divided by the estimated useful life to compute the annual depreciation expense. The annual depreciation expense is the same for each year if the asset is used for the entire year.

Original Cost	$4,000.00
Estimated salvage value	− 1,000.00
Estimated total depreciation expense	= $3,000.00
Years of estimated useful life	÷ 5
Annual depreciation expense	= $ 600.00

The original cost of a plant asset minus accumulated depreciation is called the **book value of a plant asset**. An alternate method for calculating the book value is to subtract the annual depreciation expense from the beginning book value. The beginning book value for a year is the ending book value of the prior year.

Beginning Book Value	−	Annual Depreciation	=	Ending Book Value
$2,800.00	−	$600.00	=	$2,200.00

Annual depreciation expense can also be calculated using an annual percentage rate. In the preceding example, the plant asset has an estimated useful life of five years. Therefore, the annual depreciation rate is 20% (100% divided by 5 equals 0.20, or 20%). Estimated total depreciation expense, $3,000.00, times the depreciation rate, 20%, equals the annual depreciation expense, $600.00.

Two of the three values used to compute depreciation are estimates.

Remember

Calculating Depreciation Expense for Part of a Year

A calendar month is the smallest unit of time typically used to calculate depreciation. A plant asset may be placed in service at a date other than the first day of a fiscal period. In such cases, depreciation expense can be calculated to the nearest first of a month. To calculate depreciation expense for part of a year, the annual depreciation expense is divided by 12 to determine depreciation expense for a month. The monthly depreciation is then multiplied by the number of months the plant asset was used that year.

Vaughn Distributors bought a copy machine on August 2, 20X1. The annual straight-line depreciation expense is $240.00. The depreciation expense for the part of the year that Vaughn Distributors used the copy machine (August through December equals 5 months) is $100.00.

Annual depreciation expense		$240.00
Months in a year	÷	12
Monthly depreciation expense	=	$ 20.00
Number of months asset is used	×	5
Partial year's depreciation expense	=	$100.00

Alternate Methods for Partial-Year Depreciation

Other methods of recording a partial year's depreciation are accepted. A method that recognizes one half of a year's depreciation in the year of acquisition is called the **half-year convention**. Regardless of when the plant asset is purchased, one half of the annual depreciation is recorded in the first year. Using the half-year convention, Vaughn would record $120.00 ($240.00 annual depreciation expense ÷ 2) for the copy machine in 20X1.

A method that recognizes a full year's depreciation if the asset is acquired in the first half of the year is called the **modified half-year convention**. If the asset is acquired in the second half of the year, no depreciation is recorded in the first year. Using the modified half-year convention, Vaughn would not record any depreciation for the copy machine in 20X1.

Whatever method a business selects, it should be used consistently from year to year. **>> App A: Consistent Reporting** Changing methods could result in material changes in depreciation expense that would not allow the financial statements to be comparable.

THINK LIKE AN ACCOUNTANT

Calculating Depreciation Expense

Auditors must perform their audits in accordance with standards set by the profession and by government agencies. The auditor's report states:

> Those standards require that we plan and perform the audit to obtain reasonable assurance about whether the financial statements are free of material misstatement. An audit includes examining, on a test basis, evidence supporting the amounts and disclosures in the financial statements.

Recalculation is one method of examining evidence. In the area of plant assets, an auditor should recalculate the client's depreciation expense.

Assume that you are preparing to join an audit team, and you will be responsible for testing plant assets. Create a straight-line depreciation schedule, assuming that the client has two classes of plant assets. For one class, first-year depreciation is calculated to the nearest month. For the other class, the half-year convention is used.

OPEN THE SPREADSHEET TLA_CH07

The worksheet contains an incomplete depreciation schedule. Follow the steps on the Instructions tab and answer the questions:

1. Complete the depreciation schedule for a $36,400.00 car purchased on April 16 of the current year. The car is assigned a five-year useful life and is estimated to have a $4,000.00 salvage value. Calculate depreciation to the nearest month. What is the amount of depreciation in the first year?

2. Modify the depreciation of the car in question 1 to use the half-year convention. What is the amount of depreciation in the first year?

3. Prepare an e-mail to be sent to your colleagues, promoting the use of assigning names to certain cells in a worksheet.

Recording Depreciation LO5

Vaughn Distributors records annual depreciation expense in two places for each plant asset:

1. On the plant asset record.
2. As part of the adjusting entries that are posted to general ledger accounts.

Recording Depreciation on Plant Asset Records

PLANT ASSET RECORD No. __215__   General Ledger Account No. ____1230____

Description ____Copy machine____   General Ledger Account __Office Equipment__

Date Bought __August 2, 20--__   Serial Number __642-34632-63C__   Original Cost ____$1,400.00____

Estimated Useful Life __5 years__   Estimated Salvage Value __$200.00__   Depreciation Method __Straight-line__

Disposed of: Discarded _____   Sold _____   Traded _____

Date _____   Disposal Amount _____

Year	Annual Depreciation Expense	Accumulated Depreciation	Ending Book Value
20X1	$100.00	$ 100.00	$1,300.00
20X2	240.00	340.00	1,060.00
20X3	240.00	580.00	820.00
20X4	240.00	820.00	580.00
20X5	240.00	1,060.00	340.00
20X6	140.00	1,200.00	200.00

Depreciation Expense   Accumulated Depreciation   Book Value

On December 31, Vaughn Distributors recorded the annual depreciation expense on each plant asset record. The plant asset record for a copy machine used as office equipment is shown above.

In section 3 of the plant asset record, the year is recorded in the Year column. The depreciation expense for the plant asset is recorded in the Annual Depreciation Expense column. The amount recorded in the Annual Depreciation Expense column is $100.00, the depreciation expense for the months that the copy machine was used in 20X1. For a full year, the annual depreciation expense is $240.00. The amount of accumulated depreciation is recorded in the Accumulated Depreciation column. The accumulated depreciation is the sum of the previous year's accumulated depreciation and the annual depreciation expense for the current year. A new book value is calculated and recorded in the Ending Book Value column.

20X3 Depreciation Expense	+	20X2 Accumulated Depreciation	=	20X3 Accumulated Depreciation
$240.00	+	$340.00	=	$580.00

20X3 Beginning Book Value	−	20X3 Annual Depreciation	=	20X3 Ending Book Value
$1,060.00	−	$240.00	=	$820.00

At the end of the estimated useful life, the copy machine should be depreciated down to its estimated salvage value. At the end of the sixth year, the ending book value is equal to the estimated salvage value, $200.00.

The calculation for depreciation uses an estimated useful life. The copy machine's actual useful life may exceed the estimate made when the asset was put into use. If a plant asset is used longer than the estimated useful life, depreciation is not recorded once the book value equals the estimated salvage value.

Journalizing Depreciation Expense

GENERAL JOURNAL

PAGE **16**

	DATE	ACCOUNT TITLE	DOC. NO.	POST. REF.	DEBIT	CREDIT	
1		*Adjusting Entries*					1
22	31	*Depreciation Expense—Office Equipment*			12 0 8 0 00		22
23		*Accumulated Depreciation—Office Equipment*				12 0 8 0 00	23
24							24

After depreciation expense is recorded on the plant asset records, depreciation amounts for the year are totaled.

An adjusting entry is made to record the total depreciation expense for the fiscal year for each category of plant assets. Vaughn Distributors records separate adjusting entries for office equipment, store equipment, warehouse equipment, and building. The adjusting entry for office equipment is shown above.

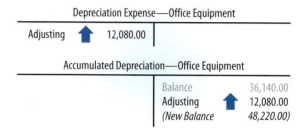

Depreciation Expense—Office Equipment

Adjusting 12,080.00

Accumulated Depreciation—Office Equipment

Balance 36,140.00
Adjusting 12,080.00
(New Balance 48,220.00)

Journalizing Repair and Maintenance Payments LO5, 6

When a long-term asset is purchased, it is recorded at its historical cost, the actual amount paid for the asset. There are some circumstances when that historical cost could change over the life of the asset.

After an asset is put into service, expenditures might be required to maintain, repair, or replace a part of the asset. The accountant will have to decide if the payment qualifies as a repair or an improvement. The decision determines the accounts affected by the transaction.

If the expenditure merely maintains the asset in its normal operation, it should be treated as an expense in the period the payment is made. This category would include painting the inside or outside of a building, minor repairs on a delivery truck, regular maintenance on a piece of factory equipment, repairing gutters, and engine tune-ups. These costs typically bring the asset back to its original condition. Therefore, the entry to record the payment of $500.00 for an engine tune-up would include a debit to Repair Expense.

If the expenditure adds to the value or extends the useful life of the asset, it must be added to the cost of the asset instead of treated as an immediate expense. This category would include adding a wing to a building, upgrading the power of the engine in a vehicle, and redoing the ventilation system of a building to include a state-of-the art air purification system. Therefore, the entry to record the payment of $10,000.00 to add an air purification system would include a debit to Building. By increasing the cost of the asset, the amount of depreciation to be recorded during the remaining useful life of the asset will also change.

Remember

The accounts used to record depreciation expense are the same regardless of the depreciation method used.

LO3 Identify the three items often used in calculating depreciation.

LO4 Calculate depreciation expense using the straight-line method.

LO5 Record depreciation expense.

LO6 Describe how to account for repair and maintenance payments.

TERMS REVIEW

salvage value

straight-line method of depreciation

book value of a plant asset

half-year convention

modified half-year convention

Audit your understanding LO3, 4, 5, 6

1. Which accounting concept is being applied when depreciation expense is recorded for plant assets?
2. Why is annual depreciation for land not recorded?
3. What three factors are used to calculate a plant asset's annual depreciation expense?
4. What is the smallest unit of time used to calculate depreciation?
5. What three amounts are recorded in the bottom section on a plant asset record?
6. What factor determines whether a repair and maintenance payment should be expensed or recorded as an asset?
7. Should the installation of an elevator in a retail store be accounted for as a repair or an addition to the historical cost of the building?

Work together 7-2 LO4, 5
Calculating and journalizing depreciation

Use the plant asset records from Work Together 7-1. Depreciation tables and a general journal are provided in the *Working Papers*. Your instructor will guide you through the following examples.

1. Complete the depreciation table for each asset using the straight-line depreciation method. If the asset was not purchased at the beginning of the year, compute the depreciation expense for the part of year 1 that the company owned the asset.
2. Complete each plant asset record for 20X1 through 20X4.
3. Journalize the adjusting entries to record depreciation expense for 20X1. Save your work to complete Work Together 7-3.

On your own 7-2 LO4, 5
Calculating and journalizing depreciation

Use the plant asset records from On Your Own 7-1. Depreciation tables and a general journal are provided in the *Working Papers*. Work this problem independently.

1. Complete the depreciation table for each asset using the straight-line depreciation method. If the asset was not purchased at the beginning of the year, compute the depreciation expense for the part of year 1 that the company owned the asset.
2. Complete each plant asset record for 20X1 through 20X4.
3. Journalize the adjusting entries to record depreciation expense for 20X1. Save your work to complete On Your Own 7-3.

LO7 Journalize the disposal of plant assets.

Disposing of Plant Assets LO7

Plant Assets may be disposed of in several ways, such as discarding, selling, or trading. Each disposal method is treated differently.

Vaughn Distributors usually disposes of plant assets in one of three ways:

1. The plant asset is discarded because the asset is no longer usable.
2. The plant asset is sold because it is no longer needed, even though it might still be usable.
3. The plant asset is traded for another plant asset of the same kind.

Discarding a Plant Asset with No Book Value

	DATE	ACCOUNT TITLE	DOC. NO.	POST. REF.	DEBIT	CREDIT	
7	4	Accumulated Depreciation—Office Equipment	M4		1 2 4 5 00		7
8		Office Equipment				1 2 4 5 00	8

GENERAL JOURNAL — PAGE 1

Journalize Disposal

PLANT ASSET RECORD No. **9**   General Ledger Account No. **1230**

Description **Notebook computer**   General Ledger Account **Office Equipment**

Disposed of: Discarded ✓   Sold _____ Traded _____

Date **January 4, 20X6**   Disposal Amount **zero**

Date, Amount, and Type of Disposal

Year	Annual Depreciation Expense	Accumulated Depreciation	Ending Book Value
20X4	249.00	996.00	249.00
20X5	249.00	1,245.00	0.00

If a plant asset has a salvage value of zero and its total accumulated depreciation is equal to the original cost, the plant asset has no book value. When a plant asset with no book value is discarded, a journal entry removes the original cost of the plant asset and its related accumulated depreciation.

> **January 4, 20X6.** Discarded a notebook computer: original cost, $1,245.00; total accumulated depreciation through December 31, 20X5, $1,245.00. Memorandum No. 4.

Accumulated Depreciation—Office Equipment

Disposal	1,245.00	Balance	1,245.00
		(New Balance	0.00)

Office Equipment

Balance	1,245.00	Disposal	1,245.00
(New Balance	0.00)		

Discarding a Plant Asset with a Book Value

	DATE	ACCOUNT TITLE	DOC. NO.	POST. REF.	DEBIT	CREDIT	
10	28	Depreciation Expense—Office Equipment	M92		4 0 00		10
11		Accumulated Depreciation—Office Equipment				4 0 00	11
12	28	Accumulated Depreciation—Office Equipment	M92		4 0 0 00		12
13		Loss on Plant Assets			3 0 0 00		13
14		Office Equipment				7 0 0 00	14
15							15

GENERAL JOURNAL   PAGE 4

Journalize ❶ Partial Year's Depreciation

❹ Journalize Disposal

Disposed of: Discarded ✓   Sold _____   Traded _____
Date __April 28, 20X4__   Disposal Amount __zero__

❸ Date, Amount, and Type of Disposal

Year	Annual Depreciation Expense	Accumulated Depreciation	Ending Book Value
20X1	$120.00	$120.00	$580.00
20X2	120.00	240.00	460.00
20X3	120.00	360.00	340.00
20X4	40.00	400.00	300.00

❷ Partial Year's Depreciation

A plant asset may be sold or disposed of at any time during its useful life. When a plant asset is disposed of, its depreciation from the beginning of the current year to the date of disposal is recorded as shown above.

When an asset with a book value is discarded, a journal entry is recorded to (1) remove the original cost of the plant asset and its related accumulated depreciation and (2) recognize the loss on disposal of the asset.

> April 28, 20X4. Discarded office table: original cost, $700.00; total accumulated depreciation through December 31, 20X3, $360.00; additional depreciation to be recorded through April 28, 20X4, $40.00. Memorandum No. 92.

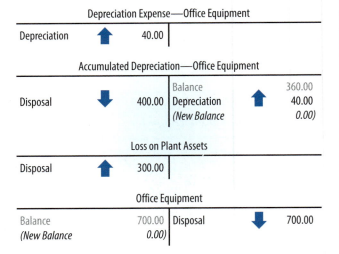

The loss from discarding a plant asset with a book value is equal to the asset's book value. The loss is not an operating expense. Therefore, Loss on Plant Assets is classified as an Other Expense.

▶▶ Discarding a Plant Asset

❶ Record a partial year's depreciation expense, **$40.00**, by debiting **Depreciation Expense— Office Equipment** and crediting **Accumulated Depreciation—Office Equipment**.

❷ Record the partial year's depreciation expense, **$40.00**, in section 3 of the plant asset record.

❸ Check the type of disposal, **Discarded**, and write the date, **April 28, 20X4**, and the disposal amount, **zero**, on the plant asset record.

❹ Record an entry to remove the original cost, **$700.00**, from **Office Equipment** and **$400.00** from **Accumulated Depreciation—Office Equipment**. Record the loss on disposal, **$300.00**, as a debit to **Loss on Plant Assets**.

Selling a Plant Asset

Journalize Sale of Plant Asset ③

Proceeds from sale		$13,400.00	① **Calculate Gain or Loss on Sale of Plant Asset**
Book value of asset sold:			
Original cost	$26,000.00		
Accumulated depreciation	(12,000.00)	14,000.00	
Gain (loss) on sale or disposal		$ (600.00)	

CASH RECEIPTS JOURNAL

PAGE 1

	DATE	ACCOUNT TITLE	DOC. NO.	POST. REF.	GENERAL DEBIT	GENERAL CREDIT	ACCOUNTS RECEIVABLE CREDIT	SALES CREDIT	SALES TAX PAYABLE CREDIT	SALES DISCOUNT DEBIT	CASH DEBIT	
2	3	Accum. Depr.—Warehouse Equip.	R2		12 0 0 0 00						13 4 0 0 00	2
3		Loss on Plant Assets			6 0 0 00							3
4		Warehouse Equipment				26 0 0 0 00						4

Disposed of:	Discarded _____	Sold ✓ _____	Traded _____	② **Date, Amount, and Type of Disposal**
Date **January 3, 20X4**		Disposal Amount **$13,400.00**		

Year	Annual Depreciation Expense	Accumulated Depreciation	Ending Book Value
20X1	$4,000.00	$ 4,000.00	$22,000.00
20X2	4,000.00	8,000.00	18,000.00
20X3	4,000.00	12,000.00	14,000.00

When a plant asset is sold, a journal entry is recorded to:

1. Remove the original cost of the plant asset and its related accumulated depreciation.
2. Recognize the cash received.
3. Recognize the gain or loss on disposal of the asset.

> January 3, 20X4. Received cash from sale of a packing machine, $13,400.00: original cost, $26,000.00; total accumulated depreciation through December 31, 20X3, $12,000.00. Receipt No. 2.

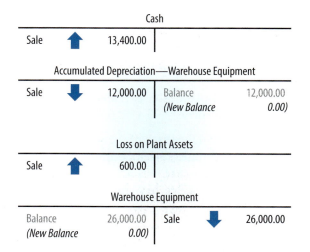

The amount of gain or loss is calculated by subtracting the book value from the cash received. The $600.00 loss on disposal is recorded as a debit to Loss on Plant Assets as shown in the next column.

The sale of plant assets is not a normal operating activity of Vaughn Distributors. A loss from the sale of plant assets is classified as Other Expense.

>> Selling a Plant Asset

① Compute the gain or loss, **$600.00** loss, by subtracting the book value of the asset, **$14,000.00**, from the cash received, **$13,400.00**.

② Check the type of disposal, **Sold**, and write the date, **January 3, 20X4**, and the disposal amount, **$13,400.00**, on the plant asset record.

③ Record an entry in the cash receipts journal to remove the original cost, **$26,000.00**, from **Warehouse Equipment** and **$12,000.00** from **Accumulated Depreciation—Warehouse Equipment**. Record the loss the on sale, **$600.00**, as a debit to **Loss on Plant Assets**.

Trading a Plant Asset

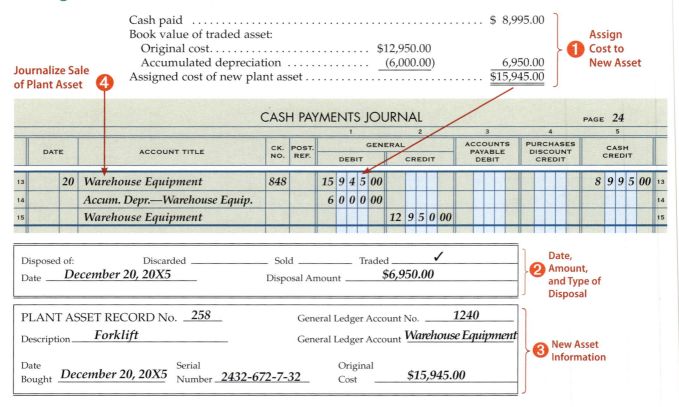

Cash paid .... $ 8,995.00

Book value of traded asset:

Original cost $12,950.00

Accumulated depreciation .... (6,000.00)   6,950.00

Journalize Sale of Plant Asset ④

Assigned cost of new plant asset $15,945.00

① Assign Cost to New Asset

	DATE	ACCOUNT TITLE	CK. NO.	POST. REF.	GENERAL DEBIT	GENERAL CREDIT	ACCOUNTS PAYABLE DEBIT	PURCHASES DISCOUNT CREDIT	CASH CREDIT	
13	20	Warehouse Equipment	848		15 9 4 5 00				8 9 9 5 00	13
14		Accum. Depr.—Warehouse Equip.			6 0 0 0 00					14
15		Warehouse Equipment				12 9 5 0 00				15

CASH PAYMENTS JOURNAL   PAGE 24

Disposed of: Discarded _____ Sold _____ Traded ____✓____

Date __December 20, 20X5__   Disposal Amount __$6,950.00__

② Date, Amount, and Type of Disposal

PLANT ASSET RECORD No. __258__   General Ledger Account No. __1240__

Description __Forklift__   General Ledger Account __Warehouse Equipment__

Date Bought __December 20, 20X5__   Serial Number __2432-672-7-32__   Original Cost __$15,945.00__

③ New Asset Information

Vaughn Distributors needed a new forklift. The vendor agreed to take cash and an old forklift in trade. The new plant asset's original cost equals the cash actually paid plus the book value of the asset traded. >> App A: Historical Cost

When an old plant asset is traded for a new plant asset, the journal entry:

1. Removes the original cost of the old plant asset and its related accumulated depreciation.

> December 20, 20X5. Paid cash, $8,995.00, plus old forklift for new forklift: original cost of old forklift, $12,950.00; total accumulated depreciation through December 20, 20X5, $6,000.00. Check No. 848.

2. Recognizes the cash paid.
3. Records the new plant asset at its original cost.

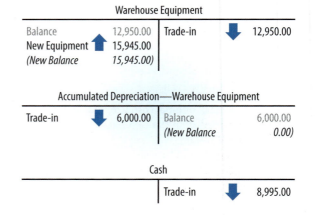

❶ Compute the original cost of the new asset, $15,945.00, by adding the book value of the asset traded, $6,950.00, and the cash paid, $8,995.00.

❷ Check the type of disposal, Traded, and write the date, December 20, 20X5, and the disposal amount, $6,950.00, on the plant asset record of the traded asset.

❸ Complete section 1 of the plant asset record for the new asset.

❹ Record the journal entry to reflect the trade in of the original plant asset, original cost, $12,950.00, from Warehouse Equipment and $6,000.00 from Accumulated Depreciation—Warehouse Equipment. Record the value assigned to the new asset, $15,945.00, as a debit to Warehouse Equipment.

Selling Land and Buildings

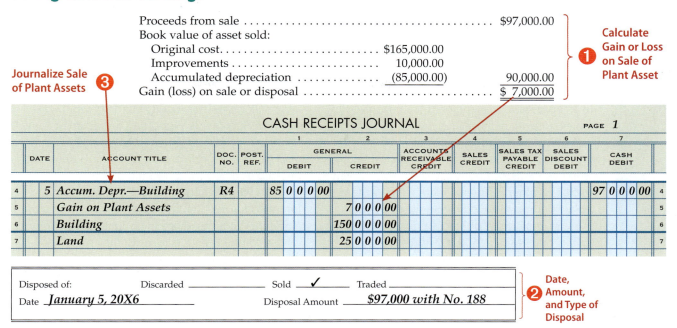

Proceeds from sale			$97,000.00	Calculate Gain or Loss on Sale of Plant Asset ❶
Book value of asset sold:				
Original cost		$165,000.00		
Improvements		10,000.00		
Accumulated depreciation		(85,000.00)	90,000.00	
Gain (loss) on sale or disposal			$ 7,000.00	

Journalize Sale of Plant Assets ❸

CASH RECEIPTS JOURNAL — PAGE 1

					GENERAL		ACCOUNTS RECEIVABLE CREDIT	SALES CREDIT	SALES TAX PAYABLE CREDIT	SALES DISCOUNT DEBIT	CASH DEBIT
	DATE	ACCOUNT TITLE	DOC. NO.	POST. REF.	DEBIT	CREDIT					
4	5	Accum. Depr.—Building	R4		85 0 0 0 00						97 0 0 0 00
5		Gain on Plant Assets				7 0 0 0 00					
6		Building				150 0 0 0 00					
7		Land				25 0 0 0 00					

Disposed of: Discarded _____   Sold ✓ _____   Traded _____

Date **January 5, 20X6**   Disposal Amount **$97,000 with No. 188**

Date, Amount, and Type of Disposal ❷

> **January 5, 20X6.** Fidelity Company sold land with a building for $97,000.00 cash; original cost of land, $25,000.00; original cost of building, $140,000.00; improvements to prepare the building for sale, $10,000.00; total accumulated depreciation on building through December 31, 20X5, $85,000.00. Receipt No. 4.

Land is considered to be a permanent plant asset. Therefore, its useful life is not estimated, and annual depreciation is not recorded for it. The book value of land is its original cost. **>> App A: Historical Cost**

Land is seldom discarded (abandoned). Usually, land is sold when the buildings on it are sold. A separate plant record is maintained for the land and the building. Each record is updated when a sale is made.

Improvements that merely maintain the asset in its normal operation should be expensed. Expenditures that improve the asset should be added to the cost of the asset.

The journal entry:

1. Removes the original cost of the land and building and the building's related accumulated depreciation.

2. Recognizes the cash received.
3. Recognizes the gain on disposal of the plant assets.

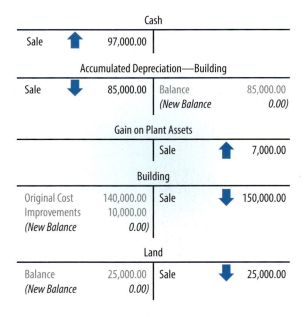

>> Selling Land and Building

❶ Compute the gain on the sale of plant assets, **$7,000.00**, by subtracting the book value of the land and buildings, **$90,000.00**, from the cash received, **$97,000.00**.

❷ Check the type of disposal, **Sold**, and write the date, **January 5, 20X6**, and the disposal amount, **$97,000.00**, on the plant asset record. Include a reference to the other plant asset included in the sale.

❸ Record an entry on the cash receipts journal to remove the cost of existing plant assets: **Land**, **$25,000.00**, and **Building**, **$150,000.00**, and to remove **$85,000.00** from **Accumulated Depreciation—Building**. Record the gain on sale, **$7,000.00**, as a credit to **Gain on Plant Assets**.

A Pyramid Scheme at Equity Funding

Equity Funding Corporation of America collapsed 13 years after its founding, a victim of an aggressive management team resolved to achieve growth at all costs.

Equity Funding's principal line of business was selling life insurance. As was typical in the insurance industry, Equity Funding would sell its policies to other insurance carriers. In exchange, Equity Funding received a one-time payment as its fee for selling the policy. For example, John Stanton purchases a $100,000 life insurance policy from Equity Funding. The policy requires that John pay an annual premium of $600. Equity Funding sells the policy to Excel Life Insurance (ELI) for $1,000. John continues to pay his $600 annual premium to Equity Funding, who remits the premium to ELI. Should John die while the policy is in force, ELI would be responsible for paying his estate $100,000.

Equity Funding first sold its stock to the public in 1964. At that time, the company earned a modest $0.6 million on assets of $9 million. The 1969 appointment of Fred Levin as the top executive of life insurance operations was a turning point for the company. Mr. Levin had a reputation for being a ruthless manager who could achieve results. His reputation was well founded, as the company's 1972 income soared to $26 million on assets of $500 million. Equity Funding had quickly become one of the nation's top life insurance companies.

These dramatic results were achieved with the help of an elaborate pyramid scheme. Equity Funding began selling fake insurance policies to other insurance companies. Equity Funding would instantly earn revenue from the one-time payment by the insurance carrier. But Mr. Levin faced two problems in maintaining the fraud. First, the insurance carriers would expect to receive the annual premiums from the fake policyholders. Thus, Equity Funding had to sell more fake policies to obtain the cash to pay the annual premiums. Using the example above, Equity Funding would have to sell two policies to pay John Stanton's $600 premium and have enough cash left over to report the continued growth in sales that Mr. Levin demanded.

Second, ELI would be alerted that something was unusual if none of the Equity Funding policies were ever collected. Thus, Equity Funding had to create fake documents supporting the death of some of the policyholders. The number of policies that had to be sold grew larger every year, a trend that resembles an inverted pyramid.

The scheme unraveled in 1973, when a disgruntled former employee blew the whistle on the scheme. When insurance investigators took control of the company and its records, they soon learned that Equity Funding used a special code to distinguish fake from real policies. The fake policies began with the digits 99.

ACTIVITY

Blaylock Insurance opened its doors in 2001 with a single office in Vermont. The company sells term life insurance to customers who, due to their medical history, have been turned down by traditional insurance companies.

Through internal growth and a series of acquisitions, the company quickly expanded its footprint to cover most of the continental United States. To help manage its growth, the company has been organized into six divisions.

OPEN THE TABLEAU WORKBOOK TLA_CH07

The Tableau workbook contains summary sales data from the period 2001 to 2018. Read the caption above each chart to understand the data presented. Use the charts to answer the following questions.

1. Review the Policies by Division worksheet. How would you describe the trend in sales?

2. Examine the Number of Policies worksheet. Does there appear to be any significant trends in the number of policies sold by any division?

3. Analyze the Sales Trends chart using the Division filter. Does any evidence exist to suggest that any division is falsifying its reported sales?

Sources: Called to Account: Financial Frauds That Shaped the American Accounting Profession, 2e, Paul M. Clikeman, Routledge (New York, New York), 2013. Contemporary Auditing, 6e, Michael C. Knapp, Cengage Learning (Mason, Ohio), 2007.

LO7 Journalize the disposal of plant assets.

Audit your understanding LO7

1. What is recorded on a plant asset record for a plant asset that has been discarded?
2. When an asset is disposed of after the beginning of the fiscal year, what entry may need to be recorded before an entry is made for a discarded plant asset?
3. What is the formula to compute the gain or loss on the sale of a plant asset?
4. When cash is paid and old store equipment is traded for new store equipment, what is the formula for calculating the new equipment's original cost?

Work together 7-3 LO7

Recording the disposal of plant assets

Use the plant asset records from Work Together 7-2. A general journal, cash receipts journal, cash payments journal, and additional plant asset records are provided in the *Working Papers*. The following transactions occurred in 20X5. Source documents are abbreviated as follows: check, C; memorandum, M; receipt, R. Your instructor will guide you through the following examples.

Transactions:

Jan.   6. Discarded printer, no. 321. M165.

Mar. 29. Received cash for sale of conveyor table, no. 326, $500.00. M182 and R321.

June 25. Received cash for sale of a desk, no. 289, $600.00. M195 and R467.

Dec. 27. Paid cash, $23,000.00, plus old truck, no. 332, for new truck, no. 392. M256 and C887.

       29. Sold a warehouse, nos. 341 and 342, for $273,400.00. M258 and R687.

1. Journalize additional depreciation, if needed. Journalize the disposal of each plant asset.
2. Make appropriate notations in the plant asset records.

On your own 7-3 LO7

Recording the disposal of plant assets

Use the plant asset records from On Your Own 7-2. A general journal, cash receipts journal, cash payments journal, and additional plant asset records are provided in the *Working Papers*. The following transactions occurred in 20X5. Source documents are abbreviated as follows: check, C; memorandum, M; receipt, R. Work this problem independently.

Transactions:

Mar. 23. Paid cash, $3,000.00, plus old point-of-sale system, no. 410, for a new system, no. 501. M89 and C753.

       27. Received cash, $300.00, for an office chair, no. 460. M91 and R699.

June 17. Received cash for sale of a display case, no. 233, $3,300.00. M103 and R789.

Aug.   8. Discarded a tablet computer, no. 403. M117.

Oct.   3. Sold land, no. 449, and a building, no. 448, for $175,000.00. M143 and R884.

1. Journalize additional depreciation, if needed. Journalize the disposal of each plant asset.
2. Make appropriate notations in the plant asset records.

LO8 Calculate depreciation expense using the declining-balance method.
LO9 Calculate depreciation expense using the units-of-production method.
LO10 Calculate depreciation expense for income tax reporting.
LO11 Compare annual depreciation expense for three depreciation methods.
LO12 Calculate depletion of a natural resource.

Declining-Balance Method of Depreciation LO8

DEPRECIATION TABLE

Plant Asset:	Automobile		Original Cost:	$37,000.00
Depreciation Method:	Double-declining balance		Estimated Salvage Value:	$4,000.00
			Estimated Useful Life:	5 years

Year	Beginning Book Value	Declining-Balance Rate	Annual Depreciation	Ending Book Value
1	$37,000.00	40%	$14,800.00	$22,200.00
2	22,200.00	40%	8,880.00	13,320.00
3	13,320.00	40%	5,328.00	7,992.00
4	7,992.00	40%	3,196.80	4,795.20
5	4,795.20	---	795.20	4,000.00

Double Declining-Balance Rate   Annual Depreciation Expense   Final Year's Depreciation Expense

Many plant assets depreciate more in the early years of useful life than in the later years. Charging more depreciation expense in the early years of a plant asset may be more accurate than charging the same amount each year.

A type of accelerated depreciation that multiplies the book value of an asset by a constant depreciation rate to determine annual depreciation is called the **declining-balance method of depreciation**.

The declining-balance depreciation rate is based on the straight-line rate. Using a depreciation rate that is twice the straight-line rate is referred to as the *double declining-balance method*. For example, a plant asset with an estimated useful life of five years would have a depreciation rate of 40%. The rate is used each year of the asset's useful life.

	Total depreciation expense		100%
÷	Estimated useful life	÷	5 years
=	Straight-line rate	=	20%
×	Double the rate	×	2
=	Double declining-balance rate	=	40%

The annual depreciation expense is calculated using the beginning book value for each year. As shown in the depreciation table above, the beginning book value equals its original cost in the first year. In later years, the beginning book value is the same as the ending book value from the previous year.

	Beginning Book Value	×	Depreciation Rate	=	Annual Depreciation Expense
Year 3	$13,320.00	×	40%	=	$5,328.00

Using this formula, the annual depreciation in year 5 would be $1,918.08 ($4,795.20 book value multiplied by the 40% depreciation rate). This amount would cause the book value of the plant asset to be less than its estimated salvage value. Therefore, in the last year, only enough depreciation expense is recorded to reduce the book value of the plant asset to its salvage value.

	Beginning Book Value	−	Salvage Value	=	Annual Depreciation Expense
Year 5	$4,795.20	−	$4,000.00	=	$795.20

Units-of-Production Method of Depreciation LO9

DEPRECIATION TABLE

Plant Asset: Van
Depreciation Method: Units-of-Production
Original Cost: $24,200.00
Estimated Salvage Value: $5,000.00

Estimated Total Depreciation: $19,200.00
Estimated Useful Life: 120,000 miles
Depreciation Rate: $0.16 per mile

Year	Beginning Book Value	Miles Driven	Annual Depreciation	Ending Book Value
1	$24,200.00	22,600	$3,616.00	$20,584.00
2	20,584.00	24,300	3,888.00	16,696.00
3	16,696.00	28,100	4,496.00	12,200.00
4	12,200.00	20,400	3,264.00	8,936.00
5	8,936.00	16,200	2,592.00	6,344.00

Annual Depreciation Expense   Unit Depreciation Rate

Sometimes the useful life of a plant asset depends on how much the asset is used. For example, an automobile will wear out faster if it is driven 80,000 miles a year rather than 60,000 miles. Calculating the estimated annual depreciation expense based on the amount of production expected from a plant asset is called the **units-of-production method of depreciation**.

Mariah Delivery Service owns a delivery van. The van originally cost $24,200.00 and had an estimated salvage value of $5,000.00 and an estimated useful life of 120,000 miles. The depreciation rate for the truck is calculated by dividing the estimated total depreciation expense by the estimated useful life.

Depreciation expense for each year of the truck's estimated useful life is calculated at 16 cents per mile driven.

	Original cost	$24,200.00
−	Estimated salvage value	− 5,000.00
=	Total depreciation expense	= $19,200.00
÷	Estimated useful life	÷ 120,000 miles
=	Unit depreciation rate	= $ 0.16

The annual depreciation expense for the truck is calculated by multiplying the total number of miles driven by the depreciation rate. After five years, $17,856.00 of depreciation has been expensed, as shown above. Additional depreciation expense will be recorded in future years as the truck approaches its 120,000 miles of useful life.

	Total Miles Driven	×	Unit Depreciation Rate	=	Annual Depreciation Expense
Year 3	28,100	×	$0.16	=	$4,496.00

> **FYI**
> A company can select any generally accepted depreciation method. Once it has selected a method, however, the company cannot change the method unless it can show that the new method would better report the company's financial activities.

Calculating Depreciation Expense for Income Tax Reporting LO10

DEPRECIATION TABLE

Plant Asset:	Computer		Original Cost:	$1,800.00
Depreciation Method:	MACRS		Property Class:	5-year

Year	Beginning Book Value	Depreciation Rate	Annual Depreciation	Ending Book Value
1	$1,800.00	20.00%	$360.00	$1,440.00
2	1,440.00	32.00%	576.00	864.00
3	864.00	19.20%	345.60	518.40
4	518.40	11.52%	207.36	311.04
5	311.04	11.52%	207.36	103.68
6	103.68	5.76%	103.68	0.00

MACRS Depreciation Rate

Annual Depreciation Expense

Most businesses use one of the generally accepted accounting methods to calculate depreciation for financial reporting purposes. A depreciation method required by the Internal Revenue Service to be used for income tax calculation purposes for most plant assets is called the **Modified Accelerated Cost Recovery System (MACRS)**.

MACRS is a depreciation method with prescribed periods for nine classes of plant assets. A property is assigned to a specified class based on its characteristics and general life expectancy. The two most common classes, other than real estate, are the five- and seven-year property classes. The five-year property class includes cars, general-purpose trucks, computers, manufacturing equipment, and office machinery. The seven-year property class includes office furniture and fixtures.

To calculate depreciation using MACRS, the Internal Revenue Service has prescribed methods that use

3-, 5-, 7-, 10-, 15-, and 20-Year Property Half-Year Convention

Year	Depreciation rate for recovery period					
	3-year	5-year	7-year	10-year	15-year	20-year
1	33.33%	20.00%	14.29%	10.00%	5.00%	3.750%
2	44.45	32.00	24.49	18.00	9.50	7.219
3	14.81	19.20	17.49	14.40	8.55	6.677
4	7.41	11.52	12.49	11.52	7.70	6.177
5		11.52	8.93	9.22	6.93	5.713
6		5.76	8.92	7.37	6.23	5.285
7			8.93	6.55	5.90	4.888
8			4.46	6.55	5.90	4.522
9				6.56	5.91	4.462
10				6.55	5.90	4.461
11				3.28	5.91	4.462
12					5.90	4.461
13					5.91	4.462
14					5.90	4.461
15					5.91	4.462
16					2.95	4.461
17						4.462
18						4.461
19						4.462
20						4.461
21						2.231

annual percentage rates to determine depreciation for each class of plant asset. These rates are applied to the total cost of the plant asset without considering a salvage value.

The depreciation rate for six asset classes is shown on the previous page. The rates assume the use of the half-year convention. As a result, an asset is depreciated over one year more than its asset class. For example, the five-year property class depreciation is spread over six years.

The rates shown in the table are based on two depreciation methods. The double declining-balance method is used for most of an asset's useful life. The depreciation method switches to the straight-line method as the asset approaches the end of its useful life. The switch can be seen in the 11.52% rates for years 4 and 5 of the five-year class. The next year's depreciation rate, 5.76%, is half of the 11.52% straight-line rate. In the sixth year, assets in this class are only depreciated for half of the year.

Annual depreciation is calculated by multiplying the plant asset's original cost times the depreciation rate for its specific class. A computer is classified as five-year property.

	Original Cost	×	Depreciation Rate	=	Annual Depreciation Expense
Year 3	$1,800.00	×	19.20%	=	$345.60

The remaining three MACRS asset classes apply to different types of real property. MACRS requires these plant assets to be depreciated using the straight-line method over useful lives ranging from 25 to 39 years.

Comparison of Depreciation Methods LO11

Original Cost: $4,000.00
Estimated Salvage Value: $350.00
Estimated Useful Life: 5 years

Year	Straight-Line Method	Double Declining-Balance Method	MACRS
1	$ 730.00	$1,600.00	$ 800.00
2	730.00	960.00	1,280.00
3	730.00	576.00	768.00
4	730.00	345.60	460.80
5	730.00	168.40	460.80
6	—	—	230.40
Total Depreciation	$3,650.00	$3,650.00	$4,000.00

A business can elect to use one depreciation method for financial reporting and MACRS depreciation for its federal tax return. Each year, the depreciation expense and accumulated depreciation will differ between the two methods. Thus, the business must maintain depreciation records for each depreciation method.

A comparison of three depreciation methods for an asset having a five-year useful life is shown above. The comparison assumes that the asset was purchased at the beginning of the fiscal year. The total depreciation differs because only the MACRS method ignores the asset's salvage value.

Each of these depreciation methods conforms to generally accepted accounting principles. The straight-line method results in the same amount of depreciation expense recorded for each of the five years of estimated life. The double declining-balance method records a larger depreciation expense in the early years than the straight-line method.

MACRS uses percentages provided by the Internal Revenue Service. MACRS is based on a combination of the double declining-balance and straight-line methods. Because MACRS uses the half-year convention, a five-year asset is depreciated over six years.

Calculating Depletion on Natural Resources LO12

DEPLETION TABLE

Plant Asset:	Coal Mine	Estimated Total Depletion:	$2,100,000.00
Depreciation Method:	Units-of-Production	Estimated Useful Life:	800,000 tons
Original Cost:	$2,500,000.00	Depletion Rate:	$2.625
Estimated Salvage Value:	$400,000.00		

Year	Beginning Book Value	Tons Recovered	Annual Depletion	Ending Book Value
1	$2,500,000.00	69,000	$181,125.00	$2,318,875.00
2	2,318,875.00	125,000	328,125.00	1,990,750.00
3	1,990,750.00	162,000	425,250.00	1,565,500.00
4	1,565,500.00	185,000	485,625.00	1,079,875.00
5	1,079,875.00	92,500	242,812.50	837,062.50

Annual Depletion Expense   Depletion Rate

Some plant assets decrease in value because part of these plant assets is physically removed in the operation of a business. For example, a lumber business owns land on which many trees grow. The business removes the trees to use for lumber. The land with the trees still growing on it is more valuable than the land from which the trees have been removed. The decrease in the value of a plant asset because of the removal of a natural resource is called **depletion**.

Powerland Company owns land on which a coal mine is located. The land with the coal has an original cost of $2,500,000.00. The company's experts estimate that the land contains 800,000 tons of recoverable coal. The estimated value of the remaining land after the coal is removed is $400,000.00. Therefore, each ton of coal taken from the land decreases the land's value by $2.625.

	Original cost	$2,500,000.00
−	Estimated salvage value	− 400,000.00
=	Estimated value of coal	= $2,100,000.00
÷	Estimated tons of coal	÷ 800,000
=	Depletion rate	= $ 2.625

In the third year of operations, the business removed 162,000 tons of coal. The depletion expense for the third year is $425,250.00 as shown. Powerland uses the general ledger accounts Mine, Accumulated Depletion—Mine, and Depletion Expense—Mine to record depletion. Rather than using a contra account, a business can elect to credit the asset account. Regardless of the method used, the amount reported on the balance sheet would reflect the book value of the land.

	Tons Recovered	×	Depletion Rate	=	Annual Depletion Expense
Year 3	162,000	×	$2.625	=	$425,250.00

FYI

Depletion is used to charge the cost of a variety of natural resources, including oil, gas, coal, gravel, minerals, and timber.

TERMS REVIEW

declining-balance method of depreciation

units-of-production method of depreciation

Modified Accelerated Cost Recovery System (MACRS)

depletion

Audit your understanding LO8, 9, 10, 11, 12

1. How is the depreciation rate calculated for the declining-balance method of depreciation?
2. How is the last year's depreciation expense calculated using the declining-balance method of depreciation?
3. What is the basis for the units-of-production method of calculating depreciation?
4. Describe the types of assets in the MACRS five- and seven-year property classes.
5. Which depreciation method ignores the estimated salvage value?
6. How does a mining company calculate the amount of depletion for a year?

Work together 7-4 LO8, 9, 10, 12

Computing depreciation using various depreciation methods and calculating depletion

1. The following information relates to a machine purchased on January 8, 20X1. Depreciation tables are provided in the *Working Papers*. Your instructor will guide you through the following examples.

		Production Hours	
Original cost	$24,000.00	20X1	2,880
Estimated salvage value	$3,000.00	20X2	3,220
Estimated useful life	5 years or 16,000 hours	20X3	3,150
MACRS property class	5-year	20X4	2,800

Complete depreciation tables showing depreciation expense calculated using the double declining-balance, units-of-production, and MACRS methods of depreciation. Round the double declining-balance depreciation rate to two decimal places. Round the units-of-production depreciation rate to the nearest cent.

2. The following data relate to a gas well owned by Southern Energy, Inc. The amount of gas taken from the well is measured in million cubic feet (MCF). A depletion table is provided in the *Working Papers*.

		MCF Recovered	
Original cost	$840,000.00	20X1	22,600
Estimated salvage value	$60,000.00	20X2	24,300
Estimated MCF of recoverable gas	800,000 MCF	20X3	28,100
		20X4	20,400

Complete a table showing depletion expense calculated using the units-of-production method. Round the depletion rate to the nearest cent.

On your own 7-4 LO8, 9, 10, 12

Computing depreciation using various depreciation methods and calculating depletion

1. The following information relates to a truck purchased on January 12, 20X1. Depreciation tables are provided in the *Working Papers*. Work independently to complete the following problem.

		Miles Driven	
Original cost	$38,000.00	20X1	79,500
Estimated salvage value	$2,500.00	20X2	62,800
Estimated useful life	3 years or 300,000 miles	20X3	52,800
MACRS property class	5-year	20X4	66,900

Complete tables showing depreciation expense calculated using the double declining-balance, units-of-production, and MACRS methods of depreciation. Round the double declining-balance depreciation rate to two decimal places. Round the units-of-production depreciation rate to the nearest cent.

2. The following data relate to a mineral mine owned by Bachmann Enterprises.

		Tons Mined	
Original cost	$420,000.00	20X1	33,500
Estimated salvage value	$80,000.00	20X2	42,500
Estimated tons of recoverable minerals	120,000 tons	20X3	25,600
		20X4	10,600

Complete a depletion table for this mine; show depletion expense calculated using the units-of-production method. Round the depletion rate to the nearest cent.

A Look at **Accounting** Software

Applying Depreciation

Vaughn Distributors, Inc., uses a manual system for calculating and recording depreciation. The company has elected to use straight-line depreciation for all plant assets, for both corporate analysis and tax reporting. Imagine that Vaughn Distributors uses a computerized accounting system. The speed and efficiency of an automated system enables a company to more simply keep two sets of financial records—one for its corporate use, retaining the straight-line method, and the other to meet the requirements of the IRS for accelerated depreciation.

Once the settings are made, plant assets can be depreciated by category or in total simply by clicking on Depreciate.

Vaughn records depreciation and produces financial statements just once at the end of the year. Most companies prefer to see financial statements at least quarterly to better manage their business activity. Since the IRS requires quarterly estimated payments of a company's annual tax liability, it is assumed here that Vaughn calculates and records depreciation at the end of every quarter so it can prepare financial reports for the period.

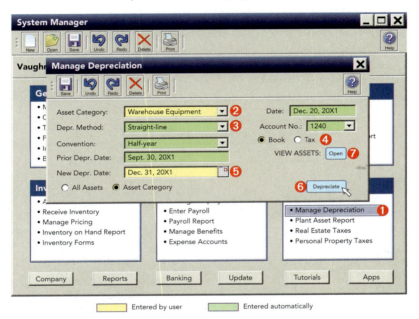

Entered by user   Entered automatically

❶ The accountant clicked on the **Manage Depreciation** option from the System Manager, and a dialog box opened that is used to set the depreciation variables for each plant asset category. Once those variables are set, the accountant can elect to depreciate all plant assets or to select a category of assets.

❷ The accountant has selected the Warehouse Equipment category for depreciation.

❸ Prior settings for depreciation method and convention are displayed along with the account number and prior depreciation date.

❹ The default setting for financial records is Book. Clicking **Tax** would display different settings such as double-declining balance or MACRS.

❺ The accountant has set December 31 as the next posting date for depreciation amounts.

❻ The choice was made to depreciate just the Warehouse Equipment category of assets and the **Depreciate** button was clicked. On December 31 the system will calculate and post the depreciation for each item of warehouse equipment and will post a journal entry for the total depreciation of all warehouse equipment.

❼ To see the status of a specific asset, the accountant would click the **Open** button.

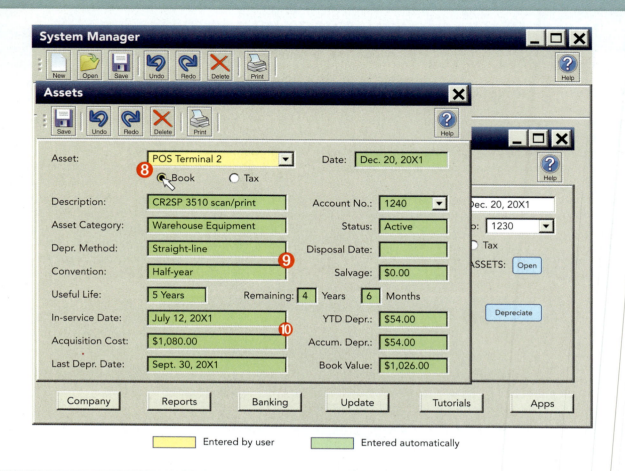

Entered by user	Entered automatically

8 When the **Open** button is clicked, a second dialog box is opened, allowing the accountant to select a specific plant asset and to choose whether to view depreciation for corporate or tax purposes. All other fields in this window are display only—no changes can be made. The accountant has opened this item to verify the accuracy of the data for an audit.

9 The system displays the depreciation settings, as in the first dialog box, as well as the status of the item. If the item is inactive, the disposal date would be displayed.

10 The system displays the current depreciation status of that asset including the remaining useful life.

The process of setting up depreciation in an automated system can be complex for a business with operations in multiple countries. Individual countries have different tax laws that affect how different assets can be depreciated. As a result of these laws, the business may need to provide each government with financial statements using GAAP, international financial reporting standards, and quarterly and annual income tax reports.

Accountants responsible for managing automated accounting systems should consider gaining certifications sponsored by the software vendor. The certification process typically requires completing a specified level of training and passing a certification exam. Certification guides the accountant in obtaining skills necessary to operate the accounting software. Similar to accounting certifications (see Explore Accounting, page 30), software certification demonstrates expertise in accounting software and enhances accountants' career opportunities. In addition, many software vendors sponsor annual conferences that enhance skill development and interaction with other software users.

Similar certifications are available for application software, such as Excel and Tableau. Microsoft offers an extensive selection of certifications for its Office, Windows, and other software. Tableau Software offers two certifications that require candidates to complete specific courses, pass an exam, and demonstrate up to a year of experience using the software.

CHAPTER SUMMARY

Plant assets, such as land, buildings, and equipment, are expected to help the business earn a profit for more than one year. The historical cost of each plant asset and related information is recorded on a plant asset record.

Except for land, a plant asset is depreciated over its estimated useful life. The original cost, estimated salvage value, and estimated useful life are used to calculate a plant asset's annual depreciation expense. Several depreciation methods conform to generally accepted accounting principles. The straight-line method of depreciation charges an equal amount of depreciation expense each year of a plant asset's useful life. The straight-line method is the easiest of the depreciation methods to calculate.

Accelerated depreciation methods depreciate more in the early years of a plant asset's useful life than in the later years. The double declining-balance method depreciates a plant asset at twice the straight-line rate. The useful life of some plant assets depends on how much

the assets are used. The units-of-production method of depreciation can be used for plant assets, such as trucks and machines. This method is also used to account for the depletion of natural resources, such as gas and mineral reserves.

The Modified Accelerated Cost Recovery System (MACRS) is used for income tax purposes. For equipment in the five- and seven-year property classes, MACRS is based on the half-year convention using an accelerated depreciation method with a switch to the straight-line method later in the asset's useful life.

When a plant asset is sold, the accumulated depreciation of the asset is brought up to date. Any gain or loss on the sale is determined by subtracting the updated book value of the asset from the sale price. If the asset is traded for a similar asset, the purchase price of the new asset is the book value of the old asset plus any additional money paid to the seller.

Tax Laws Encourage Plant Asset Purchases

The primary purpose of federal income tax laws is to guide the government's collection of tax revenue. However, Congress also uses income tax law to influence business activities. To promote economic development, Congress provides businesses with financial incentives to purchase plant assets. A business that purchases plant assets will likely hire more employees, purchase additional raw materials, and earn a higher net income—all resulting in increasing economic activity and income tax revenues.

Tax law allows businesses to expense certain plant assets in the year the assets are purchased. Assets that qualify for this election are known as *Section 179 property*, named for the applicable section of the Internal Revenue Code. In general, a business can expense up to one million dollars of

Section 179 property purchases during a tax year. Many exceptions to this tax law can increase or limit the amount a particular business can deduct. Thus, tax accountants with a thorough knowledge of the current tax law must be consulted.

Section 179 property includes tangible personal property (e.g., computers, office desks, store displays) and manufacturing equipment. Thus, most buildings and storage structures do not qualify as Section 179 property.

INSTRUCTIONS

Obtain a copy of IRS Form 4562, *Depreciation and Amortization*. Identify the parts of the form. Prepare a list of amounts and other required information to report Section 179 property and MACRS depreciation.

APPLY YOUR UNDERSTANDING

INSTRUCTIONS: Download problem instructions for Excel, QuickBooks, and Sage 50 from the textbook companion website at www.C21accounting.com.

7-1 Application Problem — Journalizing asset purchase transactions LO1, 2

McKenzie Corporation depreciates all plant assets using the straight-line method. Plant asset records, a general journal, and a cash payments journal are provided in the *Working Papers*. Source documents are abbreviated as: check, C; memorandum, M.

Transactions:

Jan. 12. Wrote a $2,400.00 check to purchase a copy machine (plant asset no. 116, serial no. 46-36364). McKenzie believes the machine will have a five-year useful life and a $200.00 salvage value. C525.

Aug. 22. Bought a store shelving unit (plant asset no. 121, serial number GE-25BK) on account from Harris Supply for $4,800.00. Payment terms of the sale are n/30. The unit is expected to last for five years and has been assigned a salvage value of $1,000.00. M77.

Sept. 27. Purchased a storage building for $225,000.00 from Platte Industries. A licensed appraiser set the value of the building at $200,000.00 and the land at $50,000.00. McKenzie depreciates buildings over a 25-year useful life. The estimated salvage value of the building is set at $60,000.00. Assign the assets numbers 133 and 134. C722.

Instructions:

1. Journalize the transactions completed during 20X1. General ledger accounts are: Land, 1210; Building, 1220; Office Equipment, 1230; Store Equipment, 1240; and Transportation Equipment, 1250.

2. Complete section 1 of a plant asset record for new asset purchases. Save your work to complete Problem 7-2.

3. Assume that McKenzie Corporation uses IFRS to depreciate plant assets. McKenzie purchased a truck for $69,000.00. The truck had a sticker price of $79,000.00. The major items on the sticker include: engine, $31,600.00; transmission, $19,750.00; tires, $3,950.00; and frame (and remaining sticker items), $23,700.00. Determine the assigned cost to each item.

7-2 Application Problem — Calculating and journalizing depreciation LO4, 5

Use the plant asset records from Problem 7-1. Depreciation tables and a general journal are provided in the *Working Papers*.

Instructions:

1. Complete the depreciation table for each asset using the straight-line depreciation method. If the asset was not purchased at the beginning of 20X1, compute the depreciation expense for the part of 20X1 that the company owned the asset.

2. Complete each plant asset record for 20X1 through 20X4.

3. Journalize the adjusting entries to record depreciation expense for 20X1. Save your work to complete Problem 7-3.

7-3 Application Problem | Recording the disposal of plant assets LO7

sage 50

1. Journalize and post transactions related to recording the disposal of plant assets to the cash receipts journal.
2. Journalize and post depreciation entries related to the disposal of plant assets to the general journal.
3. From the menu bar, select Reports & Forms; Accounts Receivable.
4. Print the cash receipts journal.

1. Journalize and post transactions related to recording the disposal of plant assets to the journal.
2. Journalize and post depreciation entries related to the disposal of plant assets to the journal.
3. From the menu bar, select Reports; Accountant & Taxes.
4. Print the Journal.

X

1. Journalize transactions related to recording the disposal of plant assets to the cash receipts, cash payments, and general journals.
2. Print the worksheets.

Use the plant asset records from Problem 7-1. A general journal, cash receipts journal, cash payments journal, and additional plant asset records are provided in the *Working Papers*. The following transactions occurred in 20X5. Source documents are abbreviated as follows: check, C; memorandum, M; receipt, R.

Transactions:

Feb. 7. Sold a storage building, including the related land, to Esterine Corporation for $194,500.00, receiving a check for the total amount. Plant assets no. 133 and 134. M201 and R445.

June 25. Sold a desk, no. 289, to Second Act for $600.00. M222 and R687.

July 12. Received a $2,000.00 check for the sale of a shelving unit, no. 121, to Gaston Nursery. M244 and R884.

Oct. 6. A copy machine, no. 116, was beyond repair and has been discarded. M277.

Dec. 27. Traded in a truck, no. 332, and paid $23,000.00 to Nelson's Auto Mart on a new truck, no. 392. M280 and C887.

Instructions:

1. Journalize additional depreciation, if needed. Journalize the disposal of each plant asset.
2. Make appropriate notations in the plant asset records.

7-4 Application Problem | Computing depreciation using various depreciation methods and calculating depletion LO8, 9, 10, 12

Instructions:

1. The following information relates to a car purchased on January 8, 20X1. Depreciation tables are provided in the *Working Papers*.

		Miles Driven	
Original cost	$40,000.00	20X1	28,600
Estimated salvage value	$5,000.00	20X2	22,600
Estimated useful life	5 years or 100,000 miles	20X3	23,800
MACRS property class	5-year	20X4	25,900

Complete depreciation tables showing depreciation expense calculated using the double declining-balance, units-of-production, and MACRS methods of depreciation. Round the double declining-balance depreciation rate to two decimal places. Round the units-of-production depreciation rate to the nearest cent.

(Continued on next page)

2. The following data relate to a mineral mine owned by Chester Mining Company. A depletion table is provided in the *Working Papers*.

		Tones Mined	
Original cost	$825,000.00	20X1	86,600
Estimated salvage value	$100,000.00	20X2	92,500
Estimated tons of recoverable minerals	700,000 tons	20X3	105,900

Complete a table showing depletion expense calculated using the units-of-production method. Round the depletion rate to the nearest cent.

7-M Mastery Problem — Recording entries for plant assets LO1, 2, 4, 5, 7, 8, 10

sage 50

1. Journalize and post transactions related to recording the disposal of plant assets to the cash receipts journal.
2. Journalize and post depreciation entries related to the disposal of plant assets to the general journal.
3. From the menu bar, select Reports & Forms; Accounts Receivable.
4. Print the cash receipts journal.

QB
Quick Books

1. Journalize and post transactions related to recording the disposal of plant assets to the journal.
2. Journalize and post depreciation entries related to the disposal of plant assets to the journal.
3. From the menu bar, select Reports; Accountant & Taxes.
4. Print the Journal.

[X]

1. Journalize transactions related to recording the disposal of plant assets to the cash receipts, cash payments, and general journals.
2. Print the worksheets.

Eastern, Inc., uses the straight-line method of calculating depreciation expense. The plant asset records, depreciation schedules, and journals for Eastern are given in the *Working Papers*.

Transactions:

Mar. 2, 20X1 — Paid cash, $660.00, and traded in an old computer, plant asset no. 233, for a new computer; serial no. C23656M, plant asset no. 315. The new computer has been assigned a three-year useful life and has an estimated salvage value of $300.00. M270 and C722.

Sept. 6, 20X3 — Sold a computer, plant asset no. 315, to an employee for $400.00. M399 and R935.

Sept. 9, 20X3 — Purchased an apartment complex from Williams Communities. The $900,000.00 purchase price includes six apartment buildings and an office. The complex was appraised for $1,000,000.00, with $820,000.00 assigned to the buildings. Eastern, Inc., paid $50,000.00 down and financed the remainder, signing a note with First American Bank. C839.

Instructions:

1. Journalize the transactions. Journalize an entry for additional depreciation expense if needed. Use page 3 of a general journal, page 9 of a cash receipts journal, and page 3 of a cash payments journal. Source documents are abbreviated as follows: check, C; memorandum, M; receipt, R.

2. Make needed notations on plant asset records 233 and 315.

3. Prepare double declining-balance and MACRS depreciation schedules for a $2,900.00 office desk purchased on January 10 of the current year. The desk has an estimated salvage value of $300.00 and a useful life of seven years. Round the double declining-balance depreciation rate to two decimal places.

4. Eastern has elected to begin using IFRS to depreciate plant assets. On September 22, 20X5, Eastern purchased a warehouse for $240,000.00, paying $50,000.00 down and signing a note with the seller for the remainder. The warehouse has an appraised value of $250,000.00, of which 45% is attributed to the land. The warehouse is structurally sound but requires significant repairs to the roof. Thus, the costs attributed to the building are estimated as follows: structure, 35%; electrical systems, 12%; roof, 5%; and landscaping, 3%. Determine the cost assigned to each item.

The following data relate to a coal mine owned by Platson Resources. A depletion table is provided in the *Working Papers*.

			Tons Mined	
Original cost	$720,000.00	20X1	54,200	
Estimated salvage value	$50,000.00	20X2	69,500	
Estimated tons of recoverable minerals	326,000 tons	20X3	62,800	

Instructions:

1. Complete a table showing depletion expense calculated using the units-of-production method. Round the depletion rate to the nearest cent.

2. In January 20X4, Platson Resources discovered a significant coal seam below the depths analyzed to determine its initial estimate of 326,000 tons. The company now estimates the mine still has 210,000 tons remaining to be recovered. Adjust the depletion rate and record depletion of 72,300 tons in 20X4 and 74,300 tons in 20X5.

21st Century Skills

A Salvage Title—Junk or Gem?

Theme: Financial, Economic, Business, and Entrepreneurial Literacy

Skills: Creativity and Innovation, Critical Thinking and Problem Solving, Communication and Collaboration, ICT Literacy

PARTNERSHIP FOR
21ST CENTURY SKILLS

You find the car of your dreams, and better yet, the price is too good to be true! Chances are it may have a salvage title, a branded title given by the state motor vehicle agency. It might be a good deal for someone thrifty. However, caution should be taken when purchasing a car with a salvage title.

Vehicles that have been in an accident, flood, or hailstorm; vandalized; or (in some states) previously stolen are issued a salvage title when the cost of repair exceeds the value of the car. Usually, the insurance company sells these cars to a salvage yard that dismantles and sells the parts. Other times, the car may be sold to someone who wants to make the needed repairs and resell the car. The salvage title protects future owners, so that they are aware of the damaged vehicle's history.

Purchasing a car with a salvage title can have potential problems. Repairs may not have been completed in their entirety by a reputable mechanic or body shop. Insurance companies may not insure the vehicle for the amount needed, and auto dealerships may be reluctant to take vehicles with salvage titles as trade-ins.

Sometimes, people take a car with a salvage title to another state, where it may be given a "clean" title. To avoid getting stuck with a car that has had its title "washed," the Edmunds automotive website recommends ordering a vehicle history report, which spans states and looks into the vehicle's entire history

If you don't mind having an imperfect car, one with a salvage title can save you a lot of money!

APPLICATION

1. Search the Internet and create a visual comparing and contrasting the following types of vehicle titles: salvage, clean, and clear.

2. a. Go to the website of the National Motor Vehicle Title Information System (NMVTIS). Research and explain the five key indicators of a NMVTIS Vehicle History Report.

   b. With a partner, create a poster informing others about the importance of obtaining a Vehicle History Report.

On May 5, 20X1, Tolstore, Inc., purchased a new drill press for use in its factory. The machine cost $9,600.00, has an estimated salvage value of $1,000.00, and an estimated useful life of seven years. Tolstore used the double declining-balance method of depreciation and the modified half-year convention. The bookkeeper prepared the following plant asset record.

PLANT ASSET RECORD No. __516__   General Ledger Account No. _____1240_____

Description _____*Drill press*_____   General Ledger Account *Production Equipment*

| Date Bought *January 14, 20X1* | Serial Number *26-32674-75* | Original Cost *$9,600.00* |
| Estimated Useful Life *7 years* | Estimated Salvage Value *$1,000.00* | Depreciation Method *Double declining-balance* |

Disposed of: Discarded _____ Sold _____ Traded _____

Date _____   Disposal Amount _____

Year	Annual Depreciation Expense	Accumulated Depreciation	Ending Book Value
20X1	$2,457.02	$2,457.02	$7,142.98

1. Find the error in the plant asset record.
2. Write a written explanation of the error to the bookkeeper. In your explanation, give the correct calculation.

Analyzing Home Depot's Financial Statements

An income statement is a financial statement prepared on an accrual basis. A statement of cash flows is a financial statement prepared on a cash basis. It shows how and where the company received cash and spent cash. On a statement of cash flows, outflows of cash are usually shown in parentheses. Inflows of cash are shown as positive amounts. These inflows and outflows of cash are organized into three categories—operating activities, investing activities, and financing activities. Buying and selling plant assets are classified as investing activities.

INSTRUCTIONS

1. Go to the Consolidated Statements of Cash Flows for Home Depot in Appendix B on page B-9. Find the heading "Cash flows from investing activities." How much cash has been used to purchase property and equipment over the last three years?

2. How much cash has been received from the sale of property and equipment over the last three years?

3. Using Note 1, beginning on page B-10, identify the method Home Depot uses to depreciate its buildings, furniture, fixtures, and equipment.

8

Accounting for Notes Payable, Prepaid Expenses, and Accrued Expenses

LEARNING OBJECTIVES

After studying Chapter 8, in addition to defining key terms, you will be able to:

LO1 Journalize transactions for notes payable.

LO2 Journalize adjusting and reversing entries for prepaid expenses.

LO3 Compare prepaid expense accounting procedures.

LO4 Journalize adjusting and reversing entries for accrued expenses.

LO5 Journalize warranty accruals and payments.

LO6 Compare the accounting principles supporting the recognition of warranty expense and uncollectible accounts expense.

© GOIR/SHUTTERSTOCK.COM

One Liberty Properties, Inc.

ACCOUNTING IN THE REAL WORLD

When you complete your education and are ready to enter the workforce, chances are you won't have the financial resources to purchase a house. Renting an apartment will be a logical alternative. Your search for the right apartment will take you to apartment complexes with interesting or inviting names, such as Forest Hills Chateaus or Ocean View Flats.

Once you have chosen an apartment, you will be required to sign a contract with the company that manages the apartments. If you read the fine print in your contract, you may learn that the apartment complex is owned by One Liberty Properties (OLP). OLP is a real estate investment trust (REIT), a special type of business that owns and leases real estate to other businesses.

REITs own land and buildings, commonly referred to as "properties," that are rented to businesses to operate apartments, restaurants, furniture stores, health and fitness centers, and industrial properties. Some REITs own and operate shopping center properties. OLP owns over 115 properties in 30 states.

A review of OLP's balance sheet reveals that nearly 90% of its assets are made up of rental property. A large portion of this $750 million investment is funded through proceeds from mortgage loans secured by the related properties. Investors seeking to understand OLP's financial condition need more information about these mortgages and their impact on OLP's future operations. The annual report contains the number of mortgages, average interest rate, and average maturity in years at the end of the fiscal year. The notes to the financial statements present a list of every new property acquired during the fiscal year, including any mortgage that was incurred to obtain it. The notes include a schedule of the long-term debt that must be paid in each of the next five years.

Source: 1liberty.com.

CRITICAL THINKING

Assume your business is considering renting space in a shopping center owned and operated by a REIT.

1. Why would the business be interested in the REIT's financial condition?
2. What ratio could provide a measure of REIT's effectiveness in operating its properties?

KEY TERMS

debt financing	maturity date	interest expense	prime interest rate
promissory note	lump-sum payment	maturity value	prepaid expense
notes payable	interest	interest-bearing note	reversing entry
date of a note	interest rate	noninterest-bearing note	accrued expenses
principal	current liabilities	line of credit	

LO1 Journalize transactions for notes payable.

Accounting for Notes Payable LO1

A business needs an adequate supply of cash to pay its operating expenses, buy inventory, and purchase plant assets. It is not unusual for a profitable business to be short of cash. When this occurs, the business must obtain additional capital to fund its operations. Obtaining capital by borrowing money for a period of time is called **debt financing**. A common way of obtaining debt financing is to get a loan from a financial institution.

Borrowing Money with a Note Payable

A written and signed promise to pay a sum of money at a specified time is called a **promissory note**. Promissory notes signed by a business and given to a creditor are called

notes payable. An example of a promissory note is shown below. Although the format of a promissory note may vary, each note will contain certain important information. The day a note is issued is called the **date of a note**. The original amount of a note is called the **principal**.

The date on which the principal of a note is due to be repaid is called the **maturity date**. A note paid in full with a single payment at the end of the maturity date is called a **lump-sum payment**.

An amount paid for the use of money for a period of time is called **interest**. The percentage of the principal that is due for the use of the funds secured by a note is called the **interest rate**.

PROMISSORY NOTE

NOTE NO.: 6142   DATE: _____March 8_____ , 20 - -

NAME: Vaughn Distributors, Inc.

ADDRESS: 1523 Fuller Drive

Trenton, NJ 08604

For the value received, the signer promises to pay to the order of **First American Banking** of Trenton, New Jersey, _____180_____ days from date, the principal sum of _____$25,000.00_____ . Twenty five thousand and xx/100 —————— Dollars with interest from the date at an annual rate of _____8%_____ per year, due on _____September 4, 20--_____ . This promissory note may be paid with interest, in total or in part, without penalty.

SIGNEE: M. David Vaughn   WITNESS: Mary T. Gattis, Trenton, NJ

President   Rayford P. Vicks, Trenton, NJ

Vaughn Distributors, Inc.

CASH RECEIPTS JOURNAL

PAGE 3

	DATE	ACCOUNT TITLE	DOC. NO.	POST. REF.	GENERAL DEBIT	GENERAL CREDIT	ACCOUNTS RECEIVABLE CREDIT	SALES CREDIT	SALES TAX PAYABLE CREDIT	SALES DISCOUNT DEBIT	CASH DEBIT	
7	8	Notes Payable	R98			25 000 00					25 000 00	7
8												8
9												9

March 8. Signed a 180-day, 8% note, $25,000.00. R98.

Liabilities due within a short time, usually within a year, are called **current liabilities**. A note payable that will be repaid during the next fiscal year should be recorded in an account classified as a current liability. A note payable scheduled to mature in later fiscal periods should be classified as a long-term liability.

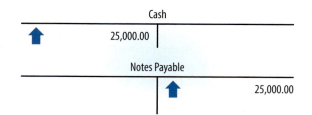

Cash

↑	
25,000.00	

Notes Payable

↑	25,000.00

The Boss Made Me Do It

Rosario Estevez was busy completing the financial information section of a bank loan application when the corporation's president entered her office. "We're not going to be able to get the loan with our balance sheet," bemoaned the president. "Add $100,000 to plant assets and stockholders' equity. That will report our plant assets at their fair market value." Rosario tried to explain that stating the plant assets at fair market value violated GAAP, but the president wouldn't listen. "Just do it, Rosario. I'll take

responsibility should anyone question it. I expect that document in the mail today. The future of this corporation and its 300 jobs depends on this loan."

INSTRUCTIONS

Using the ethical model, provide Rosario with guidance on whether she should mail the bank loan application with the altered financial statement information. Assume the corporation has yet to adopt a code of conduct.

Calculating the Maturity Date

	Days from the Month	Days Remaining
Term of the Note		180
March 8–March 31	*23*	*157*
April	*30*	*127*
May	*31*	*96*
June	*30*	*66*
July	*31*	*35*
August	*31*	*4*
September 1–September 4	*4*	*0*

❶ Days in First Month

❷ Days Remaining from Prior Month

❸ Lesser of Days Remaining and Days of the Month

❹ Days Remaining in Last Month

The number of days in each month during the term of a note impacts the maturity date. The maturity date for Vaughn Distributors' 180-day, March 8 note payable is September 4. The maturity date is determined as shown above.

>> Calculating the Maturity Date

❶ Compute the number of days in the first month, 23, by subtracting the date of the note, 8, from the number of days in the month the note was signed, 31.

❷ For each month, calculate the days remaining by subtracting the days from the month from the days remaining from the previous month. For example, the days from May, 31, are subtracted from the days remaining after April, 127, to calculate the days remaining after May, 96.

❸ For each month, enter the lesser of the number of days in the month or the number of days remaining after the previous month. For example, the number of days in June, 30, is less than the days remaining after May, 96.

❹ When the number of days in the month is greater than the days remaining after the previous month, enter the days remaining. Because 4 is less than the number of days in September, add only 4 days in September.

Calculating Interest

Principal	×	Interest Rate	×	Time as a Fraction of Year	=	Interest for Fraction of Year
$25,000.00	×	8%	×	180/365	=	$986.30

The interest rate of the note is stated as an annual rate. The interest paid on the note is calculated by applying the annual rate for the portion of the year that the note is outstanding as shown above. Vaughn's bank uses a 365-day year to calculate interest.

A financial institution may calculate its interest using a 360-day year. The loan agreement will specify whether interest is calculated using a 360-day or 365-day year. A 360-day year results in a slightly higher amount of interest. For the 180-day note shown above, the interest would be $1,000.00 ($25,000.00 × 8% × 180/360). Interest calculations in this textbook are assumed to use a 365-day year, unless the use of the 360-day year is noted.

The term of a note can be stated in months or years. For example, a six-month note dated March 2 matures on September 2. The number of days between March 2 and September 2 must be determined in interest calculations.

Paying a Note Payable

CASH PAYMENTS JOURNAL — PAGE *18*

	DATE		ACCOUNT TITLE	CK. NO.	POST. REF.	1 GENERAL DEBIT	2 GENERAL CREDIT	3 ACCOUNTS PAYABLE DEBIT	4 PURCHASES DISCOUNT CREDIT	5 CASH CREDIT	
14		4	*Notes Payable*	*667*		*25 000 00*				*25 986 30*	14
15			*Interest Expense*			*986 30*					15

Interest accrued on borrowed funds is called **interest expense**. On the maturity date, the borrower pays both the principal of the note payable and the interest expense. The interest on short-term notes payable is typically paid at the maturity date. The payment of the note is recorded in the cash payments journal as shown on the previous page. The amount that is due on the maturity date of a note is called the **maturity value**. Vaughn Distributors pays the maturity value of its note on the maturity date.

> September 4. Paid cash for the maturity value of the March 8 note: principal, $25,000.00, plus interest, $986.30; total, $25,986.30. Check No. 667.

Operating expenses, such as salaries and advertising, are incurred to support the normal operations of the business, which is sales. In contrast, the amount of interest expense is influenced by how the business elects to obtain its working capital. For this reason, Interest Expense is listed as an Other Expense on Vaughn Distributors' chart of accounts. Only expenses that are incurred to conduct normal business activities are classified as operating expenses. This method of reporting interest expense enables the comparison of operating income between companies in the same industry.

Noninterest-Bearing Notes

A note having a stated interest rate is called an **interest-bearing note**. On the maturity date, the borrower pays the face value of the note plus interest at the stated interest rate. An alternative type of note does not require a stated interest rate. The proceeds of the note are less than the maturity value of the note. The maturity value less the note proceeds equals the amount of interest. A note that deducts interest from the face value of the note is called a **noninterest-bearing note**.

Vaughn Distributors purchased $36,096.51 of merchandise from Jenkins Industries, signing a 60-day noninterest-bearing note for $36,500.00. The amount of interest Vaughn Distributors pays is the difference, $403.49. Although the note does not have a stated interest rate, an implied rate of interest can be calculated as follows:

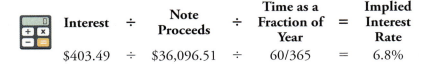

	Interest	÷	Note Proceeds	÷	Time as a Fraction of Year	=	Implied Interest Rate
	$403.49	÷	$36,096.51	÷	60/365	=	6.8%

EXPLORE ACCOUNTING

Alternative Note Payment Options

A business should ideally only borrow the amount of funds necessary to adequately fund its operations. The business incurs interest expense each day a note payable is outstanding. As the cash necessary to repay the note is accumulated, a business could reduce its interest expense by repaying a portion of the note principal.

An advantage of a lump-sum note payable is that accounting for the note is relatively simple. A lump-sum note payable may only require the recording of three types of accounting transactions:

1. Record the liability for the amount of the principal when the note is signed.
2. Make periodic interest payments, if required.
3. Pay the principal at the maturity date.

The disadvantage of a lump-sum note is that the business continues to incur interest on the full note principal for the entire term of the note.

INSTALLMENT NOTES

An alternative method of financing operations is to sign a note that requires periodic principal payments. The outstanding balance of the note decreases over time, resulting in lower interest expenses each period. These types of notes are referred to as an *installment note* or a *periodic payment note*.

Installment notes are commonly used for consumers and businesses to finance the purchase of buildings and vehicles. Installment notes typically require monthly payments. Each month the customer makes a payment

(continued)

consisting of interest and principal. On April 1 Whiley purchased a vehicle for $52,000.00, signing a 60-month 5.0% installment note. The dealer provided Whiley with a payment schedule that identifies the monthly payment and the portion of each a payment dedicated toward interest and principal. A portion of the payment schedule is shown below.

Payment Schedule				
Purchase Price:	$52,000.00		Interest Rate:	5.0%
Monthly Payment:	$981.30		Term:	60 Months
Month	Beginning Principal Balance	Interest Expense	Principal Payment	Ending Principal Balance
5/1	$ 52,000.00	$ 216.67	$ 764.63	$ 51,235.37
6/1	51,235.37	213.48	767.82	50,467.55
7/1	50,467.55	210.28	771.02	49,696.53
8/1	49,696.53	207.07	774.23	48,922.30
9/1	48,922.30	203.84	777.46	48,144.84
10/1	48,144.84	200.60	780.70	47,364.14

Each month's interest expense is calculated using the same formula used to calculate interest for a lump-sum note. The calculation of interest for the July 1 payment is shown below.

$$\text{Principal Balance} \times \text{Interest Rate} \times \text{Time as a Fraction of Year} = \text{Interest Expense}$$

$$\$50,467.55 \times 5.0\% \times 1/12 = \$210.28$$

The excess of the monthly payment over the interest reduces the outstanding principal balance.

$$\text{Monthly Payment} - \text{Interest Expense} = \text{Principal Payment}$$

$$\$981.30 - \$210.28 = \$771.02$$

The payment schedule shows the benefit of an installment note. The amount of the interest expense decreases each month, enabling the customer to more quickly reduce its outstanding note balance.

DISCOUNTING NOTES PAYABLE

Accounting for an installment note becomes more complex when the interest rate of the note is significantly different from the market interest rate. Assume that Whiley was able to purchase the vehicle taking advantage of a special dealer promotion of 0% interest. Both Whiley and the dealer understand that the interest is reflected in the purchase price. Generally accepted accounting principles require that the vehicle and note be recorded in the accounting records at a discounted amount that enables interest to be recognized at a market rate. The procedures for determining these amounts and the accounting for the periodic payments are covered in chapter 12, Accounting for Bonds.

Drawing from a Line of Credit

					GENERAL		ACCOUNTS RECEIVABLE CREDIT	SALES CREDIT	SALES TAX PAYABLE CREDIT	SALES DISCOUNT DEBIT	CASH DEBIT
	DATE	ACCOUNT TITLE	DOC. NO.	POST. REF.	DEBIT	CREDIT					
10	20	Line of Credit	R129			8 4 0 0 00					8 4 0 0 00
11											
12											

CASH RECEIPTS JOURNAL — PAGE 5

The process of submitting and having a loan application approved can take days, even weeks. A business may need more immediate access to cash. A bank loan agreement that provides immediate short-term access to cash is called a **line of credit**, or *credit line*. The loan agreement sets the maximum amount that can be borrowed, the interest rate, and the repayment terms. The business can draw any amount it needs within the terms of the loan agreement.

> **May 20. Drew $8,400.00 on a line of credit. Receipt No. 129.**

The interest rate for a note payable is fixed for the term of the loan. In contrast, the interest rate on a line of credit can change based on market interest rates. The interest rate charged to a bank's most creditworthy customers is called the **prime interest rate**. Line-of-credit interest rates are often based on the prime interest rate. For example, a line of credit may have an interest rate of 1.5% over the prime interest rate. This rate would be stated as *prime plus 1.5%*.

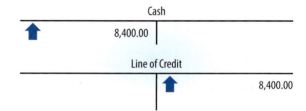

Paying a Line of Credit

					GENERAL		ACCOUNTS PAYABLE DEBIT	PURCHASES DISCOUNT CREDIT	CASH CREDIT
	DATE	ACCOUNT TITLE	CK. NO.	POST. REF.	DEBIT	CREDIT			
23	31	Line of Credit	722		1 0 0 0 00				1 0 9 2 60
24		Interest Expense			9 2 60				
25									

CASH PAYMENTS JOURNAL — PAGE 10

A business can repay a portion of the outstanding principal of a line of credit at any time. Vaughn's line of credit requires monthly payments of interest and a partial principal payment.

> **May 31. Paid cash for the principal and interest on the line of credit: principal, $1,000.00, plus interest, $92.60; total, $1,092.60. Check No. 722.**

Interest on a line of credit is typically calculated daily because the principal amount and interest rate can change during a month. The amount of interest due at the end of the month is obtained from the bank.

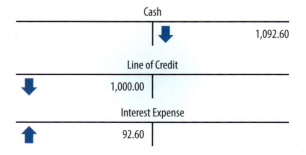

TERMS REVIEW

debt financing

promissory note

notes payable

date of a note

principal

maturity date

lump-sum payment

interest

interest rate

current liabilities

interest expense

maturity value

interest-bearing note

noninterest-bearing note

line of credit

prime interest rate

Audit your understanding LO1

1. What method of reporting interest expense enables the comparison of operating income between companies in the same industry?
2. Why is interest on a line of credit calculated daily?
3. What advantage does a business gain by having a line of credit versus signing a promissory note?

Work together 8-1 LO1

Journalizing notes payable transactions

A cash receipts journal and a cash payments journal are provided in the *Working Papers*. Source documents are abbreviated as: check, C; receipt, R. Your instructor will guide you through the following examples.

1. Using the current year, journalize the following transactions.

    Transactions:

    June 4. Signed a 90-day, 10% note with Second National Bank, $5,000.00. R223.

    July 15. Signed a 120-day, 8% note with Commerce Bank, $8,000.00. R240.

    Dec. 6. Drew $5,600.00 from a line of credit. R368.

2. Calculate the maturity date of each note payable and the total amount of interest due at the maturity date.
3. Journalize the following transactions. Use the maturity dates and interest amounts calculated in the previous instruction.

    Transactions:

    Paid cash for the maturity value of the $5,000.00 note. C345.

    Paid cash for the maturity value of the $8,000.00 note. C652.

    Dec. 31. Paid cash on the line of credit: principal, $500.00; December interest, $46.00. C887.

On your own 8-1 LO1

Journalizing notes payable transactions

A cash receipts journal and a cash payments journal are provided in the *Working Papers*. Source documents are abbreviated as: check, C; receipt, R. Work this problem independently.

1. Using the current year, journalize the following transactions.

    Transactions:

    May 16. Signed a 180-day, 10% note with First National Bank, $16,000.00. R335.

    Aug. 8. Signed a 120-day, 9% note with American Bank, $20,000.00. R456.

    Dec. 3. Drew $16,900.00 from a line of credit. R615.

2. Calculate the maturity date of each note payable and the total amount of interest due at the maturity date.
3. Journalize the following transactions. Use the maturity dates and interest amounts calculated in the previous instruction.

    Transactions:

    Paid cash for the maturity value of the $16,000.00 note. C668.

    Paid cash for the maturity value of the $20,000.00 note. C702.

    Dec. 31. Paid cash on the line of credit: principal, $1,500.00; December interest, $138.00. 722.

Prepaid Expenses

LO2 Journalize adjusting and reversing entries for prepaid expenses.

LO3 Compare prepaid expense accounting procedures.

Journalizing Entries for Prepaid Expenses LO2

Most expenses occur in the same period in which a cash payment is made for the expense. Some expenses, such as insurance and advertising, require a payment before the benefit is received. Thus, a cash payment for these expenses may occur in the fiscal period before the related expense should be recognized.

Cash paid for an expense in one fiscal period that is not used until a later period is called a **prepaid expense**. Prepaid expenses include items such as supplies,

insurance, and advertising. Only that portion of cash payment for expenses that have been used in the current fiscal period should be reported as an expense in that fiscal period. **>>** App. A: Matching Expenses with Revenue. Prepaid expenses may be recorded initially as assets or as expenses. Both procedures require that the account balances be adjusted before financial statements are prepared. In Part 1, Whiley Outdoor Living, Inc., initially recorded its prepaid expenses as assets.

WHY ACCOUNTING?

Cost of ADA Implementation

Business Management & Administration

The Americans with Disabilities Act (ADA) of 1990 and the ADA Amendments Act (ADAAA) of 2008 prohibit discrimination based on disability. Under these acts, the definition of disability is an "impairment that substantially limits one or more major life activities…, a record of such an impairment, or being regarded as having such an impairment."

ADA has broad implications in the workplace. It requires an employer to "provide reasonable accommodation" to an employee with a disability. Examples of typical accommodations are modifying equipment, adjusting the work schedule, reassigning the person to another position, and restructuring the job.

These accommodations may have a cost attached to them. In companies that are departmentalized, the cost may be assigned to the overall company, allocated in total to the department, or split between the company and the

department. If any of this cost is allocated to the department, it will affect the net income of that department. The manager of the department should understand the cost of the accommodation and the portion of that cost that will be allocated to the department.

CRITICAL THINKING

Assume you are the manager of a department. Ken, an employee, has a job which requires him to stand near a machine. Ken has developed a back problem and must be able to sit while working.

1. What accommodations might you investigate in order to allow Ken to remain employed?

2. How would you estimate the cost of these accommodations?

Source: U.S. Department of Justice, Americans with Disabilities Act (www.ada.gov).

Supplies Initially Recorded as an Expense

Prepaid expenses are assets until they are actually used. For example, Vaughn Distributors has a quantity of supplies on hand on any given day during the year. The company will use these supplies in the current and future fiscal periods. Vaughn initially records its prepaid expenses in expense accounts. Thus, the amount recorded in the account Supplies Expense prior to the fiscal year-end adjustments represents a mixture of an expense (supplies already used) and an asset (supplies not yet used).

Adjusting Entry

Debit the Asset Account

	DATE		ACCOUNT TITLE	DOC. NO.	POST. REF.	DEBIT	CREDIT	
1			*Adjusting Entries*					1
4		31	*Supplies*			7 6 0 00		4
5			*Supplies Expense*				7 6 0 00	5
6								6

GENERAL JOURNAL — PAGE 16

Credit the Expense Account

Vaughn records an adjusting entry to recognize as an expense only those supplies used. This adjusting entry is made when financial statements need to be prepared. ▶▶ App. A: Full Disclosure Vaughn records adjustments on December 31, the end of its fiscal year.

When Vaughn Distributors buys supplies, Supplies Expense is debited and Cash is credited. The $4,850.00 debit balance of Supplies Expense represents the amount of the beginning supplies inventory plus the total amount of all supplies bought during the fiscal period. Nothing has been recorded in Vaughn's Supplies account during the fiscal year.

On December 31, Vaughn takes a physical count of the supplies on hand. It determines that the supplies ending inventory is $760.00 and records the necessary adjusting entry as shown above.

The new balance of Supplies, $760.00, represents the ending supplies inventory on December 31. The new balance of Supplies Expense, $4,090.00, recognizes the amount of supplies used during the current year.

Closing Entry

To prepare a general ledger for the next fiscal period, closing entries are journalized and posted. After the closing entry is recorded, the Supplies Expense account balance is zero. The debit balance of $760.00 in Supplies represents the amount of supplies on hand on December 31.

Reversing Entry

Debit the Expense Account

	DATE		ACCOUNT TITLE	DOC. NO.	POST. REF.	DEBIT	CREDIT	
1			*Reversing Entries*					1
2	Jan. 20--	1	**Supplies Expense**			7 6 0 00		2
3			**Supplies**				7 6 0 00	3
4								4

GENERAL JOURNAL   PAGE *1*

Credit the Asset Account

Vaughn initially records the amount of all supplies bought in an expense account. On December 31, the amount of Vaughn's supplies inventory, $760.00, is the debit balance of Supplies. To prepare the general ledger accounts for the next year, the $760.00 should be returned as a debit in Supplies Expense. The $760.00 debit can then be added to the amount of supplies bought during the next year.

Businesses that initially record prepaid items as expenses reverse the adjusting entries for prepaid expenses at the beginning of each fiscal period. An entry made at the beginning of one fiscal period to reverse an adjusting entry made in the previous fiscal period is called a **reversing entry**. Thus, a reversing entry is the exact opposite of the related adjusting entry.

Vaughn initially records supplies as expenses and, therefore, needs to record reversing entries. Accountants use the following rule of thumb to determine whether a reversing entry is needed: *If an adjusting entry creates a balance in an asset or a liability account, the adjusting entry is reversed.* This rule applies to expenses that will be used early during the next fiscal year.

Because Vaughn's adjusting entry for supplies created a balance in Supplies, a reversing entry is needed. The reversing entry is shown above.

After the reversing entry is posted, the cost of the supplies inventory, $760.00, is recorded in Supplies Expense. Vaughn expects these supplies will be used during the next fiscal year. Thus, the supplies will be expensed in the same fiscal year they are used to earn revenue. **>> App. A: Matching Expenses with Revenue** The balance of Supplies is zero, as it was before the adjusting entry.

Supplies Expense			
Balance	4,850.00	Adjusting	760.00
Reversing	760.00	Closing	4,090.00
(New Balance	760.00)		

Supplies			
Adjusting	760.00	Reversing	760.00
(New Balance	0.00)		

Remember Most adjustments that create an asset or a liability should be reversed.

© KINGA/SHUTTERSTOCK.COM

Advertising Initially Recorded as an Asset

During May of a prior fiscal year, Vaughn Distributors entered into an endorsement contract with a celebrity. Vaughn paid the celebrity $100,000.00 for the right to use the celebrity's image in its advertising and on its website. During the five-year contract, the celebrity must also make an appearance at an annual trade show.

Adjusting Entry

Debit the Expense Account

	DATE		ACCOUNT TITLE	DOC. NO.	POST. REF.	DEBIT	CREDIT	
1			*Adjusting Entries*					1
8	31		*Advertising Expense*			25 0 0 0 00		8
9			*Prepaid Advertising*				25 0 0 0 00	9
10								10

GENERAL JOURNAL — PAGE 16

Credit the Asset Account

Vaughn uses a different procedure for accounting for this prepaid expense. The procedure is the same as that used by Whiley Outdoor Living in Part 1. Expenditures are initially recorded in a prepaid asset account. At the end of the fiscal year, Vaughn records an adjusting entry to expense the portion of the prepaid expense used during the current fiscal year. Vaughn uses this procedure since, unlike supplies, the prepaid expense will be expensed over several fiscal years.

Vaughn initially recorded the $100,000.00 payment in Prepaid Advertising. During prior fiscal years, $40,000.00 of the payment was adjusted to Advertising Expense. The $60,000.00 balance in Prepaid Advertising represents the value of the endorsement payment to be expensed in future fiscal years.

Vaughn expenses the $100,000.00 payment evenly over the five years of the endorsement contract. An adjusting entry of $20,000.00 ($100,000.00 ÷ 5 years) is necessary to account for the advertising expense incurred during the current fiscal year.

After recording the adjustment, the new balance of Prepaid Advertising, $40,000.00, is the value of the endorsement contract to be received during the next two years.

Closing Entry

To prepare a general ledger for the next fiscal period, closing entries are journalized and posted.

The adjusting entry did not create a balance in an asset account. Therefore, no reversing entry is required.

Vaughn can use either procedure for recording prepaid expenses. Regardless of the procedure used, the financial statements must reflect the same value of prepaid expenses.

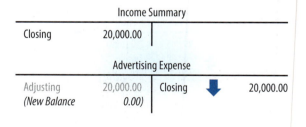

Comparison of Prepaid Expense Accounting Procedures LO3

A business can elect to initially record a prepaid expense as an expense or as an asset. Both procedures require that the account balances be adjusted before financial statements are prepared. Each procedure requires that the expense account be closed at the end of the accounting period.

The adjusting, closing, and reversing entries Vaughn recorded for supplies are shown in the left column of the following illustration. Vaughn initially records prepaid expenses as an expense. The adjusting entry recognized that $760.00 of supplies were on hand at the end of the fiscal period. The remaining balance in Supplies Expense, $4,090.00, represents the value of supplies used during the fiscal year. After accounts were closed, the balance in Supplies was reversed, resulting in a $760.00 debit in Supplies Expense.

The right side of the illustration shows the adjusting and closing entries for Vaughn if it initially records prepaid expenses as assets. The adjusting entry recognized that $4,090.00 of supplies were used during the fiscal period. The remaining balance in Supplies, $760.00, represents the value of supplies on hand at the end of the fiscal year. Because the adjusting entry did not create a balance in an asset or a liability account, no reversing entry is required.

Note that the adjusted balances of Supplies and Supplies Expense are identical, regardless of the procedure used. As a result, the entry to close Supplies Expense is also identical. Only the procedure that initially records prepaid expenses to an expense account requires that a reversing entry be recorded.

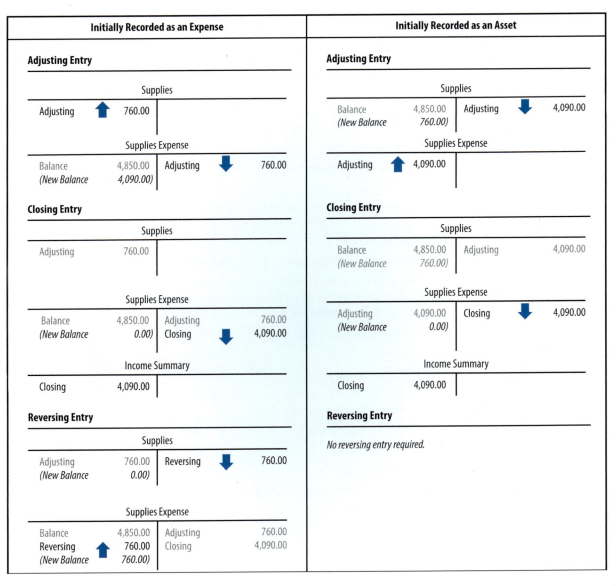

Audit your understanding LO2, 3

1. Which accounting concept is being applied when an adjusting entry is recorded for prepaid expenses?
2. Why is an adjusting entry made for supplies at the end of a fiscal period?
3. What rule of thumb can accountants follow to determine whether a reversing entry is needed?
4. How does the procedure used to account for prepaid expenses affect the expense reported in the financial statements?
5. Identify the similarities and differences between the adjusting, closing, and reversing entries of the two methods used to account for prepaid expenses.

Work together 8-2 LO2

Journalizing adjusting and reversing entries for prepaid expenses

Praxson, Inc., has the following general ledger account balances on December 31 of the current year before it records adjusting entries. A general journal is provided in the *Working Papers*. Your instructor will guide you through the following examples.

Supplies Expense	$ 3,200.00
Insurance Expense	8,000.00
Prepaid Advertising	80,000.00

1. Using the following adjustment information, journalize the adjusting entries on December 31 of the current year.

Supplies inventory	$ 400.00
Value of prepaid insurance	600.00
Advertising used	30,000.00

2. Journalize the reversing entries on January 1 of the next year.

On your own 8-2 LO2

Journalizing adjusting and reversing entries for prepaid expenses

WRP Industries has the following general ledger account balances on December 31 of the current year before it records adjusting entries. A general journal is provided in the *Working Papers*. Work this problem independently.

Insurance Expense	$ 8,600.00
Rent Expense	13,000.00
Prepaid Advertising	20,000.00

1. Using the following adjustment information, journalize the adjusting entries on December 31 of the current year.

Value of prepaid insurance	$ 900.00
Value of prepaid rent	1,000.00
Advertising used	6,000.00

2. Journalize the reversing entries on January 1 of the next year.

Accrued Expenses

LO4 Journalize adjusting and reversing entries for accrued expenses.

LO5 Journalize warranty accruals and payments.

LO6 Compare the accounting principles supporting the recognition of warranty expense and uncollectible accounts expense.

Journalizing Entries for Accrued Interest Expense LO4

Expenses incurred in one fiscal period but not paid until a later fiscal period are called **accrued expenses**. A business may need to record several accrued expenses, such as payroll, payroll taxes, and income taxes. The same procedure is used to record any accrued expense. With one exception, the transaction to record an accrued expense is the same as the transaction to record the payment of the expense. Rather than recording a credit to Cash, the credit is recorded to a liability account.

Adjusting Entry

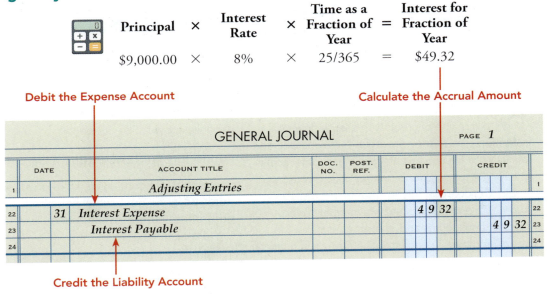

	Principal	×	Interest Rate	×	Time as a Fraction of Year	=	Interest for Fraction of Year
	$9,000.00	×	8%	×	25/365	=	$49.32

Debit the Expense Account

Calculate the Accrual Amount

GENERAL JOURNAL   PAGE *1*

	DATE	ACCOUNT TITLE	DOC. NO.	POST. REF.	DEBIT	CREDIT	
1		*Adjusting Entries*					1
22	31	Interest Expense			4 9 32		22
23		Interest Payable				4 9 32	23
24							24

Credit the Liability Account

On December 31, Vaughn Distributors has a 60-day, 8% note payable for $9,000.00, dated December 6. Vaughn owes the bank for interest on the note from December 6 to the end of the month. On December 31, Vaughn owes 25 days' worth of accrued interest on the note, $49.32. However, Vaughn will not pay any interest on this note until its maturity date.

The accrued interest expense for this note should be reported in the current fiscal period. **>> App. A: Matching Expenses with Revenue** The adjusting entry

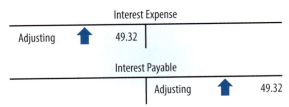

Interest Expense		
Adjusting ⬆ 49.32	

Interest Payable		
	Adjusting ⬆ 49.32

shown above records the accrued interest adjustment. Vaughn uses the account titled Interest Payable to account for accrued interest. Another account title commonly used is Accrued Interest.

Reversing Entry

Debit the Liability Account →

	DATE		ACCOUNT TITLE	DOC. NO.	POST. REF.	DEBIT	CREDIT	
1			Reversing Entries					1
20		1	Interest Payable			4 9 32		20
21			Interest Expense				4 9 32	21
22								22

GENERAL JOURNAL   PAGE 1

← Credit the Expense Account

After preparing its financial statements, Vaughn Distributors journalizes and posts closing entries. To prepare the accounts for the next year, Vaughn records a reversing entry for accrued interest expense, as shown above. Vaughn's adjusting entry for accrued interest expense creates a balance in a liability account. Accountants generally reverse an adjusting entry that creates a balance in a liability account.

When Vaughn pays the note on February 4 of the following year, the total interest expense payment is $118.36. The total interest expense should be divided between the two fiscal periods. Interest for the prior year, $49.32, is charged for the 25 days the note was outstanding in that year. Interest for the current period, $69.04, relates to the 35 days from the start of the fiscal year to the maturity date.

THINK LIKE AN ACCOUNTANT

Calculating Accrued Interest

For years, BLT Corporation maintained a $1 million line of credit with a large financial institution. The money drawn from the line of credit was used to finance inventory and accounts receivable for the corporation's primary selling season.

BLT Corporation has 30 locations across the nation. BLT generally locates its manufacturing plants in small towns and, therefore, is often the largest employer in each town. A new chief financial officer has directed that the corporation begin borrowing from banks in the towns in which the corporation has plants. BLT believes that doing business with local banks is part of being a good community citizen and helps each local economy.

The corporation regularly has 20 to 30 notes outstanding at any time. Because the corporation prepares monthly financial statements, monthly calculations of accrued interest expense are required. You have been assigned the task of creating a schedule to calculate the interest for each note and

the total amount to be used in the monthly interest expense accrual.

OPEN THE SPREADSHEET TLA_CH08

The worksheet contains a list of outstanding notes payable. Follow the steps on the Instructions tab to complete the schedule. Answer these questions:

1. What is the amount of the interest accrual for November 30, 2018?

2. Delete from the list all notes that matured during December 2018. On December 2, 2018, the corporation signed an 80-day, $50,000.00, 7.8% note with Mitchell National Bank of Mitchell, Iowa. What is the total amount of the interest accrual for December 31, 2018?

3. What other features could be added to the spreadsheet to provide more information to management regarding its notes payable?

Payment of a Note At Maturity

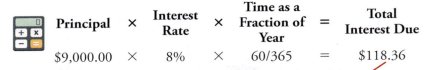

	Principal	×	Interest Rate	×	Time as a Fraction of Year	=	Total Interest Due
	$9,000.00	×	8%	×	60/365	=	$118.36

CASH PAYMENTS JOURNAL									PAGE 1	
				1	2	3	4	5		
DATE	ACCOUNT TITLE	CK. NO.	POST. REF.	GENERAL DEBIT	GENERAL CREDIT	ACCOUNTS PAYABLE DEBIT	PURCHASES DISCOUNT CREDIT	CASH CREDIT		
4	*Notes Payable*	855		9 0 0 0 00				9 1 1 8 36		5
	Interest Expense			1 1 8 36						6
										7
										8

On the maturity date, Vaughn Distributors writes a check for the maturity value of $9,118.36.

This transaction to pay the maturity of a note is the same as illustrated in Lesson 9-1. Notes Payable will be decreased by a debit for $9,000.00, the principal of the note. The debit entry to Interest Expense is for $118.36, the interest for the entire term of the note.

The $118.36 debit entry to Interest Expense, less the $49.32 credit balance created by the reversing entry, equals the $69.04 interest expense for the current period.

Notes Payable

Payment (New Balance	9,000.00 0.00)	Balance	9,000.00

Interest Expense

Payment (New Balance	118.36 69.04)	Reversing	49.32

Cash

		Payment	9,118.36

> **February 4. Paid cash for the maturity value of the December 6 note: principal, $9,000.00, plus interest, $118.36; total, $9,118.36. Check No. 855.**

Fun with FAFSA

Each year, the U.S. Congress budgets billions of dollars to help students with financing for college. One of the most important steps for students is completing the U.S. Department of Education's *Free Application for Federal Student Aid (FAFSA)*. This application is required for federal and state financial aid programs and should be completed annually regardless of admission status.

The FAFSA application is evaluated using the Department of Education's special formula to determine a family's financial situation. The result is the Expected Family Contribution, or EFC. The EFC measures the eligibility for federal student aid, since many of these programs are based on financial need. Schools use the EFC to determine the financial package offered, including eligibility for institutional scholarships and grants.

Other options, such as private loans, are also available. However, private loans generally come with higher interest rates.

ACTIVITIES

Go to the website www.studentaid.ed.gov and answer the following questions:

1. What are the three types of Federal Student Aid programs?

2. List at least five basic eligibility requirements to receive student aid.

3. a. Compare and contrast the features of the following: grant, loan—subsidized and unsubsidized, scholarship, and work-study.

   b. Indicate which programs require a promissory note.

   c. **Optional:** Prepare a spreadsheet comparing your findings.

Careers In Accounting

Judy Romano
Tax Preparer/Tax Advisor

Judy Romano started her career as a tax preparer. She worked for a major tax preparation company. In the beginning, she prepared tax returns for individuals and small businesses. Although many of the tax returns only required basic tax knowledge, some tax returns were more challenging. In these instances, Ms. Romano would need to research tax bulletins, published by the Internal Revenue Service, to ensure that the tax return was completed correctly.

Ms. Romano took additional classes offered by her company and began preparing tax returns for small corporations. She enjoyed working with these clients. However, she soon realized that many of her clients were paying more federal income tax than necessary because they were not aware of ways to lessen their tax liability. In her position, she did not have the opportunity to educate her clients on tax law and how to use it to their advantage.

At that point, Ms. Romano decided to open her own tax advice and preparation service. A major portion of her work was to study her client's prior tax returns and give them ideas on how to legally reduce their tax liability. When her clients follow her advice, it is rewarding for her to see results in the form of lower taxes for those clients.

When Ms. Romano started as a tax preparer, there were very few laws or restrictions covering paid tax return preparers. Now, the federal government and several state governments have established rules for paid tax preparers, including having a practitioner tax identification number (PTIN).

Salary Range: The median salary for a tax preparer is $38,730 per year.

Qualifications: Paid tax preparers (other than certified public accountants, attorneys, and enrolled agents) have to pass a competency test to become a registered tax return preparer. Finally, all registered tax return preparers must complete continuing education requirements each year.

Occupational Outlook: The career area of tax preparers is expected to experience faster than average growth (from 10% to 14%) from 2016 to 2026.

Source: www.onetonline.org.

Journalizing Entries for Warranty Expense LO5

Any business that offers customers a warranty on its merchandise must account for the cost of repairs and replacements. Jackson Sports offers its customers a two-year warranty on its golf carts. Jackson Sports makes all repairs resulting from defective parts free of charge to the customer.

Adjusting Entry

Debit the Expense Account

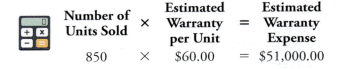

	DATE	ACCOUNT TITLE	DOC. NO.	POST. REF.	DEBIT	CREDIT	
1		*Adjusting Entries*					1
24	31	Warranty Expense			51 0 0 0 00		24
25		Accrued Warranty Liability				51 0 0 0 00	25
26							26

GENERAL JOURNAL — PAGE **1**

Credit the Liability Account

When Jackson Sports sells a golf cart, it does not know the extent of repairs that will be required during the warranty period. Some carts have no problems; other carts may require extensive repairs. Jackson Sports estimates that it spends an average of $60.00 on warranty repairs for each cart.

Warranty Expense		
Adjusting ⬆ 51,000.00		

Accrued Warranty Liability		
Balance 620.00	Adjusting ⬆ 51,000.00	
	(New Balance 50,380.00)	

The expenses associated with earning revenue should be recorded in the same accounting period. Thus, repair costs during the warranty period should be expensed in the same period as the cart sale. **>> App. A: Matching Expenses with Revenue** Jackson Sports sold 850 carts during the fiscal year. The business estimates that $51,000.00 of repairs will be required for these carts during the warranty period.

	Number of Units Sold	×	Estimated Warranty per Unit	=	Estimated Warranty Expense
	850	×	$60.00	=	$51,000.00

Jackson Sports began the current year with a $49,000.00 credit balance in Accrued Warranty Liability. During the year $49,620.00 of warranty claims was paid, resulting in a $620.00 debit balance in the accrual account. Accountants must periodically review the estimates used to calculate accruals to determine if changes are necessary.

© ISTOCKPHOTO.COM/STILLFX

Remember — Although Whiley Outdoor Living and Vaughn Distributors use different procedures, both correctly separate and record the asset and expense portions of the cost of supplies. Both procedures meet the requirements of the *Matching Expenses with Revenue* concept.

Warranty Payments

	DATE	ACCOUNT TITLE	CK. NO.	POST. REF.	GENERAL DEBIT	GENERAL CREDIT	ACCOUNTS PAYABLE DEBIT	PURCHASES DISCOUNT CREDIT	CASH CREDIT	
17	16	Accrued Warranty Liability	225		1 2 5 00				1 2 5 00	17
18										18
19										19

Jackson Sports accrues its warranty costs when it sells a golf cart. When cash is paid to make repairs, the payment reduces the estimated future warranty liability.

January 16. Paid cash to replace a defective battery, $125.00. Check No. 225.

Accountants must periodically analyze the Accrued Warranty Liability account. If the actual costs incurred are significantly more or less than the $60.00 per cart, a new warranty expense estimate is computed.

Accrued Warranty Liability

Payment	⬇	125.00	Balance	50,380.00
			(New Balance	*50,255.00)*

Cash

		Payment	⬇	125.00

With each sale on account, there is a chance that Jackson Sports will incur warranty costs. An estimate of these expenses is recorded in the same fiscal period as the sale. No expense is recorded when Jackson Sports incurs a warranty expenditure.

Accounting for Warranty Expense and Uncollectible Accounts Expense LO6

The accounting concept that supports the accounting for uncollectible accounts also applies to the accounting for warranty expenses. The *Matching Expenses with Revenue* principle requires that expenses associated with earning revenue be recorded in the same accounting period.

With each sale on account, there is a chance that the customer will not pay its account. There is also a chance that the business will be required to incur repairs or replace items in a future fiscal period. These expenses should be recorded in the same fiscal period as the revenue. The exact amount of each expense is not known at the time the sale is recorded. Thus, accountants must estimate these expenses and regularly evaluate the adequacy of their estimates.

Accrued Warranty Liability and Allowance for Uncollectible Accounts each have natural credit balances. These credit balances recognize that future, but unknown, expenses exist. The reporting for these accounts differs slightly. Allowance for Uncollectible Accounts has a related asset account and, therefore, is reported on the balance sheet as a contra asset account. In contrast, Warranty Payable does not have a related asset. As a result, Accrued Warranty Liability is reported as a liability on the balance sheet.

Accountants generally reverse an adjusting entry that creates a balance in a liability account. The accounting for uncollectible accounts and warranty expenses is an exception to this rule. Neither of the adjustments to estimate uncollectible accounts or warranty expenses is reversed.

TERM REVIEW

accrued expenses

Audit your understanding LO4, 5, 6

1. What are the three steps to accrue an expense?
2. How do accountants determine if an adjusting entry for an accrued expense should be reversed?
3. When should the cost of repairing an item under warranty be expensed?
4. Identify the similarities and differences between the accounting for warranty costs and uncollectible accounts.

Work together 8-3 LO4, 5
Journalizing adjusting and reversing entries for accrued expenses

General journals and a cash payments journal are provided in the *Working Papers*. Your instructor will guide you through the following examples.

1. Use the following information to journalize the adjusting entries for interest, payroll, payroll taxes, and warranties on December 31 of the current year.

   a. One note is outstanding on December 31: 90-day, 10% note with First Commercial Bank, $30,000.00, dated November 16.

   b. Payroll information for December 28 to December 31 is as follows:

Payroll and Employee Payroll Taxes		Employer Payroll Taxes	
Salaries	$3,200.00	Social security tax	$198.40
Federal income tax withheld	180.00	Medicare tax	46.40
Social security tax	198.40	Federal unemployment tax	4.80
Medicare tax	46.40	State unemployment tax	32.40

   c. Estimated warranty costs per item sold, $8.00. Units sold, 18,900.
2. Journalize the appropriate reversing entries on January 1 of the next year.
3. Journalize the following transactions.

   Transactions:

   Feb. 2. Paid cash to Electronic Service & Repair for warranty work performed for the company during January, $325.00. Check No. 667.

   Paid cash for the maturity value of the November 16 note. Check No. 675.

On your own 8-3 LO4, 5
Journalizing adjusting and reversing entries for accrued expenses

General journals and a cash payments journal are provided in the *Working Papers*. Work independently to complete the following problem.

1. Use the following information to journalize the adjusting entries for accrued interest, federal income tax, and warranties on December 31 of the current year.

   a. One note is outstanding on December 31: 120-day, 8% note with First American Bank, $16,000.00, dated September 20.

   b. The company owes additional federal income tax, $4,569.00.

   c. Estimated warranty costs per item sold, $2.25. Units sold, 32,600.
2. Journalize the appropriate reversing entries on January 1 of the next year.
3. Journalize the following transactions.

   Transactions:

   Jan. 12. Paid cash to D&D Service for warranty work performed for the company, $168.00. Check No. 552.

   Paid cash for the maturity value of the September 20 note. Check No. 560.

A Look at **Accounting** Software

Drawing on a Line of Credit

Vaughn Distributors, Inc., has negotiated a line of credit with its bank. Within the terms of this agreement, Vaughn can draw cash against its line of credit as needed. The way a draw on the line of credit is handled is similar in a manual accounting system and an automated accounting system. In either case, the transaction likely takes place on the bank's web site and is recorded with a journal entry in the financial records.

One difference between a manual system and an automated system might be the method of accessing the bank's web site. In Vaughn's computerized accounting system, the banking module links directly to the bank's web site. Another difference is that the transaction is entered into the automated accounting system instead of recording a journal entry manually on paper.

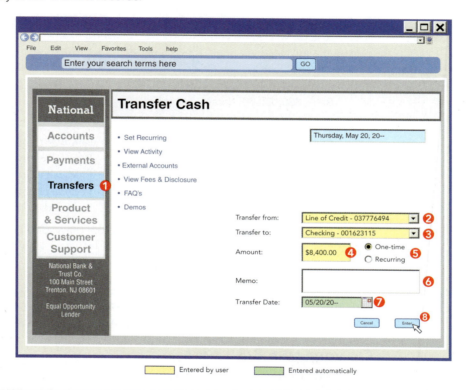

● After logging into the banking module, the accountant viewed a menu of options. **Transfers** was selected, opening the Transfer Cash web page.

❷ The accountant selected the Line of Credit account from the drop-down list labeled **Transfer from**.

❸ In **Transfer to**, the checking account was selected.

❹ The accountant entered the amount of the draw.

❺ The default choice is for a one-time transaction, but the web site offers the company the option of setting up recurring transactions. If a recurring

transaction had been set up, the bank would send a confirmation to the company via text message or email each time it executed the transfer.

❻ The accountant could have entered a brief description of the transaction in the **Memo** field.

❼ The accountant can change the default date to a future date.

❽ Upon clicking Enter, a new page would open, giving the accountant the opportunity to print or download a confirmation statement. The confirmation would be used as the source document for a journal entry to record the draw.

CHAPTER SUMMARY

A business needing capital to fund its operations may elect to obtain debt financing. One of the most common methods of debt financing is to sign a note payable with a financial institution. The interest on a note payable is calculated using the principal, annual interest rate, and the term of the note. Interest Expense is classified as Other Expense on the income statement.

A line of credit is a bank loan agreement that provides immediate short-term access to cash. The interest rate can change based on changes in market interest rates. Although a business can repay a line of credit at any time, monthly payments of principal and interest are typically required.

A prepaid expense is an expense paid in one fiscal period but not reported as an expense until a later fiscal period. Prepaid expenses may be recorded initially as assets or as expenses. In either case, an adjusting entry is required to recognize the expenses used during the current fiscal period. The adjusting entry creates a balance in an asset account. If an adjusting entry creates a balance in an asset or a liability account, the adjusting entry is reversed. This procedure is used when the prepaid expense will be used early in the next fiscal period.

The payment of an expense that will be used over several fiscal periods is initially recorded as an asset. An adjusting entry is required to recognize the portion of the expense used during the current fiscal period. However, no reversing entry is required.

An accrued expense is incurred in one fiscal period but not paid until a later fiscal period. An adjusting entry records the expense and creates a liability. Similar to prepaid expenses, accrued liabilities that will be paid early in the next fiscal period are reversed. A liability that extends over several periods is initially recorded as a liability. The procedure is similar to the accounting for uncollectible accounts receivable.

EXPLORE ACCOUNTING

Impact of Changes in Foreign Exchange Rates on a Note Payable

U.S. companies often purchase products from foreign suppliers. Any changes in foreign exchange rates can have an impact on a firm's accounts payable and notes payable.

Suppose AmCorp, a U.S. company, gives ChiCorp, a Chinese corporation, a 12-month, 5% note payable for 1,000,000 yuan. Including the interest of 50,000 yuan (1,000,000 yuan × 5%), AmCorp will pay ChiCorp 1,050,000 yuan when the note matures. If the exchange rate at the beginning and at the end of the note remains the same (one yuan = $0.14), 1,050,000 yuan will cost $147,000 (1,050,000 yuan × $0.14).

Suppose, however, that during the 12-month period, the exchange rate between the yuan and the dollar declines from $0.14 to $0.13. Since a yuan costs less, AmCorp can now purchase 1,050,000 yuan for $136,500 (1,050,000 yuan × $0.13). Due to the one-cent decline in the exchange rate, AmCorp realizes a gain of $10,500 ($147,000 − $136,500) through the currency exchange process. AmCorp accounts for the gain on accounts payable using the entry below.

Notes Payable	140,000	
Interest Expense	7,000	
Cash		136,500
Gain or Loss on Foreign Currency Exchange		10,500

INSTRUCTIONS

An American company, Fashion Clothiers, purchases men's clothing on account from a Canadian firm, Delmar, Inc., for 50,000 Canadian dollars. At the time of the sale, the exchange rate is one Canadian dollar equals 0.78 U.S. dollar. Thirty days later, when Fashion Clothiers pays the 50,000 Canadian dollars, the exchange rate has risen. One Canadian dollar can now be exchanged for 0.80 dollars. How much will it cost Fashion Clothiers to purchase Canadian dollars at the new rate? Use T accounts to show the impact on Fashion Clothiers.

APPLY YOUR UNDERSTANDING

INSTRUCTIONS: Download problem instructions for Excel, QuickBooks, and Sage 50c from the textbook companion website at www.C21accounting.com.

8-1 Application Problem | Journalizing notes payable transactions LO1

A cash receipts journal and a cash payments journal are provided in the *Working Papers*. Source documents are abbreviated as: check, C; memorandum, M; receipt, R.

Instructions:

1. Using the current year, journalize the following transactions in the cash receipts journal.

Transactions:

May 16. Obtained a note from Farmers Bank. The $10,000.00 is due in 180 days and has a 10% interest rate. R445.

June 23. Negotiated a 90-day, 9% note with American Bank. The $4,500.00 proceeds were deposited in the corporation's checking account. R490.

Dec. 12. Used an Internet banking site to transfer $6,000.00 from its line of credit to its checking account. R580.

2. Calculate the maturity date of each note payable and the total amount of interest due at the maturity date.

3. Journalize the following transactions in the cash payments journal. Use the maturity dates and interest amounts calculated in the previous instruction to journalize the payments of the notes payable.

Transactions:

Wrote Check No. 446 to pay the maturity value of the $4,500.00 note.

Paid cash for the maturity value of the $10,000.00 note. C588.

Dec. 31. Used the Internet banking site to pay the December interest, $67.25 plus $500.00 of principal on its line of credit. M71 (enter the memorandum number in the Check No. column).

8-2 Application Problem | Journalizing adjusting and reversing entries for prepaid expenses LO2

West River, Inc., has the following general ledger account balances on December 31 of the current year before it records adjusting entries. A general journal is provided in the *Working Papers*.

Supplies Expense	$ 5,900.00
Insurance Expense	16,000.00
Prepaid Advertising	90,000.00

Instructions:

1. Using the following adjustment information, journalize the adjusting entries on December 31 of the current year.

Supplies inventory	$ 940.00
Value of prepaid insurance	1,200.00
Advertising used	40,000.00

2. Journalize the reversing entries on January 1 of the next year.

8-3 Application Problem | Journalizing adjusting and reversing entries for accrued expenses LO4, 5

General journals and a cash payments journal are provided in the *Working Papers*.

Instructions:

1. Use the following information to journalize the adjusting entries for accrued interest, accrued payroll, accrued employer payroll taxes, warranties, and federal income tax on December 31 of the current year.

a. One note is outstanding on December 31: 180-day, 9% note with Windstar Bank, $50,000.00, dated October 10.

b. Payroll information for December 29 to December 31:

Payroll and Employee Payroll Taxes		Employer Payroll Taxes	
Salaries	$2,850.00	Social security tax	$176.70
Federal income tax withheld	140.00	Medicare tax	41.33
Social security tax	176.70	Federal unemployment tax	3.60
Medicare tax	41.33	State unemployment tax	24.30

c. Estimated warranty costs per item sold, $30.00. Units sold during fiscal year, 6,900.

d. The company owes additional federal income tax, $3,248.00.

2. Journalize the appropriate reversing entries on January 1 of the next year.

3. Journalize the following transaction.

Transactions:

Mar. 12. Paid cash to John Patterson for parts he purchased to repair an item under warranty, $89.95. Check No. 334.
Paid cash for the maturity value of the October 10 note: principal, $50,000.00, plus interest. Check No. 401.

---

sage 50

1. Journalize and post adjusting and reversing entries to the general journal.

2. From the menu bar, select Reports & Forms; General Ledger.

3. Print the general journal and general ledger trial balance.

QB Quick Books

1. Journalize and post adjusting and reversing entries to the journal.

2. From the menu bar, select Reports; Accountant & Taxes.

3. Print the journal and trial balance.

1. Journalize adjusting and reversing entries to the general journal.

2. Journalize warranty payments to the cash payments journal.

3. Print the worksheets.

8-M Mastery Problem

Journalizing notes payable transactions and adjusting and reversing entries LO1, 2, 4, 5

sage 50

1. Journalize and post notes payable transactions to the cash receipts journal.

2. Journalize and post adjusting and reversing entries to the general journal.

3. From the menu bar, select Reports & Forms; General Ledger.

4. Print the general journal and general ledger trial balance.

QB Quick Books

1. Journalize and post notes payable transactions to the cash receipts journal.

2. Journalize and post adjusting and reversing entries to the journal.

3. From the menu bar, select Reports & Forms; General Ledger.

4. Print the journal and general ledger trial balance.

Roberts, Inc., completed the following transactions during the current year. Roberts initially records supplies and insurance as expenses and maintains a liability account for estimated warranty expenses. Source documents are abbreviated as follows: check, C; memorandum, M; receipt, R.

Instructions:

1. Journalize the following transactions in a cash receipts journal.

Transactions:

Aug. 10. Agreed to a 180-day, 8% note with National Bank for $20,000.00. R123.

Oct. 20. Received $25,000.00 from First American Bank, signing a 90-day, 10% note. R149.

Nov. 5. Signed a $13,000.00, 90-day, 9% note with First Commerce Bank. R152.

Dec. 9. Drew $6,200.00 from its First American Bank line of credit. The bank deposited the funds directly to its checking account. R165.

2. Use the following information to journalize adjusting entries for prepaid expenses and accrued expenses on December 31 of the current year. Include the adjusting entry for the accrued interest on the outstanding notes payable.

Supplies inventory	$ 480.00
Value of prepaid insurance	2,400.00
Advertising used	20,000.00
Additional federal income tax owed	875.00

1. Journalize notes payable transactions to the cash receipts journal.
2. Journalize warranty payments to the cash payments journal.
3. Journalize adjusting and reversing entries to the general journal.
4. Print the worksheets.

3. Journalize the appropriate reversing entries on January 1 of the next year.
4. Calculate the maturity date for each note payable and the total amount of interest due at the maturity date.
5. Journalize the following transactions on a cash payments journal. For the payment of each note payable, use the maturity dates calculated in the prior step.

Transactions:

Jan. 12. Wrote a check to John Patterson for parts he purchased to repair an item under warranty, $89.95. C394.

Issued Check No. 405 for the maturity value of the First American Bank note, plus interest.

31. Used the bank's Internet site to pay $1,000.00 plus $75.69 interest on its line of credit. M84 (enter the memorandum number in the Check No. column).

Paid the maturity value of the First Commerce Bank note, plus interest. C423.

Wrote Check No. 428 to pay off the National Bank note, plus interest. C428.

8-C Challenge Problem   Accruing for self-insurance losses LO4

Presto Pizza operates a pizza delivery business. An unfortunate cost of operating the business is that customers may sue the company if they get sick after eating its pizza. Presto Pizza believes that most of these claims are unfounded. There is rarely ever any evidence that the pizza, rather than other factors, caused the customers to get sick.

For years, Pesto Pizza carried insurance coverage to protect it against these claims. However, the insurance premiums had risen dramatically in recent years, despite Presto Pizza filing fewer and fewer claims. To save money, Presto Pizza has decided to drop its insurance coverage effective January 1, 20X6. Instead, Presto Pizza will self-insure against these claims. Any future claims will be paid directly by Presto Pizza.

The following table presents information related to sales, product claims, and insurance premiums for the past five fiscal years.

	20X1	20X2	20X3	20X4	20X5
Sales	$823,632	$856,528	$896,800	$928,540	$970,463
Product claims	4,637	4,454	4,314	4,243	4,173
Insurance premiums	6,000	7,000	9,000	9,000	12,000

Instructions:

1. Identify accounts to be used to accrue the expense of product claims beginning in 20X6. Create a T account for each account. Use the forms in the *Working Papers*.
2. Use the T accounts to record the following transactions:

Transactions:

Feb. 6. Paid Family Medical Clinic $450 for the treatment of a customer who claimed the pizza made her sick.

June 9. Agreed to settle Mary Stephenson's lawsuit for $3,600.

Oct. 15. Wrote a check to Davidson County Hospital for the treatment of a customer who claimed there were foreign objects in her pizza, $489.

3. Record an adjusting entry for the expense of product claims. Use the form in the *Working Papers* to calculate the past ratios of claims to sales. Use this information to calculate an accrual for product claims. Sales for 20X6 were $1,093,267.

21st Century Skills

Student Loan Debt Crisis

Theme: Financial, Economic, Business, and Entrepreneurial Literacy

Skills: Critical Thinking and Problem Solving, Communication and Collaboration

PARTNERSHIP FOR
21ST CENTURY SKILLS

Obtaining student loans is not easy, but many websites and organizations are available to assist students in obtaining student loans and other financial aid. What many students find more difficult is paying back the loans once they are out of college.

As of 2018, it is estimated that student loan debt in the United States totals $1.5 trillion. This amount is second only to total mortgage debt. More than 44 million people in the United States have student debt, averaging over $37,000 per person.

As student debt has increased, so has the number of people who have difficulty repaying the debt. A student loan is considered delinquent the first day after the borrower misses a payment. For many loans, if the payment is more than 90 days overdue, the delinquency will be reported to the three major credit bureaus, which will lower the borrower's credit score. Many student loans are considered to be in default if the borrower fails to make a payment for 270 days. The current default rate is almost 11%.

While most kinds of debt can be discharged in bankruptcy, meaning that the debt does not have to be repaid, student debt is rarely discharged. Current law states that in order for the court to discharge student debt in bankruptcy, the borrower must prove that repaying the debt will cause "undue hardship" to the borrower. The law, however, does not clearly define the phrase "undue hardship."

The undue hardship clause makes it very difficult for most borrowers to get relief from student debt through bankruptcy. Therefore, before taking out a loan for college, realize that you will have to pay it back someday.

APPLICATION

Use the Internet to answer the following questions:

1. When a law is unclear, court cases are commonly used to clarify the law. Have recent court cases clearly defined the definition of "undue hardship?"
2. If student debt cannot be discharged in bankruptcy, a borrower may ask for a deferment or forbearance. What are the definitions for "deferment" and "forbearance" as they relate to student debt?
3. Some courts use the "Brunner Test" to determine "undue hardship." What three criteria must be met in the Brunner Test?
4. Do you think it is good for borrowers to have student debt discharged in bankruptcy?

Sources: www.studentaid.ed.gov; Zack Friedman, "Student Loan Debt Statistics in 2018: A $1.5 Trillion Crisis," Forbes, June 13, 2018.

Analyzing Home Depot's Financial Statements

An investor interested in learning how much Home Depot spends on advertising must read beyond its Consolidated Statement of Earnings. Home Depot's advertising expense is not listed separately on the statement but is included in selling, general, and administrative expenses. Information regarding advertising can be obtained in the Notes to Consolidated Financial Statements. Note 1, Summary of Significant Accounting Policies, beginning on page B-10 in Appendix B, contains two sections that reveal how Home Depot accounts for advertising expenses.

INSTRUCTIONS

1. In the section Advertising Expense, when are the costs of producing television advertising recognized as an expense?
2. Identify the gross advertising expense for each fiscal year presented.
3. In the section Vendor Allowances, what are vendor allowances, and how does Home Depot account for these allowances?

9

Accounting for Unearned Revenue, Accrued Revenue, and Installment Notes Receivable

LEARNING OBJECTIVES

After studying Chapter 9, in addition to defining key terms, you will be able to:

LO1 Journalize the adjusting and reversing entries for unearned revenue.

LO2 Journalize the adjusting and reversing entries for accrued revenue.

LO3 Journalize transactions for gift cards.

LO4 Journalize the adjusting entry for gift card breakage.

LO5 Describe how gift card breakage is reported in the financial statements.

LO6 Journalize transactions for installment notes receivable.

LO7 Journalize the reclassification and reversing entries for installment notes receivable.

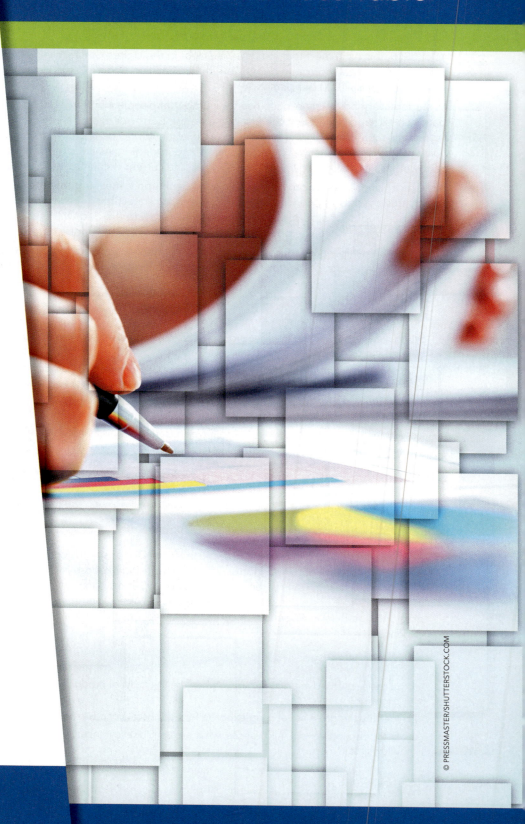

© PRESSMASTER/SHUTTERSTOCK.COM

Ford Motor Company

Few products have the brand recognition of the F-150, Ford Motor Company's iconic "half-ton" pickup truck. Ford proudly boasts that its F-series has been the U.S. truck leader for over 40 years.

But even the best-built truck can experience problems that require service at a local dealer. To improve customer satisfaction, Ford sells every vehicle with a warranty that covers repairs performed during the warranty period. Ford records an estimate of warranty claims as an expense when each vehicle is sold, using the matching revenue with expenses concept.

Ford estimates its warranty expense by using "historical information regarding the nature, frequency, and average cost of claims for each vehicle line by model year." Recording the warranty expense creates a liability reported on Ford's balance sheet in the *Other liabilities and deferred revenue* category. When Ford pays a repair claim submitted by an authorized dealer, the claim reduces the liability account. Then, Ford uses the actual claim information to adjust its assumptions.

A note to the financial statements includes a schedule that reports changes in the warranty liability. The liability balance is reduced by actual warranty payments made during the year, increased by additions for vehicles sold during the year, and adjusted for changes in the estimates related to pre-existing warranties.

Source: www.ford.com.

CRITICAL THINKING

1. Ford offers a 3-year or 36,000-mile bumper-to-bumper warranty for a particular line of vehicles. What entry would be used to record the payment of a warranty claim submitted by an authorized dealer?

2. Assume that Ford records a $400 warranty expense for a new F-150 model. The trucks carry a 5-year or 60,000-mile powertrain warranty. During the first year the average warranty claim is only $30. Should this information result in a change in the warranty expense assumptions for next year's model? Explain your answer.

KEY TERMS

unearned revenue	breakage	amortization schedule
accrued revenue	installment note	reclassification entry

Unearned and Accrued Revenue

LO1 Journalize the adjusting and reversing entries for unearned revenue.
LO2 Journalize the adjusting and reversing entries for accrued revenue.

Journal Entries for Unearned Revenue LO1

Cash received for goods or services which have not been provided is called **unearned revenue**. Unearned revenue is also known as *deferred revenue*.

Unearned revenue may be recorded initially as a liability or as revenue. Vaughn Distributors, Inc., rents part of its building to Keller Construction. During the year, Vaughn receives four checks from Keller, each for the next three months' rent. Most of these rental payments will be earned during the current fiscal year. For this reason, Vaughn has elected to record rent receipts initially as revenue.

Adjusting Entry

Debit Rent Income

		GENERAL JOURNAL				PAGE 13	
	DATE	ACCOUNT TITLE	DOC. NO.	POST. REF.	DEBIT	CREDIT	
1		*Adjusting Entries*					1
12	31	Rent Income			5 000 00		12
13		Unearned Rent				5 000 00	13

Credit Unearned Rent

On December 1, Vaughn Distributors received $7,500.00 from Keller Construction ($2,500.00 per month for December, January, and February rent).

The receipt was recorded initially as rent income and is included in the $35,000.00 balance of Rent Income.

Sharing Nonpublic Information

Juanita Suarez, CPA, is a financial analyst for Natural Stores. The company manufactures a line of organic and gluten-free snack foods. As a result, Natural Stores purchases large quantities of corn and rice. Juanita's job is to track production costs and provide management with projections of future grain prices.

While attending a tailgate party before a football game, Juanita's friends were involved in a spirited conversation about the rising cost of going to the supermarket. "Have you seen what's happened to cereal prices lately?" bemoaned one friend. "Just another example of big business padding their wallets at our expense!" added another friend.

Juanita could not stay quiet any longer. "Oh, quit complaining. So much of the grain supply is being diverted for the production of alternative fuels. Our grain costs have skyrocketed. We're only passing part of the cost on to the consumer. People are going to be surprised when we report earnings."

INSTRUCTIONS

Access *A Champion's Code of Conduct* of General Mills. Use this code as a guide and the ethical model to help determine whether Juanita's comments demonstrate ethical behavior. Does this statement represent the disclosure of nonpublic information?

Rent Income				
Adjusting	⬇	5,000.00	Balance	35,000.00
			(New Balance	*30,000.00)*

Unearned Rent		
	Adjusting ⬆	5,000.00

Unearned Rent is classified as a current liability, since the rent will be earned during the next fiscal period. Because Vaughn Distributors is not in the business of renting buildings, Rent Income is classified as Other Revenue.

Only that part of the rent actually earned should be recorded as revenue in a fiscal period. An adjusting entry is recorded to separate the earned and unearned portions of the rent recorded in Rent Income, as shown above. The January and February rent is unearned and should be reported in Unearned Rent.

The $5,000.00 balance of Unearned Rent, a liability account, represents the value of two months of rental use owed to Keller Construction. The new balance of Rent Income, $30,000.00, correctly reflects 12 months of rent at $2,500.00 per month.

© MONKEY BUSINESS IMAGES/SHUTTERSTOCK.COM

Reversing Entry

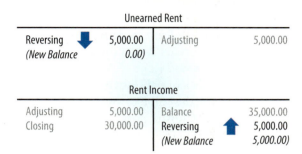

Debit Unearned Rent

	DATE	ACCOUNT TITLE	DOC. NO.	POST. REF.	DEBIT	CREDIT	
		GENERAL JOURNAL				PAGE **1**	
1		*Reversing Entries*					1
10	1	*Unearned Rent*			5 0 0 0 00		10
11		*Rent Income*				5 0 0 0 00	11

Credit Rent Income

On December 31, Rent Income is closed as part of Vaughn Distributors' closing entries. After closing entries are posted, the balance in Rent Income is zero and ready to record transactions in the next fiscal period.

Reversing entries for prepaid and accrued expenses are described in Chapter 8. If an adjusting entry creates a balance in an asset or liability account, the adjusting entry is normally reversed. Reversing entries for unearned revenue are made for the same reason as for prepaid expenses. The amount of unearned revenue must be returned to the account in which it was recorded initially.

Vaughn Distributors' adjusting entry created a balance in the liability account, Unearned Rent. Therefore, Vaughn Distributors needs to make a reversing entry for unearned rent on January 1, as shown above.

Unearned Rent

Reversing	5,000.00	Adjusting	5,000.00
(New Balance	0.00)		

Rent Income

Adjusting	5,000.00	Balance	35,000.00
Closing	30,000.00	Reversing	5,000.00
		(New Balance	5,000.00)

On January 1, after the reversing entry is posted, the new balance of Unearned Rent is zero, as it was before the adjusting entry. Rent Income has a $5,000.00 credit balance. The rent received in advance for January and February, $5,000.00, is part of the rent revenue earned in the new fiscal period.

GLOBAL AWARENESS

Legal Rights in Foreign Countries

While traveling, working, or living in a foreign country, U.S. citizens are expected to obey the laws of that country. Some of these laws may be very different from those in the United States. The punishment for a specific crime in a foreign country may be much harsher than that for the same crime in the United States.

A U.S. citizen arrested for a crime in a foreign country must follow that country's legal process for being charged with a crime, convicted, or sentenced, and for appealing a conviction. Usually, however, the U.S. citizen does not have to go through this process without help.

The United States has embassies in many countries. These embassies as well as the U.S. Department of State (the State Department) provide help to U.S. citizens who have been jailed in a foreign country. The website for the Department of State notes that "The State Department is committed to

ensuring fair and humane treatment for American citizens imprisoned overseas … within the limits of our authority in accordance with international law."

The State Department website gives specific information for many countries. This information includes a description of the country and its political climate, entry/exit requirements for U.S. citizens, and other information.

CRITICAL THINKING

Go to the website for the U.S. Department of State (www.state.gov). Pick a country you would like to visit. Search the site for specific information about that country. Summarize your findings in the following categories:

a. Country description.

b. City and phone number of one U.S. embassy in this country.

c. Alerts for U.S. travelers to this country.

Journal Entries for Accrued Interest Income LO2

Revenue earned in one fiscal period but not received until a later fiscal period is called **accrued revenue**. For example, a business accepts a 30-day note on December 15. During December, the business earned interest for 16 days. However, the business will not receive any of the interest until the note's maturity in January. Interest for the first 16 days must be recorded in the current fiscal period. ➤➤ App A: Matching Expenses with Revenue

Adjusting Entry

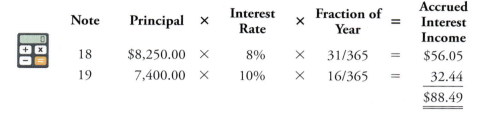

	Note	Principal	×	Interest Rate	×	Fraction of Year	=	Accrued Interest Income
	18	$8,250.00	×	8%	×	31/365	=	$56.05
	19	7,400.00	×	10%	×	16/365	=	32.44
								$88.49

Debit Interest Receivable

GENERAL JOURNAL   PAGE 13

	DATE	ACCOUNT TITLE	DOC. NO.	POST. REF.	DEBIT	CREDIT	
1		*Adjusting Entries*					1
17	31	*Interest Receivable*			8 8 49		17
18		*Interest Income*				8 8 49	18

Credit Interest Income

Vaughn Distributors periodically accepts a note from a customer who is unable to pay its account. On December 31, Vaughn Distributors has two notes receivable outstanding.

- Note Receivable No. 18, a 60-day, 8% note dated November 30, $8,250.00.
- Note Receivable No. 19, a 90-day, 10% note dated December 15, $7,400.00.

Accrued interest for each note is calculated from the date of the note through the end of the fiscal period, as shown above.

The accrued interest for all notes is totaled to compute the adjusting entry amount. The adjusting entry increases the balance of Interest Income to include interest that has been earned but not received in cash. Interest Income is reported in the Other Revenue section of the income statement.

The amount of interest owed to the company is reported as Interest Receivable. Interest Receivable is reported in the Current Assets section of the balance sheet.

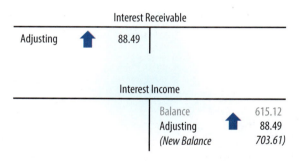

Interest Receivable

Adjusting ⬆ 88.49	

Interest Income

	Balance ⬆ 615.12
	Adjusting 88.49
	(New Balance 703.61)

© DENISNATA/SHUTTERSTOCK.COM

Reversing Entry

Debit Interest Income

	DATE		ACCOUNT TITLE	DOC. NO.	POST. REF.	DEBIT	CREDIT	
			GENERAL JOURNAL				PAGE **1**	
1			*Reversing Entries*					1
2	Jan.²⁰⁻⁻	1	*Interest Income*			8 8 49		2
3			*Interest Receivable*				8 8 49	3
4								4

Credit Interest Receivable

Interest Income

		Balance	615.12
Closing	703.61	Adjusting	88.49
Reversing	88.49		
(New Balance	*88.49)*		

Interest Receivable

Adjusting	88.49	Reversing	88.49
(New Balance	*0.00)*		

Interest Income is closed as part of Vaughn Distributors' closing entries. After closing entries are posted, Interest Income has a zero balance. The $88.49 balance in Interest Receivable represents interest that Vaughn Distributors has earned but has not yet received in cash.

The adjusting entry for accrued interest income created a balance in the asset account Interest Receivable. Therefore, on January 1, Vaughn Distributors needs to reverse the adjusting entry that created the balance in Interest Receivable, as shown above.

The new balance of Interest Receivable is zero, as it was before the adjusting entry. The new debit balance, $88.49, in Interest Income is not the normal balance in that account. When cash is received on the maturity date of each note, a credit to Interest Income will offset the debit balance.

© KONSTANTIN CHAGIN/SHUTTERSTOCK.COM

LO1 Journalize the adjusting and reversing entries for unearned revenue.

LO2 Journalize the adjusting and reversing entries for accrued revenue.

TERMS REVIEW

unearned revenue

accrued revenue

Audit your understanding LO1, 2

1. What is another term used to describe unearned revenue?
2. Why might a business receiving rent payments initially record the receipts as Rent Income?
3. How is the account Unearned Rent classified on the financial statements?
4. What is the rule for determining whether an adjusting entry should be reversed?
5. How does the adjusting entry for accrued interest impact the balance sheet?
6. In which section of the income statement is the account Interest Income reported?

Work together 9-1 LO1, 2

Journalizing adjusting and reversing entries for unearned and accrued revenue

Winston, Inc., is preparing its December 31 financial statements for the current year. On December 1, the company received a $4,200.00 rent payment from Youngston Company. The payment is the $1,400.00 per month rent for December of the current year through February of the next year. Winston records rent receipts initially as revenue. General journal pages are provided in the *Working Papers*. Your instructor will guide you through the following examples.

Winston, Inc., has two notes receivable outstanding on December 31 of the current year.

Note No.	Interest Rate	Term	Principal	Date
22	8%	60 days	$6,000.00	November 22
23	9%	90 days	$5,000.00	December 8

1. Journalize the adjusting entries for unearned rent and accrued interest income. Use page 13 of a general journal.
2. Journalize the reversing entries for unearned rent and accrued interest income. Use page 14 of a general journal.

On your own 9-1 LO1, 2

Journalizing adjusting and reversing entries for unearned and accrued revenue

K-109 Radio is preparing its December 31 financial statements for the current year. On October 30, City Recycling paid $3,500.00 to K-109 Radio for advertising. The advertising contract requires K-109 to provide City Recycling with $700.00 of advertising time per month for November of the current year through March of the next year. K-109 records advertising receipts initially as revenue. General journal pages are provided in the *Working Papers*. Work this problem independently.

K-109 Radio has two notes receivable outstanding on December 31 of the current year.

Note No.	Interest Rate	Term	Principal	Date
16	10%	120 days	$2,300.00	November 6
17	8%	60 days	$1,800.00	December 2

1. Journalize the adjusting entries for unearned advertising revenue and accrued interest income. Use page 19 of a general journal.
2. Journalize the reversing entries for unearned advertising revenue and accrued interest income. Use page 20 of a general journal.

LO3 Journalize transactions for gift cards.

LO4 Journalize the adjusting entry for gift card breakage.

LO5 Describe how gift card breakage is reported in the financial statements.

Journal Entries for Gift Cards LO3

Retailers have traditionally accepted cash, check, or credit card for payment of a sale. Debit card use has increased as technology has enabled customers convenient access to their checking accounts. Sales paid for with a debit card are processed and accounted for like a credit card. Thus, no new accounting procedures are required.

The use of gift cards has increased recently. Retailers often issue gift cards as credit for returned merchandise. Gift cards resemble credit and debit cards—a plastic card with a magnetic strip where the card balance can be stored. Websites and smartphones enable gift cards, also called *virtual gift cards* or *eGift cards*, to be purchased and redeemed electronically.

Sale of a Gift Card

CASH RECEIPTS JOURNAL — PAGE 7

Credit Gift Cards Outstanding   Debit Cash

Although they may look like credit and debit cards, gift cards require very different accounting treatment. The sale of a gift card does not result in revenue. The retailer receives cash and promises to allow the cardholder to purchase merchandise at some time in the future. Until the card is redeemed, the outstanding balance of the card is unearned revenue.

Riverside Lighting sells gift cards at its store and through its website. The company records the sale of gift cards in Gift Cards Outstanding, a current liability account.

April 1. Received cash for the sale of gift cards, $625.00. Receipt No. 522.

Gift cardholders expect they can redeem the full amount of the card at any future date. The Credit Card Accountability Responsibility and Disclosure Act of 2009 (Credit CARD Act) includes provisions designed to protect the value of gift cards. Retailers are not allowed to charge fees on unredeemed cards for 12 months. Unredeemed cards cannot be canceled until five years after the date of issuance.

Gift Cards Outstanding

Debit Decreases | Credit Increases

Sale Using a Gift Card

Debit Gift Cards Outstanding

	DATE		ACCOUNT TITLE	DOC. NO.	POST. REF.	DEBIT	CREDIT	
	GENERAL JOURNAL						PAGE 8	
1	Aug. 20--	2	Gift Cards Outstanding	M325		3 3 9 20		1
2			Sales				3 2 0 00	2
3			Sales Tax Payable				1 9 20	3

Credit Sales   **Credit Sales Tax Payable**

A sale is recorded when a customer pays for merchandise using a gift card. Riverside Lighting's point-of-sale system records the daily amount of sales paid for with a gift card.

> **August 2.** Customers redeemed gift cards for the sale of merchandise, $320.00, plus sales tax, $19.20. Memorandum No. 325.

The redemption of a gift card reduces the amount of gift cards outstanding. The debit to Gift Cards Outstanding reduces the balance of this liability account.

Gift Cards Outstanding

339.20

Sales

320.00

Sales Tax Payable

19.20

The unused balance of a gift card can be electronically recorded on the card's magnetic strip or updated in the point-of-sale system. The balance of a virtual gift card is updated in the retailer's computer system.

WHY ACCOUNTING?

Buying What They Want to Sell

CareerClusters®
PATHWAYS TO COLLEGE & CAREER READINESS
Architecture & Construction

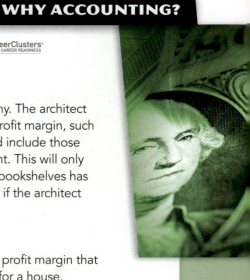

Many people dream of designing a home that is perfect for their needs. When designing a house, an architect must listen to the wants and needs of the client and reflect these in the drawings. The architect must have good communications skills and know how to ask questions that will get clients to explain their expectations clearly.

The architect has quite a bit of influence over the items chosen by the clients. If the architect understands the concept of net income, he or she can also have a large influence on the bottom line of the construction company. The architect can choose items with a high profit margin, such as handmade bookshelves, and include those items in the drawings for a client. This will only be successful if the cost of the bookshelves has been calculated accurately and if the architect understands accounting.

CRITICAL THINKING

Make a list of items with a high profit margin that could be included in the plans for a house.

Accounting for Unredeemed Gift Cards LO4

	DATE	ACCOUNT TITLE	DOC. NO.	POST. REF.	DEBIT	CREDIT	
		GENERAL JOURNAL				PAGE 13	
1		*Adjusting Entries*					1
22	31	*Gift Cards Outstanding*			8 2 9 0 00		22
23		*Breakage Revenue*				8 2 9 0 00	23

Some gift cards are never redeemed. A cardholder may lose the card or discard a card having a very small remaining value. The cardholder of a virtual gift card may forget about the card or be unable to remember login, password, and security questions necessary to redeem the card's value.

The value of unredeemed gift cards is called **breakage**. When a business concludes that a gift card will never be redeemed, the value of the card is no longer a liability.

Gift Cards Outstanding	
Adjusting ⬇ 8,290.00	

Breakage Revenue	
	Adjusting ⬆ 8,290.00

Depending on state laws, the card value may be recognized as revenue or be paid to the state government. An adjusting entry records the gift card breakage. The adjusting entry reduces Gift Cards Outstanding to reflect the amount the business expects cardholders to redeem in the future. Vaughn operates in a state that allows it to recognize revenue from gift card breakage. The adjusting entry increases Breakage Revenue for the amount of the gift cards the business estimates will never be redeemed.

Breakage revenue is an estimate. Similar to the accounting for uncollectible accounts and the depreciation of plant assets, the business must use a generally accepted method consistently for making an unbiased estimate. >> App A: Neutrality At a minimum, a business should allow several years to pass before recognizing gift card breakage as revenue.

Reporting of Gift Card Breakage LO5

Riverside Lighting uses the account Breakage Revenue to record unredeemed cards. The account is included in the Net Sales section of the income statement, as shown below.

Breakage revenue is a normal part of business operations. Most businesses elect to include breakage revenue with other sales accounts instead of including the amount as other revenue. Breakage Revenue is listed separately on the income statement to allow users to compare the amount of revenue from sales with the related cost of merchandise sold. The notes to the financial statements include the policies for how and when breakage revenue is recognized, the amount of unredeemed cards, and how gift-card-related accounts are presented on the financial statements.

Riverside Lighting			
Income Statement			
For Year Ended December 31, 20--			
Operating Revenue:			
Sales			2101 8 6 4 17
Less: Sales Discounts	21 8 4 2 16		
Sales Returns and Allowances	16 4 9 7 14	38 3 3 9 30	
Revenue from Sales		2063 5 2 4 87	
Breakage Revenue		32 0 8 4 00	
Net Sales		2095 6 0 8 87	

LO3 Journalize transactions for gift cards.

LO4 Journalize the adjusting entry for gift card breakage.

LO5 Describe how gift card breakage is reported in the financial statements.

TERM REVIEW

breakage

Audit your understanding LO3, 4, 5

1. How is the sale of a gift card reported on the balance sheet and income statement?
2. When is a sale recorded from the issuance of a gift card?
3. What account is credited when a business recognizes that gift cards will never be redeemed?
4. In what section of the income statement is the account Breakage Revenue reported?
5. Identify information related to gift cards that is disclosed in the notes to the financial statements.

Work together 9-2 LO3, 4
Journalizing gift card transactions

Salter Stores uses gift cards to help increase its sales. A cash receipts journal and general journals are provided in the *Working Papers*. Your instructor will guide you through the following examples.

1. Record the following transactions on page 24 of a cash receipts journal and page 18 of a general journal. Salter Stores uses the accounts Gift Cards Outstanding and Breakage Revenue to account for gift card transactions. Source documents are abbreviated as follows: memorandum, M; receipt, R.

   Transactions:

   Dec. 29. Received cash for the sale of gift cards, $450.00. R456.
   29. Customers redeemed gift cards for the sale of merchandise, $148.15, plus $8.89 sales tax. M334.
   30. Received cash for the sale of gift cards, $550.00. R457.
   30. Customers redeemed gift cards for the sale of merchandise, $92.68, plus $5.56 sales tax. M335.

2. Salter Stores estimates that $4,525.00 of gift cards will never be redeemed. Record the adjusting entry on page 19 of a general journal.

On your own 9-2 LO3, 4
Journalizing gift card transactions

Main Street Gifts sells gift cards at its store and via a website. A cash receipts journal and general journals are provided in the *Working Papers*. Work this problem independently.

1. Record the following transactions on page 18 of a cash receipts journal and page 14 of a general journal. Main Street Gifts uses the accounts Gift Cards Outstanding and Breakage Revenue to account for gift card transactions. Source documents are abbreviated as follows: memorandum, M; receipt, R.

   Transactions:

   Dec. 28. Received cash for the sale of gift cards, $920.00. R888.
   28. Customers redeemed gift cards for the sale of merchandise, $895.44, plus $62.68 sales tax. M167.
   31. Customers redeemed gift cards for the sale of merchandise, $1,648.07, plus $115.36 sales tax. M170.
   31. Received cash for the sale of gift cards, $625.00. R914.

2. Main Street Gifts estimates that $3,150.00 of gift cards will never be redeemed. Record the adjusting entry on page 15 of a general journal.

Accounting for Installment Notes Receivable

LO6 Journalize transactions for installment notes receivable.
LO7 Journalize the reclassification and reversing entries for installment notes receivable.

Journal Entries for an Installment Note Receivable LO6

To promote sales, some businesses must offer customers the opportunity to sign a note extending their payment over time. Retailers who sell expensive items, such as cars, boats, and recreational vehicles, typically finance their customers' purchases. Customers are generally required to make monthly payments over the term of the loan.

A note resulting from a sale that requires monthly payments of principal and interest is called an **installment note**. The procedures used to account for installment notes receivable must ensure that interest earned on the note is recorded in the correct accounting period. The business must also ensure that the total principal of outstanding notes is properly reported on the balance sheet.

Issuing an Installment Note Receivable

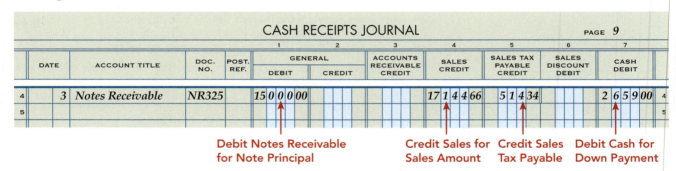

					GENERAL		ACCOUNTS RECEIVABLE CREDIT	SALES CREDIT	SALES TAX PAYABLE CREDIT	SALES DISCOUNT DEBIT	CASH DEBIT	
	DATE	ACCOUNT TITLE	DOC. NO.	POST. REF.	DEBIT	CREDIT						
4	3	Notes Receivable	NR325		15 000 00			17 144 66	5 14 34		2 659 00	4
5												5

CASH RECEIPTS JOURNAL — PAGE 9

Debit Notes Receivable for Note Principal — **Credit Sales for Sales Amount** — **Credit Sales Tax Payable** — **Debit Cash for Down Payment**

Candor Auto Mart sells previously owned cars obtained from car rental companies. Candor offers creditworthy customers the opportunity to finance up to 90% of the purchase price of any car. Past experience has taught Candor that customers who can make a significant down payment are more likely to make their monthly payments.

Similar to sales on account, the sale is recorded as revenue at the time of sale, regardless of when the payment is made. **>> App A: Realization of Revenue**

> **May 3.** Sold a car to Mark Carver for $17,144.66 plus sales tax of $514.34, receiving a $2,659.00 down payment and accepting a 60-month, 10% installment note receivable for the balance, $15,000.00. Note Receivable No. 325.

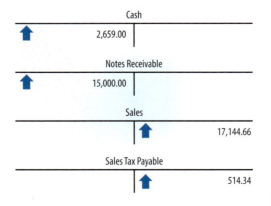

FYI A company that accepts a large number of notes might benefit from using a ledger system that enables management to identify the amount of notes outstanding with any customer. Thus, management could make informed decisions about extending additional credit to a particular customer.

Receiving a Monthly Payment

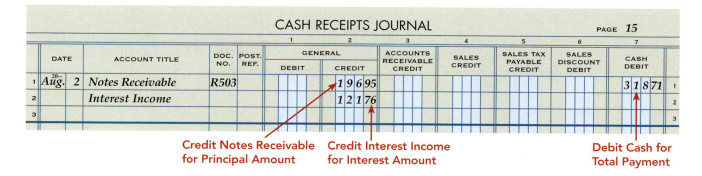

					GENERAL		ACCOUNTS RECEIVABLE CREDIT	SALES CREDIT	SALES TAX PAYABLE CREDIT	SALES DISCOUNT DEBIT	CASH DEBIT	
	DATE	ACCOUNT TITLE	DOC. NO.	POST. REF.	DEBIT	CREDIT						
1	Aug. 2	Notes Receivable	R503			1 9 6 95					3 1 8 71	1
2		Interest Income				1 2 1 76						2
3												3

Credit Notes Receivable for Principal Amount   **Credit Interest Income for Interest Amount**   **Debit Cash for Total Payment**

Candor Auto Mart provides its customers with a note agreement that includes a payment schedule. A schedule of the periodic payments on a note is called an **amortization schedule**. Mark Carver purchased the car on May 3. Thus, the note agreement requires that he make a payment by the third day of every month.

> **August 2. Received cash for Mark Carver's August payment, $196.95, and interest, $121.76; total, $318.71. Receipt No. 503.**

Mark Carver is required to pay $318.71 each month. A portion of the payment is interest on the outstanding balance of the loan. The remaining amount reduces the outstanding loan principal. The monthly payment will enable Mark Carver to repay the loan fully by the end of the 5 years (60 months). Candor Auto Mart uses a 360-day year to prepare its amortization schedules.

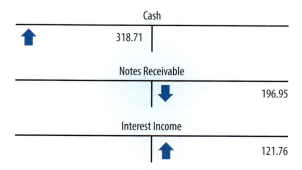

Amount Borrowed	$15,000.00
Term of Note (Months)	60
Annual Interest Rate	10%
Monthly Payment	$318.71
Monthly Due Date	3rd

Payment Number	Month	Beginning Balance	Interest	Principal	Ending Balance
1	June	$15,000.00	$125.00	$193.71	$14,806.29
2	July	$14,806.29	$123.39	$195.32	$14,610.97
3	August	$14,610.97	$121.76	$196.95	$14,414.02
4	September	$14,414.02	$120.12	$198.59	$14,215.43
5	October	$14,215.43	$118.46	$200.25	$14,015.18
6	November	$14,015.18	$116.79	$201.92	$13,813.26
7	December	$13,813.26	$115.11	$203.60	$13,609.66
8	January	$13,609.66	$113.41	$205.30	$13,404.36

Journal Entries for Reclassifying an Installment Note Receivable LO7

At the end of a fiscal period, a company records adjusting entries to bring account balances up to date. Adjusting entries change the balances of revenue and expense accounts. An entry that transfers account balances between accounts on one financial statement is called a **reclassification entry**.

Reclassification Entry

Debit Current Portion of Notes Receivable

	DATE		ACCOUNT TITLE	DOC. NO.	POST. REF.	DEBIT	CREDIT	
1			*Reclassification Entries*					1
2	20-- Dec.	31	*Current Portion of Notes Receivable*			175 2 1 2 00		2
3			*Notes Receivable*				175 2 1 2 00	3
4								4

GENERAL JOURNAL — PAGE 14

Credit Notes Receivable

Candor Auto Mart reports new installment notes receivable initially in Notes Receivable, as a noncurrent asset. When a balance sheet is prepared, Candor determines the total principal payments it expects to collect during the next fiscal period. A reclassification entry is recorded to transfer the amount from Notes Receivable to Current Portion of Notes Receivable, a current asset.

On December 31, Candor has $584,040.00 of notes receivable. Of that amount, $175,212.00 is expected to be collected during the next fiscal period. The total is reclassified from a noncurrent asset account to a current asset account. The entry has no effect on total assets or net income.

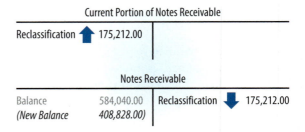

The impact of the reclassification entry is shown in the following section from Candor's balance sheet. Current Portion of Notes Receivable appears in the Current Assets section. Notes Receivable, the noncurrent portion of future principal payments, is presented after plant assets.

Candor Auto Mart			
Balance Sheet			
December 31, 20--			
Inventory	648 1 5 3 00		
Current Portion of Notes Receivable	175 2 1 2 00		
Other Current Assets	21 4 9 5 00		
Total Current Assets		914 6 1 3 00	
Property and Equipment, net		159 1 4 8 00	
Notes Receivable		408 8 2 8 00	
Other Assets		32 0 8 4 00	
Total Assets		1514 6 7 3 00	

Reversing Entry

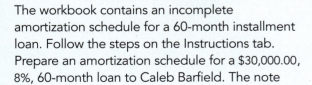

GENERAL JOURNAL   PAGE 1

Debit Notes Receivable ↓

	DATE	ACCOUNT TITLE	DOC. NO.	POST. REF.	DEBIT	CREDIT	
1		*Reversing Entries*					1
4	Jan. 1	Notes Receivable			175 212 00		4
5		Current Portion of Notes Receivable				175 212 00	5
6							6

Credit Current Portion of Notes Receivable ↑

The recording of customer note payments is simplified by using a single account to credit principal payments. Candor Auto Mart reverses the reclassification entry after the financial statements are prepared. After the reversing entry is posted, the balance of **Notes Receivable** represents the total outstanding principal of installment notes receivable.

Current Portion of Notes Receivable

Reclassification	175,212.00	Reversing ↓	175,212.00
(New Balance	*0.00)*		

Notes Receivable

Balance	584,040.00	Reclassification	175,212.00
Reversing ↑	175,212.00		
(New Balance	*584,040.00)*		

THINK LIKE AN ACCOUNTANT

Creating an Amortization Schedule

Hwy 66 RVs sells recreational vehicles. The business has been purchasing a license for software to prepare loan agreements. The owner, who prepares the loan documents, believes that the cost of the software outweighs its benefits. The owner also believes that using Microsoft Office products to prepare the documents would reduce administrative expenses. The owner has created a loan agreement in word processing but does not know how to create an amortization schedule.

OPEN THE SPREADSHEET TLA_CH09

The workbook contains an incomplete amortization schedule for a 60-month installment loan. Follow the steps on the Instructions tab. Prepare an amortization schedule for a $30,000.00, 8%, 60-month loan to Caleb Barfield. The note

was signed on November 1, 2018. Answer the following questions.

1. What are the interest and principal amounts for the December 2019 payment?

2. Mandy Everson is buying a pre-owned $35,000.00 recreational vehicle. Prepare an amortization schedule for a 5%, 60-month loan, using today's date. What are the date, monthly payment, and the interest and principal amounts for the 48th payment?

3. Hwy 66 RVs is considering having a special financing sale. Customers would be offered 10% off the sale price, but the interest rate would be increased by 1%. Modify Mandy Everson's loan as a method of analyzing the impact on the company. Would you recommend Hwy 66 RVs adopt this plan?

A Royal Disaster

*R*estatement may be one of the most feared words in the financial community. A restatement occurs when a corporation must publish revised financial statements due to a misstatement in previously published financial statements. A restatement often results in the corporation reporting a reduction in sales and net income. More importantly, a restatement brings into question the competency and integrity of management.

The restatement of Royal Ahold's financial statements in 2003 was a financial disaster for its home country, the Netherlands. The roots of Ahold can be traced back to a grocery store opened by Albert Heijn in 1887. Within 10 years, the business had expanded to 23 stores and had created its own brand of products. Thus, a corporate culture of expansion was established early in Ahold's history. Over the next 100 years, Ahold expanded into new markets, often acquiring entire grocery chains in other countries. By the late 20th century, Ahold had become a global leader in the grocery industry.

A pivotal event in Ahold's history was its 2000 acquisition of U.S. Foodservice. To inflate its earnings, U.S. Foodservice was fraudulently misstating payments from food manufacturers, an industry practice known as *promotional allowances*. Ahold was also incorrectly including in its financial statements the sales of other corporations in which it was part owner.

In 2003, Ahold announced the restatement of its financial statements for fiscal years 1999 to 2001. The restatement resulted in a $25.8 billion reduction in sales and a $1.1 billion reduction in operating income. Four corporate executives were forced to resign amid accusations they were involved in the frauds and concealed information from external auditors.

Fortunately, Ahold survived the scandal and remains a vibrant business today. However, the corporation was required to sell several of its acquisitions.

ACTIVITY

Helman Auto Mart has been struggling over the past several years. The auto market has declined, hurting Helman's sales and having a negative impact on its balance sheet. Helman's primary bank loan requires the company to maintain at least a 1.5 ratio of current assets to current liabilities. If the actual ratio drops below 1.5, the bank can immediately demand repayment of the loan.

The bank received a tip that Helman might be misstating its financial statements. Taking advantage of a provision of its loan agreement, the bank sent an audit team to review the statements.

As a member of that audit team, you have been instructed to examine the support for Helman's reclassification entry for the current portion of its installment notes receivable. The worksheet contains a list of Helman's installment notes receivable and the calculations supporting the reclassification entry.

INSTRUCTIONS

Open the spreadsheet FA_CH09 and complete the steps on the Instructions tab. Use your analysis to answer the following questions.

1. What is the difference, if any, between the reported and audited totals of outstanding notes receivable?

2. What evidence suggests that Helman's management may have intentionally misstated the outstanding balances?

3. Helman's worksheet calculated the current portion of installment notes receivable to be $271,170.09. How did the change in the outstanding balances affect this amount?

Sources: www.sec.gov/news/press/2004-144.htm; www.ahold.com.

TERMS REVIEW

installment note

amortization schedule

reclassification entry

Audit your understanding LO6, 7

1. When would the sale of a boat financed with an installment note be recorded as revenue?
2. What dollar amounts are presented for each month on an amortization schedule?
3. Over the term of an installment note, what changes occur to the monthly payment, interest, and principal?
4. What amount of installment notes receivable should be classified as a current asset?

Work together 9-3 LO6, 7

Journalizing installment notes receivable transactions

The journals and a loan payment schedule for Danny's Used Cars are given in the *Working Papers*. Your instructor will guide you through the following examples.

1. Using May of the current year, journalize these transactions. Refer to the amortization schedule when journalizing the May 9 transaction. Source documents are abbreviated as follows: note receivable, NR; receipt, R.

   Transactions:

   May 7. Sold a car to Jill Shelton for $14,860.00 plus $445.80 sales tax, receiving a $2,305.80 down payment and accepting a 60-month, 8% installment note receivable for the balance, $13,000.00. NR369.

   9. Received cash for Daniel Toney's May payment, $243.32. R787.

2. On December 31, $93,467.00 of the installment notes receivable of Danny's Used Cars is expected to be collected during the next fiscal period. Record the reclassification entry using page 15 of a general journal.

3. Use page 16 of a general journal to journalize the reversing entry of the December 31 reclassification entry for installment notes receivable.

On your own 9-3 LO6, 7

Journalizing installment notes receivable transactions

The journals and a loan payment schedule for Riverside Marine are given in the *Working Papers*. Work these problems independently.

1. Using June of the current year, journalize these transactions. Refer to the amortization schedule when journalizing the June 10 and 16 transactions. Source documents are abbreviated as follows: note receivable, NR; receipt, R.

   Transactions:

   June 7. Sold a boat to Tyesha Anderson for $3,550.00 plus $177.50 sales tax, receiving a $527.50 down payment and accepting a 36-month, 9% installment note receivable for the balance, $3,200.00. NR283.

   10. Received cash for Wayne Wood's June payment, $120.84. R490.

   16. Received cash for Patrick Morgan's June payment, $127.20. R498.

   24. Sold a boat to Marie Mims for $4,000.00 plus $200.00 sales tax, receiving a $600.00 down payment and accepting a 36-month, 9% installment note receivable for the balance, $3,600.00. NR285.

2. On December 31, $48,475.00 of the installment notes receivable of Riverside Marine is expected to be collected during the next fiscal period. Record the reclassification entry using page 18 of a general journal.

3. Use page 19 of a general journal to journalize the reversing entry of the December 31 reclassification entry for installment notes receivable.

Setting Up a Note Receivable

Merchandising companies, especially those that deal in high-priced goods, will generally provide customers options for financing their purchases. Most often, the financing is done by another company that specializes in making loans. The merchandiser simply takes an application, seeks approval from the finance company, and then completes the transaction. The customer makes payments directly to the financing company. When a sale is financed by another company, the transaction is accounted for as a cash sale, with a corresponding account receivable from the finance company entered.

Merchandisers will sometimes extend credit themselves. The merchandiser may choose to hold a note to maturity or sell it to a finance company to raise cash. In this example, Candor Auto Mart has completed the sale of an automobile to Mark Carver and is financing the sale itself.

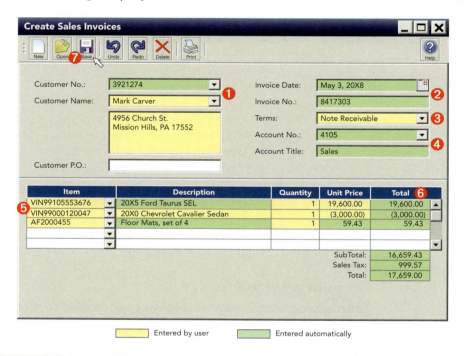

Entered by user | Entered automatically

❶ The finance manager at Candor Auto Mart has entered an auto sale to Mark Carver. The customer number was entered in sequence automatically by the system. If Mark were an existing customer, his account could have been selected from the customer list by name or number.

❷ The invoice date and number were entered automatically by the system.

❸ Since Candor is financing this sale, Notes Receivable was selected from the **Terms** drop-down list.

❹ The default general ledger account is Sales. It could be changed if needed.

❺ Mark is purchasing a Ford Taurus, trading in a Chevy Cavalier, and buying new floor mats for the Taurus.

The Taurus and floor mats are inventory items; so when their stock numbers were selected, their descriptions and prices were automatically entered by the system. Here, the price of the Taurus was changed, probably due to negotiation. The Chevy is not an inventory item, so its description and trade-in value had to be entered.

❻ The system calculated and entered all totals.

❼ The system is programmed to request loan origination information whenever Note Receivable is selected in **Terms**. When the finance manager clicked **Save,** the system opened the Notes Receivable window.

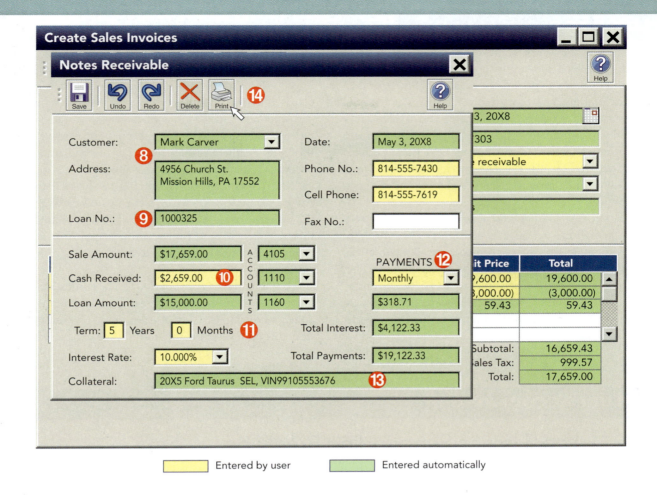

Entered by user | Entered automatically

⑧ The customer name and address were entered automatically by the system. Phone numbers were entered by the finance manager.

⑨ The loan number was entered in sequence by the system.

⑩ The sale amount was brought forward automatically. The finance manager entered the amount of the down payment and the system calculated and entered the loan amount. Account numbers were entered by default, but could be changed.

⑪ The finance manager has entered the term of the note and selected the interest rate.

⑫ After the frequency of payments (Monthly) was selected, the system calculated and entered the monthly payment, the total interest, and the total payments.

⑬ Candor assumes that each note receivable will be collateralized with the vehicle sold. That means that if Mr. Carver fails to make payments as agreed, Candor can repossess the vehicle. The system automatically enters the vehicle's description.

⑭ The finance manager has saved the information and will print out the note so it can be signed. An amortization schedule can also be printed for the customer.

CHAPTER SUMMARY

Revenue received in one fiscal period but not earned until the next fiscal period is called *unearned revenue*. An adjusting entry is recorded to recognize as income only that amount that is earned during the fiscal period. The adjustment creates a liability equal to the amount of revenue to be earned during the next fiscal period. A business that records the cash receipt initially as revenue will record a reversing entry at the start of the next fiscal period.

Revenue earned in one fiscal period but not received until a later fiscal period is called *accrued revenue*. An adjusting entry is recorded to recognize as income the amount that is earned during the fiscal period. The adjustment creates a receivable equal to the amount owed to the business. A business that records accrued revenue will record a reversing entry at the start of the next fiscal period.

The proceeds from the sale of gift cards are recorded initially in an unearned revenue account, such as Gift Cards Outstanding. Revenue is recognized when the customer redeems the gift card. Some gift cards are never redeemed. The value of unredeemed gift cards is called *breakage*. At the end of a fiscal period, the amount of breakage is generally recorded as revenue.

Many retailers offer financing to their customers. An installment note enables the customer to pay for the amount owed over a period of time. An amortization schedule is used to determine the portion of each monthly payment recognized as interest income and principal.

At the end of a fiscal period, a reclassification entry records as a current asset the principal payments to be collected during the next fiscal period. The reclassification entry is reversed at the start of the next fiscal period.

EXPLORE ACCOUNTING

Legal Issues Surrounding Breakage

Accountants of a retail business that issues gift cards need to understand state laws related to unclaimed property. All states have rules that govern the ownership of all unclaimed property. Unclaimed property ranges from land to cars to checking accounts. Once all efforts to identify the owner have been exhausted, the unclaimed property becomes the property of the state.

Unredeemed gift cards represent a new form of unclaimed property. Some states have enacted legislation that exempts gift cards from unclaimed property rules. In these states, the issuing retailer can claim the unclaimed property, recording the breakage as revenue.

In all other states, the retailer must turn over the value of unclaimed property to the state. The state that receives the property is determined by the last known address of the cardholder. If the owner's address is unknown, the state where the retailer is located has the right to the unclaimed property.

The form of the gift card has a significant impact on the application of unclaimed property

rules. No personal information of the cardholder is obtained when a plastic card is purchased at a retail store. Thus, there is no way to identify the last known address of the cardholder. Information about the cardholder is obtained at the time a virtual card is purchased. However, unless a cardholder notifies the retailer of any address change, the information stored by the retailer may be out of date.

INSTRUCTIONS

1. Danover Stores sold a $50.00 virtual gift card five years ago. The card has never been used. Danover has the name, address, phone number, and e-mail address of the cardholder. What efforts would be considered reasonable to contact the cardholder? Assuming those efforts are unsuccessful, identify the journal entry that would be required to account for unredeemed gift cards in a state that claims unclaimed property.

2. Research breakage laws in your state. How do your findings change the answers to question 1?

APPLY YOUR UNDERSTANDING

INSTRUCTIONS: Download problem instructions for Excel, QuickBooks, and Sage 50c from the textbook companion website at www.C21accounting.com.

9-1 Application Problem — Journalizing adjusting and reversing entries for unearned and accrued revenue LO1, 2

JMB Properties is preparing its December 31 financial statements for the current year. On September 30, Mixon & Sheppard, LLP, paid $12,000.00 to JMB Properties for the rental of office space. The payment is the monthly rent for October of the current year through March of the next year. JMB Properties records rent receipts initially as revenue. General journal pages are provided in the *Working Papers*.

Instructions:

1. Journalize the adjusting entry for unearned rent revenue. Use page 16 of a general journal.
2. Journalize the reversing entry for unearned rent revenue. Use page 17 of a general journal.

JMB Properties has two notes receivable outstanding on December 31 of the current year.

Note No.	Interest Rate	Term	Principal	Date
16	10%	120 days	$2,300.00	October 22
17	8%	60 days	$1,800.00	November 26

3. Journalize the adjusting entry for accrued interest income. Use page 16 of a general journal.
4. Journalize the reversing entry for accrued interest income. Use page 17 of a general journal.

9-2 Application Problem — Journalizing gift card transactions LO3, 4

Discount Hardware sells $25.00 and $50.00 gift cards. A cash receipts journal and general journals are provided in the *Working Papers*.

Instructions:

1. Record the following transactions on page 16 of a cash receipts journal and page 12 of a general journal. Discount Hardware uses the accounts Gift Card Outstanding and Breakage Revenue to account for gift card transactions. Source documents are abbreviated as follows: memorandum, M; receipt, R.

Transactions:

Dec. 28. Customers redeemed gift cards for the sale of merchandise, $315.08, plus $18.90 sales tax. M223.

29. Received cash for the sale of gift cards, $250.00. R789.

30. Customers redeemed gift cards for the sale of merchandise, $221.67, plus $13.30 sales tax. M226.

30. Received cash for the sale of gift cards, $150.00. R792.

2. Discount Hardware estimates that $1,721.00 of gift cards will never be redeemed. Record the adjusting entry on page 13 of a general journal.

9-3 Application Problem

Journalizing installment notes receivable transactions LO6, 7

sage 50

1. Journalize and post notes receivable transactions to the cash receipts journal.
2. Journalize and post the reclassification entry to the general journal.
3. Journalize and post the reversing entry to the general journal.

1. Journalize and post notes receivable transactions to the Journal.
2. Journalize and post the reclassification entry and reversing entry to the journal.

1. Journalize notes receivable transactions to the cash receipts journal.
2. Journalize the reclassification entry and reversing entry to the general journals.

The journals and a loan payment schedule for Maben RV Center are given in the *Working Papers.*

Instructions:

1. Using July of the current year, journalize these transactions on page 7 of a cash receipts journal. Refer to the amortization schedule when journalizing the July 3 and 12 transactions. Source documents are abbreviated as follows: note receivable, NR; receipt, R.

Transactions:

July 3. Received cash for Berk Hyde's July payment, $1,264.23. R369.
   6. Sold a recreational vehicle to Blair Jordan for $53,350.00 plus $2,667.50 sales tax, receiving a $7,667.50 down payment and accepting a 60-month, 7% installment note receivable for the balance, $48,350.00. NR172.
   12. Received cash for Altoria Johnwick's July payment, $985.84. R378.
   16. Sold a recreational vehicle to Matt Payne for $61,450.00 plus $3,072.50 sales tax, receiving an $11,572.50 down payment and accepting a 48-month, 7% installment note receivable for the balance, $52,950.00. NR173.

2. On December 31, Maben RV Center has $675,474.90 of installment notes receivable outstanding. Of that amount, $134,643.00 is expected to be collected during the next fiscal period. Record the reclassification entry using page 20 of a general journal.

3. Journalize the reversing entry of the December 31 reclassification entry for installment notes receivable. Record the reversing entry using page 21 of a general journal.

9-M Mastery Problem

Journalizing unearned revenue, accrued revenue, and gift card and installment note receivable transactions LO1, 2, 3, 4, 6, 7

sage 50

1. Journalize and post transactions to the cash receipts journal.
2. Journalize and post the reclassification entry to the general journal.
3. Journalize and post the adjusting and reversing entries to the general journal.

QB

1. Journalize and post transactions to the journal.
2. Journalize and post the reclassification entry to the general journal.
3. Journalize and post adjusting and reversing entries to the journal.

Marist Entertainment completed the following transactions during December of the current year. Marist records unearned items initially as revenue. The company uses the accounts Gift Cards Outstanding and Breakage Revenue to account for gift card transactions. The sales tax rate is 7.0%. A cash receipts journal and general journals are provided in the *Working Papers.*

Instructions:

1. Journalize the following transactions. Refer to the amortization schedule when journalizing cash receipts on installment notes receivable.

Transactions:

Dec. 19. Sold an entertainment system to Donna Tuttle for $3,000.00 plus $210.00 sales tax, receiving a $510.00 down payment and accepting a 36-month, 12% installment note receivable for the balance, $2,700.00. NR226.
   20. Received cash for the sale of gift cards, $650.00. R820.
   22. Received cash for Lisa Renfroe's December payment, $88.02. R825.
   23. Customers redeemed gift cards for the sale of merchandise, $168.95. M301.
   27. Received cash for the sale of gift cards, $150.00. R834.
   29. Received cash for Rose Cribbs' December payment, $108.94. R841.
   30. Customers redeemed gift cards for the sale of merchandise, $2,180.68. M312.
   31. Sold a home theatre system to Rocky Holman for $4,762.50 plus $333.38 sales tax, receiving an $833.38 down payment and accepting a 36-month, 12% installment note receivable for the balance, $4,262.50. NR227.

1. Journalize transactions in the cash receipts journal.
2. Journalize the reclassification entry to the general journal.
3. Journalize the adjusting and reversing entries to the general journals.

2. Use the following information to record adjusting entries on December 31 of the current year. Use page 21 of a general journal.

   a. On November 1, Marist Entertainment received $5,400.00 from Logistic Games for advertising of its electronic games. The payment is to pay for $1,800.00 of monthly advertising for November, December, and January. Marist Entertainment records advertising receipts initially as revenue.

   b. Marist Entertainment periodically loans money to employees. The company has two notes outstanding to employees on December 31.

Note No.	Interest Rate	Term	Principal	Date
E31	6%	120 days	$3,500.00	October 23
E32	5%	180 days	$1,800.00	November 4

   c. Marist Entertainment estimates that $5,820.00 of gift cards will never be redeemed.

3. On December 31, Marist Entertainment has $42,675.50 of installment notes receivable outstanding. Of that amount, $22,365.00 is expected to be collected during the next fiscal period. Record the reclassification entry using page 22 of a general journal.

4. Journalize any adjusting or reclassification entries that should be reversed. Use page 23 of a general journal.

9-C Challenge Problem — Journalizing sales and gift card transactions from a point-of-sale system LO3

The point-of-sale system for Teton Designs prepares a terminal summary that summarizes all cash and sales transactions, including transactions involving gift cards. Teton Designs records the amounts from the terminal summary in a single entry in the cash receipts journal. To provide a history of gift card transactions in the Gift Cards Outstanding account, the amounts of sales and redemptions of gift cards are listed individually in the journal entry.

Instructions:

Record the following transactions that occurred during August of the current year. Use page 5 of a cash receipts journal.

Transactions:

Aug. 4. Recorded the output of the terminal summary: cash and credit card sales, $2,532.55; sales tax, $145.34; sales of gift cards, $625.00; redemptions of gift cards, $208.34. Terminal Summary No. 28.

11. Recorded the output of the terminal summary: cash and credit card sales, $2,842.04; sales tax, $184.15; sales of gift cards, $200.00; redemptions of gift cards, $489.12. Terminal Summary No. 29.

Prepaid Debit Cards

Theme: Financial, Economic, Business, and Entrepreneurial Literacy

Skills: Critical Thinking and Problem Solving, Communication and Collaboration, ICT Literacy

PARTNERSHIP FOR
21ST CENTURY SKILLS

Consumers are turning to prepaid debit cards as a convenient way to manage money. Prepaid debit cards are not credit cards. Credit cards allow the user to spend money first and pay for it later. Prepaid debit cards require payment up front. Only the money paid in advance can be spent.

While credit cards are convenient, many people find themselves in excessive debt due to overspending. Prepaid cards are appealing because they enable the user to avoid debt. They are offered by banks, with recognizable brand names like Visa and MasterCard.

Prepaid debit cards are also different than a bank account debit card. Bank account debit cards are linked to a checking account. Prepaid debit cards do not require a checking account relationship. In fact, many users of prepaid debit cards use them as a replacement for a traditional checking account. Some bank account debit cards allow you to overspend your account, which often results in an overdraft fee. This cannot happen with a prepaid debit card.

Prepaid debit cards are often easier to obtain, especially for people with a negative banking history. In addition to not requiring a related checking account, they do not require a credit check. All the user has to do is pay cash up front in the desired amount.

Prepaid debit cards have fewer consumer protections than bank account debit cards do. Generally, there is no protection against unauthorized transactions. Also, the fee structure is not always clearly stated on the outside of the card's packaging. This means that when purchasing a prepaid debit card for the first time, the purchaser does not have any way to compare prepaid cards before purchasing one. Fees associated with prepaid debit cards can include an activation fee, a reloading fee, monthly fees, and even a fee for each transaction.

New laws have been approved that would give prepaid debit cards more protections, similar to those of debit cards, such as limited liability for unauthorized transactions, limits on overdraft fees for cards that allow overdrafts, and the requirement that fee information must be available to the consumer and clearly stated on the outside of the package. These laws were originally scheduled to go into effect on October 1, 2017. At the time of publication of this textbook, the implementation of these laws was delayed until April 1, 2019.

APPLICATION

1. Search the Internet to determine if new laws have been put in place to give more protection to prepaid debit card holders. If so, briefly summarize the laws.
2. Using the Internet, research three prepaid debit cards. Compare and contrast the following for each card: activation fee, monthly fee, ATM withdrawal fee, maximum deposit balance, ATM balance inquiry fee, inactivity fee, closed account fee, card replacement fee, and one other interesting fact learned.
3. Select a presentation method and share your findings from question 2 as a comparison.

Source: www.consumerfinance.gov.

Analyzing Home Depot's Financial Statements

Like most national retailers, Home Depot offers its customer the opportunity to purchase gift cards. The cash received from the sale of gift cards is recorded in Deferred Revenue on Home Depot's Consolidated Balance Sheet.

INSTRUCTIONS

Refer to the Notes to Consolidated Financial Statements beginning on page B-10 to answer the following questions:
1. In which account does Home Depot record the redemption of gift cards?
2. How does Home Depot estimate the amount of gift card breakage?
3. Identify the amount of gift card breakage recognized in the three years presented on the Consolidated Statements of Earnings on page B-6.
4. How does Home Depot report breakage income?

Reinforcement Activity 2

Processing Accounting Data for a Corporation

    sage 50   QB Quick Books

This activity reinforces selected learning from Part 2, Chapters 5 through 9.

Franklin Auto Parts, Inc.

Franklin Auto Parts, Inc. (Franklin), a merchandising business, is organized as a corporation. The business sells a complete line of automotive parts to businesses and individuals. The business owns the land and building where its store is located.

Franklin's fiscal year ends on December 31. Franklin uses the chart of accounts shown on page 289. The journals used by Franklin are similar to those used in Part 2.

Franklin uses the following accounting policies:

- The allowance method of accounting for uncollectible accounts is used.
- The last-in, first-out and lower of cost or market costing methods are used.
- The straight-line method is used to calculate depreciation expense.
- Supplies, insurance, and advertising are initially recorded as expenses.
- A liability account is maintained for estimated warranty expenses.
- Receipts received in advance of sales are initially recorded as revenue.
- A liability account is maintained for outstanding gift cards.
- Gift card breakage is recorded as revenue.
- Interest on bank notes is calculated using a 365-day year. Amortization schedules for installment notes receivable are based on a 360-day year.

Recording Transactions

INSTRUCTIONS

1. Use the appropriate journal to record the following transactions completed during December of the current year. The sales tax rate is 6.0%. Journals and selected note amortization schedules are given in the *Working Papers*. Source documents are abbreviated as follows: check, C; memorandum, M; receipt, R; note receivable, NR.

Transactions:

Dec. 2. Drew $19,200.00 from its First Commerce Bank line of credit. The bank deposited the funds directly to Franklin's checking account. R892.

3. Received cash for the sale of gift cards, $860.00. R893.

Dec. 4. Received an e-mail from James Daniels, the legal counsel for Mattre Enterprises, stating that Mattre has filed for bankruptcy. Mr. Daniels stated that it will likely take several years for the bankruptcy proceedings to be completed. Even then, there is little chance that Franklin will receive any payment from Mattre. The Mattre account of $2,486.31 is over 180 days past due. M135.

5. Discarded an office desk: original cost, $1,650.00; estimated salvage value, $250.00; estimated useful life, 7 years; total accumulated depreciation through December 31 of last year, $900.00. M136.

7. Customers redeemed gift cards for merchandise, $548.68, plus $27.43 sales tax. M137.

9. Purchased at auction the store of a bankrupt merchandising business. The $380,000.00 purchase price included land appraised for $180,000.00 and a building appraised for $270,000.00. Franklin paid $80,000.00 down and financed the remainder by signing a note with First Commerce Bank. C769.

12. May Stenson, owner of May's Mints, stated that she does not intend to pay the remaining $45.50 of her bill. May maintains that she did not receive all the items listed on the sales invoice. Although your records clearly indicate the correct number of items was delivered, your manager believes that further efforts to collect this account could damage your relationship with a valued customer. M138.

13. GPR Landscape dishonored its $500.00, 60-day, 10% note due today. M139.

14. Paid the maturity value of a $25,000.00, 180-day, 7.5% note with First Commerce Bank, plus interest. C770.

16. Wrote a check to City Handyman for parts and labor to repair equipment under warranty, $155.95. C771.

18. Earlier in the year, Franklin wrote off the $1,662.95 balance of Dan's Garage. The account was over 210 days past due and collection seemed doubtful. Today, Franklin received a $1,000.00 check from Dan's Garage. M140 and R894.

Reinforcement Activity 2 (continued)

Processing Accounting Data for a Corporation

Dec. 19. Sold merchandise to David Anderson for $2,000.00 plus $100.00 sales tax, receiving a $350.00 down payment and accepting a 12-month, 12% installment note receivable for the balance, $1,750.00. NR226.

20. Received cash for the sale of gift cards, $1,590.00. R895.

21. Received the December note payment from Danielle Petrus on her $4,200.00, 12-month, 10.0% note. R896.

22. Received $32,000.00 from First American Bank, signing a 180-day, 8% note. R897.

23. Paid cash, $1,460.00, and traded in an old copy machine for a new copy machine. The old copy machine had an original cost of $2,500.00, an estimated salvage value of $400.00, and a useful life of 5 years. Total accumulated depreciation recorded on the copy machine through December 31 of last year was $980.00. M141 and C772.

27. Received cash from the sale of a notebook computer, $360.00: original cost, $1,400.00; estimated salvage value, $200.00; useful life, 3 years; total accumulated depreciation through December 31 of last year, $700.00. M142 and R898.

28. Received the December note payment from David Lander on his $2,480.00, 12-month, 12.0% note. R899.

29. Customers redeemed gift cards for merchandise, $2,195.47, plus $109.77 sales tax. M143.

30. Paid the December payment on a $40,000.00 installment note with Platt Equipment. C773.

31. Used the bank's Internet site to pay $2,000.00 plus $134.95 interest on its line of credit. M144.

2. Journalize the adjusting entry for uncollectible accounts expense on December 31 of the current year. Franklin estimates that the amount of uncollectible accounts expense is equal to 0.9% of its net sales on account. The following information was obtained from Franklin's accounting records for the current year:

	January 1	December 31
Accounts Receivable	$ 58,161.32	$67,218.49
Allowance for Doubtful Accounts	4,671.34	265.22
Net Sales (on account)	644,787.46	

3. Franklin uses the perpetual inventory system. On December 31, the unadjusted balance of Merchandise Inventory was $22,330.01. On December 31, Franklin took a physical inventory to determine the actual quantity of each item in inventory. Using the forms in the *Working Papers*, determine the FIFO value of these items and the lower-of-cost-or-market value of total inventory. Units in the December 31 inventory and the market prices are shown below.

Stock Item	Quantity of Units on Hand	Market Price per Item
C-362	26	$ 35.50
A-342	42	84.50
B-164	16	1,062.25

Prepare an adjusting entry for inventory.

4. Use the following information to journalize adjusting entries on December 31 of the current year.

a. Current values of selected expense items are shown below.

Supplies inventory	$ 689.00
Value of unexpired insurance	2,800.00
Unused advertising	3,500.00

b. Warranty expense is estimated to be 1.5% of total sales. Total sales for the current fiscal year are $1,345,675.34.

c. Gift cards that will never be redeemed are estimated to be $1,920.00.

d. Interest revenue earned but not yet recorded on notes receivable is estimated to be $690.00.

e. No payment has been made on the $32,000.00 note payable with First American Bank, signed on December 22.

f. After recording all adjusting entries, Franklin determines that it owes additional federal income tax of $5,092.00.

Franklin Auto Parts, Inc., Chart of Accounts

General Ledger

Balance Sheet Accounts

(1000) ASSETS

1100 Current Assets
1110 Cash
1115 Petty Cash
1120 Accounts Receivable
1125 Allowance for Uncollectible Accounts
1135 Interest Receivable
1140 Merchandise Inventory
1150 Supplies
1160 Prepaid Insurance
1165 Prepaid Advertising
1200 Plant Assets
1210 Land
1220 Building
1225 Accumulated Depreciation—Building
1230 Office Equipment
1235 Accumulated Depreciation—Office Equipment
1240 Store Equipment
1245 Accumulated Depreciation—Store Equipment

(2000) LIABILITIES

2100 Current Liabilities
2105 Accounts Payable
2110 Salaries Payable
2115 Accrued Warranty Liability
2120 Unearned Rent
2125 Gift Cards Outstanding
2130 Employee Income Tax Payable
2135 Social Security Tax Payable
2140 Medicare Tax Payable
2145 Unemployment Tax Payable—Federal
2150 Unemployment Tax Payable—State
2160 Federal Income Tax Payable
2170 Line of Credit
2180 Notes Payable
2190 Interest Payable
2200 Long-Term Liability
2205 Mortgage Payable

(3000) STOCKHOLDERS' EQUITY

3105 Capital Stock
3110 Retained Earnings
3115 Dividends
3120 Income Summary

Income Statement Accounts

(4000) OPERATING REVENUE

4105 Sales
4110 Sales Discount
4115 Sales Returns and Allowances
4120 Breakage Revenue

(5000) COST OF MERCHANDISE

5105 Purchases
5110 Purchases Discount
5115 Purchases Returns and Allowances

(6000) OPERATING EXPENSE

6105 Advertising Expense
6110 Depreciation Expense—Building
6115 Depreciation Expense—Office Equipment
6120 Depreciation Expense—Warehouse Equipment
6125 Insurance Expense
6130 Miscellaneous Expense
6135 Payroll Taxes Expense
6140 Property Tax Expense
6145 Salary Expense
6150 Supplies Expense
6155 Uncollectible Accounts Expense
6160 Warranty Expense

(7000) OTHER REVENUE

7105 Gain on Plant Assets
7110 Interest Income
7115 Rent Income

(8000) OTHER EXPENSES

8105 Interest Expense
8110 Loss on Plant Assets

(9000) INCOME TAX

9105 Federal Income Tax Expense

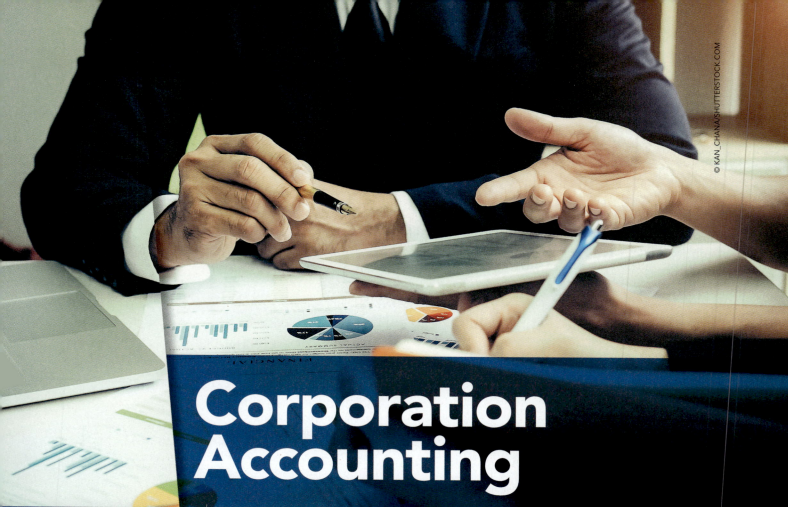

Corporation Accounting

FOREST EQUIPMENT, INC.

Forest Equipment, Inc., is a corporation that sells farming and logging equipment. It purchases equipment from manufacturers to sell to a variety of agricultural businesses. Forest also has a store that sells to retail customers.

Chart of Accounts
FOREST EQUIPMENT, INC.

GENERAL LEDGER

Balance Sheet Accounts

(1000) ASSETS

1100 Current Assets
1105 Cash
1110 Petty Cash
1115 Marketable Securities
1120 Accounts Receivable
1125 Allowance for Uncollectible Accounts
1130 Merchandise Inventory
1140 Supplies—Store
1145 Supplies—Administrative
1150 Prepaid Insurance
1155 Prepaid Interest
1160 Notes Receivable
1165 Interest Receivable
1200 Long-Term Investments
1205 Investment Securities
1300 Plant Assets
1310 Land
1320 Building
1325 Accumulated Depreciation—Building
1330 Office Equipment
1335 Accumulated Depreciation—Office Equipment
1340 Store Equipment
1345 Accumulated Depreciation—Store Equipment
1400 Intangible Assets
1405 Trademarks

(2000) LIABILITIES

2100 Current Liabilities
2105 Accounts Payable
2110 Sales Tax Payable
2115 Salaries Payable
2120 Employee Income Tax Payable
2125 Social Security Tax Payable
2130 Medicare Tax Payable
2135 Unemployment Tax Payable—Federal
2140 Unemployment Tax Payable—State
2145 Medical Insurance Payable
2150 Retirement Plan Payable
2155 Federal Income Tax Payable
2160 Dividends Payable
2165 Interest Payable
2170 Notes Payable
2175 Current Portion of Long-Term Debt
2200 Long-Term Liabilities
2205 Bonds Payable
2210 Discount on Bonds Payable
2215 Premium on Bonds Payable

(3000) STOCKHOLDERS' EQUITY

3105 Capital Stock—Common
3110 Paid-In Capital in Excess of Par Value—Common *(continued)*

3115 Capital Stock—Preferred
3120 Paid-In Capital in Excess of Par Value—Preferred
3125 Treasury Stock
3130 Paid-In Capital from Sale of Treasury Stock
3135 Retained Earnings
3140 Dividends—Common
3145 Dividends—Preferred
3150 Income Summary

Income Statement Accounts

(4000) OPERATING REVENUE

4105 Sales
4110 Sales Discount
4115 Sales Returns and Allowances

(5000) COST OF MERCHANDISE

5105 Purchases
5110 Purchases Discount
5115 Purchases Returns and Allowances

(6000) OPERATING EXPENSES

6100 Selling Expenses
6105 Advertising Expense
6110 Credit Card Fee Expense
6115 Depreciation Expense—Store Equipment
6120 Miscellaneous Expense—Sales
6125 Salary Expense—Sales
6130 Supplies Expense—Sales
6200 Administrative Expenses
6205 Depreciation Expense—Building
6210 Depreciation Expense—Office Equipment
6215 Insurance Expense
6220 Miscellaneous Expense—Administrative
6225 Payroll Taxes Expense
6230 Property Tax Expense
6235 Salary Expense—Administrative
6240 Supplies Expense—Administrative
6245 Uncollectible Accounts Expense
6250 Utilities Expense

(7000) OTHER REVENUE

7105 Gain on Plant Assets
7110 Interest Income

(8000) OTHER EXPENSES

8105 Interest Expense
8110 Loss on Plant Assets

(9000) INCOME TAX

9105 Federal Income Tax Expense

The chart of accounts for Forest Equipment, Inc., is illustrated above for ready reference as you study Part 3 of this textbook.

Organizing a Corporation

LEARNING OBJECTIVES

After studying Chapter 10, in addition to defining key terms, you will be able to:

LO1 Describe the process for forming a corporation.

LO2 Describe the two basic kinds of stock.

LO3 Identify advantages and disadvantages of the corporate form of business.

LO4 Journalize the issuances of par-value, no-par-value, and stated-value common stock.

LO5 Describe the process for taking a corporation public.

LO6 Journalize the issuance of preferred stock.

LO7 Explain how to account for convertible preferred stock.

© GOD4ATHER/SHUTTERSTOCK.COM

ARMO BIOSCIENCES

ARMO BioSciences, Inc.

ACCOUNTING IN THE REAL WORLD

Exploiting the Body's Immune System to Treat a Broa
Range of Diseases

ARMO Biosciences, a wholly owned subsidiary of Eli Lilly and Company

Driving down a busy city street you notice a new location of your favorite fast food chain ready to open its doors. The building is complete, the parking lot is nearly paved, and food trucks are arriving to stock the kitchen. Have you ever wondered where the business obtained the money needed to open the store?

A well-established business typically can fund expansions using retained earnings. Bank loans can be arranged if a little extra financing is required. However, small businesses without a proven track record of earnings may find it difficult to qualify for a bank loan. For these businesses, an investment from a venture capital firm may be an option. A venture capital firm seeks to invest in small businesses with high growth potential and provides management expertise as well as needed financial capital. Another method of funding business expansion is issuing stock to the public. This option is especially viable if the current stockholders lack funds to invest in the corporation. To protect the investing public, the corporation is required to register the stock with the Securities and Exchange Commission. The registration document includes a profile the corporation, audited financial statements, risk factors, and the intended use of the funds generated by the stock sale.

In 2018, ARMO BioSciences, Inc., (ARMO) issued stock for public purchase on a national stock exchange. ARMO develops prescription drugs designed to activate a patient's natural immune system to fight cancer. Prior to 2018, ARMO's stock had not been traded on a public market. According to the registration document, ARMO expected to generate as much as $103.3 million from the stock sale. The corporation intends to use a majority of the funds for the development and clinical trials of drugs. The remaining funds are to be used for additional personnel, capital expenditures, and other operating costs.

Source: ARMO BioSciences, Inc. Amendment No 1 to Form S-1.

CRITICAL THINKING

1. Research a business classified as a venture capital firm. Summarize the mission of the firm. Discuss the role of a venture capital firm in the economy.

2. Research a corporation that recently sold stock for the first time on a national stock exchange. How did the corporation expect to use the generated funds?

KEY TERMS

corporation
share of stock
stockholder
board of directors
articles of incorporation
charter
common stock
preferred stock
stock certificate

par value
par-value stock
no-par-value stock
stated-value stock
proprietorship
partnership
double taxation
limited liability corporation
privately held corporation

initial public offering
publicly held corporation
registration statement
conversion option
conversion ratio
convertible preferred stock
conversion price

LO1   Describe the process for forming a corporation.
LO2   Describe the two basic kinds of stock.
LO3   Identify advantages and disadvantages of the corporate form of business.
LO4   Journalize the issuances of par-value, no-par-value, and stated-value common stock.

Corporate Form of Business Ownership   LO1

Selecting the form of business ownership is an important decision of new business owners. An organization with the legal rights of a person which many persons or other corporations may own is called a **corporation**. >> App. A: Business Entity A corporation is organized by law to exist separately and apart from its owners. Corporations differ from other forms of businesses principally in the nature of ownership and management.

A corporation's ownership is divided into units. A unit of ownership in a corporation is called a **share of stock**. The total shares of ownership in a corporation is known as *capital stock*. The owner of one or more shares of stock is called a **stockholder**. A stockholder is also referred to as a *shareholder*.

Stockholders share in a corporation's earnings. Many corporations distribute a portion of their earnings to stockholders by paying a dividend. Corporations may retain some or all of their earnings to finance future business expansion and improvement.

ETHICS IN ACTION

Good Investing or Insider Trading?

The discovery of alternative fuels has led most oil companies to become involved in the search for natural gas in shale located throughout the United States. As a geological engineer for ExxonMobil Corporation, Trent Hendrix has been working to develop estimates of the amount of natural gas reserves in a recent discovery in the Marcellus Shale.

Trent's findings are nothing short of spectacular. His data indicate the reserves are four times any previously published estimates. This discovery could increase ExxonMobil's earnings by as much as 3% a year for the next ten years.

Trent purchases $400.00 of ExxonMobil stock every month through a payroll deduction program. He is considering using a large portion of his savings to buy additional shares. Since you are the ethics officer of the company, he has asked your opinion on his proposed stock purchase.

INSTRUCTIONS

Access the *Standards of Business Conduct* of ExxonMobil Corporation. Using this code of conduct as a guide, provide Trent with guidance on his proposed stock purchase. Can Trent continue his monthly purchases?

ARTICLES OF INCORPORATION
OF
FOREST EQUIPMENT, INC.

ARTICLE I – NAME

The name of this corporation is Forest Equipment, Inc.

ARTICLE II – NATURE OF BUSINESS

This corporation may engage in or transact any and all lawful activities or business permitted under the laws of the United States and of the State of Alabama.

ARTICLE III – CAPITAL STOCK

The maximum authorized capital stock is:
Common stock: 10,000,000 shares, $1.00 par value
Preferred stock: 500,000 shares, 6%, $100.00 par value

ARTICLE IV – ADDRESS

The present street address of the principle office of this corporation is 15320 Shellhorn Road, Troy, Alabama, 36079.

ARTICLE V – TERM OF EXISTENCE

The duration of the corporation is perpetual unless otherwise stated.

ARTICLE VI – DIRECTORS

M. Dale Pearson	725 Garden Lane	Troy, AL 36079
Matthew H. Tillman	4362 University Ave.	Troy, AL 36079
Stephen P. Pearson	326 Woodside Circle	Montgomery, AL 36117
Mary E. McMullan	1634 Three Notch St.	Troy, AL 36079
Jeannie P. Donovan	9304 Briarwood Dr.	Troy, AL 36079

ARTICLE VII – INCORPORATORS

M. Dale Pearson	725 Garden Lane	Troy, AL 36079
Betty H. Pearson	725 Garden Lane	Troy, AL 36079
Stephen P. Pearson	326 Woodside Circle	Montgomery, AL 36117

IN WITNESS THEREOF, the undersigned incorporator executed these Articles of Incorporation on this the 31st day of March, 20--.

M. Dale Pearson

M. Dale Pearson

A corporation may have many owners. In many small corporations, the owners often participate in the management of the business. Members of a single family often own these businesses. In contrast, the owners of large national and international corporations do not participate in the management of the business. A group of persons elected by the stockholders to govern a corporation is called a **board of directors**. A board of directors represents the stockholders' interests and monitors the management of the corporation.

Legal Requirements for Forming a Corporation

Persons seeking to form a corporation must submit an application to the state in which the company is to be incorporated. A legal document that identifies basic characteristics of a corporation, which is a part of the application submitted to a state to become a corporation, is called the **articles of incorporation**. Some articles of incorporation are submitted to the federal government, but most are submitted to a state government. A state approves the formation of a corporation by issuing a **charter**, the legal right for a business to conduct operations as a corporation. The articles of incorporation submitted for Forest Equipment, Inc., are shown above.

Forest Equipment, Inc., is a corporation that sells farming and logging equipment. However, Article II of its articles of incorporation describes the nature of the business in broad, general terms. This broad purpose enables Forest to expand into other kinds of business activities, if it desires, without applying for a new charter.

Capital Stock LO2

No. 00001   Shares 20,000

FOREST EQUIPMENT, INC.

This Certifies that ___M. Dale Pearson___ *is the registered holder of* _20,000_ *shares of the Common Stock transferable only on the books of the Corporation by the holder hereof in person of by Attorney upon surrender of this Certificate properly endorsed.*

In Witness Whereof, the said Corporation has caused this Certificate to be signed by its duly authorized officers this 2nd day of April, A.D. 20--.

___M. Dale Pearson___   ___Matthew H. Tillman___

___M. Dale Pearson___   ___Matthew H. Tillman___

Chairman of the Board   Secretary

Corporations may issue two basic kinds of stock. Stock that does not give stockholders any special preferences is called **common stock**. A class of stock that gives preferred shareholders preference over common shareholders in dividends along with other rights is called **preferred stock**. Forest is authorized to issue both common and preferred stock as described in Article III of the illustration on the previous page.

Most common stockholders have three basic rights.

1. To vote at stockholders' meetings, unless an exception is made for holders of a particular kind of stock.
2. To share in a corporation's earnings.
3. To share in the distribution of the assets of the corporation if it ceases operations and sells all its assets.

Written evidence of the number of shares that each stockholder owns in a corporation is called a **stock certificate**. A corporation issues a stock certificate when it receives full payment for the stock. A stock certificate, such as the one shown above, usually states the issue date, certificate number, number of shares, and name of the stockholder.

A stock certificate was once the only way of documenting ownership of a stock. Electronic recording of stock ownership has gradually eliminated the need for a corporation to issue stock certificates. Most large corporations now only issue a stock certificate on the request of the stockholder. Small corporations may still elect to issue stock certificates to their stockholders.

A corporation keeps a record of stock issued to each stockholder. A stockholder may later decide to sell some or all shares of stock owned. Changing ownership of stock is referred to as a *stock transfer*. Some corporations handle the issuing and transferring of stock certificates as well as the recording of stock ownership. Most corporations, however, engage a transfer agent, such as a bank, to maintain stock ownership records.

Value of Stock

Shares of stock are frequently assigned a value. A value assigned to a share of stock and printed on the stock certificate is called the **par value**. The par value has no relationship to the market value of the stock. The par value is set based on other factors, including state laws. A share of stock that has par value is called **par-value stock**.

A share of stock that has no authorized value printed on the stock certificate is called **no-par-value stock**. Some states require that no-par-value stock be assigned a stated or specific value. No-par-value stock that is assigned a value by a corporation is called **stated-value stock**. Stated-value stock is similar to par-value stock except that the value is not printed on the stock certificates.

Common Stock

If a corporation issues only one type of stock, that stock is common stock. If a corporation issues only common stock, the common stockholders are entitled to all of the dividends. In most corporations, only owners of common stock have a right to vote on matters brought before the stockholders. The most common matters voted on by common stockholders are the members of the board of directors and the appointment of the independent auditor. Forest is authorized to issue $1.00 par-value common stock.

Preferred Stock

To attract more investors, a corporation may offer preferred stock with preferences beyond the basic stockholders' rights. Preferred stockholders usually do not have voting rights and cannot influence when and how much is paid in dividends. Therefore, a typical preference given to preferred stockholders is to receive dividends before common stockholders. Other preferences granted preferred stockholders might include the following:

1. Unpaid dividends may accumulate and be paid in a later quarter. Accumulated preferred dividends must be paid before any common stock dividends are paid.
2. Dividends may be shared with common stockholders above a stated percentage or amount. Once the dividend to common stockholders equals the stated percentage of the preferred stock, additional dividends may be shared between preferred and common stockholders.

Every preference granted to preferred stockholders comes at the expense of common stockholders. For example, if preferred stockholders share in dividends above a stated percentage, common stockholders give up a right to some dividends. However, regardless of the type of stock issued, no stockholder is entitled to dividends until a corporation's board of directors votes to pay dividends.

Preferred stock dividends may be stated as an annual percentage of par value or as an amount per share. For example, Forest has authorized the issuance of 6%, $100.00 par-value preferred stock. Preferred stockholders will expect Forest to pay them a $6.00 (6% × $100.00) dividend per share.

Capital Accounts of a Corporation

Because of the number of owners, a corporation does not keep a separate capital account for each stockholder. Instead, it maintains a single summary general ledger capital account for each kind of stock issued. When a corporation issues only common stock, the value of all stock issued is recorded in a single capital stock account. When a corporation issues both common and preferred stock, separate capital stock accounts are used for common and preferred stock.

A corporation's net income is recorded in the capital account Retained Earnings. Using this account keeps the net income separate from the recorded values of issued capital stock. A net income is credited and a net loss is debited to Retained Earnings.

FYI Most stock issued today is common stock.

Advantages and Disadvantages of Corporations LO3

A corporation is only one of several forms of business. Several factors influence the form of business that is best at any particular time. Many businesses start as a **proprietorship**, a business owned by one person. As the business grows, the owner may need the expertise and financial resources of others. The form of ownership must change to account for multiple owners. A **partnership** is a business in which two or more persons combine their assets and skills. Most successful businesses will ultimately elect to adopt a corporate form of business.

Each form of business has advantages and disadvantages. The most significant difference is the extent to which the owner is responsible for the debts, taxes, and losses of the business. The personal assets of the owners of a proprietorship and partnership can be taken to satisfy the debts of the business.

The corporate form of business organization has several advantages over a proprietorship and a partnership:

- **Ease of formation.** Organizing a corporation is as simple as filing an application with the appropriate state agency. The approved application establishes the corporation as a legal entity, giving the corporation many of the same legal rights and risks as individuals have, including owning assets, borrowing money, paying taxes, and being sued.
- **Limited liability.** The liability of stockholders is limited to their investment in the corporation.
- **Supply of capital.** Individuals are more willing to invest in a corporation because their personal assets are protected by limited liability. Reporting requirements by government agencies reduce the perceived risk to investors.
- **Term of existence.** A corporation has a life independent of its owners. Most corporations have a perpetual term of existence.
- **Transfer of ownership.** Shares of stock can be bought and sold directly between individuals. The stock of some corporations can be traded on stock markets. The value of these shares is more readily available to help individuals make investment decisions. Individual investors can trade stock using Internet trading sites.

There are also some disadvantages to a corporation:

- **Regulation.** Corporations that issue stock to the public must follow the reporting requirements of the Securities and Exchange Commission (SEC) and the Public Company Accounting Oversight Board (PCAOB).
- **Loss of decision making.** Stockholders delegate the governance and decision making to the board of directors and executive officers. Some business decisions require approval of the stockholders. Although stockholders have the right to vote, most small investors have little chance of influencing the outcome of the vote.
- **Shared profits.** The earnings of the corporation are divided among the stockholders. The board of directors decides what portion of earnings is returned to the stockholders as a dividend.
- **Taxation.** The earnings of a corporation may be subject to federal and state income taxes. When the earnings of the corporation are distributed to the stockholders, individual stockholders may also have to pay income taxes on the dividends. The taxation of earnings to the corporation and to the stockholders when they receive dividends is called **double taxation**.

To help promote business development, many states now allow a form of business that combines certain characteristics of partnerships and corporations. A **limited liability corporation**, or LLC, offers its owners (known as members) the limited liability afforded to corporate stockholders. However, an LLC does not pay taxes on its earnings. Like a proprietorship or partnership, the earnings are divided among its members. The earnings are only taxed on the members' personal tax returns, thus eliminating the disadvantage of double taxation.

Many accounting firms operate as limited liability partnerships (LLPs). LLPs have the same advantages of limited liability and taxation as LLCs. LLPs are used when the business operates in states that do not recognize LLCs.

FYI A business operating as a limited liability corporation must include the letters LLC in its formal business name.

Journal Entries for Issuing Common Stock LO4

Forest's charter is its legal authorization to begin business in the name of the corporation. The first step for Forest to begin operations is to raise the capital needed to purchase inventory, rent a building, and hire employees. It obtains capital by issuing stock to the incorporators.

Common Stock with a Par Value

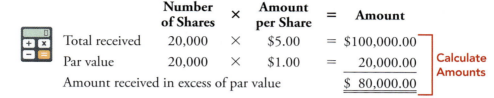

	Number of Shares	×	Amount per Share	=	Amount	
Total received	20,000	×	$5.00	=	$100,000.00	Calculate Amounts
Par value	20,000	×	$1.00	=	20,000.00	
Amount received in excess of par value					$ 80,000.00	

Credit the Capital Stock Account for the Par Value

Credit the Paid-In Capital Account for the Excess Over Par Value

Debit Cash

When the corporation is formed, each of Forest's incorporators agreed to buy a minimum of 10,000 shares of common stock at $5.00 per share.

Common stock par values are arbitrary amounts that rarely have any relationship to the market value of the stock. Most issues of common stock are for an amount in excess of the par value.

The excess of proceeds from the issue of stock over the par value is recorded in the account Paid-In Capital in Excess of Par Value—Common. This account is an equity account and has a normal credit balance.

> **April 2.** Received cash from M. Dale Pearson for 20,000 shares of $1.00 par-value common stock, valued at $5.00 per share, $100,000.00. Receipt No. 1.

Cash is debited for $100,000.00. Capital Stock—Common is credited for $20,000.00, the number of shares issued multiplied by the par value. The excess of the amount received over the par value of the stock issued, $80,000.00, is credited to Paid-In Capital in Excess of Par Value—Common.

Paid-In Capital in Excess of Par Value—Common

Debit Decreases | Credit Increases

> **FYI** International Financial Reporting Standards (IFRS) use the title *Share Premium* for Paid-In Capital in Excess of Par Value.

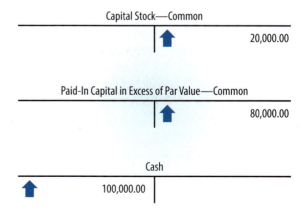

Common Stock with No Par Value

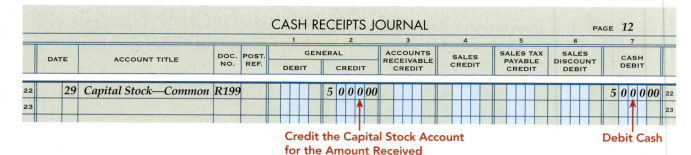

	DATE	ACCOUNT TITLE	DOC. NO.	POST. REF.	GENERAL DEBIT	GENERAL CREDIT	ACCOUNTS RECEIVABLE CREDIT	SALES CREDIT	SALES TAX PAYABLE CREDIT	SALES DISCOUNT DEBIT	CASH DEBIT	
22	29	Capital Stock—Common	R199			5 0 0 0 00					5 0 0 0 00	22
23												23

CASH RECEIPTS JOURNAL   PAGE *12*

Credit the Capital Stock Account for the Amount Received

Debit Cash

Common stock sometimes has no par value assigned to it. With no-par-value stock, the entire amount paid by an investor is recorded in the capital stock account. Wheeler, Inc., issues no-par-value common stock. The journal entry to record the transaction is shown above.

> December 29. Received cash from Elizabeth Griffin for 1,000 shares of no-par-value common stock at $5.00 per share, $5,000.00. Receipt No. 199.

Cash is debited for $5,000.00. Capital Stock—Common is credited for $5,000.00, the total amount received for the 1,000 shares of stock.

FINANCIAL LITERACY

Making Cents of Dollar-Cost Averaging

Investing in the stock market can be tricky. Some people are uncomfortable determining the best time to invest, and then they become concerned because the investment fluctuates over a short period.

Dollar-cost averaging is a technique whereby one places the same amount of money in the same investment consistently, regardless of the performance of the investment. It does not guarantee a profit. However, it is a beneficial technique for those who are not skilled in investing or those who find it difficult to save consistently over time. Dollar-cost averaging allows you to buy more shares when the prices are lower and fewer shares when the prices are higher.

Below is an example of dollar-cost averaging, assuming you plan to invest $100.00 per month.

June 28: Widgets cost $1 each. You buy 100 widgets.

July 27: Widgets now cost 75 cents each. You buy 133 widgets.

August 28: Widgets drop to 65 cents each. You buy 153 widgets.

September 27: Widgets cost $1.25 each. You buy 80 widgets.

At the end of September, you own 466 widgets. The cost of the units is now $1.25, so your total investment is worth $582.50. The cost of the 466 widgets over the four months was $400.00, so the average cost of each widget was 86 cents. Your investment increased from $400.00 to $582.50.

ACTIVITY

Using the following information, calculate the number of shares bought and the average cost per share. The monthly investment is $150.00. Round to two decimal places.

Date of Investment	Investment Amount	Cost per Share	Shares Bought*
January	$150.00	$12	
February	150.00	10	
March	150.00	8	
April	150.00	13	
TOTAL			

*Calculated by dividing investment by number of shares bought.

Common Stock with a Stated Value

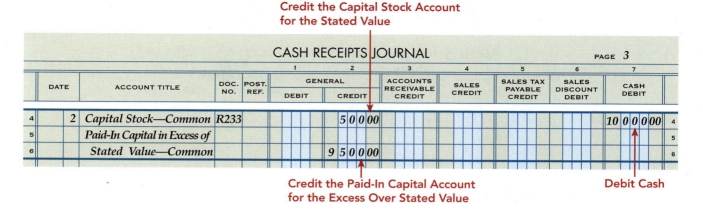

Credit the Capital Stock Account for the Stated Value

				DOC. NO.	POST. REF.	GENERAL		ACCOUNTS RECEIVABLE CREDIT	SALES CREDIT	SALES TAX PAYABLE CREDIT	SALES DISCOUNT DEBIT	CASH DEBIT	
	DATE	ACCOUNT TITLE				1 DEBIT	2 CREDIT	3	4	5	6	7	

CASH RECEIPTS JOURNAL   PAGE 3

4	2	Capital Stock—Common	R233			50000					1000000	4
5		Paid-In Capital in Excess of										5
6		Stated Value—Common				950000						6

Credit the Paid-In Capital Account for the Excess Over Stated Value

Debit Cash

Corporations may assign a value to common stock. The value is known as the *stated value*. A stated value serves the same function as par value. Therefore, no-par-value common stock with a stated value is recorded using the same procedures as par-value stock.

Lampkin Corporation's common stock has a stated value of $10.00 per share. Lampkin issued 50 shares of common stock to Alice Blake for $200.00 a share. The excess of the amount per share is recorded in Paid-In Capital in Excess of Stated Value—Common. This account is similar to the account used by Forest Equipment, except the description includes "Stated Value" rather than "Par Value."

> **March 2.** Received cash from Alice Blake for 50 shares of $10.00 stated-value common stock at $200.00 per share, $10,000.00. Receipt No. 233.

Cash is debited for $10,000.00, the total amount received. Capital Stock—Common is credited for $500.00, the total stated value of the 50 shares. Paid-In Capital in Excess of Stated Value—Common is credited for $9,500.00, the amount received in excess of the stated value.

THINK LIKE AN ACCOUNTANT

Charting the Capital Structure

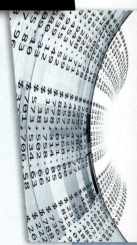

The board of directors of P&J Industries begins each meeting with an overview of the corporation's financial condition. The board consists of a diverse group of individuals, including a banker, a lawyer, a rancher, an educator, and a philanthropist. Each member brings unique talents and perspectives that have enabled the board to direct the corporation effectively. However, that diversity comes with a price. Some of the board members have little experience with reading financial statements.

To communicate the corporation's financial condition effectively to all board members, the Accounting Department prepares a report containing a series of charts. The controller recently learned of a new chart type and wants it incorporated into this quarter's report. The chart is known as a *pie of pie chart*. Unlike a single pie chart, a secondary chart shows the components of a single slice of the primary pie chart.

OPEN THE SPREADSHEET TLA_CH10

The worksheet contains a table containing the liability and stockholders' equity accounts of the balance sheet. Follow the steps on the Instructions tab to prepare two charts, and answer the following questions:

1. What percent is the stockholders' equity of the total liabilities and stockholders' equity?

2. What percent of the accounts are presented in the secondary chart?

3. Each chart could be improved by reducing the number of items in the chart. Suggest changes in the items included in the charts.

4. Describe the charts that could communicate effectively the information provided on an income statement.

LO1 Describe the process for forming a corporation.

LO2 Describe the two basic kinds of stock.

LO3 Identify advantages and disadvantages of the corporate form of business.

LO4 Journalize the issuances of par-value, no-par-value, and stated-value common stock.

TERMS REVIEW

corporation

share of stock

stockholder

board of directors

articles of incorporation

charter

common stock

preferred stock

stock certificate

par value

par-value stock

no-par-value stock

stated-value stock

proprietorship

partnership

double taxation

limited liability corporation

Audit your understanding LO1, 2, 3

1. What are three steps necessary to receive a charter?
2. What are the responsibilities of a corporation's board of directors?
3. What two basic kinds of stock may a corporation issue?
4. What three basic rights do stockholders usually have?
5. In place of a general ledger capital account for each owner, how does a corporation show stock ownership?
6. What is the most significant advantage of a corporation over a proprietorship or partnership?
7. How are the earnings of a corporation subject to double taxation?
8. How does a limited liability corporation differ from a traditional corporation?

Work together 10-1 LO4
Issuing common stock

Page 6 of a cash receipts journal is provided in the *Working Papers*. The source document is abbreviated as follows: receipt, R. Your instructor will guide you through the following examples.

> Transaction:
>
> June   5.   Harold Davis purchased 6,000 shares of GlassTown, Inc., common stock for $8.00 per share. R242.

Journalize the transaction using each of the following assumptions regarding the common stock:
a. $1.00 par-value common stock.
b. No-par-value common stock.
c. $1.00 stated-value common stock.

On your own 10-1 LO4
Issuing common stock

Page 15 of a cash receipts journal is provided in the *Working Papers*. The source document is abbreviated as follows: receipt, R. Work this problem independently.

> Transaction:
>
> Aug.   9.   Mandy Reston purchased 500 shares of First National Bank common stock for $14.00 per share. R334.

Journalize the transaction using each of the following assumptions regarding the common stock:
a. $5.00 par-value common stock.
b. No-par-value common stock.
c. $5.00 stated-value common stock.

LO5 Describe the process for taking a corporation public.
LO6 Journalize the issuance of preferred stock.
LO7 Explain how to account for convertible preferred stock.

Publicly Held Corporations LO5

As a corporation grows, it may require additional capital to finance its expansion. The portion of a corporation's net income not paid to stockholders as dividends is a primary source of additional capital. However, retained earnings may not provide an adequate source of capital for a corporation. Both new and existing corporations may require a large increase in capital to finance rapid expansion. Thus, a corporation can acquire additional capital by issuing stock to investors, borrowing money, or both.

Usually, the articles of incorporation permit a corporation to issue more shares of stock than it sells to initial investors. As the need arises for more capital, a corporation can issue some of the remaining authorized stock.

Three members of the Pearson family incorporated Forest Equipment, Inc. A corporation owned by a small number of individuals is called a **privately held corporation**. Many of today's largest corporations began as small, privately held corporations. As these businesses grew, the need to raise additional capital required them to issue stock to the public. The initial issue of a security on a public exchange is called an **initial public offering**. An initial public offering is commonly referred to as an *IPO*. A corporation having its stock traded on public exchanges is called a **publicly held corporation**. The process of issuing an IPO is commonly referred to as *taking a company public*. Although the initial investors may retain a large portion of the outstanding stock, a corporation with stock traded on a public exchange is a publicly held corporation.

A publicly held corporation is required to file its financial statements with the Securities and Exchange Commission. The document submitted to the SEC for permission to sell a security on a public exchange is called a **registration statement**. The registration statement contains an extensive description of the corporation, its financial condition, and the expected use of the proceeds from the stock sale. The statement identifies the number and type of stock (common or preferred) to be issued and the expected price per share.

Once a corporation becomes publicly held, it must submit many documents to the SEC. The two statements most commonly used by investors are the 10-Q (quarterly) and 10-K (annual) reports. Each statement contains financial statements and other financial information. These statements are available free to the public on the SEC's and the corporation's Internet sites.

Journal Entries for Issuing Preferred Stock LO6

Preferred stock are always issued with a par or stated value. Dividends on preferred stock are based on this value. Whether the stock is issued for cash or some other asset, the transactions are similar to the issuance of common stock having a par value.

Preferred Stock at Par Value

Credit the Capital Stock Account for the Par Value

				GENERAL		ACCOUNTS RECEIVABLE CREDIT	SALES CREDIT	SALES TAX PAYABLE CREDIT	SALES DISCOUNT DEBIT	CASH DEBIT	
DATE	ACCOUNT TITLE	DOC. NO.	POST. REF.	DEBIT	CREDIT						
Nov. 2	Capital Stock—Preferred	R235			30 0 0 0 00					30 0 0 0 00	1
											2

Debit Cash

Forest Equipment is authorized by its charter to issue a total of 10,000,000 shares of common stock and 500,000 shares of preferred stock. However, Forest initially issued only 65,000 shares of common stock to its three stockholders. Thus, Forest may issue some of the remaining shares of common or some shares of preferred stock to raise additional capital.

Forest's three initial stockholders, all members of the Pearson family, want to retain full management control. Selling common stock to another investor, or taking the company public, would cause the Pearson family to lose some of its control over the business. In addition, Forest does not want to incur the cost and effort required to file its financial statements with the SEC.

After weighing its options, Forest elects to issue preferred stock to a small number of local investors. Issuing this stock will not cause Forest to become a publicly held corporation. Forest's preferred stock does not offer any voting rights. Thus, the current stockholders can retain management control of the business.

Forest negotiated an issue of 300 preferred shares of preferred stock at par value to Zach Ruston.

Capital Stock—Preferred

Debit Decreases | Credit Increases

November 2. Received cash from Zach Ruston for 300 shares of 6%, $100.00 par-value preferred stock at par value, $30,000.00. Receipt No. 235.

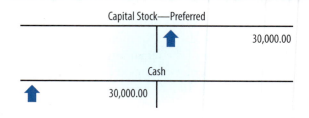

Capital Stock—Preferred — 30,000.00

Cash — 30,000.00

Cash is debited for $30,000.00, the total amount received. Capital Stock—Preferred is credited for $30,000.00, the total par value of the preferred stock issued.

WHY ACCOUNTING?

Getting Paid to Communicate

CareerClusters
PATHWAYS TO COLLEGE & CAREER READINESS
Arts, A/V Technology & Communications

A major in communications can lead to a variety of career fields such as broadcasting, journalism, government, public relations, arbitration, grant writing, and education.

Many public relations (PR) positions require more than good communication skills. For example, a PR director for a company that makes pacemakers may be the one to announce a research breakthrough or to explain why the company's income statement is being restated. He or she should have some knowledge of medicine and an understanding of how revenues and expenses are measured.

CRITICAL THINKING

Using the Internet or the "Help Wanted" section of a local newspaper, find a job opening in the communications/public relations area. List the education and work experience requirements for the position.

Preferred Stock Above Par Value

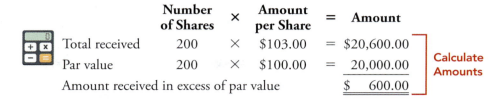

	Number of Shares	×	Amount per Share	=	Amount
Total received	200	×	$103.00	=	$20,600.00
Par value	200	×	$100.00	=	20,000.00
Amount received in excess of par value					$ 600.00

Calculate Amounts

Credit the Capital Stock Account for the Par Value

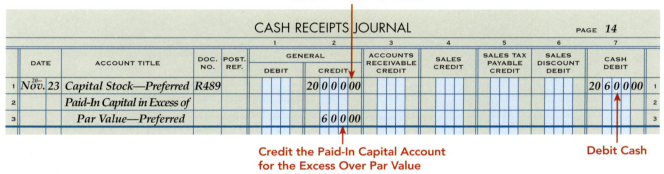

CASH RECEIPTS JOURNAL
PAGE **14**

				1	2	3	4	5	6	7	
DATE	ACCOUNT TITLE	DOC. NO.	POST. REF.	GENERAL DEBIT	GENERAL CREDIT	ACCOUNTS RECEIVABLE CREDIT	SALES CREDIT	SALES TAX PAYABLE CREDIT	SALES DISCOUNT DEBIT	CASH DEBIT	
Nov. 23	Capital Stock—Preferred	R489			20 000 00					20 600 00	1
	Paid-In Capital in Excess of										2
	Par Value—Preferred				6 00 00						3

Credit the Paid-In Capital Account for the Excess Over Par Value

Debit Cash

Investors purchase preferred stock to earn the dividend. A preferred stock's dividend rate can be compared to the rate of interest earned on alternative investments. As a result, the value of a preferred stock is dependent on market interest rates and the investor's confidence that the dividend will be paid without interruption. These factors may cause the preferred stock to be issued at a price other than its par value.

Market interest rates fluctuate based on many economic factors. When market interest rates fall below the preferred stock's dividend rate, investors will pay more than the par value. When market interest rates rise above the preferred stock's dividend rate, investors will pay less than the par value.

Paid-In Capital in Excess of Par Value—Preferred

Debit Decreases	Credit Increases

The payment of preferred dividends is not guaranteed. A company in financial distress may not generate enough cash to pay the dividend. Thus, investors must attempt to predict the future economic health of the company. Investors should evaluate the financial statements, research the expertise and experience of management, and consider the future market for the company's products and services.

The excess of proceeds from the issue of preferred stock over the par value is recorded in the account Paid-In Capital in Excess of Par Value—Preferred. This account is an equity account and has a normal credit balance.

Forest negotiated an issue of 200 preferred shares to Sophia Sanchez. Market interest rates had declined since the preferred stock was first issued. Thus, Sophia is willing to pay $103.00 per share.

> **November 23. Received cash from Sophia Sanchez for 200 shares of 6%, $100.00 par-value preferred stock at $103.00 per share, $20,600.00. Receipt No. 489.**

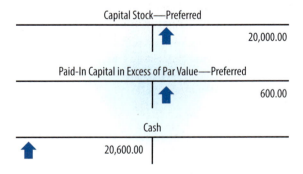

Cash is debited for $20,600.00, the total amount received. Capital Stock—Preferred is credited for $20,000.00, the total par value of the preferred stock issued. Paid-In Capital in Excess of Par Value—Preferred is credited for $600.00, the amount received in excess of the par value. Regardless of the amount received, the credit to the capital stock account always equals the total par or stated value of the stock issued.

Preferred Stock Issued for Assets Other than Cash

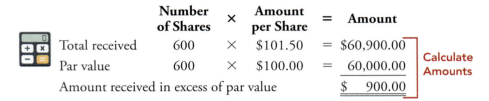

	Number of Shares	×	Amount per Share	=	Amount	
Total received	600	×	$101.50	=	$60,900.00	Calculate Amounts
Par value	600	×	$100.00	=	60,000.00	
Amount received in excess of par value					$ 900.00	

Debit the Asset Accounts for the Assets Received

GENERAL JOURNAL   PAGE 13

DATE	ACCOUNT TITLE	DOC. NO.	POST. REF.	DEBIT	CREDIT	
16	Inventory	M53		45 300 00		11
	Store Equipment			15 600 00		12
	Capital Stock—Preferred				60 000 00	13
	Paid-In Capital in Excess of					14
	Par Value—Preferred				900 00	15

Credit the Capital Stock Account

Credit the Paid-In Capital Account for the Excess Over Par Value

Occasionally, corporations issue capital stock in exchange for assets other than cash. When other assets are used to pay for capital stock, the investor and corporation must agree on the value of the assets and the capital stock.

BSF Supply is going out of business and has agreed to sell selected assets to Forest Equipment for $60,900.00. BSF Supply agreed to accept 600 shares of preferred stock in exchange for its inventory and store equipment.

> **December 16.** Received inventory and store equipment from BSF Supply at agreed values of $45,300.00 for inventory and $15,600.00 for store equipment. Forest Equipment issued 600 shares of 6%, $100.00 par-value preferred stock. Memorandum No. 53.

Inventory is debited for $45,300.00. Store Equipment is debited for $15,600.00. Capital Stock—Preferred

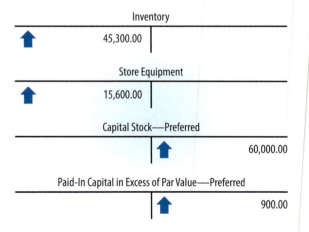

is credited for $60,000.00, the total par value of the preferred stock issued. Paid-In Capital in Excess of Par Value—Preferred is credited for $900.00, the amount received in excess of the par value.

FYI International Financial Reporting Standards (IFRS) use the title *Ordinary Shares* for Common Stock *and Preferred Shares* for Preferred Stock.

Convertible Preferred Stock LO7

A preferred stock is a contractual agreement between the corporation and the stockholder. The stockholder agrees to permanently invest an amount of money with the corporation. In exchange, the corporation gives preferred stockholders the right to receive any declared dividends before common stockholders receive dividends.

When preparing to issue preferred stock, a corporation has to balance two naturally conflicting objectives:

1. Maximize the price that investors are willing to pay for the preferred stock.
2. Minimize the amount of dividends that might be declared in the future.

A provision that helps a corporation achieve both objectives is a one that lets the stockholder trade preferred stock for common stock. The ability of a security to be traded for a specified number of shares of another security is called a **conversion option**. The number of shares of common stock received when a security is converted is called the **conversion ratio**. Preferred stock that can be exchanged for a specified number of common shares is called **convertible preferred stock**.

Convertible preferred stock gives the stockholder the ability to share in the income of the corporation through an increase in the market price of the common stock. Thus, this option adds value to the preferred stock and enables the corporation to issue the stock with a lower dividend rate.

Five years ago, Chandler Corporation issued 1,000 shares of $100.00 par-value, 4.5% preferred stock. The preferred stock has a conversion option, allowing the stockholder to convert each preferred share into five shares of common stock. The par or stated value of the preferred stock divided by the conversion ratio is called the **conversion price**. The conversion price of Chandler's preferred stock is $20.00, as shown below.

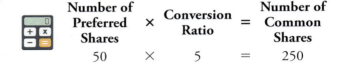

Par Value of Preferred Stock	÷	Conversion Ratio	=	Conversion Price
$100.00	÷	5	=	$20.00

Agnes Moreland purchased 50 of Chandler's preferred shares when its common stock had a market value of $8.00 per share. Since the market price of the common stock is less than $20.00, Agnes should hold her preferred shares and receive any dividends. However, when the common stock increases to $20.00 or more

per share, Agnes has a decision to make. She can hold her preferred shares and continue to receive the 4.5% dividend, or she can elect to convert her 50 shares to common stock. Upon conversion, Agnes would receive 250 shares of common stock, as shown below.

Number of Preferred Shares	×	Conversion Ratio	=	Number of Common Shares
50	×	5	=	250

Agnes will only benefit from converting her preferred shares if the market value of the common stock increases by at least 4.5% each year, less the effect of any dividends paid on common stock.

The conversion affects the corporation in two ways. After the conversion, dividends can be declared to common stockholders without having to first pay preferred stockholders. However, the earnings of the corporation and any declared dividends must now be shared among a larger number of shares.

Neither the corporation nor potential investors can predict the future market price of the common stock. Thus, the ultimate value of the conversion option is difficult to determine. If the market price never reaches $20.00, the conversion option is worthless to the stockholders. However, if Chandler sets the conversion price too high, such as $60.00, investors may not perceive the conversion option to be of any value.

Careers In Accounting

Edward O'Brien
Financial Planner

© SMARTPHOTOLAB/SHUTTERSTOCK.COM

Edward O'Brien is a financial planner. He works with individuals and families to help them develop financial objectives, form a plan for reaching those objectives, and implement the plan. His clients hire him for a variety of tasks over a wide range of areas.

Many clients only want help in relation to tax strategies or estate planning. However, Mr. O'Brien offers a broad range of services, including cash flow management, investments, insurance and risk management, budgeting, saving for educational costs, and planning for retirement.

Before Mr. O'Brien can help a client make financial decisions, he must understand the client's goals and the client's comfort with the risk related to various investments. He must also have a good understanding of the client's current financial position and other nonfinancial factors that may affect the achievement of the client's goals.

Mr. O'Brien feels that excellent communications skills are extremely important in his work. He needs to make his clients feel comfortable sharing personal information with him. He also needs to ask the right questions in the right way to ensure that he and his client establish appropriate goals and objectives.

Most states and countries do not highly regulate the financial planning career field. In many states, people can call themselves financial planners with little or no education or experience in the field. In order for his clients to have more trust in him, Mr. O'Brien completed the requirements to be called a Certified Financial Planner (CFP). These requirements include earning a bachelor's degree, completing educational requirements in the financial planning area, passing an examination, and acquiring work experience.

Salary Range: Salary varies greatly, depending on how many clients a financial planner has and how successful the financial planner is. In 2017, the median wage for a financial planner was $90,640.

Qualifications: As stated above, the qualifications to be a financial planner vary from state to state. In order to sell services as a CFP, one must have completed the requirements of that certification. However, it is possible to sell services as a financial planner with only a high school education.

Occupational Outlook: The growth for financial planner positions is projected to be much faster than average (15% or higher) through 2026.

Sources: www.onetonline.org; www.cfp.net.

TERMS REVIEW

privately held corporation

initial public offering

publicly held corporation

registration statement

conversion option

conversion ratio

convertible preferred stock

conversion price

Audit your understanding LO5, 6, 7

1. To finance rapid expansion, how can a corporation acquire additional capital?
2. Must all corporations file their financial statements with the SEC?
3. How can a business issue stock without causing the voting rights of current common stockholders to be diminished?
4. What is the relationship between an investor's desired dividend rate and the price at which a preferred stock is issued?
5. Why does a conversion option add value to preferred stock?
6. A 6%, $100.00 par-value preferred stock has a conversion ratio of 10. The corporation's common stock is currently valued at $12.00. Should preferred stockholders convert their stock?

Work together 10-2 LO6

Journalizing preferred stock transactions

Journalize each transaction completed during the current year. A general journal and a cash receipts journal are provided in the *Working Papers*. Your instructor will guide you through the following examples.

Transactions:

Mar. 17. Received cash from Lataya Davis for 200 shares of 6%, $50.00 par-value preferred stock at par value, $10,000.00. Receipt No. 443.

May 2. Received cash from Richard Estes for 100 shares of 6%, $50.00 par-value preferred stock at $53.00 per share, $5,300.00. Receipt No. 589.

July 12. Received office equipment from Isabella Hubbard at an agreed-upon value of $7,300.00 for 130 shares of 6%, $50.00 par-value preferred stock. Memorandum No. 133.

On your own 10-2 LO6

Journalizing preferred stock transactions

Journalize each transaction completed during the current year. A general journal and a cash receipts journal are provided in the *Working Papers*. Work independently to complete the following problem.

Transactions:

Feb. 6. Received inventory from Ella McMurtry at an agreed-upon value of $6,210.00 for 60 shares of 8%, $100.00 par-value preferred stock. Memorandum No. 87.

Apr. 12. Received cash from HGL Investments for 700 shares of 8%, $100.00 par-value preferred stock at par value, $70,000.00. Receipt No. 233.

May 22. Received cash from Lashundra Green for 150 shares of 8%, $100.00 par-value preferred stock at $102.50 per share, $15,375.00. Receipt No. 279.

A Look at **Accounting** Software

Maintaining Shareholder Records

This chapter covered the accounting transactions recorded by a corporation when stock is issued. The initial sale of issued shares is just a small step in the process of accounting for capital stock. The corporation must notify shareholders of stockholder meetings, elections of directors, declaration and payment of dividends, and regulatory filings. Thus, a corporation must have records of all its shareholders—how to contact them, how many shares each holds, and the dates of their stock purchases and sales.

Small corporations, often closely held, are usually able to maintain these records in a spreadsheet. Large corporations may have thousands or even millions of shareholders. The largest corporations, especially those that are publicly traded, contract with agents to manage record keeping for,

and communications with, their shareholders. Many corporations, though, are able to maintain these records with the help of specially designed accounting programs, generally referred to as *shareholder accounting software*.

Since shareholder accounting software is not often included with accounting software packages, it is usually necessary to purchase it separately. Add-on programs like these are called *modules* or *applications*, and they may function separately from the company's main accounting system or be integrated with it.

In this feature, it is assumed that the shareholder software is a fully integrated module that is launched from the System Manager. The Main Menu illustrates the functions performed by this module.

① The user clicked the **Apps** button, which brought up a dialog box showing the icons of all add-on modules.

② The user then clicked on the **Shareholder Accounting** icon to open that module's main menu.

③ To record a sale of stock from one shareholder to another, the user clicked on **Stock Transfers**, and the system opened the Stock Transfers window.

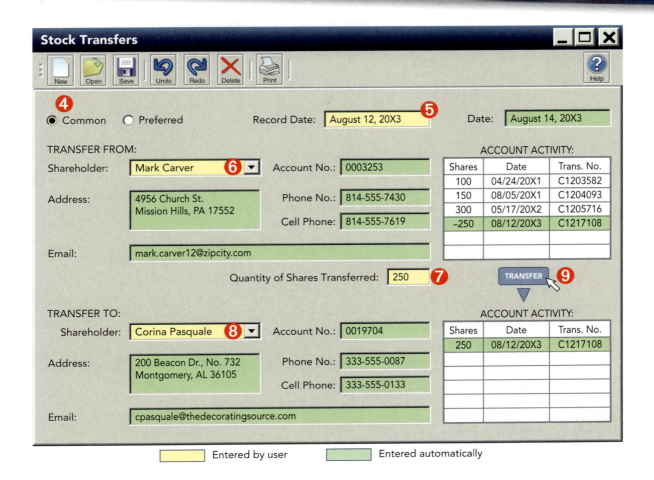

Stock Transfers ☐ ▢ ✕

New Open Save Undo Redo Delete Print Help

❹
◉ Common ○ Preferred   Record Date: [August 12, 20X3] ❺   Date: [August 14, 20X3]

TRANSFER FROM:

		ACCOUNT ACTIVITY:		
Shareholder: [Mark Carver ❻ ▾] Account No.: [0003253]

Shares	Date	Trans. No.
100	04/24/20X1	C1203582
150	08/05/20X1	C1204093
300	05/17/20X2	C1205716
–250	08/12/20X3	C1217108

Address: [4956 Church St. Mission Hills, PA 17552] Phone No.: [814-555-7430] Cell Phone: [814-555-7619]

Email: [mark.carver12@zipcity.com]

Quantity of Shares Transferred: [250] ❼   [TRANSFER] ❾

TRANSFER TO:

Shareholder: [Corina Pasquale ❽ ▾] Account No.: [0019704]

ACCOUNT ACTIVITY:

Shares	Date	Trans. No.
250	08/12/20X3	C1217108

Address: [200 Beacon Dr., No. 732 Montgomery, AL 36105] Phone No.: [333-555-0087] Cell Phone: [333-555-0133]

Email: [cpasquale@thedecoratingsource.com]

▭ Entered by user   ▭ Entered automatically

❹ Forest Equipment has issued both common and preferred shares, so the type of shares to be transferred must be selected. Since there is more activity in the company's common shares, **Common** is the default setting.

❺ The record date is the date on which the sale of the stock actually took place. The date on which the transaction is entered may be later, as it is here.

❻ The user selected the account of Mark Carver, the shareholder who sold some of his shares. His account number, address, phone numbers, e-mail address, and account activity were entered automatically by the system.

❼ The user entered **250** in the Quantity of Shares Transferred field.

❽ Corina Pasquale was selected as the purchaser of Mark Carver's shares. If she were a new shareholder, the user would first have had to use the Account Maintenance feature on the main menu to set up an account for her. The amount paid for the shares is of no consequence to the corporation. Forest Equipment is only interested in knowing how to contact Corina and where to send her dividends. If she elected to have dividends automatically deposited, that information would also appear in her account.

❾ The user clicked the **Transfer** button, and the system automatically assigned a transaction number and recorded the entries in the shareholder accounts.

CHAPTER SUMMARY

A corporation is created by filing articles of incorporation with a state agency. Upon receiving its charter, the corporation can issue up to its authorized number of common and preferred shares. Although some stockholders may receive a stock certificate, most stock ownership is maintained in electronic records.

A stock can be a par-value, no-par-value, or stated-value stock. The value has no relationship to the stock's market value. Common stockholders have the right to the earnings of the corporation and the right to vote on matters brought before the stockholders. Preferred stock usually does not have voting rights. However, preferred stockholders may have (1) the right to receive unpaid dividends and (2) the right to participate in dividends equal to the common stockholders.

A corporate form of business provides several advantages and disadvantages over a proprietorship or partnership. A corporation limits the liability of its stockholders to their investment in the corporation. However, the earnings of a corporation are subject to double taxation. A publicly held corporation also incurs significant costs to file its financial statements with the Securities and Exchange Commission. A limited liability corporation is a form of business that retains the limited liability of stockholders while eliminating the disadvantage of double taxation.

The stock issued above its par value results in a credit to a capital stock account. The excess of the amount over the par value is credited to a paid-in capital in excess of par value account. The accounting for stated-value stock is similar. All proceeds from the issue of no-par stock are credited to the capital stock account.

A corporation can lower the dividend rate of its preferred stock by including a conversion option. Preferred stockholders can elect to convert their stock for common stock. Stockholders benefit when the market price of common stock exceeds the conversion price and the annual increase in the price of common stock is expected to exceed the preferred stock dividend rate.

EXPLORE ACCOUNTING

A Delaware Corporation

In 1960, Sam Walton opened his first store in Rogers, then a small town of 5,700 in northwest Arkansas. Initially, members of the Walton family owned the new company. When the company's stock was listed on the New York Stock Exchange in 1972, Wal-Mart Stores, Inc., had grown to 51 stores in five states: Arkansas, Missouri, Oklahoma, Kansas, and Louisiana. The corporation is headquartered in Bentonville, Arkansas.

Readers of Wal-Mart's annual 10-K report filed with the Securities and Exchange Commission are likely to notice something unusual on the cover page. Wal-Mart is incorporated in the state of Delaware.

Since the early 1900s, Delaware has been a popular state in which to incorporate. Nearly half of all public corporations in the United States are incorporated in Delaware. These corporations do not have to be headquartered in Delaware. They do not even have to do business or have a bank account in the state. Delaware is only their legal home. The only requirement is that the corporation maintain a registered agent in the state.

By drafting corporation-friendly laws, Delaware has attracted corporations in the United States and across the world. Delaware corporations pay an annual tax known as a *franchise tax*. There are two methods to calculate this tax. For most corporations, the tax is calculated based on the amount of total assets, the number of authorized and issued shares of stock, and the par value of the stock. There is also a limit on what a corporation must pay.

These taxes provide a significant amount of funds to operate the state government. The amount of legal activity in the state also employs many Delaware residents. Thus, like any business that provides a service, the state of Delaware is eager to encourage corporations around the world to call Delaware home.

INSTRUCTIONS

Conduct research on the Internet to answer the following questions.

1. How does the Division of Corporations for the state of Delaware advertise Delaware's interest in attracting incorporation in the state?

2. What are the requirements of a registered agent?

3. Identify any negative events that have occurred that might suggest that Delaware's laws of incorporation may be too liberal.

Sources: http://corp.delaware.gov/; Why Corporations Choose Delaware, Lewis J. Black, Jr., Delaware Department of State, Division of Corporations, 2007.

APPLY YOUR UNDERSTANDING

INSTRUCTIONS: Download problem instructions for Excel, QuickBooks, and Sage 50c from the textbook companion website at www.C21accounting.com.

10-1 Application Problem | Issuing common stock LO4

A cash receipts journal is provided in the *Working Papers*. The source document is abbreviated as follows: receipt, R.

Transaction:

July   2.   John Abrams purchased 4,000 shares of GDT Tractors common stock for $6.00 per share. R553.

Instructions:

Journalize the transaction using each of the following assumptions regarding the common stock:

A. $0.10 par-value common stock.

B.   No-par-value common stock.

C. $0.10 stated-value common stock.

10-2 Application Problem | Journalizing preferred stock transactions LO6

sage 50

1. Journalize and post preferred stock transactions to the cash receipts journal.
2. Journalize and post issuance of preferred stock for store equipment to the general journal.
3. Print the cash receipts journal, general journal and general ledger trial balance.

QB Quick Books

1. Journalize and post preferred stock transactions to the journal.
2. Print the journal and trial balance.

X

1. Journalize preferred stock transactions to the cash receipts journal and general journal.
2. Print the spreadsheets.

Instructions:

Journalize each transaction completed during the current year. A cash receipts journal and a general journal are provided in the *Working Papers*. Source documents are abbreviated as follows: memorandum, M; receipt, R.

Transactions:

Jan.   7.   Received cash from Kelly Everland for 400 shares of $25.00 par-value preferred stock at par value, $10,000.00. R199.

Mar. 12.   Received cash from Brienna Terrell for 300 shares of $25.00 par-value preferred stock at $27.00 per share, $8,100.00. R274.

Apr.   6.   Received store equipment from Weldon Bester at an agreed-upon value of $5,800.00 for 220 shares of $25.00 par-value preferred stock. M93.

June   3.   Received cash from Cliff Jemison for 400 shares of $25.00 par-value preferred stock at $26.50 per share, $10,000.00. R433.

Organizing a Corporation   **Chapter 10**   313

10-M Mastery Problem — Journalizing stock transactions LO4, 6

sage 50

1. Journalize and post preferred stock transactions to the cash receipts journal.
2. Journalize and post issuance of preferred stock for store equipment to the general journal.
3. Print the cash receipts journal, general journal and general ledger trial balance.

QB Quick Books

1. Journalize and post preferred stock transactions to the journal.
2. Print the journal and trial balance.

X

1. Journalize preferred stock transactions to the cash receipts journal and general journal.
2. Print the spreadsheets.

After operating as a partnership for several years, Temika Clark and Terry Friesen decided to incorporate their business, Modern Landscapes. The new corporation received its charter on March 31 of the current year. The corporation is authorized to issue 150,000 shares of $1.00 stated-value common stock and 50,000 shares of 4.5%, $100.00 par-value preferred stock.

Instructions:

Journalize the following transactions. A general journal and a cash receipts journal are provided in the *Working Papers*. Source documents are abbreviated as follows: memorandum, M; receipt, R.

Transactions:

Apr. 1. Received cash from Temika Clark for 10,000 shares of common stock at $5.00 per share, $50,000.00. Receipt No. 1.

2. Received cash from Harris Financial Advisors for 800 shares of preferred stock at par value. Receipt No. 2.

3. Received cash from Terry Friesen for 25,000 shares of common stock at $5.00 per share, $125,000.00. Receipt No. 3.

4. Received equipment from Marshall Glenn at an agreed-upon value of $27,600.00 in exchange for 250 shares of preferred stock. M3.

28. Received cash from State Retirement Fund for 500 shares of preferred stock at $103.00 per share, $51,500.00. Receipt No. 16.

10-C Challenge Problem — Journalizing stock transactions LO4, 6, 7

Tullos Technologies is authorized to issue 100,000 shares of $1.00 par-value common stock and 80,000 shares of 5%, $100.00 par-value preferred stock. The preferred stock has a conversion option that allows one share to be exchanged for five shares of common stock.

Instructions:

Journalize the following transactions. A general journal and a cash receipts journal are provided in the *Working Papers*. Source documents are abbreviated as follows: memorandum, M; receipt, R.

Transactions:

Feb. 11. Received land from Development Partners at an agreed-upon value of $155,600.00 in exchange for 9,540 shares of common stock. M33.

Mar. 7. Received cash from Salmar Equity Partners for 2,000 shares of preferred stock at $102.00 per share. R56.

July 4. Lisle Motors exchanged 300 shares of preferred stock for common stock. M47.

Aug. 13. Received $68,900.00 from Melton Pension Fund for 625 shares of preferred stock. R196.

Sept. 22. Salmar Equity Partners exchanged its 2,000 shares of preferred stock for common stock. M156.

The Dow … and How

Theme: Financial, Economic, Business, Entrepreneurial Literacy, and History

Skills: Critical Thinking and Problem Solving, Communication and Collaboration, ICT Literacy, Life and Career Skills

PARTNERSHIP FOR
21ST CENTURY SKILLS

If you read or listen to investment news, you might hear that the Dow is up or the Dow is down. Upward trends are referred to as *bull markets*, and downward trends are referred to as *bear markets*. These terms give us the pulse of the stock market. The Dow Jones Industrial Average, called *Dow* for short, is the oldest index and probably the most widely followed stock market index in the world.

With an index, the number is not important. What is important is the percentage of change over time from an original value. The movement of the index, up or down, tells you how companies traded on the stock market are doing, in general.

Charles Dow and Edward Jones created the Dow Jones Industrial Average (DJIA) in 1896. It represented the average stock price of companies in 12 industries, including cotton, sugar, tobacco, gas, electric, coal, iron, leather, and rubber. The average was calculated as a simple average.

The companies of the DJIA have changed 48 times in its history. Today, the Dow's 30 stocks reflect a portion of the actual industries in the market, including technology and fast-food companies. These stocks are averaged using a special formula. To be included in the index, a stock must be a leader in its industry. General Electric held the longest continuous place in the Dow. Initially listed in 1896, it was replaced by Walgreens Boots Alliance in June, 2018.

APPLICATION

1. Use the Internet with a partner and research the performance of the Dow over the last 100 years. Create a timeline depicting historical events that influenced gains or losses in the market.

2. Use the Internet and obtain a list of the 30 companies currently listed in the DJIA. Select one company to research. Write a one-page paper describing how the company was started, when and why it went public, when it became a part of the DJIA, a history of its stock performance, and events that affected its performance. Present your findings to the class. **Optional:** Create a sample page on social media, outlining this information for a company of your choice.

3. Look over the list of 30 companies currently listed in the DJIA. If one company could be replaced, explain what public company you would add, describe its industry, and justify your reason.

Analyzing Home Depot's Financial Statements

Home Depot is authorized to issue one class of common stock. The corporation has only issued a fraction of the number of shares authorized. Information about the par value of the stock and the number of shares authorized, issued, and outstanding can be found in the Equity section of Home Depot's balance sheet.

INSTRUCTIONS

Use Home Depot's Consolidated Balance Sheets and Consolidated Statements of Stockholders' Equity on pages B-5 and B-8 to answer the following questions:

1. What is the par value of Home Depot's common stock?

2. How many shares of common stock are authorized, issued, and outstanding as of January 28, 2018?

3. Determine the dollar amount of common stock issued under employee stock plans during the 2017 fiscal year.

Corporate Dividends and Treasury Stock

© VINTAGE TONE/SHUTTERSTOCK.COM

LEARNING OBJECTIVES

After studying Chapter 11, in addition to defining key terms, you will be able to:

LO1 Journalize the declaration and payment of a cash dividend.

LO2 Journalize the declaration and payment of a stock dividend.

LO3 Describe the impact of a stock dividend.

LO4 Explain why a corporation would purchase its own stock.

LO5 Journalize entries for buying and selling treasury stock.

LO6 Journalize the purchase and sale of the capital stock of other corporations.

Wells Fargo & Company

ACCOUNTING IN THE REAL WORLD

© SUNDRY PHOTOGRAPHY/SHUTTERSTOCK.COM

Wells Fargo is one of most well-known financial institutions based in the United States. Like most financial institutions, Wells Fargo has faced numerous challenges over its 165-year history. Most recently the Great Recession of 2007–2009 required the government to provide temporary financial support to many banks, including Wells Fargo. The recession prompted Congress to enact sweeping regulatory reforms that included new capital requirements. The new regulations require banks to maintain a higher minimum ratio of stockholders' equity relative to total assets.

Although Wells Fargo remained profitable during the recession, its earnings declined significantly in 2008. In addition to the new capital requirements, Wells Fargo was forced to reduce its annual dividend. From a high of $1.30 in 2008, the dividend was cut to a low of $0.20 in 2010. Not until 2014 did the annual dividend recover to its pre-recession level.

One of Wells Fargo's goals is to create long-term value for its stockholders. The board of directors must monitor the bank's income to determine how much value to return to stockholders. The board must first make certain that the bank meets the government's minimum capital requirement. The board can then determine the amount to distribute to stockholders. The board has two options for returning value to its stockholders: (1) declaring dividends, and (2) repurchasing stock. Dividends are a direct cash distribution to the stockholders. Stock repurchases reduce the number of

outstanding shares, which increases the value of the remaining outstanding shares.

The board uses two payout ratios to monitor the level of value returned to stockholders.

Dividend payout: Total dividends ÷ net income.

Payout ratio: (Total dividends + share repurchases) ÷ net income.

In 2017 Wells Fargo's ratios were dividend payout ratio 38% and payout ratio 72%.

Source: www.wellsfargo.com.

CRITICAL THINKING

1. Wells Fargo must have an adequate supply of cash to pay a dividend. What other factors should management consider when determining the portion of earnings to pay as a dividend?

2. What factor may motivate the board to distribute value to stockholders using a stock repurchase rather than declaring a dividend?

3. Work in a small group to identify three corporations that have a large amount of cash. Based on your knowledge of the dividend payout ratio, why do you think the corporations are not using this cash to pay dividends? Do you think any of the corporations should begin paying or increasing their dividends?

KEY TERMS

declaring a dividend
date of declaration

date of record
date of payment

stock dividend
treasury stock

buyback

LO1 Journalize the declaration and payment of a cash dividend.

LO2 Journalize the declaration and payment of a stock dividend.

LO3 Describe the impact of a stock dividend.

Cash Dividends LO1

A primary goal of a corporation's board of directors is to increase stockholder wealth. A corporation can achieve this goal in two ways. It can reinvest its earnings to finance growth, causing the stock price to increase. It can distribute a portion of its earnings to its stockholders. Corporate earnings distributed to stockholders are known as *dividends*. The board of directors must weigh the financing needs of the business against the desire of its stockholders to receive a dividend.

Declaring a Cash Dividend

Action by a board of directors to distribute corporate earnings to stockholders is called **declaring a dividend**. The board determines when and what amount of the

retained earnings will be distributed. Three dates are involved in distributing a dividend:

1. **Date of declaration:** The date on which a board of directors votes to distribute a dividend.

2. **Date of record:** The date that determines which stockholders are to receive dividends. Only persons listed as stockholders on the date of record will receive dividends.

3. **Date of payment:** The date on which dividends are actually to be paid to stockholders. Ordinarily, the date of payment occurs several weeks after the date of record, giving a corporation time to determine who is entitled to receive dividends.

ETHICS IN ACTION

Exercising Stock Options

Corporations often compensate executives with more than a salary. The compensation package often includes **stock options**—the right to purchase company stock at a specified price. The option price typically is set higher than the current market price. If the stock price increases above the option price, the option enables the executive to purchase the stock at less than the market price. If the stock's market price never exceeds the option price, the option is worthless.

Four years ago, Mena Corp. offered its new chief executive officer, Emily Tillman, an annual salary of $500,000 plus 200,000 stock options at $30. The stock was selling for $18 at the time. Emily successfully

improved the corporation's profitability. When the stock reached $40 per share, Emily exercised the stock options and purchased 200,000 shares of stock from Mena Corp. for $6 million. She later sold the stock for an average price of $42 per share.

Mena Corp.'s code of conduct states, "Employees should receive compensation consistent with their contributions toward our strategic objectives."

INSTRUCTIONS

Use the ethical model to analyze whether the corporation's use of stock options as executive compensation demonstrates ethical behavior.

Calculating a Dividend

When a board of directors declares a dividend, the corporation is obligated to pay it. At the date of declaration, the corporation incurs a liability that must be recorded.

The board of directors of Hariton, Inc., has decided to declare a quarterly dividend of $10,000.00. On December 31, the date of record, the corporation has issued 2,000 shares of 8%, $100.00 par-value preferred stock and 64,000 shares of $10.00 par-value common stock. The par value of preferred stock is used to calculate the dividend on preferred stock. The amount of the $10,000.00 distributed to the preferred stock is calculated as follows:

Number of Preferred Shares	×	Par Value	=	Par Value of Preferred Stock
2,000	×	$100.00	=	$200,000.00

Par Value of Preferred Stock	×	Quarterly Dividend Rate	=	Preferred Dividend Amount
$200,000.00	×	8%/4	=	$4,000.00

The dividend rate on preferred stock is stated as an annual rate. The annual rate is divided by 4 to calculate a quarterly dividend. Any dividends above the amount paid to preferred stock are available for common stock.

Total Amount Available for Dividends	−	Preferred Dividend Amount	=	Amount Available for Common Dividends
$10,000.00	−	$4,000.00	=	$6,000.00

In subsequent years, Hariton may elect to increase its quarterly dividend. Hariton's preferred stock dividend will never exceed an annual rate of 8% of its par value. Therefore, additional dividends will be distributed to common stock.

Importing and Exporting Goods

Many businesses, large and small, operate in the global market. Some companies import goods to sell or to use in manufacturing, and other companies export goods to foreign markets. These companies must adhere to government regulations in both the importing and the exporting country.

When shipping goods overseas, appropriate documentation must accompany the package to verify its contents. Customs officials will read the documentation and may open the packages. If the documentation is incomplete or inaccurate, the shipment may be delayed or returned to the sender.

All major trading nations use the Harmonized Commodity Description and Coding System (HS). HS allows all products to be classified and more easily identified. HS establishes a single ten-digit code for each type of commodity, and this code is included on all paperwork connected with a shipment. This helps customs officials in both countries determine if the product is subject to import/export restrictions or special duties.

The World Customs Organization (WCO) maintains HS. The WCO is an international intergovernmental organization. Its goal is to "improve the effectiveness and efficiency" of international customs to support global trade while maintaining security. By encouraging international standards for imports and exports, the WCO also supports developing nations with their global trade. WCO membership consists of customs administrators from 176 countries.

CRITICAL THINKING

Go to the website for the World Customs Organization (www.wcoomd.org). Search for information about the WCO to answer the following questions:

1. List five countries (other than the United States) that belong to the WCO.

2. List the name of the secretary general of the WCO and one item of information from the secretary general's biography.

Declaration of a Dividend

Debit Each Dividend Account

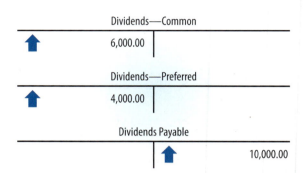

	DATE	ACCOUNT TITLE	DOC. NO.	POST. REF.	DEBIT	CREDIT	
16	Dec. 15	Dividends—Common	M456		6 0 0 0 00		16
17		Dividends—Preferred			4 0 0 0 00		17
18		Dividends Payable				10 0 0 0 00	18

GENERAL JOURNAL — PAGE 24

Credit Dividends Payable

A journal entry is recorded on the date the dividend is declared.

> **December 15. Hariton's board of directors declared an annual dividend of $10,000.00. Memorandum No. 456.**

The journal entry creates a current liability for the total amount of the dividends declared. The action of the board of directors creates an obligation to pay the dividend on January 15, the payment date.

No journal entry is recorded on December 31, the date of record. Stockholders owning the stock on the date of record receive the declared dividend. On the next day, a buyer would purchase the shares *ex-dividend* (without the dividend).

Dividends—Common
6,000.00

Dividends—Preferred
4,000.00

Dividends Payable
10,000.00

Payment of a Dividend

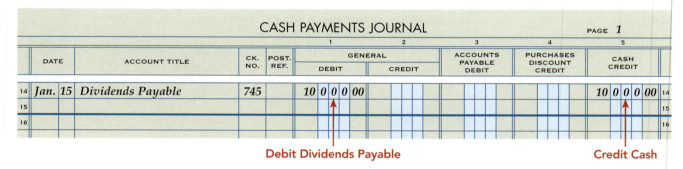

CASH PAYMENTS JOURNAL — PAGE 1

	DATE	ACCOUNT TITLE	CK. NO.	POST. REF.	GENERAL DEBIT	GENERAL CREDIT	ACCOUNTS PAYABLE DEBIT	PURCHASES DISCOUNT CREDIT	CASH CREDIT	
14	Jan. 15	Dividends Payable	745		10 0 0 0 00				10 0 0 0 00	14
15										15
16										16

Debit Dividends Payable   **Credit Cash**

On January 15, Hariton issued a single check for $10,000.00, the total amount of the dividends to be paid.

> **January 15. Paid cash for annual dividend declared on December 15, $10,000.00. Check No. 745.**

The dividend check is issued to an agent who handles the details of preparing and mailing stockholders'

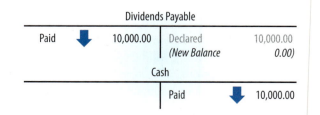

Dividends Payable
Paid   10,000.00 | Declared   10,000.00
                   (New Balance   0.00)

Cash
         | Paid   10,000.00

checks. The agent writes a separate check to each eligible stockholder. This procedure avoids a large number of entries in Hariton's cash payments journal.

Stock Dividends LO2

A company may prefer to issue its stockholders additional shares of stock instead of issuing a cash dividend. The payment of a dividend with the stock of the corporation is called a **stock dividend**. Similar to cash dividends, transactions are recorded on the declaration date and the payment date.

Declaring a Stock Dividend

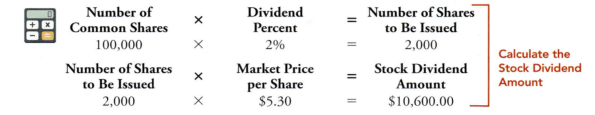

Number of Common Shares	×	Dividend Percent	=	Number of Shares to Be Issued
100,000	×	2%	=	2,000

Number of Shares to Be Issued	×	Market Price per Share	=	Stock Dividend Amount
2,000	×	$5.30	=	$10,600.00

Calculate the Stock Dividend Amount

Credit Stock Dividends Distributable

	DATE		ACCOUNT TITLE	DOC. NO.	POST. REF.	DEBIT	CREDIT	
1	June	1	Stock Dividends	M235		10 6 0 0 00		1
2			Stock Dividends Distributable				2 0 0 00	2
3			Paid-In Capital in Excess of Par Value—Common				10 4 0 0 00	3

GENERAL JOURNAL — PAGE 6

Debit Stock Dividends   Credit Paid-In Capital in Excess of Par Value—Common

Stock Dividends

Debit Increases | Credit Decreases

The debit portion of the journal entry to record the declaration of a stock dividend is similar to that used for a cash dividend. To distinguish between cash and stock dividends, the amount of the stock dividend is debited to Stock Dividends rather than Dividends. Stock Dividends is a temporary equity account and has a normal debit balance. The amount of the stock dividend is based on the market price of the stock.

Stock Dividends Distributable

Debit Decreases | Credit Increases

The credit part of the journal entry resembles the issuance of common stock. Because the stock will not be issued until the payment date, the par value of the stock to be issued is credited to Stock Dividends Distributable rather than Common Stock. Stock Dividends Distributable is an equity account and has a normal credit balance.

> June 1. Abraham Corporation's board of directors declared a 2% stock dividend, payable on June 30. The corporation has 100,000 shares of $0.10 par-value common stock outstanding. The current market price of the stock is $5.30. Memorandum No. 235.

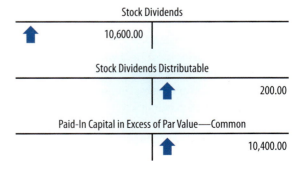

Stock Dividends
10,600.00

Stock Dividends Distributable
200.00

Paid-In Capital in Excess of Par Value—Common
10,400.00

Paying a Stock Dividend

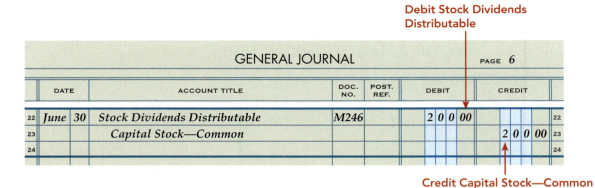

Debit Stock Dividends Distributable

	DATE		ACCOUNT TITLE	DOC. NO.	POST. REF.	DEBIT	CREDIT	
22	June	30	*Stock Dividends Distributable*	M246		2 0 0 00		22
23			*Capital Stock—Common*				2 0 0 00	23
24								24

GENERAL JOURNAL   PAGE 6

Credit Capital Stock—Common

Abraham Corporation declared a 2% stock dividend on June 1. The company had 100,000 of its $0.10 par-value stock outstanding. The stock dividend will result in the issuance of 2,000 shares (100,000 shares × 2%). On the declaration date, the par value of the 2,000 shares, $200.00, was debited to Stock Dividends Distributable.

> **June 30.** Abraham Corporation issued 2,000 shares of common stock in payment of its June 1 stock dividend, $200.00. Memorandum No. 246.

Stock Dividends Distributable

Issued	⬇	200.00	Declared	200.00
			(New Balance	*0.00)*

Capital Stock—Common

	Issued	⬆	200.00

The journal entry removes the balance from Stock Dividends Distributable to Capital Stock—Common.

WHY ACCOUNTING?

How the Bottom Line Can Affect Jail Sentences

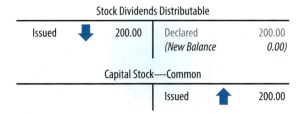

CareerClusters®
PATHWAYS TO COLLEGE & CAREER READINESS
Law, Public Safety, Corrections & Security

Many prison and jail systems throughout the United States are dealing with the issue of overcrowding. In California, a gymnasium is being used to house 213 prisoners. Bunk beds are aligned in rows and columns. The tight living arrangements are being blamed for numerous riots and fights that occur at the facility.

One way to solve overcrowding is to build more facilities. Because of the high cost to build more jails, many jurisdictions are taking a different approach. Instead of raising taxes to build jails, they are releasing prisoners who have lesser offenses. In many cases, these prisoners will be in monitored probation programs, increasing the costs to administer these programs.

Administrators of jails and prisons need to adhere to budgets that usually are set by governmental organizations. When trying to keep expenses within the budget, they have to analyze the costs of different options. Knowledge of how to identify and measure costs is essential.

CRITICAL THINKING

1. Search the Internet to find information about the prison population in your state or a neighboring state. Summarize the information in a short report.

2. Not all decisions are based on costs alone. What other items should be considered when making a decision to release inmates rather than build new jails?

Impact of a Stock Dividend LO3

		GENERAL JOURNAL						PAGE 15		
	DATE	ACCOUNT TITLE	DOC. NO.	POST. REF.	DEBIT		CREDIT			
1		*Closing Entries*							1
23	Dec. 31	*Retained Earnings*			10 6 0 0 00				23
24		*Stock Dividends*					10 6 0 0 00		24

Stock Dividends

Declared	10,600.00	Closing	10,600.00
(New Balance	0.00)		

Stock Dividends Distributable

Issued	200.00	Declared	200.00
		(Balance	0.00)

Paid-In Capital in Excess of Par—Common

		Declared	10,400.00

Capital Stock—Common

		Issued	200.00

Retained Earnings

Closing	10,600.00

All dividends, whether for cash or stock, are closed to Retained Earnings at the end of the fiscal period. The impact of declaring and paying a stock dividend on the accounts of Abraham Corporation is shown in the T accounts.

The stock dividend has no impact on the assets or liabilities of the corporation. The journal entries simply transfer amounts among equity accounts. Retained Earnings is reduced by the amount of the dividend.

Common Stock and Paid-In Capital in Excess of Par—Common, together, increase by the amount of the dividend.

Because the corporation gives nothing of value, the stockholders do not receive anything of value. The transaction increases the number of shares outstanding. Each stockholder retains his or her share of the corporation. For example, Gail Winston owned 4,000, or 4%, of Abraham's 100,000 shares prior to the stock dividend. She receives 80 shares with the 2% stock dividend. After the stock dividend, she owns 4,080 of the 102,000 shares outstanding, still exactly 4%.

If stockholders receive nothing of value, why would a corporation pay a stock dividend? Two common reasons are:

- A corporation's stockholders may expect a dividend, but the corporation lacks the necessary funds to pay a cash dividend. A stock dividend allows the corporation to pay a dividend without using any financial resources.
- A stock dividend will cause an immediate decline in the market price per share. The total market value of the corporation remains constant, while the number of shares increases. Abraham's 2% stock dividend should cause the market price to drop from $5.30 to $5.20 per share as shown below.

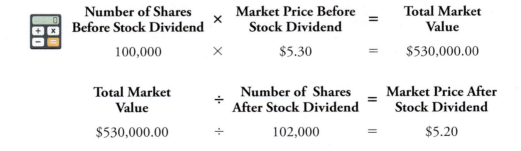

	Number of Shares Before Stock Dividend	×	Market Price Before Stock Dividend	=	Total Market Value
	100,000	×	$5.30	=	$530,000.00

Total Market Value	÷	Number of Shares After Stock Dividend	=	Market Price After Stock Dividend
$530,000.00	÷	102,000	=	$5.20

A stock dividend helps to maintain investor demand for a stock. As a corporation continues to grow, its stock market price will also grow. An investor who perceives the stock price to be too expensive might not consider buying the stock. The stock dividend is an effective tool for the corporation to keep its stock price within a desired price range.

TERMS REVIEW

declaring a dividend
date of declaration
date of record
date of payment
stock dividend

Audit your understanding LO1, 2, 3

1. Who determines when and what amount of retained earnings a corporation will distribute as dividends?
2. Why does a corporation record a liability when a dividend is declared?
3. What transaction is recorded on the date of record?
4. What term is used to describe a stock purchased after the date of record?
5. What is the normal balance of the account Stock Dividends Distributable?
6. Describe the effect of a stock dividend on (a) the stockholders and (b) the corporation.

Work together 11-1 LO1, 2

Journalizing dividend transactions

On April 1 of the current year, Western Tours, Inc., had 8,000 shares of 6%, $100.00 par-value preferred stock and 50,000 shares of $1.00 par-value common stock outstanding.

   Journalize each transaction completed during the current year. Page 5 of a general journal and page 7 of a cash payments journal are provided in the *Working Papers*. Source documents are abbreviated as follows: check, C; memorandum, M. Your instructor will guide you through the following examples.

Transactions:

Apr.   1.   The board of directors declared a quarterly cash dividend of $25,000.00, payable on April 30. M32.

      30.   Paid the April 1 dividend. C533.

July   1.   An economic downturn made it impossible for Western Tours to declare its regular quarterly cash dividend. In lieu of a cash dividend, the board of directors declared a 5% stock dividend on common stock. The market price of the common stock on July 1 was $6.90. M57.

      31.   Issued the July 1 stock dividend. M68.

On your own 11-1 LO1, 2

Journalizing dividend transactions

On July 1 of the current year, TPE Industries had 10,000 shares of 8%, $50.00 par-value preferred stock and 60,000 shares of $0.10 par-value common stock outstanding.

   Journalize each transaction completed during the current year. Page 7 of a general journal and page 12 of a cash payments journal are provided in the *Working Papers*. Source documents are abbreviated as follows: check, C; memorandum, M. Work this problem independently.

Transactions:

July   1.   The board of directors declared a quarterly cash dividend of $30,000.00, payable on August 1. M66.

Aug.   1.   Paid the July 1 dividend. C765.

      15.   In an effort to reduce its stock price, the board of directors declared a 10% stock dividend on common stock. The market price of the common stock was $78.60. M87.

Sept. 15.   Issued the August 15 stock dividend. M99.

LESSON 11-2

Treasury Stock Transactions

LO4 Explain why a corporation would purchase its own stock.
LO5 Journalize entries for buying and selling treasury stock.

Treasury Stock LO4

A corporation with a significant amount of excess cash has several options. The corporation can invest in plant assets, purchase other businesses, issue or increase the dividend, or pay down outstanding debt.

Another option is to purchase its own stock. A corporation's own stock that has been issued and reacquired is called **treasury stock**. When a corporation buys treasury stock, it reduces the number of shares outstanding. A corporation usually intends to use the treasury stock for a specific purpose. For example, a corporation may acquire treasury stock to be given to employees as bonus payments.

A program approved by a board of directors authorizing the corporation to repurchase its stock is called a **buyback**. A buyback often occurs when a corporation believes that its stock is undervalued by the stock market. Remaining stockholders benefit because the net income of the corporation is divided among a fewer number of shares.

Journal Entries for Treasury Stock LO5

Capital stock accounts have normal credit balances. Treasury Stock is a contra capital stock account and therefore has a normal debit balance.

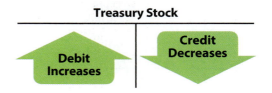

Treasury Stock

Debit Increases | Credit Decreases

Buying Treasury Stock

				CASH PAYMENTS JOURNAL				PAGE 3
				1	2	3	4	5
DATE	ACCOUNT TITLE	CK. NO.	POST. REF.	GENERAL DEBIT	GENERAL CREDIT	ACCOUNTS PAYABLE DEBIT	PURCHASES DISCOUNT CREDIT	CASH CREDIT
5	Feb. 3	Treasury Stock	887		18 0 0 0 00				18 0 0 0 00	5
6										6

Debit Treasury Stock   Credit Cash

Forest Equipment's board of directors authorizes the corporation to repurchase up to 10,000 shares of its common stock. Treasury stock is recorded at the price paid, regardless of the stock's par or stated value. **>>** App. A: Historical Cost

> **February 3. Paid cash to Kate Mason for 2,000 shares of $5.00 par-value common stock at $9.00 per share, $18,000.00. Check No. 887.**

Treasury Stock
18,000.00

Cash
18,000.00

Selling Treasury Stock for More Than Original Cost

	No. of Shares	×	Value per Share	=	Value	
Total received	300	×	$16.00	=	$4,800.00	Calculate the Amounts to Be Recorded
Original cost	300	×	$ 9.00	=	2,700.00	
Amount received in excess of original cost					$2,100.00	

Credit Treasury Stock for Its Cost

CASH RECEIPTS JOURNAL

PAGE 16

	DATE	ACCOUNT TITLE	DOC. NO.	POST. REF.	GENERAL DEBIT	GENERAL CREDIT	ACCOUNTS RECEIVABLE CREDIT	SALES CREDIT	SALES TAX PAYABLE CREDIT	SALES DISCOUNT DEBIT	CASH DEBIT	
13	Aug. 6	Treasury Stock	R657			2 7 0 0 00					4 8 0 0 00	13
14		Paid-In Capital from										14
15		Sale of Treasury Stock				2 1 0 0 00						15

Credit the Paid-In Capital Account for the Excess over Cost of Treasury Stock

Debit Cash

August 6. Received cash from DeMarcus Long for 300 shares of treasury stock at $16.00 per share, $4,800.00. Treasury stock was bought on February 3 for $9.00 per share. Receipt No. 657.

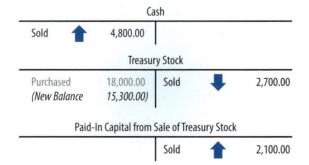

A corporation needing to raise additional capital may elect to sell its treasury stock rather than issue additional shares.

Cash is debited for $4,800.00, the total amount received from the sale of the treasury stock. Treasury Stock is credited for $2,700.00, the original cost of the 300 shares of treasury stock. Paid-In Capital from Sale of Treasury Stock is credited for $2,100.00, the amount received in excess of the treasury stock's original cost.

Treasury stock is not an asset of a corporation. Since treasury stock is not owned by a stockholder, the stock does not involve voting rights. Dividends are not paid on treasury stock. Once treasury stock is given or sold to a stockholder, it ceases to be treasury stock and is again capital stock outstanding.

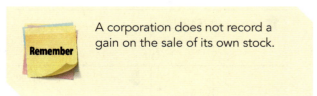

A corporation does not record a gain on the sale of its own stock.

Remember

Selling Treasury Stock for Less Than Original Cost

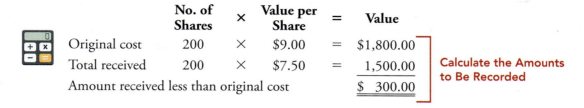

	No. of Shares	×	Value per Share	=	Value	
Original cost	200	×	$9.00	=	$1,800.00	**Calculate the Amounts to Be Recorded**
Total received	200	×	$7.50	=	1,500.00	
Amount received less than original cost					$ 300.00	

Credit Treasury Stock for Its Cost

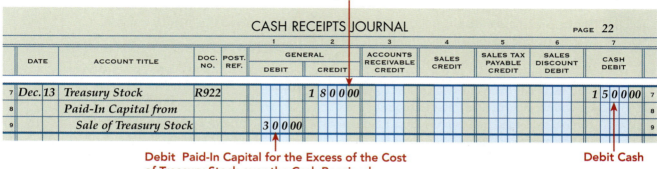

					CASH RECEIPTS JOURNAL						PAGE 22	
					1	2	3	4	5	6	7	
DATE	ACCOUNT TITLE	DOC. NO.	POST. REF.	GENERAL DEBIT	GENERAL CREDIT	ACCOUNTS RECEIVABLE CREDIT	SALES CREDIT	SALES TAX PAYABLE CREDIT	SALES DISCOUNT DEBIT	CASH DEBIT	
7	Dec. 13	Treasury Stock	R922		1 8 0 0 00						1 5 0 0 00	7
8		Paid-In Capital from										8
9		Sale of Treasury Stock		3 0 0 00								9

Debit Paid-In Capital for the Excess of the Cost of Treasury Stock over the Cash Received

Debit Cash

A corporation with excess cash may purchase its stock when it believes the stock is undervalued by the market. Like many investors, the corporation cannot always predict future stock prices. The market price of the stock may continue to decline. If the corporation needs to sell treasury stock to raise capital, the sales price may be less than the cost of the treasury stock.

> **December 13. Received cash from Granger Hollins for 200 shares of treasury stock at $7.50 per share, $1,500.00. Treasury stock was bought originally on February 3 at $9.00 per share. Receipt No. 922.**

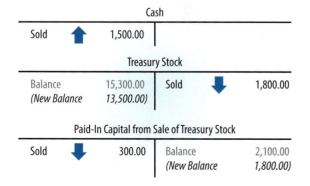

Cash is debited for $1,500.00, the total amount of cash received. Treasury Stock is credited for $1,800.00, the original cost. Paid-In Capital from Sale of Treasury Stock is debited for $300.00, the amount received that is less than the treasury stock's original cost.

Treasury stock is still considered to be issued stock. When treasury stock transactions occur, no entry is made in Capital Stock—Common. The difference between the balance of the capital stock account and the treasury stock account is the value of outstanding stock. After recording the entry on December 13 for the sale of treasury stock, the number of outstanding shares of common stock is calculated as follows:

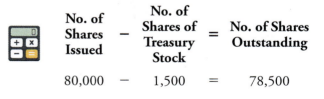

	No. of Shares Issued	−	No. of Shares of Treasury Stock	=	No. of Shares Outstanding
	80,000	−	1,500	=	78,500

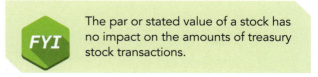

FYI The par or stated value of a stock has no impact on the amounts of treasury stock transactions.

Insider Trading

Martha Stewart has built a media empire by selling a distinct lifestyle. Martha Stewart Living Omnimedia offers a wide range of products, from recipe books to cookware, furniture to paint, and towels to bedding. Stewart shares cooking, decorating, gardening, and craft ideas through magazines, books, radio and television shows, and social media.

During one period, Martha Stewart's name was in the media for the wrong reason. In 2003, the Securities and Exchange Commission (SEC) filed securities fraud charges against Stewart and her former stockbroker, Peter Bacanovic. The complaint alleged that the receipt of insider information motivated Stewart to sell her shares of a biopharmaceutical company, ImClone Systems, Inc. Subsequently, during the SEC investigation, she attempted to conceal facts.

In 2001, investors were awaiting the government's decision to approve ImClone's new cancer drug Erbitux. ImClone chief executive officer, Sam Waksal, knew that the government was about to reject Erbitux. Waksal instructed his stockbroker, Peter Bacanovic, to sell all his ImClone stock that was held by Bacanovic's firm, Merrill Lynch. Waksal used his insider information to his benefit, which resulted in his being convicted of violating insider trading laws.

Bacanovic was also Stewart's stockbroker. On December 27, 2001, Bacanovic executed a sale of all of Stewart's shares in ImClone. The next day, ImClone publicly announced that the government did not approve Erbitux. ImClone's stock price dropped instantly. By selling her shares before the official announcement, Stewart avoided losses of $45,673.

Stewart was not convicted of using this insider information. However, she was accused of lying to investigators, stating that she did not recall anyone telling her that Waksal was selling his stock. Stewart was convicted of obstruction of justice and served five months in prison.

ACTIVITY

Blanchard Corporation's common stock is traded publicly. To avoid any appearance of insider trading, Blanchard has a code of conduct that restricts how its employees can buy and sell its stock. Employees may only purchase Blanchard stock by scheduling monthly purchases, thus avoiding any appearance of using insider information to make purchase decisions. Employees must provide a 30-day written notice of their intent to sell any of their shares. These rules apply to the employees and members of their immediate family.

Blanchard's internal auditors have obtained from its stock agent a listing of all stock transactions during the past fiscal year. The list does not include scheduled employee purchases. No employees submitted written requests for the sale of stock.

INSTRUCTIONS

Open the spreadsheet FA_CH11 and complete the steps on the Instructions tab. Write an e-mail to the chief financial officer, describing any information that seems to indicate that an employee used insider information to execute stock trades.

Source: www.sec.gov/news/press/2003-69.htm.

TERMS REVIEW

treasury stock

buyback

Audit your understanding LO4, 5

1. What is the normal balance of the Treasury Stock account?
2. What often causes a corporation to authorize a buyback?
3. How do remaining stockholders benefit from a buyback?
4. How does treasury stock affect the amount of dividends paid by the corporation?

Work together 11-2 LO5

Journalizing treasury stock transactions

Journalize each transaction completed during the current year. Page 12 of a cash receipts journal and page 2 of a cash payments journal are provided in the *Working Papers*. Source documents are abbreviated as follows: check, C; receipt, R. Your instructor will guide you through the following examples.

Transactions:

Jan. 25. Paid cash to Mike Straton for 400 shares of $1.00 par-value common stock at $16.00 per share, $6,400.00. C688.

May 7. Received cash from Patti Edwards for 200 shares of treasury stock at $16.50 per share, $3,300.00. R456.

19. Received cash from Kathryn Welch for 50 shares of treasury stock at $15.00 per share, $750.00. R468.

On your own 11-2 LO5

Journalizing treasury stock transactions

Journalize each transaction completed during the current year. Page 16 of a cash receipts journal and page 4 of a cash payments journal are provided in the *Working Papers*. Source documents are abbreviated as follows: check, C; receipt, R. Work independently to complete the following problem.

Transactions:

Feb. 14. Paid cash to Jill Goforth for 3,000 shares of $10.00 stated-value common stock at $24.00 per share, $72,000.00. C554.

Aug. 2. Received cash from Chandra Gunter for 600 shares of treasury stock at $24.50 per share, $14,700.00. R732.

13. Received cash from Dewey Jaynes for 300 shares of treasury stock at $23.25 per share, $6,975.00. R748.

LO6 Journalize the purchase and sale of the capital stock of other corporations.

Investing in the Stock of Other Corporations LO6

A corporation that earns a net income usually generates a positive cash flow. The corporation must decide what to do with the cash. Alternative uses of the cash include reinvesting in the business, paying a dividend, or reducing liabilities.

A period often exists between the time a corporation generates the cash and when the cash will be used. During this time, the corporation should attempt to earn a return on its cash assets. Depositing the cash in a bank is an easy and safe method to earn interest. A corporation can also make a temporary investment by purchasing the capital stock of another corporation.

Purchasing Marketable Securities

														CASH PAYMENTS JOURNAL												PAGE 2	
									1				2			3			4			5		
	DATE		ACCOUNT TITLE		CK. NO.	POST. REF.	GENERAL						ACCOUNTS PAYABLE DEBIT			PURCHASES DISCOUNT CREDIT			CASH CREDIT			
							DEBIT			CREDIT													
4	Jan. 23	Marketable Securities		268		52 0 0 0 00												52 0 0 0 00					4
5																						5
6																						6

Debit Marketable Securities   Credit Cash

The purchase of the capital stock of another corporation is recorded in the account Marketable Securities. This account is a current asset that has a normal debit balance. Forest uses Marketable Securities to account for short-term investments and Investment Securities to account for long-term investments.

> **January 23.** Purchased 2,000 shares of Ellisville Steel at the current market price of $26.00 per share, $52,000.00. Check No. 268.

Marketable Securities

| Debit Increases | Credit Decreases |

Forest Equipment, Inc., has excess cash it intends to use to purchase new store equipment. However, the equipment will not be purchased for several months. Thus, Forest decides to make a temporary investment in the stock market. After an evaluation of alternative investments, the board of directors approved the purchase of the common stock of Ellisville Steel. On the date of purchase, the market price of the stock is $26.00 per share.

The debit to Marketable Securities is the number of shares purchased, 2,000, multiplied by the market price of the stock, $26.00. Cash is credited for the total amount of the purchase, $52,000.00.

Purchasing the capital stock of publicly held corporations is a common method of investing excess cash. The corporation can sell its investment quickly and easily on a national stock exchange.

Business Combinations

The primary goal of a business is to earn a profit for its owners. The amount of profit is expected to increase over time. To accomplish this goal, a business can adopt one or more of the following strategies:

1. Expand its market by introducing new products or services in new geographic areas.
2. Expand its physical operations with new manufacturing plants, distribution centers, and or retail stores.
3. Minimize product costs and operating expenses.

One way of implementing these profit-optimizing strategies is for two businesses to combine their operations. Businesses of any size and structure can enter into a business combination. A common combination involves two sole proprietors forming a partnership. The partners share expertise to provide more goods and services to customers while reducing operating expenses such as utilities and advertising. Thus, the synergy of the two businesses operating as one should produce financial results greater than what businesses could achieve operating independently.

The business combinations reported by financial news sources typically involve publicly-held corporations. Most business combinations occur when the board of directors of one corporation, referred to as the acquirer, submits a combination offer to the board of another corporation, referred to as the target. A board of directors continually should be alert to combination opportunities that enable the corporation to maximize value for its stockholders.

MERGERS AND ACQUISITIONS

Three methods of structuring a business combination exist.

- **Statutory merger** The combination of two corporations where only one corporation continues as a legal entity. The acquirer obtains the assets and assumes the liabilities of the target. Target stockholders sell their stock to the acquirer for a combination of cash and acquirer stock. The target is then dissolved.

- **Statutory consolidation** The combining of two independent corporations into a new single entity. Stockholders of each corporation surrender its stock in exchange for stock in the new corporation. The two original corporations are then dissolved.

- **Acquisition** The combination of two corporations where the acquirer purchases a significant percentage of the target's stock. Each corporation continues to operate independently and retains its corporate structure. The level of the acquirer's ownership influences the degree that it can influence the operations of the acquired corporation. By achieving a majority of the target's stock, the acquirer gains complete control of the target's operations.

HOSTILE TAKEOVERS

The combination of two corporations is a complex process. Changes must be made in the management structure, computer systems, production methods, sales strategies, etc. This process is simplified when each corporation recognizes the advantage of the combination. Unfortunately, in some cases, the target's board of directors may not believe that the terms of the acquirer's offer provides adequate value to its stockholders. A business combination achieved without the approval of the board of directors of the target corporation is referred to as a *hostile takeover*.

When the target's board of directors votes against the combination, the acquirer may contact the stockholders directly. An offer extended to a target corporation's stockholders to purchase their stock is referred to as a *tender offer*. The tender offer price is typically significantly above the market price, thus enticing stockholders to surrender their stock against the recommendation of management.

A hostile takeover is not the ideal path to completing a merger or acquisition. As the quantity of available stock declines and word of a possible takeover become common knowledge, the acquirer will often be forced to pay a higher price for the target's stock. The target's management is less likely to continue with the acquirer, resulting in lost expertise and leadership.

INSTRUCTIONS

Identify two publicly-traded corporations that you believe could benefit from a business combination. Assuming the role of the chief executive officer (CEO) of the acquirer, write a letter to the CEO of the target inviting the CEO of a target to enter into negotiations for a business combination. What form of business combination would you recommend?

Receiving a Dividend on a Marketable Security

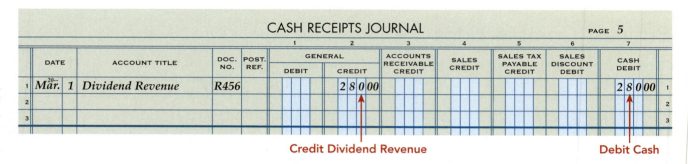

CASH RECEIPTS JOURNAL   PAGE 5

	DATE	ACCOUNT TITLE	DOC. NO.	POST. REF.	GENERAL DEBIT	GENERAL CREDIT	ACCOUNTS RECEIVABLE CREDIT	SALES CREDIT	SALES TAX PAYABLE CREDIT	SALES DISCOUNT DEBIT	CASH DEBIT	
1	Mar. 1	Dividend Revenue	R456			2 8 0 00					2 8 0 00	1
2												2
3												3

Credit Dividend Revenue   Debit Cash

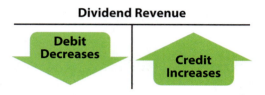

Dividend Revenue

Debit Decreases | Credit Increases

Like individual stockholders, a corporation may receive a dividend on capital stock owned as a temporary investment. Dividends earned on marketable securities are recorded in Dividend Revenue. This account is classified as an other revenue account and has a normal credit balance.

The credit to Dividend Revenue is the number of shares owned, 2,000, multiplied by the dividend per share, $0.14. Cash is debited for the amount received, $280.00.

> March 1. Forest Equipment received a $0.14 per share dividend on its 2,000 shares of Ellisville Steel, $280.00. Receipt No. 456.

Dividend Revenue | 280.00

Cash | 280.00

THINK LIKE AN ACCOUNTANT

Evaluating a Stock Buyback Program

A corporation must make important decisions, such as how to spend the cash generated from earning net income. Many corporations invest the cash in additional plant assets to expand the business. Others use the cash to pay down long-term liabilities. Cash is also used to pay dividends.

Hillman Corporation recently sold its international operations, resulting in a one-time increase in cash. After fully funding its expansion plans, reducing the level of debt, and paying annual dividends, Hillman Corporation still has $40 million more than its normal cash balance. The board of directors is meeting to debate what, if anything, should be done with this unusual amount of available cash. One idea that has been suggested is for the corporation to implement its first stock buyback program.

The board of directors has requested an analysis of the impact of a $20 million buyback or using $20 million to increase the annual dividend.

OPEN THE SPREADSHEET TLA_CH11

The worksheet contains the structure required to prepare the analysis. Follow the steps on the Instructions tab to create the formulas required to calculate the requested information. Answer these questions:

1. How many shares of stock could be repurchased?

2. What effect would the buyback have on the current amount of the total annual dividends?

3. The board has expressed concern over increasing the dividend above a level it could not sustain for at least eight years. Recommend a new amount for the annual dividend.

Selling a Marketable Security

Credit Marketable Securities

	DATE	ACCOUNT TITLE	DOC. NO.	POST. REF.	1 GENERAL DEBIT	2 GENERAL CREDIT	3 ACCOUNTS RECEIVABLE CREDIT	4 SALES CREDIT	5 SALES TAX PAYABLE CREDIT	6 SALES DISCOUNT DEBIT	7 CASH DEBIT	
10	May 4	Marketable Securities	R677			52 0 0 0 00					54 4 0 0 00	10
11		Gain on Sale of Investments				2 4 0 0 00						11
12												12

CASH RECEIPTS JOURNAL — PAGE 9

Credit Gain on Sale of Investments   **Debit Cash**

Gain on Sale of Investments

Debit Decreases | **Credit Increases**

A corporation sells its temporary investments when cash is needed for use in the business. Any gain on the sale of marketable securities is recorded in Gain on Sale of Investments. The account is classified as an other revenue account and has a normal credit balance.

Any loss from the sale of temporary investments would be recorded in Loss on Sale of Investments.

Forest Equipment is beginning its purchase of new store equipment. Since the common stock of Ellisville Steel has reached its highest market price of the year, Forest decides to sell its shares in the corporation.

The credit to Marketable Securities is the original purchase price of the stock, $52,000.00. The stock was sold for $27.20 per share, a $1.20 gain over the original cost of $26.00 per share. The resulting gain of $2,400.00 is credited to Gain on Sale of Investments. Cash is debited for the amount received, $54,400.00.

> **May 4. Forest Equipment sold its investment in Ellisville Steel, 2,000 shares at $27.20 per share, $54,400.00. Receipt 677.**

Marketable Securities

Purchased	52,000.00	Sold	52,000.00
(New Balance	0.00)		

Gain on Sale of Investments

		Sold	2,400.00

Cash

Sold	54,400.00		

© TRAVIS WOLFE/SHUTTERSTOCK.COM

LO6 Journalize the purchase and sale of the capital stock of other corporations.

Audit your understanding LO6

1. Why would a corporation purchase the capital stock of another corporation?
2. How is the account Marketable Securities classified?
3. How is the account Dividend Revenue classified?
4. How is the account Gain on Sale of Investments classified?

Work together 11-3 LO6

Journalizing the purchase and sale of the capital stock of other corporations

MPL Industries has decided to purchase stock of Rowen Corporation as a temporary investment of excess cash.

Journalize each transaction completed during the current year. Page 3 of a cash payments journal and page 8 of a cash receipts journal are provided in the *Working Papers*. Source documents are abbreviated as follows: check, C; receipt, R. Your instructor will guide you through the following examples.

Transactions:

Feb. 8. MPL purchased 3,000 shares of Rowen Corporation at $16.80 per share, $50,400.00. C258.

Apr. 2. Received a $0.12 per share cash dividend from Rowen Corporation, $360.00. R322.

June 13. MPL sold its 3,000 shares of Rowen Corporation for $19.40 per share, $58,200.00. R367.

On your own 11-3 LO6

Journalizing the purchase and sale of the capital stock of other corporations

Keller Mining's board of directors approved the use of excess cash to purchase stock in HPC Equipment.

Journalize each transaction completed during the current year. Page 1 of a cash payments journal and page 6 of a cash receipts journal are provided in the *Working Papers*. Source documents are abbreviated as follows: check, C; receipt, R. Work this problem independently.

Transactions:

Jan. 23. Keller Mining purchased 700 shares of HPC Equipment with a current market price of $56.25 per share, $39,375.00. C456.

Mar. 15. Received a $0.25 per share cash dividend from HPC Equipment, $175.00. R443.

May 22. Keller Mining sold all of its shares of HPC Equipment for $62.90 per share, $44,030.00. R532.

Stock Splits

The method for trading stock has changed dramatically since 1990. The Internet led to the founding of numerous online trading sites allowing individual investors to trade any number of shares for a fixed fee. Despite these changes, many corporations continue to manage their stock prices. At a point during 2018, the average stock price of the 30 stocks comprising the Dow Jones Industrial Average was $112.

To reduce the market price, a corporation can increase the number of shares outstanding by dividing each outstanding share into two or more shares. Dividing a share of stock into a larger number of shares is called a **stock split**. In a 2-for-1 stock split, the company doubles the number of shares and reduces each share's par value by half. Thus, an investor holding 100 shares of $10 par-value stock then owns 200 shares of $5 par-value stock. More importantly, the market price of the stock, once at $60 per share, immediately drops to $30 per share.

Similar to a stock dividend, a stock split does not increase stockholders' ownership in the company and the value of their investment. Before the stock split, the investor owned 100 shares of $60 stock valued at $6,000. After the stock split, the investor owns 200 shares of $30 stock, also valued at $6,000. Because all stockholders now own twice the number of shares, each investor's percentage ownership in the corporation remains the same.

Stock split information is available from a variety of sources. The following stock split information for The Coca-Cola Company was obtained from the Investor Relations section of its website.

HISTORY OF STOCK SPLITS FOR THE COCA-COLA COMPANY

Record Date	Activity	Cumulative Shares
07/27/2012	2-for-1 Stock Split	9,216
05/01/1996	2-for-1 Stock Split	4,608
05/01/1992	2-for-1 Stock Split	2,304
05/01/1990	2-for-1 Stock Split	1,152
06/16/1986	3-for-1 Stock Split	576
05/09/1977	2-for-1 Stock Split	192
05/13/1968	2-for-1 Stock Split	96
01/22/1965	2-for-1 Stock Split	48
01/22/1960	3-for-1 Stock Split	24
11/15/1935	4-for-1 Stock Split	8
04/25/1927	1-for-1 Stock Dividend	2
09/05/1919		1

Source: www.coca-colacompany.com/investors/stock-history/investors-info-splits.

Suppose an investor purchased 100 shares of The Cola-Cola Company on March 1, 1990, for $73.60 per share.

Assuming a current market price of $50 per share, the 100 shares initially purchased for $7,360 are now worth $80,000 ($50 × 1,600).

Without any stock splits, the 100 shares would likely have a market price $800 per share ($80,000/100 shares) with a cost basis of $73.60 per share.

Record Date	Split	Number of Shares	Cost Basis	Total Cost
07/27/2012	2-for-1	1,600	$ 4.60	$7,360
05/01/1996	2-for-1	800	$ 9.20	$7,360
05/01/1992	2-for-1	400	$18.40	$7,360
05/01/1990	2-for-1	200	$36.80	$7,360
Initial investment		100	$73.60	$7,360

INSTRUCTIONS

Assume an investor purchased 100 shares of The Coca-Cola Company on July 1, 1985, for $72.00 per share. Determine the current value of the shares, assuming a $50.00 market price. How many shares would the investor own?

CHAPTER SUMMARY

A cash dividend distributes a corporation's earnings to its stockholders. A corporation incurs a liability when the board of directors declares a dividend. Stockholders who own the stock on the date of record receive the dividend. A stock dividend results in the issuance of additional shares of stock, but does not provide stockholders with anything of value. A corporation may issue a stock dividend to reduce the stock's market price.

Treasury stock is a corporation's own stock that has been issued and reacquired. A corporation may approve a program to buy treasury stock if it believes that its stock is undervalued by the stock market. Treasury stock may later be sold. Any gain or loss from the sale of treasury stock is recorded in stockholders' equity.

A corporation may make a temporary investment in the capital stock of another corporation. Dividends earned and any gain from the sale of the investment are classified as other revenue on the income statement.

APPLY YOUR UNDERSTANDING

INSTRUCTIONS: Download problem instructions for Excel, QuickBooks, and Sage 50c from the textbook companion website at www.C21accounting.com.

11-1 Application Problem — Journalizing dividend transactions LO1, 2

On January 1 of the current year, Southeast Supply had 5,000 shares of 6%, $100.00 par-value preferred stock and 200,000 shares of $10.00 par-value common stock outstanding.

Instructions:

Journalize each transaction completed during the current year. Page 1 of a general journal and page 2 of a cash payments journal are provided in the *Working Papers*. Source documents are abbreviated as follows: check, C; memorandum, M.

Transactions:

Jan. 1. The board of directors declared a quarterly cash dividend of $40,000.00, payable on January 31. M3.

      31. Paid the January 1 dividend. C223.

Apr. 1. The board of directors raised its quarterly cash dividend to $42,000.00, payable on April 30. M23.

      30. Paid the April 1 dividend. C345.

May 15. The board of directors declared a 2% stock dividend on common stock. The market price of the common stock on May 15 was $84.00. M78.

June 15. Issued the May 15 stock dividend. M93.

11-2 Application Problem — Journalizing treasury stock transactions LO5

HPT Corporation has 50,000 shares of $1.00 par stock outstanding.

Instructions:

Journalize each transaction completed during the current year. Page 12 of a cash receipts journal and page 2 of a cash payments journal are provided in the *Working Papers*. Source documents are abbreviated as follows: check, C; receipt, R.

Transactions:

Jan. 6. Paid cash to Debra Joiner for 600 shares of common stock at $24.00 per share, $14,400.00. C325.

June 2. Received cash from Imani Locke for 200 shares of treasury stock at $24.60 per share, $4,920.00. R628.

      12. Received cash from Bernard Laws for 100 shares of treasury stock at $23.80 per share, $2,380.00. R634.

      29. Received cash from Lynda Lann for 150 shares of treasury stock at $24.90 per share, $3,735.00. R651.

11-3 Application Problem

Journalizing the purchase and sale of the capital stock of other corporations LO6

SkyFore Corporation invests excess cash in the stock market.

Instructions:

Journalize each transaction completed during the current year. Page 15 of a cash payments journal and page 10 of a cash receipts journal are provided in the *Working Papers*. Source documents are abbreviated as follows: check, C; receipt, R.

Transactions:

Aug. 30. SkyFore purchased 1,100 shares of Plancing Corporation for $35.40 per share, $38,940.00. C664.

Oct. 15. Received a $0.60 per share cash dividend from Plancing Corporation, $660.00. R621.

Nov. 3. SkyFore sold all of its shares of Plancing Corporation at the current market price of $36.50 per share, $40,150.00. R764.

11-M Mastery Problem

Journalizing dividend, treasury stock, and investment transactions LO1, 2, 5, 6

sage 50

1. Journalize and post corporate dividend and treasury stock transactions to the cash disbursements journal.
2. Journalize and post stock dividend transactions to the general journal.
3. Print the cash disbursements journal, cash receipts journal, and general journal.

QB Quick Books

1. Journalize and post corporate dividend and treasury stock transactions in the Write Checks window.
2. Journalize and post stock dividend transactions to the journal.
3. Print the check detail and journal.

X

1. Journalize corporate stock dividend and treasury stock transactions to the general, cash payments, and cash receipts journals.
2. Print the spreadsheets.

TA Post Corporation has 35,000 shares of $1.00 stated-value common stock and 250 shares of 8%, $100.00 par-value preferred stock outstanding.

Instructions:

Journalize each transaction completed during the current year. Page 4 of a general journal, page 6 of a cash receipts journal, and page 7 of a cash payments journal are provided in the *Working Papers*. Source documents are abbreviated as follows: check, C; memorandum, M; receipt, R.

Transactions:

July 1. The board of directors declared a quarterly cash dividend of $3,000.00, payable on July 31. M22.

31. Paid the July 1 dividend. C55.

Aug. 6. The board of directors declared a 1% stock dividend on common stock. An independent appraisal service has estimated that the common stock has a market value of $16.50 on August 6. M31.

9. Purchased 300 shares of MXZ Corporation for $52.00 per share, $15,600.00. C68.

23. Paid cash to Darius Henderson for 250 shares of the corporation's common stock at $17.00 per share, $4,250.00. C79.

Sept. 6. Issued the August 6 stock dividend. M42.

30. Received a $0.38 per share cash dividend from MXZ Corporation, $114.00. R69.

Oct. 12. Sold all of its shares of MXZ Corporation for $54.30 per share, $16,290.00. R81.

25. Received cash from Tatyanna Jamley for 150 shares of treasury stock at $19.00 per share, $2,850.00. R92.

sage 50

1. Journalize and post corporate dividend and treasury stock transactions to the cash disbursements journal.
2. Journalize and post stock dividend transactions to the general journal.
3. Print the cash disbursements journal, cash receipts journal, and general journal.

QB
Quick Books

1. Journalize and post corporate dividend and treasury stock transactions in the Write Checks window.
2. Journalize and post stock dividend transactions to the journal.
3. Print the check detail and journal.

[X]

1. Journalize corporate stock dividend and treasury stock transactions to the general, cash payments, and cash receipts journals.
2. Print the spreadsheets.

KCL Stores began the current year with the following capital stock outstanding: 82,000 shares of $1.00 par-value common stock and 12,000 shares of 7.5%, $50.00 par-value preferred stock. KCL's preferred stock has the right to receive unpaid dividends from previous quarters before common stockholders can share in any future cash dividends.

Instructions:

Journalize the following transactions. Page 1 of a general journal, page 4 of a cash receipts journal, and page 3 of a cash payments journal are provided in the *Working Papers*. Source documents are abbreviated as follows: check, C; memorandum, M; receipt, R.

Transactions:

Jan.	5.	The board of directors, concerned over the company's cash flows, decided to limit the quarterly dividend to $10,000.00, payable on January 31. M4.
	5.	The board of directors declared a 5% stock dividend on common stock. An independent appraisal service estimated that the common stock has a market value of $62.50 on January 5. M31.
	31.	Paid the January 5 cash dividend. C298.
Feb.	2.	Issued the January 5 stock dividend. M42.
Apr.	1.	With cash flow problems continuing, the board of directors decided to suspend any dividends during the current quarter.
	2.	Received cash for the sale of 3,000 shares of preferred stock for $52.00 per share, $156,000.00. R234.
July	1.	The board of directors decided to resume a quarterly cash dividend, declaring a $25,000.00 dividend payable on July 31. M62.
	31.	Paid the July 1 cash dividend. C334.
Oct.	1.	The board of directors declared a quarterly cash dividend of $25,000.00, payable on October 31. M83.
	31.	Paid the October 1 cash dividend. C456.

Build Wealth DRIP by DRIP

Theme: Financial, Economic, Business, and Entrepreneurial Literacy

Skills: Critical Thinking and Problem Solving, Information Literacy, Creativity and Innovation, and Communication and Collaboration

PARTNERSHIP FOR
21ST CENTURY SKILLS

Many corporations sell stock only through brokers, with a hefty minimum investment and service charges. However, many quality corporations offer direct stock purchase plans (DSPP). An individual share of stock can be purchased from the company with minimal or no fees and commissions. It is not uncommon for this transaction to be administered by a third party, hired by the company. DSPP are regulated by the Securities and Exchange Commission (SEC), similar to stock purchases handled by brokerage firms. This makes investing more affordable for those with small amounts of money to invest. The company benefits by being able to attract those investors who don't have large sums to invest.

Another program that an investor can participate in is direct reinvestment programs (DRIPS). Instead of receiving cash dividends, over one thousand companies offer DRIPS. DRIPS allow the investor to reinvest cash dividends by purchasing additional company stock. The investor can watch his or her shares and investment grow.

DSPP and DRIPS are ideal for young people just starting to invest. With very little money, one can learn the value of investing through these programs.

APPLICATION

1. Using the Internet, find three companies that offer direct stock plans. List the names of the companies, the minimum initial purchase, the minimum purchase, the maximum purchase, and the fees, if any, to purchase the stock.

2. Using the Internet, research DSPP and DRIPS. What are the conditions for a minor (someone under age 18) to purchase a share of stock?

3. Create a public service announcement using print or video to educate young investors about DSPP and DRIPS. Be sure to include the names of at least three companies that offer these plans and that would also be familiar to students.

Analyzing Home Depot's Financial Statements

A corporation's board of directors decides the dividend policy for the corporation. Home Depot has paid a quarterly dividend since 1987. During fiscal year 2017, Home Depot raised its fourth quarter dividend from $0.89 to $1.03 per share.

A ratio of interest to stockholders is the dividend yield. It is calculated as the dividend per share divided by the market price per share.

INSTRUCTIONS

1. Use Home Depot's Consolidated Balance Sheets in Appendix B on page B-5 to determine the number of shares of common stock issued and outstanding as of January 28, 2018.

2. In fiscal year 2017, Home Depot's board of directors declared dividends of $3.56 per share of common stock. Using the number of shares of common stock that were issued and outstanding at the end of fiscal year 2017, estimate the total dividends Home Depot would have paid that year.

3. Use Home Depot's Consolidated Statements of Cash Flows, on page B-9, and locate the dollar amount of cash dividends actually paid during fiscal year 2017. How does your amount of total dividends calculated in part (2) compare with the actual cash dividends paid? Why do you think the two amounts are different?

4. During fiscal year 2017, Home Depot's stock reached a high of $207.23 per share. Use this market price to determine the dividend yield for fiscal year 2017.

12

Accounting for Bonds

LEARNING OBJECTIVES

After studying Chapter 12, in addition to defining key terms, you will be able to:

LO1 Explain why and how a corporation issues bonds.

LO2 Journalize the issue of bonds at a discount and at a premium.

LO3 Journalize interest payments for bonds issued at a discount and a premium.

LO4 Journalize the retiring of a bond issue.

LO5 Journalize the early redemption of a bond issue.

LO6 Explain how to account for convertible bonds.

LO7 Journalize the purchase of an investment in bonds.

LO8 Journalize the receipt of interest on bonds purchased at a discount and a premium.

LO9 Journalize the sale of a bond investment.

© BLEAKSTAR/SHUTTERSTOCK.COM

Port of New Orleans

ACCOUNTING IN THE REAL WORLD

© ED METZ/SHUTTERSTOCK.COM

By the late 18th century the Spanish colony of Louisiana had become a significant entry point for goods. New Orleans's location at the mouth of the Mississippi River provided a cost-effective transportation method for the import and export of commodities within the heartland of a growing United States. When a treaty with Spain that allowed free passage through the Port of New Orleans expired in 1798, Americans in the country's interior complained that they could not survive without access to the port. The problem was solved when, in 1803, the United States purchased Louisiana from France.

Today the Port of New Orleans continues to be a significant port of entry for goods that will be transported to the middle of the United States. The port moves over 36 million tons of cargo each year. It also serves as a point of departure for cruise ships that serve more than one million passengers annually.

The Port of New Orleans is an independent government agency within the state of Louisiana. It is governed by a board of commissioners that acts similarly to the board of directors of a corporation. And just like a corporation, the port frequently needs to borrow money to expand its operations.

One source of funds for expansions are notes called revenue bonds. Revenue bonds are issued by a government agency to finance income-producing projects such as a cruise terminal. The funds can be used for the specified purpose only, and the revenue from the project must be used to pay interest and principal on the notes. In many cases, the stated purpose of the funds is to pay off revenue bonds issued at higher interest rates. These notes typically have terms of 20 years or more. In recent years the port has issued several revenue bonds.

CRITICAL THINKING

1. What advantage is gained by the Port of New Orleans operating independently of the State of Louisiana?

2. What role do accountants have in the decision to finance the port's expansions using revenue bonds?

Source: www.portnola.com.

KEY TERMS

bond	bond amortization	call option
bond issue	carrying value	callable bond
face value	retiring a bond issue	institutional investors
stated interest rate	term bonds	
effective interest rate	serial bonds	

LO1 Explain why and how a corporation issues bonds.

LO2 Journalize the issue of bonds at a discount and at a premium.

Corporate Bonds Payable LO1

For a growing business, the capital needed to expand may come from three sources:

1. Using retained earnings.
2. Issuing additional capital stock.
3. Borrowing the funds.

A business's management team may find that capital needed for expansion could be accumulated from retained net income during the next five to ten years. However, the business may need the additional capital within the next year. A corporation's board of directors must decide whether to raise the needed capital by issuing additional stock or by borrowing the money.

An advantage of issuing stock is that the additional capital becomes part of a corporation's permanent capital. Permanent capital does not have to be returned to stockholders as long as the business continues to operate. Another advantage is that dividends do not have to be paid to stockholders unless the earnings are sufficient to warrant such payments. A disadvantage of issuing more stock to raise additional capital is that the ownership is spread over more shares and more owners.

An advantage of borrowing the additional capital is that stockholders' equity is not spread over additional shares of stock. A disadvantage is that interest must be paid on the loan, which decreases the net income. This decrease in net income decreases the amount available for dividends.

Another disadvantage of borrowing additional capital is that the amount borrowed must be repaid in the future.

Large loans are sometimes difficult to obtain for short periods. Corporations frequently borrow needed capital with the provision that the loan be repaid several years in the future. Therefore, the loan can be paid out of future earnings accumulated over several years.

Large loans may also be difficult to obtain from one bank or one individual. A long-term promise to pay a specified amount on a specified date and to pay interest at stated intervals is called a **bond**. Bonds are similar to notes payable because both are written promises to pay. However, most notes payable are for one year or less, but bonds generally run for a long period of time, such as 5, 10, or 20 years. Also, bonds payable tend to be issued for larger amounts than notes payable.

All bonds representing the total amount of a loan are called a **bond issue**. A corporation usually sells an entire bond issue to a securities dealer, who sells individual bonds to the public.

Comparison of Capital Stock and Bonds as a Source of Corporate Capital

Decisions of how to obtain capital can impact a corporation's future significantly. A board of directors must consider the short- and long-term impact of the following qualities of capital stock and bonds:

	Capital Stock	Bonds
Status of security holder	Corporate owners	Creditors
Account classification	Stockholders' equity	Liability
Claim on corporate assets	Secondary claim	Primary claim
Nature of periodic payments	Dividends	Interest expense
Requirement to make periodic payments	Optional, subject to adequate net income and board approval	Required; payment of interest does not depend on net income
Length of access to capital	Permanent unless corporation implements a buyback plan	Must be repaid to the bondholders on the bonds' maturity date

Issuing Bonds Payable LO2

It can take several months for a company to issue bonds. The registration process begins when the company determines what type of security it will issue. Public accountants are hired to audit the information that will be included in the registration statement filed with the Securities and Exchange Commission. The amount to be paid to a bondholder at the bond maturity date is called the **face value**. The face value is also known as *par value*, *principal*, or *maturity value*. The rate of interest used to calculate periodic interest payments on a bond is called the **stated interest rate**.

As the registration process nears conclusion, the corporation will decide on the number, face value, interest rate, and term of the bonds. The company must then arrange for a securities dealer, known as an *underwriter*, to sell the bonds. This final process may require several weeks.

A corporation will attempt to assign a stated interest rate that approximates the current market rate of interest. That rate, however, rarely equals the market interest rate on the day the bonds are issued. Two factors cause this difference. Unlike market interest rates, the stated interest rate is often a rounded percentage, such as 6.0%, 6.5%, or 7.0%. During the final weeks of the registration process, market interest rates can be expected to change.

Investors will adjust the price they are willing to pay for the bond, based on the current market interest rate. If the market interest rate is above the stated interest rate, investors are not willing to pay full price for a bond that yields a below-market rate. Thus, the bond will be issued at a discount. However, if the market interest rate is below the stated interest rate, investors are willing to pay extra to earn an above-market rate. This bond will be issued at a premium.

Issuing Bonds at a Discount

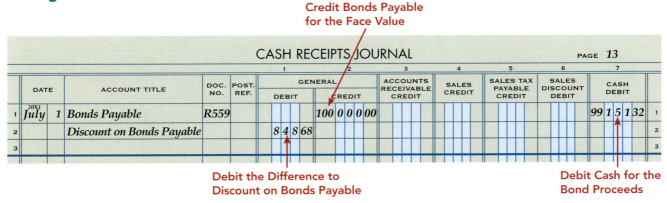

Credit Bonds Payable for the Face Value

Debit the Difference to Discount on Bonds Payable

Debit Cash for the Bond Proceeds

A securities dealer purchases the bonds at a price that yields the market interest rate. As a result, the bonds are almost always issued for an amount above or below the bonds' face value. Regardless of the amount received, the face value of the bonds is credited to Bonds Payable. Bonds issued for an amount below the face value are accounted for using a contra account, Discount on Bonds Payable. Because it is a contra account to a liability account, Discount on Bonds Payable has a normal debit balance.

Discount on Bonds Payable

| Debit Increases | Credit Decreases |

Forest Equipment issued bonds to finance the expansion of its store. The market interest rate on the bond issue date was above the bonds' stated interest rate.

July 1, 20X1. Received cash for 100 five-year, 6.0%, $1,000.00 face-value bonds, issued to yield 6.2%, $99,151.32. Receipt No. 559.

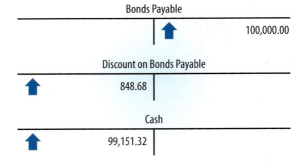

Bonds Payable is credited for $100,000.00, the face value of the bonds. Cash is debited for $99,151.32, the proceeds from the issuance of the bonds. The difference, $848.68, is debited to Discount on Bonds Payable.

Issuing Bonds at a Premium

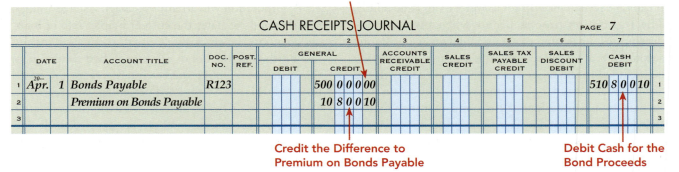

Credit Bonds Payable for the Face Value

Credit the Difference to Premium on Bonds Payable

Debit Cash for the Bond Proceeds

	DATE	ACCOUNT TITLE	DOC. NO.	POST. REF.	GENERAL DEBIT	GENERAL CREDIT	ACCOUNTS RECEIVABLE CREDIT	SALES CREDIT	SALES TAX PAYABLE CREDIT	SALES DISCOUNT DEBIT	CASH DEBIT	
1	Apr. 1	Bonds Payable	R123			500 000 00					510 800 10	1
2		Premium on Bonds Payable				10 800 10						2
3												3

CASH RECEIPTS JOURNAL — PAGE 7

A bond may be issued to yield an interest rate below the market rate. The proceeds from the issue will be greater than the face value of the bonds. Bonds issued for an amount above the face value are accounted for using the account Premium on Bonds Payable. This account has a normal credit balance.

TYP Corporation issued bonds to finance the purchase of a competing corporation. The market interest rate on the bond issue date was below the bonds' stated interest rate.

> April 1. Received cash for 500 five-year, 6.0%, $1,000.00 face-value bonds, issued to yield 5.5%, $510,800.10. Receipt No. 123.

Bonds Payable is credited for $500,000.00, the face value of the bonds. Cash is debited for $510,800.10, the proceeds from the issuance of the bonds.

The difference, $10,800.10, is credited to Premium on Bonds Payable.

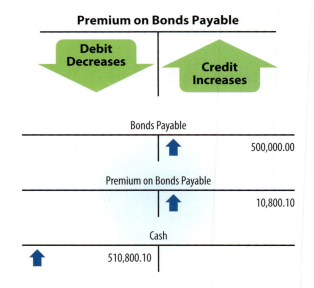

Premium on Bonds Payable

Debit Decreases | Credit Increases

Bonds Payable — 500,000.00

Premium on Bonds Payable — 10,800.10

Cash — 510,800.10

ETHICS IN ACTION

Reporting Ethics Violations

What should employees do when they witness another employee possibly violating a law or the company's code of conduct? Many companies instruct their employees to report the possible violation to an ethics officer or a compliance department. The company may have a phone number or "hotline" that allows an individual to provide confidential information regarding possible ethics violations.

For a hotline to be effective, employees must have confidence that their information is being treated seriously. One way that FedEx achieves this goal is to provide the callers with a control number. Callers can use the control number to receive updates on the status of their reported violation.

INSTRUCTIONS

1. Access the FedEx *Code of Business Conduct and Ethics*. Describe how an employee is instructed to contact the hotline. How is the call answered?

2. Write a script that a hotline employee would use to give callers confidence that their information will remain confidential.

LO1 Explain why and how a corporation issues bonds.

LO2 Journalize the issue of bonds at a discount and at a premium.

TERMS REVIEW

bond
bond issue
face value
stated interest rate

Audit your understanding LO1, 2

1. What are two advantages of raising needed capital by issuing stock?
2. What is an advantage of raising additional capital by borrowing?
3. What is a disadvantage of borrowing additional capital?
4. What are three names for the face value of a bond?
5. What are two reasons why the stated interest rate of a bond will vary from the market interest rate?
6. What amount is recorded in the Bonds Payable account when the bonds are sold at a premium or discount?

Work together 12-1 LO2

Journalizing bond transactions

Journalize the following transactions. Page 7 of a cash receipts journal is provided in the *Working Papers*. Your instructor will guide you through the following examples.

Transactions:

July 1, 20X1.   Received cash for 50 five-year, 7.0%, $5,000.00 face-value bonds, issued to yield 6.7%, $253,142.42. Receipt 291.

July 1, 20X6.   Received cash for 600 five-year, 6.5%, $1,000.00 face-value bonds, issued to yield 6.6%, $595,658.06. Receipt 888.

On your own 12-1 LO2

Journalizing bond transactions

Journalize the following transactions. Page 8 of a cash receipts journal is provided in the *Working Papers*. Work independently to complete the following problem.

Transactions:

July 1, 20X1.   Received cash for 40 five-year, 8.0%, $5,000.00 face-value bonds, issued to yield 8.25%, $197,984.83. Receipt 334.

July 1, 20X6.   Received cash for 300 five-year, 7.5%, $1,000.00 face-value bonds, issued to yield 7.0%, $310,659.31. Receipt 986.

LO3 Journalize interest payments for bonds issued at a discount and a premium.

Journal Entries for Paying Interest on Bonds Payable LO3

Forest Equipment issued $100,000.00 of bonds with a stated interest rate of 6.0%. As with most bonds, Forest is required to pay semiannual interest payments. Forest pays the interest amount to a trustee, who handles the payments to each individual bondholder. The total payment is calculated using the face value of the bonds and the stated interest rate, as shown below.

Calculating Bond Interest

Amortization Schedule					
Face Value: $100,000.00			Bond Proceeds: $99,151.32		
Stated Interest Rate: 6.0%			Effective Interest Rate: 6.2%		
Term of Bonds: 5 years			Bond Discount: $848.68		
Interest Payments: semiannual					
Period	Beginning Carrying Value	Interest Expense	Interest Payment	Amortization of Bond Discount	Ending Carrying Value
1	$99,151.32	$3,073.69	$3,000.00	$73.69	$ 99,225.01
2	99,225.01	3,075.98	3,000.00	75.98	99,300.99
3	99,300.99	3,078.33	3,000.00	78.33	99,379.32
4	99,379.32	3,080.76	3,000.00	80.76	99,460.08
5	99,460.08	3,083.26	3,000.00	83.26	99,543.34
6	99,543.34	3,085.84	3,000.00	85.84	99,629.18
7	99,629.18	3,088.50	3,000.00	88.50	99,717.68
8	99,717.68	3,091.25	3,000.00	91.25	99,808.93
9	99,808.93	3,094.08	3,000.00	94.08	99,903.01
10	99,903.01	3,096.99	3,000.00	96.99	100,000.00

Forest issued its bonds for $99,151.32, an $848.68 discount. The stated interest rate of 6.0% was below the market interest rate on the date the bonds were issued. As a result, investors were not willing to pay the face value for the bonds. The discounted bonds were issued at a price that will earn investors a 6.2% return, the market interest rate on the issue date. The market interest rate at the time bonds are issued is called the **effective interest rate**. When the bonds are retired, the bondholders will receive $848.68 more than they paid for the bonds. This payment, equal to the discount, is the extra interest that enables the bondholders to earn an effective interest rate above the stated interest rate.

Face Value of Bonds	×	Stated Interest Rate	×	Time as Fraction of a Year	=	Interest Payment
$100,000.00	×	6.0%	×	1/2	=	$3,000.00

Generally accepted accounting principles require that a portion of the bond discount or premium be expensed over the term of the bonds. Reducing the amount of a bond discount or premium over time is called **bond amortization**. The face value of a bond adjusted for any unamortized discount or premium is called the **carrying value**.

Interest expense is calculated based on the carrying value of the bonds multiplied by the effective interest rate. The amount of the first semiannual interest expense is calculated below.

The amortization schedule on the previous page shows the changes in the amount of interest expense recognized each period. The amortization of the discount reduces the balance in Discount on Bonds Payable, thus increasing the carrying value of the bonds. The amount of interest expense on bonds issued at a discount will increase each year. At the maturity date of the bonds, the carrying value is equal to the face value of the bonds.

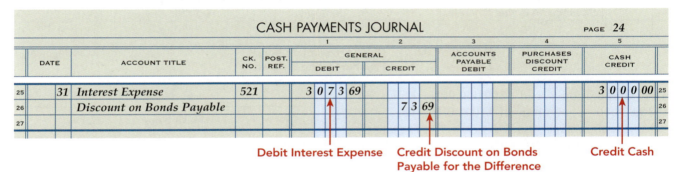

	Carrying Value of Bonds	×	Effective Interest Rate	×	Time as Fraction of a Year	=	Interest Expense
	$99,151.32	×	6.2%	×	1/2	=	$3,073.69

The calculation of interest expense is similar for an installment note payable. The note's carrying value is multiplied by the market rate of interest and fraction of the year to calculate interest expense. The remainder of the periodic payment reduces the carrying value.

Paying Interest on Bonds Issued at a Discount

		CASH PAYMENTS JOURNAL							PAGE 24
					1	2	3	4	5
	DATE	ACCOUNT TITLE	CK. NO.	POST. REF.	GENERAL DEBIT	GENERAL CREDIT	ACCOUNTS PAYABLE DEBIT	PURCHASES DISCOUNT CREDIT	CASH CREDIT
25	31	Interest Expense	521		3 0 7 3 69				3 0 0 0 00	25
26		Discount on Bonds Payable				7 3 69				26
27										27

Debit Interest Expense   Credit Discount on Bonds Payable for the Difference   Credit Cash

Forest Equipment issued its $100,000.00 bonds for $99,151.32. The discount of $848.68 will be amortized over the ten semiannual interest payments. The amortization schedule on the previous page provides the amounts to be recorded for each payment.

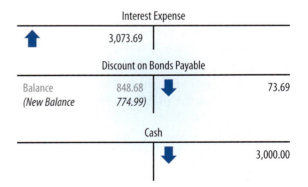

Interest Expense
3,073.69

Discount on Bonds Payable
Balance 848.68   73.69
(New Balance 774.99)

Cash
3,000.00

> **December 31, 20X1.** Paid cash to trustee for first semiannual interest payment on bond issue, $3,000.00. Check No. 521.

Interest Expense is debited for $3,073.69. Discount on Bonds Payable is credited for $73.69. Cash is credited for $3,000.00.

After the interest payment is posted, the new balance of Discount on Bonds Payable is $774.99. The new carrying value of the bonds, $99,225.01, is calculated as shown at the right. The new carrying value matches the ending carrying value for period 1, as shown in the amortization schedule.

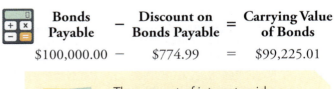

Bonds Payable	−	Discount on Bonds Payable	=	Carrying Value of Bonds
$100,000.00	−	$774.99	=	$99,225.01

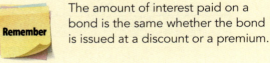

Remember The amount of interest paid on a bond is the same whether the bond is issued at a discount or a premium.

Paying Interest on Bonds Issued at a Premium

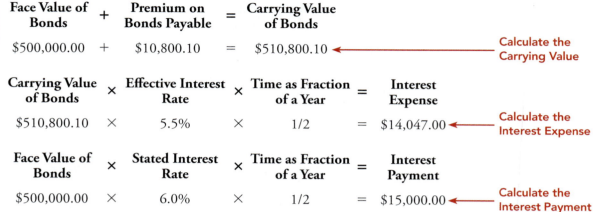

Face Value of Bonds	+	Premium on Bonds Payable	=	Carrying Value of Bonds	
$500,000.00	+	$10,800.10	=	$510,800.10	← Calculate the Carrying Value

Carrying Value of Bonds	×	Effective Interest Rate	×	Time as Fraction of a Year	=	Interest Expense	
$510,800.10	×	5.5%	×	1/2	=	$14,047.00	← Calculate the Interest Expense

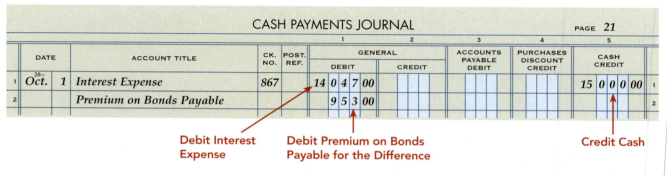

Face Value of Bonds	×	Stated Interest Rate	×	Time as Fraction of a Year	=	Interest Payment	
$500,000.00	×	6.0%	×	1/2	=	$15,000.00	← Calculate the Interest Payment

CASH PAYMENTS JOURNAL

PAGE 21

	DATE	ACCOUNT TITLE	CK. NO.	POST. REF.	GENERAL DEBIT	GENERAL CREDIT	ACCOUNTS PAYABLE DEBIT	PURCHASES DISCOUNT CREDIT	CASH CREDIT	
1	Oct. 1	Interest Expense	867		14 047 00				15 000 00	1
2		Premium on Bonds Payable			953 00					2

Debit Interest Expense   **Debit Premium on Bonds Payable for the Difference**   **Credit Cash**

TYP Corporation issued $500,000.00 of bonds for $510,800.10, a premium of $10,800.10. The 6.0% stated-value bonds were issued to yield 5.5%. The interest expense is calculated using the current carrying value of the bonds, multiplied by the effective interest rate, as shown above.

> **October 1.** Paid cash to trustee for first semiannual interest payment on bond issue, $15,000.00. Check No. 867.

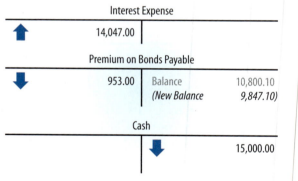

Interest Expense	
14,047.00	

Premium on Bonds Payable		
953.00	Balance	10,800.10
	(New Balance	9,847.10)

Cash	
	15,000.00

When the bonds are issued, their carrying value is the face value plus the premium, or $510,800.10. As shown in the partial amortization schedule below, the carrying value is reduced each period. As a result, the amount of interest expense declines each period.

Amortization Schedule

Face Value:	$500,000.00	Bond Proceeds:	$510,800.10
Stated Interest Rate:	6.0%	Effective Interest Rate:	5.5%
Term of Bonds:	5 years	Bond Premium:	$10,800.10
Interest Payments:	semiannual		

Period	Beginning Carrying Value	Interest Expense	Interest Payment	Amortization of Bond Premium	Ending Carrying Value
1	$510,800.10	$14,047.00	$15,000.00	$ (953.00)	$509,847.10
2	509,847.10	14,020.80	15,000.00	(979.20)	508,867.90
10	501,216.55	13,783.45	15,000.00	(1,216.55)	500,000.00

LO3 Journalize interest payments for bonds issued at a discount and a premium.

TERMS REVIEW

effective interest rate

bond amortization

carrying value

Audit your understanding LO3

1. What is the formula for calculating periodic interest expense on a bond?
2. How does the effective interest rate impact the amount of interest paid on bonds with semiannual interest payments?
3. How does the amount of interest expense change over the term of a bond issued at a discount?
4. How does the amount of the carrying value change over the term of a bond issued at a premium?

Work together 12-2 LO3

Journalizing bond interest payments

Journalize each transaction completed during the current year. Round calculated amounts to two decimal places. Page 20 of a cash payments journal is provided in the *Working Papers*. Your instructor will guide you through the following examples.

Transactions:

June 30. Paid cash to trustee for the semiannual interest payment on a $300,000.00, 6.0% bond issue having a carrying value of $296,190.63 and a 6.3% effective interest rate. Check No. 654.

Dec. 31. Paid cash to trustee for the semiannual interest payment on a $500,000.00, 6.5% bond issue having a carrying value of $506,365.13 and a 6.2% effective interest rate. Check No. 776.

On your own 12-2 LO3

Journalizing bond interest payments

Journalize each transaction completed during the current year. Round calculated amounts to two decimal places. Page 12 of a cash payments journal is provided in the *Working Papers*. Work independently to complete the following problem.

Transactions:

June 30. Paid cash to trustee for the semiannual interest payment on a $400,000.00, 7.0% bond issue having a carrying value of $396,690.07 and a 7.2% effective interest rate. Check No. 543.

Dec. 31. Paid cash to trustee for the semiannual interest payment on a $300,000.00, 6.0% bond issue having a carrying value of $303,868.15 and a 5.7% effective interest rate. Check No. 622.

LO4 Journalize the retiring of a bond issue.

LO5 Journalize the early redemption of a bond issue.

LO6 Explain how to account for convertible bonds.

Retiring a Bond Issue LO4

				CK. NO.	POST. REF.	GENERAL		ACCOUNTS PAYABLE DEBIT	PURCHASES DISCOUNT CREDIT	CASH CREDIT	
	DATE		ACCOUNT TITLE			DEBIT	CREDIT				

CASH PAYMENTS JOURNAL — PAGE 13

Columns: 1 GENERAL DEBIT, 2 GENERAL CREDIT, 3 ACCOUNTS PAYABLE DEBIT, 4 PURCHASES DISCOUNT CREDIT, 5 CASH CREDIT

	DATE	ACCOUNT TITLE	CK. NO.	POST. REF.	GENERAL DEBIT	GENERAL CREDIT	ACCOUNTS PAYABLE DEBIT	PURCHASES DISCOUNT CREDIT	CASH CREDIT	
1	20X6 July 1	Bonds Payable	954		100 0 0 0 00				100 0 0 0 00	1
2										2
3										3

Debit Bonds Payable **Credit Cash**

When Forest's bonds are due, the corporation issues a single check to a trustee for the total maturity value of the bonds. The trustee writes checks to individual bondholders. Paying the amounts owed to bondholders for a bond issue is called **retiring a bond issue**.

> July 1, 20X6. Retired a bond issue at its face value, $100,000.00. Check No. 954.

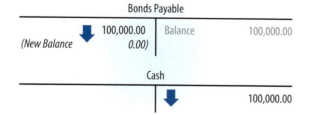

Bonds Payable

(New Balance	100,000.00 0.00)	Balance	100,000.00

Cash

			100,000.00

Bonds Payable is debited for $100,000.00, the total amount of the bond issue. Cash is credited for $100,000.00. After this entry is posted, Bonds Payable has a zero balance.

All of Forest's bond issue matures on the same date. Bonds that all mature on the same date are called **term bonds**. Sometimes portions of a bond issue mature on different dates. Portions of a bond issue that mature on different dates are called **serial bonds**. For example, a 10-year bond issue with one-tenth of the bonds maturing every year is a serial bond issue. An advantage of serial bonds is that interest does not have to be paid on the total bond issue for the total 10 years.

Calling a Bond Issue at a Loss LO5

A corporation can benefit from having the legal right to repurchase outstanding bonds. The right of a corporation to repurchase its security for a specified price is called a **call option**. A bond that can be called before its maturity date is called a **callable bond**.

A corporation sets the stated interest rate of a bond issue to approximate the current market interest rates. Without a call option, the corporation is obligated to pay the stated interest rate for the term of the bond. If market interest rates increase, the corporation benefits

Debit Bonds Payable

	DATE		ACCOUNT TITLE	CK. NO.	POST. REF.	GENERAL		ACCOUNTS PAYABLE DEBIT	PURCHASES DISCOUNT CREDIT	CASH CREDIT	
						DEBIT	CREDIT				
1	20-- July	1	Bonds Payable	622		500 0 0 0 00				525 0 0 0 00	1
2			Discount on Bonds Payable				20 0 0 0 00				2
3			Loss on Redemption of Bonds			45 0 0 0 00					3

CASH PAYMENTS JOURNAL   PAGE 9

Debit Loss on Redemption of Bonds   **Credit Discount on Bonds Payable**   **Credit Cash**

from having issued bonds at lower rates. If current market interest rates fall, the corporation is burdened by having to pay higher-than-market interest rates.

A call option protects a corporation from declines in market interest rates. Chandler Corporation issued $500,000.00 of 10.5%, 20-year callable bonds. Five years later, the market interest rate dropped to 7.0%. Thus, Chandler is paying more in interest each year than it would if it could pay current interest rates.

Chandler has decided to call its bond issue. The bond issue requires bondholders be paid 105% of the bonds'

face value. Thus, Chandler will have to pay $525,000.00 to call the bonds.

The redemption amount is almost always above the carrying value, resulting in a loss. The loss is recorded in Loss on Redemption of Bonds. This account is classified as an Other Expense on the income statement.

Loss on Redemption of Bonds

Debit Increases

Credit Decreases

Financing a Takeover

Kelsay Corporation is the fourth largest security service provider in its region. Recently, the market has been consolidating, with smaller corporations being purchased by larger competitors. Kelsay's management is considering acquiring one of its larger competitors.

Kelsay's board has a proposal to generate the $7.5 million necessary to buy one of its competitors. The proposal calls for a 7%, 5-year, $2,000,000 bank note, issuing 60,000 shares of 5%, $50.00 preferred stock, and issuing 100,000 shares of common stock at the current market price of $25.00. The proposal does not include the issuance of any bonds.

Three board members subsequently submitted different proposals:

Proposal A: Obtain a 7%, 6-year, $2,000,000 bank note and issue 220,000 shares of common stock.

Proposal B: Obtain an 8%, 3-year, $500,000 bank note and issue 5,000 of 6%, 20-year, $1,000 bonds, 10,000 shares of preferred stock, and 60,000 shares of common stock.

Proposal C: Issue 5,000 of 6%, 20-year, $1,000 bonds and 50,000 shares of preferred stock.

OPEN THE SPREADSHEET TLA_CH12

The workbook contains a detailed 10-year projection of Kelsay's cash flows from purchasing its competitor. Follow the steps on the Instructions tab to prepare an analysis. Answer these questions:

1. Which of the four proposals results in the highest total projected income available to common stockholders?

2. Prepare a statement for the board of directors, explaining the results of the analysis.

> July 1. Chandler Corporation redeemed its $500,000.00 bond issue with a call option of 105%, $525,000.00. The bonds have a carrying value of $480,000.00. Check 622.

Bonds Payable

⬇	500,000.00	Balance	500,000.00
		(New Balance	0.00)

Discount on Bonds Payable

Balance	20,000.00	⬇	20,000.00
(New Balance	0.00)		

Loss on Redemption of Bonds

⬆	45,000.00

Cash

⬇	525,000.00

Bonds Payable is debited for $500,000.00. Discount on Bonds Payable is credited for $20,000.00. Cash is credited for $525,000.00. The difference, $45,000.00, is debited to Loss on Redemption of Bonds.

Chandler is willing to incur a loss of $45,000.00 in the current year to eliminate the annual $17,500.00 overpayment of interest for the remaining 15 years of the bond term.

The redemption of a bond issue with a premium would be journalized using similar steps. The entry would include a debit to Premium on Bonds Payable.

Face Value of Bond Issue	×	Call Option	=	Redemption Amount
$500,000.00	×	105%	=	$525,000.00

Redemption Amount	−	Carrying Value of Bond Issue	=	Loss on Redemption
$525,000.00	−	$480,000.00	=	$45,000.00

Accounting for Convertible Bonds LO6

Similar to preferred stock, bonds can be issued with a conversion option. If the market price of the corporation's common stock rises above the conversion price, bondholders may elect to convert their bonds to common stock. Investors are willing to pay more for a bond issue that has a conversion option. As a result, the conversion option reduces the corporation's interest expense.

Bennett Corporation needed to raise $800,000.00 of capital to finance a major expansion. The corporation was relatively young and had only become profitable in the past year. As a result, management knew that it would have to offer investors additional incentives to purchase its bonds.

Bennett elected to issue 800, $1,000.00, 7.5%, 10-year convertible bonds at a premium, $820,000.00. The bonds have a conversion rate of 20 shares of common stock for each bond. Thus, the conversion price is $50.00.

Par Value of Bonds	÷	Conversion Ratio	=	Conversion Price
$1,000.00	÷	20	=	$50.00

Prior to issuing the bonds, Bennett's underwriter projected that the bonds would be sold at $750,000.00, which is a $50,000.00 discount without the conversion option. Thus, investors were willing to pay $70,000.00 more for the bonds with the conversion option.

Generally Accepted Accounting Principles

As illustrated earlier in the chapter, generally accepted accounting principles require the bonds to be recorded at face value, $800,000.00, with the premium being recorded in Premium on Bonds Payable. The following journal entry illustrates the issuance of a convertible bond at a premium:

Cash	820,000.00	
Bonds Payable		800,000.00
Premium on Bonds Payable		20,000.00

International Financial Reporting Standards

IFRS account for bond issuance transactions differently. IFRS recognize the estimated value of the conversion option. The estimated value of the bonds without the conversion option is recorded in Bonds Payable. The estimated value of the conversion option is recorded in a stockholders' equity account, Conversion Option. IFRS consider the value of the conversion option to be a contribution to stockholders' equity.

Cash	820,000.00	
Bonds Payable		750,000.00
Conversion Option		70,000.00
(Stockholders' Equity)		

Careers In Accounting

Olguita Mendez
Tax Examiner/Collector

Olguita Mendez works for the Internal Revenue Service (IRS) as a tax examiner. She has held this position since she graduated from college three years ago with a degree in accounting. Her main activity in this position is to verify the accuracy of tax returns. When she first started, she focused on the tax returns of individuals. In the last year, she has been working on business tax returns.

In her position, Ms. Mendez must have a good understanding of the federal tax code. She had extensive training when she was first hired by the IRS, and she is required to attend classes every year in order to stay current.

When verifying a tax return, Ms. Mendez may find that the return is not complete. A document, a supplemental schedule, or a signature may be missing. In that case, she corresponds with the taxpayer or business, seeking to obtain the missing information or document. If an error is found, she will correct the error and recalculate the taxes due, again contacting the taxpayer to request the amount due.

Most of Ms. Mendez's time is spent in a local office of the IRS. Occasionally, she finds a return that contains questionable data. She then may inform the taxpayer that she will be performing an audit. Audits are usually performed in the home of an individual taxpayer or in the office of a representative of a business.

Although Ms. Mendez enjoys the challenges of her job, she is training to be a tax collector. A tax collector contacts individuals and businesses who owe back taxes and negotiates a plan for the payment of these taxes. A tax collector almost exclusively works out in the field, in contact with taxpayers and businesses.

Salary: The median wage for tax examiners is $53,130.

Qualifications: Most positions require training in a vocational school or an associate's degree. A four-year degree in accounting is helpful.

Occupational Outlook: The growth for tax examiner positions is projected to have little or no change (−1% to 1%) for the period from 2016 to 2026.

Source: www.onetonline.org.

LO4 Journalize the retiring of a bond issue.

LO5 Journalize the early redemption of a bond issue.

LO6 Explain how to account for convertible bonds.

TERMS REVIEW

retiring a bond issue

term bonds

serial bonds

call option

callable bond

Audit your understanding LO4, 5, 6

1. What amount is debited to the Bonds Payable account when a bond is retired?
2. What is the primary difference between a term bond and a serial bond?
3. What would encourage a corporation to call a bond issue?
4. How is a loss on calling a bond issue reported in the financial statements?
5. What is the conversion price of a $5,000.00 bond having a conversion ratio of 25?
6. A corporation issues $600,000.00 of convertible bonds for $610,000.00. The underwriters projected that the bonds would be sold for $585,000.00, until the corporation added a conversion option. What amount should be recorded in Bonds Payable, using GAAP? IFRS?

Work together 12-3 LO4, 5

Redeeming and calling a bond issue

Journalize each transaction completed during the current year. Page 6 of a cash payments journal is provided in the *Working Papers*. Your instructor will guide you through the following examples.

Transactions:

Apr. 1. Retired a bond issue at its face value, $250,000.00. Check No. 558.

July 1. Redeemed an $800,000.00 bond issue with a call option of 103%. The bonds have a carrying value of $765,000.00. Check No. 740.

Oct. 1. Redeemed a $600,000.00 bond issue with a call option of 105%. The bonds have a carrying value of $610,000.00. Check No. 941.

On your own 12-3 LO4, 5

Redeeming and calling a bond issue

Journalize each transaction completed during the current year. Page 10 of a cash payments journal is provided in the *Working Papers*. Work independently to complete the following problem.

Transactions:

July 1. Retired a bond issue at its face value, $200,000.00. Check No. 621.

Oct. 1. Redeemed a $700,000.00 bond issue with a call option of 105%. The bonds have a carrying value of $732,000.00. Check No. 842.

Nov. 1. Redeemed a $600,000.00 bond issue with a call option of 106%. The bonds have a carrying value of $584,000.00. Check No. 969.

LO7 Journalize the purchase of an investment in bonds.

LO8 Journalize the receipt of interest on bonds purchased at a discount and a premium.

LO9 Journalize the sale of a bond investment.

Purchasing Bonds LO7

DATE	ACCOUNT TITLE	CK. NO.	POST. REF.	GENERAL DEBIT	GENERAL CREDIT	ACCOUNTS PAYABLE DEBIT	PURCHASES DISCOUNT CREDIT	CASH CREDIT	
				1	2	3	4	5	
1	July 1 Investment Securities	754		24 7 8 7 75				24 7 8 7 75	1
2									2
3									3

(CASH PAYMENTS JOURNAL — PAGE 7)

Debit Investment Securities   Credit Cash

A corporation uses an underwriter to sell its bonds to the public. The underwriter can sell the bonds to individual investors or to other corporations. However, most bonds are sold to organizations that manage the investments of individual investors. These organizations are called **institutional investors**. Mutual funds and pension plans are examples of institutional investors.

In an effort to maximize the return of its investments, an institutional investor will generally purchase a variety of investments. Short-term investments usually consist of capital stock. Long-term investments usually consist of capital stock and bonds. Bonds tend to provide the institutional investor with a stable and predictable return on its investment.

A bond issued at a discount or premium is also purchased at a discount or premium. Bonds purchased by an institutional investor are recorded in Investment Securities. Unlike the issuing corporation, the buyer does not record the discount or premium in a separate account.

On July 1, Forest Equipment issued 100, five-year, 6.0%, $1,000.00 face-value bonds for $99,151.32. Thus, each bond was issued for $991.51 ($99,151.32 ÷ 100 bonds). The Albreck Investment Fund purchased 25 of Forest's bonds for $24,787.75 ($991.51 × 25 bonds). The fund intends to hold the bonds for several years.

July 1. The Albreck Investment Fund purchased 25 of Forest Equipment's $1,000 face-value bonds at $991.51 each. Check No. 754.

Investment Securities is debited for $24,787.75, the total amount paid for the bonds. Cash is credited for $24,787.75.

The market price of capital stock can change significantly over a short period of time. In contrast, a change in the market price of bonds tends to be more gradual. As a result, an institutional investor is unlikely to make a short-term investment in bonds.

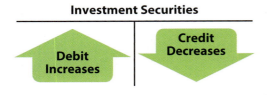

Investment Securities

Debit Increases | Credit Decreases

Superman and Savings Bonds

Paying for the American Revolutionary War was the start of the country's debt. To help the government pay for World War I, Americans bought *Liberty Bonds*. In 1935, *U.S. Savings Bonds* were first sold. These bonds were designed so that the owners could *lend* money to the government and be paid interest for the use of their money. During World War II, U.S. Savings bonds became known as *War Bonds*. After September 11, 2001 and until December 2011, U.S. Savings Bonds were sold as *Patriot Bonds* to help fight the war on global terrorism.

Savings bonds can be owned by anyone, including children, and are unique because they cannot be sold by brokers or dealers to other people in the secondary market. Initially, savings bonds could be purchased at financial institutions and through the mail. Smart investors would store their savings bonds in a safe place, such as a safe deposit box, until the bonds matured. In 2012, the Treasury Department discontinued the practice of selling paper savings bonds. They can be purchased through the U.S. Government Treasury Direct website, making it easier for individuals to loan money to the federal government.

Savings bonds are purchased at face value and can be bought for as little as $25. They are often referred to as an "All American Investment" because they are an easy way to save money safely and receive a low interest rate. In addition, they are considered very safe, since they are "backed by the full faith and credit of the U.S. Government."

ACTIVITIES

1. There are two different types of U.S. Savings Bonds. The most common is the Series EE. There is also another, called the Series I Bond. Using the library or the Internet, research the differences. Then, compose a letter to a classmate, comparing and contrasting Series EE and Series I Savings Bonds available for purchase.

2. Different media have been used over the years to persuade people to buy bonds. Go to http://www.treasurydirect.gov/kids/art/art.htm and view some of the posters, newspaper ads, and commercials used by the government. Choose and create an advertising medium to convince your classmates to buy savings bonds today. Research at least three advantages of buying bonds, and be sure to use these advantages as well as creativity and a persuasive tone in your advertisement.

Source: www.treasurydirect.gov.

Journalizing Entries for Interest Received on Bond Investments LO8

A business that issues a bond for a discount or premium must record interest expense using the effective rate of interest. A business that purchases a bond as a marketable security must account for its interest revenue using the same effective interest rate.

Receiving Interest on Bonds Purchased at a Discount

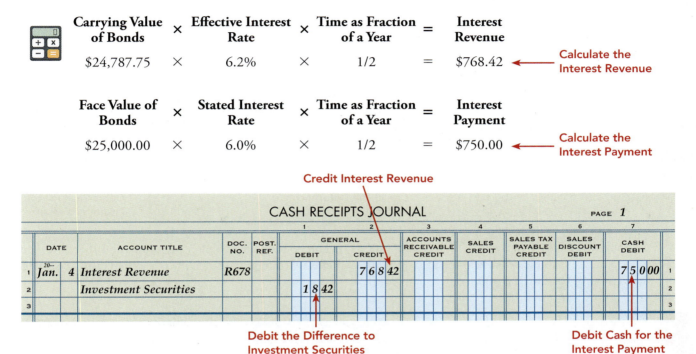

Carrying Value of Bonds	×	Effective Interest Rate	×	Time as Fraction of a Year	=	Interest Revenue	
$24,787.75	×	6.2%	×	1/2	=	$768.42	← Calculate the Interest Revenue

Face Value of Bonds	×	Stated Interest Rate	×	Time as Fraction of a Year	=	Interest Payment	
$25,000.00	×	6.0%	×	1/2	=	$750.00	← Calculate the Interest Payment

Credit Interest Revenue

CASH RECEIPTS JOURNAL — PAGE 1

	DATE	ACCOUNT TITLE	DOC. NO.	POST. REF.	GENERAL DEBIT	GENERAL CREDIT	ACCOUNTS RECEIVABLE CREDIT	SALES CREDIT	SALES TAX PAYABLE CREDIT	SALES DISCOUNT DEBIT	CASH DEBIT	
1	Jan. 4	Interest Revenue	R678			768 42					750 00	1
2		Investment Securities			18 42							2
3												3

Debit the Difference to Investment Securities **Debit Cash for the Interest Payment**

Forest Equipment issued its 6.0% bonds to yield 6.2%. The calculation of the first period's semiannual interest payment is shown above. The interest revenue is calculated using the current carrying value of the bonds multiplied by the effective interest rate.

Interest Revenue is credited for $768.42. Cash is debited for $750.00. The difference, $18.42, is debited to Investment Securities.

The carrying value of the bonds increased by $18.42. If the fund keeps the bonds until maturity, the carrying value will gradually increase to equal the bonds' total face value of $25,000.00.

> **January 4.** The Albreck Investment Fund received the semiannual interest payment on 25 bonds of Forest Equipment, $750.00. Receipt No. 678.

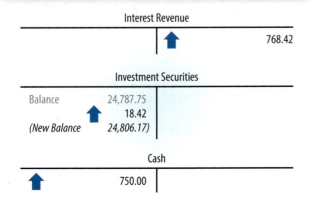

Interest Revenue

	768.42

Investment Securities

Balance	24,787.75	
	18.42	
(New Balance	24,806.17)	

Cash

750.00	

The calculation method is the same for interest revenue and interest expense.

Receiving Interest on Bonds Purchased at a Premium

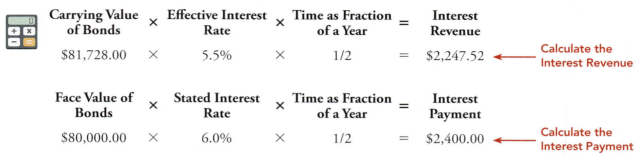

Carrying Value of Bonds	×	Effective Interest Rate	×	Time as Fraction of a Year	=	Interest Revenue
$81,728.00	×	5.5%	×	1/2	=	$2,247.52

← Calculate the Interest Revenue

Face Value of Bonds	×	Stated Interest Rate	×	Time as Fraction of a Year	=	Interest Payment
$80,000.00	×	6.0%	×	1/2	=	$2,400.00

← Calculate the Interest Payment

Credit Interest Revenue

CASH RECEIPTS JOURNAL — PAGE 20

	DATE	ACCOUNT TITLE	DOC. NO.	POST. REF.	GENERAL DEBIT	GENERAL CREDIT	ACCOUNTS RECEIVABLE CREDIT	SALES CREDIT	SALES TAX PAYABLE CREDIT	SALES DISCOUNT DEBIT	CASH DEBIT	
1	Oct. 3	Interest Revenue	R544			2 247 52					2 400 00	1
2		Investment Securities				152 48						2
3												3

Credit the Difference to Investment Securities

Debit Cash for the Interest Payment

TYP Corporation issued 500, five-year, 6.0%, $1,000.00 face-value bonds. The bonds were sold for $510,800.10, or $1,021.60 ($510,800.10 ÷ 500 bonds) per bond.

The bonds were sold at a premium, and therefore, the effective interest rate of 5.5% is less than the 6.0% stated interest rate.

WHY ACCOUNTING?

CareerClusters®
PATHWAYS TO COLLEGE & CAREER READINESS
Marketing

How Marketing Can Use Accounting Ratios

The American Marketing Association defines marketing as "… the activity, set of institutions, and processes for creating, communicating, delivering, and exchanging offerings that have value for customers, clients, partners, and society at large."

The Marketing Department may develop and implement a marketing campaign, but how does it determine if the campaign was effective? The Accounting Department may be able to provide the data needed to measure the effectiveness of the plan. One way to measure this would be to determine the ratio of advertising expense to net sales before and after the campaign. While the Accounting Department would produce the calculations, Marketing Department personnel must understand what is being measured and how to interpret the results. For example, if sales are recorded on the accrual basis, the receipt of cash from a sale in the previous period would not be

included in the measurement. Without this knowledge, the Marketing Department may misinterpret the results.

CRITICAL THINKING

The Accounting Department provided the following data measuring the items before and after a sales promotion:

	Before the Promotion	After the Promotion
Sales	$130,000.00	$145,000.00
Advertising expense	1,300.00	2,175.00

1. Calculate the ratio of advertising expense to sales before the promotion and after the promotion. Put your answer in the form of a percentage, rounded to the nearest tenth (0.1).

2. What does the answer for question 1 indicate?

Source: www.marketingpower.com.

The Albreck Investment Fund purchased 80 of these bonds, paying $81,728.00 ($1,021.60 × 80 bonds). The calculation of the first period's semiannual interest payment is shown on the previous page. The interest revenue is calculated using the current carrying value of the bonds multiplied by the effective interest rate.

Interest Revenue is credited for $2,247.52. Cash is debited for $2,400.00. The difference, $152.48, is credited to Investment Securities.

The carrying value of the bonds decreased by $152.48. If the fund keeps the bonds until maturity, the carrying value will gradually decrease to equal the bonds' total face value of $80,000.00.

October 3. The Albreck Investment Fund received the semiannual interest payment on 80 bonds of TYP Corporation, $2,400.00. Receipt No. 544.

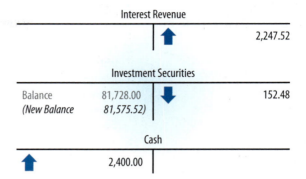

Selling A Bond Investment LO9

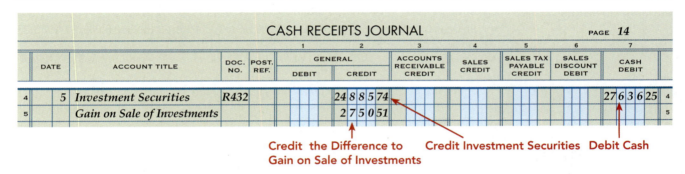

CASH RECEIPTS JOURNAL   PAGE 14

					1 GENERAL DEBIT	2 GENERAL CREDIT	3 ACCOUNTS RECEIVABLE CREDIT	4 SALES CREDIT	5 SALES TAX PAYABLE CREDIT	6 SALES DISCOUNT DEBIT	7 CASH DEBIT	
4	5	*Investment Securities*	R432			24 885 74					27 636 25	4
5		*Gain on Sale of Investments*				2 750 51						5

Credit the Difference to Gain on Sale of Investments   Credit Investment Securities   Debit Cash

The Albreck Investment Fund held its 25 bonds of Forest Equipment for several years. On the receipt of each semiannual interest payment, a debit was recorded that included an increase in the carrying value of the bonds. After three years, the carrying value of the bonds had increased to $24,885.74.

After receiving the latest interest payment, the Albreck Investment Fund decided to sell the bonds. Changes in market interest rates have caused the market value of the bonds to increase $1,105.45 per bond.

Investment Securities is credited for $24,885.74, the current carrying value of the bonds. Cash is debited for $27,636.25, the total amount received from the sale. The difference, $2,750.51, is credited to Gain on Sale of Investments.

July 1. The Albreck Investment Fund sold its 25 bonds of Forest Equipment for $1,105.45 per bond. Receipt No. 432.

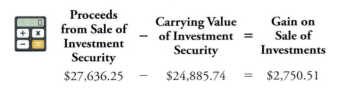

Proceeds from Sale of Investment Security	−	Carrying Value of Investment Security	=	Gain on Sale of Investments
$27,636.25	−	$24,885.74	=	$2,750.51

An institutional investor is in the business of purchasing and selling securities to earn a return for its investors. The gains and losses from the sale of investments are reported in a special section of its income statement. In contrast, most corporations are not in the business of purchasing and selling securities. Any gain or loss from the sale of investments is reported by the corporation as Other Revenue or Other Expense.

LO7 Journalize the purchase of an investment in bonds.

LO8 Journalize the receipt of interest on bonds purchased at a discount and a premium.

LO9 Journalize the sale of a bond investment.

TERM REVIEW

institutional investors

Audit your understanding LO7, 8, 9

1. What account is debited when an institutional investor purchases a bond?
2. How does the accounting for a bond discount differ between the issuing corporation and an institutional investor?
3. What amounts are used to calculate the amount of interest revenue earned on a bond investment?
4. At the maturity date of a bond investment, what will be the amount in the Investment Securities account?
5. How would a corporation in the retail industry report a gain or loss on the sale of a bond investment?

Work together 12-4 LO7, 8, 9

Journalizing bond investment transactions

FTR Investments specializes in investing retirement funds for teachers. On January 1, FTR Investments has the following bond investments:

- PlatMat Corporation, $75,000.00 of 5.0% bonds, purchased to yield 5.2%; $74,588.27 carrying value.
- OpeLin Industries, $120,000.00 of 6.0% bonds, purchased to yield 5.9%; $120,422.07 carrying value.

Journalize each transaction completed during the current year. Page 5 of a cash payments journal and page 3 of a cash receipts journal are provided in the *Working Papers*. Source documents are abbreviated as follows: check, C; receipt, R. Your instructor will guide you through the following examples.

Transactions:

June 30. Purchased 40 of Mason Electronic Corporation's $5,000.00 face-value bonds at $5,158.16 each, totaling $206,326.40. C624.

July 1. Received the semiannual interest payment on the PlatMat Corporation bonds. R642.

1. Received the semiannual interest payment on the OpeLin Industries bonds. R643.

1. Sold the OpeLin bonds, $122,754.00. R644.

On your own 12-4 LO7, 8, 9

Journalizing bond investment transactions

Davidson Securities has the following bond investments as of January 1:

- Greatlin Industries, $50,000.00 of 6.0% bonds, purchased to yield 5.8%; $50,271.76 carrying value.
- PESC Corporation, $90,000.00 of 6.5% bonds, purchased to yield 6.8%; $89,068.12 carrying value.

Journalize each transaction completed during the current year. Page 7 of a cash payments journal and page 4 of a cash receipts journal are provided in the *Working Papers*. Source documents are abbreviated as follows: check, C; receipt, R. Work independently to complete the following problem.

Transactions:

July 1. Received the semiannual interest payment on the Greatlin Industries bonds. R599.

1. Received the semiannual interest payment on the PESC Corporation bonds. R600.

1. Sold the PESC Corporation bonds, $89,900.00. R601.

14. Purchased 50 of Larsson Corporation's $1,000.00 face-value bonds at $998.60 each, totaling $49,930.00. C591.

CHAPTER SUMMARY

A corporation may elect to acquire capital by issuing bonds. Bonds enable the corporation to obtain a large amount of debt for an extended period of time. A bond is typically identified by its stated interest rate, term, and face value, such as 6%, 20-year, $5,000.00 bonds. A bond with a callable option can be redeemed by the corporation prior to the maturity date. An early redemption typically results in a loss that is recorded as an Other Expense.

Changes in market interest rates may cause bonds to be issued at a discount or a premium. The effective interest rate is the rate that will be earned by the bondholder over the term of the bond. The discount or premium is amortized over the remaining term of the bond. The amount of interest expense recorded is based on the carrying value of the bonds and the effective interest rate. The amount of the interest payment is based on the face value and the stated interest rate of the bonds. The interest payment amount is the same, regardless of the price at which the bonds were issued.

Institutional investors, such as mutual funds and pension plans, are significant buyers of corporate bonds. Unlike the issuing corporation, institutional investors record investments in Investment Securities, net of any premium or discount. The interest revenue earned on a bond is calculated using the same method the corporation uses to determine interest expense—the carrying value of the bonds multiplied by the effective interest rate.

Bond Sinking Funds

To assure bondholders that the bond issue will be paid at maturity, some bonds require the corporation to make periodic payments to a restricted fund. The fund is referred as a *bond sinking fund*. The payments are made to a trustee, which is a person or an institution given legal authorization to administer property for the benefit of the property owners.

Each time the corporation pays interest on the bonds, it also makes a payment into the bond sinking fund. The amount of the payment is typically the total face value of the bond issue divided by the number of payments. Thus, a corporation that issues $100,000.00 of 20-year bonds would be required to make $5,000.00 semiannual payments.

Although the trustee has control over the funds, the bond sinking fund is an asset of the corporation. The trustee is expected to invest the balance of the bond sinking fund on behalf of the corporation. Any interest earned reduces the amount the corporation must deposit. For example, Porterville Corporation is responsible for making a $5,000.00 payment into the bond sinking fund. The fund has earned $400.00 of interest since the last payment. The journal entry to record the deposit into the bond sinking fund would be as follows:

Bond Sinking Fund	5,000.00	
Interest Income		400.00
Cash		4,600.00

As the bond sinking fund balance increases, the amount of interest earned in a year usually increases. Thus, the amount the corporation must deposit each year will generally decrease. At the maturity date of the bonds, the trustee uses the bond sinking fund to pay the maturity value to the bondholders.

INSTRUCTIONS

Assume your corporation is planning to issue bonds that will contain a sinking fund provision. The bond trustee will be required to invest sinking fund cash in short-term (one year or less) bank certificates of deposit. Research how the sinking fund will be disclosed on the financial statements. Do you agree with the findings of your research?

APPLY YOUR UNDERSTANDING

INSTRUCTIONS: Download problem instructions for Excel, QuickBooks, and Sage 50c from the textbook companion website at www.C21accounting.com.

12-1 Application Problem — Journalizing bond transactions LO2

Instructions:

Journalize the following transactions. Page 8 of a cash receipts journal is provided in the *Working Papers*.

Transactions:

July 1, 20X1.   Received cash for 200 five-year, 6.5%, $1,000.00 face-value bonds, issued to yield 6.8%, $197,492.34. Receipt 450.

July 1, 20X6.   Received cash for 400 five-year, 6.0%, $1,000.00 face-value bonds, issued to yield 5.85%, $404,494.34. Receipt 890.

12-2 Application Problem — Journalizing bond interest payments LO3

Instructions:

Journalize each transaction completed during the current year. Page 18 of a cash payments journal is provided in the *Working Papers*.

Transactions:

July   1.   Paid cash to trustee for the semiannual interest payment on a 6.0%, $500,000.00 bond issue having a carrying value of $502,138.00 and a 5.9% effective interest rate. Check No. 446.

Aug.   1.   Paid cash to trustee for the semiannual interest payment on a 6.5%, $800,000.00 bond issue having a carrying value of $794,965.73 and a 6.65% effective interest rate. Check No. 538.

12-3 Application Problem — Redeeming and calling a bond issue LO4, 5

After making its semiannual interest payments, Cutform Corporation elected to call three of its bond issues.

Instructions:

Journalize each transaction completed during the current year. Page 9 of a cash payments journal is provided in the *Working Papers*.

Transactions:

Apr.   1.   Redeemed a $900,000.00 bond issue with a call option of 104%. The bonds have a carrying value of $889,000.00. Check No. 554.

June   1.   Retired a bond issue at face value, $300,000.00. Check No. 721.

July   1.   Redeemed an $800,000.00 bond issue with a call option of 106%. The bonds have a carrying value of $821,000.00. Check No. 763.

12-4 Application Problem — Journalizing bond investment transactions LO7, 8, 9

Betterson Mutual Funds has the following bond investments as of January 1:

- Ocean Import, $100,000.00 of 6.0% bonds, purchased to yield 5.9%; $100,271.32 carrying value.
- Washington Corporation, $60,000.00 of 5.5% bonds, purchased to yield 5.7%; $59,576.14 carrying value.

Betterson Mutual Funds accrued earned but unpaid interest income on its December 31 financial statements. These accruals were reversed at the start of the current fiscal year.

Instructions:

Journalize each transaction completed during the current year. Page 5 of a cash payments journal and page 3 of a cash receipts journal are provided in the *Working Papers*. Source documents are abbreviated as follows: check, C; receipt, R.

Transactions:

Mar.	1.	Purchased 50 of PC Corporation's $1,000.00 face-value bonds at $998.60 each, totaling $49,930.00. C591.
	1.	Received the semiannual interest payment on the Ocean Import bonds. R289.
Apr.	1.	Received the semiannual interest payment on the Washington Corporation bonds. R325.
	1.	Sold the Ocean Import bonds, $102,100.00. R326.

12-M Mastery Problem — Journalizing bond transactions LO2, 3, 4, 5, 7, 8, 9

sage 50

1. Journalize and post bond transactions to the cash receipts journal and cash disbursements journal.
2. Print the cash receipts journal and cash disbursements journal.

QB Quick Books

1. Journalize and post bond transactions to the journal.
2. Journalize and post bond transactions in the Write Checks window.
3. Print the journal and check detail.

X ⊞

1. Journalize bond transactions to the cash receipts journal and cash payments journal.
2. Print the spreadsheets.

TA Post Corporation has the following bonds outstanding as of January 1:

- 6%, 10-year, $1,000 face-value bonds, $500,000.00, issued at a 5.9% effective interest rate, callable at 105%.
- 6.5%, 20-year, $5,000 face-value bonds, $750,000.00, issued at a 6.7% effective interest rate.

The corporation accrued interest income and interest expense when preparing its December 31 financial statements. These accruals were reversed at the start of the current fiscal year.

Instructions:

Journalize each transaction completed during the current year. Page 6 of a cash receipts journal and page 3 of a cash payments journal are provided in the *Working Papers*. Source documents are abbreviated as follows: check, C; receipt, R.

Transactions:

Apr.	1.	Purchased ten of DRB Corporation's 6.25% $1,000.00 face-value bonds at $1,008.52 each, resulting in a yield of 6.05%. C445.
	27.	Paid cash to trustee for the semiannual interest payment on the $750,000.00 bond issue, which has a carrying value of $749,274.31. C468.
May	1.	Paid cash to trustee to retire the $750,000.00 bond issue at its face value. C492.
June	1.	Received cash for 400 ten-year, 5.0%, $1,000.00 face-value bonds, issued to yield 5.2%, $396,517.20. R161.
July	1.	Paid cash to trustee for the semiannual interest payment on the $500,000.00 bond issue, which has a carrying value of $501,560.51. C589.
	1.	Redeemed the $500,000.00 bond issue with a call option of 105%. C590.
Oct.	1.	Received the semiannual interest payment on its DRB Corporation bonds. R268.
	1.	Sold its investment in DRB Corporation bonds for $1,025.00 per bond. R269.

sage 50

1. Journalize and post bond transactions to the cash disbursements journal.
2. Print the cash disbursements journal.

QB
QuickBooks

1. Journalize and post bond transactions in the Write Checks window.
2. Print the check detail.

1. Journalize bond transactions to the cash payments journal.
2. Print the spreadsheets.

PR&K Corporation has 480 of its 7.5%, ten-year, $1,000 face-value bonds outstanding. The bonds were issued to yield a 7.2% effective interest rate. The bonds pay interest on April 1 and October 1 each year and have a call option at 104%.

PR&K Corporation called the bonds on June 23 of the current year. Bond transactions that occur during a semiannual period require that accrued interest be recorded.

Instructions:

Journalize each transaction. Page 3 of a cash payments journal is provided in the *Working Papers*.

Transactions:

Apr. 1. Paid cash to trustee for the semiannual interest payment on the $480,000.00 bond issue, which has a carrying value of $483,241.65. Check No. 654.

June 23. Paid cash to trustee for the interest accrued on the $480,000.00 bond issue since the last semiannual interest payment. Check No. 728.

  23. Redeemed the $480,000.00 bond issue. Check No. 729.

Bond Investment Options

Theme: Financial, Economic, Business, and Entrepreneurial Literacy

Skills: Critical Thinking and Problem Solving, Information Literacy, ICT Literacy

PARTNERSHIP FOR
21ST CENTURY SKILLS

Bonds are issued as a way to raise capital. An investor who purchases bonds lends money in return for a promise to be paid a fixed rate of interest plus the principal at a future date. Bonds can be purchased online or through a broker or a bank.

Most bonds are issued by one of three groups. First, the U.S. government issues Treasury bonds to finance the national debt and the ongoing business of the federal government. State and local governments also issue bonds to raise money for public projects, such as schools, bridges, and roads. These bonds, called *municipal bonds* or *munis*, offer special tax exemptions that attract investors.

Corporations issue bonds to help finance major purchases or ongoing activities. Corporate bonds are the most lucrative, but have greater risk.

Bonds are given credit ratings, much like grades, that range from AAA to DDD. These ratings help the investor determine the credit risk of the bond. Bonds with lower ratings usually pay a higher yield, or rate of return, due to their higher risk. Treasury bonds are considered the safest bond investment, since the government has less risk of defaulting than a corporation.

APPLICATION

1. Using the Internet, find the names of the three main rating agencies for bonds.
2. Using websites like www.bondsonline.com, compare and contrast the bond rating definitions of the three rating agencies. Create a spreadsheet or other visual to share your findings.
3. Some bonds are referred to as "junk" bonds. Using the Internet, explain the meaning of junk bonds. Explain why an investor would buy a bond called "junk."

Analyzing Home Depot's Financial Statements

Home Depot uses a variety of financial instruments to finance its operations and fund its expansion. As of January 28, 2018, Home Depot had bond issues outstanding with due dates ranging from 2018 to 2056 and interest rates ranging from 1.80% to 5.95%.

INSTRUCTIONS

Use Home Depot's Consolidated Balance Sheets and Consolidated Statements of Cash Flows found in Appendix B on pages B-5 and B-9 to answer the following questions:

1. What were the proceeds from long-term debt for each of the three fiscal years?
2. Identify the amount of payments of long-term debt for each fiscal year.
3. For each year presented on the Consolidated Balance Sheets, determine the amount of long-term debt as a percent of total liabilities and stockholders' equity. Include the current installments of long-term debt.

Financial Reporting and Analysis for a Corporation

LEARNING OBJECTIVES

After studying Chapter 13, in addition to defining key terms, you will be able to:

LO1 Identify the users of financial statement analysis.

LO2 Identify the objectives of financial statement analysis.

LO3 Analyze the short-term financial strength of a business.

LO4 Analyze the long-term financial strength of a business.

LO5 Analyze the profitability of a business.

LO6 Perform efficiency analysis of a business.

LO7 Calculate the market ratios of a business.

LO8 Calculate permanent and temporary differences in net income and taxable income.

LO9 Identify the components of comprehensive income.

LO10 Identify where non-recurring items appear on the income statement.

Kohl's Corporation

What started as a single department store in 1962 is now a major department store chain with over 1,100 stores in 49 states. (The only state that does not have a Kohl's department store is Hawaii.)

As a consumer, you may be mostly concerned with the style and quality of merchandise available at Kohl's. The company knows that their customers prefer popular brands, so they have recently partnered with Nike and Skechers and offer exclusive lines of goods from Tony Hawk and Vera Wang.

As an investor, you may be interested in more than name-brand merchandise. You may want to study Kohl's financial statements to compare them with other investments. Many financial ratios can be calculated using the financial statements of the company. Other measures may require some research.

One measure used by company management and by investors is known as *comparable sales*. Comparable sales is used to evaluate sales trends at individual store locations. This measure requires that the company separately measure sales of stores by the length of time the store has been open. According to its 2018 annual report, Kohl's "store sales are included in comparable sales after the store has been open for 12 full months."

Companies strive to generate consistent increases in comparable sales. Popular methods of increasing sales include expanding merchandise options, offering exclusive items, increasing prices, and even offering groceries at some stores.

In 2017, Kohl's comparable sales grew 1.5%, which is an increase over its 2016 negative growth of −2.4%. Kohl's 2018 annual report states, "The increase in comparable sales reflects higher average transaction values as increases in selling prices were only partially offset by decreases in units per transaction." Kohl's also tracks comparable sales by department in order to evaluate each department's performance.

It is risky for a business to implement price increases. The company might lose customers to other similar stores. Customers might make fewer trips to Kohl's. However, at Kohl's, the number of transactions improved even as some prices increased.

CRITICAL THINKING

1. Why might a Kohl's customer continue choosing Kohl's despite price increases?

2. If a business does not report its comparable sales growth, would an investor be able to calculate it by using published financial statements?

Sources: www.kohls.com; www.washingtonpost.com ("Kohl's has a new plan to get you into its stores: Groceries," March 1, 2018).

KEY TERMS

comparative financial statements	EBIT	earnings per share (EPS)
cash equivalents	interest coverage ratio	market value of a share of stock
working capital	gross margin	price-earnings ratio
current ratio	operating margin	dividend yield
quick assets	rate earned on average total assets	permanent difference
quick ratio	rate earned on average	temporary difference
debt ratio	stockholders' equity	comprehensive income
equity ratio	free cash flow	
common equity per share	capital expenditures	

LO1 Identify the users of financial statement analysis.
LO2 Identify the objectives of financial statement analysis.
LO3 Analyze the short-term financial strength of a business.
LO4 Analyze the long-term financial strength of a business.

Financial Statement Analysis LO1

Financial statements contain all information necessary to understand a business's financial condition. **>> App: Full Disclosure** The structure of these statements is similar from company to company in order to meet the requirements of the Securities and Exchange Commission (SEC). Congress established the SEC in 1933. The SEC was given the authority to develop accounting principles and rules.

To ensure that information provided to external users is accurate and complete, the SEC requires public companies to submit quarterly and annual reports. These reports must include specific disclosures and discussions. The SEC makes these reports available to all current and potential investors through an online database called EDGAR (the Electronic Data Gathering, Analysis, and Retrieval system).

Financial statements are prepared for both internal and external users. Managers use financial information to identify areas for improving the profitability of their corporation. Banks and lending agencies use the information to decide whether to loan money to a business. Owners and potential owners use the information to decide whether to buy, sell, or keep their investment. Each group uses the financial information in a different way to assist with decision making.

Although financial statements provide useful information, they can be difficult to understand. For example, is a significant increase in the cost of merchandise sold an unfavorable trend? This question cannot be answered without considering information provided by other financial statement items, such as net sales. Financial statement analysis provides this information, since it calculates the relationships among financial statement items.

Financial Analysis Objectives LO2

Financial analysis objectives are determined by a business's characteristics and achievements that are important to the analyst. Information is analyzed to obtain more knowledge about the business's strengths and weaknesses. Common objectives for analyzing financial information are to determine (1) financial strength, (2) profitability (3) efficiency, and (4) market value.

Financial statements, with supporting schedules, are the primary information sources to be analyzed. A statement showing two or more years' information permits a reader to compare year-to-year differences. Financial statements that provide information for multiple fiscal periods are known as **comparative financial statements**. To be useful, financial statements must be prepared by using the same accounting principles in each period. **>> App A: Consistent Reporting**

© ISTOCKPHOTO.COM/NANO

Comparative financial statements for Forest Equipment, Inc., are shown below and on the next several pages. These financial statements will be used as the basis for the financial analysis discussed in this chapter.

Income Statement

Forest Equipment, Inc. Income Statement For Years Ended December 31, 20X3, 20X2, and 20X1	20X3	20X2	20X1
Net Sales	646 0 1 7 54	645 2 1 2 32	642 5 7 8 45
Cost of Merchandise Sold:	391 0 3 5 52	398 6 0 0 20	395 4 5 2 15
Gross Profit	254 9 8 2 02	246 6 1 2 12	247 1 2 6 30
Operating Expenses:			
Selling, General and Administrative	109 4 3 5 14	105 2 6 5 14	104 6 9 8 20
Depreciation and Amortization	26 0 5 3 00	22 4 2 1 30	21 5 3 5 28
Total Operating Expenses	135 4 8 8 14	127 6 8 6 44	126 2 3 3 48
Income from Operations	119 4 9 3 88	118 9 2 5 68	120 8 9 2 82
Other Revenue and Expenses:			
Interest Income	1 0 8 7 50	1 0 9 5 54	9 8 9 54
Dividend Revenue	3 0 0 0 00	2 5 0 0 00	1 5 0 0 00
Gain on Sale of Investments	5 7 0 0 00	6 5 0 0 00	—
Interest Expense	(11 7 0 8 33)	(7 8 5 0 00)	(4 5 5 4 25)
Total Other Revenue and Expenses	(1 9 2 0 83)	2 2 4 5 54	(2 0 6 4 71)
Net Income before Federal Income Tax	117 5 7 3 05	121 1 7 1 22	118 8 2 8 11
Less: Federal Income Tax Expense	24 6 9 0 34	25 4 4 5 96	24 9 5 3 90
Net Income	92 8 8 2 71	95 7 2 5 26	93 8 7 4 21

The income statement is presented in an abbreviated format normally used in annual reports. The cost of merchandise sold section has been reduced to a single line, and the operating expenses are divided into two categories: selling, general and administrative expenses and depreciation and amortization expenses.

ETHICS IN ACTION

Client Referrals

Feng Entertainment Group asked its public accounting firm, Aquino, Mendoza & Ruett, to develop a comprehensive health and retirement program. Aquino, Mendoza & Ruett conducts Feng Entertainment's annual audit. Knowing that it lacked the expertise needed to perform these services, Halina Aquino, a CPA and the managing partner of the accounting firm, refers Feng Entertainment to another firm, Moreno and Cote. In appreciation for the referral, Moreno and Cote gives Halina Aquino an all-expense-paid trip to St. Thomas. Neither accounting firm informs Feng Entertainment of the trip.

INSTRUCTIONS

Determine whether the referral was made in accordance with the AICPA *Code of Professional Conduct.*

Statement of Stockholders' Equity

Forest Equipment, Inc. Statement of Stockholders' Equity For Years Ended December 31, 20X3, 20X2, and 20X1	20X3	20X2	20X1
Paid-In Capital:			
Common Stock, $1.00 Par Value:			
Balance, January 1	65 000 00	65 000 00	65 000 00
Additional Common Stock Issued			
Balance, December 31	65 000 00	65 000 00	65 000 00
Preferred Stock, 6%, $100.00 Par Value:			
Balance, January 1	127 500 00	50 000 00	50 000 00
Additional Preferred Stock Issued		77 500 00	
Balance, December 31	127 500 00	127 500 00	50 000 00
Total Value of Capital Stock Issued	192 500 00	192 500 00	115 000 00
Additional Paid-In Capital:			
Paid-In Capital in Excess of Par Value—Common	100 000 00	100 000 00	100 000 00
Paid-In Capital in Excess of Par Value—Preferred	6 000 00	6 000 00	1 500 00
Paid-In Capital from Sale of Treasury Stock	1 000 00		
Total Additional Paid-In Capital	107 000 00	106 000 00	101 500 00
Total Paid-In Capital	299 500 00	298 500 00	216 500 00
Retained Earnings:			
Balance, January 1, 20--	153 541 14	82 365 88	6 441 67
Net Income after Federal Income Tax	92 882 71	95 725 26	93 874 21
Less Preferred Dividends Declared	(7 650 00)	(7 650 00)	(3 000 00)
Less Common Dividends Declared	(14 950 00)	(16 900 00)	(14 950 00)
Balance, December 31	223 823 85	153 541 14	82 365 88
Treasury Stock			
Balance, December 31	(22 000 00)	(30 000 00)	(18 000 00)
Total Stockholders' Equity, December 31, 20--	501 323 85	422 041 14	280 865 88
Common Shares Outstanding	65 000 00	65 000 00	65 000 00
Preferred Shares Outstanding	1 275 00	1 275 00	500 00
Treasury Shares	250 00	350 00	200 00

Forest's statement of stockholders' equity is presented for three years. When beginning and ending balances are shown, the ending balance for one period is equal to the beginning balance for the following period. A comparative statement allows the user to identify changes over several accounting periods.

Remember

Businesses present abbreviated financial statements in the annual report. Major subtotals are given, but details of individual accounts are not.

Balance Sheet

	20X3	20X2
Assets		
Current Assets:		
Cash and Cash Equivalents	47 2 7 7 30	45 3 7 8 52
Accounts Receivable, net	66 7 0 6 43	55 6 4 7 10
Merchandise Inventory	144 0 6 6 40	95 2 1 4 25
Other Receivables	8 2 5 0 00	8 5 3 1 40
Other Current Assets	70 6 9 4 98	71 4 5 6 21
Total Current Assets	336 9 9 5 11	276 2 2 7 48
Total Plant Assets, net	397 6 5 0 00	366 4 8 0 00
Intangible Assets	1 4 4 0 00	1 4 4 0 00
Total Assets	736 0 8 5 11	644 1 4 7 48
Liabilities		
Current Liabilities:		
Accounts Payable	52 9 3 9 05	54 2 2 5 68
Accrued Salaries and Related Expenses	26 1 8 3 69	25 7 0 0 40
Sales Tax Payable	1 6 1 6 05	1 5 4 5 22
Federal Income Tax Payable	5 1 0 3 49	4 8 3 0 06
Other Current Liabilities	50 0 2 0 30	49 6 2 1 45
Total Current Liabilities	135 8 6 2 58	135 9 2 2 81
Long-Term Liabilities:		
Bonds Payable, net	98 8 9 8 68	86 1 8 3 53
Total Liabilities	234 7 6 1 26	222 1 0 6 34
Stockholders' Equity		
Paid-In Capital	299 5 0 0 00	298 5 0 0 00
Retained Earnings	223 8 2 3 85	153 5 4 1 14
Treasury Stock	(22 0 0 0 00)	(30 0 0 0 00)
Total Stockholders' Equity	501 3 2 3 85	422 0 4 1 14
Total Liabilities and Stockholders' Equity	736 0 8 5 11	644 1 4 7 48

Forest Equipment, Inc.
Balance Sheet
December 31, 20X3 and 20X2

Forest's balance sheet is also presented in an abbreviated format. Short-term, liquid investments that are readily convertible to cash and which mature in three months or less are called **cash equivalents**. Cash and cash equivalents are summarized on the first line of the balance sheet. Accounts receivable are shown at net realizable value. Plant assets are shown at net book value and are presented as a total on one line of the balance sheet. Bonds payable are shown net of any bond premium or bond discount.

Remember Comparative financial statements allow the reader to compare results and determine trends more easily.

Statement of Cash Flows

	20X3	20X2
Cash flows from operating activities:		
Cash receipts from:		
Sales	598 8 1 6 56	604 4 3 9 88
Interest	4 2 2 10	6 5 0 42
Total cash receipts	599 2 3 8 66	605 0 9 0 30
Cash payments for:		
Inventory purchases	(355 6 5 4 12)	(342 3 3 6 89)
Salaries and wages	(68 9 3 7 82)	(69 3 1 2 25)
Insurance	(12 0 0 0 00)	(10 6 5 0 00)
Interest	(11 6 9 0 10)	(6 4 8 9 33)
Taxes	(29 4 5 2 47)	(30 0 1 5 45)
Other operating expenses	(102 0 0 5 37)	(95 4 0 0 25)
Total cash payments	(579 7 3 9 88)	(554 2 0 4 17)
Net cash provided/(used) by operating activities	19 4 9 8 78	50 8 8 6 13
Cash flows from investing activities:		
Sale of investment securities	12 0 0 0 00	20 0 0 0 00
Purchase of office equipment	(15 0 0 0 00)	(35 2 1 4 00)
Purchase of store equipment	(16 0 0 0 00)	(87 6 3 9 00)
Net cash provided/(used) by investing activities	(19 0 0 0 00)	(102 8 5 3 00)
Cash flows from financing activities:		
Issuance of bonds	15 0 0 0 00	
Issuance of preferred stock		82 0 0 0 00
Sale of treasury stock	9 0 0 0 00	
Purchase of treasury stock		(12 0 0 0 00)
Payment of cash dividends	(22 6 0 0 00)	(24 5 5 0 00)
Net cash provided/(used) by financing activities	1 4 0 0 00	45 4 5 0 00
Net change in cash	1 8 9 8 78	(6 5 1 6 87)
Cash balance, January 1	45 3 7 8 52	51 8 9 5 39
Cash balance, December 31	47 2 7 7 30	45 3 7 8 52

Forest Equipment, Inc.
Statement of Cash Flows
For Years Ended December 31, 20X3 and 20X2

Forest's statement of cash flows is presented in comparative format for two periods. The ending cash balance for 20X2 is equal to the beginning balance for 20X3. The comparative format allows the user to compare sources and uses of cash over two accounting periods.

Remember

The statement of cash flows reports all cash flows in and out of the company.

Short-Term Financial Strength LO3

A successful business needs adequate capital. A business gets capital from two sources: (1) owners' investments and retained earnings and (2) loans. Some capital, either owned or borrowed, will be used for long periods. Some capital is borrowed for short periods. A business can invest capital in assets (such as equipment and buildings) for long periods. A business also invests in assets (such as merchandise) that will be converted back to cash in a short period. Short-term assets are referred to as current assets because they are consumed in a business's daily activities or exchanged for cash. Long-term assets are referred to as *plant assets* and are used over a long period.

Forest uses three measures to analyze its short-term financial strength: (1) working capital, (2) current ratio, and (3) quick ratio.

Working Capital

	Total Current Assets	–	Total Current Liabilities	=	Working Capital
20X3	$336,995.11	–	$135,862.58	=	$201,132.53
20X2	$276,227.48	–	$135,922.81	=	$140,304.67

The amount of total current assets less total current liabilities is known as **working capital**. Working capital, stated in dollars, is the amount of current assets available to the business after current liabilities are paid. It is not the amount of cash available to the business. Comparing the amount of working capital from year to year reveals trends.

Forest's working capital for December 31, 20X3, and December 31, 20X2, is calculated as shown above, using information from the balance sheet (page 371). Forest's working capital increased from $140,304.67 to $201,132.53, a favorable trend. A review of other financial information suggests that part of the reason for the lower working capital in 20X2 was the company's fast expansion. Frequently, when a business expands rapidly, it borrows money to buy more inventory and pay more employees. The rate of increased costs for merchandise and payroll may be initially greater than the rate of increase in sales and net income. In 20X3, Forest increased its current assets more than its current liabilities by increasing long-term liabilities and paying out less dividends.

Current Ratio

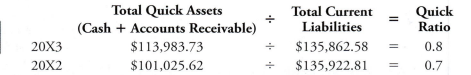

		Total Current Assets	÷	Total Current Liabilities	=	Current Ratio
	20X3	$336,995.11	÷	$135,862.58	=	2.5
	20X2	$276,227.48	÷	$135,922.81	=	2.0

A ratio that measures the relationship of current assets to current liabilities is called the **current ratio**. Normally, current liabilities are expected to be paid from cash on hand and cash soon to be received from other current assets.

The current ratio is calculated by dividing total current assets by total current liabilities. Forest's current ratios for 20X3 and 20X2 are calculated as shown above, using information from the balance sheet (page 371). The 20X3 current ratio of 2.5 means that Forest owns $2.50 in current assets for each $1.00 needed to pay current liabilities.

Forest wants to maintain a current ratio between 2.0 and 3.0. Industry experience has shown that a business with a current ratio of less than 2.0 has difficulty raising cash to pay current liabilities on time. At the same time, industry experience shows that a current ratio can be too high. If the current ratio is 3.0 or higher, the business has more capital invested in current assets than is needed to run the business.

In 20X2, Forest's current ratio of 2.0 was at the low end of the desired range. However, the 20X3 ratio, 2.5, is at the midpoint of the target range and a favorable indication of its financial strength. Forest's expansion may also have contributed to the lower current ratio in 20X2. In 20X3, Forest increased its current assets while its current liabilities remain unchanged.

Quick Ratio

		Total Quick Assets (Cash + Accounts Receivable)	÷	Total Current Liabilities	=	Quick Ratio
	20X3	$113,983.73	÷	$135,862.58	=	0.8
	20X2	$101,025.62	÷	$135,922.81	=	0.7

Cash and other current assets that can be converted quickly into cash are called **quick assets**. Quick assets include cash, accounts receivable, and marketable securities, but not merchandise inventory or prepaid expenses. On Forest's balance sheet, cash and cash equivalents and accounts receivable are quick assets. A ratio that measures the relationship of quick assets to current liabilities is called the **quick ratio**. The quick ratio is also called the *acid-test* ratio. This ratio shows the ability of a business to pay all its current liabilities almost immediately, if necessary.

Forest's quick ratios for 20X3 and 20X2 are calculated as shown above. The 20X3 ratio of 0.8 indicates that for each $1.00 needed to pay current liabilities, Forest has $0.80 available in quick assets. For companies similar to Forest, the desired industry standard for a quick ratio is between 0.9 and 1.3. Therefore, Forest's quick ratio for 20X3 is slightly lower than desired.

Forest's quick ratio has increased from 0.7 to 0.8. While this is a favorable trend, Forest must do more to increase its quick ratio. This could be accomplished by increasing cash from the sale of capital stock or by borrowing for a long term to pay off current liabilities.

> **FYI** A favorable trend occurs when a ratio moves closer to the midpoint of the target range, even if the ratio is outside the target range.

Long-Term Financial Strength LO4

Businesses that are successful and are able to continue operating through both strong and weak economic periods usually have long-term financial strength. Long-term financial strength requires a balance between stockholders' capital and borrowed capital. A profitable business can be even more profitable by using borrowed capital wisely. However, borrowed capital must be repaid with interest. Continuing operation of a business with a large percentage of borrowed capital may be jeopardized if net income declines and it cannot make loan payments. In addition, creditors are reluctant to loan additional money to companies with a high level of liabilities. A well-managed company monitors its long-term financial strength to ensure that it maintains a reasonable balance between stockholders' capital and borrowed capital.

Forest uses four measures to analyze long-term financial strength: (1) debt ratio, (2) equity ratio, (3) equity per share, and (4) interest coverage ratio.

Debt Ratio

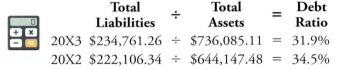

	Total Liabilities	÷	Total Assets	=	Debt Ratio
20X3	$234,761.26	÷	$736,085.11	=	31.9%
20X2	$222,106.34	÷	$644,147.48	=	34.5%

Total liabilities divided by total assets is called the **debt ratio**. This ratio shows the percentage of assets that are financed with borrowed capital (liabilities).

Forest's debt ratios for 20X3 and 20X2 are calculated as shown above, using information from the balance sheet (page 371). The 20X3 ratio of 31.9% indicates that for each $1.00 of assets owned by Forest, the company has borrowed 31.9 cents.

Forest has determined that the debt ratio should be between 29.0% and 33.0%. Forest's debt ratio for 20X2 was above the target range. Rapid growth over the past two or three years, financed primarily through borrowed capital, caused the unfavorable liabilities level. However, Forest's 20X3 debt ratio has decreased from 20X2, and is now within the target range. The company should consider increasing assets without increasing liabilities by issuing more capital stock. This action would reduce the debt ratio even further.

Equity Ratio

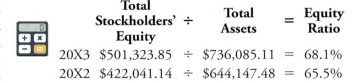

	Total Stockholders' Equity	÷	Total Assets	=	Equity Ratio
20X3	$501,323.85	÷	$736,085.11	=	68.1%
20X2	$422,041.14	÷	$644,147.48	=	65.5%

The ratio found by dividing stockholders' equity by total assets is called the **equity ratio**. This ratio shows the percentage of assets that are provided by stockholders' equity.

Forest's equity ratios for 20X3 and 20X2 are calculated as shown above, using information from the statement of stockholders' equity (page 370) and the balance sheet (page 371). Forest's ratio for 20X3, 68.1%, indicates that for each $1.00 of assets owned by the company, 68.1 cents' worth was acquired with stockholders' capital. Forest desires an equity ratio between 67.0% and 71.0%. The trend is favorable, and Forest's equity ratio for 20X3 is within the target range.

The debt and equity ratios show the mix of capital provided by capital borrowed and capital provided by stockholders. The sum of the two ratios equals 100%, as shown here because total liabilities and stockholders' equity represent the source of all asset ownership.

	20X3	20X2
Debt Ratio	31.9%	34.5%
Equity Ratio	68.1%	65.5%
Totals	100.0%	100.0%

Due to rapid expansion, Forest's 20X2 equity ratio declined to an unfavorable level, and its debt ratio increased to an unfavorable level. In 20X3, both ratios have improved and are within the target range. Forest can continue efforts to increase its equity ratio by reducing liabilities and issuing additional stock.

FYI An unfavorable ratio in one year may be balanced by previous actual positive results and future expected positive results. The trend in a ratio may be more important than the ratio for a particular year.

Equity Per Share of Common Stock

	Total Stockholders' Equity	_	Preferred Stockholders' Share of Stockholders' Equity	=	Common Stockholders' Share of Stockholders' Equity
20X3	$501,323.85	−	$127,500.00	=	$373,823.85
20X2	$422,041.14	−	$127,500.00	=	$294,541.14

	Common Stockholders' Share of Stockholders' Equity	÷	Shares of Capital Stock Outstanding	=	Common Equity per Share
20X3	$373,823.85	÷	65,000	=	$5.75
20X2	$294,541.14	÷	65,000	=	$4.53

The amount of common stockholders' equity belonging to a single share of common stock is known as **common equity per share**. When a company has both common and preferred stock outstanding, the preferred stockholders' share of stockholders' equity must be subtracted from the total stockholders' equity. The preferred stockholders' share of stockholders' equity is equal to the par value of the preferred stock multiplied by the number of preferred shares outstanding.

Forest's common equity per share for 20X3 and 20X2 is calculated as shown above, using information from the statement of stockholders' equity (page 370). Forest's common equity per share in 20X3, $5.75, indicates that on December 31, 20X3, each share of common stock represents ownership in $5.75 of the assets.

Common equity per share tells stockholders how much ownership of the company each share represents. For example, Forest's common stockholders know that each share represents a $5.75 equity in the total company assets. This ownership has increased from $4.53 per share in 20X2, a significant increase and a favorable trend.

Interest Coverage Ratio and EBIT

	EBIT	÷	Interest Expense	=	Interest Coverage Ratio
20X3	$129,281.38	÷	$11,708.33	=	11.0
20X2	$129,021.22	÷	$ 7,850.00	=	16.4
20X1	$123,382.36	÷	$ 4,554.25	=	27.1

Earnings before interest expense and taxes is called **EBIT** (pronounced ē - bĭt). EBIT is used in the calculation of several financial ratios. The easiest way to calculate EBIT is to start with net income and add interest expense and taxes. EBIT for 20X3 is is $129,281.38 ($92,882.71 + $11,708.33 + $24,690.34).

The number of times a company can cover its interest expense with its earnings is called the **interest coverage ratio**. The interest coverage ratio is also referred to as the "times interest-earned ratio." Forest's interest coverage ratios for the most recent three years are shown at the bottom of the first column, using information from the income statement (page 369). Forest's interest coverage ratio of 11.0 for 20X3 means that Forest's earnings can cover its interest expense 11.0 times.

Forest has been increasing its debt as it experiences rapid growth and increases in inventory. With increased debt comes increased interest expense. While Forest's net income has been relatively stable, its interest expense has grown each of the past two years. This growth has caused Forest's interest coverage ratio to decrease dramatically. However, it is still well above the acceptable ratio of 2.5.

If a company's interest coverage ratio falls below 2.5, it runs the risk of not being able to pay its annual interest expense. When this happens, banks may hesitate to loan additional funds to the company.

LO1 Identify the users of financial statement analysis.

LO2 Identify the objectives of financial statement analysis.

LO3 Analyze the short-term financial strength of a business.

LO4 Analyze the long-term financial strength of a business.

TERMS REVIEW

comparative financial statements

cash equivalents

working capital

current ratio

quick assets

quick ratio

debt ratio

equity ratio

common equity per share

EBIT

interest coverage ratio

Audit your understanding LO1, 2, 3, 4

1. List three groups that may use financial statement analysis.
2. What are four objectives for analyzing financial information?
3. What three measures can be used to analyze short-term financial strength?
4. What four measures are used to analyze the long-term financial strength of a business?

Work together 13-1 LO3, 4

Analyzing short- and long-term financial strength

Information taken from S & T Company's comparative income statement and balance sheet and a form for completing this problem are provided in the *Working Papers*. Your instructor will guide you through the following examples.

1. Calculate the following financial strength ratios for the current year and the prior year. Round ratios to the nearest tenth.
   a. Working capital
   b. Current ratio
   c. Quick ratio
   d. Debt ratio
   e. Equity ratio
   f. Common equity per share
   g. Interest coverage ratio
2. Compare each ratio to S & T Company's target range. Identify whether each ratio indicates a favorable trend and a favorable result.
3. List two ways that S & T Company can increase its interest coverage ratio.

On your own 13-1 LO3, 4

Analyzing short- and long-term financial strength

Information taken from OfficeWorld Supply Company's comparative income statement and balance sheet and a form for completing this problem are provided in the *Working Papers*. Work independently to complete the following problem.

1. Calculate the following financial strength ratios for the current year and the prior year. Round ratios to the nearest tenth.
   a. Working capital
   b. Current ratio
   c. Quick ratio
   d. Debt ratio
   e. Equity ratio
   f. Common equity per share
   g. Interest coverage ratio
2. Compare each ratio to S & T Company's target range. Identify whether each ratio indicates a favorable trend and a favorable result.
3. List one way that OfficeWorld Supply Company can decrease its debt ratio.

LO5 Analyze the profitability of a business.

Profitability Analysis LO5

The amounts and consistency of earnings are important measures of a business's success. The earnings of a business must be satisfactory to continue operations. ≫ App A: Going Concern Consequently, managers, owners, and creditors are interested in an analysis of the profitability of the company. Forest calculates five profitability measures for the three most recent years: (1) gross margin, (2) operating margin, (3) rate earned on average total assets, (4) rate earned on average stockholders' equity, and (5) free cash flow.

Gross Margin

		Gross Profit	÷	Net Sales	=	Gross Margin
	20X3	$254,982.02	÷	$646,017.54	=	39.5%
	20X2	$246,612.12	÷	$645,212.32	=	38.2%
	20X1	$247,126.30	÷	$642,578.45	=	38.5%

The ratio of the money earned relative to the amount of the investment is known as the *return on investment.* There are several measures used to analyze return on investment. The measures differ as to the investment that is identified and the dollar amount used for the earnings.

Gross profit as a percent of net sales is called **gross margin**. Forest's gross margins for 20X3 and the two prior years are calculated as shown above, using information from the income statement (page 369). The 39.5% gross margin for 20X3 indicates that for each $1.00 of sales, Forest earns 39.5 cents in gross profit. The remaining amount from the sales dollar, 60.5 cents ($1.00 − $0.395), represents the cost of merchandise sold. Gross profit must be high enough to cover operating expenses, other expenses, taxes, and profit. Gross margin can be improved by increasing sales at a faster rate than the cost of merchandise sold.

Forest's gross margin decreased from 20X1 to 20X2, even though net sales increased significantly. This decrease was the result of the cost of merchandise sold increasing at a faster rate than net sales. Forest's gross margin increased from 20X2 to 20X3. Net sales increased only slightly during this period, but the cost of merchandise sold actually decreased. Forest was able to lower its cost of merchandise sold, possibly due to lower employee costs or finding a less expensive inventory source.

Forest feels that an acceptable gross margin target range is 40% to 41%. The trend for the last year is favorable, but the result is still outside the acceptable range. Forest must try to increase its gross margin in the future.

© ZHU DIFENG/SHUTTERSTOCK.COM

Operating Margin

		Income from Operations	÷	Net Sales	=	Operating Margin
	20X3	$119,493.88	÷	$646,017.54	=	18.5%
	20X2	$118,925.68	÷	$645,212.32	=	18.4%
	20X1	$120,892.82	÷	$642,578.45	=	18.8%

Income from operations as a percent of net sales is called **operating margin**. This ratio is also referred to as the *rate of return on sales*. Forest's operating margins for 20X3 and the two prior years are calculated as shown above, using information from the income statement (page 369).

Forest's 18.5% operating margin for 20X3 indicates that for each $1.00 of sales, it earns 18.5 cents in operating income. This amount is available to cover other expenses, taxes, and profit.

Operating margin is used by investors to determine how effective a business is at earning a profit from its normal operations. Investors can compare Forest's operating margin with that for other companies in the same industry. This measure of a company's profitability is better than a ratio using net income because the managers of a company have more control over income from operations. Net income is affected by the income statement category "Other Revenues and Expenses" and by taxes. The items included in Other Revenues and Expenses do not reflect the normal operations of the business, and managers cannot easily control the amount of taxes paid to the government.

Forest has set a target range of between 18% and 22%. Therefore, even though Forest's gross margin is at the lower end of the target range, the company has done a very good job of controlling operating expenses and has an operating margin that is acceptable.

© NICOELNINO/SHUTTERSTOCK.COM

Channel Stuffing

It seems to happen earlier every year. Retail store shelves have barely been cleared of their Halloween candy when gifts and supplies for the important Thanksgiving through New Year's Day selling season begin to appear.

Commonly, retailers take delivery of seasonal items well before the selling season. In fact, it is a business necessity. Items for sale in December might be ordered during the spring and be delivered in October. Retailers and suppliers both benefit from early ordering. The retailer is assured that the merchandise will be available for sale and will be delivered at the desired time. A supplier can plan its production schedules better, ensuring that it has an adequate supply of raw materials and labor.

Suppose that a supplier offers customers a 20% discount to order and pay for merchandise a full 12 months before the selling season. In exchange, the supplier will warehouse the merchandise until requested by each retailer.

When should the supplier record the sale? When the order is received, when the merchandise is produced, when the merchandise is delivered, or when cash is exchanged? Generally accepted accounting principles (GAAP) require that the sale be recorded when the merchandise is transferred between the parties. The transfer most often occurs when the goods are delivered.

Sunbeam, a maker of household appliances, began to offer its customers similar terms in 1997. Customers were offered discounts for ordering merchandise well before it was needed. Sunbeam would hold the items until the normal delivery date. However, contrary to GAAP, Sunbeam recorded the sales when the orders were received. This practice, known as *channel stuffing*, is illegal because it fraudulently inflates sales by recording future sales in the current period. Channel stuffing was just one of several schemes Sunbeam used to inflate earnings. When Sunbeam's fraudulent financial statements were revealed, the reported net income of $109.4 million was reduced to $38.3 million. As sales continued to decline, Sunbeam's stock price plummeted.

ACTIVITY

The latest quarterly income statement of Chopra Novelties reported a sharp increase in sales. This was the "break-out" quarter that the new chief executive officer had been promising. As a member of the board of directors, you are pleased with this higher level of sales. Yet, you wonder whether some imaginative accounting could have been used to achieve these results. Thus, you direct the internal auditor to perform some basic tests related to the timing of sales and to look specifically for signs of channel stuffing.

Chopra's customers consist of retail businesses such as gift, grocery, and book stores. Customers place orders with their assigned sales representative and specify a desired delivery date. Since most retailers have limited space to store extra inventory, Chopra often receives orders having requested delivery dates several months after the order is placed. For example, novelty items related to Valentine's Day may be ordered in November but not delivered until the middle of January. Sales representatives strive to ship their customers' orders one to three days before the requested delivery date.

INSTRUCTIONS   ⊕ +ableau·

The Tableau workbook FA_CH13 contains charts that show the relationships between the order, requested delivery, and actual delivery dates. Read the caption above each chart to gain an understanding of the data presented. Use the charts to answer the following questions:

1. Examine the Order to Actual worksheet. Are the days between the customers' orders and actual delivery dates consistent among the three sales representatives?

2. The Actual to Requested worksheet shows the number of days between the actual and requested delivery dates. Is there any evidence that Chopra's delivery policy is being violated?

3. Does the Early Shipments worksheet provide any evidence of channel stuffing? Support your answer. What additional evidence could be obtained?

Source: Paul M. Clikeman, Called to Account: Financial Frauds That Shaped the Accounting Profession, *2nd ed., (New York, NY: Routledge), 2013.*

Rate Earned on Average Total Assets

$$\left[\begin{array}{c}\text{January 1, 20X3} \\ \text{Total Assets}\end{array} + \begin{array}{c}\text{December 31, 20X3} \\ \text{Total Assets}\end{array}\right] \div 2 = \begin{array}{c}\text{Average} \\ \text{Total Assets}\end{array} \text{ ❶}$$

$$\left[\$644,147.48 + \$736,085.11\right] \div 2 = \$690,116.30$$

$$\begin{array}{c}\text{Net} \\ \text{Income}\end{array} \div \begin{array}{c}\text{Average} \\ \text{Total Assets}\end{array} = \begin{array}{c}\text{Rate Earned on} \\ \text{Average Total Assets}\end{array} \text{ ❷}$$

$$\$92,882.71 \div \$690,116.30 = 13.5\%$$

A business uses its assets to earn net income. If a business uses all assets as efficiently as possible, it should earn the best possible net income. The relationship between net income and average total assets is called the **rate earned on average total assets**. This rate is also referred to as *return on assets* (*ROA*), and it shows how well a business is using its assets to earn net income. Forest's rate earned on average total assets is calculated as shown above, using income statement and balance sheet information.

>> Calculating the Rate Earned on Average Total Assets

❶ Calculate average total assets. Average total assets is the average amount of assets held during a year.

   a. Add January 1 total assets and December 31 total assets. (Total assets for January 1 are the same as the total assets on the prior year's December 31 balance sheet.)

   b. Divide the total by 2.

❷ Divide net income by average total assets to determine the rate earned on average total assets.

A 13.5% rate earned on average total assets means that for each $1.00 of assets, the business earned 13.5 cents.

A table comparing this result to the rate for 20X2 is shown below.

	20X3	20X2*
Net income	$ 92,882.71	$ 95,725.26
January 1 total assets	644,147.48	645,298.12
December 31 total assets	736,085.11	644,147.48
Average total assets	690,116.30	644,722.80
Rate earned on average total assets	13.5%	14.8%

*Some information for 20X2 is taken from financial statements that are not illustrated.

Forest compares this rate to rates of return on alternative investments. Forest's goal is to earn a rate of return that is at least as high as other types of investments. For example, if Forest can earn more by placing extra cash in government bonds, the company is not meeting its earnings goal.

Investment sources available to Forest are earning between 13.0% and 13.4%. Although both years' rates of return are above this goal, the rate earned on average total assets for 20X3 has dropped significantly from 20X2. Forest must take measures to ensure that this trend does not continue. To increase this rate, Forest must either earn more net income with the same amount of assets or earn the same amount of income with less invested assets.

Rate Earned on Average Stockholders' Equity

$$\left[\begin{array}{c}\text{January 1, 20X3}\\\text{Stockholders' Equity}\end{array} + \begin{array}{c}\text{December 31, 20X3}\\\text{Stockholders' Equity}\end{array}\right] \div 2 = \begin{array}{c}\text{Average}\\\text{Stockholders' Equity}\end{array} \; \mathbf{1}$$

$$\left[\$422,041.14 \quad + \quad \$501,323.85\right] \quad \div \quad 2 \quad = \quad \$461,682.50$$

$$\text{Net Income} \div \begin{array}{c}\text{Average}\\\text{Stockholders' Equity}\end{array} = \begin{array}{c}\text{Rate Earned on}\\\text{Average Stockholders' Equity}\end{array} \; \mathbf{2}$$

$$\$92,882.71 \quad \div \quad \$461,682.50 \quad = \quad 20.1\%$$

Investors use financial measures to compare businesses to determine the best investment. The relationship between net income and average stockholders' equity is called the **rate earned on average stockholders' equity**. Forest's rate earned on average stockholders' equity is calculated as shown above.

>> Calculating the Rate Earned on Average Stockholders' Equity

1 Calculate average stockholders' equity.

   a. Add January 1 stockholders' equity and December 31 stockholders' equity. (Stockholders' equity for January 1 is the same as the stockholders' equity on the prior year's December 31 balance sheet.)

   b. Divide the total by 2.

2 Divide net income by average stockholders' equity to determine the rate earned on average stockholders' equity.

A 20.1% rate earned on average stockholders' equity means that for each $1.00 of stockholders' equity, the business earned 20.1 cents. The following table compares the 20X3 rate to the 20X2 rate.

	20X3	20X2*
Net income	$ 92,882.71	$ 95,725.26
January 1 stockholders' equity	422,041.14	280,865.88
December 31 stockholders' equity	501,323.85	422,041.14
Average stockholders' equity	461,682.50	351,453.51
Rate earned on average stockholders' equity	20.1%	27.2%

*Some information for 20X2 is taken from financial statements that are not illustrated.

Forest's rate is well above the industry standard of 13.0%. However, its rate has decreased significantly from 27.2% to 20.1%. Even though a comparison with industry standards shows that Forest achieved a satisfactory rate earned on average stockholders' equity, the trend is one that should be investigated. Forest does not want this trend to continue. To keep the rate from decreasing, Forest must maintain the level of net income with the same amount of stockholders' equity.

Free Cash Flow

	Cash Flow from Operating Activities	−	Capital Expenditures	=	Free Cash Flow
20X3	$19,498.78	−	$31,000.00	=	($11,501.22)
20X2	$50,886.13	−	$122,853.00	=	($71,966.87)

Cash flow data are important information for company managers, creditors, and investors. If a company cannot pay its bills by their due date, it must arrange for short-term loans or cash advances. **Free cash flow** is a measure equal to cash flows from operations less cash used for capital expenditures. **Capital expenditures** are purchases of plant assets used in the operation of a business. Forest's free cash flow for 20X3 and 20X2 is calculated as shown above, using information from the statement of cash flows (page 372). For Forest, capital expenditures are the purchases of office equipment and store equipment.

Forest's free cash flow is negative for both years. This means that each year Forest used more cash for purchases of equipment than the cash flow from operating activities. The negative free cash flow for 20X3 ($11,501.22) is considerably less than the negative cash flow for 20X2 ($71,966.87). Even though cash flow from operating activities decreased from 20X2 to 20X3, capital expenditures decreased by a much greater amount.

While a negative free cash flow is not acceptable in the long run, Forest was aware of the need to invest in capital items. Over the last three years, company managers took steps to increase cash flows by issuing bonds and selling preferred stock.

World Trade Organization

A company looking to expand its business can try to sell its goods and services in foreign markets. Goods or services shipped out of a seller's home country to another country are known as *exports*.

Companies can also buy products from foreign markets. A foreign company may sell materials, component parts, or finished goods at a lower price than a domestic company. Goods or services shipped into the buyer's home country from another country are known as *imports*.

Doing business in a foreign country can help a company grow, but it also brings potential challenges. Business practices can vary from country to country. In some countries, the government can block imports to or exports from specific countries. In other countries, the government can institute tariffs on imports or exports.

An organization that works "to ensure that trade flows as smoothly, predictably and freely as possible" between nations is the World Trade Organization (WTO). The WTO states on its website that it "is the only international organization dealing with the global rules of trade between nations." The WTO was established on January 1, 1995. At the time of publication, the WTO had 164 member countries.

The basis for smooth, predictable, and free trade flows is a WTO trading agreement. A country signs such an agreement and is then bound to follow it. The WTO supports the negotiation and enforcement of these agreements. If a country is not adhering to a trade agreement, the WTO will oversee a dispute settlement process.

The WTO also focuses efforts on helping developing countries, which are given some leeway in implementing trade agreements. Most trade agreements also contain measures to increase the trading opportunities of developing countries.

CRITICAL THINKING

Visit the WTO website at www.wto.org to answer these questions.

1. Find the current list of WTO member countries. List three countries that joined the WTO on January 1, 1995. List the newest member of the WTO and the date it became a member.

2. List the name of the director-general and when his or her term as director-general ends.

3. Why might the government of a country limit the importing of goods to that country?

LO5 Analyze the profitability of a business.

TERMS REVIEW

gross margin

operating margin

rate earned on average total assets

rate earned on average stockholders' equity

free cash flow

capital expenditures

Audit your understanding LO5

1. What five measures can be used to analyze the profitability of a business?
2. What does the rate earned on average total assets show?
3. What does the rate earned on average stockholders' equity show?

Work together 13-2 LO5
Calculating profitability measures

Information taken from KL Marketing Group's financial statements and a form for completing this problem are provided in the *Working Papers*. Your instructor will guide you through the following examples.

1. Calculate the following profitability measures for the current year and the prior year. Round percentage calculations to the nearest 0.1% and dollar amounts to the nearest $0.01.

    a. Gross margin

    b. Operating margin

    c. Rate earned on average total assets

    d. Rate earned on average stockholders' equity

    e. Free cash flow

2. Compare each measure to KL's target range. Identify whether each measure indicated a favorable trend and a favorable result.

3. Explain what its operating margin from the current year tells KL Marketing Group.

On your own 13-2 LO5
Calculating profitability measures

Information taken from GreenWay Corporation's financial statements and a form for completing this problem are provided in the *Working Papers*. Work independently to complete the following problem.

1. Calculate the following profitability measures for the current year and the prior year. Round percentage calculations to the nearest 0.1% and dollar amounts to the nearest $0.01. Your instructor will guide you through the examples.

    a. Gross margin

    b. Operating margin

    c. Rate earned on average total assets

    d. Rate earned on average stockholders' equity

    e. Free cash flow

2. Compare each measure to GreenWay's target range. Identify whether each measure indicated a favorable trend and a favorable result.

3. Explain what the gross margin from the current year tells GreenWay Corporation.

Calculating and Analyzing Efficiency Measures and Market Ratios

LO6 Perform efficiency analysis of a business.
LO7 Calculate the market ratios of a business.

Analyzing Efficiency LO6

The profitability and continued growth of a business are influenced by how efficiently the business utilizes its assets. The operating cycle of a merchandising business consists of three phases: (1) purchasing merchandise, (2) selling merchandise (frequently on account), and (3) collecting the accounts receivable. Much of a business's assets are in accounts receivable and merchandise inventory. The faster a business can convert these assets to cash and begin another operating cycle, the more efficient and profitable the business will be.

Accounts Receivable Turnover Ratio

Calculate average book value of accounts receivable

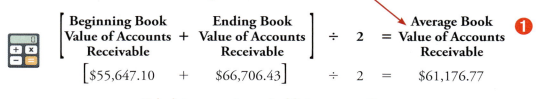

Calculate accounts receivable turnover ratio

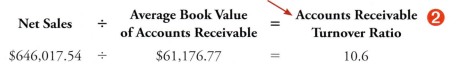

A business accepts accounts receivable to encourage sales. However, the earnings process is not complete until the business receives cash for sales on account. Thus, an efficient company closely monitors the length of time required to collect its receivables. The number of times the average amount of accounts receivable is collected during a specified period is known as the *accounts receivable turnover ratio*. This ratio monitors a business's accounts receivable collection efficiency.

Forest's accounts receivable turnover ratio for 20X3 is calculated as shown above, using the information from the balance sheet and income statement. Forest's turnover ratio indicates that accounts are being collected 10.6 times a year.

Days' Sales in Accounts Receivable

The average period of time to collect an account receivable is known as *days' sales in accounts receivable*.

Calculate days' sales in accounts receivable

The days' sales in accounts receivable is calculated above.

The accounts receivable turnover ratio for 20X2 was 11.4. The days' sales in accounts receivable was 32 days. Forest's credit terms are n/30. Thus, the company's goal is to collect accounts receivable in 30 days or less. Neither year's results meet that goal. In addition, the ratio has decreased from 11.4 to 10.6. This unfavorable trend may be a result of Forest's growth and should be monitored carefully so that it does not continue. The unfavorable trend could also result from a relaxation of credit restrictions.

Inventory Turnover Ratio

Calculate average merchandise inventory **1**

$$\left[\begin{array}{ccc} \text{January 1} & & \text{December 31} \\ \text{Merchandise} & + & \text{Merchandise} \\ \text{Inventory} & & \text{Inventory} \end{array}\right] \div\ 2\ =\ \begin{array}{c}\text{Average Merchandise}\\\text{Inventory}\end{array}$$

$$\left[\$95,\!214.25\ +\ \$144,\!066.40\right]\ \div\ 2\ =\ \$119,\!640.33$$

Calculate inventory turnover ratio **2**

$$\begin{array}{c}\text{Cost of}\\\text{Merchandise Sold}\end{array} \div \begin{array}{c}\text{Average Merchandise}\\\text{Inventory}\end{array} = \begin{array}{c}\text{Inventory Turnover}\\\text{Ratio}\end{array}$$

$$\$391,\!035.52\ \div\ \$119,\!640.33\ =\ 3.3$$

A company earns income when it sells merchandise. The faster it sells its inventory, the more efficient and generally the more profitable the business. The number of times the average amount of merchandise inventory is sold during a specific period is known as the *inventory turnover ratio*. This ratio can be used to monitor merchandise inventory efficiency.

Forest's inventory turnover ratio for 20X3 is calculated as shown above, using information from the income statement and balance sheet. The turnover ratio of 3.3 indicates that the inventory is being sold 3.3 times in a year.

Days' Sales in Inventory

Calculate days' sales in inventory

$$\begin{array}{c}\text{Days}\\\text{in Year}\end{array} \div \begin{array}{c}\text{Inventory}\\\text{Turnover Ratio}\end{array} = \begin{array}{c}\text{Days' Sales in}\\\text{Inventory}\end{array}$$

$$365\ \div\ 3.3\ =\ 111\ \text{days}$$

The time needed to sell an average amount of merchandise inventory is known as *days' sales in inventory*. The days' sales in inventory is calculated in the column to the left.

The inventory turnover ratio for 20X2 was 3.2. The days' sales in inventory was 114 days. An optimum merchandise inventory turnover ratio is determined by two factors: (1) amount of sales and (2) number of days needed to replenish the inventory. Previous experience indicates that Forest needs to maintain an inventory turnover ratio between 3.3 and 3.6. Forest's inventory turnover ratio is at the low end of the target range. A turnover ratio considerably lower than the acceptable range would indicate too much inventory on hand. A turnover ratio considerably higher than the acceptable range would mean that Forest is at risk for lost sales because some items could be out of stock before new inventory is received. Overall, Forest's current inventory level is satisfactory.

Market Ratios LO7

Most ratios classified as market ratios relate an amount from the financial statements of a company with the market price of the company's stock. Market ratios, therefore, are somewhat objective because the market price of a stock is determined by the marketplace.

Earnings Per Share

		Net Income		Preferred Dividends		Shares of Common Stock Outstanding		Earnings per Share
20X3	[	$92,882.71	–	$7,650.00] ÷		65,000	=	$1.31
20X2	[	$95,725.26	–	$7,650.00] ÷		65,000	=	$1.36
20X1	[	$93,874.21	–	$3,000.00] ÷		65,000	=	$1.40

Net income after federal income tax divided by the number of outstanding shares of stock is known as **earnings per share (EPS)**. Stockholders and management frequently use earnings per share as a measure of success. As earnings per share increase, more people become interested in buying stock. This demand for stock causes stock prices to go up. The company then finds it easier to issue stock or borrow money.

Forest's earnings per share for 20X3 and the two prior years are calculated as shown on page 386, using information from the income statement and the statement of stockholders' equity. Although net income increased from 20X1 to 20X2, earnings per share decreased from $1.40 to $1.36. This was caused by an increase in preferred dividends due to more preferred shares outstanding. More dividends paid to preferred stockholders decreased the amount of net income available to common shareholders. Earnings per share decreased again in 20X3, due to a decrease in net income. Forest knows that a positive trend is important to the company and must try to increase its earnings per share in the future.

Forest Equipment, Inc., has what is called a *simple capital structure*. This means that it does not have any convertible preferred stock or convertible bonds payable or stock options outstanding. If a company has convertible preferred stock or bonds or stock options, it is considered to have a *complex capital structure*, and it must complete additional calculations for earnings per share. Earnings per share calculated as if all convertible securities and stock options are converted to shares of common stock is called *diluted earnings per share*.

For example, assume that during 20X3, Forest Equipment, Inc., issued bonds that could be converted to 5,000 shares of common stock. Even though the bonds were not converted during 20X3, the company would have to calculate and disclose diluted earnings per share in addition to regular (or basic) earnings per share. The only part of the calculation that would change would be the number of shares of common stock outstanding. For calculating diluted earnings per share, it is assumed that all 5,000 shares of common stock have been issued. Forest's diluted earnings per share would be $1.22 [($92,882.71 – $7,650.00) ÷ 70,000 = $1.22]. Notice that this calculation indicates that each share only earned $1.22 instead of $1.31. Diluted earnings per share gives the stockholder a "worst-case scenario of earnings. This lower earnings per share would only come true if everyone holding the convertible bonds converted his or her shares.

THINK LIKE AN ACCOUNTANT

Charting Earnings per Share

LMP Technology has been a privately held corporation since its inception. A major source of the corporation's capital has been the sale of preferred stock to venture capitalists. The corporation also manages a stock incentive program that awards its 20 employees with stock in lieu of competitive market salaries.

The corporation's strategies have worked well. The corporation has grown to become a major supplier of computer networking equipment. At the urging of its venture capitalist investors, LMP has decided it is time to take the corporation public.

LMP's Accounting Department has been charged with creating the documents required to file an initial public offering with the Securities and Exchange Commission. The Accounting Department was also given responsibility for creating a presentation that management would deliver to various brokerage firms and institutional investors to raise awareness of, and demand for, LMP's common stock. Charts showing the growth in earnings per share would be critical to communicating the success of the corporation.

OPEN THE SPREADSHEET TLA_CH13

The workbook contains ten years of earnings and stock information. Follow the steps on the Instructions tab to prepare two charts. Answer these questions:

1. Describe the growth in earnings per share over the past ten years.

2. Compare and contrast the two charts. Identify what charting options should be selected to create the chart for the presentation.

Price-Earnings Ratio

	Market Price per Share	÷	Earnings per Share	=	Price-Earnings Ratio
20X3	$ 9.50	÷	$1.31	=	7.3
20X2	$10.00	÷	$1.36	=	7.4
20X1	$ 9.00	÷	$1.40	=	6.4

The price at which a share of stock may be sold on the stock market at any given time is called the **market value of a share of stock**. The market price of a share of stock is determined by the amount that investors are willing to pay for it. Thus, the market price of a company's stock is influenced strongly by what potential investors think the company's earnings will be in the future. Market value can change frequently and dramatically for heavily traded stocks.

The relationship between the market value per share and earnings per share of a stock is called the **price-earnings ratio** (P/E ratio). Investors usually want to buy stock in companies that are earning a reasonable amount of net income. The P/E ratio can be compared to those of similar companies.

Forest's P/E ratio of 7.3 means that the price of one share of stock is 7.3 times the earnings per share. In 20X3, the decrease in the market price caused the P/E ratio to decrease. The market is not willing to pay as much per share as in the past. This may be due to several unfavorable trends revealed by an analysis of Forest's financial statements. Forest may need to try to increase earnings per share to maintain investor confidence.

It is also important to realize that Forest's P/E ratio for 20X3 would have decreased even more if not for the decrease in earnings per share from 20X2 to 20X3. Had its earnings per share stayed at $1.36, its P/E ratio would have been only 7.0.

What is a typical P/E ratio? P/E ratios vary considerably from industry to industry. When analyzing a company, it is best to compare its P/E ratio with other companies in the same industry. In addition, while a higher P/E ratio usually is considered better than a lower P/E ratio, there are some exceptions. A low P/E ratio (a low market price compared to the earnings) indicates that the market is not confident about the future of the stock. However, it could also mean that the stock is undervalued, which would indicate a good time to buy its shares. On the other hand, a high P/E ratio (a high market price compared to the earnings) indicates that the market has confidence in the future earnings of the company. However, it may mean that the stock is overpriced and ready for a correction. These considerations, plus the fact that Forest cannot directly control the market price for its stock, are the reasons why Forest has not determined a target range for earnings per share and cannot simply state whether the trend in earnings per share is favorable or unfavorable.

A smart investor will not make an investment decision based on P/E ratio alone. The P/E ratio should be used in conjunction with other financial measures and with nonfinancial data that would help one predict the future success of a company.

FYI *The Wall Street Journal* and many local newspapers report price-earnings ratios in their stock quotations.

Dividend Yield

		Common Dividends	÷	Common Shares Outstanding	=	Common Dividend per Share
	20X3	$14,950.00	÷	65,000	=	$0.23
	20X2	$16,900.00	÷	65,000	=	$0.26
	20X1	$14,950.00	÷	65,000	=	$0.23

	Common Dividend per Share	÷	Market Price per Share	=	Common Dividend Yield
20X3	$0.23	÷	$ 9.50	=	2.4%
20X2	$0.26	÷	$10.00	=	2.6%
20X1	$0.23	÷	$ 9.00	=	2.6%

The relationship between dividends per share and market price per share is called the **dividend yield**. Dividend yield can be calculated for both common and preferred stock. Forest's common dividend yield for 20X3 and the two prior years is calculated above.

Forest's common dividend yield of 2.4% for 20X3 means that stockholders are earning 2.4% on their investment in Forest stock. An investor will compare the earnings on Forest's stock with other investment opportunities. However, even though the dividend yield is low, investors who are not looking for immediate cash inflow from dividends may hold on to their Forest stock because of an expectation that the market value of the stock will increase.

		Preferred Dividends	÷	Preferred Shares Outstanding	=	Preferred Dividend per Share
	20X3	$7,650.00	÷	1,275	=	$6.00
	20X2	$7,650.00	÷	1,275	=	$6.00
	20X1	$3,000.00	÷	500	=	$6.00

	Preferred Dividend per Share	÷	Market Price per Share	=	Preferred Dividend Yield
20X3	$6.00	÷	$107.00	=	5.6%
20X2	$6.00	÷	$112.00	=	5.4%
20X1	$6.00	÷	$110.00	=	5.5%

Forest's preferred dividend yield for 20X3 and the two prior years is calculated above. Forest's preferred dividend yield of 5.6% for 20X3 means that stockholders are earning 5.6% on their investment in Forest stock.

Note that the dividend yield decreased in 20X2 because the market price of the stock increased. The dividend yield increased in 20X3 because the market price of the stock decreased.

LO6 Perform efficiency analysis of a business.

LO7 Calculate the market ratios of a business.

TERMS REVIEW

earnings per share (EPS)

market value of a share of stock

price-earnings ratio

dividend yield

Audit your understanding LO6, 7

1. What does an increase in accounts receivable turnover indicate?
2. What is the formula for the price-earnings ratio?
3. If the dividend paid remains the same from Year 1 to Year 2, but the market value of the stock decreases, how will the dividend yield be affected?

Work together 13-3 LO6, 7

Calculating and analyzing efficiency measures and market ratios

Information taken from Bonita Bay Supply's financial statements and a form for completing this problem are provided in the *Working Papers*. Your instructor will guide you through the following examples.

1. Calculate the following efficiency measures and market ratios for the current year and the prior year. Round percentage calculations to the nearest 0.1%, dollar amounts to the nearest $0.01, and the price-earnings ratio to the nearest tenth.

   a. Accounts receivable turnover ratio

   b. Days' sales in accounts receivable

   c. Inventory turnover ratio

   d. Days' sales in inventory

   e. Earnings per share

   f. Price-earnings ratio

   g. Dividend yield

2. Compare each measure to Bonita Bay Supply's target range. Identify whether each measure indicated a favorable trend and a favorable result.

3. Bonita Bay Supply's credit terms are n/30. Analyze the company's days' sales in accounts receivable in terms of its credit policy and state any trend this measure reveals.

On your own 13-3 LO6, 7

Calculating and analyzing efficiency measures and market ratios

Information taken from Morgan Enterprise's financial statements and a form for completing this problem are provided in the *Working Papers*. Work independently to complete the following problem.

1. Calculate the following efficiency measures and market ratios for the current year and the prior year. Round percentage calculations to the nearest 0.1%, dollar amounts to the nearest $0.01, and the price-earnings ratio to the nearest tenth.

   a. Accounts receivable turnover ratio

   b. Days' sales in accounts receivable

   c. Inventory turnover ratio

   d. Days' sales in inventory

   e. Earnings per share

   f. Price-earnings ratio

   g. Dividend yield

2. Compare each measure to Morgan Enterprise's target range. Identify whether each measure indicated a favorable trend and a favorable result.

3. Analyze the company's days' sales in inventory and state any trend this measure reveals.

Advanced Topics in Financial Reporting

LO8 Calculate permanent and temporary differences in net income and taxable income.

LO9 Identify the components of comprehensive income.

LO10 Identify where non-recurring items appear on the income statement.

Net Income and Taxable Income LO8

The net income reported by a company on its income statement is usually not the same amount reported on the company's tax return as "taxable income." The difference between net income and taxable income is caused by the rules that must be followed to calculate each amount.

Net income is calculated following accounting rules, called generally accepted accounting principles (GAAP). GAAP are developed by the accounting profession and are designed to provide important information that is accurate, reliable, comparable, and consistent.

Taxable income is calculated following U.S. tax laws. Tax laws are developed by Congress, enforced by the Internal Revenue Service, and designed to collect government revenue in an equitable manner. In addition, most tax laws are cash-based, where amounts are included in revenue when the cash is actually received and count as an expense when the cash is paid out.

Because two different sets of rules are followed, net income rarely equals taxable income. The differences between net income and taxable income fall into two categories: permanent differences and temporary differences.

Permanent Differences

A difference between net income and taxable income only for that year and that is never balanced out in a future year is called a **permanent difference**. An example of a permanent difference in revenues is interest revenue on a tax-exempt bond. This interest revenue is never subject to income tax. The company receiving the interest will not have to include it in its taxable income, but will include it on its income statement. Thus, its net income will be higher than its taxable income.

Company ABC bought a tax-exempt bond on January 1, 20X1, and sold the bond on December 31, 20X1. The company earned and received $1,000 of interest revenue on the bond. Before considering the interest

revenue from the bond, Company ABC's net income and taxable income both equal $50,000. What effect does the $1,000 of interest revenue have on both taxable income and net income? As shown, taxable income is not affected by the interest revenue on the tax-exempt bond. However, net income is increased by $1,000 because the interest revenue was earned in 20X1 and GAAP require that it be added to net income. The difference of $1,000 is a permanent difference because the interest revenue will never be included in taxable income.

Taxable Income	
Taxable income before interest revenue	$50,000.00
+ Taxable interest revenue	—
Taxable income	$50,000.00

Net Income	
Net income before interest revenue	$50,000.00
+ Interest revenue	1,000.00
Net Income	$51,000.00

Permanent differences include cash payments that are not deductible for tax purposes but are listed as expenses for net income calculations. Some examples are premiums paid on life insurance policies for key employees, lobbying and political expenses, fines, and one-half the cost of business meals.

Temporary Differences

A difference between net income and taxable income for more than one period that reverses out over the entire period is called a **temporary difference**. A temporary difference is also known as a *timing difference*. Once the difference has been reversed, the total net income will equal the total taxable income.

Taxable Income—20X1	
Taxable income before insurance expense	$50,000.00
– Tax deductible insurance expense	1,000.00
Taxable income	$49,000.00

Net Income—20X1	
Net income before insurance expense	$50,000.00
– Insurance expense	—
Net Income	$50,000.00

Taxable Income—20X2	
Taxable income before insurance expense	$50,000.00
– Tax deductible insurance expense	—
Taxable income	$50,000.00

Net Income—20X2	
Net income before insurance expense	$50,000.00
– Insurance expense	1,000.00
Net Income	$49,000.00

Accrued items often lead to temporary differences between taxable income and net income. These differences arise because the expenses must be recognized in net income when they are incurred, while taxable deductions are taken in the period the cash is paid. Company XYZ paid $1,000 cash for insurance on December 15, 20X1, for the next year. Before considering the insurance expense, Company XYZ's net income and taxable income both equal $50,000. What effect does the $1,000 of insurance

The largest temporary difference is often associated with depreciation. Many companies use straight-line depreciation for the calculation of net income so that the amount of depreciation is level over the life of the asset. For the same asset, the company will usually use an accelerated method of depreciation for the calculation of

expense have on taxable income and net income? As shown above, net income will not include the $1,000 as an expense in 20X1, but it will show the expense on the 20X2 income statement because the insurance premium was for 20X2. For tax purposes, the $1,000 will be a deduction against taxable income for 20X1, not 20X2.

The total taxable income and the total net income over the two-year period is the same, $99,000.00. The difference is a timing difference.

taxable income. This allows the company to pay fewer taxes in the early years of the asset, because the deductible expense is higher. The company pays more taxes in the later years of the asset, because of a lower deductible expense. Again, over the life of the asset the total amount of depreciation will be the same.

Comprehensive Income LO9

Income Statement	
Revenues	$50,000.00
Expenses	15,000.00
Income from operations	$35,000.00
Other revenues and expenses	(2,000.00)
Income before fed. income tax	$33,000.00
Federal income tax	(4,950.00)
Net income	$28,050.00

Statement of Comprehensive Income	
Net income	$28,050.00
Other comprehensive income	
Foreign currency translation	4,200.00
Unrealized loss on securities	(3,000.00)
Comprehensive Income	$29,250.00

How revenue is measured and when it is recognized is determined by GAAP. Not everyone agrees with GAAP and there is controversy about some areas of revenue recognition. Most items that increase or decrease equity are stated on the income statement. There are some items, however, that are not on the income statement but are included as increases or decreases directly to equity.

All changes in equity for the period, except changes caused by owner investments and owner distributions,

is called **comprehensive income**. Companies must disclose comprehensive income either as a separate statement or as part of the traditional income statement.

Most of these items shown above on the statement of comprehensive income are beyond the scope of this book. The illustration shows how these items can cause comprehensive income to be more or less than net income.

Non-recurring Items on the Income Statement LO10

Where an amount is placed on the income statement is important. The higher up on the statement, the more closely it is related to the purpose of the company and the more likely it is that it will recur in the future. An item that appears toward the bottom of an income statement is less closely related to the purpose of the company and is less likely to recur. It is often referred to as a non-recurring item.

For example, Forest Equipment's income statement on page 369 first lists the revenue and expenses from normal company operations. The difference between the revenues and expenses from operations is labeled "Income from Operations." This amount is directly related to the buying and selling of farming and logging equipment and the items included in this amount are expected to recur in future periods.

Below "Income from Operations," Forest Equipment lists its "Other Revenue and Expenses," such as Interest Income and Interest Expense. While these items may recur, they are not directly connected to buying and selling equipment. There are several items that a company would include in this category. Examples include a loss from a natural disaster, the writing down of the value of an asset, gains or losses from a lawsuit, and gains or losses from the sale of investments.

Income from operations and other revenues and expenses are listed before the effect of income taxes. The total from each category is calculated to determine "Net Income before Federal Income Tax." Federal income tax expense is then calculated and subtracted, resulting in Net Income.

Some income statements can contain additional sections where very specific events are reported, such as the discontinuation of a business or a large segment of the business. These events do not typically occur on a regular basis. Therefore, the revenues and expenses for the year from the discontinued operation are reported independently from income from continuing operations. The net income or loss from the discontinued operations is listed on the income statement below the federal income tax expense. Any gain or loss from the disposal of assets related to the discontinued operations is also listed in this section. This gain or loss would also affect federal income tax expense. Because this item is entered below the federal income tax line on the income statement, the amount entered would be net of federal income tax.

A partial income statement for Sullivan Manufacturing, Inc. is given below. Sullivan's income from operations, $254,698.00, reflects normal continuing operations and is expected to reoccur. Sullivan's net income is $165,792.42, which includes non-operating and non-recurring items. Understanding the difference between these two amounts is important when analyzing an income statement.

Sullivan Manufacturing, Inc. Income Statement For Year Ended December 31, 20--					
Income from Operations	254	6	9	8	00
Other Revenue and Expenses:					
Interest Income	1	2	0	0	00
Loss from Flood	(35	5	0	0	00)
Gain from Lawsuit	18	2	0	0	00
Total Other Revenue and Expenses	(16	1	0	0	00)
Net Income before Federal Income Tax	238	5	9	8	00
Less: Federal Income Tax Expense	50	1	0	5	58
Income from Continuing Operations	188	4	9	2	42
Discontinued Operations, net of tax					
Loss from Discontinued Operations	18	5	0	0	00
Loss from Disposal of Assets of Discontinued Operations	4	2	0	0	00
Net Income	165	7	9	2	42

TERMS REVIEW

permanent difference
temporary difference
comprehensive income

Audit your understanding LO8, 9, 10

1. What rules are followed to prepare the income statement?
2. What rules are followed when preparing a tax return?
3. Name the two types of differences between taxable income and net income.
4. What is included in comprehensive income?
5. How must comprehensive income be disclosed?
6. What two items must be reported when a company has discontinued a segment?

Work together 13-4 LO8

Calculating permanent and temporary differences in net income and taxable income

Klitzke Corporation had net income and taxable income of $95,000.00 for 20X1 before depreciation and interest revenue. In addition, Klitzke Corporation identified the following two items that will cause differences between net income and taxable income:

a. On January 1, 20X1, Klitzke Corporation bought office furniture for $49,000. For net income purposes, Klitzke Corporation will depreciate it using straight-line depreciation. Estimated life is 7 years. Estimated salvage value is zero. For taxable income purposes, depreciation for 20X1 is $12,250.00.

b. On December 31, 20X1, Klitzke Corporation received a check for $2,500.00 for interest earned in 20X1 on a tax-exempt bond.

1. Identify each difference between net income and taxable income as permanent or temporary.
2. Calculate the straight-line depreciation for 20X1 for the office furniture.
3. Calculate net income for Klitzke Corporation.
4. Calculate taxable income for Klitzke Corporation.

On your own 13-4 LO8

Calculating permanent and temporary differences in net income and taxable income

Hill Company had net income and taxable income of $88,000.00 for 20X1 before rent revenue and interest revenue. In addition, Hill Company identified the following two items that will cause differences between net income and taxable income:

a. On December 20, 20X1, Hill Company received a $12,000 check for rent revenue for the first six months of 20X2.

b. On December 31, 20X1, Hill Company received a check for $1,200.00 for interest earned in 20X1 on a tax-exempt bond.

1. Identify each difference between net income and taxable income as permanent or temporary.
2. Calculate net income for Hill Company.
3. Calculate taxable income for Hill Company.

CHAPTER SUMMARY

Financial statements are prepared periodically and used by company management and external users such as investors, creditors, and government agencies. The information contained in the financial statements is analyzed to help the user determine the company's financial strength, profitability, efficiency, and market value.

Short-term financial strength measures indicate the short-term liquidity of the business. These measures include working capital, the current ratio, and the quick ratio. Long-term financial strength focuses on how a company obtains long-term capital. Long-term measures are the debt ratio, the equity ratio, equity per share, and the interest coverage ratio.

Profitability analysis helps the user determine the consistency of the company's earnings. Profitability measures are gross margin, operating margin, rate of return on average total assets, rate of return on average stockholders' equity, and free cash flow. Viewing these measures over time will reveal favorable and/or unfavorable trends.

Efficiency measures indicate how the business utilizes its resources. They include measures for collection of accounts receivable and turnover of inventory. An efficient business will collect accounts receivable on a timely basis and only have enough inventory on hand to meet customer demand.

Market ratios tie together the financial statements and the stock market. The value of a share of stock not only indicates past performance, but also reflects how the market views the future of a company. Market measures include the earnings per share, the price-earnings ratio, and the dividend yield.

Net income and taxable income can be different because of permanent differences and temporary differences. Permanent differences will never balance out. Temporary differences will balance out over the term of the difference.

Comprehensive income is a more inclusive measure of income and includes all changes in equity except those resulting from owner investments or owner distributions.

EBIT and EBITDA

As described on page 376, EBIT is net earnings before interest expense and taxes. **EBITDA** (pronounced ē - bĭt - dah) is net earnings before interest expense, taxes, depreciation, and amortization. Both EBIT and EBITDA are often used in place of net income in calculations such as the rate of return on average total assets and the rate earned on average stockholders' equity. When more than one calculation is available for a financial measure, a company must decide which calculation is the best measure to use in making decisions. Once decided, the company should use the same calculation from period to period. If the same calculation is used over time, the company can compare results over the period to determine trends.

While EBIT is a generally accepted measure used by accountants and analysts, EBITDA is quite controversial. Since EBITDA begins with net earnings and then adds back not only interest expense and taxes, but also depreciation and amortization, some feel that this is an easy way to change negative earnings into a positive number. Those who

support the calculation of EBITDA say that it is a true measure of cash flows because depreciation and amortization are expenses that do not require a cash outflow.

Perhaps the biggest argument against the use of EBITDA is that it does not adhere to GAAP. It allows a company to ignore several components of net income that are required by GAAP. To add to the discussion, some companies do not want to stop at EBITDA. In recent times, companies are calculating EBITDAR, which also adds back any rent expense paid by the company.

INSTRUCTIONS

Obtain the annual reports of three public corporations. List the net earnings of each company. For each company, calculate EBIT and EBITDA. Compare the differences between the three amounts for each company. Write a paragraph describing the relationship between net earnings, EBIT, and EBITDA. State which measure you feel is most accurate.

APPLY YOUR UNDERSTANDING

INSTRUCTIONS: Download problem instructions for Excel, QuickBooks, and Sage 50c Accounting from the textbook companion website at www.C21accounting.com.

13-1 Application Problem — Analyzing short- and long-term financial strength LO3, 4

1. Create and key formulas to compute the financial strength ratios.
2. Print the Ratios worksheet.

Information taken from Rogness Corporation's comparative income statement and balance sheet and a form for completing this problem are provided in the *Working Papers*.

Instructions:

1. Calculate the following financial strength ratios for the current year and the prior year. Round ratios to the nearest tenth.

   a. Working capital
   b. Current ratio
   c. Quick ratio
   d. Debt ratio
   e. Equity ratio
   f. Common equity per share
   g. Interest coverage ratio

2. Compare each ratio to Rogness Corporation's target range. Identify whether each ratio indicated a favorable trend and a favorable result.

3. Explain any change in the quick ratio for Rogness Corporation.

13-2 Application Problem — Calculating profitability measures LO5

1. Create and key formulas to compute ratios related to profitability measures.
2. Print the Ratios worksheet.

Information taken from Emerald Resort Incorporated's financial statements and a form for completing this problem are provided in the *Working Papers*.

Instructions:

1. Calculate the following profitability measures for the current year and the prior year. Round percentage calculations to the nearest 0.1% and dollar amounts to the nearest $0.01.

   a. Gross margin
   b. Operating margin
   c. Rate earned on average total assets
   d. Rate earned on average stockholders' equity
   e. Free cash flow

2. Compare each measure to Emerald Resort Incorporated's target range. Identify whether each measure indicated a favorable trend and a favorable result.

3. Explain what free cash flow from the current year tells Emerald Resort Incorporated.

13-3 Application Problem

Calculating and analyzing efficiency measures and market ratios LO6, 7

1. Create and key formulas to analyze efficiency measures and market ratios.
2. Print the Ratios worksheet.

Information taken from Hartmann Company's financial statements and a form for completing this problem are provided in the *Working Papers*.

Instructions:

1. Calculate the following efficiency measures and market ratios for the current year and the prior year. Round percentage calculations to the nearest 0.1%, dollar amounts to the nearest $0.01, and the price-earnings ratio to the nearest tenth.

   a. Accounts receivable turnover ratio
   b. Days' sales in accounts receivable
   c. Inventory turnover ratio
   d. Days' sales in inventory

   e. Earnings per share
   f. Price-earnings ratio
   g. Dividend yield

2. Compare each measure to Hartmann Company's target range. Identify whether each measure indicated a favorable trend and a favorable result.

3. Hartmann Company's credit terms are n/30. Analyze the company's days' sales in accounts receivable in terms of its credit policy and state any trend this measure reveals.

13-4 Application Problem

Calculating permanent and temporary differences in net income and taxable income LO8

CMS Corporation had net income and taxable income of $77,000.00 for 20X1 before depreciation, interest revenue, and rent expense. In addition, CMS Corporation identified the following three items that will cause differences between net income and taxable income:

a. On January 1, 20X1, CMS Corporation bought office furniture for $40,000. For net income purposes, CMS Corporation will depreciate it using straight-line depreciation. Estimated life is five years. Estimated salvage value is zero. For taxable income purposes, depreciation for 20X1 is $10,000.00.

b. On December 31, 20X1, CMS Corporation received a check for $3,500.00 for interest earned in 20X1 on a tax-exempt bond.

c. On December 20, 20X1, CMS Corporation paid $15,000 for rent expense for the first three months of 20X2.

Instructions:

1. Identify each difference between net income and taxable income as permanent or temporary.
2. Calculate the straight-line depreciation for 20X1 for the office furniture.
3. Calculate net income for CMS Corporation.
4. Calculate taxable income for CMS Corporation.

13-M Mastery Problem | Analyzing financial statements LO3, 4, 5, 6, 7

1. Create and key formulas related to Eiler Enterprise's financial statements to calculate financial ratios and measures.
2. Print the Ratios worksheet.

Information taken from Eiler Enterprise's financial statements and a form for completing this problem are provided in the *Working Papers*.

Instructions:

1. Calculate the following ratios and measures for the current year and the prior year. Round percentage calculations to the nearest 0.01%, dollar amounts to the nearest $0.01, and ratios to the nearest tenth.

1. Working capital
2. Current ratio
3. Quick ratio
4. Debt ratio
5. Equity ratio
6. Common equity per share
7. Interest coverage ratio
8. Gross margin
9. Operating margin
10. Rate earned on average total assets
11. Rate earned on average stockholders' equity

12. Free cash flow
13. Accounts receivable turnover ratio
14. Days' sales in accounts receivable
15. Inventory turnover ratio
16. Days' sales in inventory
17. Earnings per share
18. Price-earnings ratio
19. Dividend yield

2. Compare each measure to Eller Enterprise's target range. Identify whether each measure indicated a favorable trend and a favorable result.

13-C Challenge Problem | Calculating the effect of transactions on the current ratio LO3

1. Create and key formulas to compute current ratios.
2. Print the Ratios worksheet.

Clausen Company is nearing the end of its fiscal year, and the Accounting Department has estimated that the current ratio for the current year will be 1.5, with estimated current assets of $150,000 and estimated current liabilities of $100,000. The company wants to increase the current ratio to at least 2.0 by the end of the period. It has the following options:

a. Borrow $50,000 by signing a short-term note payable, due in six months.
b. Borrow $50,000 by signing a long-term note payable, due in 18 months.
c. Sell $50,000 of common stock.
d. Pay off $25,000 of accounts payable with cash.
e. Replace $25,000 of accounts payable with a long-term note payable, due in 24 months.

Instructions:

1. For each option above, calculate the new totals for the current assets and the current liabilities, and calculate the new current ratio.
2. Identify which options would achieve the company's goal of a current ratio of 2.0.

Radio Frequency Identification Tags—Music for Inventory Turnover

Theme: Financial, Economic, Business, and Entrepreneurial Literacy

Skills: Critical Thinking and Problem Solving and Information Literacy

Every company's goal should be to optimize inventory turnover. After all, a company has a limited amount of money to invest in inventory. To pay a bill and generate a profit, the inventory must be sold. The inventory turnover rate measures how quickly a business is moving its inventory.

Understanding the market and understanding the customer are two important factors that can improve inventory turnover rates. Technology allows companies to go one step further to improve inventory turnover.

Radio frequency identification, or RFID, tags can be used to identify and track inventory. Macy's asked all of its suppliers to insert RFID tags in all merchandise. Walmart is again trying to incorporate RFID tags in its inventory after its first attempt was discontinued because of the costs involved.

Sources: www.stores.org/2017/09/11/rfid-ready-revolutionize-retail-industry; www.supplychaindive.com/news/rfid-retail-technology-implementation.

PARTNERSHIP FOR
21ST CENTURY SKILLS

APPLICATION

1. Using the Internet, research and list three new applications for the use of RFID tags.
2. Many students are opposed to the use of RFID tags for attendance purposes. Write one paragraph explaining your point of view.

Analyzing Home Depot's Financial Statements

The annual reports of publicly traded companies describe some of the financial ratios presented in this chapter. Other ratios must be calculated using the information provided in the financial statements.

Income statement amounts are the result of operations over an entire year or fiscal period. However, balance sheet amounts are the balances on a particular date. Therefore, when financial ratios use both an income statement amount and a balance sheet amount, the balance sheet amount is expressed commonly as an average of the amount at the beginning of the fiscal period and the amount at the end of the fiscal period. For example, average total assets for a company that uses the calendar year as its fiscal year would be the sum of the total assets on January 1 and the total assets on December 31, divided by 2.

Because the balance sheet contains only two years of information, investors rely on information in multiple-year summaries to obtain the required information. Home Depot's Selected Financial Data, found in Appendix B on page B-20 enables readers to calculate financial ratios for several fiscal periods.

INSTRUCTIONS

Identify or calculate the following financial ratios for the years 2017 and 2016, using the financial statements and the Selected Financial Data, as appropriate. Use amounts in millions of dollars, except for per-share data.

1. Rate earned on average total assets
2. Rate earned on average stockholders' equity
3. Diluted earnings per share
4. Working capital
5. Current ratio
6. Debt ratio
7. Free cash flow

14

Statement of Cash Flows

LEARNING OBJECTIVES

After studying Chapter 14, in addition to defining key terms, you will be able to:

LO1 Identify the uses of a statement of cash flows.

LO2 Identify the difference between the direct and indirect methods of preparing the statement of cash flows.

LO3 Calculate cash flows from operating activities using the indirect method.

LO4 Complete the operating activities section of a statement of cash flows using the indirect method.

LO5 Complete the investing activities section of a statement of cash flows.

LO6 Complete the financing activities section of a statement of cash flows.

LO7 Complete the statement of cash flows.

LO8 Calculate the operating cash flow ratio and the cash flow margin ratio.

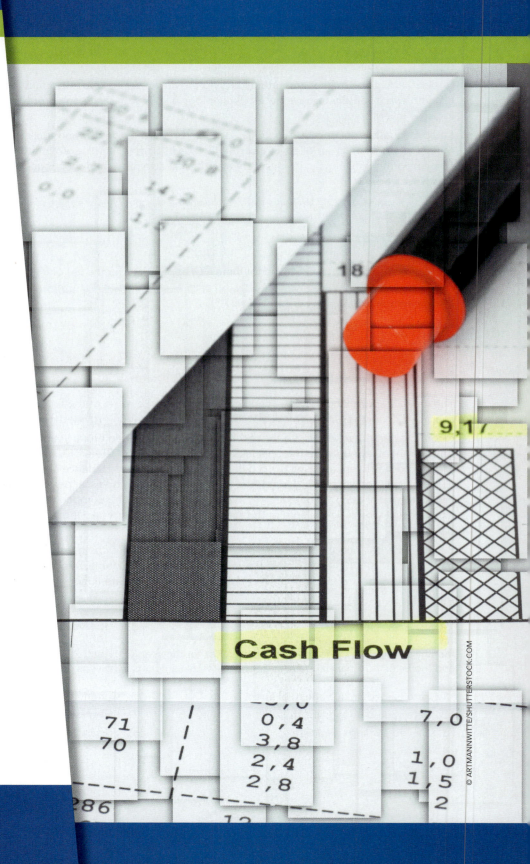

Cash Flow

© ARTMANNWITTE/SHUTTERSTOCK.COM

Apple, Inc.

ACCOUNTING IN THE REAL WORLD

© R.CLASSEN/SHUTTERSTOCK.COM

Most people know that Apple, Inc., makes wildly popular technological devices—from iPads and iPhones to Apple Watch and Apple TV. What many consumers don't know about Apple is that the company is also striving to make the world a better place. One of its major initiatives is to ensure that its suppliers share the company's values when it comes to issues such as working conditions and environmental responsibility.

Since 2007, Apple has published an annual Supplier Responsibility Progress Report. This report card grades Apple on how it has met three major goals: improve working conditions at the facilities of suppliers, achieve zero waste, and ensure that materials are obtained in a responsible manner. Apple has purposely set these goals "above and beyond accepted industry standards."

Focusing on the well-being of workers and their communities, Apple recently started a program aimed at improving health awareness for women who work for Apple suppliers around the world. The goal is to provide health education to 1 million women by 2020 with the hope that these women will bring good health practices back to their homes and communities.

Because Apple suppliers are located throughout the world, the laws protecting these workers vary greatly. To ensure that all workers are treated with dignity and respect and that they know their rights, Apple has set its workplace safety standards above those of many countries and above accepted industry standards.

Apple is working to improve conditions not only for workers but also for the environment. In 2017, Apple received certification from Underwriters Laboratories (UL) which has a certified Zero Waste Program. To achieve this certification, a company "must divert 100 percent of its waste from landfills." Apple achieved this goal in 100 percent of its final assembly facilities

for iPhones, and it is also helping its suppliers achieve this certification.

To reach its goal of responsibly sourced materials, Apple is attempting to trace materials all the way back to their source. The goal is to ensure that the methods used to obtain and process the materials are sustainable and environmentally friendly.

Apple does not have to share the report cards, but it chooses to share these goals, the processes used to achieve them, and the progress report for two reasons: (1) Apple believes that transparency will keep them accountable, and (2) Apple hopes that others will "learn and benefit" from their experience.

Like other publicly held corporations, Apple publishes an annual report that includes a statement of cash flow. Apple's statement of cash flows is prepared using one of two methods approved by GAAP. The two different methods will be discussed in this chapter.

Source: www.apple.com.

CRITICAL THINKING

1. Using the Internet, find the most recent Supplier Responsibility Progress Report for Apple, Inc. List one statistic given in the report.

2. Using the Internet, find the most recent annual report for Apple, Inc. For the most recent year, find and list the following amounts from the statement of cash flows: net cash generated by (used in) operating activities, net cash generated by (used in) investing activities, net cash generated by (used in) financing activities, and increase (decrease) in cash and cash equivalents.

3. How does the increase (decrease) in cash for the most current year compare to the same figure for the two prior years?

KEY TERMS

direct method
indirect method

LO1 Identify the uses of a statement of cash flows.

LO2 Identify the difference between the direct and indirect methods of preparing the statement of cash flows.

LO3 Calculate cash flows from operating activities using the indirect method.

LO4 Complete the operating activities section of a statement of cash flows using the indirect method.

Cash Flows   LO1

Some investors and financial analysts rely heavily on an examination of income statements and balance sheets to judge a company's performance. However, impressive profits are not always a guarantee of success in the future. For example, despite reporting a substantial net income for the year, a business may experience a cash shortage and have difficulty paying its bills. Cash flow analysis helps owners, creditors, and other interested parties:

1. Determine a company's potential to produce cash in the future.
2. Judge a company's ability to pay bills and repay debts.
3. Explain changes in the Cash account balance.
4. Evaluate a company's investment and equity transactions.

The statement of cash flows is prepared on a cash basis. It reports cash flows in and out of the company, using three categories of cash flows: operating activities, investing activities, and financing activities.

ETHICS IN ACTION

Bribing Government Officials

Companies that operate throughout the world are exposed to different cultures, social norms, and acceptable business practices. In some countries, giving bribes to government officials to gain favorable business terms is both acceptable and expected. In our society, however, giving bribes to government officials is unethical and illegal.

In 1977, Congress passed the Foreign Corrupt Practices Act, which made it illegal for U.S. companies to bribe foreign government officials.

INSTRUCTIONS

Access *Everyday Values*, the code of conduct for Harley-Davidson. What guidance does Harley-Davidson provide its employees in the following situations involving foreign government officials?

a. An employee, at the end of a business meeting with a government official, is considering paying for everyone's lunch.

b. To thank a mayor's staff for their help with a bike rally, an employee wants to give the mayor's staff Harley-Davidson hats or T-shirts.

c. An employee learns that a marketing company hired by Harley-Davidson has given a free motorcycle to a government official in thanks for closing a road to film a commercial.

d. An employee submits an expense reimbursement request that includes a $1,000 payment to a government official, a payment described as necessary to arrange for a trade agreement to allow Harley-Davidson to purchase supplies from businesses in the country.

Direct Method and Indirect Method LO2

Direct Method

Statement of Cash Flows

Cash flows from operating activities:

Cash receipts from:

Sales	xxx	
Interest	xxx	
Total cash receipts		xxx

Cash payments for:

Inventory purchases	xxx	
Salaries and wages	xxx	
Interest	xxx	
Federal income tax	xxx	
Total cash payments		xxx

Cash provided by (used for)
operating activities   xxx

Indirect Method

Statement of Cash Flows

Cash flows from operating activities:

Net income	xxx

Adjustments to net income:

Depreciation and amortization expense	xxx

Changes in current assets and liabilities:

Decrease in accounts receivable	xxx
Increase in merchandise inventory	(xxx)
Decrease in accounts payable	(xxx)
Increase in federal income tax payable	xxx
Total adjustments to net income	xxx

Cash provided by (used for)
operating activities   xxx

The operating activities section of the statement of cash flows reports the cash inflows and cash outflows resulting from the operation of a business. This section can be prepared using either of two formats. Listing cash flows from operating activities as cash receipts and cash payments is called the **direct method**. Listing cash flows from operating activities by starting with net income and adjusting for noncash items is called the **indirect method**.

Two important facts are true when comparing the direct method and the indirect method:

1. Only the cash flows from operating activities differ. The cash flows from investing activities and the cash flows from financing activities are prepared in the same manner under the two methods.
2. Regardless of the method used, the total cash provided by (used for) operating activities equals the same amount. The only thing that is different is the way the cash flows are presented.

GAAP allow either method, but prefer the direct method. The direct method is easier to understand because:

1. The direct method lists the actual cash receipts and cash payments within categories that are understood easily.
2. The indirect method starts with net income that results from using accrual-based accounting. Thus, the relationship between net income and actual cash flows is not obvious.

When the direct method is used, GAAP require that a separate schedule be prepared. This schedule reconciles net income to total cash provided by (used for) operating activities. The supplemental schedule is very similar to the format used for the indirect method. Because the direct method requires this schedule, most companies use the indirect method to prepare the statement of cash flows.

Chapter 4 focused on the direct method of preparing the statement of cash flows. This chapter will focus on the indirect method of preparing the statement of cash flows.

Determining Cash Flows from Operating Activities LO3

The cash flows from operating activities can be determined indirectly by identifying the net income for the period and making several adjustments.

Net Income

Net income presented on an income statement summarizes revenues and expenses generated by the operating activities of a business during the fiscal period. For this reason, net income is a good starting point for calculating the cash flows from operating activities.

A net income is viewed as a *source of cash*, because it brings additional money into a firm eventually. A net loss reduces the amount of money available for expenditures and is considered to be a *use of cash*.

Since the income statement is prepared using the accrual basis of accounting and the statement of cash flows is prepared using the cash basis of accounting, the recognition of revenues and expenses occurs at different times. Adjustments are made to net income to recognize the timing differences.

Adjusting Net Income for Depreciation and Amortization

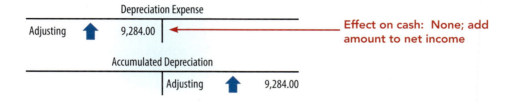

Depreciation expense is recognized on the income statement. However, it does not involve an outflow of cash. Since depreciation expense does not use cash, the amount is added back to the net income amount.

At the end of the fiscal year, Cradle Mountain Corporation uses the straight-line method of depreciation to expense an appropriate amount of the original cost of equipment. An adjusting entry is recorded by debiting Depreciation Expense and crediting Accumulated Depreciation as shown above.

Notice that the credit for this transaction is Accumulated Depreciation, not Cash. Depreciation expense does not affect the balance in the Cash account. However, depreciation expense is deducted from company revenues to determine net income. Since no cash is paid out, the amount of depreciation expense reported on the income statement must be added back to net income to determine the actual cash generated from operating activities.

The amount of total depreciation expense added back to net income is one of the adjustments to net income to determine the actual *source of cash* from operations. Amortization expense is also a noncash expense and is treated in a similar manner.

Remember Sources of cash represent cash inflows, which are added on the statement of cash flows. Uses of cash represent cash outflows, which are subtracted on the statement of cash flows.

Analyzing Changes in Current Assets

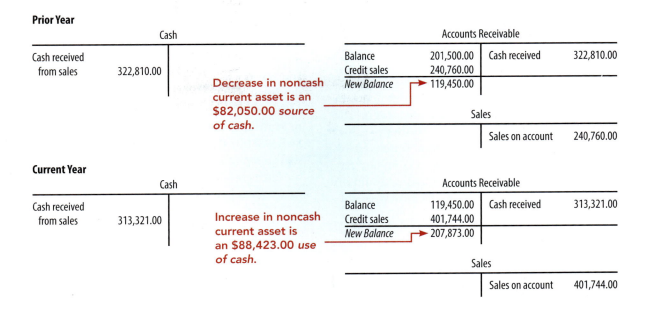

Prior Year

Cash				Accounts Receivable			
Cash received from sales	322,810.00			Balance	201,500.00	Cash received	322,810.00
				Credit sales	240,760.00		
				New Balance	119,450.00		

Decrease in noncash current asset is an $82,050.00 *source* of cash.

Sales			
		Sales on account	240,760.00

Current Year

Cash				Accounts Receivable			
Cash received from sales	313,321.00			Balance	119,450.00	Cash received	313,321.00
				Credit sales	401,744.00		
				New Balance	207,873.00		

Increase in noncash current asset is an $88,423.00 *use* of cash.

Sales			
		Sales on account	401,744.00

The second adjustment to net income involves changes in *noncash current assets* (current assets other than cash). Increases and decreases in noncash current assets affect cash flows and require an adjustment to net income. For example, an increase in the current asset Accounts Receivable indicates that not all of the sales on account reported for a period were collected. Consequently, an increase in Accounts Receivable means that cash received from sales is less than the sales amount reported on the income statement.

During the prior year, Cradle Mountain Corporation's Accounts Receivable decreased $82,050.00. Assuming that all sales were made on account, this decrease means that the actual cash inflow for sales on account was $322,810.00, which is more than the $240,760.00 reported as sales on the income statement. For this reason, net income is adjusted by adding $82,050.00 for the decrease in a current asset.

A decrease in a noncash current asset is considered to be a *source of cash*.

How can a company collect $322.810.00 of receivables if sales on account for the year are only $240,760.00? In this instance, Cradle Mountain collected a portion of the $201,500.00 balance in Accounts Receivable due from the previous year. Noncash current assets may also increase during a fiscal period. During the current year, Cradle Mountain collected $88,423.00 less than it sold on account. An increase in a noncash current asset represents a *use of cash* and is subtracted from the net income amount. This use of cash supports the company's daily operations by allowing the business to offer customers the option to buy now and pay later. A use of cash means a specified sum of money is no longer available for other business activities.

Each noncash asset account is analyzed in a similar manner to Accounts Receivable to determine cash flows from operations.

FYI Determine if the increase or decrease in an account represents a source of cash or a use of cash. If a change in an account represents a source of cash, it is always added on the statement of cash flows. If a change represents a use of cash, it is always subtracted.

Remember The cash inflows and outflows of a business are identified using the information presented on a company's financial statements.

Analyzing Changes in Current Liabilities

The third adjustment to net income involves changes in current liabilities. During the operation of a business, increases and decreases in current liabilities occur as debts are added and paid off in the process of generating revenues.

During the prior year, Cradle Mountain Corporation was extremely aggressive in paying off its debts. In fact, assuming that all purchases were on account, the company paid off $111,886.00 of accounts payable, which is $7,630.00 more than the total purchases on account of $104,256.00. Why would a company pay more than it owes? In this instance, Cradle Mountain paid a portion of the $40,000.00 accounts payable balance owed for the previous year. A decrease in a current liability represents a *use of cash* and is subtracted from net income.

The $43,940.00 increase in accounts payable at the end of the current year means that the actual cash outflow for purchases on account was $149,252.00 and not the full $193,192.00 reported as purchases on the income statement. For this reason, net income is adjusted by adding back $43,940.00 for the increase in a current liability. Since the company has use of the $43,940.00, the increase in a current liability represents a *source of cash*.

Each current liability is analyzed in a similar manner to accounts payable.

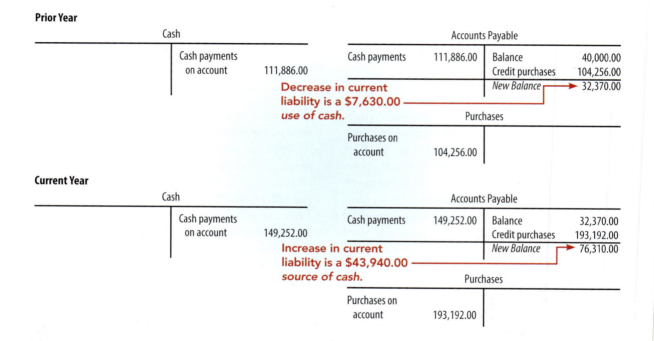

Prior Year

Cash			Accounts Payable		
Cash payments on account	111,886.00		Cash payments 111,886.00	Balance	40,000.00
				Credit purchases	104,256.00
				New Balance	32,370.00

Decrease in current liability is a $7,630.00 use of cash.

Purchases	
Purchases on account	104,256.00

Current Year

Cash			Accounts Payable		
Cash payments on account	149,252.00		Cash payments 149,252.00	Balance	32,370.00
				Credit purchases	193,192.00
				New Balance	76,310.00

Increase in current liability is a $43,940.00 source of cash.

Purchases	
Purchases on account	193,192.00

FYI

The Financial Accounting Standards Board (FASB), in Statement No. 95, classifies the interest paid on borrowed money as an operating activity. The reason for this classification is that the payment of interest expense on a loan is considered to have a direct effect on a firm's net income.

Bottom Line May Affect Theatrical Performance

CareerClusters®
PATHWAYS TO COLLEGE & CAREER READINESS
Arts, A/V Technology & Communications

The last time you went to see a play, you probably didn't wonder if the production would make a net income. You were probably more interested in the acting and the set design. However, someone does have to worry about the bottom line generated by the production. That task usually is the responsibility of the theater's general manager. He or she must make sure that all operations stay within the budget. The budget may determine how many performances are offered, the set design, and who fills each acting role. The budget is also affected by the anticipated size of the audience, the grants received, and the fundraising efforts. If any of these revenue sources are less than budgeted, decisions must be made to cut expenses during the run of the play.

CRITICAL THINKING

1. Assume that your school is putting on a play. Make a list of the costs that may be incurred.

2. List sources of revenue that could help offset these costs.

Charting the Statement of Cash Flows

A publicly held corporation must publish an annual report. The report includes its financial statements, a discussion of its operations, and other information that management considers useful to investors. Charts are often used to communicate changes in sales, income, and other key financial statement amounts.

While attending a seminar, the controller for Walthal Corporation learned about a *waterfall chart*. The seminar leader used the chart to show the source and use of an item of inventory. He demonstrated how to create the chart by using a stacked column chart design.

The controller realized that a waterfall chart is uniquely qualified to communicate the information on a statement of cash flows. The chart could show the beginning cash balance, the sources of cash, the uses of cash, and the ending cash balance. Thus, the chart quickly enables the user to see how cash was generated and used.

OPEN THE SPREADSHEET TLA_CH14

The worksheet contains Walthal's statement of cash flows. Follow the steps on the Instructions tab to prepare the chart. Answer the following questions:

1. What colors could be selected to reinforce the concepts of sources and uses of cash?

2. Prepare a statement to be included in an accounting procedures manual that provides guidance on when a waterfall chart should be selected to communicate information.

Reporting Cash Flows from Operating Activities LO4

Cradle Mountain Corporation
Comparative Income Statement
For Years Ended December 31, 20X2 and 20X1

	20X2	20X1	Increase (Decrease)
Net Sales	$401,744.00	$240,760.00	$160,984.00
Cost of Merchandise Sold	193,192.00	104,256.00	88,936.00
Gross Profit on Operations	$208,552.00	$136,504.00	$ 72,048.00
Operating Expenses:			
Depreciation Expense	$ 9,284.00	$ 8,204.00	$ 1,080.00
Other Operating Expenses	97,654.08	67,488.61	30,165.47
Total Operating Expenses	$106,938.08	$ 75,692.61	$ 31,245.47
Net Income before Federal Income Tax Expense	$101,613.92	$ 60,811.39	$ 40,802.53
Less Federal Income Tax Expense	21,338.92	12,770.39	8,568.53
Net Income after Federal Income Tax Expense	$ 80,275.00	$ 48,041.00	$ 32,234.00

Add depreciation expense. ❷

❶ Enter net income.

Cradle Mountain Corporation
Statement of Cash Flows
For Year Ended December 31, 20X2

Cash flows from operating activities:		
Net income		$ 80,275.00
Adjustments to net income:		
Depreciation expense	$ 9,284.00	
Changes in current assets and liabilities:		
Increase in accounts receivable	(88,423.00)	
Decrease in supplies	319.00	
Increase in merchandise inventory	(93,312.00)	
Increase in notes payable	31,191.00	
Increase in accounts payable	43,940.00	
Total adjustments to net income		$(97,001.00)
Cash used for operating activities		$(16,726.00)

Enter changes in current assets. ❸

Calculate cash flows from operating activities. ❺

Cradle Mountain Corporation
Comparative Balance Sheet
December 31, 20X2 and 20X1

	20X2	20X1	Increase (Decrease)
ASSETS			
Current Assets:			
Cash	$ 6,748.00	$ 10,056.00	$ (3,308.00)
Accounts Receivable (book value)	207,873.00	119,450.00	88,423.00
Supplies	1,001.00	1,320.00	(319.00)
Merchandise Inventory	248,256.00	154,944.00	93,312.00
Total Current Assets	$463,878.00	$285,770.00	$178,108.00
Plant Assets:			
Equipment	$ 66,400.00	$ 49,856.00	$ 16,544.00
Building	96,000.00	96,000.00	—
Land	48,000.00	72,000.00	(24,000.00)
Less Accum. Depr.—Equipment and Land	17,488.00	8,204.00	9,284.00
Total Plant Assets (book value)	$192,912.00	$209,652.00	$ (16,740.00)
Total Assets	$656,790.00	$495,422.00	$161,368.00
LIABILITIES			
Current Liabilities:			
Notes Payable	$ 40,602.00	$ 9,411.00	$ 31,191.00
Accounts Payable	76,310.00	32,370.00	43,940.00
Total Current Liabilities	$116,912.00	$ 41,781.00	$ 75,131.00
Long-Term Liabilities:			
Mortgage Payable	$117,162.00	$117,600.00	$ (438.00)
Total Liabilities	$234,074.00	$159,381.00	$ 74,693.00
STOCKHOLDERS' EQUITY			
Total Stockholders' Equity	$422,716.00	$336,041.00	$ 86,675.00
Total Liabilities and Stockholders' Equity	$656,790.00	$495,422.00	$161,368.00

Enter changes in current liabilities. ❹

1 Enter net income, **$80,275.00**, as shown on Cradle Mountain's comparative income statement.

2 Add the amount of depreciation expense, **$9,284.00**, to net income.

3 Enter the changes in current assets as indicated in the table below.

Change in Account	20X2	20X1	Increase (Decrease)	Source or Use of Cash
Increase in Accts. Rec.	$207,873.00	$119,450.00	$88,423.00	use of cash
Decrease in Supplies	1,001.00	1,320.00	(319.00)	source of cash
Increase in Mdse. Inv.	248,256.00	154,944.00	93,312.00	use of cash

4 Enter the changes in current liabilities as indicated in the table below.

Change in Account	20X2	20X1	Increase (Decrease)	Source or Use of Cash
Increase in Notes Pay.	$40,602.00	$ 9,411.00	$31,191.00	source of cash
Increase in Accts. Pay.	76,310.00	32,370.00	43,940.00	source of cash

5 Determine the cash provided by operating activities (if cash increases) or the cash used for operating activities (if cash decreases). After reporting the individual adjustments to net income, the statement of cash flows shows that the actual cash requirement for Cradle Mountain's operating activities exceeded net income by **$16,726.00**. This shortfall places Cradle Mountain in a very serious position regarding the company's ability to meet its short-term demands for cash.

Money Chase

A budget, or spending plan, is necessary for financial planning. Many individuals have a well-planned budget, yet find themselves unable to pay bills when due. Why? While the budget is helpful for establishing financial goals, the user may not take into account the timing and fluctuations of the inflows and outflows of cash.

Each day, financial events take place. Paychecks or other monies are received. Payments and other expenditures are made. A personal income and expenditures statement, also known as a *cash flow statement*, is helpful for analyzing the timing of inflows and outflows of cash. Once the cash flow has been determined, smart money management strategies can be used. A surplus, or positive cash flow, allows monies to be set aside for an emergency fund or an investment or to pay off debt. Managing cash helps eliminate the need for borrowing or using credit in the future.

ACTIVITIES

1. Sometimes there is a negative cash flow, or a deficit in cash. Together with a partner, list three money management strategies that could be implemented to avoid a deficit.

2. a. Using the Internet, research the difference between discretionary income and disposable income. Write a letter to a middle-school-aged student, explaining the difference.

   b. Explain what is meant by the following: "Teenagers with discretionary income determine new trends." What trends are being determined today by teenagers? What trends do you think teenagers may have impacted with discretionary income in the 1960s?

3. Many U.S. companies have expanded into China in recent years as its economy has expanded. Using the Internet, research some of the reasons why discretionary income in China is increasing at a faster rate than in the United States, in spite of Chinese workers earning lower wages than U.S. workers.

Source: www.mckinsey.com ("Meet the 2020 Chinese Consumer").

LO1 Identify the uses of a statement of cash flows.

LO2 Identify the difference between the direct and indirect methods of preparing the statement of cash flows.

LO3 Calculate cash flows from operating activities using the indirect method.

LO4 Complete the operating activities section of a statement of cash flows using the indirect method.

TERMS REVIEW

direct method

indirect method

Audit your understanding LO1, 2, 3

1. List four uses of the statement of cash flows.
2. Which section is different between the direct and indirect methods of preparing the statement of cash flows?
3. What does a decrease in the balance of supplies indicate?
4. What does an increase in the balance of merchandise inventory indicate?
5. What is the starting point for calculating the cash flow from operating activities, using the indirect method?

Work together 14-1 LO3, 4

Preparing the operating activities section of a statement of cash flows

A comparative balance sheet for Western Wear, Inc., is provided in the *Working Papers*. The income statement for 20X2 indicates that net income was $5,080.00 and depreciation expense was $13,650.00. Statement paper and a form for analyzing changes in accounts are also provided in the *Working Papers*. Your instructor will guide you through the following examples.

1. For each item listed on the form:
   a. Record the appropriate December 31 balances for 20X2 and 20X1.
   b. Classify it as a current asset or a current liability.
   c. Compute the amount of increase or decrease from 20X1.
   d. Indicate if the increase or decrease represents a source of cash or a use of cash.
2. Prepare the operating activities section of the statement of cash flows for the current year ended December 31, using the indirect method.

Save your work to complete Work Together 14-2.

On your own 14-1 LO3, 4

Preparing the operating activities section of a statement of cash flows

A comparative balance sheet for Southern Gulf Corporation is provided in the *Working Papers*. The income statement for 20X2 indicates that net income was $41,800.00 and depreciation expense was $9,800.00. Statement paper and a form for analyzing changes in accounts are also provided in the *Working Papers*. Work independently to complete the following problem.

1. For each item listed on the form:
   a. Record the appropriate December 31 balances for 20X2 and 20X1.
   b. Classify it as a current asset or a current liability.
   c. Compute the amount of increase or decrease from 20X1.
   d. Indicate if the increase or decrease represents a source of cash or a use of cash.
2. Prepare the operating activities section of the statement of cash flows for the current year ended December 31, using the indirect method.

Save your work to complete On Your Own 14-2.

LO5 Complete the investing activities section of a statement of cash flows.

LO6 Complete the financing activities section of a statement of cash flows.

LO7 Complete the statement of cash flows.

LO8 Calculate the operating cash flow ratio and the cash flow margin ratio.

Preparing the Investing Activities Section LO5

Cradle Mountain Corporation
Comparative Balance Sheet
December 31, 20X2 and 20X1

	20X2	20X1	Increase (Decrease)
ASSETS			
Plant Assets:			
Equipment	$ 66,400.00	$ 49,856.00	$ 16,544.00
Building	96,000.00	96,000.00	—
Land	48,000.00	72,000.00	(24,000.00)
Less Accum. Depr.—Equipment and Land	17,488.00	8,204.00	9,284.00
Total Plant Assets (book value).	$192,912.00	$209,652.00	$(16,740.00)

Enter changes in long-term assets. **①**

Cradle Mountain Corporation
Statement of Cash Flows
For Year Ended December 31, 20--

Determine the effect on cash from investing activities.

Cash flows from investing activities:		
Addition to equipment.	$(16,544.00)	
Proceeds from sale of property.	24,000.00	
Cash provided by investing activities		$ 7,456.00

②

Cash flows resulting from investing activities are identified by analyzing the changes in long-term assets (plant assets). Cradle Mountain's investing activities section for the statement of cash flows is shown above.

>> Reporting Cash Flows from Investing Activities

① Analyze changes in long-term assets. The **$16,544.00** increase in equipment represents a cash outflow. The **$24,000.00** decrease in the long-term asset, Land, represents a cash inflow and is a source of cash. The following table summarizes the changes.

Change in Account	20X2	20X1	Increase (Decrease)	Source or Use of Cash
Increase in Equipment	$66,400.00	$49,856.00	$ 16,544.00	use of cash
Decrease in Land	48,000.00	72,000.00	(24,000.00)	source of cash

② Determine the cash provided by investing activities (if cash increases) or the cash used for investing activities (if cash decreases). Cradle Mountain's investing activities provided **$7,456.00** in cash during the current year.

The increase in accumulated depreciation for equipment and building ($9,284.00) can be ignored. The effect of depreciation on cash flows was already accounted for under operating activities.

When calculating the cash flows from investing activities, it is useful to remember that:

- Increases in long-term assets generally result in cash outflows (*uses of cash*) that are subtracted on the statement of cash flows.
- Decreases in long-term assets generally result in cash inflows (*sources of cash*) that are added on the statement of cash flows.

Preparing the Financing Activities Section LO6

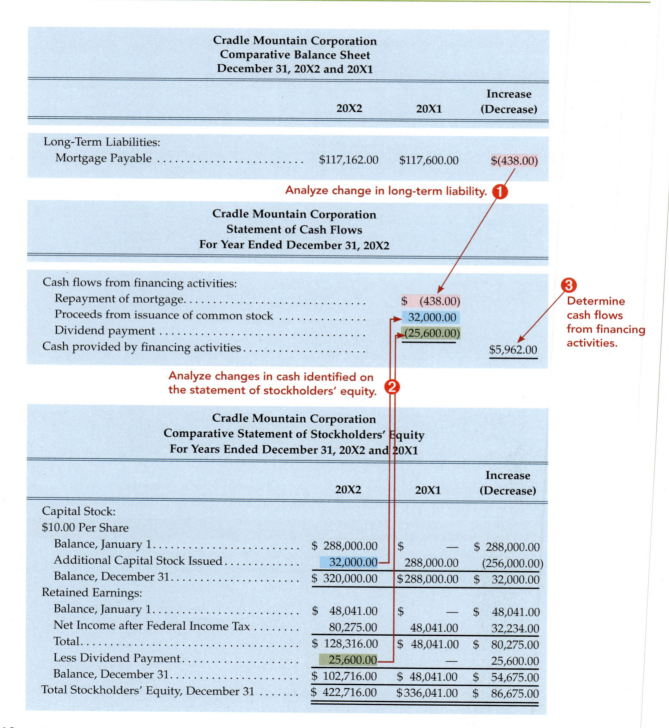

Cradle Mountain Corporation
Comparative Balance Sheet
December 31, 20X2 and 20X1

	20X2	20X1	Increase (Decrease)
Long-Term Liabilities:			
Mortgage Payable	$117,162.00	$117,600.00	$(438.00)

Analyze change in long-term liability. **1**

Cradle Mountain Corporation
Statement of Cash Flows
For Year Ended December 31, 20X2

3 Determine cash flows from financing activities.

Cash flows from financing activities:		
Repayment of mortgage.............................	$ (438.00)	
Proceeds from issuance of common stock	32,000.00	
Dividend payment	(25,600.00)	
Cash provided by financing activities..................		$5,962.00

Analyze changes in cash identified on the statement of stockholders' equity. **2**

Cradle Mountain Corporation
Comparative Statement of Stockholders' Equity
For Years Ended December 31, 20X2 and 20X1

	20X2	20X1	Increase (Decrease)
Capital Stock:			
$10.00 Per Share			
Balance, January 1.........................	$ 288,000.00	$ —	$ 288,000.00
Additional Capital Stock Issued.............	32,000.00	288,000.00	(256,000.00)
Balance, December 31......................	$ 320,000.00	$288,000.00	$ 32,000.00
Retained Earnings:			
Balance, January 1.........................	$ 48,041.00	$ —	$ 48,041.00
Net Income after Federal Income Tax	80,275.00	48,041.00	32,234.00
Total......................................	$ 128,316.00	$ 48,041.00	$ 80,275.00
Less Dividend Payment....................	25,600.00	—	25,600.00
Balance, December 31......................	$ 102,716.00	$ 48,041.00	$ 54,675.00
Total Stockholders' Equity, December 31	$ 422,716.00	$336,041.00	$ 86,675.00

❶ Analyze changes in long-term liabilities. The $438.00 decrease in Mortgage Payable represents a cash outflow.

❷ Analyze changes in cash identified on the statement of stockholders' equity. Cradle Mountain issued $32,000.00 of additional capital stock during the year. This activity resulted in a receipt of $32,000.00 from the issuance of 3,200 shares of capital stock at $10.00 per share. The sale of stock provides a source of cash. A cash dividend of $25,600.00 was paid during the year. The dividend payment represents a use of cash.

❸ Determine the cash provided by financing activities (if cash increases) or the cash used for investing activities (if cash decreases). Cradle Mountain's financing activities provided $5,962.00 in cash during the current year.

Financing activities are often used to maintain an adequate balance in the **Cash** account. These activities usually involve borrowing money from creditors and repaying the principal or acquiring capital from owners and providing a return on their investment. Cash flows originating from a company's financing activities are identified by examining the changes in long-term liabilities reported on the balance sheet and the changes in stockholders' equity reported on the statement of stockholders' equity. This analysis is shown on the previous page.

The statement of stockholders' equity also shows a change in **Retained Earnings** due to the net income of the business. Net income was the starting point for the analysis of changes in the operating activities of the business. Net income does not affect the financing activities of the business.

When calculating the cash flows from financing activities, remember that:

- Increases in long-term liabilities and the issuance of stock generally result in cash inflows (*sources of cash*) that are added on the statement of cash flows.
- Decreases in long-term liabilities and the payment of cash dividends generally result in cash outflows (*uses of cash*) that are subtracted on the statement of cash flows.

Remember Financing activities involve debt or equity transactions.

© DIZAIN/SHUTTERSTOCK.COM

Completing the Statement of Cash Flows LO7

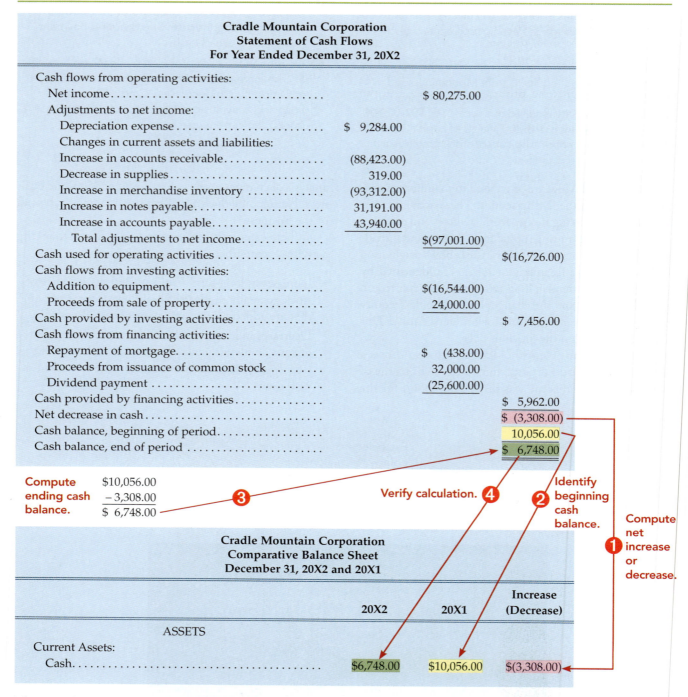

Cradle Mountain Corporation
Statement of Cash Flows
For Year Ended December 31, 20X2

Cash flows from operating activities:			
Net income		$ 80,275.00	
Adjustments to net income:			
Depreciation expense	$ 9,284.00		
Changes in current assets and liabilities:			
Increase in accounts receivable	(88,423.00)		
Decrease in supplies	319.00		
Increase in merchandise inventory	(93,312.00)		
Increase in notes payable	31,191.00		
Increase in accounts payable	43,940.00		
Total adjustments to net income		$(97,001.00)	
Cash used for operating activities			$(16,726.00)
Cash flows from investing activities:			
Addition to equipment		$(16,544.00)	
Proceeds from sale of property		24,000.00	
Cash provided by investing activities			$ 7,456.00
Cash flows from financing activities:			
Repayment of mortgage		$ (438.00)	
Proceeds from issuance of common stock		32,000.00	
Dividend payment		(25,600.00)	
Cash provided by financing activities			$ 5,962.00
Net decrease in cash			$ (3,308.00)
Cash balance, beginning of period			10,056.00
Cash balance, end of period			$ 6,748.00

Compute ending cash balance.
$10,056.00
− 3,308.00
$ 6,748.00

③ Verify calculation. ④ ② Identify beginning cash balance.
① Compute net increase or decrease.

Cradle Mountain Corporation
Comparative Balance Sheet
December 31, 20X2 and 20X1

	20X2	20X1	Increase (Decrease)
ASSETS			
Current Assets:			
Cash	$6,748.00	$10,056.00	$(3,308.00)

The completed statement of cash flows is shown above. The cash balances at the beginning and end of the period, shown on the statement of cash flows, must match the amounts shown on the comparative balance sheet.

>> Completing the Statement of Cash Flows

❶ Compute the net increase or decrease in Cash resulting from operating, investing, and financing activities.

❷ Identify the beginning cash balance from the comparative balance sheet. The beginning cash balance for the current year is the ending cash balance from the prior year, **$10,056.00**.

❸ Compute the ending cash balance, **$6,748.00** ($10,056.00 − $3,308.00 decrease in cash).

❹ Verify that the Cash balance, end of period, matches the ending cash balance shown on the comparative balance sheet.

Cash Flow Analysis LO8

The intent of the statement of cash flows is to report and explain the sources and uses of a company's cash and to clarify changes in other account balances. Cradle Mountain's statement of cash flows helps explain the difference between solid profits and a decrease in the Cash account. Among other things, the large increases in accounts receivable and merchandise inventory (uses of cash) hampered Cradle Mountain's ability to pay its bills. Studying cash flows along with analyzing the income statement, the statement of stockholders' equity, and the balance sheet provides a more accurate overview of a company's present and future financial condition.

In addition to free cash flow, which was explained in Chapter 13, additional ratios are sometimes used to analyze cash flows.

The **operating cash flow ratio** is calculated as:

$$\text{Operating Cash Flow Ratio} = \frac{\text{Cash Flows from Operating Activities}}{\text{Current Liabilities}}$$

The operating cash flow ratio for Cradle Mountain for 20X2 is calculated as:

$$(14.3) = (\$16,726.00) \div \$116,912.00$$

Similar to the current ratio, the operating cash flow ratio indicates how likely the company is to be able to pay off current liabilities with its cash flows from operations. A ratio of 1.0 or greater is desirable. Cradle Mountain's ratio of (14.3) is not desirable. It can improve its ratio by selling inventory and decreasing the receivables.

The **cash flow margin ratio** is calculated as:

$$\text{Cash Flow Margin Ratio} = \frac{\text{Cash Flows from Operating Activities}}{\text{Net Sales}}$$

The cash flow margin ratio for Cradle Mountain for 20X2 is calculated as:

$$(4.16) = (\$16,726.00) \div \$401,744.00$$

This ratio shows the cash flow from operations for every $1.00 of net sales. Net income is necessary for the long-term success of a business, but a company must also be able to pay its bills when due. The operations of a business must provide cash on a timely basis so that it can remain in business. Cradle Mountain's ratio of (4.16) is not desirable. As stated above, Cradle Mountain needs to achieve a positive cash flow from its operating activities to remain in business.

Careers In Accounting

Rebecca Martin
Financial Analyst

© STOCKLITE/SHUTTERSTOCK.COM

Rebecca Martin enjoys her job as a senior financial analyst for an investment company in New York City. She has been with the company for six years. She was promoted to her current position after three years as a junior financial analyst.

An investment company receives money from its clients. The company invests the money in stocks and other investments and charges a fee for its services. The entire set of investments is called a **portfolio**. The portfolio managers continually sell stocks from the portfolio and add new stocks to it. The clients then share in the net profits and losses of the investments.

In her position, Rebecca Martin does extensive research on potential investments. She makes recommendations on which stocks should be included in the portfolio. She also tracks funds in the portfolio and recommends when stocks should be sold.

Rebecca uses basic financial ratios and measures to analyze an investment's performance, paying attention to historic data and trends. She also needs to gather other information that could affect the value of stock. She tracks economic forecasts and reads financial newspapers and journals. She searches the Internet for data and press releases about companies. She then puts all these data together and determines the value of an investment by forecasting its future earnings.

Soon after starting in her current position, at the suggestion of her manager, Rebecca began to focus on investments in technology. She has acquired a sound understanding of the field and now analyzes only technology investments. She finds it very challenging to stay up to date on the latest developments in the ever-changing world of technology. Many weeks she works 50 to 70 hours.

When asked what she likes best about her position, Rebecca stated that she likes the fact that she can evaluate her decisions by tracking the value of the investments she recommends. She is results-oriented, and she can easily determine the results of her work.

Because technology changes quickly, Rebecca attends several conferences and seminars each year. She is also working to earn the designation of Chartered Financial Analyst (CFA). To obtain this, she must complete a program of study and pass three exams. Once she becomes a CFA, she hopes to move up to the position of portfolio manager.

A financial analyst must have excellent written and oral communications skills. The analyst must also be able to synthesize information, pay attention to details, and use critical thinking and investigative skills. Expertise in using electronic spreadsheet and presentation software is essential.

Salary Range: In 2017, the median wage for a financial analyst was $84,300 with top salaries at $165,100.

Qualifications: The minimum requirement is a bachelor's degree in a related field, such as accounting, economics, or finance. A master's degree is often preferred.

Occupational Outlook: The growth for financial analyst positions is projected to be faster than average (10% to 14%) for the period from 2016 to 2026. However, competition is strong in this career area. A graduate degree and/or certification are very helpful.

Sources: www.onetonline.org; www.cfainstitute.org.

Audit your understanding   LO5, 6, 7, 8

1. How are the cash flows resulting from a company's investing activities identified?
2. Why is an increase in accumulated depreciation on the balance sheet ignored when analyzing the cash flows from investing activities?
3. How are the cash flows originating from a company's financing activities identified?
4. How does an individual know if all cash transactions have been properly accounted for on the statement of cash flows?
5. What does the operating cash flow ratio indicate?

Work together 14-2   LO5, 6, 7, 8

Completing the statement of cash flows

Use the *Working Papers* from Work Together 14-1. A comparative balance sheet and forms for analyzing changes in long-term assets, long-term liabilities, and stockholders' equity are provided in the *Working Papers*. Your instructor will guide you through the following examples.

1. Complete the changes in the long-term assets and long-term liabilities form.
2. Prepare the investing activities section of the statement of cash flows.
3. Complete the changes in stockholders' equity form.
4. Prepare the financing activities section of the statement of cash flows.
5. Complete the statement of cash flows.
6. Calculate the following ratios:

   a. Operating cash flow ratio
   b. Cash flow margin ratio (Net sales equal $24,645.00)

On your own 14-2   LO5, 6, 7, 8

Completing the statement of cash flows

Use the Working Papers from On Your Own 14-1. A comparative balance sheet and forms for analyzing changes in long-term assets, long-term liabilities, and stockholders' equity are provided in the Working Papers. Work independently to complete the following problem.

1. Complete the changes in the long-term assets and long-term liabilities form.
2. Prepare the investing activities section of the statement of cash flows.
3. Complete the changes in stockholders' equity form.
4. Prepare the financing activities section of the statement of cash flows.
5. Complete the statement of cash flows.
6. Calculate the following ratios:

   a. Operating cash flow ratio
   b. Cash flow margin ratio (Net sales equal $70,110.00)

CHAPTER SUMMARY

The statement of cash flows can be prepared by using the direct method or the indirect method. The method used affects only the cash flows from operating activities section. The direct method lists the cash receipts and cash payments from operating activities. The indirect method begins with net income and makes adjustments for the differences between net income and actual cash flows.

When using the indirect method, the first adjustment is for depreciation and amortization. These two noncash expenses are added to net income. The second adjustment analyzes all noncash current assets. Increases in current assets are subtracted from net income. Decreases in current assets are added to net income. The third adjustment analyzes all current liabilities. Increases in current liabilities are added to net income. Decreases in current liabilities are subtracted from net income.

Cash provided by or used for operating activities is net income plus or minus all adjustments.

Cash flows from investing activities involve long-term (plant) assets. Increases in plant assets represent a use of cash. Decreases in plant assets represent a source of cash.

Cash flows from financing activities involve long-term liabilities and changes in stockholders' equity. Increases in these accounts represent a source of cash. Decreases in these accounts represent a use of cash.

The statement of cash flows is completed by netting the cash flows from operating, investing, and financing activities to determine the change in cash during the fiscal period. The change is then verified by taking the beginning cash balance and adding a cash increase or subtracting a cash decrease to arrive at the ending cash balance as found on the balance sheet.

EXPLORE ACCOUNTING

Changing GAAP

Generally accepted accounting principles (GAAP) are not subject to change frequently, but one of the more recent changes is related to revenue recognition. The new rule is a joint project of the Financial Accounting Standards Board (FASB) and the International Accounting Standards Board (IASB). The FASB develops the GAAP for financial reporting in the United States. The IASB develops International Financial Reporting Standards (IFRS). This joint proposal means that GAAP and IFRS will use the same standards to measure and record revenue.

The former GAAP contained different rules for revenue recognition in different industries. The former IFRS related to revenue recognition were difficult to use when the sales contract was complex. The new rule still provides that revenue be recognized when the transfer of goods or services is essentially complete and in the amount that the company expects to receive. It also eliminates some inconsistencies in the revenue recognition standards and provides a single model that can be used across a range of industries. The major difference between the former standards and the new rule relates to long-term contracts and to contracts that had multiple elements.

Before a new rule is passed, FASB issues a proposed draft of the new rule and invites interested parties to comment on the proposal. These comments are taken into consideration when the final version of the rule is passed. Once a new standard is passed, an effective date is announced. Companies usually need to take special steps to ensure that the new rule is followed but must also ensure that financial statements follow the consistent reporting concept.

Assume the effective date for the new revenue recognition rule was January 1, 2018. Since companies use comparative financial statements, the revenue must be measured the same way for all years shown. Therefore, companies will have to measure revenue using both methods until 2018. For financial statements before 2018, all years will be shown on financial statements using the old standard. In 2018, the current and prior years will all be shown using the new standard.

INSTRUCTIONS

Search the Internet for the Financial Accounting Standards Board. Find at least one new proposed standard. List the name of the proposed standard and write a one sentence summary of the proposal's topic.

Sources: www.ifrs.org; www.fasb.org.

APPLY YOUR UNDERSTANDING

INSTRUCTIONS: Download problem instructions for Excel, QuickBooks, and Sage 50c from the textbook companion website at www.C21accounting.com.

14-1 Application Problem — Preparing the operating activities section of a statement of cash flows LO3, 4

1. Compute the increase (decrease) of the corresponding accounts to operating activities of the statement of cash flows.
2. Print the worksheet.

The comparative income statement of NLC Corporation reveals the following net income and depreciation expense for the current year:

Net income	$182,920
Depreciation expense	25,000

The comparative balance sheet of NLC Corporation lists the following current assets and current liabilities and their ending balances for the current and prior years:

	Current Year	Prior Year
Accounts Receivable (book value)	$111,030	$ 96,000
Merchandise Inventory	236,632	242,000
Supplies	12,296	11,000
Accounts Payable	99,524	88,000

Instructions:

1. In the forms provided in the *Working Papers*, record the appropriate amount for net income. Indicate if this item represents a source of cash or a use of cash.
2. Record the appropriate amount for depreciation expense. Indicate if this item represents a source of cash or a use of cash.
3. For each current asset and current liability, write the balances for the current year and the prior year. Classify each account as a current asset or a current liability. Compute the amount of increase or decrease from the prior year. Indicate if the increase or decrease represents a source of cash or a use of cash.
4. Using the indirect method and the information collected, prepare the cash flows from operating activities section of the statement of cash flows for the current year ending December 31, 20X2. Save your work to complete Problem 14-2.

14-2 Application Problem — Completing the statement of cash flows LO5, 6, 7, 8

Use the statement of cash flows started in Problem 14-1. The comparative balance sheet of NLC Corporation lists the following long-term assets and long-term liabilities, with their ending balances for the current and prior years:

	Current Year	Prior Year
Office Equipment	$ 45,600	$ 25,000
Office Furniture	24,420	18,000
Land (decrease due to sale)	200,000	280,000
Mortgage Payable	160,200	184,000

The comparative statement of stockholders' equity of NLC Corporation reveals the following stock and dividend information for the current year:

Sale of additional common stock	$ 40,000
Payment of cash dividend	100,000

1. Compute the increase (decrease) of the corresponding accounts to investing activities and to financing activities of the statement of cash flows.
2. Complete the statement of cash flows.
3. Print the worksheets.

Instructions:

1. For each long-term asset and long-term liability, write the balances for the current year and the prior year. Compute the amount of increase or decrease from the prior year. Indicate if the increase or decrease represents a source of cash or a use of cash.

2. For each amount taken from the comparative statement of stockholders' equity, record the appropriate amount. Indicate if these activities represent a source of cash or a use of cash.

3. Using the statement of cash flows started in Problem 14-1, prepare the cash flows from investing activities section of the statement of cash flows.

4. Prepare the cash flows from financing activities section of the statement of cash flows.

5. Compute the net increase or decrease resulting from operating, investing, and financing activities.

6. Record the cash balance for the beginning of the period in the form provided. NLC Corporation started the year with a beginning cash balance of $135,860.00.

7. Compute the cash balance for the end of the fiscal period by adding the amount of increase or decrease in cash and the beginning cash amount.

8. Complete the statement of cash flows for NLC Corporation by entering the net increase or decrease in cash, the beginning cash balance, and the ending cash balance.

9. Verify the accuracy of the statement of cash flows by comparing the statement's ending cash balance with the cash balance of $313,526.00 listed for the current year on NLC's comparative balance sheet.

10. Calculate the following ratios:

    a. Operating cash flow ratio

    b. Cash flow margin ratio (Net sales equal $270,220.00)

14-M Mastery Problem   Preparing a statement of cash flows LO3, 4, 5, 6, 7, 8

Use the abbreviated comparative financial statements for Alpine Corporation in the *Working Papers*.

Instructions:

1. Review the comparative income statement and identify the amounts of net income (or net loss) and depreciation expense for the period. Indicate if each item represents a source of cash or a use of cash.

2. Analyze the comparative balance sheet and complete the following steps:

    a. Prepare a list of current assets and current liabilities.

    b. Write the balances for 20X2 and 20X1.

    c. Classify each account as a current asset or a current liability.

    d. Compute the amount of increase or decrease from 20X1.

    e. Indicate if the increase or decrease represents a source of cash or a use of cash.

3. Analyze the comparative balance sheet and complete the following steps:

    a. Prepare a list of long-term assets.

    b. Write the balances for 20X2 and 20X1.

    c. Compute the amount of increase or decrease from 20X1.

    d. Indicate if the increase or decrease represents a source of cash or a use of cash.

1. Complete the comparative income statement, the comparative statement of stockholders' equity and the comparative balance sheet.
2. Compute the increase (decrease) of the corresponding accounts to operating activities, to investing activities and to financing activities of the statement of cash flows.
3. Complete the statement of cash flows.
4. Print the worksheets.

4. Reexamine the comparative balance sheet and complete the following steps:
   a. Prepare a list of long-term liabilities.
   b. Compute the amount of increase or decrease from 20X1.
   c. Indicate if the increase or decrease represents a source of cash or a use of cash.
5. Review the comparative statement of stockholders' equity and (1) identify the amounts of any additional stock issued or cash dividends paid and (2) indicate if each item represents a source of cash or a use of cash.
6. Prepare the operating, investing, and financing activities sections of a statement of cash flows, using the indirect method.
7. Enter the cash balance at the beginning of the year as shown on the comparative balance sheet.
8. Compute the cash balance for the end of the period to complete the statement of cash flows.
9. Verify the accuracy of the statement of cash flows by comparing the statement's ending cash balance with the cash balance listed for 20X2 on Alpine's comparative balance sheet.
10. Calculate the following ratios:
    a. Operating cash flow ratio
    b. Cash flow margin ratio
11. Assume that for 20X1, Alpine Corporation's operating cash flow ratio was 0.40, and its cash flow margin ratio was 0.06. Compare the two-year trend for each calculation and write a short summary of each trend.

14-C Challenge Problem

Preparing a statement of cash flows with amortization expense LO3, 4, 5, 6, 7

1. Complete the comparative income statement, the comparative statement of stockholders' equity, and the comparative balance sheet.
2. Complete the statement of cash flows.
3. Print the worksheets.

Use the abbreviated comparative financial statements for Southwest Electronics, Inc., in the *Working Papers*. The comparative balance sheet for Southwest Electronics lists an intangible asset, Patents. The patents were granted in the first year of the business's existence. Southwest Electronics has estimated that the patents have a five-year useful life. Although the expense is recognized on the income statement under the accrual basis of accounting, it does not involve an outflow of cash. The cash was actually spent in an earlier period. Since the amortized patent expense shown on Southwest Electronics' comparative income statement does not use cash, it is handled the same way as depreciation expense. Both patents and depreciation expense are adjustments to net income (or net loss), which are presented before changes in current assets and liabilities.

Instructions:

Prepare a statement of cash flows for 20X2 for Southwest Electronics, Inc., using the indirect method.

Henry Hunter, a newly hired accountant, has prepared the following statement of cash flows. Henry has asked you to examine his statement because the ending cash balance does not equal the balance of the cash account. Prepare a list of any errors you identify in the statement and calculate the correct ending cash balance.

Westside Corporation			
Statement of Cash Flows			
Cash flows from operating activities:			
Net income		91 4 6 0 00	
Adjustments to net income:			
Depreciation expense	13 0 0 0 00		
Changes in current assets and liabilities:			
Increase in accounts receivable	7 5 1 0 00		
Decrease in merchandise inventory	(2 7 3 3 00)		
Increase in accounts payable	1 0 4 5 00		
Decrease in notes payable	(6 5 0 0 00)		
Total adjustments to net income		12 3 2 2 00	
Cash provided by operating activities			103 7 8 2 00
Cash flows from investing activities:			
Addition to machinery		(15 0 0 0 00)	
Repayment of mortgage		12 6 5 0 00	
Addition to office furniture		(3 8 0 0 00)	
Cash provided by investing activities			(6 1 5 0 00)
Cash flows from financing activities:			
Proceeds from sale of land		15 0 0 0 00	
Proceeds from issuance of common stock		(25 0 0 0 00)	
Dividend payment		50 0 0 0 00	
Cash used for financing activities			40 0 0 0 00
Net increase in cash			137 6 3 2 00
Cash balance, beginning of period			135 8 6 0 00
Cash balance, end of period			1 7 7 2 00

Dash for Cash

Theme: Financial, Economic, Business, and Entrepreneurial Literacy

Skills: Critical Thinking and Problem Solving, Communication and Collaboration

PARTNERSHIP FOR
21ST CENTURY SKILLS

If businesses were paid the instant they made a sale, they would never have a cash flow problem. Unfortunately, that does not happen. It seems simple enough to collect accounts receivable as fast as possible. However, most customers are using the same strategy of collecting receivables fast and slowing down their own accounts payable. Many companies find themselves owing payables prior to collecting receivables. Nonetheless, some top-performing companies have found strategies to help improve their cash flow by managing their accounts receivable.

To shorten the accounts receivable collection period, a good system needs to be in place. Evaluating the customer terms, the length of time it takes to be paid, and the process for contacting customers past due is a good place to begin. The whole idea is to improve the speed in which payment is received.

APPLICATION

1. Marilla Manufacturing produces screens for smartphones. It is currently experiencing a cash shortage and is having difficulty purchasing manufacturing supplies and meeting weekly payroll. It extends credit to all customers and allows them 90 days to pay on receivables. Its sales have grown dramatically this year, and it maintains outstanding relations with its customers. Marilla Manufacturing is having difficulty understanding why there is a shortage of cash. What suggestions would you offer the president of the company regarding its credit policy? What recommendations would you make in the short term to help overcome the shortage of cash? Explain your recommendations.

2. Interview two local small business owners who extend credit to customers. Create a Venn diagram on a poster to compare and contrast their credit policies and credit terms.

Analyzing Home Depot's Financial Statements

Home Depot's Comparative Statement of Cash Flows is given on page B-9 of Appendix B.

INSTRUCTIONS

Using Home Depot's statement of cash flows, answer the following questions:

1. Which method does Home Depot use for its statement of cash flows?
2. In the operating activities section, looking only at changes in assets and liabilities and ignoring the "Other" category, list by both title and amount the largest source of cash for 2017. Did this item increase or decrease during the current fiscal period?
3. For 2017, what was Home Depot's Net Cash Used in Investing Activities?
4. For 2017, what was Home Depot's largest use of cash from financing activities?

Reinforcement Activity 3

Processing and Analyzing Accounting Data for a Corporation

This activity reinforces selected learning from Part 3, Chapters 10 through 14.

Peterson Pet Supply, Inc.

Peterson Pet Supply, Inc., organized as a corporation, sells a complete line of pet supplies. Peterson owns the land and building where its store is located.

Peterson's fiscal year ends on December 31. It has recorded and posted all journal entries through December 14. It uses the chart of accounts shown on page 426.

INSTRUCTIONS

1. Use the appropriate journal to record the following selected transactions completed from December 15 through December 31, 20X3. Source documents are abbreviated as follows: check, C; memorandum, M; receipt, R.

Transactions:

Dec. 15. The board of directors declared a $2,800.00 semiannual cash dividend on preferred stock, payable on December 31. M432.

18. Received cash for 10,000 shares of common stock, $10 par value, at $12.40 per share, $124,000.00. R512.

19. Received cash for 100 shares of 8%, $100 par-value preferred stock at $120.00 per share, $12,000.00. R513.

23. Received office equipment at an agreed-upon value of $20,000.00 in exchange for 1,600 shares of common stock. M433.

31. Paid the December 15 dividend. C818.

31. Paid cash to trustee for the semiannual interest payment on a $30,000.00, 8% bond, which was issued at face value. C819.

31. Purchased 1,000 shares of Apex Corporation stock as an investment for $85.00 per share, $85,000.00. C820.

31. Received cash for 30 five-year, 6.0%, $1,000.00 bonds, issued at face value, $30,000.00. R514.

2. A comparative income, a statement of stockholders' equity, and a balance sheet for Peterson Pet Supply, Inc., are given in the *Working Papers*. Use these statements

and the following information to prepare a statement of cash flows (indirect method) for 20X3.

a. The change in the Investment Securities account is due to the cash purchase of additional investments throughout 20X3.

b. Land was sold for its cost, $25,000.00.

c. Equipment was purchased for cash as follows: office equipment, $50,000.00; store equipment, $35,000.00.

d. Bonds were issued at face value, $30,000.00.

e. Common stock was issued for $310,000.00.

f. Preferred stock was issued for $24,000.00.

g. All common and preferred dividends declared were paid in cash.

3. Using the financial statements, calculate the following ratios and measures for the years indicated. Round percentage calculations to the nearest 0.1%, dollar amounts to the nearest $0.01, and ratios to the nearest 0.1. Complete the form provided by entering the ratios and measures and indicate whether the trend and result are favorable.

a. Profitability ratios:
   (1) Gross margin
   (2) Operating margin
   (3) Rate earned on average total assets (total assets, January 1, 20X2: $975,223.55)
   (4) Rate of return on average stockholders' equity (total stockholders' equity, January 1, 20X2: $967,852.88)

b. Efficiency ratios:
   (1) Accounts receivable turnover (net accounts receivable, January 1, 20X2: $67,248.25)
   (2) Inventory turnover (total merchandise inventory, January 1, 20X2: $98,254.10)

c. Short-term financial strength ratios:
   (1) Working capital
   (2) Current ratio
   (3) Quick ratio

d. Long-term financial strength ratios:
   (1) Debt ratio
   (2) Equity ratio
   (3) Common equity per share
   (4) Interest coverage ratio

e. Market ratios:
   (1) Earnings per share
   (2) Price-earnings ratio (market for fiscal year-end 20X3, 20X2, and 20X1, respectively: $12.10, $12.00, $11.50)
   (3) Dividend yield—common stock

f. Cash ratios:
   (1) Free cash flow (20X2: cash provided by operating activities, $75,521.11; capital expenditures, $10,000.00)
   (2) Operating cash flow ratio
   (3) Cash flow margin ratio

4. Using a new journal page, journalize the following selected transactions from 20X4:

Transactions:

Jan. 1. Paid cash to Courtney Hoff for 100 shares of Peterson Pet Supply, Inc., stock at $12.00 per share, $1,200.00. C821.

   1. Received cash for 100 ten-year, 6.0%, $1,000.00 face-value bonds paying interest semiannually, issued to yield 7.0%, $92,894.20. R515.

June 30. Received a $0.75 per share cash dividend from Apex Corporation, $750.00. R586.

June 30. Paid cash to trustee for the semiannual interest payment on the bonds issued on January 1. C875.

July 1. Sold all 1,000 shares of Apex Corporation stock at $87.00 per share, $87,000.00. R587.

   1. Paid cash to trustee to retire bonds at maturity. Bonds were issued at face value, $25,000.00. C876.

Aug. 15. Received cash from Teresa Fischer for 200 shares of treasury stock at $12.50 per share, $2,500.00. This treasury stock was purchased for $10.00 per share. R598.

Dec. 31. Paid cash to trustee for the semiannual interest payment on the bonds issued on January 1. C923.

   31. Paid cash to trustee to redeem its $100,000.00 bond issue of January 1, with a call option of 101%, $101,000.00. The bonds have a carrying value of $93,405.59. C924.

Peterson Pet Supply, Inc., Chart of Accounts
General Ledger

Balance Sheet Accounts

(1000) ASSETS
1100 Current Assets
1105 Cash
1110 Petty Cash
1115 Marketable Securities
1120 Accounts Receivable
1125 Allowance for Uncollectible Accounts
1130 Merchandise Inventory
1135 Supplies—Store
1140 Supplies—Administrative
1145 Prepaid Insurance
1200 Long-Term Investments
1205 Investment Securities
1300 Plant Assets
1310 Land
1320 Building
1325 Accumulated Depreciation—Building
1330 Office Equipment
1335 Accumulated Depreciation—Office Equipment
1340 Store Equipment
1345 Accumulated Depreciation—Store Equipment

(2000) LIABILITIES
2100 Current Liabilities
2105 Accounts Payable
2110 Sales Tax Payable
2115 Salaries Payable
2120 Employee Income Tax Payable
2125 Social Security Tax Payable
2130 Medicare Tax Payable
2135 Unemployment Tax Payable—Federal
2140 Unemployment Tax Payable—State
2145 Federal Income Tax Payable
2150 Dividends Payable
2155 Interest Payable
2160 Notes Payable
2200 Long-Term Liabilities
2205 Bonds Payable
2210 Discount on Bonds Payable
2215 Premium on Bonds Payable

(3000) STOCKHOLDERS' EQUITY
3105 Capital Stock—Common
3110 Paid-In Capital in Excess of Par—Common
3115 Capital Stock—Preferred
3120 Paid-In Capital in Excess of Par—Preferred
3125 Treasury Stock

3130 Paid-In Capital from Sale of Treasury Stock
3135 Retained Earnings
3140 Dividends—Common
3145 Dividends—Preferred
3150 Income Summary

Income Statement Accounts

(4000) OPERATING REVENUE
4105 Sales
4110 Sales Discount
4115 Sales Returns and Allowances

(5000) COST OF MERCHANDISE
5105 Purchases
5110 Purchases Discount
5115 Purchases Returns and Allowances

(6000) OPERATING EXPENSE
6100 Selling Expenses
6105 Advertising Expense
6110 Cash Short and Over
6115 Depreciation Expense—Store Equipment
6120 Miscellaneous Expense—Sales
6125 Salary Expense—Sales
6130 Supplies Expense—Sales
6200 Administrative Expenses
6205 Depreciation Expense—Building
6210 Depreciation Expense—Office Equipment
6215 Insurance Expense
6220 Miscellaneous Expense—Administrative
6225 Payroll Taxes Expense
6230 Property Tax Expense
6235 Salary Expense—Administrative
6240 Supplies Expense—Administrative
6245 Uncollectible Accounts Expense
6250 Utilities Expense

(7000) OTHER REVENUE
7105 Dividend Revenue
7110 Gain on Plant Assets
7115 Gain on Sale of Investments
7120 Interest Income

(8000) OTHER EXPENSES
8105 Interest Expense
8110 Loss on Plant Assets
8115 Loss on Redemption of Bonds

(9000) INCOME TAX
9105 Federal Income Tax Expense

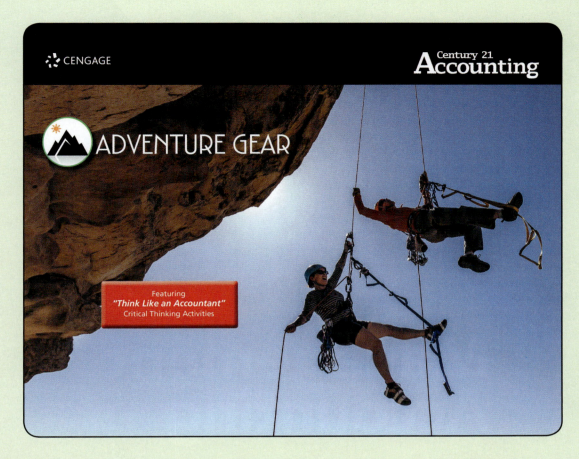

Adventure Gear is a dynamic merchandising business organized as a corporation. This business simulation covers the realistic transactions completed by Adventure Gear, which sells gear and accessories for adventure sports such as rock climbing, snowboarding, ziplining, kayaking, mountain biking, and more. The activities included in the accounting cycle for Adventure Gear are listed below.

This automated simulation is completed in the General Ledger System, available in MindTap.

The following activities are included in this simulation:

1. Recording transactions in special journals and a general journal.
2. Posting items to be posted individually to a general ledger and subsidiary ledgers.
3. Proving and ruling journals.
4. Posting column totals to a general ledger.
5. Preparing schedules of accounts receivable and accounts payable.
6. Preparing a trial balance on a work sheet.
7. Planning adjustments and completing a work sheet.
8. Preparing financial statements.
9. Journalizing and posting adjusting entries.
10. Journalizing and posting closing entries.
11. Preparing a post-closing trial balance.
12. Completing Think Like an Accountant Financial Analysis.

Management Accounting

THE BUSINESS—

TINT MY WINDOWS, INC.

Tint My Windows, Inc., the business described in Chapters 15 and 16, purchases window tinting material in large quantities and sells it to commercial businesses and individual consumers. Tint My Windows operates from a rented warehouse.

© BCFC/SHUTTERSTOCK.COM

Chart of Accounts
TINT MY WINDOWS, INC.

GENERAL LEDGER

Balance Sheet Accounts

(1000) ASSETS
1100 Current Assets
1105 Cash
1110 Petty Cash
1115 Accounts Receivable
1120 Allowance for Uncollectible Accounts
1125 Notes Receivable
1130 Interest Receivable
1135 Merchandise Inventory
1140 Supplies—Sales
1145 Supplies—Administrative
1150 Prepaid Insurance
1200 Plant Assets
1205 Equipment—Delivery
1210 Accumulated Depreciation—Delivery Equipment
1215 Equipment—Office
1220 Accumulated Depreciation—Office Equipment
1225 Equipment—Warehouse
1230 Accumulated Depreciation—Warehouse Equipment

(2000) LIABILITIES
2100 Current Liabilities
2105 Accounts Payable
2110 Sales Tax Payable
2115 Notes Payable
2120 Interest Payable
2125 Employee Income Tax Payable
2130 Social Security Tax Payable
2135 Medicare Tax Payable
2140 Unemployment Tax Payable—Federal
2145 Unemployment Tax Payable—State
2150 Federal Income Tax Payable
2155 Dividends Payable
2200 Long-Term Liabilities
2205 Bonds Payable

(3000) STOCKHOLDERS' EQUITY
3105 Capital Stock
3110 Retained Earnings
3115 Dividends
3120 Income Summary

Income Statement Accounts

(4000) OPERATING REVENUE
4105 Sales
4110 Sales Discount
4115 Sales Returns and Allowances

(5000) COST OF MERCHANDISE
5105 Purchases
5110 Purchases Discount
5115 Purchases Returns and Allowances

(6000) OPERATING EXPENSE
6100 Selling Expenses
6105 Advertising Expense
6110 Delivery Expense
6115 Depreciation Expense— Delivery Equipment
6120 Depreciation Expense— Warehouse Equipment
6125 Miscellaneous Expense
6130 Salary Expense—Commissions
6135 Salary Expense—Regular
6140 Supplies Expense—Sales
6200 Administrative Expenses
6205 Depreciation Expense—Office Equipment
6210 Insurance Expense
6215 Miscellaneous Expense—Administrative
6225 Payroll Taxes Expense
6230 Rent Expense
6235 Salary Expense—Administrative
6240 Supplies Expense—Administrative
6245 Uncollectible Accounts Expense
6250 Utilities Expense

(7000) OTHER REVENUE
7105 Interest Income
7110 Gain on Plant Asset

(8000) OTHER EXPENSES
8105 Interest Expense
8110 Loss on Plant Asset

(9000) INCOME TAX
9105 Federal Income Tax Expense

The chart of accounts for Tint My Windows, Inc., is illustrated above for reference as you study Chapters 15 and 16 of this textbook.

15

CHAPTER 15

Budgetary Planning and Control

Burlington Stores, Inc.

ACCOUNTING IN THE REAL WORLD

© KEN WOLTER/SHUTTERSTOCK.COM

You may recognize the name "Burlington Coat Factory" more than "Burlington Stores." The former name goes back to the company's first store, which opened in 1972 in Burlington, New Jersey, and featured coats as its primary product. The current name, Burlington Stores, represents an expanded line of offerings that includes women's, men's, youth, and baby apparel; accessories; footwear; coats; a home line; and gifts. Burlington Stores has grown to over 629 stores in 45 states and Puerto Rico.

The company website states that Burlington sells "current, high-quality, designer and name-brand merchandise at up to 65% off other retailers' prices." Their annual report explains that Burlington Stores, Inc., acquires its merchandise from "many suppliers, none of which accounted for more than 4% of our net purchases. . . ." Acquiring merchandise from many sources allows Burlington to avoid long-term commitments with any one supplier and to avoid being dependent on only a few major suppliers.

Even with an expanded product line, Burlington still focuses on a low-price, high-volume structure. Burlington makes up for a lower profit margin by achieving a high volume of sales. This goal of low prices and high-volume sales has a significant impact on Burlington's financial budgets. As this chapter illustrates, a company begins the budget process by setting revenue goals. Expenses are then estimated so that the company can predict its profitability for the year.

With its commitment to low prices, Burlington must do all it can to keep its costs as low as possible. One way to accomplish this is by tightly controlling the amount and type of inventory on hand. Burlington's buyers watch for trends and shop weekly for good buys on current merchandise. This helps Burlington avoid out-of-date inventory that would have to be sold at an even deeper discount.

Inventory costs are only part of the budgeting process, however. Burlington must also keep other operating costs, such as employee wages, utilities, and administrative expenses, as low as possible.

Source: www.burlington.com.

CRITICAL THINKING

1. Using the Internet, obtain the most recent annual report for Burlington Stores, Inc. Using the income statement, calculate the ratio of operating income to net sales for each of the three years given. Analyze your results and write a two- or three-sentence summary of your findings.

2. Assume that Burlington's managers are thinking of increasing its advertising budget. What should the managers consider before deciding how much, if at all, to increase this budget item?

KEY TERMS

budgeting
budget
budget period
sales budget
purchases budget

selling expenses budget
administrative expenses
   budget
other revenue and
   expenses budget

budgeted income
   statement
cash receipts budget
cash payments budget
cash budget

performance report
balanced scorecard

LO1 Identify the components of effective budget planning.
LO2 Prepare a sales budget.
LO3 Prepare a purchases budget.

Budget Planning LO1

Planning the financial operations of a business is called **budgeting**. A financial road map used by individuals and companies as a guide for spending and saving is called a **budget**. Many businesses prepare a variety of budgets, choosing those budgets that fit the needs of that company. Each budget provides managers with detailed information about a specific area of the business's operations.

A budget is a view into the future—a financial estimate of future business activities. Budget preparation begins with identifying company goals. Company goals might be to increase sales, reduce the cost of merchandise sold, or increase net income. All of these goals affect budget preparation because the budget is a business's financial plan.

Two budgets commonly prepared in businesses are the budgeted income statement and the cash budget. The budgeted income statement is a projection of a business's sales, costs, expenses, and net income for a fiscal period. It is similar to a regular income statement and is sometimes known as an *operating budget*. The cash budget is a projection of a business's cash receipts and payments for a fiscal period. It is used to manage cash and estimate cash shortages and overages.

ETHICS IN ACTION

Sharing Your Knowledge

John Oglesby is a certified public accountant who works as a computer consultant. He has just helped a local movie theater install a new ticketing system that tracks when and how often individuals come to the theater. The system will enable the theater to analyze its customers and select movies that target customers having specific movie preferences.

John has received a phone call from another theater in the same city. The theater owner explained that her business had been steadily declining over the past few years. She was particularly disturbed that her teenage daughter had received a text message containing a special movie premier offer from one of her competitors. After talking for over ten minutes, the owner finally got around to the purpose of her call—offering to hire John to evaluate her existing computer systems and to suggest any recommendations. After allowing the theater owner to present her request, John politely declined to accept the engagement.

INSTRUCTIONS

Use the AICPA *Code of Professional Conduct* to determine if John's actions are consistent with the confidentiality rule. When researching the AICPA *Code of Professional Conduct*, begin by selecting the section title that most closely relates to the issue. Consult the rule and any related interpretations.

Budget Functions

A carefully prepared budget reflects the best financial projections possible by those persons who prepare it. A completed budget shows the projected course of action for a business. A budget serves three important business functions.

1. **Planning.** In preparing a budget, managers plan actions that will meet desired goals.
2. **Operational control.** A budget projects the accomplishments of a business. It specifies the type and the amount of projected activities. By comparing actual performance with projected performance, management can judge how well a business is achieving its goals.
3. **Department coordination.** Profitable business growth requires all managers to be aware of the company's plans. A budget reflects these plans. Each phase of a business operation must be coordinated with all related phases. For example, to achieve projected sales, the Purchasing Department must know when and how much merchandise to purchase. Therefore, all management personnel must help plan and use a budget as a guide to control and coordinate sales, costs, and expenses.

Budget Period

The length of time covered by a budget is called the **budget period**. Usually, this period is one year. Some companies also prepare a long-range budget of five years or more for special projects and plant and equipment purchases. However, the annual budget is the one used to compare current financial performance with budget plans.

An annual budget is normally prepared for a company's fiscal year. The annual budget is commonly divided into quarterly and monthly budgets. Such budget subdivisions provide frequent opportunities to evaluate how actual operations compare with budgeted operations.

A budget must be prepared in sufficient time to be communicated to the appropriate managers prior to the beginning of a budget period. Large and complex companies start gathering budget information long before the beginning of a new budget year.

Sources of Budget Information

A budget cannot be exact, since it shows only projected sales, costs, and expenses. However, a company should project future operations as accurately as possible. A company uses many information sources.

Company Records

The accounting and sales records of a business contain much of the information needed to prepare budgets. Accounting information about previous years' operations is used to determine trends in sales, purchases, and operating expenses. Expected price changes, sales promotion plans, and market research studies also are important in projecting activity for a budget period.

General Economic Information

A general slowdown or acceleration in the national economy may affect budget decisions. Unusually high inflation rates affect budgeted amounts. A labor strike may affect some related industries and thus affect company operations. New product development, changes in consumer buying habits, merchandise availability, international trade, and general business conditions all must be considered when preparing budgets.

Company Staff and Managers

Sales personnel estimate the amount of projected sales. Considering projected sales for the new budget period, other department managers project budget items for their areas of responsibility in the business.

Good Judgment

Good judgment by the individuals preparing the budgets is essential to realistic budgets. Even after evaluating all available information, answers to many budget questions are seldom obvious. Since some information will conflict with other information, final budget decisions are based on good judgment.

 Remember National magazines and newspapers are a good source of information regarding general economic conditions.

Comparative Income Statement

Tint My Windows, Inc.
Comparative Income Statement
For Years Ended December 31, 20X2 and 20X1

	20X2	20X1	Increase (Decrease) Amount	Increase (Decrease) Percentage*
Operating Revenue:				
Net Sales.	$2,350,250	$2,100,000	$ 250,250	11.9
Cost of Merchandise Sold	1,343,000	1,188,000	155,000	13.0
Gross Profit on Operations	$1,007,250	$ 912,000	$ 95,250	10.4
Operating Expenses:				
Selling Expenses:				
Advertising Expense.	$ 56,400	$ 47,250	$ 9,150	19.4
Delivery Expense	188,010	175,800	12,210	6.9
Depreciation Expense—Delivery Equipment.	9,000	8,750	250	2.9
Depreciation Expense—Warehouse Equipment	13,500	13,500	0	0.0
Miscellaneous Expense—Sales	14,360	14,950	(590)	(3.9)
Salary Expense—Commissions.	94,000	85,000	9,000	10.6
Salary Expense—Regular.	42,700	35,400	7,300	20.6
Supplies Expense	14,100	13,560	540	4.0
Total Selling Expenses	$ 432,070	$ 394,210	$ 37,860	9.6
Administrative Expenses:				
Depreciation Expense—Office Equipment	$ 18,000	$ 15,000	$ 3,000	20.0
Insurance Expense	6,000	5,620	380	6.8
Miscellaneous Expense—Administrative	48,460	42,050	6,410	15.2
Payroll Taxes Expense	28,170	25,740	2,430	9.4
Rent Expense	37,500	37,500	0	0.0
Salary Expense—Administrative	97,280	94,050	3,230	3.4
Supplies Expense—Administrative	17,030	18,250	(1,220)	(6.7)
Uncollectible Accounts Expense.	14,100	12,785	1,315	10.3
Utilities Expense	12,600	9,150	3,450	37.7
Total Administrative Expenses	$ 279,140	$ 260,145	$ 18,995	7.3
Total Operating Expenses	$ 711,210	$ 654,355	$ 56,855	8.7
Income from Operations	$ 296,040	$ 257,645	$ 38,395	14.9
Other Expenses:				
Interest Expense	3,600	8,120	$ (4,520)	(55.7)
Net Income before Federal Income Tax.	$ 292,440	$ 249,525	$ 42,915	17.2
Federal Income Tax Expense.	61,413	52,401	9,012	17.2
Net Income after Federal Income Tax	$ 231,027	$ 197,124	$ 33,903	17.2
Units (sq. ft.) of Tint Sold.	671,500	600,000	71,500	11.9

*Percentages rounded to the nearest 0.1%

Preparing a budget involves analyzing available financial information. An analysis of previous years' sales, costs, and expenses is an important part of budget preparations. A comparative income statement provides the information for Tint My Windows' analysis of previous years' sales, costs, and expenses and also shows trends that may be occurring. The statement also highlights items that may be increasing or decreasing at a higher rate than other items on the statement. Tint My Windows' comparative income statement is shown above.

Annual Operational Plans and Goals

Goals for 20X3:

1. The economy is projected to remain strong throughout 20X3. Therefore, the sales goal is to increase unit sales to 700,000, about a 4.2% increase. The unit sales price will be increased in the second quarter from $3.50 to $3.70 per square foot to recover merchandise cost increases in 20X2 and projected increases in the budget year.
2. Sales distribution by quarters is projected to be consistent with prior quarters.
3. The unit cost of merchandise is projected to rise from $2.00 to $2.10 in the first quarter, a 5% increase.
4. An automated cutting machine has been ordered. It will cost $50,000 and is projected to save approximately $15,000 per year in salary expense.
5. All sales employees on salary will receive a 6.0% increase in wages. Administrative employees on salary will receive a 3.0% increase in wages.
6. An effort will be made to maintain rigid controls on all expenditures.

Good management of any project undertaken by a business requires three phases, sometimes referred to as the *management cycle*. The phases are planning, performing, and evaluating. Budgeting is one example of the management cycle. The first step in budgeting is planning, which is discussed below. Once the budget is planned, it is implemented or performed. The budget process cannot stop there, however. Evaluating is comparing the budget with actual results, which is discussed later in this chapter.

After previous years' records have been analyzed, a business sets goals, develops operational plans, and projects sales, costs, and expenses for the coming year. Annual company goals establish targets that the company will work toward in the coming year. Goals help a company coordinate the efforts of all areas toward a common direction. An operational plan provides general guidelines for achieving the company's goals. Operational plans and goals generally are determined by a planning group consisting of the company's executive officers and department managers.

At Tint My Windows, the planning group includes the president and all department managers. The planning group reviews the analysis of the previous year's comparative income statement and considers possible changes in economic conditions that may affect the

company. From these discussions, the company's operational plan and goals for the coming year are determined. After reviewing company records and considering general economic conditions, Tint My Windows' planning group develops the planning guidelines shown above.

The operational plan is converted into a more precise plan expressed in dollars by preparing a budgeted income statement. Tint My Windows prepares separate budgets for the major parts of the budgeted income statement. Separate budgets are prepared for sales, purchases, selling expenses, administrative expenses, and other revenue and expenses. To permit more frequent comparisons between actual and budgeted amounts, budgets are separated into quarterly projections.

At Tint My Windows, the Accounting Department is responsible for coordinating budget preparation. The sales manager is responsible for preparing the sales, purchases, and selling expenses budgets. The administrative manager is responsible for preparing the administrative expenses budget and the other revenue and expenses budget. The Accounting Department then prepares the budgeted income statement. The completed budgeted income statement, with attached supporting budgets, is submitted to the budget committee for approval. The budget committee consists of the president and two members of Tint My Windows' board of directors.

FYI Most budgets are based on forecasts of increases or decreases over previous years' performances. In zero-based budgeting, however, the data are prepared each year as though operations were being started for the first time.

© VALUA VITALY/SHUTTERSTOCK.COM

Sales Budget LO2

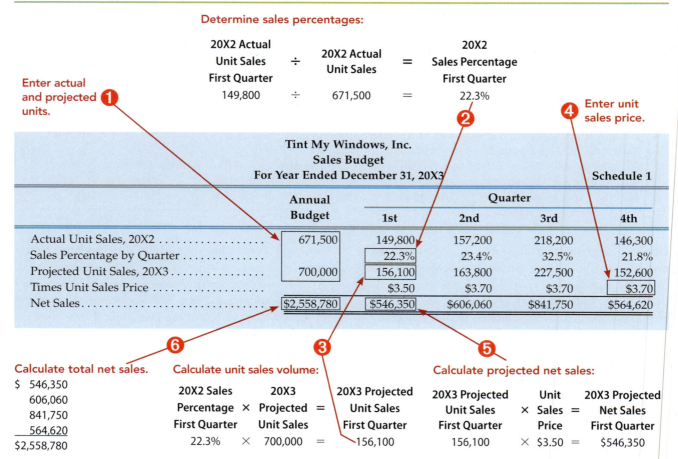

Determine sales percentages:

20X2 Actual Unit Sales First Quarter	÷	20X2 Actual Unit Sales	=	20X2 Sales Percentage First Quarter
149,800	÷	671,500	=	22.3%

Enter actual and projected units. ❶

❷ **Enter unit sales price.** ❹

Tint My Windows, Inc.
Sales Budget
For Year Ended December 31, 20X3

Schedule 1

	Annual Budget	Quarter			
		1st	2nd	3rd	4th
Actual Unit Sales, 20X2	671,500	149,800	157,200	218,200	146,300
Sales Percentage by Quarter		22.3%	23.4%	32.5%	21.8%
Projected Unit Sales, 20X3	700,000	156,100	163,800	227,500	152,600
Times Unit Sales Price		$3.50	$3.70	$3.70	$3.70
Net Sales.................................	$2,558,780	$546,350	$606,060	$841,750	$564,620

❻   ❸   ❺

Calculate total net sales.

$ 546,350
606,060
841,750
564,620
$2,558,780

Calculate unit sales volume:

20X2 Sales Percentage First Quarter	×	20X3 Projected Unit Sales	=	20X3 Projected Unit Sales First Quarter
22.3%	×	700,000	=	156,100

Calculate projected net sales:

20X3 Projected Unit Sales First Quarter	×	Unit Sales Price	=	20X3 Projected Net Sales First Quarter
156,100	×	$3.50	=	$546,350

A statement that shows the projected net sales for a budget period is called a **sales budget**. The sales budget is prepared first because the other budgets are affected by the projected net sales. Projected net sales are used to estimate the amount of merchandise to purchase and the amount that may be spent for salaries, advertising, and other selling and administrative expenses.

Tint My Windows' sales manager, with knowledge of the budget guidelines and with the assistance of sales representatives, prepares the sales budget shown above. Based on the planning group's goal of a 4.2% increase in unit sales, the budget reflects projected sales of 700,000

units. The sales manager plans to increase the unit sales price from $3.50 to $3.70 in the second quarter. The timing of this increase was planned after reviewing competitors' selling prices and analyzing projected costs of merchandise.

Accurate projections are important for effective budgeting. However, since budgets are based on estimates, most businesses round the projected amounts to simplify the budgeting process. Tint My Window rounds unit projections to the nearest hundred units and dollar projections to the nearest $10.

>> Preparing a Sales Budget

❶ Enter the number of actual units, **671,500**, and projected units, **700,000**, in the Annual Budget column.

❷ Determine the sales percentages by quarter. Dividing the annual budget into quarterly segments provides more frequent opportunities to compare actual with budgeted operations.

❸ Calculate the unit sales volume for each quarter. Tint My Windows' planning group believes that

quarterly sales percentages will remain the same. Therefore, 22.3% of annual sales are expected to occur in the first quarter.

❹ Enter the unit sales prices for each quarter.

❺ Calculate projected net sales for each quarter.

❻ Calculate total net sales for 20X3.

Purchases Budget LO3

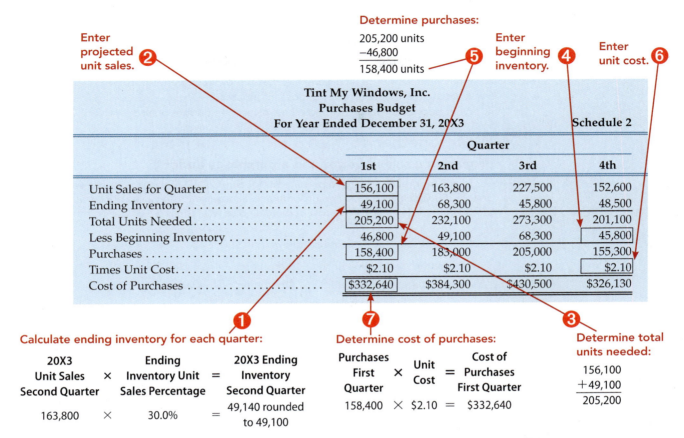

Enter projected unit sales. ②

Determine purchases:
205,200 units
−46,800
158,400 units
⑤

Enter beginning inventory. ④

Enter unit cost. ⑥

Tint My Windows, Inc.
Purchases Budget
For Year Ended December 31, 20X3
Schedule 2

	Quarter			
	1st	2nd	3rd	4th
Unit Sales for Quarter	156,100	163,800	227,500	152,600
Ending Inventory	49,100	68,300	45,800	48,500
Total Units Needed	205,200	232,100	273,300	201,100
Less Beginning Inventory	46,800	49,100	68,300	45,800
Purchases	158,400	183,000	205,000	155,300
Times Unit Cost	$2.10	$2.10	$2.10	$2.10
Cost of Purchases	$332,640	$384,300	$430,500	$326,130

① **Calculate ending inventory for each quarter:**

20X3 Unit Sales Second Quarter	×	Ending Inventory Unit Sales Percentage	=	20X3 Ending Inventory Second Quarter
163,800	×	30.0%	=	49,140 rounded to 49,100

⑦ **Determine cost of purchases:**

Purchases First Quarter	×	Unit Cost	=	Cost of Purchases First Quarter
158,400	×	$2.10	=	$332,640

③ **Determine total units needed:**

156,100
+49,100
205,200

After the planning group approves the sales budget, the remaining budgets are prepared. A statement prepared to show the projected amount of purchases that will be required during a budget period is called a **purchases budget**. The following factors are considered when projecting purchases:

1. Projected unit sales.
2. The quantity of merchandise on hand at the beginning of the budget period.

3. The quantity of merchandise needed to fill projected sales orders without having excessive inventory.
4. The price trends of merchandise to be purchased.

The sales manager prepares the purchases budget shown above. The sales manager determines that the number of units in the ending inventory should be about 30.0% of the number of units projected to be sold in the subsequent quarter.

>> Preparing a Purchases Budget

① Calculate the ending inventory for each quarter. Round estimates to the nearest hundred. Use **48,500** units for the fourth quarter's ending inventory (161,700 units projected to be sold in the first quarter of 20X4 × 30%).

② Enter projected unit sales for the quarter from the sales budget.

③ Add projected sales units and the ending inventory units to determine the total units needed per quarter.

④ Enter the beginning inventory, which is the same as the ending inventory for the preceding quarter. Tint My Windows' ending inventory of 46,800 units on

December 31, 20X2, becomes its January 1 beginning inventory.

⑤ Subtract the beginning inventory from the total units needed to determine total unit purchases for the quarter.

⑥ Enter the unit cost for each quarter. Tint My Windows' planning group has projected that materials costs will rise from $2.00 to $2.10 per unit in the first quarter of 20X3.

⑦ Multiply the unit purchases each quarter by the unit cost to determine the cost of purchases.

TERMS REVIEW

budgeting

budget

budget period

sales budget

purchases budget

Audit your understanding LO1

1. A budget serves what three important business functions?
2. What is the length of time generally covered by a company's budget?
3. What are the four sources of budget information?
4. What budget shows the projected net sales for a budget period?

Work together 15-1 LO2, 3

Preparing a sales budget and a purchases budget

Maddox Corporation wishes to prepare budgets for 20X3. Management has set a sales goal of 100,000 units. Maddox Corporation will increase its unit sales price from $14.50 to $15.00 in the first quarter. The cost of merchandise will remain $7.00 per unit throughout 20X3.

Quarterly unit sales for 20X2 are as follows:

1st quarter	17,000 units	3rd quarter	24,000 units
2nd quarter	19,000 units	4th quarter	30,000 units

The sales manager requests that 20.0% of the next quarter's unit sales be available in the prior quarter's ending inventory. Ending inventory for 20X2 is 3,800 units. Management projects that 22,600 units will be sold in the first quarter of 20X4.

A partially completed sales budget and purchases budget are given in the *Working Papers*.

1. Complete the sales budget (Schedule 1) for the four quarters ended December 31, 20X3. Maddox Corporation rounds unit amounts to the nearest hundred units, dollar amounts to the nearest $10, and percentage amounts to the nearest 0.1%.
2. Complete the purchases budget (Schedule 2) for the four quarters ended December 31, 20X3.

Save your work for use in Work Together 15-2.

On your own 15-1 LO2, 3

Preparing a sales budget and a purchases budget

Northstar, Inc., wishes to prepare budgets for 20X3. Management has set a sales goal of 220,000 units. Northstar, Inc., will increase its unit sales price from $8.00 to $8.25 in the first quarter. The cost of merchandise will increase from $3.25 to $3.50 in the first quarter of 20X3.

Quarterly unit sales for 20X2 are as follows:

1st quarter	40,000 units	3rd quarter	52,000 units
2nd quarter	48,000 units	4th quarter	60,000 units

The sales manager requests that 25.0% of the next quarter's unit sales be available in the prior quarter's ending inventory. Ending inventory for 20X2 is 11,000 units. Management projects that 48,000 units will be sold in the first quarter of 20X4.

A partially completed sales budget and purchases budget are given in the *Working Papers*.

1. Complete the sales budget (Schedule 1) for the four quarters ended December 31, 20X3. Northstar rounds unit amounts to the nearest hundred units, dollar amounts to the nearest $10, and percentage amounts to the nearest 0.1%.
2. Complete the purchases budget (Schedule 2) for the four quarters ended December 31, 20X3.

Save your work for use in On Your Own 15-2.

Expense Budgets and the Budgeted Income Statement

LO4 Prepare a selling expenses budget.
LO5 Prepare an administrative expenses budget.
LO6 Prepare an other revenue and expenses budget.
LO7 Prepare a budgeted income statement.

Selling Expenses Budget LO4

Tint My Windows, Inc. Selling Expenses Budget For Year Ended December 31, 20X3					Schedule 3
	Annual Budget	**Quarter**			
		1st	**2nd**	**3rd**	**4th**
Advertising Expense	$ 61,410	$13,110	$ 14,550	$ 20,200	$13,550
Delivery Expense	189,010	42,150	44,230	61,430	41,200
Depr. Expense—Delivery Equipment	9,000	2,250	2,250	2,250	2,250
Depr. Expense—Warehouse Equipment	16,880	3,380	4,500	4,500	4,500
Miscellaneous Expense—Sales	12,790	2,730	3,030	4,210	2,820
Salary Expense—Commissions............	102,340	21,850	24,240	33,670	22,580
Salary Expense—Regular.................	29,360	6,550	6,870	9,540	6,400
Supplies Expense—Sales	15,360	3,280	3,640	5,050	3,390
Total Selling Expenses	$436,150	$95,300	$103,310	$140,850	$96,690

A statement prepared to show projected expenditures related directly to the selling operations is called a **selling expenses budget**. The sales manager projects the information for the selling expenses budget. However, other sales personnel may provide specific information. For example, the advertising manager supplies much of the advertising expense information. After selling expenses information has been projected, a selling expenses budget is prepared.

Some selling expense items are relatively stable and require little planning. For example, depreciation expenses for delivery and warehouse equipment are reasonably stable from year to year unless new equipment is bought. On the other hand, several selling expenses increase and decrease in relation to sales increases and decreases. Tint My Windows has a seasonal business, with higher sales during the second and third quarters. The company hires more personnel and spends more for advertising and sales supplies during the heavy sales

season. All of these factors are considered when a selling expenses budget is made. Tint My Windows' selling expenses budget is shown above.

The company's sales manager uses a number of approaches to project the various selling expenses. Most selling expenses are linked closely to the amount of quarterly net sales. Management uses the following projection guides to prepare its selling expenses budget.

1. **Advertising expense.** This expense is closely related to sales and sales promotions for the year. Advertising expense for 20X2 was 2.4% ($56,400 ÷ $2,350,250) of net sales. Sales promotion emphasis will be maintained at about the same level this year. Thus, 2.4% of each quarter's projected net sales will be allocated to advertising expense. The first-quarter projected advertising expense is $13,110 (2.4% × $546,350 = $13,112, rounded to $13,110).

2. **Delivery expense.** This expense is closely related to the number of units sold and delivered. The previous year's delivery expense increased significantly because an external freight company was used for some deliveries until Tint My Windows could acquire an additional truck. Rigid cost control measures will be applied to reduce future unit delivery expenses. Delivery expense is projected to be $0.27 per unit (sq. ft.) sold times each quarter's projected unit sales. The first-quarter projected delivery expense is $42,150 ($0.27 × 156,100 units = $42,147, rounded to $42,150).

3. **Depreciation expense—delivery equipment.** No new delivery equipment will be added. Thus, depreciation expense will remain the same as for the previous year ($2,250 per quarter).

4. **Depreciation expense—warehouse equipment.** A new automated cutter will be acquired at the beginning of the second quarter, increasing quarterly depreciation expense from $3,380 to $4,500 per quarter in the second, third, and fourth quarters.

5. **Miscellaneous expense—sales.** Miscellaneous expense was 0.6% ($14,360 ÷ $2,350,250) of net sales in 20X2. Management is committed to reducing miscellaneous expense to 0.5% of net sales in 20X3. The first-quarter miscellaneous expense is projected as $2,730 (0.5% × $546,350 = $2,732, rounded to $2,730).

6. **Salary expense—commissions.** Salespersons will continue to earn a 4.0% commission on net sales. The first-quarter commissions are projected as

$21,850 (4.0% × $546,350 = $21,854, rounded to $21,850).

7. **Salary expense—regular.** Regular salary expense is determined by salary increases and changes in activity that affect the number of people employed. The new automated cutter will reduce regular salary expense by $15,000. A 6.0% raise will be added to remaining salaries. Thus, the projected annual amount is calculated as shown.

Salary Expense: 20X2 Comparative Income Statement	$42,700
Less Reduction from Automated Cutter	− 15,000
Total	$27,700
Plus 6.0% Rate Increase	+ 1,660
Projected Salary Expense—Regular	$29,360

The projected amount is allocated among the four quarters in relation to the sales percentage from the sales budget. The first-quarter regular salaries are projected as $6,550 (22.3% × $29,360 = $6,547, rounded to $6,550).

8. **Supplies expense—sales.** Supplies expense was 0.6% ($14,100 ÷ $2,350,250) of net sales in 20X2. The same percentage relationship is expected in 20X3. The first-quarter supplies expense is projected as $3,280 (0.6% × $546,350 = $3,278, rounded to $3,280).

After the quarterly amounts have been calculated and entered, the annual budget amounts are determined by totaling the quarterly amounts.

State Parks and Sources of Revenue

CareerClusters®
PATHWAYS TO COLLEGE & CAREER READINESS
Government & Public Administration

A state government must establish budgets for its revenues and operating expenses and for the services it provides to its residents. One cost item for most states is a state park system. The state governing body must allocate a specific amount of money for the operation of these parks. To do this, the governing body will rely on the specialized skills of government accountants.

If state tax revenues decrease, the governing body must make corresponding decreases in monies allocated to specific programs and services. If this happens, the state park system has two choices: decrease the budgeted costs and expenses (usually by decreasing the services offered), or identify other sources of revenue (to maintain the same level of services).

Some sources of additional revenue are user fees (such as entrance fees, camping fees, and revenue-generating activities such as zip lining, etc.), dedicated public revenue sources (such as lottery profits earmarked for state parks or the inclusion of a state park pass with the cost of vehicle licenses), philanthropy (donations by businesses and/or individual), and corporate sponsorships.

CRITICAL THINKING

For each of the sources of additional revenue categories given above, list (a) one comment supporting the revenue source and (b) one comment opposing the revenue source.

Source: www.pewtrusts.org, "State Parks Find New Ways to Save, Make Money," by Rebecca Beitsch.

Administrative Expenses Budget LO5

	Annual Budget	Quarter			
		1st	2nd	3rd	4th
Depreciation Expense—Office Equipment ..	$ 18,000	$ 4,500	$ 4,500	$ 4,500	$ 4,500
Insurance Expense	7,000	1,750	1,750	1,750	1,750
Miscellaneous Expense—Administrative ...	45,080	11,270	11,270	11,270	11,270
Payroll Taxes Expense	28,980	6,680	7,020	8,530	6,750
Rent Expense..........................	37,800	9,450	9,450	9,450	9,450
Salary Expense—Administrative	100,200	25,050	25,050	25,050	25,050
Supplies Expense—Administrative	17,900	3,820	4,240	5,890	3,950
Uncollectible Accounts Expense..........	15,360	3,280	3,640	5,050	3,390
Utilities Expense	13,630	3,040	3,190	4,430	2,970
Total Administrative Expenses............	$283,950	$68,840	$70,110	$75,920	$69,080

Tint My Windows, Inc.
Administrative Expenses Budget
For Year Ended December 31, 20X3   **Schedule 4**

A statement that shows the projected expenses for all operating expenses not directly related to selling operations is called an **administrative expenses budget**. The administrative manager prepares this budget, using information from these sources:

1. Past records.
2. Company plans.
3. Sales and selling expenses budgets.
4. Discussions with other managers.

After the administrative expenses have been projected, the administrative expenses budget is prepared. Tint My Windows' administrative expenses budget is shown above.

Most administrative expenses are known and remain the same each period. Some administrative expenses need to be budgeted as a percentage of another amount from another budget. The following information was used to prepare the administrative expenses budget.

1. **Depreciation expense—office equipment.** Recently purchased office equipment increased annual depreciation to $18,000. Annual depreciation is divided equally over the four quarters.
2. **Insurance expense.** Annual insurance is projected to increase to $7,000 primarily because of added coverage for the new automated cutting machine. An equal amount is paid each quarter.
3. **Miscellaneous expense—administrative.** This expense is based on Salary Expense—Administrative. Therefore, Salary Expense—Administrative must be calculated first. Closely related to administrative salaries, miscellaneous expense was 49.8% ($48,460 ÷ $97,280) of administrative salaries in 20X2. Management is committed to reducing

miscellaneous expense to 45.0% of projected administrative salaries in 20X3. The first-quarter miscellaneous expense is projected as $11,270 (45.0% × $25,050 = 11,273, rounded to $11,270).

4. **Payroll taxes expense.** This expense is based on the total of three salary expense amounts. Therefore, all salary expense amounts must be calculated before calculating payroll tax expense. Based on current payroll tax rates, payroll taxes expense is 12.5% of all salaries each quarter. The first-quarter salaries are projected as $53,450 (Salary Expense—Commissions, $21,850 + Salary Expense—Regular, $6,550 + Salary Expense—Administrative, $25,050). Thus, payroll taxes expense is projected as $6,680 (12.5% × $53,450 = $6,681, rounded to $6,680). Tint My Windows chooses to put all payroll tax expenses into the administrative expenses budget, even though some of these taxes relate to the sales department. Other companies may choose to list payroll taxes in both budgets.
5. **Rent expense.** Tint My Windows leases the building for a known rental fee. Rent will increase to $3,150 per month. Thus, rent expense can be projected at $9,450 each quarter.
6. **Salary expense—administrative.** No new administrative personnel will be hired. Salary expense is projected as $100,200, equal to the 20X2 amount, $97,280, adjusted for a 3.0% salary increase. An equal amount is paid each quarter. Thus, each quarter's salary expense is projected as $25,050 ($100,200 ÷ 4).

7. **Supplies expense—administrative.** Supplies expense was 0.7% ($17,030 ÷ $2,350,250) of net sales for 20X2. The same percentage will be used in 20X3. The first-quarter supplies expense is projected as $3,820 (0.7% × $546,350 = $3,824, rounded to $3,820).

8. **Uncollectible accounts expense.** Closely related to net sales, uncollectible accounts expense was 0.6% ($14,100 ÷ $2,350,250) of net sales in 20X2. The first-quarter uncollectible accounts expense is

projected as $3,280 (0.6% × $546,350 = $3,278, rounded to $3,280).

9. **Utilities expense.** Utilities expense is based on the amount of power, heat, telephone, and other utilities used in 20X2. Costs are projected to increase by 8.2%, consisting of a 4.2% projected increase in activity and a 4.0% increase in rates. The utilities expense by quarter in 20X2 is multiplied by 108.2% (100.0% + 8.2%) and 20X3's projected utilities expense is calculated as follows:

	20X2 Actual Utilities Expense	×	108.2%	=	20X3 Projected Utilities Expense
1st Quarter	$ 2,810	×	108.2%	=	$ 3,040
2nd Quarter	2,950	×	108.2%	=	3,190
3rd Quarter	4,095	×	108.2%	=	4,430
4th Quarter	2,745	×	108.2%	=	2,970
Total	$12,600	×	108.2%	=	$13,630

Other Revenue and Expenses Budget LO6

Tint My Windows, Inc. Other Revenue and Expenses Budget For Year Ended December 31, 20X3					Schedule 5
	Annual Budget	Quarter			
		1st	2nd	3rd	4th
Other Expenses:					
Interest Expense	$2,820	$940	$940	$940	

Budgeted revenue and expenses from activities other than normal operations are shown in a statement called the **other revenue and expenses budget**. Typical items in this budget are interest income, interest expense, and gains or losses on the sale of plant assets. Tint My Windows' other revenue and expenses budget is shown above. Tint My Windows has only one other expense item and no other revenue items.

Tint My Windows' administrative manager is responsible for projecting the information in the other revenue and expenses budget. The projected interest expense is based on the interest due on a $25,000 loan used to acquire the automated cutter. Since Tint My Windows plans to repay the $25,000 loan at the beginning of the fourth quarter, the budget shows interest expense for only three quarters.

Remember Even though budgets are based on estimates, much care is taken to ensure that the estimates are as accurate as possible.

Budgeted Income Statement LO7

	Annual Budget	Quarter 1st	Quarter 2nd	Quarter 3rd	Quarter 4th
Tint My Windows, Inc. **Budgeted Income Statement** **For Year Ended December 31, 20X3**					Schedule 6
Operating Revenue:					
Net Sales (Schedule 1)	$2,558,780	$546,350	$606,060	$841,750	$564,620
Cost of Merchandise Sold:					
Beginning Inventory.	$ 93,600	$ 93,600	$103,110	$143,430	$ 96,180
Purchases (Schedule 2).	1,473,570	332,640	384,300	430,500	326,130
Total Merchandise Available.	$1,567,170	$426,240	$487,410	$573,930	$422,310
Less Ending Inventory	101,850	103,110	143,430	96,180	101,850
Cost of Merchandise Sold	$1,465,320	$323,130	$343,980	$477,750	$320,460
Gross Profit on Sales.	$1,093,460	$223,220	$262,080	$364,000	$244,160
Operating Expenses:					
Selling Expenses (Schedule 3).	$ 436,150	$ 95,300	$103,310	$140,850	$ 96,690
Administrative Expenses (Schedule 4) . . .	283,950	68,840	70,110	75,920	69,080
Total Operating Expenses	$ 720,100	$164,140	$173,420	$216,770	$165,770
Income from Operations	$ 373,360	$ 59,080	$ 88,660	$147,230	$ 78,390
Other Expenses (Schedule 5).	2,820	940	940	940	—
Net Income before Federal Income Tax.	$ 370,540	$ 58,140	$ 87,720	$146,290	$ 78,390
Federal Income Tax Expense.	77,810	12,210	18,420	30,720	16,460*
Net Income after Federal Income Tax	$ 292,730	$ 45,930	$ 69,300	$115,570	$ 61,930

*Rounded so that the sum of the quarterly amounts equal the Annual Budget amount.

1. Beginning inventory:
46,800 units × $2.00 = $93,600

2. Ending inventory:
49,100 units × $2.10 = $103,110

A statement that shows a company's projected sales, costs, expenses, and net income is called a **budgeted income statement**. Since the five budgets contain detailed items, Tint My Windows prepares a shortened budgeted income statement and attaches the supporting budgets. Tint My Windows' budgeted income statement is shown above.

The first-quarter beginning inventory is calculated using the 20X2 unit cost, $2.00. Other inventory amounts are calculated using the unit cost for 20X3, $2.10.

© LJUPCO SMOKOVSKI/SHUTTERSTOCK.COM

Amounts from the five supporting budgets allow Tint My Windows to project net income before federal income tax. Estimated federal income taxes are calculated using the corporate tax rate of 21% as shown below. Since Tint My Windows has an estimated net income before federal income tax for each quarter, that amount is used to calculate the estimated federal income tax for that quarter. As with other budgeted amounts, Federal Income Tax is rounded to the nearest $10. Due to this rounding in quarters 1, 2, and 3, an adjustment may be required in the fourth quarter in order to ensure that the sum of the four quarterly amounts equals 21% of the estimated total net income before Federal Income Tax.

Net Income before Federal Income Taxes	×	Tax Rate	=	Federal Income Tax Expense
$370,540	×	21%	=	$77,813.40 rounded to $77,810

At this point, the net income has been estimated by quarter for the next fiscal year. Tint My Windows' management must analyze these results to determine if the estimated net income is adequate for current stockholders and to attract new investors. If not, management must adjust the supporting budgets by either increasing revenue or decreasing expenses.

Charting Financial Ratios

Aretha Johnson, the owner of Johnson Stores, was ready to retire but faced a serious problem. None of her children had any interest in operating her farming supply stores. Wanting to retain an equity interest in the business to benefit her grandchildren, she elected to recruit a partner, Wayne Hillman. Mr. Hillman purchased a 40% stake in the business and set in motion a five-year plan to improve its financial performance.

Mr. Hillman set targets for six financial ratios that he considered critical measures of success. He has requested a chart that shows the three-year progress in meeting those targets. He intends to use the information to assist in preparing the budgets for the coming year.

OPEN THE SPREADSHEET TLA_CH15

The worksheet contains a schedule of six financial ratios. The schedule presents the actual ratios for the past three years and Mr. Hillman's target ratios. Follow the steps on the Instructions tab to prepare a chart. Answer these questions:

1. Explain why the chart does not effectively communicate the trend in all of the financial ratios.

2. Each set of bars communicates the change in the actual ratios relative to the target ratios. What two questions can be answered by evaluating each set of bars?

3. Is Johnson Stores making progress in achieving its five-year targets? Support your answer.

4. Is there a ratio where the message communicated by the chart is inconsistent with the other ratios? How would you correct this problem?

LO4 Prepare a selling expenses budget.

LO5 Prepare an administrative expenses budget.

LO6 Prepare an other revenue and expenses budget.

LO7 Prepare a budgeted income statement.

TERMS REVIEW

selling expenses budget

administrative expenses budget

other revenue and expenses budget

budgeted income statement

Audit your understanding LO4, 5, 6, 7

1. Which budget shows projected expenditures related directly to the selling operations?
2. What sources of information are used in preparing an administrative expenses budget?
3. What items are typically included in the other revenue and expenses budget?
4. If the budgeted income statement does not show adequate net income, what must be done?

Work together 15-2 LO4, 5, 6, 7

Preparing budgets for selling expenses, administrative expenses, and other expenses and preparing a budgeted income statement

Use the information given and the budgets prepared in Work Together 15-1. Additional information is given below. Expenses for 20X3 are projected as follows: Except where noted, percentages are based on projected net sales. For these items, calculate each quarter's amount by multiplying the percentage times that quarter's net sales. Calculate the annual total by adding the four quarterly amounts. When a dollar amount is given, the total amount should be divided equally among the four quarters.

Selling Expenses	
Advertising Expense	2.5%
Delivery Expense	5.0%
Depreciation Expense—Delivery Equipment	$8,000.00
Depreciation Expense—Warehouse Equipment	$5,000.00
Miscellaneous Expense—Sales	4.0%
Salary Expense—Sales	6.0%
Supplies Expense—Sales	2.0%

Administrative Expenses	
Depreciation Expense—Office Equipment	$4,000.00
Insurance Expense	$6,000.00
Miscellaneous Expense—Administrative	$3,000.00
Payroll Taxes Expense	12.0% of total salaries
Rent Expense	$24,000.00
Salary Expense—Administrative	$20,000.00
Supplies Expense—Administrative	$8,000.00
Uncollected Accounts Expense	0.5%
Utilities Expense	2.5%

Interest Expense is estimated to be $2,520.00. Federal income taxes are calculated at 21% of net income before federal income tax for each quarter. Partially completed budget forms are given in the *Working Papers*.

1. Complete the selling expenses budget (Schedule 3) for the four quarters ended December 31, 20X3. Maddox Corporation rounds all amounts to the nearest $10.
2. Complete the administrative expenses budget (Schedule 4) for the four quarters ended December 31, 20X3.
3. Complete the other revenue and expenses budget (Schedule 5) for the four quarters ended December 31, 20X3.
4. Complete the budgeted income statement for the four quarters ended December 31, 20X3. Save your work for use in Work Together 15-3.

On your own 15-2 LO4, 5, 6, 7

Preparing budgets for selling expenses, administrative expenses, and other expenses and preparing a budgeted income statement

Use the information given and the budgets prepared in On Your Own 15-1. Additional information is given below. Expenses for 20X3 are projected as follows: Except where noted, percentages are based on projected net sales. For these items, calculate each quarter's amount by multiplying the percentage times that quarter's net sales. Calculate the annual total by adding the four quarterly amounts. When a dollar amount is given, the total amount should be divided equally among the four quarters.

Selling Expenses	
Advertising Expense	4.0%
Delivery Expense	6.5%
Depreciation Expense—Delivery Equipment	$10,000.00
Depreciation Expense—Warehouse Equipment	$20,000.00
Miscellaneous Expense—Sales	5.0%
Salary Expense—Sales	7.0%
Supplies Expense—Sales	2.0%

Administrative Expenses	
Depreciation Expense—Office Equipment	$15,000.00
Insurance Expense	$12,000.00
Miscellaneous Expense—Administrative	$8,000.00
Payroll Taxes Expense	12.0% of total salaries
Rent Expense	$24,000.00
Salary Expense—Administrative	$35,000.00
Supplies Expense—Administrative	$14,400.00
Uncollected Accounts Expense	0.4%
Utilities Expense	6.0%

Interest Expense is estimated to be $4,000.00. Federal income taxes are calculated at 21% of net income before federal income tax for each quarter. Partially completed budget forms are given in the *Working Papers*.

1. Complete the selling expenses budget (Schedule 3) for the four quarters ended December 31, 20X3. Northstar, Inc., rounds all amounts to the nearest $10.

2. Complete the administrative expenses budget (Schedule 4) for the four quarters ended December 31, 20X3.

3. Complete the other revenue and expenses budget (Schedule 5) for the four quarters ended December 31, 20X3.

4. Complete the budgeted income statement for the four quarters ended December 31, 20X3. Save your work for use in On Your Own 15-3.

LO8 Prepare a cash receipts budget.
LO9 Prepare a cash payments budget.
LO10 Prepare a cash budget.

Cash Receipts Budget LO8

Tint My Windows, Inc. Cash Receipts Budget For Year Ended December 31, 20X3				Schedule A
	Quarter			
	1st	**2nd**	**3rd**	**4th**
Cash Receipts from Sales:				
Prior Year's 4th-Quarter Sales ($512,050) ...	$150,540			
1st-Quarter Sales ($546,350)............	382,450	$160,630		
2nd-Quarter Sales ($606,060)...........		424,240	$178,180	
3rd-Quarter Sales ($841,750)			589,230	$247,470
4th-Quarter Sales ($564,620)				395,230
Total Cash Receipts from Sales..........	$532,990	$584,870	$767,410	$642,700
Cash Receipts from Other Sources:				
Note Payable to Bank..................	25,000			
Total Cash Receipts...................	$557,990	$584,870	$767,410	$642,700

Collection Percentage	×	First-Quarter Sales	=	Second-Quarter Cash Receipts
29.4%	×	$546,350	=	$160,627, rounded to $160,630

Collection Percentage	×	Second-Quarter Sales	=	Second-Quarter Cash Receipts
70.0%	×	$606,060	=	$424,242, rounded to $424,240

Good cash management requires planning and controlling cash so that it will be available to meet obligations when they come due. Tint My Windows prepares a cash budget to help analyze cash inflows and cash outflows. The treasurer prepares Tint My Windows' cash budget in consultation with the budget committee. A treasurer is a corporate officer who is usually responsible for planning the corporation's requirement for and use of cash. The treasurer analyzes:

1. Projected receipts from cash sales, customers on account, and other sources.
2. Projected cash payments for ordinary expenses, such as rent, payroll, and payments to vendors on account.
3. Other cash payments for assets, such as plant assets or supplies.

Projected cash receipts for a budget period are reported on a statement called a **cash receipts budget**. Tint My Windows' cash receipts budget is shown above. To prepare a cash receipts budget, projections are composed of the following:

1. Quarterly cash sales.
2. Quarterly collections on account from customers. The amounts received from customers will not be the same as the amount of sales on account. Normally, cash is received for sales on account made during the previous one or two months. In addition, some sales returns and allowances and uncollectible accounts are likely.
3. Cash to be received quarterly from other sources.

Analysis of Cash Receipts

An analysis of Tint My Windows' sales for previous years shows the following pattern of net sales per quarter:

1. About 40.0% are cash sales.
2. About 30.0% are sales on account collected in the same quarter. Thus, 70.0% of a quarter's net sales are collected during the same quarter.
3. About 29.4% are collected in the following quarter.
4. About 0.6% prove to be uncollectible.

As shown in the cash receipts budget, the total cash receipts from sales in the first quarter ($532,990) include $105,540 from 20X2's fourth-quarter sales on account (29.4% × $512,050 = $150,543, rounded to $150,540) plus $382,450 from 20X3's first-quarter sales (70.0% × $546,350 = $382,445, rounded to $382,450). Cash sales and collections on account provide most of the cash receipts. If additional cash is needed, other sources of cash should be planned. For example, Tint My Windows' treasurer determines that cash on hand will be reduced in the first quarter to an unusually low level. This condition could prevent the company from making timely payments for its expenditures. Therefore, the treasurer arranges to borrow $25,000 during the first quarter.

GLOBAL AWARENESS

Foreign Corrupt Practices Act

In the United States, it is illegal for any person or business to bribe a government official in order to have that official act or fail to act in a manner that benefits the person or business. However, in some countries, bribery is a legal, accepted way to conduct business.

During investigations by the Securities and Exchange Commission (SEC) in the mid-1970s, more than 400 U.S. companies admitted to such bribery. As a result, the Foreign Corrupt Practices Act (FCPA) was enacted by Congress and signed into law in 1977. The purpose of the FCPA was to stop corrupt practices, "create a level playing field" for businesses so that honest competition could prevail, and restore the public's trust in the marketplace.

The FCPA focuses on two methods of preventing corruption. First, it prohibits individuals and firms from engaging in the bribery of foreign officials. Second, it requires specific control measures to prevent the falsifying of accounting records or the failure to use a system of internal control. A 1998 amendment to the FCPA extends the prohibition of bribery to foreign individuals and firms doing business in the United States.

A company found guilty of violating the FCPA could be required to pay back with interest any illegally acquired profits and be subject to penalties. In addition, it may have to be overseen by a consultant. The total financial loss could be substantial and could include the loss of exporting rights.

The Department of Justice (DOJ) and the SEC have developed guidelines for implementing the FCPA. These guidelines cover to whom the act applies, what actions are prohibited, and what sanctions may be enforced, and they include an outline of an effective compliance program.

CRITICAL THINKING

1. Go to the website for either the DOJ or the SEC. Search for the FCPA and find a recent case brought against a U.S. company. List the name of the company and how it violated the FCPA.

2. Using the case found in Part 1, list several ways in which bribery is bad for business.

Sources: www.justice.gov; www.sec.gov.

Cash Payments Budget LO9

<table>
<tr><td colspan="5" align="center">Tint My Windows, Inc.
Cash Payments Budget</td></tr>
<tr><td colspan="4" align="center">For Year Ended December 31, 20X3</td><td align="right">Schedule B</td></tr>
<tr><td></td><td colspan="4" align="center">Quarter</td></tr>
<tr><td></td><td>1st</td><td>2nd</td><td>3rd</td><td>4th</td></tr>
<tr><td>From Purchases:</td><td></td><td></td><td></td><td></td></tr>
<tr><td>Prior Year's 4th Quarter ($276,800) ......</td><td>$ 83,040</td><td></td><td></td><td></td></tr>
<tr><td>1st-Quarter Purchases ($332,640) ....</td><td>232,850</td><td>$ 99,790</td><td></td><td></td></tr>
<tr><td>2nd-Quarter Purchases ($384,300) ....</td><td></td><td>269,010</td><td>$115,290</td><td></td></tr>
<tr><td>3rd-Quarter Purchases ($430,500) ....</td><td></td><td></td><td>301,350</td><td>$129,150</td></tr>
<tr><td>4th-Quarter Purchases ($326,130) ....</td><td></td><td></td><td></td><td>228,290</td></tr>
<tr><td>Total Payments from Purchases ....</td><td>$315,890</td><td>$368,800</td><td>$416,640</td><td>$357,440</td></tr>
<tr><td>For Operating Expenses:</td><td></td><td></td><td></td><td></td></tr>
<tr><td>Cash Selling Expenses ....</td><td>$ 89,670</td><td>$ 96,560</td><td>$134,100</td><td>$ 89,940</td></tr>
<tr><td>Cash Administrative Expenses..........</td><td>61,060</td><td>61,970</td><td>66,370</td><td>61,190</td></tr>
<tr><td>Total Cash Operating Expenses ....</td><td>$150,730</td><td>$158,530</td><td>$200,470</td><td>$151,130</td></tr>
<tr><td>Other Cash Payments:</td><td></td><td></td><td></td><td></td></tr>
<tr><td>Federal Income Tax Expense............</td><td>$ 12,210</td><td>$ 18,420</td><td>$ 30,720</td><td>$ 16,460</td></tr>
<tr><td>Fixed Asset Purchases ....</td><td>50,000</td><td></td><td></td><td></td></tr>
<tr><td>Cash Dividend.......................</td><td></td><td>55,000</td><td></td><td>55,000</td></tr>
<tr><td>Investment ....</td><td></td><td></td><td></td><td>100,000</td></tr>
<tr><td>Note Payable and Interest ....</td><td></td><td></td><td></td><td>27,500</td></tr>
<tr><td>Total Other Cash Payments............</td><td>$ 62,210</td><td>$ 73,420</td><td>$ 30,720</td><td>$198,960</td></tr>
<tr><td>Total Cash Payments ....</td><td>$528,830</td><td>$600,750</td><td>$647,830</td><td>$707,530</td></tr>
</table>

Projected cash payments for a budget period are reported on a statement called a **cash payments budget**. Tint My Windows' cash payments budget is shown above. To prepare the cash payments budget, the accountant and treasurer make the following projections:

1. Quarterly cash payments for accounts payable or notes payable to vendors.
2. Quarterly cash payments for each expense item. This projection requires an analysis of the selling expenses, administrative expenses, and other revenue and expenses budgets.
3. Quarterly cash payments for buying equipment and other assets.
4. Quarterly cash payments for dividends.
5. Quarterly cash payments for investments.

Tint My Windows' treasurer uses the following guides to prepare the cash payments budget.

1. **Cash payments for merchandise.** An analysis of past records for payments to vendors on account shows the following pattern of purchases in a quarter:
   a. About 20.0% are cash purchases.
   b. About 50.0% are on account and are paid for in the quarter. Thus, 70.0% (20.0% + 50.0%) of a quarter's purchases are paid for during the same quarter.
   c. The remaining 30.0% are purchases on account paid for in the following quarter.

   Cash payments are calculated using the same procedure used for cash receipts. Purchase amounts are from the purchases budget. The first-quarter cash payments for the first-quarter purchases are $232,850 (70.0% × $332,640 = $232,848 rounded to $232,850).

2. Cash payments for operating expenses. Cash payments for most operating expenses are made in the quarter the expense is incurred. However, the selling expenses budget, shown on page 439, and the administrative expenses budget, page 441, include some projected items for which cash will not be paid. For example, cash is not paid for depreciation and uncollectible accounts expenses. Therefore, these amounts are not included in the cash payments budget. The first quarter's cash payments for selling expenses and for administrative expenses are calculated as follows:

Selling Expenses		$95,300
Less: Depr. Exp. —Delivery Equip.	$2,250	
Depr. Exp. —Warehouse Equip.	3,380	5,630
Cash Payments for Selling Exp.		$89,670
Administrative Expenses		$68,840
Less: Depr. Exp. —Office Equip.	$4,500	
Uncollectible Accts. Exp.	3,280	7,780
Cash Payment for Admin. Exp.		$61,060

3. Other cash payments. Tint My Windows also plans for cash payments other than for merchandise, selling expenses, and administrative expenses. Federal income tax payments equal the quarterly federal income tax expense amounts on the budgeted income statement. Tint My Windows also plans to buy a new automated cutting machine for $50,000 at the end of the first quarter. The company expects to pay a $55,000 cash dividend to stockholders in the second and fourth quarters. Since a large cash balance is projected for the third quarter, Tint My Windows plans a $100,000 interest-earning investment in the fourth quarter. In addition, plans call for repaying the promissory note plus interest, $27,500, at the beginning of the fourth quarter.

The last line of the cash payments budget shows the total cash payments projected each quarter. This total indicates the minimum amount of cash that must be available each quarter.

Cash Budget LO10

Tint My Windows, Inc.
Cash Budget
For Year Ended December 31, 20X3

	Quarter			
	1st	**2nd**	**3rd**	**4th**
Cash Balance—Beginning	$ 26,220	$ 55,380	$ 39,500	$159,080
Cash Receipts Budget (Schedule A).	557,990	584,870	767,410	642,700
Cash Available.	$584,210	$640,250	$806,910	$801,780
Less Cash Payments (Schedule B)	528,830	600,750	647,830	707,530
Cash Balance—Ending.	$ 55,380	$ 39,500	$159,080	$ 94,250

A statement that shows for each month or quarter a projection of a company's beginning cash balance, cash receipts, cash payments, and ending cash balance is called a **cash budget**. Tint My Windows' cash budget, shown above, is prepared from the information in the cash receipts budget and the cash payments budget. The first-quarter beginning cash balance is taken from the balance sheet on December 31, 20X2.

At the end of each quarter of a budget period, Tint My Windows compares the actual cash balance with the projected cash balance shown on the cash budget.

If the actual cash balance is less than the projected balance, the reasons for the decrease are determined and action is taken to correct the problem. One reason may be that some customers are not paying their accounts when they should. Another may be that expenses are exceeding budget projections. If the decrease continues, the company could have a quarter in which there is not enough cash to make all the required cash payments. If this shortage does occur, the business will have to borrow money until receipts and payments are brought into balance.

LO8 Prepare a cash receipts budget.

LO9 Prepare a cash payments budget.

LO10 Prepare a cash budget.

TERMS REVIEW

cash receipts budget

cash payments budget

cash budget

Audit your understanding LO8, 9, 10

1. What is the goal of good cash management?
2. What projections are needed to prepare a cash receipts budget?
3. What projections are needed to prepare a cash payments budget?
4. At the end of a period, if the actual cash balance is less than the projected cash balance, what should be done?

Work together 15-3 LO8, 9, 10

Preparing a cash receipts budget, a cash payments budget, and a cash budget

Use the information given and the budgets prepared in Work Together 15-1 and 15-2. Additional information is given below. Round all amounts to the nearest $10.

a. 20X2: Fourth quarter sales = $435,000.00; purchases = $168,000.00.
b. The balance of cash on hand on January 1, 20X3, is $9,500.00.
c. Each quarter, cash sales are 15.0% and collections of accounts receivable are 50.0% of the projected net sales for that quarter. Collections from the preceding quarter's net sales are 34.5% of that quarter. Uncollectible accounts expense is 0.5% of net sales.
d. Each quarter, cash payments for cash purchases are 10.0% and for accounts payable 50.0% of the purchases for that quarter. Cash payments for purchases of the preceding quarter are 40.0% of that quarter.
e. In the first quarter, Maddox will borrow $20,000.00 on a promissory note and will purchase equipment costing $55,000.00 for cash. In each quarter, dividends of $2,500.00 will be paid in cash. In the fourth quarter, the promissory note plus interest will be paid in cash, $22,500.00.
f. Income tax payments equal the quarterly federal income tax expense amounts on the budgeted income statement.

Partially completed budget forms are given in the *Working Papers*. For the four quarters ended December 31, 20X3, complete the following: (1) Cash receipts budget (Schedule A), (2) Cash payments budget (Schedule B), (3) Cash budget.

On your own 15-3 LO8, 9, 10

Preparing a cash receipts budget, a cash payments budget, and a cash budget

Use the information given and the budgets prepared in On Your Own 15-1 and 15-2. Additional information is given below. Round all amounts to the nearest $10.

a. 20X2: Fourth quarter sales = $480,000.00; purchases = $146,250.00.
b. The balance of cash on hand on January 1, 20X3, is $7,250.00.
c. Each quarter, cash sales are 10.0% and collections of accounts receivable are 45.0% of the projected net sales for that quarter. Collections from the preceding quarter's net sales are 44.6% of that quarter. Uncollectible accounts expense is 0.4% of net sales.
d. Each quarter, cash payments for cash purchases are 20.0% and for accounts payable 45.0% of the purchases for that quarter. Cash payments for purchases of the preceding quarter are 35.0% of that quarter.
e. In the first quarter, Northstar will borrow $30,000.00 on a promissory note and will purchase equipment costing $100,000.00 for cash. In each quarter, dividends of $6,000.00 will be paid in cash. In the fourth quarter, the promissory note plus interest will be paid in cash, $34,000.00.
f. Income tax payments equal the quarterly federal income tax expense amounts on the budgeted income statement.

Partially completed budget forms are given in the *Working Papers*. For the four quarters ended December 31, 20X3, complete the following budgets: (1) Cash receipts budget (Schedule A), (2) Cash payments budget (Schedule B), (3) Cash budget.

LO11 Prepare a performance report.
LO12 Identify performance measures in a balanced scorecard system.

Preparing a Performance Report LO11

Tint My Windows, Inc.
Performance Report
For Quarter Ended March 31, 20X3

	Budget	Actual	Over (Under) Amount	Over (Under) Percentage
Unit Sales	156,100	157,800	1,700	1.1
Operating Revenue:				
Net Sales..............................	$546,350	$552,300	$ 5,950	1.1
Cost of Merchandise Sold	323,130	331,380	8,250	2.6
Gross Profit on Operations	$223,220	$220,920	$ (2,300)	(1.0)
Operating Expenses:				
Selling Expenses:				
Advertising Expense..................	$ 13,110	$ 13,000	$ (110)	(0.8)
Delivery Expense	42,150	42,606	456	1.1
Depr. Expense—Delivery Equipment ..	2,250	2,250	—	—
Depr. Expense—Warehouse Equipment..	3,380	3,380	—	—
Miscellaneous Expense—Sales	2,730	2,750	20	0.7
Salary Expense—Commissions........	21,850	22,092	242	1.1
Salary Expense—Regular.............	6,550	6,550	—	—
Supplies Expense—Sales	3,280	3,200	(80)	(2.4)
Total Selling Expenses	$ 95,300	$ 95,828	$ 528	0.6
Administrative Expenses:				
Depr. Expense—Office Equipment.....	$ 4,500	$ 4,500	$ —	—
Insurance Expense	1,750	1,750	—	—
Miscellaneous Expense—Administrative	11,270	11,250	(20)	(0.2)
Payroll Taxes Expense	6,680	6,712	32	0.5
Rent Expense......................	9,450	9,450	—	—
Salary Expense—Administrative	25,050	25,050	—	—
Supplies Expense—Administrative	3,820	3,780	(40)	(1.0)
Uncollectible Accounts Expense.......	3,280	3,200	(80)	(2.4)
Utilities Expense	3,040	3,200	160	5.3
Total Administrative Expenses........	$ 68,840	$ 68,892	$ 52	0.1
Total Operating Expenses	$164,140	$164,720	$ 580	0.4
Income from Operations	$ 59,080	$ 56,200	$ (2,880)	(4.9)
Other Expenses	940	940	—	—
Net Income before Federal Income Tax.....	$ 58,140	$ 55,260	$ (2,880)	(5.0)
Federal Income Tax Expense.............	12,210	11,605	(605)	(5.0)
Net Income after Federal Income Tax	$ 45,930	$ 43,655	$ (2,275)	(5.0)

At the end of each quarter, a business prepares an income statement that compares actual amounts with the budgeted income statement for the same period. This comparison shows variations between actual and projected items. A report showing a comparison of projected and actual amounts for a specific period is called a **performance report**.

The quarterly performance report for Tint My Windows is shown on the previous page. This report is sent to the sales manager and the administrative manager. Knowing about significant differences between projected and actual income statement amounts helps the managers identify areas that need to be reviewed. By identifying large variations early, managers may be able to make changes that will correct negative effects on net income for the year. If conditions change significantly, the budget for the remainder of the year can be revised.

Preparation of a performance report is similar to preparation of a comparative income statement. However, a performance report compares actual amounts with projected amounts for the same period. A comparative income statement compares actual amounts of one period with actual amounts of a prior period.

The first amount column of the performance report shows the amounts projected for the first quarter. The second amount column shows the actual sales, costs, and expenses for the quarter. The third amount column shows how much the actual amount varies from the projected amount. For example, actual net sales, $552,300, *less* projected net sales, $546,350, *equals* the actual over

projected amount, $5,950. The fourth column shows the percentage that the actual amount was over or under the projected amount. For example, the net sales increase, $5,950, *divided by* projected net sales, $546,350, *equals* the percentage by which actual exceeds projected, 1.1%. Percentages are rounded to the nearest 0.1%.

An analysis is made of all significant differences to determine why the differences occurred. Normally, Tint My Windows only considers changes of 5.0% or more to be significant. However, because the items influencing gross profit are large dollar amounts, small percentage changes affect net income significantly. Therefore, Tint My Windows' sales manager reviews changes in net sales and the cost of merchandise sold, regardless of the amount of change.

Tint My Windows' performance report indicates that three items should be reviewed:

1. Net sales.
2. Cost of merchandise sold.
3. Utilities expense.

Managers should determine what actions, if any, could correct the unfavorable situations, such as the 5.3% overage in utilities expense. If the utility service cost has increased, the manager cannot change that. However, if power is being wasted, procedures may need to be changed.

Managers should also determine what actions caused favorable results, such as the 1.1% overage in net sales, and encourage a continuation of those favorable actions.

Balanced Scorecard LO12

The performance report presented in this lesson focuses solely on financial data. While financial data are important, some managers feel that only using financial measures ignores other possible measures and feedback that may improve the efficiency and effectiveness of a business. This focus on financial data is said to be "out of balance." A more balanced approach is to include other nonfinancial data when measuring performance.

A **balanced scorecard** is a planning and measurement system developed by R. S. Kaplan and D. P. Norton[1] to use multiple performance measures to ensure that a company's vision and strategy are reflected in its goals and activities. The balanced scorecard develops performance

measures in four areas: learning and growth, internal business, customer service, and financial.

Learning and Growth

Learning and growth includes both research and development of company products or services as well as education of employees and customers. Learning and growth performance measures would answer the question, "To achieve our vision, how will we sustain our ability to change and improve?" Typical learning and growth performance measures could include the number of new products introduced, employee turnover, employee satisfaction ratings, the number of classes completed, and the number of employees trained for more than one task.

---

[1] R. S. Kaplan and D. P. Norton, *The Balanced Scorecard: Translating Strategy into Action,* published by Harvard Business School Press, 1996.

Internal Business

Internal business includes the basic processes for providing a product or service that has value to customers and creates value for shareholders. Internal business performance measures would answer the question, "To satisfy our shareholders and customers, at what business processes must we excel?" Typical internal business performance measures could include the amount of materials wasted in a manufacturing process, the percentage of defective units produced, the time to produce a product, machinery down time due to lack of routine maintenance, and the number of sales returns.

Customer Service

Customer service includes identifying customers and providing the products and/or services they desire. Customer service performance measures would answer the question, "To achieve our vision, how should we appear to our customers?" Typical customer service performance measures could include percentage of repeat customers, the percentage of customer referrals, and market share.

Financial

Financial, which businesses usually measure, includes traditional ratios and measures already discussed in this textbook. Financial performance measures would answer the question, "To succeed financially, how should we appear to our shareholders?" Typical financial performance measures could include earnings per share, the current ratio, the price/earnings ratio, the debt/equity ratio, return on investment, and profit margin.

Objectives, Measures, Targets, and Initiatives

The balanced scorecard system is more than just setting performance objectives. Within each area, a company should identify its objectives, determine how outcomes will be measured, set target goals, and develop an initiative to help ensure its objectives are met. For example, in the customer service area, one objective could be to increase customer satisfaction. The measure used could be a follow-up survey that rates customer satisfaction on a scale of five to one. The target goal would be to receive a score of five from 75% of the surveys taken. An initiative to help ensure success would be to hold training classes on customer service.

The balanced scorecard system emphasizes that there is a cause-and-effect relationship between the four focus areas. Employees who are trained better will have a positive effect on internal business practices. Better and more efficient business practices will have a positive effect on customers. Satisfied customers will have a positive effect on the financial results of the company.

The balanced scorecard for Masonville College is shown below.

Performance Measure	Objective	How Measured	Target Goal
Learning/ Growth	Increase the awareness and observance of confidentiality laws.	Number of employees who complete an online course on confidentiality laws.	25% of employees complete the online course each year.
	Improve employee use of computerized purchase order system.	Percent of purchase orders that are submitted electronically.	No less than 25% increase in percent of purchases orders submitted electronically each year.
Internal Business	Increase the number of applicants for faculty positions.	Average number of applications received for faculty positions.	No less than 10% increase in average number of applications received for faculty positions.
	Update faculty computers.	Number of new computers put into service.	No less than 20% of faculty computers replaced each year.
Customer Service	Decrease the number of days to process entrance applications that are complete.	Number of days from receipt of complete application to sending approval or non approval to applicant.	90% of applicants will have a response within 10 business days.
	Decrease the number of books returned to bookstore because the wrong book was purchased.	Number of returns processed because the wrong book was purchased.	No more than 6% of books purchased are returned because the incorrect book was purchased.
Financial	Increase the total credit hours enrolled by students.	Total credit hours of tuition paid.	No less than a 2% increase in total credit hours per semester.
	Decrease utilities costs.	Total utilities costs incurred.	No less than a 5% decrease in utilities cost by the end of the fiscal period.

Shell Companies

Joseph Wells may be the most recognized name in forensic accounting. As the founder of the Association of Certified Fraud Examiners, Mr. Wells has led the charge to heighten accountants' and managers' awareness of the damage that fraud can have on business organizations. One method Mr. Wells uses to share his knowledge is to publish articles in the *Journal of Accountancy*, the monthly publication of the American Institute of Certified Public Accountants.

In a series of *Journal of Accountancy* articles, Mr. Wells identified several tests that auditors should perform to search for the signs, or "red flags," of expenditure fraud. With improper accounting controls, an employee may be able to create a false vendor and issue checks to the vendor. These false vendors are often referred to as "shell companies." A common red flag of a shell company includes an address consisting of a post office box. Because a shell company does not have a physical address, it must have a location for the check to be delivered. A fraudster can easily rent a post office box.

ACTIVITY

Malcolm Promotions has hired Webb & Associates, a public accounting firm, to perform the annual audit of its financial statements. Sari Mariza, a first-year staff auditor, has been assigned the task of performing tests on Malcolm's vendor data file. The file has been provided to Sari as a tab delimited text file. Thus, Sari must first import the data into Excel before searching for any red flags of a shell company. Each data item, such as company name and address, is separated by a tab. Excel uses the tabs to identify the data items and place them in the appropriate columns.

INSTRUCTIONS

Open the spreadsheet FA_CH15 and complete the steps on the Instructions tab.

Answer the following questions:

1. How many vendors are selected with the initial test using a wildcard filter?

2. Why were some vendors selected that do not contain a post office box address?

3. How could the filter be modified to prevent the unintended results from being included in the list?

LO11 Prepare a performance report.

LO12 Identify performance measures in a balanced scorecard system.

TERMS REVIEW

performance report
balanced scorecard

Audit your understanding LO11, 12

1. Why is knowing about significant differences between projected and actual income statement amounts important?
2. How does a performance report differ from a comparative income statement?
3. A balanced scorecard system develops performance measures in what four areas?
4. In addition to identifying objectives in each of the four areas, what else is required by a balanced scorecard system?

Work together 15-4 LO11

Completing a performance report

A partially completed performance report for Maddox Corporation is in the *Working Papers.*

Maddox Corporation has just completed its first quarter of the fiscal year ended December 31, 20X3. Management is interested in identifying significant favorable and unfavorable differences between projected and actual amounts. Maddox only considers changes of 5.0% or more to be significant. Management reviews changes in net sales and cost of merchandise regardless of the amount of change.

1. Complete the performance report by calculating the increase (decrease) from budget and percentage increase (decrease) from budget.
2. Place an asterisk (*) in the right margin by every item that is significant.

On your own 15-4 LO11

Completing a performance report

A partially completed performance report for Northstar, Inc., is in the *Working Papers.*

Northstar has just completed its first quarter of the fiscal year ended December 31, 20X3. Management is interested in identifying significant favorable and unfavorable differences between projected and actual amounts. Northstar, Inc., only considers changes of 5.0% or more to be significant. Management reviews changes in net sales and cost of merchandise regardless of the amount of change.

1. Complete the performance report by calculating the increase (decrease) from budget and percentage increase (decrease) from budget.
2. Place an asterisk (*) in the right margin by every item that is significant.

Preparing Budgets Using Open Database Connectivity (ODBC)

The *A Look at Accounting Software* feature illustrates generally the advantages of automated accounting systems compared to the manual systems presented in the content of a chapter. With analytical activity such as budgeting, however, spreadsheet software improves the efficiency of both manual and automated accounting systems. While it is possible to create detailed budgets in automated systems, the database structure of accounting software doesn't allow the kind of "what if" analysis that can be done in a spreadsheet. Still, it is important to have budget numbers in the automated accounting system so that reports can be created to compare actual performance with budgeted expectations.

One solution for creating spreadsheets for budgets is to use open database connectivity (ODBC) to export financial data from the accounting system. Using an ODBC transfer, data from the accounting system (e.g., end-of-period balances from the general ledger) are downloaded to a spreadsheet, where complex analysis can be performed as budgets are finalized. After the budgeting process is completed, the budget data are uploaded to the accounting system. If a budget needs to be modified, changes can be made directly in the accounting system or revised in the spreadsheet and uploaded again.

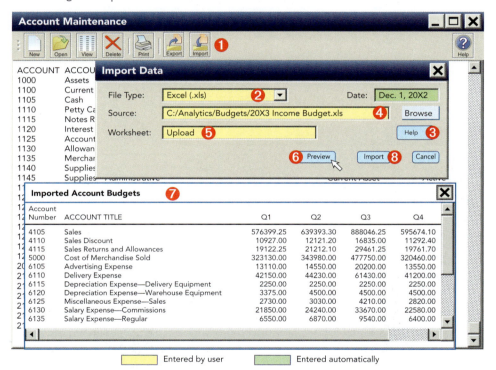

□ Entered by user   □ Entered automatically

❶ The controller for Tint My Windows, Inc., began working on budgets for the coming year (20X3) by exporting data from the accounting system to Excel. The controller and company management completed the budgets and are in the process of importing the budgets into the company's accounting system. On December 1, 20X2, the controller accessed the **Account Maintenance** window. The system displayed all accounts in the chart of accounts. Next, the controller clicked on the **Import** button. That action opened the Import Data dialog box.

❷ The accounting system allows users to import data in several different formats. The controller selected Excel as the file type.

❸ Before data can be imported, it must be precisely formatted, so that the system knows how to enter the data to the proper accounts and budget periods. The Help button provides detailed guidance on how to format spreadsheet data.

❹ The controller browsed to the Excel file containing the 20X3 income budget.

(Continued on next page)

5 Since the budget spreadsheet is made up of several worksheets, it was necessary to tell the system which worksheet contained the budget data.

6 The controller clicked the **Preview** button to verify that the formats were correct and the data would be imported correctly.

7 The system opened a pop-up display showing each account affecting the income budget with the quarterly budget amounts set by management.

8 After verifying that the data would import correctly, the controller clicked the **Import** button to bring the data into the accounting system.

9 Budgeting is an ongoing process. After the budget data were imported into the accounting system, management continued to analyze its business opportunities and risks. Management determined that sales would be improved in the first and second quarters if the company took advantage of a unique advertising opportunity. On December 10, the controller accessed the **Account Maintenance** window again to modify a budget number. By scrolling down and clicking on account **6105**, the controller opened the **View/Edit Account** window displaying the advertising expense account.

10 The controller clicked the **Budget** button, which opened the Account Budget Maintenance window.

11 Budget year **20X3** was selected.

12 As you learned in this chapter, several budgets commonly are prepared. The controller selected the **Income Budget**.

13 The accounting system offers several options for calculating and entering budget amounts. For example, to set the budget for this account, the controller could choose to increase last year's budgeted amounts by some percentage. Or, the new budget could be set up as a percentage increase over the prior year's actual

expense. In this case, the controller simply wanted to change one number and selected **Set Amount**. That option enabled the controller to enter or change each number.

14 The system displayed the quarterly budget amounts that were imported earlier, and the controller increased the Q1 advertising expense budget from $13,110.00 to $14,500.00.

15 After making the change, the controller must click **Save** to enter the new budget number.

A budget is an estimate of the financial future of a business. Preparing a budget requires a known set of company goals. Once a budget is developed, it should be communicated to all employees. Two major budgets are the budgeted income statement and the cash budget. Supporting budgets are used to develop the two major budgets.

Budgets are usually prepared for a one-year period and are prepared ahead of time, so that they can be communicated to the appropriate managers. Sources of budget information include company records, general economic information, and company staff and managers. Managers also need to use good judgment.

Once goals are determined, the budgets are developed in the following order: sales budget, purchases budget, selling expenses budget, administrative expenses budget, other revenue and expenses budget, budgeted income statement, cash receipts budget, cash payments budget, and the cash budget.

A performance report compares the budgeted and the actual revenues and expenses for a budget period. It calculates the differences between budgeted amounts and actual amounts, both on a dollar basis and a percentage basis. A performance report helps identify problem areas while there is still time to make adjustments.

The balanced scorecard is a method used to provide a more balanced approach to performance evaluation. A company using the balanced scorecard will determine performance objectives in four areas: learning and growth, internal business, customer service, and financial. In addition to setting objectives, the company will identify the measure to be used to determine if the objective is met, determine a target score to be achieved, and develop an initiative to help ensure success.

EXPLORE ACCOUNTING

Contingent Liabilities

Business transactions affect the accounts of a business and are reflected in journal entries, which are posted to accounts. However, other items that can affect the financial position of the company are not entered into the books automatically.

One such item is called a **contingent liability**. A contingent liability is a possible future obligation that arises from a current condition and is dependent upon a future event occurring. One example of a contingent liability is a pending lawsuit against a company. The possible future obligation is the chance that the company may lose the lawsuit and have to pay a penalty or fine. The current condition is the fact that the lawsuit has already been filed. The future event is the ruling of the court. Depending on the court ruling, the company may or may not have a financial obligation.

The accountant must analyze each contingent liability to determine if it must be included in the financial statements. The first step is to determine how likely it is that a loss will occur in the future. GAAP list three possibilities: probable, possible, and remote. If it is probable that the loss will occur and if the loss can be reasonably estimated, the company must add a liability to the balance sheet in the amount of the probable loss. At the same time, a loss must be shown on the income statement.

If it is probable that the loss will occur but the loss cannot be reasonably estimated, the company does not have to add a liability to its balance sheet. However, the company must disclose the possible loss in the notes that accompany the financial statements.

If the chance of loss is possible, the company must treat the possibility in the same way it would treat a probable loss. If the chance of loss is remote, the company does not have to do anything.

A company must budget for the actual payment of such a liability—if it is deemed to be a probable loss. Depending on the amount of the probable loss, a company may have to arrange to borrow money or sell other assets.

INSTRUCTIONS

For each of the following activities, state if a liability must be added to the balance sheet, if the company must disclose the activity in the notes, or if no reporting of the activity is required.

1. The company is involved in a lawsuit. The legal team thinks it is probable that the company will lose the case, but it has no idea of the amount of probable loss.

2. The company has published a $1-off coupon in the local paper. The company has estimated that 35% of the coupons will be redeemed.

INSTRUCTIONS: Download problem instructions for Excel, QuickBooks, and Sage 50c from the textbook companion website at www.C21accounting.com.

15-1 Application Problem

Preparing a sales budget and a purchases budget LO2, 3

1. Complete the sales budget.
2. Complete the purchases budget.
3. Print the worksheets.

Craine Corporation wishes to prepare a sales budget and a purchases budget for 20X3. Management has set a sales goal of 500,000 units. After reviewing price trends, the sales manager projects that Craine Corporation will need to increase its unit sales price from $12.50 to $14.00 in the first quarter.

The sales manager, after checking with the company's merchandise suppliers, projects that the cost of merchandise will increase from $7.00 to $7.50 per unit in the first quarter of 20X3.

Quarterly unit sales for 20X2 are as follows:

1st quarter	117,000 units	3rd quarter	137,800 units
2nd quarter	125,400 units	4th quarter	87,800 units

After considering the time required to reorder merchandise, the sales manager requests that 30.0% of the next quarter's unit sales be available in the prior quarter's ending inventory. Ending inventory for 20X2 is 54,400 units. Management projects that 130,000 units will be sold in the first quarter of 20X4.

Instructions:

1. Prepare a sales budget (Schedule 1) for the four quarters ended December 31, 20X3. Craine Corporation rounds unit amounts to the nearest hundred units, dollar amounts to the nearest $10, and percentage amounts to the nearest 0.1%.
2. Prepare a purchases budget (Schedule 2) for the four quarters ended December 31, 20X3.
   Save your work for use in Problem 15-2.

15-2 Application Problem

Preparing budgets for selling expenses, administrative expenses, and other expenses and preparing a budgeted income statement LO4, 5, 6, 7

1. Complete the selling expenses budget.
2. Complete the administrative expense budget.
3. Complete the budgeted income statement.
4. Print the worksheets.

Use the information given and the budgets prepared in Problem 15-1. Additional information is given below.

Expenses for 20X3 are projected as follows: Except where noted, percentages are based on projected net sales. For these items, calculate each quarter's amount by multiplying the percentage times that quarter's net sales. Calculate the annual total by adding the four quarterly amounts. When a dollar amount is given, the total amount should be divided equally among the four quarters.

Selling Expenses

Advertising Expense	4.5%
Delivery Expense	2.0%
Depreciation Expense—Delivery Equipment	$75,000.00
Depreciation Expense—Warehouse Equipment	$84,000.00
Miscellaneous Expense—Sales	5.5%
Salary Expense—Sales	7.0%
Supplies Expense—Sales	4.0%

(Continued on next page)

Administrative Expenses

Depreciation Expense—Office Equipment	$44,000.00
Insurance Expense	$14,400.00
Miscellaneous Expense—Administrative	$16,000.00
Payroll Taxes Expense	12.0% of total salaries
Rent Expense	$72,000.00
Salary Expense—Administrative	$64,400.00
Supplies Expense—Administrative	$30,000.00
Uncollectible Accounts Expense	0.5%
Utilities Expense	8.0%

Interest Expense is estimated to be $20,000.00. Federal income taxes are calculated at 21% of net income before federal income tax.

Instructions:

1. Prepare a selling expenses budget (Schedule 3) for the four quarters ended December 31, 20X3. Craine Corporation rounds all amounts to the nearest $10.

2. Prepare an administrative expenses budget (Schedule 4) for the four quarters ended December 31, 20X3.

3. Prepare an other revenue and expenses budget (Schedule 5) for the four quarters ended December 31, 20X3.

4. Prepare a budgeted income statement for the four quarters ended December 31, 20X3.

    Save your work for use in Problem 15-3.

15-3 Application Problem

Preparing a cash receipts budget, a cash payments budget, and a cash budget LO8, 9, 10

1. Complete the cash receipts budget.
2. Complete the cash payments budget.
3. Complete the cash budget.
4. Print the worksheets.

Use the information given and the budgets prepared in Problems 15-1 and 15-2. Additional information is given below.

a. Actual amounts for the fourth quarter of 20X2: sales, $1,229,200.00; purchases, $369,600.00.

b. The balance of cash on hand on January 1, 20X3, is $122,500.00.

c. In each quarter, cash sales are 15.0% and collections of accounts receivable are 35.0% of the projected net sales for the current quarter. Collections from the preceding quarter's net sales are 49.5% of that quarter. Uncollectible accounts expense is 0.5% of net sales.

d. In each quarter, cash payments for cash purchases are 20.0% and for accounts payable 65.0% of the purchases for the current quarter. Cash payments for purchases of the preceding quarter are 15.0% of that quarter.

e. In the first quarter, Craine will borrow $200,000.00 on a promissory note and will purchase equipment costing $350,000.00 for cash. In each quarter, dividends of $15,000.00 will be paid in cash. In the fourth quarter, the promissory note plus interest will be paid in cash, $220,000.00.

f. Income tax payments equal the quarterly federal income tax expense amounts on the budgeted income statement.

Instructions:

1. Prepare a cash receipts budget (Schedule A) for the four quarters ended December 31, 20X3. Round all amounts to the nearest $10.

2. Prepare a cash payments budget (Schedule B) for the four quarters ended December 31, 20X3.

3. Prepare a cash budget for the four quarters ended December 31, 20X3.

15-4 Application Problem   Completing a performance report LO11

1. Complete the Performance Report.
2. Print the worksheet.

A partially completed performance report for Craine Corporation is in the *Working Papers*.

Craine Corporation has just completed its first quarter of the fiscal year ended December 31, 20X3. Management is interested in identifying significant favorable and unfavorable differences between projected and actual amounts. Craine only considers changes of 5.0% or more to be significant. Management reviews changes in net sales and cost of merchandise regardless of the amount of change.

Instructions:

1. Complete the performance report by calculating the increase (decrease) from budget and percentage increase (decrease) from budget.

2. Place an asterisk (*) in the right margin by every item that is significant.

15-M Mastery Problem   Preparing a budgeted income statement and a cash budget with supporting budgets LO2, 3, 4, 5, 6, 7, 8, 9, 10

1. Complete the sales budget and the purchases budget.
2. Complete the selling expenses budget and the administrative expenses budget.
3. Complete the budgeted income statement and the cash receipts budget.
4. Complete the cash payments budget and the cash budget.
5. Print the worksheets.

On December 31, 20X2, the accounting records of ZZZ Company show the following unit sales for 20X2:

1st quarter	44,000 units	3rd quarter	69,600 units
2nd quarter	68,800 units	4th quarter	57,600 units

The following are additional actual amounts for the 4th quarter of 20X2:

Sales (57,600 units @ $5.60)	$322,560
Purchases (52,800 units @ $4.00)	$211,200
Ending inventory	25,000 units

Management has established a unit sales goal of 260,000 units for 20X3 and 48,000 units for the first quarter of 20X4. The sales manager, after reviewing price trends and checking with the company's merchandise suppliers, projects that the unit cost of merchandise will increase from $4.00 to $4.25 in the first quarter of 20X3. Because of the increase in costs, the company will need to increase its unit sales price from $5.60 to $6.00 in the first quarter of 20X3.

After considering the time required to reorder merchandise, the sales manager requests that 40.0% of each quarter's unit sales be available in the prior quarter's ending inventory.

Expenses are projected as shown below. Except where noted, percentages are based on quarterly projected net sales. For these items, calculate each quarter's amount by multiplying the percentage times that quarter's net sales. Calculate the annual total by adding the four quarterly amounts. When a dollar amount is given, the total amount should be divided equally among the four quarters.

Interest expense for each quarter is projected to be $2,500.

Federal income taxes are calculated at 21% of net income before federal income tax for each quarter. Income tax payments equal the quarterly federal income tax expense amounts on the budgeted income statement.

Additional information is as follows:

a. The balance of cash on hand on January 1, 20X3, is $83,200.

b. In each quarter, cash sales are 10.0% and collections of accounts receivable are 40.0% of the projected net sales for the current quarter. Collections from the preceding quarter's net sales are 49.4% of that quarter. Uncollectible accounts expense is 0.6% of net sales.

Selling Expenses

Advertising Expense	1.2%
Delivery Expense	0.6%
Depreciation Expense—Delivery Equipment	$ 4,800
Depreciation Expense—Warehouse Equipment	$13,360
Miscellaneous Expense—Sales	0.4%
Salary Expense—Sales	5.0%
Supplies Expense—Sales	0.8%

Administrative Expenses

Depreciation Expense—Office Equipment	$7,200
Insurance Expense	$8,400
Miscellaneous Expense—Administrative	$6,000
Payroll Taxes Expense	12.0% of salaries
Rent Expense	$19,200
Salary Expense—Administrative	$50,400
Supplies Expense—Administrative	$5,600
Uncollectible Accounts Expense	0.6%
Utilities Expense	1.8%

c. In each quarter, cash payments for cash purchases are 10.0% and for accounts payable 55.0% of the purchases for the current quarter. Cash payments for purchases of the preceding quarter are 35.0% of that quarter.

d. In the first quarter, $80,000 will be borrowed on a promissory note, and equipment costing $60,000 will be purchased for cash. In each quarter, dividends of $20,000 will be paid in cash. In the fourth quarter, the promissory note plus interest will be paid in cash, $90,000.

Instructions:

Prepare the following budgets for the year ended December 31, 20X3. Round percentage amounts to the nearest 0.1%, unit amounts to the nearest 100 units, and dollar amounts to the nearest $10.

1. Prepare a sales budget (Schedule 1).
2. Prepare a purchases budget (Schedule 2).
3. Prepare a selling expenses budget (Schedule 3).
4. Prepare an administrative expenses budget (Schedule 4).
5. Prepare an other revenue and expenses budget (Schedule 5).
6. Prepare a budgeted income statement (Schedule 6).
7. Prepare a cash receipts budget (Schedule A).
8. Prepare a cash payments budget (Schedule B).
9. Prepare a cash budget.

15-C Challenge Problem   Balanced scorecard LO12

Superior Bicycles is implementing a balanced scorecard system. It has developed the following performance measures:

Increase the number of cross-trained employees

Increase the return on investment

Decrease the returns on parts purchased by Superior Bicycles

Decrease the number of times parts are out of stock

Improve employee turnover

Decrease the number of returned bicycles

Decrease operating costs

Decrease the time from sale to delivery of bicycle to customer

Use the form provided in the *Working Papers*. The first performance measure has been completed as an example.

Instructions:

1. Identify two performance measures for each of the four scorecard areas, and write them in the form next to the appropriate area (Learning/Growth, Internal Business, Customer Service, and Financial).

2. For each performance measure, list one way it could be measured and a possible target goal.

21st Century Skills

Avoid the Payday Trap

Theme: Financial, Economic, Business, and Entrepreneurial Literacy

Skills: ICT Literacy, Communication and Collaboration, Critical Thinking and Problem Solving

PARTNERSHIP FOR
21ST CENTURY SKILLS

Making wise financial decisions and sticking to a budget are the best ways to be prepared for unexpected financial emergencies. However, actual spending is not always the same as planned on a personal budget.

To help bridge the gap when temporary cash shortfalls result, some people turn to quick alternatives, such as short-term payday loans. These loans, also referred to as *cash advances*, provide quick cash without a credit check or collateral. These short-term loans are intended to carry one through to the next paycheck.

Payday loans are legal and regulated in many states, but they are illegal in some states, primarily due to the interest rates charged. At first, the interest rates may not appear to be excessive. However, when the rate is applied to the term of the loan, the borrower may be paying an interest rate of more than 500%. Many people have difficulty paying back these loans in the required time, and they begin a cycle of loan traps.

APPLICATION

1. The Consumer Federation of America has created a website, www.paydayloaninfo.org, to help educate consumers about payday loans in each state.

   a. Using this website or others found through research, identify five states that prohibit payday loans and five states that permit payday loans.

   b. Prepare a spreadsheet with the following headings: Name of State, Legal Status, Maximum Amount per Loan, APR for 14-Day Loan on $100, Maximum Number of Outstanding Loans per Year.

2. Write a paragraph in which you compare and contrast the data obtained for the ten states.

Source: www.paydayloaninfo.org.

Analyzing Home Depot's Financial Statements

From net sales to the average amount of each sales ticket, the Selected Financial Data on page B-20 of Appendix B in this textbook provides a historical perspective to Home Depot's growth. This data reports trends that are an important input in the budgeting process. The first step of the budgeting process is to establish operational goals.

INSTRUCTIONS

Use the information in the Selected Financial Data report to suggest operational goals for Home Depot for 2018. For each of the following items, examine the trend from 2013–2017 and decide what operational goal you believe Home Depot should attempt to achieve in 2018. State each goal in terms of a range and be prepared to defend your goals in class.

1. What percent increase in comparable store sales will Home Depot achieve during 2018?

2. Home Depot will control product costs and achieve what gross profit percentage in 2018? (*Hint:* Gross profit percentage and gross margin are similar terms.)

3. What average ticket price will Home Depot achieve in 2018? (*Hint:* Calculate the percent increase in the average ticket price each year.)

16

CHAPTER 16

Management Decision Making Using Cost-Volume-Profit Analysis

LEARNING OBJECTIVES

After studying Chapter 16, in addition to defining key terms, you will be able to:

LO1 Identify fixed and variable costs.

LO2 Prepare an income statement reporting contribution margin.

LO3 Calculate the contribution margin per unit.

LO4 Calculate contribution margin rate.

LO5 Calculate the breakeven point.

LO6 Prepare a breakeven income statement.

LO7 Calculate the sales dollars and sales units required to earn a planned amount of net income.

LO8 Determine the effect of changes in sales volume, unit costs, and unit sales prices on net income.

LO9 Calculate a sales mix.

© BOATSHIRO/SHUTTERSTOCK.COM

Samsung Electronics, Co., Ltd.

ACCOUNTING IN THE REAL WORLD

When you hear the word "Samsung," you may think of electronics. You may even think of appliances. You probably don't think of the exportation of dried fish from Korea to China. However, the roots of current-day Samsung Electronics can be traced back to 1938 to an exporting company. Since then, Samsung businesses have been involved in a variety of industries that have sold products and services throughout the world. These businesses included a sugar refinery, a woolen mill, a construction business, a department store, insurance sales, and chemical, paper, and electronics businesses. Eventually, the businesses split into completely independent groups.

The group that eventually focused on electronics, Samsung Electronics, started selling black-and-white televisions in 1969. Since that time, the group has reorganized several times and has added semiconductors, networks, appliances, mobile phones and other electronics, colored televisions, financial services, and biopharmaceuticals to its product offerings. Samsung Electronics entered the global market in the late 1970s.

As a leader in the electronics industry, Samsung is serious and intentional about being an "admired company." It has established five business principles to help maintain this status. The principles are as follows:

1. We comply with laws and ethical standards.
2. We maintain a clean organizational culture.
3. We respect customers, shareholders, and employees.
4. We care for the environment, safety, and health.
5. We are a socially responsible corporate citizen.

From its early days, Samsung employed diversification strategies to grow the company. This strategy included moving into new industries and investing in research and development to broaden the company's existing line of goods by making them faster and able to do more tasks better.

When a company considers expanding its product line, it must determine whether the company will benefit financially. Will the new product be profitable enough to make a net profit? If so, how many units will have to be sold in order to make a specified amount of net profit? To answer these questions, managers need to understand the relationship between expected revenues and costs.

CRITICAL THINKING

1. Not all new products are successful. Identify a company that was unsuccessful in introducing a new product, and describe the unsuccessful product.
2. Does increasing sales automatically translate to higher net income? Explain.

Sources: www.businessinsider.com; www.britannica.com; www.samsung.com.

KEY TERMS

cost-volume-profit (CVP) analysis	variable costs	breakeven point
total costs	fixed costs	breakeven analysis
unit cost	contribution margin	sales mix

LO1 Identify fixed and variable costs.
LO2 Prepare an income statement reporting contribution margin.
LO3 Calculate the contribution margin per unit.
LO4 Calculate the contribution margin rate.

Cost Characteristics LO1

Managers use financial statements, including the income statement, to make business decisions. An income statement includes information about operating revenue, the cost of merchandise sold, the gross profit on operations, operating expenses, and the net income or net loss. A method used to determine how changes in costs and volume affect a company's profit is called **cost-volume-profit (CVP) analysis**.

Managers can increase net income by increasing sales and/or decreasing costs and expenses. Managers, with the advice and assistance of accountants, use CVP analysis to analyze the relationships among sales, costs, and expenses to:

1. Determine the level of sales necessary to achieve planned net income.
2. Evaluate the impact of changes in sales volume, unit sales prices, and unit costs on net income.
3. Identify the strengths and weaknesses of a company.

ETHICS IN ACTION

Fraud Awareness

The Association of Certified Fraud Examiners (ACFE) estimates that the typical organization loses 5% of its revenues to fraud. The ACFE periodically conducts an extensive survey of organizations to learn the impact of fraud, how fraud was detected, and what organizations are doing to combat fraud.

Every business owner can benefit by studying the findings of this survey. The information is particularly valuable to small business owners. The survey indicates that smaller organizations suffer greater losses than larger organizations. Most small organizations do not have the financial resources to segregate duties properly, a fundamental method for preventing fraud. Small organizations are also less likely to have formal anti-fraud controls.

An awareness of how fraud occurs, who is most likely to commit fraud, and how fraud can be detected enables business owners to implement controls that can help reduce the negative impact of fraud. Accountants need to take an active role in fraud prevention and detection.

INSTRUCTIONS

Access the *Report to the Nations* to answer the following questions:

1. What is the median dollar amount lost to fraud?
2. What is the most common type of occupational fraud?
3. What is the most common method used to detect frauds?
4. Identify another interesting fact from the survey.

Source: http://www.acfe.com.

Total Cost versus Unit Cost

Tint My Windows, Inc.		
Income Statement		
For Month Ended July 31, 20--		
Operating Revenue:		
Net Sales..		$269,500.00
Cost of Merchandise Sold		161,700.00
Gross Profit on Operations		$107,800.00
Operating Expenses:		
Selling Expenses	$46,950.00	
Administrative Expenses......................	24,430.00	
Total Operating Expenses		71,380.00
Income from Operations		$ 36,420.00
Other Expenses		300.00
Net Income.....................................		$ 36,120.00

CVP analysis requires a thorough understanding of the costs of a company. Costs have many characteristics. All costs for a specific period of time are called **total costs**. The abbreviated income statement above shows that the total cost of the merchandise sold by Tint My Windows, Inc., during July was $161,700.00. Total selling expenses were $46,950.00. These totals show how much money was spent for these activities during a specific period. >> App A: Accounting Period Cycle

An amount spent for one unit of a specific product or service is called a **unit cost**. Tint My Windows sold 77,000 square feet of tinting materials during July at a total cost of $161,700.00. The unit cost of each square foot of material is calculated as follows:

Total Cost of Merchandise Sold	÷	Units Sold	=	Unit Cost of Merchandise Sold
$161,700.00	÷	77,000	=	$2.10

Units may be expressed in many different terms. However, units should be expressed in terms that are meaningful to the people who are responsible for the costs. Some examples of other unit terms are gallons, liters, pounds, kilograms, inches, yards, meters, and hours. Knowing unit costs can be helpful to a manager in setting unit selling prices and in planning cost control.

© STOCK-ASSO/SHUTTERSTOCK.COM

Variable Cost Characteristics

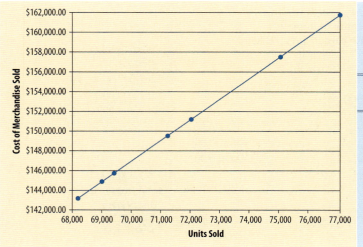

Tint My Windows, Inc. Cost of Merchandise Sold For Period January 1–July 31, 20--			
Month	Units Sold	Unit Cost per Sq. Ft.	Total Cost
January	68,200	$2.10	$ 143,220.00
February	69,400	2.10	145,740.00
March	69,000	2.10	144,900.00
April	72,000	2.10	151,200.00
May	71,200	2.10	149,520.00
June	75,000	2.10	157,500.00
July	77,000	2.10	161,700.00
	501,800		$1,053,780.00

Costs may be separated into two parts: variable and fixed. Costs that change in direct proportion to a change in the number of units are called **variable costs**. The *total* variable cost *varies* with a change in the number of units. As the number of units increases, the cost increases. The *unit* variable cost *remains the same* regardless of the number of units.

For example, a business buys 1 hour of radio advertising for $300.00. Later, the business buys 10 more hours of advertising for $3,000.00 (10 × $300.00). Regardless of the number of hours purchased, the unit cost of an hour of advertising is $300.00 per hour. Thus, radio advertising is a variable cost.

Tint My Windows' materials purchases for the months of January through July are shown above. The volume of materials purchased ranges from a low of 68,200 square feet in January to a high of 77,000 square feet in July. However, the price paid per square foot (unit cost) remained at $2.10 throughout the seven-month period. Therefore, these costs have the characteristics of variable costs.

Tint My Windows' monthly costs for materials purchases are plotted on the graph above. The line between the plotted points indicates the relationship between the number of square feet of materials purchased and the total cost of materials. The straight, upward-sloping line shows that as the quantity of materials increases, the total cost also increases. The line is straight because Tint My Windows' unit cost per square foot remained the same, although the number of units purchased per month varied.

Fixed Costs

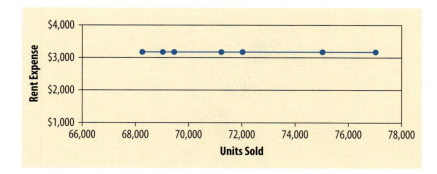

Costs that remain constant regardless of a change in business activity are called **fixed costs**. For example, Tint My Windows' rent is $3,150.00 per month. Rent is *fixed* because the amount has been set at $3,150.00 per month regardless of how many square feet of materials are purchased. If each monthly rental cost is plotted on a graph and the points are connected, the chart will appear as shown here. The fixed cost line is a straight line parallel to the base of the graph.

FYI Businesses such as airlines, public utilities, and railroads have large fixed costs. These businesses may be considered riskier because much of their revenue is devoted to paying these fixed costs.

Gross Profit and Contribution Margin Income Statements LO2

Tint My Windows, Inc.
Income Statement
For Month Ended July 31, 20--

Operating Revenue:		
Net Sales (77,000 sq. ft. @ $3.50)		$269,500.00
Cost of Merchandise Sold (77,000 sq. ft. @ $2.10)		161,700.00
Gross Profit on Sales		$107,800.00
Operating Costs:		
Selling Costs:		
Sales Commissions (77,000 sq. ft. @ $0.14)	$10,780.00	
Delivery Expense (77,000 sq. ft. @ $0.27)	20,790.00	
Other Variable Selling Costs (77,000 sq. ft. @ $0.12)	9,240.00	
Other Fixed Selling Costs	6,140.00	$46,950.00
Administrative Costs:		
Rent Expense	$ 3,150.00	
Insurance Expense	580.00	
Other Variable Administrative Costs (77,000 sq. ft. @ $0.03)	2,310.00	
Other Fixed Administrative Costs	18,390.00	24,430.00
Total Operating Expenses		71,380.00
Income from Operations		$ 36,420.00
Other Expenses		300.00
Net Income		$ 36,120.00

Tint My Windows, Inc.
Income Statement
For Month Ended July 31, 20--

Operating Revenue:		
Net Sales (77,000 sq. ft. @ $3.50)		$269,500.00
Variable Costs:		
Cost of Merchandise Sold (77,000 sq. ft. @ $2.10)	$161,700.00	
Sales Commissions (77,000 sq. ft. @ $0.14)	10,780.00	
Delivery Expense (77,000 sq. ft. @ $0.27)	20,790.00	
Other Variable Selling Costs (77,000 sq. ft. @ $0.12)	9,240.00	
Other Variable Administrative Costs (77,000 sq. ft. @ $0.03)	2,310.00	
Total Variable Costs		204,820.00
Contribution Margin		$ 64,680.00
Fixed Costs:		
Rent Expense	$ 3,150.00	
Insurance Expense	580.00	
Other Fixed Selling Costs	6,140.00	
Other Fixed Administrative Costs	18,390.00	
Other Expenses	300.00	
Total Fixed Costs		28,560.00
Net Income		$ 36,120.00

An income statement reports operating revenue, the cost of merchandise sold, gross profit on operations, operating expenses, and the net income or net loss. Gross profit is determined by subtracting the cost of merchandise sold from net sales. On a typical income statement, as shown in the top portion of the illustration above, costs are shown as the cost of merchandise sold, selling expenses, and administrative expenses.

Income determined by subtracting all variable costs from net sales is called the **contribution margin**. Tint My Windows' income statement, shown in the bottom portion of the illustration above, reports the contribution margin and the net income by grouping costs into two categories: variable costs and fixed costs.

Contribution Margin Per Unit LO3

The concept of contribution margin is important to managers because it allows them to determine the income available to cover fixed costs and provide a profit. Tint My Windows' managers can determine from this income statement that the contribution margin in July was $64,680.00. The contribution margin per unit is calculated as follows:

	Contribution Margin	÷	Units Sold	=	Per Unit Contribution Margin
	$64,680.00	÷	77,000	=	$0.84

Thus, Tint My Windows determined that it will earn an $0.84 contribution margin for each square foot of tinting materials sold. The managers also know that the company will have $28,560.00 of fixed costs each month, regardless of the number of square feet of tinting materials sold. In July, therefore, Tint My Windows earned net income of $36,120.00.

Contribution Margin Rate LO4

	Contribution Margin	÷	Net Sales	=	Contribution Margin Rate
	$64,680.00	÷	$269,500.00	=	0.24 or 24%

The contribution margin rate measures the relationship between the contribution margin and net sales. The formula for the contribution margin rate is shown above, with the amounts taken from the financial statements. The rate for Tint My Windows means that for every $1.00 of new sales, $0.24 is contribution margin. The contribution margin rate is the portion of each dollar of revenue that is available to pay for fixed costs and provide a net income.

FINANCIAL LITERACY

House Poor

Fixed expenses for individuals include rent or house payments, insurance, and car payments. Variable expenses include electricity, water, and food.

Individuals who spend a large portion of their income on a house payment, leaving little for other variable expenses, may become "house poor." According to lenders, the monthly mortgage, taxes, and insurance should be less than 28% of the monthly gross income. In addition, monthly debt payments, such as car loan, mortgage, and credit card payments, should not exceed 36% of the monthly gross income.

ACTIVITIES

Tony and Lauren are thinking about purchasing a home. Their combined gross monthly income is $5,200. Their fixed expenses total $3,240, which includes rent of $925. Variable expenses are $2,260.

1. According to lenders, what is the maximum amount that Tony and Lauren should spend on a monthly mortgage payment, taxes, and insurance?

2. Assuming that Tony and Lauren's monthly payment for mortgage, taxes, and insurance is equal to the maximum calculated in #1, explain whether they can afford to purchase a home at this time.

Sources: www.forbes.com; www.investopedia.com.

LO1 Identify fixed and variable costs.

LO2 Prepare an income statement reporting contribution margin.

LO3 Calculate the contribution margin per unit.

LO4 Calculate the contribution margin rate.

TERMS REVIEW

cost-volume-profit analysis

total costs

unit cost

variable costs

fixed costs

contribution margin

Audit your understanding LO1, 2

1. If total monthly variable costs for a company were plotted on a graph for ten months during a period of increasing sales, would the line drawn between the plotted points be parallel to the base or sloping? Explain why.
2. How does the contribution margin differ from the gross profit?

Work together 16-1 LO1, 2, 3, 4

Preparing an income statement with contribution margin

A blank income statement form for Fullman Flooring is included in the *Working Papers*. Your instructor will guide you through the following examples.

1. Use the following information to prepare Fullman Flooring's January income statement reporting contribution margin. The February information will be used to complete On Your Own 16-1.

	January	February
Net sales	104,000 square feet	99,000 square feet
Unit sales price	$8.00 per square foot	$8.00 per square foot
Cost of merchandise sold	$4.50 per square foot	$4.55 per square foot
Selling expenses:		
Sales commission	$0.64 per square foot	$0.64 per square foot
Delivery cost	$1.00 per square foot	$1.00 per square foot
Other variable selling expenses	$0.70 per square foot	$0.70 per square foot
Other fixed selling expenses	$14,240.00	$14,240.00
Administrative expenses:		
Rent expense	$7,600.00	$7,600.00
Insurance expense	$900.00	$900.00
Other variable administrative expenses	$0.60 per square foot	$0.62 per square foot
Other fixed administrative expenses	$25,080.00	$25,080.00

2. Calculate the contribution margin per unit.
3. Calculate the contribution margin rate.

On your own 16-1 LO1, 2, 3, 4

Preparing an income statement with contribution margin

Use the February information from Work Together 16-1. A blank income statement form for Fullman Flooring is included in the *Working Papers*. Work independently to complete this problem.

1. Prepare Fullman Flooring's February income statement reporting contribution margin.
2. Calculate the contribution margin per unit.
3. Calculate the contribution margin rate.

Determining Breakeven

LO5 Calculate the breakeven point.
LO6 Prepare a breakeven income statement.

Calculating the Breakeven Point LO5

| Contribution Margin | ÷ | Net Sales | = | Contribution Margin Rate | ❶ |
| $64,680.00 | ÷ | $269,500.00 | = | 0.24 or 24% | |

| Total Fixed Costs | ÷ | Contribution Margin Rate | = | Sales Dollar Breakeven Point | ❷ |
| $28,560.00 | ÷ | 0.24 or 24% | = | $119,000.00 | |

| Sales Dollar Breakeven Point | ÷ | Unit Sales Price | = | Unit Sales Breakeven Point | ❸ |
| $119,000.00 | ÷ | $3.50 | = | 34,000 | |

If a manager is to make decisions that yield a favorable net income for a company, the manager needs two important types of information:

1. The amount of merchandise or services the company must sell to earn a favorable net income.
2. The factors that contribute most to net income.

The amount of sales at which net sales is equal to total costs is called the **breakeven point**. Using CVP techniques to determine a company's breakeven point is called **breakeven analysis**. At the breakeven point, neither a net income nor a net loss occurs. At sales levels above the breakeven point, a net income occurs. Conversely, at sales levels below the breakeven point, a net loss occurs. Knowing the breakeven point allows managers to determine the amount of sales needed to start earning a profit. The breakeven point can be stated in sales dollars or in unit sales, as shown above.

> **>> Calculating a Breakeven Point**

❶ Using the second income statement on page 471, calculate the contribution margin rate. Variable costs change in direct proportion to changes in sales activity. Therefore, for every $1.00 of revenue, $0.76 is required for variable costs.

❷ Calculate the sales dollar breakeven point by dividing the total fixed costs by the contribution margin rate. Tint My Windows uses total amounts rounded to the nearest $10 in breakeven point calculations. The sales dollar breakeven point is the amount of sales at which the entire contribution margin is used to pay for fixed costs. Tint My Windows must have total sales of $119,000.00 just to recover its variable and fixed

costs. Sales must be more than $119,000.00 if the company is to earn a net income. At a sales level of exactly $119,000, total costs are $119,000 (fixed costs are $28,560 and variable costs are $90,440 [$119,000 × 0.76]), and Tint My Windows has no net income. Any sales level less than $119,000 results in a net loss.

❸ Calculate the unit sales breakeven point by dividing the sales dollar breakeven point by the unit sales price. The unit sales breakeven point indicates the number of square feet of tinting materials that Tint My Windows must sell at $3.50 per square foot to achieve breakeven sales.

Breakeven Income Statement LO6

Tint My Windows, Inc.
Breakeven Income Statement
For Month Ended July 31, 20--

Operating Revenue:		
Net Sales (34,000 sq. ft. @ $3.50)		$119,000.00
Variable Costs:		
Cost of Merchandise Sold (34,000 sq. ft. @ $2.10)	$71,400.00	
Sales Commissions (34,000 sq. ft. @ $0.14)	4,760.00	
Delivery Expense (34,000 sq. ft. @ $0.27).	9,180.00	
Other Variable Selling Costs (34,000 sq. ft. @ $0.12)	4,080.00	
Other Variable Administrative Costs (34,000 sq. ft. @ $0.03) . . .	1,020.00	
Total Variable Costs		90,440.00
Contribution Margin		$ 28,560.00
Fixed Costs:		
Rent Expense	$ 3,150.00	
Insurance Expense	580.00	
Other Fixed Selling Costs	6,140.00	
Other Fixed Administrative Costs	18,390.00	
Other Expenses	300.00	
Total Fixed Costs.		28,560.00
Net Income.		$ 0.00

The breakeven income statement above shows the proof for Tint My Windows' breakeven point for materials sales. If the breakeven point is accurate, the net income is zero.

The breakeven income statement is a projection of sales and costs under specific assumptions. Tint My Windows reports projected amounts to the nearest $10. Total sales, *$119,000.00*, is equal to the sales dollar breakeven point. Each variable cost is calculated by multiplying the unit sales breakeven point, *34,000 units*, by the unit variable cost of each cost item. The amount of each fixed cost is taken from the July income statement. The contribution margin, *$28,560.00*, is 24% of net sales, *$119,000.00*. This verifies Tint My Windows' contribution margin rate of 24%.

WHY ACCOUNTING?

Computerized Breakeven Analysis

CareerClusters®
PATHWAYS TO COLLEGE & CAREER READINESS
Information Technology

Members of the Information Technology (IT) Department of any business need to have a basic understanding of the operations they support. For example, in a manufacturing firm, the Accounting Department may have specific data it needs to gather to track production costs. In addition, the controller may want the data presented in a specific format. A member of the IT Department may need to rewrite the software program used by the Accounting Department so that reports will gather the data and print out a report in the desired format.

To accomplish this, the IT person needs to have an understanding of what is included in the costs of production. Good communication skills are also necessary when consulting with other departments about their needs.

CRITICAL THINKING

Assume that you work in the IT Department of a company that sells a variety of cellular phones. Explain how the understanding of variable costs and fixed costs can help you in your position.

Careers In Accounting

Kumar Khan
Loan Officer

Kumar Khan likes helping people achieve their goals. His position as a loan officer at a mid-size bank gives him the opportunity to do this every day.

Mr. Khan meets with bank customers who wish to apply for a loan. He explains the different types of loans, credit options, and payment schedules that are available. Kumar feels one of the most important tasks he performs is listening to the applicant's needs and matching those needs to the best loan option.

Once the applicant has determined the best option and has submitted an application, Mr. Khan will review the application for completeness and accuracy. A loan officer also verifies the financial status of the applicant to determine if the application is likely to be approved. The application may be sent to a credit analyst, who will report on the completeness of the application and/or ask for additional information. Mr. Khan's bank requires that all loan applications be presented to a loan committee for approval. Once approved, the loan officer completes the final paperwork and presents it to the applicant for signing.

In addition to processing loan applications, loan officers may also attempt to collect past-due loans. This might include setting up a revised payment plan with the borrowers. If the borrower fails to make payments, the loan officer may need to arrange to repossess the property used as collateral for the loan. This property is then sold to pay off the loan.

In large financial institutions, loan officers may specialize in specific types of loans, such as commercial or agricultural. Some loan officers, especially those who specialize in the mortgage market, may work evenings and weekends in order to meet customer schedules. Most loan officers spend some time outside the financial institution calling on businesses and meeting potential new customers.

Salary Range: In 2017, the median wage for a loan officer was $64,660.00. In some markets, compensation includes commissions on loans acquired.

Qualifications: Minimum requirement is a high school diploma. Most openings prefer an associate's degree or vocational school training. Some loan officers work their way up to the position, starting as tellers or in customer service.

Occupational Outlook: The growth for loan officer positions is projected to be faster than average (10% to 14%) for the period from 2016 to 2026.

Source: www.onetonline.org.

Calculating the Breakeven Point for New Products

	Unit Sales Price	−	Variable Cost per Unit	=	Contribution Margin per Unit	
	$38.00	−	$18.00	=	$20.00	**1**

Total Fixed Costs	÷	Contribution Margin per Unit	=	Unit Sales Breakeven Point	
$25,000.00	÷	$20.00	=	1,250	**2**

Unit Sales Breakeven Point	×	Unit Sales Price	=	Sales Dollar Breakeven Point	
1,250	×	$38.00	=	$47,500.00	**3**

When a business plans to introduce a new product, management is interested in knowing how many units the company must sell to break even. Unfortunately, no financial statements exist from which sales and cost information can be obtained. Therefore, an alternative method of calculating the breakeven point is using the *contribution margin per unit* rather than the *contribution margin rate*.

Tint My Windows is considering selling seat covers at $38.00 per unit. Management expects variable costs of $18.00 per unit, with fixed costs of $25,000.00 per month. From the analysis, Tint My Windows determines that it must sell more than 1,250 seat covers per month before the company begins to make a net income. Thus, management will begin selling seat covers if it believes it can sell more than 1,250 per month.

This alternative method is also useful for calculating the breakeven point for existing products when complete financial statements are not available.

>> Calculating a Breakeven Point for a New Product

1 Calculate the contribution margin per unit by subtracting the variable cost per unit from the unit sales price. The contribution margin per unit represents the amount available per unit to cover fixed costs and earn a profit.

2 Calculate the unit sales breakeven point by dividing the total fixed costs by the contribution margin per unit. The unit sales breakeven point indicates the number of units that must be sold at the projected unit sales price to cover all variable and fixed costs. If Tint My Windows sells exactly 1,250 units, it will earn no net income, nor will it incur a net loss.

3 Calculate the sales dollar breakeven point by multiplying the unit sales breakeven point by the unit sales price. This calculation gives the revenue earned by selling 1,250 units at the projected sales price, $38.00 per unit.

LO5 Calculate the breakeven point.

LO6 Prepare a breakeven income statement.

TERMS REVIEW

breakeven point
breakeven analysis

Audit your understanding LO5

1. In what two ways can the breakeven point be stated?
2. What is the result of sales above the breakeven point?
3. What is the result of sales below the breakeven point?
4. If no historic information exists from which sales and cost information can be obtained, how can management calculate a breakeven point?
5. What is the simplest way to verify the accuracy of a breakeven calculation?

Work together 16-2 LO5,6

Calculating breakeven in sales dollars and unit sales and preparing a breakeven income statement

An income statement for July and blank forms for Cathy's Cakes are included in the *Working Papers*. Your instructor will guide you through the following examples.

1. Use the income statement to calculate the breakeven point in sales dollars and in unit sales for July.
2. Prepare a breakeven income statement for July of the current year. Save your work to complete Work Together 16-3.

On your own 16-2 LO5,6

Calculating breakeven in sales dollars and unit sales and preparing a breakeven income statement

An income statement for August and blank forms for Cathy's Cakes are included in the *Working Papers*. Work independently to complete this problem.

1. Use the income statement to calculate the breakeven point in sales dollars and in unit sales for August.
2. Prepare a breakeven income statement for August of the current year. Save your work to complete On Your Own 16-3.

Decisions That Affect Net Income

LO7 Calculate the sales dollars and sales units required to earn a planned amount of net income.
LO8 Determine the effect of changes in sales volume, unit costs, and unit sales prices on net income.
LO9 Calculate a sales mix.

Calculating Sales to Earn a Planned Net Income LO7

Total Fixed Costs	+	Planned Net Income	=	Required Contribution Margin ❶
$28,560.00	+	$10,500.00	=	$39,060.00

Required Contribution Margin	÷	Contribution Margin Rate	=	Sales Dollars ❷
$39,060.00	÷	0.24 or 24%	=	$162,750.00

Sales Dollars	÷	Unit Sales Price	=	Sales Units ❸
$162,750.00	÷	$3.50	=	46,500

Breakeven analysis provides management with important information about the relationship of sales, variable costs, and fixed costs. Businesses do not, however, operate merely to break even. Managers need information that will assist them in achieving a planned net income. CVP analysis can be used to calculate the dollar and unit sales needed to earn a specified amount of a planned net income.

>> **Calculating Sales to Earn Planned Net Income**

❶ Calculate the required contribution margin. The sum of the total fixed costs and the planned net income is the contribution margin necessary to cover fixed costs and to earn the planned amount of net income. Tint My Windows' managers want to know the amount of total sales required to earn $10,500.00 of net income.

❷ Calculate the amount of sales dollars by dividing the required contribution margin by the contribution margin rate. Thus, Tint My Windows must sell $162,750.00 of tinting materials in order to earn a net profit of $10,500.00.

❸ Calculate unit sales by dividing the sales dollars by the unit sales price. Thus, Tint My Windows must sell 46,500 square feet of tinting materials ($162,750.00 total sales *divided by* the unit sales price of $3.50) to earn $10,500.00 of net income.

There is another way to calculate the sales units required to make this profit. The required contribution margin, $39,060.00, divided by the contribution margin per unit, $0.84, is 46,500 units.

Calculating the Effect of Changes on Net Income LO8

CVP analysis can be used to determine the change in net income that would result from changes in the relationship of sales, variable costs, and fixed costs. Tint My Windows' managers desire answers to questions such as these:

1. What would net income be if sales increase or decrease?

2. Would it be profitable to change production methods?

3. What would be the effect on net income of a decrease in unit sales price and an increase in sales volume?

Effect of Volume Changes on Net Income

	Per Unit	Number of Units		
		30,000	34,000	38,000
Net sales	$3.50	$105,000.00	$119,000.00	$133,000.00
Variable costs	2.66	79,800.00	90,440.00	101,080.00
Contribution margin.	$0.84	$ 25,200.00	$ 28,560.00	$ 31,920.00
Fixed costs		28,560.00	28,560.00	28,560.00
Income from operations . . .		$ (3,360.00)	$ 0.00	$ 3,360.00

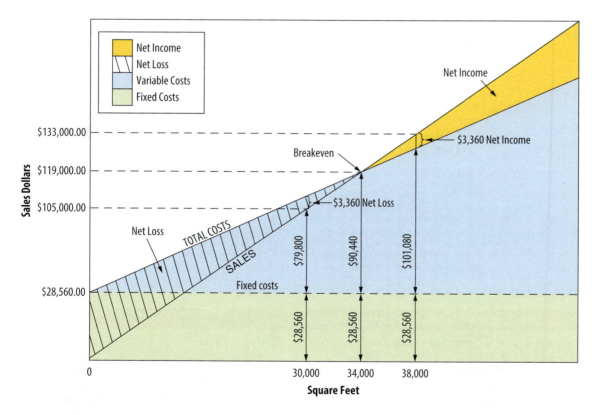

Tint My Windows has calculated its unit breakeven point to be 34,000 square feet. The table above shows how net income changes for a decrease or an increase of 4,000 units. For each square foot of tinting materials that Tint My Windows sells, $0.84 of contribution margin is available for fixed costs and net income. At the 34,000-unit breakeven point, the $28,560.00 contribution margin pays for fixed costs, leaving no remaining amount for net income. For each square foot of tinting materials sold above 34,000 units, the $0.84 per square foot contribution margin increases net income. Therefore, when 38,000 square feet of tinting materials are sold, net income is expected to be $3,360.00 (4,000 square feet × $0.84 contribution margin per unit).

If only 30,000 square feet of tinting materials are sold during the month, the contribution margin of $25,200.00 would not cover the fixed costs of $28,560.00. At this sales volume, a net loss of $3,360.00 would result.

The graph on the previous page shows the relationship of sales, costs, and net income as the volume changes. The sales line, beginning at zero, represents the unit sales price times the number of units sold. The total cost line, starting at $28,560.00 (total fixed costs), represents the total fixed and variable costs for the number of units sold. No matter what the sales volume is, the fixed costs remain constant. The variable cost area represents 76% of sales ($2.66 ÷ $3.50), regardless of volume.

At the breakeven point, the sales and total cost lines intersect, indicating that neither a net income nor a net loss will occur. If 38,000 square feet of tinting materials are sold, the sales line is above the total cost line. At this sales volume, $133,000.00 of sales is higher than the sum of the fixed costs ($28,560.00) and the variable costs ($101,080.00), resulting in a net income of $3,360.00. If the sales volume is below 34,000 square feet, the total cost line is above the sales line, indicating a net loss.

Effect of Cost Changes at Average Volume

	Alternative 1 Manual Cutting			Alternative 2 Automated Cutting		
	Per Unit	Units Sold	Total	Per Unit	Units Sold	Total
Net sales	$3.50	38,000	$133,000.00	$3.50	38,000	$133,000.00
Variable costs	2.66	38,000	101,080.00	2.50	38,000	95,000.00
Contribution margin.	$0.84	38,000	$ 31,920.00	$1.00	38,000	$ 38,000.00
Fixed costs			28,560.00			34,640.00
Income from operations. . .			$ 3,360.00			$ 3,360.00

Two types of costs, variable and fixed, influence the decisions a company may make. Total variable costs increase or decrease as sales increase or decrease. Total fixed costs remain constant regardless of sales.

Tint My Windows' management is concerned that the relatively low contribution margin rate makes increasing the net income difficult. Tint My Windows is searching for ways to improve its percentage of net income per sales dollar. An alternate production method is being considered. The new method would automate the cutting of tinting materials. A cost comparison of the two methods, Alternative 1 and Alternative 2, is shown above and described below.

- *Alternative 1: Manual Cutting.* Variable costs per square foot of tinting materials are $2.66. Tint My Windows currently pays a crew to cut the tinting materials to dimensions ordered by its customers. Of the total variable costs, $0.16 per square foot represents the cost of this crew. Fixed costs are $28,560.00 per month.

- *Alternative 2: Automated Cutting.* The company buys an automated cutter and assigns the cutting crew to process orders of new product lines. The variable costs of the tinting materials decrease by $0.16 per square foot to $2.50 per square foot. However, the new method requires buying the automated cutter and employing an experienced cutter at a fixed salary. Thus, fixed costs increase by $6,080.00 per month, to a total of $34,640.00.

Sales have been averaging about 38,000 square feet of tinting materials per month. At a 38,000-unit sales level, net income is the same for both alternatives. With Alternative 2, the contribution margin is higher, but fixed costs also are higher. Thus, the higher fixed costs cancel the higher contribution margin.

Effect of Cost Changes at Above-Average Volume

	Alternative 1 Manual Cutting			Alternative 2 Automated Cutting		
	Per Unit	Units Sold	Total	Per Unit	Units Sold	Total
Net sales...............	$3.50	42,000	$147,000.00	$3.50	42,000	$147,000.00
Variable costs............	2.66	42,000	111,720.00	2.50	42,000	105,000.00
Contribution margin......	$0.84	42,000	$ 35,280.00	$1.00	42,000	$ 42,000.00
Fixed costs			28,560.00			34,640.00
Income from operations...			$ 6,720.00			$ 7,360.00

Tint My Windows is planning to increase unit sales. A cost comparison with a sales volume of 42,000 units is shown above. With the increased sales volume,

Alternative 2 earns a higher net income. If Tint My Windows expects a permanent sales increase, Alternative 2 would be more profitable than Alternative 1.

Effect of Changes in Costs on the Contribution Margin Rate

	Alternative 1 Manual Cutting		Alternative 2 Automated Cutting	
	Dollars	Percent	Dollars	Percent
Net sales..............	$133,000	100.0%	$133,000	100.0%
Variable costs..........	101,080	76.0%	95,000	71.4%
Contribution margin....	$ 31,920	24.0%	$ 38,000	28.6%

As long as sales increase as expected, Alternative 2 will be favored. However, if sales do not increase, the results will be much different. If the number of units actually sold falls below 38,000, the results will favor Alternative 1.

What is the reason for the change in favorable alternatives? The contribution margin rate favors Alternative 2. The illustration above shows that the contribution margin rate for Alternative 1 is 24.0% versus 28.6% for Alternative 2. This means that for every $1.00 of sales from Alternative 1, $0.24 is available for fixed costs and net income. However, for every $1.00 of sales from Alternative 2, $0.286 is available for fixed costs and net income.

A higher contribution margin rate is usually desirable. However, fixed costs must also be reasonable, since the contribution margin must cover the fixed

costs before any net income is earned. The contribution margin rate, 28.6%, for the automated cutting method is more favorable. However, fixed costs are $34,640.00−$6,080.00 more than the fixed costs for the manual cutting method. If the sales volume declines, the increased contribution margin is not enough to recover the increased fixed costs. Therefore, a reduction in the net income occurs.

A logical conclusion is "Everything else being equal, the activity with the higher contribution margin rate is more profitable." If "everything else" is equal, selecting the more profitable choice is very simple. However, alternatives are seldom that simple, because fixed costs probably differ for each alternative. Therefore, an effective manager looks for the best combination of fixed and variable costs.

Effect of a Change in the Sales Price

	Current Price			Price Reduction and Sales Volume Increase		
	Per Unit	Units Sold	Total	Per Unit	Units Sold	Total
Net sales	$3.50	38,000	$133,000.00	$3.25	45,600	$148,200.00
Variable costs	2.66	38,000	101,080.00	2.66	45,600	121,296.00
Contribution margin	$0.84	38,000	$ 31,920.00	$0.59	45,600	$ 26,904.00
Fixed costs			28,560.00			28,560.00
Income from operations . . .			$ 3,360.00			$ (1,656.00)

Setting the sales price of a product is extremely important. If the price is set too high, potential customers will buy from another business. If the price is set too low, the company may not earn enough money to cover costs and may suffer a loss. The objective is to set sales prices that provide a reasonable amount of net income, while keeping prices competitive. Determining how the price affects net income is often referred to as *sensitivity analysis*.

Tint My Windows earned a record net income in July, selling 38,000 units. Unfortunately, Tint My Windows' managers believe that a price reduction is necessary to sustain this sales volume. Management is considering a plan to reduce the unit sales price by $0.25 (from $3.50 to $3.25). Management projects that the price decrease will result in an increase in the average number of units sold (from 38,000 to 45,600 units). Should Tint My Windows implement this price reduction? The illustration above shows the effect of this price change on the sales volume and the net income.

Price cutting can be dangerous. In July, Tint My Windows had an $0.84 contribution margin per square foot of materials sold. The average sales of 38,000 units resulted in a $31,920.00 total contribution margin. A unit sales price reduction of $0.25 per unit to $3.25 per unit reduces the contribution margin to $0.59. The potential results of a price cut can be calculated. The unit sales required to maintain the net income using the new contribution margin is calculated as follows:

Contribution Margin	÷	New Contribution Margin per Unit	=	Unit Sales Required to Maintain Planned Net Income
$31,920.00	÷	$0.59	=	54,101.69 (Rounded to 54,100)

A decrease in unit sales price from $3.50 to $3.25 is projected to increase average sales from 38,000 to 45,600 units. However, at $3.25, the company would have to sell a total of 54,100 units to maintain the same net income as current sales at the $3.50 price. Reducing the unit sales price by $0.25 would not be a profitable decision if the company can sell only 45,600 units.

FYI Spreadsheet software is an ideal tool to use for calculating breakeven and for analyzing the effect of price, cost, and sales mix changes. An effective spreadsheet identifies the variables used in an analysis, for example, units sold, price per unit, variable costs, and fixed costs. The analysis is built by creating formulas that reference these variables. When the amounts of the variables are changed, the spreadsheet instantly recalculates the analysis and displays the results.

Using CVP Analysis to Plan a Sales Mix LO9

Wicklund Appliances
Income Statement
For the Month Ended May 31, 20--

Operating Revenue:

Net Sales

Refrigerators (320 @ $1,000.00)	$320,000.00	
Dishwashers (800 @ $600.00)	480,000.00	$800,000.00

Variable Costs

Refrigerators (320 @ $750.00)	$240,000.00	
Dishwashers (800 @ $500.00)	400,000.00	640,000.00
Contribution Margin		$160,000.00
Fixed Costs		150,000.00
Income from Operations		$ 10,000.00

	Product Sales	÷	Net Sales	=	Sales Mix	
Refrigerators	$320,000.00	÷	$800,000.00	=	40.0%	❶
Dishwashers	$480,000.00	÷	$800,000.00	=	60.0%	

Contribution Margin	÷	Net Sales	=	Contribution Margin Rate	
$160,000.00	÷	$800,000.00	=	20.0%	❷

Total Fixed Costs	+	Planned Income from Operations	=	Required Contribution Margin	
$150,000.00	+	$15,000.00	=	$165,000.00	❸

Required Contribution Margin	÷	Contribution Margin Rate	=	Total Sales Dollars	
$165,000.00	÷	20.0%	=	$825,000.00	❹

	Sales Mix	×	Total Sales Dollars	=	Product Sales Dollars	
Refrigerators	40.0%	×	$825,000.00	=	$330,000.00	❺
Dishwashers	60.0%	×	$825,000.00	=	$495,000.00	

	Product Sales Dollars	÷	Unit Sales Price	=	Product Unit Sales	
Refrigerators	$330,000.00	÷	$1,000.00	=	330	❻
Dishwashers	$495,000.00	÷	$ 600.00	=	825	

The relative distribution of sales among various products is called the **sales mix**. The sales mix must be calculated to determine the breakeven point for a company that sells more than one product. Wicklund Appliances sells refrigerators and dishwashers. The income statement on the previous page reports Wicklund's sales and cost information for the month ended May 31.

Wicklund expects the relationship of refrigerator sales to dishwasher sales to remain relatively stable in future months. However, management has indicated its objective to improve monthly net income to $15,000.00. How many refrigerators and dishwashers should Wicklund plan to purchase and sell?

The procedures used to calculate the sales to earn a planned net income are similar to those previously described in this chapter.

Managers of the Refrigerators and Dishwashers departments can now plan to accomplish these sales objectives. For example, the Dishwashers Department manager knows that the department must sell 25 more dishwashers ($825 - 800 = 25$) each month. Thus, the manager can plan to increase purchases and devise new sales promotion and advertising campaigns to sell the increased number of dishwashers.

>> Sales Mix Needed to Earn a Planned Net Income

1 Calculate the sales mix using information from the income statement. The sales amounts for each product are divided by net sales. The total product mix must equal 100%.

2 Calculate the contribution margin rate by dividing the contribution margin by net sales.

3 Add the total fixed costs and the planned net income to determine the required contribution margin.

4 Divide the required contribution margin by the contribution margin rate to determine the total sales dollars.

5 Multiply the sales mix percentage by the total sales dollars to determine the sales dollars needed for each product.

6 Divide the product sales dollars by the unit sales price to determine the product unit sales. The unit sales prices are found on the income statement. The product unit sales indicate the number of units of each product that must be sold to achieve the planned net income of $15,000.00.

Analyzing Relationships to Predict Sales

Denisa Cortez operates a coffee shop in a resort village in Colorado. Her instincts tell her that sales vary according to the weather. Since most of her sales occur before 10:00 A.M., Denisa believes the morning low temperature is a good predictor of sales.

Denisa wants to get more precise with her predictions in an effort to control inventory and employee hours better.

Your analysis will rely on a statistical method known as *regression*. The regression yields an equation containing constant and variable amounts. Assume that the relationship between sales and temperature is determined to be $400.00 + $2.00X$. Given a temperature of 25, sales would be predicted to be $450.00 [$400.00 + ($2.00 \times 25)]$.

The ability of the equation to make an accurate prediction is measured by the R^2 (R squared) statistic. R^2 is a value between zero and one. An R^2 near zero indicates that the equation has no predictive value. An R^2 near 1 indicates that the equation can generate very accurate predictions.

OPEN THE TABLEAU WORKBOOK TLA_CH16

+tableau

The Tableau workbook TLA_CH16 contains charts that show one year of sales for each product—coffee, frozen drinks, cappuccinos, doughnuts, and muffins. Individual charts for each product include a trend line based on a regression analysis. Read the caption above each chart to understand the data presented. Use the charts to answer the following questions:

1. Based on the Daily Sales worksheet, what products, if any, have a significant trend over time?

2. Review each chart on the Low Temperatures worksheet. Do sales appear to be related to the daily low temperature?

3. Which of the five product charts contains a trend line that is most effective in predicting sales?

4. Using the five product charts, estimate unit sales assuming a predicted low temperature of 30 degrees.

LO7 Calculate the sales dollars and sales units required to earn a planned amount of net income.

LO8 Determine the effect of changes in sales volume, unit costs, and unit sales prices on net income.

LO9 Calculate a sales mix.

TERM REVIEW

sales mix

Audit your understanding LO7, 8

1. To earn a planned net income, the contribution margin must equal what two amounts?
2. At the breakeven point on a graph, what is true about the sales total costs lines?
3. What is true about total variable costs as sales increase?
4. What is true about total fixed costs as sales increase?

Work together 16-3 LO7, 8, 9

Calculating sales to earn a planned net income, the effect of volume and sales price changes, and sales mix

Use your work and the data from Work Together 16-2. Forms are provided in the *Working Papers*. Your instructor will guide you through the examples.

1. Calculate the amount of sales dollars needed to achieve a net income of $6,000 for July.
2. Determine the net income or net loss if: (a) 4,000 units are sold; (b) 5,000 units are sold; (c) 6,000 units are sold.
3. Cathy's Cakes normally sells 7,500 cakes in July. If the selling price is reduced by $1.00, Cathy's Cakes expects to sell 9,000 cakes. Calculate this change's effect on net income.
4. In September, Cathy's Cakes expanded to sell pies at $20.00 each. Use the following results from September to calculate the product sales dollars and product unit sales necessary for Cathy's Cakes to earn a planned net income of $36,000.00.

	Cakes	Pies	Totals
Net sales	$120,000.00	$80,000.00	$200,000.00
Variable costs	105,000.00	45,000.00	150,000.00
Total contribution margin			$ 50,000.00
Fixed costs			19,000.00
Income from operations			$ 31,000.00

On your own 16-3 LO7, 8, 9

Calculating sales to earn a planned net income, the effect of volume and sales price changes, and sales mix

Use your work and the data from On Your Own 16-2. Forms are provided in the *Working Papers*. Work independently to complete this problem.

1. Calculate the sales dollars needed to achieve a net income of $6,000 for August.
2. Determine the net income or net loss if: (a) 7,000 units are sold; (b) 8,000 units are sold; (c) 9,000 units are sold.
3. Cathy's Cakes normally sells 10,000 cakes in August. Calculate the change in net income of reducing the selling price by $1.00, assuming unit sales will fall to 9,500 units.
4. In October, Cathy's Cakes' sales mix changed. Because of rising variable costs for cakes, Cathy's had to increase the price of cakes by $0.50 (to $16.50). Cathy's was able to decrease the variable costs for pies, so it decreased the price of pies by $1.00 (to $19.00). However, Cathy's sold fewer cakes and more pies. Fixed increased expenses by $5,000 (to $24,000). Use the following results to calculate the product sales dollars and product unit sales necessary for Cathy's to continue earning a net income of $36,000.00. Round percentage calculations to one decimal place.

	Cakes	Pies	Totals
Net sales	$82,500.00	$123,500.00	$206,000.00
Variable costs	72,700.00	71,500.00	144,200.00
Total contribution margin			$ 61,800.00
Fixed costs			24,000.00
Income from operations			$ 37,800.00

CVP analysis helps managers evaluate the impact of changes in sales volume, unit sale prices, unit costs, and sales mix on the net income of a company. Costs can be separated into two kinds: variable and fixed. Total variable costs increase as sales volume increases. Total fixed costs stay the same, regardless of sales volume.

The contribution margin can be used to assist in calculating the effect on net income of changes in costs and sales. The contribution margin is also useful in calculating the breakeven point in sales dollars or in sales units. Another useful calculation that uses the contribution margin is the sales required to earn a planned net income.

Companies that sell more than one product also must be concerned about the sales mix of the products sold. Since each product may have a different contribution margin, the sales mix of the units sold will produce differing results. If changes are to be made in sales volume, selling price, or costs, the relative sales mix must be considered in order to produce accurate predictions.

EXPLORE ACCOUNTING

The High-Low Method

A cost having both fixed and variable characteristics is called a *mixed cost*. For example, the electricity use in a factory is a mixed cost. As production increases, the cost of electricity for the production machinery increases. This is the variable portion of electricity expense. The cost of lights, which are on regardless of how many units of product are being manufactured, is the fixed portion of electricity expense. A graph of mixed costs is shown below.

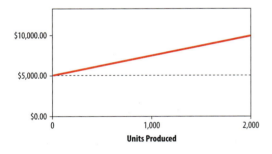

The fixed portion ($5,000.00) of the mixed cost is represented by the dotted horizontal line that is parallel to the base of the graph. The variable portion of the mixed cost is the space between the fixed cost line and the red line. The red line represents the total mixed cost.

When applying what-if scenarios to mixed costs, the fixed and variable components of these costs must be determined. Several measures can be used for this purpose, including the scattergraph, high-low, and least-squares regression methods. Regardless of the method used, a formula can be used to calculate the mixed cost. This formula, based on a fixed cost plus an amount per unit of output, is usually stated as:

Total Mixed Cost = Fixed Cost + (Variable Rate × Output)

The high-low method, while not the most accurate, is the easiest to use without the help of a computer. Using the electricity example, the high-low method requires tracking total electricity expense and units of production for past periods. Assume the following data:

	Expense	Units
January	$2,830.00	560
February	2,580.00	500
March	2,740.00	540
April	2,150.00	400
May	2,488.00	480

Identifying the months having the highest and lowest units, the variable rate is calculated using the formula:

$$\frac{\text{Highest Cost} - \text{Lowest Cost}}{\text{Highest Units} - \text{Lowest Units}} = \frac{\$2,830 - \$2,150}{560 - 400}$$

$$= \$4.25 \text{ per unit}$$

The variable cost of electricity is $4.25 per unit of production.

The fixed cost is determined by using either the high or low production point and solving for total fixed costs:

$$\$2,830 = X + (\$4.25 \times 560), \text{ or}$$
$$X = \$450$$

The cost of electricity can be estimated by solving the formula for any level of production:

Total Cost of Electricity = $450 + ($4.25 × X)

INSTRUCTIONS

Use the following data to develop the formula for total delivery expense:

Delivery Expense	Miles Driven
$10,000	70,000
9,498	65,000
8,705	57,000
9,802	68,000
8,500	55,000

INSTRUCTIONS: Download problem instructions for Excel, QuickBooks, and Sage 50c from the textbook companion website at www.C21accounting.com.

16-1 Application Problem

Preparing an income statement with contribution margin LO1, 2, 3, 4

1. Complete the income statement with contribution margin.
2. Calculate the contribution margin per unit and contribution margin rate.
3. Print the worksheets.

A blank income statement for Adams Paint Supply, Inc., is included in the *Working Papers*.

Instructions:

1. Use the following information to prepare Adams Paint Supply's March income statement reporting contribution margin.

	March	
Net sales	2,875,000	gallons
Unit sales price	$10.00	per gallon
Cost of merchandise sold	$5.00	per gallon
Selling expenses:		
Sales commission	$0.15	per gallon
Delivery cost	$0.50	per gallon
Other variable selling expenses	$0.10	per gallon
Other fixed selling expenses	$650,000.00	
Administrative expenses:		
Rent expense	$107,600.00	
Insurance expense	$72,000.00	
Other variable administrative expenses	$0.25	per gallon
Other fixed administrative expenses	$85,000.00	

2. Calculate the contribution margin per unit.
3. Calculate the contribution margin rate.

16-2 Application Problem

Calculating breakeven in sales dollars and unit sales and preparing a breakeven income statement LO5, 6

1. Complete the income statement.
2. Calculate the contribution margin per unit and contribution margin rate.
3. Complete the breakeven income statement.
4. Print the worksheets.

An income statement for September and blank forms for Bountiful Boards, Inc., are included in the *Working Papers*.

Instructions:

1. Use the income statement to calculate the breakeven point in sales dollars and in unit sales for September.
2. Prepare a breakeven income statement for September of the current year. Save your work to complete Problem 16-3.

16-3 Application Problem

Calculating sales, sales mix, and the effect of volume and price changes LO7, 8, 9

1. Calculate income from operations under three separate scenarios in step 2.
2. Analyze the impact on September net income by reducing the unit selling price.
3. Complete the worksheet to calculate a planned net income of $302,000.00 with the added product of snowboards.
4. Print the worksheets.

Use the *Working Papers* and data from Problem 16-2. Forms for completing this problem are provided in the *Working Papers*.

Instructions:

1. Assume that Bountiful Boards wants a net income of $324,000.00 for September. Calculate the amount of sales dollars needed to achieve this net income.

2. Determine the net income or net loss if: (a) 4,500 units are sold; (b) 5,500 units are sold; (c) 6,500 units are sold.

3. Assume that Bountiful Boards normally sells 4,000 skateboards in September. If the selling price is reduced by $5.00, Bountiful Boards expects to sell 4,500 skateboards. Calculate this change's effect on net income.

4. In November, Bountiful Boards expanded to sell snowboards at $500.00 each. Use the following results from November to calculate the product sales dollars and product unit sales necessary for Bountiful Boards to earn a planned net income of $302,000.00.

	Skateboards	Snowboards	Totals
Net sales	$400,000.00	$100,000.00	$500,000.00
Variable costs	160,000.00	60,000.00	220,000.00
Total contribution margin			$280,000.00
Fixed costs			6,000.00
Income from operations			$274,000.00

16-M Mastery Problem

Calculating breakeven and the sales required for a desired income LO2, 3, 4, 5, 6, 7

1. Complete the income statement.
2. Calculate unit sales for April.
3. Print the worksheets.

A blank income statement for Candle Scents, Inc., is included in the *Working Papers*.

Instructions:

1. Use the following information to prepare Candle Scents' income statement reporting contribution margin.

	April
Net sales	6,000 gallons
Unit sales price	$5.00 per gallon
Cost of merchandise sold	$2.00 per gallon
Selling expenses:	
Sales commission	$0.50 per gallon
Delivery cost	$0.10 per gallon
Other variable selling expenses	$0.15 per gallon
Other fixed selling expenses	$1,000.00
Administrative expenses:	
Rent expense	$1,200.00
Insurance expense	$200.00
Other variable administrative expenses	$0.25 per gallon
Other fixed administrative expenses	$3,000.00

2. Calculate the contribution margin per unit and the contribution margin rate.

3. Use the income statement to calculate the breakeven point in sales dollars and in unit sales for April.

4. Assume that Candle Scents wants a net income of $7,500.00 for April. Calculate the amount of sales dollars and unit sales needed to achieve this net income.

16-C Challenge Problem | Using contribution margin to analyze sales mix with constraint LO3, 9

ABC Corporation makes two briefcases, Models X and Y. ABC Corporation is trying to determine the optimal sales mix for its products. The following per-unit data have been compiled by the Accounting Department:

	Model X	Model Y
Unit selling price	$200.00	$300.00
Unit variable expense	50.00	80.00
Unit contribution margin	$150.00	$220.00
Unit demand	25,000	15,000
Stitching time (minutes)	3	5

Since the unit contribution margin of Model Y is higher than that of Model X, it may appear that ABC Corporation should focus its efforts on Model Y. However, another issue must be considered.

A point in a system that limits the output of the entire system is called a *constraint* or *bottleneck*. ABC Corporation's constraint is its stitching machine, which is run 40 hours per week, 50 weeks of the year. The *theory of constraints* concept states that in order to optimize profits, a company should produce the product that gives the company the highest amount of contribution margin per unit of the constraint.

The formula for calculating the contribution margin per unit of constraint is:

$$\text{Contribution Margin per Unit of Constraint} = \frac{\text{Contribution Margin per Unit}}{\text{Amount of Constraint Required per Unit}}$$

The contribution margin per minute of stitching for Model X is calculated as follows:

$$\$50.00 = \frac{\$150.00}{3 \text{ minutes}}$$

Therefore, ABC Corporation earns $50.00 of contribution margin per minute while Model X is being stitched.

Instructions:

1. Calculate the contribution margin per minute for Model Y.

2. Which model earns the higher contribution margin per minute?

3. The theory of constraints states that the product with the higher contribution margin per unit of constraint should be produced up to its total demand. Any additional units of constraint should be used to produce the product with the lower contribution margin per unit of constraint. Using your results from parts (1) and (2) how many units of Models X and Y should ABC Corporation produce in a year? (*Hint:* ABC Corporation has only 120,000 minutes of stitching available per year.)

21st Century Skills

Pursue the Passion?

Theme: Financial, Economic, Business, and Entrepreneurial Literacy

Skills: Communication and Collaboration, Critical Thinking and Problem Solving, and Life and Career Skills

Entrepreneurship plays a vital role in the U.S. economy. New ideas and opportunities create jobs, allow for global competition, create economic growth, and improve the quality of life. Entrepreneurs must investigate what consumers want in order to identify new ideas and opportunities. A good place to start is to look at trends, unmet needs, customer frustrations, or even their own experiences that could create business opportunities.

There is no guarantee that a new business venture will be profitable, or if it will break even. Entrepreneurs cannot assume that their great ideas will translate into profits. Therefore, all entrepreneurs should calculate the breakeven point before investing time and money in a new business.

APPLICATION

With a partner, answer the following:

1. **Many households are very busy with jobs and family**. Identify a need that house-holds described by this statement would have. Then list three business opportunities that could be created due to this need.
2. Select one of the above business opportunities.
   a. List the fixed and variable costs that would be incurred by this business venture.
   b. Prepare a breakeven analysis.
3. Many service businesses have relatively low fixed costs and high variable costs, while manufacturers have relatively high fixed costs and low variable costs. Explain.
4. What types of service businesses might have high fixed costs?

Analyzing Home Depot's Financial Statements

Home Depot's Consolidated Statements of Earnings can be found in Appendix B on page B-6. Assume that Home Depot's fixed costs equal 75% of selling, general, and administrative expenses and 100% of depreciation and amortization and that Home Depot's variable costs consist only of 100% of the cost of sales plus 25% of the selling, general, and administrative expenses. Ignore all other costs.

INSTRUCTIONS

For 2017, calculate the following. Round dollar amounts to whole dollars. Round percents to one decimal place.

1. Total fixed expenses.
2. Total variable expenses.
3. Contribution margin.
4. Contribution margin rate.
5. Breakeven sales dollars.

Management Decision Making Using Cost-Volume-Profit Analysis **Chapter 16** **491**

17

Job Order Costing

CHAPTER 17

LEARNING OBJECTIVES

After studying chapter 17, in addition to defining key terms, you will be able to:

LO1 Classify manufacturing costs.

LO2 Prepare ledgers and cost sheets for a manufacturing business.

LO3 Maintain records for materials purchased and used in production.

LO4 Prepare journal entries for materials purchased and used in production.

LO5 Maintain records for labor costs used in production.

LO6 Prepare journal entries for labor costs used in production.

LO7 Maintain records for factory overhead.

LO8 Prepare journal entries for factory overhead.

LO9 Maintain records for finished goods.

LO10 Journalize the transfer of work in process to finished goods.

LO11 Journalize a sale and the related cost of goods sold.

LO12 Prepare a statement of cost of goods manufactured.

LO13 Identify the differences on the financial statements for a manufacturing business.

LO14 Identify standard costs.

LO15 Calculate and analyze variances related to direct materials.

LO16 Calculate and analyze variances related to direct labor.

© GOIR/SHUTTERSTOCK.COM

Donnelly Custom Manufacturing

ACCOUNTING IN THE REAL WORLD

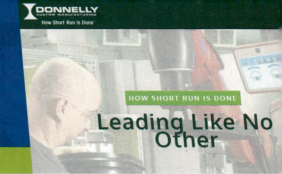

HOW SHORT RUN IS DONE

Leading Like No Other

SOURCE: DONNELLY CUSTOM MANUFACTURING

Donnelly Custom Manufacturing, located in Alexandria, Minnesota, is a midsize company that makes plastic-molded parts and assemblies. They specialize in smaller orders, called short-run work. In fact, their tagline is "How Short Run Is Done."

Under normal manufacturing conditions, short runs are very expensive to produce. Machines must be set up and processes prepared before the first part is made. Doing this setup for a small number of parts makes the cost per part high. Each additional part that is made using that same setup decreases the cost per part. In order to accurately track costs, small- to mid-sized manufacturing companies like Donnelly may use a job-order costing system as described in this chapter.

Short-run expenses must be passed on to the customer, so Donnelly focuses on cutting costs, or lean processes, in order to provide short-run work at the lowest possible price. Donnelly states on its website that their production process "allows us to repeatedly and reliably deliver high-quality, highly engineered parts on time to customers in 30 states and 15 countries." The company adds, "That's why we set new standards when it comes to quality and efficiency. We do things right the first time."

One way the company keeps its costs low is by using robots. Part-removal robots were the first successful use of robots at Donnelly. These robots remove finished parts from the injection molding machine and set them on a conveyor for an operator to package. This repetitive task used to require one employee for each machine, but, with the assistance of robots, one employee can now monitor two or three machines. The robots save labor costs and allow employees to do more challenging and interesting tasks. Another robot, named Baxter, packs finished goods into boxes, counting each unit. Like the part-removal robots, Baxter works efficiently and can be operated 24 hours a day.

Donnelly's focus on efficiency has not come at the cost of quality. The company has been through an assessment process which certifies that its production system meets standards established by the International Organization for Standardization. (See Explore Accounting on page 525 for more information on this certification).

Sources: www.donnmfg.com, www.minnesotabusiness.com.

CRITICAL THINKING

1. Some workers are opposed to the use of robots. Working in groups, list two advantages and two disadvantages of using robots from the viewpoint of an employee.

2. Working in the same group, list two advantages and two disadvantages of using robots from the viewpoint of an employer.

KEY TERMS

direct materials	process costing	statement of cost of goods manufactured	labor price standard
direct labor	materials ledger	standard	total materials variance
factory overhead	cost ledger	standard costing system	materials price variance
indirect materials	finished goods ledger	materials quantity standard	materials quantity variance
indirect labor	applied overhead	materials price standard	total labor variance
work in process	underapplied overhead	labor quantity standard	labor price variance
finished goods	overapplied overhead		labor quantity variance
job order costing			

THE BUSINESS—

CUSTOM CYCLERY CORPORATION

Custom Cyclery Corporation, a custom bicycle manufacturing business, buys wheels, tires, frames, gears, and other materials.

Chart of Accounts
CUSTOM CYCLERY CORPORATION

Balance Sheet Accounts

(1000) ASSETS
1100 Current Assets
1105 Cash
1110 Petty Cash
1115 Accounts Receivable
1120 Allowance for Uncollectible Accounts
1125 Materials
1130 Work in Process
1135 Finished Goods
1140 Supplies—Factory
1145 Supplies—Sales
1150 Supplies—Administrative
1155 Prepaid Insurance
1200 Plant Assets
1205 Factory Equipment
1210 Accumulated Depreciation—Factory Equipment
1215 Office Equipment
1220 Accumulated Depreciation—Office Equipment
1225 Store Equipment
1230 Accumulated Depreciation—Store Equipment
1235 Building
1240 Accumulated Depreciation—Building
1245 Land

(2000) LIABILITIES
2100 Current Liabilities
2105 Accounts Payable
2110 Employee Income Tax Payable
2115 Social Security Tax Payable
2120 Medicare Tax Payable
2125 Salaries Payable
2130 Unemployment Tax Payable—Federal
2135 Unemployment Tax Payable—State
2140 Federal Income Tax Payable
2145 Dividends Payable
2200 Long-Term Liabilities
2205 Mortgage Payable

(3000) STOCKHOLDERS' EQUITY
3105 Capital Stock
3110 Retained Earnings
3115 Dividends
3120 Income Summary

Income Statement Accounts

(4000) OPERATING REVENUE
4105 Sales

(5000) COST OF SALES
5105 Cost of Goods Sold

(5500) MANUFACTURING COSTS
5505 Factory Overhead
5510 Depreciation Expense—Factory Equipment
5515 Depreciation Expense—Building
5520 Heat, Light, and Power Expense
5525 Insurance Expense—Factory
5530 Miscellaneous Expense—Factory
5535 Payroll Taxes Expense—Factory
5540 Property Tax Expense—Factory
5545 Supplies Expense—Factory

(6000) OPERATING EXPENSE
6100 Selling Expenses
6105 Advertising Expense
6110 Delivery Expense
6115 Depreciation Expense—Store Equipment
6120 Miscellaneous Expense—Sales
6125 Salary Expense—Sales
6130 Supplies Expense—Sales
6200 Administrative Expenses
6205 Depreciation Expense—Office Equipment
6210 Insurance Expense—Administrative
6215 Miscellaneous Expense—Administrative
6220 Payroll Tax Expense—Administrative
6225 Property Tax Expense—Administrative
6230 Salary Expense—Administrative
6235 Supplies Expense—Administrative
6240 Uncollectible Accounts Expense
6245 Utilities Expense—Administrative

(7000) OTHER REVENUE
7105 Gain on Plant Assets
7110 Miscellaneous Revenue

(8000) OTHER EXPENSES
8105 Interest Expense
8110 Loss on Plant Assets

(9000) INCOME TAX
9105 Federal Income Tax Expense

The chart of accounts for Custom Cyclery Corporation is illustrated above for reference as you study Chapters 17 through 19 of this textbook.

LO1 Classify manufacturing costs.
LO2 Prepare ledgers and cost sheets for a manufacturing business.
LO3 Maintain records for materials purchased and used in production.
LO4 Prepare journal entries for materials purchased and used in production.
LO5 Maintain records for labor costs used in production.
LO6 Prepare journal entries for labor costs used in production.

Manufacturing Costs and Inventories for a Manufacturing Businesses LO1

The three general types of businesses are service, merchandising, and manufacturing. Service businesses provide a needed service for their customers. Examples of service business are accounting firms, law firms, and medical practices.

Merchandising businesses sell products to customers. A merchandising business purchases products and, without changing the products' forms, sells those products to customers. Department stores and grocery stores are examples of merchandising businesses.

A manufacturing business buys materials and uses labor and machinery to change the materials into a finished product. A manufacturing business generally sells the finished product to a merchandising business, which then sells the product to customers.

Custom Cyclery Corporation, a custom bicycle manufacturing business, buys wheels, tires, frames, gears, and other materials. Using labor and machinery, Custom Cyclery combines the materials to make bicycles. Merchandising businesses buy the bicycles from Custom Cyclery for resale to customers.

A service business needs to know the cost of providing services to be able to calculate net income. A merchandising business needs to know the cost of merchandise sold to calculate net income. For the same reason, a manufacturing company needs to know the costs required to produce the finished products that it sells. To know how much finished products cost, Custom Cyclery keeps records of all costs involved in making the products.

Can a CPA Earn a Commission?

Karen Schwartz is a CPA whose practice focuses on computer applications in business. Karen helps her clients to select, install, and manage computerized accounting systems. Karen was recently engaged to help the internal audit staff of Golden Hotels to purchase and install AuditTech, a database designed specifically for auditors to search for the red flags of errors and fraud in accounting data. In addition, Karen will provide regular training to the audit staff.

AuditTech Software, Inc., provides monetary awards to consultants who refer new customers. The 20 software licenses purchased by Golden Hotels enabled Karen to reach the 100-license level of sales, earning her a $1,000 credit at a popular electronics store.

INSTRUCTIONS

Determine whether the referral was made in accordance with the AICPA *Code of Professional Conduct*.

Three Manufacturing Cost Elements

The manufacturing cost of any finished product includes three elements: (1) direct materials, (2) direct labor, and (3) factory overhead.

Direct Materials

Materials that are of significant value in the cost of a finished product and that become an identifiable part of the product are called **direct materials**. Direct materials include all items used in the manufacturing process that have sufficient value to justify charging the cost directly to the product. **>> App. A: Materiality** The Materiality concept states that business activities creating dollar amounts large enough to affect business decisions should be recorded and reported as separate items. Dollar amounts that are small and not considered important in decision making may be combined with other amounts. For example, frames, wheels, gears, and seats used to manufacture bicycles are considered direct materials and accounted for separately. Screws, nuts, and glue used in the manufacture of bicycles are parts with a small enough dollar value that they are grouped together and only their total value is recorded in the accounting records.

Direct Labor

Salaries of factory workers who make a product are called **direct labor**. Direct labor includes wages and salaries only of persons working directly on a product. Wages and salaries of supervisors, maintenance workers, and others whose efforts do not apply directly to the manufacture of a product are not considered to be direct labor.

Factory Overhead

All expenses other than direct materials and direct labor that apply to making products are called **factory overhead**. Some materials used in manufacturing a product cost a very small amount for each unit produced. Materials used in the completion of a product that are of insignificant value to justify accounting for separately are called **indirect materials**. Indirect materials may include such items as screws, glue, solder, and nuts. Materials and supplies used by the factory, such as cleaning supplies and lubricants for the machinery, are also classified as indirect materials.

Some factory workers devote their time to supervisory, clerical, and maintenance tasks necessary to operate the factory. Such workers include time clerks, supervisors, maintenance people, receiving clerks, and inspectors. Salaries paid to factory workers who are not actually making products are called **indirect labor**.

Other costs incurred in the manufacturing process include: (1) depreciation of factory buildings and equipment; (2) repairs to factory buildings and equipment; (3) insurance on building, equipment, and stock; (4) taxes on property owned; and (5) heat, light, and power. All of these expenses, along with indirect materials and indirect labor, make up factory overhead.

Inventories for a Manufacturing Business

A merchandising business normally has one general ledger account for merchandise inventory. However, a manufacturing business has three inventory accounts related to the products manufactured: (1) Materials; (2) Work in Process; and (3) Finished Goods. These accounts are classified as Current Assets of Custom Cyclery Corporation.

A Materials inventory account shows the cost of materials on hand that have not yet been used in making a product. Products that are being manufactured but are not yet complete are called **work in process**. A Work in Process inventory account shows all costs that have been spent on products that are not yet complete. Manufactured products that are fully completed are called **finished goods**. A Finished Goods inventory account shows the cost of completed products still on hand and unsold.

FYI Robots and advanced electronic systems are used to manufacture products in many factories. The use of automated equipment to perform routine, repetitive manufacturing tasks is often referred to as "computer integrated manufacturing" (CIM).

Cost Records LO2

Manufacturing businesses keep detailed cost records for three purposes: (1) to determine accurate costs for each product made, (2) to provide specific cost information to managers who must identify high cost areas so that corrective action can be taken, and (3) to provide cost summary information for journal entries.

Two general methods are used to measure manufacturing costs. Measuring the manufacturing costs of a specific order or batch as it goes through the production process is called **job order costing**. The end result is a total cost for that order or batch and a per-unit cost for each unit in the batch. Job order costing, illustrated in this chapter, is used when a company manufactures smaller batches of products that are significantly different from each other.

Measuring the manufacturing costs of similar goods as they flow continuously from one production process to another is called **process costing**. At the end of a period, costs are collected from each process to determine an average per-unit cost. Process costing is used when a company manufactures homogenous goods in a continuous process.

Subsidiary Cost Ledgers

Three subsidiary ledgers provide the detailed cost information for the three manufacturing inventory accounts.

1. **Materials Ledger.** Custom Cyclery uses a perpetual inventory system for direct and indirect materials. A perpetual inventory record provides detailed cost information about each type of material. A ledger containing all records of materials is called a **materials ledger**.
2. **Cost Ledger.** Custom Cyclery keeps a record of all charges for direct materials, direct labor, and factory overhead for each job. The record is known as a *cost sheet*. A cost sheet is maintained for each manufacturing job. A ledger containing all cost sheets for products in the process of being manufactured is called a **cost ledger**.
3. **Finished Goods Ledger.** The company keeps a record of each kind of finished good to provide a perpetual inventory of each product produced and its cost. A ledger containing records of all finished goods on hand is called a **finished goods ledger**. This ledger is similar to a materials ledger.

WHY ACCOUNTING?

Limited Resources

Many of the calculations in this chapter are based on the units that the manufacturer produces. Generally speaking, the more units a manufacturer can produce and sell, the greater the profit that will be achieved. However, most resources involved in production are limited. Machines can only produce so many units, which is why sales mix is so important. Materials may be limited, in that there is not always an endless supply.

Labor also has limits. Adding labor to produce more units may not always contribute to higher profits. Assume that a production process, operating 40 hours a week, can produce 10,000 widgets. The demand for widgets is 15,000. The company can obtain the raw materials necessary

to produce 15,000 widgets. The issue is direct labor. Should the company ask current employees to work overtime? Should the company put on a second shift? Could the company save money by operating two shifts of part-time workers?

Most of these questions can be answered by the Accounting Department and the Production Department working together and understanding the issues that affect the ultimate decision.

CRITICAL THINKING

List three issues that need to be considered when deciding to increase production to 15,000 widgets.

Manufacturing Cost Flows

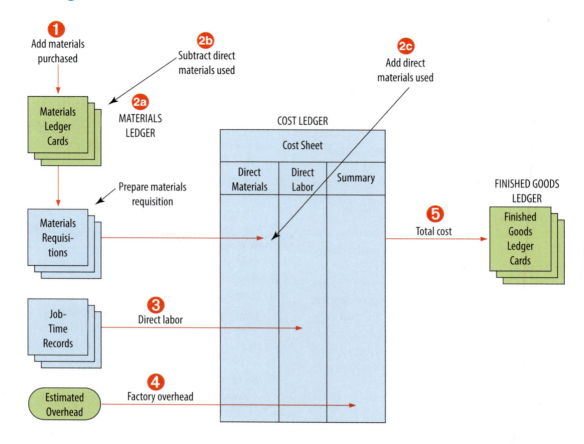

Some manufacturing costs are recorded as the products flow through the production system. Others are estimated and added at the completion of a job. Various forms are used to track the costs associated with a job. The flow of manufacturing costs is illustrated above.

>> Recording Manufacturing Costs

① Record the number and cost of each kind of material purchased on materials ledger cards. This step is performed for both direct and indirect materials.

② a. Prepare a materials requisition to use when direct materials are issued for use in the factory.

  b. The amount of direct materials issued is recorded as a reduction on the materials ledger card.

  c. The amount of direct materials issued is recorded as an increase in the Direct Materials column of the cost sheet.

③ Prepare job-time records when direct labor is used. Time record amounts are recorded in the Direct Labor column of the cost sheet.

④ Estimate and record the amount of factory overhead when a product is completed. The amount of factory overhead is recorded in the Summary column of the cost sheet. Estimating factory overhead is described later in this chapter.

⑤ Total all costs on the cost sheet when a product is completed. Transfer the total to a finished goods ledger card.

Remember Only the cost of direct materials and direct labor are recorded separately on the cost sheet for each job. Indirect materials and indirect labor are recorded as part of the estimated overhead recorded on the cost sheet.

Records for Materials LO3

A manufacturing business keeps a record of materials used in the manufacturing process. The business should have on hand sufficient materials so that the manufacturing process will not be interrupted. However, too large a stock of materials requires needless investment in inventory. To provide a perpetual inventory and detailed cost information about materials, Custom Cyclery keeps a materials ledger card for each type of material.

Materials Acquisitions

1 Open a materials ledger card.

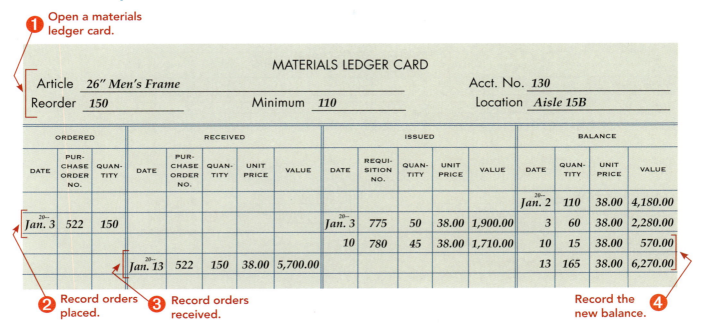

2 Record orders placed.   **3** Record orders received.   **4** Record the new balance.

Notice that the materials ledger card also shows items that have been issued. The issuing of materials will be discussed later in the chapter. The total value for all the materials ledger cards equals the balance of the Materials general ledger account. The relationship of the general ledger accounts to the forms and ledgers will also be discussed later in the chapter.

›› Opening a Materials Ledger Card and Recording Materials Ordered

1 Open a materials ledger card for each type of material kept in the storeroom.
  a. Enter the name and account number of the item.
  b. Determine and record the reorder quantity and minimum quantities to be kept in stock. When the number on hand equals the minimum, the materials clerk notifies the purchasing agent to place a new order.

2 Record the date of an order, Jan. 3, the purchase order number, 522, and the quantity ordered, 150, in the Ordered columns. The data are recorded from a purchase order. The purchase order authorizes a seller to deliver goods with payment to be made later. The order was placed because the quantity on hand, 110 units, equaled the minimum level at which a new order is placed. Note that the quantity ordered equals the reorder quantity shown at the top of the ledger card.

3 When the items ordered are received, record the date, Jan. 13, the purchase order number, 522, the quantity, 150, the unit price, 38.00, and the total value of the order, 5,700.00, in the Received columns of the materials ledger card. The total value is the quantity, 150, multiplied by the unit price, $38.00.

4 Add the quantity and value to the previous balances and extend the amounts to the Balance columns.

Recording Direct Materials on a Cost Sheet

COST SHEET

Job. No. **644**   Date **January 17, 20--**

Item **Model SFM Bicycle**   Date wanted **January 26, 20--**

No. of items **25**   Date completed _____

Ordered for **Stock**

① Open a cost sheet for each job.

REQ. NO.	DIRECT MATERIALS AMOUNT	DIRECT LABOR DATE	AMOUNT	DATE	AMOUNT	SUMMARY ITEM	AMOUNT
796	$ 85.00						
802	950.00						

④ Record the issuance of direct materials.

MATERIALS REQUISITION

☒ Direct ☐ Indirect

Requisition No. **802**   Date **January 17, 20--**

Requisitioned by: **Cameron Wright**   Position **Supervisor**

② Prepare a materials requisition.

JOB NO.	QUANTITY	DESCRIPTION	UNIT PRICE	TOTAL COST
644	25	26" Men's Frame	38.00	950.00

Materials Issued **January 17, 20--**   Recorded:

By **GFG**

Materials Clerk

③ Update the materials ledger card.

MATERIALS LEDGER CARD

Article **26" Men's Frame**   Acct. No. **130**

Reorder **150**   Minimum **110**   Location **Aisle 15B**

ORDERED DATE	PUR-CHASE ORDER NO.	QUAN-TITY	RECEIVED DATE	PUR-CHASE ORDER NO.	QUAN-TITY	UNIT PRICE	VALUE	ISSUED DATE	REQUI-SITION NO.	QUAN-TITY	UNIT PRICE	VALUE	BALANCE DATE	QUAN-TITY	UNIT PRICE	VALUE
			Jan. 13 20--	522	150	38.00	5,700.00						13	165	38.00	6,270.00
								Jan. 17 20--	802	25	38.00	950.00	17	140	38.00	5,320.00

During the manufacturing process, all costs of making a product must be recorded. All charges for direct materials, direct labor, and factory overhead for a particular job are recorded on a cost sheet, such as the one shown above.

When direct materials are needed for a job, they are requested from the storeroom using a materials requisition form. A materials requisition form is used to authorize transfer of items from the storeroom to the factory. When materials are issued to the factory from the storeroom, the materials ledger card is updated.

1 Open a new cost sheet for each job started. When the Cost Accounting Department receives a request from the Factory Department supervisor for a job number, it assigns the number and prepares a new job cost sheet. To open a new job cost sheet:

a. Enter the Job No., **644**.

b. Enter the stock number and the description of the product, **Model SFM Bicycle**.

c. Enter the number of items to be manufactured, **25**.

d. Enter the customer that ordered the item. In this case, the product will replenish Custom Cyclery's stock of the bicycle. Therefore, **Stock** is entered on the Ordered for line.

e. Enter the date the job number is assigned, **January 17, 20--**.

f. Enter the date the item is wanted, **January 26, 20--**.

2 Prepare a materials requisition in triplicate. One copy of a materials requisition is kept in the factory. Two copies are sent to the materials storeroom.

a. Enter the requisition number, **802**. Requisitions are numbered in order. The next available number is assigned.

b. Enter the name of the person who is making the requisition, **Cameron Wright**.

c. Check the appropriate box to indicate whether the requisition is for direct or indirect materials. In this case, a bicycle frame is a major part of the finished product. Therefore, the Direct box is checked.

d. Enter the date of the requisition, **January 17, 20--**.

e. Enter the position of the person making the requisition, **Supervisor**. Usually, a supervisor or a manager has the authority to make the requisition.

f. Enter the job number to which the materials are being issued, **644**.

g. Enter the quantity requisitioned, **25**.

h. Enter the description, **26" Men's Frame**.

i. Enter the unit price of the materials, **38.00**.

j. Enter the total cost of the materials being issued, **950.00**. The total cost is determined by multiplying the quantity by the unit price (25 × $38.00 = $950.00).

k. Record the date on which the materials are issued to the factory, **January 17, 20--**.

l. The materials clerk initials the requisition to show that the materials have been issued. One copy of the completed materials requisition is kept in the storeroom. The original requisition is sent to the Cost Accounting Department.

3 Update the materials ledger card. When the materials requisition is received by the Cost Accounting Department, an entry is made in the materials ledger.

a. Enter the date the materials are issued to the factory, **Jan. 17, 20--**, in the Date column of the Issued section of the materials ledger card.

b. Enter the requisition number, **802**.

c. Enter the quantity issued, **25**.

d. Enter the unit price, **38.00**.

e. Enter the total value of the materials issued, **950.00**.

f. Enter the date in the Balance Date column.

g. Enter the new quantity of the material, **140**, in the Balance Quantity column. Subtract the quantity issued from the current quantity in inventory (165 − 25 = 140) to determine the new quantity.

h. Enter the unit price, **38.00**.

i. Enter the total value of the materials, **5,320.00** (140 units × $38.00 = $5,320.00).

4 Record the issuance of direct materials on the cost sheet. When the Cost Accounting Department receives the materials requisition, an entry is made on the cost sheet.

a. Enter the requisition number, **802**, in the Req. No. column.

b. Enter the total value of the materials issued, **950.00**, in the Direct Materials Amount column.

It Just Doesn't Add Up

For years, Crown Sports used the same employee-intensive process to produce its aluminum bats. When new owners purchased the company, they instructed Rob Jenkins, the manager of the Bat Department, to investigate alternative production methods. Rob submitted an analysis containing estimates of fixed and variable costs for the existing process, compared to installing new equipment to automate the process. (The automated process would result in the termination of many employees.) The analysis also included an option to subcontract the production of the bats from another vendor.

The units available for sale using each method differ. New automated equipment would be able to produce more bats. As more bats become available, Rob believes that the unit sales price must change to ensure that the higher quantity can be sold. The new owners met with Rob and concurred with the estimates in his analysis. Fortunately for Crown's employees, the analysis demonstrated that the current employee-intensive production process generates the highest net income of $19,296. This is compared to only $4,110 for the automated process, and $14,165 for subcontracting.

ACTIVITY

A year has passed since the decision was made to maintain the employee-intensive production method. But, the owners are puzzled over the Bat Department's poor performance. The department had failed to achieve the net income projected in Rob's analysis. The owners have observed the production process and interviewed the employees in an effort to identify a cause for the income shortfall. Nothing remarkable has been identified to explain the department's failure to earn the projected net income.

Frustrated that they can't correct a problem they can't identify, the owners have asked you to examine Rob's analysis. Your first step is to check its accuracy.

INSTRUCTIONS

Open the spreadsheet FA_CH17 and complete the steps on the Instructions tab.

Answer the following questions:

1. Identify and correct the errors in the analysis.
2. Based on the corrected analysis, would the owners have made a different decision?
3. Do you believe that Rob committed a fraud by intentionally misstating the analysis? Explain your answer.

Journalizing Materials Purchases and Usage LO4

Custom Cyclery records the amount of direct and indirect materials purchased and issued in the general ledger account Materials. Custom Cyclery uses a perpetual inventory in the factory that permits the company to charge the cost of direct materials to a job as materials are issued. **>> App. A: Matching Expenses with Revenue**

Journalizing Materials Purchases

	DATE		ACCOUNT CREDITED	PURCH. NO.	POST. REF.	MATERIALS DR. ACCTS. PAY. CR.	
1	Jan.	3	Schwindley Gear Company	501		3 2 7 8 85	1
23		31	Total			174 2 9 3 20	23

MATERIALS PURCHASES JOURNAL — PAGE 1

Custom Cyclery uses a special materials purchases journal to record all materials purchases. All purchases are made on account; therefore, the journal has a single amount column. An entry in the materials purchases journal is shown above.

At the end of a month, the total of the materials purchases journal is posted to Materials and Accounts Payable in the general ledger.

In the Materials account, the January 1 debit balance, $87,255.41, is the materials inventory at the beginning of the month. The January 31 debit, $174,293.20, is the total posted from the materials purchases journal. This represents the total cost of direct and indirect materials purchased during the month.

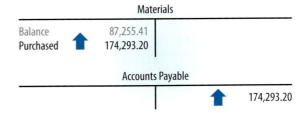

Journalizing Materials Requisitions

	DATE		ACCOUNT TITLE	DOC. NO.	POST. REF.	DEBIT	CREDIT	
1	Jan.	31	Work in Process	M312		143 8 7 6 00		1
2			Factory Overhead			15 2 2 1 00		2
3			Materials				159 0 9 7 00	3
4								4

GENERAL JOURNAL — PAGE 1

A materials requisition is prepared for direct materials issued for a specific job. After materials are issued, the requisition amount is recorded on a cost sheet and the requisition is filed. At the end of a month, the total value of all direct materials issued to specific jobs must be transferred from Materials to Work in Process.

A materials requisition is also prepared for indirect materials used in the factory. After the indirect materials are issued to the factory, the requisition is filed. At the end of the month, the total value of all indirect materials issued is transferred from Materials to Factory Overhead.

Custom Cyclery prepares a memorandum with monthly summary information of the direct materials requisitions and the indirect materials totals. The general journal entry to transfer these amounts is shown above.

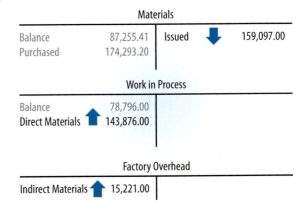

Direct Labor on a Cost Sheet LO5

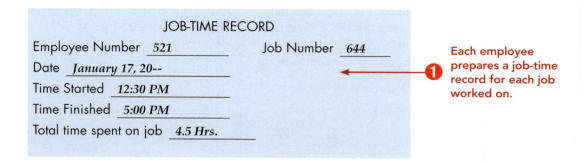

JOB-TIME RECORD

Employee Number __521__   Job Number __644__

Date __January 17, 20--__

Time Started __12:30 PM__

Time Finished __5:00 PM__

Total time spent on job __4.5 Hrs.__

1 Each employee prepares a job-time record for each job worked on.

COST SHEET

Job. No. __644__   Date __January 17, 20--__

Item __Model SFM Bicycle__   Date wanted __January 26, 20--__

No. of items __25__   Date completed _____

Ordered for __Stock__

DIRECT MATERIALS		DIRECT LABOR				SUMMARY	
REQ. NO.	AMOUNT	DATE	AMOUNT	DATE	AMOUNT	ITEM	AMOUNT
796	$ 85.00	Jan. 17	$270.00				
802	950.00						

2 Record the total of all the job-time records for the job.

Factory employees may work on a number of different jobs each day. Therefore, a job-time record is kept to indicate the amount of time spent on each job. At the end of each day, all job-time records are summarized. The total direct labor cost for each job is recorded on each job's cost sheet.

A job-time record for one Custom Cyclery employee working 4.5 hours on Job No. 644 is shown above. All the direct labor costs for Job No. 644 are recorded in the Direct Labor columns of the cost sheet shown above.

>> Assigning Direct Labor to Jobs

Each factory employee:

1 Prepares a job-time record for each job worked on during the day. The record includes employee number, job number, date, time started, and time finished. The employee calculates and records the total time spent on the job.

Accounting Department:

2 Totals the time on job-time records for each job and records the cost in the Direct Labor column of the cost sheet.

Journal Entries to Record Factory Payroll for a Month LO6

1

	DATE	ACCOUNT TITLE	CK. NO.	POST. REF.	GENERAL DEBIT	GENERAL CREDIT	ACCOUNTS PAYABLE DEBIT	PURCHASES DISCOUNT CREDIT	CASH CREDIT	
1	Jan. 15	Work in Process	1221		44 2 2 0 00				41 9 4 4 88	1
2		Factory Overhead			7 3 4 1 00					2
3		Employee Income Tax Payable				5 6 7 1 71				3
4		Social Security Tax Payable				3 1 9 6 78				4
5		Medicare Tax Payable				7 4 7 63				5
18	31	Work in Process	1260		42 8 7 5 00				39 9 9 3 29	18
19		Factory Overhead			6 2 8 7 00					19
20		Employee Income Tax Payable				5 4 0 7 82				20
21		Social Security Tax Payable				3 0 4 8 04				21
22		Medicare Tax Payable				7 1 2 85				22

CASH PAYMENTS JOURNAL   PAGE 1

2   **3**

Custom Cyclery pays all factory employees twice each month. A separate payroll register is prepared for factory employees. A cash payments journal entry is prepared for each factory payroll. The journal entries for the January 15 and January 31 factory payroll for Custom Cyclery are shown above.

>> Recording Factory Payroll

1 Debit Work in Process for direct labor and Factory Overhead for indirect labor.

2 Credit Employee Income Tax Payable, Social Security Tax Payable, and Medicare Tax Payable for the amounts withheld from employees.

3 Credit Cash for the net pay.

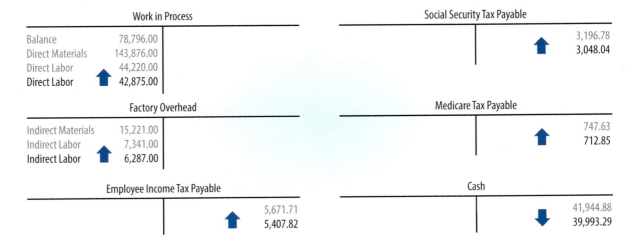

Work in Process	
Balance	78,796.00
Direct Materials	143,876.00
Direct Labor	44,220.00
Direct Labor	42,875.00

Factory Overhead	
Indirect Materials	15,221.00
Indirect Labor	7,341.00
Indirect Labor	6,287.00

Employee Income Tax Payable	
	5,671.71
	5,407.82

Social Security Tax Payable	
	3,196.78
	3,048.04

Medicare Tax Payable	
	747.63
	712.85

Cash	
	41,944.88
	39,993.29

The balance in Work in Process, $78,796.00, represents the costs associated with products that were in production at the end of the prior period. The other debits represent the total amounts of direct labor and direct materials used for all jobs during the month.

The debits to Factory Overhead represent the total amounts of indirect materials issued and indirect labor used during the month.

LO1 Classify manufacturing costs.

LO2 Prepare ledgers and cost sheets for a manufacturing business.

LO3 Maintain records for materials purchased and used in production.

LO4 Prepare journal entries for materials purchased and used in production.

LO5 Maintain records for labor costs used in production.

LO6 Prepare journal entries for labor costs used in production.

TERMS REVIEW

direct materials

direct labor

factory overhead

indirect materials

indirect labor

work in process

finished goods

job order costing

process costing

materials ledger

cost ledger

finished goods ledger

Audit your understanding LO1, 2, 3, 4, 5, 6

1. What are the three manufacturing cost elements of a finished product?
2. What term is used to describe products that are being manufactured but are not yet complete?
3. What is the purpose of a cost sheet?
4. What is the purpose of a materials requisition?
5. At the end of the month, the total value of all direct materials issued to specific jobs is transferred to what account?
6. What is recorded on a job-time record?
7. What accounts are used to record direct and indirect labor costs?

Work together 17-1 LO1, 2, 3, 4, 5, 6

Classifying manufacturing costs; recording and journalizing materials and labor costs

Wooddale Products Corporation manufactures furniture. A list of manufacturing costs, a cost sheet, and blank journals are included in the *Working Papers*. Your instructor will guide you through the following examples. Save your work for use in Work Together 17-2.

1. For each cost, determine whether the cost should be classified as direct materials, direct labor, or factory overhead.
2. Record the following items on the cost sheet for Job No. 218:
   a. Materials Requisition No. 335, for $200.00 of direct materials for Job No. 218.
   b. April 25 total of all Job-Time Records for Job No. 218 for the day, $250.00.
3. Journalize the following transactions for April of the current year:

Transactions:

Apr. 30. Requisitioned $2,350.00 of direct materials and $1,700.00 of indirect materials for the Production Department. M265.

30. Paid employees their semimonthly pay. Gross (pretax) direct labor costs were $13,200.00. Gross indirect labor costs were $8,950.00. Employee income tax was $2,436.50. Social Security tax was 6.2% and Medicare tax was 1.45% of gross wages. C354.

On your own 17-1 LO1, 2, 3, 4, 5, 6

Classifying manufacturing costs; recording and journalizing materials and labor costs

Morganstern Corporation manufactures gas grills. A list of manufacturing costs, a cost sheet, and blank journals are included in the *Working Papers*. Work independently to complete the following problems. Save your work for use in On Your Own 17-2.

1. For each cost, determine whether the cost should be classified as direct materials, direct labor, or factory overhead.
2. Record the following items on the cost sheet for Job No. 587:
   a. Materials Requisition No. 422, for $750.00 of direct materials for Job No. 587.
   b. May 28 total of all Job-Time Records for Job No. 587 for the day, $600.00.
3. Journalize the following transactions for May of the current year:

Transactions:

May 28. Requisitioned $8,425.00 of direct materials and $4,623.00 of indirect materials for the Production Department. M381.

31. Paid employees their semimonthly pay. Gross (pretax) direct labor costs were $14,500.00. Gross indirect labor costs were $6,000.00. Employee income tax was $2,255.00. Social Security tax was 6.2% and Medicare tax was 1.45% of gross wages. C533.

LO7 Maintain records for factory overhead.
LO8 Prepare journal entries for factory overhead.

Calculating and Recording Factory Overhead LO7

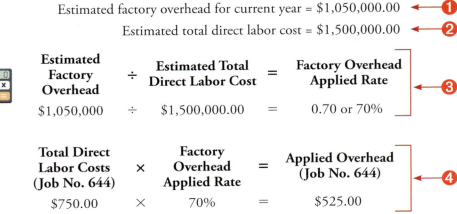

Estimated factory overhead for current year = $1,050,000.00 ← **❶**
Estimated total direct labor cost = $1,500,000.00 ← **❷**

Estimated Factory Overhead	÷	Estimated Total Direct Labor Cost	=	Factory Overhead Applied Rate	
$1,050,000	÷	$1,500,000.00	=	0.70 or 70%	← **❸**

Total Direct Labor Costs (Job No. 644)	×	Factory Overhead Applied Rate	=	Applied Overhead (Job No. 644)	
$750.00	×	70%	=	$525.00	← **❹**

Some factory overhead expenses occur regularly throughout a fiscal period, and others occur irregularly. Many factory overhead expenses are not known until the end of a fiscal period. Therefore, factory overhead expenses normally are charged to jobs by using an application rate based on a known cost such as direct labor. This method applies factory overhead expenses to all jobs and permits a company to record overhead on a cost sheet when a job is completed. Generally, three factors are considered in estimating factory overhead: (1) amount of factory overhead for the past several fiscal periods, (2) number of products the factory expects to produce in the next fiscal period, and (3) expected change in unit costs of factory overhead items. Base units are usually cost items that can

be identified easily. Direct labor cost, direct labor hours, and direct materials costs are common bases. A base unit should be selected that most closely relates to the actual overhead costs. Custom Cyclery uses direct labor cost as a base unit because there is a close relationship between the amount of direct labor cost and factory overhead costs. The estimated amount of factory overhead recorded on cost sheets is called **applied overhead**. The applied overhead is calculated for Job No. 644 as shown above.

Applied overhead is recorded on cost sheets during the fiscal period and before all factory overhead for the current period is known. **≫ App. A: Matching Expenses with Revenue** Therefore, the factory overhead applied rate is calculated before the fiscal period begins.

≫ Determining a Factory Overhead Applied Rate

❶ Estimate the amount of factory overhead costs for the next fiscal period. Custom Cyclery expects to produce 50,000 bicycles during the coming year. Considering this volume, the previous years' overhead, and anticipated cost increases, Custom Cyclery estimates factory overhead as $1,050,000.00.

❷ Estimate the number of base units that will be used in the next fiscal period. Custom Cyclery estimates next year's direct labor cost as $1,500,000.00 (50,000 x 2 x $15.00).

❸ Calculate the factory overhead applied rate. Divide estimated factory overhead costs by the estimated base unit. Custom Cyclery's factory overhead applied rate is 70% of direct labor cost.

❹ Calculate and record the amount of applied overhead, *$525.00*, on the cost sheet for Job No. 644 (total direct labor for Job No. 644, $750.00, multiplied by the factory overhead rate, 70%).

Completing a Job Cost Sheet

COST SHEET

Job. No. __644__

Item __Model SFM Bicycle__

No. of items __25__

Ordered for __Stock__

Date __January 17, 20--__

Date wanted __January 26, 20--__

Date completed __January 19, 20--__

DIRECT MATERIALS		DIRECT LABOR					SUMMARY		
REQ. NO.	AMOUNT	DATE	AMOUNT	DATE	AMOUNT		ITEM	AMOUNT	
796	$ 85.00	Jan. 17	$270.00				Direct Materials	$1,250.00	
802	950.00	18	195.00				Direct Labor	750.00	
810	215.00	19	285.00				Factory Overhead		
	$1,250.00		$750.00				(70% of direct		
							labor costs)	525.00	
							Total Cost	$2,525.00	
							No. of units finished	25	
							Cost per unit	$ 101.00	

3. Transfer amounts to Summary columns.

4. Calculate applied factory overhead.

5. Determine total job cost.

1. Total direct materials.

2. Total direct labor.

6. Determine cost per unit.

Total Costs (Job No. 644)	÷	No. of Units	=	Cost per Unit
$2,525.00	÷	25	=	$101.00

The completed cost sheet for Job No. 644 is shown above. When a job is completed, its total costs are calculated and recorded in the Summary columns of the cost sheet. Direct Materials and Direct Labor columns on the cost sheet are totaled and the totals are recorded in the Summary columns. Then factory overhead is applied to the job. A cost per unit is determined for each job.

Job No. 644 was completed on January 19. At the end of a fiscal period, cost sheets will also exist for jobs that have not been completed. The total value for all cost sheets for work still in process equals the balance of the Work in Process account in the general ledger. Thus, at the end of a fiscal period, cost sheets for work in process are totaled to determine the ending inventory for the general ledger account Work in Process.

FYI At the end of a fiscal period, factory overhead is applied to all jobs that are still in process. Therefore, the Work in Process account reflects direct materials, direct labor, and factory overhead costs for work still in process.

© ISTOCKPHOTO.COM/JASANTISO

Journalizing Factory Overhead LO8

Factory overhead includes various indirect factory expenses such as indirect labor, indirect materials, taxes, depreciation, and insurance. Actual factory overhead expenses are summarized in an account titled Factory Overhead.

Actual Factory Overhead

	DATE	ACCOUNT TITLE	DOC. NO.	POST. REF.	DEBIT	CREDIT	
4	31	Factory Overhead	M313		32 3 5 4 00		4
5		Depreciation Expense—Factory Equipment				4 6 0 0 00	5
6		Depreciation Expense—Building				4 0 0 0 00	6
7		Heat, Light, and Power Expense				4 6 0 0 25	7
8		Insurance Expense—Factory				7 5 0 00	8
9		Miscellaneous Expense—Factory				1 6 7 9 75	9
10		Payroll Taxes Expense—Factory				11 2 5 0 30	10
11		Property Tax Expense—Factory				3 5 4 3 70	11
12		Supplies Expense—Factory				1 9 3 0 00	12
13							13

GENERAL JOURNAL — PAGE 1

Indirect labor and indirect materials are posted directly to Factory Overhead from the entries shown on pages 503 and 505. Other indirect expenses are recorded throughout the month in other manufacturing expense accounts. At the end of each month, these indirect expense account balances are transferred to Factory Overhead. The actual factory overhead can then be compared with the estimated amount of factory overhead recorded on the job cost sheets. Recall that factory overhead is estimated (applied) so that a company can record overhead on a cost sheet as soon as a job is completed.

Factory Overhead

Indirect Materials	15,221.00
Indirect Labor	7,341.00
Indirect Labor	6,287.00
Overhead Expense	32,354.00
(New Balance	61,203.00)

Adjusting entries are made at the end of a fiscal period. These adjusting entries include debits to Depreciation Expense, Insurance Expense, and Supplies Expense. The closing entry to transfer actual overhead expenses to Factory Overhead is shown above.

After postings are completed, all actual factory overhead expense accounts are summarized in the Factory Overhead account.

Applied Overhead

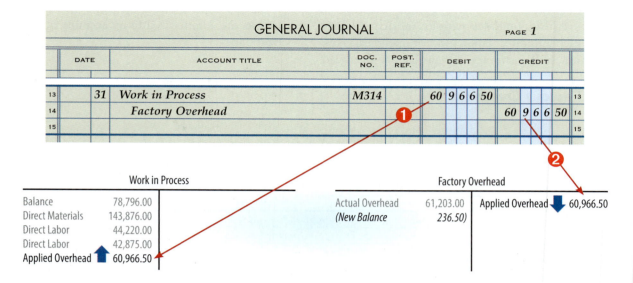

Custom Cyclery applies factory overhead to each job at the rate of 70% of direct labor charges. At the end of each month, Custom Cyclery totals the applied factory overhead recorded on all job cost sheets. Its applied factory overhead for January is $60,966.50. The journal entry to record applied factory overhead is shown above.

The Factory Overhead debit, $61,203.00, is the actual factory overhead expense for the month. The credit, $60,966.50, is the applied factory overhead for the month. The account's $236.50 ending debit balance results from recording less applied factory overhead than the amount of actual factory overhead expenses for the month.

Disposing of Overapplied and Underapplied Factory Overhead Balances

	DATE		ACCOUNT TITLE	DOC. NO.	POST. REF.	DEBIT	CREDIT	
15		31	Income Summary	M315		2 3 6 50		15
16			Factory Overhead				2 3 6 50	16
17								17

GENERAL JOURNAL — PAGE 1

The rate used to calculate applied factory overhead is only an estimate. Therefore, Factory Overhead may have an ending balance. The amount by which applied factory overhead is less than actual factory overhead is called **underapplied overhead**. The debit balance, $236.50, in Custom Cyclery's account indicates underapplied overhead for January. The journal entry to close Factory Overhead at the end of January is shown above.

A credit balance indicates that applied factory overhead is more than actual factory overhead. The amount by which applied factory overhead is more than actual factory overhead is called **overapplied overhead**. If Factory Overhead has a credit balance, Factory Overhead is debited and Income Summary is credited for the overapplied overhead amount.

Overhead may be overapplied or underapplied for two reasons: (1) actual expenses may be higher or lower than normal, an event that requires closer control over expenditures; (2) the factory overhead applied rate may be inaccurate. If the rate is found to be inaccurate, a revised rate is determined. The revised rate is used in the next fiscal period.

LO7 Maintain records for factory overhead.

LO8 Prepare journal entries for factory overhead.

TERMS REVIEW

applied overhead
underapplied overhead
overapplied overhead

Audit your understanding LO7, 8

1. When is applied overhead recorded on cost sheets?
2. After factory overhead has been applied to work in process, what does a credit balance in Factory Overhead indicate?
3. Explain the difference between actual factory overhead and applied factory overhead.

Work together 17-2 LO7, 8
Completing a cost sheet and journalizing entries for overhead

Use the cost sheet and journals used in Work Together 17-1. Your instructor will guide you through the following examples. Save your work for use in Work Together 17-3.

1. Job No. 218 was completed on April 30. Complete the cost sheet for Job No. 218. Factory overhead is applied based on direct labor hours. Estimated factory overhead for the period was $35,000.00. The number of estimated direct labor hours was 1,750. A total of 29 direct labor hours was used on Job No. 218.
2. Journalize the following transactions for April of the current year:

Transactions:

Apr. 30. Obtained factory costs for the month: depreciation on building, $800.00; depreciation on equipment, $850.00; insurance, $640.00; property taxes, $710.00; utilities, $1,600.00. M266. Assume that these expenses have already been properly accounted for and now need to be closed.

   30. Applied overhead at the rate of $20.00 per direct labor hour, with 1,740 direct labor hours worked this period. M267.

   30. Closed the Factory Overhead account. Actual total overhead costs for the period were $35,700.00. M268.

On Your Own 17-2 LO7, 8
Completing a cost sheet and journalizing entries for overhead

Use the cost sheet and journals used in On Your Own 17-1. Work independently to complete the following problems. Save your work for use in On Your Own 17-3.

1. Job No. 587 was completed on May 28. Complete the cost sheet for Job No. 587. Factory overhead is applied to each job as a percentage of direct labor charges. Estimated factory overhead for the year is $280,000.00. Estimated direct labor cost for the year is $350,000.00.
2. Journalize the following transactions for May of the current year:

Transactions:

May 31. Obtained factory costs for the month: depreciation on building, $750.00; depreciation on equipment, $200.00; insurance, $400.00; property taxes, $950.00; utilities, $2,600.00. M385. Assume that these expenses have already been properly accounted for and now need to be closed.

   31. Applied overhead at the rate determined in part 1 above. Total direct labor cost for the month is $29,000.00. M386.

   31. Closed the Factory Overhead account. Actual total overhead costs for the period were $23,000.00. M387.

Accounting for Finished Goods and Cost of Goods Sold and Financial Reporting for a Manufacturing Business

LO9 Maintain records for finished goods.
LO10 Journalize the transfer of work in process to finished goods.
LO11 Journalize a sale and the related cost of goods sold.
LO12 Prepare a statement of cost of goods manufactured.
LO13 Identify the differences on financial statements for a manufacturing business.

Finished Goods Ledger Card LO9

① Complete the Manufactured/Received columns. ② Enter existing inventory balance.

FINISHED GOODS LEDGER CARD

Description *Bicycle* Stock No. *SFM*
Minimum *75* Location *Aisle 22L*

MANUFACTURED/RECEIVED					SHIPPED/ISSUED					BALANCE			
DATE	JOB NO.	QUANTITY	UNIT COST	TOTAL COST	DATE	SALES INVOICE NO.	QUAN-TITY	UNIT COST	TOTAL COST	DATE	QUANTITY	UNIT COST	TOTAL COST
										20-- Jan. 1	106	98.00	10,388.00
					17	622	20	98.00					
							30	100.00	4,960.00	17	70	100.00	7,000.00
19	644	25	101.00	2,525.00						19	70	100.00	
											25	101.00	9,525.00

③ Extend data for Job 644. Calculate total cost. ④

When a job is completed, summary information from the cost sheet is recorded on the finished goods ledger card. Job No. 644 is recorded on the finished goods ledger card shown above.

The total value for all finished goods ledger cards equals the Finished Goods inventory balance in the general ledger. After Custom Cyclery's Job No. 644 is completed and recorded, the company has 95 SFM bicycles on hand at a total cost of $9,525.00. This amount will be added to the total costs of all other finished goods still on hand to determine the balance of Finished Goods inventory in the general ledger.

›› Completing a Finished Goods Ledger Card

❶ Complete the Manufactured/Received columns of the finished goods ledger card. (a) Record the date the finished goods are transferred to the finished goods inventory, **19**; (b) enter the Job No., **644**; (c) enter the quantity, **25**; (d) enter the unit cost, **101.00**; (e) enter the total cost, **2,525.00**.

❷ Enter the existing inventory in the Balance columns. (a) Enter the date, **19**; (b) enter the previous quantity of fax machines in inventory, **70**, and the unit cost, **100.00**.

❸ Extend the quantity, **25**, and the unit cost, **101.00**, for Job 644.

❹ Calculate the total cost of all goods in inventory, **9,525.00** [(70 × $100.00) + (25 × $101.00)]. The total cost balance is combined for all units in the finished goods inventory. Custom Cyclery uses the first-in, first-out inventory method. Thus, the cost recorded first is the cost removed from inventory first when units are sold.

Recording Finished Goods Transactions LO10

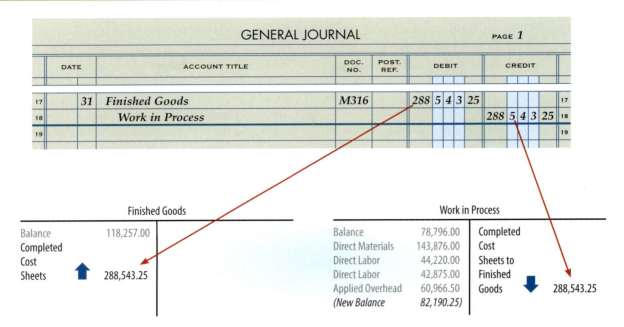

Custom Cyclery totals the cost sheets for all jobs completed during the month. Its January total, $288,543.25, is the cost of work finished during the month. This amount is transferred from Work in Process to Finished Goods. The journal entry to record this transaction is shown above.

The balance in Finished Goods, $118,257.00, represents the beginning inventory. The January 31

debit to Finished Goods and credit to Work in Process, $288,543.25, represents the cost of finished goods transferred from the factory to the stockroom. The Work in Process balance, $82,190.25, is the total amount of direct labor, direct materials, and applied factory overhead charged to the jobs in the ending inventory of work in process.

Recording Sales and Cost of Goods Sold LO11

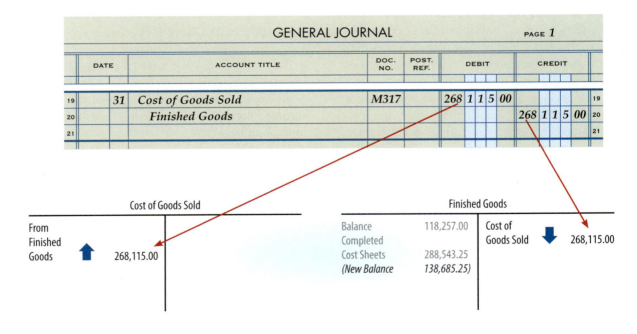

Custom Cyclery uses a perpetual inventory, one in which a continuous record is kept of increases and decreases to inventory accounts. Therefore, a different procedure is used to determine and record the cost of goods sold. A copy of each sales invoice is sent to the Accounting Department to record the sale. For each invoice, the unit cost of each product shipped and the total cost of all products shipped are calculated and recorded on the sales invoice copy.

At the end of the month, cost information on all sales invoices is totaled. The total costs recorded for Custom Cyclery's January sales, $268,115.00, is the cost of goods sold for the month. This number represents the total cost of products sold, not the revenue derived from sales (which is determined by the selling price). This total cost is transferred from the inventory account Finished Goods to the cost account Cost of Goods Sold, as shown on the previous page.

The debit to Cost of Goods Sold, $268,115.00, is the cost of goods sold during the month. The credit to Finished Goods, $268,115.00, is the cost of finished goods sold during the month and removed from inventory. The Finished Goods balance, $138,685.25, is the ending inventory of finished goods.

Statement of Cost of Goods Manufactured LO12

Custom Cyclery Corporation
Statement of Cost of Goods Manufactured
For Month Ended January 31, 20--

Direct Materials.	$143,876.00
Direct Labor	87,095.00
Factory Overhead Applied	60,966.50
Total Cost of Work Placed in Process.	$291,937.50
Work in Process Inventory, Jan. 1, 20--	78,796.00
Total Cost of Work in Process During January.	$370,733.50
Less Work on Process Inventory, Jan. 31, 20--	82,190.25
Cost of Goods Manufactured	$288,543.25

Enter direct materials, direct labor, and factory overhead applied for the period.

Total the cost of work placed in process.

Add beginning work in process inventory.

Subtract ending work in process inventory.

A manufacturing business prepares an income statement, a statement of stockholders' equity, and a balance sheet. These statements are similar to those previously described for other kinds of businesses. A statement showing details about the cost of finished goods is called a **statement of cost of goods manufactured**. It is also referred to as a *schedule of cost of goods manufactured*. This statement shows the amounts of the cost elements—materials, direct labor, and factory overhead—spent on the goods completed in a fiscal period. A statement of cost of goods manufactured supplements the income statement. Custom Cyclery's statement of cost of goods manufactured is shown above.

The direct materials amount, $143,876.00, is the amount debited to Work in Process in the general journal on page 503. The direct labor amount, $87,095.00, is the total direct labor entered in the cash payments journal, page 505. The factory overhead amount, $60,966.50, is the total of the applied factory overhead recorded on the cost sheet and recorded in the general journal on page 510.

Financial Statements for a Manufacturing Business LO13

Custom Cyclery Corporation
Partial Income Statement
For Month Ended January 31, 20--

			% of Net Sales
Operating Revenue:			
Sales..		$413,000.00	100.0%
Cost of Goods Sold:			
Finished Goods Inventory, Jan. 1, 20--.............	$118,257.00		
Cost of Goods Manufactured	288,543.25		
Total Cost of Finished Goods Available for Sale	$406,800.25		
Less Finished Goods Inventory, Jan. 31, 20--	138,685.25		
Cost of Goods Sold............................	$268,115.00		
Underapplied Overhead	236.50		
Net Cost of Goods Sold		268,351.50	65.0%
Gross Profit on Operations		$144,648.50	35.0%

Income Statement for a Manufacturing Business

The income statement for a manufacturing business differs in two ways from the income statements of merchandising businesses shown in previous chapters:

1. Cost of goods manufactured is used instead of purchases. This amount is taken from the statement of cost of goods manufactured.
2. The amount of underapplied overhead, $236.50, is added to the cost of goods sold. The amount is added because applied overhead is less than the actual overhead. The cost of goods manufactured, shown

on the previous page, includes the applied overhead amount rather than the actual amount. The income statement must be adjusted to reflect actual factory overhead costs. Theoretically, the underapplied or overapplied overhead should be apportioned among the Work in Process inventory, Finished Goods inventory, and Cost of Goods Sold accounts. However, since the amount is small, it is charged entirely to Cost of Goods Sold. The partial income statement for Custom Cyclery Corporation, with these differences, is shown above. After Gross Profit on Operations, the remaining income statement is the same as those shown in previous chapters.

Balance Sheet for a Manufacturing Business

Custom Cyclery Corporation
Partial Balance Sheet
January 31, 20--

ASSETS		
Current Assets:		
Cash...		$185,269.21
Petty Cash		200.00
Accounts Receivable..........................	$234,112.75	
Less Allowance for Uncollectible Accounts ...	7,035.25	227,077.50
Materials.....................................		102,451.61
Work in Process		82,190.25
Finished Goods................................		138,685.25
Supplies—Factory.............................		7,871.00
Supplies—Sales		7,258.50
Supplies—Administrative		1,945.00
Prepaid Insurance		3,500.00
Total Current Assets...........................		$756,448.32

A partial balance sheet prepared by Custom Cyclery Corporation on January 31 of the current year is shown on the previous page.

Except for the list of inventories, the balance sheet of a manufacturing business is similar to the balance sheet of a merchandising business. In a manufacturing business, the Current Assets section of the balance sheet lists three types of inventories: (1) materials, (2) work in process, and (3) finished goods.

A statement of stockholders' equity and a statement of cash flows for a manufacturing business are similar to those of a merchandising business described in previous chapters.

GLOBAL AWARENESS

Why Do Foreign Exchange Rates Change?

When a business transaction is completed between companies in different countries, one of the companies will be dealing with foreign currency. The price of the goods being sold will have to be stated in the currency of one of the countries. As discussed in Chapter 8 (p. 257), if the exchange rate changes between the time of the sale and the payment date, one company will report a foreign currency loss and the other company will report a foreign currency gain.

The exchange rate between two countries is based on the relative value of each country's currency in terms of supply and demand. For example, if the demand for Country A's currency is low compared to the currency for Country B, the value of Country A's currency will decrease. Thus, it will take more of Country A's currency to buy imported goods from Country B, so the demand for local goods in Country A will increase. In addition, it will take less of Country B's currency to buy goods from Country A, increasing the demand for exports to Country B.

What causes a country's currency to change value? While many factors influence the value of a currency, three major factors are commonly cited: balance of trade, inflation, and interest rates.

The difference between the value of a country's exports and the value of its imports is called its balance of trade. A *trade surplus* exists when exports exceed imports. A *trade deficit* exists when imports exceed exports. When a country has a trade surplus, the demand for its currency is high and, therefore, the value of its currency will increase. A trade deficit causes a decrease in the demand for the currency and a decrease in the currency's value.

Countries with a high inflation rate will produce products with a higher price, which will discourage exports. Products from countries with a lower inflation rate will have a lower cost, which will encourage imports. Therefore, inflation affects the balance of trade, which affects the value of a country's currency.

As the interest rates increase in a country, the interest rates on new bonds will also increase. This increases the demand for that country's bonds, which will increase the value of its currency. As interest rates decrease in a country, the value of its currency will also decrease.

CRITICAL THINKING

Prior to 2005, China had a fixed exchange rate. This can happen when a government buys or sells its own currency in order to have it maintain a fixed value. In 2005, China discontinued its fixed exchange rate. What impact would this have on the value of the Chinese currency?

Summary Flowchart of Journal Entries for a Manufacturing Business

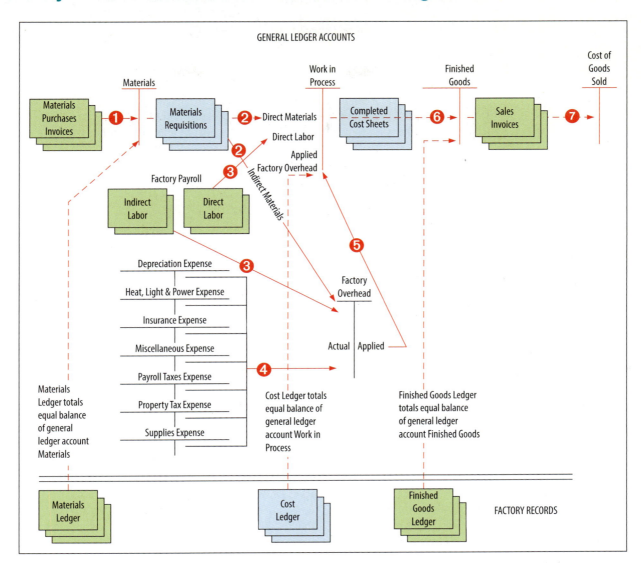

All manufacturing costs flow through the manufacturing accounts. These costs are recorded through each phase of the manufacturing process. Summary journal entries update general ledger accounts for costs incurred in completing jobs, as shown above. Thus, end-of-fiscal-period inventory adjustments are not required.

>> Recording Journal Entries for Manufacturing Accounts

1. Purchase materials.
2. Issue direct and indirect materials to the factory.
3. Record factory payroll.
4. Close individual manufacturing expense accounts.
5. Record applied overhead.
6. Record cost of products completed.
7. Record cost of products sold.

LO9 Maintain records for finished goods.

LO10 Journalize the transfer of work in process to finished goods.

LO11 Journalize a sale and the related cost of goods sold.

LO12 Prepare a statement of cost of goods manufactured.

LO13 Identify the differences on the financial statements for a manufacturing business.

TERM REVIEW

statement of cost of goods manufactured

Audit your understanding LO9, 10, 11, 12, 13

1. What should the Finished Goods account balance equal?
2. What is the journal entry to record goods that are finished?
3. What is the journal entry to record the cost of goods sold?
4. What statement shows the details about the cost of finished goods?
5. How is overapplied overhead accounted for on an income statement?
6. In which section of the balance sheet are the three inventory accounts of a manufacturing business listed?

Work together 17-3 LO9, 10, 11

Updating a finished goods ledger card; journalizing entries for finished goods and cost of goods sold

Use the forms and journals used in Work Together 17-2. Your instructor will guide you through the following examples.

1. Using the cost sheet for Job No. 218, update the finished goods ledger card for Desk G-78.
2. Journalize the following transactions for April of the current year:

Transactions:

Apr. 30. Transferred products costing $74,600.00 to finished goods during the month. M269.

30. Sold products costing $69,700.00 during the month. M270.

On your own 17-3 LO9, 10, 11

Updating a finished goods ledger card; journalizing entries for finished goods and cost of goods sold

Use the forms and journals used in On Your Own 17-2. Work independently to complete the following problems.

1. Using the cost sheet for Job No. 587, update the finished goods ledger card for grill Model SS412.
2. Journalize the following transactions for May of the current year:

Transactions:

May 31. Transferred products costing $92,500.00 to finished goods during the month. M388.

31. Sold products costing $89,700.00 during the month. M389.

LO14 Identify standard costs.
LO15 Calculate and analyze variances related to direct materials.
LO16 Calculate and analyze variances related to direct labor.

Standard Costs LO14

To increase net income, management must control costs. Since direct materials and direct labor can comprise a large portion of total costs, these two items are often the focus of cost controls. Dixon Molding Corporation, a manufacturer of molded plastic items, makes plastic cell phone cases. Dixon management wants to determine if the cost of each cell phone case is as low as possible in terms of direct materials and direct labor.

One way of evaluating this is for Dixon to determine how much plastic should be used for each case, how much that plastic should cost, how much direct labor should be employed for each case, and how much that direct labor should cost. An estimated amount of direct materials or direct labor, usually in price or quantity, established for each unit produced is called a **standard**. A **standard costing system** is a system of setting standards for each cost of production. The estimated amount of direct materials to be used per unit of output is called the **materials quantity standard**. The estimated cost per unit of direct materials is called the **materials price standard**. The estimated amount of direct labor needed to produce one unit of output is called the **labor quantity standard**.

The labor quantity standard is also referred to as the *labor efficiency standard*. The estimated cost per hour of direct labor is called the **labor price standard**. The labor price standard is also referred to as the *labor rate standard*.

Once standards are established, they can be compared to actual results to evaluate the efficiency of the manufacturing process. A standard costing system assists company management in planning and controlling company performance.

Dixon's management has established the following standards:

Material quantity standard	4 ounces per cell phone case
Material price standard	$0.03 per ounce
Labor quantity standard	0.1 hour per cell phone case
Labor price standard	$15.00 per hour

Using these standards, Dixon can calculate the total standard cost of one cell phone case as follows:

	Quantity Standard	×	Price Standard	=	Total
Direct materials	4 ounces	×	$0.03	=	$0.12
Direct labor	0.1 hour	×	$15.00	=	1.50
Total cost				=	$1.62

Total Materials Variance LO15

$$
\begin{aligned}
\text{Total Materials Variance} &= & \text{Actual Cost} & \quad - \quad & \text{Standard Cost} \\
&= & (\text{AP} \times \text{AQ}) & \quad - \quad & (\text{SP} \times \text{SQ}) \\
&= & (\$0.028 \times 890{,}000) & \quad - \quad & (\$0.03 \times 800{,}000) \\
&= & \$24{,}920.00 & \quad - \quad & \$24{,}000.00 \\
&= & \$920.00 & & \text{Unfavorable}
\end{aligned}
$$

Where:

AP = Actual Price
AQ = Actual Quantity
SP = Standard Price
SQ = Standard Quantity

The difference between the actual cost of materials and the expected standard cost of materials is called the **total materials variance**. Using the standard costs listed on page 519, Dixon Molding Corporation can calculate its total materials variance.

Assume that Dixon produced 200,000 cell phone cases in March. Dixon purchased and used 890,000 ounces of plastic at a cost of $24,920.00, or $0.028 per ounce ($24,920.00 ÷ 890,000 ounces). According to its materials quantity standard, Dixon should have used 800,000 ounces of plastic (200,000 units × 4 ounces *per* unit).

Filling in the above formula, the actual price per ounce of plastic purchased is $0.028. The actual quantity purchased and used in production is 890,000 ounces of plastic. The standard price per ounce of plastic is $0.03. The standard quantity is 800,000 ounces. Therefore, the actual cost is $24,920.00, and the standard cost for 200,000 units is $24,000.00. Since the actual cost is more than the standard cost, the $920.00 variance is said to be *unfavorable*. This unfavorable variance means that Dixon paid $920.00 more for materials than it should have according to the materials price and quantity standards.

Materials Price Variance

$$\begin{aligned}
\text{Materials Price Variance} &= \text{AQ} \times (\text{AP} - \text{SP}) \\
&= 890{,}000 \times (\$0.028 - \$0.03) \\
&= 890{,}000 \times \$0.002 \\
&= \$1{,}780.00 \quad \text{Favorable}
\end{aligned}$$

Where:

AQ = Actual Quantity
AP = Actual Price
SP = Standard Price

The total materials variance of $920.00 can have one of two causes: (1) the quantity used is different from the standard quantity at that level of production or (2) the price paid for plastic is different from the standard price. To understand the cause of the variance in more detail, Dixon calculates two additional materials variances.

The difference between the actual price paid for materials and the materials price standard at the actual quantity purchased and used is called the **materials price variance**.

Using the standards and the actual amounts previously given, Dixon calculates its materials price variance as shown above.

The actual quantity of plastic purchased and used in production is 890,000 ounces. The actual price paid for the plastic is $0.028 per ounce. The standard price for plastic is $0.03 per ounce. Because the actual price paid for plastic is less than the standard price for plastic, the $1,780.00 variance is said to be *favorable*.

Materials Quantity Variance

$$\begin{aligned}
\text{Materials Quantity Variance} &= \text{SP} \times (\text{AQ} - \text{SQ}) \\
&= \$0.03 \times (890{,}000 - 800{,}000) \\
&= \$0.03 \times 90{,}000 \\
&= \$2{,}700.00 \quad \text{Unfavorable}
\end{aligned}$$

Where:

SP = Standard Price
AQ = Actual Quantity
SQ = Standard Quantity

The difference between the actual quantity of materials purchased and used in production and the standard quantity of materials for that level of production at the standard price is called the **materials quantity variance**.

Dixon calculates its materials quantity variance as shown above. The standard price of plastic is $0.03 per ounce. The actual quantity of material used to produce 200,000 units is 890,000 ounces. The standard quantity is 800,000 ounces. Because the actual quantity used is more than the standard quantity, the $2,700.00 variance is said to be *unfavorable*.

The difference between the materials quantity variance ($2,700.00 Unfavorable) and the materials price variance ($1,780.00 Favorable) is equal to the total materials variance of $920.00 Unfavorable.

Dixon's management will want to investigate these variances to determine what actions need to be taken. Was the lower materials cost due to obtaining material of lesser quality? Were waste and spoilage higher than normal because of these materials? If so, since the total materials variance was unfavorable, it indicates that the less expensive plastic saved Dixon less money than the added cost caused by inferior materials. Are material costs decreasing? If so, Dixon may need to review the materials price standard to reflect new, lower costs.

Total Labor Variance LO16

$$
\begin{aligned}
\text{Total Labor Variance} &= & \text{Actual Cost} &\quad - &\text{Standard Cost} \\
&= & (\text{AP} \times \text{AQ}) &\quad - &(\text{SP} \times \text{SQ}) \\
&= & (\$15.10 \times 19{,}000) &\quad - &(\$15.00 \times 20{,}000) \\
&= & \$286{,}900.00 &\quad - &\$300{,}000.00 \\
&= & \$13{,}100.00 & &\text{Favorable}
\end{aligned}
$$

Where:

AP	=	Actual Price
AQ	=	Actual Quantity
SP	=	Standard Price
SQ	=	Standard Quantity

The difference between the actual cost of labor and the expected standard cost of labor is called the **total labor variance**. Using the standard costs listed on page 519, Dixon Molding Corporation can calculate its total labor variance.

Assume, again, that Dixon produced 200,000 cell phone cases in March. Dixon used 19,000 hours of direct labor at a cost of $286,900.00, or $15.10 per hour ($286,900.00 ÷ 19,000). According to its labor quantity standard, Dixon should have used 20,000 hours of direct labor (200,000 × 0.1 hour per unit).

Filling in the above formula, the actual price per hour of direct labor is $15.10. The actual quantity of labor is 19,000 hours. The standard price of labor is $15.00 per hour. The standard quantity of labor is 20,000 hours. Therefore, the actual cost of labor is $286,900.00, and the standard cost of labor for 200,000 units is $300,000.00. Since the actual cost is less than the standard cost, the $13,100.00 variance is said to be *favorable*. This favorable variance means that Dixon paid $13,100.00 less for labor than it should have according to the labor price and quantity standards.

THINK LIKE AN ACCOUNTANT

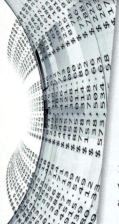

Measuring Material Variances

Management accountants are responsible for monitoring the costs of production. Accountants establish standards for the quantity and price of the material that should be used for each unit produced. For example, Dutch Bakery expects to use 3 cups of flour for each loaf of bread. Each cup of flour is expected to cost $0.30. These amounts are known as *standards*. Any variance from the standards should be investigated and appropriate actions taken.

Dutch Bakery used 48,600 pounds of flour last week to produce 16,200 loaves of bread. The company should have spent $14,580 for the flour. The job cost records indicate that the company used 52,900 cups of flour having a total cost of $15,606, or $0.295 per cup. Thus, the company spent $1,026 more on flour than it expected.

OPEN THE SPREADSHEET TLA_CH17

The workbook contains an incomplete materials variance analysis. Follow the steps on the Instructions tab to calculate what portion of the total variance can be attributed to the quantity and the price of material used.

1. Determine the materials price variance and materials usage variance for the flour used in last week's bread production.

2. During the same week, Dutch Bakery used 7,050 cups of the same flour to produce 2,900 pound cakes. The company expected to use 2.5 cups of flour for each cake. Calculate the materials price and material usage variances.

3. How can a favorable materials price or material usage variance require managers to take corrective actions?

Labor Price Variance

$$\begin{aligned}
\text{Labor Price Variance} &= \text{AQ} \times (\text{AP} - \text{SP}) \\
&= 19{,}000 \times (\$15.10 - \$15.00) \\
&= 19{,}000 \times \$0.10 \\
&= \$1{,}900.00 \quad \text{Unfavorable}
\end{aligned}$$

Where:

AQ = Actual Quantity

AP = Actual Price

SP = Standard Price

The total labor variance of $13,100.00 can be caused by two reasons: (1) the quantity used is different from the standard quantity at that level of production or (2) the price paid for labor is different from the standard price. To understand the cause of the variance in more detail, Dixon calculates two additional labor variances.

The difference between the actual price paid for labor and the labor price standard at the actual quantity used is called the **labor price variance**. Using the standards and the actual amounts previously given, Dixon calculates its labor price variance as shown above.

The actual quantity of labor used in production is 19,000 hours. The actual price paid for labor is $15.10 per hour. The standard price for labor is $15.00 per hour. Because the actual price paid for labor is more than the standard price for labor, the $1,900.00 variance is said to be *unfavorable*.

Labor Quantity Variance

$$\begin{aligned}
\text{Labor Quantity Variance} &= \text{SP} \times (\text{AQ} - \text{SQ}) \\
&= \$15.00 \times (19{,}000 - 20{,}000) \\
&= \$15.00 \times 1{,}000 \\
&= \$15{,}000.00 \quad \text{Favorable}
\end{aligned}$$

Where:

SP = Standard Price

AQ = Actual Quantity

SQ = Standard Quantity

The difference between the actual quantity of labor used in production and the standard quantity of labor for that level of production at the standard price is called the **labor quantity variance**.

Dixon calculates its labor quantity variance as shown above. The standard price of labor is $15.00 per hour. The actual quantity of labor used to produce 200,000 units is 19,000 hours. The standard quantity is 20,000 hours. Because the quantity used is less than the standard quantity, the $15,000.00 variance is said to be *favorable*.

The difference between the labor quantity variance ($15,000.00 Favorable) and the labor price variance ($1,900.00 Unfavorable) is equal to the total labor variance of $13,100.00 Favorable.

Even though the total labor variance is favorable, Dixon's management will want to investigate the labor variances to determine the cause of the variances. Are labor costs rising? If so, the labor price standard may have to be changed. Did Dixon employ more experienced workers than normal? If so, are these more experienced workers more efficient, causing the favorable variance for labor quantity? Should more experienced workers be used for this process in the future?

Labor variances may be related to materials variances. Any possible connection should be investigated. Did Dixon have to assign more experienced workers to the process because lesser quality materials were purchased? Would more materials have been used if less experienced workers were employed?

TERMS REVIEW

standard

standard costing system

materials quantity standard

materials price standard

labor quantity standard

labor price standard

total materials variance

materials price variance

materials quantity variance

total labor variance

labor price variance

labor quantity variance

Audit your understanding LO14, 15, 16

1. What two cost items are often the focus of control?
2. What is another name for the labor quantity standard?
3. What is the formula for total materials variance?
4. If the actual materials cost is less than the standard cost, is the variance favorable or unfavorable?
5. How can the total materials variance be related to the total labor variance?
6. What is the formula for total labor variance?

Work together 17-4 LO14, 15, 16

Calculating variances for materials and labor

Glommen Corporation makes jeans. Glommen's management has established the following standards:

Material quantity standard	3 yards per pair of jeans
Material price standard	$6.00 per yard
Labor quantity standard	1 hour per pair of jeans
Labor price standard	$12.00 per hour

Glommen actually produced 150,000 pairs of jeans this month. It purchased and used 445,000 yards of denim at a total cost of $2,714,500.00. A total of 151,200 hours of direct labor were used at a total cost of $1,829,520.00. Forms are provided in the *Working Papers*. Your instructor will guide you through the following examples.

1. Calculate the total materials variance, the materials price variance, and the materials quantity variance. Comment on your results.
2. Calculate the total labor variance, the labor price variance, and the labor quantity variance. Comment on your results.

On your own 17-4 LO14, 15, 16

Calculating variances for materials and labor

Northstar, Inc., produces wooden bird feeders. Northstar's management has established the following standards:

Material quantity standard	2 board feet per feeder
Material price standard	$1.50 per board foot
Labor quantity standard	0.5 hour per feeder
Labor price standard	$10.00 per hour

Northstar actually produced 1,000,000 bird feeders this year. It purchased and used 2,020,000 board feet of wood at a total cost of $2,949,200.00. A total of 480,000 hours of direct labor were used at a total cost of $4,790,400.00. Forms are provided in the *Working Papers*. Work independently to complete the following problems.

1. Calculate the total materials variance, the materials price variance, and the materials quantity variance. Comment on your results.
2. Calculate the total labor variance, the labor price variance, and the labor quantity variance. Comment on your results.

The cost of a manufactured product consists of three cost elements: (1) direct materials, (2) direct labor, and (3) factory overhead. Direct materials are those materials that have significant value and become an identifiable part of the finished product. Direct labor is the cost of labor connected directly to the manufacture of the product. Factory overhead consists of all other manufacturing costs, such as indirect materials, indirect labor, cleaning supplies, factory depreciation, and insurance.

A manufacturing business uses three inventory accounts: (1) Materials, (2) Work in Process, and (3) Finished Goods. As these materials and labor costs flow through the manufacturing process, the related costs must flow through the accounts via journal entries. Overhead costs are recorded by using a predetermined overhead rate. At the end of the period, overapplied overhead or underapplied overhead must be transferred to Cost of Goods Sold.

The cost of each job order must also be recorded. A cost sheet is used to collect the direct materials, direct labor, and factory overhead costs for each job. When the job is complete, the total cost is known and a per-unit cost can be calculated.

The statement of cost of goods manufactured is used by a manufacturing company to calculate the cost of goods manufactured, which replaces the purchases line on the income statement. On the balance sheet, a manufacturing company must report all three inventory accounts.

Standard costs are established in a standard costing system. These standard costs can then be used to evaluate the performance of a company in terms of materials used, the price paid for materials, the labor hours employed, and the cost of labor through variance calculation and analysis.

EXPLORE ACCOUNTING

ISO 9001 Certification

A manufacturing company can make all of its component parts or purchase some of those parts from other companies. If the company purchases components from another company, it needs assurance about the quality of the parts. Rather than personally examining each supplier's manufacturing process, the purchasing company can require its suppliers to be ISO 9001 certified. ISO 9001 certification assures customers that the company has an effective quality management system that continually evaluates and improves the production process.

The ISO certification program was developed by the International Organization of Standardization (ISO), a worldwide federation of national standards organizations. ISO's role includes programs that certify the manufacturing process. To become ISO 9001 certified, a company must follow ISO's standards for various phases of the production process, including design, development, production, inspection, and servicing. The company must maintain an information system to record its compliance with ISO standards. Finally, the company must hire an independent organization to audit its initial and continuing compliance with ISO standards. ISO 9001 certification does not assure or guarantee

the production of quality products. However, ISO 9001 certification does make a positive statement about a company's commitment to quality.

Other than helping to control costs, how does ISO 9001 certification impact accounting? Accountants assist in designing and operating the information system necessary to collect ISO 9001 compliance data. Accountants in public accounting firms are also involved in ISO 9001 certification. These firms can either assist a client to prepare for the ISO 9001 certification process or be the independent organization that audits the client and awards ISO 9001 certification.

INSTRUCTIONS

1. How is ISO certification similar to financial statement audits?

2. Several types of ISO certification are available. Explain the purpose of the ISO 14000 family of standards.

3. An acronym for the International Organization of Standardization would logically be "IOS." Explain why the ISO title is used for the organization and its certifications.

Source: www.iso.org.

APPLY YOUR UNDERSTANDING

INSTRUCTIONS: Download problem instructions for Excel, QuickBooks, and Sage 50c from the textbook companion website at www.C21accounting.com.

17-1.1 Application Problem — Completing a materials ledger card and journalizing entries in a materials purchases journal LO2, 3, 4

Wold Appliance makes all appliances, but specializes in washing machines and dryers. A partially completed materials ledger card and a materials purchases journal are given in the *Working Papers*.

Instructions:

1. Record the following transactions for FL7500 Washer Tubs on the materials ledger card. The price for this tub is $24.00 per unit. Update the balance when necessary.

Transactions:

Jan. 3. Recorded Purchase Order No. 613 for 200 units.
  3. Recorded Requisition No. 775, moving 10 tubs into production.
  10. Recorded Requisition No. 782, moving 45 tubs into production.
  13. Received Purchase Order No. 613.

2. Record the following purchases in a materials purchases journal.

Transactions:

Jan. 3. Purchased materials on account from KB Manufacturing, $3,212.00. P610.
  5. Purchased materials on account from Northend Motors, $21,567.00. P611.
  12. Purchased materials on account from Gateway Gear, Inc., $6,765.00. P612.
  13. Purchased materials on account from Washington Corporation, $4,800.00. P613.

17-1.2 Application Problem — Recording and journalizing materials and labor costs LO2, 3, 4, 5, 6

sage 50

1. Journalize and post transactions related to manufacturing materials and labor costs to the general journal and the case disbursements journal.
2. Print the general journal and trial balance.

QB QuickBooks

1. Journalize and post transactions related to manufacturing materials and labor costs to the journal.
2. Print the journal and the trial balance.

Lake Country Manufacturing produces plastic gears. A cost sheet and blank journals are included in the *Working Papers*.

Instructions:

1. Record the following items on the cost sheet for Job No. 335:
   a. Materials Requisition No. 230 for $1,900.00 of direct materials for Job No. 335.
   b. June 29 total of all Job-Time Records for Job No. 335 for the day, $2,725.00.

2. Journalize the following transactions:

Transactions:

June 30. Requisitioned $24,000.00 of direct materials and $20,000.00 of indirect materials for the Production Department. M421.
  30. Paid employees their semimonthly pay. Gross (pretax) direct labor costs were $52,500.00. Gross indirect labor costs were $9,500.00. Employee income tax was $6,820.00. Social Security tax was 6.2% and Medicare tax was 1.45% of gross wages. C574.

Save your work for use in Problem 17-2.

17-2 Application Problem — Completing a cost sheet and journalizing entries for overhead LO7, 8

Use the cost sheet and journals used in Problem 17-1.2.

Instructions:

1. Job No. 335 was completed on June 30. Complete the cost sheet for Job No. 335. Factory overhead is applied based on direct labor hours. Estimated factory overhead for the year was $600,000.00. The number of estimated direct labor hours for the year was 60,000. A total of 415 direct labor hours was used on Job No. 335.

2. Journalize the following transactions:

Transactions:

June 30. Obtained factory costs for the month: depreciation on building, $1,650.00; depreciation on equipment, $1,950.00; insurance, $1,750.00; property taxes, $2,250.00; utilities, $2,400.00. M422. Assume that these expenses have already been properly accounted for and now need to be closed.

30. Applied overhead at the rate of $10.00 per direct labor hour, with 5,000 direct labor hours worked this period. M423.

30. Closed the Factory Overhead account. Actual total overhead costs for the period were $49,500.00. M424.

Save your work for use in Problem 17-3.1.

17-3.1 Application Problem — Updating a finished goods ledger card; journalizing entries for finished goods and cost of goods sold LO9, 10, 11

Use the forms and journals used in Problem 17-2.

Instructions:

1. Using the cost sheet for Job No. 335, update the finished goods ledger card for Magnetic Gear MEG3.

2. Journalize the following transactions:

Transactions:

June 30. Transferred products costing $135,000.00 to finished goods during the month. M425.

30. Sold products costing $118,550.00 during the month. M426.

17-3.2 Application Problem — Preparing a statement of cost of goods manufactured and completing financial statements for a manufacturing business LO12, 13

The Accounting Department at Medford Manufacturing has compiled the following data for the month of April of the current year.

Cost of direct labor	$ 95,120.00
Direct materials issued into production	268,300.00
Factory overhead applied	122,600.00
Finished goods beginning inventory	63,540.00
Finished goods ending inventory	59,420.00
Materials ending inventory	32,690.00
Overapplied overhead	2,100.00
Work in process beginning inventory	63,250.00
Work in process ending inventory	61,720.00

Forms are provided in the *Working Papers*.

Instructions:

1. Prepare a statement of cost of goods manufactured for the month of April.
2. Complete the partial income statement through gross profit on operations for the month of April.
3. Complete the partial balance sheet through total current assets for April 30, 20--.

Arneson Corporation makes hand-dipped candles. Arneson's management has established the following standards for one of its candles:

Material quantity standard	10 ounces of wax
Material price standard	$0.20 per ounce
Labor quantity standard	0.25 hour per candle
Labor price standard	$15.00 per hour

Arneson actually produced 7,000 candles this month. It purchased and used 71,000 ounces of wax at a total cost of $13,490.00. A total of 1,700 hours of direct labor were used at a total cost of $25,840. Forms are provided in the *Working Papers*.

1. Calculate the total materials variance, the materials price variance, and the materials quantity variance. Comment on your results.

2. Calculate the total labor variance, the labor price variance, and the labor quantity variance. Comment on your results.

17-M Mastery Problem Preparing cost records and journalizing entries that summarize cost records at the end of a fiscal period
LO2, 3, 4, 5, 6, 7, 8, 9, 10, 11

sage 50

1. Journalize and post transactions related to manufacturing materials and labor costs to the general journal.
2. Print the general journal and trial balance.

QB Quick Books

1. Journalize and post transactions related to manufacturing materials and labor costs to the journal.
2. Print the journal and the trial balance.

X

1. Complete the cost sheet and finished good ledger card.
2. Journalize transactions to the general journal and cash payments journal.
3. Print the worksheets.

Mercury manufactures boots. The company records manufacturing costs by job number and uses a factory overhead applied rate to charge overhead costs to its products. The company estimates Mercury will manufacture 50,000 boots next year. For this amount of production, total factory overhead is estimated to be $797,600.00. Estimated direct labor costs for next year are $997,000.00.

The following information is taken from the records of Mercury on May 31 of the current year.

a. The total factory payroll for the month according to the payroll register is $154,860.00, distributed as follows.

Work in Process	$116,320.00	Employee Income Tax Payable	$17,255.00
Factory Overhead	38,540.00	Social Security Tax Payable	9,601.32
Cash	125,758.21	Medicare Tax Payable	2,245.47

b. The total of all requisitions of direct materials issued during the month is $128,688.00. The total of all requisitions of indirect materials issued during the month is $11,670.00.

c. Manufacturing expense accounts and their balances for the month are as follows:

Depreciation Expense—Factory Equipment	$ 2,947.20	Miscellaneous Expense	$ 640.00
Depreciation Expense—Building	1,440.00	Payroll Taxes Expense—Factory	21,680.40
Heat, Light, and Power Expense	4,620.00	Property Tax Expense—Factory	3,624.00
Insurance Expense—Factory	768.00	Supplies Expense—Factory	8,016.00

d. The total of all cost sheets completed during the month is $332,850.00.

e. The total of costs recorded on all sales invoices for May is $517,410.00.

Instructions:

1. Calculate Mercury's factory overhead applied rate for next year as a percentage of direct labor cost.

2. On May 3, Mercury began work on Job No. 283. The order is for 150 pairs of No. 52L boots for stock; date wanted May 13. Open a cost sheet for Job No. 283 and record the following items.

Transactions:

May	3.	Direct materials, $1,725.00. Materials Requisition No. 392.
	3.	Direct labor, $258.00. Daily summary of job-time records.
	4.	Direct labor, $496.00. Daily summary of job-time records.
	5.	Direct materials, $945.00. Materials Requisition No. 399.
	5.	Direct labor, $350.00. Daily summary of job-time records.
	6.	Direct labor, $384.00. Daily summary of job-time records.
	7.	Direct labor, $590.00. Daily summary of job-time records.
	10.	Direct materials, $720.00. Materials Requisition No. 428.
	10.	Direct labor, $330.00. Daily summary of job-time records.
	11.	Direct labor, $304.00. Daily summary of job-time records.
	12.	Direct labor, $248.00. Daily summary of job-time records.

3. Complete the cost sheet, recording factory overhead at the rate calculated in part (1).

4. Prepare a finished goods ledger card for Stock No. 52L boots. Minimum quantity is set at 100. Inventory location is Area C-50.

5. Record on the finished goods ledger card the beginning balance on May 1: 140 units at a unit cost of $60.90. Mercury uses the first-in, first-out method to record inventory costs.

6. Record the following transactions on the finished goods ledger card for 52L boots.

Transactions:

May	5.	Sold 60 pairs of 52L boots. Sales Invoice No. 633.
	12.	Received 150 pairs of 52L boots. Record cost from cost sheet for Job No. 283.
	18.	Sold 30 pairs of 52L boots. Sales Invoice No. 652.

7. Journalize the factory payroll entry on page 10 of a cash payments journal. C711.

8. Journalize the following entries on page 5 of a general journal.

a. An entry to transfer the total of all direct materials requisitions to Work in Process and indirect materials to Factory Overhead. M211.

b. An entry to close all individual manufacturing expense accounts to Factory Overhead. M212.

c. An entry to record applied factory overhead to Work in Process. M213.

9. Continue using page 5 of the general journal. Journalize the entry to close the balance of the Factory Overhead account to Income Summary. M214.

10. Journalize the entry to transfer the total of all cost sheets completed from Work in Process to Finished Goods. M215.

11. Journalize the entry to transfer the cost of products sold from Finished Goods to Cost of Goods Sold. M216.

Owatonna, Inc., has made the following estimates for the current year: total factory overhead, $400,000.00; direct material costs, $1,000,000.00; direct labor costs, $1,600,000.00; direct labor hours, 50,000. It is trying to determine which method of applying an overhead rate is most accurate: (a) direct materials cost, (b) direct labor cost, or (c) direct labor hours.

Instructions:
1. Calculate Owatonna's factory overhead applied rate for each of the three bases.
2. Assume the following for Job No. 444: total direct materials, $150,000.00; total direct labor, $130,000.00; direct labor hours, 5,000; 4,000 units produced. Calculate the total cost and the per-unit cost for Job No. 444 using each of the three bases for factory overhead.
3. How should Owatonna decide which overhead basis to use to apply overhead?
4. What is the danger in using an inaccurate overhead basis to apply overhead?

Auditing for Errors   LO1

East End Manufacturing is a new company that will produce a line of high-quality wood computer desks. The company's management is working on its accounting system and has prepared the following policy for classifying manufacturing costs. Determine whether any item in the policy violates generally accepted accounting principles.

Description	Direct Materials	Direct Labor	Indirect Material	Indirect Labor	Other
Advertising and promotion					X
Delivery of finished goods to customer		X			
Depreciation of machinery					X
Utilities					X
Inspector wages		X			
Insurance on factory					X
Maintenance wages				X	
Packing materials			X		
Production wages		X			
Sandpaper	X				
Screws			X		
Supervisor salaries				X	
Varnish	X				
Wood	X				

Are Manufacturing Jobs Coming Back to America?

Theme: Financial, Economic, Business, Entrepreneurial Literacy, and Global Awareness

Skills: Information Literacy and Critical Thinking and Problem Solving

PARTNERSHIP FOR
21ST CENTURY SKILLS

There has been much controversy about manufacturing jobs in the United States. At the peak of American manufacturing, over 19.5 million jobs were factory work. In 2010, that number had dropped to approximately 11.5 million, but since then the number has increased somewhat. At the time of publication, the Bureau of Labor Statistics estimated that there were 12.6 million U.S. manufacturing jobs.

The controversy centers around two topics: (1) What portion of those jobs were lost to U.S. companies moving their production to foreign countries, and what portion were lost to robots? (2) Are manufacturing jobs continuing to return to the United States?

Historically, inexpensive labor costs have made foreign countries attractive to the American manufacturer. This fact seems to be changing, however. As wages increase in countries such as China and automation increases in the United States, direct labor costs tend to be less of a reason to produce overseas.

APPLICATION

1. It is said that American technology and innovative leadership should give U.S. companies the advantage in automation. Using the Internet, research companies that have brought manufacturing back to the United States. Write a report of your findings. Include the names of the companies, the number of jobs returning, and the reasons why the jobs are coming back.

2. Using the Internet, research technology manufacturing jobs. Write a report of your findings. Include names of companies and their locations, educational and/or skill requirements, and salaries.

Sources: www.bls.gov; www.money.cnn.com

Analyzing Home Depot's Financial Statements

This chapter discussed the accounting for a manufacturing business and how the financial statements for a manufacturer are different from those for a service business or a merchandising business.

INSTRUCTIONS

1. Is Home Depot a service business, a merchandising business, or a manufacturing business?

2. If Home Depot were a manufacturing business, it would list three inventory accounts on its balance sheet. Review Home Depot's Consolidated Balance Sheets on page B-5 and list its inventory account(s).

CHAPTER 18

Management Decision Making Using Differential Analysis

© ONE PHOTO/SHUTTERSTOCK.COM

Macy's

ACCOUNTING IN THE REAL WORLD

"Everyone loves a parade" is a quote often repeated, but there is no firm explanation for its origin. Parades come in many sizes and styles and are viewed by crowds large and small. One of the more famous parades is the Macy's Thanksgiving Day Parade, held on Thanksgiving Day in New York City. The parade is known for its gigantic balloons, which require several "balloon pilots" just to keep them from floating away. The first parade was held in 1924 and since then has been cancelled only three times—the years 1942 to 1944 because of helium and rubber shortages during World War II.

Macy's is more than the organizer of an annual parade, however. Since its first store opened in 1858, with first-day sales totaling $11.06, the retail store has grown to be one of the largest retailers in the world. Macy's 2017 Fact Book states that the company has approximately 140,000 employees and more than 700 stores. Macy's annual report for the fiscal year ending February 3, 2018, lists net sales of $24.8 billion, which is over $68 million a day.

Macy's overall success doesn't mean that it hasn't faced hard times. In fact, it continues to struggle to meet competition from Internet retail websites such as Amazon. Macy's isn't alone in this struggle. Many companies that have only brick and mortar stores have closed thousands of locations in order to reduce costs to match reduced revenue. Others have simply gone out of business.

Macy's has closed over 200 stores and, at the time of publication, intends to close even more. What Macy's did that many of the other companies have not been able to accomplish is to grow its online clothing site in an effort to counteract the drop in in-store sales. In fact, Macy's was recently named the top e-commerce clothing store in the United States.

When deciding which stores to close, Macy's has to consider several factors. Downward trends in the number of customers that enter a store and the average sales per square foot might be considered. The tools discussed in this chapter could help company management in its decision-making process.

Sources: www.macysinc.com; www.time.com/money.

CRITICAL THINKING

1. Search the Internet to see how many Macy's stores are currently open. Based on this number, comment on the success or failure of Macy's strategy.

2. Under what conditions might Macy's elect to keep a store open that has shown a steady decline in the number of customers that enter the store?

KEY TERMS

differential analysis
relevant revenues
relevant costs
sunk cost
joint products

split-off point
joint costs
payback period
time value of money
future value

compounding
present value
annuity
future value of
  an annuity

present value of
  an annuity
net cash flows
net present value

LO1 Define costs associated with differential analysis.
LO2 Use differential analysis for make or buy decisions.
LO3 Use differential analysis for special order decisions.
LO4 Use differential analysis for discontinuing a segment decisions.
LO5 Use differential analysis for sell or process further decisions.
LO6 Calculate the payback period of an investment.

Differential Analysis LO1

Management makes many decisions in the course of operating a company. These decisions can affect the financial performance of the company for a few days or for many years. When comparing two options, management may look at the total revenues and expenses relating to each alternative. However, if some revenues and expenses are the same regardless of the alternative chosen, looking at total revenues and expenses may not be the best method. Analyzing only the differences between the revenues and expenses resulting from each of two options is called **differential analysis**. Differential analysis is useful for short-term management decisions.

Revenues that are different between two options are called **relevant revenues**. Costs that are different between two options are called **relevant costs**. Differential analysis considers only relevant revenues and relevant costs.

Relevant costs must be both future costs and costs that differ between alternatives. A cost that occurred in the past and cannot be recovered by a future decision is called a **sunk cost**. A sunk cost can never be a relevant cost. An example of a sunk cost is the depreciation incurred by an asset purchased three years ago. When considering whether to replace the asset, the depreciation associated with that asset is a sunk cost and, therefore, is not a relevant cost.

ETHICS IN ACTION

It's Just a Day or Two

Binata Barnes arrived for work on January 3 to find that MDK Industries had faxed a signed contract the day before. Binata had been working for months to land this contract. Excited that the deal was now official, she shared the news with Dan Smith, her supervisor.

"This is great! This contract will keep the plant working at full speed for months," Dan replied. "But for purposes of awarding annual bonuses, it needs to be included in last year's activity. None of us will get our bonuses without it."

"But what can we do? The contract is dated January 2," replied Binata. "Just change the date to December 30," Dan instructed. We have an informal policy whereby we can adjust contract dates by up to a week. We do it all the time."

"Why don't I just ask the customer to sign another contract with a new date?" Binata asked, a little concerned with being asked to alter the contract. "One thing you need to remember—never give a customer a second chance to sign a contract," Dan replied.

INSTRUCTIONS

Using the ethical model, provide Binata with guidance on whether she should mail the revised contract. Assume the only guidance in the company's code of conduct states: "We strive to present information fairly to customers, vendors, and all other parties with which we conduct business."

Source: Adapted with permission from October 29, 2012, presentation by Walt Pavlo.

Make or Buy Decision LO2

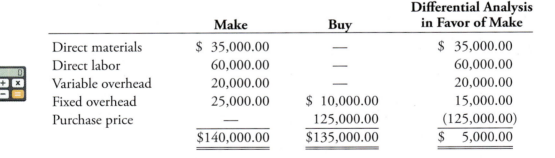

	Make	Buy	Differential Analysis in Favor of Make
Direct materials	$ 35,000.00	—	$ 35,000.00
Direct labor	60,000.00	—	60,000.00
Variable overhead	20,000.00	—	20,000.00
Fixed overhead	25,000.00	$ 25,000.00	—
Purchase price	—	125,000.00	(125,000.00)
	$140,000.00	$150,000.00	$ (10,000.00)

Custom Cyclery Corporation has been purchasing 10,000 brake assemblies from an outside source at a cost of $12.50 per assembly. Since Custom Cyclery has excess capacity, it is considering making the brake assemblies in its own factory. No new machinery or equipment will need to be purchased. Custom Cyclery has idle machines and no other use for them.

Custom Cyclery's Accounting Department has estimated the costs associated with making 10,000 brake assemblies, as shown above.

The variable overhead consists of indirect materials, indirect labor, and other expenses that are connected with making the brake assemblies. These costs will not exist if Custom Cyclery continues buying the assemblies. The fixed overhead consists of depreciation and other

expenses that are allocated to each product. If Custom Cyclery continues to buy the assemblies, these costs will remain and will be allocated to other products manufactured.

The first step in the analysis is to determine relevant revenues and relevant costs. Direct materials, direct labor, and variable overhead costs are all relevant because they are different between the two options. Fixed overhead costs, however, are not relevant. Once the relevant costs have been determined, the costs are totaled.

As shown above, it will cost Custom Cyclery $140,000.00 to make 10,000 brake assemblies. It will cost Custom Cyclery $150,000.00 to buy 10,000 brake assemblies. Therefore, it should make the assemblies.

Avoidable Fixed Overhead

	Make	Buy	Differential Analysis in Favor of Make
Direct materials	$ 35,000.00	—	$ 35,000.00
Direct labor	60,000.00	—	60,000.00
Variable overhead	20,000.00	—	20,000.00
Fixed overhead	25,000.00	$ 10,000.00	15,000.00
Purchase price	—	125,000.00	(125,000.00)
	$140,000.00	$135,000.00	$ 5,000.00

Assume the same cost structure as above, but that only $10,000.00 of the fixed overhead will remain if the assemblies are purchased. Now, only $10,000.00 of fixed overhead is not relevant. The $15,000.00 of fixed

overhead that can be avoided if Custom Cyclery buys the assemblies is a relevant cost. The differential analysis now shows that Custom Cyclery will save $5,000.00 by buying the assemblies from an outside source.

Special Orders LO3

	Accept Special Order	Reject Special Order	Differential Analysis in Favor of Acceptance
Sales revenue	$110.00	—	$110.00
Direct materials	(60.00)	—	(60.00)
Direct labor	(35.00)	—	(35.00)
Variable overhead ($8.00 – $3.00)	(5.00)	—	(5.00)
Special emblem	(0.50)	—	(0.50)
Fixed costs	NR	NR	NR
Net increase	$ 9.50	$0.00	$ 9.50

Custom Cyclery was approached by a potential customer to make a special edition of a bicycle. The bicycle will have the retailer's name embossed on it. The retailer would like to buy 100 bicycles and will pay $110.00 for each bicycle. Custom Cyclery has ample excess capacity, and it can make 100 additional bicycles without affecting its normal production. Custom Cyclery calculates its per-unit cost to be $100.50, which includes $0.50 per unit for the cost of the special emblem. Excluded from the variable overhead costs are $1.00 for sales commissions and $2.00 for other selling expenses that will not have to be paid on this special order. The total fixed overhead costs for Custom Cyclery will remain the same whether the special order is accepted or rejected.

This particular model of bicycle usually sells for $150.00. However, the retailer is in a different region of the country, so the additional 100 bicycles will not impact Custom Cyclery's normal sales. Should Custom Cyclery accept this special order?

This special order decision can be analyzed on a per-unit basis or on a total revenue basis. The per-unit basis is used in the differential analysis shown above. Relevant revenue is $110.00 per unit. This is revenue that would not be received if the special order is rejected. Relevant costs include direct materials ($60.00), direct labor ($35.00), variable overhead ($5.00), and the special emblem ($0.50). Thus, Custom Cyclery will make an additional $9.50 per unit if it accepts the special order.

If this special order would affect normal sales for Custom Cyclery or if it had to decrease normal production in order to accept the special order, the differential analysis would have to include those relevant revenues and costs. Another potentially negative result of accepting the special order would be Custom Cyclery's normal customers learning about the special order and becoming upset that they are paying $150.00 for the same bicycle.

Discontinue a Segment LO4

Cartwright sells children's clothing and shoes. It is considering dropping its children's shoes because of disappointing results over the last few years. Financial data for the last year are as follows:

	Clothing	Shoes	Total Company
Sales	$200,000.00	$120,000.00	$320,000.00
Variable expenses	90,000.00	95,000.00	185,000.00
Contribution margin	$110,000.00	$ 25,000.00	$135,000.00
Fixed costs	48,000.00	32,000.00	80,000.00
Operating income	$ 62,000.00	$ (7,000.00)	$ 55,000.00

Further analysis reveals that the $32,000.00 of fixed costs for shoes includes $12,000.00 allocated for insurance, electricity, and taxes. If shoes are discontinued, these costs will remain and will all be allocated to clothing. The remaining $20,000.00 is the cost of salaries, which will be eliminated if the shoes are discontinued.

Cartwright management completes the following differential analysis:

	Keep Shoe Department	Drop Shoe Department	Differential Analysis in Favor of Keeping Shoe Department
Sales	$320,000.00	$200,000.00	$120,000.00
Variable expenses	185,000.00	90,000.00	95,000.00
Contribution margin	$135,000.00	$110,000.00	$ 25,000.00
Fixed costs	80,000.00	60,000.00	20,000.00
Operating income	$ 55,000.00	$ 50,000.00	$ 5,000.00

Since $12,000.00 of fixed costs will remain, it is not profitable for Cartwright to discontinue shoes. If it does, its operating income will decrease $5,000.00.

If the analysis indicated that it would be profitable for Cartwright to discontinue shoes, management would also have to consider other items. Will clothing sales be affected by discontinuing shoes? If Cartwright's customers desire the convenience of buying clothing and shoes in one stop, sales of clothing may actually be less than $200,000.00.

Sell or Process Further LO5

Cruthers Corporation makes lumber. It gets timber from a saw mill, dries it, and cuts it into standard size boards. At that point, Cruthers can sell it to lumber yards or process it further into window frames.

The window frames can be sold to a local window manufacturer.

The following costs have been compiled. These costs are based on the original purchase of 1,000 board feet of timber.

Item or Process	Number of Board Feet	Unit Cost or Selling Price
Purchase timber logs	1,000	$0.25
Kiln dry the logs	1,000	0.05
Cut to standard size	900	0.12
Sell as lumber	900	0.60
Process to window frames	500	0.60
Sell as window frames	500	2.00

Two or more products that are produced simultaneously with the same processes and costs and are inseparable up to a certain point are called **joint products**. The point where joint products are separable into identifiable products is called the **split-off point**. The costs of processing joint products to their split-off point are called **joint costs**.

For Cruthers, the lumber and the window frames are joint products from the time the logs are purchased, through the kiln-drying process and through the cutting process. The split-off point is when Cruthers must decide to sell the lumber or process it further into window frames. The joints costs are those associated with kiln-drying the lumber and cutting it into standard sizes. Since these joint costs are past costs that cannot be recovered by a future decision, they are also sunk costs. Since a sunk cost can never be a relevant cost, none of the joint costs in this example are relevant. Thus, differential analysis of the decision to sell the lumber or process it further begins at the split-off point. This analysis is shown on page 538.

	Process Further	Sell at Split-Off Point	Differential Analysis in Favor of Processing Further
Revenue	$1,000.00	$540.00	$460.00
Cost to process further	300.00	—	300.00
Operating income	$ 700.00	$540.00	$160.00

If the lumber is processed further, it can be sold for $1,000.00 (500 board feet × $2.00). If the lumber is sold at the split-off point, it can be sold for $540.00 (900 board feet × $0.60). The cost to process the lumber into window frames is $300.00 (500 board feet × $0.60). There is no added cost to sell the lumber at the split-off point. Since the difference in revenue is greater than the additional processing costs, Cruthers should process the lumber into window frames. If the difference in revenue is less than the additional processing costs, Cruthers should sell the lumber at the split-off point.

Payback Period LO6

Another method used to make a decision on investments is to analyze how long it takes to recoup the cost of the investment. The amount of time required to recover the cost of an investment is called the **payback period**. The payback method requires an estimate of the additional revenue earned or costs saved by the investment.

Patton Corporation is considering purchasing a milling machine at a cost of $100,000.00. Patton estimates that the new machine is more efficient and will increase revenue by $20,000.00 per year. The formula for calculating the payback period is shown below.

$$\text{Cost of Investment} \div \text{Annual Increase In Revenue} = \text{Payback Period (in years)}$$

$$\$100,000.00 \div \$20,000.00 = 5.0 \text{ years}$$

The payback period for purchasing the new machine is 5 years. This means it will take Patton 5 years to recover the cost of the machine. Instead of purchasing a new machine, Patton Corporation could update its current machine, which would decrease costs instead of increasing revenue. The payback period for updating the current machine is 6.5 years. Using the payback period alone to evaluate the decision, Patton would purchase the new milling machine because it has a shorter payback period.

TERMS REVIEW

differential analysis

relevant revenues

relevant costs

sunk cost

joint products

split-off point

joint costs

payback period

Audit your understanding LO1, 2, 3, 4, 5, 6

1. What two features are necessary for a cost to be a relevant cost?
2. In a make or buy decision, how is an avoidable fixed cost treated?
3. Besides differential analysis, what other factors should a company consider when deciding whether to accept or reject a special order?
4. How are fixed costs treated when deciding if a department should be discontinued?
5. In a sell or process further decision, if the difference in revenue is less than the additional processing costs, what should the company do?
6. An investment costing $60,000.00 will save $20,000.00 per year in expenses. What is the payback period for the investment?

Work together 18-1 LO2, 4

Determining relevant amounts

Forms are provided in the *Working Papers*. List the amount of each item that is relevant and irrelevant. Your instructor will guide you through each situation.

1. Bayfront Corporation is considering making a component part that it has been buying for $500,000.00. Bayfront has idle machines that have no other use. Costs to make the part include: direct materials, $125,000.00; direct labor, $150,000.00; and variable overhead, $75,000.00. Fixed costs of $80,000.00 have been allocated to the production of the part; these costs will remain and will be allocated to other products.
2. Carey Corporation sells canoe and paddleboard paddles. It is considering dropping its line of canoe paddles and has compiled the following data.

	Paddleboard Paddles	Canoe Paddles	Total Company
Sales	$420,000.00	$200,000.00	$620,000.00
Variable expenses	121,000.00	135,000.00	256,000.00
Contribution margin	$299,000.00	$ 65,000.00	$364,000.00
Fixed costs	130,000.00	70,000.00	200,000.00
Operating income	$169,000.00	$ (5,000.00)	$164,000.00

Further analysis shows that $15,000.00 of the fixed costs is allocated. If canoe paddles are discontinued, these costs will remain and be allocated to paddleboard paddles. The remaining $55,000.00 will be eliminated if canoe paddles are discontinued.

On your own 18-1 LO3, 5

Determining relevant amounts

Forms are provided in the *Working Papers*. For each situation, list the amount of each item that is relevant and irrelevant. Work these problems independently.

1. Cosgrove Corporation sells safety glasses for $10.00 per pair. It is considering accepting a special order for $7.00 per pair. It has excess capacity. The special order will not affect sales. Cosgrove has determined that the variable costs for each pair of glasses are: direct materials, $2.00; direct labor, $2.50; and overhead, $3.50. Variable overhead includes $1.50 for selling expenses, which will not be incurred for this special order. At its normal level of production, fixed costs per unit are $0.75. These fixed costs will remain the same whether the order is accepted or not.
2. Deercreek Creamery gets milk from dairy farms and pasteurizes it. It can then sell it as whole milk or process it further into ice cream. Deercreek can sell whole milk for $3.00 per gallon. It can sell ice cream for $7.00 per gallon. The cost to pasteurize the milk is $1.50 per gallon. Processing it further into ice cream costs an additional $3.25 per gallon.

LESSON 18-2

Future and Present Value of Money

LO7 Explain the time value of money.
LO8 Calculate the future value of an amount.
LO9 Calculate the present value of an amount.
LO10 Calculate the future value of an annuity.
LO11 Calculate the present value of an annuity.

Time Value of Money LO7

Bank customers deposit their money in savings accounts and certificates of deposit to earn interest and increase their wealth. The expectation that invested money will increase over time is called the **time value of money**. Because of the time value of money, the promise of receiving $100.00 in three years is not worth $100.00 today. A bank customer would expect to deposit less than $100.00 today on the promise of receiving $100.00 in three years.

Like bank customers, managers must consider the time value of money when investing in plant assets. A business invests in plant assets, such as buildings, trucks, computers, and computer networks, to expand its operations and increase profits. When deciding whether to purchase a plant asset, managers should compare the asset's cost to the additional profits that will be earned in the future. If future profits exceed the cost, then management should purchase the asset.

When profits are earned is an important factor in an asset purchase decision. The value of a dollar earned several years from now should not be compared directly to the cost of the asset today. Managers must consider the time value of money when comparing future profits to today's costs.

WHY ACCOUNTING?

Selling Waste Products for a Profit?

Many manufacturing companies are finding new revenue sources in their waste products. Items that at one time cost money to be hauled away to a landfill are now finding new markets and are being sold. One of the original examples is used vegetable oil, a waste product of many restaurants and fast-food outlets. Instead of paying to have this oil disposed of in an environmentally safe way, the oil can be sold. One use for this oil is to fuel vehicles that have been adapted to run on vegetable oil. Other items that have a resale value include leather scrap, PVC pipe, and carpet.

Besides increasing net income, selling waste products is also environmentally friendly. Many companies are striving to move from "less waste" to "zero waste." Zero waste means that nothing is added to landfills. There are organizations that provide assistance to match sellers and buyers of commercial waste.

CRITICAL THINKING

1. Use the Internet to find an organization that helps match sellers and buyers of waste products. Give two examples of waste products that are currently for sale on the site.

2. Investigate a company that has achieved the goal of zero waste. Write a brief summary of how it achieved zero-waste status. Include one interesting fact about the company's achievement.

Sources: www.recyclematch.com; www.tradingwaste.com.

Future Value of Money LO8

	1/1/X1	12/31/X1	12/31/X2	12/31/X3	12/31/X4
		$1,000.00	$1,100.00	$1,210.00	$1,331.00
		× 10%	× 10%	× 10%	× 10%
		$ 100.00	$ 110.00	$ 121.00	$ 133.10

Individuals and businesses expect invested money to grow over time. The value of money invested today at some point in the future is called **future value**. The figure above shows how the value of a $1,000.00 investment on January 1, 20X1, at 10% annual interest will grow over time. The future value of $1,000.00 invested today at 10% interest is $1,464.10 in four years.

The interest earned each year is calculated by multiplying the current investment value by the interest rate. The calculation of interest earned in the third year is shown as follows:

Current Investment Value on 12/31/X2	×	Interest Rate	=	Interest Earned in 20X3
$1,210.00	×	10%	=	$121.00

Current Investment Value on 12/31/X2	+	Interest Earned in 20X3	=	Balance on 12/31/X3
$1,210.00	+	$121.00	=	$1,331.00

Each year, the interest earned increases the value of the investment. As the investment value increases, the amount of interest earned each year also increases. Interest earned in the fourth year, $133.10, is greater than the $121.00 interest earned in the third year. Earning interest on previously earned interest is called **compounding**. Compounding interest causes the annual interest earned to increase each year.

Future Value of $1					
	Interest Rate				
Period	4%	6%	8%	10%	12%
1	1.040	1.060	1.080	1.100	1.120
2	1.082	1.124	1.166	1.210	1.254
3	1.125	1.191	1.260	1.331	1.405
4	1.170	1.263	1.361	1.464	1.574
5	1.217	1.338	1.469	1.611	1.762
6	1.265	1.419	1.587	1.772	1.974
7	1.316	1.504	1.714	1.949	2.211
8	1.369	1.594	1.851	2.144	2.476
9	1.423	1.690	1.999	2.358	2.773
10	1.480	1.791	2.159	2.594	3.106
15	1.801	2.397	3.172	4.177	5.474
20	2.191	3.207	4.661	6.728	9.647

Rather than having to calculate the future value of an amount, tables can be used. This is especially helpful with calculations that go out more than a few years into the future. Notice that the above table is titled "Future Value of $1." The amounts in the tables are known as *future value factors*. This table can be used to determine the future value of any amount by multiplying the amount by the factor at the intersection of the appropriate interest rate and the number of compounding periods.

The formula to calculate the future value of $1,000.00 invested on January 1, 20X1, at 10% for four years is:

Current value	$1,000.00
Future value factor	× 1.464
Future value	$1,464.00

Using the future value of $1 table, the investment will grow to $1,464.00 by December 31, 20X4. The manual calculation, presented on the previous page, shows the future value of this investment to be $1,464.10. The $0.10 difference between the two calculations is due to the rounding of the table factors to three places after the decimal point.

FYI A bank may advertise that its certificates of deposit earn "5% interest compounded annually." Each year, the bank calculates interest earned on 5% of the outstanding account balance and adds this amount to the account. The more often (daily, monthly, or quarterly) interest is compounded, the more quickly the account balance will grow. For example, a $1,000.00 investment at 10% interest compounded semiannually (twice each year) will grow to $1,628.90 in four years—$164.80 more than the $1,464.10 future value illustrated on the previous page.

Careers In Accounting

Deborah Gluzman
Enterprise Resource Planning Project Manager

Deborah Gluzman works for an enterprise resource planning (ERP) consulting firm. ERP is an enterprise-wide system of integrating core business processes. It is achieved through the use of integrated software to manage the business.

As an ERP project manager, Ms. Gluzman works with a company through the entire process of ERP. She begins by developing an ERP plan for the business with which she is working. This involves gaining an understanding of the company's operations, such as production, processing, inventory management, human resources, sales, accounting, and customer support.

Once Ms. Gluzman acquires this information, she develops a proposed enterprise resource plan for the company. This plan will integrate all systems, so that data can be shared with other related functional areas. This usually includes a common database that is shared throughout the enterprise.

If the plan is accepted, the next step is to develop a plan for its implementation. This includes bringing the software onboard and providing the training necessary to operate and implement the software. The plan is then implemented under Ms. Gluzman's supervision. She sets deadlines, assigns responsibilities, and monitors the progress of the implementation to ensure that the plan is fully operational.

The project manager's work does not stop here, however. Ms. Gluzman also works with the company to analyze the ERP system. This includes evaluating and recommending changes to the system as the company's needs change.

Immediately out of college, Ms. Gluzman's first position with the company was as part of the implementation team. As she acquired more experience, she took on more supervisory positions. She now enjoys being a project manager and overseeing the work of the ERP team.

ERP project managers must have excellent communications skills as well as a basic understanding of a broad range of management areas, including technology, accounting, production management, human resources, and customer sales and support.

Salary Range: The average salary for an ERP project manager is $132,140. The range is from $116,500 to $147,000.

Qualifications: Most positions with ERP require a college degree in a related business area. Higher-level positions, such as project manager, also require work experience in enterprise resource planning.

Occupational Outlook: The growth for computer and information systems managers, including ERP project managers, is projected to average 10% to 14% for the period from 2016 to 2026.

Sources: www.onetonline.org; www.salary.com.

Present Value of Money LO9

Present Value of $1					
	Interest Rate				
Period	4%	6%	8%	10%	12%
1	0.962	0.943	0.926	0.909	0.893
2	0.925	0.890	0.857	0.826	0.797
3	0.889	0.840	0.794	0.751	0.712
4	0.855	0.792	0.735	0.683	0.636
5	0.822	0.747	0.681	0.621	0.567
6	0.790	0.705	0.630	0.564	0.507
7	0.760	0.665	0.583	0.513	0.452
8	0.731	0.627	0.540	0.467	0.404
9	0.703	0.592	0.500	0.424	0.361
10	0.676	0.558	0.463	0.386	0.322
15	0.555	0.417	0.315	0.239	0.183
20	0.456	0.312	0.215	0.149	0.104

The current value of a future cash payment or receipt is called a **present value**. At 10% interest, $1,000.00 invested today will be worth $1,464.10 in four years. Therefore, $1,000.00 is the present value of $1,464.10 in four years at 10% interest.

Present value tables enable managers to calculate the present value of any future amount. The amounts in the tables are known as *present value factors*. The present value factor is determined by finding the intersection of the interest rate in the columns and the number of years in the rows. The calculation of the present value of $1,464.10 is shown in the next column.

Projected net cash flows	$1,464.10
Present value factor	× 0.683
Present value	$ 999.98

Again, the slight difference in the amounts is due to the present value factors in the table being rounded to three decimal places. Calculating the present value of $1,464.10 using a rounded present value factor results in a $0.02 rounding error. Such minor rounding errors are acceptable when managers are using present values to make business decisions.

© FREEDOMZ/SHUTTERSTOCK.COM

Future Value of an Annuity LO10

	Future Value of an Annuity of $1				
	Interest Rate				
Period	4%	6%	8%	10%	12%
1	1.000	1.000	1.000	1.000	1.000
2	2.040	2.060	2.080	2.100	2.120
3	3.122	3.184	3.246	3.310	3.374
4	4.247	4.375	4.506	4.641	4.779
5	5.416	5.637	5.867	6.105	6.353
6	6.633	6.975	7.336	7.716	8.115
7	7.898	8.394	8.923	9.487	10.089
8	9.214	9.898	10.637	11.436	12.300
9	10.583	11.491	12.488	13.580	14.776
10	12.006	13.181	14.487	15.937	17.549
15	20.024	23.276	27.152	31.773	37.280
20	29.778	36.786	45.762	57.275	72.052

Some business transactions result in equal net cash flows each year. A series of equal cash flows is called an **annuity**. The future value of an equal series of investments over equal time periods at a given interest rate is called the **future value of an annuity**.

The future value of an annuity of $1 table shown above makes one very important assumption. It assumes that all payments are made at the end of each year. An example would be that a company knows that it will be receiving $1,000.00 at the end of each year, for four years, beginning at the end of the current year. On a timeline, the payments and investments would be:

If the company invests the money when it is received and earns 10% interest on it, how much will be in the investment account immediately after the fourth payment has been deposited?

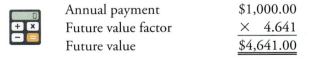

Annual payment	$1,000.00
Future value factor	× 4.641
Future value	$4,641.00

The balance in the investment account immediately after the fourth payment will be $4,641.00.

Present Value of an Annuity LO11

Present Value of an Annuity of $1					
	Interest Rate				
Period	4%	6%	8%	10%	12%
1	0.962	0.943	0.926	0.909	0.893
2	1.886	1.833	1.783	1.736	1.690
3	2.775	2.673	2.577	2.487	2.402
4	3.630	3.465	3.312	3.170	3.037
5	4.452	4.212	3.993	3.791	3.605
6	5.242	4.917	4.623	4.355	4.111
7	6.002	5.582	5.206	4.868	4.564
8	6.733	6.210	5.747	5.335	4.968
9	7.435	6.802	6.247	5.759	5.328
10	8.111	7.360	6.710	6.145	5.650
15	11.118	9.712	8.559	7.606	6.811
20	13.590	11.470	9.818	8.514	7.469

An amount invested at a given interest rate that supports the payments of an annuity is called the **present value of an annuity**. Assume that a company wants to invest enough money at the beginning of the current year so that it earns enough interest to make a payment of $1,000.00 at the end of each year for the next five years.

The present value of an annuity of $1 table shown above makes two important assumptions. The present value is calculated for the beginning of the current year, and the payments will be made at the end of the current year and each following year. On a timeline, the payments and investment would be:

How much money does the company have to invest today (beginning of Year 1), at a 10% interest rate, to withdraw $1,000.00 at the end of each year for five years?

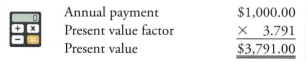

Annual payment	$1,000.00
Present value factor	× 3.791
Present value	$3,791.00

The company must invest $3,791.00 today.

LO7 Explain the time value of money.

LO8 Calculate the future value of an amount.

LO9 Calculate the present value of an amount.

LO10 Calculate the future value of an annuity.

LO11 Calculate the present value of an annuity.

TERMS REVIEW

time value of money

future value

compounding

present value

annuity

future value of an annuity

present value of an annuity

Audit your understanding LO7, 8, 9, 10, 11

1. Explain what is meant by "the time value of money."
2. Why does the amount of interest earned on an investment increase each year?
3. When is the present value of $1 table used?
4. What is an annuity?
5. What table is used to calculate the current value of a series of equal payments over equal time periods?

Work together 18-2 LO8, 9, 10, 11

Calculating future and present values

Forms are provided in the *Working Papers*. Use the tables illustrated in this lesson. Your instructor will guide you through the following examples.

1. Calculate the future value of a one-time $3,000.00 investment in four years at 6%.
2. Calculate the present value of $20,000.00 received in five years at a 4% rate of return.
3. John's grandparents are going to put $1,000.00 in a savings account for John at the end of this year and each following year for a total of 20 deposits. If the savings account earns 8% per year, what will be the balance in the account immediately after the last deposit?
4. Jerry and Laurie Hoffman would like to deposit enough money today to allow their daughter to withdraw $5,000.00 at the end of each year for four years. The investment will earn 4% interest. How much do the Hoffmans have to invest today?

On your own 18-2 LO8, 9, 10, 11

Calculating future and present values

Forms are provided in the *Working Papers*. Use the tables illustrated in this lesson. Work these problems independently.

1. Calculate the future value of a one-time $20,000.00 investment in five years at 10%.
2. Calculate the present value of $80,000.00 received in six years at a 6% rate of return.
3. The Greenstein family is hoping to take a family vacation in five years. They feel they can invest $3,000.00 per year at the end of this year and each of the next four years. If the investment earns 8% interest, how much will be in the account immediately after the last deposit?
4. Congratulations, you won the lottery! The lottery will be paid over 20 years, with a payment of $300,000.00 at the end of each year. You can invest each payment at 6%. What is the present value of the annuity payment?

Long-Term Management Decisions Using Net Present Value

LO12 Use net present value of an annuity to evaluate business decisions.
LO13 Use net present value of unequal cash flows to evaluate business decisions.
LO14 Use net present value to evaluate a lease or buy decision.

Calculating the Net Present Value of an Investment LO12

As a measure of the worth of an investment, managers typically focus on the cash receipts and cash payments connected with the investment. The difference between the cash receipts and cash payments is called the **net cash flows**.

Differential analysis and payback period, discussed earlier in this chapter, are commonly used in making short-term decisions. One shortcoming of differential analysis and payback period, however, is that they do not consider the time value of money. While the time value of money is not critical for short-term decisions, it should be considered when making long-term decisions.

Custom Cyclery Corporation is considering purchasing equipment for $25,000.00. The equipment will enable the company to generate net cash flows of $5,000.00 annually over the equipment's six-year useful life. Management expects assets to yield an 8% rate of return. Using the present value of an annuity of $1 table, the calculation of the present value of an annuity of $5,000 is shown below.

Annual net cash flows	$ 5,000.00
Present value factor	× 4.623
Present value of an annuity	$23,115.00

The difference between the present value of the cash flows of the investment and the amount of the investment is called the **net present value**. The net present value is the amount the business expects to earn above the desired rate of return on the investment. The net present value of the decision to purchase new equipment is calculated below.

Annual net cash flows	$ 5,000.00
Present value factor	× 4.623
Present value of an annuity	$ 23,115.00
Investment	(25,000.00)
Net present value	$ (1,885.00)

The net present value is a negative $1,885.00, and therefore, the investment fails to achieve the desired 8% rate of return.

Should management purchase the equipment? It may appear logical to purchase the equipment, since the net cash flows of $30,000 ($5,000.00 per year multiplied by 6 years) are greater than the cost of the equipment. However, effective managers will not purchase equipment that does not yield a positive net present value. Rather, they will continue to search for alternative uses of the $25,000.00 investment that will achieve the desired rate of return.

Managers may state that a future amount has been "discounted" to the present value.

Calculating the Net Present Value with an Unequal Net Cash Flow LO13

Year	Net Cash Flows		Present Value Factor		Present Value of Net Cash Flow
1	$ 500.00	×	0.926	=	$ 463.00
2	1,500.00	×	0.857	=	1,285.50
3	2,000.00	×	0.794	=	1,588.00
4	2,000.00	×	0.735	=	1,470.00
5	1,500.00	×	0.681	=	1,021.50
6	1,000.00	×	0.630	=	630.00
Present value of net cash flows					$ 6,458.00
Investment					(6,000.00)
Net present value					$ 458.00

Custom Cyclery Corporation is considering purchasing an assembly machine for $6,000.00. The expected net cash flows during the machine's six-year useful life are shown above. Management approves investments only if they earn an 8% rate of return. Since the cash flows are not equal, the present value of an annuity of $1 table cannot be used. Instead, each year's cash flow is discounted using present value factors for 8%.

For example, in Year 1, the first year the assembly machine is used, the net cash flow is estimated to be $500.00. The present value factor for this year is one period at 8%—0.926. The next net cash flow will be for two periods. The sum of the present values for each year is the total present value of the investment.

The investment in the assembly machine is expected to earn a net present value of $458.00. Custom Cyclery should invest in the machine because the net present value is positive. The discounted cash flows exceed the desired 8% rate of return.

THINK LIKE AN ACCOUNTANT

Evaluating Projects with the Internal Rate of Return

Power Contractors, Inc. (PCI), specializes in providing the cranes used in the construction of gas-fired power plants. PCI custom designs and builds each crane based on the needs of the customer and the physical constraints of the project, such as space restrictions, uneven terrain, and harsh weather. Because the cranes are only used at various stages of the project, PCI's contracts provide for unequal payments at specific dates. The amount of each payment is based on the time the crane is used and the complexity of the work at each state of construction. For example, PCI often receives 10% of the total contract price at the end of the second month when the foundation work is complete.

An alternative method for evaluating the profitability of a project is the internal rate of return. The method determines the rate of return of a series of cash flows that will yield a net present value of zero. PCI's management requires that projects earn a minimum internal rate of return of 10%.

OPEN THE SPREADSHEET TLA_CH18

The workbook contains the cost estimates and proposed payments of a contract proposal being submitted to a power company. Follow the steps on the Instructions tab to calculate the internal rate of return for the proposal. Answer these questions:

1. What are the rate of return and the total payments of the project as it is currently proposed?

2. After receiving the proposal, the power company is demanding a 3% reduction in the total project cost. Modify the proposal to increase the amount of early payments and reduce later payments, maintaining a minimum 10% rate of return. What are the rate of return and total payments of the revised project?

3. Compare the increase in the early stage payments relative to the later stage projects.

Lease or Buy Decision LO14

Custom Cyclery would like to acquire a new machine which will increase net income $50,000 per year. It is considering buying or leasing the machine. Additional expenses for repairs and maintenance of the machine will average $3,000.00 per year.

If purchased, the price of the machine is $200,000.00. Custom Cyclery will pay $50,000.00 down and issue $150,000.00 of five-year, 10% bonds. The company will only use the machine for five years, although its useful life is 7 years. After five years, Custom Cyclery will sell the machine at its estimated value of $40,000.00.

Straight-line depreciation will be used to depreciate the machine. Custom Cyclery's tax rate is 21%, and it uses 6% in present value calculations.

If Custom Cyclery leases the machine, lease payments of $45,000.00 are due at the end of each of five years. In order to analyze this decision, Custom Cyclery will need to calculate the net present value of the cash flows connected with buying the machine and leasing the machine. The alternative with the higher positive (or lower negative) net present value of cash flows is the better choice.

Cash Flows for Buying Option

Buy the machinery:

	Now	Years 1–5	Year 5
Down payment	$(50,000.00)		
Bond interest, net of tax savings		$(11,850.00)	
Tax savings due to depreciation		6,720.00	
Retirement of bonds			$(150,000.00)
Sale of asset			40,000.00
Net cash flows	$(50,000.00)	$ (5,130.00)	$(110,000.00)

The cash flows from the buying option are listed above. The down payment (−$50,000.00) must be paid when the machine is purchased. At the end of Years 1 through 5, Custom Cyclery will have cash flows connected with the payment of interest on the bonds (−$11,850.00) and with depreciation (+$6,720.00), which are explained more fully below. At the end of Year 5, Custom Cyclery will repay the bond (−$150,000.00) and sell the machine (+$40,000.00).

The additional net income and the additional repair and maintenance expenses will be generated whether the machine is bought or leased. Therefore, these costs are not relevant to the decision and are excluded from the calculation of net cash flows for both options.

The annual interest paid on the bond is $15,000.00 ($150,000.00 × 10%). Bond interest is a tax-deductible

expense. The $15,000.00 interest payment will cause a tax savings of $3,150.00 ($15,000.00 × 21%). Therefore, the net cash flow from the interest payment is only $11,850.00 ($15,000.00 − $3,150.00).

Even though depreciation expense does not cause a cash flow, the tax savings as a result of depreciation does affect cash flows. Annual depreciation on the machine is $32,000.00 [($200,000.00 − $40,000.00) ÷ 5]. Depreciation expense of $32,000.00 per year saves Custom Cyclery $6,720.00 ($32,000.00 × 21%) in taxes each year. Therefore, the net cash flow effect from depreciation expense is a *positive (inflow)* of $6,720.00.

The net present value of the net cash flows connected with buying the machine is calculated as shown below.

Year	Net Cash Flows		Present Value of $1 Factor	Present Value of an Annuity Factor		Present Value of Net Cash Flow
0	$ (50,000.00)	×	1.000		=	$ (50,000.00)
1–5	(5,130.00)	×		4.212	=	(21,607.56)
5	(110,000.00)	×	0.747		=	(82,170.00)
Present value of net cash flows						$(153,777.56)

The $50,000.00 down payment, paid immediately, has a present value of $50,000.00. The net cash flows in Years 1 through 5 are equal payments, multiplied by the present value of an annuity factor of 4.212 (5 years, 6%). The cash flows connected with retiring the bonds and

selling the machine is a single cash flow, multiplied by the present value of $1 factor of 0.747 (5 years, 6%). The present values are added together for a total of −$153,777.56 as the present value of the net cash flows for buying the machine.

Cash Flows for Leasing Option

Lease the machinery:

	Now	Years 1–5	Year 5
Lease payment, net of tax		$(35,550.00)	
Net cash flows	$—	$(35,550.00)	$—

There is only one cash flow connected with leasing the machine, the $45,000.00 annual lease payment. However, since the lease payment is a tax-deductible expense, it will cause a tax savings of $9,450.00 ($45,000.00 × 21%). Therefore, the net cash flow connected with the lease payment is $35,550.00 ($45,000.00 − $9,450.00).

The net present value of the net cash flows connected with leasing the machine is calculated as shown below.

Year	Net Cash Flows	Present Value Factor	Present Value of an Annuity Factor	Present Value of Net Cash Flow
1–5	$(35,550.00) ×		4.212 =	$(149,736.60)
Present value of net cash flows				$(149,736.60)

The net cash flows in Years 1 through 5 are equal payments, multiplied by the present value of an annuity factor of 4.212 (5 years, 6%). The present value of net cash flows for leasing the machine is −$149,736.60.

Since the present value of the net cash flows for leasing is a lower negative value than that for buying, Custom Cyclery should lease the machine.

Costs of Lost Productivity

Lowering direct labor costs is a necessity for thriving in any economic environment. Cross training, job sharing, the use of robots, and cutting the standard workweek are all efforts that companies are implementing to reduce labor costs.

Absenteeism costs billions of dollars per year due to wages paid to absent employees, to replacement workers, and to those who train the replacement workers. Longer production times, poor quality of goods caused by understaffing, safety issues, and employee error, as well as poor morale, add to the indirect and invisible costs of labor.

ACTIVITIES

1. An estimate of the cost of turnover for hourly employees is 25% of their annual salaries. Assume that you own a small clothing boutique.

Calculate the cost of turnover for each of the following employees who leave your company. The yearly salary is based on the employee being paid for working 40 hours per week, 50 weeks per year.

a. Anthony makes $10 per hour. Calculate the cost of turnover if Anthony leaves abruptly without giving notice.

b. Shannon makes $20 per hour. Calculate the cost of turnover if Shannon leaves for another position in her field, after she gives a 2-week notice.

2. Clement earns $4,000 per month, based on working 220 days per year. He was absent 7 days this year, but he was paid because he used sick time. How much did his 7 absences cost the company in lost productivity?

TERMS REVIEW

net cash flows

net present value

Audit your understanding LO12, 13, 14

1. Why is net present value used for long-term decisions?
2. If the cash flows from an investment are equal and occur at the end of each year, which present value table is used to determine a factor?
3. If the cash flows from an investment are unequal and occur at the end of each year, which present value table is used to determine a factor?
4. When using net present value to decide whether to lease or buy equipment, which option is the better choice?

Work together 18-3 LO13, 14

Using net present value to make business decisions

Forms are provided in the *Working Papers*. Your instructor will guide you through the following examples.

1. Robshaw Corporation is considering the purchase of equipment costing $30,000.00 that will have a six-year useful life. Projected net cash flows from the investment are shown below. Determine the net present value of the investment, assuming a rate of return of 10%. Should the company purchase the equipment?

Year	Cash Flows
1	$ 1,000.00
2	8,000.00
3	13,000.00
4	15,000.00
5	6,000.00
6	6,000.00

2. Spring Grove Corporation must replace a machine in its production facility. If purchased, the price of the machine is $150,000.00, which will be paid in cash. The machine will be used for 4 years, after which it will be sold for $20,000.00. Spring Grove uses straight-line depreciation, and its tax rate is 21%. If Spring Grove leases the machine, lease payments of $37,000.00 would be due at the end of each of four years. Spring Grove uses 4% in present value calculations. Should Spring Grove buy or lease the machine?

On your own 18-3 LO12, 14

Using net present value to make business decisions

Forms are provided in the *Working Papers*. Work these problems independently.

1. Cedar Corporation is considering purchasing equipment for $38,000.00. The equipment will enable the company to generate net cash flows of $8,000.00 annually over the equipment's five-year useful life. Management expects assets to yield a 6% rate of return. Should the company purchase the equipment?
2. Cedar Corporation must replace a machine. If purchased, the price of the machine is $250,000.00, which will be paid in cash. The machine will be used for 5 years, after which it will be sold for $25,000.00. Cedar uses straight-line depreciation, and its tax rate is 21%. If Cedar leases the machine, lease payments of $37,000.00 would be due at the end of each of five years. Cedar uses 6% in present value calculations. Should Cedar buy or lease the machine?

CHAPTER SUMMARY

Good decision making is critical for the success of a business. Some decisions have short-term effects, and some will affect the net income of the company for many years. Differential analysis helps simplify decision making by eliminating those revenues and expenses that are the same for all options being analyzed. Those revenues and costs that are different between options are said to be relevant to the decision and are included in the analysis.

In differential analysis, allocated fixed costs should be examined carefully. Some parts of allocated fixed costs are avoidable, meaning that they will go away if one of the options is chosen. Some parts of allocated fixed costs will remain, regardless of the decision made. Allocated fixed costs that will not go away will need to be allocated among the remaining units.

The time value of money should be considered when making long-term decisions. The timing of payments or receipts of cash are affected by the interest that can be earned. The value of an amount today is less than the value of an amount to be received three years in the future because money received today can be invested to grow to a higher amount in three years. The amount of the growth depends on the interest the investment can be expected to earn. Tables can assist in calculating present and future values.

Net present value calculations take into account the time value of money. The cash inflows and outflows of various investment options are determined, and the net cash flows are used to calculate the total net present value of the flows. The investment option with the higher positive (or lower negative) net present value is the better option.

The Power of Compounding

Investing early in your life enables the power of compounding interest to increase your investment portfolio. Consider the example of two individuals: Sally Early and Jim Late. Sally began investing $1,000.00 every year, beginning at the age of 18. For many years, this was a struggle for her as she paid for college, started her career, established a home, and raised her children. Jim did not begin investing until he was 48, after his children were out of college. But Jim believed he could catch up by investing $4,000.00 annually.

By age 58, both Sally and Jim had invested $40,000 and were beginning to think about retirement. How well will their investments support their retirement? The graph compares how their investment portfolios grew over the 40 years.

At 8% interest, Sally's portfolio has grown to $279,781, whereas Jim's portfolio is only $62,581.95. Why is there such a significant difference? Because of the power of compounding, money earning 8% interest will double every 9 years. That means that Sally's first $1,000.00 investment at age 18 doubled to $2,000.00 by age 27, $4,000.00 by age 36, $8,000.00 by age 45, and $16,000.00 by age 54. The original $1,000.00 will reach $32,000.00 by age 63.

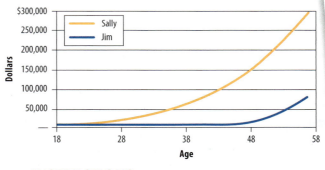

INSTRUCTIONS

Using an electronic spreadsheet, create a schedule to calculate the future value of annual investments. The headings and formulas for the first two years are shown below.

	A	B	C	D	E	F
1	Age	Investment	Balance on January 1	Interest Rate	Interest Earned	Balance on December 31
2	18	1,000.00	=+B2	0.06	=+C2*D2	=+C2+E2
3	=+A2+1	=+B2	=+B3+F2	=+D2	=+C3*D3	=+C3+E3

Copy the Year 2 formulas for the remaining years. Change the age in A2, annual investment in B2, and interest rate in D2 to develop a realistic plan that will guide you toward saving $1,000,000 for your retirement.

APPLY YOUR UNDERSTANDING

INSTRUCTIONS: Download problem instructions for Excel from the textbook companion website at www.C21accounting.com.

18-1.1 Application Problem — Calculations for a make or buy decision LO2

Clarksville Corporation is considering making a component part that it has been buying for $220,000.00 from an outside supplier. No new machinery will need to be purchased, and Clarksville has idle machines that have no other use. Costs to make the part include: direct materials, $75,000.00; direct labor, $90,000.00; and variable overhead, $45,000.00. In addition, total fixed overhead costs for this part are $48,000. Variable overhead is directly related to making the part and will not exist if Clarksville continues to buy it. Fixed overhead includes $18,000.00 of costs that are directly related to buying the part. The remaining fixed costs are allocated to each product made by Clarksville. If Clarksville continues to buy the part, these costs will remain and will be allocated to other products.

Instructions:

Forms are provided in the *Working Papers*. Should Clarksville make the part or continue buying it?

18-1.2 Application Problem — Calculating relevant costs for a special order LO3

Worldwide Manufacturing, Inc., makes and sells suitcases. A particular model sells for $150.00. It is considering accepting a special order by a customer who offered to pay $125.00 per unit. Worldwide has determined that the variable costs for each suitcase are: direct materials, $40.00; direct labor, $45.00; and variable overhead, $10.00. Variable overhead includes $2.50 for commissions and selling expenses, which will not be incurred for this special order. A special emblem will be added to each suitcase at a cost of $0.25. At its normal level of production, fixed costs per unit are $38.00. These fixed costs will remain the same whether the order is accepted or not.

Instructions:

Should Worldwide accept the special order?

18-1.3 Application Problem — Calculating relevant costs for a decision to discontinue a segment LO4

Pierson, Inc., sells women's and men's clothing. It is considering dropping its line of men's clothing and has compiled the following data:

	Women's Clothing	Men's Clothing	Total Company
Sales	$210,000.00	$100,000.00	$310,000.00
Variable expenses	60,500.00	67,500.00	128,000.00
Contribution margin	$149,500.00	$ 32,500.00	$182,000.00
Fixed costs	65,000.00	35,000.00	100,000.00
Operating income	$ 84,500.00	$ (2,500.00)	$ 82,000.00

Further analysis shows that $7,500.00 of the fixed costs for men's clothing is allocated. If the Men's Clothing Department is discontinued, these costs will remain and be allocated to the Women's Clothing Department. The remaining $27,500.00 will be eliminated if the Men's Clothing Department is discontinued.

Instructions:

Should the department be discontinued?

18-1.4 Application Problem — Calculating relevant costs for a sell or process further decision LO5

Kato Cotton Corporation gets raw cotton and processes it into cotton material. It can sell the material or process it further into bed sheets. Kato can sell 100 yards of material for $300.00. It can use those 100 yards of material to make 40 bed sheets, which it can sell for a total of $800.00. The cost to process cotton into 100 yards of material is $200.00. Processing the material further into bed sheets costs an additional $550.00.

Instructions:

Should Kato sell the material or process it further?

18-2 Application Problem — Calculating future and present values LO8, 9, 10, 11

Forms are provided in the *Working Papers*. Use the tables illustrated in this lesson.

Instructions:

1. Calculate the future value of a one-time $5,000.00 investment in 10 years at 12%.
2. You won a contest and can choose between collecting $65,000.00 today or $100,000.00 five years from now. Current interest rates for a similar investment are 10%. Which option has the higher present value?
3. Sherry Greenstein is saving money for a down payment on a house. She can deposit $5,000.00 per year at the end of this year and each of the following 9 years. If her investment account earns 6% interest, how much will be in the account immediately after the last deposit?
4. You are selling a machine. You have received an offer to buy the machine and receive seven equal annual payments of $6,500.00, beginning one year from now. Assume an interest rate of 8%. What is the present value of this offer?

18-3 Application Problem — Using net present value to make business decisions LO12, 13, 14

Fireside Company is considering the purchase of several assets. You have been asked to analyze the following alternatives independently of each other. Forms are provided in the *Working Papers*.

Instructions:

1. Purchase installation equipment for $45,000.00. The equipment will enable the company to generate net cash flows of $9,000.00 annually over the equipment's six-year useful life. Management expects assets to yield a 4% rate of return. Should the company purchase the equipment?
2. Purchase a truck costing $21,000.00. The truck will have a five-year useful life. Projected net cash flows from the investment are shown below. Determine the net present value of the investment, assuming a rate of return of 4%. Should the company purchase the equipment?

Year	Cash Flows
1	$2,000.00
2	4,000.00
3	6,000.00
4	4,000.00
5	7,000.00

3. Fireside must replace a machine in its production facility. If purchased, the price of the machine is $400,000.00. Fireside will pay $5,000.00 down and issue $395,000.00 of five-year, 6% bonds. The machine will be used for five years, after which it will be sold for its estimated value of $275,000.00. Fireside uses straight-line depreciation, and its tax rate is 21%. If Fireside leases the machine, lease payments of $50,000.00 would be due at the end of each of five years. Fireside uses 4% in present value calculations. Should Fireside buy or lease the machine?

1. Calculate the net present value of each potential purchase.
2. Print the worksheet.

Clinton Company is evaluating the purchase of equipment from two vendors. Differences in the technology and labor requirements to operate the equipment of each vendor affect the projected net cash flows. The equipment purchased from Abbott Industries would cost $97,250.00 and is projected to generate total net cash flows of $168,000.00. The equipment from Costello Manufacturing would cost $135,200.00 and is projected to generate net cash flows totaling $235,000.00. The net cash flows for each year follow.

Year	Abbott Industries	Costello Manufacturing
1	$30,000.00	$10,000.00
2	28,000.00	20,000.00
3	26,000.00	30,000.00
4	24,000.00	40,000.00
5	22,000.00	50,000.00
6	20,000.00	60,000.00
7	18,000.00	25,000.00

Instructions:

1. Assuming that Clinton Company wants to earn a 12% rate of return, calculate the net present value of each equipment purchase.

2. Would you purchase the equipment and, if so, from which vendor?

1. Calculate the net present value of the equipment purchase from each company.
2. Print the worksheet.

Lee Foods processes beef into ground beef. It can sell the regular ground beef or process it further into lean or extra-lean ground beef. Lee Foods can sell 10 pounds of regular ground beef for $15.00. The same amount of regular ground beef can be processed into 8 pounds of lean ground beef, which can be sold for $3.00 per pound or into 7 pounds of extra-lean ground beef, which can be sold for $4.00 per pound. The cost to process 10 pounds of regular ground beef into 8 pounds of lean ground beef is $1.00 per pound. The cost to process 10 pounds of regular ground beef into 7 pounds of extra-lean ground beef is $2.00 per pound.

Instructions:

Should Lee Foods sell regular ground beef, lean ground beef, or extra-lean ground beef?

21st Century Skills

Making Green by Going Green

Theme: Financial, Economic, Business, and Entrepreneurial and Environmental Literacy

Skills: Creative Thinking and Problem Solving

Many entrepreneurs are looking for business opportunities that help preserve environmental quality. Organic foods, alternative energy, energy efficiency, and green products and services are examples of business opportunities in an industry that is taking steps to protect our natural resources.

PARTNERSHIP FOR
21ST CENTURY SKILLS

Green transportation is growing around the world in an effort to reduce carbon emissions. Many U.S. cities and college campuses are offering bike sharing as an alternative form of transportation. Traditional automobiles not only release greenhouse gases into the atmosphere, but also create smog, which can affect overall public health.

APPLICATION

Assume you are going to start your own bike-share business, which will enhance your local school or community and will impact the environment positively. Your business will also provide bike repair services.

1. What would be the major costs of your business? Classify the costs as direct materials, direct labor, factory overhead, and selling and administrative expenses (if applicable).

2. Create a job cost sheet that includes estimates of the costs of serving one of your customers in bike rental or repair. What amount would you need to charge to cover all the costs for the service and make a profit for yourself?

Auditing for Errors   LO11

Bachmann Corporation has the opportunity to purchase new machinery that will save the company $24,000.00 per year in manufacturing costs. The $124,000.00 of machinery is expected to be useful for 8 years, after which it could be sold for $5,000.00. The company requires an 8% return on investments. Eduardo Lopez, an accountant, prepared the following analysis and concluded that the company should purchase the equipment.

	Cash Flows	Present Value Factors	Present Values
Annual savings	$24,000.00	5.747	$ 137,928.00
Salvage value	5,000.00	0.540	2,700.00
Total present value			$ 140,628.00
Investment			(124,000.00)
Net present value			$ 16,628.00

Evaluate Eduardo's analysis to determine whether it is accurate. Did Eduardo make the correct decision?

Analyzing Home Depot's Financial Statements

Numerous accounting principles require companies to discount future cash flows when estimating amounts that are reported on financial statements. For example, the present value of a $10,000 account receivable expected to be collected in two years should be reported on the balance sheet as $8,570, assuming an 8% discount rate.

Accounting principles require companies to write down the value of plant assets if the fair value of the assets is less than the recorded book value. When establishing these principles, the Financial Accounting Standards Board (FASB) considered how present value should be applied to this situation. Home Depot presents its application of the FASB rules in the section Property and Equipment, including Capitalized Lease Assets of Note 1 on page B-11 in Appendix B of this text.

1. Does the FASB require Home Depot to discount future cash flows related to asset impairment? Support your answer.

2. Did Home Depot write down any plant assets during the period 2016 to 2017?

Process Costing, Activity-Based Costing, and Product Pricing

LEARNING OBJECTIVES

After studying Chapter 19, in addition to defining key terms, you will be able to:

LO1 Compare job order costing and process costing.

LO2 Calculate equivalent units of production.

LO3 Journalize the transfer of costs in a process costing system.

LO4 Describe a cost of production report.

LO5 Identify problems associated with the traditional method of allocating overhead.

LO6 Use activity-based costing to allocate overhead costs.

LO7 Compare traditional and activity-based methods of allocating overhead.

LO8 Use cost-based pricing to calculate the price of a product.

LO9 Use target costing to calculate the cost of a product.

© PJ AUN/SHUTTERSTOCK.COM

General Mills

ACCOUNTING IN THE REAL WORLD

To help support education, many students and schools across the nation have participated in a program called Box Tops for Education. The program started in 1996 as a test program in California. Special box tops were printed on a few Big G (General Mills) cereals, and each box top was worth ten cents for the school. You may remember cutting out the box top from Cheerios or Lucky Charms.

The program was quickly considered a success and was launched across the nation. Box Tops for Education coupons began appearing on many more General Mills products, and within eight years more than $100 million was raised by over 82,000 schools. But the program did not stop growing there.

Non-food items, including Ziploc, Kleenex, and Scott products, have been added to the Box Tops for Education family. The program has also kept up with technology and offers bonus points via the Box Tops for Education Bonus App, online sweepstakes, email registration, receipt scanning, and retailer loyalty programs. Each organization can earn up to $20,000 per year from the regular box top clipping program. Additional money can be earned through eBox Tops or Bonus Box Tops. The Box Tops for Education website currently states that "American schools have earned over $868 million and you can find Box Tops on hundreds of products throughout the grocery store and online."

The Box Tops for Education program is sponsored by General Mills, a multinational food producer. General Mills produces a variety of popular brands including Old El Paso, Hamburger Helper, Betty Crocker, Pillsbury, Yoplait, and Häagen-Dazs. The company has roots that go back over 150 years to the banks of the Mississippi River in Minneapolis, Minnesota, where Cadwallader Washburn built the largest flour mill west of Buffalo, New York. The mill was referred to as "Washburn's Folly" because it was thought that it could produce more flour than could ever be sold. That thinking was incorrect. General Mills still produces flour and had net sales of over $15.7 billion in the fiscal year that ended May 27, 2018.

Sources: www.generalmills.com; www.boxtops4education.com.

CRITICAL THINKING

1. Job order costing was introduced in Chapter 17. Think about the manufacturing process for General Mills' Cheerios. What is different about processing Cheerios that makes job order costing inappropriate for tracking its manufacturing costs?

2. What are two advantages of the Box Tops for Education program to General Mills?

KEY TERMS

equivalent units of production (EUP)	activity-based costing (ABC)	facility-sustaining level costs	activity rate
	unit-level costs		cost-based pricing
conversion costs	batch-level costs	cost pool	value-based pricing
cost of production report	product-level costs	cost driver	target costing

19-1

Process Costing

LO1 Compare job order costing and process costing.
LO2 Calculate equivalent units of production.
LO3 Journalize the transfer of costs in a process costing system.
LO4 Describe a cost of production report.

Comparing Job Order Costing and Process Costing LO1

In Chapter 17, Custom Cyclery used a job order costing system to determine the cost of each bicycle produced. Job order costing is used when a company produces individual orders of different products in smaller quantities. In job order costing, the costs for each job are tracked and recorded.

Process costing is used when a single process with a continuous flow of inputs produces the same product. Process costing tracks the costs of the inputs added in each process or department of the facility. Costs are determined and recorded each period for all units produced in that period.

ETHICS IN ACTION

The Bad Pizza

Devon Stewart, an internal auditor for NBD Foods, loves to golf. Neither poor weather nor lack of a playing partner has ever kept Devon from his regular Friday afternoon round of golf. On one particular day, Devon was paired with three other men whom he had never met. As the men played, they shared information about their families and professions.

When Andy Foster, one of the golfers, learned that Devon worked for NBD Foods, he commented that his family used to love its frozen pizzas. "That was until a supreme pizza made the whole family sick. I missed two days of work!" Andy did not

seem distressed over the event and proceeded to sink a 30-foot putt. As the men celebrated, Devon pondered whether he should tell anyone at work about the conversation. After all, there could have been other things that caused Andy's family to get sick. By the time Devon reached the 18th green, he had put Andy's comment out of his mind.

INSTRUCTIONS

Access *The Blue Book*, the code of conduct for Pfizer. Using this code as a guide, determine if Devon's actions were ethical.

Calculating Equivalent Units LO2

Financial statements must be prepared at the end of a fiscal period. **>> App A: Accounting Period Cycle** Preparing these statements can present unique challenges in a process accounting system. Premium Paints, a paint manufacturing company has two process departments, Mixing and Packaging. At Premium Paints, gallons of paint are continuously being produced. Therefore, not all processes will be complete at the end of a month. Gallons of unfinished paint will remain in the system at the end of the month. These units must be accounted for.

No Beginning Balance in Work in Process

The data at the top of the next column are for the month of June for the Mixing Department at Premium Paints.

Units in beginning work in process	0
Units started this period	500,000
Units completed this period	495,000
Units in ending work in process (60% complete)	5,000

How should Premium Paints account for the 5,000 gallons of paint that are still in the Mixing Department at the end of the month? An estimate must be made of how complete these units are. An estimate of the amount of direct materials, direct labor, and overhead that have already been incurred on partially finished units, stated in terms of fully completed units, is called the **equivalent units of production (EUP)**.

Premium Paints calculates EUP as shown:

		Equivalent Units of Production	
	Actual Units	**Direct Materials**	**Conversion Costs**
Beginning WIP	0		
Units started	500,000		
Total units processed	500,000		
Beginning WIP	0	0	0
Units started and completed	495,000	495,000	495,000
Ending WIP (60% complete)	5,000	5,000	3,000
Units accounted for	500,000	500,000	498,000

At Premium Paints, all materials used to produce paint are added at the beginning of the process in the Mixing Department. Therefore, the 5,000 gallons of paint included in the ending work in process in the Mixing Department are 100% complete as to materials. However, these same 5,000 gallons are only 60% complete as to direct labor and overhead. The sum of the costs for direct labor and overhead are called **conversion costs**. At the end of the period, EUP must be calculated separately for direct materials and for conversion costs.

The EUP for direct materials is 5,000 units (5,000 units × 100%). The EUP for conversion cost is 3,000 units (5,000 units × 60%).

In the illustration, total units processed equals units accounted for. These two amounts must always be equal, which verifies that all units put into production are accounted for. In this example, the top calculation shows that 500,000 units must be accounted for. The bottom calculation accounts for the 500,000 units by showing that 495,000 units are complete and 5,000 are still in WIP.

Beginning Balance in Work in Process

In July, the 5,000 units of paint will be completed and more units will be introduced into production. Of the new units started during July, some will remain unfinished at the end of the month. On July 31, Premium Paints will have to calculate EUP again. The following data are for the month of July.

Units in beginning work in process (60% complete)	5,000
Units started this period	480,000
Units completed this period	475,000
Units in ending work in process (30% complete)	10,000

The EUP for July is calculated as follows:

	Actual Units	Equivalent Units of Production	
		Direct Materials	Conversion Costs
Beginning WIP	5,000		
Units started.	480,000		
Total units processed	485,000		
Beginning WIP (60% complete)	5,000	0	2,000
Units started and completed.	470,000	470,000	470,000
Ending WIP (30% complete).	10,000	10,000	3,000
Units accounted for.	485,000	480,000	475,000

The calculation of EUP with a beginning balance in WIP is more challenging. Since the 5,000 units in beginning WIP were 100% complete as to materials, no additional direct materials were added to those units. Therefore, EUP for direct materials is 0. However, conversion costs were added; therefore, an EUP must be calculated. Since the units were 60% complete at the end of June, only 40% (100% − 60%) of conversion costs were added in July to complete the units. The EUP for conversion costs is 2,000 units (5,000 × 40%).

The EUP for the ending WIP for July is calculated in the same manner as the ending WIP for June. The 10,000 units of paint are 100% complete as to materials, so the EUP for direct materials is 10,000 (10,000 units × 100%). These 10,000 units are only 30% complete as to conversion cost, so the EUP for conversion cost is 3,000 (10,000 × 30%). Note that the total units processed, 485,000, equals the units accounted for.

The EUP calculation for the Packaging Department is similar to the EUP calculation for the Mixing Department.

Journalizing the Transfer of Goods LO3

The journal entries for a process costing system are very similar to those for a job order costing system, with one exception. When goods are transferred to the next department, all costs from the former department flow with the product to the next department.

Transfer of Goods from One Department to the Next

How costs are recorded in a Work in Process (WIP) account is different in job order costing and process costing. In job order costing, one WIP account is used. In process costing, a WIP account is used for each department or process. Premium Paints would have a Work in Process—Mixing account and a Work in Process—Packaging account.

		GENERAL JOURNAL				PAGE 6	
	DATE	ACCOUNT TITLE	DOC. NO.	POST. REF.	DEBIT	CREDIT	
22	30	Work in Process—Packaging	M485		100 0 0 0 00		22
23		Work in Process—Mixing				100 0 0 0 00	23
24							24

June 30. Recorded the transfer of goods from the Mixing Department to the Packaging Department, $100,000.00. M485.

Work in Process—Mixing is credited for $100,000.00 to decrease the account. Work in Process—Packaging is debited for $100,000.00 to increase the account. Notice that all costs incurred in the Mixing Department flow with the goods to the Packaging Department.

Transfer of Goods to Finished Goods

	DATE	ACCOUNT TITLE	DOC. NO.	POST. REF.	DEBIT	CREDIT	
24	30	*Finished Goods*	M486		225 0 0 0 00		24
25		*Work in Process—Packaging*				225 0 0 0 00	25
26							26

GENERAL JOURNAL   PAGE 6

At the end of a period, the cost of finished goods is transferred from the final department to the Finished Goods account.

Finished Goods is debited for the total costs of the units produced, $225,000.00. Work in Process—Packaging is credited for $225,000.00.

> **June 30. Recorded the transfer of finished goods out of the Packaging Department, $225,000.00. M486.**

GLOBAL AWARENESS

Repatriation of Profits Earned Abroad

"Repatriation," as it relates to money, is the act of converting foreign currency into the currency of one's own country. For example, when you change a foreign currency back into U.S. dollars, you are repatriating the currency.

Repatriation of profits is a similar concept. The profits earned by U.S. corporations in a foreign country would be subject to U.S. tax, just as though they were earned here.

Under prior U.S. tax law, profits earned by U.S. corporations in foreign countries were not subject to U.S. income taxes if the U.S. company claimed that these profits had been "permanently reinvested" in the foreign country. In addition to the tax effect, this action decreased domestic investment, which resulted in fewer American jobs. An additional negative effect was that the expenses incurred to earn these profits may have been tax deductible. This means that a company could claim the expenses in order to lower its tax liability, but it did not have to claim the income related to those expenses, until the income was repatriated.

The tax law was changed in December 2017. The new law includes a one-time repatriation tax on foreign profits earned prior to 2018. Under the former law, the repatriation tax was 35%. Under the new law, the rate drops to either 8% or 15.5% depending on whether the profit is held as cash or as other assets. Profits earned after 2017 will be taxed by the foreign nation and will usually not be taxed by the U.S.

It is estimated that U.S. companies were holding over $1 trillion in cash overseas. It is felt that the new tax law may encourage companies to bring future foreign profits back to the United States.

CRITICAL THINKING

1. Who benefits the most from the new repatriation tax, and who is hurt the most?

2. Why would the U.S. government encourage U.S. companies to bring foreign profits back to the United States?

Source: Center on Budget and Policy Priorities (www.cbpp.org); Tax Reform–Overseas Cash and Repatriation Implications (www.wellsfargofunds.com).

Cost of Production Report LO4

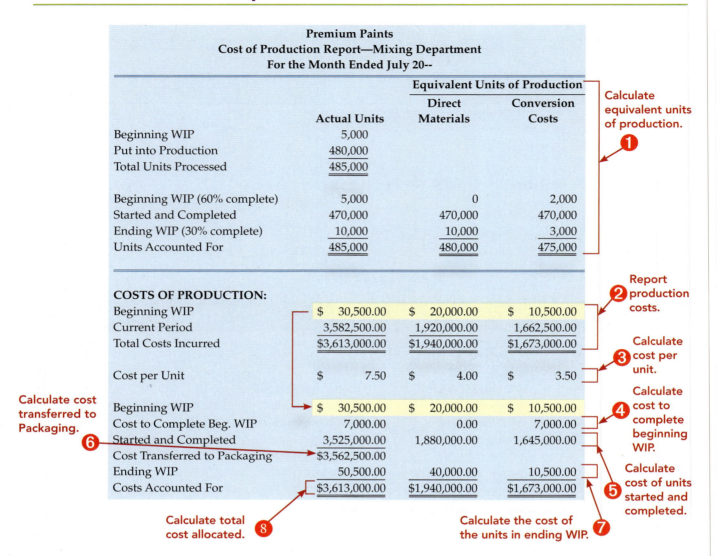

Premium Paints
Cost of Production Report—Mixing Department
For the Month Ended July 20--

| | | Equivalent Units of Production | |
	Actual Units	Direct Materials	Conversion Costs
Beginning WIP	5,000		
Put into Production	480,000		
Total Units Processed	485,000		
Beginning WIP (60% complete)	5,000	0	2,000
Started and Completed	470,000	470,000	470,000
Ending WIP (30% complete)	10,000	10,000	3,000
Units Accounted For	485,000	480,000	475,000
COSTS OF PRODUCTION:			
Beginning WIP	$ 30,500.00	$ 20,000.00	$ 10,500.00
Current Period	3,582,500.00	1,920,000.00	1,662,500.00
Total Costs Incurred	$3,613,000.00	$1,940,000.00	$1,673,000.00
Cost per Unit	$ 7.50	$ 4.00	$ 3.50
Beginning WIP	$ 30,500.00	$ 20,000.00	$ 10,500.00
Cost to Complete Beg. WIP	7,000.00	0.00	7,000.00
Started and Completed	3,525,000.00	1,880,000.00	1,645,000.00
Cost Transferred to Packaging	$3,562,500.00		
Ending WIP	50,500.00	40,000.00	10,500.00
Costs Accounted For	$3,613,000.00	$1,940,000.00	$1,673,000.00

Annotations on the report:
- ① Calculate equivalent units of production.
- ② Report production costs.
- ③ Calculate cost per unit.
- ④ Calculate cost to complete beginning WIP.
- ⑤ Calculate cost of units started and completed.
- ⑥ Calculate cost transferred to Packaging.
- ⑦ Calculate the cost of the units in ending WIP.
- ⑧ Calculate total cost allocated.

A report that shows unit information and cost information for a department using a process costing system is called a **cost of production report**. A cost of production report is completed by each department. The top section of the cost of production report shows actual units and EUP. Calculating EUP is the first section of the cost of production report for the month. The costs incurred in each department must also be calculated so that a per-unit cost can be assigned for each unit produced. The per-unit cost will be used in the journal entry to show the transfer of products from the Mixing Department to the Packaging Department and from the Packaging Department to Finished Goods.

The bottom section of the cost of production report explains the costs incurred by the department and the per-unit cost. The per-unit cost is used to allocate costs to completed units, which are transferred to the next department, and the units remaining in the ending WIP. Notice that the total costs incurred must equal the costs accounted for on this report.

The cost of production report can be prepared using the average cost method or the first-in, first-out (FIFO) method. The difference between the two methods is how the costs of the beginning inventory are treated. The average cost method averages the costs of the beginning inventory with the costs of the units put into production. The FIFO method keeps the costs of the beginning inventory separate from the costs of the units put into production. Only the FIFO method will be discussed here.

❶ Calculate equivalent units of production, as shown on the previous page.

❷ Report and total the production costs. These costs are gathered by the Accounting Department. Premium Paints' production costs for July are Beginning WIP: Direct Materials, $20,000.00, and Conversion Costs, $10,500.00. Current period costs: Direct Materials, $1,920,000.00; Conversion Costs, $1,662,500.00.

❸ In the FIFO method of preparing the cost of production report, the equivalent cost per unit for direct materials is calculated as:

$$\frac{\text{Cost per Unit,}}{\text{Direct Materials}} = \frac{\text{Current Cost of Direct Materials}}{\text{Total Equivalent Units of Production}} = \frac{\$1,920,000.00}{480,000} = \$4.00$$

The cost per unit for conversion is calculated in the same manner:

$$\frac{\text{Cost per Unit,}}{\text{Conversion}} = \frac{\text{Current Cost of Conversion}}{\text{Total Equivalent Units of Production}} = \frac{\$1,662,500.00}{475,000} = \$3.50$$

The total equivalent cost per unit is $7.50 ($4.00 + $3.50).

❹ Steps 4 through 7 will allocate the total costs incurred to either cost transferred to packaging or to ending WIP. All costs must be allocated. The cost transferred to packaging consists of the costs of the beginning WIP units, the costs incurred to complete these units, and the cost of units started and completed this period. Calculate the cost to complete the beginning WIP. Since all the direct materials had already been entered into the ending WIP, the cost to complete these 5,000 units consists only of conversion costs. Completing the 5,000 units, which were 60% complete at the beginning of July, cost $7,000.00 (2,000 EUP × $3.50 cost per unit).

❺ Calculate the cost of the units started and completed in July. The direct materials cost is calculated as:

470,000 EUP × $4.00 direct materials cost per unit = $1,880,000.00.

Conversion costs are calculated as:

470,000 EUP × $3.50 conversion costs per unit = $1,645,000.00

❻ Add the totals for items from Steps 4 through 6 to determine the production costs for the units transferred to the Packaging Department. The total costs, $3,562,500.00, will be debited to WIP—Packaging and credited to WIP—Mixing to remove the costs from the Mixing Department and pass the costs on to the Packaging Department along with the physical units of product.

❼ Calculate the cost of the units in the ending WIP. Direct materials cost is:

10,000 EUP × $4.00 direct materials cost per unit = $40,000.00

Conversion costs are calculated as:

3,000 EUP × $3.50 conversion costs per unit = $10,500.00

❽ Calculate the total cost allocated. This total must equal the total costs incurred, calculated in Step 2 above.

Remember A cost of production report is completed by each department each period. The top section of the report shows actual units and equivalent units of production.

LO1 Compare job order costing and process costing.

LO2 Calculate equivalent units of production.

LO3 Journalize the transfer of costs in a process costing system.

LO4 Describe a cost of production report.

TERMS REVIEW

equivalent units of production (EUP)

conversion costs

cost of production report

Audit your understanding LO1, 2, 3, 4

1. When is process costing used?
2. Why is the equivalent units of production calculation necessary?
3. What accounts are debited and credited to journalize the transfer of goods from the Processing Department to the Shipping Department?
4. What is contained in the first section of the cost of production report?
5. What is contained in the bottom section of the cost of production report?

Work together 19-1 LO2, 3

Calculating equivalent units of production and completing journal entries in process costing

Schnieder Snacks, Inc., produces a variety of flavored potato chips. Schnieder uses a process costing system to record costs. On September 1, Schnieder had 10,000 units of potato chips in the Processing Department. The chips were 90% complete as to direct materials and 35% complete as to conversion costs. The following data were gathered on September 30:

Units started this period	560,000
Units completed this period	555,000
Units in ending work in process (50% complete as to direct materials and 25% complete as to conversion costs)	15,000

Partially completed forms and a blank general journal are provided in the *Working Papers*. Your instructor will guide you through the following examples.

1. Calculate equivalent units of production for the Processing Department for September.
2. Record the following transactions:
   a. Sept. 30. Recorded the transfer of goods from the Processing Department to the Packaging Department, $544,200.00. M666.
   b. Sept. 30. Recorded the transfer of finished goods out of the Packaging Department, $615,000.00. M667.

On your own 19-1 LO2, 3

Calculating equivalent units of production and completing journal entries in process costing

Northstar Industries produces snack-size cupcakes. Northstar uses a process costing system to record costs. On March 1, Northstar had 90,000 units in the Mixing Department. The cupcakes were 40% complete as to direct materials and 30% complete as to conversion costs. The following data were gathered on March 31:

Units started this period	880,000
Units completed this period	870,000
Units in ending work in process (60% complete as to direct materials and 50% complete as to conversion costs)	100,000

Partially completed forms and a blank general journal are provided in the *Working Papers*. Work independently to complete the following problem.

1. Calculate equivalent units of production for the Mixing Department for March.
2. Record the following transactions:
   a. Mar. 31. Recorded the transfer of goods from the Mixing Department to the Baking Department, $850,000.00. M771.
   b. Mar. 31. Recorded the transfer of finished goods out of the Baking Department, $925,000.00. M772.

LO5 Identify problems associated with the traditional method of allocating overhead.
LO6 Use activity-based costing to allocate overhead costs.
LO7 Compare traditional and activity-based methods of allocating overhead.

Issues with Allocating Overhead LO5

Both product costing and process costing methods use a predetermined overhead rate to allocate overhead costs. The predetermined overhead rate is commonly based on a cost element, such as direct labor hours, direct labor costs, or machine hours. These methods of allocating overhead costs are effective when there is a direct connection between the cost element and overhead costs.

Technology improvements may decrease the proportion of direct labor and materials used in production, while, at the same time, increase the proportion of indirect costs. This shift may decrease the effectiveness of using direct materials or direct labor to allocate overhead costs.

Using activity bases may be more effective for allocating factory overhead costs. Allocating factory overhead based on the level of major activities is called **activity-based costing (ABC)**.

Example of Traditional Overhead Allocation

	Simple Product	Complex Product	Total Costs
Quantity	1,900	100	
Direct materials	$15,000.00	$12,000.00	$ 27,000.00
Direct labor	13,000.00	16,000.00	29,000.00
Overhead allocated on machine hours	47,500.00	2,500.00	50,000.00
Total cost	$75,500.00	$30,500.00	$106,000.00
Per unit cost	$ 39.74	$ 305.00	

Assume that Midwest Manufacturing Company produces 1,900 units of Simple Product and 100 units of Complex Product. The factory overhead allocation is based on a predetermined rate of $50.00 per machine hour. Both products require 0.5 machine hour per unit. Therefore, Simple Product uses 950 machine hours and Complex Product uses 50 machine hours. The direct materials, direct labor, and allocated overhead costs are shown above. The total factory overhead costs for Midwest are $50,000.00. Simple Product is allocated $47,500.00 of overhead (950 machine hours × $50.00 per machine hour). Complex Product is allocated $2,500.00 of overhead (50 machine hours × $50.00 per machine hour). Using a traditional method of overhead allocation, Midwest's costs per unit for Simple Product and Complex Product are $39.74 and $305.00, respectively. Simple Product sells for $50.00 per unit, and Complex Product sells for $400.00 per unit.

Midwest has been losing business for Simple Product to its competitors, which are selling a similar product for $30.00 per unit. Midwest's sales of Complex Product are brisk.

Implementing Activity-Based Costing LO6

If Midwest were to use activity-based costing, it would first need to identify the activities that are required to manufacture both products. An analysis of activities reveals that both products require the use of at least one machine. Each machine used requires a setup. Both products require at least one quality test. Complex Product also requires storage between production steps.

Types of Costs

Type of Cost	Examples of Costs
Unit-level	Electricity to run machines, indirect materials, machine and equipment depreciation, storage
Batch-level	Machine setup, ordering materials, quality testing
Product-level	Product design, consumer testing, inventory management, design changes
Facility-sustaining level	Building depreciation, factory supervisor's salary, property taxes, insurance

The costs associated with these activities can be classified into a hierarchy of costs: unit-level, batch-level, product-level, and facility-sustaining level.

Resources used on activities connected with each individual unit produced are called **unit-level costs**. Resources used on activities connected with a group of products are called **batch-level costs**. Resources used to support the entire product line are called **product-level costs**. Resources used to support the entire company and production process are called **facility-sustaining level costs**. Examples of each type of cost are given above.

THINK LIKE AN ACCOUNTANT

Evaluating Production Efficiency

Superior, Inc., manufactures office furniture in six plants. Each style of furniture requires different raw materials, production equipment, and employee skills. Each completed item is inspected for quality. Any item having a flaw is returned to the department for repair, called *rework*. Most reworked items ultimately pass inspection. A small number with problems that cannot be easily corrected are sold as "seconds."

Nothing is currently being done to combine daily production information into a single report. Superior's chief executive officer has asked the Accounting Department to collect production information and provide upper management with daily feedback.

OPEN THE TABLEAU WORKBOOK TLA_CH19

The Tableau workbook TLA_CH19 contains charts that show the production results for all plants. Read the caption above each chart to gain an understanding of the data presented. Use the charts to answer the following questions:

1. Using the Style by Plant worksheet, which are the most and least productive plants?
2. Examine the Style Production worksheet. For which styles did the company appear to require a high level of rework to produce good units?
3. Review the Plant Production worksheets. At what plant and for what style does management need to take action to improve the rate at which good units are produced?
4. Which of the Plant Production worksheets (unscaled or scaled) provides management with better information regarding the extent to which units must be reworked or sold as seconds? Support your answer.

Cost Pools and Cost Drivers

Cost Pool	Cost Driver
Machine setup	Number of machine setups
Machining	Machine hours
Quality testing	Number of tests performed
Storage	Number of times product is stored

A group of costs related to a specific activity is called a **cost pool**. The cost pools for Simple Product and Complex Product are machine setup, machining, quality testing, and storage. All the costs for each pool are gathered together under that pool. Midwest next needs to determine what item most closely affects the costs in the pool.

The factor that affects the cost of an activity is called a **cost driver**. Midwest has found that the cost driver for machine setups is the number of machine setups each product requires. The cost driver for each cost pool is listed in the table above.

Activity Rates

	Total Activity Costs	Simple Product	Complex Product	Totals
Quantity		1,900	100	
Direct materials costs		$15,000.00	$12,000.00	$27,000.00
Direct labor costs		$13,000.00	$16,000.00	$29,000.00
Machine setups	$17,000.00	1	3	4
Machine hours	$5,000.00	950	50	1,000
Testing	$12,000.00	1	2	3
Storage	$16,000.00	0	4	4

The next step is to calculate the estimated total cost of each activity. As the above table illustrates, Manufacturing Company has estimated that the four machine setups will cost a total of $17,000.00. Using the data

for each cost driver, Manufacturing will determine a price for each unit of activity, called an **activity rate**. The activity rate for the machine setup driver is calculated as:

$$\text{Activity Rate} = \frac{\text{Activity Cost}}{\text{Total Activity Useage}} = \frac{\$17,000.00}{4} = \$4,250.00 \text{ per setup}$$

Therefore, for each machine setup required by a product, that product will be allocated $4,250.00. An activity rate must be calculated for each cost driver.

Midwest has calculated the following activity rate for each cost driver:

Cost Driver	Activity Rate
Machine setups	$4,250.00
Machine hours	$ 5.00
Quality testing	$4,000.00
Storage	$4,000.00

Vacations Prevent Lapping

One of the basic controls within an accounting system is the segregation of duties. The duties of having the authority to execute a transaction, the custody of the assets involved, and the responsibility for recording the transaction in the accounting records should be segregated.

Small businesses often find it difficult to segregate these duties. A lack of a sufficient number of staff in the accounting function often requires an individual to perform two or more of these duties. When this lack of segregation exists, other controls can help prevent or detect a fraud.

It may seem funny, but one such control requires employees in control positions to take extended vacations. The logic of this control is that another individual will need to perform the absent employee's duties. Many frauds require constant maintenance. Forcing another individual to perform an employee's duties, even for just two weeks, has a good chance of detecting fraudulent activities. Employees who know they will be unable to maintain a fraud are less likely to commit the fraud.

A fraud in the cash receipts and accounts receivable area that requires constant maintenance is known as *lapping*. This fraud involves the misuse of cash received from sales on account. The cash receipts clerk takes a check and deposits the check in his or her personal account. No entry is made in the customer's account in the accounts receivable ledger. When another check is received, the check is deposited in the company's account, but the first customer's account is credited in the accounts receivable ledger. As more checks are redirected to the clerk's account, the work required to maintain this fraud makes it impossible for the clerk to take an extended vacation.

ACTIVITY

Marshall Corporation provides services to companies involved in oil exploration. All sales are on account, and most customers use checks to submit their payments. Marshall employs two cash receipts clerks. The clerks are responsible for opening the mail, preparing the checks to be deposited, taking the deposits to the bank, and recording the transactions in the accounts receivable subsidiary ledger.

Amanda Stillman has worked for the company for over twenty years and handles payroll duties. Desha Davis has only worked for the company for two years. She is responsible for maintaining the company's extensive investment in plant assets. When either clerk takes an extended vacation, Jonas LaGrange, the accounts payable clerk, substitutes as a cash receipts clerk.

For the first time, Marshall Corporation has hired an accounting firm to perform an audit. Its accounting policy manual clearly states that all accounting personnel are required to take a two-week vacation. While reviewing accounting procedures with employees, a staff auditor learned that Jonas LaGrange had only substituted for Desha Davis. "Amanda has never asked me to substitute for her," he stated. "Maybe someone else took her place?"

In an earlier conversation, Amanda had stated that she did take an extended vacation. Given the inconsistency in the employees' stories, the staff auditor decided to analyze cash receipts records. The analysis would attempt to determine if there are any significant gaps in the dates that each cash receipts clerk processed a cash receipt. A large gap would indicate the clerk took the required extended vacation.

INSTRUCTIONS

Open the spreadsheet FA_CH19 and complete the steps on the Instructions tab. Provide answers to the following questions, supporting your answers.

1. How many rows of data have a large or unusual gap in days?
2. For each flagged row, complete a table with the following information: Date, User ID, Gap in Days, and Explanation. Use the transactions before and after each flagged row to explain the gap in days.
3. Does the evidence suggest either cash receipts clerk is involved in lapping?

Allocating Overhead Costs Using Activity-Based Costing

Activity Pool	Simple Product	Complex Product	Total
Machine setups.....................	$ 4,250.00	$12,750.00	$17,000.00
Machining.........................	4,750.00	250.00	5,000.00
Testing...........................	4,000.00	8,000.00	12,000.00
Storage...........................	0.00	16,000.00	16,000.00
Overhead allocated	$13,000.00	$37,000.00	$50,000.00

Simple Product is allocated $4,250.00 of overhead cost for machine setups ($4,250.00 activity rate × 1 setup). Complex Product is allocated $12,750.00 of overhead cost for machine setups ($4,250.00 × 3 setups). Each

activity pool is calculated in a similar manner. Simple Product is allocated $13,000.00 of total overhead, and Complex Product is allocated $37,000.00 of total overhead.

Calculating Total Product Cost Using Activity-Based Costing

	Simple Product	Complex Product	Total Costs
Quantity	1,900	100	
Direct materials	$15,000.00	$12,000.00	$ 27,000.00
Direct labor	13,000.00	16,000.00	29,000.00
Overhead allocated	13,000.00	37,000.00	50,000.00
Total cost	$41,000.00	$65,000.00	$106,000.00
Per-unit cost	$ 21.58	$ 650.00	

The total cost of each product is the sum of the direct materials, direct labor, and allocated overhead for that product. The cost per unit for each product can

also be calculated: for Simple Product, $21.58, and for Complex Product, $650.00.

Comparison of Traditional and Activity-Based Methods of Allocating Overhead LO7

	Simple Product	Complex Product
Per-unit cost, traditional method	$39.74	$305.00
Per-unit cost, ABC method	21.58	650.00
Current selling price	50.00	400.00

When Midwest Manufacturing Company used the traditional method of overhead allocation, it overestimated its production costs for Simple Product and underestimated its production costs for Complex Product. This could be the reason that it has been losing sales of Simple Product to its competitors, who are charging $30.00 for a similar product. In addition, according to the

ABC method, Midwest is selling each unit of Complex Product for less than its cost.

How does Midwest determine which costing method to use? It should use the method that more accurately reflects the actual cost of each product. This is determined by finding the method that most closely matches actual overhead costs with the activity that causes those costs.

FYI Activity-based costing works equally well in service businesses and in companies that sell products.

Advantages and Disadvantages of Activity-Based Costing

Activity-based costing offers several advantages over other costing methods. One advantage is that once activities are identified and a cost for each activity is determined, the company can use this information to identify inefficient activities. A high-cost activity is a good candidate for reducing costs by simplifying the activity. Nonessential activities can be minimized or eliminated.

If there is a strong relationship between cost pools and cost drivers, ABC can ensure that the company is accurate in costing its products. It can eliminate the risk of charging too little or too much for its products because of inaccurate costing.

ABC can also be used effectively in service businesses, such as banking and health services. A service business uses ABC in order to determine what it should charge a customer for the service provided. In an online environment, the bank can determine the cost of providing a service online versus using bank personnel to perform the same activity.

A disadvantage of ABC is the initial cost and effort required to implement it. When identifying activities and cost pools, it is important to identify all major activities. However, a company that identifies too many cost pools may make the overall system cumbersome and inefficient. Many companies find it necessary to hire a consultant to implement an ABC system.

ABC does not conform to generally accepted accounting principles (GAAP). Therefore, it cannot be used for external reporting. If a company chooses to use ABC for internal decision-making purposes, it must also track costs by using a method that is in conformity with GAAP.

Not all product costs can be associated with activities. These costs usually relate to higher-order product-level costs and facility-sustaining level costs.

WHY ACCOUNTING?

College Marketing

Marketing is an important part of most business plans. Few industries have the luxury of not having to market to customers. This has not always been true in the marketing of colleges and universities.

In a time when there were more than enough students, a GI bill covering education costs for those serving in the military, and relatively low college costs, universities did not need to have efficient marketing programs to attract as many students as they could enroll. Times have changed.

Marketing is now an essential activity at most institutions of higher learning. College fairs, career fairs, and state fairs are just some of the more traditional places you can find colleges and universities marketing their programs. New methods include technology and social media. Colleges are buying names of students from college testing services such as SAT and ACT, using Snapchat and Instagram, offering virtual tours of campus, and ensuring that their college gets a high listing in Google searches. The colleges take care to make their website mobile friendly, intuitive, and easy to navigate.

How does a college develop a marketing plan and, more importantly, how does a college determine if the plan is effective? Any evaluation of a marketing plan should include the cost of the items within the plan, such as the cost of an actual campus tour versus a virtual tour, or the cost of a visit to a high school by a college recruiter versus a booth at a college fair.

CRITICAL THINKING

What are some of the costs that would be incurred to set up a booth at a college fair?

Source: www.theatlantic.com.

TERMS REVIEW

activity-based costing (ABC)

unit-level costs

batch-level costs

product-level costs

facility-sustaining level costs

cost pool

cost driver

activity rate

Audit your understanding LO5, 6, 7

1. When is it effective to allocate overhead costs on the basis of direct labor hours?
2. What effect might technology have on production costs?
3. Identify the four types of costs in an activity-based costing system.
4. How does a company determine which costing method to use to allocate overhead costs?
5. List two major disadvantages of activity-based costing.

Work together 19-2 LO6

Calculating activity rates and allocating costs

Wilkerson Corporation uses activity-based costing. It bases its activity rates on yearly estimates of cost and activity. The Materials Department has made the following estimates for the current year:

Activity Pool	Cost Driver	Estimated Cost	Estimated Activity
Preparing purchase orders	Number of purchase orders	$ 50,000.00	25,000 purchase orders
Receiving materials	Number of boxes received	100,000.00	100,000 boxes
Storage of materials	Cubic foot per day of storage	10,000.00	50,000 cubic foot storage days
Issuing materials to production	Number of materials requisitions	200,000.00	20,000 requisitions

Forms are provided in the *Working Papers*. Your instructor will guide you through the following examples.

1. Calculate the activity rate for each cost driver.
2. Allocate the materials handling costs for Job No. 455, which requires five purchase orders, 50 boxes of materials received, 100 cubic feet of storage for 25 days, and 3 materials requisitions.

On your own 19-2 LO6

Calculating activity rates and allocating costs

Medford Manufacturing uses activity-based costing. It bases its activity rates on yearly estimates of cost and activity. The Accounting Department has made the following estimates for the current year:

Activity Pool	Cost Driver	Estimated Cost	Estimated Activity
Machine setups	Number of machine setups	$600,000.00	10,000 machine setups
Machine processing	Number of machine hours	200,000.00	50,000 machine hours
Shipping of product	Number of boxes shipped	75,000.00	25,000 boxes shipped

Forms are provided in the *Working Papers*. Work independently to complete the following problem.

1. Calculate the activity rate for each cost driver.
2. Allocate the overhead production costs for Job No. 388, which requires 6 machine setups, 100 machine hours, and 15 boxes shipped.

LO8 Use cost-based pricing to calculate the price of a product.

LO9 Use target costing to calculate the cost of a product.

Cost-Based Product Pricing LO8

The selling price of a product must be high enough to cover all of the costs of the product and administrative expenses of the company. The price must also provide an adequate profit for the capital invested in the company. Varieties of methods are used to set the price of a product or service. A method of establishing a price for a product or service in which a fixed percentage or a fixed sum is added to the cost of the product or service is called **cost-based pricing**. Cost-based pricing is also known as *markup pricing*.

In Chapter 17, Custom Cyclery tracked the total and per-unit cost to produce a model SFM bicycle. The bicycle had production costs of $101.00 per unit. Assuming that Custom Cyclery uses a 50% markup on its product, the selling price of model SFM is calculated as shown below. The total cost, $101.00, is multiplied by the percentage markup, 50%, to obtain the amount of the markup, $50.50. The markup is then added to the cost of the bicycle to obtain the selling price of the bicycle, $151.50.

$$\text{Selling Price} = \text{Total Cost of the Product} + (\text{Total Cost of the Product} \times \text{Percentage Markup})$$
$$= \$101.00 + (\$101.00 \times 50\%)$$
$$= \$151.50$$

Advantages and Disadvantages of Cost-Based Product Pricing

An advantage of the cost-based method of product pricing is that it is easy to calculate and use. Software can calculate the selling price for each product. The markup can be set at any percentage desired by the company. The higher the markup, the greater the company profits.

The cost-based method of product pricing has several disadvantages. It focuses on the company and the company costs, instead of on the customer. It may lead to prices that are too high or too low. Perhaps the biggest disadvantage is that it provides no incentive to keep costs under control. This is especially true if software automatically tracks the cost of the product and calculates the selling price. Management must take measures to monitor costs and selling prices

periodically. Finally, if the costs of the product change and the accounting software does not automatically calculate a new selling price, the profit margin on the product will change.

Percentage Markup Versus Gross Profit Margin

Care should be taken not to confuse the percentage markup with the gross profit margin. The percentage markup will always be greater than the gross profit margin. As shown previously, if the cost of model SFM is $101.00 and the selling price is $151.50, the markup is 50%.

The gross profit margin on model SFM is 33.33%, calculated as shown below. Therefore, when the markup is 50%, the gross profit margin is only 33.33%.

$$\text{Gross Profit Margin} = \frac{\text{Gross Profit}}{\text{Selling Price}} = \frac{\$50.50}{\$151.50} = 33.33\%$$

Differences Between Cost-Based Pricing and Value-Based Pricing

A method of establishing a price for a product or service based on the value the product or service has to its customer is called **value-based pricing**. To use value-based pricing, the company must have a good understanding of its customers and the value the product or service gives to the customer. There is no formula for calculating a value-based price. Value-based pricing is effective in products or services that have emotional value, are in high demand and/or low supply, will increase efficiency or improve health, and where there is little or no competition for a product or service that is necessary. Artwork, pharmaceuticals, and new technology are some examples of industries that may use value-based pricing.

Value-based pricing focuses on the customer instead of the company or the company's costs. In the long term, value-based pricing always results in a higher-priced product than does cost-based pricing. This is because if the value of the product is less than the cost of the product, the company cannot generate a profit by producing and selling the product. Either the cost of the product must be decreased or the company will stop making the product.

Target Costing LO9

A method of establishing a price for a product or service, based on the price the customer is willing to pay and controlling the cost of the product so that the company still makes a profit, is called **target costing**. This method requires that management knows how much their customers are willing to pay for a product and the amount of profit the company requires.

Using the model SFM bicycle and assuming that customers are willing to pay $150.00 for the product and Custom Cyclery expects a 33.33% profit, the target cost of the bicycle is calculated as follows:

	Target Cost per Unit	=	Desired Selling Price per Unit	−	Required Profit per Unit
		=	$150.00	−	$150.00 × 33.33%
	$100.00	=	$150.00	−	$50.00

Target costing indicates that the model SFM bicycle can cost no more than $100.00. At a cost of $100.00, Custom Cyclery can sell the bicycle for $150.00 and earn a $50.00 profit per unit. Since the current cost of model SFM is $101.00, the company will have to investigate the production process and determine how to cut $1.00 off the cost of the bicycle.

Target costing focuses on the price customers are willing to pay and the cost of producing the product, so that the required profit can be achieved on each unit sold. Since this method focuses on a maximum selling price, company management realizes that the only way to increase profit margin is to lower the production costs. Target costing is especially helpful when products are in the design stages. The product developers estimate the selling price and the desired profit. The company can then determine if the product can be produced for the target cost. If the estimated cost of the product is higher than the target cost, design changes can be made more easily at this stage than after production actually begins.

FYI — Value-based pricing can take advantage of emotional issues. How can one put a value on a drug that promises a cure for cancer?

Remember — The percentage markup on a product is not the same as the gross profit margin on the product.

LO8 Use cost-based pricing to calculate the price of a product.

LO9 Use target costing to calculate the cost of a product.

TERMS REVIEW

cost-based pricing

value-based pricing

target costing

Audit your understanding LO8, 9

1. List four disadvantages of cost-based pricing.
2. Name four cases where value-based pricing is effective.
3. What is the formula for calculating target cost?

Work together 19-3 LO8, 9

Calculating cost-based pricing and target costs

Holdger Manufacturing Company makes furniture. Your instructor will guide you through the following examples.

1. The costs and markups for several products are given in the *Working Papers*. For each item, calculate the following:

   a. Dollar amount of markup

   b. Selling price

   c. Profit margin

2. Holdger is in the process of designing an entertainment center. The company believes that the selling price cannot exceed $2,500.00, and it requires a profit of 40% per unit. What is the target cost for the entertainment center?

On your own 19-3 LO8, 9

Calculating cost-based pricing and target costs

Unique Design Company makes jewelry and watches. Work independently to complete the following problem.

1. The costs and markups for several products are given in the *Working Papers*. For each item, calculate the following:

   a. Dollar amount of markup

   b. Selling price

   c. Profit margin

2. Unique Design is in the process of designing an anniversary pendant. The company believes that the selling price cannot exceed $1,800.00, and it requires a profit of 80% per unit. What is the target cost for the pendant?

CHAPTER SUMMARY

Process costing is used when a company produces similar products in a continuous flow of inputs. Costs are recorded for each process for each financial period. Units produced are also measured so that a per-unit cost can be calculated. At the end of each fiscal period, some units of product are only partially completed. In order to include the cost of partially completed units, the company must calculate equivalent units of production for each process or department. The costs of totally and partially completed units are reported for each process or department in a cost of production report. A major difference between process costing and job order costing is that, in process costing, a separate work in process account is used for each process or department.

Activity-based costing is a method of allocating factory overhead costs based on the activities required to produce goods or provide a service. Cost pools and cost drivers are identified. An activity rate is calculated for each activity. This activity rate is used to calculate the overhead to be allocated. An activity-based costing system is expensive to establish, but it may allocate overhead costs more accurately than traditional overhead allocation methods.

A common method for calculating the price of a product is to base the price on the cost of the product. Typically, a specific percentage is used for each group of products. Cost-based pricing is easy to implement. Caution should be used to ensure that the price of a product changes as the costs of that product change. Target costing establishes the price for a product or service, based on the price the customer is willing to pay. It requires the company to control the cost of the product so that the company earns a specific level of profit. This method is most effective if used during the design stage of a product, when costs are more easily controlled.

EXPLORE ACCOUNTING

Responsibility Centers

Accountability is a term used in relation to organizations and people. It means that the person or organization must justify or be responsible for actions taken and decisions made. Assigning control of revenues, costs, and expenses to a specific manager is known as *responsibility accounting*. The unit of the business over which a manager has control is called a *responsibility center*. There are four kinds of responsibility centers: cost centers, revenue centers, profit centers, and investment centers.

A responsibility center in which the manager is only responsible for costs is called a *cost center*. The cost center manager is not responsible for revenues and, in many cases, does not provide a revenue-producing product or service. In most companies, the Accounting Department would be a cost center. It does not bring revenue into the company. Many production departments are also cost centers. Managers of a cost center are held accountable for the costs incurred in the department. Upper management may set quantity and price standards, which are used to evaluate the effectiveness of the cost center.

A responsibility center in which the manager is only responsible for revenues is called a *revenue center*. The revenue center manager is not responsible for costs. A revenue center is usually responsible for selling finished goods or services offered by a company. It may be able to set the selling price, and it is evaluated based on meeting sales goals set by upper management.

A responsibility center in which the manager is responsible for both costs and revenues is called a *profit center*. The profit center manager is not responsible for capital investments purchased by the company, but does have authority in decisions related to costs and revenues. Therefore, a profit center is both a cost center and a revenue center. The profit center manager may be evaluated based on such measures as gross margin, return on sales, and operating margin.

A responsibility center in which the manager is responsible for both the profits of the unit and the investments of the unit is called an *investment center*. In addition to those measures used to evaluate a profit center manager, the investment center manager may also be evaluated on profit margin and return on investments.

INSTRUCTIONS

Identify each of the following business units as a cost, revenue, profit, or investment center:

a. A corporation's subsidiary that is independent and whose manager makes decisions regarding capital investments.

b. Sales Department that is not responsible for costs.

c. Customer Service Department.

d. Bank branch that does not have the authority to make investment decisions.

APPLY YOUR UNDERSTANDING

INSTRUCTIONS: Download problem instructions for Excel, QuickBooks, and Sage 50c from the textbook companion website at www.C21accounting.com.

19-1 Application Problem — Calculating equivalent units of production and completing journal entries in process costing LO2, 3

1. Calculate equivalent units of production to complete the worksheet.
2. Journalize transactions to the general journal.
3. Print the worksheets.

Jutko Corporation produces leather gloves. Jutko uses a process costing system to record costs. On December 1, Jutko had 15,000 gloves in the Cutting Department. The gloves were 80% complete as to direct materials and 40% complete as to conversion costs. The following data were gathered on December 30:

Units started this period	320,000
Units completed this period	325,000
Units in ending work in process (70% complete as to direct materials and 30% complete as to conversion costs)	10,000

Partially completed forms and a blank general journal are provided in the *Working Papers*.

Instructions:

1. Calculate equivalent units of production for the Cutting Department for December.
2. Record the following transactions:
   a. Dec. 31. Recorded the transfer of goods from the Cutting Department to the Stitching Department, $421,500.00. M524.
   b. Dec. 31. Recorded the transfer of finished goods out of the Stitching Department, $734,800.00. M525.

19-2 Application Problem — Calculating activity rates and allocating costs LO6

Regions Corporation uses activity-based costing. It bases its activity rates on yearly estimates of cost and activity. The Production Department has made the following estimates for the current year:

Activity Pool	Cost Driver	Estimated Cost	Estimated Activity
Cutting machine setups	Number of setups	$400,000.00	10,000 setups
Cutting machine usage	Machine minutes	500,000.00	125,000 minutes
Moving	Distance in feet	200,000.00	400,000 boxes
Storage	Cubic foot of storage	440,000.00	2,200,000 cubic feet
Assembly	Number of pieces in one unit	400,000.00	40,000 pieces

Forms are provided in the *Working Papers*.

Instructions:

1. Calculate the activity rate for each cost driver.
2. Allocate the materials handling costs for Job No. 220, which requires three machine setups, 50 minutes of machine usage, 300 feet of moving, 200 cubic feet of storage, and 18 pieces.

TravelRight Corporation makes suitcases. Your instructor will guide you through the following examples.

Instructions:

1. The costs and markups for several products are given in the *Working Papers*. For each item, calculate the following:
   a. Dollar amount of markup
   b. Selling price
   c. Profit margin

2. TravelRight is in the process of designing a protective computer case. The company believes that the selling price cannot exceed $150.00, and it requires a profit of 60% per unit. What is the target cost for the computer case?

19-M Mastery Problem
Calculating equivalent units of production and completing journal entries in process costing LO2, 3, 8, 9

sage 50

1. Journalize and post transactions to the general journal.
2. Print the general journal and trial balance.

QB
Quick Books

1. Journalize and post transactions to the journal.
2. Print the journal and trial balance.

1. Calculate equivalent units of production to complete the worksheet.
2. Journalize transactions to the general journal.
3. Print the worksheets.

Voeller Corporation produces ketchup. Voeller uses a process costing system to record costs. On October 1, Voeller had 18,000 bottles of ketchup in the Processing Department. The bottles were 100% complete as to direct materials and 30% complete as to conversion costs. The following data were gathered on October 31:

Units started this period	620,000
Units completed this period	618,000
Units in ending work in process (100% complete as to direct materials and 60% complete as to conversion costs)	20,000

Partially completed forms and a blank general journal are provided in the *Working Papers*.

Instructions:

1. Calculate equivalent units of production for the Processing Department for October.

2. Record the following transactions:
   a. Oct. 31. Recorded the transfer of goods from the Processing Department to the Bottling Department, $365,000.00. M357.
   b. Oct. 31. Recorded the transfer of goods out of the Bottling Department to the Packaging Department, $398,000. M358.
   c. Oct. 31. Recorded the transfer of finished goods out of the Packaging Department, $420,000. M359.

3. Using the cost information in Instruction 2c, assume that 560,000 bottles of ketchup were transferred to finished goods. If Voeller uses 20% as its percentage of markup, calculate the following per bottle:
   a. Cost
   b. Dollar amount of markup
   c. Selling price
   d. Profit margin

4. Voeller is in the process of developing a Cajun specialty sauce. The company believes that the selling price cannot exceed $3.00, and it requires a profit of 20% per unit. What is the target cost for the specialty sauce?

Memorial Hospital uses activity-based costing. It bases its activity rates on yearly estimates of cost and activity. The Radiology Department has made the following estimates for the current year:

Activity Pool	Cost Driver	Estimated Cost	Estimated Activity
Patient intake processing	Number of intakes	$ 2,500,000.00	25,000 intakes
X-rays	Number of X-rays	750,000.00	10,000 X-rays
CT scan—scans	Number of scans	3,010,000.00	14,000 scans
CT scan—minutes	Length of scan, in minutes	25,000,000.00	250,000 minutes
MRI—images	Number of images	3,750,000.00	15,000 images
MRI—minutes	Length of test, in minutes	17,600,000.00	220,000 minutes

Forms are provided in the *Working Papers.*

Instructions:

1. Calculate the activity rate for each cost driver.
2. Allocate the costs for the following patients:
   a. Patient 03016598: One patient intake; 2 CT scans, total 30 minutes; 1 MRI image, total 15 minutes.
   b. Patient 10415423: One patient intake; 1 X-ray; 3 MRI images, total 40 minutes.

21st Century Skills

Think Like the Customer

Theme: Financial, Economic, Business, and Entrepreneurial Literacy, and Global Awareness

Skills: Critical Thinking and Problem Solving

PARTNERSHIP FOR
21ST CENTURY SKILLS

A common pricing mistake is setting prices simply by marking up costs. While it is easy to implement, this type of pricing does not take into consideration the amount that customers are willing to pay, nor does it evaluate the potential for additional profit. Prices should not be set too high for customers who cannot afford a needed product, or too low for customers willing to pay more for a product's benefits.

Value-based pricing is used in businesses that try to think like the customer to determine how much the products are worth to their customers. Who would be willing to buy? Why is this product unique? What is the next best alternative? Answering these questions can help assess the product's worth to the customer. Attributes that differentiate products include brand, quality, physical attributes, service, ease of purchase, style, and perhaps even timing. An amusement park that sets its umbrella prices when it looks like rain probably understands the value that a customer places on the product. A customer who prefers warm gloves from a department store instead of a thrift store probably values the brand or style more than the practicality of the gloves.

APPLICATION

1. The cost of airline tickets for the week of Thanksgiving is often 100% more than for a different week of November. Describe the value perceived from this pricing strategy.
2. Select a product of your choice. Research the price of the product from three different retailers. Explain the likely pricing strategy used by each of the retailers.
3. List three products that you have purchased recently, realizing that you likely paid a premium based on the value you placed on the product. Explain the value that you gained from purchasing each of these products.
4. List two examples of companies that likely use their brands to add value to price.

Analyzing Home Depot's Financial Statements

Home Depot must determine a price for each item it sells. For the majority of items it sells, Home Depot will use a cost-based pricing method. This chapter identified the difference between gross profit margin and percentage markup.

INSTRUCTIONS

Use Home Depot's Consolidated Statements of Earnings on page B-6 of Appendix B to answer the following questions. Round answers to the nearest 0.0%.

1. Calculate Home Depot's gross profit margin for 2017, 2016, and 2015.
2. Calculate the percentage markup for Home Depot for 2017, 2016, and 2015.

Reinforcement Activity 4

Processing and Analyzing Cost Accounting Data for a Manufacturing Business

This activity reinforces selected learning from Chapters 17 through 19.

Alexandria Corporation

Alexandria Corporation manufactures custom plastic products. The company uses a job order cost accounting system to record manufacturing costs.

Part A: Recording Cost Accounting Activities

In Part A of this activity, Alexandria's daily cost accounting activities for one month will be recorded. Alexandria uses the chart of accounts shown on page 587. The journals and ledgers used by Alexandria are similar to those illustrated in Chapter 17. The job cost sheets, selected general ledger accounts, and other accounting records or forms are provided in the *Working Papers*.

The January 31 general ledger balances have been recorded. These balances are the result of posting completed during January. Note that Accounts Payable has a debit balance for this reason. Also, the balances of the payroll liability accounts are the amounts posted for sales and administrative salaries for January.

INSTRUCTIONS

1. Calculate the factory overhead applied rate based on direct labor costs. The estimated annual factory overhead costs for the current year are $612,000.00. The estimated direct labor hours to be used during the current year are 34,000 hours at an estimated rate of $15.00 per hour.

2. Record the following transactions completed during January of the current year. Recording instructions, when necessary, are provided only for the first occurrence of each kind of transaction. Source documents are abbreviated as follows: check, C; memorandum, M; materials requisition, MR; purchase order, PO; sales invoice, S.

Transactions:

Jan. 3. Opened a cost sheet for Job No. 232, with 250 C200 book racks ordered for stock. Date wanted, January 12.

Jan. 3. Issued direct materials to factory for Job No. 232, $10,200.00. MR750.

Materials list:
    6,000 pounds of resin @ $0.40 per pound
    6,000 pounds of polymer @ $1.20 per pound
    187.5 ounces of dye @ $3.20 per ounce
Record the direct materials in the materials ledger and the cost ledger.

5. Opened a cost sheet for Job No. 233, with 200 P150 shelving units ordered for stock. Date wanted, January 17.

5. Issued direct materials to factory for Job No. 233, $6,800.00. MR751.
Materials list:
    4,000 pounds of resin @ $0.40 per pound
    4,000 pounds of polymer @ $1.20 per pound
    125 ounces of dye @ $3.20 per ounce

5. Ordered 30,000 pounds of resin. PO520.
Record the purchase order in the materials ledger only at this time, so that it is clear the materials have been ordered. Once the materials are received, the transaction will be journalized in the materials purchases journal.

5. Ordered 20,000 pounds of polymer. PO521.

7. Ordered 1,600 connectors. PO522.

7. Issued direct materials to factory for Job No. 232, $2,500.00. MR752.
Materials list:
    1,000 connectors @ $2.50 each

7. Ordered 1,000 sets of hinges. PO523.

7. Recorded weekly summary of time records to the cost ledger.
Job No. 232: $6,600.00
Job No. 233: 2,250.00

7. Ordered 1,000 ounces of dye. PO524.

10. Issued direct materials to factory for Job No. 233, $2,400.00. MR753.
Materials list:
    800 connectors @ $2.50 each
    200 sets of metal glides @ $2.00 per set

10. Ordered 300 sets of metal glides. PO525.

Jan. 10. Sold 100 C200 book racks to Office Mart. S323. Record only the cost in the finished goods ledger. Alexandria uses the first-in, first-out inventory method. Thus, the cost recorded first is the cost removed from inventory first when units are sold.

10. Ordered 1,000 fasteners. PO526.

10. Received at the materials stockroom 20,000 pounds of polymer @ $1.20 per pound. Materials were purchased on account from Palmdale Plastics, $24,000.00. PO521.

Record all receipts of materials in the materials ledger and materials purchases journal.

11. Completed Job No. 232. Interim summary of time records for Job No. 232, $2,775.00. When jobs are completed in the middle of a week, Alexandria makes a special interim summary of time records for these jobs. Therefore, direct labor costs will be complete. Apply factory overhead to job. Use the rate calculated in Instruction 1. Complete the cost sheet. Record the finished goods in the finished goods ledger.

12. Opened a cost sheet for Job No. 234, with 120 E400 inline skate boots ordered for stock. Date wanted, January 18.

12. Issued direct materials to factory for Job No. 234, $10,200.00. MR754.

Materials list:
6,000 pounds of resin @ $0.40 per pound
6,000 pounds of polymer @ $1.20 per pound
187.5 ounces of dye @ $3.20 per pound

12. Received at the materials stockroom 30,000 pounds of resin @ $0.40 per pound. Materials were purchased on account from Woodcrest, Inc., $12,000.00. PO520.

12. Received at the materials stockroom 1,600 connectors @ $2.50 each. Materials were purchased on account from Westmore Corporation, $4,000.00. PO522.

12. Received at the materials stockroom 300 sets of metal glides @ $2.00 per set. Materials were purchased on account from Smythe Company, $600.00. PO525.

14. Opened a cost sheet for Job No. 235, with 150 V110 benches ordered for stock. Date wanted, January 27.

Jan. 14. Issued direct materials to factory for Job No. 235, $4,080.00. MR755.

Materials list:
2,400 pounds of resin @ $0.40 per pound
2,400 pounds of polymer @ $1.20 per pound
75 ounces of dye @ $3.20 per ounce

14. Recorded weekly summary of time records to cost ledger.
Job No. 233: $3,750.00
Job No. 234: 3,600.00
Job No. 235:   450.00

14. Completed Job No. 233.

17. Paid cash for semimonthly factory payroll, $22,257.36 (direct labor, $19,425.00, and indirect labor, $7,935.00, less deductions: employee income tax, $3,009.60; Social Security tax, $1,696.32; Medicare, $396.72. C782.

Record the payroll entry in the cash payments journal. Post the general debit and general credit amounts.

17. Recorded employer factory payroll taxes, $3,734.64, for the semimonthly pay period ended January 15. Taxes owed are Social Security tax, $1,696.32; Medicare, $396.72; federal unemployment tax, $164.16; state unemployment tax, $1,477.44. M308.

Record the entry in the general journal. Post the amounts.

17. Sold 150 P150 shelving units to CompuFurnishings. S324.

18. Issued direct materials to factory for Job No. 234, $840.00. MR756.

Materials list:
240 sets of hinges @ $2.00 per set
240 fasteners @ $1.50 each

18. Opened a cost sheet for Job No. 236, with 200 B160 vertical bookcases ordered for stock. Date wanted, January 28.

18. Issued direct materials to factory for Job No. 236, $13,600.00. MR757.

Materials list:
8,000 pounds of resin @ $0.40 per pound
8,000 pounds of polymer @ $1.20 per pound
250 ounces of dye @ $3.20 per ounce

Jan. 19. Completed Job No. 234. Interim summary of time record for Job No. 234, $3,600.00.

20. Sold 60 T120 serving carts to Office Mart. S325.

21. Issued direct materials to factory for Job No. 235, $1,650.00. MR758.
Materials list:
300 sets of metal glides @ $2.00 per set
300 sets of hinges @ $2.00 per set
300 fasteners @ $1.50 each

21. Received at the materials stockroom 1,000 ounces of dye @ $3.20 per ounce. Materials were purchased on account from Colton Dyes, $3,200.00. PO524.

21. Received at the materials stockroom 1,000 fasteners @ $1.50 each. Materials were purchased on account from Smythe Company, $1,500.00. PO526.

21. Ordered 300 sets of metal glides. PO527.

21. Posted weekly summary of time records to cost ledger.
Job No. 235: $2,250.00
Job No. 236: 4,500.00

24. Ordered 20,000 pounds of polymer. PO528.

24. Received at the materials stockroom 1,000 sets of hinges @ $2.00 per set. Materials were purchased on account from Smythe Company, $2,000.00. PO523.

25. Issued direct materials to factory for Job No. 236, $1,400.00. MR759.
Materials list:
400 sets of hinges @ $2.00 per set
400 fasteners @ $1.50 each

25. Opened a cost sheet for Job No. 237, with 160 T120 serving carts ordered for stock. Date wanted, January 31.

25. Issued direct materials to factory for Job No. 237, $3,808.00. MR760.
Materials list:
2,240 pounds of resin @ $0.40 per pound
2,240 pounds of polymer @ $1.20 per pound
70 ounces of dye @ $3.20 per ounce

26. Sold 90 E400 inline skate boots to BizFurn. S326.

27. Completed Job No. 235. Interim summary of time records for Job No. 235, $1,800.00.

Jan. 27. Sold 200 V110 benches to CompuFurnishings. S327.

28. Issued direct materials to factory for Job No. 237, $1,600.00. MR761.
Materials list:
640 connectors @ $2.50 each

28. Opened a cost sheet for Job No. 238, with 200 C200 book racks ordered for stock. Date wanted, February 8.

28. Issued direct materials to factory for Job No. 238, $8,160.00. MR762.
Materials list:
4,800 pounds of resin @ $0.40 per pound
4,800 pounds of polymer @ $1.20 per pound
150 ounces dye @ $3.20 per ounce

28. Posted weekly summary of job-time records to cost ledger.
Job No. 236: $4,500.00
Job No. 237: 2,880.00
Job No. 238: 1,260.00

28. Completed Job No. 236.

28. Sold 120 B160 bookcases to CompuFurnishings. S328.

31. Received at the materials stockroom 300 metal glides @ $2.00 per set. Materials were purchased on account from Smythe Company, $600.00. PO527.

31. Received at the materials stockroom indirect materials (bolts, screws, and nails). Materials were purchased on account from Greenleaf Manufacturing Supplies, $2,400.00. PO519. (Record indirect materials purchases only in the materials purchases journal.)

31. Posted summary of time records for January 31 to cost ledger.
Job No. 237: $ 720.00
Job No. 238: 1,260.00
(Only Job No. 238 is still in process on January 31.)

31. Sold 200 C200 book racks to Straight Arrow, Inc., S329.

31. Paid cash for semimonthly factory payroll, $26,088.64 (direct labor, $22,770.00, and indirect labor, $9,300.00, less deductions: employee income tax, $3,528.00; Social Security tax, $1,988.34; Medicare tax, $465.02). C856.

Jan. 31. Recorded employer factory payroll taxes, $4,377.56, for the semimonthly pay period ended January 31. Taxes owed are Social Security tax, $1,988.34; Medicare tax, $465.02; federal unemployment tax, $192.42; state unemployment tax, $1,731.78. M345.

Completing Cost Records:

3. In the Summary column with the item description *Factory Overhead for January*, record the factory overhead for the job not completed on January 31 and the explanation of how it was calculated. Apply the factory overhead rate to the direct labor costs recorded on the cost sheet for work in process.

4. Total and rule the materials purchases journal. Post the total. Do not post the individual amounts. The abbreviation for the materials purchases journal is MP.

5. Prove and rule the cash payments journal. Do not post the total of the Cash Credit column.

6. Record the following entries. Continue using page 1 of the general journal. Use January 31 as the date. Post after journalizing each entry.

   a. Transfer the total of all direct materials requisitions to Work in Process and indirect materials to Factory Overhead. The total of all requisitions of direct materials issued during January is $67,238.00. The total of all requisitions of indirect materials issued is $2,362.00. M346.

   b. Close all individual manufacturing expense accounts to Factory Overhead. M347.

   c. Record the applied factory overhead to Work in Process (sum of factory overhead applied to cost sheets for the month). M348.

7. Continue using page 1 of the general journal. Journalize and post the entry to close the balance of the Factory Overhead account to Income Summary. M349.

8. Journalize and post the entry to transfer the total of all cost sheets completed from Work in Process to Finished Goods. M350.

9. Journalize and post the entry to transfer the cost of products sold from Finished Goods to Cost of Goods Sold. The total cost recorded on all sales invoices for January is $122,275.00. M351.

10. Prove the subsidiary ledgers as follows:

    a. Add the ending balances in the materials ledger. The ending balance of the indirect materials is $2,738.00. The total of the materials ledger must equal the ending balance of Materials in the general ledger.

    b. Add the costs recorded on all cost sheets in the cost ledger that have not been completed. This total must equal the ending balance of Work in Process in the general ledger.

    c. Add the ending balances in the finished goods ledger. This total must equal the ending balance of Finished Goods in the general ledger.

11. Prepare a statement of cost of goods manufactured for Alexandria for the month ended January 31 of the current year.

Part B: Analyzing Costs and Using Cost Data for Decision Making

12. Alexandria Corporation sets standards for both materials and labor for many of its products. These standards are analyzed annually. However, Alexandria spot-checks the standards each month, using specific job orders. The quantity standard for labor for the book racks on Job No. 232 is 2 ¼ hours per unit. The price standard for labor for the book racks is $15.50 per hour. Job No. 232 required 625 total labor hours. Using the data collected in Part A, calculate the following variances for Job No. 232 and summarize your findings:

    a. Total labor
    b. Labor price
    c. Labor quantity

13. Alexandria has been purchasing 30,000 connectors per year from an outside source at a cost of $2.50 each. Since Alexandria has excess capacity, it is considering making the connector in its own factory. No new machinery or equipment will need to be purchased. Alexandria has idle machines and no other use for them. Costs to make the part include direct materials, $25,500.00; direct labor, $24,000.00; and variable overhead, $23,500.00. In addition, the total fixed overhead allocated to the connectors is $5,000.00. Fixed overhead costs that are allocated

to each product will remain and will be allocated to other products. Variable overhead is related directly to making the connectors and will not exist if Alexandria continues to buy the connector. Using differential analysis, determine whether Alexandria should make the connectors or continue to buy them.

14. Alexandria is considering purchasing equipment for $35,000. The equipment will enable the company to generate net cash flows of $10,000.00 annually over the equipment's four-year useful life. Management expects assets to yield an 8% rate of return. Using the present value tables from Chapter 18, determine if Alexandria Corporation should purchase the equipment.

15. Alexandria uses cost-based pricing for all its products. Using the cost records from January and the form given in the *Working Papers*, calculate the following for each item:
    a. Dollar amount of markup
    b. Selling price
    c. Profit margin

16. Alexandria is in the process of designing a locker organizer. It believes that the selling price cannot exceed $30.00, and it requires a profit of 30% per unit. What is the target cost for the locker organizer?

17. Alexandria uses a job order costing system. How would its chart of accounts differ if it used a process costing system?

Alexandria Corporation Chart of Accounts

General Ledger

Balance Sheet Accounts

(1000) ASSETS

1100 Current Assets
1105 Cash
1110 Petty Cash
1115 Accounts Receivable
1120 Allowance for Uncollectible Accounts
1125 Materials
1130 Work in Process
1135 Finished Goods
1140 Supplies—Factory
1145 Supplies—Sales
1150 Supplies—Administrative
1155 Prepaid Insurance
1200 Plant Assets
1205 Factory Equipment
1210 Accumulated Depreciation—Factory Equipment
1215 Office Equipment
1220 Accumulated Depreciation—Office Equipment
1225 Store Equipment
1230 Accumulated Depreciation—Store Equipment
1235 Building
1240 Accumulated Depreciation—Building
1245 Land

(2000) LIABILITIES

2100 Current Liabilities
2105 Accounts Payable
2110 Employee Income Tax Payable
2115 Federal Income Tax Payable
2120 Social Security Tax Payable
2125 Medicare Tax Payable
2130 Unemployment Tax Payable—Federal
2135 Unemployment Tax Payable—State
2140 Dividends Payable
2200 Long-Term Liability
2205 Mortgage Payable

(3000) STOCKHOLDERS' EQUITY

3105 Capital Stock
3110 Retained Earnings
3115 Dividends
3120 Income Summary

Income Statement Accounts

(4000) OPERATING REVENUE

4105 Sales

(5000) COST OF SALES

5105 Cost of Goods Sold

(5500) MANUFACTURING COSTS

5505 Factory Overhead
5510 Depreciation Expense—Factory Equipment
5515 Depreciation Expense—Building
5520 Heat, Light, and Power Expense
5525 Insurance Expense—Factory
5530 Miscellaneous Expense—Factory
5535 Payroll Taxes Expense—Factory
5540 Property Tax Expense—Factory
5545 Supplies Expense—Factory

(6000) OPERATING EXPENSE

6100 Selling Expenses
6105 Advertising Expense
6110 Delivery Expense
6115 Depreciation Expense—Store Equipment
6120 Miscellaneous Expense—Sales
6125 Salary Expense—Sales
6130 Supplies Expense—Sales
6200 Administrative Expenses
6205 Depreciation Expense—Office Equipment
6210 Insurance Expense—Administrative
6215 Miscellaneous Expense—Administrative
6220 Payroll Taxes Expense—Administrative
6225 Property Tax Expense—Administrative
6230 Salary Expense—Administrative
6235 Supplies Expense—Administrative
6240 Uncollectible Accounts Expense
6245 Utilities Expense—Administrative

(7000) OTHER REVENUE

7105 Gain on Plant Assets
7110 Miscellaneous Revenue

(8000) OTHER EXPENSES

8105 Interest Expense
8110 Loss on Plant Assets

(9000) INCOME TAX

9105 Federal Income Tax Expense

Internal Control and Other Organizational Structures

588

CASTILLO LIQUIDATORS, INC.

Castillo Liquidators is a retail merchandising business organized as a corporation. The business purchases discontinued and overstocked hardware for sale to homeowners. Jason Castillo got the idea for the company while working in his uncle's hardware store. He witnessed how the hardware store struggled to sell new models of power tools while it still had older models in stock. His idea was to encourage manufacturers to ask their customers to return discontinued items and allow him to sell them out of a low-cost warehouse.

Chart of Accounts
CASTILLO LIQUIDATORS, INC.

GENERAL LEDGER

Balance Sheet Accounts

(1000) ASSETS
1100 Current Assets
1105 Cash
1110 Petty Cash
1115 Merchandise Inventory
1120 Supplies
1125 Prepaid Insurance

1200 Plant Assets
1205 Land
1210 Building
1215 Accumulated Depreciation—Building
1220 Office Equipment
1225 Accumulated Depreciation—Office Equipment
1230 Warehouse Equipment
1235 Accumulated Depreciation—Warehouse Equipment

(2000) LIABILITIES
2100 Current Liabilities
2105 Vouchers Payable
2110 Salaries Payable
2115 Employee Income Tax Payable
2120 Social Security Tax Payable
2125 Medicare Tax Payable
2130 Unemployment Tax Payable—Federal
2135 Unemployment Tax Payable—State

(3000) STOCKHOLDERS' EQUITY
3105 Capital Stock
3110 Retained Earnings
3115 Dividends
3120 Income Summary

Income Statement Accounts

(4000) OPERATING REVENUE
4105 Sales
4110 Sales Returns and Allowances

(5000) COST OF MERCHANDISE
5105 Purchases
5110 Purchases Discount
5115 Purchases Returns and Allowances

(6000) OPERATING EXPENSE
6105 Advertising Expense
6110 Depreciation Expense—Building
6115 Depreciation Expense—Office Equipment
6120 Depreciation Expense—Warehouse Equipment
6125 Insurance Expense
6130 Miscellaneous Expense
6135 Payroll Taxes Expense
6140 Property Tax Expense
6145 Salary Expense
6150 Supplies Expense

(7000) INCOME TAX
7105 Federal Income Tax Expense

The chart of accounts for Castillo Liquidators, Inc., is illustrated above for ready reference as you study Chapter 20 of this textbook.

Internal Control

LEARNING OBJECTIVES

After studying Chapter 20, in addition to defining key terms, you will be able to:

LO1 List the purpose of accounting control systems.

LO2 Identify the different types of fraud.

LO3 Identify the five components of an internal control structure.

LO4 Identify the tasks that should be segregated in an accounting system.

LO5 Prepare a flowchart to document an accounting process.

LO6 Journalize data from vouchers in a voucher register.

LO7 Journalize voucher payment transactions in a check register.

LO8 Identify the key controls of a voucher system.

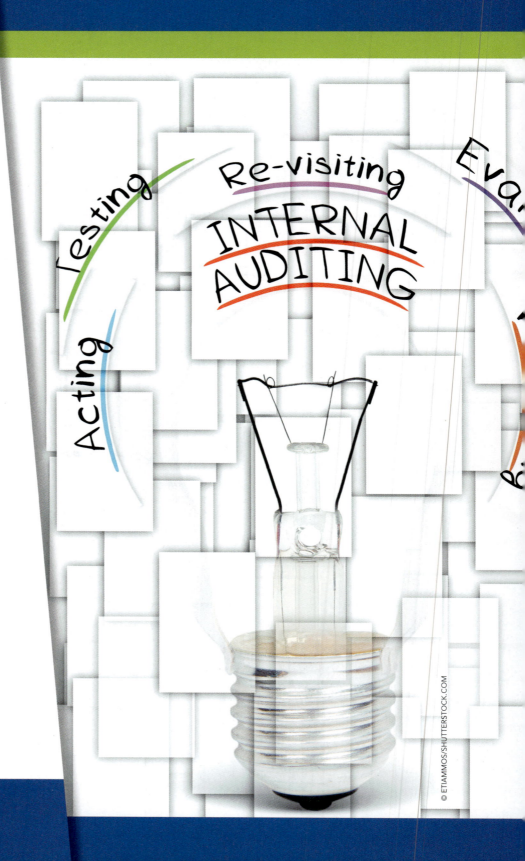

acl

Why we do what we do.

Changing the way organizations operate to make a better world.

ACL.COM

ACL Services Ltd.

ACCOUNTING IN THE REAL WORLD

"What keeps you up at night?" This is a rather casual question to be asking business managers. Yet when they consider the question seriously, managers are pointed to legitimate concerns their companies must face if they are to survive. They need to ask, for example, what forces exist in the economy, society, technology, or politics that could have a negative impact on the business tomorrow, next year, even 20 years in the future? Grappling with these hard questions is a central part of a process of identifying and avoiding negative financial risk, a process known as *risk management*.

Risk management begins with the collection of information, such as surveys completed by upper-level managers that identify risks they observe within their individual business units. As an example, a manager in a foreign country is in an ideal position to sense consumer behavior changes that may affect sales in that country. Data generated by the accounting system, the Internet, communication systems, and social media is another valuable source of information.

For over 30 years, ACL Services Ltd. has provided managers and accountants with database software designed specifically for the analysis of business data. The earliest version of the software, Audit Command Language, helped auditors test large data sets so they didn't have to rely solely on testing random samples. The database software can easily analyze data sets, such as 200 million sales, that are too large for electronic spreadsheets. Known today simply as ACL, modern versions of the software include powerful tools that assist businesses in collecting information that is useful in risk assessment.

For a business, risk assessment should be a continuous process rather than a periodic event. To aid in that process, ACL provides tools that enable managers to continuously monitor data. Managers enter goals or limits, known as *key performance indicators* (KPIs), into the software, and ACL instantly alerts them when a KPI has been reached.

Source: www.acl.com.

CRITICAL THINKING

1. Identify risks faced by a clothing retailer.
2. Select a large corporation with international sales. Assuming you are a member of upper-level management, identify three risk factors you believe the corporation faces.
3. Identify a business that failed to react to risks and subsequently went out of business. Explain.

KEY TERMS

internal controls	control environment	authority	requisition
error	risk assessment	custody	purchase order
fraud	control activities	recording	receiving report
occupational fraud	information and	narrative	invoice
financial statement	communication	flowchart	voucher register
misstatement	monitoring	voucher	voucher check
internal control structure	segregation of duties	voucher system	check register

20-1 Internal Control Structure

LO1 List the purpose of accounting control systems.
LO2 Identify the different types of fraud.
LO3 Identify the five components of an internal control structure.
LO4 Identify the tasks that should be segregated in an accounting system.

Controlling Accounting Systems LO1

Accountants are responsible for designing accounting systems that produce accurate financial statements and other reports. Accountants are also responsible for ensuring that the assets of the business are secure and are used only as authorized by management.

Processes and procedures employed within a business to ensure that its operations are conducted ethically, accurately, and reliably are called **internal controls**. Consider the following internal controls presented in this textbook:

Posting. Writing the posting references in journals and ledgers helps to ensure that all transactions are posted.

Bank Reconciliation. The bank reconciliation helps to detect an incorrect posting of a check or deposit.

Petty Cash. A petty cash system helps to ensure that small cash payments are recorded in the accounting records on a timely basis.

Proving a Special Journal. Proving the totals of the debit and credit columns of a special journal helps to ensure that all transactions were journalized accurately.

Trial Balance. Comparing the totals of the debits and credits helps ensure that all transactions have been posted.

Note that the explanation of each procedure included the word *help*. Any one internal control rarely provides absolute assurance that a transaction is recorded accurately. For example, proving the cash payments journal would not detect a cash payment for $930.00 recorded as $390.00. Fortunately, a bank reconciliation would detect the error.

ETHICS IN ACTION

Reporting Violations

What should employees do when they witness another employee possibly violating a law or the company's code of conduct? A small business may direct its employees to discuss the matter with the owner or manager. Larger companies may instruct employees to report it to an ethics officer or a compliance department. Public companies are required to establish procedures for employees to report complaints regarding questionable accounting, internal accounting controls, or auditing matters. These companies must provide a phone number or "hotline" that allows an individual to provide confidential information regarding possible ethics violations. The hotline must ensure that employee reports are anonymous.

For a hotline to be effective, employees must also have confidence that their information is being treated seriously. One way that FedEx achieves this goal is to provide callers with a control number. Callers can use the control number to receive updates on the status of their reported violation.

INSTRUCTIONS

1. Access the FedEx *Code of Business Conduct and Ethics*. Describe how an employee is instructed to contact the hotline. How is the call answered?

2. Write a script that a hotline employee would use to give callers confidence that their information will remain confidential.

Types of Fraud LO2

Internal controls are usually effective in detecting an **error**, an unintentional mistake. They are less effective in detecting a **fraud**, the theft of assets by employees or the intentional misstatement of financial information.

Occupational fraud is the theft of assets by an employee. Occupational fraud is also referred to as *embezzlement* or *asset misappropriation*. Cash and inventory are common targets of occupational fraud. Employees can also use plant equipment for unauthorized uses. Occupational frauds are the most common form of business fraud. The amounts stolen can range from hundreds to millions of dollars.

Financial statement misstatement is the manipulation of amounts reported on a financial statement. Overstating revenues is the most common form of this kind of fraud. Although financial statement misstatement occurs with less frequency than occupational fraud, its impact is usually more damaging. An occupational fraud rarely causes a business to fail. In contrast, financial statement misstatement often results in a business failure, as in the case of Enron and WorldCom. Investors and creditors lost billions of dollars when these corporations failed.

Laws and Regulations LO3

For over one hundred years, a few notable accounting frauds have caused the accounting profession to re-evaluate its accounting and auditing rules. In some cases, the frauds involved individual companies, such as Enron and WorldCom. In others, the frauds involved many companies in a particular industry.

Committee of Sponsoring Organizations

In 1985, five major financial and accounting organizations established the Committee of Sponsoring Organizations to study the factors that lead to fraudulent financial reporting. The organization was a reaction to a financial crisis in the savings and loan industry.

The commission's report broadened the accounting profession's perception of internal controls. The commission established a model that required accountants to consider more than internal control procedures. The **internal control structure** is a process designed to achieve effectiveness and efficiency of operations, reliability of financial reporting, and compliance with applicable laws and regulations. These control goals are best achieved by addressing each of the five components of the internal control structure.

Control Environment. The attitude and actions of management that indicate its commitment to strong internal controls and ethical standards are called the **control environment**. The control environment is often referred to as the *tone at the top*. Management must establish and enforce policies that ensure fair financial reporting and encourage employees to make ethical decisions. A corporation should have a code of conduct and regularly train its employees on how to make ethical decisions. Managers must follow the rules in the code of conduct if they expect their employees to follow the same rules.

Risk Assessment. The process of determining whether an error or fraud could occur is called **risk assessment**. A mistake in calculating employer payroll taxes could go undetected unless another employee verifies the amounts. Since cash is hard to trace and easy to use, it is most often the target of employees committing an occupational fraud. Recording false sales is the most effective way of increasing reported net income.

Control Activities. The policies and procedures designed to prevent or detect errors or fraud are called **control activities**. Verifying the work of an employee is a control activity. A point-of-sale system that prevents a salesclerk from changing sales prices without management approval is a control activity.

Information and Communication. The processes used to collect information about how the business is achieving its control goals are called **information and communication**. This information is generated at the operations level and reported to management. For example, the information technology staff should send management periodic reports on the number of hacking attempts on the company's website.

Monitoring. The process management uses to determine whether its policies are operating effectively is called **monitoring**. Management can employ internal auditors to observe procedures and collect information to ensure that policies are being followed.

Sarbanes-Oxley

Congress has generally allowed the accounting profession to develop standards to improve accounting and auditing rules. After Enron and WorldCom failed in the same year, Congress passed the Sarbanes-Oxley Act of 2002 (SOX). This act set higher standards for the development and auditing of internal control systems.

SOX created the Public Company Accounting Oversight Board (PCAOB) with the power to set auditing standards. PCAOB standards apply to any business having publicly traded stocks or bonds. Unlike standards previously set by the accounting profession, PCAOB standards are law. Failure to adhere to PCAOB standards can result in penalties, including jail time.

SOX requires management to assess the quality of its internal controls. This process begins with the design of an effective internal control system. The business must also maintain comprehensive documentation of its system. Two methods of documenting an internal control system are presented later in the chapter.

Management must also document how it tests the effectiveness of its internal control system. This process enables the chief executive and chief financial officers to certify the internal controls of the business. These officers are personally responsible for the accuracy of their financial statements.

Segregation of Duties LO4

The most fundamental control activity is having one employee oversee or approve the work of another. This requires dividing the tasks of the accounting system among employees in different functions. This division of accounting tasks is called **segregation of duties**. For any single transaction, the following three functions should be segregated:

Authority is the ability of an employee to authorize a transaction. Authority would include:

- Selling merchandise.
- Requesting the purchase of merchandise.
- Accepting a customer's sales return.
- Authorizing the write-off of a customer account.
- Approving documents, such as invoices and checks.

Custody is the physical access to the assets involved in a transaction. Custody would include:

- Having access to merchandise.
- Having access to checks and petty cash funds.
- Receiving or shipping merchandise.

Recording is the entry of a transaction in the financial records. Recording would include:

- Journalizing a transaction in a journal.
- Entering a transaction in a computerized accounting system.

Segregation of duties requires that two or more employees be involved in every transaction. The risk of error or fraud increases when a single employee is given any two of these duties. The following situation illustrates a system common in small businesses.

> Mary works in a local yogurt shop. When a customer arrives, she prepares the requested item using the yogurt machines behind the counter. Mary gives the customer the yogurt and presses a cash register button for the type of item purchased. She asks the customer for the amount of the sale and makes any necessary change.
>
> At the end of the day, the owner arrives at the shop to count the money in the cash register. She compares the amount of cash with a sales record printed by the cash register. The amount of money on hand must equal the amount printed on the sales record. The owner has always been able to reconcile Mary's cash to the sales record.

Accountants begin their analysis by gaining an understanding of the system. Then they assess the risk of error or fraud by answering questions such as:

What business resources are at risk? Cash is a risky asset. Cash is difficult to trace and easy to convert to other goods or services. Although the yogurt is also at risk, it is more difficult for an employee to steal or use a large quantity of yogurt.

Could the cash from sales be incorrectly counted? The system ensures the proper accounting for every sale entered in the cash register. The cash collected is reconciled to sales according to the cash register.

Does Mary have motivation to perform a fraud? Most fraudsters steal assets because they already have a financial hardship. Accountants would need to talk with Mary, her coworkers, and the business owner to learn whether Mary is experiencing any financial problems.

How could Mary perform a fraud without the knowledge of the owner? Mary has both authority and custody functions. She has the authority to sell the yogurt and access to the yogurt machines and toppings. This lack of segregation of duties could enable several frauds, including:

1. Mary can give yogurt to her friends. She could dispense the yogurt as usual and then simply not enter the sale in the cash register.
2. Mary can sell yogurt to her friends at a reduced price. She could prepare a $5.00 item but select a $3.00 item in the cash register.
3. Mary can enter a lower-priced item in the cash register but ask the customer for the full price. She could serve a $5.00 item but select a $3.00 item in the cash register, pocketing the extra $2.00.

Knowing the risks to the system, accountants can design control activities to prevent or detect any possible errors or frauds.

Careers In Accounting

Lisa Rodriguez
Partner in an Accounting Firm

Lisa Rodriguez is a partner in a regional accounting firm. She has been working for the same firm for over 20 years. Ms. Rodriguez started with the firm the summer before her last year in college. She started as an intern and was hired full-time after she graduated.

Ms. Rodriguez has followed a rather traditional career path to obtain her current position. She started as a junior accountant in the auditing area and earned her designation as a certified public accountant. She soon moved to senior accountant and to manager. Her promotions gave her more responsibility, and she supervised more people. She managed the audits of major customers and worked hard to bring in new business to the firm.

Ms. Rodriguez's duties shifted again when she was promoted to partner. She managed the local office of the firm and spent more time on administrative duties. As a partner, she is also expected to market the firm and its services.

When Ms. Rodriguez became a partner in the firm, she invested a rather large sum of money in the firm. In exchange for this investment, she shares in the profits of the firm. In addition, if the firm does well, the value of her ownership of the firm will increase.

Ms. Rodriguez worked very hard to achieve the position of partner. Most accountants in public accounting firms leave within three to five years to move into corporate accounting. Only a very small percentage of accountants rise to the level of partner. Ms. Rodriguez has always enjoyed public accounting and plans to stay with her firm for many more years.

Salary Range: The range in salary for a partner varies greatly, depending on the size and geographic location of the firm. The range can be from a few hundred thousand to several million dollars per year. The partner also gains from increases in the value of the firm.

Qualifications: Audit partners usually have at least a four-year accounting degree and have earned the designation "certified public accountant."

Occupational Outlook: As a career area, accounting is expected to experience faster than average growth (10% to 14%) from 2016 to 2026. Although only a very small percentage of accountants achieve the level of partner, the number of partners should grow as accounting positions grow.

Source: www.onetonline.org.

TERMS REVIEW

internal controls

error

fraud

occupational fraud

financial statement
 misstatement

internal control structure

control environment

risk assessment

control activities

information and
 communication

monitoring

segregation of duties

authority

custody

recording

Audit your understanding LO1, 2, 3, 4

1. What is the purpose of accounting control systems?
2. What is the primary difference between an error and a fraud?
3. Which type of fraud is more likely to result in a business failure?
4. What component of the internal control structure is often referred to as the *tone at the top*?
5. What organization has the power to set auditing standards for publicly traded companies?
6. What is the first step accountants should perform when analyzing an accounting system?

Work together 20-1 LO3, 4

Classify internal controls

Use the forms provided in the *Working Papers*. Your instructor will guide you through the following examples.

1. For each item, indicate the component of the internal control structure: control environment, risk assessment, control activities, information and communication, or monitoring. The first item is completed as an example.

Item	Description	Component of the Internal Control Structure
1	A manager approves an employee's time card.	Control activities

2. For each item, indicate whether the action is an authority, custody, or recording function. The first item is completed as an example.

Item	Description	Function
1	A department store clerk processes a customer sale.	Authority

On your own 20-1 LO3, 4

Classify internal controls

Use the forms provided in the *Working Papers*. Complete this problem independently.

1. For each item, indicate the component of the internal control structure: control environment, risk assessment, control activities, information and communication, or monitoring.
2. For each item, indicate whether the action is an authority, custody, or recording function.

LO5 Prepare a flowchart to document an accounting process.

Documentation Methods LO5

Effective internal controls begin with good documentation. Documenting the procedures of an accounting system forces a business to evaluate its processes and identify areas of weakness.

The simplest form of documentation to prepare is a written description of the system. A **narrative** is a written description of the flow of documents and information between employees, departments, and external parties. Although an effective tool for a simple system, a narrative can become confusing as the system becomes complex.

Many businesses also create diagrams of their accounting systems. A diagram that uses symbols and connecting lines to represent a process is called a **flowchart**. Flowcharting is a form of language. Understanding a foreign language requires an understanding of its words and their use in a sentence. In the same manner,

flowcharting requires an understanding of the symbols and rules used. An explanation of three important components of a flowchart follows.

Segregated Functions. Dashed lines segregate the tasks of each primary employee, department, or external party.

Symbols. Each symbol represents an object, such as a document or process. Castillo Distributors also color-codes its symbols to assist the user in identifying like objects. For example, all documents are shaded in green. A solid line connects the symbols and represents the flow of information through the system.

Style. The flow of documents and information generally moves from the upper left to lower right corner of a flowchart.

▽	**Manual File.** A folder or file containing paper documents.
▭	**Document.** Any document, including time cards, sales invoices, and checks. A symbol may represent one document or many copies of the same document.
▭	**Process.** An accounting process, such as creating a form, comparing forms, journalizing a transaction, or signing a form.
▱	**Accounting Record.** Any accounting journal or ledger, such as a purchases journal, payroll register, or general ledger.
▭	**Terminate Process.** The beginning or end of a process. The symbol is often used to show a document being received from or sent to a department or external party not represented in the flowchart.
⌐→	**Information Flow.** The transfer of information or the movement of a document between departments. The arrow indicates the direction of the transfer.
🔒	**Control.** Identifies a key control to ensure that accounting transactions are recorded accurately. Numbers under the symbol identify each control.
🔓	**Risk.** Identifies that a process is subject to the risk of error or fraud. Numbers under the symbol identify each risk.

A flowchart communicates a small segment of the internal control structure. A process may begin on one flowchart and continue on other flowcharts. Thus, even a small business could require 20 or more

flowcharts to document a single system, such as sales and cash receipts. Inadequate segregation of duties is particularly visible when a process is documented in a flowchart.

Documenting a Cash Receipts System

Deposit of Cash Receipts by Mail

Mailroom. Customers submit payments in specially marked envelopes. A mailroom clerk opens each envelope, matches the amount of the check to the enclosed receipt, and endorses the check. The receipt is the bottom section of the invoice sent to the customer. The clerk prepares a two-part cash receipts report that includes the number and total dollar amount of checks received. The customer checks and a cash receipts report are sent to the cashier. The receipts are sent to accounts receivable. The original copy of the cash receipts report is sent to accounting.

Cashier. The cashier totals the checks and compares the total to the summary report. The clerk prepares a deposit slip and deposits the checks in the bank. The clerk forwards the validated deposit slip to accounting.

Accounting. An accounting clerk compares the amount on the validated deposit slip to the cash receipts report. The total of checks received is journalized in the cash receipts journal.

Castillo Distributors has always maintained narratives of its accounting systems. The narrative above describes Castillo's system for the deposit of cash received in the mail. After the passage of the Sarbanes-Oxley Act, the business elected to improve the quality of its documentation by preparing flowcharts of its accounting systems. The flowchart representing Castillo's system for the deposit of cash receipts by mail is shown below. Examples of flowchart components are highlighted.

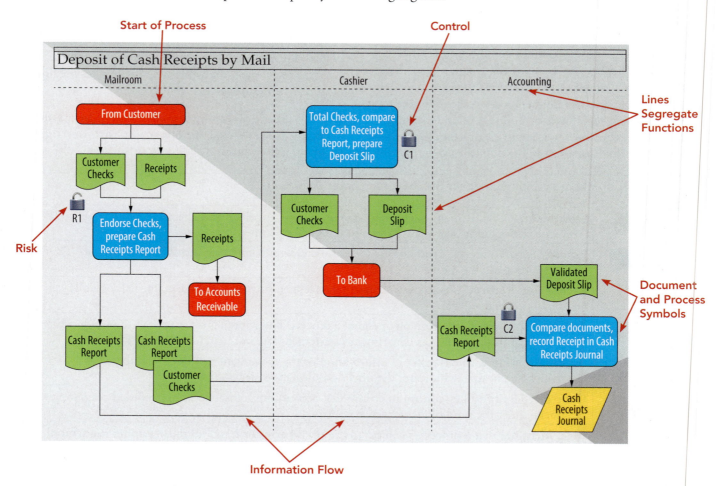

The flowchart shows the location of key risks and internal controls designed to protect the business against the risk of errors and fraud. Castillo has elected to highlight one risk and two key controls in this flowchart. These risks and controls are discussed on the next page.

Performing a Risk Assessment

Risk/Control Symbol	Risk Assessment	Control Activity
R1	Any employee that has access to a check could steal the check, cash it, and take the proceeds. A mail clerk can steal a check before the cash receipts report is prepared.	Monthly statements (shown on another flowchart) are sent to customers. A customer not receiving credit for a check can be expected to alert the company.
C1	The mailroom may deliver checks to the cashier that do not total to the amount on the cash receipts report.	The cashier totals the checks and compares the amount to the cash receipts report before preparing the bank deposit slip.
C2	The cashier can steal a check, cash the check, and keep the proceeds.	An accounting clerk compares the validated deposit slip to the cash receipts report received directly from the mailroom. Any check stolen by the cashier would cause these amounts to differ.

A flowchart enables a business to identify risks and determine if adequate internal controls exist to prevent or detect an error or a fraud. A business should document how it identifies and evaluates key risks and controls.

Castillo recognizes that a mailroom clerk could steal a check. The risk is noted by the R1 symbol in the flowchart on the previous page. The analysis above indicates that Castillo has an internal control in place. Each month, the business sends statements to its customers. A stolen check would not have been credited to the customer's account. Castillo is assuming the customer will question why the check has been cashed but not credited to its account. When the customer contacts Castillo to question its statement, the theft of the check would be quickly detected.

Management must determine if this internal control is adequate. Other controls could be implemented to prevent or detect the fraud on a timelier basis. For example, a second employee could be present for the processing of the checks in the mailroom. Only management can decide whether reducing the risk of this fraud is offset by the added cost of the control. By noting this as a risk, Castillo is recognizing that its risk in this process needs to be corrected.

Clergy

CareerClusters
PATHWAYS TO COLLEGE & CAREER READINESS
Human Services

Usually, people who consider a career as a religious leader do not do so because they like the area of business administration. They consider such a career because they feel called to support and promote the doctrine of their religion. While each individual may have plans for how to accomplish this mission, most of these plans require financial resources.

Being the leader of a religious organization is similar to running a corporation. Budgets must be developed, employees must be hired and trained, and financial reports must be prepared. When new facilities are required, the organization may have to hold a capital fund-raising campaign. Yet few religious training institutions offer courses in business administration or accounting as part of their curriculum.

CRITICAL THINKING

Assume a religious organization is trying to balance its budget for next year. The executive committee, including the religious leaders, has determined that only four budget categories can be decreased. The four categories are (a) Building costs, (b) Training/ Education of lay members, (c) Conferences/Seminars for religious leaders, and (d) Advertising (which includes publishing the date/time of scheduled classes and activities in local newspapers). For each category, list at least one negative aspect of decreasing the budgeted amount.

LO5 Prepare a flowchart
to document an
accounting process.

TERMS REVIEW

narrative

flowchart

Audit your understanding LO5

1. What is the simplest form of documentation of an accounting system?
2. Where is the beginning point of the processes presented in a flowchart?
3. What is indicated by a line with an arrow?
4. How does management decide whether to implement additional internal controls?

Work together 20-2 LO5
Preparing flowcharts

Use the forms provided in the *Working Papers*. For each statement, prepare a flowchart to represent the process described. Your instructor will guide you through the following examples.

a. An employee approves and signs a check by reviewing information on an invoice.
b. An employee posts sales return transactions from the general journal to the accounts receivable ledger.
c. A warehouse manager approves time cards and forwards the time cards to the Payroll Department.
d. A mailroom clerk receives customer checks, endorses the checks, and forwards the checks to the cashier. The cashier uses the checks to prepare a deposit slip.

On your own 20-2 LO5
Preparing flowcharts

Use the forms provided in the *Working Papers*. For each statement, prepare a flowchart to represent the process described. Work this problem independently.

a. An employee uses the accounts receivable ledger to prepare a schedule of accounts receivable.
b. An employee sorts a group of shipping orders in numerical order.
c. A credit manager prepares a receivables adjustment form. The accounting clerk uses the information on the form to journalize the write-off of an account receivable.
d. A sales representative prepares a sales order. The form is forwarded to a salesclerk, who prepares the sales invoice that is sent to the customer.

LESSON
20-3

Cash Payments Using a Voucher System

LO6 Journalize data from vouchers in a voucher register.
LO7 Journalize voucher payment transactions in a check register.

A Voucher System LO6

An accounting system includes procedures for recording and reporting accurate and up-to-date financial information. An accounting system should also include procedures to assist management in controlling a company's daily operations. Management is particularly concerned with procedures and records to control and protect assets. One asset that should be controlled and protected is cash. Cash is the asset most likely to be misused because its ownership is easily transferred. In addition, transactions generally affect the **Cash** account more often than other general ledger accounts. Many businesses, therefore, use specific cash control procedures.

Among the procedures used to control cash are storing it in a safe place, making bank deposits regularly, and approving all cash payments. Approving cash payments ensures that the goods or services were ordered, they have been received, and the amounts due are correct. In small businesses, the owner or manager usually approves cash payments. In large businesses, several persons may have authority to approve cash payments. A collection of documents used to authorize a cash payment is called a **voucher**. A set of procedures for controlling cash payments by preparing and approving vouchers before payments are made is called a **voucher system**.

Stash the Cash

A bank or a credit union will provide a secure location for your cash. Both may offer checking and savings accounts, investment accounts, loans, and credit cards. However, their business structures set them apart.

An account holder at a credit union is called a *member*. Credit unions are not-for-profit organizations owned by their members. The members are usually a group formed by common interests, such as an employer or a geographic area. Credit unions have some advantages over banks. They often do not have advertising costs, typically pay higher interest rates on savings accounts, offer lower rates on loans, provide free checking accounts, and have fewer penalties like overdrafts and late payments.

A bank is a business formed to generate profits, which result from loaning money and earning interest off the loan. A bank offers some advantages over a credit union. Membership is not required, and banks typically offer more products, such as investments. Banks may also offer more options, such as several types of checking accounts.

Some differences between banks and credit unions are disappearing. For example, banks used to offer more ATMs than credit unions did. Now credit unions are joining together to enlarge their network of available ATMs.

ACTIVITIES

1. Make a list of two banks and two credit unions in your area. Provide the criteria for membership for the credit unions.

2. Compare the products and services offered by the organizations you researched for question 1. Select which institution is best for you, and provide the criteria used to make your decision.

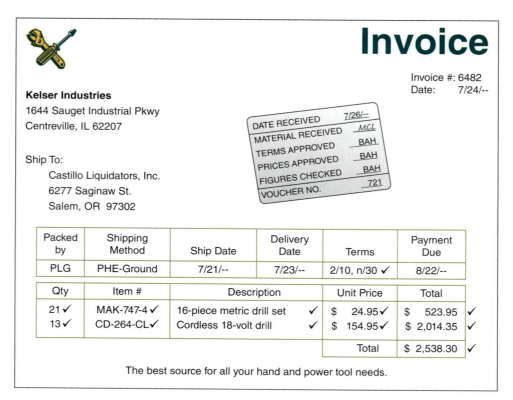

Invoice

Invoice #: 6482
Date: 7/24/--

Kelser Industries
1644 Sauget Industrial Pkwy
Centreville, IL 62207

Ship To:

    Castillo Liquidators, Inc.
    6277 Saginaw St.
    Salem, OR 97302

DATE RECEIVED	7/26/--
MATERIAL RECEIVED	MCL
TERMS APPROVED	BAH
PRICES APPROVED	BAH
FIGURES CHECKED	BAH
VOUCHER NO.	721

Packed by	Shipping Method	Ship Date	Delivery Date	Terms	Payment Due
PLG	PHE-Ground	7/21/--	7/23/--	2/10, n/30 ✓	8/22/--

Qty	Item #	Description		Unit Price	Total	
21 ✓	MAK-747-4 ✓	16-piece metric drill set	✓	$ 24.95 ✓	$ 523.95	✓
13 ✓	CD-264-CL ✓	Cordless 18-volt drill	✓	$ 154.95 ✓	$ 2,014.35	✓
				Total	$ 2,538.30	✓

The best source for all your hand and power tool needs.

The process of ordering merchandise begins when an authorized employee submits a purchase request. A form requesting the purchase of merchandise is called a **requisition**. The requisition includes a description of the merchandise to be ordered, the quantity to be purchased, and the required delivery date. Requisitions generally require management approval.

An approved requisition is submitted to another employee, who is responsible for placing an order with the supplier that provides the best combination of quality and price. A form requesting that a vendor sell merchandise to a business is called a **purchase order**. The purchase order lists the number, description, quantity, and unit price of each item ordered. The vendor uses the purchase order to (1) approve the sale and (2) process the order. No transaction occurs until the customer receives the goods from the vendor. Thus, no journal entry is recorded when a purchase order is prepared or sent to the vendor.

When the order is received, the Receiving Department prepares a document to identify the qualities of the items received. A form that lists the item received from a vendor is called a **receiving report**.

The requisition, purchase order, and receiving report are submitted to an accounts payable clerk. A transaction is not recorded until the vendor submits an **invoice**, a form describing the goods or services sold, the quantity, the price, and the terms of sale. The accounts payable clerk compares the information on the invoice with the other documents to ensure that the business has only been invoiced for the goods it ordered and received.

A Voucher

The requisition, purchase order, receiving report, and invoice provide a historical account of the transaction. Together these documents comprise a voucher. The methods used to organize these documents vary. Some businesses prepare a prenumbered form that summarizes the information to be recorded in the accounting records. This form can be stapled with the documentation or assembled in a folder. Other businesses use the invoice as the cover document of the voucher. Castillo's accounts payable clerk stamps the invoice and records a voucher number. The other forms are stapled to the invoice.

The voucher stamp lists important steps required to verify the voucher. On the receiving report, Michael C. Langston identified the quantities of items received. His initials, MCL, are written in the stamp. Beth Ann Harris, the accounts payable clerk, signs her initials, BAH, on the tasks she performs. She also places check marks next to the items verified on the invoice. This process ensures that every step is performed. The voucher shows the employee responsible for each step in the verification process.

Journalizing a Voucher in a Voucher Register's Special Columns

| | | | | PAID | | | SUPPLIES— | SUPPLIES— | GENERAL | | | |
DATE	PAYEE	VCHR. NO.	DATE	CK. NO.	VOUCHERS PAYABLE CREDIT	PURCHASES DEBIT	SALES DEBIT	ADMIN. DEBIT	ACCOUNT TITLE	POST. REF.	DEBIT	CREDIT
23	26	Kelser Industries	721			2 5 3 8 30	2 5 3 8 30						
24												

The voucher is recorded in the accounting records after it has been approved. A journal used to record vouchers is called a **voucher register**. A voucher register is similar to and replaces a purchases journal. The accounts payable clerk assigns sequential numbers to the vouchers. A missing voucher number shows that a voucher has not been recorded.

In a voucher system, the liability account Vouchers Payable is used to record all amounts to be paid by check. Castillo's voucher register has special columns for Vouchers Payable Credit, Purchases Debit, Supplies— Sales Debit, and Supplies—Administrative Debit. For accounts with no special amount columns, information is recorded in the General columns. Voucher 721 is recorded on line 23 of the voucher register.

> **July 26.** Purchased merchandise on account from Kelser Industries, $2,538.30. Voucher No. 721.

The purchase of merchandise results in a debit to Purchases and a credit to Vouchers Payable. Similar to a purchases journal, a voucher register has special columns that are used to record this transaction. After a voucher is journalized, the voucher is filed in an unpaid vouchers file. The vouchers are placed in this file according to the expected payment date. Filing the vouchers by payment date makes it easier to determine which vouchers need to be paid each day. This method helps ensure payment of invoices within the discount period. To ensure the check will arrive at Kelser Industries by the 10th day, the accounts payable clerk files the voucher under the date on which it is to be paid, August 1. Payment of a voucher is described later in this lesson.

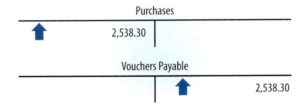

Purchases

2,538.30

Vouchers Payable

2,538.30

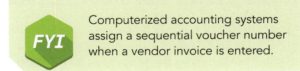

> **FYI**
>
> Computerized accounting systems assign a sequential voucher number when a vendor invoice is entered.

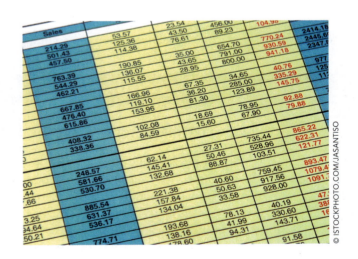

© ISTOCKPHOTO.COM/JASANTISO

Journalizing a Voucher in a Voucher Register's General Column

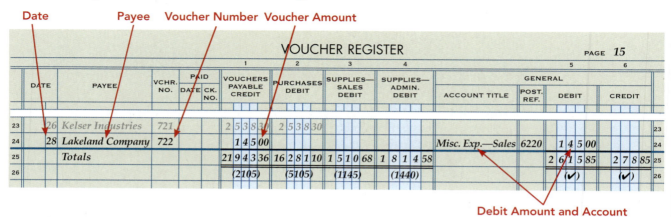

Date   Payee   Voucher Number   Voucher Amount

VOUCHER REGISTER   PAGE **15**

			PAID		VOUCHERS PAYABLE CREDIT	PURCHASES DEBIT	SUPPLIES— SALES DEBIT	SUPPLIES— ADMIN. DEBIT	GENERAL			
DATE	PAYEE	VCHR. NO.	DATE	CK. NO.					ACCOUNT TITLE	POST. REF.	DEBIT	CREDIT
26 Kelser Industries		721			2 5 3 8 30	2 5 3 8 30						
28 Lakeland Company		722			1 4 5 00				Misc. Exp.—Sales	6220	1 4 5 00	
Totals					21 9 4 3 36	16 2 8 1 10	1 5 1 0 68	1 8 1 4 58			2 6 1 5 85	2 7 8 85
					(2105)	(5105)	(1145)	(1440)			(✔)	(✔)

Debit Amount and Account

Only two of the special journals illustrated in previous parts of this textbook contain General Debit and Credit columns—the cash receipts and cash payments journals. If no cash is involved, the transaction is recorded in a general journal.

> **July 28.** Received an invoice for a sales miscellaneous expense from Lakeland Company, $145.00. Voucher No. 722.

A voucher register contains general columns that enable the business to record all transactions on account.

Because no special column exists for miscellaneous expenses, this transaction is recorded in the General Debit column.

Proving, Ruling, and Posting a Voucher Register

The voucher register is proved, ruled, and posted, using the same steps as other special journals. Separate amounts recorded in the General Debit and General Credit columns of a voucher register are posted individually during the month. As each amount is posted, the account number is written in the Post. Ref. column of the voucher register.

At the end of each month, Castillo's voucher register is proved and ruled. The totals of special amount columns are posted to the general ledger accounts listed in the column headings. Totals of General Debit and General Credit amount columns are not posted.

THINK LIKE AN ACCOUNTANT

Documenting Cash Collections

Lancing Brick sells its products directly to contractors for the construction of both residential housing and commercial buildings. The company offers contractors 2/10, n/30 payment terms. Customers are sent an invoice on the same day the bricks are delivered to the construction site. A remittance advice and a pre-stamped envelope are included with the invoice. All of Lancing's customers pay their accounts by writing a check.

A narrative describing the procedures for receiving customer payments is presented in the worksheet.

OPEN THE SPREADSHEET TLA_CH20

The worksheet contains an incomplete flowchart of Lancing's cash receipts procedures. Follow the steps on the Instructions tab to complete the flowchart.

Paying a Voucher LO7

CASTILLO LIQUIDATORS, INC.	DATE 8/1/20--			No. 915

PAYEE	Kelser Industries			
ACCOUNT	**TITLE**	**VOUCHER**	**VENDOR INVOICE**	**AMOUNT**
2105	Purchases	721	6482	2,538.30
5110	Purchases Discount			50.77

CASTILLO LIQUIDATORS, INC.
6277 Saginaw St.
Salem, OR 97302

FIRST AMERICAN BANK
101 S. Marion Street
Salem, OR 97302

No. 915

GENERAL ACCOUNT

DATE
8/1/20--

AMOUNT
$ 2,487.53

Two thousand four hundred eighty seven and 53/100 _____ Dollars
FOR CLASSROOM USE ONLY

PAY TO THE
ORDER OF

Kelser Industries
1644 Sauget Industrial Pkwy
Centreville, IL 62207

Gerald C. Andrews

⑆063260364⑆ 02⑈5643⑈64⑈ 0915

In a voucher system, a check cannot be issued without a properly authorized voucher. Castillo prepares a check for the amount of each voucher less any purchases discount. The check and voucher are presented to a person authorized to approve payment. A check with a detachable check stub, or *voucher*, that contains detailed information about the cash payment is called a **voucher check**. Castillo prepares voucher checks in duplicate.

On August 1, vouchers to be paid on that day are removed from the unpaid vouchers file. Included in this group is Voucher No. 721. Castillo's cash payments clerk prepares the voucher checks.

Castillo uses the detachable section of the voucher check to record details about the cash payment. On Check No. 915, the information includes the following items:

1. Castillo's voucher number, 721.
2. The vendor's invoice number, 6482.
3. The account debited and the amount of the invoice, $2,538.30.

4. The amount of the purchases discount, $50.77.
5. The net amount for which the check is written, $2,487.53.

The check signer, Gerald C. Andrews, verifies that the information on the check and on the voucher agrees and is accurate. After verification, he signs the check. The duplicate of the voucher check is attached to the voucher. The check signer cancels each voucher document to ensure the documents cannot be submitted for payment a second time. Documents are cancelled by using a stamp or a machine that punches holes spelling PAID or CANCELLED. The check is given or sent to the payee by the check signer.

The cancelled voucher is returned to the accounts payable clerk. Information about this payment is recorded in the voucher register. The date on which this voucher is paid, *8/1/--*, and the check number, *915*, are written in the Paid columns of the voucher register. The cancelled voucher is filed in the paid vouchers file according to the name of the vendor.

	DATE	PAYEE	VCHR. NO.	PAID		VOUCHERS PAYABLE CREDIT	
				DATE	CK. NO.		
23	26	Kelser Industries	721	8/1/--	915	2,538.30	23
24	28	Lakeland Company	722			145.00	24

Journalizing Checks in a Check Register

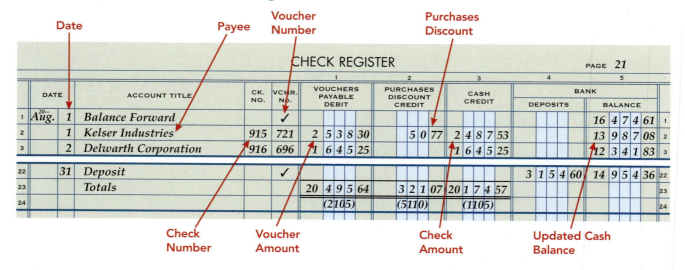

Date **Payee** **Voucher Number** **Purchases Discount**

CHECK REGISTER

PAGE **21**

	DATE	ACCOUNT TITLE	CK. NO.	VCHR. NO.	VOUCHERS PAYABLE DEBIT	PURCHASES DISCOUNT CREDIT	CASH CREDIT	BANK DEPOSITS	BANK BALANCE	
1	Aug. 1	Balance Forward		✓					16 4 7 4 61	1
2	1	Kelser Industries	915	721	2 5 3 8 30	5 0 77	2 4 8 7 53		13 9 8 7 08	2
3	2	Delwarth Corporation	916	696	1 6 4 5 25		1 6 4 5 25		12 3 4 1 83	3
22	31	Deposit		✓				3 1 5 4 60	14 9 5 4 36	22
23		Totals			20 4 9 5 64	3 2 1 07	20 1 7 4 57			23
24					(2105)	(5110)	(1105)			24

Check Number **Voucher Amount** **Check Amount** **Updated Cash Balance**

A journal used in a voucher system to record cash payments is called a **check register**. The check register is similar to and replaces a cash payments journal.

Castillo prepares a voucher for each approved cash payment. Therefore, each check is issued in payment of a voucher. Checks are recorded in the check register in the order they are written.

Castillo's check register has only three special amount columns: Vouchers Payable Debit, Purchases Discount Credit, and Cash Credit. Each check is recorded in a check register as a debit to the liability account, Vouchers Payable, and a credit to the asset account, Cash. If a discount is taken for prompt payment, the discount amount is recorded as a credit to the contra cost account, Purchases Discount.

Castillo's procedures for posting from its check register are the same as those previously described for special journals. However, no separate amounts are posted individually because the check register does not have a General Debit or General Credit column.

> **August 1. Paid cash to Kelser Industries, $2,487.53, covering Voucher No. 721 for $2,538.30, less 2% discount, $50.77. Check No. 915.**

The liability account, Vouchers Payable, is debited for $2,538.30. The contra cost account, Purchases Discount, is credited for $50.77. Cash is credited for the net amount paid, $2,487.53. Castillo's procedures for posting from its check register are the same as those previously described for special journals. However, no separate amounts are

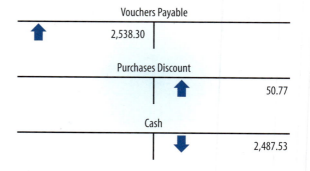

posted individually because the check register does not have a General Debit or General Credit column.

Maintaining Bank Columns in a Check Register

Castillo uses a check register to maintain the checking account balance. The check register has two Bank columns, Deposits and Balance. The Bank Deposits column is used to record the amounts deposited in the checking account. The Bank Balance column shows the checking account balance after each check and each deposit are recorded in the check register.

A deposit in the checking account is shown on line 22 above. The Deposits column does not need to be totaled and posted because each cash receipt is recorded in the cash receipts journal and posted from that journal. At the end of each month, cash is proved by comparing the last amount in the Balance column of the check register with the balance in the general ledger cash account. The two Bank columns are used to summarize the status of the checking account balance. These two columns are neither ruled nor posted.

LO6 Journalize data from vouchers in a voucher register.

LO7 Journalize voucher payment transactions in a check register.

TERMS REVIEW

voucher

voucher system

requisition

purchase order

receiving report

invoice

voucher register

voucher check

check register

Audit your understanding LO6, 7

1. In a voucher system, what general ledger account is used to record all amounts to be paid by check?
2. A voucher register is similar to and replaces what journal?
3. What account is debited for each check recorded in a check register?

Work together 20-3 LO6, 7

Journalizing transactions in a voucher system

The following transactions of Kelley's Crafts were completed during July of the current year. A voucher register and check register are provided in the *Working Papers*. Your instructor will guide you through the following examples. Source documents are abbreviated as follows: voucher, V; check, C.

Transactions:

July 1. Purchased merchandise on account from Dickens Company, $754.60. V63.
    3. Paid cash to LPG Industries, $1,635.00, covering V62. C121.
    5. Bought sales supplies on account from College Supplies, $350.00. V64.
    11. Paid cash to Dickens Company, $754.60, less 2% discount, covering V63. C122.
    13. Paid cash to College Supplies, $350.00, less 2% discount, covering V64. C123.
    16. Received an invoice from City Bagel for a miscellaneous expense, $65.00. V65.
    24. Made a deposit in the checking account, $1,943.68.
    29. Received an invoice for August rent from LaMure Co., $1,200.00. V66.

1. Record the bank balance brought forward on July 1, $8,265.66.
2. Journalize the transactions completed during July of the current year. Use page 7 of a voucher register and page 8 of a check register and check register.
3. Prove and rule the voucher register and check register.

On your own 20-3 LO6, 7

Journalizing transactions in a voucher system

The following transactions of Electronic Innovations were completed during September of the current year. A voucher register and check register are provided in the *Working Papers*. Work this problem independently. Source documents are abbreviated as follows: voucher, V; check, C.

Transactions:

Sept. 4. Received an invoice from James Peterson for a miscellaneous expense, $132.00. V124.
    5. Paid cash to Danstin Corporation, $6,245.00, covering V123. C147.
    9. Bought administrative supplies on account from Burrough Supplies, $234.00. V125.
    14. Paid cash to James Peterson, $132.00, covering V124. C148.
    16. Made a deposit in the checking account, $2,643.11.
    18. Paid cash to Burrough Supplies, $234.00, less 2% discount, covering V125. C149.
    25. Purchased merchandise on account from Clarmore Company, $1,375.75. V126.
    26. Received an invoice for rent from Office Properties, $1,400.00. V127.

1. Record the bank balance brought forward on September 1, $6,417.35.
2. Journalize the transactions completed during September of the current year. Use page 9 of a voucher register and page 11 of a check register.
3. Prove and rule the voucher register and check register.

LO8 Identify the key controls of a voucher system.

Key Controls of a Voucher System LO8

Accounting systems share common documents and processes. Most voucher systems will use requisitions and purchase orders. However, a business will modify a system to meet its individual needs. A business with a single location will have a different voucher system than a multinational corporation. The extent that a business has adopted computerized accounting systems will determine whether vouchers are in paper or electronic format.

Accountants must be able to understand the unique processes, forms, and controls of each system. Documentation is critical in helping accountants understand and evaluate accounting systems. Castillo Liquidators' accountants prepared the narrative below to document a segment of its voucher processing. A flowchart and a risk analysis of this system are presented on the following pages.

Narrative of a Voucher System

Accounts Payable/Cash Payments System

Departments. Authorized managers may complete a requisition to request the purchase of goods and services. The requisition is forwarded to the Purchasing Department.

Purchasing. A purchasing employee identifies the best source for purchasing the good or service by (1) reviewing the price lists of approved vendors or (2) advertising requests for competitive bids. Upon approving a completed purchase order, a purchasing manager sends the purchase order to the selected vendor. Copies of the purchase order are also sent to the Receiving and Accounts Payable departments.

Receiving. Upon receiving goods, a Receiving Department employee matches the vendor's documentation with the purchase order to ensure the goods were ordered. The goods are counted and recorded on the purchase order copy, which serves as the receiving report. The receiving report is sent to the Accounts Payable Department.

Accounts Payable. When the vendor's invoice is received, the accounts payable clerk prepares a voucher. The documents are compared for consistency. The approved voucher is recorded in the voucher register and filed until its expected payment date. If the purchase is for services, no receiving report will exist. The invoice is sent to the appropriate manager for approval, providing support that the services were received.

Treasury. On the assigned date, approved vouchers are sent to the Treasury Department for payment. A treasury clerk prepares the check based on the information on the voucher. The check and voucher are forwarded to the check signer. After reviewing the documentation and signing the check, the signed check is sent to the vendor. The transaction is recorded in the check register. The voucher is cancelled and returned to the Accounts Payable Department.

Accounts Payable. The Accounts Payable Department records the check information in the voucher register. The cancelled vouchers are filed in the paid vouchers file according to the name of the vendor.

Flowchart of a Voucher System

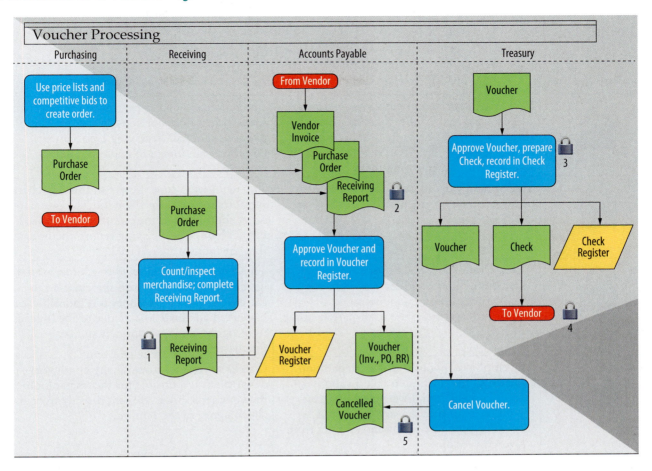

The flowchart representing a portion of Castillo's voucher processing is presented above. Two common flowchart writing styles are illustrated on this flowchart.

When multiple documents join together, a single flowchart symbol can be used to represent the documents. The flowchart illustrates how three documents—vendor invoice, purchase order, and receiving report—transform into a single document, a voucher. Castillo uses a stamp on the vendor invoice to document the verification of the voucher. The purchase order and receiving report are stapled to the invoice. Under the process in the Accounts Payable Department, the

document *Voucher (Inv., PO, RR)* alerts the reader that the voucher consists of the three documents. Later in the flowchart, the documents are denoted only as *Voucher*.

A change in a document can be reflected by a change in the symbol label. Castillo's Treasury Department cancels the documents in the voucher. The document symbol entering the *Cancel Voucher* process is labeled *Voucher*. After the process, the document symbol label is changed to *Cancelled Voucher*. The change in the label reflects the change in the document.

Five key controls are identified on the flowchart. The controls are discussed on the next page.

Risk Assessment of Voucher Processing

Castillo identified five key controls in this portion of its voucher processing system. The flowchart shows the location of key internal controls designed to protect the business against the risk of errors or fraud.

Control Symbol	Risk Assessment	Internal Control
1	Receiving Department employees need to make an accurate count of goods received. If the employees know the number ordered, they may simply check off that the goods are received without counting them.	The purchase order copy sent to the Receiving Department does not contain the quantity of goods ordered. Receiving Department employees are forced to count the items received.
2	The company could pay for an item it does not need, did not order, or did not receive.	The requisition (not shown on this flowchart) supports the need for the item. The purchase order supports that the company authorized its purchase. The receiving report documents that the items were received.
3	Checks could be issued for unauthorized purchases of goods and services. A check could be prepared for an amount or a vendor different from the information in the voucher.	The check signer reviews the accuracy of the voucher and compares this information to the check. The check signer is responsible for having an adequate knowledge of the business to recognize and question any unusual purchases or vendors.
4	Any employee involved in the preparation of any voucher document could submit a false document. Employees could request the purchase of unnecessary goods and services or purchase goods and services from a favored vendor.	Checks are not returned to any employee or department responsible for the preparation of the voucher. Checks are sent directly from the check signer to the vendor.
5	A document could be used to support multiple payments of a voucher.	The check signer cancels every document in the voucher before it is returned to Accounts Payable for filing. If the document was submitted to support another cash payment, the check signer should see the cancelled document when the vouchers are approved.

LO8 Identify the key controls of a voucher system.

Audit your understanding LO8

1. Who prepares a requisition?
2. What happens to a check after it is signed by the check signer?
3. How does a business ensure that the Receiving Department counts the items received?
4. How does a business ensure that voucher documents are only used once to support a cash payment?

Work together 20-4 LO8

Performing a risk assessment

Perform a risk assessment of Glaston Company's voucher processing system. A portion of a flowchart documenting the system and a form are provided in the *Working Papers*. Use the control symbols on the form to mark the flowchart location of three significant risks. In the Internal Control column, describe how the system should be changed to prevent or detect errors or frauds. Your instructor will guide you through completing this problem.

On your own 20-4 LO8

Performing a risk assessment

Perform a risk assessment of Lamier Company's voucher processing system. A portion of a flowchart documenting the system and a form are provided in the *Working Papers*. Use the control symbols on the form to mark the flowchart location of four significant risks. In the Internal Control column, describe how the system should be changed to prevent or detect errors or frauds. Work this problem independently.

A Look at **Accounting** Software

Setting User Access Privileges

The principles you learned in this chapter related to internal controls are as important in a company using a computerized accounting system as in a manual accounting environment. To provide for internal control, automated accounting systems are designed to limit each user to specific types of access to the system. Defining and setting user access privileges are control activities. These settings determine which windows and reports users can open on their computers.

It is very important to understand that these system controls are only as good as the overall control system. For example, an employee might seek out a computer where another user with greater access privileges is logged in. That employee could then access and control the system in ways not allowed with his or her own login. Therefore, additional control measures need to be implemented and

enforced. Users who are logged on to the system might be required to put their computers in sleep mode if they will be out of sight of their computer for more than a few minutes. Sleep mode leaves the computer running but requires the user to log back in. Of course, if the employee had learned the password of the other user, the computer could still be accessed. Another control measure, then, would be to require that passwords be changed periodically.

Controlling user access to any automated system is a function of the system administrator. Generally, only a few highly trusted individuals are made system administrators, since they require complete access to the system. Administrators of a company's computerized accounting system would usually be under the direction of the chief financial officer, vice president of operations, or information systems director.

1 The system administrator has accessed the Company Information tab on the Enter/Edit Company Information window and selected **Users** in the System Setup field.

2 Information describing the user of an automated system is commonly called the **user profile**. The administrator has selected Dabne Coulter's user profile for editing. The User ID is an important feature for system control. Whenever users log on to the system, their User ID and the system date are attached to every entry they make. This feature makes it possible to hold users accountable for their entries and changes.

3 One part of the system control process is establishing user classifications and setting default access privileges for each class. Some classifications that might be listed would be Administrator, Accounting Manager, Executive Assistant—Sales, Sales Representative, Warehouse Manager, etc. These classifications define a user's level of authority and the type of access required to perform the user's job. Dabne Coulter's classification is Accounting Staff.

4 Not all users will be company employees. Outside users might include the company's CPA firm and external technical support staff. The Affiliation field identifies the user as an employee or an outside resource.

5 All users must enter a valid password to access the system. Longer passwords and those containing a variety of character types (alphabet, numbers, and symbols) increase the level of security because they make it more difficult for an unauthorized individual to guess the password. It is a common requirement that users change their passwords periodically. Occasionally, a user will forget a password or discover that it is no longer a secret. In that case, the administrator can reset the password.

6 The administrator clicked on the **Privileges** button to edit Dabne's access privileges. The system opened the User Access Privileges dialog box where privileges are set. The default profile for the Accounting Staff classification is displayed by the system. Users may be limited to only viewing certain types of information, they may be given the privilege of entering or editing data, or they may be prevented from accessing certain types of information.

7 When this system was originally set up, zones of access were established. Different types of data fields were linked to these zone labels. Access controls enable the system to limit the types of information users can view, enter, or change.

8 The administrator clicked on the second **check box** next to Plant Assets to change Dabne's access privilege from View to Enter Edit.

9 Note that neither check box for Employee Records or Payroll Transactions has been checked. Since Dabne has no payroll responsibilities, he should not have any access to employee records.

10 The administrator would click **OK** to close the dialog box and then click **Save** on the User Setup menu bar to keep the change.

CHAPTER SUMMARY

Internal controls are a collection of procedures designed to reduce the risk of errors and fraud. An error is an unintentional mistake. In contrast, a fraud is the theft of assets or the intentional misstatement of financial statements.

Frauds during the early 1980s led to the creation of the Committee of Sponsoring Organizations (COSO) to study the factors that lead to fraudulent financial reporting. The result was an expanded view of the accounting profession's perception of internal controls. The internal control structure consists of the control environment, risk assessment, control activities, information and communication, and monitoring. Accountants use the internal control structure to guide their assessment of whether an accounting system is subject to error or fraud. One of the most basic internal controls is the segregation of the authority, custody, and recording functions of a transaction.

The frauds that caused the failures of Enron and WorldCom forced Congress to enact the Sarbanes-Oxley Act of 2002 (SOX). SOX created the Public Company Accounting Oversight Board (PCAOB) with the power to set auditing standards. SOX requires publicly held corporations to document their accounting systems and related internal controls.

Narratives and flowcharts are two common methods of documenting accounting systems. A flowchart is a collection of symbols and connecting lines that diagram the documents and the flow of information in an accounting system. A flowchart enables accountants to assess the risk that an error or fraud could occur.

A voucher system is an example of an accounting system with numerous control activities. A voucher is a group of documents that support a transaction. Approved vouchers are entered in a voucher register. When the assigned time to pay the voucher arrives, the documents are used to support the writing of a check. The check is recorded in a check register. Control activities help ensure that the business only pays authentic vendors for those items ordered and received.

EXPLORE ACCOUNTING

Preventive and Detective Control Activities

Control activities are often classified as preventive, detective, and corrective. A preventive control prevents an error or fraud from occurring. A computer system that prevents an accounts receivable clerk from entering a sale is a preventive control. The system does not allow the clerk to access the window required to enter the sale. A detective control detects an error or fraud after it has occurred. A bank reconciliation is a detective control. A check incorrectly recorded in a cash payments journal or a check register should be detected by a bank reconciliation. A corrective control enables the business to correct the damage caused by an error or fraud. Insurance is the most common type of corrective control. Insurance covering key employees can reimburse a business for stolen assets.

Effective internal controls are designed to provide reasonable, but not absolute, assurance that errors and frauds are prevented or detected on a timely basis. There are many reasons why a well-designed control activity can fail. Most of the reasons involve people. Many control activities rely on one employee checking the work of another employee. For example, a payroll clerk totals the overtime hours reported on a time card. A manager performs the same process to ensure the amount of overtime hours is accurate. If the payroll clerk makes an error, the possibility exists that the manager will fail to detect the error. This chance increases if the manager is busy or not dedicated to performing control activities.

Suppose a salesclerk can only obtain sold merchandise by presenting a warehouse employee with a sales ticket. The sales ticket proves that the sale was recorded in the point-of-sale system. However, if the employees work together to commit a fraud, the control activity no longer exists. If the salesclerk can obtain merchandise without a sales ticket, the clerk and the warehouse employee can steal merchandise without being detected.

Two or more employees working together to commit a fraud is referred to as *collusion*. Most control activities are designed assuming that employees perform their assigned control activities. Knowing that collusion can occur, accountants must continually monitor the accounting systems to look for signs of fraudulent activities.

INSTRUCTIONS

Write a paragraph explaining a control activity that you have observed. Consider tasks you observed on a job or as a volunteer for a school or civic event. Describe how two individuals could collude to commit a fraud.

APPLY YOUR UNDERSTANDING

INSTRUCTIONS: Download problem instructions for Excel, QuickBooks, and Sage 50c from the textbook companion website at www.C21accounting.com.

20-1 Application Problem | Classify internal controls LO3, 4

Use the forms provided in the *Working Papers*.

Instructions:

1. For each item, indicate the component of the internal control structure: control environment, risk assessment, control activities, information and communication, or monitoring.
2. For each item, indicate whether the action is authority, custody, or recording function.

20-2 Application Problem | Preparing flowcharts LO5

Use the form provided in the *Working Papers*.

Instructions:

For each statement, prepare a flowchart to represent the process described.

a. A human resource manager approves an employee's vacation request form.
b. An employee journalizes a credit memorandum in the general ledger.
c. A warehouse employee records the quantity of items on a picking ticket and sends the form to the Shipping Department employee who compares the picking ticket with the number of items received from the warehouse.
d. A receptionist opens the mail and prepares a list of checks received. The list of checks is sent to an accounting clerk, who posts the total in a cash receipts journal.

20-3 Application Problem | Journalizing transactions in a voucher system LO6, 7

sage 50

1. Journalize and post transactions related to a voucher system to the general journal.
2. Journalize and post transactions related to a voucher system in the Write Checks window.
3. Print the general journal, cash disbursements journal, and the trial balance.

QB Quick Books

1. Journalize and post transactions related to a voucher system to the journal.
2. Journalize and post transactions related to a voucher system in the Write Checks window.
3. Print the journal, check detail, and trial balance.

[Excel]

1. Journalize transactions related to a voucher system in the general journal.
2. Journalize transactions related to a voucher system in the cash payments journal.
3. Print the worksheets.

The following transactions of Marlon's Ceramics were completed during June of the current year. A voucher register and cash register are provided in the *Working Papers*. Source documents are abbreviated as follows: voucher, V; check, C.

Transactions:

June 4. Paid cash to Baker Company, $3,670.00, covering V206. C234.
6. Purchased merchandise on account from Marsh Industries, $1,635.00. V208.
10. Received an invoice from Lynch Catering for a miscellaneous expense, $265.00. V209.
11. Paid cash to Marsh Industries, $1,635.00, less 2% discount, covering V208. C235.
14. Made a deposit in the checking account, $3,844.75.
18. Bought sales supplies on account from B&L Supplies, $450.00. V210.
22. Purchased merchandise on account from Abram Corp., $995.75. V211.
26. Paid cash to B&L Supplies, $450.00, less 2% discount, covering V210. C236.

Instructions:

1. Record the bank balance brought forward on June 1, $10,618.60.
2. Journalize the transactions completed during June of the current year. Use page 6 of a voucher register and page 9 of a check register.
3. Prove and rule the voucher register.
4. Prove and rule the check register.

A portion of a flowchart documenting Quitman Company's voucher processing system and a form are provided in the *Working Papers*.

Instructions:

Perform a risk assessment of Quitman's voucher processing system. Use the control symbols on the form to mark the flowchart location of four significant risks. In the Internal Control column, describe how the system should be changed to prevent or detect errors or frauds.

20-M Mastery Problem

Analyzing a voucher system and journalizing transactions in a voucher system LO5, 6, 7, 8

sage 50

1. Journalize and post transactions related to a voucher system to the general journal.
2. Journalize and post transactions related to a voucher system in the Write Checks window.
3. Print the general journal, cash disbursements journal, and the trial balance.

QB Quick Books

1. Journalize and post transactions related to a voucher system to the journal.
2. Journalize and post transactions related to a voucher system in the Write Checks window.
3. Print the journal, check detail and trial balance.

X

1. Journalize transactions related to a voucher system in the general journal.
2. Journalize transactions related to a voucher system in the cash payments journal.
3. Print the worksheets.

Avery Company is a small business that cannot employ the number of individuals required to separate adequately the duties in voucher processing. Its voucher processing is described in the following narrative.

Marcus Garran, store manager, is responsible for ordering the items required to maintain the store's merchandise inventory. He uses distributor websites to place the orders. When the merchandise arrives at the store, any available store employee is asked to receive the shipment. The employee compares the quantity of items received with the invoice included in the shipment and notes any differences. The goods are sent to the store floor and the invoice is sent to Patti Schmidt, the bookkeeper. She places the invoice in an Unpaid Invoices folder by the date the check should be written.

Each morning, Ms. Schmidt removes the invoices to be paid that day. She prepares a check for each invoice, attaches the check to the invoice, and records the checks in a cash payments journal. The documents are forwarded to Daniel Avery, the owner, for signing. He inspects the documents, signs the checks, and mails the checks to the vendors. A copy of the check is stapled to the invoice. The documents are returned to Ms. Schmidt for filing by vendor in the Paid Invoices file.

Instructions:

1. Prepare a flowchart of Avery Company's voucher system. Use a triangle ∇ to represent the Unpaid Invoices and Paid Invoices folders.
2. Identify four risks in the system. Complete the Risk Assessment and Internal Control columns of the form provided in the *Working Papers*. Use the control symbols on the form to mark the flowchart location of the risks.
3. Journalize the following transactions completed during August of the current year. Use page 8 of a voucher register and page 12 of a check register provided in the *Working Papers*.

Transactions:

Aug. 2. Paid cash to O'Leary Company, $1,689.00, covering V613, no discount. C704.
 3. Made a deposit in the checking account, $4,185.66.
 4. Received an invoice from Kellogg Marketing for advertising, $3,500.00. V622.
 9. Purchased merchandise on account from NTY Industries, $2,380.00. V623.
 12. Paid cash to Kellogg Marketing, $3,500.00, less 2% discount, covering V622. C705.
 16. Bought administrative supplies on account from Lakeland Supply, $485.00. V624.
 18. Paid cash to NTY Industries, $2,380.00, less 1% discount, covering V623. C706.
 4. Prove and rule the voucher register.
 5. Prove and rule the check register.

The Certified Public Accountant examination often requires candidates to complete a flowchart. The flowchart is complete with the exception of selected symbol descriptions. Candidates must use their knowledge of the accounting systems and flowchart symbols to describe the symbols. Candidates must also be able to assign a meaning to an unfamiliar symbol by understanding how that symbol is used elsewhere in the flowchart.

A flowchart for a portion of Velcar Corporation's sales processing system is shown below. Velcar uses a computerized accounting system.

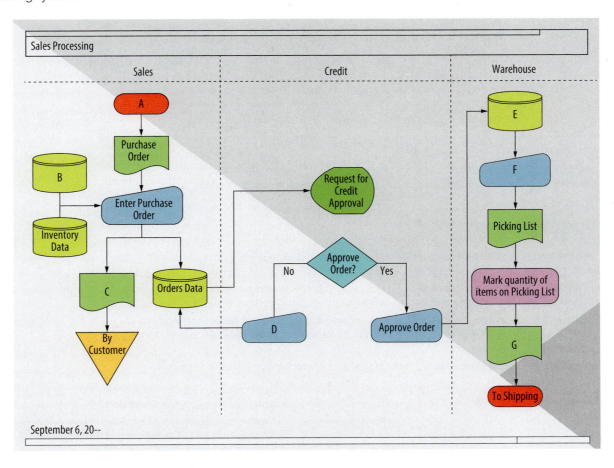

Instructions:

Complete the form provided in the *Working Papers*. The first item is completed as an example.

Symbol	Description
A	From customer

21st Century Skills

Controls for Social Media

Theme: Financial, Economic, Business, and Entrepreneurial Literacy

Skills: Creativity and Innovation, Critical Thinking and Problem Solving, Communication and Collaboration

PARTNERSHIP FOR
21ST CENTURY SKILLS

Facebook has over 2.2 billion users; Twitter, 330 million; and Instagram, 813 million. It comes as no surprise that social media is presenting new opportunities for conducting business.

Corporate blogs, fan pages on Facebook, and image- and video-sharing sites like YouTube have helped companies find new customers and increase customer loyalty. These trends are also forcing internal auditors to evaluate risks associated with social media.

A lack of control over content poses a risk. Deciphering what information can be distributed to the public and identifying responsible parties for posting on behalf of the company can minimize the risk. Data leaks, viruses, and unfavorable comments can be consumed by millions of recipients within seconds and affect company performance and reputation.

Businesses should embrace the benefits of social media. However, internal controls must be established so employees know the expectation and the impact of not following procedures.

APPLICATION

1. Player's Choice, a new sporting goods company, has decided to jump on the social media bandwagon.

   a. Determine three examples of social media that you feel would be effective for a sporting goods company wanting to advertise products for sale. Explain why.

   b. Create a social media policy that focuses on user behavior for employees using (1) Facebook, (2) YouTube, and (3) Twitter. Include at least three internal control procedures for each.

2. Compare the similarities of a social media policy and a voucher system used for a business.

Source: www.statista.com.

Analyzing Home Depot's Financial Statements

The financial statement frauds at Enron and WorldCom involved corporate officers at the highest levels. In response, Congress passed the Sarbanes-Oxley Act of 2002 in an effort to reduce the possibility of similar financial disasters. This act holds corporate officers more accountable for the accuracy of their corporation's financial statements. The new rules require select corporate officers to take personal responsibility for the accuracy of the financial statements.

INSTRUCTIONS

Refer to pages B-3 and B-4 in Appendix B to answer the following questions:

1. Who is responsible for the preparation of Home Depot's financial statements?
2. Who is responsible for ensuring that the corporation has an adequate system of internal controls?
3. Which corporate officers are specifically mentioned as being involved in the corporation's evaluation of its internal control and signing the report?
4. Who audited the effectiveness of Home Depot's internal control over financial reporting?

21

Organizational Structure of a Partnership

LEARNING OBJECTIVES

After studying Chapter 21, in addition to defining key terms, you will be able to:

LO1 Compare the organization structures of a partnership and corporation.

LO2 Explain how a partnership is organized.

LO3 Journalize transactions related to the formation of a partnership.

LO4 Journalize transactions to admit a new partner to an existing partnership.

Ernst & Young LLP

ACCOUNTING IN THE REAL WORLD

Ernst & Young (EY) is one of the largest public accounting firms in the world. Like many public accounting firms, EY earns a significant portion of its revenue by performing financial statement audits of other companies and organizations. In addition, they offer services that include preparing client tax returns, assisting clients with tax planning, and providing a wide range of business consulting services.

An accountant who conducts an audit is known as an auditor. A single auditor is capable of auditing a small business, but a team of auditors is needed to audit larger businesses. The audit team will consist of auditors having different levels of experience and expertise.

Public accounting firms have highly structured methods for promoting professional staff. The method used by many accounting firms follows this common route: new college accounting graduates begin their careers as staff auditors, and after two to three years of experience they are promoted to senior auditors. Staff and senior auditors perform the majority of the procedures involved in an audit, and the senior auditors are also responsible for supervising staff auditors.

After five to six years of experience, an auditor is promoted to manager. Managers have primary responsibility for the audit and approve the work of the staff and senior auditors. Managers must possess a high level of competence in generally accepted accounting principles and auditing standards. To be promoted to partner, managers also must demonstrate the ability to recruit and secure new clients. After 11 to 13 years of working with the firm, managers may be admitted as partners in the firm.

Partners are responsible for the management of the firm and are ultimately responsible for the quality of all work performed by the accounting firm. Partners devote significant time to obtaining new clients, referred to as practice development. In recent years a new position of director has emerged as a way of retaining talented individuals who are not selected for partner or who choose not to be admitted to the partnership.

Source: www.ey.com.

CRITICAL THINKING

1. What skills must a manager possess to be effective in recruiting new clients?
2. Why do you think a partnership is an attractive form of organization for a firm like EY?
3. Why might an individual choose not to be admitted as a partner in the firm?

KEY TERMS

partnership agreement
mutual agency

fair market value balance sheet
goodwill

intangible asset

LAMOR LEARNING CENTER

Lamor Learning Center is a service business organized as a partnership. The business provides tutoring services to students of all ages and specializes in preparing candidates to excel on standardized tests.

Chart of Accounts
LAMOR LEARNING CENTER

Balance Sheet Accounts

(1000) ASSETS
1100	Current Assets
1105	Cash
1110	Petty Cash
1115	Accounts Receivable
1120	Allowance for Uncollectible Accounts
1125	Supplies—Educational
1130	Supplies—Office
1135	Prepaid Insurance
1200	Plant Assets
1205	Equipment
1210	Accumulated Depreciation—Equipment
1215	Car
1220	Accumulated Depreciation—Car

(2000) LIABILITIES
2100	Current Liabilities
2105	Accounts Payable

(3000) OWNERS' EQUITY
3105	LaDonna Alford, Capital
3110	LaDonna Alford, Drawing
3115	Morgan Colvin, Capital
3120	Morgan Colvin, Drawing
3125	Income Summary

(4000) OPERATING REVENUE
4105	Sales

(5000) OPERATING EXPENSES
5105	Advertising Expense
5110	Depreciation Expense—Equipment
5115	Depreciation Expense—Car
5120	Insurance Expense
5125	Miscellaneous Expense
5130	Rent Expense
5135	Supplies Expense—Educational
5140	Supplies Expense—Office
5145	Truck Expense
5150	Uncollectible Accounts Expense
5155	Utilities Expense

The chart of accounts for Lamor Learning Center is illustrated above for reference as you study Chapters 21 and 22 of this textbook.

LO1 Compare the organizational structures of a partnership and corporation.
LO2 Explain how a partnership is organized.
LO3 Journalize transactions related to the formation of a partnership.

Organizational Structure of a Partnership LO1

A business in which two or more persons combine their assets and skills is known as a *partnership*. Each member of a partnership is known as a *partner*. Partnerships generally have only a few owners (partners), unlike a corporation that typically has many owners (stockholders). The partners' ownership is recorded in equity accounts for each of the partners. In contrast, a corporation records all stockholders' ownership in a single set of accounts. Except for recording owners' equity and income taxes, accounting procedures for a partnership are similar to those for a corporation.

A partnership has a limited life, unlike a corporation, which has an unlimited life. Any change in the number of partners terminates an existing partnership. When a new partner is admitted, the partners sign a new partnership agreement. The old partnership's accounting records are often continued for the new partnership. As a result, initial investment journal entries for all partners are not always needed. Journal entries are needed, however, to show clearly how the partners' equity has changed. One or both of the following journal entries may be needed:

1. To show how much the new partner invests.
2. To show how the new partner's admission affects existing partners' capital accounts.

Serving as an Expert Witness

Paul Rackley and Edward Miller were once the best of friends. However, the failure of their partnership resulted in allegations of mismanagement and fraud. The dispute made it to court, where Brittney Sellers, a certified fraud examiner, was being questioned by Amy Pratt, Mr. Rackley's legal counsel.

Amy: Ms. Sellers, you examined the financial records of the partnership. Did you find any evidence that Mr. Miller, the defendant, misused the assets of the partnership?

Brittney: In a detailed review of cash disbursements, I discovered that a large number of checks were written to Jenson Advertising. Jenson Advertising is owned by Mr. Miller's sister, April Miller Jenson.

Amy: I assume these expenditures were for advertising?

Brittney: That was the purpose stated on the invoices. Specifically, the invoices were for Internet advertising on social media sites. However, I confirmed with those sites that no advertising contracts were ever signed with either the partnership or Jenson Advertising.

Amy: So you believe these checks were fraudulent?

Brittney: Jenson Advertising does not even maintain an office—only a post office box. This is a clear case of a shell company, a fictitious business set up for the sole purpose of committing a fraud.

Amy: Thank you, Ms. Sellers. No further questions.

INSTRUCTIONS

Access the *Code of Ethics* of the Association of Certified Fraud Examiners. Using this code as a guide, use the ethical model to help determine whether Brittney's testimony demonstrates ethical behavior.

Organizing a Partnership LO2

A partnership is created when two or more persons agree orally or in writing to start a business, using the partnership form of organization. As in other forms of business, a partnership's financial records are kept separate from those of the partners. >> App. A: Business Entity

LaDonna Alford and Morgan Colvin agree to form a partnership called Lamor Learning Center. Prior to forming the partnership, Morgan owned a similar business and LaDonna was employed as a teacher.

Lamor Learning Center provides tutoring services and standardized test preparation classes. The business does not sell merchandise. For this reason, it does not need general ledger accounts for merchandise inventory, purchases, purchases discount, and purchases returns and allowances. Its clients cannot return a service and the business does not offer a sales discount. Thus, no sales returns and allowances or sales discount accounts are needed. The partners, who provide all the services to the clients, are not employees of the partnership. The Internal Revenue Service does not consider the money that partners receive from a partnership to be salaries. Therefore, until the growth of the business demands that it hire employees, the business does not need accounts for recording salaries and payroll taxes.

A written agreement setting forth the conditions under which a partnership is to operate is called a **partnership agreement**. A partnership agreement is also known as the *articles of partnership*. A partnership's life is limited to the length of time agreed on by the partners. A partnership is terminated by the partners' mutual agreement, death of a partner, withdrawal of one partner, or admission of a new partner.

Each partner can bind a partnership to any contract. The right of all partners to contract for a partnership is called **mutual agency**. Each partner is an agent of the partnership unless restricted by agreement.

Legally, a partnership agreement may be either written or oral. However, to avoid misunderstandings, a partnership agreement should be in writing. Some but not all states require that a partnership agreement be in writing. With an attorney's assistance, LaDonna and Morgan prepare their partnership agreement, shown on the next page.

Partnership Capital Accounts

The owners' equity division of a partnership's general ledger has two capital accounts for each partner.

1. An account in which to record a partner's equity includes the word *Capital* in the title. The two equity accounts in Lamor's general ledger are LaDonna Alford, Capital and Morgan Colvin, Capital.

2. An account in which the earnings taken out of the partnership during the fiscal period are recorded includes the word *Drawing* in the title. Assets taken out of a business for the owner's personal use are known as *withdrawals*. The two accounts in Lamor's general ledger used to record withdrawals are titled LaDonna Alford, Drawing and Morgan Colvin, Drawing.

Partners' withdrawals can be a cause of misunderstandings. For this reason, most partnership agreements include a statement controlling withdrawals. Lamor's partnership agreement has a controlling statement in Article VI of the partnership agreement.

PARTNERSHIP AGREEMENT

THIS CONTRACT is made and entered into this __28th__ day of __February 20--__, by and between __LaDonna Alford__ and __Morgan Colvin__ of __Plano, Texas__.

WITNESSETH: That the said parties have this date formed a partnership to engage in and conduct a business under the following stipulations that are a part of this contract. The partnership will begin operation on __March 1, 20--__.

ARTICLE I: The business shall be conducted under the name of Lamor Learning Center, located initially at 1910 15th Street, Plano, TX 75023-5233.

ARTICLE II: The investment of each partner is: Morgan Colvin: Equity in a business located at 1910 15th Street, Plano, TX 75023-5233, and as shown in a fair market value balance sheet to be agreed upon by both partners prior to February 28, 20--. Total investment, $45,760.00. LaDonna Alford: Cash equal to the initial investment of Ms. Colvin. Total investment $22,800.00.

ARTICLE III: Both partners are to (a) participate in all general policy-making decisions, (b) devote full time and attention to the partnership business, and (c) engage in no other business enterprise without the written consent of the other partner. Ms. Colvin is to be general manager of the business's operations.

ARTICLE IV: Neither partner is to become a surety or bonding agent for anyone without the written consent of the other partner.

ARTICLE V: The partners' share in earnings and losses of the partnership are: Ms. Colvin: 5% interest on equity as of January 1 of each year; salary, $20,000.00 per year; remaining income or loss, 50%. Ms. Alford: 5% interest on equity as of January 1 of each year; salary, $15,000.00 per year; remaining income or loss, 50%.

ARTICLE VI: No partner is to withdraw assets in excess of the agreed-upon interest and salary without the other partner's written consent.

ARTICLE VII: All partnership transactions are to be recorded in accordance with standard and generally accepted accounting procedures and concepts. The partnership records are to be open at all times for inspection by either partner.

ARTICLE VIII: In case of either partner's death or legal disability, the equity of the partners is to be determined as of the time of the death or disability of the one partner. The continuing partner is to have first option to buy the deceased/disabled partner's equity at recorded book value.

ARTICLE IX: This partnership agreement is to continue indefinitely unless (a) terminated by the death of one partner, (b) terminated by giving the other partner written notice at least ninety (90) days prior to the termination date, or (c) terminated by written mutual agreement signed by both partners.

ARTICLE X: At the termination of this partnership agreement, the partnership's assets, after all liabilities are paid, will be distributed according to the balance in partners' capital accounts.

IN WITNESS WHEREOF, the parties to this contract have set their hands and seals on the date and year written.

Signed: *LaDonna Alford*   (Seal) Date: __February 28, 20--__

Signed: *Morgan Colvin*   (Seal) Date: __February 28, 20--__

Currency Manipulation

When the free market works correctly, foreign exchange rates can change almost daily. Many governments purchase or sell a currency on an exchange market with the intention of stabilizing the currency's exchange rate in the short run, which will help attract investors and free market trade. Usually, this action is not controversial.

In recent years, however, there has been some discussion about the ability of a government to manipulate foreign exchange rates to its country's advantage on a long-term basis. Currency manipulation, which is somewhat controversial, has been defined as:

> ". . . when a government buys or sells foreign currency to push the exchange rate of its currency away from its equilibrium value or to prevent the exchange rate from moving toward its equilibrium value.[1]"

Buying foreign currency tends to hold down the value of the domestic currency, which increases demand in the goods market as well as in the financial markets. This action has the opposite effect on the competing country's currency, which increases in value. In the long term, this action keeps the two currencies at those values artificially. The country whose currency is higher than it should be suffers from a deficit trade balance, which can cost that country jobs and hurt its economy.

The Articles of Agreement of the International Monetary Fund (IMF) prohibit the manipulation of currency values. However, the IMF has no procedures in place to stop or punish the country doing the manipulation. Also, it is difficult to prove the motive of a country that is buying foreign currency. Some think that the World Trade Organization (WTO) should respond to countries charged with currency manipulation. How can the United States counterbalance currency manipulation by other countries? One suggestion is to have Congress label the manipulation of currency as an illegal subsidy. Such action would allow duties to be placed on products shipped to the United States from that country. This would have the effect of increasing the price of those products, which would discourage their importation. This action is controversial, however, in that it could start a tariff war between the two countries.

CRITICAL THINKING

Search the Internet to find an article relating to the WTO and currency manipulation. Summarize any action taken by the WTO or proposed action rejected by this organization.

---

[1]"Combating Widespread Currency Manipulation," by Joseph E. Gagnon; Peterson Institute for International Economics, Policy Brief, Number PB12-19, July 2012. The equilibrium value of currency is the value at which the currency would remain without outside interference.

Partners' Initial Investments

Colvin Tutoring Center
Fair Market Value Balance Sheet
March 1, 20--

ASSETS

Current Assets:			
Cash...		$18,268.40	
Accounts Receivable.............................	$3,895.88		
Less Allowance for Uncollectible Accounts...........	120.00	3,775.88	
Supplies—Educational............................		4,380.00	
Supplies—Office		1,800.00	
Prepaid Insurance................................		235.00	
Total Current Assets			$28,459.28
Plant Assets:			
Equipment		$21,700.00	
Car..		9,800.00	
Total Plant Assets			31,500.00
Total Assets			$59,959.28

LIABILITIES

Accounts Payable			$14,199.28

OWNER'S EQUITY

Morgan Colvin, Capital...........................			45,760.00
Total Liabilities and Owner's Equity....................			$59,959.28

Morgan invests the assets of her existing business in the new partnership. According to Article II of the partnership agreement, she must provide financial information for her existing business.

Morgan's investment in the partnership includes cash and other assets, less liabilities, from her prior existing business. A balance sheet prepared in accordance with GAAP may not adequately report the value of the owner's contribution to the partnership. For example, although the book value of Morgan's car is $5,200.00, its market value is $9,800.00. She should be given credit for contributing $9,800.00 to the partnership.

A financial statement that presents the fair market value of a company's assets, liabilities, and owner's equity is called a **fair market value balance sheet**. The partners must agree on the current market value of the assets and liabilities being contributed. Some values, such as cash, accounts receivable, and accounts payable, are simple to verify with accounting records. Other values, such as inventory and plant assets, can be estimated using information available from independent sources. Finally, the partners must analyze available information and use judgment when agreeing on accounts, such as allowance for uncollectible accounts.

A copy of the fair market value balance sheet from Morgan's previous business, shown above, is attached to a receipt to provide needed details for the journal entry.
>> App. A: Objective Evidence

FYI The use of several individuals' names in the name of a business is often an indication of a partnership.

Journal Entries to Record Partners' Initial Investments LO3

Write Account Title | **Debit Asset Amounts** | **Credit Liability and Owners' Equity Amounts** | **Debit Cash**

CASH RECEIPTS JOURNAL

PAGE 1

	DATE	ACCOUNT TITLE	DOC. NO.	POST. REF.	GENERAL DEBIT	GENERAL CREDIT	ACCOUNTS RECEIVABLE CREDIT	SALES CREDIT	SALES TAX PAYABLE CREDIT	SALES DISCOUNT DEBIT	CASH DEBIT	
1	20-- Mar. 1	LaDonna Alford, Capital	R1			22 88 0 00					22 88 0 00	1
2	1	Accounts Receivable	R2		3 89 5 88						18 26 8 40	2
3		Supplies—Educational			4 38 0 00							3
4		Supplies—Office			1 80 0 00							4
5		Prepaid Insurance			2 35 00							5
6		Equipment			21 70 0 00							6
7		Car			9 80 0 00							7
8		Allow. for Uncoll. Accounts				1 2 0 00						8
9		Accounts Payable				14 19 9 28						9
10		Morgan Colvin, Capital				45 76 0 00						10

The two partners agree on a value for all invested assets on the date the partnership begins, March 1. LaDonna's initial investment is cash of $22,880.00. Morgan's initial investment is $45,760.00, the agreed-upon value of her equity in her previous business, Colvin Tutoring Center.

A separate journal entry is made for each partner's initial investment as shown above.

> March 1, 20--. Received cash from partner, LaDonna Alford, as an initial investment, $22,880.00. Receipt No. 1.

Cash is debited for $22,880.00. LaDonna Alford, Capital is credited for $22,880.00.

> March 1, 20--. Accepted assets and liabilities of Morgan Colvin's existing business, Colvin Tutoring Center, as an initial investment, $45,760.00. Receipt No. 2.

All asset amounts on the balance sheet are debited. Allowance for Uncollectible Accounts and Accounts Payable are credited. Morgan Colvin, Capital is credited for the capital in her existing business, $45,760.00.

THINK LIKE AN ACCOUNTANT

Improving Efficiency with Templates

Sandra Evans and three of her close friends have started a small business that assists parents in planning and conducting birthday parties. Her friends are responsible for contacting potential clients and rendering the services. Sandra's responsibility is to handle the accounting duties.

The new partnership has very little capital and cannot afford to have custom source documents printed. Yet the partners want to present a professional image. Sandra has asked you to help her create these documents.

Excel contains templates for a wide variety of source documents that can be downloaded and modified. Use a template to create a sample invoice for Sandra's approval. Complete the invoice, using imaginary information about the company, the client, and the services provided.

OPEN THE SPREADSHEET TLA_CH21

The worksheet contains instructions for downloading a template containing a simple sales invoice. Follow the steps on the Instructions tab to modify the template. Answer these questions:

1. Select four other templates that Sandra might find useful in operating her new partnership. Draft an e-mail to Sandra that would explain why she should use each template.

2. Select a template containing an income statement. How might the income statement need to be modified to be used by a partnership?

TERMS REVIEW

partnership agreement

mutual agency

fair market value balance sheet

Audit your understanding LO1, 2

1. What is the difference between the equity accounts of a partnership and corporation?
2. What happens to a partnership with any change in the number of partners?
3. Why should a partnership agreement be in writing?
4. What happens to an existing partnership if a partner dies?
5. What does mutual agency mean?
6. Why is a balance sheet prepared in accordance with GAAP not appropriate to support a partner's contribution to a partnership?

Work together 21-1 LO3

Forming a partnership

A cash receipts journal is provided in the *Working Papers*. Your instructor will guide you through the following examples.

Ming Han and Keel Milner agree to form a partnership on May 1 of the current year. The partnership assumes the assets and liabilities of Keel's existing business. Ming invests cash equal to Keel's investment. Partners share equally in all changes in equity. The May 1 balance sheet for Keel's existing business is shown in the *Working Papers*. Source documents are abbreviated as follows: receipt, R.

Journalize the transactions in a cash receipts journal.

> Transactions:
>
> May 1. Received cash from partner, Ming Han, as an initial investment, $60,000.00. R1.
>
> 1. Accepted assets and liabilities of Keel Milner's existing business as an initial investment, $60,000.00. R2.

On your own 21-1 LO3

Forming a partnership

A cash receipts journal is provided in the *Working Papers*. Work independently to complete the following problem.

Willie Tribble and Janey Stapp agree to form a partnership on July 1 of the current year. The partnership assumes the assets and liabilities of Janey's existing business. Willie invests cash equal to Janey's investment. Partners share equally in all changes in equity. The July 1 balance sheet for Janey's existing business is shown in the *Working Papers*. Source documents are abbreviated as follows: receipt, R.

Journalize the transactions in a cash receipts journal.

> Transactions:
>
> July 1. Received cash from partner, Willie Tribble, as an initial investment, $38,000.00. R1.
>
> 1. Accepted assets and liabilities of Janey Stapp's existing business as an initial investment, $38,000.00. R2.

LO4 Journalize transactions to admit a new partner to an existing partnership.

Admitting a New Partner LO4

A partnership should consider every opportunity to expand its business. One method is to admit a new partner to the partnership. The new partner can help the partnership in several ways, such as adding a unique expertise, contributing new capital, or allowing the business to expand into new geographic regions. Although the existing partners will own a smaller share of the partnership, the value of their capital should increase as the business expands.

The transaction for admitting a new partner depends on the value of assets the new partner contributes to the business relative to the equity of the existing partners.

No Change in Total Equity

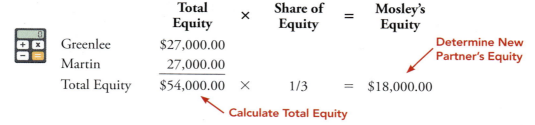

	Total Equity	×	Share of Equity	=	Mosley's Equity
Greenlee	$27,000.00				
Martin	27,000.00				
Total Equity	$54,000.00	×	1/3	=	$18,000.00

Determine New Partner's Equity

Calculate Total Equity

GENERAL JOURNAL   PAGE **4**

	DATE		ACCOUNT TITLE	DOC. NO.	POST. REF.	DEBIT	CREDIT	
1	20-- Jan.	1	Joy Greenlee, Capital	M22		9 0 0 0 00		1
2			Dwaylon Martin, Capital			9 0 0 0 00		2
3			Jesse Mosley, Capital				18 0 0 0 00	3
4								4

Redistribute Capital

Joy Greenlee and Dwaylon Martin are partners in an existing business. The partners agree to admit Jesse Mosley as a new partner. However, the business does not need additional capital now. Therefore, Joy and Dwaylon agree to sell part of their existing equity to Jesse.

The existing partners each have $27,000.00 equity in the existing partnership. The three partners agree that Jesse is to pay $18,000.00 for a one-third equity in the new partnership. Joy and Dwaylon receive cash from Jesse for equity in the partnership. The partnership does not receive the cash from the sale of equity.

The two existing partners are each entitled to one-half of the price Jesse pays for one-third of the equity of the partnership. Therefore, Jesse pays $9,000.00 each to Joy and Dwaylon. Also, on the partnership's records, $18,000.00 of the existing equity is transferred to Jesse.

> January 1, 20--. Journalized the personal sale of equity to a new partner, Jesse Mosley, for a one-third equity in the business, $18,000.00. Memorandum No. 22.

The receipt of cash, a personal transaction among Joy, Dwaylon, and Jesse, is not recorded on the partnership's records. However, the redistribution of capital is a partnership entry and is journalized.

Equity Equal to New Partner's Investment

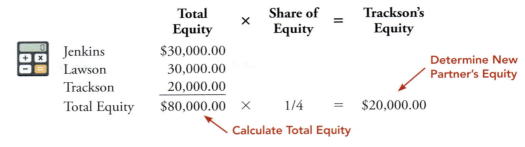

	Total Equity	×	Share of Equity	=	Trackson's Equity
Jenkins	$30,000.00				
Lawson	30,000.00				
Trackson	20,000.00				
Total Equity	$80,000.00	×	1/4	=	$20,000.00

Determine New Partner's Equity

Calculate Total Equity

CASH RECEIPTS JOURNAL   PAGE 3

					1 GENERAL	2 GENERAL	3 ACCOUNTS RECEIVABLE CREDIT	4 SALES CREDIT	5 SALES TAX PAYABLE CREDIT	6 SALES DISCOUNT DEBIT	7 CASH DEBIT	
	DATE	ACCOUNT TITLE	DOC. NO.	POST. REF.	DEBIT	CREDIT						
1	Feb. 1	Rosean Trackson, Capital	R120			20 000 00					20 000 00	1
2												2
3												3

Record Additional Capital

Partnerships often seek to increase their total equity to allow the business to grow. Partnerships may seek to expand their current markets, move into new markets, or sell new types of merchandise. Additional capital gives partnerships added financial strength as the business grows.

John Jenkins and Natalia Lawson are partners in an existing partnership. Each partner's equity is $30,000.00, for a total equity of $60,000.00. The existing partners

agree to admit Rosean Trackson as a partner with a one-fourth interest for a $20,000.00 cash investment. Rosean's equity is calculated as shown above. Rosean's investment does not change John's or Natalia's equity.

> February 1, 20--. Received cash from new partner, Rosean Trackson, for a one-fourth equity in the business, $20,000.00. Receipt No. 120.

Changing Services to Match the Times

CareerClusters
PATHWAYS TO COLLEGE & CAREER READINESS
Hospitality & Tourism

The origin of the modern-day travel agency, which may be organized as a partnership, can be traced to the United Kingdom in the 19th century. Twenty-five years ago, the most common way to book an airline flight was to go through a travel agent, who had access to airline information. The agent could search for the lowest cost or best travel times for the customer and book the ticket. The agent would get a commission from the airlines for processing the booking.

The rise of the Internet drastically changed how flights are booked. Today, a traveler can search the Internet and actually book the ticket. If a travel agent does book a flight, the agency will often charge the traveler a fee for the service.

Travel agents still do many of the bookings for cruises and travel packages, which continue to pay commissions. To stay in business, the travel agent must be aware of how much time it takes to service each customer and the amount of commission to be earned on the sale. The source of such information is accurate accounting records.

CRITICAL THINKING

Contact a travel agency by phone or via the Internet and determine what services the agency offers free and what services are offered for a fee. Ask the agent how the commission structure has changed in the last 10 to 15 years and what the implications of this change are for the profitability of the agency.

Equity Greater Than New Partner's Investment

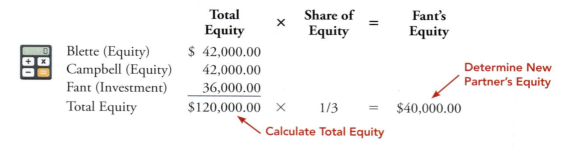

	Total Equity	×	Share of Equity	=	Fant's Equity
Blette (Equity)	$ 42,000.00				
Campbell (Equity)	42,000.00				
Fant (Investment)	36,000.00				
Total Equity	$120,000.00	×	1/3	=	$40,000.00

Determine New Partner's Equity

Calculate Total Equity

CASH RECEIPTS JOURNAL — PAGE 7

	DATE	ACCOUNT TITLE	DOC. NO.	POST. REF.	GENERAL DEBIT	GENERAL CREDIT	ACCOUNTS RECEIVABLE CREDIT	SALES CREDIT	SALES TAX PAYABLE CREDIT	SALES DISCOUNT DEBIT	CASH DEBIT	
1	May 1	Klaire Fant, Capital	R106			36 0 0 0 00					36 0 0 0 00	1
2												2
3												3

Record Additional Capital

GENERAL JOURNAL — PAGE 6

	DATE	ACCOUNT TITLE	DOC. NO.	POST. REF.	DEBIT	CREDIT	
1	May 1	Kelsay Blette, Capital	M45		2 0 0 0 00		1
2		Marge Campbell			2 0 0 0 00		2
3		Klaire Fant, Capital				4 0 0 0 00	3
4							4

Redistribute Capital

Kelsay Blette and Marge Campbell both have equity of $42,000.00 in an existing partnership. The existing partners agree to admit Klaire Fant as a partner with a one-third interest for a $36,000.00 cash investment. Klaire's equity is calculated as shown above.

> May 1, 20--. Received cash from new partner, Klaire Fant, for a one-third equity in the business, $36,000.00. Existing equity is redistributed as follows: from Kelsay Blette, $2,000.00; from Marge Campbell, $2,000.00. Receipt No. 106 and Memorandum No. 45.

Two journal entries are required to record this transaction. (1) The receipt of cash is recorded. (2) The redistribution of existing equity is recorded.

When Goodwill Is Recognized

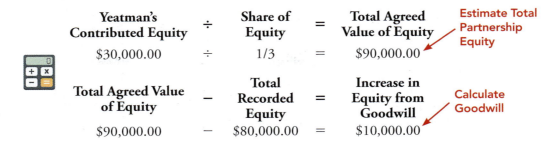

Yeatman's Contributed Equity	÷	Share of Equity	=	Total Agreed Value of Equity	Estimate Total Partnership Equity
$30,000.00	÷	1/3	=	$90,000.00	

Total Agreed Value of Equity	−	Total Recorded Equity	=	Increase in Equity from Goodwill	Calculate Goodwill
$90,000.00	−	$80,000.00	=	$10,000.00	

CASH RECEIPTS JOURNAL — PAGE 9

	DATE	ACCOUNT TITLE	DOC. NO.	POST. REF.	GENERAL DEBIT	GENERAL CREDIT	ACCOUNTS RECEIVABLE CREDIT	SALES CREDIT	SALES TAX PAYABLE CREDIT	SALES DISCOUNT DEBIT	CASH DEBIT	
1	July 1	Marshall Yeatman, Capital	R344			30 0 0 0 00					30 0 0 0 00	1
2												2
3												3

Record Additional Capital

GENERAL JOURNAL — PAGE 7

	DATE	ACCOUNT TITLE	DOC. NO.	POST. REF.	DEBIT	CREDIT	
1	July 1	Goodwill	M89		10 0 0 0 00		1
2		Kenya Norris, Capital				5 0 0 0 00	2
3		Tawanya Elrod, Capital				5 0 0 0 00	3
4							4

Record Goodwill and Redistribute Capital

The fair value of the assets may not be the best measure of the value of the business. The value of a business can also be valued based on the amount of revenue the business can generate. For example, the assets of a public accounting firm are relatively small, consisting primarily of office furniture and computers. The value of these assets is relatively small compared to the fees that the accountants earn by performing professional services. In this case, the transaction to admit a new partner needs to account for the full value of the business.

Kenya Norris and Tawanya Elrod are partners in an existing business. Each partner's equity is $25,000.00, for a total equity of $50,000.00. The existing partners agree to admit Marshall Yeatman as a partner with a one-third interest for a $30,000.00 cash investment. Based on the past revenue earned by the business, Marshall believes the total equity value is worth $90,000.00 after his investment.

The value of a business in excess of the total investment of owners is called **goodwill**. The partners agree that Marshall's willingness to pay $30,000.00 for a one-third interest is evidence that goodwill exists. The

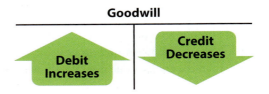

Goodwill

Debit Increases	Credit Decreases

value of goodwill is calculated as shown above. The total recorded equity, $80,000.00, is the equity of the existing partners, $50,000.00, plus the amount to be contributed by Marshall, $30,000.00.

> July 1, 20--. Received cash from new partner, Marshall Yeatman, for a one-third equity in the business, $30,000.00. Goodwill, $10,000.00, is distributed as follows: Kenya Norris, $5,000.00; Tawanya Elrod, $5,000.00. Receipt No. 344 and Memorandum No. 89.

Two journal entries are required for this transaction. (1) The receipt of cash is recorded. (2) The distribution of goodwill is recorded. The $10,000.00 amount of equity in excess of the total recorded investment of the three partners is the value of the goodwill.

Equity Accounts After Goodwill is Recognized

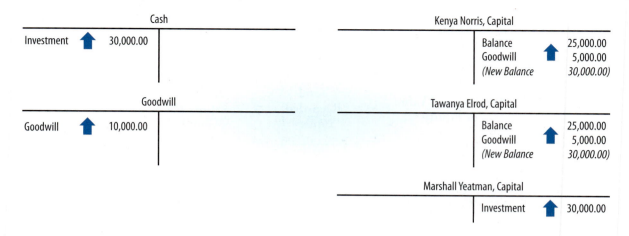

	Cash	
Investment ⬆ 30,000.00		

	Goodwill	
Goodwill ⬆ 10,000.00		

Kenya Norris, Capital

	Balance ⬆ 25,000.00
	Goodwill 5,000.00
	(New Balance 30,000.00)

Tawanya Elrod, Capital

	Balance ⬆ 25,000.00
	Goodwill 5,000.00
	(New Balance 30,000.00)

Marshall Yeatman, Capital

	Investment ⬆ 30,000.00

	Recorded Equity	+	Share of Goodwill	=	New Equity
Norris	$25,000.00	+	$ 5,000.00	=	$30,000.00
Elrod	25,000.00	+	5,000.00	=	30,000.00
Yeatman	30,000.00	+	—	=	30,000.00
Totals	$80,000.00	+	$10,000.00	=	$90,000.00

The analysis of the investment of cash by Marshall Yeatman and the distribution of goodwill is shown in the T accounts above. None of the goodwill is recorded in Marshall's capital account. He invested $30,000.00 for a one-third share of the business. One-third of the total equity, $90,000.00, equals the current balance of Marshall's capital account, $30,000.00.

Goodwill may be recorded only at the time of a change in ownership of business. An ongoing business may be worth more than the equity value stated in the accounting records. However, goodwill may not be recorded without some evidence of its value. This evidence is provided by the willingness of an investor to pay a premium for an ownership interest in the business.

An asset that does not have physical substance is called an **intangible asset**. Unlike most other asset accounts, the amount of goodwill cannot be related to a physical asset, such as inventory, or to a legal right, such as accounts receivable. Therefore, the account Goodwill is located in a general ledger's Intangible Assets section.

Improper Revenue Recognition

John Parchman has been trying to persuade his friend, Taylor Duke, to purchase his equity interest in Freshland Distributing, a business that operates in the food services industry. The business is organized as a partnership and currently has five other partners.

Every quarter, John sends Taylor a copy of Freshland's financial statements. The statements have shown a constant level of sales, despite the fact that the economy entered a recession a year ago. Taylor believes the business has the potential for significant growth, once the recession is over. After being courted by John for over a year, Taylor is about ready to make the investment.

At a New Year's social, Taylor was sharing his intent to purchase John's equity interest in Freshland. Marshall Edmonds, a CPA, was listening to Taylor explain how the business had maintained its sales despite the current state of the economy. Marshall jokingly interjected, "I hope they haven't been keeping the books open." Although Taylor seemed to ignore the comment, he was bothered by Marshall's facial expression, and he did not understand what was meant by "keeping the books open."

The first thing the next morning, Taylor was in Marshall's office seeking more information. "A few years ago," said Marshall, "I investigated a company that inflated its quarterly sales. The manager would record sales from the first few days of April, for example, as March sales. The first quarter's sales looked better than they should have. Of course, at the end of the next quarter, the manager had to do the same thing, just to keep sales from going down. To inflate that quarter's sales, even more July sales had to be recorded in June. After a few quarters, the fraud was totally out of control."

ACTIVITY

Taylor has obtained a data file of Freshland's sales and asked Marshall to search for fraud. Marshall has assigned you the task of analyzing the data to search for any "red flag" of improper revenue recognition. "This company's daily sales should be reasonably consistent," he stated. "Look for any sharp increase in daily sales at the end of a quarter, accompanied by a sharp decrease in daily sales right after the new quarter begins."

INSTRUCTIONS

Open the spreadsheet FA_CH21 and complete the steps on the Instructions tab. Provide answers to the following questions, supporting your answers.

1. Calculate the average daily sales.

2. Does the chart effectively provide evidence of a fraud?

3. Do the columns near the end of each quarter provide evidence of a fraud?

LO4 Journalize transactions to admit a new partner to an existing partnership.

TERMS REVIEW

goodwill

intangible asset

Audit your understanding LO4

1. When admitting a new partner, how is the new partner's equity calculated?
2. Why might a partnership seek an investment from a new partner?
3. What accounts are debited and credited to record the distribution of goodwill when a new partner is admitted?

Work together 21-2 LO4

Admitting partners to existing partnerships

Four independent situations of an existing partnership admitting a new partner are given below. The partners share equally in all changes in equity. For each situation, prepare the appropriate journal entries to admit a new partner on June 1 of the current year. A cash receipts journal and a general journal are provided in the *Working Papers*. Source documents are abbreviated as follows: memorandum, M; receipt, R. Your instructor will guide you through the following examples.

1. Charles Fulton and Davis Stewart each have equity of $18,000.00. Each partner agrees to sell $6,000.00 of his equity to Moses Tate and to give Moses a one-third share of ownership. Moses is to pay the money directly to the two original partners. M42.
2. Kennedy Davies and Kelly Andrews each have equity of $60,000.00. Mason Wood will pay $60,000.00 cash to the partnership for a one-third equity in the business. R121.
3. Marie Henson and Bobby Edwards each have $40,000.00 of equity. Cindy Yates will pay the partnership $34,000.00 cash for a one-third share in the business. R135 and M38.
4. Tyrone Wegner and Brodie Thomas each have equity of $36,000.00. Sue Shinn will pay $42,000.00 cash to the partnership to purchase a one-third share in the partnership. R79 and M24.

On your own 21-2 LO4

Admitting partners to existing partnerships

Four independent situations of an existing partnership admitting a new partner are given below. The partners share equally in all changes in equity. For each situation, prepare the appropriate journal entries to admit a new partner on May 1 of the current year. A cash receipts journal and a general journal are provided in the *Working Papers*. Work independently to complete the following examples.

1. Churna Knox and Mack Daniels each have equity of $36,000.00. Each partner agrees to sell $12,000.00 in equity to Paola Diaz and to give her a one-third share of ownership. Paola is to pay the money directly to the two original partners. M52.
2. Barry Sales and Jeff Rhea each have $62,000.00 of equity. Murray Price will pay $62,000.00 to the partnership to purchase a one-third share in the partnership. R192.
3. Scott Polk and Erica Morgan each have equity of $40,000.00. Tiffany Macri will pay the partnership $34,000.00 for a one-third equity in the business. R160 and M44.
4. Avaline Laird and Ethel Howe each have $38,000.00 of equity. Shelly Harmon will pay $45,000.00 to the partnership for a one-third share in the business. R223 and M111.

CHAPTER SUMMARY

A partnership is a business that is usually formed by a small group of individuals. Except for recording transactions involving owners' equity and income taxes, accounting procedures for a partnership are similar to those for a corporation. Each partner has two accounts: (1) a capital account to record contributions to the partnership and (2) a drawing account to record withdrawals. Partners are not employees of the partnership. Each partner's share of the income of the partnership is reported as income on that partner's individual tax return.

A written partnership agreement sets forth the conditions under which a partnership is to operate, including the addition or withdrawal of partners. A partnership's life is limited to the length of time agreed on by the partners and is terminated with any change in ownership. Unless limited by the partnership agreement, each partner has the authority to enter into transactions on behalf of the partnership.

A partner can contribute cash or other assets. The fair market value of assets contributed to a partnership should be determined and agreed upon by the partners. A fair market value balance sheet reports the value of an existing business's assets and liabilities that are contributed to the partnership.

The accounting for changes in the ownership of a partnership depends on (1) whether the new partner contributes assets to the partnership, (2) the amount contributed, and (3) the ownership percentage acquired. The addition of a new partner may require the recognition of goodwill when the amount of assets contributed exceeds the equity value of the partnership acquired. The goodwill increases the capital accounts of the existing partners.

Limited Liability Partnerships

The organizational structure of a corporation differs from a partnership in four ways.

1. *Continuity of life.* A partnership ends upon the death or withdrawal of an owner. Stockholders of a corporation buy and sell stock without affecting the life of the corporation.

2. *Centralization of management.* A partnership generally is managed by one or more of its partners. A corporation generally is managed by professional managers employed by the stockholders.

3. *Limited liability.* All partners are liable for contracts and liabilities incurred by the partnership. Because a corporation is treated as a separate legal entity, stockholders are not liable for the contracts or liabilities of the corporation.

4. *Free transferability of interest.* Generally, a partnership ends if a partner dies or withdraws. In addition, other partners must agree before a partner can sell his/her interest to another person. Stockholders can buy and sell shares of a corporation without consulting other stockholders.

Most states allow a special kind of partnership, called a *limited liability partnership* and frequently referred to as an *LLP*. An LLP must file articles of organization with the state. The operating agreement is similar to a traditional partnership agreement. The LLP must be managed by the members or a group of managers who are elected by the members. To qualify to be taxed as a partnership, the partnership can have no more than two of the characteristics of a corporation. Most LLPs retain the two characteristics of centralization of management and limited liability.

The attractiveness of an LLP is twofold. (1) Partners can be taxed as a partnership (net income is reported on the individual partner's tax return). (2) Partners have limited liability for the actions of the partnership, much like stockholders of a corporation. For these reasons, many partnerships have changed to an LLP.

INSTRUCTIONS

1. Identify your state's process and requirements for registering to become an LLP.

2. After reading more about LLPs or interviewing local partners of an LLP, determine other advantages and disadvantages of an LLP.

APPLY YOUR UNDERSTANDING

INSTRUCTIONS: Download problem instructions for Excel, QuickBooks, and Sage 50c from the textbook companion website at www.C21accounting.com.

21-1 Application Problem   Forming a partnership LO3

Crystal Foote and Lillie Classen agree to form a partnership on May 1 of the current year. The partnership assumes the assets and liabilities of Lillie's existing business. Crystal invests cash equal to Lillie's investment. Partners share equally in all changes in equity. The May 1 fair market value balance sheet for Lillie's existing business is as follows. A cash receipts journal is given in the *Working Papers*.

Lil's Gifts
Fair Market Value Balance Sheet
May 1, 20--

ASSETS			
Current Assets:			
Cash		$ 3,676.52	
Accounts Receivable	$10,531.68		
Less Allowance for Uncollectible Accounts	4,400.00	6,131.68	
Inventory		32,150.00	
Supplies		830.00	
Total Current Assets			$42,788.20
Plant Assets:			
Equipment			24,800.00
Total Assets			$67,588.20
LIABILITIES			
Accounts Payable			$ 9,481.36
OWNER'S EQUITY			
Lillie Classen, Capital			58,106.84
Total Liabilities and Owner's Equity			$67,588.20

Instructions:

Journalize the transactions. Source documents are abbreviated as follows: receipt, R.

Transactions:

May 1. Received cash from partner, Crystal Foote, as an initial investment, $58,106.84. R1.

    1. Accepted assets and liabilities of Lillie Classen's existing business as an initial investment, $58,106.84. R2.

Four independent situations are given below. The existing partners are Sadie Ryals and Shelly Perry. The new partner is Vergie Lowry. A general journal and cash receipts journal are given in the *Working Papers*. For each situation, prepare the appropriate journal entries to admit the new partner.

Instructions:

Journalize the transactions. Source documents are abbreviated as follows: memorandum, M; receipt, R.

Transactions:

1. Sadie Ryals and Shelly Perry have equity of $32,400.00 each in an existing partnership. On February 1 of the current year, the two partners agree to admit Vergie Lowry as a one-third partner. Each partner agrees to sell Vergie $21,600.00 in equity and to give her a one-third share of ownership. Vergie is to pay the money directly to the two original partners.

    Feb. 1. Journalized personal sale of equity to new partner, Vergie Lowry, $21,600.00, distributed as follows: from Sadie Ryals, $10,800.00; from Shelly Perry, $10,800.00. M30.

2. Sadie Ryals and Shelly Perry have equity of $34,280.00 each in the partnership. Partners share equally in all changes in equity. On February 1 of the current year, the two partners agree to admit Vergie as a partner with a one-third share of the total equity.

    Feb. 1. Received cash from new partner, Vergie Lowry, for a one-third equity in the business, $34,280.00. R222.

3. Sadie Ryals and Shelly Perry have equity of $24,250.00 each in an existing partnership. The partners share equally in all changes in equity. On February 1 of the current year, the existing partners agree to admit Vergie with a one-third share of the total equity.

    Feb. 1. Received cash from new partner, Vergie Lowry, for a one-third equity in the business, $22,000.00. Existing equity is redistributed as follows: from Sadie Ryals, $750.00; from Shelly Perry, $750.00. R175 and M27.

4. Sadie Ryals and Shelly Perry each have $32,650.00 equity in an existing business. The partners share equally in all changes in equity. On February 1 of the current year, Vergie is admitted as a new partner with a one-third share of the total equity.

    Feb. 1. Received cash from new partner, Vergie Lowry, for a one-third equity in the business, $40,000.00. Goodwill, $14,700.00, is distributed as follows: Sadie Ryals, $7,350.00; Shelly Perry, $7,350.00. R150 and M25.

sage 50

1. Journalize and post transactions related to admitting a new partner to the general journal.
2. Journalize and post transactions related to admitting a new partner in the Receipts window.
3. Print the general journal and cash receipts journal.

QB Quick Books

1. Journalize and post transactions related to admitting a new partner to the journal.
2. Print the journal and the transaction detail by account report.

X

1. Journalize transactions related to admitting a new partner to the general journal.
2. Journalize transactions related to admitting a new partner to the cash receipts journal.
3. Print the worksheets.

On May 1 of the current year, Tamra Hamby and Sharunda Massey form a partnership. The partners share equally in all changes in equity. The partnership assumes the assets and liabilities of Sharunda's existing business. Tamra invests cash equal to Sharunda's investment. A general journal and cash receipts journal are given in the *Working Papers*. The May 1 fair market value balance sheet for Sharunda's existing business is as follows.

Massey Specialty Shop
Fair Market Value Balance Sheet
May 1, 20--

ASSETS			
Current Assets:			
Cash..		$ 5,028.26	
Accounts Receivable...........................	$6,185.36		
Less Allowance for Uncollectible Accounts	1,000.00	5,185.36	
Inventory		24,100.00	
Supplies		1,050.00	
Total Current Assets			$35,363.62
Plant Assets:			
Equipment			12,600.00
Total Assets			$47,963.62
LIABILITIES			
Accounts Payable			$25,483.62
OWNER'S EQUITY			
Sharunda Massey, Capital			22,480.00
Total Liabilities and Owner's Equity..............			$47,963.62

Instructions:

Journalize the following transactions. Source documents are abbreviated as follows: memorandum, M; receipt, R.

Transactions:

May 　1. Received cash from partner, Tamra Hamby, as an initial investment, $22,480.00. R1.

　　　1. Accepted assets and liabilities of Sharunda Massey's existing business as an initial investment, $22,480.00. R2.

Aug. 　9. Journalized personal sale of equity to new partner, Emma Laws, $14,000.00. Each existing partner has a current equity balance of $21,000.00. M8.

Oct. 　3. Received cash from new partner, Antonio McKay, for a one-fourth equity in the business, $17,250.00. Each existing partner has a current equity balance of $17,250.00. R151.

　　12. Received cash from new partner, Luis Soto, for a one-fifth equity in the business, $21,300.00. Each existing partner has a current equity balance of $22,425.00. R158 and M42.

Dec. 　8. Received cash from new partner, Octavia Ruffin, for a one-sixth equity in the business, $28,000.00. Goodwill is distributed evenly among the existing partners. Each existing partner has a current equity balance of $24,800.00. R184 and M48.

---

sage 50

1. Journalize and post transactions related to a partnership to the general journal.
2. Journalize and post transactions related to a partnership in the Receipts window.
3. Print the general journal and cash receipts journal.

QB Quick Books

1. Journalize and post transactions related to a partnership to the journal.
2. Print the journal and the transaction detail by account report.

x

1. Journalize transactions related to a partnership to the general journal.
2. Journalize transactions related to a partnership to the cash receipts journal.
3. Print the worksheets.

College friends Dennis Brock, Joe Miller, and Kelly Mann operate a sporting goods store as a partnership. As a result of several transactions, the equity balances are as follows:

Dennis Brock	$40,000.00
Joe Miller	35,000.00
Kelly Mann	25,000.00

Partners share in all equity changes based on their relative equity balances.

Instructions:

Journalize the following transactions using the cash receipts journal and general journal provided in the *Working Papers*. Source documents are abbreviated as follows: memorandum, M; receipt, R.

Transactions:

Mar. 9. Received cash from new partner, Marilyn Pace, for a 10% equity ownership in the business, $15,000.00. R24 and M85. Each of the existing partners sold 10% of their equity to Ms. Pace. R215 and M35.

Aug. 14. Kelly Mann announced his desire to leave the partnership. Marilyn Pace purchased Kelly's equity interest for $32,000.00. M75.

Dec. 9. Danielle King closed her business and contributed inventory valued at $9,000.00 for a 5% equity ownership in the business. M92.

Auditing for Errors   LO4

James Mangione, Carl Nelson, and Marris Trevathon are partners in an existing business. Each partner's equity is $42,000, for a total equity of $126,000. The partners agree to admit Kelly Russell as a partner with a one-fourth interest for contributing $32,000 of inventory. The firm's bookkeeper made the following entry in the partnership's general journal:

	GENERAL JOURNAL			PAGE 7		
DATE	ACCOUNT TITLE	DOC. NO.	POST. REF.	DEBIT	CREDIT	
1	July 1	Inventory	M23		32 0 0 0 00		1
2		Goodwill			10 0 0 0 00		2
3		Kelly Russell, Capital				42 0 0 0 00	3
4							4

What entry would you make to correct the bookkeeper's entry? Explain your answer.

Causes and Consequences

Theme: Financial, Economic, Business, and Entrepreneurial Literacy

Skills: Communication and Collaboration, Critical Thinking and Problem Solving, ICT Literacy, and Initiative and Self-Direction

PARTNERSHIP FOR
21ST CENTURY SKILLS

When a company is acquired for a higher price than its book value, the excess is considered the value of the company and is recorded on the company's balance sheet under Goodwill. For example, a company's assets may be $1 million, but if someone is willing to pay $5 million for the company, the value of the company has increased $4 million due to goodwill.

Goodwill can be based on such factors as reputation, customer loyalty, products, executives, or ability to increase future revenue. However, if a company's reputation has suffered in any way, a company's value can be impaired and is noted on the balance sheet. Stock value could decrease, but a poor reputation could affect the company's bottom line for an extended period. Companies must work aggressively to protect the goodwill value that often takes years to build.

APPLICATION

1. Using the Internet, find two companies that have incurred an event that could have impacted the company's value. For each company, explain the event and how it could cause an impairment of goodwill.

2. With a partner, combine your results and create a poster depicting the company names, the events, and how the events could cause an impairment of goodwill.

Analyzing Home Depot's Financial Statements

Financial statements are interrelated and connected to one another. A change on one financial statement will have an impact on other financial statements. For example, if a corporation neglected to record a $10,000 cash payment for July rent, the cash amount reported on the balance sheet would be overstated. On the income statement, the net income would also be overstated, due to the $10,000 missing in the Rent Expense account. Since net income increases the retained earnings, the amount of retained earnings listed on the statement of stockholders' equity would be incorrect. Finally, since the amount of net income and year-end cash balance are reported on the statement of cash flows, that financial statement would be incorrect as well.

INSTRUCTIONS

Refer to Home Depot's financial statements shown on pages B-5 through B-9 in Appendix B of this text-book to answer the following questions:

1. Identify the amount of net income (earnings) reported on the Consolidated Statements of Earnings for the year ended January 28, 2018.

2. Locate the dollar amount in question 1 on Home Depot's Consolidated Statements of Stockholders' Equity. Identify the title of the section containing the amount.

3. Locate the dollar amount in question 1 on Home Depot's Consolidated Statements of Cash Flows. Identify the title of the section containing the amount.

4. Can you locate the dollar amount in question 1 on Home Depot's Consolidated Balance Sheets? Explain.

5. List the financial statements that would be affected by a failure to account for a $100,000 cash purchase of equipment in the first month of a fiscal year.

22

Financial Reporting for a Partnership

LEARNING OBJECTIVES

After studying Chapter 22, in addition to defining key terms, you will be able to:

LO1 Calculate the distribution of partnership earnings.

LO2 Journalize entries for the withdrawal of partnership earnings.

LO3 Complete end-of-period work for a partnership.

LO4 Journalize entries for liquidating a partnership.

© PRESSMASTER/SHUTTERSTOCK.COM.

Valero Energy Partners LP

ACCOUNTING IN THE REAL WORLD

Driving down the highway, you may pass a convenience store and recognize the name Valero on the gas pumps. Even if the name is familiar, you might not know much about the business itself. Based in San Antonio, Valero began as a natural gas transportation business. Through internal growth and acquisitions, the company expanded to operate oil refineries, pipelines, and gas stations. In 2013, Valero initiated a strategy to modify its organizational structure, and its retail business was spun off to create CST Brands Inc. Later that year, Valero spun off its oil and gas pipelines, terminals, and other transportation assets to Valero Energy Partners LP (VLP).

VLP is a publicly traded limited partnership. This type of partnership issues limited partnership units rather than stock. The units are traded on the New York Stock Exchange, just like the stock of a corporation. A limited partnership is a form of business organization that has one general partner and can have many limited partners. The general partner manages the business and has the same rights and obligations of a typical partner. Valero is the general partner for VLP. Only the general partner, not the limited partners, is personally responsible for the debts of the partnership. The financial loss of a limited partner is limited to the value of his or her investment.

Individual state laws establish the ability of a business to form as a limited partnership. The federal government taxes a limited partnership like other partnerships—the income of the partnership is distributed, or passes through, to its partners. For this reason, a partnership is often referred to as a pass-through entity. The partnership issues a Schedule K-1 that reports each partner's share of partnership net income. This amount must be reported as income on the partner's individual tax return.

Source: www.valeroenergypartners.com.

CRITICAL THINKING

1. Why would a business choose to be organized as a limited partnership rather than a corporation?
2. Should the ticker symbols of limited liability partnerships denote that the business is not a corporation?

KEY TERMS

distribution deficit
owners' equity statement

liquidation of a partnership
realization

Distribution and Withdrawal of Partnership Earnings

LO1 Calculate the distribution of partnership earnings.

LO2 Journalize entries for the withdrawal of partnership earnings.

Distribution of Partnership Earnings LO1

Most end-of-fiscal-period work is similar for corporations, proprietorships, and partnerships. Two major procedures are different. (1) A corporation calculates and pays income tax on its net income, but partnerships and proprietorships do not. (2) A corporation maintains separate accounts for contributed capital (**Capital Stock**) and earned capital (**Retained Earnings**). Partnerships and proprietorships combine contributed and earned capital in one account for each owner.

A corporation may distribute some, but usually not all, of its earnings to stockholders as dividends. Partnerships, like proprietorships, distribute all earnings

of the business to the owners' capital accounts. The owners may then withdraw the earnings or leave them in the business.

All of the net income of a partnership is distributed to the partners. Five methods are commonly used for calculating the distribution of partnership earnings.

1. Fixed percentage.
2. Percentage of total equity.
3. Interest on equity.
4. Salaries.
5. Combination of methods.

ETHICS IN ACTION

The Client Is Not Always Right

For over ten years, Susan, a CPA, had prepared the tax returns for Oliver, an art dealer from Beverly Hills. Oliver often referred his clients to Susan and, thus, had been instrumental in building her tax practice.

While preparing Oliver's 2007 tax return, Susan noted a $1.3 million cash deposit that he had not reported. When questioned, Oliver told Susan that the money was from the sale of a painting from his collection. Relying on Oliver's response, Susan recorded the transaction on the proper tax form and filed the return.

Months later, IRS agents were at Susan's door, quizzing her about the transaction. Susan told the agents the details of her phone conversation with Oliver. She soon found herself testifying before a grand jury. Each time, Susan truthfully recounted her conversation with Oliver.

Unknown to Susan, Oliver had stolen money from the sale of a client's Picasso. However, in an attempt to avoid prosecution, Oliver was telling IRS agents a very different story. Oliver and his lawyer met with

Susan and pressured her to change her story. Oliver even threatened legal action against Susan. Feeling trapped and wanting to satisfy an important client, Susan reluctantly signed a document stating that she *may have* misunderstood what Oliver told her.

That seemingly simple act would change her life. She had now recounted two different versions of the conversation to the IRS agents. In their eyes, she had lied. Federal law provides for up to 20 years in prison for making false statements to a government agency. Susan ultimately pled guilty and was sentenced to nine months in prison.

INSTRUCTIONS

Susan was placed in a position where she was forced to make an instant decision, a decision that violated her moral values. What could Susan have done to prepare herself better for this situation?

Source: Justin M. Paperny, Ethics in Motion, *Encino, California: APS Publishing, 2010.*

Fixed Percentage

	Total Net Income	×	Fixed Percentage	=	Share of Net Income
Derrick Bigham	$56,000.00	×	60%	=	$33,600.00
Ethan Ming	$56,000.00	×	40%	=	22,400.00
Total					$56,000.00

The basis on which a partnership's earnings are distributed is usually stated in the partnership agreement. If a partnership agreement does not indicate how to divide the earnings, most state laws stipulate that partners share the earnings equally. The law applies regardless of differences in the partners' investments, abilities, or time devoted to the business.

Derrick Bigham and Ethan Ming are partners. The partnership agreement states that Derrick is to receive 60% and Ethan is to receive 40% of the net income or net loss. The distribution of net income is calculated as shown above.

Percentage of Total Equity

	Partner's Equity	÷	Total Equity	=	Percentage of Total Equity
Derrick Bigham	$42,000.00	÷	$60,000.00	=	70.0%
Ethan Ming	18,000.00	÷	$60,000.00	=	30.0%
	$60,000.00				

	Total Net Income	×	Percentage of Total Equity	=	Share of Net Income
Derrick Bigham	$56,000.00	×	70.0%	=	$39,200.00
Ethan Ming	$56,000.00	×	30.0%	=	16,800.00
Total					$56,000.00

Partners often agree to use capital account balances on the first day of a fiscal year as the basis for calculating the distribution of partnership earnings. On January 1, Derrick's equity was $42,000.00, and Ethan's equity was $18,000.00. If Derrick and Ethan had agreed to use this method, referred to as the *percentage of total equity method*, each partner's share of net income would have been calculated as shown above.

FYI Limited partnerships include owners who have limited liability and limited operating responsibilities. Limited partnerships are sometimes formed for special projects, such as Broadway plays.

© ISTOCKPHOTO.COM/PHOTOTALK

Interest on Equity

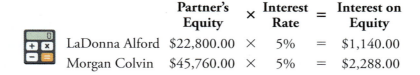

	Partner's Equity	×	Interest Rate	=	Interest on Equity
LaDonna Alford	$22,800.00	×	5%	=	$1,140.00
Morgan Colvin	$45,760.00	×	5%	=	$2,288.00

Interest on equity is often used as a method to distribute earnings when partners invest different amounts in a partnership. Partners often agree to use capital account balances on the first day of a fiscal year as the basis for this income distribution method. The partnership agreement states the interest rate.

Lamor Learning Center's partnership agreement, Article V, shown in Chapter 21, stipulates that each partner is to receive a 5% interest on equity. On January 1, LaDonna Alford's equity is $22,800.00, and Morgan Colvin's equity is $45,760.00. The interest on equity is calculated as shown above.

When the interest on equity method is used, the remaining net income or net loss is distributed using a combination of methods.

Salaries

Salaries are often used as a method to distribute earnings when partners contribute different amounts of personal service or bring different prior experiences to a partnership. The amount of salary for each partner is stated in the partnership agreement.

Lamor's partnership agreement states that salaries are to be paid as follows: LaDonna Alford, $15,000.00; Morgan Colvin, $20,000.00. When salaries are used, the remaining net income or net loss is distributed using a combination of methods.

THINK LIKE AN ACCOUNTANT

Analyzing Partnership Distributions

Four friends from college own and operate Fun N' Sun, a water and amusement park. For years, the partners have distributed a portion of the partnership income as interest on each partner's equity. The partners initially agreed to use capital account balances on the first day of a fiscal year as the basis for calculating the interest on equity. The partnership agreement provides for an interest rate of 8% and states that partners cannot withdraw more than the balance in their equity accounts.

Over the years, two of the partners have become dissatisfied with the current method of distributing income. One of the other partners regularly withdraws capital soon after the start of the year. The partnership often has to borrow money to fund this withdrawal, causing the partnership to incur additional interest expense.

The partners have asked you to analyze the impact of a distribution method based on a partner's average capital balance. They have provided you with a list of all partner distributions for the prior year, as well as the beginning capital balances.

OPEN THE SPREADSHEET TLA_CH22

The workbook contains the withdrawal transactions and the January 1 capital balances. Follow the steps on the Instructions tab to create the formulas required to calculate the requested information. Answer these questions:

1. Describe the withdrawal patterns of each partner.
2. What would the distribution amounts have been if the prior year's interest were calculated on average equity?
3. Which distribution method do you believe is the most equitable? Support your answer.

Combination of Methods

	Interest on Equity	Salary	Distribution of Remaining Net Income or Net Loss
LaDonna Alford	5%	$5,000.00	50.0%
Morgan Colvin	5%	$3,000.00	50.0%

	LaDonna Alford	Morgan Colvin	Distribution
Total net income			$54,800.00
Interest on equity	$ 1,140.00	$ 2,288.00	
Salary	5,000.00	3,000.00	
Total	$ 6,140.00	$ 5,288.00	11,428.00
Remaining net income			$43,372.00
Distribution of remaining net income	21,686.00	21,686.00	
Total distribution	$27,826.00	$26,974.00	$54,800.00

A combination of income distribution methods may be used for distributing partnership earnings. Lamor's partnership agreement states the earnings distribution as shown above. Each partner receives 5% on her January 1 equity. Then each partner is given a salary. The amount of net income remaining, $43,372.00, is distributed using the fixed percentage method.

Should We Buy Another Mill?

CareerClusters®
PATHWAYS TO COLLEGE & CAREER READINESS
Agriculture, Food & Natural Resources

Two brothers, John and Joe, are partners in a sawmill located in the Northwest. They harvest logs and mill them down to lumber. John is the logging/milling specialist. Joe is the salesperson. Both do their jobs well. In fact, Joe is actually selling more lumber than John can mill. "Buy another mill!" replies Joe when John tells him he cannot meet the demand for orders. "The more lumber we mill, the more money we make!" Joe adds.

John increases the number of logs he cuts by 50%. Running two mills, more lumber is produced and sold. They are meeting the demand for lumber and cannot wait until they see the increased profits from the investment. However, when their accountant prepares year-end financial statements, the brothers are disappointed to learn that they had less net income this year than in the prior year.

CRITICAL THINKING

1. Name three possible reasons for the partnership's decrease in net income.
2. If Joe had taken an accounting class, how could it have helped him in this business decision?

Distribution of Net Income Showing a Distribution Deficit

	Interest on Equity	Partner's Equity	Salary	Distribution of Remaining Net Income or Net Loss
Daniel Davis	10%	$60,000.00	$30,000.00	40.0%
Malorie Franks	10%	$14,000.00	$40,000.00	60.0%

	Daniel Davis	Malorie Franks	Distribution
Total net income			$74,600.00
Interest on equity	$ 6,000.00	$ 1,400.00	
Salary	30,000.00	40,000.00	
Total	$36,000.00	$41,400.00	77,400.00
Distribution deficit			$ (2,800.00)
Distribution of distribution deficit	(1,120.00)	(1,680.00)	
Total distribution	$34,880.00	$39,720.00	$74,600.00

Distribute the Distribution Deficit   Distribute Interest on Equity and Salaries   Calculate the Distribution Deficit

When salaries or interest on equity are stipulated, the amounts are allowed whether or not sufficient net income is available. D&F Landscaping's distributions of interest and salaries total $77,400.00, which is $2,800.00 more than the partnership's total net income of $74,600.00. A negative balance that remains after partner salaries and interest are subtracted from total income is called a **distribution deficit**. D&F Landscaping has a distribution deficit of $2,800.00 that is distributed to the partners by using the fixed percentage method.

A distribution deficit should not be confused with a net loss. A partnership with a net income can have a distribution deficit while calculating net income distributions. The distribution deficit simply reduces the amount of net income distributed to each partner.

Withdrawal of Partnership Earnings LO2

A partner often needs a portion of the annual net income before the end of a fiscal year when the actual net income is known. During a fiscal year, partners take assets out of the partnership in anticipation of the net income for the year. Assets taken out of a business for the owner's personal use are known as *withdrawals*. The partnership agreement should limit the amount of assets that may be withdrawn.

Withdrawal of Cash

						CASH PAYMENTS JOURNAL					PAGE 10	
						1	2	3	4	5		
	DATE	ACCOUNT TITLE	CK. NO.	POST. REF.		GENERAL DEBIT	GENERAL CREDIT	ACCOUNTS PAYABLE DEBIT	PURCHASES DISCOUNT CREDIT	CASH CREDIT		
25	20-- June 28	LaDonna Alford, Drawing	123			1 0 0 0 00				1 0 0 0 00		25
26												26
27												27

Withdrawals are recorded to the partner's contra equity account.

June 28, 20--. LaDonna Alford, partner, withdrew cash for personal use, $1,000.00. Check No. 123.

LaDonna Alford, Drawing
↑ 1,000.00

Cash
↓ 1,000.00

Withdrawal of Assets Other Than Cash

	DATE		ACCOUNT TITLE	DOC. NO.	POST. REF.	DEBIT	CREDIT	
1	July	2	Morgan Colvin, Drawing	M33		1 5 0 00		1
2			Supplies—Office				1 5 0 00	2
3								3

GENERAL JOURNAL — PAGE 9

A partner may elect to take partnership assets instead of cash. Assets such as office supplies withdrawn for personal use are not a business expense. This transaction reduces the partnership's office supplies inventory, and therefore, **Supplies—Office** is credited.

The withdrawal is a reduction of the partner's equity in the partnership. Rather than debiting Morgan Colvin's capital account, the transaction is debited to **Morgan Colvin, Drawing**. The accounting procedure of debiting withdrawals to a drawing account is consistent with accounting for a proprietorship.

July 2, 20—. Morgan Colvin, partner, withdrew office supplies for personal use, $150.00. Memorandum No. 33.

Morgan Colvin, Drawing

↑ 150.00

Supplies—Office

↓ 150.00

Signing Away the Future

We have all heard stories about business partnerships failing. Unfortunately, it is estimated that over half of all business partnerships fail. At the same time, many business partnerships have thrived. Evan Williams and Biz Stone of Twitter, Ben Cohen and Jerry Greenfield of Ben & Jerry's, and William Procter and James Gamble of Procter & Gamble all discovered that planning and assessing potential risks are keys to preventing partnership pitfalls.

A planned exit strategy allows one of the partners to walk away from the partnership. A non-compete agreement is an agreement not to pursue business from existing clients or compete against the existing business. Non-compete agreements usually include terms such as length of time and proximity. Some companies even require new employees to sign a non-compete agreement to protect the interests of the business.

ACTIVITIES

1. Jackson was employed as a salesperson for a uniform supply company. He obtained a job with another company that supplied rental equipment in addition to uniforms. After six months, Jackson's employer told him that they would have to let him go due to a non-compete agreement with his former employer. What could Jackson have done to avoid termination on this job? Explain.

2. Imara was required to sign a non-compete agreement for a term of one year after leaving her fast-food employer. She received an offer from another fast-food restaurant for more pay. Do you think the non-compete agreement will be enforced? Explain.

TERM REVIEW

distribution deficit

Audit your understanding LO1, 2

1. What are five methods commonly used to distribute partnership earnings?
2. Where should the method of distributing partnership earnings be stated?
3. When does a distribution deficit occur?
4. What account is debited when a partner withdraws cash for personal use?
5. How is the accounting for owner withdrawals the same for partnerships and proprietorships?

Work together 22-1 LO1, 2

Calculating partnership earnings and journalizing partnership withdrawals

Jen Turner and Lavenia Hogan are partners in a business. On January 1 of the current year, the partners' equities are Jen, $23,000.00, and Lavenia, $39,000.00. Forms are provided in the *Working Papers*. Your instructor will guide you through the following examples.

1. For each of the following independent cases, calculate how the net income of $50,000.00 will be distributed to the two partners.

    a. Each partner receives a share of net income based on a percentage of equity.

    b. Each partner receives 10% interest on equity and an equal share of remaining net income.

2. Calculate how net income of $40,000.00 will be distributed to the two partners. Jen receives 8% interest on equity and a salary of $18,000.00. Lavenia receives 8% interest on equity and a salary of $20,000.00. The partners share remaining net income, net loss, or distribution deficit as follows: Jen, 60% and Lavenia, 40%.

3. Record the following transactions in the appropriate journal.

    Transactions:

    July 20. Jen Turner, partner, withdrew cash for personal use, $750.00. Check No. 146.
         23. Lavenia Hogan, partner, withdrew office supplies for personal use, $45.00. Memorandum No. 33.

On your own 22-1 LO1, 2

Calculating partnership earnings and journalizing partnership withdrawals

Greg Judson and Pauline Malone are partners in a business. On January 1 of the current year, the partners' equities are Greg, $30,000.00, and Pauline, $18,000.00. Forms are provided in the *Working Papers*. Work independently to complete the following problem.

1. For each of the following independent cases, calculate how the net income of $60,000.00 will be distributed to the two partners.

    a. Each partner receives a share of net income based on a percentage of equity.

    b. Each partner receives 6% interest on equity and an equal share of remaining net income.

2. Calculate how net income of $70,000.00 will be distributed to the two partners. Greg receives 10% interest on equity and a salary of $34,000.00. Pauline receives 10% interest on equity and a salary of $42,000.00. The partners share remaining net income, net loss, or distribution deficit as follows: Greg, 65% and Pauline, 35%.

3. Record the following transactions in the appropriate journal.

    Transactions:

    Aug. 12. Greg Judson, partner, withdrew store supplies for personal use, $80.00. Memorandum No. 62.
         15. Pauline Malone, partner, withdrew cash for personal use, $500.00. Check No. 206.

LO3 Complete end-of-period work for a partnership.

End-of-Period Work for a Partnership LO3

The end-of-period work for a partnership is similar to that for a proprietorship or a corporation. An unadjusted trial balance assists accountants in preparing adjusting entries. The adjusting entries are posted, and then an adjusted trial balance provides the amounts necessary for preparing the financial statements.

Income Statement

Lamor Learning Center Income Statement For the Year Ended December 31, 20--		
		% of Sales*
Operating Revenue:		
Sales..	$98,156.25	100.0
Operating Expenses:		
Advertising Expense..........................	$ 2,185.00	2.2
Depreciation Expense—Equipment...........	5,460.00	5.6
Depreciation Expense—Car..................	4,800.00	4.9
Insurance Expenses..........................	3,500.00	3.6
Miscellaneous Expense	6,153.50	6.3
Rent Expense................................	10,800.00	11.0
Supplies Expense—Educational...............	2,452.60	2.5
Supplies Expense—Office	1,984.80	2.0
Uncollectible Accounts Expense..............	2,405.00	2.5
Utilities Expense	3,615.35	3.7
Total Operating Expenses	43,356.25	44.2
Net Income..................................	$54,800.00	55.8

*Rounded to the nearest 0.1%.

With one exception, Lamor Learning Center's income statement is the same as that of any small business that provides a service. Unlike a corporation, however, a partnership does not pay federal income taxes. As described later in this chapter, partnership net income is reported on the partners' personal tax returns. Thus, Lamor's income statement does not contain references to net income before federal income tax, federal income tax expense, or net income after federal income tax.

Lamor's income statement contains vertical analysis ratios for every amount. Each ratio is calculated by dividing each amount by sales. The partners use this information to determine if each amount is within its target range. Any ratios that are outside the target range should be investigated, and if necessary, corrective action should be taken.

Owners' Equity Statement

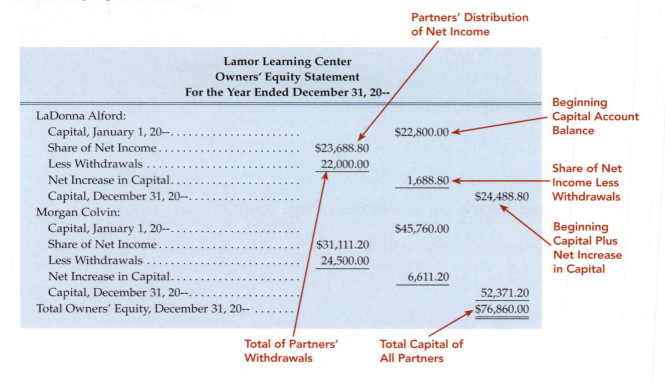

Lamor Learning Center
Owners' Equity Statement
For the Year Ended December 31, 20--

LaDonna Alford:

Capital, January 1, 20--........................		$22,800.00
Share of Net Income........................	$23,688.80	
Less Withdrawals	22,000.00	
Net Increase in Capital......................		1,688.80
Capital, December 31, 20--....................		$24,488.80

Morgan Colvin:

Capital, January 1, 20--........................		$45,760.00
Share of Net Income........................	$31,111.20	
Less Withdrawals	24,500.00	
Net Increase in Capital......................		6,611.20
Capital, December 31, 20--....................		52,371.20
Total Owners' Equity, December 31, 20--		$76,860.00

Partners' Distribution of Net Income

Beginning Capital Account Balance

Share of Net Income Less Withdrawals

Beginning Capital Plus Net Increase in Capital

Total of Partners' Withdrawals

Total Capital of All Partners

A corporation's equity is reported on a statement of stockholders' equity. A similar statement is prepared for a partnership. A financial statement that summarizes the changes in owners' equity during a fiscal period is called an **owners' equity statement**.

This statement reports the changes in each partner's equity. The partner's share of net income, less any withdrawals, is added to the partner's beginning capital balance to calculate the partner's equity balance on the statement date.

Balance Sheet

Lamor Learning Center
Balance Sheet
December 31, 20--

OWNERS' EQUITY		
LaDonna Alford, Capital	$24,488.80	
Morgan Colvin, Capital	52,371.20	
Total Owners' Equity		76,860.00
Total Liabilities and Owners' Equity		$92,154.35

The asset and liability sections of a balance sheet are the same for a proprietorship, a partnership, and a corporation. The owners' equity section of a partnership's balance sheet, however, is different. On a partnership balance sheet, each partner's ending capital is reported under the heading Owners' Equity. Each partner's capital amount is obtained from the owners' equity statement.

Adjusting and Closing Entries

GENERAL JOURNAL

PAGE 16

	DATE	ACCOUNT TITLE	DOC. NO.	POST. REF.	DEBIT	CREDIT	
1		*Closing Entries*					1
23	31	Income Summary			54 8 0 0 00		23
24		LaDonna Alford, Capital				23 6 8 8 80	24
25		Morgan Colvin, Capital				31 1 1 1 20	25
26	31	LaDonna Alford, Capital			22 0 0 0 00		26
27		LaDonna Alford, Drawing				22 0 0 0 00	27
28	31	Morgan Colvin, Capital			24 5 0 0 00		28
29		Morgan Colvin, Drawing				24 5 0 0 00	29
30							30
31							31

Close Income Summary (rows 23–25)
Close Drawing Accounts (rows 26–29)

The adjusting entries are similar for a proprietorship, a partnership, and a corporation. Only a corporation records federal income tax expenses.

The entries to close revenue and expense accounts are the same for all businesses. One entry closes all temporary accounts having a credit balance. A second entry closes all temporary accounts having a debit balance. Each closing entry results in a debit or a credit to Income Summary.

The entries to close Income Summary and temporary equity accounts are different for each form of organization. A partnership closes Income Summary to the partners' capital accounts. The amount recorded to each partner's capital account is determined using the distribution methods presented in the previous lesson. Each partner's drawing account is closed to the partner's capital account.

Federal Income Taxes

Lamor's distribution of net income includes salaries for each of the partners. However, the Internal Revenue Service does not consider partners to be employees of the partnership. The IRS classifies the partners as self-employed persons, whose salaries are not an expense of the partnership. Therefore, partners' salaries and withdrawals are considered the withdrawals of partnership equity, not expenses.

A partnership does not pay income tax on its earnings. However, a partnership does submit to the IRS a partnership tax return that reports the earnings distributed to each partner. This type of return is known as an *information return*. The partnership tax return is filed on Form 1065. Each partner receives a Schedule K-1 that reports the partner's capital balances and share of partnership net income. The partners include their respective share of the partnership net income or net loss on their personal income tax returns.

As self-employed persons, partners are entitled to old-age, survivors, disability, and hospitalization insurance benefits known collectively as Social Security and Medicare. Each partner personally pays a self-employment tax to qualify for Social Security and Medicare coverage. Therefore, the self-employment tax rate is double that of an employed individual's Social Security and Medicare tax rates. Thus, the same total amount of Social Security and Medicare taxes are paid for both self-employed persons and employees. The self-employment taxes are personal expenses of the partners, not of the partnership. Therefore, partners' self-employment Social Security and Medicare taxes are not recorded on partnership records. **>> App. A: Business Entity**

Post-Closing Trial Balance

Lamor Learning Center Post-Closing Trial Balance December 31, 20--		
Account Title	Debit	Credit
Cash..	$ 8,568.45	
LaDonna Alford, Capital.....................		24,488.80
Morgan Colvin, Capital......................		52,371.20
	$93,354.35	$93,354.35

After adjusting and closing entries have been posted, Lamor prepares a post-closing trial balance. Lamor's post-closing trial balance is similar to that of a corporation, with the exception of the partners' capital accounts.

TERM REVIEW

owners' equity statement

Audit your understanding LO3

1. Why does a partnership not record an adjusting entry for federal income taxes?
2. What is the purpose of the owners' equity statement?
3. Are partners taxed on their distributions or withdrawals? Explain.
4. How are Social Security and Medicare taxes paid on partners' distributions?

Work together 22-2 LO3

End-of-period work for a partnership

Jeffrey Lowe and Mona Ray are partners in a business. On January 1 of the current year, the partners' equities were Jeffrey, $46,000.00, and Mona, $34,000.00. The net income for the year is $70,000.00. Statement paper and a general journal are provided in the *Working Papers*. Your instructor will guide you through the following examples.

1. For the fiscal year ended December 31, 20--, prepare an owners' equity statement. Each partner is to receive 8% interest on January 1 equity. Also, partners' salaries are Jeffrey, $36,500.00, and Mona, $24,500.00. The remaining net income, net loss, or distribution deficit is shared equally. During the year, Jeffrey withdrew cash of $29,000.00 and Mona withdrew cash of $22,000.00.
2. Journalize the entries to close Income Summary and the owners' equity accounts.

On your own 22-2 LO3

End-of-period work for a partnership

Kim Peters and Mitzi West are partners in a business. On January 1 of the current year, the partners' equities were Kim, $63,000.00, and Mitzi, $15,000.00. The net income for the year is $89,000.00. Statement paper and a general journal are provided in the *Working Papers*. Work independently to complete the following problem.

1. For the fiscal year ended December 31, 20--, prepare an owners' equity statement. Each partner is to receive 10% interest on January 1 equity. Also, partners' salaries are Kim, $25,000.00, and Mitzi, $12,500.00. The remaining net income, net loss, or distribution deficit is shared 80% to Kim and 20% to Mitzi. During the year, Kim withdrew cash of $52,600.00 and Mitzi withdrew cash of $8,000.00.
2. Journalize the entries to close Income Summary and the owners' equity accounts.

Liquidation of a Partnership

LO4 Journalize entries for liquidating a partnership.

Liquidating a Partnership LO4

If a partnership elects or is forced to go out of business, its assets are distributed to the creditors and the partners. The process of paying a partnership's liabilities and distributing remaining assets to the partners is called **liquidation of a partnership**.

Cash received from the sale of assets during liquidation of a partnership is called **realization**. Typically, when a partnership is liquidated, the noncash assets are sold, and the available cash is used to pay the creditors. Any remaining cash is distributed to the partners according to each partner's total equity.

Recognizing a Gain on Realization

Value of Asset Received	–	Book Value of Asset Sold	=	Gain on Realization
		Cost $18,000.00		
		Acc. Depr. 12,000.00		
Cash $8,400.00	–	Book Value $ 6,000.00	=	$2,400.00

CASH RECEIPTS JOURNAL PAGE **14**

					1	2	3	4	5	6	7	
					GENERAL		ACCOUNTS RECEIVABLE CREDIT	SALES CREDIT	SALES TAX PAYABLE CREDIT	SALES DISCOUNT DEBIT	CASH DEBIT	
	DATE	ACCOUNT TITLE	DOC. NO.	POST. REF.	DEBIT	CREDIT						
1	20-- Nov. 3	Accum. Depr.—Equipment	R845		12 0 0 0 00						8 4 0 0 00	1
2		Equipment				18 0 0 0 00						2
3		Gain or Loss on Realization				2 4 0 0 00						3
4												4
5												5

On November 1, Janice Rona and Ira Barnes began the process of liquidating their partnership. At that time, financial statements were prepared and adjusting and closing entries were journalized and posted.

Noncash assets might be sold for more than the recorded book value. When this happens, the amount received in excess of the book value is recorded as a gain on realization. The gain is recorded as a credit in an account titled Gain or Loss on Realization.

November 3, 20--. Received cash from sale of equipment, $8,400.00; original cost, $18,000.00; total accumulated depreciation recorded to date, $12,000.00. Receipt No. 845.

Remember In a partnership liquidation, remaining cash is distributed according to the balance in each partner's equity account—not according to the ratio by which they share income and losses.

Gain or Loss on Realization

Loss on Realization	Gain on Realization

The account balances before liquidation and the November 3 transaction to liquidate equipment are shown below. After the equipment is sold, the balance of the Equipment and Accumulated Depreciation—Equipment accounts are zero.

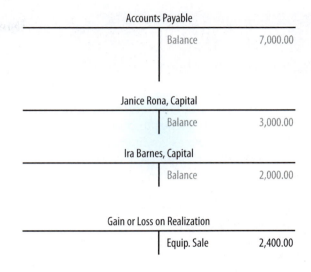

Recognizing a Loss on Realization

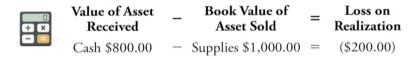

	Value of Asset Received	−	Book Value of Asset Sold	=	Loss on Realization
	Cash $800.00	−	Supplies $1,000.00	=	($200.00)

CASH RECEIPTS JOURNAL PAGE 14

					1	2	3	4	5	6	7	
	DATE	ACCOUNT TITLE	DOC. NO.	POST. REF.	GENERAL DEBIT	GENERAL CREDIT	ACCOUNTS RECEIVABLE CREDIT	SALES CREDIT	SALES TAX PAYABLE CREDIT	SALES DISCOUNT DEBIT	CASH DEBIT	
4	6	Gain or Loss on Realization	R846		2 0 0 00						8 0 0 00	4
5		Supplies				1 0 0 0 00						5
6												6

Sometimes during liquidation, the sale of an asset brings in less cash than the recorded book value.

> **November 6, 20-- Received cash from sale of supplies, $800.00; balance of supplies account, $1,000.00. Receipt No. 846.**

The supplies were sold for $200.00 less than the recorded value, resulting in a loss on realization. The loss is recorded as a debit to Gain or Loss on Realization.

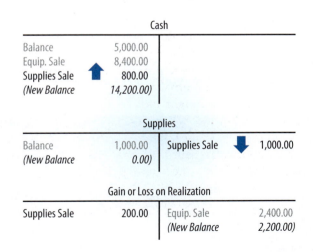

Careers In Accounting

Emma Shoquist
Credit Analyst

Emma Shoquist is a credit analyst for a large bank with branches throughout the United States. In her role as credit analyst, she assists loan officers and other bank employees in granting loans to customers. Once a loan officer has met with the client and helped the client prepare the loan application, the application and all supporting documents are sent to Ms. Shoquist. She will analyze the application, credit bureau reports, financial statements, and other documentation. She will evaluate the client's financial position to determine the degree of risk the bank would take on by granting the loan. She will also compare the client's degree of risk with that of other companies in the same industry.

At times, Ms. Shoquist communicates with the client directly. For example, when Ms. Shoquist receives a credit bureau report that indicates the client is past due on several accounts, she will notify the client, who may disagree with the credit bureau report. She will work with the client to verify the accuracy of the report. Once she feels she has an accurate picture of the client, she will prepare a report for the loan committee, stating her appraisal of the creditworthiness of the application.

When Ms. Shoquist first started working at the bank, she evaluated loan applications primarily for individuals. As she acquired more experience, she moved to the commercial side of the bank, where she only analyzes credit applications for commercial loans.

Ms. Shoquist uses computers every day. Many of the reports she gathers are computer-generated. She also uses a spreadsheet program to calculate common accounting ratios when analyzing financial statements. She feels computers make her work more efficient and more accurate.

Ms. Shoquist likes working with her fellow employees and directly with clients. Her college personal communications classes prepared her to communicate ideas and findings in a clear manner. Her accounting classes taught her to evaluate financial statements. She feels that to be successful as a credit analyst, she must be comfortable making a decision—often involving hundreds of thousands of dollars.

Salary Range: In 2017, the median wage for a loan officer was $71,290.00.

Qualifications: Most jobs in the credit analyst field require a bachelor's degree. Course work and experience in finance and accounting are helpful.

Occupational Outlook: The growth for loan officer positions is projected to be average (5% to 9%) for the period from 2016 to 2026.

Source: www.onetonline.org.

Liquidating Liabilities

CASH PAYMENTS JOURNAL PAGE 18

	DATE	ACCOUNT TITLE	CK. NO.	POST. REF.	GENERAL DEBIT	GENERAL CREDIT	ACCOUNTS PAYABLE DEBIT	PURCHASES DISCOUNT CREDIT	CASH CREDIT	
1	Nov. 10	Hillside Supply	921				3 0 0 0 00		3 0 0 0 00	1
2	10	Mentory Industries	922				4 0 0 0 00		4 0 0 0 00	2
3										3

The partnership's available cash is used to pay creditors. The checks prepared to pay each creditor are recorded in the cash payments journal.

> November 10, 20--. Paid cash to all creditors for the amounts owed, Check No. 921 to Hillside Supply for $3,000.00, and Check No. 922 to Mentory Industries for $4,000.00.

Liquidating liabilities does not typically result in a gain or loss on liquidation. However, sometimes debtors are willing to settle their accounts for less than the recorded amount. In this case, a gain on liquidation would be recorded.

Cash

Balance	5,000.00	Paid Creditor	3,000.00
Equip. Sale	8,400.00	Paid Creditor	4,000.00
Supplies Sale	800.00		
(New Balance	7,200.00)		

Accounts Payable

Paid Creditor	3,000.00	Balance	7,000.00
Paid Creditor	4,000.00	(New Balance	0.00)

Account Balances After Liquidation of Noncash Assets and Liabilities

Cash

Balance	5,000.00	Paid Creditor	3,000.00
Equip. Sale	8,400.00	Paid Creditor	4,000.00
Supplies Sale	800.00		
(New Balance	7,200.00)		

Supplies

Balance	1,000.00	Supplies Sale	1,000.00
(New Balance	0.00)		

Equipment

Balance	18,000.00	Equip. Sale	18,000.00
(New Balance	0.00)		

Accumulated Depreciation—Equipment

Equip. Sale	12,000.00	Balance	12,000.00
		(New Balance	0.00)

Accounts Payable

Paid Creditor	3,000.00	Balance	7,000.00
Paid Creditor	4,000.00	(New Balance	0.00)

Janice Rona, Capital

		Balance	3,000.00

Ira Barnes, Capital

		Balance	2,000.00

Gain or Loss on Realization

Supplies Sale	200.00	Equip. Sale	2,400.00
		(New Balance	2,200.00)

The transactions recorded for the sale of assets and the liquidation of liabilities are shown in the T accounts. When these transactions have been journalized and posted, the partnership has only four general ledger accounts with balances: Cash, Gain or Loss on Realization, and the two partners' capital accounts.

Distributing a Gain or Loss on Realization to Partners

	Balance of Gain or Loss on Realization	×	Equity Percentage	=	Share of Gain or Loss on Realization
Rona	$2,200.00	×	60%	=	$1,320.00
Barnes	$2,200.00	×	40%	=	880.00
Total					$2,200.00

GENERAL JOURNAL — PAGE 12

	DATE	ACCOUNT TITLE	DOC. NO.	POST. REF.	DEBIT	CREDIT	
9	15	Gain or Loss on Realization	M211		2 2 0 0 00		9
10		Janice Rona, Capital				1 3 2 0 00	10
11		Ira Barnes, Capital				8 8 0 00	11
12							12

When all creditors have been paid, the balance of Gain or Loss on Realization is distributed to the partners. A credit balance indicates a gain on realization. A debit balance indicates a loss. The distribution is based on the method of distributing net income or net loss as stated in the partnership agreement. The percentages for Janice Rona and Ira Barnes are 60.0% and 40.0%, respectively.

> November 15, 20--. Recorded distribution of gain on realization: to Janice Rona, $1,320.00; to Ira Barnes, $880.00. Memorandum No. 211.

If a loss on realization is distributed to the partners, Gain or Loss on Realization is credited to close the account. Each partner's capital account is debited for the partner's share of the loss on realization.

Distributing Remaining Cash to Partners

CASH PAYMENTS JOURNAL — PAGE 18

	DATE	ACCOUNT TITLE	CK. NO.	POST. REF.	GENERAL DEBIT	GENERAL CREDIT	ACCOUNTS PAYABLE DEBIT	PURCHASES DISCOUNT CREDIT	CASH CREDIT	
3	Nov. 17	Janice Rona, Capital	923		4 3 2 0 00				4 3 2 0 00	3
4	17	Ira Barnes, Capital	924		2 8 8 0 00				2 8 8 0 00	4
5										5

Any cash remaining after the partnership assets are sold and the liabilities are paid is distributed to the partners. The cash is distributed according to each partner's capital account balance, regardless of the method used to distribute net income or net loss.

> November 17, 20--. Recorded the final distribution of remaining cash to partners: to Janice Rona, $4,320.00; to Ira Barnes, $2,880.00. Check Nos. 923 and 924.

After this entry is journalized and posted, all of the partnership's general ledger accounts will have zero balances. The partnership is liquidated.

LO4 Journalize entries for liquidating a partnership.

TERMS REVIEW

liquidation of a partnership

realization

Audit your understanding LO4

1. What accounting procedures must be completed before the partnership liquidation process begins?
2. What accounts are debited when distributing remaining cash to partners during liquidation?

Work together 22-3 LO4

Liquidation of a partnership

Mandi Stokes and Dustin Mann agreed to liquidate their partnership on March 15 of the current year. On that date, after financial statements were prepared and the closing entries were posted, the general ledger accounts had the balances shown in the *Working Papers*.

Journalize the transactions. A cash receipts journal, a cash payments journal, and a general journal are provided in the *Working Papers*. Source documents are abbreviated as follows: check, C; memorandum, M; receipt, R. Your instructor will guide you through the following examples.

Transactions:

Mar. 16. Received cash from sale of equipment, $5,000.00. R486.
     17. Received cash from sale of supplies, $650.00. R487.
     18. Paid cash on account to Daniel Supply, $450.00. C626.
     19. Received cash from sale of truck, $12,500.00. R488.
     20. Paid cash on account to PFG Consultants, $1,800.00. C627.
     23. Distributed the balance of Gain or Loss on Realization to Mandi Stokes, 60%; to Dustin Mann, 40%. M211.
     24. Distributed remaining cash to partners. C628 and C629.

On your own 22-3 LO4

Liquidation of a partnership

Petre Oakley and Jamal Beck agreed to liquidate their partnership on June 20 of the current year. On that date, after financial statements were prepared and the closing entries were posted, the general ledger accounts had the balances shown in the *Working Papers*.

Journalize the following transactions. A cash receipts journal, a cash payments journal, and a general journal are provided in the *Working Papers*. Source documents are abbreviated as follows: check, C; memorandum, M; receipt, R. Work independently to complete the following problem.

Transactions:

July 4. Received cash from sale of equipment, $8,000.00. R845.
     5. Paid cash on account to N&T Supply Co., $445.00. C921.
     8. Received cash from sale of supplies, $600.00. R846.
     10. Paid cash on account to Ullman Associates, $430.00. C922.
     12. Received cash from sale of truck, $10,500.00. R847.
     14. Distributed the balance of Gain or Loss on Realization to Petre Oakley, 70%; to Jamal Beck, 30%. M292.
     15. Distributed remaining cash to partners. C923 and C924.

CHAPTER SUMMARY

The end-of-period work is similar for proprietorships, partnerships, and corporations. The differences result from the structure of the owners' equity accounts and income tax policies. A partnership maintains a capital account and a drawing account for each partner. A partnership does not maintain a Retained Earnings account; rather, the net income retained in the partnership is included in the partners' capital accounts.

A partnership does not pay income tax on its net income, as does a corporation. The income of a partnership is reported on the partners' individual tax returns, regardless of the amount of income that is withdrawn by the partners.

Five methods are commonly used for calculating the distribution of partnership earnings. Distributions based on a fixed percentage, a percentage of total equity, interest on equity, and salaries are made first. These distributions do not depend on the amount of net income. The

distributions are deducted from net income to determine the remaining net income to be distributed. If these distributions exceed the amount of net income, the remainder is called a distribution deficit. The remainder can be distributed to the partners by using a fixed percentage or a percentage of equity.

Some differences exist between the financial reporting of a partnership and corporation. The owners' equity statement reports the changes in each partner's capital account over the fiscal period. No income tax expense is reported on the income statement of a partnership. The capital structure of the partnership's balance sheet shows the capital balance of each partner.

A partnership may elect or be forced to liquidate. After the assets of the business are sold and all liabilities are paid, any remaining cash is distributed to the partners, using the distribution method specified in the partnership agreement.

EXPLORE ACCOUNTING

Determining the Value of a Partnership

When a partnership decides to add another partner or an existing partner wants to withdraw, the value of a partnership must be determined. The book value of a partnership is not necessarily an equitable value to the new partner or the existing partners. Therefore, before admitting a new partner or retiring one, a current equitable value should be determined for the partnership. Three common methods used to value a partnership are (1) comparable sales, (2) appraisal, and (3) income capitalization.

Comparable sales method. This method attempts to compare other comparable businesses that have been sold recently with the partnership business being valued. Factors to be considered in selecting comparable businesses are type, size, and location of the business. If a comparable business recently sold for $500,000.00, a sound basis for valuing the partnership is $500,000.00, regardless of the book value of the partnership.

Appraisal method. This method estimates the current fair market value of each of the assets and liabilities. A professional appraiser would be employed to determine the value of the assets and the liabilities of the business.

Income capitalization method. This method places most emphasis on the expected future earnings capacity of the business. The buyer of a share of a partnership probably is making the investment for the anticipated future earnings of the business. This method values the business based on those expected future earnings.

INSTRUCTIONS

Assume that you are a doctor. You have been offered a one-quarter interest in a growing medical practice partnership located in a fast-growth area. Which method of valuing the existing partnership would you prefer? Explain the reason for your choice.

APPLY YOUR UNDERSTANDING

INSTRUCTIONS: Download problem instructions for Excel, QuickBooks, and Sage 50c from the textbook companion website at www.C21accounting.com.

22-1 Application Problem — Calculating partnership earnings and journalizing partnership withdrawals LO1, 2

Ann Marsh and Beth White are partners in a business. On December 31 of the current year, the partners' equities are Ann, $42,000.00, and Beth, $18,000.00. The net income for the year is $70,000.00. A form for calculating distribution of partners' earnings, a cash payments journal, and a general journal are provided in the *Working Papers*.

Instructions:

1. For each of the following independent cases, calculate how the $70,000.00 net income will be distributed to the two partners.
   a. Each partner receives a fixed percentage of 50% of net income.
   b. Each partner receives a percentage of net income based on the percentage of total equity.
   c. Each partner receives 6% interest on equity. The partners share remaining net income, net loss, or distribution deficit equally.
   d. Ann receives a salary of $30,000.00; Beth receives a salary of $35,000.00. The partners share remaining net income, net loss, or distribution deficit in a fixed percentage of Ann, 45%, and Beth, 55%.
   e. Ann is to receive 10% interest on equity and a salary of $32,000.00. Beth is to receive 12% interest on equity and a salary of $28,000.00. The partners share remaining net income, net loss, or distribution deficit equally.
   f. Ann and Beth are to receive salaries of $38,000.00 and $36,000.00, respectively. The partners share remaining net income, net loss, or distribution deficit equally.
2. Record the following transactions in the appropriate journal.

Transactions:

May 12. Ann Marsh, partner, withdrew store supplies for personal use, $120.00. Memorandum No. 92.

20. Beth White, partner, withdrew cash for personal use, $2,000.00. Check No. 433.

22-2 Application Problem — End-of-period work for a partnership LO3

Sherra Gray and Tynisha Banks are partners in Sherra's Home Health. The net income for the year is $48,000.00. On January 1 of the current year, the partners' equities were Sherra, $12,000.00, and Tynisha, $60,000.00. Source documents are abbreviated as follows: check, C; memorandum, M; receipt, R. Statement paper and a general journal are provided in the *Working Papers*.

Instructions:

1. Calculate the distribution of net income to the partners. Partners' salaries are Sherra, $25,000.00, and Tynisha, $15,000.00. Each partner is to receive 12% interest on her January 1 equity. The remaining net income, net loss, or distribution deficit is shared as follows: Sherra, 60%, and Tynisha, 40%.
2. Prepare an owners' equity statement. During the year, Sherra withdrew cash of $30,000.00 and Tynisha withdrew cash of $25,000.00.
3. Journalize the entries to close Income Summary and the owners' equity accounts.

Janie Brooks and Duwanda Morris agreed to liquidate their partnership on July 22 of the current year. On that date, after financial statements were prepared and closing entries were posted, the general ledger accounts had the following balances:

Cash	$ 2,200.00
Supplies	600.00
Equipment	11,000.00
Accumulated Depreciation—Equipment	5,800.00
Truck	18,000.00
Accumulated Depreciation—Truck	13,200.00
Accounts Payable	650.00
Janie Brooks, Capital	6,150.00
Duwanda Morris, Capital	6,000.00

Instructions:

Journalize the following transactions. Source documents are abbreviated as follows: check, C; memorandum, M; receipt, R. A cash receipts journal, a cash payments journal, and a general journal are provided in the *Working Papers*.

Transactions:

Aug. 5. Received cash from sale of equipment, $4,800.00. R546.

7. Received cash from sale of truck, $3,500.00. R547.

8. Paid cash on account to Justin Enterprises, $650.00. C992.

9. Received cash from sale of supplies, $450.00. R548.

12. Distributed the balance of Gain or Loss on Realization to Janie Brooks, 35%; to Duwanda Morris, 65%. M198.

14. Distributed remaining cash to partners. C993 and C994.

Mastery Problem   Completing end-of-period work for a partnership **LO1, 3**

sage 50

1. Journalize and post transactions related to a partnership to the general journal.
2. Print the general journal.

1. Journalize and post transactions related to a partnership to the journal.
2. Print the journal.

Marcie Davies and Dean Elmore are partners in Dean's Gym. On January 1 of the current year, the partners' equities were Marcie, $26,250.00, and Dean, $22,500.00. The net income for the year is $72,350.00. Statement paper and a general journal are provided in the *Working Papers*.

Instructions:

1. Calculate the distribution of net income to the partners. Each partner is to receive 10% interest on January 1 equity. Also, partners' salaries are Marcie, $35,000.00, and Dean, $22,000.00. The remaining net income, net loss, or distribution deficit is shared 68% to Marcie and 32% to Dean.
2. Prepare an owners' equity statement. During the year, Marcie withdrew cash of $32,600.00 and Dean withdrew cash of $25,300.00.
3. Journalize the entries to close Income Summary and the owners' equity accounts.

22-C Challenge Problem   Completing end-of-period work for a partnership **LO1, 3**

1. Use the account information from the adjusted trial balance to prepare the required financial statements.
2. Print the worksheets.

Johan Copeland and Lou Newell are partners in C&N Plumbing. The partnership's adjusted trial balance for the year ended December 31 of the current year is provided in the *Working Papers*. Statement paper is provided in the *Working Papers*.

Instructions:

1. Prepare an income statement. Calculate and record the component percentages for the cost of merchandise sold, gross profit on operations, total operating expenses, and net income or net loss. Round percentage calculations to the nearest 0.1%. If there is a net loss, use a minus sign with the component percentage.
2. Calculate the distribution of net income to the partners. Each partner is to receive 10% interest on January 1 equity. The January 1 equity is Johan, $32,450.60, and Lou, $28,457.74. Also, partners' salaries are Johan, $25,000.00, and Lou, $36,000.00. The remaining net income, net loss, or distribution deficit is shared equally.
3. Prepare an owners' equity statement.
4. Prepare a balance sheet.

Purposeful Partners

Theme: Financial, Economic, Business, Entrepreneurial Literacy, and Global Awareness

Skills: Communication and Collaboration, Critical Thinking and Problem Solving, Creativity and Innovation

The selection process for finding a business partner should begin with asking why you want a partner. If you think finding someone who thinks just like you is like hitting the lottery, think again! A business partner should be someone who has skills that you do not have, so that you can expand as a team.

After finding that perfect partner whose skills and abilities complement your own, you can think about the legal agreement. Although business partnership agreements are not legally required, they are highly recommended. An example was shown in the previous chapter.

APPLICATION

1. Decide on a business that you would like to start in a foreign country. Explain the business and the country in which you would like to operate. Describe at least five qualities that you would seek in a business partner from that country. Explain why these qualities are important to you.

2. Using the Internet, research the requirements for forming a partnership in the country you selected. Draw a Venn diagram to compare and contrast establishing a partnership in this country and one in the United States.

3. With another classmate, write and perform a skit about your proposed partnership and its partners. Be sure to include the negotiation of at least five important terms in the partnership agreement and how partnership earnings will be distributed.

Analyzing Home Depot's Financial Statements

A corporation that does business in the United States must pay federal income taxes based on its net income. The amount of income tax varies from year to year, based on net income, corporate tax brackets, tax legislation, and changing tax regulations. The effective tax rate for a corporation can be calculated by dividing the "provision for income taxes" amount by the "earnings before provision for income taxes" amount. An awareness of the effective tax rate can help a corporation prepare budgets for future years.

INSTRUCTIONS

Refer to Home Depot's Consolidated Statements of Earnings on page B-6 of Appendix B in this textbook and complete the following items.

1. List the "provision for income taxes" amounts for each of the three years presented.
2. Calculate the effective tax rates for each of the three fiscal years.
3. Assume the management of Home Depot expects the corporation to earn $15,000 million before income taxes during the next fiscal year. What amount would you recommend be included in the budget for the provision for income taxes?

Budgeting and Accounting for a Not-for-Profit Organization

LEARNING OBJECTIVES

After studying Chapter 23, in addition to defining key terms, you will be able to:

LO1 Describe the characteristics of not-for-profit organizations.

LO2 Describe the differences between financial reporting for profit and not-for-profit organizations.

LO3 Describe the process used to develop an operating budget for a governmental organization.

LO4 Journalize budget transactions for a governmental organization.

LO5 Journalize revenues for a governmental organization.

LO6 Journalize expenditures, encumbrances, and other transactions for a governmental organization.

LO7 Journalize financing and investing transactions for a governmental organization.

© MARTA DESIGN/SHUTTERSTOCK.COM

MARTA

ACCOUNTING IN THE REAL WORLD

© REANC/SHUTTERSTOCK.COM

Providing mass transit services to a growing city is not an easy task. Take, for example, the development of Atlanta's MARTA system. The groundwork for MARTA began in the 1950s, but it wasn't until the 1960s that a commission issued a report recommending the addition of a rail system. Another seven years were needed to gain the necessary legislative and voter support to begin the process of laying track and constructing rail stations. During this lengthy planning stage, bus service remained the sole means of public transportation.

It's almost impossible to imagine the complexity and cost of laying underground track through the heart of downtown Atlanta, but the first rail service that provided access to the east side of Atlanta was finally operational in 1979. The present-day rail service, which reaches all four sides of Atlanta, was not completed until 1996. MARTA's system now includes 48 miles of rail that serve the downtown area, airport, and surrounding communities.

MARTA prepares an annual report that contains financial information of its operations. Unlike a corporation, MARTA's mission is not to make a profit. As a result, its financial reports are slightly different from a corporation's. For example, its statement showing assets and liabilities is titled a statement of net position. MARTA's annual report also contains significant operational data. The population served, size of the area served in miles, on time performance, and annual rail passenger miles are just a few of the reported statistics.

Accountants play a pivotal role in MARTA's operations because they are involved in developing budgets for daily operations to service expansion projects. In addition, advancements in technology have required that accountants upgrade the accounting system to process fares from automated machines to mobile apps.

Source: www.itsmarta.com.

CRITICAL THINKING

1. Obtain MARTA's most recent annual report. Examine the statement of cash flows to identify the amount of funds received from the federal government.

2. Do taxpayers and society benefit from the government's annual subsidy of MARTA's operations? Explain your answer.

3. Why would MARTA's annual report contain a 10-year history of (a) expense per passenger mile, (b) number of employees for the top ten corporate employers, and (c) population growth?

KEY TERMS

not-for-profit organization
fund
expenditure
statement of revenues, expenditures, and changes in fund balance

fund equity
operating budget
appropriations
tax levy
encumbrance

general fixed assets
certificate of deposit

LO1 Describe the characteristics of not-for-profit organizations.
LO2 Describe the differences between financial reporting for profit and not-for-profit organizations.
LO3 Describe the process used to develop an operating budget for a governmental organization.
LO4 Journalize budget transactions for a governmental organization.

Characteristics of Not-for-Profit Organizations LO1

The main objective of proprietorships, partnerships, and corporations is to earn a profit. Some organizations, however, are formed for purposes other than earning a profit. An organization providing goods or services with neither a conscious motive nor an expectation of earning a profit is called a **not-for-profit organization**. Not-for-profit organizations are also referred to as *nonprofit organizations*. These organizations are formed to provide needed goods or services to a group of individuals without regard to earning a profit.

ETHICS IN ACTION

Evaluating Auditor Independence

Teresa Stafford is a manager in the accounting firm of Turner & Avant. She has worked on the RBH Industries audit engagement since joining the firm seven years ago. RBH Industries is a family-owned business that processes wood products. Her younger brother Robbie, a junior accounting major at Macon University, has been offered a six-month internship with RBH Industries. Robbie is being recruited to work in the Tax Compliance Department. In the accounting profession, it is common for college interns to receive offers for full-time employment.

INSTRUCTIONS

Refer to the *Code of Professional Conduct* of the American Institute of Certified Public Accountants. Read Section 1.200 related to independence and selected definitions in Section 0.400. Can Teresa's accounting firm continue to perform the audit if her brother is hired as an intern? What if Robbie is hired for a full-time position?

Source: www.AICPA.org.

Types of Not-For-Profit Organizations

Not-for-profit organizations may differ as to the types of goods or services they provide, their sources of revenues, or the procedures they use to select their leaders or managers. The major types of not-for-profit organizations are as follows.

1. Governmental, such as federal, state, county, city, town, and village.
2. Educational, such as elementary, secondary, and postsecondary schools.
3. Health, such as hospitals and nursing homes.
4. Charitable, such as United Way, United Fund, and American Red Cross.
5. Foundational, including trusts and corporations organized for charitable and educational purposes, such as the Carnegie Foundation and the Ford Foundation.
6. Religious, such as churches and other religious groups.

Since not-for-profit organizations have a common objective, they share many of the same needs for financial information. Thus, the accounting system and many of the financial reports are similar for all not-for-profit organizations. However, because of differences in goods or services provided, sources of revenues, or methods of leadership selection, their accounting procedures and reports are modified for the specific type of organization.

Purpose of Governmental Organizations

All individuals are affected by or are members of one or more governmental organizations. Also, more individuals are employed by governmental organizations than any other type of not-for-profit organization. Therefore, Chapters 23 and 24 emphasize accounting for local governmental organizations.

A governmental organization's purpose is normally to provide needed goods or services that would be impossible for individuals to provide for themselves. For example, the federal government provides national defense for all citizens of the nation. Individual states and cities would find it difficult and very inefficient to provide for their own defense from foreign pressures. Similarly, cities provide police and fire protection that would be very expensive and inefficient for individuals to provide for themselves.

Charitable Giving Watchdogs

Many not-for-profit organizations rely on contributions as their major source of revenue. Some organizations get most of their contributions from large corporations. Others rely on donations by individuals. Not-for-profit organizations are competing with each other for a limited number of donated dollars. In the United States, the total number of dollars donated each year remains relatively constant, even in years of economic downturn.

Each organization develops a plan for how it will raise money. Contributions can be obtained through grants, donations, fund-raising events, and online crowd-funding sites. Not all donated dollars go to the mission of the charitable organization. The organization incurs expenses for administrative salaries, maintaining an office, and fund-raising. What remains can be used to support the charity's mission, which could be hunger, animal rights, medical research, the arts, the environment, education, or youth programs.

As a donor with limited dollars, you want to contribute to those organizations that operate most efficiently so that a high percentage of your donation actually supports the mission. It is important that not-for-profit organizations keep accurate records of donations and expenses. A variety of watchdog groups evaluate not-for-profit spending.

CRITICAL THINKING

1. Search the Internet for two charitable giving watchdog organizations. Summarize how each organization rates charitable organizations.

2. Choose which one of the two watchdog organizations you feel has a better evaluation method. Defend your choice in a short paragraph.

Source: www.charitynavigator.org.

Characteristics of Governmental Organizations and Accounting Systems

A governmental organization has several major characteristics that affect its accounting system. First, a government has no profit motive. A business's success can be measured by whether or not it earns a profit. A business that is inefficient, or not competitive, will not earn a profit. Without profits, a business will not be able to continue operations. However, since a governmental organization does not intend to earn a profit, success is much more difficult to measure. As long as money is available, a governmental organization can continue to operate, regardless of its efficiency or inefficiency.

Policy-making bodies of governmental organizations are generally elected by a popular vote of the group's members. Thus, the leadership depends on the political process and may change frequently. Policies and long-range goals may change when the leadership changes. These frequent changes make effective long-range planning difficult.

Revenues for governmental organizations are provided primarily by taxation on property, retail sales, or income. Organization members who have the greatest amount of property or income provide the greatest amount of revenues. However, the goods or services are normally provided to all members of the organization based on need. The amount that individuals pay is not related directly to the benefits they receive. Therefore, individuals have decreased incentive for ensuring that services are administered efficiently.

No direct relationship exists between who pays for and who receives the services provided by a governmental organization. Therefore, individuals generally support the organizational objective that is most advantageous to them. For example, some citizens of a city may give the construction of a library a high priority. Others who seldom use a library may give this project a low priority. Consequently, services provided by a governmental organization are usually determined through negotiation and compromise among the different interest groups. This procedure does not necessarily provide for the best services or the most efficiency.

The characteristics of governmental organizations have affected the development of governmental accounting systems. Therefore, numerous financial and legal regulations for determining the source and amount of revenues and for planning and executing expenditures of funds must be followed. These characteristics of a governmental organization compared to a corporation are summarized as follows:

Characteristic	Governmental Organization	Corporation
Profit motive	None	Maximize profits
Measure of success	Subjective evaluation of the quality of service provided	Earning a consistent profit indicates customer satisfaction with service
Ability to continue operations	Not dependent on effectiveness or efficiency—can continue as long as funding is available	Requires earning a consistent profit
Leadership	Changes frequently; elected by public or appointed by other government officials	Relatively stable; board of directors elected by stockholders
Effective long-term planning	Difficult due to frequent changes in leadership	Stable leadership in board of directors and management enables long-term planning
Objectives	Established through negotiation among both uses of services and taxpayers	Determined by management
Payment for services	Users of services rarely pay for service received	Customers pay for services or goods received
Source of funding	Taxes on property, retail sales, and/or income	Revenue from customers

Six accounting practices are similar for business and governmental organizations.

1. The accounting equation (assets equal liabilities plus equities) is applied.
2. An appropriate chart of accounts is prepared.
3. Transactions are analyzed into debit and credit elements.
4. Transactions are journalized and posted to ledgers.
5. Financial statements are prepared for each fiscal period.
6. Most of the same accounting concepts are applied.

The characteristics of governmental organizations and the conditions in which they operate create information and control requirements that differ from those of businesses. Because of these differences, governmental accounting and financial reporting differ in several ways from business accounting and financial reporting.

Financial Reporting for a Not-for-Profit Organization LO2

The accounting system for a business includes a single accounting entity. That is, all accounts used to record accounting transactions for the entire business are part of a single set of accounts. Within this set of accounts, assets must equal liabilities plus equities. A governmental accounting entity with a set of accounts in which assets always equal liabilities plus equities is called a **fund**. A governmental unit, such as a city, may have several different funds.

Fund Accounting Balance Sheet

Westburg General Fund	
ASSETS	
Cash.....................................	$425,000.00
Taxes Receivable	60,000.00
Total Assets	$485,000.00
LIABILITIES AND FUND EQUITY	
Liabilities:	
Accounts Payable	$ 45,000.00
Fund Equity:	
Fund Balance........................	440,000.00
Total Liabilities and Fund Equity........	$485,000.00

Westburg Library Fund	
ASSETS	
Cash...................................	$94,200.00
Late Fees Receivable...................	800.00
Total Assets	$95,000.00
LIABILITIES AND FUND EQUITY	
Liabilities:	
Accounts Payable	$ 6,000.00
Fund Equity:	
Fund Balance........................	89,000.00
Total Liabilities and Fund Equity........	$95,000.00

A fund accounting system emphasizes strong controls on the use of funds. The amount in a fund can be spent only for the specified purpose of the fund. Different funds may be created for different purposes. For example, the town of Westburg has two funds: (1) a general fund and (2) a library fund. Balance sheets for the two funds are shown above.

The town of Westburg has total assets of $580,000.00 (general fund, $485,000.00, plus library fund, $95,000.00). However, the assets are accounted for separately. Assets in the library fund may be used only for library purposes. General fund assets may be used for other authorized town expenditures. Each fund is kept as a separate set of accounts.

The fund equity, similar to owners' equity for a business, is the net amount of assets available for use. For example, Westburg's library fund equity is $89,000.00 (assets, $95,000.00, less liabilities, $6,000.00). If $7,000.00 cash is spent for library salaries, total assets available for spending would be reduced to $88,000.00 ($95,000.00 less $7,000.00). The fund equity account, Fund Balance, would be reduced to $82,000.00 (assets, $88,000.00, less liabilities, $6,000.00). Total Liabilities and Fund Equity would be recalculated as $88,000.00. After this transaction, the governmental accounting equation, assets equal liabilities plus fund equity, is in balance.

Types of funds vary with the type of not-for-profit organization and the types of goods or services provided. A unique set of funds normally is used for each type of organization—federal government, state and local governments, hospitals, or schools.

Modified Accrual Accounting

Most businesses use accrual accounting so that revenue and expenses incurred during a fiscal period determine the resulting net income for the period. **>> App. A: Matching Expenses with Revenue** Governmental organizations use modified accrual accounting. In modified accrual accounting, revenues are recorded in the accounting period in which they become measurable and available. For example, property taxes become measurable and available as soon as the amount is determined and tax statements are sent to property owners. However, sales taxes cannot be determined until sales are made. Thus, sales tax revenue is recognized when the taxes are received from merchants.

 FYI As with the general fund, modified accrual accounting would be used for a library fund.

Difference Between Expenses and Expenditures

Cash disbursements and liabilities incurred for the cost of goods delivered or services rendered are called **expenditures**. In modified accrual accounting, expenditures are generally recognized when a liability is incurred. Therefore, governmental organizations record expenditures rather than expenses.

An important distinction is made between expenditures and expenses. Businesses emphasize matching expenses with revenue in each fiscal period. An expense is recorded when an asset is used or a service is rendered in the process of earning revenue. However, governmental accounting emphasizes determining and controlling revenues and expenditures during a fiscal period. For example, if a business buys a truck, Plant Asset or Truck is debited and Cash or Notes Payable is credited. No expense is incurred until the truck is used. If a governmental organization buys a truck out of its general fund, Expenditure is debited and Cash or Notes Payable is credited. The amount of money spent or the liability incurred is recorded, not the expense. Thus, expenditures are decreases in net financial resources. Emphasis is placed on the control of the net financial resources, not on matching expenses with revenue. Modified accrual accounting is used to measure the financial position and operating results of the general funds of governmental organizations.

Financial Reporting Emphasis

Both business and governmental organizations prepare financial statements at the end of a fiscal period. **>> App. A: Accounting Period Cycle** However, because the organizations have different objectives, their charts of accounts and statements differ. The chart of accounts for Lindville appears on the next page.

The two most common financial statements prepared by businesses are the income statement and the balance sheet. Businesses prepare income statements to report the amount of net income earned during a fiscal period. Earning a net income is not an objective of governmental organizations. Rather, identifying and controlling the sources of revenues and the expenditure of funds are part of the control process. Therefore, government organizations prepare a different statement than do businesses. A statement that reports the sources of revenues and the expenditure of funds of a government organization is called a **statement of revenues, expenditures, and changes in fund balance**.

A business's balance sheet reports the assets, liabilities, and owners' equity of the business at the end of a fiscal period. A governmental organization's balance sheet (described in Chapter 24) also reports the current assets and liabilities of the organization at the end of a period. However, no specific ownership of a governmental organization exists. The amount of assets less liabilities of a governmental organization is called **fund equity**.

Budgeting LO3

Both businesses and governmental organizations prepare budgets. The primary purpose of all budgets is planning and control. During a business's fiscal period, budgeted amounts are compared with actual amounts to provide information to management about the effectiveness of cost control. For a governmental organization, however, an approved budget becomes (1) a legal authorization to spend and (2) a legal limit on the amount that can be spent.

FYI The Governmental Accounting Standards Board (GASB) establishes generally accepted accounting principles for city and state government financial reporting.

The town of Lindville serves as the center of retail commerce for a three-county area. The town provides its residents with many basic services, such as police and fire protection. Located at the foothills of the Greystone Mountains, Lindville is the center of numerous recreational opportunities for residents and visitors.

Chart of Accounts
TOWN OF LINDVILLE GENERAL FUND

Balance Sheet Accounts

(1000) ASSETS
1010 Cash
1020 Taxes Receivable—Current
1030 Allowance for Uncollectible Taxes—Current
1040 Taxes Receivable—Delinquent
1050 Allowance for Uncollectible Taxes—Delinquent
1060 Interest Receivable
1070 Allowance for Uncollectible Interest
1080 Inventory of Supplies
1090 Investments—Short Term

(2000) LIABILITIES
2010 Accounts Payable
2020 Notes Payable

(3000) FUND EQUITY
3010 Unreserved Fund Balance
3020 Reserve for Encumbrances— Current Year
3030 Reserve for Encumbrances— Prior Year
3040 Reserve for Inventory of Supplies

Revenue and Expenditure Accounts

(4000) REVENUES
4010 Property Tax Revenue
4020 Interest Revenue
4030 Other Revenue

(5000) EXPENDITURES
5100 GENERAL GOVERNMENT
5110 Expenditure—Personnel, General Government
5120 Expenditure—Supplies, General Government
5130 Expenditure—Other Charges, General Government
5140 Expenditure—Capital Outlays, General Government

5200 PUBLIC SAFETY
5210 Expenditure—Personnel, Public Safety
5220 Expenditure—Supplies, Public Safety
5230 Expenditure—Other Charges, Public Safety
5240 Expenditure—Capital Outlays, Public Safety

5300 FIRE PROTECTION
5310 Expenditure—Personnel, Fire Protection
5320 Expenditure—Supplies, Fire Protection

5330 Expenditure—Other Charges, Fire Protection
5340 Expenditure—Capital Outlays, Fire Protection

5400 RECREATION
5410 Expenditure—Personnel, Recreation
5420 Expenditure—Supplies, Recreation
5430 Expenditure—Other Charges, Recreation
5440 Expenditure—Capital Outlays, Recreation

Budgetary Accounts

(6000) BUDGETARY
6010 Estimated Revenues
6020 Appropriations
6030 Budgetary Fund Balance

6100 GENERAL GOVERNMENT
6110 Encumbrance—Personnel, General Government
6120 Encumbrance—Supplies, General Government
6130 Encumbrance—Other Charges, General Government
6140 Encumbrance—Capital Outlays, General Government

6200 PUBLIC SAFETY
6210 Encumbrance—Personnel, Public Safety
6220 Encumbrance—Supplies, Public Safety
6230 Encumbrance—Other Charges, Public Safety
6240 Encumbrance—Capital Outlays, Public Safety

6300 FIRE PROTECTION
6310 Encumbrance—Personnel, Fire Protection
6320 Encumbrance—Supplies, Fire Protection
6330 Encumbrance—Other Charges, Fire Protection
6340 Encumbrance—Capital Outlays, Fire Protection

6400 RECREATION
6410 Encumbrance—Personnel, Recreation
6420 Encumbrance—Supplies, Recreation
6430 Encumbrance—Other Charges, Recreation
6440 Encumbrance—Capital Outlays, Recreation

The chart of accounts for Lindville is illustrated above for reference as you study Chapters 23 and 24 of this textbook.

Governmental Operating Budget

<table>
<tr><td colspan="3" align="center">**Town of Lindville**
Annual Operating Budget—General Fund
For Year Ended December 31, 20--</td></tr>
<tr><td colspan="3" align="center">ESTIMATED REVENUES</td></tr>
<tr><td>Property Tax</td><td>$1,675,000.00</td><td></td></tr>
<tr><td>Interest</td><td>12,000.00</td><td></td></tr>
<tr><td>Other</td><td>4,500.00</td><td></td></tr>
<tr><td>Total Estimated Revenues</td><td></td><td>$1,691,500.00</td></tr>
<tr><td colspan="3" align="center">ESTIMATED EXPENDITURES AND BUDGETARY FUND BALANCE</td></tr>
<tr><td>General Government</td><td></td><td></td></tr>
<tr><td> Personnel</td><td>$ 271,100.00</td><td></td></tr>
<tr><td> Supplies</td><td>15,400.00</td><td></td></tr>
<tr><td> Other Charges</td><td>114,400.00</td><td></td></tr>
<tr><td> Capital Outlays</td><td>23,900.00</td><td></td></tr>
<tr><td> Total General Government</td><td></td><td>$ 424,800.00</td></tr>
<tr><td>Public Safety</td><td></td><td></td></tr>
<tr><td> Personnel</td><td>$ 597,500.00</td><td></td></tr>
<tr><td> Supplies</td><td>28,800.00</td><td></td></tr>
<tr><td> Other Charges</td><td>157,500.00</td><td></td></tr>
<tr><td> Capital Outlays</td><td>96,000.00</td><td></td></tr>
<tr><td> Total Public Safety</td><td></td><td>879,800.00</td></tr>
<tr><td>Fire Protection</td><td></td><td></td></tr>
<tr><td> Personnel</td><td>$ 115,500.00</td><td></td></tr>
<tr><td> Supplies</td><td>13,400.00</td><td></td></tr>
<tr><td> Other Charges</td><td>50,200.00</td><td></td></tr>
<tr><td> Capital Outlays</td><td>57,200.00</td><td></td></tr>
<tr><td> Total Fire Protection</td><td></td><td>236,300.00</td></tr>
<tr><td>Recreation</td><td></td><td></td></tr>
<tr><td> Personnel</td><td>$ 63,300.00</td><td></td></tr>
<tr><td> Supplies</td><td>6,600.00</td><td></td></tr>
<tr><td> Other Charges</td><td>28,900.00</td><td></td></tr>
<tr><td> Capital Outlays</td><td>19,300.00</td><td></td></tr>
<tr><td> Total Recreation</td><td></td><td>118,100.00</td></tr>
<tr><td>Total Estimated Expenditures</td><td></td><td>$1,659,000.00</td></tr>
<tr><td>Budgetary Fund Balance</td><td></td><td>32,500.00</td></tr>
<tr><td>Total Estimated Expenditures and Budgetary Fund Balance</td><td></td><td>$1,691,500.00</td></tr>
</table>

A plan of current expenditures and the proposed means of financing those expenditures is called an **operating budget**. A governmental fund's annual operating budget authorizes and provides the basis for controlling financial operations during a fiscal year. Since each governmental fund is a separate accounting entity, an operating budget is normally prepared to show the estimated revenues, estimated expenditures, and budgetary fund balance for each fund. The operating budget shown above was prepared for the general fund of the town of Lindville.

Lindville organizes revenue accounts by source of revenue. Expenditure accounts are organized by department and type of expenditure. Some organizations maintain subsidiary accounts for each of the general ledger accounts to provide more detail about the sources of revenues and types of expenditures. Because of its small size, Lindville maintains only the general ledger accounts listed in its chart of accounts.

Single Audits

A not-for-profit organization may receive funds from several agencies of the federal government. For example, a school district might receive funds from the Department of Education, the Department of Agriculture, and the National Science Foundation. An award of funds to an organization for a specified purpose is known as a *grant*. The organization and agency will sign a grant agreement, a legal document that identifies the purpose of the grant and how the funds must be spent. Every agency wants to ensure that its funds are used for only the intended purpose. Therefore, agencies may require the organization to be audited.

The Office of Management and Budget (OMB) has issued special rules for accountants auditing any organization that receives more than $750,000 of federal funds. These audits must be performed following the guidance of the Single Audit Act and OMB Circular A-133, *Audits of States, Local Governments and Non-Profit Organizations*, as amended. An audit performed using this guidance is commonly known as a *single audit*.

Auditors aren't the only individuals who are involved in an audit. An organization's accounting staff must devote time to obtaining requested documents, preparing detailed schedules, and discussing issues with the auditors, all while performing their normal job responsibilities.

Prior to the issuance of OMB Circular A-133, an organization might be audited by every federal agency from which it received federal funds. Having to work with two or more auditors placed an unfair burden on the organization and its accounting staff. To solve the problem, the OMB allows the organization to have a single audit. Every federal agency must accept the results of the one audit.

A single audit expands the scope of tests performed by auditors in a normal financial statement audit. OMB Circular A-133 requires additional tests designed to ensure that the organization has complied with the regulations of the grants received from each of the funding agencies. For example, a grant may limit the types of expenses that can be paid with grant funds.

ACTIVITY

Farris & Talbot, a public accounting firm, is performing a single audit of a State Department of Education. One of the grants requires education counselors to travel to schools across the state to meet with special-needs students. The counselors are reimbursed after each trip for their expenses, including travel, lodging, and meals.

Farris & Talbot has designed an extensive list of audit tests to ensure the accuracy and appropriateness of counselor reimbursements. The first test is a Benford's Law test on reimbursement checks. Benford's Law states that select digits of numbers from a natural data set should match a specific frequency. For example, 30.1% of the first digit of each amount should begin with the number 1, whereas only 4.6% of the first digits of amounts should begin with the number 9. The law is based on the mathematics of logarithms and can be applied to most data sets. However, the law does not apply to data that has limits, such as test grades, or have significant digits, such as zip codes and phone numbers.

The auditors expect the frequency of the first digit of each check amount to follow percentages of Benford's Law. If the actual frequency of digits is significantly different, the auditors are alerted that some bias exists. Additional audit tests are required to determine if the bias is natural for the organization or the result of a fraud.

INSTRUCTIONS

Open the spreadsheet FA_CH23 and complete the steps on the Instructions tab.

1. Summarize the findings of the Benford's Law analysis.

2. Does the chart provide any evidence that a fraud has occurred?

3. What additional procedures in Excel could be performed to better understand the data?

Preparing an Annual Operating Budget

Some basic procedures are followed in preparing an annual governmental operating budget.

1. Departments of the governmental organization submit budget requests to the chief executive of the organization. Requests are based on an analysis of expenditures for the previous year and expected changes in expenditures for the coming year.
2. The chief executive reviews budget requests with department heads. When budget requests are acceptable to the chief executive, departmental requests are consolidated into a single budget request for the organization. The chief executive then submits the operating budget to the legislative body. The legislative body is a group of persons normally elected by the citizens/members of the organization and granted authority to make laws for the organization.
3. The legislative body approves the operating budget. The approved operating budget becomes an authorization to spend the amounts listed in the budget. Before the operating budget can be approved, revenues plus the available amount of fund equity must be at least as great as the expenditures. If the expenditures are more than the total of expected revenues and available fund equity, the expected sources of revenue must be increased or the expenditures decreased.

Lindville is a small town with a town manager and five town council members. The council members are elected to their positions. One member of the council serves as mayor. The council serves as the legislative body for Lindville. The council appoints the town manager who works full-time as chief executive of the town. Lindville has three department heads: Public Safety Director, Fire Protection Director, and Recreation Director. Because Lindville is small and most of its revenues come from property taxes, the accounting system contains only one fund—a general fund.

At the request of the town manager, Lindville's three department heads analyze the current year's expenditures and expected changes and then prepare budget requests for the next year. The town manager reviews the budget requests and prepares a single operating budget for Lindville's general fund for the next year. The operating budget is submitted to the town council.

The town council represents the interests of all the town's citizens. Thus, the council should evaluate the operating budget from at least four perspectives. (1) Are adequate services being provided? (2) Are the services desired by a majority of citizens? (3) Are the amounts requested sufficient to provide the desired level of services? (4) Does the city have the financial capacity to support the budget?

The approved operating budget determines the amount of revenues needed for the year. The town's tax rate necessary to provide the needed funds for the approved operating budget is then determined.

After completing its review, the Lindville council formally approves next year's governmental operating budget. The approval provides legal authorization for the town manager and the department heads to make expenditures for specified purposes. Authorizations to make expenditures for specific purposes are called **appropriations**. Lindville's approved operating budget has appropriations that authorize expenditures up to the amounts stated in the budget.

The tax rate is set at a rate that will raise at least enough revenue to cover the appropriations. Many governmental organizations restrict the amount that taxes can be increased. Public hearings may be required before taxes can be increased. A formal vote in an election may also be required. If a proposed operating budget exceeds the amount of taxes and other estimated revenue, the budget may need to be reduced to the level of available revenues.

© PRESSMASTER/SHUTTERSTOCK.COM

Journalizing an Approved Annual Budget LO4

							GENERAL				CASH			
	DATE		ACCOUNT TITLE	DOC. NO.	POST. REF.		DEBIT		CREDIT		DEBIT		CREDIT	
1	Jan.	2	*Estimated Revenues*	M1			1691 5 0 0 00							1
2			*Appropriations*						1659 0 0 0 00					2
3			*Budgetary Fund Balance*						32 5 0 0 00					3
4														4

JOURNAL — PAGE 1

As an additional control measure, Lindville journalizes its approved operating budget as shown above. Budgetary accounts are for control purposes and are closed at the end of a fiscal period.

Governmental organizations, like businesses, record accounting transactions initially in a journal. Source documents are the basis for the journal entries. Governmental organizations may use a multicolumn journal, a general journal, or special journals adapted to the organization's needs. Lindville uses a multicolumn journal.

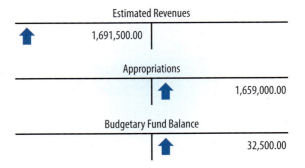

Estimated Revenues
1,691,500.00

Appropriations
1,659,000.00

Budgetary Fund Balance
32,500.00

> **January 2. Recorded Lindville's approved operating budget: estimated revenues, $1,691,500.00; appropriations, $1,659,000.00; budgetary fund balance, $32,500.00. Memorandum No. 1.**

Estimated Revenues is increased by a debit for the budgeted revenues, $1,691,500.00. Estimated Revenues has a normal debit balance, opposite the normal credit balance of an actual revenue account. Appropriations is increased by a credit for Lindville's budgeted expenditures, $1,659,000.00. Appropriations has a normal credit balance, opposite the normal debit balance of the actual expenditure accounts. Budgetary Fund Balance is increased by a credit, $32,500.00 (estimated revenues, $1,691,500.00, less appropriations, $1,659,000.00).

A separate revenue account will be credited as revenues are earned. Balances of the two accounts, Estimated Revenues and Revenues, can be reviewed to compare the amount of actual revenues earned and the amount of revenues estimated to be earned. If actual revenues are not as great as expected, expenditures may

need to be reduced to avoid exceeding available funds. Recording the estimated revenues in the budgetary account Estimated Revenues provides this planning and control information.

Separate expenditure accounts will be debited as actual expenditures are made. Ensuring that expenditures do not exceed the appropriations (budgeted expenditures) is essential for governmental organizations. Periodically, the appropriations account balance can be compared with the total of expenditure account balances to avoid overspending appropriations. Appropriations less total expenditures is the amount still available for spending. Recording appropriations in the budgetary account Appropriations provides this additional control information. Each department also keeps records of its appropriated and expended amounts to ensure that no department exceeds its appropriation amounts.

If appropriations exceed estimated revenues, Budgetary Fund Balance is debited to make the total debits equal the total credits. However, most governmental organizations normally set their revenue sources slightly above appropriations to avoid exceeding appropriations.

LO1 Describe the characteristics of not-for-profit organizations.

LO2 Describe the differences between financial reporting for profit and not-for-profit organizations.

LO3 Describe the process used to develop an operating budget for a governmental organization.

LO4 Journalize budget transactions for a governmental organization.

TERMS REVIEW

not-for-profit organization

fund

expenditure

statement of revenues, expenditures, and changes in fund balance

fund equity

operating budget

appropriations

Audit your understanding LO1, 2, 3

1. How does a lack of a profit motive affect a governmental organization's measure of success and its ability to continue operations?
2. List the accounting practices that are similar for businesses and governmental organizations.
3. Why do governmental organizations use a fund accounting system?
4. What is the difference between an expenditure and an expense?
5. What is the purpose of a governmental operating budget?
6. What is achieved by a city council approving an operating budget?
7. What accounts are debited and credited to journalize a governmental organization's approved operating budget?

Work together 23-1 LO4

Journalizing governmental operating budgets

The town of Lindforde approved its annual general fund operating budgets effective January 1 of the current year. A journal is provided in the *Working Papers*. Your instructor will guide you through the following example.

Journalize the entry to record the following operating budget for the town of Lindforde. The source document is Memorandum No. 1.

Estimated Revenues	Appropriations	Budgetary Fund Balance
$943,700.00	$936,800.00	$6,900.00

On your own 23-1 LO4

Journalizing governmental operating budgets

The town of Portsburg approved its annual general fund operating budgets effective January 1 of the current year. A journal is provided in the *Working Papers*. Work independently to complete the following problem.

Journalize the entry to record the following operating budget for the town of Portsburg. The source document is Memorandum No. 1.

Estimated Revenues	Appropriations	Budgetary Fund Balance
$1,987,300.00	$1,945,000.00	$42,300.00

Journalizing Revenues

LO5 Journalize revenues for a governmental organization.

Revenue Transactions for a Governmental Organization LO5

Governmental fund revenues are recorded in the accounting period in which the revenues become measurable and available. Authorized action taken by a governmental organization to collect taxes by legal authority is called a **tax levy**. When tax rates have been set and tax amounts calculated, taxes are levied on all taxable property. Levied property taxes are considered measurable and available because they become a legal obligation of

property owners. Therefore, when the levy is enacted, a journal entry to record property tax revenue is prepared, as shown below.

Although tax levies are legal obligations, some property owners do not pay their taxes. Legal action may eventually be taken against these property owners in an effort to collect the taxes. Even with these actions, a government generally does not collect all the taxes levied.

Journalizing Current Property Tax Revenues

					GENERAL		CASH	
	DATE	ACCOUNT TITLE	DOC. NO.	POST. REF.	DEBIT	CREDIT	DEBIT	CREDIT
4	2	*Taxes Receivable—Current*	M2		1699 0 0 0 00			
5		*Allowance for Uncollectible Taxes—Current*				24 0 0 0 00		
6		*Property Tax Revenue*				1675 0 0 0 00		
7								

JOURNAL   PAGE **1**

Total Taxes Levied   **Revenue Recognized from Tax Levy**   **Estimated Losses for Taxes Not Collected**

On January 2, Lindville authorized its tax levy and sent out tax statements to property owners. Lindville estimated that $24,000.00 of property taxes will not be collected.

> **January 2.** Recorded property tax levy: taxes receivable—current, $1,699,000.00; allowance for uncollectible taxes—current, $24,000.00; property tax revenue, $1,675,000.00. Memorandum No. 2.

Taxes Receivable—Current is debited for the total tax levied, $1,699,000.00. This amount is the total of the tax statements sent to taxpayers. The contra asset account, Allowance for Uncollectible Taxes—Current, is credited for the estimated loss, $24,000.00. The

credit to the revenue account Property Tax Revenue, $1,675,000.00, is the revenue presented on Lindville's annual operating budget for the general fund.

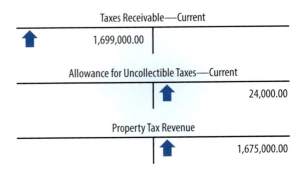

Taxes Receivable—Current

1,699,000.00

Allowance for Uncollectible Taxes—Current

24,000.00

Property Tax Revenue

1,675,000.00

Collection of Current Property Taxes

DATE	ACCOUNT TITLE	DOC. NO.	POST. REF.	GENERAL DEBIT	GENERAL CREDIT	CASH DEBIT	CASH CREDIT	
7	10	Taxes Receivable—Current	R1		206 000 00	206 000 00		7
8								8
9								9

Tax collections reduce the amount of taxes to be received from taxpayers. Similar to a partnership or corporation, the receipt of cash from a receivable does not result in the recognition of revenue.

> **January 10.** Received cash for current taxes receivable, $206,000.00. Receipt No. 1.

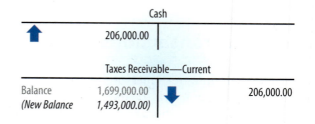

The outstanding balance of Taxes Receivable—Current is reduced by the amount of cash received.

Other Revenue

DATE	ACCOUNT TITLE	DOC. NO.	POST. REF.	GENERAL DEBIT	GENERAL CREDIT	CASH DEBIT	CASH CREDIT	
8	12	Other Revenue	R2		125 00	125 00		8
9								9
10								10

Some revenues, such as fines, inspection charges, parking meter receipts, and penalties, are normally not known and, thus, are not measurable until cash is received. A journal entry to record such revenues, therefore, is generally made only when cash is received.

> **January 12.** Received cash from a traffic fine, $125.00. Receipt No. 2.

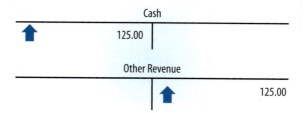

Unlike property taxes, no receivables account was established for this source of revenue. Therefore, Other Revenue is credited when the cash is collected.

Remember Other Revenue is used to account for cash receipts that are not measurable until received.

Accounting for Delinquent Property Taxes

Establish Balances in Deliquent Receivable Accounts

JOURNAL

PAGE 5

	DATE		ACCOUNT TITLE	DOC. NO.	POST. REF.	GENERAL DEBIT	GENERAL CREDIT	CASH DEBIT	CASH CREDIT	
1	Mar. 20--	1	Taxes Receivable—Delinquent	M15		74 2 0 0 00				1
2			Allowance for Uncollectible Taxes—Current			24 0 0 0 00				2
3			Taxes Receivable—Current				74 2 0 0 00			3
4			Allowance for Uncollectible Taxes—Delinquent				24 0 0 0 00			4
15		20	Taxes Receivable—Delinquent	R32			5 0 0 0 00	5 0 0 0 00		15

Remove Balances in Current Receivable Accounts

Tax payments specify the date that property taxes are due and payable. Taxes not paid by the specified date are reclassified as delinquent. Lindville's property taxes are due on February 28. On March 1, taxes not paid are considered delinquent. On that date, a journal entry is made to transfer uncollected taxes from current to delinquent status as shown above.

Taxes that Lindville expects to collect are accounted for by using two accounts, Taxes Receivable—Current and Allowance for Uncollectible Taxes—Current. Delinquent taxes are accounted for using two accounts, Taxes Receivable—Delinquent and Allowance for Uncollectible Taxes—Delinquent. A journal entry transfers the balances of the two current accounts to the two delinquent accounts.

> March 1. Recorded reclassification of current taxes receivable to delinquent status, $74,200.00, and the accompanying allowance for uncollectible accounts, $24,000.00. Memorandum No. 15.

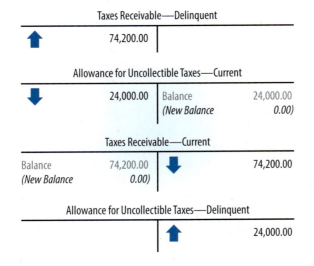

Collection of Delinquent Property Taxes

Although some taxes become delinquent, Lindville continues efforts to collect these taxes. Cash received for delinquent taxes reduces Taxes Receivable—Delinquent as shown in line 15 of the journal above.

> March 20. Received cash for delinquent taxes receivable, $5,000.00. Receipt No. 32.

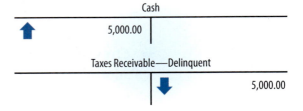

TERM REVIEW

tax levy

Audit your understanding LO5

1. When is the journal entry to record property tax revenue prepared?
2. What accounts are affected, and how, when a taxpayer pays current property taxes?
3. What accounts are affected, and how, when a taxpayer pays property taxes two months after the due date?

Work together 23-2 LO5

Journalizing governmental revenue transactions

Tomeville's town council recently approved the town's general fund operating budget for the current year. A journal is provided in the *Working Papers*. Source documents are abbreviated as follows: check, C; receipt, R; memorandum, M. Your instructor will guide you through the following examples.

Journalize the following transactions.

Transactions:

Jan. 2. Recorded property tax levy: taxes receivable—current, $2,723,000.00; allowance for uncollectible taxes—current, $30,000.00; property tax revenue, $2,693,000.00. M22.

15. Received cash from traffic fines, $1,488.00. R94. (Other Revenue)

Feb. 12. Received cash for current taxes receivable, $669,000.00. R103.

Mar. 1. Recorded reclassification of current taxes receivable to delinquent status, $89,200.00, and the accompanying allowance for uncollectible accounts, $30,000.00. M44.

13. Received cash for delinquent taxes receivable, $21,300.00. R137.

On your own 23-2 LO5

Journalizing governmental revenue transactions

Missville's town council recently approved the town's general fund operating budget for the current year. A journal is provided in the *Working Papers*. Source documents are abbreviated as follows: check, C; receipt, R; memorandum, M. Work independently to complete the following problem.

Journalize the following transactions.

Transactions:

Jan. 3. Recorded property tax levy: taxes receivable—current, $1,267,000.00; allowance for uncollectible taxes—current, $13,000.00; property tax revenue, $1,254,000.00. M15.

Feb. 2. Received cash for current taxes receivable, $948,200.00. R45.

14. Received cash from parking meter receipts, $1,060.00. R67. (Other Revenue)

Mar. 1. Recorded reclassification of current taxes receivable to delinquent status, $32,600.00, and the accompanying allowance for uncollectible accounts, $13,000.00. M34.

28. Received cash for delinquent taxes receivable, $16,920.00. R100.

Journalizing Expenditures, Encumbrances, and Other Transactions

LO6 Journalize expenditures, encumbrances, and other transactions for a governmental organization.

LO7 Journalize financing and investing transactions for a governmental organization.

Expenditure Transactions for a Governmental Organization LO6

A primary objective of governmental accounting is to control the financial resources. Governmental accounting focuses on measuring changes in financial resources rather than determining net income. Therefore, in governmental accounting, expenditures rather than expenses are recorded.

Journalizing Expenditures

		JOURNAL							PAGE 1	
						1	2	3	4	
						GENERAL		CASH		
	DATE	ACCOUNT TITLE	DOC. NO.	POST. REF.		DEBIT	CREDIT	DEBIT	CREDIT	
10	14	*Expenditure—Supplies, Fire Protection*	C234			1 2 0 00			1 2 0 00	10
11										11
12										12

The use of two special accounting procedures enhances the control of expenditures.

1. Expenditures are classified into categories to assign specific responsibility for and to analyze the purpose of the expenditure. For example, Expenditure—Personnel, Fire Protection, is one of Lindville's expenditure accounts. Personnel indicates the type of expenditure (salaries for personnel). Fire Protection indicates the department for which the personnel expenditures were made.

2. Budgetary accounts are used to record estimated amounts of expenditures to protect against overspending the budgeted amounts. To accomplish this control procedure, encumbrance accounts are used. A commitment to pay for goods or services that have been ordered but not yet provided is called an **encumbrance**. When an order that will require a future expenditure is placed, a budgetary encumbrance account is debited for the estimated amount. This entry reduces the fund balance and ensures that commitments and expenditures will not be greater than the funds available.

Exact amounts of some expenditures are known as soon as the obligation is determined. For example, the amount and due date of payment for supplies is known when the department employee purchases the supplies at a local retailer. The entry to record the expenditure is shown above.

> **January 14. Paid cash for supplies in the Fire Department, $120.00. Check No. 234.**

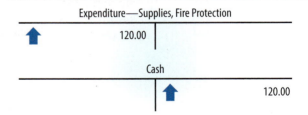

The major control of expenditures is achieved by holding department heads accountable for expenditures in their departments. Classification of expenditures is used to analyze major types of expenditures within each department. For Lindville, each department's expenditures are recorded in one of four classifications: personnel, supplies, other charges, or capital outlays. The other charges classification is used for all expenditures except salaries and related personnel expenditures, supplies expenditures, and capital outlays. Capital outlays is used for expenditures that will benefit future years.

Journalizing Encumbrances

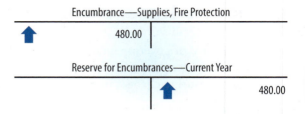

	DATE	ACCOUNT TITLE	DOC. NO.	POST. REF.	GENERAL DEBIT	GENERAL CREDIT	CASH DEBIT	CASH CREDIT	
4	16	Encumbrance—Supplies, Fire Protection	M8		4 8 0 00				4
5		Reserve for Encumbrances—Current Year				4 8 0 00			5
6									6

To avoid spending more resources than are available, encumbrance accounts are used. When goods or services are ordered that will be provided at a later date, an obligation for a future expenditure is made. Resources have not yet been used, but there is a promise to give up those resources when ordered goods or services are delivered. Encumbering resources is a way of setting aside the amount estimated to be needed to pay for the goods or services. When the goods or services are delivered, the estimated amount is removed from the encumbrance account and the exact amount of the expenditure is journalized in an expenditure account.

January 16. Encumbered estimated amount for supplies in Fire Protection Department, $480.00. Memorandum No. 8.

The budgetary account Encumbrance—Supplies, Fire Protection is increased by a debit for the amount of the order, $480.00. The fund equity account Reserve for Encumbrances—Current Year is increased by a credit for the supplies order, $480.00, as shown above.

Encumbrance—Supplies, Fire Protection

| 480.00 | |

Reserve for Encumbrances—Current Year

| | 480.00 |

This account serves as an offsetting account for the encumbrance account and shows that this amount of the fund equity is reserved for an encumbrance.

Expenditures plus encumbrances for a specific account equal the total commitment that has been made against the appropriated amount for that account. The appropriated amount less the encumbrances and expenditures equals the amount that can still be spent. For example, Lindville appropriated $13,400.00 for supplies for the Fire Protection Department. If expenditures are $120.00 and encumbrances are $480.00, then $12,800.00 is still available for fire protection supplies expenditures.

Appropriated for Supplies	−	Expenditures	−	Encumbrances	=	Amount Still Available
$13,400.00	−	$120.00	−	$480.00	=	$12,800.00

Remember

Governmental organizations record expenditures rather than expenses.

Journalizing Expenditures for Amounts Encumbered

JOURNAL

PAGE 2

	DATE	ACCOUNT TITLE	DOC. NO.	POST. REF.	GENERAL DEBIT	GENERAL CREDIT	CASH DEBIT	CASH CREDIT	
16	28	Reserve for Encumbrances—Current Year	M19		4 8 0 00				16
17		Encumbrance—Supplies, Fire Protection				4 8 0 00			17
18	28	Expenditure—Supplies, Fire Protection	C246		4 6 5 00			4 6 5 00	18

When goods or services that have been encumbered are received, two entries must be made.

1. The encumbrance entry is reversed to remove the estimated amount from the encumbrance and the reserve for encumbrance accounts.
2. The expenditure is recorded.

These entries are illustrated above.

> **January 28. Paid cash for Fire Protection Department supplies, $465.00, encumbered January 16 per Memorandum No. 8. Memorandum No. 19 and Check No. 246.**

The first entry cancels the encumbrance entry by removing the estimated amount from the encumbrance and the reserve for encumbrance accounts. The encumbrance is no longer needed, since it is no longer outstanding. The encumbrance was for an estimated amount, $480.00.

The actual amount of an expenditure sometimes differs from the amount estimated when an order is placed. When the supplies were delivered, the actual cost was

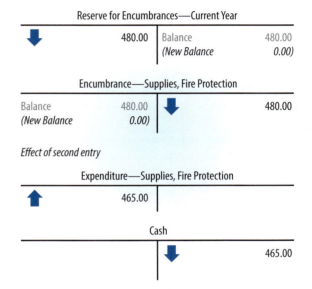

Effect of first entry

Reserve for Encumbrances—Current Year

↓	480.00	Balance	480.00
		(New Balance	0.00)

Encumbrance—Supplies, Fire Protection

Balance	480.00	↓	480.00
(New Balance	0.00)		

Effect of second entry

Expenditure—Supplies, Fire Protection

↑	465.00

Cash

	↓ 465.00

$465.00. Expenditure—Supplies, Fire Protection is debited for the actual cost of supplies, $465.00.

Journalizing Expenditures Benefiting Future Periods

JOURNAL

PAGE 5

	DATE	ACCOUNT TITLE	DOC. NO.	POST. REF.	GENERAL DEBIT	GENERAL CREDIT	CASH DEBIT	CASH CREDIT	
7	10	Expenditure—Capital Outlays, Gen. Gov't.	C269		2 9 0 00			2 9 0 00	7
8									8
9									9

Governmental organizations are formed to provide services that their members need, not to earn a profit. A business records the cost of property, such as a computer, as an asset. The business then depreciates the asset over its useful life. The depreciation expense is matched with revenue earned in each fiscal period. In contrast, a governmental fund does not record assets or depreciation. However, controlling the expenditure of funds is important. When money is spent for capital outlays, the amount is recorded as an expenditure in the period spent, even though the item may benefit several accounting periods.

On March 10, Lindville's General Government Department bought a new wireless router.

> March 10. Paid cash for a wireless router for General Government Department, $290.00. Check No. 269.

Expenditure—Capital Outlays, General Government is increased by a debit for the cost of the router, $290.00. Cash is decreased by a credit for the same amount, $290.00. The journal entry is shown on page 689.

Governmental properties that benefit future periods are called **general fixed assets**. Most governmental organizations keep a record of general fixed assets. This record helps to safeguard the government's ownership of the property. Lindville keeps a card file with information about each general fixed asset.

Financing and Investing Transactions for a Governmental Organization LO7

Governmental organizations may need to borrow cash for short periods until tax money is received. At other times, these organizations have cash to invest for short periods until the cash is needed to pay expenditures.

Journalize the Issuance of Liabilities

		JOURNAL							PAGE 2
					GENERAL		CASH		
	DATE	ACCOUNT TITLE	DOC. NO.	POST. REF.	DEBIT	CREDIT	DEBIT	CREDIT	
1	20-- Jan. 15	Notes Payable	NP3			60 000 00	60 000 00		1
2									2

Lindville sends tax statements to property owners on January 1 each year. Taxes can be paid between January 1 and February 28. Consequently, the town may need to borrow cash until taxes are received.

> January 15. Issued a 30-day, 9% note, $60,000.00. Note Payable No. 3.

Cash is increased by a debit for the amount received, $60,000.00. Notes Payable is increased by a credit for the same amount, $60,000.00. The journal entry to record this transaction is shown above.

Journalize the Payment of Liabilities

		JOURNAL							PAGE 4
					GENERAL		CASH		
	DATE	ACCOUNT TITLE	DOC. NO.	POST. REF.	DEBIT	CREDIT	DEBIT	CREDIT	
1	20-- Feb. 14	Notes Payable	C370		60 000 00			60 450 00	1
2		Expenditure—Other Charges, Gen. Gov't.			450 00				2

When Lindville's note payable is due on February 14, the amount of the note plus interest expense is paid to the bank. The bank uses a 360-day year when calculating interest.

> February 14. Paid cash for the maturity value of NP3: principal, $60,000.00, plus interest, $450.00; total, $60,450.00. Check No. 370.

Notes Payable is decreased by a debit, $60,000.00. Expenditure—Other Charges, General Government is increased by a debit for the interest expense, $450.00. Cash is decreased by a credit for the total amount paid, $60,450.00. The journal entry is shown above.

Investing in Short-Term Investments

	DATE		ACCOUNT TITLE	DOC. NO.	POST. REF.	GENERAL DEBIT	GENERAL CREDIT	CASH DEBIT	CASH CREDIT	
			JOURNAL						PAGE 9	
1	May	4	Investments—Short Term	C603		300 0 0 0 00			300 0 0 0 00	1
2										2
3										3

Most of Lindville's property taxes, the major portion of the town's revenue, are collected by March 1 each year. Cash that will not be needed for several months is placed in short-term investments. Interest on these investments provides additional revenue.

> **May 4. Paid cash for a 120-day, 2.5% certificate of deposit, $300,000.00. Check No. 603.**

A document issued by a bank as evidence of money invested with the bank is called a **certificate of deposit**. The time and interest rate to be paid are included on the certificate.

Investments—Short Term is increased by a debit for the amount of the certificate, $300,000.00. Cash is decreased by a credit for the same amount, $300,000.00. The journal entry is shown above.

THINK LIKE AN ACCOUNTANT

Organizational Structure

Within the past year, Alexander County residents had suffered the loss of property and life as a result of a hurricane and two tornadoes. Unhappy with the timeliness and breadth of the response by federal agencies, the county supervisors decided to organize their own disaster response agency.

The job of organizing the Alexander County Taskforce (ACT) was assigned to Sandi Franklin and funded by a small grant from the county. Sandi assembled a group of individuals who would assume leadership roles. As ACT began operations, Sandi knew that ACT would need to seek significant financial support from local corporations.

Dennis Sparks, a CPA, accepted the role of development officer. Dennis would be responsible for obtaining ACT's financial support. His first task is to prepare a funding proposal to submit to corporations. The proposal needs to demonstrate

that ACT is a legitimate organization deserving financial support. As a part of this proposal, Dennis decided to include a profile of each leader in the organization. At his request, Sandi prepared a document containing an alphabetical list of ACT leaders.

OPEN THE SPREADSHEET TLA_CH23

The workbook contains a description of the individuals who accepted ACT's leadership positions. Follow the steps on the Instructions tab to create a graphic image of ACT's organizational structure. Answer these questions:

1. How does an organizational chart help the corporations understand ACT's organizational structure?

2. What recommendation would you give Dennis to improve the organizational chart?

Receiving Cash from Short-Term Investments

	DATE		ACCOUNT TITLE	DOC. NO.	POST. REF.	GENERAL DEBIT	GENERAL CREDIT	CASH DEBIT	CASH CREDIT	
			JOURNAL						PAGE **20**	
1	Sept. 20--	1	Investments—Short Term	R172			300 0 0 0 00	302 5 0 0 00		1
2			Interest Revenue				2 5 0 0 00			2
3										3

When the certificate of deposit is due on September 1, cash is received for the original cost of the investment plus interest revenue earned.

> September 1. Received cash for the maturity value of certificate of deposit due today: principal, $300,000.00, plus interest, $2,500.00; total, $302,500.00. Receipt No. 172.

Cash is increased by a debit for the cash received, $302,500.00. Investments—Short Term is decreased by a credit for the certificate of deposit's original cost, $300,000.00. Interest Revenue is increased by a credit for the interest earned, $2,500.00. The journal entry is shown above.

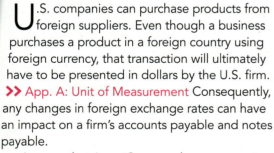

Foreign Currency Exchange Gains or Losses

U.S. companies can purchase products from foreign suppliers. Even though a business purchases a product in a foreign country using foreign currency, that transaction will ultimately have to be presented in dollars by the U.S. firm. **>> App. A: Unit of Measurement** Consequently, any changes in foreign exchange rates can have an impact on a firm's accounts payable and notes payable.

Assume that AmeriCom purchases computer cables from ChinaCom on account and agrees to pay a total of $120,000 yuan, the Chinese currency, in 60 days. At the time of the purchase, one yuan is equal to $0.14 American cents. Therefore, AmeriCom credits Accounts Payable for $16,800.00 (120,000 yuan × $0.14).

During the 60-day credit period, however, the exchange rate for the yuan rises to $0.16. Now it will cost AmeriCom $19,200.00 to purchase 120,000 yuan. Due to the 2-cent increase in the exchange rate, AmeriCom will

spend an extra $2,400.00 through the currency exchange process. AmeriCom accounts for the loss on accounts payable with the entry below. The account Gain or Loss on Foreign Currency Exchange is classified as an other revenue account.

Accounts Payable/ChinaCom . . 16,800.00
Gain or Loss on Foreign
    Currency Exchange 2,400.00
       Cash 19,200.00

CRITICAL THINKING

1. Assume that instead of increasing during the 60-day credit period, the exchange rate for the yuan decreases to $0.13. Will AmeriCom realize a gain or a loss on the transaction?

2. Indicate the accounts and amounts debited and credited when AmeriCom records the payment.

LO6 Journalize expenditures, encumbrances, and other transactions for a governmental organization.

LO7 Journalize financing and investing transactions for a governmental organization.

TERMS REVIEW

encumbrance

general fixed assets

certificate of deposit

Audit your understanding LO6, 7

1. What is an encumbrance?
2. What two entries are required when goods or services that have been encumbered are received?
3. Why does a governmental organization not record depreciation expense?
4. What is a certificate of deposit?

Work together 23-3 LO6, 7

Journalizing governmental encumbrances, expenditures, and other transactions

The town of Crystal Falls records expenditures by type of expenditure and by department. The four categories of expenditures are personnel, supplies, other charges, and capital outlays. Departments are General Government, Public Safety, Fire Protection, and Recreation.

A journal is provided in the *Working Papers*. Source documents are abbreviated as follows: memorandum, M; check, C; notes payable, NP. Your instructor will guide you through the following examples. Interest is calculated using a 360-day year.

Journalize the transactions completed during the current year.

Transactions:

Jan. 12. Paid cash for electrical service in Fire Protection Dept., $692.00. C382.
17. Encumbered estimated amount for supplies for the Public Safety Department, $250.00. M18.
20. Issued a 30-day, 5% note, $120,000.00. NP5.
28. Paid cash for Public Safety Department supplies, $256.00, encumbered January 17 per M18. M22 and C397.
Feb. 7. Paid cash for printer for General Government Department, $625.00. C420. (Capital Outlays)
19. Paid cash for the maturity value of NP5: principal, $120,000.00, plus interest, $500.00; total, $120,500.00. C438.
Mar. 17. Paid cash for a 90-day, 3% certificate of deposit, $150,000.00. C467.
June 15. Received cash for the maturity value of certificate of deposit due today; principal, $150,000.00, plus interest, $1,125.00; total, $151,125.00. R212.

On your own 23-3 LO6, 7

Journalizing governmental encumbrances, expenditures, and other transactions

The town of Emandale uses the same categories and departments as Crystal Falls in the Work Together 23-3 problem. Journalize the transactions completed during the current year.

Transactions:

Jan. 10. Paid cash for consultant's services in Recreation Department, $332.00. C113. (Personnel)
15. Encumbered estimated amount for supplies in Fire Protection Department, $1,800.00. M12.
18. Issued a 30-day, 4% note, $45,000.00. NP3.
26. Paid cash for Fire Protection Department supplies, $1,726.00, encumbered January 15 per M12. M19 and C156.
Feb. 17. Paid cash for the maturity value of NP3: principal, $45,000.00, plus interest, $150.00; total, $45,150.00. C178.
Mar. 15. Paid cash for a 90-day, 3% certificate of deposit, $92,000.00. C210.
June 13. Received cash for the maturity value of certificate of deposit due today; principal, $92,000.00, plus interest, $690.00; total, $92,690.00. R97.

CHAPTER SUMMARY

The goal of a not-for-profit organization is to provide goods or services rather than to earn a profit. Most government agencies are organized as not-for-profit organizations. A governmental organization has four major characteristics that affect the accounting system: (1) No profit motive exists. (2) Leadership is subject to frequent change. (3) Users of services do not necessarily pay for the services. (4) Conflicting pressures for differing objectives exist.

Government agencies use fund accounting systems. A governmental unit, such as a city, may have several different funds. The amount in a fund can be spent only for the specified purpose of the fund.

A governmental fund's annual operating budget authorizes and provides the basis for control of financial operations during a fiscal year. Appropriations are authorizations to make expenditures for specified purposes. As a control, the expected sources of revenues and appropriations are journalized in the fund's accounting system.

Accounting transactions are recorded using modified accrual accounting. Revenues are recorded in the accounting period in which they become measurable and available. To protect against overspending, government organizations use encumbrance accounts to record estimates of ordered goods or services not yet received. When the goods or services are received, the encumbrance is reversed and the actual cost is recorded as an expenditure. Governmental organizations record expenditures rather than expenses. Capital outlays, such as the purchase of equipment, are recorded as expenditures in the period when the liability is incurred.

EXPLORE ACCOUNTING

Accounting Opportunities in Not-for-Profit Organizations

When asked to think about accounting careers available in the not-for-profit sector, most people think about city, county, and state positions. Most often, these positions involve completing the accounting and reporting tasks required by these governmental agencies. However, there are other exciting and challenging accounting-related careers in the not-for-profit sector. These careers include working for the Federal Bureau of Investigation (FBI), the Internal Revenue Service (IRS), and/or insurance companies in an area called "forensic accounting."

Forensic accounting is the investigation of accounting records and reports when fraud and/or embezzlement is suspected. Forensic accountants may help investigate crimes such as extortion, fraud, and embezzlement.

FBI agents may use interview and research techniques to investigate crimes. Requirements for employment as an FBI special agent working in the accounting field include a four-year accounting degree from an accredited school and at least three years of professional work experience. In addition, an agent must be a citizen of the United States between the ages of 23 and 36 and in good physical condition.

The IRS also employs accountants in various areas. Internal revenue agents are accountants who, by looking at the accounting records and the tax returns of a business, determine if the business owes taxes and, if so, how much. The IRS also employs accountants as special agents. A special agent investigates potential criminal violations of tax laws. Requirements for employment within the IRS vary, but most do include a four-year degree with some experience in the accounting field.

Insurance companies also hire accountants to assist in investigating cases involving suspected insurance fraud. States employ accountants to audit the accounting systems and financial statements of state and local agencies, school systems, and other government agencies.

INSTRUCTIONS

Access the employee recruitment section of a federal or state agency's Internet site. Search for detailed information on job opportunities, requirements, and application procedures. Report your findings in written form.

Source: www.fbijobs.gov.

INSTRUCTIONS: Download problem instructions for Excel, QuickBooks, and Sage 50c from the textbook companion website at www.C21accounting.com.

23-1 Application Problem Journalizing governmental operating budgets LO4

Three towns have approved their annual general fund operating budgets effective January 1 of the current year. A journal is provided in the *Working Papers*.

Instructions:

Journalize the entry to record the operating budgets for each of the three towns for the current year.

	Estimated Revenues	Appropriations	Budgetary Fund Balance
Westville	$1,831,000.00	$1,814,800.00	$16,200.00
Amberville	2,208,600.00	2,184,000.00	24,600.00
Smithburg	3,186,000.00	3,154,000.00	32,000.00

23-2 Application Problem Journalizing governmental revenue transactions LO5

Milltown's town council recently approved the town's general fund operating budget for the current year. A journal is provided in the *Working Papers*.

Instructions:

Journalize the transactions for the current year.

Transactions:

Jan. 1. Recorded property tax levy: taxes receivable—current, $1,985,000.00; allowance for uncollectible taxes—current, $35,000.00; property tax revenue, $1,950,000.00. M99.

16. Received cash for current taxes receivable, $514,000.00. R155.

28. Received cash from traffic fines, $2,150.00. R164.

Feb. 23. Received cash for current taxes receivable, $725,000.00. R189.

Mar. 1. Recorded reclassification of current taxes receivable to delinquent status, $129,300.00, and the accompanying allowance for uncollectible accounts, $35,000.00. M128.

26. Received cash for delinquent taxes receivable, $45,300.00. R222.

23-3 Application Problem

Journalizing governmental encumbrances, expenditures, and other transactions LO6, 7

sage 50

1. Journalize and post transactions related to governmental encumbrances to the general journal.
2. Print the general journal and the trial balance.

QB

1. Journalize and post transactions related to governmental encumbrances to the journal.
2. Print the journal and the trial balance.

[Excel]

1. Journalize transactions related to governmental encumbrances to the journal.
2. Print the worksheet.

The town of Templeton uses a general fund for all financial transactions. Expenditures are recorded by type of expenditure and by department. The four categories of expenditures are personnel, supplies, other charges, and capital outlays. Departments are General Government, Public Safety, Fire Protection, and Recreation.

Instructions:

Journalize the transactions for the current year. Use page 1 of a journal. Interest is calculated using a 360-day year.

Transactions:

Jan. 6. Paid cash for supplies in Public Safety Department, $625.00. C244.

12. Encumbered estimated amount for the purchase of a police car, $32,250.00. M44.

22. Issued a 30-day, 6% note, $125,000.00. NP12.

25. Encumbered estimated amount for supplies in the Fire Department, $4,320.00. M42.

Feb. 3. Paid cash of $33,120.00 for the police car encumbered January 12 per M44. M55 and C320.

21. Paid cash for the maturity value of NP12: principal, $125,000.00, plus interest. C356.

28. Paid cash for a 30-day, 2% certificate of deposit, $25,000.00. C369.

Mar. 6. Paid cash of $4,260.00 for supplies encumbered January 25 per M42. M67 and C406.

30. Received cash for the maturity value of certificate of deposit due today: principal, $25,000.00, plus interest. R334.

23-M Mastery Problem

Journalizing governmental transactions LO4, 5, 6, 7

sage 50

1. Journalize and post governmental transactions to the general journal.
2. Print the general journal and the trial balance.

QB

1. Journalize and post governmental transactions to the journal.
2. Print the journal and the trial balance.

[Excel]

1. Journalize governmental transactions to the journal.
2. Print the worksheet.

The town of Lanceburg uses a general fund for all financial transactions. Expenditures are recorded by type of expenditure and by department. The four categories of expenditures are personnel, supplies, other charges, and capital outlays. Departments are General Government, Public Safety, Fire Protection, and Recreation. Interest is calculated using a 360-day year.

Instructions:

Journalize the transactions for the current year.

Transactions:

Use page 1 of a journal.

Jan. 2. Recorded current year's approved operating budget: estimated revenues, $2,200,000.00; appropriations, $2,162,000.00; budgetary fund balance, $38,000.00. M32.

2. Recorded current year's property tax levy: taxes receivable—current, $2,225,000.00; allowance for uncollectible taxes—current, $25,000.00; property tax revenue, $2,200,000.00. M33.

14. Received cash for current taxes receivable, $268,500.00. R95.

22. Paid cash for supplies in the General Government Department, $1,648.00. C198.

24. Issued a 45-day, 6% note, $500,000.00. NP6.

30. Encumbered estimated amount for supplies in the Fire Department, $3,415.00. M42.

Feb. 2. Received cash from traffic fines, $4,158.00. R164. (Other Revenue)

6. Paid cash for car parts for the Police Department, $339.00. C226.

14. Paid cash for Fire Department supplies, $3,559.00, encumbered January 30 per M42. M50 and C240.

19. Encumbered estimated amount for equipment purchases by the Recreation Department, $2,269.00. M63.

Mar. 1. Recorded reclassification of current taxes receivable to delinquent status, $148,300.00, and the accompanying allowance for uncollectible accounts, $25,000.00. M80.

Use page 2 of a journal.

Mar. 10. Paid cash for the maturity value of NP6: principal, $500,000.00, plus interest. C255.

11. Paid cash for a 60-day, 2.5% certificate of deposit, $100,000.00. C278.

12. Paid cash for Recreation Department equipment, $2,315.00, encumbered February 19 per M63. M92 and C290.

16. Received cash for delinquent taxes receivable, $61,800.00. R223.

23. Paid cash for consultant's services in Public Safety Department, $680.00. C301. (Personnel)

May 10. Received cash for the maturity value of certificate of deposit due today: principal, $100,000.00, plus interest. R240.

23-C Challenge Problem   Determining the increase, decrease, and normal balance of accounts LO4, 5, 6

Instructions:

Complete a table to provide an easy reference tool to help new accounting clerks accurately record journal entries and calculate general ledger balances. For each account, enter "+" (for an increase) or "−" (for a decrease) in the appropriate Debit and Credit column to show the impact of a debit or credit to each account's balance. Enter Dr. or Cr. in the last column to indicate the normal balance for each account. Use the table in the *Working Papers* to complete this problem. The Cash account is provided as an example.

Account Title	Debit	Credit	Normal Balance
Cash	+	−	Dr.

Nonprofits Benefit from Kaizen

PARTNERSHIP FOR
21ST CENTURY SKILLS

Theme: Financial, Economic, Business, and Entrepreneurial Literacy

Skills: Communication and Collaboration, Critical Thinking and Problem Solving, Creativity and Innovation, Leadership and Responsibility

Whether a CEO, an accountant, a software developer, or a musician, all workers need to find ways to improve processes in order to be successful and competitive. Improving processes means finding ways to minimize problems, eliminate waste and excess work, and increase productivity and performance.

Toyota is known for its continuous improvement, and the philosophy of kaizen is one of Toyota's core values and keys for success. *Kaizen* is a Japanese word that means *improvement* or *change for the best*. Kaizen in Toyota's organization means that all members of the organization are looking constantly for ways to improve operations.

Toyota took its kaizen philosophy to one of the country's largest anti-hunger nonprofit organizations, the Food Bank of New York City. Here, Toyota engineers found a solution to the problem of long lines for this soup kitchen. Guests would often find themselves waiting as long as 90 minutes. However, kaizen paid off. Toyota's focus on efficiency trimmed the wait time for dinner down to 18 minutes.

Source: www.nytimes.com.

APPLICATION

1. Make a list of three processes that could be changed at your school. Look for ways to improve wait time or performance, or cut down on waste. Practice the kaizen philosophy by recommending a solution to improve each of the three processes. Share your answers with the class.

2. Visit a local charity and look for ways that processes could be improved to provide services more efficiently. Compose a letter to this organization explaining your recommendation and why it might improve its process to provide a better result.

Analyzing Home Depot's Financial Statements

Corporations seeking to expand into a new country often elect to purchase a similar business in the target country. Acquiring an existing business prevents the corporation from having to "start from scratch." The existing business already has the physical assets necessary to conduct business: merchandise, buildings, and equipment.

The intangible assets of the existing business are often the most valuable: an experienced management team, trained employees, and loyal customers. Thus, a corporation will often pay more than the value of the physical assets of the existing business. The price paid in excess of the physical assets purchased is recorded as goodwill and reported on the balance sheet. This amount is an estimate that represents the value of the intangible assets. As long as the benefit of these intangible assets is perceived to have value, the recorded balance in the goodwill account will not change.

INSTRUCTIONS

Refer to Home Depot's financial statements shown in Appendix B of this textbook to answer the following questions:

1. Identify the amount of goodwill for each year reported on the Consolidated Balance Sheets on page B-5.
2. Refer to the Goodwill and Other Intangible Assets section of Note 1 on page B-11. What term is used to describe a loss in the perceived value of goodwill?
3. Did Home Depot recognize any loss in the value of goodwill during fiscal 2017?
4. How does Home Depot estimate the fair value of its goodwill in the United States, Canada, and Mexico?

Financial Reporting for a Not-for-Profit Organization

© ZADOROZHNYI VIKTOR/SHUTTERSTOCK.COM

LEARNING OBJECTIVES

After studying Chapter 24, in addition to defining key terms, you will be able to:

LO1 Prepare adjusting entries for a general fund.

LO2 Prepare financial statements for a general fund.

LO3 Prepare closing entries for a general fund.

LO4 Prepare a post-closing trial balance.

LO5 Describe the components of a comprehensive annual financial report.

City of Tulsa

ACCOUNTING IN THE REAL WORLD

The city Tulsa was founded in 1898 and, with a population of over 400,000 residents, is the second most populous city in Oklahoma. The city's annual revenues for its fiscal year ending on June 30, 2017, were greater than $610 million. Tulsa boasts an economy that includes concentrations in aerospace, oil and gas, and machine manufacturing. The city offers businesses a cost of doing business 11% below the national average and individuals a cost of living 8% below the national average.

Tulsa uses numerous funds to account for typical city-government services—public safety and protection, public works and transportation, and culture and recreation. In fiscal 2017, over 67% of the city's revenue for these governmental funds was generated from taxes: sales, property, franchise, and use taxes. The remaining revenue was collected from grants and from individuals and businesses as payment for services and fees, including building permits, traffic tickets, and court fees.

The accounting rules used for funds that charge fees for providing services are different from governmental funds. Tulsa accounts for the transactions of its convention centers, technology centers, athletic stadiums, and golf courses using accounting rules that are more consistent with for-profit businesses. In fiscal 2017, these business-related funds generated over $57.4 million in revenues and experienced a $9.7 million operating loss. Financial statements provide the city's leaders information needed to make important decisions about the city's effectiveness and financial health.

Source: www.cityoftulsa.org.

CRITICAL THINKING

1. If you were a city manager or a city council member, what suggestions might you recommend for increasing revenues?

2. If you were a city manager or a city council member, what suggestions might you recommend for decreasing expenditures? Your recommendation should reflect the best interests of your district's constituents.

3. What circumstances would likely justify the city incurring an operating loss from its business-related funds?

KEY TERMS

comprehensive annual financial report

governmental fund proprietary fund

fiduciary fund

LO1 Prepare adjusting entries for a general fund.

Preparing Adjusting Entries LO1

Both businesses and not-for-profit organizations prepare financial statements periodically to report the results of financial activities. **≫ App A: Accounting Period Cycle** However, financial information for not-for-profit organizations differs from that needed for businesses. A business measures performance primarily through determining the amount of net income. Thus, the accounting records are designed to emphasize the measurement of net income, and the income statement reports the net income.

A not-for-profit organization's performance is measured primarily by the services provided and the efficiency with which resources are used. A not-for-profit

organization does not prepare an income statement. Instead, it prepares a statement of revenues, expenditures, and changes in fund balance. A not-for-profit organization's financial statements are designed to provide information for the following purposes:

1. To make decisions about the use of resources.
2. To assess services provided and the ability to provide those services.
3. To assess management's financial accountability and performance.
4. To determine the assets, liabilities, and fund equity of the organization.

Ethics in Government

Jacob Estrada was a well-known history professor before entering the world of politics. What began with helping a friend get elected to a state office has evolved into serving as the chief of staff of the president of the United States.

It is now six months before the national elections. Jacob is extraordinarily busy organizing the president's reelection campaign, in addition to his normal duties as chief of staff. However, a phone call from a former colleague makes him cast aside all thoughts of his current duties.

Jacob has received a high honor—an invitation to be the keynote speaker at a national meeting of a prestigious association of historians. The

requested topic is the origin of the two-party system. Jacob would be reimbursed for his travel expenses and receive a $10,000 honorarium. The meeting is scheduled for one month before the election, right in the middle of the most intense period of the campaign.

INSTRUCTIONS

Obtain the *Standards of Ethical Conduct for Employees of the Executive Branch*, issued by the U.S. Office of Government Ethics. Unlike the codes of conduct for corporations, these standards are "codified," meaning that the code is law. Using the ethical model, provide Jacob with guidance on whether he should accept the invitation.

Preparing an Unadjusted Trial Balance

General Ledger Accounts Other Than Encumbrances

Town of Lindville
Unadjusted Trial Balance
December 31, 20--

ACCOUNT TITLE	DEBIT	CREDIT
Cash	62 1 8 0 00	
Taxes Receivable—Current		
Allowance for Uncollectible Taxes—Current		
Taxes Receivable—Delinquent	21 6 6 0 00	
Allowance for Uncollectible Taxes—Delinquent		16 7 4 0 00
Interest Receivable		
Allowance for Uncollectible Interest		
Inventory of Supplies		
Accounts Payable		28 9 3 0 00
Notes Payable		
Unreserved Fund Balance		13 6 0 0 00
Reserve for Encumbrances—Current Year		2 1 9 0 00
Reserve for Encumbrances—Prior Year		
Reserve for Inventory of Supplies		
Property Tax Revenue		1675 0 0 0 00
Interest Revenue		10 8 6 0 00
Other Revenue		6 1 4 0 00
Expenditure—Personnel, General Government	273 2 0 0 00	
Expenditure—Supplies, General Government	14 9 0 0 00	
Expenditure—Other Charges, General Government	118 3 8 0 00	
Expenditure—Capital Outlays, General Government	22 9 5 0 00	
Expenditure—Personnel, Public Safety	598 6 5 0 00	
Expenditure—Supplies, Public Safety	28 7 9 0 00	
Expenditure—Other Charges, Public Safety	150 8 0 0 00	
Expenditure—Capital Outlays, Public Safety	99 3 5 0 00	
Expenditure—Personnel, Fire Protection	123 3 0 0 00	
Expenditure—Supplies, Fire Protection	14 2 0 0 00	
Expenditure—Other Charges, Fire Protection	51 3 5 0 00	
Expenditure—Capital Outlays, Fire Protection	53 9 5 0 00	
Expenditure—Personnel, Recreation	62 6 0 0 00	
Expenditure—Supplies, Recreation	7 0 5 0 00	
Expenditure—Other Charges, Recreation	26 4 8 0 00	
Expenditure—Capital Outlays, Recreation	21 4 8 0 00	
Estimated Revenues	1691 5 0 0 00	
Appropriations		1659 0 0 0 00
Budgetary Fund Balance		32 5 0 0 00
Encumbrance—Supplies, Public Safety	2 1 9 0 00	
Totals	3444 9 6 0 00	3444 9 6 0 00

Encumbrances Accounts with a Balance

Column Totals

The town of Lindville begins the process of preparing financial statements by creating an unadjusted trial balance. The unadjusted trial balance provides accountants with the information needed to plan adjusting entries.

Adjustment for Inventory of Supplies

						GENERAL		CASH	
	DATE	ACCOUNT TITLE	DOC. NO.	POST. REF.	DEBIT	CREDIT	DEBIT	CREDIT	
1		*Adjusting Entries*							1
2	20-- Dec. 31	*Inventory of Supplies*			2 7 5 0 00				2
3		*Reserve for Inventory of Supplies*				2 7 5 0 00			3
4									4

JOURNAL — PAGE 20

Some general ledger accounts for general funds need to be brought up to date before financial statements are prepared. However, since a general fund reports expenditures and not expenses, no adjustments are needed for expense accounts. The actual amounts that have been spent and recorded as expenditures are reported.

Lindville makes adjustments to three accounts: (1) Inventory of Supplies, (2) Interest Revenue, and (3) Reserve for Encumbrances—Current Year.

When supplies are bought, an expenditure account is debited. Some supplies may be unused at the end of a fiscal period. These unused supplies should be reported as an asset. **>> App A: Full Disclosure** Thus, an adjustment is made at the end of a period to record the remaining amount of supplies inventory as an asset. Expenditure accounts debited when supplies were bought are not adjusted. When an expenditure is made during a fiscal period, the expenditure is reported regardless of the purpose.

The total account balances of a general fund represent the equity of that fund. Thus, assets less liabilities equals total fund equity, which, unless reserved for a specified purpose, should represent resources that are available for appropriations and spending. The inventory of supplies, however, will be used by the organization. Therefore, this asset is not available for spending. To show that this asset, Inventory of Supplies, is not available for other uses, an equal amount of fund equity is reserved. Thus, the amount is credited to a restricted fund equity account titled Reserve for Inventory of Supplies.

Inventory of Supplies is increased by a debit for the amount of supplies on hand, $2,750.00. Reserve for Inventory of Supplies is increased by a credit for the same amount, $2,750.00.

Inventory of Supplies

Adjusting ↑ 2,750.00	

Reserve for Inventory of Supplies

	Adjusting ↑ 2,750.00

THINK LIKE AN ACCOUNTANT

Improving Your Efficiency

The accountant for the city of Grassville prepares a special monthly financial statement for the mayor. The financial statement shows year-to-date, prior month, and current month revenue and expenditures for the general fund. The accountant uses an Excel worksheet to create the financial statement.

Each month, the accountant must perform a series of repetitive tasks to prepare the worksheet for the next month. Having performed these tasks for many months, the accountant finally had enough. "I have more important things to do!" she exclaimed. So she decided it was time to automate the process. Rather than manually performing the command each month, she wants

to run a macro to execute all the commands with a single click.

OPEN THE SPREADSHEET TLA_CH24

The workbook contains the financial statement. Follow the steps on the Instructions tab to create a macro to prepare the statement for entering the next month's financial results. Use the knowledge you gain to answer these questions:

1. What advantages are gained by storing a repetitive task in a macro?

2. Identify a workbook from this textbook. What repetitive task could be stored effectively as a macro?

Adjustments for Interest Revenue and Reserve for Encumbrances

	DATE	ACCOUNT TITLE	DOC. NO.	POST. REF.	GENERAL DEBIT	GENERAL CREDIT	CASH DEBIT	CASH CREDIT	
4	31	Interest Receivable			3 2 0 0 00				4
5		Allowance for Uncollectible Interest				1 2 8 0 00			5
6		Interest Revenue				1 9 2 0 00			6
7	31	Reserve for Encumbrances—Current Year			2 1 9 0 00				7
8		Reserve for Encumbrances—Prior Year				2 1 9 0 00			8
9									9
10									10
11									11
12									12

JOURNAL — PAGE 20

Since a general fund recognizes revenues when the revenues become measurable and available, an adjustment may be needed to record some revenues. Interest is assessed on all delinquent taxes. Interest on delinquent taxes becomes measurable and available when it is assessed. Thus, to bring the accounts up to date and record revenue earned but not collected at the end of the year, an adjustment is made.

Lindville's interest earned but not yet collected on December 31 is $3,200.00. Experience has shown that approximately 40% of this amount, $1,280.00 ($3,200.00 × 40%), will not be collected. Thus, the amount expected to be collected, $1,920.00 ($3,200.00 − $1,280.00), is recorded as revenue.

At the end of a fiscal year, a governmental organization may have outstanding encumbrances—orders that have not yet been delivered. When goods are delivered that were encumbered against the preceding year's appropriations, the amount should not be recorded as an expenditure of the current period. Therefore, at the end of a period, the amount of encumbrances outstanding in the balance of Reserve for Encumbrances—Current Year should be reclassified to prior-year status. Then, when the prior year's orders arrive, they are debited to Reserve for Encumbrances—Prior Year, which prevents charging expenditures of one year to another year's appropriations.

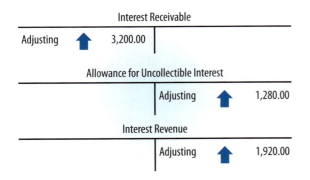

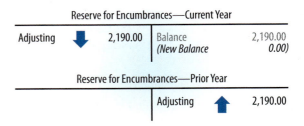

Adjusting entries are posted to the general ledger. The adjusted balances are used to prepare an adjusted trial balance.

FYI

Governments often issue bonds to pay for large construction projects, such as schools and highways. Investors are generally not required to pay federal income tax on the interest income on these bonds.

LO1 Prepare adjusting entries for a general fund.

Audit your understanding LO1

1. How do the measures of performance differ between businesses and not-for-profit organizations?
2. What accounts are not included on the unadjusted trial balance of a general fund?
3. What adjusting entries for expenses are made by a general fund?
4. In what account would a general fund record the amount of interest on delinquent taxes that it expects to collect?

Work together 24-1 LO1

Preparing adjusting entries for a general fund

The town of Kellerville uses a general fund. Adjustment information for December 31 is presented below. Analyze the adjustment information and prepare adjusting entries. A journal is provided in the *Working Papers*. Your instructor will guide you through the following examples.

Supplies inventory	$4,925.00
Interest revenue due but not collected	5,490.00

An estimated 30% of the interest revenue due will not be collected. The reserve for encumbrances for the current year has a credit balance of $12,534.00.

On your own 24-1 LO1

Preparing adjusting entries for a general fund

The town of Harris City uses a general fund. Adjustment information for December 31 is presented below. Analyze the adjustment information and prepare adjusting entries. A journal is provided in the *Working Papers*. Work independently to complete the following problem.

Supplies inventory	$1,890.00
Interest revenue due but not collected	2,260.00

An estimated 40% of the interest revenue due will not be collected. The reserve for encumbrances for the current year has a credit balance of $9,360.00.

LO2 Prepare financial statements for a general fund.
LO3 Prepare closing entries for a general fund.
LO4 Prepare a post-closing trial balance.
LO5 Describe the components of a comprehensive annual financial report.

Financial Statements for a General Fund LO2

Financial statements are prepared for each fund.
>> App A: Full Disclosure Two of the financial statements that Lindville prepares for its general fund are

(1) the statement of revenues, expenditures, and changes in fund balance—budget and actual and (2) the balance sheet.

Statement of Revenues, Expenditures, and Changes in Fund Balance—Budget and Actual

Town of Lindville General Fund
Statement of Revenues, Expenditures, and Changes in Fund Balance—Budget and Actual
For Year Ended December 31, 20--

	Budget	Actual	Variance— Favorable (Unfavorable)
Revenues:			
Property Tax Revenue	$1,675,000.00	$1,675,000.00	$ —
Interest Revenue	12,000.00	12,780.00	780.00
Other Revenue	4,500.00	6,140.00	1,640.00
Total Revenue	$1,691,500.00	$1,693,920.00	$ 2,420.00
Expenditures:			
General Government	$ 424,800.00	$ 429,430.00	$(4,630.00)
Public Safety	879,800.00	877,590.00	2,210.00
Fire Protection	236,300.00	242,800.00	(6,500.00)
Recreation	118,100.00	117,610.00	490.00
Total Expenditures	$1,659,000.00	$1,667,430.00	$(8,430.00)
Excess of Revenues Over Expenditures	$ 32,500.00	$ 26,490.00	$(6,010.00)
Less Outstanding Encumbrances, Dec. 31, 20--	—	2,190.00	(2,190.00)
Increase in Unreserved Fund Balance for Year	$ 32,500.00	$ 24,300.00	$(8,200.00)
Unreserved Fund Balance, Jan. 1, 20--	13,600.00	13,600.00	—
Unreserved Fund Balance, Dec. 31, 20--	$ 46,100.00	$ 37,900.00	$(8,200.00)

Lindville's general fund statement of revenues, expenditures, and changes in fund balance—budget and actual reports the amount of revenues earned and expenditures made for a fiscal period. Departments are responsible for controlling expenditures through budgeting and appropriations of specific amounts for each department. Thus, to aid the control process, amounts actually spent are reported for each responsible department. The total expenditures for the whole fund are also shown on the statement.

Any outstanding encumbrances for the current year are deducted from the excess of revenues over expenditures. Outstanding encumbrances are not deducted in figuring the excess of revenues over expenditures. However, funds will be required in the future when the goods for which the encumbrances were made are delivered. Therefore, the current year's encumbrances should be reported as a reduction in the current year's excess of revenues, rather than in the next year when the payment for goods is made. Because no amount is budgeted for the encumbrances, the amount shown in the Budget column is zero. The report concludes with an analysis of the change in the unreserved fund balance from the beginning to the end of the fiscal period.

The Variance column reports the difference between the budget and actual amounts for the item. For example, the variance for **Other Revenue** is $1,640.00 (actual, $6,140.00, less budget, $4,500.00). Variances are considered favorable if actual results are better than the amount budgeted for that item. When actual revenues are more than budgeted revenues, variances are favorable. When actual revenues are less than budgeted revenues, variances are unfavorable. When actual expenditures are less than budgeted expenditures, variances are favorable. When actual expenditures are more than budgeted expenditures, variances are unfavorable. A reserve for encumbrances variance has the same effect as an expenditure variance. Because encumbrances are not budgeted, any variance will be unfavorable, since an actual encumbrance will cause an increase. Unfavorable variances are indicated by placing the amounts in parentheses.

FINANCIAL LITERACY

Domino Effect in Detroit

At one time, Detroit was an industrial giant at the center of the automotive industry. It had a large population and a low unemployment rate. Over time, increased automotive competition greatly reduced the job opportunities. Many people were unemployed or on welfare. Others left for jobs in the suburbs, leaving Detroit starved for tax revenues. With fewer people paying taxes and city expenses on the rise, Detroit ran out of money to pay its creditors.

Detroit is not unlike San Bernardino, California, or Harrisburg, Pennsylvania. It just happens to be the largest municipality to file Chapter 9 bankruptcy. A Chapter 9 bankruptcy is a court proceeding that gives a municipality a fresh start while trying to arrange some form of repayment to its creditors.

ACTIVITY

Individuals, like municipalities, may find themselves drowning in debt due to medical expenses or a loss of income. However, filing bankruptcy remains on your credit report for up to ten years. Use the Internet to research answers to the following:

1. How can filing bankruptcy affect your goals in life? Explain.

2. Why do you think the United States allows bankruptcy, when some countries imprison debtors?

3. Research a Chapter 7 and a Chapter 13 bankruptcy. Create a visual public service announcement, or write a letter comparing and contrasting the two types of bankruptcies for individuals. Include the dangers and the consequences of filing bankruptcy.

Balance Sheet

Town of Lindville General Fund
Balance Sheet
December 31, 20--

ASSETS

Cash...		$62,180.00
Taxes Receivable—Delinquent	$21,660.00	
Less Allowance for Uncollectible Taxes—Delinquent............	16,740.00	4,920.00
Interest Receivable	$ 3,200.00	
Less Allowance for Uncollectible Interest....................	1,280.00	1,920.00
Inventory of Supplies.......................................		2,750.00
Total Assets		$71,770.00

LIABILITIES AND FUND BALANCE

Liabilities:		
Accounts Payable		$28,930.00
Fund Balance:		
Unreserved Fund Balance	$37,900.00	
Reserve for Encumbrances—Prior Year.......................	2,190.00	
Reserve for Inventory of Supplies	2,750.00	
Total Fund Balance		42,840.00
Total Liabilities and Fund Balance..........................		$71,770.00

A general fund balance sheet reports information about assets, liabilities, and fund equity for a specific date, usually the last day of a fiscal period. **>> App A: Full Disclosure** Assets and liabilities on a general fund balance sheet have characteristics similar to those on a corporation's balance sheet. However, a general fund does not have specific owners. Therefore, a general fund has no Owners' Equity section. Instead, the difference between assets and liabilities is reported as fund equity. Thus, unless restricted, fund equity represents the amount that is available for expenditures or encumbrances.

On December 31, Lindville's fund equity, consisting of three fund equity account balances, is $42,840.00. The Unreserved Fund Balance, $37,900.00, represents fund equity that has no restrictions (Total fund equity, $42,840.00, less Reserve for Encumbrances—Prior Year, $2,190.00, and less Reserve for Inventory of Supplies, $2,750.00). With proper authorization, Lindville may appropriate this amount for expenditures.

The other two fund equity account balances are reserved for specific purposes. The Reserve for Encumbrances—Prior Year, $2,190.00, is an amount of equity set aside for an encumbrance outstanding on December 31 of the prior year. Recording the payment for an order that was encumbered in a prior year closes the reserve for encumbrances account.

The Reserve for Inventory of Supplies, $2,750.00, represents the equity in the inventory of supplies. Although supplies are assets, they are available for use, not spending. Therefore, part of the fund equity is reserved for the amount of supplies on hand. This reserve avoids appropriating the amount of equity that is represented by the supplies.

On a general fund balance sheet, total assets must equal total liabilities and fund equity. Lindville's balance sheet has total assets of $71,770.00. The total of the liabilities and fund balance accounts is also $71,770.00.

	DATE		ACCOUNT TITLE	DOC. NO.	POST. REF.	GENERAL DEBIT	GENERAL CREDIT	CASH DEBIT	CASH CREDIT	
1			*Closing Entries*							1
2	Dec.	31	Property Tax Revenue			1675 0 0 0 00				2
3			Interest Revenue			12 7 8 0 00				3
4			Other Revenue			6 1 4 0 00				4
5			Unreserved Fund Balance				1693 9 2 0 00			5
6		31	Unreserved Fund Balance			1667 4 3 0 00				6
7			Expend.—Personnel, Gen., Gov't.				273 2 0 0 00			7
8			Expend.—Supplies, Gen., Gov't.				14 9 0 0 00			8
9			Expend.—Other Chgs., Gen., Gov't.				118 3 8 0 00			9
10			Expend.—Cap. Outlays, Gen., Gov't.				22 9 5 0 00			10
11			Expend.—Personnel, Public Safety				598 6 5 0 00			11
12			Expend.—Supplies, Public Safety				28 7 9 0 00			12
13			Expend.—Other Chgs., Pub. Safety				150 8 0 0 00			13
14			Expend.—Cap. Outlays, Pub. Safety				99 3 5 0 00			14
15			Expend.—Personnel, Fire Protection				123 3 0 0 00			15
16			Expend.—Supplies, Fire Protection				14 2 0 0 00			16
17			Expend.—Other Chgs., Fire Protection				51 3 5 0 00			17
18			Expend.—Cap. Outlays, Fire Protection				53 9 5 0 00			18
19			Expend.—Personnel, Recreation				62 6 0 0 00			19
20			Expend.—Supplies, Recreation				7 0 5 0 00			20
21			Expend.—Other Chgs., Recreation				26 4 8 0 00			21
22			Expend.—Cap. Outlays, Recreation				21 4 8 0 00			22
23		31	Appropriations			1659 0 0 0 00				23
24			Budgetary Fund Balance			32 5 0 0 00				24
25			Estimated Revenues				1691 5 0 0 00			25
26		31	Unreserved Fund Balance			2 1 9 0 00				26
27			Encum.—Supplies, Public Safety				2 1 9 0 00			27

Information needed for the closing entries is obtained from the adjusted trial balance. Four closing entries are made:

1. Close all revenue accounts to the Unreserved Fund Balance account.
2. Close all expenditure accounts to the Unreserved Fund Balance account.
3. Close the budgetary accounts. At the beginning of the fiscal year, estimated revenues and appropriations were recorded based on the approved operating budget. At the end of the fiscal year, these budgetary accounts are closed. This entry is the opposite of the original entry to record the operating budget.
4. Close the outstanding encumbrance accounts to the Unreserved Fund Balance account. This entry

reduces the Unreserved Fund Balance account by the amount of the outstanding encumbrance for supplies, public safety, $2,190.00. Reserve for Encumbrances—Prior Year is a fund equity account. This account balance now is the amount of total fund equity that is reserved for outstanding encumbrances.

After posting the closing entries, all temporary accounts have zero balances and are prepared for a new fiscal period. The difference between revenues and expenditures has been transferred to the Unreserved Fund Balance account. Fund equity amounts that are not available for appropriations are recorded in reserve accounts.

Post-Closing Trial Balance LO4

Town of Lindville General Fund Post-Closing Trial Balance December 31, 20--		
Cash	$62,180.00	
Taxes Receivable—Delinquent	21,660.00	
Allowance for Uncollectible Taxes—Delinquent		$16,740.00
Interest Receivable	3,200.00	
Allowance for Uncollectible Interest		1,280.00
Inventory of Supplies	2,750.00	
Accounts Payable		28,930.00
Unreserved Fund Balance		37,900.00
Reserve for Encumbrances—Prior Year		2,190.00
Reserve for Inventory of Supplies		2,750.00
	$89,790.00	$89,790.00

After all end-of-fiscal-period activities are complete, a post-closing trial balance is prepared to prove the equality of debits and credits in the account balances, as shown above. Because the debit and credit balance totals equal, the general ledger accounts are ready for the new fiscal period. >> App A: Accounting Period Cycle

>> App A: Accounting Period Cycle

WHY ACCOUNTING?

CareerClusters®
PATHWAYS TO COLLEGE & CAREER READINESS
Government & Public Administration

Campaign Financing

Have you ever thought about running for a political office? Maybe you know someone who has been a candidate for election. Whether involved in a small city election or a large federal election, there are laws that you must follow. There are laws related to how and when you can campaign, who can endorse a political candidate, and where you can place campaign literature and signs.

Most of the laws relate to campaign donations and spending limits. These laws vary, depending on the jurisdiction covering the election. The laws cover limits on who can donate to the campaign, how much can be donated, and whether the donations are tax deductible.

Federal, state, and city laws also cover financial reports that must be filed. These reports require that the candidate or the campaign staff keep accurate financial records. The purpose of these records is to have full disclosure of who is supporting which candidate. Even in small city elections, the campaign treasurer may have to disclose the names and addresses of all donors, their places of employment, and the amounts of their donations.

CRITICAL THINKING

1. Why is it important to have full disclosure of who is supporting a political candidate?

2. Research the laws of your local government. Is there a limit on the amount a contributor can donate? If so, what is the limit?

Sources: www.fec.gov; www.completecampaigns.com.

Comprehensive Annual Financial Report LO5

Comprehensive Annual Financial Report	Individual Fund Financial Statements		
	Governmental Funds	Proprietary Funds	Fiduciary Funds
Accrual	Modified Accrual	Accrual	Accrual
Statement of Activities	Statement of Revenues, Expenditures, and Changes in Fund Balance	Statement of Revenues, Expenses, and Changes in Net Position	Statement of Changes in Fiduciary Net Position
Statement of Net Assets	Balance Sheet	Statement of Net Position	Statement of Fiduciary Net Position

Governmental accounting is governed by the Governmental Accounting Standards Board (GASB). The GASB's mission is to establish and improve standards of financial accounting and reporting for governmental entities.

Generally accepted accounting principles (GAAP) require that financial statements be prepared on a full accrual basis. This accounting method requires that plant assets be capitalized and depreciated. Amounts owed in future fiscal years are reported as liabilities. Users accustomed to GAAP financial statements may be confused over the lack of plant assets and long-term liabilities on the balance sheet of a general fund prepared on a modified accrual basis.

To address this confusion, the GASB requires state and local governments to prepare financial statements for each major fund as well as prepare combined financial statements. The detailed financial report of a governmental agency is called a **comprehensive annual financial report** (CAFR). The basic financial statements in the CAFR include (1) government-wide financial statements, (2) individual fund financial statements, and (3) notes to the financial statements.

Three types of funds are reported in the CAFR:

Governmental Funds: A fund that accounts for the tax-supported activities of a government agency is called a **governmental fund**. A government agency can establish a governmental fund to account for the revenues or expenditures of each special activity and project. All activities not accounted for in a special governmental fund are accounted for in a general fund. Individual financial statements of a governmental fund are accounted for on a modified accrual basis.

Proprietary Funds: A fund that accounts for the financial transactions of a government organization that operates as a for-profit enterprise is called a **proprietary fund**. Unlike a governmental fund, a proprietary fund earns most of its revenue from fees charged to individuals and businesses using its services. Examples of proprietary funds include water and sewer, sanitation,

and power utilities. Individual financial statements of a proprietary fund are prepared on a full accrual basis.

Fiduciary Funds: A fund that reports assets held by a government agency to benefit a specific group of individuals is called a **fiduciary fund**. A common type of fiduciary fund is a pension plan for government employees. Financial statements of a fiduciary fund are prepared on a full accrual basis.

Adjusting from Modified to Full Accrual Accounting

The financial statements presented in this chapter do not report fixed assets and long-term liabilities. The individual financial statements of governmental funds, including the general fund, continue to be reported on a modified accrual basis. The fixed assets and long-term liabilities of a governmental fund are reported when the financial information for every fund is combined into the government-wide financial statements.

GASB standards have little impact on how cities and states record the daily accounting transactions of their governmental funds. However, fixed assets and long-term liabilities are not recorded in a general ledger. Rather, most cities and states record fixed assets (including accumulated depreciation and depreciation expense) and long-term liabilities (including interest expense) as reclassification entries. These entries only impact the trial balance used to prepare the government-wide financial statements and are not posted to general ledger accounts of the governmental funds.

To help readers understand the difference between statements, the GASB created slightly different names for government-wide financial statements. Instead of a balance sheet prepared for governmental funds, the similar government-wide financial statement is called a "statement of net position." The equivalent of a statement of revenues, expenditures, and changes in fund balance prepared for governmental funds is called a "statement of activities" for a government-wide financial statement.

Careers In Accounting

Adwin Ballo
Municipal Treasurer

© EL NARIZ/SHUTTERSTOCK.COM

Adwin Ballo is a city treasurer in a West Coast suburban municipality with a population of just over 25,000. As the treasurer, Mr. Ballo is responsible for all aspects of the city's cash. He oversees the collection of all property and business taxes, the primary source of revenue for the city. These receipts must be safeguarded while in the city's custody.

Since property taxes are paid once a year, Mr. Ballo must estimate the cash needs of the city and determine if there is enough cash available to pay current liabilities. If the supply of cash is insufficient, he must arrange for short-term borrowing to cover debt obligations. If excess cash exists, he must invest it, seeking as high an interest rate as possible for the level of risk the city is willing to take.

Long-term debt is also Mr. Ballo's responsibility. The city council authorizes the debt. Mr. Ballo leads the negotiations on the amount of debt, the interest, and the repayment plan, as well as oversees the actual repayment of the debt.

Mr. Ballo must have a firm understanding of fund accounting in order to ensure that all fund accounting policies are followed. He also oversees all payments made by the city, including payroll and related items, and he prepares a variety of budgets and monitors them throughout the year.

As a city treasurer, Mr. Ballo needs excellent management, communication, and leadership skills. In addition, he must have the ability to work with a broad range of people, including elected and appointed city officials, employees, community organizations, and the citizens of the community. One of the challenges of his position is that elected officials, such as the city council, can change with each election. Since the city council appoints many taskforce members, the taskforce leaders may change after each election. Mr. Ballo must be able to adjust to new city representatives and provide training on fund accounting systems and financial statements.

In the future, Mr. Ballo would like to be a city treasurer in a large city. He is hoping to earn the designation of Certified Public Finance Officer (CPFO), which is governed by the Government Finance Officers Association (GFOA). To obtain this certification, he must pass a series of five exams.

Salary Range: Salaries vary widely, depending on the size of the governmental unit. Salaries in midsize cities range from $110,000 to over $200,000.

Qualifications: A minimum of a bachelor's degree in accounting, finance, or a related field is required, as well as previous experience with fund accounting systems.

Occupational Outlook: The growth for treasurer positions is projected to be faster than average (15% or higher) for the period from 2016 to 2026.

Source: www.onetonline.org.

LO2 Prepare financial statements for a general fund.

LO3 Prepare closing entries for a general fund.

LO4 Prepare a post-closing trial balance.

LO5 Describe the components of a comprehensive annual financial report.

TERMS REVIEW

comprehensive annual
    financial report
governmental fund
proprietary fund
fiduciary fund

Audit your understanding LO2, 3, 4, 5

1. Where is the prior-year fund balance on the statement of revenues, expenditures, and changes in fund balance—budget and actual obtained?
2. A city's expenditures are greater than its revenues. How will this difference be labeled on the statement of revenues, expenditures, and changes in fund balance?
3. When actual expenditures are more than budgeted expenditures, is the variance favorable or unfavorable?
4. Into what account are revenue and expenditure accounts closed?
5. Which of the following accounts will appear on a post-closing trial balance?

   | Appropriations | Reserve for Encumbrances—Prior Year |
   | Property Tax Revenue | Taxes Receivable—Delinquent |

6. Identify the three sections of a comprehensive annual financial report.
7. What is the primary factor that determines whether a government organization is accounted for as a governmental fund or a proprietary fund?

Work together 24-2 LO2, 3, 4
Preparing financial statements for a governmental organization

The city of River Springs uses a general fund. The operating budget for the current year, an adjusted trial balance, and a journal are provided in the *Working Papers*. Your instructor will guide you through the following examples.

1. Prepare a statement of revenues, expenditures, and changes in fund balance—budget and actual for the year ended December 31 of the current year.
2. Prepare a balance sheet for December 31 of the current year.
3. Journalize the closing entries.
4. Prepare a post-closing trial balance.

On your own 24-2 LO2, 3, 4
Preparing financial statements for a governmental organization

The town of Parson uses a general fund. The operating budget for the current year, an adjusted trial balance, and a journal are provided in the *Working Papers*. Work independently to complete the following problem.

1. Prepare a statement of revenues, expenditures, and changes in fund balance—budget and actual for the year ended December 31 of the current year.
2. Prepare a balance sheet for December 31 of the current year.
3. Journalize the closing entries.
4. Prepare a post-closing trial balance.

CHAPTER SUMMARY

Both businesses and not-for-profit organizations prepare financial statements periodically to report the results of financial activities. A business measures performance primarily through determining the amount of net income. In contrast, a not-for-profit organization's performance is measured primarily by the quality of services provided and the efficiency with which resources are used.

The process of preparing financial statements is similar to that for a business. An unadjusted trial balance is prepared from all accounts in the general ledger, except for encumbrance accounts with a zero balance. Adjusting entries are made to record supplies on hand, to accrue interest revenue, and to reclassify current-year encumbrances as prior-year encumbrances. The adjusted trial balance provides the information required to prepare the financial statements.

The financial statements for a governmental fund include a statement of revenues, expenditures, and changes in fund balance. The assets, liabilities, and fund balance of a governmental fund are reported on a balance sheet.

Government agencies, such as city and state governments, typically have two types of funds. Governmental funds account for activities funded through taxes and grants that provide services, with little if any charge. Proprietary funds account for activities funded through fees paid by those individuals and businesses that use the services provided. Some cities and states may also have fiduciary funds to account for the assets held to benefit a specific group of individuals.

Government agencies are required to prepare a comprehensive annual financial report (CAFR) that includes financial statements for the combined funds as well as detailed reports for major funds. Financial statements for governmental funds are presented on a modified accrual basis. The financial statements for proprietary and fiduciary funds are presented on a full accrual basis.

Components of a Comprehensive Annual Financial Report

Any individual or business seeking to relocate to a new city should first research the city's financial stability. The comprehensive annual financial report (CAFR) provides a wealth of information about the city. Many of the reports provide financial information in more detail than presented in the financial statements. Other reports contain nonfinancial information. A sample of questions that might be answered using a CAFR follows.

1. *How likely is it that my taxes are going to increase?* A report presents the city's property tax rates for the past ten years.

2. *What would happen if a major employer closed?* A report presents the total property value and percent of the city's total taxes paid by the top ten taxpayers during the current year and nine years ago.

3. *Does the city do a good job in collecting its taxes?* A report shows, for the past ten years, the dollar amount and percent of taxes collected in the current and subsequent years.

4. *What major employers are located in the city?* A report shows the number of people employed by the top ten employers. The report includes the percentage of the county's workers employed by each employer.

5. *Are the city's residents financially stable?* A report shows the city's population and per capita personal income for the past ten years. The report also includes the unemployment rate for each year.

INSTRUCTIONS

Prepare answers to the following questions:

1. Prepare three additional questions for which you would like to obtain the answers before moving to a new city.

2. Obtain a copy of the CAFR of a nearby city. Use the information in the Statistical section to obtain, for the current year, answers to the five questions just presented. Search the CAFR to determine if it contains the answers to your questions.

INSTRUCTIONS: Download problem instructions for Excel, QuickBooks, and Sage 50c from the textbook companion website at www.C21accounting.com.

24-1 Application Problem — Preparing adjusting entries for a governmental organization LO1

The town of Ellieville uses a general fund. Adjustment information for December 31 is presented below.

Supplies inventory	$1,648.00
Interest revenue due but not collected	990.00

An estimated 25% of the interest revenue due will not be collected.
The reserve for encumbrances for the current year has a credit balance of $2,950.00.

Instructions:

Analyze the adjustment information and prepare adjusting entries. A journal is provided in the *Working Papers*.

24-2 Application Problem — Preparing financial statements for a governmental organization LO2, 3, 4

sage 50

1. Journalize and post closing entries related to a governmental organization to the general journal.
2. Print the general journal and trial balance.

QB *QuickBooks*

1. Journalize and post closing entries related to a governmental organization to the journal.
2. Print the journal and trial balance.

1. Use the adjusted trial balance to prepare the required financial statements.
2. Print the worksheets.

The city of Proffit Bluff uses a general fund. The operating budget for the current year, an adjusted trial balance, and a journal are provided in the *Working Papers*.

Instructions:

1. Prepare a statement of revenues, expenditures, and changes in fund balance—budget and actual for the year ended December 31 of the current year.
2. Prepare a balance sheet for December 31 of the current year.
3. Journalize the closing entries.
4. Prepare a post-closing trial balance.

24-M Mastery Problem — Completing the end-of-period work for a governmental organization LO1, 2, 3, 4

sage 50

1. Journalize and post closing entries related to a governmental organization to the general journal.
2. Print the general journal and trial balance.

The city of Moserville uses a general fund. An operating budget for the current year, an adjusted trial balance, a journal, and forms are provided in the *Working Papers*. Save your work to complete Challenge Problem 24-C. The following adjustment information is available.

Adjustment Information, December 31

Supplies inventory	$2,590.00
Interest revenue due but not collected	2,160.00

An estimated 20% of the interest revenue due will not be collected.
The reserve for encumbrances for the current year has a credit balance of $5,250.00.

1. Journalize and post closing entries related to a governmental organization to the journal.
2. Print the journal and trial balance.

1. Use the adjusted trial balance to prepare the required financial statements.
2. Print the worksheets.

Instructions:

1. Analyze the adjustment information and record adjusting entries in the journal.
2. Prepare a statement of revenues, expenditures, and changes in fund balance—budget and actual for the year ended December 31 of the current year.
3. Prepare a balance sheet for December 31 of the current year.
4. Journalize the closing entries.
5. Prepare a post-closing trial balance.

24-C Challenge Problem   Completing the end-of-period work for a governmental organization LO5

To prepare its statement of net assets, the information presented in Moserville's general fund balance sheet must be modified to the full accrual basis. The city maintains separate records of its assets and long-term liabilities. Use the general journal in the *Working Papers* to prepare the reclassification entries necessary to modify the financial information to full accrual accounting. The impact on the fund balance should be reported as a single item, Invested in Capital Assets, Net of Related Debt, on the statement.

Adjustment Information, December 31

Land, at cost	$ 343,000.00
Buildings and equipment, at cost	1,637,000.00
Accumulated depreciation	521,000.00
Outstanding balance on a building mortgage	640,000.00

Instructions:

Use the balance sheet from Mastery Problem 24-M. A journal is provided in the *Working Papers*.

1. Record the reclassification entries in the journal.
2. Prepare a statement of net position.

21st Century Skills

The True Cost of Credit

Theme: Financial, Economic, Business, and Entrepreneurial Literacy

Skill: Information Literacy

In recent years, bankruptcy filings have increased, often due to indebtedness from credit card borrowing. Credit cards have increasingly become a more convenient method of payment; however, many people do not understand the impact of using credit cards. For example, some people do not pay their credit cards in full each month, or they are unaware of the long-term consequences of making low monthly payments.

Buying a car, tires, or a laptop all seem like great items to buy now and pay for later. Credit card companies advertise "low minimum payments" that appear to make the purchase affordable for most anyone. Before buying on credit, consider not only what you will pay on a monthly basis, but also the total cost. Understanding the true cost before making a credit card purchase may save money in the long run.

PARTNERSHIP FOR
21ST CENTURY SKILLS

Lauren would like to buy a high-performance laptop for her job. Her credit card allows her to make minimum payments equivalent to 2% of the balance. Using the Internet, go to www.bankrate.com or a comparable website with credit card calculators. Answer the following:

1. Use the card minimum payment calculator to determine how long it will take Lauren to pay off a laptop costing $2,500, with a credit card annual percentage rate (APR) of 18%, assuming she makes the minimum payment and does not purchase anything additional on her credit card.

2. Use the "How long will it take to pay off my credit card" calculator, or an equivalent, to determine how long it will take Lauren to pay off the laptop if she makes a $50-per-month payment.

3. Use a calculator to determine the total amount that Lauren will pay for the laptop that originally cost $2,500 if she makes the minimum monthly payment. Then, determine the total amount paid if she makes a $50-per-month payment.

4. Consider that the average lifetime of a laptop is five years. What advice would you give Lauren regarding the purchase of a laptop? What other considerations might be made if she must use her credit card?

Analyzing Home Depot's Financial Statements

Every publicly traded company is required to have an annual audit of its financial statements. Independent auditors—accountants from outside the company—examine how a company records transactions and prepares its financial statements. Auditors examine the records that support the financial records of a business to ensure that generally accepted accounting principles are followed. The auditors then issue an opinion that states whether the financial statements "present fairly, in all material respects, the financial position" of the company. The auditors' opinion gives external users confidence in the financial statement information. With this confidence, individuals and other companies are more likely to enter into business transactions with the company.

INSTRUCTIONS

Using Appendix B in this textbook, refer to Home Depot's Report of Independent Registered Public Accounting Firm on page B-4 to answer the following questions:

1. List the five financial statements that were audited by the independent public accounting firm.

2. Identify the fiscal periods examined by the independent public accounting firm.

3. State whether auditing standards require the independent public accounting firm to obtain "total and absolute" assurance that the financial statements are free of material misstatement.

4. State whether the independent public accounting firm examines every business transaction conducted by Home Depot.

5. Name the independent public accounting firm and which office is responsible for the audit of Home Depot's financial statements.

Accounting Concepts

Since 1973, the Financial Accounting Standards Board (FASB) has assumed responsibility for setting financial accounting standards known as *Generally Accepted Accounting Principles* (GAAP). One of the first tasks of the FASB was to establish a framework that describes the concepts underlying GAAP. That framework continues to guide the FASB's development of new standards.

In the United States, GAAP serves as a guide for reporting and interpreting accounting information. The accounting principles described in this textbook are based on the application of the concepts underlying GAAP. These concepts are described below and referenced throughout the textbook.

In 1973, the international financial community formed an organization with the ambitious goal of creating a universal set of accounting standards. Similar to the FASB, the International Accounting Standards Board (IASB) uses a framework to develop its standards, known as *International Financial Reporting Standards* (IFRS, pronounced ī′-fers).

The FASB and IASB are committed to merging GAAP and IFRS to achieve one universal set of accounting standards. At the time this textbook was written, the FASB and IASB were working to establish a common framework. That framework will provide the foundation for development of accounting standards to be used around the world.

Accounting Period Cycle

Changes in financial information are reported for a specific period of time in the form of financial statements.

Financial statements summarize the financial information that a business records. The time period for which financial statements are prepared depends on the needs of the business. An accounting period may be one month, three months, six months, or one year.

An accounting period of one year is a fiscal year. Publicly held corporations must prepare fiscal year financial statements. For tax purposes, every business prepares financial statements at the end of each year.

Business Entity

Financial information is recorded and reported separately from the owner's personal financial information.

A business exists separately from its owners. A business's records must not be mixed with an owner's personal records and reports. For example, a business owner may buy insurance to protect the business and insurance to protect the owner's home. Only the insurance obtained for the business is recorded in the business' financial records. Insurance purchased for the owner's personal home is recorded in the owner's personal financial records. One bank account is used for the business and another for the owner.

Consistent Reporting

The same accounting principles must be followed in the same way in each accounting period.

Business decisions are based on the financial information reported on financial statements. Some decisions require a comparison of current financial statements with previous financial statements. If accounting information is recorded and reported differently each accounting period, comparisons from one accounting period to another may not be possible. If a business were to include $100,000 of supply purchases as a cost of merchandise sold in one period and as an operating expense in the next period, a user of this information could not adequately compare the two accounting periods. Therefore, unless a change is necessary to make information more easily understood, accounting information is reported in a consistent way every accounting period.

Full Disclosure

Financial statements contain all information necessary to understand a business's financial condition.

Owners, managers, lenders, and investors rely on financial statements to make informed decisions. All relevant financial information must be adequately and completely disclosed on financial statements.

Assume a business only reports total liabilities of $200,000 on its balance sheet. If that total includes $75,000 in current liabilities, then the balance sheet does not adequately disclose the nature of the liabilities. The critical information not disclosed is that $75,000 is due within the current fiscal year. Full disclosure requires an income statement, a balance sheet, a statement of owners' equity, a statement of cash flows, and the notes to the financial statements.

Going Concern

Financial statements are prepared with the expectation that a business will remain in operation indefinitely.

New businesses are started with the expectation that they will be successful. Accounting records and financial statements are designed as though businesses will continue indefinitely. For example, a business buys store equipment for $80,000. After yearly depreciation is recorded and reported based on the expected life of the equipment, the equipment's book value (cost less accumulated depreciation) is $44,000. If the business ended operations and the equipment had to be sold, the amount received might be less or more than the $44,000. However, accounting records are maintained with the expectation that the business will remain in operation indefinitely and that the cost will be allocated over the useful life of the equipment. The equipment value, therefore, is $44,000 on the records regardless of what it may be worth when sold.

Historical Cost

The actual amount paid for merchandise or other items bought is recorded.

The actual amount paid for an item in a business transaction may be different from its market value. For example, a business purchases a delivery truck that is advertised for sale at $28,500. The truck has a market value of $30,000. The business negotiated a purchase price of just $27,000. The amount recorded in accounting records for the delivery truck is the "historical" cost, $27,000—the actual amount paid.

Matching Expenses with Revenue

The revenue from business activities and the expenses associated with earning that revenue are recorded in the same accounting period.

Business activities for an accounting period are summarized in financial statements. To adequately report how a business performed during an accounting period, all revenue earned as a result of business operations must be reported. Likewise, all expenses incurred in producing the revenue during the same accounting period must be reported. Matching expenses with revenue gives a true picture of business operations for an accounting period. The timing of when cash is exchanged does not impact when a transaction is recorded as either revenue or expense.

For example, in February, a business performs $50,000 of services and uses $5,000 of supplies that were purchased in the prior fiscal year. Matching expenses with revenue results in net income of $45,000. Including all required expenses gives readers of the financial statements a more complete picture of the financial condition of the business.

Materiality

Business activities creating dollar amounts large enough to affect business decisions should be recorded and reported as separate items in accounting records and financial statements.

Business transactions are recorded in accounting records and reported in financial statements in dollar amounts. How the amounts are recorded and reported depends on the amount involved and the relative importance of the item in making business decisions. Dollar amounts that are large will generally be considered in making decisions about future operations. A separate accounting record is kept for items with dollar amounts large enough to be considered in making decisions about future operations. Dollar amounts that are small and not considered important in decision making may be combined with other amounts in the accounting records and financial statements.

Neutrality

The process of making accounting estimates is free from bias.

Many accounting functions require a business to use estimates. These include the estimation of uncollectible accounts receivable and the assignment of a useful life and salvage value for a plant asset. A business must not set or alter these estimates to achieve some other goal, such as reducing net income to avoid income taxes. For example, a business could raise its estimate of uncollectible accounts receivable to reduce its operating income subject to income tax. However, in compliance with the neutrality principle, the book value of accounts receivable in the financial accounts must always be a reasonable and unbiased estimate of the money the business expects to collect in the future.

Objective Evidence

A source document is prepared for each transaction.

A source document is an original business paper indicating that a transaction did occur and that the amounts recorded in the accounting records are accurate and true. For example, a check is the original business paper for cash payments. The original business paper for purchases on account is the purchase invoice. When accounting information reported on the financial statements needs to be verified, an accountant will first check the accounting record. If the details of an entry need further checking, an accountant will then check the business papers as objective evidence that the transaction did occur as recorded.

Many transactions in modern computerized accounting systems are entered directly into the system. Although no paper document is ever prepared, an electronic version of the document is available in the system. The electronic record provides the same objective evidence of the transaction as would a paper record.

Realization of Revenue

Revenue is recorded at the time goods or services are sold.

A business may sell goods or services or both. Cash may be received at the time of sale, or the business may agree to receive payment at a later date. Regardless of when cash is actually received, the sale amount is recorded in the accounting records at the time of sale. For example, merchandise is sold for $3,500. The business agrees to an initial payment of $500 with the remaining balance to be divided in four monthly payments of $750 each. The full $3,500 of revenue is recorded at the time of the sale even though $3,000 will be collected later.

Unit of Measurement

Business transactions are reported in numbers that have common values—that is, using a common unit of measurement.

All transactions are recorded in accounting records in terms of money. Useful nonfinancial information may also be recorded to describe the nature of a business transaction. If part of the information in the accounting records is financial and part is nonfinancial, the financial statements will not be clear. For example, if a business states its sales in number of units sold (nonfinancial) and its expenses in dollars (financial), net profit cannot be calculated. Instead, total expenses (financial) are subtracted from the money taken in through sales (financial) to determine net profit.

FORM 10-K
(Annual Report)

for the Period Ending 01/28/2018

UNITED STATES
SECURITIES AND EXCHANGE COMMISSION
WASHINGTON, D.C. 20549

FORM 10-K

☒ **ANNUAL REPORT PURSUANT TO SECTION 13 OR 15(d) OF THE SECURITIES EXCHANGE ACT OF 1934**

For the fiscal year ended January 28, 2018

OR

☐ **TRANSITION REPORT PURSUANT TO SECTION 13 OR 15(d) OF THE SECURITIES EXCHANGE ACT OF 1934**

Commission File Number 1-8207

THE HOME DEPOT, INC.
(Exact name of registrant as specified in its charter)

DELAWARE	**95-3261426**
(State or other jurisdiction of incorporation or organization)	(I.R.S. Employer Identification No.)
2455 PACES FERRY ROAD, ATLANTA, GEORGIA 30339	Registrant's Telephone Number, Including Area Code:
(Address of principal executive offices) (Zip Code)	**(770) 433-8211**

SECURITIES REGISTERED PURSUANT TO SECTION 12(b) OF THE ACT:

TITLE OF EACH CLASS	**NAME OF EACH EXCHANGE ON WHICH REGISTERED**
Common Stock, $0.05 Par Value Per Share	New York Stock Exchange

SECURITIES REGISTERED PURSUANT TO SECTION 12(g) OF THE ACT: **None**

Indicate by check mark if the Registrant is a well-known seasoned issuer, as defined in Rule 405 of the Securities Act. Yes ☒ No ☐

Indicate by check mark if the Registrant is not required to file reports pursuant to Section 13 or Section 15(d) of the Act. Yes ☐ No ☒

Indicate by check mark whether the Registrant (1) has filed all reports required to be filed by Section 13 or 15(d) of the Securities Exchange Act of 1934 during the preceding 12 months (or for such shorter period that the Registrant was required to file such reports), and (2) has been subject to such filing requirements for the past 90 days. Yes ☒ No ☐

Indicate by check mark whether the Registrant has submitted electronically and posted on its corporate Web site, if any, every Interactive Data File required to be submitted and posted pursuant to Rule 405 of Regulation S-T during the preceding 12 months (or for such shorter period that the Registrant was required to submit and post such files). Yes ☒ No ☐

Indicate by check mark if disclosure of delinquent filers pursuant to Item 405 of Regulation S-K is not contained herein, and will not be contained, to the best of Registrant's knowledge, in definitive proxy or information statements incorporated by reference in Part III of this Form 10-K or any amendment to this Form 10-K. ☐

Indicate by check mark whether the Registrant is a large accelerated filer, an accelerated filer, a non-accelerated filer, smaller reporting company, or an emerging growth company. See the definitions of "large accelerated filer," "accelerated filer," "smaller reporting company," and " emerging growth company" in Rule 12b-2 of the Exchange Act. (Check one):

Large accelerated filer ☒   Accelerated filer ☐   Non-accelerated filer ☐   Smaller reporting company ☐

Emerging growth company ☐   If an emerging growth company, indicate by check mark if the registrant has elected not to use the extended transition period for complying with any new or revised financial accounting standards provided pursuant to Section 13(a) of the Exchange Act. ☐

Indicate by check mark whether the Registrant is a shell company (as defined in Rule 12b-2 of the Exchange Act). Yes ☐ No ☒

The aggregate market value of the common stock of the Registrant held by non-affiliates of the Registrant on July 30, 2017 was $176.5 billion.

The number of shares outstanding of the Registrant's common stock as of March 2, 2018 was 1,157,269,522 shares.

DOCUMENTS INCORPORATED BY REFERENCE

Portions of the Registrant's proxy statement for the 2018 Annual Meeting of Shareholders are incorporated by reference in Part III of this Form 10-K to the extent described herein.

Management's Report on Internal Control Over Financial Reporting

Our management is responsible for establishing and maintaining adequate internal control over financial reporting, as such term is defined in Rule 13a-15(f) promulgated under the Exchange Act. Under the supervision and with the participation of our management, including our Chief Executive Officer and Chief Financial Officer, we conducted an evaluation of the effectiveness of our internal control over financial reporting as of January 28, 2018 based on the framework in *Internal Control – Integrated Framework (2013)* issued by the Committee of Sponsoring Organizations of the Treadway Commission. Based on our evaluation, our management concluded that our internal control over financial reporting was effective as of January 28, 2018 in providing reasonable assurance regarding the reliability of financial reporting and the preparation of financial statements for external purposes in accordance with GAAP. The effectiveness of our internal control over financial reporting as of January 28, 2018 has been audited by KPMG LLP, an independent registered public accounting firm, as stated in their report which is included herein.

/s/ CRAIG A. MENEAR

Craig A. Menear

Chairman, Chief Executive Officer and President

/s/ CAROL B. TOMÉ

Carol B. Tomé

Chief Financial Officer and Executive Vice President – Corporate Services

Report of Independent Registered Public Accounting Firm

The Stockholders and Board of Directors
The Home Depot, Inc.:

Opinion on the Consolidated Financial Statements

We have audited the accompanying Consolidated Balance Sheets of The Home Depot, Inc. and Subsidiaries as of January 28, 2018 and January 29, 2017, and the related Consolidated Statements of Earnings, Comprehensive Income, Stockholders' Equity, and Cash Flows for each of the fiscal years in the three-year period ended January 28, 2018 and the related notes (collectively, the "Consolidated Financial Statements"). In our opinion, the Consolidated Financial Statements present fairly, in all material respects, the financial position of The Home Depot, Inc. and Subsidiaries as of January 28, 2018 and January 29, 2017, and the results of their operations and their cash flows for each of the fiscal years in the three-year period ended January 28, 2018, in conformity with U.S. generally accepted accounting principles.

We also have audited, in accordance with the standards of the Public Company Accounting Oversight Board (United States) ("PCAOB"), The Home Depot, Inc.'s internal control over financial reporting as of January 28, 2018, based on criteria established in *Internal Control – Integrated Framework (2013)* issued by the Committee of Sponsoring Organizations of the Treadway Commission, and our report dated March 22, 2018 expressed an unqualified opinion on the effectiveness of the Company's internal control over financial reporting.

Basis for Opinion

These Consolidated Financial Statements are the responsibility of the Company's management. Our responsibility is to express an opinion on these Consolidated Financial Statements based on our audits. We are a public accounting firm registered with the PCAOB and are required to be independent with respect to the Company in accordance with the U.S. federal securities laws and the applicable rules and regulations of the Securities and Exchange Commission and the PCAOB.

We conducted our audits in accordance with the standards of the PCAOB. Those standards require that we plan and perform the audit to obtain reasonable assurance about whether the Consolidated Financial Statements are free of material misstatement, whether due to error or fraud. Our audits included performing procedures to assess the risks of material misstatement of the Consolidated Financial Statements, whether due to error or fraud, and performing procedures that respond to those risks. Such procedures included examining, on a test basis, evidence regarding the amounts and disclosures in the Consolidated Financial Statements. Our audits also included evaluating the accounting principles used and significant estimates made by management, as well as evaluating the overall presentation of the Consolidated Financial Statements. We believe that our audits provide a reasonable basis for our opinion.

/s/KPMG LLP

We have served as the Company's auditor since 1979.

Atlanta, Georgia
March 22, 2018

The Home Depot, Inc. Consolidated Balance Sheets

in millions, except per share data	January 28, 2018	January 29, 2017
Assets		
Current assets:		
Cash and cash equivalents	$ 3,595	$ 2,538
Receivables, net	1,952	2,029
Merchandise inventories	12,748	12,549
Other current assets	638	608
Total current assets	18,933	17,724
Net property and equipment	22,075	21,914
Goodwill	2,275	2,093
Other assets	1,246	1,235
Total assets	$ 44,529	$ 42,966
Liabilities and Stockholders' Equity		
Current liabilities:		
Short-term debt	$ 1,559	$ 710
Accounts payable	7,244	7,000
Accrued salaries and related expenses	1,640	1,484
Sales taxes payable	520	508
Deferred revenue	1,805	1,669
Income taxes payable	54	25
Current installments of long-term debt	1,202	542
Other accrued expenses	2,170	2,195
Total current liabilities	16,194	14,133
Long-term debt, excluding current installments	24,267	22,349
Deferred income taxes	440	296
Other long-term liabilities	2,174	1,855
Total liabilities	43,075	38,633
Common stock, par value $0.05; authorized: 10,000 shares; issued: 1,780 shares at January 28, 2018 and 1,776 shares at January 29, 2017	89	88
Paid-in capital	10,192	9,787
Retained earnings	39,935	35,519
Accumulated other comprehensive loss	(566)	(867)
Treasury stock, at cost, 622 shares at January 28, 2018 and 573 shares at January 29, 2017	(48,196)	(40,194)
Total stockholders' equity	1,454	4,333
Total liabilities and stockholders' equity	$ 44,529	$ 42,966

See accompanying notes to consolidated financial statements.

The Home Depot, Inc. Consolidated Statements of Earnings

in millions, except per share data	Fiscal 2017	Fiscal 2016	Fiscal 2015
Net sales	$100,904	$ 94,595	$ 88,519
Cost of sales	66,548	62,282	58,254
Gross profit	34,356	32,313	30,265
Operating expenses:			
Selling, general and administrative	17,864	17,132	16,801
Depreciation and amortization	1,811	1,754	1,690
Total operating expenses	19,675	18,886	18,491
Operating income	14,681	13,427	11,774
Interest and other (income) expense:			
Interest and investment income	(74)	(36)	(166)
Interest expense	1,057	972	919
Interest and other, net	983	936	753
Earnings before provision for income taxes	13,698	12,491	11,021
Provision for income taxes	5,068	4,534	4,012
Net earnings	$ 8,630	$ 7,957	$ 7,009
Basic weighted average common shares	1,178	1,229	1,277
Basic earnings per share	$ 7.33	$ 6.47	$ 5.49
Diluted weighted average common shares	1,184	1,234	1,283
Diluted earnings per share	$ 7.29	$ 6.45	$ 5.46

See accompanying notes to consolidated financial statements.

The Home Depot, Inc. Consolidated Statements of Comprehensive Income

in millions	Fiscal 2017	Fiscal 2016	Fiscal 2015
Net earnings	$ 8,630	$ 7,957	$ 7,009
Other comprehensive income (loss):			
Foreign currency translation adjustments	311	(3)	(412)
Cash flow hedges, net of tax	(1)	34	(34)
Other	(9)	—	—
Total other comprehensive income (loss)	301	31	(446)
Comprehensive income	$ 8,931	$ 7,988	$ 6,563

See accompanying notes to consolidated financial statements.

The Home Depot, Inc. Consolidated Statements of Stockholders' Equity

in millions, except per share data	Fiscal 2017	Fiscal 2016	Fiscal 2015
Common Stock:			
Balance at beginning of year	$ 88	$ 88	$ 88
Shares issued under employee stock plans	1	—	—
Balance at end of year	89	88	88
Paid-in Capital:			
Balance at beginning of year	9,787	9,347	8,885
Shares issued under employee stock plans	132	76	73
Tax effect of stock-based compensation	—	97	145
Stock-based compensation expense	273	267	244
Balance at end of year	10,192	9,787	9,347
Retained Earnings:			
Balance at beginning of year	35,519	30,973	26,995
Net earnings	8,630	7,957	7,009
Cash dividends ($3.56 per share in fiscal 2017, $2.76 per share in fiscal 2016, and $2.36 per share in fiscal 2015)	(4,212)	(3,404)	(3,031)
Other	(2)	(7)	—
Balance at end of year	39,935	35,519	30,973
Accumulated Other Comprehensive Income (Loss):			
Balance at beginning of year	(867)	(898)	(452)
Foreign currency translation adjustments	311	(3)	(412)
Cash flow hedges, net of tax	(1)	34	(34)
Other	(9)	—	—
Balance at end of year	(566)	(867)	(898)
Treasury Stock:			
Balance at beginning of year	(40,194)	(33,194)	(26,194)
Repurchases of common stock	(8,002)	(7,000)	(7,000)
Balance at end of year	(48,196)	(40,194)	(33,194)
Total stockholders' equity	$ 1,454	$ 4,333	$ 6,316

See accompanying notes to consolidated financial statements.

The Home Depot, Inc. Consolidated Statements of Cash Flows

in millions	Fiscal 2017	Fiscal 2016	Fiscal 2015
Cash Flows from Operating Activities:			
Net earnings	$ 8,630	$ 7,957	$ 7,009
Reconciliation of net earnings to net cash provided by operating activities:			
Depreciation and amortization	2,062	1,973	1,863
Stock-based compensation expense	273	267	244
Gain on sales of investments	—	—	(144)
Changes in assets and liabilities, net of acquisition effects:			
Receivables, net	139	(138)	(181)
Merchandise inventories	(84)	(769)	(546)
Other current assets	(10)	(48)	(5)
Accounts payable and accrued expenses	352	446	888
Deferred revenue	128	99	109
Income taxes payable	29	109	154
Deferred income taxes	92	(117)	15
Other	420	4	(33)
Net cash provided by operating activities	12,031	9,783	9,373
Cash Flows from Investing Activities:			
Capital expenditures, net of non-cash capital expenditures	(1,897)	(1,621)	(1,503)
Proceeds from sales of investments	—	—	144
Payments for businesses acquired, net	(374)	—	(1,666)
Proceeds from sales of property and equipment	47	38	43
Other investing activities	(4)	—	—
Net cash used in investing activities	(2,228)	(1,583)	(2,982)
Cash Flows from Financing Activities:			
Proceeds from short-term debt, net	850	360	60
Proceeds from long-term debt, net of discounts	2,991	4,959	3,991
Repayments of long-term debt	(543)	(3,045)	(39)
Repurchases of common stock	(8,000)	(6,880)	(7,000)
Proceeds from sales of common stock	255	218	228
Cash dividends	(4,212)	(3,404)	(3,031)
Other financing activities	(211)	(78)	4
Net cash used in financing activities	(8,870)	(7,870)	(5,787)
Change in cash and cash equivalents	933	330	604
Effect of exchange rate changes on cash and cash equivalents	124	(8)	(111)
Cash and cash equivalents at beginning of year	2,538	2,216	1,723
Cash and cash equivalents at end of year	$ 3,595	$ 2,538	$ 2,216
Supplemental Disclosures:			
Cash paid for interest, net of interest capitalized	$ 991	$ 924	$ 874
Cash paid for income taxes	4,732	4,623	3,853
Non-cash capital expenditures	150	179	165

See accompanying notes to consolidated financial statements.

Notes to Consolidated Financial Statements

1. Summary of Significant Accounting Policies

Business

The Home Depot, Inc., together with its subsidiaries (the "Company," "Home Depot," "we," "our" or "us"), is a home improvement retailer that sells a wide assortment of building materials, home improvement products, lawn and garden products, and décor items and provides a number of services, in stores and online. We operate in the U.S., including the Commonwealth of Puerto Rico and the territories of the U.S. Virgin Islands and Guam, Canada, and Mexico.

Consolidation and Presentation

Our consolidated financial statements include our accounts and those of our wholly-owned subsidiaries. All significant intercompany transactions have been eliminated in consolidation. Certain amounts in prior fiscal years have been reclassified to conform with the presentation adopted in the current fiscal year. Our fiscal year is a 52- or 53-week period ending on the Sunday nearest to January 31. Fiscal 2017, 2016, and 2015 each included 52 weeks.

Use of Estimates

We have made a number of estimates and assumptions relating to the reporting of assets and liabilities, the disclosure of contingent assets and liabilities, and reported amounts of revenues and expenses in preparing these financial statements in conformity with GAAP. Actual results could differ from these estimates.

Cash Equivalents

We consider all highly liquid investments purchased with original maturities of three months or less to be cash equivalents. Our cash equivalents are carried at fair market value and consist primarily of money market funds.

Receivables

The components of receivables, net, follow.

in millions	January 28, 2018	January 29, 2017
Card receivables	$ 734	$ 729
Rebate receivables	609	625
Customer receivables	261	216
Other receivables	348	459
Receivables, net	$ 1,952	$ 2,029

Card receivables consist of payments due from financial institutions for the settlement of credit card and debit card transactions. Rebate receivables represent amounts due from vendors for volume and co-op advertising rebates. Receivables due from customers relate to credit extended directly to customers by certain subsidiaries in the ordinary course of business. The valuation reserve related to accounts receivable was not material to our consolidated financial statements at the end of fiscal 2017 or 2016.

Merchandise Inventories

The majority of our merchandise inventories are stated at the lower of cost (first-in, first-out) or market, as determined by the retail inventory method. As the inventory retail value is adjusted regularly to reflect market conditions, the inventory valued using the retail method approximates the lower of cost or market. Certain subsidiaries, including retail operations in Canada and Mexico, and distribution centers, record merchandise inventories at the lower of cost or market, as determined by a cost method. These merchandise inventories represent approximately 30% of the total merchandise inventories balance. We evaluate the inventory valued using a cost method at the end of each quarter to ensure that it is carried at the lower of cost or net realizable value. The valuation allowance for merchandise inventories valued under a cost method was not material to our consolidated financial statements at the end of fiscal 2017 or 2016.

Independent physical inventory counts or cycle counts are taken on a regular basis in each store and distribution center to ensure that amounts reflected in merchandise inventories are properly stated. Shrink (or in the case of excess inventory, "swell") is the difference between the recorded amount of inventory and the physical inventory. We calculate shrink based on actual inventory losses occurring as a result of physical inventory counts during each fiscal period and estimated inventory losses occurring between physical inventory counts. The estimate for shrink occurring in the interim period between physical inventory counts is calculated on a store-specific basis based on recent shrink results and current trends in the business.

Property and Equipment, including Capitalized Lease Assets

Buildings, furniture, fixtures, and equipment are recorded at cost and depreciated using the straight-line method over their estimated useful lives. Leasehold improvements are amortized using the straight-line method over the original term of the lease or the useful life of the improvement, whichever is shorter. The estimated useful lives of our property and equipment follow.

	Life
Buildings	5 – 45 years
Furniture, fixtures and equipment	2 – 20 years
Leasehold improvements	5 – 45 years

We capitalize certain costs related to the acquisition and development of software and amortize these costs using the straight-line method over the estimated useful life of the software, which is three to six years. Certain development costs not meeting the criteria for capitalization are expensed as incurred.

We evaluate our long-lived assets each quarter for indicators of potential impairment. Indicators of impairment include current period losses combined with a history of losses, our decision to relocate or close a store or other location before the end of its previously estimated useful life, or when changes in other circumstances indicate the carrying amount of an asset may not be recoverable. The evaluation for long-lived assets is performed at the lowest level of identifiable cash flows, which is generally the individual store level. The assets of a store with indicators of impairment are evaluated for recoverability by comparing its undiscounted future cash flows with its carrying value. If the carrying value is greater than the undiscounted future cash flows, we then measure the asset's fair value to determine whether an impairment loss should be recognized. If the resulting fair value is less than the carrying value, an impairment loss is recognized for the difference between the carrying value and the estimated fair value. Impairment losses are recorded as a component of SG&A. When a leased location closes, we also recognize, in SG&A, the net present value of future lease obligations less estimated sublease income. Impairments and lease obligation costs on closings and relocations were not material to our consolidated financial statements in fiscal 2017, 2016, or 2015.

Goodwill and Other Intangible Assets

Goodwill represents the excess of purchase price over the fair value of net assets acquired. We do not amortize goodwill, but assess the recoverability of goodwill in the third quarter of each fiscal year, or more often if indicators warrant, by determining whether the fair value of each reporting unit supports its carrying value. Each fiscal year, we may assess qualitative factors to determine whether it is more likely than not that the fair value of each reporting unit is less than its carrying amount as a basis for determining whether it is necessary to complete quantitative impairment assessments, with a quantitative assessment completed at least once every three years. We completed our last quantitative assessment in fiscal 2016.

In fiscal 2017, we completed our annual assessment of the recoverability of goodwill for the U.S., Canada, and Mexico reporting units. We performed qualitative assessments, concluding that the fair value of the reporting units substantially exceeded the respective reporting unit's carrying value, including goodwill. As a result, there were no impairment charges related to goodwill for fiscal 2017, 2016, or 2015.

Changes in the carrying amount of our goodwill follow.

in millions	Fiscal 2017	Fiscal 2016	Fiscal 2015
Goodwill, balance at beginning of year	$ 2,093	$ 2,102	$ 1,353
Acquisitions	164	—	788
Other [1]	18	(9)	(39)
Goodwill, balance at end of year	$ 2,275	$ 2,093	$ 2,102

(1) Primarily reflects the impact of foreign currency translation.

We amortize the cost of other intangible assets over their estimated useful lives, which range up to 12 years, unless such lives are deemed indefinite. Intangible assets with indefinite lives are tested in the third quarter of each fiscal year for impairment, or more often if indicators warrant. Intangible assets are included in other assets.

Debt

Any premiums or discounts, as the case may be, associated with an issuance of long-term debt are recorded as a direct addition or deduction to the carrying value of the related senior notes and amortized over the term of those notes using the effective interest rate method. Debt issuance costs associated with an issuance of long-term debt are recorded as a direct deduction to the carrying value of the related senior notes and amortized over the term of those notes using the effective interest rate method.

Derivatives

We use derivative financial instruments in the management of our interest rate exposure on long-term debt and our exposure to foreign currency fluctuations. For derivatives that are designated as hedges, changes in their fair values that are considered effective are either accounted for in earnings or recognized in other comprehensive income (loss) until the hedged item is recognized in earnings, depending on the nature of the hedge. Any ineffective portion of a derivative's change in fair value is immediately recognized in earnings. Financial instruments that do not qualify for hedge accounting are recorded at fair value with unrealized gains or losses reported in earnings. All qualifying derivative financial instruments are recognized at their fair values in either assets or liabilities at the balance sheet date and are reported on a gross basis. The fair values of our derivative financial instruments are discussed in Note 4 and Note 7.

Insurance

We are self-insured for certain losses related to general liability (including product liability), workers' compensation, employee group medical, and automobile claims. We recognize the expected ultimate cost for claims incurred (undiscounted) at the balance sheet date as a liability. The expected ultimate cost for claims incurred is estimated based upon analysis of historical data and actuarial estimates. We also maintain network security and privacy liability insurance coverage to limit our exposure to losses such as those that may be caused by a significant compromise or breach of our data security. Insurance related expenses are included in SG&A.

Treasury Stock

Treasury stock is reflected as a reduction of stockholders' equity at cost. We use the weighted-average purchase cost to determine the cost of treasury stock that is reissued.

Revenues

We recognize revenue, net of estimated returns and sales tax, at the time the customer takes possession of merchandise or when a service is performed. The liability for sales returns, including the impact to gross profit, is estimated based on historical return levels.

Net sales include services revenue generated through a variety of installation, home maintenance, and professional service programs. In these programs, the customer selects and purchases material for a project, and we provide or arrange professional installation. These programs are offered through our stores and in-home sales programs. Under certain programs, when we provide or arrange the installation of a project and the subcontractor provides material as part of the installation, both the material and labor are included in services revenue. We recognize this revenue when the service for the customer is complete.

When we receive payment from customers before the customer has taken possession of the merchandise or the service has been performed, the amount received is recorded as deferred revenue until the sale or service is complete. We also record deferred revenue for the sale of gift cards and recognize this revenue upon the redemption of gift cards in net sales. Gift card breakage income is recognized based upon historical redemption patterns and represents the balance of gift cards for which we believe the likelihood of redemption by the customer is remote.

Gift card breakage income, which is recognized as a reduction to SG&A, follows.

in millions	Fiscal 2017	Fiscal 2016	Fiscal 2015
Gift card breakage income	$ 39	$ 34	$ 27

Cost of Sales

Cost of sales includes the actual cost of merchandise sold and services performed; the cost of transportation of merchandise from vendors to our distribution network, stores, or customers; shipping and handling costs from our stores or distribution network to customers; the operating cost and depreciation of our sourcing and distribution network and online fulfillment centers; and the cost of deferred interest programs offered through our PLCC programs.

Cost of Credit

We have agreements with third-party service providers who directly extend credit to customers, manage our PLCC program, and own the related receivables. We have evaluated the third-party entities holding the receivables under the program and concluded that they should not be consolidated. The agreement with the primary third-party service provider for our PLCC program expires in 2028, with us having the option, but no obligation, to purchase the receivables at the end of the agreement. The deferred interest charges we incur for our deferred financing programs offered to our customers are included in cost of sales. The interchange fees charged to us for our customers' use of the cards and any profit sharing with the third-party service providers are included in SG&A. The sum of these three components is referred to as the cost of credit of the PLCC program.

Vendor Allowances

Vendor allowances primarily consist of volume rebates that are earned as a result of attaining certain purchase levels and co-op advertising allowances for the promotion of vendors' products that are typically based on guaranteed minimum amounts with additional amounts being earned for attaining certain purchase levels. These vendor allowances are accrued as earned, with those allowances received as a result of attaining certain purchase levels accrued over the incentive period based on estimates of purchases.

Volume rebates and certain co-op advertising allowances earned are initially recorded as a reduction in merchandise inventories and a subsequent reduction in cost of sales when the related product is sold. Certain co-op advertising allowances that are reimbursements of specific, incremental, and identifiable costs incurred to promote vendors' products are recorded as an offset against advertising expense in SG&A and were as follows:

in millions	Fiscal 2017	Fiscal 2016	Fiscal 2015
Specific, incremental, and identifiable co-op advertising allowances	$ 198	$ 166	$ 129

Advertising Expense

Television and radio advertising production costs, along with media placement costs, are expensed when the advertisement first appears. Gross advertising expense is included in SG&A. Certain co-op advertising allowances are recorded as an offset against advertising expense.

in millions	Fiscal 2017	Fiscal 2016	Fiscal 2015
Gross advertising expense	$ 995	$ 955	$ 868

Income Taxes

Income taxes are accounted for under the asset and liability method. We provide for federal, state, and foreign income taxes currently payable, as well as for those deferred due to timing differences between reporting income and expenses for financial statement purposes versus tax purposes. Deferred tax assets and liabilities are recognized for the future tax consequences attributable to temporary differences between the financial statement carrying amounts of existing assets and liabilities and their respective tax bases. Deferred tax assets and liabilities are measured using enacted income tax rates expected to apply to taxable income in the years in which those temporary differences are expected to be recovered or settled. The effect of a change in income tax rates is recognized as income or expense in the period that includes the enactment date.

We recognize the effect of income tax positions only if those positions are more likely than not of being sustained. Recognized income tax positions are measured at the largest amount that is greater than 50% likely of being realized. Changes in recognition or measurement are reflected in the period in which the change in judgment occurs.

We file a consolidated U.S. federal income tax return which includes certain eligible subsidiaries. Non-U.S. subsidiaries and certain U.S. subsidiaries, which are consolidated for financial reporting purposes, are not eligible to be included in our consolidated U.S. federal income tax return. Separate provisions for income taxes have been determined for these entities. For unremitted earnings of our non-U.S. subsidiaries, we are required to make an assertion regarding reinvestment or repatriation for tax purposes. For any earnings that we do not make a permanent reinvestment assertion, we recognize a provision for deferred income taxes. For earnings where we have made a permanent reinvestment assertion, no provision is recognized. See Note 5 for further discussion.

Comprehensive Income

Comprehensive income includes net earnings adjusted for certain gains and losses that are excluded from net earnings under GAAP, which consists primarily of foreign currency translation adjustments.

Foreign Currency Translation

Assets and liabilities denominated in a foreign currency are translated into U.S. dollars at the current rate of exchange on the last day of the reporting period. Revenues and expenses are translated using average exchange rates for the period and equity transactions are translated using the actual rate on the day of the transaction.

Recently Adopted Accounting Pronouncements

ASU No. 2016-09. In the first quarter of fiscal 2017, we adopted ASU No. 2016-09, "Compensation-Stock Compensation (Topic 718): Improvements to Employee Share-Based Payment Accounting." Upon adoption of this update, all excess tax benefits or deficiencies related to share-based payment awards are recognized in the provision for income taxes in the period in which they occur. Previously these amounts were reflected in paid-in capital. In addition, upon adoption, these amounts are classified as an operating activity in our consolidated statements of cash flows in the period in which they occur. Previously, these amounts were reflected as a financing activity. Cash paid to tax authorities when directly withholding shares for tax withholding purposes will continue to be classified as a financing activity in our consolidated statements of cash flows. Stock-based compensation expense will continue to reflect estimated forfeitures of share-based awards. We have adopted the applicable provisions of ASU No. 2016-09 prospectively.

As a result of the adoption of ASU No. 2016-09, we recognized $106 million of excess tax benefits related to share-based payment awards in our provision for income taxes during fiscal 2017. The recognition of these benefits contributed $0.09 to diluted earnings per share in fiscal 2017.

Recently Issued Accounting Pronouncements

ASU No. 2018-02. In February 2018, the FASB issued ASU No. 2018-02, "Income Statement - Reporting Comprehensive Income (Topic 220): Reclassification of Certain Tax Effects from Accumulated Other Comprehensive Income," which allows for an optional reclassification from accumulated other comprehensive income to retained earnings for stranded tax effects as a result of the Tax Act. ASU No. 2018-02 is effective for us in the first quarter of fiscal 2019 and early adoption is permitted. Two transition methods are available: at the beginning of the period of adoption, or retrospective to each period in which the income tax effects of the Tax Act related to items remaining in accumulated other comprehensive income are recognized. We are evaluating the effect that ASU No. 2018-02 will have on our consolidated financial statements and related disclosures.

ASU No. 2017-12. In August 2017, the FASB issued ASU No. 2017-12, "Derivatives and Hedging (Topic 815): Targeted Improvements to Accounting for Hedging Activities," which amends the hedge accounting recognition and presentation requirements. ASU No. 2017-12 eliminates the concept of recognizing periodic hedge ineffectiveness for cash flow and net investment hedges and allows an entity to apply the shortcut method to partial-term fair value hedges of interest rate risk. ASU No. 2017-12 is effective for us in the first quarter of fiscal 2019. Early adoption is permitted in any interim period after issuance of this update. We are evaluating the effect that ASU No. 2017-12 will have on our consolidated financial statements and related disclosures.

ASU No. 2017-04. In January 2017, the FASB issued ASU No. 2017-04, "Intangibles–Goodwill and Other (Topic 350): Simplifying the Test for Goodwill Impairment," which simplifies how an entity is required to test goodwill for impairment. The amendments in ASU No. 2017-04 require goodwill impairment to be measured using the difference between the carrying amount and the fair value of the reporting unit and require the loss recognized to not exceed the total amount of goodwill allocated to that reporting unit. ASU No. 2017-04 should be applied on a prospective basis and is effective for our annual goodwill impairment tests beginning in the first quarter of fiscal 2020. Early adoption is permitted. We have evaluated the effect that ASU No. 2017-04 will have on our consolidated financial statements and related disclosures and noted no material impact.

ASU No. 2016-16. In October 2016, the FASB issued ASU No. 2016-16, "Income Taxes (Topic 740): Intra-Entity Transfers of Assets Other Than Inventory," which requires an entity to recognize the income tax consequences of an intercompany transfer of assets other than inventory when the transfer occurs. An entity will continue to recognize the income tax consequences of an intercompany transfer of inventory when the inventory is sold to a third party. ASU No. 2016-16 is effective for us in the first quarter of fiscal 2018 using a modified retrospective approach. We are evaluating the effect that ASU No. 2016-16 will have on our consolidated financial statements and related disclosures.

ASU No. 2016-02. In February 2016, the FASB issued ASU No. 2016-02, "Leases (Topic 842)," which requires an entity that is a lessee to recognize the assets and liabilities arising from leases on the balance sheet. ASU No. 2016-02 also requires disclosures about the amount, timing, and uncertainty of cash flows arising from leases. ASU No. 2016-02 is effective for us in the first quarter of fiscal 2019 using a modified retrospective approach. Early adoption is permitted.

We are evaluating and planning for the adoption and implementation of ASU No. 2016-02. We believe that ASU No. 2016-02 will have a material impact on our financial position, as a result of the requirement to recognize right-of-use assets and lease liabilities on our consolidated balance sheets. The impact to our results of operations is being evaluated, and we do not believe there will be a material impact to our cash flows upon adoption of ASU No. 2016-02.

ASU No. 2014-09. In May 2014, the FASB issued a new ASU related to revenue recognition. Under ASU No. 2014-09, "Revenue from Contracts with Customers (Topic 606)," revenue is recognized when a customer obtains control of promised goods or services in an amount that reflects the consideration the entity expects to receive in exchange for those goods or services. In addition, ASU No. 2014-09 requires disclosure of the nature, amount, timing, and uncertainty of revenue and cash flows arising from contracts with customers. ASU No. 2014-09 permits two methods of adoption: retrospectively to each prior reporting period presented (full retrospective method), or retrospectively with the cumulative effect of initially applying the guidance recognized at the date of initial application (modified retrospective method). ASU No. 2014-09 is effective for us in the first quarter of fiscal 2018.

We will adopt ASU No. 2014-09 in the first quarter of fiscal 2018 using the modified retrospective method. This adoption will not materially impact our consolidated financial statements or related disclosures. Under ASU No. 2014-09, we will change the presentation of certain expenses and cost reimbursements associated with our PLCC program, certain expenses related to the sale of our gift cards to customers, and gift card breakage income. We will also change our recognition of gift card breakage income to be recognized proportionately as redemption occurs, rather than based on historical redemption patterns. We are in the process of implementing changes to our processes, controls and systems in support of our adoption of ASU No. 2014-09.

Recent accounting pronouncements pending adoption not discussed above are either not applicable or are not expected to have a material impact on us.

2. Segment Reporting

We currently conduct our retail operations in the U.S., Canada, and Mexico, each of which represents one of our three operating segments. Our operating segments reflect the way in which internally-reported financial information is used to make decisions and allocate resources. For disclosure purposes, we aggregate these three operating segments into one reportable segment due to their similar operating and financial characteristics and how the business is managed.

The assets of each of our operating segments primarily consist of net property and equipment and merchandise inventories. Long-lived assets, classified by geography, follow.

in millions	January 28, 2018	January 29, 2017	January 31, 2016
Long-lived assets – in the U.S.	$ 19,526	$ 19,519	$ 19,846
Long-lived assets – outside the U.S.	2,549	2,395	2,345
Total long-lived assets	$ 22,075	$ 21,914	$ 22,191

No sales to an individual customer or country other than the U.S. accounted for more than 10% of revenue during any of the last three fiscal years. Net sales, classified by geography, follow.

in millions	Fiscal 2017	Fiscal 2016	Fiscal 2015
Net sales – in the U.S.	$ 92,413	$ 86,615	$ 80,550
Net sales – outside the U.S.	8,491	7,980	7,969
Net sales	$ 100,904	$ 94,595	$ 88,519

Net sales by products and services follow.

in millions	Fiscal 2017	Fiscal 2016	Fiscal 2015
Net sales – products [1]	$ 95,956	$ 90,028	$ 84,130
Net sales – services [1]	4,948	4,567	4,389
Net sales	$ 100,904	$ 94,595	$ 88,519

(1) Certain sales were reclassified from products to services in fiscal 2017. Prior year amounts have been reclassified to conform with the current year presentation.

Major product lines and the related merchandising departments (and related services) follow.

Major Product Line	Merchandising Departments
Building Materials	Building Materials, Electrical, Lighting, Lumber, Millwork, and Plumbing
Décor	Appliances, Décor, Flooring, Kitchen and Bath, and Paint
Hardlines	Hardware, Indoor Garden, Outdoor Garden, and Tools

Net sales by merchandising department (and related services) follow.

	Fiscal 2017		Fiscal 2016		Fiscal 2015	
dollars in millions	Net Sales	% of Net Sales	Net Sales	% of Net Sales	Net Sales	% of Net Sales
Appliances	$ 8,147	8.1	$ 7,362	7.8	$ 6,539	7.4
Building Materials	7,342	7.3	6,774	7.2	6,416	7.2
Décor	3,057	3.0	2,906	3.1	2,730	3.1
Electrical [1]	5,037	5.0	4,561	4.8	4,291	4.8
Flooring	7,078	7.0	6,477	6.8	6,215	7.0
Hardware	5,891	5.8	5,629	6.0	5,296	6.0
Indoor Garden	9,639	9.6	9,204	9.7	8,227	9.3
Kitchen and Bath	7,377	7.3	7,184	7.6	6,909	7.8
Lighting [1]	4,409	4.4	4,423	4.7	4,249	4.8
Lumber	7,790	7.7	6,828	7.2	6,284	7.1
Millwork	5,382	5.3	5,139	5.4	4,937	5.6
Outdoor Garden	7,030	7.0	6,789	7.2	6,505	7.3
Paint	7,990	7.9	7,666	8.1	7,497	8.5
Plumbing	7,356	7.3	6,985	7.4	6,364	7.2
Tools	7,379	7.3	6,668	7.0	6,060	6.8
Total	$ 100,904	100.0%	$ 94,595	100.0%	$ 88,519	100.0%

Note: Certain percentages may not sum to totals due to rounding.

(1) Certain products were reclassified from Electrical to Lighting in fiscal 2017. Prior year amounts have been reclassified to conform with the current year presentation.

3. Property and Leases

Net Property and Equipment

The components of net property and equipment follow.

in millions	January 28, 2018	January 29, 2017
Land	$ 8,352	$ 8,207
Buildings	18,073	17,772
Furniture, fixtures and equipment	11,506	11,020
Leasehold improvements	1,637	1,519
Construction in progress	538	739
Capital leases	1,308	1,169
Property and equipment, at cost	41,414	40,426
Less accumulated depreciation and amortization	19,339	18,512
Net property and equipment	$ 22,075	$ 21,914

Leases

We lease certain retail locations, office space, warehouse and distribution space, equipment, and vehicles. While most of the leases are operating leases, certain locations and equipment are leased under capital leases. As leases approach maturity, we consider various factors such as market conditions and the terms of any renewal options that may exist to determine whether we will renew or replace the lease. Short-term and long-term obligations for capital leases are included in the applicable long-term debt category based on maturity.

Assets under capital leases (net of amortization) recorded in net property and equipment follow.

in millions	January 28, 2018	January 29, 2017
Capital leases, net	$ 821	$ 730

Certain lease agreements include escalating rents over the lease terms. Real estate taxes, insurance, maintenance, and operating expenses applicable to the leased property are our obligations under the lease agreements. We expense rent on a straight-line basis over the lease term, which commences on the date we have the right to control the property. The cumulative expense recognized on a straight-line basis in excess of the cumulative payments is included in other accrued expenses and other long-term liabilities.

Our total rent expense follows.

in millions	Fiscal 2017	Fiscal 2016	Fiscal 2015
Total rent expense	$ 1,053	$ 984	$ 922

The approximate future minimum lease payments under capital and operating leases at January 28, 2018 follow.

in millions	Operating Leases	Capital Leases
Fiscal 2018	$ 921	$ 147
Fiscal 2019	869	142
Fiscal 2020	786	156
Fiscal 2021	696	132
Fiscal 2022	580	132
Thereafter through fiscal 2097	3,286	1,044
	$ 7,138	1,753
Less imputed interest		769
Net present value of capital lease obligations		984
Less current installments		52
Long-term capital lease obligations, excluding current installments		$ 932

The Home Depot, Inc. Selected Financial Data

amounts in millions, except per share data or where noted	Fiscal 2017	Fiscal 2016	Fiscal 2015	Fiscal 2014	Fiscal 2013
STATEMENT OF EARNINGS DATA					
Net sales	$100,904	$94,595	$88,519	$83,176	$78,812
Net sales increase (%)	6.7	6.9	6.4	5.5	5.4
Earnings before provision for income taxes ($)	13,698	12,491	11,021	9,976	8,467
Net earnings ($)	8,630	7,957	7,009	6,345	5,385
Net earnings increase (%)	8.5	13.5	10.5	17.8	18.7
Diluted earnings per share ($)	7.29	6.45	5.46	4.71	3.76
Diluted earnings per share increase (%)	13.0	18.1	15.9	25.3	25.3
Diluted weighted average number of common shares	1,184	1,234	1,283	1,346	1,434
Gross profit – % of sales	34.0	34.2	34.2	34.1	34.2
Total operating expenses – % of sales	19.5	20.0	20.9	21.5	22.5
Interest and other, net – % of sales	1.0	1.0	0.9	0.6	0.9
Net earnings – % of sales	8.6	8.4	7.9	7.6	6.8
BALANCE SHEET DATA AND FINANCIAL RATIOS					
Total assets	$44,529	$42,966	$41,973	$39,449	$39,996
Working capital ($)	2,739	3,591	3,960	3,589	4,050
Merchandise inventories ($)	12,748	12,549	11,809	11,079	11,057
Net property and equipment ($)	22,075	21,914	22,191	22,720	23,348
Long-term debt, excluding current installments ($)	24,267	22,349	20,789	16,786	14,615
Stockholders' equity ($)	1,454	4,333	6,316	9,322	12,522
Long-term debt-to-equity (%)	1,669.0	515.8	329.1	180.1	116.7
Total debt-to-equity (%)	1,858.9	544.7	335.9	183.6	117.0
Current ratio	1.17:1	1.25:1	1.32:1	1.32:1	1.38:1
Inventory turnover	5.1x	4.9x	4.9x	4.7x	4.6x
Return on invested capital (%)	34.2	31.4	28.1	25.0	20.9
STATEMENT OF CASH FLOWS DATA					
Depreciation and amortization	$2,062	$1,973	$1,863	$1,786	$1,757
Capital expenditures ($)	1,897	1,621	1,503	1,442	1,389
Cash dividends per share ($)	3.56	2.76	2.36	1.88	1.56
STORE AND OTHER SALES DATA					
Number of stores	2,284	2,278	2,274	2,269	2,263
Square footage at fiscal year-end	237	237	237	236	236
Average square footage per store (in thousands)	104	104	104	104	104
Comparable sales increase (%) [1]	6.8	5.6	5.6	5.3	6.8
Sales per square foot ($) [1]	417.02	390.78	370.55	352.22	334.35
Customer transactions [1]	1,579	1,544	1,501	1,442	1,391
Average ticket ($) [1]	63.06	60.35	58.77	57.87	56.78
Number of associates at fiscal year-end (in thousands)	413	406	385	371	365

Note: This information should be read in conjunction with MD&A and our consolidated financial statements.

(1) These amounts do not include the results for Interline, which was acquired in the third quarter of fiscal 2015.

Answers to Audit Your Understanding

Chapter 1, Lesson 1-1, page 12

1. The chart of accounts must contain departmental accounts for significant types of transactions, such as purchases, sales, and salary expense.
2. Assets = Liabilities + Owners' Equity.
3. Debits are entered in the left column; credits are entered in the right column.
4. Journals are used to record transactions in chronological order.
5. When only one kind of transaction is being recorded.
6. Asset, debit; revenue, credit.
7. The total of the accounts payable subsidiary ledger accounts should equal the balance of the Accounts Payable general ledger account.
8. Revenue, 4; Direct Expenses, 6.

Chapter 1, Lesson 1-2, page 19

1. For a business having multiple departments, a departmental accounting systems allows management to decide whether a department's performance is acceptable or unacceptable.
2. Purchases—Grills is debited; Accounts Payable is credited.
3. Accounts Payable is debited; Purchases Returns and Allowances—Furniture is credited.

Chapter 1, Lesson 1-3, page 27

1. Accounts Payable is debited; Cash and Purchases Discount—Furniture are credited.
2. In the General Debit and Credit columns of the cash payments journal.
3. When the transaction is recorded in the cash payments journal.

Chapter 2, Lesson 2-1, page 46

1. Information such as departmental gross profit from operations can help business managers decide if each department is earning an appropriate profit.
2. A tax-exempt customer is not required to pay sales tax. Examples include federal, state, and local government agencies; not-for-profit educational institutions; and certain religious and charitable organizations.
3. An invoice.
4. Sales are recorded at the time of sale, regardless of when payment is received.
5. A credit memorandum is issued by a vendor to show the amount deducted from the customer's account for returns and allowances.

Chapter 2, Lesson 2-2, page 54

1. To encourage early payment of its accounts receivable.
2. A 2% sales discount may be deducted if sales on account are paid within 10 days of the invoice date. All sales on account must be paid within 30 days of the invoice date.
3. None. A sales discount only reduces the amount due from the customer.
4. Both cash sales and credit card sales result in an immediate increase in the bank account balance.
5. Individual amounts in the Accounts Receivable Credit column are posted in individual customer accounts on the same date that the transaction is recorded in the cash receipts journal. This procedure keeps the customer accounts up to date. The total of the Accounts Receivable column is posted to the controlling account in the general ledger when the journal is full or at the end of the month.

Chapter 3, Lesson 3-1, page 74

1. Employees can be paid one or more of the following: wage, salary, commission, cost-of-living adjustment, a share of profits, or a bonus.
2. Federal income tax, Social Security tax, and Medicare tax.
3. Calculate the number of overtime hours by subtracting 40 from the hours worked. Multiple the overtime hours by the regular rate multiplied by 1.5.
4. To encourage employees to increase sales.
5. As a percentage of net sales.
6. By consulting withholding tax tables provided by the Internal Revenue Service.
7. Total Earnings − Total Deductions = Net Pay.
8. Total earnings for the pay period.

Chapter 3, Lesson 3-2, page 83

1. The business deposits the total net pay in the payroll bank account. Checks are written to the employees from the payroll bank account.
2. It has no change.
3. Cash.
4. a. Employer Social Security tax.
   b. Employer Medicare tax.
   c. Federal unemployment tax.
   d. State unemployment tax.
5. a. Employer Social Security tax.
   b. Federal unemployment tax.
   c. State unemployment tax.

Chapter 4, Lesson 4-1, page 107

1. Ensure that all transactions are journalized, ensure that all journals have been posted, and perform bank reconciliations.
2. Outstanding deposits are added to the bank balance. Outstanding checks are deducted from the bank balance.
3. Schedule of accounts receivable and schedule of accounts payable.
4. To bring certain general ledger accounts up to date.
5. Subtract the total of the income statement accounts having a debit balance, except for Federal Income Tax Expense, from the total of the income statement accounts having a credit balance. Include any debit or credit balances of income summary accounts.

Chapter 4, Lesson 4-2, page 111

1. a. Each manager is assigned responsibility for those revenues, costs, and expenses for which the manager can make decisions and affect the outcome.
   b. The revenues, costs, and expenses must be readily identifiable with the manager's unit.
2. Revenue, cost of merchandise sold, and direct expenses.
3. Subtract the cost of merchandise sold from net sales.
4. By dividing the amount on each line by the amount of departmental net sales.
5. Favorable. The ratio increased toward 32.8%, the middle of the target range.
6. Unfavorable. The ratio increased, moving away from 22.1%, the middle of the target range.

Chapter 4, Lesson 4-3, page 116

1. Account titles and balances are obtained from the adjusted trial balance.
2. Totals are obtained from the departmental margin statements.
3. The totals of capital stock and retained earnings are obtained from the statement of stockholders' equity.

Chapter 4, Lesson 4-4, page 122

1. To prepare temporary accounts for the new fiscal period.
2. a. Income statement accounts having credit balances.
   b. Income statement accounts having debit balances.
   c. The Income Summary account.
   d. The Dividends account.
3. To prove the equality of the debits and credits in the general ledger after all closing entries have been posted.
4. Asset, liability, and owners' equity accounts.
5. a. Transactions
   b. Adjusting entries
   c. Closing entries
6. Prepare an adjusted trial balance.

Chapter 5, Lesson 5-1, page 150

1. a. Cost of the beginning merchandise inventory.
   b. Cost of the net purchases added to the inventory during the fiscal year.
2. Understated.

3. The price paid to the vendor for the merchandise and the cost of getting the merchandise in the business ready for sale.
4. Title passes to the buyer when the vendor delivers the goods to a shipping company. The buyer pays for the shipping costs.
5. a. By physically counting the items.
   b. By keeping a continuous record showing the number purchased and sold for each item.

Chapter 5, Lesson 5-2, page 158
1. The last-in, first-out (LIFO) method.
2. a. Total cost of beginning inventory and all purchases.
   b. Total units in beginning inventory and all purchases.
3. The first-in, first-out (FIFO) method.
4. To qualify to use the LIFO method for tax reporting, a business must also use LIFO for its preparation of financial statements using GAAP. Since IFRS do not allow LIFO for preparing financial statements, a business may be unable to use LIFO for its tax reporting.
5. The LIFO method.
6. a. The cost of the inventory using the FIFO, LIFO, or weighted-average method.
   b. The current market price of the inventory.

Chapter 5, Lesson 5-3, page 162
1. That a continuing relationship exists between gross profit and net sales.
2. Separate records of both cost and retail prices for net purchases, net sales, and the beginning merchandise inventory.
3. An inventory ratio of 5.0 means the business sold its average merchandise inventory 5 times during the current year.
4. On average, each item in merchandise inventory is sold 60 days after it is purchased.

Chapter 6, Lesson 6-1, page 177
1. When a customer's account is believed to be uncollectible, it should be written off because it is no longer an asset of the business.
2. Uncollectible Accounts Expense is debited; Accounts Receivable is credited. The customer's account in the accounts receivable ledger is also credited.

3. The account is reopened to provide a complete history of the customer's credit activities.

Chapter 6, Lesson 6-2, page 185
1. The direct write-off method can be used when the difference between the accounts receivable reported on the balance sheet, using the two methods, is immaterial.
2. a. Percentage of sales method.
   b. Percentage of accounts receivable method.
3. Net sales times the percentage expected to be uncollectible equals the estimated uncollectible accounts expense.
4. a. Compute an estimate for each age group by multiplying the amount of each group by the percentage estimate.
   b. Compute the total of the uncollectible estimates for all age groups.
   c. Subtract the current credit balance or add the current debit balance to the balance of Allowance for Uncollectible Accounts to determine the addition to the account.
5. There is no impact on Accounts Receivable Expense. The expense is recorded when an estimate is recorded to Allowance for Uncollectible Accounts.
6. The journal entries are identical except for the credit recorded to reopen the account. With the direct write-off method, the credit is to Uncollectible Accounts Expense. With the allowance method, the credit is to Allowance for Uncollectible Accounts.

Chapter 6, Lesson 6-3, page 188
1. Net sales on account divided by average book value of accounts receivable equals accounts receivable turnover ratio.
2. Customers took an average of 50 days to pay their accounts in full.
3. Customers are taking about 60 days to pay their accounts. The business needs to encourage prompter payment in order to reduce the number of days to receive payment to 30 days.
4. Business can be lost as some customers may buy from competitors with less restrictive credit terms.

Chapter 7, Lesson 7-1, page 204

1. All costs necessary to get the plant asset ready for its intended use are included in the cost of a plant asset.
2. The cost is allocated to individual plant assets based on their appraised values.
3. a. General information completed when the asset is purchased.
   b. Disposal section completed when the asset is discarded, sold, or traded.
   c. Section to record annual depreciation expense.
4. The assessed value of the property is multiplied by the millage rate of the governmental unit.
5. Components of the plant asset having different useful lives are assigned a cost and recorded in different plant asset accounts.

Chapter 7, Lesson 7-2, page 210

1. Matching Expenses with Revenue.
2. Because of its permanent nature, depreciation is not recorded for land.
3. Original cost, estimated salvage value, and estimated useful life.
4. A calendar month.
5. Annual depreciation expense, accumulated depreciation, and ending book value.
6. If the payment maintains the asset in its normal operation, the payment should be expensed. If the payment adds value or extends the useful life of the asset, the payment should be added to the cost of the asset.
7. The cost of the elevator should be added to the historical cost of the building. The addition adds to the value of the building.

Chapter 7, Lesson 7-3, page 217

1. The date, type, and amount of disposal.
2. Depreciation Expense will be debited and Accumulated Depreciation will be credited to bring the accounts up to date before the disposal.
3. Cash received minus the book value of the asset sold.
4. Cash plus the book value of the store equipment traded equals the book value of the new store equipment.

Chapter 7, Lesson 7-4, page 223

1. The straight-line rate (100% divided by the useful life) multiplied by the declining rate (commonly 2).
2. The book value less the salvage value.

3. The amount of use the asset receives, measured in hours, units, weight, or volume.
4. The five-year property class includes cars, general-purpose trucks, computers, manufacturing equipment, and office machinery. The seven-year property class includes office furniture and fixtures.
5. MACRS.
6. Tons of material mined times the depletion rate equals annual depletion expense. The depletion rate is calculated by dividing the estimated total value of the mineral resource by the estimated number of tons of the mineral to be recovered.

Chapter 8, Lesson 8-1, page 242

1. Reporting interest expense as Other Expense enables the comparison of operating income between companies in the same industry.
2. Interest on a line of credit is typically calculated daily because the principal amount and interest range can change during a month.
3. A line of credit provides the business with immediate access to cash; it may require days, even weeks, to arrange a note.

Chapter 8, Lesson 8-2, page 248

1. Matching Expenses with Revenue.
2. To record the amount of supplies used during the period as an expense.
3. If an adjusting entry creates a balance in an asset or liability account, the adjusting entry is reversed.
4. The balance of the prepaid expense and related expense accounts should be the same, regardless of the procedure used.
5. Similarities:
   - The ending balances in the asset and related expense accounts are identical.
   - The closing entries are identical.
   Differences:
   - The amounts of the adjusting entries are different.
   - The debit and credit accounts of the adjusting entries are reversed.
   - Only the procedure that initially debits prepaid expenses to an expense account requires a reversing entry.

Chapter 8, Lesson 8-3, page 255

1. a. Determine the amounts of the accrual.
   b. Record the expense accounts.
   c. Record the liability accounts.

2. Accountants generally reverse an adjusting entry that creates a balance in a liability account.
3. In the fiscal period in which the item is sold.
4. Similarities: With each sale on account, there is a chance that the business will incur warranty costs and that the customer will not pay its account. An estimate of these expenses is recorded in the same fiscal period as the sale.
Differences: Allowance for Uncollectible Accounts has a related asset account and is reported on the balance sheet as a contra asset account. Accrued Warranty Payable does not have a related asset and is reported as a liability on the balance sheet.

Chapter 9, Lesson 9-1, page 269
1. Deferred revenue.
2. Most of the payments will be earned during the fiscal year.
3. As a current liability.
4. If an adjusting entry creates a balance in an asset or liability account, the adjusting entry is normally reversed.
5. Creates a balance in Interest Receivable that is reported as a current asset.
6. In the Other Revenue section.

Chapter 9, Lesson 9-2, page 273
1. The sale increases a liability and increases cash on the balance sheet. The sale is not recorded on the income statement.
2. A sale is recorded when a customer pays for merchandise using a gift card.
3. Breakage Revenue.
4. Other Revenue.
5. The notes to the financial statements include the policies for how and when breakage revenue is recognized, the amount of unredeemed cards, and how gift-card-related accounts are presented on the financial statements.

Chapter 9, Lesson 9-3, page 279
1. At the time of sale.
2. Beginning balance, interest, principal, and ending balance.
3. The monthly payment does not change, the interest decreases, and the principal increases.
4. The total principal payments expected to be collected during the next fiscal period.

Chapter 10, Lesson 10-1, page 302
1. a. Submit an application to the state in which the company is to be incorporated.
   b. Prepare an articles of incorporation.
   c. Organize a board of directors.
2. A board of directors determines corporate policies and selects corporate officers to supervise the day-to-day management of the corporation.
3. Common and preferred.
4. a. To vote at stockholders' meetings, unless an exception is made for holders of a particular kind of stock.
   b. To share in a corporation's earnings.
   c. To share in the distribution of the assets of the corporation if it ceases operations and sells all its assets.
5. A single summary general ledger capital account is used for each kind of stock issued.
6. The extent to which the owner is responsible for the debts, taxes, and losses of the business.
7. The earnings of a corporation may be subject to federal and state income taxes. When the earnings of the corporation are distributed to the stockholders, individual stockholders may also have to pay income taxes on the dividends.
8. The earnings of an LLC are divided among its members. The earnings are only taxed on the members' personal tax returns.

Chapter 10, Lesson 10-2, page 309
1. By selling stock to investors or borrowing money.
2. No. Only publicly held corporations are required to file their financial statements with the Securities and Exchange Commission.
3. By issuing preferred stock that does not offer voting rights.
4. An investor willing to accept a dividend rate lower than that offered by the preferred stock will pay more than the par value. An investor demanding a dividend rate higher than that offered by the preferred stock will pay less than the par value.
5. The conversion option enables the corporation to issue the stock with a lower dividend rate. Convertible preferred stock gives the stockholder the ability to share in the income of the corporation through an increase in the market price of the common stock.
6. Stockholders should convert their stock if they believe the market price of the common stock will increase by more than 6% per year, less the effect of any dividends paid on common stock.

Chapter 11, Lesson 11-1, page 324

1. The board of directors.
2. When a board of directors declares a dividend, the corporation is obligated to pay it.
3. No transaction is recorded on the date of record.
4. Ex-dividend.
5. Credit.
6. a. The stockholders do not receive anything of value. The transaction increases the number of shares outstanding. Each stockholder retains his or her share of the corporation.
   b. The stock dividend transfers amounts among equity accounts. The market price per share of the stock will decline.

Chapter 11, Lesson 11-2, page 329

1. Debit.
2. A corporation believes that its stock is undervalued by the stock market.
3. The net income of the corporation is divided among fewer shares.
4. Dividends are not paid on treasury stock.

Chapter 11, Lesson 11-3, page 334

1. To earn a return on its cash assets until the cash is required for reinvesting in the business, paying a dividend, or reducing liabilities.
2. As a Current Asset.
3. As an Other Revenue account.
4. As an Other Revenue account.

Chapter 12, Lesson 12-1, page 345

1. a. Additional capital becomes part of a corporation's permanent capital.
   b. Dividends do not have to be paid to stockholders unless the earnings are sufficient.
2. Stockholders' equity is not spread over additional shares of stock.
3. Interest must be paid on the loan, which decreases the net income, and the loan principal must be repaid.
4. Principal, maturity value, and par value.
5. a. The stated interest rate is often a rounded percentage.
   b. Market interest rates change daily.
6. The face value of the bonds.

Chapter 12, Lesson 12-2, page 349

1. Carrying Value × Effective Interest Rate × Time as Fraction of a Year.
2. The effective interest rate has no impact on the amount of semiannual interest payments.
3. The amount of interest expense increases.
4. The carrying value decreases.

Chapter 12, Lesson 12-3, page 354

1. The liability is eliminated when a bond is retired. The debit to Bonds Payable reduces the account by the face value of the bonds.
2. Term bonds mature on the same date, while serial bonds are portions of a bond issue that mature on different dates.
3. If market interest rates fall, the corporation can be relieved of the burden of paying higher-than-market interest rates.
4. As a Loss on Redemption of Bonds reported as an Other Expense.
5. $5,000.00/25 = $200.00.
6. GAAP, $600,000.00; IFRS, $585,000.00.

Chapter 12, Lesson 12-4, page 360

1. Investment Securities.
2. Unlike the issuing corporation, the institutional investor does not record the discount or premium in a separate account.
3. Carrying value of the bonds multiplied by the effective interest rate, multiplied by time as a fraction of a year.
4. The total face value of the bonds.
5. As Other Revenue or Other Expense.

Chapter 13, Lesson 13-1, page 377

1. Managers, banks and lending agencies, and owners and potential owners.
2. Financial strength, profitability, efficiency, and market value.
3. Working capital, current ratio, and quick ratio.
4. Debt ratio, equity ratio, common equity per share, and interest coverage ratio.

Chapter 13, Lesson 13-2, page 384

1. Gross margin, operating margin, rate earned on average total assets, rate earned on average stockholders' equity, and free cash flow.

2. How well a business is using its assets to earn net income.
3. How much net income the stockholders' investment is earning.

Chapter 13, Lesson 13-3, page 390
1. That the company is, on average, collecting its accounts receivable in fewer days.
2. Market price per share divided by earnings per share.
3. Dividend yield will increase.

Chapter 13, Lesson 13-4, page 394
1. Generally accepted accounting principles (GAAP).
2. Tax laws developed by Congress.
3. Permanent differences and temporary differences.
4. All changes in equity for the period except changes caused by owner investments and owner distributions.
5. Comprehensive income must be disclosed either as a separate statement or as part of the traditional income statement.
6. The net income or loss from operations for the discontinued segment and any gain or loss from the disposal of the assets of the discontinued segment.

Chapter 14, Lesson 14-1, page 410
1. a. Determine a company's potential to produce cash in the future;
   b. Judge a company's ability to pay bills and repay debts;
   c. Explain changes in the Cash account balance;
   d. Evaluate a company's investment and equity transactions.
2. Operating Activities section.
3. A company did not replace all the supplies it used during the year. Therefore, cash was saved by not spending it on replacement supplies.
4. A company bought more merchandise inventory than it sold. Therefore, more cash was used to buy inventory than was shown on the income statement for cost of merchandise sold. The company has more cash tied up in inventory than it did at the end of the previous period.
5. Net income (net loss).

Chapter 14, Lesson 14-2, page 417
1. By analyzing the changes in long-term assets (plant assets) on the comparative balance sheet.
2. The increase in accumulated depreciation matches the depreciation expense that was recorded on the income statement. The effect on cash flows due to depreciation expense was already accounted for under operating activities.
3. By examining the changes in long-term liabilities on the balance sheet and reviewing the statement of stockholders' equity.
4. If the cash balance, end of period, shown on the statement of cash flows equals the current year's cash balance reported on the comparative balance sheet.
5. How likely the company is to be able to pay off current liabilities with its cash flows from operations.

Chapter 15, Lesson 15-1, page 438
1. Planning, operational control, and department coordination.
2. One year.
3. Company records, general economic information, company staff and managers, and good judgment.
4. Sales budget.

Chapter 15, Lesson 15-2, page 445
1. Selling expenses budget.
2. Past records, company plans, sales and selling expenses budgets, and discussions with other managers.
3. Interest income, interest expense, and gains or losses on the sale of plant assets.
4. Management must adjust the supporting budgets by either increasing revenue or decreasing expenses.

Chapter 15, Lesson 15-3, page 451
1. Good cash management requires the planning and controlling of cash so that cash will be available to meet obligations when due.
2. Quarterly cash sales, quarterly collections on account from customers, and cash to be received quarterly from other sources.

3. Quarterly cash payments for accounts payable or notes payable; each selling, administrative, and other expense item; equipment purchases; cash dividends; and investments.
4. The reasons for the decrease should be determined and action should be taken to correct the problem.

Chapter 15, Lesson 15-4, page 456
1. It helps managers identify areas that need to be reviewed, allows managers to make changes that will correct negative effects on net income for the year, and provides the opportunity to revise the budget if necessary.
2. A performance report compares actual amounts with projected amounts for the same period. A comparative income statement compares actual amounts of one period with actual amounts of a prior period.
3. Learning and growth, internal business, customer service, and financial.
4. Determine how the outcomes will be measured, set target goals, and develop an initiative to help ensure that the objectives are met.

Chapter 16, Lesson 16-1, page 473
1. The line would be sloping because the total variable costs will increase as the number of units increase.
2. Gross profit is determined by subtracting only the cost of merchandise sold from net sales. Contribution margin is determined by subtracting all variable costs from net sales.

Chapter 16, Lesson 16-2, page 478
1. In sales dollars and unit sales.
2. A net income for the company.
3. A net loss for the company.
4. By using the contribution margin per unit.
5. Prepare an income statement using the breakeven point numbers. If the breakeven point is accurate, net income will be zero.

Chapter 16, Lesson 16-3, page 486
1. Total fixed costs plus planned net income.
2. They intersect.
3. Total variable costs will increase.
4. Total fixed costs will remain the same.

Chapter 17, Lesson 17-1, page 506
1. a. Direct materials.
   b. Direct labor.
   c. Factory overhead.
2. Work in process.
3. To keep a record of all charges for direct materials, direct labor, and factory overhead for each specific job.
4. To authorize transfer of items from the storeroom to the factory.
5. Work in Process.
6. The amount of time spent by each employee on each job.
7. Work in Process and Factory Overhead.

Chapter 17, Lesson 17-2, page 511
1. During the fiscal period before all factory overhead for the current period is known.
2. Overapplied overhead.
3. Applied factory overhead is only an estimate used to assign factory overhead to jobs. The amount of actual factory overhead is determined at the end of the period. It consists of the actual costs for indirect labor, indirect materials, and other factory expenses.

Chapter 17, Lesson 17-3, page 518
1. The total value for all finished goods ledger cards.
2. Debit Finished Goods, credit Work in Process.
3. Debit Cost of Goods Sold, credit Finished Goods.
4. Statement of cost of good manufactured.
5. Overapplied overhead is subtracted from the cost of goods sold.
6. Current Assets.

Chapter 17, Lesson 17-4, page 524
1. Direct materials and direct labor.
2. Labor efficiency standard.
3. Total Materials Variance = Actual Cost − Standard Cost.
4. Favorable.
5. Answers will vary. Some examples: Spending less on materials may require more labor hours in rework, and spending more on materials may allow the use of less experienced workers.
6. Total Labor Variance = Actual Cost − Standard Cost.

Chapter 18, Lesson 18-1, page 539

1. A relevant cost must be a future cost, and it must differ between alternatives.
2. As a relevant cost.
3. If the special order will affect sales for the product and if normal customers will be upset by the discounted price of the special order.
4. Fixed costs must be analyzed to determine if they will remain or be discontinued. If they will remain, they must be added to the fixed costs of the other departments. If they will be discontinued, that amount is a relevant cost and should be included in the analysis.
5. Sell the product at the split-off point.
6. Three years.

Chapter 18, Lesson 18-2, page 547

1. There is an expectation that invested money will increase over time.
2. Compounding interest causes the annual interest earned to increase each year.
3. When the problem is to determine the present value of an amount to be received in the future.
4. A series of equal cash flows.
5. Present value of an annuity table.

Chapter 18, Lesson 18-3, page 552

1. Net present value takes into account the time value of money.
2. Present value of an annuity of $1.
3. Present value of $1.
4. The option with the higher positive (or lower negative) net present value.

Chapter 19, Lesson 19-1, page 566

1. When a single process with a continuous flow of inputs produces the same product.
2. An estimate must be made of the cost connected with goods still in production.
3. Debit Work in Process—Shipping; credit Work in Process—Processing.
4. The actual units processed and the equivalent units of production.
5. The total costs of production and the per unit costs of production.

Chapter 19, Lesson 19-2, page 573

1. When there is a direct connection between direct labor hours and overhead costs.
2. Technology may decrease the proportion of direct labor and direct materials costs while increasing the proportion of indirect costs.
3. Unit-level, batch-level, product-level, and facility-sustaining level.
4. Companies should use the method that most accurately reflects the actual cost of each product.
5. Activity-based costing requires initial cost and effort to implement, and it does not conform to GAAP.

Chapter 19, Lesson 19-3, page 576

1. Cost-based pricing focuses on company costs instead of the customer; it may lead to prices that are too high or too low; it provides no incentive to contain costs; and if the cost of the product changes and the price is not changed, the profit margin will change.
2. When products or services have emotional value, are in high demand/low supply, will increase efficiency or improve health, and there is little or no competition for a product or service that is necessary.
3. Target cost equals desired selling price per unit minus required profit per unit.

Chapter 20, Lesson 20-1, page 596

1. The purpose of accounting control systems is to produce accurate financial statements and other reports and to ensure that the assets of the business are secure and are used only as authorized by management.
2. Intent. An error is unintentional, whereas a fraud is intentional.
3. Financial statement misstatement.
4. Control environment.
5. Public Company Accounting Oversight Board (PCAOB).
6. Gain an understanding of the system.

Chapter 20, Lesson 20-2, page 600

1. A written description or narrative.
2. Upper left corner of the page.

3. The transfer of information or the movement of a document.
4. If the added cost of the control is offset by the benefit of reducing the risk of fraud.

Chapter 20, Lesson 20-3, page 607
1. Vouchers Payable.
2. Purchases journal.
3. Vouchers Payable.

Chapter 20, Lesson 20-4, page 611
1. Authorized managers.
2. The check is sent to the vendor.
3. The purchase order copy sent to the Receiving Department does not contain the quantity of goods ordered.
4. The documents are cancelled by the check signer.

Chapter 21, Lesson 21-1, page 629
1. A partnership has equity accounts for each partner; in contrast, a corporation records all stockholder's ownership in a single set of accounts.
2. The existing partnership is terminated and a new partnership is formed.
3. To avoid misunderstandings. Some states require that partnership agreements be in writing.
4. The existing partnership is terminated.
5. The right of all partners to contract for a partnership.
6. A balance sheet may not report adequately the value of the owner's contribution to the partnership. Assets such as inventory and plant assets should be valued at their current market value.

Chapter 21, Lesson 21-2, page 636
1. The existing partnership is terminated.
2. Total equity (including the investment by the new partner) multiplied by the new partner's share of equity equals the new partner's equity.
3. Goodwill is debited; the existing partners' capital accounts are credited.

Chapter 22, Lesson 22-1, page 652
1. a. Fixed percentage
   b. Percentage of total equity
   c. Interest on equity

d. Salaries
e. Combination of methods
2. In the partnership agreement.
3. When the amount of guaranteed distributions exceeds the amount of net income available for distribution.
4. The partner's drawing account.
5. Withdrawals are debited to a drawing account.

Chapter 22, Lesson 22-2, page 657
1. Because a partnership does not pay federal income tax.
2. The statement reports the changes in each partner's equity.
3. Partners are personally taxed on their share of partnership net income. In contrast, withdrawals are considered the withdrawals of partnership equity and are not subject to income taxes.
4. Each partner personally pays both the employee and employer portion of Social Security and Medicare taxes on his or her share of partnership net income.

Chapter 22, Lesson 22-3, page 663
1. Noncash assets are sold, and available cash is used to pay the creditors.
2. The partners' capital accounts.

Chapter 23, Lesson 23-1, page 682
1. A governmental organization must use a subjective evaluation of the quality of the service provided. Its ability to continue operations is not dependent on its effectiveness or efficiency as long as funding is available.
2. a. The accounting equation is applied.
   b. An appropriate chart of accounts is prepared.
   c. Transactions are analyzed into debit and credit elements.
   d. Transactions are journalized and posted to ledgers.
   e. Financial statements are prepared for each fiscal period.
   f. Most of the same accounting concepts are applied.
3. A fund accounting system emphasizes strong controls on the use of funds. The amount in a fund can be spent only for the specified purpose of the fund.

4. Expenditures are recorded when a cash disbursement or liability is incurred. An expense is recorded when an asset is used or a service is rendered in the process of earning revenue.
5. The governmental operating budget is used to authorize and provide the basis for control of financial operations during a fiscal year.
6. The approved budget impacts the tax rate and provides authorization for managers to make expenditures for specified purposes.
7. Estimated Revenues is debited; Appropriations and Budgetary Fund Balance are credited.

Chapter 23, Lesson 23-2, page 686
1. When property taxes are levied.
2. Cash is debited; Taxes Receivable—Current is credited.
3. Cash is debited; Taxes Receivable—Delinquent is credited.

Chapter 23, Lesson 23-3, page 693
1. A commitment to pay for goods or services that have been ordered but not yet provided.
2. a. The encumbrance entry is reversed to remove the estimated amount from the encumbrance and the reserve for encumbrance accounts.
   b. The expenditure is recorded.
3. Because the organization does not earn a net income, it has no need for expense information. Expenditures rather than expenses are recorded. The primary objective is to control financial resources rather than determine net income.

4. A certificate of deposit (or CD) is a document with the maturity date and interest to be paid by a bank and is issued as evidence of money invested with the bank.

Chapter 24, Lesson 24-1, page 706
1. A business measures performance primarily through determining the amount of net income. A not-forprofit organization's performance is measured primarily by the services provided and the efficiency with which resources are used.
2. Encumbrance accounts with zero balances.
3. None. A governmental fund has expenditures rather than expenses.
4. Interest Revenue.

Chapter 24, Lesson 24-2, page 714
1. The prior year's balance sheet.
2. Excess of expenditures over revenues.
3. Unfavorable.
4. Unreserved Fund Balance.
5. Reserve for Encumbrances—Prior Year and Taxes Receivable—Delinquent.
6. The basic financial statements in the CAFR include (1) government-wide financial statements, (2) individual fund financial statements, and (3) notes to the financial statements.
7. Whether the government organization obtains most of its revenue from fees charged to individuals and businesses using its services.

GLOSSARY

A

Account A record that summarizes all the transactions pertaining to a single item in the accounting equation. (p. 9)

Accounting cycle The series of accounting activities included in recording financial information for a fiscal period. (p. 121)

Accounting equation An equation showing the relationship among assets, liabilities, and owners' equity. (p. 7)

Accounts receivable turnover ratio The number of times the average amount of accounts receivable is collected during a specified period. (p. 186)

Accrued expenses Expenses incurred in one fiscal period, but not paid until a later fiscal period. (p. 249)

Accrued revenue Revenue earned in one fiscal period but not received until a later fiscal period. (p. 267)

Acquisition the combination of two corporations where the acquirer purchases a significant percentage of the target's stock. (p. 331)

Activity rate The price for each unit of activity, determined by Manufacturing. (p. 569)

Activity-based costing (ABC) Allocating factory overhead based on the level of major activities. (p. 567)

Adjusted trial balance A trial balance prepared after adjusting entries are posted. (p. 103)

Adjusting entries Journal entries recorded to update general ledger accounts at the end of a fiscal period. (p. 98)

Administrative expenses budget A statement that shows the projected expenses for all operating expenses not directly related to selling operations. (p. 441)

Aging accounts receivable Analyzing accounts receivable according to when they are due. (p. 180)

Allowance method Crediting the estimated value of uncollectible accounts to a contra account. (p. 178)

Amortization schedule A schedule of the periodic payments on a note. (p. 275)

Annuity A series of equal cash flows. (p. 545)

Applied overhead The estimated amount of factory overhead recorded on cost sheets. (p. 507)

Appropriations Authorizations to make expenditures for specific purposes. (p. 680)

Articles of incorporation A legal document that identifies basic characteristics of a corporation, which is a part of the application submitted to a state to become a corporation. (p. 294)

Assessed value The value of an asset determined by tax authorities for the purpose of calculating taxes. (p. 202)

Asset Anything of value that is owned. (p. 7)

Authority The ability of an employee to authorize a transaction. (p. 594)

Automatic check deposit Depositing payroll checks directly to an employee's checking or savings account. (p. 76)

B

Balance sheet A financial statement that reports assets, liabilities, and owners' equity on a specific date. (p. 114)

Balanced scorecard A planning and measurement system developed by R. S. Kaplan and D. P. Norton to use multiple performance measures to ensure that a company's vision and strategy are reflected in its goals and activities. (p. 453)

Batch-level costs Resources used on activities connected with a group of products. (p. 568)

Board of directors A group of persons elected by the stockholders to govern a corporation. (p. 295)

Bond A long-term promise to pay a specified amount on a specified date and to pay interest at stated intervals. (p. 342)

Bond amortization Reducing the amount of a bond discount or premium over time. (p. 347)

Bond issue All bonds representing the total amount of a loan. (p. 342)

Book value The difference between an asset's account balance and its related contra account balance. (p. 178)

Book value of a plant asset The original cost of a plant asset minus accumulated depreciation. (p. 206)

Breakage The value of unredeemed gift cards. (p. 272)

Breakeven analysis Using cost-volume-profit (CVP) techniques to determine a company's breakeven point. (p. 474)

Breakeven point The amount of sales at which net sales is equal to total costs. (p. 474)

Budget A financial road map used by individuals and companies as a guide for spending and saving. (p. 432)

Budget period The length of time covered by a budget. (p. 433)

Budgeted income statement A statement that reports a company's projected sales, costs, expenses, and net income. (p. 443)

Budgeting Planning the financial operations of a business. (p. 432)

Buyback A program approved by a board of directors authorizing the corporation to repurchase its stock. (p. 325)

C

Call option The right of a corporation to repurchase its security for a specified price. (p. 350)

Callable bond A bond that can be called before its maturity date. (p. 350)

Capital expenditures Purchases of plant assets used in the operation of a business. (p. 383)

Capital stock The total shares of ownership in a corporation. (p. 113)

Carrying value The face value of a bond adjusted for any unamortized discount or premium. (p. 347)

Cash budget A statement that shows for each month or quarter a projection of a company's beginning cash balance, cash receipts, cash payments, and ending cash balance. (p. 450)

Cash discount A deduction that a vendor allows on the invoice amount to encourage prompt payment. (p. 20)

Cash equivalents Short-term, liquid investments that are readily convertible to cash and which mature in three months or less. (p. 371)

Cash flow The cash receipts and cash payments of a company. (p. 115)

Cash payments budget A statement that reports projected cash payments for a budget period. (p. 449)

Cash receipts budget A statement that reports projected cash receipts for a budget period. (p. 447)

Certificate of deposit A document issued by a bank as evidence of money invested with the bank. (p. 691)

Charter The legal right for a business to conduct operations as a corporation. (p. 295)

Check register A journal used in a voucher system to record cash payments. (p. 606)

Closing entries Journal entries used to prepare temporary accounts for a new fiscal period. (p. 117)

Common equity per share The amount of common stockholders' equity belonging to a single share of common stock. (p. 376)

Common stock Stock that does not give stockholders any special preferences. (p. 296)

Comparative financial statements Financial statements that provide information for multiple fiscal periods. (p. 368)

Compounding Earning interest on previously earned interest. (p. 541)

Comprehensive annual financial report The detailed financial report of a governmental agency. (p. 712)

Comprehensive income All changes in equity for the period, except changes caused by owner investments and owner distributions. (p. 392)

Consignee The person or business that receives goods on consignment. (p. 146)

Consignment Goods that are given to a business to sell but for which title remains with the vendor. (p. 146)

Consignor The person or business that gives goods on consignment. (p. 146)

Contra account An account that reduces a related account on a financial statement. (p. 18)

Contribution margin Income determined by subtracting all variable costs from net sales. (p. 471)

Control activities The policies and procedures designed to prevent or detect errors or fraud. (p. 593)

Control environment The attitude and actions of management that indicate its commitment to strong internal controls and ethical standards. (p. 593)

Controlling account An account in a general ledger that summarizes all accounts in a subsidiary ledger. (p. 11)

Conversion costs The sum of the costs for direct labor and overhead. (p. 561)

Conversion option The ability of a security to be traded for a specified number of shares of another security. (p. 307)

Conversion price The par or stated value of the preferred stock divided by the conversion ratio. (p. 307)

Conversion ratio The number of shares of common stock received when a security is converted. (p. 307)

Convertible preferred stock Preferred stock that can be exchanged for a specified number of common shares. (p. 307)

Corporation An organization with the legal rights of a person which many persons or other corporations may own. (p. 294)

Cost driver The factor that affects the cost of an activity. (p. 569)

Cost ledger A ledger containing all cost sheets for products in the process of being manufactured. (p. 497)

Cost of production report A report that shows unit information and cost information for a department using a process costing system. (p. 564)

Cost pool A group of costs related to a specific activity. (p. 569)

Cost-based pricing A method of establishing a price for a product or service in which a fixed percentage or a fixed sum is added to the cost of the product or service. Also known as *markup pricing*. (p. 574)

Cost-volume-profit (CVP) analysis A method used to determine how changes in costs and volume affect a company's profit. (p. 468)

Credit memorandum A form prepared by the vendor showing the amount deducted for sales returns and allowances. (p. 43)

Current assets Cash and other assets expected to be exchanged for cash or consumed within a year. (p. 198)

Current liabilities Liabilities that are due within a short time, usually a year. (p. 237)

Current ratio A ratio that measures the relationship of current assets to current liabilities. (p. 374)

Custody The physical access to the assets involved in a transaction. (p. 594)

D

Date of a note The day a note is issued. (p. 236)

Date of declaration The date on which a board of directors votes to distribute a dividend. (p. 318)

Date of payment The date on which dividends are actually to be paid to stockholders. (p. 318)

Date of record The date that determines which stockholders are to receive dividends. (p. 318)

Days' sales in accounts receivable The average period of time to collect an account receivable. (p. 186)

Days' sales in inventory The time needed to sell an average amount of merchandise inventory. (p. 161)

Debit memorandum A form prepared by the customer showing the price deduction taken by the customer for a return or an allowance. (p. 17)

Debt financing Obtaining capital by borrowing money for a period of time. (p. 236)

Debt ratio Total liabilities divided by total assets. (p. 375)

Declaring a dividend Action by a board of directors to distribute corporate earnings to stockholders. (p. 318)

Declining-balance method of depreciation A type of accelerated depreciation that multiplies the book value of an asset by a constant depreciation rate to determine annual depreciation. (p. 218)

Deflation The rate at which the price for goods and services decreases over time. (p. 155)

Departmental accounting system An accounting system showing accounting information for two or more departments. (p. 13)

Departmental margin The revenue earned by a department less its cost of merchandise sold and less its direct expenses. (p. 109)

Departmental margin statement A statement that reports departmental margin for a specific department. (p. 109)

Depletion The decrease in the value of a plant asset because of the removal of a natural resource. (p. 222)

Depreciation expense The portion of a plant asset's cost that is transferred to an expense account in each fiscal period during that asset's useful life. (p. 102)

Differential analysis Analyzing only the differences between the revenues and expenses resulting from each of two options. (p. 534)

Direct expense An operating expense identifiable with and chargeable to the operation of a specific department. (p. 108)

Direct labor Salaries of factory workers who make a product. (p. 496)

Direct materials Materials that are of significant value in the cost of a finished product and that become an identifiable part of the product. (p. 496)

Direct method Listing cash flows from operating activities as cash receipts and cash payments. (p. 403)

Direct write-off method Recording uncollectible accounts expense only when an amount is actually known to be uncollectible. (p. 175)

Distribution deficit A negative balance that remains after partner salaries and interest are subtracted from total income. (p. 650)

Dividend yield The relationship between dividends per share and market price per share. (p. 389)

Dividends Earnings distributed to stockholders. (p. 113)

Double taxation The taxation of earnings when earned by a corporation and again when dividends are received by stockholders. (p. 298)

Double-entry accounting The recording of debit and credit parts of a transaction. (p. 8)

E

Earnings per share (EPS) Net income after federal income tax divided by the number of outstanding shares of stock. (p. 387)

EBIT Earnings before interest expense and taxes. (p. 376)

Effective interest rate The market interest rate at the time bonds are issued. (p. 346)

Electronic funds transfer (EFT) A computerized cash payments system that transfers funds without the use of checks, currency, or other paper documents. (p. 76)

Employee earnings record A business form used to record details of an employee's earnings and deductions. (p. 73)

Encumbrance A commitment to pay for goods or services that have been ordered but not yet provided. (p. 687)

Equities Financial rights to the assets of a business. (p. 7)

Equity ratio The ratio found by dividing stockholders' equity by total assets. (p. 375)

Equivalent units of production (EUP) An estimate of the amount of direct materials, direct labor, and overhead that have already been incurred on partially finished units, stated in terms of fully completed units. (p. 561)

Error An unintentional mistake. (p. 593)

Expenditures Cash disbursements and liabilities incurred for the cost of goods delivered or services rendered. (p. 676)

F

Face value The amount to be paid to a bondholder at the bond maturity date. (p. 343)

Facility-sustaining level costs Resources used to support the entire company and production process. (p. 568)

Factory overhead All expenses other than direct materials and direct labor that apply to making products. (p. 496)

Fair market value balance sheet A financial statement that presents the fair market value of a company's assets, liabilities, and owner's equity. (p. 627)

Fiduciary fund A fund that reports assets held by a government agency to benefit a specific group of individuals. (p. 712)

File maintenance The procedure for arranging accounts in a general ledger, assigning account numbers, and keeping records current. (p. 11)

Financial ratio A comparison between two components of financial information. (p. 110)

Financial statement misstatement The manipulation of amounts reported on a financial statement. (p. 593)

Financing activities Cash receipts and payments involving debt or equity transactions. (p. 115)

Finished goods Manufactured products that are fully completed. (p. 496)

Finished goods ledger A ledger containing records of all finished goods on hand. This ledger is similar to a materials ledger. (p. 497)

First-in, first-out inventory costing method Using the price of merchandise purchased first to calculate the cost of merchandise sold first. (p. 151)

Fiscal period The length of time for which a business summarizes its financial information and reports its financial performance. (p. 96)

Fiscal year A fiscal period consisting of 12 consecutive months. (p. 96)

Fixed costs Costs that remain constant regardless of a change in business activity. (p. 470)

Flowchart A diagram that uses symbols and connecting lines to represent a process. (p. 597)

Fraud The theft of assets by employees or the intentional misstatement of financial information. (p. 593)

Free cash flow A measure equal to cash flows from operations less cash used for capital expenditures. (p. 383)

Fund A governmental accounting entity with a set of accounts in which assets always equal liabilities plus equities. (p. 675)

Fund equity The amount of assets less liabilities of a governmental organization. (p. 676)

Future value The value of money invested today at some point in the future. (p. 541)

Future value of an annuity The future value of an equal series of investments over equal time periods at a given interest rate. (p. 545)

G

General fixed assets Governmental properties that benefit future periods. (p. 690)

General ledger A ledger that contains all accounts needed to prepare financial statements. (p. 11)

Generally accepted accounting principles The standards and rules that accountants follow while recording and reporting financial activities. (p. 151)

Goodwill The value of a business in excess of the total investment of owners. (p. 633)

Governmental fund A fund that accounts for the tax-supported activities of a government agency. (p. 712)

Gross margin Gross profit as a percent of net sales. (p. 378)

Gross profit The operating revenue remaining after cost of merchandise sold has been deducted. (p. 109)

Gross profit method of estimating inventory Estimating inventory by using the previous year's percentage of gross profit on operations. (p. 159)

H

Half-year convention A method that recognizes one half of a year's depreciation in the year of acquisition. (p. 207)

Hostile takeover A combination achieved without the approval of the board of directors of the target corporation. (p. 331)

I

Income statement A financial statement showing the revenue and expenses for a fiscal period. (p. 113)

Indirect expense An operating expense chargeable to overall business operations and not identifiable with a specific department. (p. 108)

Indirect labor Salaries paid to factory workers who are not actually making products. (p. 496)

Indirect materials Materials used in the completion of a product that are of insignificant value to justify accounting for separately. (p. 496)

Indirect method Listing cash flows from operating activities by starting with net income and adjusting for non-cash items. (p. 403)

Inflation The rate at which the price for goods and services increases over time. (p. 154)

Information and communication The processes used to collect information about how the business is achieving its control goals. (p. 593)

Initial public offering The initial issue of a security on a public exchange. Also called *IPO*. (p. 303)

Installment note A note resulting from a sale that requires monthly payments of principal and interest. (p. 274)

Institutional investors Organizations that manage the investments of individual investors. (p. 355)

Intangible asset An asset that does not have physical substance. (p. 634)

Interest An amount paid for the use of money for a period of time. (p. 236)

Interest coverage ratio The number of times a company can cover its interest expense with its earnings. (p. 376)

Interest expense Interest accrued on borrowed funds. (p. 239)

Interest rate The percentage of the principal that is due for the use of the funds secured by a note. (p. 236)

Interest-bearing note A note having a stated interest rate. (p. 239)

Internal control structure A process designed to achieve effectiveness and efficiency of operations, reliability of financial reporting, and compliance with applicable laws and regulations. (p. 593)

Internal controls Processes and procedures employed within a business to ensure that its operations are conducted ethically, accurately, and reliably. (p. 592)

International financial reporting standards A set of accounting standards being adopted across the world. (p. 156)

Inventory record A form used during a physical inventory to record information about each item of merchandise on hand. (p. 148)

Inventory turnover ratio The number of times the average amount of merchandise inventory is sold during a specific period of time. (p. 161)

Investing activities Cash receipts and cash payments involving the sale or purchase of assets used to earn revenue over a period of time. (p. 115)

Invoice A form describing the goods or services sold, the quantity, the price, and the terms of sale. (p. 602)

J

Job order costing Measuring the manufacturing costs of a specific order or batch as it goes through the production process. (p. 497)

Joint costs The costs of processing joint products to their split-off point. (p. 537)

Joint products Two or more products that are produced simultaneously with the same processes and costs and are inseparable up to a certain point. (p. 537)

Journal A form for recording transactions in chronological order. (p. 8)

L

Labor price standard The estimated cost per hour of direct labor. Also referred to as the *labor rate standard*. (p. 519)

Labor price variance The difference between the actual price paid for labor and the labor price standard at the actual quantity used. (p. 523)

Labor quantity standard The estimated amount of direct labor needed to produce one unit of output. Also referred to as the *labor efficiency standard*. (p. 519)

Labor quantity variance The difference between the actual quantity of labor used in production and the standard quantity of labor for that level of production at the standard price. (p. 523)

Last-in, first-out inventory costing method Using the price of merchandise purchased last to calculate the cost of merchandise sold first. (p. 152)

Ledger A group of accounts. (p. 11)

Liability An amount owed by a business. (p. 7)

Limited liability corporation A type of corporation that does not pay taxes on its earnings. The earnings are divided among its members and are only taxed on the members' personal tax returns, thus eliminating the disadvantage of double taxation. Also called *LLC*. (p. 298)

Line of credit A bank loan agreement that provides immediate short-term access to cash. (p. 241)

Liquidation of a partnership The process of paying a partnership's liabilities and distributing remaining assets to the partners. (p. 658)

Lower of cost or market inventory costing method Using the lower of cost or market price to calculate the cost of the ending merchandise inventory. (p. 157)

M

Market value of a share of stock The price at which a share of stock may be sold on the stock market at any given time. (p. 388)

Materials ledger A ledger containing all records of materials. (p. 497)

Materials price standard The estimated cost per unit of direct materials. (p. 519)

Materials price variance The difference between the actual price paid for materials and the materials price standard at the actual quantity purchased and used. (p. 521)

Materials quantity standard The estimated amount of direct materials to be used per unit of output. (p. 519)

Materials quantity variance The difference between the actual quantity of materials purchased and used in production and the standard quantity of materials for that level of production at the standard price. (p. 521)

Maturity date The date on which the principal of a note is due to be repaid. (p. 236)

Maturity value The amount that is due on the maturity date of a note. (p. 239)

Merchandising business A business that purchases and sells goods. (p. 13)

Millage rate The tax rate used to calculate property taxes. (p. 202)

Modified Accelerated Cost Recovery System (MACRS) A depreciation method required by the Internal Revenue Service to be used for income tax calculation purposes for most plant assets. (p. 220)

Modified half-year convention A method that recognizes a full year's depreciation if the asset is acquired in the first half of the year. (p. 207)

Monitoring The process management uses to determine whether its policies are operating effectively. (p. 593)

Mutual agency The right of all partners to contract for a partnership. (p. 624)

N

Narrative A written description of the flow of documents and information between employees, departments, and external parties. (p. 597)

Net cash flows The difference between the cash receipts and cash payments. (p. 548)

Net present value The difference between the present value of the cash flows of the investment and the amount of the investment. (p. 548)

Net realizable value See *book value*.

Noninterest-bearing note A note that deducts interest from the face value of the note. (p. 239)

No-par-value stock A share of stock that has no authorized value printed on the stock certificate. (p. 297)

Notes payable Promissory notes signed by a business and given to a creditor. (p. 236)

Not-for-profit organization An organization providing goods or services with neither a conscious motive nor an expectation of earning a profit. Also referred to as *nonprofit organizations*. (p. 672)

O

Occupational fraud The theft of business assets by an employee. It is also referred to as *embezzlement* or *asset misappropriation*. (p. 593)

Operating activities The cash receipts and payments necessary to operate a business on a day-to-day basis. (p. 115)

Operating budget A plan of current expenditures and the proposed means of financing those expenditures. (p. 678)

Operating margin Income from operations as a percent of net sales. (p. 379)

Other revenue and expenses budget A statement that shows budgeted revenue and expenses from activities other than normal operations. (p. 442)

Overapplied overhead The amount by which applied factory overhead is more than actual factory overhead. (p. 510)

Owners' equity The amount remaining after the value of all liabilities is subtracted from the value of all assets. (p. 7)

Owners' equity statement A financial statement that summarizes the changes in owners' equity during a fiscal period. (p. 654)

P

Par value A value assigned to a share of stock and printed on the stock certificate. (p. 296)

Partnership A business in which two or more persons combine their assets and skills. (p. 298)

Partnership agreement A written agreement setting forth the conditions under which a partnership is to operate. Also known as the *articles of partnership*. (p. 624)

Par-value stock A share of stock that has par value. (p. 296)

Pay period The number of days or weeks of work covered by an employee's paycheck. (p. 64)

Payback period The amount of time required to recover the cost of an investment. (p. 538)

Payroll The total amount earned by all employees for a pay period. (p. 64)

Payroll register An accounting form that summarizes the earnings, deductions, and net pay of all employees for one pay period. (p. 68)

Payroll taxes Taxes based on the payroll of a business. (p. 64)

Performance report A report showing a comparison of projected and actual amounts for a specific period. (p. 453)

Permanent difference A difference between net income and taxable income only for that year that is never balanced out in a future year. (p. 391)

Personal property All property not classified as real property. (p. 202)

Petty cash An amount of cash kept on hand and used for making small payments. (p. 25)

Plant asset record An accounting form on which a business records information about each plant asset. (p. 202)

Plant assets Physical assets that will be used for a number of years in the operation of a business. (p. 102)

Point-of-sale (POS) terminal A specialized computer used to collect, store, and report all the information about a sales transaction. (p. 49)

Post-closing trial balance A trial balance prepared after the closing entries are posted. (p. 120)

Posting Transferring transaction information from a journal entry to a ledger account. (p. 15)

Preferred stock A class of stock that gives preferred shareholders preference over common shareholders in dividends along with other rights. (p. 296)

Prepaid expense Cash paid for an expense in one fiscal period that is not used until a later period. (p. 243)

Present value The current value of a future cash payment or receipt. (p. 544)

Present value of an annuity An amount invested at a given interest rate that supports the payments of an annuity. (p. 546)

Price-earnings ratio The relationship between the market value per share and earnings per share of a stock. (p. 388)

Prime interest rate The interest rate charged to a bank's most creditworthy customers. (p. 241)

Principal The original amount of a note. (p. 236)

Privately held corporation A corporation owned by a small number of individuals. (p. 303)

Process costing Measuring the manufacturing costs of similar goods as they flow continuously from one production process to another. (p. 497)

Product-level costs Resources used to support the entire product line. (p. 568)

Promissory note A written and signed promise to pay a sum of money at a specified time. (p. 236)

Proprietary fund A fund that accounts for the financial transactions of a government organization that operates as a for-profit enterprise. (p. 712)

Proprietorship A business owned by one person. (p. 298)

Publicly held corporation A corporation having its stock traded on public exchanges. (p. 303)

Purchase order A form requesting that a vendor sell merchandise to a business. (p. 602)

Purchases budget A statement that shows the projected amount of purchases that will be required during a budget period. (p. 437)

Purchases discount When a company that has purchased merchandise on account takes a cash discount. (p. 20)

Q

Quick assets Cash and other current assets that can be converted quickly into cash. (p. 374)

Quick ratio A ratio that measures the relationship of quick assets to current liabilities. (p. 374)

R

Rate earned on average stockholders' equity The relationship between net income and average stockholders' equity. (p. 382)

Rate earned on average total assets The relationship between net income and average total assets. (p. 381)

Real property Land and anything attached to it; also called *real estate*. (p. 202)

Realization Cash received from the sale of assets during liquidation of a partnership. (p. 658)

Receiving report A form that lists the item received from a vendor. (p. 602)

Reclassification entry An entry that transfers account balances between accounts on one financial statement. (p. 276)

Recording The entry of a transaction in the financial records. (p. 594)

Registration statement The document submitted to the SEC for permission to sell a security on a public exchange. (p. 303)

Relevant costs Costs that are different between two options. (p. 534)

Relevant revenue Revenues that are different between two options. (p. 534)

Requisition A form requesting the purchase of merchandise. (p. 602)

Responsibility accounting Assigning control of revenues, costs, and expenses to a specific manager. (p. 108)

Responsibility statements Financial statements reporting revenue, costs, and direct expenses under a specific department's control. (p. 109)

Retail method of estimating inventory Estimating inventory by using a percentage based on both cost and retail prices. (p. 160)

Retained earnings An amount earned by a corporation and not yet distributed to stockholders. (p. 113)

Retiring a bond issue Paying the amounts owed to bondholders for a bond issue. (p. 350)

Reversing entry An entry made at the beginning of one fiscal period to reverse an adjusting entry made in the previous fiscal period. (p. 245)

Risk assessment The process of determining whether an error or fraud could occur. (p. 593)

S

Salary A fixed annual sum of money divided among equal pay periods. (p. 64)

Sales budget A statement that shows the projected net sales for a budget period. (p. 436)

Sales discount A cash discount on a sale taken by the customer. (p. 47)

Sales mix The relative distribution of sales among various products. (p. 485)

Salvage value The amount that will be received for an asset at the time of its disposal. (p. 205)

Schedule of accounts payable A listing of vendor accounts, account balances, and the total amount due all vendors. Some businesses call this listing an accounts payable trial balance. (p. 97)

Schedule of accounts receivable A listing of customer accounts, account balances, and total amount due from all customers. (p. 97)

Segregation of duties Dividing the tasks of the accounting system among employees in different functions. (p. 594)

Selling expenses budget A statement that shows projected expenditures related directly to the selling operations. (p. 439)

Serial bonds Portions of a bond issue that mature on different dates. (p. 350)

Share of stock A unit of ownership in a corporation. (p. 294)

Source document A business paper from which information is obtained for a journal entry. (p. 7)

Special journal A journal used to record only one kind of transaction. (p. 8)

Split-off point The point where joint products are separable into identifiable products. (p. 537)

Standard An estimated amount of direct materials or direct labor, usually in price or quantity, established for each unit produced. (p. 519)

Standard costing system A system of setting standards for each cost of production. (p. 519)

Stated interest rate The rate of interest used to calculate periodic interest payments on a bond. (p. 343)

Stated-value stock No-par-value stock that is assigned a value by a corporation. Stated-value stock is similar to par-value stock except that the value is not printed on the stock certificates. (p. 297)

Statement of cash flows A financial statement that summarizes cash receipts and cash payments resulting from business activities during a fiscal period. (p. 115)

Statement of cost of goods manufactured A statement showing details about the cost of finished goods. (p. 514)

Statement of revenues, expenditures, and changes in fund balance A statement that reports the sources of revenues and the expenditure of funds of a government organization. (p. 676)

Statement of stockholders' equity A financial statement that shows changes in a corporation's ownership for a fiscal period. (p. 113)

Statutory consolidation The combining of two independent corporations into a new single entity. (p. 331)

Statutory merger The combination of two corporations where only one corporation continues as a legal entity. (p. 331)

Stock certificate Written evidence of the number of shares that each stockholder owns in a corporation. (p. 296)

Stock dividend The payment of a dividend with the stock of the corporation. (p. 321)

Stock ledger A file of stock records for all merchandise on hand. (p. 147)

Stock record A form used to show the type of merchandise, quantity received, quantity sold, and balance on hand. (p. 147)

Stockholder The owner of one or more shares of stock. (p. 294)

Stockholders' equity The owners' equity in a corporation. (p. 7)

Straight-line method of depreciation Recording an equal amount of depreciation expense for a plant asset in each year of its useful life. (p. 206)

Subsidiary ledger A ledger that is summarized in a single general ledger account. (p. 11)

Sunk cost A cost that occurred in the past and cannot be recovered by a future decision. (p. 534)

T

Target costing A method of establishing a price for a product or service, based on the price the customer is willing to pay and controlling the cost of the product so that the company still makes a profit. (p. 575)

Tax base The maximum amount of earnings on which a tax is calculated. (p. 65)

Tax levy Authorized action taken by a governmental organization to collect taxes by legal authority. (p. 683)

Temporary difference A difference between net income and taxable income for more than one period that reverses out over the entire period. (p. 391)

Term bonds Bonds that all mature on the same date. (p. 350)

Terminal summary The report that summarizes the cash and credit card sales of a point-of-sale terminal. (p. 49)

Time value of money The expectation that invested money will increase over time. (p. 540)

Total costs All costs for a specific period of time. (p. 469)

Total labor variance The difference between the actual cost of labor and

the expected standard cost of labor. (p. 522)

Total materials variance The difference between the actual cost of materials and the expected standard cost of materials. (p. 520)

Treasury stock A corporation's own stock that has been issued and reacquired. (p. 325)

Trial balance A proof of the equality of debits and credits in a general ledger. (p. 98)

U

Unadjusted trial balance A trial balance prepared before adjusting entries are posted. (p. 98)

Uncollectible accounts Accounts receivable that cannot be collected. (p. 174)

Underapplied overhead The amount by which applied factory overhead is less than actual factory overhead. (p. 510)

Unearned revenue Cash received for goods or services which have not been provided. (p. 264)

Unit cost An amount spent for one unit of a specific product or service. (p. 469)

Unit-level costs Resources used on activities connected with each individual unit produced. (p. 568)

Units-of-production method of depreciation Calculating the estimated annual depreciation expense based on the amount of production expected from a plant asset. (p. 219)

V

Value-based pricing A method of establishing a price for a product or service based on the value the product or service has to its customer. (p. 575)

Variable costs Costs that change in direct proportion to a change in the number of units. (p. 470)

Vertical analysis Reporting an amount on a financial statement as a percentage of another item on the same financial statement. (p. 110)

Voucher A collection of documents used to authorize a cash payment. (p. 601)

Voucher check A check with a detachable check stub, or *voucher*, that contains detailed information about the cash payment. (p. 605)

Voucher register A journal used to record vouchers. (p. 603)

Voucher system A set of procedures for controlling cash payments by preparing and approving vouchers before payments are made. (p. 601)

W

Wage The amount paid to an employee for every hour worked. (p. 64)

Weighted-average inventory costing method Using the average cost of the beginning inventory plus merchandise purchased during a fiscal period to calculate the cost of merchandise sold. (p. 153)

Withholding allowance A deduction from total earnings for each person legally supported by a taxpayer, including the employee. (p. 65)

Work in process Products that are being manufactured but are not yet complete. (p. 496)

Work sheet A columnar accounting form used to summarize the general ledger information needed for preparing financial statements. (p. 132)

Working capital The amount of total current assets less total current liabilities. (p. 373)

Writing off an account Canceling the balance of a customer account because the customer does not pay. (p. 174)

GLOSARIO

A

Account *Cuenta* Un registro que da un resumen de toda la información que pertenece a un solo artículo en la ecuación de contabilidad. (p. 9)

Accounting cycle *Ciclo contable* La serie de actividades de contabilidad que se incluyen en el registro de la información financiera en un período fiscal. (p. 121)

Accounting equation *Ecuación de contabilidad* Una ecuación que muestra la relación entre activos, pasivos y capital propio. (p. 7)

Accounts receivable turnover ratio *Índice de rotación de cuentas por cobrar* El número de veces que la cantidad promedia de cuentas por cobrar se recibe durante un período específico. (p. 186)

Accrued expenses *Gastos acumulados* Los gastos incurridos durante un período fiscal, pero pagados en otro período fiscal posterior. (p. 249)

Accrued revenue *Ingreso acumulado* Ingresos ganados en un período fiscal, pero no recibido hasta un período fiscal posterior. (p. 267)

Acquisition *La adquisición* La combinación de dos corporaciones en las que el adquirente adquiere un porcentaje significativo de la reserva del objetivo. (p. 331)

Activity rate *Tarifa de actividad* El precio de cada unidad de actividad. (p. 569)

Activity-based costing (ABC) *Determinación de costo por actividad (costeo ABC)* Asignar los gastos generales de la fábrica basados en el nivel de actividades mayores. (p. 567)

Adjusted trial balance *Balance de comprobación ajustado* Un balance de comprobación después de registrarse los asientos de ajuste. (p. 103)

Adjusting entries *Asientos de ajuste* Asientos registrados para poner al corriente las cuentas del libro mayor al final de un período fiscal. (p. 98)

Administrative expenses budget *Presupuesto de gastos administrativos* Una declaración que muestra la proyección de los gastos de todos los gastos operativos que no están directamente relacionados con las operaciones de ventas. (p. 441)

Aging accounts receivable *Antigüedad de cuentas por cobrar* Analizar las cuentas por cobrar de acuerdo a cuando se deben de pagar. (p. 180)

Allowance method *Método de concesión* Acreditar el valor estimado de las cuentas incobrables a una contra cuenta. (p. 178)

Amortization schedule *Plan de amortización* Un plan de los pagos regulares de un pagaré. (p. 275)

Annuity *Anualidad* Una serie de flujos de efectivo equitativos. (p. 545)

Applied overhead *Gastos fijos aplicados* La cantidad estimada de gastos fijos mostrada en las hojas de gastos. (p. 507)

Appropriations *Distribución de recursos* Autorizaciones para hacer gastos para propósitos específicos. (p. 680)

Articles of incorporation *Acta constitutiva de una sociedad* Un documento legal que identifica las características básicas de una corporación, el cual es parte de la solicitud sometida al estado para volverse una corporación. (p. 294)

Assessed value *Valor fiscal* El valor de un activo determinado por las autoridades de impuestos para calcular los impuestos. (p. 202)

Asset *Activo* Cualquier cosa de valor que se posee. (p. 7)

B

Authority *Autoridad* La habilidad de un empleado de autorizar una transacción. (p. 594)

Automatic check deposit *Depósito automático* Depositar los cheques de nómina de un empleado directamente a su cuenta de cheques o de ahorros. (p. 76)

B

Balance sheet *Balance general* Un estado financiero que informa sobre los activos, las obligaciones y el capital propio en una fecha específica. (p. 114)

Balanced scorecard *Cuadro de Mando Integral* Un sistema de medición y planeación desarrollado por R. S. Kaplan y D. P. Norton de utilizar varias medidas de desempeño para asegurar que la visión y estrategia de una compañía estén reflejadas en sus metas y actividades. (p. 453)

Batch-level costs *Costos a nivel de lote* Los recursos utilizados en las actividades relacionadas con un grupo de productos. (p. 568)

Board of directors *Consejo directivo* Un grupo de personas elegidas por los accionistas para dirigir una corporación. (p. 295)

Bond amortization *Amortización de bono* Reducir la cantidad de descuento o prima de un bono con el paso del tiempo. (p. 347)

Bond *Bono* Una promesa de largo plazo de pagar una cantidad específica en una fecha específica y de pagar interés a intervalos estipulados. (p. 342)

Bond issue *Emisión de bonos* Todos los bonos que representan la cantidad total de un préstamo. (p. 342)

Book value *Valor contable* La diferencia entre el saldo de cuenta de un activo y el saldo de su contra cuenta relacionada. (p. 178)

Book value of a plant asset *Valor contable de un activo fijo* El costo original de un activo fijo menos la depreciación acumulada. (p. 206)

Breakage *Tarjetas no redimidas* El valor de las tarjetas de regalo sin redimir. (p. 272)

Breakeven analysis *Análisis equilibrio-* Usando técnicas de costo-volumen-beneficio para determinar el punto de equilibrio de una empresa. (p.474)

Breakeven point *Punto de equilibrio* La cantidad de ventas en la cual las ventas netas igualan el gasto total. (p. 474)

Budget *Presupuesto* Una guía financiera utilizada por los individuos y compañías como una guía de gastos y ahorros. (p. 432)

Budget period *Período presupuestario* El plazo de tiempo cubierto por un presupuesto. (p. 433)

Budgeted income statement *Declaración de ingresos presupuestado* Una declaración que informa las proyecciones de las ventas, gastos, costos, e ingresos netos de una compañía. (p. 443)

Budgeting *Preparación del presupuesto* La planeación de las operaciones financieras de un negocio. (p. 432)

Buyback *Recompra* Un programa aprobado por el consejo directivo que autoriza a la compañía de readquirir sus acciones. (p. 325)

C

Call option *Opción de compra* El derecho de una corporación de readquirir sus valores bursátiles a un precio especificado. (p. 350)

Callable bond *Bono rescatable* Un bono que puede ser rescatado antes de su fecha de vencimiento. (p. 350)

Capital expenditures *Gastos de capital* Las compras de activos fijos utilizados en la operación de un negocio. (p. 383)

Capital stock *Capital social* El número total de acciones de propiedad en una corporación. (p. 113)

Carrying value *Valor contable* El valor nominal de un bono ajustado por cualquier descuento o prima no amortizado. (p. 347)

Cash budget *Presupuesto de efectivo* Un informe que muestra por mes o trimestre una proyección del balance inicial, recibos, pagos, y balance final de efectivo de una compañía. (p. 450)

Cash discount *Descuento de efectivo* Un descuento que un vendedor permite en una factura para motivar un pago rápido. (p. 20)

Cash equivalents *Equivalentes de caja* Inversiones disponibles de corto plazo que se pueden convertir rápidamente en efectivo y que se vencen en tres meses o menos. (p. 371)

Cash flow *Flujo de caja* Los recibos y pagos de efectivo de una compañía. (p. 115)

Cash payments budget *Presupuesto de pagos en efectivo* Un informe que muestra la proyección de pagos en efectivo de un período presupuestario. (p. 449)

Cash receipts budget *Presupuesto de recibos en efectivo* Un informe que muestra la proyección de recibos en efectivo de un período presupuestario. (p. 447)

Certificate of deposit *Certificado de depósito* Un documento emitido por un banco como evidencia del dinero invertido con el banco. (p. 691)

Charter *Acta constitutiva* El derecho legal para que un negocio lleve a cabo sus operaciones como una corporación. (p. 295)

Check register *registro de cheque* Un diario que se utiliza en un sistema de comprobantes para registrar pagos en efectivo. (p. 606)

Closing entries *Asientos de cierre* Los asientos en el diario que se usan para preparar cuentas temporales para un período fiscal nuevo. (p. 117)

Common equity per share *Capital ordinario por acción* La cantidad de capital propio de un accionista común que pertenece a una sola unidad de acción común. (p. 376)

Common stock *Acción ordinaria* Acciones que no dan preferencia especial a los accionistas. (p. 296)

Comparative financial statements *Estados financieros comparativos* Informes financieros que proveen información de múltiples períodos fiscales. (p. 368)

Compounding *Intereses compuestos* Ganar intereses sobre los intereses previamente ganados. (p. 541)

Comprehensive annual financial report *Informe financiero anual completo* El informe financiero detallado de una agencia gubernamental. (p. 712)

Comprehensive income *Ingreso total* Todos los cambios de capital por el período, con la excepción de los cambios causados por las inversiones y distribuciones del dueño. (p. 392)

Consignee *Consignatario* La persona o negocio que recibe bienes a consignación. (p. 146)

Consignment *Consignación* Los bienes que se otorgan a un negocio para vender pero que la titularidad permanece con el vendedor. (p. 146)

Consignor *Consignador* La persona o negocio que otorga bienes a consignación. (p. 146)

Contra account *Contra cuenta* Cuenta que reduce una cuenta relacionada en un estado financiero. (p. 18)

Contribution margin *Margen de contribución* Los ingresos determinados al restar todos los gastos variables de las ventas netas. (p. 471)

Control activities *Actividades de control* Las pólizas y procedimientos diseñados para prevenir o detectar errores o fraude. (p. 593)

Control environment *Ambiente de control* Las acciones y actitudes de la gerencia que indica su compromiso a los controles firmes internos y estándares de ética. (p. 593)

Controlling account *Cuenta de control* Una cuenta en el libro mayor general que da un resumen de todas las cuentas de un libro mayor auxiliar. (p. 11)

Conversion costs *Costos de conversión* La suma de los gastos fijos y los gastos de mano de obra directa. (p. 561)

Conversion option *Opción de conversión* La habilidad de poder intercambiar un valor bursátil por un número específico de acciones de otro valor bursátil. (p. 307)

Conversion price *Precio de conversión* El valor nominal de una acción preferida dividida por el índice de conversión. (p. 307)

Conversion ratio *Índice de conversión* El número de acciones comunes recibidas cuando un valor es convertido. (p. 307)

Convertible preferred stock *Acción preferente convertible* Acciones preferentes que se pueden intercambiar por un número específico de acciones comunes. (p. 307)

Corporation *Corporación* Una organización con los derechos legales de una persona y de la cual varias personas u otras corporaciones son dueñas. (p. 294)

Cost driver *Origen del costo* El factor que afecta el costo de una actividad. (p. 569)

Cost ledger *Libro mayor de costos* Un libro mayor que contiene todas las hojas de costos de los productos que están en el proceso de fabricación. (p. 497)

Cost of production report *Informe sobre el costo de producción* Un informe que muestra la información de unidades y costos de un departamento que utiliza un proceso de sistema de costeo. (p. 564)

Cost pool *Agrupación de costos* Un grupo de costos relacionados con una actividad específica. (p. 569)

Cost-based pricing *Fijación de precios según costo* Un método para establecer el precio de un producto o servicio en el cual se añade un porcentaje fijo o una cantidad fija al costo del producto o servicio. (p. 574)

Cost-volume-profit (CVP) analysis *Análisis de costo-volumen-beneficio* Un método utilizado para determinar cómo los cambios en los costes y el volumen afectan al beneficio de una empresa. (p. 468)

Credit memorandum *Memorándum de crédito* Un documento preparado por el vendedor que muestra la cantidad deducida por las devoluciones de ventas y concesiones. (p. 43)

Current assets *Activos actuales* El efectivo y otros activos que se espera que se intercambien por efectivo o que se consuman dentro de un año. (p. 198)

Current liabilities *Obligaciones actuales* Las obligaciones que se deben dentro de un corto plazo, generalmente dentro de año. (p. 237)

Current ratio *Índice actual* Un índice que mide la relación actual de los activos actuales con las obligaciones actuales. (p. 374)

Custody *Custodia* El acceso físico a los activos involucrados en una transacción. (p. 594)

D

Date of a note *Fecha del pagaré* El día que un pagaré es emitido. (p. 236)

Date of declaration *Fecha de declaración* La fecha en la que el consejo directivo vota para distribuir un dividendo. (p. 318)

Date of payment *Fecha de pago* La fecha actual en la cual se pagan dividendos a los accionistas. (p. 318)

Date of record *Fecha de registro* La fecha que determina cuales accionistas recibirán dividendos. (p. 318)

Days' sales in accounts receivable *Días promedio de Cuentas por cobrar* El período de tiempo promedio para cobrar una cuenta por cobrar. (p. 186)

Days' sales in inventory *Días promedio en inventario* El tiempo necesario para vender una cantidad promedia de mercancía en inventario. (p. 161)

Debit memorandum *Memorándum de débito* Un documento preparado por el cliente que muestra la deducción de precio tomada por el cliente por una devolución o concesión. (p. 17)

Debt financing *Financiamiento de deuda* Obteniendo capital al pedir prestado por un período de tiempo. (p. 236)

Debt ratio *Índice de deuda* El total de las obligaciones dividido por el total de los activos. (p. 375)

Declaring a dividend *Declaración de dividendos* La acción tomada por el consejo directivo para distribuir las ganancias de la corporación a los accionistas. (p. 318)

Declining-balance method of depreciation *Método de depreciación de saldo decreciente* Un tipo de depreciación acelerada que multiplica el valor contable de un activo por un índice de depreciación constante para determinar su depreciación. (p. 218)

Deflation *Deflación* El índice al cual el precio de bienes y servicios disminuye con el paso del tiempo. (p. 155)

Departmental accounting system *Sistema de contabilidad departamental* Un sistema de contabilidad que muestra la información contable de dos o más departamentos. (p. 13)

Departmental margin *Margen departamental* Los ingresos de un departamento menos sus gastos directos y de la mercancía vendida. (p. 109)

Departmental margin statement *Informe del margen departamental* Un informe que muestra el margen departamental de un departamento específico. (p. 109)

Depletion *Agotamiento* La depreciación en valor de un activo fijo debido a la extracción de un recurso natural. (p. 222)

Depreciation expense *Gasto de depreciación* La porción del costo de un activo fijo que es transferida a una cuenta de gastos cada período fiscal durante la vida útil de ese activo. (p. 102)

Differential analysis *Análisis diferencial* Analizar solamente las diferencias entre los ingresos y los gastos que resultan de cada uno de dos opciones. (p. 534)

Direct expense *Gasto directo* Un gasto operativo que se identifica y es cobrable a la operación de un departamento específico. (p. 108)

Direct labor *Mano de obra directa* Los salarios de los obreros de la fábrica quienes hacen un producto. (p. 496)

Direct materials *Materia prima directa* Los materiales que son de valor significativo en el costo de un producto terminado y los cuales se vuelven una parte identificable del producto. (p. 496)

Direct method *Método directo* Una lista de flujos de caja de las actividades operativas tales como los recibos y pagos de efectivo. (p. 403)

Direct write-off method *Método de pérdida directa* Registrar los gastos de cuentas incobrables solamente cuando en verdad se sabe que una cantidad es incobrable. (p. 175)

Distribution deficit *Déficit distributivo* Un balance negativo que queda después de que los sueldos de los socios y el interés son descontados del ingreso total. (p. 650)

Dividend yield *Rendimiento de dividendo* La relación entre los dividendos por acción y el precio del mercado de cada acción. (p. 389)

Dividends *Dividendos* Las ganancias que se distribuyen a los accionistas. (p. 113)

Double taxation *Tributación doble* La imposición de impuestos sobre las ganancias de una corporación y nuevamente cuando los dividendos son recibidos por los accionistas. (p. 298)

Double-entry accounting *Contabilidad de partida doble* El registro de las partes de débito y crédito de una transacción. (p. 8)

E

Earnings per share (EPS) *Ganancia por acción (GPA)* Ganancias netas después del impuesto fiscal dividido por la cantidad pendiente de acciones. (p. 387)

EBIT *BAII* Beneficios antes de intereses e impuestos. (p. 376)

Effective interest rate *Tasa de interés vigente* La tasa de interés de mercado cuando los bonos son emitidos. (p. 346)

Electronic funds transfer (EFT) *Transferencia electrónica de fondos (TEF)* Un sistema computarizado de pagos de efectivo, el cual transfiere fondos sin el uso de cheques, moneda, u otro documento de papel. (p. 76)

Employee earnings record *Registro de ganancias de los empleados* Un documento de negocios que registra todos los detalles de las ganancias y deducciones de un empleado. (p. 73)

Encumbrance *Gravamen* El compromiso de pagar por los bienes o servicios que han sido ordenados pero que todavía no han sido proveídos. (p. 687)

Equities *Derechos de propiedad* Los derechos financieros a los activos de un negocio. (p. 70)

Equity ratio *Proporción de capital* La proporción que es el resultado de dividir el capital de un accionista por el total de activos. (p. 375)

Equivalent units of production (EUP) *Unidades equivalentes de producción* Una estimación de la cantidad de materia prima directa, la mano de obra directa, y los gastos fijos que ya han sido incurridos en las unidades parcialmente terminadas, declarados en términos de unidades ya completadas. (p. 561)

Error *Error* Una equivocación no intencional. (p. 593)

Expenditures *Gastos* La distribución de efectivo y las obligaciones incurridas por el costo de los bienes entregados o los servicios otorgados. (p. 676)

F

Face value *Valor nominal* La cantidad a ser pagada a un obligacionista en la fecha de vencimiento del bono. (p. 343)

Facility-sustaining level costs *Gastos de producción y mantenimiento* Los recursos utilizados para el sustentamiento de la compañía y el proceso de producción. (p. 568)

Factory overhead *Gastos fijos de fábrica* Todos los gastos aparte de la materia prima y mano de obra directa que aplican para fabricar productos. (p. 496)

Fair market value balance sheet *Estado de cuenta del valor justo de mercado* Una declaración financiera que presenta el valor justo de mercado de los activos, obligaciones, y el capital social de una compañía. (p. 627)

Fiduciary fund *Fondo fiduciario* Un fondo que informa sobre los activos de una agencia gubernamental para el beneficio de un grupo específico de individuos. (p. 712)

File maintenance *Mantenimiento de archivos* El procedimiento de ordenar cuentas en un libro mayor general, asignando números de cuenta y manteniendo los registros al corriente. (p. 11)

Financial ratio *Proporción financiera* Una comparación entre dos componentes de información financiera. (p. 110)

Financial statement misstatement *Declaración falsa del estado de cuenta* La manipulación de las cantidades reportadas en un estado de cuenta financiero. (p. 593)

Financing activities *Actividades financieras* Recibos y pagos de efectivo que involucran transacciones de deuda o patrimonio neto. (p. 115)

Finished goods *Bienes terminados* Los productos fabricados que están completamente terminados. (p. 496)

Finished goods ledger *Libro mayor de bienes terminados* Un libro mayor que contiene los registros de todos los bienes terminados a la mano. Este libro mayor es similar a un libro mayor de materiales. (p. 497)

First-in, first-out inventory costing method *Método de costos de inventario de primero en entrar, primero en salir* Utilizando el precio de la mercancía comprada primero para calcular el costo de la mercancía que se vende primero. (p. 151)

Fiscal period *Período fiscal* El plazo de tiempo en el cual un negocio da un resumen de su información financiera y reporta su desempeño financiero. (p. 96)

Fiscal year *Año fiscal* Un período fiscal que consiste de doce meses consecutivos. (p. 96)

Fixed costs *Gastos fijos* Los gastos que permanecen constantes independientes de un cambio en las actividades de negocio. (p. 470)

Flowchart *Diagrama de flujo* Un diagrama que utiliza símbolos y conexiones para representar un proceso. (p. 597)

Fraud *Fraude* El robo de activos por empleados o la declaración falsa intencional de la información financiera. (p. 593)

Free cash flow *Flujo libre de caja* Una medida igual a los flujos de efectivo de las operaciones menos el efectivo utilizado en los gastos de capital. (p. 383)

Fund *Fondo* Una entidad contable gubernamental con una colección de cuentas en las cuales los activos siempre igualan las obligaciones más los valores. (p. 675)

Fund equity *Capital de fondo* La cantidad de activos menos las obligaciones de una organización gubernamental. (p. 676)

Future value *Valor futuro* El valor futuro del dinero que es invertido hoy en día. (p. 541)

Future value of an annuity *Valor futuro de una anualidad* El valor futuro de una serie de inversiones iguales sobre plazos de tiempo iguales a una tasa de interés determinada. (p. 545)

G

General fixed assets *Activos fijos generales* Propiedades gubernamentales que benefician a períodos futuros. (p. 690)

General ledger *Libro mayor general* Un libro mayor que contiene todas las cuentas necesarias para preparar estados financieros. (p. 11)

Generally accepted accounting principles *Principios de Contabilidad Generalmente Aceptados* Los estándares y normas que los contadores siguen mientras que registran y reportan actividades financieras. (p. 151)

Goodwill *Fondo de comercio* El valor de un negocio en exceso de la inversión total de los dueños. (p. 633)

Governmental fund *Fondo gubernamental* Un fondo que justifica las actividades de una agencia gubernamental financiadas por impuestos. (p. 712)

Gross margin *Margen bruto* Ganancia bruta como un porcentaje de ventas netas. (p. 378)

Gross profit *Ganancia bruta* El ingreso operativo restante después de deducir el costo de la mercancía vendida. (p. 109)

Gross profit method of estimating inventory *Método de ganancia bruta para estimar un inventario* Estimando del inventario mediante el uso de los porcentajes de ganancia bruta de operaciones en años anteriores. (p. 159)

H

Half-year convention *Convención de medio año* Un método que reconoce medio año de la depreciación anual en el año en que se adquiere. (p. 207)

Hostile takeover *Toma de posesión hostil* Una combinacion adquirida sin la aprobacion de la mesa de directivos de una corporación objetivo. (p. 331)

I

Income statement *Estado de ingresos* Un estado financiero que muestra los gastos e ingresos durante un período fiscal. (p. 113)

Indirect expense *Gasto indirecto* Un gasto operativo facturable a las operaciones en general del negocio y que no se identifica con un departamento específico. (p. 108)

Indirect labor *Mano de obra indirect* Los salarios pagados a los obreros de la fábrica que no están haciendo los productos. (p. 496)

Indirect materials *Materia prima indirecta* Los materiales utilizados para completar un producto que tienen un valor insignificante para justificarlos por separado. (p. 496)

Indirect method *Método indirecto* Hacer una lista de flujos de efectivo de las actividades operativas comenzando con los ingresos netos y ajustando por los artículos no monetarios. (p. 403)

Inflation *Inflación* El índice al cual el precio de bienes y servicios aumenta con el paso del tiempo. (p. 154)

Information and communication *Información y comunicación* El proceso utilizado para recolectar información sobre como el negocio está logrando sus metas de control. (p. 593)

Initial public offering *Oferta pública inicial* La emisión inicial de valores para el mercado público. También llamado IPO. (p. 303)

Installment note *Pagaré a plazos* Un pagaré que resulta de una venta y que requiere de pagos mensuales de principal e interés. (p. 274)

Institutional investors *Inversionistas institucionales* Organizaciones que administran las inversiones de los inversionistas individuales. (p. 355)

Intangible asset *Activo intangible* Un activo que no tiene forma física. (p. 634)

Interest *Interés* Una cantidad que se paga por el uso de dinero durante un período de tiempo. (p. 236)

Interest coverage ratio *Índice de cobertura de intereses* El número de veces que una compañía puede cubrir sus gastos de interés con las ganancias. (p. 376)

Interest expense *Gastos de interés* El interés que se acumula en dinero que se ha tomado prestado. (p. 239)

Interest rate *Tasa de interés* El porcentaje del capital que se debe por el uso de los fondos garantizados por un pagaré. (p. 236)

Interest-bearing note *Pagaré con intereses* Un pagaré con una tasa de interés estipulado. (p. 239)

Internal control structure *Estructura de control interno* Un proceso diseñado para lograr operaciones eficientes y efectivas, la confiabilidad de informes financieros, y el cumplimiento con las leyes y regulaciones aplicables. (p. 593)

Internal controls *Controles internos* Los procesos y procedimientos utilizados dentro de un negocio para asegurar que sus operaciones son manejadas con ética, precisión, y confiabilidad. (p. 592)

International financial reporting standards *Normas Internacionales de Información Financiera (NIIF)* Un conjunto de normas de contabilidad adoptadas por todo el mundo. (p. 156)

Inventory record *Registro de inventario* Un formulario que se usa durante un inventario físico para registrar información acerca de cada artículo de mercancía a la mano. (p. 148)

Inventory turnover ratio *Índice de rotación de inventario* El número de veces que la cantidad promedia de mercancía en inventario es vendida durante un período de tiempo específico. (p. 161)

Investing activities *Actividades de inversión* Recibos y pagos de efectivo que involucran la venta o compra de activos utilizados para generar ingresos sobre un período de tiempo. (p. 115)

Invoice *Factura* Un formulario que describe los bienes o servicios vendidos, la cantidad, el precio, y los términos de venta. (p. 602)

J

Job order costing *Costeo por orden de fabricación* Calculando el costo de fabricación de una orden o lote en específico mientras pasa por el proceso de producción. (p. 497)

Joint costs *Costos conjuntos* El costo de fabricar productos conjuntos hasta su punto de separación. (p. 537)

Joint products *Productos conjuntos* Dos o más productos que son fabricados simultáneamente con los mismos procesos y costos y que son inseparables hasta cierto punto. (p. 537)

Journal *Diario* Un formulario para registrar transacciones en orden cronológico. (p. 80)

L

Labor price standard *Precio estándar de mano de obra* El costo estimado por hora de mano de obra directa. También se le refiere como el *estándar de la tarifa laboral*. (p. 519)

Labor price variance *Variación en el precio de mano de obra* La diferencia entre el precio actual pagado por la mano de obra y el precio estándar de mano de obra en la cantidad utilizada actualmente. (p. 523)

Labor quantity standard *Cantidad estándar de mano de obra* La cantidad estimada de mano de obra directa necesaria para fabricar una unidad de producción. También referido como el *estándar de productividad de mano de obra*. (p. 519)

Labor quantity variance *Variación en la cantidad de mano de obra* La diferencia entre la cantidad actual de mano de obra utilizada durante la fabricación y la cantidad estándar de mano de obra por el nivel de producción al precio estándar. (p. 523)

Last-in, first-out inventory costing method *Método de inventario de costos del último en entrar, primero en salir* Se usa el precio de la mercancía que se compra al último para calcular el costo de la mercancía que se vende primero. (p. 152)

Ledger *Libro mayor* Un grupo de cuentas. (p. 11)

Liability *Obligación* Una cantidad que debe un negocio. (p. 7)

Limited liability corporation *Corporación con responsabilidad legal limitada* El tipo de corporación que no paga impuestos sobre sus ganancias.

Las ganancias son divididas entre sus miembros y solamente son sujetas a impuestos en las declaraciones de impuestos personales de los miembros, así eliminando la desventaja de tributación doble. También conocido como *LLC*. (p. 298)

Line of credit *Línea de crédito* Un acuerdo de préstamo bancario que provee acceso inmediato de corto plazo a efectivo. (p. 241)

Liquidation of a partnership *Disolución de una sociedad* El proceso de pagar las obligaciones de la sociedad y distribuir los activos restantes entre los socios. (p. 658)

Lower of cost or market inventory costing method *Método de inventario de costo de mercado del menor costo* Utilizando el más bajo del costo o del valor de mercado para calcular el costo del inventario final de mercancías. (p. 157)

M

Market value of a share of stock *Valor de mercado de una unidad de acción* El precio al cual una acción pude ser vendida en la bolsa de valores en cualquier momento. (p. 388)

Materials ledger *Libro mayor de materiales* Un libro mayor que contiene todos los registros de los materiales. (p. 497)

Materials price standard *Precio estándar de materia prima* El costo estimado de cada unidad de materia prima directa. (p. 519)

Materials price variance *Variación en precio de material* La diferencia entre el precio actual pagado por materiales y el precio estándar de materiales en la cantidad comprada y utilizada actualmente. (p. 521)

Materials quantity standard *Calidad de material estándar* El costo estimado de materia prima directa utilizada por cada unidad producida. (p. 519)

Materials quantity variance *Variación en la calidad de material* La diferencia entre la cantidad actual de materiales comprados y utilizados durante la fabricación y la cantidad estándar de materiales por el nivel de producción al precio estándar. (p. 521)

Maturity date *Fecha de vencimiento* La fecha en la cual el capital de un pagaré se debe pagar. (p. 236)

Maturity value *Valor de vencimiento* La cantidad que se debe en la fecha de vencimiento de un pagaré. (p. 239)

Merchandising business *Negocio mercantil* Un negocio que compra y revende bienes. (p. 13)

Millage rate *Tasa de la milésima* La tasa de impuestos utilizada para calcular los impuestos de propiedad. (p. 202)

Modified Accelerated Cost Recovery System (MACRS) *Sistema Modificado de Recuperación Acelerada de Costo (MACRS)* Un método de depreciación requerida por el Servicio de Impuestos Internos que se utiliza para el propósito de calcular los impuestos sobre los ingresos de la mayoría de los activos fijos. (p. 220)

Modified half-year convention *Convención de medio año modificado* Un método que reconoce la depreciación de un año completo si el activo se adquiere en la primera mitad del año. (p. 207)

Monitoring *Monitorear* El proceso que utiliza la gerencia para determinar si sus políticas están funcionando eficazmente. (p. 593)

Mutual agency *Agencia mutualista* El derecho de todos los socios de solicitar una sociedad. (p. 624)

N

Narrative *Narrativa* Una descripción por escrito de la circulación de documentos e información entre empleados, departamentos, y personas exteriores. (p. 597)

Net cash flows *Flujo de caja neto* La diferencia entre los recibos y pagos de efectivo. (p. 548)

Net present value *Valor actual neto* La diferencia entre el valor actual de los flujos de efectivo de la inversión y la cantidad de la inversión. (p. 548)

Net realizable value *Valor neto realizable* Véase *Valor contable*.

Noninterest-bearing note *Pagaré sin intereses* Un pagaré que resta el interés del valor nominal del pagaré. (p. 239)

No-par-value stock *Acción sin valor nominal* Una acción que no indica un valor autorizado en el certificado de acciones. (p. 297)

Notes payable *Pagarés pendientes* Pagarés firmados por un negocio y otorgados a un acreedor. (p. 236)

Not-for-profit organization *Organización sin fines de lucro* Una organización que provee bienes o servicios sin ningún motivo deliberado o alguna expectativa de generar una ganancia. (p. 672)

O

Occupational fraud *Fraude ocupacional* El robo de activos del negocio por parte de un empleado. También se le refiere como *desfalco* o *apropiación indebida de activos*. (p. 593)

Operating activities *Actividades operativas* Los recibos de efectivo y pagos necesarios para operar un negocio día a día. (p. 115)

Operating budget *Presupuesto operativo* Un plan de gastos actuales y los recursos sugeridos para financiar esos gastos. (p. 678)

Operating margin *Margen operativo* Los ingresos operativos como un porcentaje de las ventas netas. (p. 379)

Other revenue and expenses budget *Presupuesto de otros gastos e ingresos* Una declaración que muestra los ingresos y gastos presupuestados de las actividades que no son parte de las operaciones normales. (p. 442)

Overapplied overhead *Gastos fijos sobre aplicados* La cantidad por la cual los gastos fijos de fábrica son más que los gastos fijos actuales de fábrica. (p. 510)

Owners' equity *Capital propio* La cantidad que queda después que el valor de las obligaciones es restada del valor de los activos. (p. 7)

Owners' equity statement *Estado de cuenta de capital propio* Un estado financiero que resume los cambios en el capital propio durante un período fiscal. (p. 654)

P

Par value *Valor nominal* Un valor asignado a una acción e impreso en el certificado de acciones. (p. 296)

Partnership *Sociedad* Un negocio en el cual dos o más personas combinan sus activos y sus habilidades. (p. 296)

Partnership agreement *Convenio de sociedad* Un acuerdo por escrito que establece las condiciones bajo las cuales opera una sociedad. También conocido como *los artículos de sociedad*. (p. 624)

Par-value stock *Acción con valor nominal* Una unidad de acción que tiene valor nominal. (p. 298)

Pay period *Período de pago* El número de días o semanas laborales cubiertas en un cheque de nómina del empleado. (p. 64)

Payback period *Periodo de repago* La cantidad de tiempo requerido para recuperar el costo de una inversión. (p. 538)

Payroll *Nómina* La cantidad total que ganan todos los empleados durante un período de pago. (p. 64)

Payroll register *Registro de nomina* Un formulario de contabilidad que resume las ganancias, deducciones, y pago neto de todos los empleados por un período de pago. (p. 68)

Payroll taxes *Impuestos de nómina* Impuestos basados en la nómina de un negocio. (p. 64)

Performance report *Informe de desempeño* Un informe que muestra la comparación de las cantidades proyectadas y las actuales de un período específico. (p. 453)

Permanent difference *Diferencia permanente* Una diferencia entre los ingresos netos y los ingresos sujetos a impuestos solamente por aquel año que no es balanceado en un año futuro. (p. 391)

Personal property *Propiedad personal* Toda la propiedad no clasificada como propiedad inmueble. (p. 202)

Petty cash *Caja chica* Una cantidad de efectivo que se tiene a la mano y se usa para hacer pagos menores. (p. 25)

Plant asset record *Registro de activo fijo* Un formulario de contabilidad en el cual se registra la información de cada activo fijo de un negocio. (p. 202)

Plant assets *Activos fijos* Activos físicos que se usarán durante un número de años en la operación de un negocio. (p. 102)

Point-of-sale (POS) terminal *Terminal de punto de venta* Un computadora especializada que se usa para recolectar, guardar, y reportar toda la información de una transacción de venta. (p. 49)

Post-closing trial balance *Balance de comprobación posterior al cierre* Un balance de comprobación preparado después de pasar los asientos de cierre. (p. 120)

Posting *Pasar asientos* Transferir información de las transacciones de un asiento diario a una cuenta del libro mayor. (p. 15)

Preferred stock *Acción preferente* Un tipo de acción que les da preferencia a los accionistas privilegiados sobre los accionistas comunes en cuanto a los dividendos y otros derechos. (p. 296)

Prepaid expense *Gasto pre pagado* Efectivo pagado por un gasto en un período fiscal el cual no es utilizado hasta otro período después. (p. 243)

Present value *Valor actual* El valor actual de un pago o recibo de efectivo en el futuro. (p. 544)

Present value of an annuity *Valor actual de una anualidad* La cantidad invertida a una tasa de interés determinada que sustenta los pagos de una anualidad. (p. 546)

Price-earnings ratio *Índice de ganancias sobre precio* La relación entre el valor de mercado por acción y las ganancias por acción de una inversión. (p. 388)

Prime interest rate *Tase de interés preferencial* La tasa de interés que se les cobra a los clientes más dignos de crédito de un banco. (p. 241)

Principal *Principal* La cantidad original de una pagaré. (p. 236)

Privately held corporation *Corporación privada* Una corporación de la cual son dueños un pequeño número de individuos. (p. 303)

Process costing *Costeo del proceso* Calculando el costo de fabricación de bienes similares mientras se mueven continuamente de un proceso de fabricación a otra. (p. 497)

Product-level costs *Costo al nivel de producto* Los recursos utilizados para sustentar toda la línea de fabricación. (p. 568)

Promissory note *Pagaré* Una promesa por escrito y firmado para pagar una suma de dinero a una fecha específica. (p. 236)

Proprietary fund *Fondo propietario* Un fondo que justifica las transacciones financieras de una agencia gubernamental la cual opera como una empresa con fines de lucro. (p. 712)

Proprietorship *Empresa de propietario único* Un negocio cuyo dueño es una sola persona. (p. 298)

Publicly held corporation *Corporación públicamente comercializada* Una corporación cuyas acciones son cotizadas en las bolsas de valores. (p. 303)

Purchase order *Orden de compra* Un documento que solicita que un proveedor le venda mercancía a un negocio. (p. 602)

Purchases budget *Presupuesto de compras* Una declaración que muestra la cantidad de compras proyectadas que serán requeridas durante el período presupuestado. (p. 437)

Purchases discount *Descuento de compras* Cuando una compañía que compra mercancía a cuenta toma un descuento de efectivo. (p. 20)

Q

Quick assets *Activos realizables* Efectivo y otros activos actuales que se pueden convertir rápidamente en efectivo. (p. 374)

Quick ratio *Índice de realización* Un índice que mide la relación de los activos realizables a las responsabilidades actuales. (p. 374)

R

Rate earned on average stockholders' equity *Índice ganado sobre el promedio de capital del accionista* La relación entre los ingresos netos y el promedio del capital del accionista. (p. 382)

Rate earned on average total assets *Índice ganado sobre el promedio del total de activos* La relación entre los ingresos netos y el promedio del total de activos. (p. 381)

Real property *Propiedad de inmuebles* Terreno y cualquier cosa unida al terreno; también llamado *bienes raíces*. (p. 202)

Realization *Ganancia* Efectivo recibido de la venta de activos durante la disolución de una sociedad. (p. 658)

Receiving report *Informe de recibido* Un formulario que muestra los artículos recibidos de un proveedor. (p. 602)

Reclassification entry *Asiento de reclasificación* Un asiento que transfiere saldos entre cuentas en un solo informe financiero. (p. 276)

Recording *asentar* El asiento de una transacción en los registros financieros. (p. 594)

Registration statement *Declaración de registro* El documento presentado a la SEC para obtener permiso de vender valores en la bolsa de valores. (p. 303)

Relevant costs *Costos relevantes* Los costos que son diferentes entre dos opciones. (p. 534)

Relevant revenues *Ingresos relevantes* Los ingresos que son diferentes entre dos opciones. (p. 534)

Requisition *Requisición* Un documento solicitando la compra de mercancía. (p. 602)

Responsibility accounting *Contabilidad por áreas de responsabilidad* La asignación de control de ingresos, costos, y gastos a un gerente en particular. (p. 108)

Responsibility statements *Declaraciones por áreas de responsabilidad* Declaraciones financieras que informan sobre los ingresos, costos, y gastos directos que están bajo el control de un departamento en particular. (p. 109)

Retail method of estimating inventory *Método ventas al detalle para estimar inventario* La estimación de inventario utilizando un porcentaje basado en costos y precios minoristas. (p. 160)

Retained earnings *Ganancias retenidas* Una cantidad que gana una corporación y aún no ha sido distribuida entre los accionistas. (p. 113)

Retiring a bond issue *Retirar la emisión de un bono* El pago de la cantidad adeudada al tenedor de bonos por la emisión de un bono. (p. 350)

Reversing entry *Asiento revertido* Un asiento hecho al principio de un período fiscal para revertir un asiento de ajuste hecho en el período fiscal anterior. (p. 245)

Risk assessment *Evaluación de riesgo* El proceso de determinar si pudiera ocurrir un error o fraude. (p. 593)

S

Salary *Sueldo* Una suma fija de dinero dividida igualmente entre los períodos de pago. (p. 64)

Sales budget *Presupuesto de ventas* Una declaración que muestra las ventas netas proyectadas durante el período presupuestado. (p. 436)

Sales discount *Descuento de venta* Un descuento en el precio de una venta por el cliente. (p. 47)

Sales mix *Ventas mixtas* La distribución relativa de ventas entre varios productos. (p. 485)

Salvage value *Valor de recuperación* La cantidad que será recibida por un activo al tiempo de su eliminación. (p. 205)

Schedule of accounts payable *Plan de cuentas por pagar* Una lista de cuentas de proveedores, saldos de las cuentas, y la cantidad total que se debe a todos los proveedores. A esto algunos negocios le llaman balance de comprobación de cuentas por pagar. (p. 97)

Schedule of accounts receivable *Plan de cuentas por cobrar* Una lista de cuentas de clientes, saldos de las cuentas y la cantidad total que deben todos los clientes. (p. 97)

Segregation of duties *División de responsabilidades* La división de tareas del sistema de contabilidad entre empleados con diferentes funciones. (p. 594)

Selling expenses budget *Presupuesto de los gastos de ventas* Una declaración que muestra las proyecciones de gastos directamente relacionados con las operaciones de ventas. (p. 439)

Serial bonds *Bonos de vencimiento escalonado* Porciones de una emisión de bonos que se vencen en fechas diferentes. (p. 350)

Share of stock *Unidad de acción* Una unidad de titularidad en una corporación. (p. 294)

Source document *Documento original* Un documento de negocios del cual se obtiene información para asentar en un diario. (p. 7)

Special journal *Diario especial* Un diario que se usa para registrar solamente un tipo de transacción. (p. 8)

Split-off point *Punto de separación* El punto en el cual los productos conjuntos son separables en productos identificables. (p. 537)

Standard *Estándar* Una cantidad estimada por lo general en precio o cantidad de materia prima directa o mano de obra directa, establecida por cada unidad fabricada. (p. 519)

Standard costing system *Sistema de costeo estándar* Un sistema de establecer estándares por cada unidad de producción. (p. 519)

Stated interest rate *Tasa de interés especificada* La tasa de interés que se usa para calcular los pagos de interés periódicos de un bono. (p. 343)

Stated-value stock *Acción de valor contable* Acciones sin valor nominal a las cuales una corporación les asigna un valor. Una acción de valor contable es similar a una acción de valor nominal con la excepción de que el valor no está indicado en los certificados. (p. 297)

Statement of cash flows *Declaración de flujo de efectivo* Un estado financiero que resume los recibos y pagos de efectivo que resultan de las actividades de negocios durante un período fiscal. (p. 115)

Statement of cost of goods manufactured *Declaración del costo de bienes fabricados* Una declaración que muestra los detalles sobre el costo de bienes terminados. (p. 514)

Statement of revenues, expenditures, and changes in fund balance *Declaración de ingresos, gastos, y cambios en el balance de fondos* Una declaración que informa las fuentes de ingresos y los gastos de los fondos de una agencia gubernamental. (p. 676)

Statement of stockholders' equity *Estado financiero del capital de accionistas* Un estado financiero que muestra los cambios en la titularidad de una corporación durante un período fiscal. (p. 113)

Statutory consolidation *Consolidación estatutaria-* La combinación de dos corporaciones independientes en una nueva entidad única. (p. 331)

Statutory merger *Fusión estatutaria-* La combinación de dos corporaciones donde sólo una corporación sigue como una entidad legal. (p. 331)

Stock certificate *Certificado de acciones* Evidencia por escrito del número de acciones que tiene cada accionista en una corporación. (p. 296)

Stock dividend *Dividendo en acciones* El pago de dividendos con acciones de la compañia. (p. 321)

Stock ledger *Libro mayor de inventario* Un archivo para el registro del inventario de la mercancía a la mano. (p. 147)

Stock record *Registro de existencias* Un documento que se usa para mostrar la clase de mercancía, cantidad recibida, cantidad vendida y cantidad a la mano. (p. 147)

Stockholder *Accionista* Dueño de una o más acciones en una corporación. (p. 294)

Stockholders' equity *Capital del accionista* El capital propio de un dueño en una corporación. (p. 7)

Straight-line method of depreciation *Método de depreciación de línea directa* El registro de una cantidad igual de gasto de depreciación para un activo fijo en cada año de su vida útil. (p. 206)

Subsidiary ledger *Libro mayor auxiliar* Un libro mayor que esta resumida en una sola cuenta del libro mayor general. (p. 11)

Sunk cost *Costo hundido* Un gasto que ocurrió en el pasado y no se puede recuperar con una decisión en el futuro. (p. 534)

T

Target costing *Costeo objetivo* Un método de establecer un precio por un producto o servicio basado en el precio que el consumidor está dispuesto a pagar, y controlar el precio de los productos para que la compañía todavía pueda generar una ganancia. (p. 575)

Tax base *Base de impuestos* La cantidad máxima de ganancias sobre la cual se calculan los impuestos. (p. 65)

Tax levy *Recaudación de impuestos* La acción autorizada por una agencia de gobierno para cobrar impuestos por medio de una autoridad legal. (p. 683)

Temporary difference *Diferencia temporal* Una diferencia entre los ingresos netos y los ingresos sujetos a impuestos por más de un período, la cual se equilibra con el paso completo del período. (p. 391)

Term bonds *Bonos a plazo* Bonos que se vencen en la misma fecha. (p. 350)

Terminal summary *Resumen de terminal* El informe que resume las ventas en efectivo y de crédito de una terminal de punto de venta. (p. 49)

Time value of money *Valor del dinero con el tiempo* La expectativa de que el dinero invertido crecerá con el paso del tiempo. (p. 540)

Total costs *Gasto total* Todos los gastos de un período de tiempo específico. (p. 469)

Total labor variance *Variación de mano de obra total* La diferencia entre el costo actual de mano de obra y el costo estándar anticipado de mano de obra. (p. 522)

Total materials variance *Variación del material total* La diferencia entre el costo actual de materiales y el costo estándar anticipado de materiales. (p. 520)

Treasury stock *Acciones de tesorería* Las acciones propias de una corporación que han sido emitidas y readquiridas. (p. 325)

Trial balance *Balance de comprobación* Una prueba de la igualdad de débitos y créditos en el libro mayor general. (p. 98)

U

Unadjusted trial balance *Balance de comprobación no ajustado* Un balance de comprobación antes de que los asientos de ajuste sean registrados. (p. 98)

Uncollectible accounts *Cuentas incobrables* Cuentas por cobrar que no pueden ser cobradas. (p. 174)

Underapplied overhead *Ajuste de gastos fijos* La cantidad por la cual los gastos fijos de fábrica es menor que los gastos fijos actuales de fábrica. (p. 510)

Unearned revenue *Ingreso no ganados* Efectivo recibido por bienes y servicios que aún no han sido proveídos. (p. 264)

Unit cost *Costo por unidad* La cantidad gastada por una unidad de un producto o servicio específico. (p. 469)

Unit-level costs *Costos a nivel de unidad* Los recursos utilizados en las actividades relacionadas con cada unidad individual fabricada. (p. 568)

Units-of-production method of depreciation *Método de depreciación por unidades de fabricación* Calculando el gasto estimado de la depreciación anual basado en la cantidad de producción anticipada de un activo fijo. (p. 219)

Value-based pricing *Fijación de precios según valor* Un método para establecer el precio de un producto o servicio basado en el valor que tiene el producto o servicio para el consumidor. (p. 575)

Variable costs *Costos variables* Los costos que cambian en proporción directa con un cambio en el número de unidades. (p. 470)

Vertical analysis *Análisis vertical* Reportar una cantidad en un estado financiero como un porcentaje de otro artículo en el mismo estado financiero. (p. 110)

Voucher *Comprobante* Una colección de documentos utilizados para autorizar un pago. (p. 601)

Voucher check *Comprobante de cheque* Un cheque que tiene un talón desprendible, o comprobante, que contiene información detallada sobre el pago de efectivo. (p. 605)

Voucher register *Registro de comprobantes* Un libro mayor utilizado para registrar comprobantes. (p. 603)

Voucher system *Sistema de comprobantes* Un conjunto de procedimientos para controlar pagos de efectivo al preparar y aprobar comprobantes antes de que se realicen los pagos. (p. 601)

Wage *Salario* La cantidad que se le paga a un empleado por cada hora laboral. (p. 64)

Weighted-average inventory costing method *Método de inventario de costo promedio* Utilizando el costo promedio del inventario inicial más las mercancías compradas durante un período fiscal para calcular el costo de la mercancía vendida. (p. 153)

Withholding allowance *Deducción en la retención de impuestos* Una deducción del ingreso total por cada persona legalmente mantenida por el contribuyente, incluyendo al empleado. (p. 65)

Work in process *Trabajo en proceso* Productos que están en el proceso de fabricación que todavía no han sido terminados. (p. 496)

Work sheet *Hoja de trabajo* Un formulario de contabilidad que contiene columnas que se usa para resumir la información del libro general mayor que es necesario para preparar estados financieros. (p. 132)

Working capital *Capital de trabajo* La cantidad del total de los activos actuales menos el total de las obligaciones actuales. (p. 373)

Writing off an account *Anulación de una cuenta* Cancelar el saldo de la cuenta de un cliente por incumplimiento de pago. (p. 174)

INDEX

A

ABC. *See* Activity-based costing
Access privileges, setting user, 612–613
Account(s), 9
buying plant asset on, 200
cash payments on, 20
cash receipts on, 47
departmental sales on, 38–45
journalizing purchases on, 14
journalizing sales on, 40
normal balances of, 9
payroll bank, 76
uncollectible, 174
using accounting software for receiving payment on, 55–56
writing off an, 174
See also Chart of accounts
Account balance, 9
after liquidation of noncash assets and liabilities, 661
Accountability, 577
Accounting certifications, 30
Accounting cycle, 121
Accounting equation, 7
Accounting firm, partner in an, 595
Accounting opportunities in not-for-profit organizations, 694
Accounting principles and records, 6–12
Accounting ratios and marketing, 358
Accounting records, 7–11, 597
Accounting software
applying depreciation, 225–226
drawing on line of credit, 256
maintaining shareholder records, 310–311

managing employee information, 84–85
modifying a report, 123–125
preparing budgets using open database connectivity (ODBC), 457–458
receiving payment on account, 55–56
setting credit limits, 189–190
setting prices using, 163–165
setting up a note receivable, 280–281
setting up accounts for corporation, 28–29
setting user access privileges, 612–613
Accounting systems
controlling, 592–593
documenting of, 597–599
Accounts payable
schedule of, 97
trial balance, 97
Accounts receivable
days' sales in, 186, 385
financial analysis of, 186–187
schedule of, 97
Accounts receivable ledger, posting from sales journal to, 41
Accounts receivable ratios, analyzing, 187
Accounts receivable turnover ratio, 186, 385
Accredited in Business Valuation, 30
Accrual accounting
adjusting from modified to full, 712
modified, 675
Accrued expenses, 249, 249–254
procedure for recording, 249–251
Accrued interest
calculating, 250
reversing entry for, 250

Accrued interest expense, journalizing of, 249–251
Accrued interest income
adjusting entry for, 267
reversing entry for, 268
Accrued revenue, 264–268, 267
ACFE. *See* Association of Certified Fraud Examiners
Acid-test ratio, 374
ACL Services Ltd., 591
Acquisition, 331
Activity rate, 569
Activity-based costing (ABC), 567–572
advantages and disadvantages of, 572
allocating overhead costs using, 571
calculating total product cost using, 571
implementing, 568–571
Actual factory overhead, journalizing, 509
ADA Amendments Act (ADAAA), 243
Adjusted trial balance, 103
completing, 106
preparing, 103
Adjusting entries, 98, 655
accrued interest income, 267
advertising initially recorded as an asset, 246
preparing, 702
supplies initially recorded as an expense, 244
unearned revenue, 264–265
Adjustment information, 99–102
Adjustment using
aging of accounts receivable, 180
percentage of accounts receivable, 181
percentage of sales method, 179

Drawing, 624
Duties, segregation of, 594

E

Earnings
  calculating employee, 66
  distribution and withdrawal of
    partnership, 646–651
Earnings per share (EPS), 386–387
EBIT, 376, 395
EBITDA, 395
EDGAR (Electronic Data
    Gathering, Analysis, and
    Retrieval system), 368
EDI (electronic data interchange),
    166
Education, Department of, 251
Effective interest rate, 346
Efficiency
  measures, calculating and
    analyzing, 385–389, 568
EFT (Electronic funds transfer),
    76
EFTPS (Electronic Federal Tax
    Payment System), 80
Electronic data interchange
    (EDI), 166
Electronic Federal Tax Payment
    System (EFTPS), 80
Electronic funds transfer (EFT),
    76
Embezzlement, 10, 593
Employee(s)
  calculating earnings of, 66
  paying, 64
  payroll records for earnings and
    deductions of, 64–73
  pretax benefits, 86
  using accounting software for
    managing information of,
    84–85
Employee earnings record, 73
Employer payroll taxes, 77
  calculating, 78
  journalizing, 79
Encumbrance, 687
  journalizing, 688–689
End-of-period financial reporting,
  preparing for, 96–97

End-of-period work for
  departmentalized business,
    117–121
  partnership, 653–656
Enrolled Agent, 30
Equities, 7
Equity
  admitting a partner with no
    change in total, 630
  equal to new partner's
    investment, admitting a
    partner with, 631
  greater than new partner's
    investment, admitting a
    partner with, 632
  interest on, 648
  percentage of total, 647
Equity accounts after goodwill is
  recognized, 634
Equity funding, pyramid scheme
  at, 216
Equity Funding Corporation of
  America, 216
Equity per share on common
  stock, 376
Equity ratio, 375
Equivalent units of production
  (EUP), 561
  calculating, 561–562
Ernst & Young LLP, 621
Error, 593
  in costing merchandise
    inventory, effects of, 145
Estimated salvage value, 205
Estimated useful life, 205
Estimating inventory, 159–161
  gross profit method of, 159
  retail method of, 160
Estimating uncollectible accounts
  expense, 178–183
Ethics, codes of, 6
Ethics violations, reporting of, 344
EUP. See equivalent units of
  production
Ex Works (EXW), 18
Exception reports, 126
Expected Family Contribution
  (EFC), 251
Expenditures, 676
  differences between expenses
    and, 676
  journalizing, 687

Expense
  accrued, 249
  adjusting entry for supplies
    initially recorded as, 244
  closing entry for supplies, 244
  depreciation, 102
  interest, 239
  journalizing warranty, 253–254
  prepaid, 243
  reversing entry for supplies
    initially recorded as, 245
Expense budgets and budgeted
  income statement,
    439–444
Expenses and expenditures,
  difference between, 676
Exporting and importing goods,
  319
EXW (Ex Works), 18
ExxonMobil, 37

F

Face value, 343
Facility-sustaining level costs,
  568
Factory overhead, 496
  accounting for, 507–510
  calculating and recording,
    507–508
  journalizing actual, 509
FAFSA (Free Application for
    Federal Student Aid),
    251
Fair market value balance sheet,
  627
FASB. See Financial Accounting
  Standards Board
FCPA. See Foreign Corrupt
  Practices Act
Federal income tax, 656
  calculating adjustment, 104–105
  journalizing payment of
    liabilities, 80
  withholding tables, 70–71
Federal unemployment tax
    liability, journalizing
    payment of, 81
FICO score, 191
Fiduciary fund, 712

FIFO. *See* First-in, first-out inventory costing method
File maintenance, 11
Financial Accounting Standards Board (FASB), 418
Financial analysis
   accounts receivable, 186–187
   merchandise inventory, 161
   objectives, 368–372
Financial information, preparing for departmentalized business, 96–106
Financial ratio, 110
Financial reporting
   advanced topics in, 391–393
   for departments, 6–7
   emphasis, 676
   for a manufacturing business, 512–517
   preparing for end-of-period, 96–97
Financial statement analysis, 368
Financial statement misstatement, 593
Financial statements
   for departmental merchandising business, 112–115
   preparing for a governmental organization, 707–712
   using work sheet to prepare, 106
Financial strength
   long-term, 375–376
   measuring and analyzing, 368–376
   short-term, 373–374
Financing a takeover, 351
Financing activities, 115
   analyzing cash flows from, 413
   section, preparing, 412–413
Finished goods, 496
   accounting for, 512–517
   card, 512
   transactions, recording, 513
Finished goods ledger, 497–498
First-in, first-out inventory costing method (FIFO), 151
Fiscal period, 96
Fiscal year, 96
Fixed assets, 198
Fixed costs, 470

Fixed overhead, avoidable, 535
Fixed percentage, 647
Flowchart, 597
   of a voucher system, 609
FOB destination, 146
FOB shipping point, 146
Ford Motor Company, 263
Foreign Corrupt Practices Act (FCPA), 448
Foreign countries, legal rights in, 266
Foreign currency exchange gains or losses, 692
Foreign exchange rates, 516
   impact of on note payable, 257
Formation, ease of, 298
Franchise tax, 312
Fraud, 593
   awareness, 468
   types of, 593
Free Application for Federal Student Aid (FAFSA), 251
Free cash flow, 383
Fund, 675
Fund accounting balance sheet, 675
Fund equity, 676
FUTA earnings, 78
Future value, 541
   factors, 542
Future value of an annuity, 545
Future value of money, 541–542

G

GAAP. *See* Generally accepted accounting principles
GASB. *See* Governmental Accounting Standards Board
Gain on realization
   to partners, distributing a, 662
   in a partnership liquidation, recognizing of, 658–659
General economic information, 433
General fixed assets, 690
General journal, 8
   posting from, 45
General ledger, 9, 11
General ledger account, posting from sales journal to, 42

General Mills, 559
General partner, 645
Generally accepted accounting principles (GAAP), 151, 203, 352, 391–392, 403, 418, 572, 712
Gift card breakage, reporting of, 272
Gift cards
   accounting for, 270–272
   accounting for unredeemed, 272
   recording of sale with, 271
   recording sale of, 270
Goals and plans, annual operational, 435
Goods, 146
   on consignment, 146
   importing and exporting of, 319
   journalizing transfer from one department to the next, 562
   journalizing transfer to finished goods, 563
   in transit, 146
Goodwill, 633
   admitting a partner when goodwill is recognized, 633
   equity accounts after goodwill is recognized, 634
Government, ethics in, 702
Governmental Accounting Standards Board (GASB), 712
Governmental fund, 712
Governmental operating budget, developing an annual, 678
Governmental organizations
   adjusting entries for general fund, 702–705
   characteristics of accounting systems and, 674
   expenditure transactions for, 687–690
   financing and investing transactions for, 690–692
   preparing financial statements for, 707–712
   purpose of, 673
   revenue transactions for, 683–685

FEATURES INDEX

A LOOK AT ACCOUNTING SOFTWARE

CAREERS IN ACCOUNTING

ETHICS IN ACTION

EXPLORE ACCOUNTING

FINANCIAL LITERACY

FORENSIC ACCOUNTING

GLOBAL AWARENESS

THINK LIKE AN ACCOUNTANT

WHY ACCOUNTING?